# THE ENCYCLOPEDIA OF
# MIDDLE EAST WARS

# THE ENCYCLOPEDIA OF MIDDLE EAST WARS

## The United States in the Persian Gulf, Afghanistan, and Iraq Conflicts

VOLUME III: M–S

Spencer C. Tucker

Editor

Priscilla Mary Roberts

Editor, Documents Volume

Dr. Paul G. Pierpaoli Jr.

Associate Editor

Colonel Jerry D. Morelock, USAR (retired)
Major General David Zabecki, USAR (retired)
Dr. Sherifa Zuhur

Assistant Editors

FOREWORD BY
General Anthony C. Zinni, USMC (retired)

ABC CLIO

Santa Barbara, California   Denver, Colorado   Oxford, England

Library of Congress Cataloging-in-Publication Data

The encyclopedia of Middle East wars : the United States in the Persian Gulf, Afghanistan, and Iraq conflicts / Spencer C. Tucker, editor ; Priscilla Mary Roberts, editor, documents volume.
    v.  cm.
  Includes bibliographical references and index.
    ISBN 978-1-85109-947-4 (hard copy : alk. paper) — ISBN 978-1-85109-948-1 (ebook)
    1. Middle East—History, Military—20th century—Encyclopedias.   2. Middle East—History, Military—21st century—Encyclopedias.
3. Middle East—Military relations—United States—Encyclopedias.   4. United States—Military relations—Middle
East—Encyclopedias.   5. Persian Gulf War, 1991—Encyclopedias.   6. Afghan War, 2001—Encyclopedias.   7. Iraq War, 2003—
Encyclopedias.   I. Tucker, Spencer, 1937–   II. Roberts, Priscilla Mary.
  DS63.1.E453 2010
  355.00956'03—dc22

2010033812

13 12 11 10 9   1 2 3 4 5

This book is also available on the World Wide Web as an ebook.
Visit abc-clio.com for details.

ABC-CLIO, LLC
130 Cremona Drive, P.O. Box 1911
Santa Barbara, California 93116–1911

This book is printed on acid-free paper ∞
Manufactured in the United States of America

# About the Editors

**Spencer C. Tucker**, PhD, graduated from the Virginia Military Institute and was a Fulbright scholar in France. He was a U.S. Army captain and intelligence analyst in the Pentagon during the Vietnam War, then taught for 30 years at Texas Christian University before returning to his alma mater for 6 years as the holder of the John Biggs Chair of Military History. He retired from teaching in 2003. He is now Senior Fellow of Military History at ABC-CLIO. Dr. Tucker has written or edited 36 books, including ABC-CLIO's award-winning *The Encyclopedia of the Cold War* and *The Encyclopedia of the Arab-Israeli Conflict* as well as the comprehensive *A Global Chronology of Conflict*.

**Priscilla Mary Roberts** received her PhD from Cambridge University and is an associate professor of history and an honorary director of the Centre of American Studies at the University of Hong Kong. Dr. Roberts has received numerous research awards and was the documents editor of *The Encyclopedia of the Cold War* and *The Encyclopedia of the Arab-Israeli Conflict*, published by ABC-CLIO. She spent 2003 as a visiting Fulbright scholar at the Institute for European, Russian, and Eurasian Studies at the George Washington University in Washington, D.C.

# Contents

# List of Entries

# List of Maps

# General Maps

# MIDDLE EAST

# TOPOGRAPHY OF THE MIDDLE EAST

KAZAKHSTAN

RUSSIA

*Black Sea*

*Caspian Sea*

UZBEKISTAN

GEORGIA

ARMENIA AZERBAIJAN

TURKMENISTAN

40°N

TURKEY

CYPRUS

SYRIA

AFGHANISTAN

LEBANON

*Mediterranean Sea*

IRAQ

I R A N

ISRAEL

JORDAN

30°N

KUWAIT

PAKISTAN

*Persian Gulf*

EGYPT

BAHRAIN

QATAR

UNITED ARAB EMIRATES

*Red Sea*

SAUDI ARABIA

OMAN

*Arabian Sea*

20°N

SUDAN

ERITREA

YEMEN

*INDIAN*

DJIBOUTI

*OCEAN*

SOMALIA

ETHIOPIA

40°E

50°E

**Elevation (in feet)**

10,000 +
7,000–10,000
5,000–7,000
2,000–5,000
1,000–2,000
500–1,000
0–500
Below sea level

0   100   200 mi

0  100  200 km

# COALITION AGAINST IRAQ, AUGUST 2, 1990–FEBRUARY 28, 1991

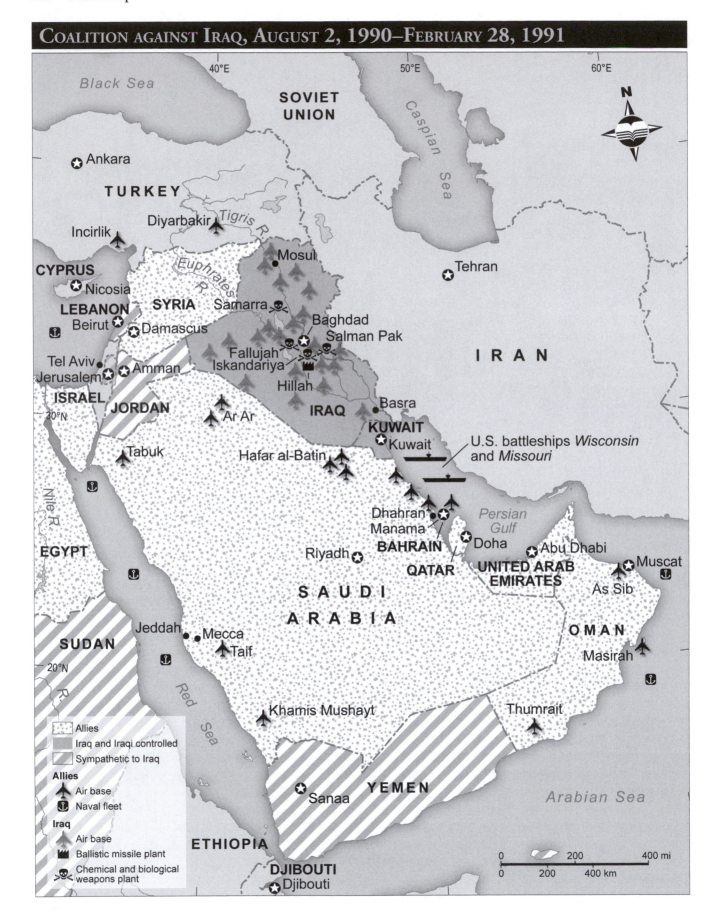

Black Sea

SOVIET UNION

Caspian Sea

40°E          50°E          60°E

N

Ankara

TURKEY

Diyarbakir

Incirlik              Tigris R.

CYPRUS                    Mosul

Nicosia              Euphrates R.

SYRIA        Samarra

LEBANON
Beirut              Damascus

Tehran

IRAN

Tel Aviv              Amman
Jerusalem

Baghdad
Salman Pak
Fallujah
Iskandariya
Hillah

ISRAEL        JORDAN

30°N                                    IRAQ          Basra

Ar Ar                          KUWAIT

Tabuk                                    Kuwait

Hafar al-Batin                    U.S. battleships *Wisconsin*
and *Missouri*

Dhahran
Manama                    Persian
Gulf

BAHRAIN        Doha        Abu Dhabi        Muscat

Riyadh              QATAR        UNITED ARAB
EMIRATES              As Sib

EGYPT

SAUDI
ARABIA              OMAN

Nile R.

Jeddah    Mecca
Taif                          Masirah

20°N

SUDAN

Red Sea        Khamis Mushayt        Thumrait

**Allies**

.·.·. Allies

▓ Iraq and Iraqi controlled

╱╱ Sympathetic to Iraq

**Allies**

✈ Air base

⚓ Naval fleet

**Iraq**

✈ Air base

▲ Ballistic missile plant

☠ Chemical and biological
weapons plant

ETHIOPIA

Sanaa              YEMEN        Arabian Sea

DJIBOUTI
Djibouti

0        200        400 mi
0    200    400 km

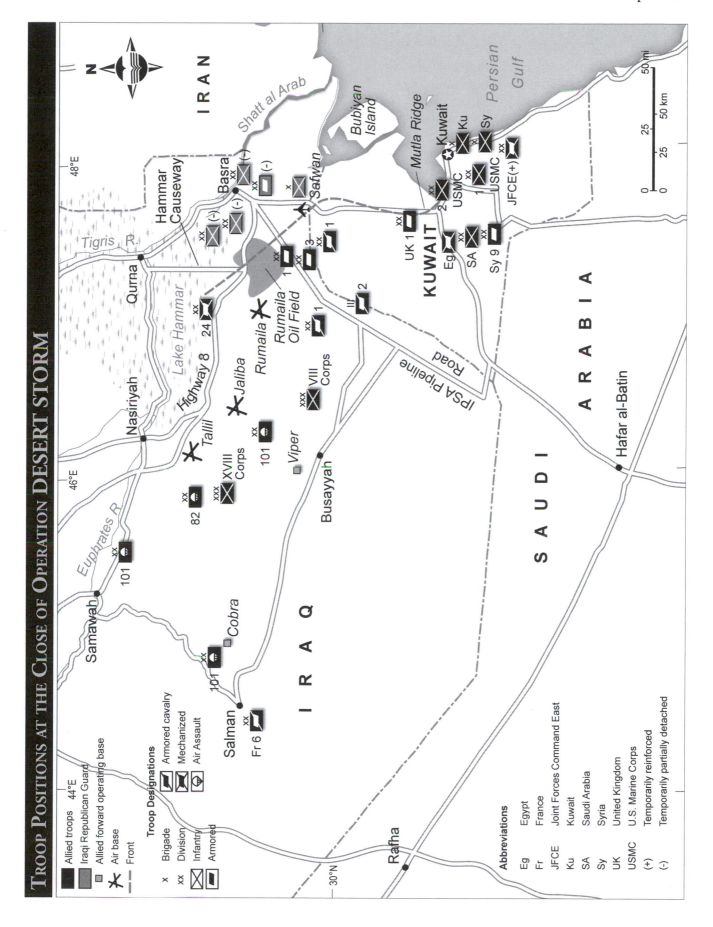

TROOP POSITIONS AT THE CLOSE OF OPERATION DESERT STORM

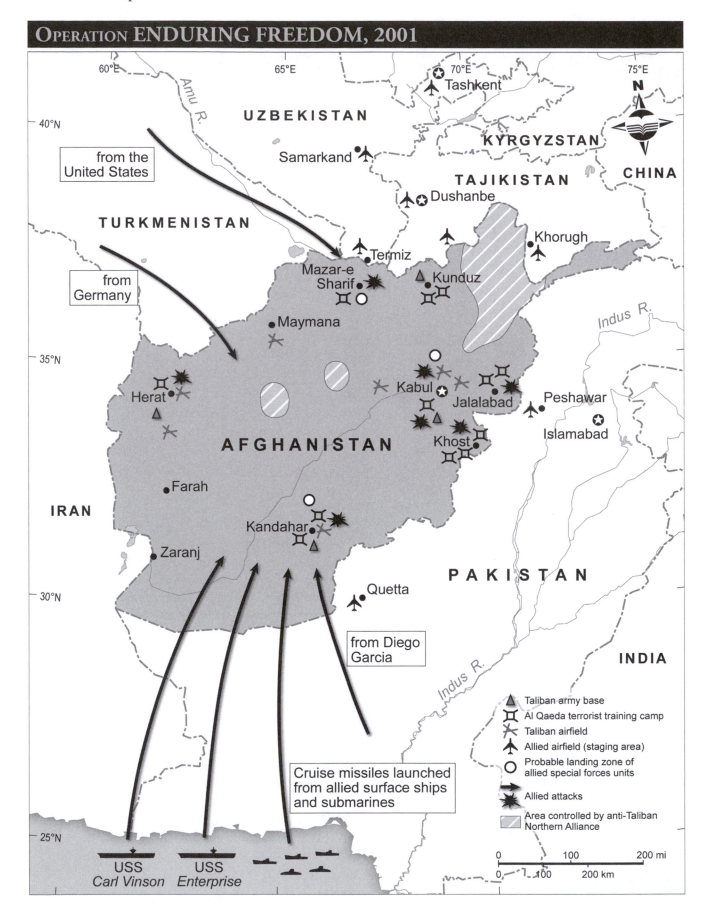

## OPERATION ENDURING FREEDOM, 2001

# DISPOSITION OF FORCES ON THE EVE OF THE 2003 IRAQ WAR

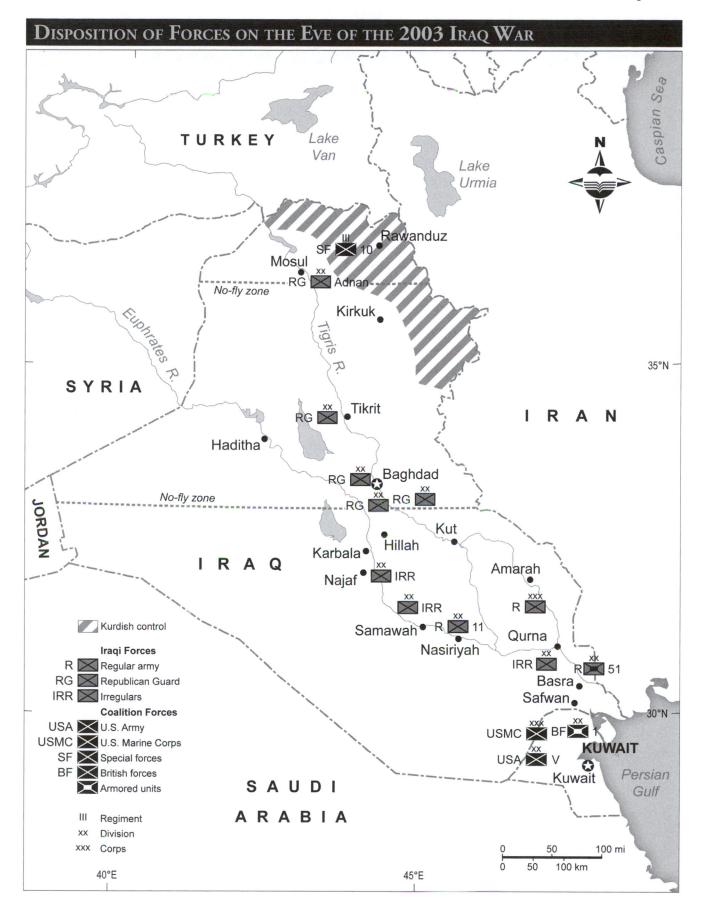

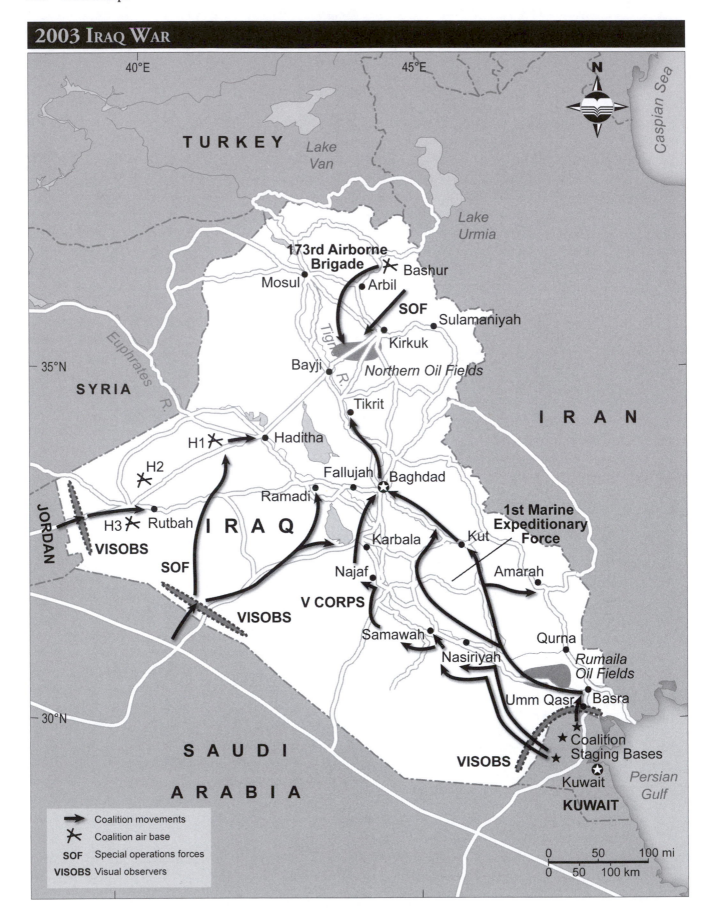

## 2003 IRAQ WAR

Coalition movements
Coalition air base
SOF  Special operations forces
VISOBS  Visual observers

# M

## M1A1 and M1A2 Abrams Main Battle Tanks

The M1A1 and M1A2 Abrams is the most powerful U.S. tank and one of the top main battle tanks (MBTs) in the world. Designed to replace the M60 (which had entered service in 1960), the M1 began as a project by the Federal Republic of Germany (FRG, West Germany) and the United States for an MBT able to engage and defeat the vast number of tanks that the Soviet Union and its satellites might field in an invasion of Central Europe. Designated the MBT-70, the new tank was centered on the Shillelagh gun/missile launcher and a 1,500-horsepower engine, neither of which, however, worked out as planned.

Collapse of the MBT-70 project and cancellation of the follow-on XM803 program led to a brand new program, begun from the ground up, in 1972. That same year the U.S. Army came up with a concept of what it wanted in the new MBT, and two companies—Chrysler Defense and the Detroit Diesel division of General Motors—built prototypes of what was then designated the XM1 MBT. Both were tested in early 1976, and that November the army declared Chrysler the winner. Following manufacture of a number of test vehicles, the first production model M1 tank came off the assembly line in February 1980. The new tank was named for General Creighton Abrams, armor tank battalion commander in World War II, commander of allied forces in Vietnam, and then army chief of staff.

The M1 was a revolutionary design and a sharp departure from previous U.S. tanks, with their rounded surfaces and relatively high profile. The M1 was more angular, with flat-plate composite Chobham-type armor and armor boxes that can be opened and the armor changed according to the threat. It was also considerably lower (8 feet) than the M60 (10 feet 9 inches).

From the start the army's intention was to arm the M1 with the 105-millimeter (mm) gun. As a result of a program aimed at securing a common main armament for U.S., British, and West German tanks, the army made the decision, after initial M1 production had begun, to arm the M1 with a German-designed Rheinmetall 120-mm smoothbore gun. But that gun was still under development when the tank was ready, so the army decided to continue with the 105-mm M68 gun utilized in the M60. The 120-mm M256 gun, essentially the German-designed gun with a U.S. breech, was available in 1984, and the first M1A1 with this new armament came off the production line in August 1985. The M1A1HA introduced a new steel-encased depleted uranium armor, which is virtually impenetrable but also dramatically increased the tank's weight to nearly 146,000 pounds. A total of 3,273 M1s were produced for the U.S. Army.

The M1A1, produced beginning in 1985, mounts the 120-mm main gun, and the next modification was the introduction of almost-impenetrable steel-encased depleted-uranium armor, designated HA (heavy armor). Prior to the 1991 Persian Gulf War, upgrades were carried out in Saudi Arabia on all in-theater M1A1 tanks to bring them to M1A1HA status.

A total of 4,796 M1As were produced for the U.S. Army. The U.S. Marine Corps received 221, along with 403 M1s transferred from the army, to replace its more than 700 M60A1s. Kuwait also purchased 218 Abrams tanks, and Saudi Arabia bought 315. Egypt also arranged to produce 551 of them under a coproduction arrangement in which they were built in Egypt by the Halwan Tank Plant. In 2006–2007 the Australian Army took delivery of 59 M1A1s. In July 2008 Iraq issued a formal request to purchase 140 upgraded M1A1Ms from the United States.

In the Persian Gulf War, the M1A1 Abrams and British Challenger proved their great superiority over their Soviet counterparts,

An M1A1 Abrams tank provides area security alongside a street intersection in Iraq, 2005. (U.S. Marine Corps)

especially in night fighting. Of some 600 M1A1 Abrams that saw combat, only 18 were disabled by enemy action. None were penetrated by an enemy round, but 3 were struck by depleted uranium shells fired from other M1s, although none of these were permanently disabled, and there were no crew fatalities. This reflected the survivability features built into the tank, including armored bulkheads to deflect blasts outward. Conversely, the M1A1's 120-mm gun proved lethal to Iraqi MBTs. The M1A1 could engage Iraqi armor at some 3000 yards, twice the Iraqi effective range, and its superior fire-control system could deliver a first-round hit while on the move. The depleted uranium penetrators could almost guarantee a kill.

The M1A2 was first produced in 1986. Most changes are internal. These include a thermal viewer for the tank commander, a new land navigation system, and the Inter-Vehicular Information System (IVIS). The latter is a datalink compatible with other advanced armored fighting vehicles (AFVs) and helicopters. Although only 77 M1A2s were delivered new, more than 500 M1A1s were upgraded to M1A2s. The M1A2 weighs some 139,000 pounds, mounts a 120-mm main gun and three machine guns: two M-240 7.62-mm (.30-caliber), one for the loader and the other mounted coaxially to the right of the main gun, and one M-2 12–7-mm (.50-caliber) mounted on the tank commander's cupola. A six-barrel smoke grenade launcher is located on each side of the

turret, and the tank can also lay a smokescreen by an engine-operated system.

During the Iraq War, no Abrams tanks were disabled by enemy action during the initial battles in March and April 2003. During the occupation that followed, some 80 Abrams were knocked out of action as of March 2005. Five crew members have been killed inside their tanks when the vehicles were hit by large improvised explosive devices (IEDs) using explosively formed penetrators (EFPs). Ten crew members also died after being hit while riding partially exposed in open hatches.

Production of the M1A2 was completed in 1996 but can be renewed if necessary. The M1A2 is also in service in Kuwait and Saudi Arabia.

SPENCER C. TUCKER

**See also**

Antitank Weapons; Armored Warfare, Persian Gulf and Iraq Wars; Challenger Main Battle Tanks; Improvised Explosive Devices; T-54/55 Series Main Battle Tank; T-62 Main Battle Tank; T-72 Main Battle Tank

**References**

Foss, Christopher F., ed. *The Encyclopedia of Tanks and Armored Fighting Vehicles.* San Diego: Thunder Bay, 2002.

Tucker, Spencer C. *Tanks: An Illustrated History of Their Impact.* Santa Barbara, CA: ABC-CLIO, 2004.

# M-113 Armored Personnel Carrier

The M-113 armored personnel carrier (APC) originated in a 1954 U.S. Army requirement for an air-deliverable armored personnel carrier. The Food Machinery Corporation (FMC), later United Defense and BAE Systems, began production in 1960. The requirement was to deliver a squad of 11 infantry to a battle area in an armored vehicle. The crew would be comprised of a track commander (who was also the infantry squad leader) and a driver, and the vehicle would be armed with a .50-caliber machine gun and 2,000 rounds of ammunition. The first model was a gasoline-powered tracked vehicle that was basically a box protected by rolled aluminum armor on three sides and had a sloped front.

The armor on the sloped front was 1.5 inches thick, while the thickness of the armor on the sides and floor varied from 1.125 inches to 1.75 inches. The engine was an 8-cylinder Chrysler V-8 with 209 horsepower. The 80-gallon internal fuel tank allowed a range of 200 miles and a speed up to 40 miles per hour (mph). Air-droppable weight was 18,600 pounds, while the combat weight was 22,900 pounds. The M-113 was 15 feet 11 inches long, 8 feet 10 inches wide, and 8 feet 2 inches high. It had a ground clearance of 16.1 inches and could ascend a 60 percent grade, cross a 66-inch-wide trench, and move in water at 3.5 mph, powered by the tracks. The M-113 would prove to be one of the most popular armored vehicles in the American inventory, from the conflict in Vietnam to current conflicts in Iraq and Afghanistan.

The M-113 has gone through four major upgrades, with more possible. Approximately 80,000 have been produced in the United States and under license in Italy. More than 50 nations include the M-113 in their force structures. The M-113 has become a Family of Vehicles (FOV), with numerous variants adapted to specialized missions. Among the variants are several mortar carriers, smoke-generator carriers, command-post carriers, a medical evacuation vehicle, and other specialized-use vehicles, including Soviet-looking vehicles used for training at the National Training Center at Fort Irwin, California. The many nations using the M-113 have also made their own specialized versions.

The first upgrade was FMC's M-113A1 in 1964. This vehicle had a General Motors 6-cylinder diesel engine that produced 212 horsepower. There were no changes in armor or dimensions, but there were a modest increase in weight and an increase in range to 300 miles, partially accounted for by a fuel tank capable of holding 95 gallons. The M-113A2 in 1979 moved the fuel tank to armored external tanks, along with providing improvements in engine cooling and suspension and smoke grenade launchers. Moving the fuel tanks freed up 16 cubic feet of space inside the vehicle and reduced the hazards to the occupants from explosion of fuel due to enemy fire. The new model, also produced by FMC, weighed about 200 pounds more but was still capable of swimming, although this was no longer a requirement and was eliminated from training. This model was the one most used in Operation DESERT STORM, with deployment of 762 such vehicles with U.S. forces and significant numbers with coalition forces. The M113A2 was the most numerous of all APCs in DESERT STORM.

FMC introduced the M-113A3 in 1987, and some participated in Operation DESERT STORM along with the older models. In January 1991 the U.S. Army possessed 972 M-113s of all models. Lieutenant General Frederick Franks, commander of the VII Corps, chose the A3 model as his command track. The turbo supercharged diesel engine produced 275 horsepower, while speed increased to 41 mph, allowing it to keep pace with the M1 Abrams tank. The transmission was improved, and the more powerful engine allowed application of an external armor kit to enhance protection. A traditional steering wheel replaced the lever controls that controlled each track and, along with improved braking, made the new model easier to drive. Although some M-113s were able to keep up with the Abrams tank, many could not, and after-action reports noted this problem.

As each new model of the M-113 came on line, earlier models cycled through the U.S. Army depot system, such as the Anniston Army Depot, to be refitted by depot personnel and United Defense contractors, including modern electronics. There are also programs to use the M-113 as a platform for a variety of new models of APCs. United Defense has proposed stretching the M-113 from five to six road wheels to add 34 inches to the length of the vehicle. As M-113 chasses become available by replacement by newer vehicles, three variations are being considered. One is the M113 A3+ Mobile Tactical Vehicle Light, a demonstration vehicle upon which variations can be adapted. More specialized is the M113 A3+ Engineering Squad Vehicle designed to transport an eight-man engineering squad with all its equipment and also accommodate a mine dispenser and a pathfinder marking system, and tow a trailer with engineering equipment. Another idea is the Infantry Fighting Vehicle Light with a turret with a 25-mm gun, a 400-horsepower engine, and upgraded armor. Also being developed is a Hazardous Materials Recovery Vehicle, with a bulldozer blade and an external mechanical arm. This vehicle, which could have civilian use, would have an overpressure closed-circuit life support system for operating in chemically and biologically contaminated environments.

All of these vehicles will be able to roll on and off the Lockheed C-130 Hercules air transport aircraft. The U.S. Army continues to have the M-113 in its inventory and employs them both in Afghanistan and Iraq. The initial force deployed by air to northern Iraq during Operation IRAQI FREEDOM included 10 M-113s and 4 M-1094 20-mm mortars on the M-113 chassis. Small numbers have been used elsewhere in Iraq, and about 20 have been lost to combat.

The proliferation of improvised explosive devices (IEDs) in Iraq and Afghanistan, which are becoming increasingly lethal, has led to a program of sending M-113A1s to Iraq to provide more protection against IEDs. U.S. representative Ike Skelton (D-Miss.) proposed this in December 2004, noting that there were more than 700 M-113s in Kuwait that would provide better protection for infantry patrols than the Humvees in current use. In early 2005 the U.S. Army began an $84 million program to enhance the armor of 734 M-113A3s and the command vehicle counterpart. The armor upgrade, with parts made in the United States and installed in Kuwait, includes steel side armor, a slat-armor cage that bolts to the steel armor and provides protection from rocket-propelled grenades, and antimine armor at the bottom of the vehicle. This program will give the M-113 a lease on life for a time longer, but the army intends to phase out the M-113s in favor of the Bradley fighting vehicle and the wheeled Stryker combat vehicle.

DANIEL E. SPECTOR

**See also**

Bradley Fighting Vehicle; Franks, Frederick Melvin, Jr.; High Mobility Multipurpose Wheeled Vehicle; Improvised Explosive Devices; M1A1 and M1A2 Abrams Main Battle Tanks

**References**

Cordesman, Anthony H., and Abraham R. Wagner. *The Lessons of Modern War,* Vol. 4, *The Gulf War.* Boulder, CO: Westview, 1996.

Hogg, Ian V. *The Greenhill Armoured Fighting Vehicles Data Book.* London: Greenhill Books, 2002.

Scales, Robert H. *United States Army in the Gulf War: Certain Victory.* Washington, DC: U.S. Army, 1993.

Thompson, Loren B., Lawrence J. Korb, and Caroline Wadhams. *Army Equipment after Iraq.* Arlington, VA: Center for American Progress Lexington Institute, 2006.

## Macedonia, Republic of, Role in Afghanistan and Iraq Wars

Former Yugoslav republic and Balkan nation, independent since 1991. With a 2008 population of 2.06 million people, Macedonia is a landlocked country bordered by Albania to the west, Bulgaria to the east, Serbia to the north, and Greece to the south. The small nation covers just 9,780 square miles. Macedonia has been a member of the United Nations (UN) since 1993. In 2005 Macedonia became a candidate for entry into the European Union (EU) and has also applied for membership to the North Atlantic Treaty Organization (NATO). Not surprisingly, Macedonia's foreign policy since independence has been oriented toward Western Europe and the United States. Macedonia's government is a representative parliamentary democracy with a president as head of government and a prime minister who is chosen by the unicameral legislature. The president is elected popularly to a five-year term and may not serve more than two terms. The multiparty political landscape features broad political coalitions that share legislative power. The major political parties include the Social Democratic Union of Macedonia, the International Macedonian Revolutionary Organization, the Democratic Union for Integration, and the Democratic Party of Albanians.

Macedonia's economy moved steadily to embrace free-market capitalism in the 1990s, and by 2006 it was among the best performers of the 178 nations in the world monitored by the World Bank. By 2007 Macedonia's annual gross domestic product (GDP) growth was estimated to be 5.5 percent. About one-third of the nation's population is Muslim, giving it Europe's fourth-largest Muslim population (by percentage). Although Macedonia was not involved in the devastating Balkan Wars of the 1990s, in 2001 the Macedonian government fought a brief conflict with Albanian minority insurgents in the northern and western parts of the nation. In June 2001 a NATO-brokered cease-fire took effect, and the government agreed to allow more autonomy to its Albanian minority. To date, there have been only sporadic and isolated incidents of violence stemming from the conflict.

Hoping to gain entrance into the EU and NATO and recognizing that global terrorism was a growing concern, Macedonia has participated—albeit in a very minor role—in both the Afghanistan War and the Iraq War. In mid-2003 Macedonia signaled its willingness to send a small troop deployment to Afghanistan and since then has maintained some 130 military personnel in the war-torn nation. They have served chiefly in support roles alongside U.S. and NATO forces as part of the International Security Assistance Force–Afghanistan (ISAF). In July 2003 after major combat operations ended in Iraq, Macedonia provided approximately 50 noncombat personnel to work with U.S.-led forces there as part of the Multi-National Force–Iraq. Macedonia's deployment peaked at 77 personnel, all of whom were withdrawn upon consultation with the United States and other allies in November 2008. Macedonia has suffered no fatalities to date.

PAUL G. PIERPAOLI JR.

**See also**

Afghanistan, Coalition Combat Operations in, 2002–Present; International Security Assistance Force; IRAQI FREEDOM, Operation, Coalition Ground Forces; Multi-National Force–Iraq; North Atlantic Treaty Organization in Afghanistan

**References**

Cockburn, Patrick. *The Occupation: War and Resistance in Iraq.* New York: Verso, 2007.

Keegan, John. *The Iraq War: The Military Offensive, from Victory in 21 Days to the Insurgent Aftermath.* New York: Vintage, 2005.

## Madrasahs

The term "madrasah" is simply the Arabic word for school. It can also mean a more advanced academy or college of Islamic studies. In the past, the lower-level school of Islamic study was called a *kuttab,* where memorization of the Qur'an is taught, but in modern times a *kuttab* is sometimes confused with a madrasah as in the general meaning of the word. Mosques, or *masajid,* may also have a *halaqat,* or study circle. Early in Islamic history, madrasahs were attached to mosques. Those as separate institutions came later. Nizam al-Mulk, an 11th-century ruler, is said to have institutionalized the system by building a great school, the Nizamiyah, that was then copied by others.

These separately established madrasahs were primarily created to teach Islamic law but included subjects other than *fiqh* (jurisprudence), such as Arabic, *tafsir* (study of the interpretation of the Qur'an), mysticism, and hadith science. They were open to traveling students, often from the poorer classes in society. Typically, these madrasahs were endowed to give stipends to students who might live there and to provide salaries to the faculty. The fortunes of the madrasahs rose and fell depending on the times. Thus, the madrasahs of Mecca were not as well endowed in the 19th century as later.

Particularly in the wake of the terrorist attacks on the United States on September 11, 2001, the entire system of Islamic education was heavily criticized in the West and blamed for the rise of the Taliban, for example. Certainly many, although not all, of the Taliban did come from the madrasahs in Pakistan, but the critique of all madrasahs as institutions teaching hatred for the West or seeking to institute a radical form of Islam is misinformed. Most acts of Islamic terrorism around the world have been the product of individuals trained outside of the madrasah system. Nevertheless, it is true that some madrasahs in Pakistan have provided jihadists to the Taliban and Kashmiri militant groups. At least two of the suicide bombers who struck the London transportation system on July 7, 2005, had spent time at a Pakistani madrasah. However, it is also true that one cannot obtain advanced Islamic training outside of the Islamic education system, as the requisite subjects are not taught at all in universities or Western seminaries.

In some areas the madrasahs are being subjected to reforms imposed by the state, as in Saudi Arabia. In other countries they have long been under attack or even shut down by the government, as in Turkey. In Egypt's renowned al-Azhar University system, the madrasah curriculum has evolved steadily, although this has not satisfied all critics of al-Azhar's broader educational system, which includes primary and secondary schools. In Iraq in the holy cities of Karbala and Najaf, the madrasah system is presided over by the Hawzah al-Ilmiyya (the certified Islamic scholars). In general, clerics of the Hawzah support a separation of the life and work of the Muslim scholar from politics, which is why clerics such as Ayatollah Sistani resist being identified with political parties and may express views divergent from the government.

Many of the madrasahs in Pakistan, Afghanistan, and areas outside of the Arab heartland maintain a connection with the Arab Middle East, both through idealizing the history and legacy of Islamic studies and by religious and educationally related travel. Hence, connections with Saudi Arabia, for example, are to some degree unavoidable and not necessarily radicalizing. On the other hand, Muslim state governments are now keeping a close watch on pilgrims and those who travel for religious studies. Realization that many suicide bombers and other terrorists involved in terrorist attacks are not products of the madrasah system could contribute to critical thinking about the modern phenomenon of Islamist terrorism.

CLARE M. LOPEZ AND SHERIFA ZUHUR

**See also**

Afghanistan; Islamic Radicalism; Jihad; Pakistan; September 11 Attacks, International Reactions to; Taliban

**References**

Ahitsaari, Martii, ed. *Pakistan: Madrasas, Extremism, and Militarism.* Darby, PA: Diane Publishing, 2002.

Fair, C. Christine. "Militant Recruitment in Pakistan: A New Look at the Militancy-Madrasah Connection." *Asia Policy* 4 (July 2007): 107–134.

Faruqi, Ziu ul-Husan. *The Deoband School and the Demand for Pakistan.* London: Asia Publishing House, 1963.

Sageman, Marc. *Understanding Terror Networks.* Philadelphia: University of Pennsylvania Press, 2004.

Tibawi, A. L. *Islamic Education: Its Traditions and Modernizations into the Arab Nationalist Systems.* London: Luzac, 1979.

# Madrid Attacks
## Event Date: March 11, 2004

Terrorist bombing attacks in Madrid, Spain, on March 11, 2004, also referred to as 3/11. The attacks were launched in the morning against the city's commuter train system, killing an announced 191 people and wounding 1,755 others. Later estimates, after reexamination of the remains of the victims, reduced the death toll to 190. The victims included citizens of 17 countries.

The attacks took place during the morning rush hour on four commuter trains traveling between Alcala des Henares and the Atocha Station in Madrid in an obvious effort to inflict the greatest amount of casualties possible. Thirteen bombs, hidden in backpacks, were placed on the trains, and 10 of these exploded within a two-minute period beginning at 7:37 a.m. Two of the 3 additional bombs were detonated by a police bomb squad, as was a suspicious package found near the Atocha Station. An additional unexploded bomb was brought intact to a police facility and later dismantled. This unexploded bomb provided evidence for the investigation and subsequent trial of the terrorists.

In the immediate aftermath of the attacks, the Spanish government blamed the attacks on Euskadi Ta Askatasuna (Basque Homeland and Freedom, or ETA), the Basque separatist movement that had launched terrorist attacks in the past. Investigators quickly absolved ETA of the attacks, however, and the blame shifted to the terrorist group Al Qaeda, which had perpetrated the September 11, 2001, attacks against the United States. Spanish authorities have claimed that the attackers were a loosely knit group of radical Muslims primarily from Morocco, Syria, and Algeria. A number of Spanish nationals were also involved, mainly by selling the explosives to the terrorists.

The Partido Popular (Popular Party, PP), which then formed the government of Spain, was defeated in national elections held three days later, replaced in power by the left-leaning Partido Socialista Obrero Españo (Spanish Socialist Workers' Party, PSOE). While Al Qaeda later claimed that the attacks had led to

Rescue workers remove victims from the destroyed passenger car of a bomb-damaged train at Atocha Station in Madrid, Spain, on March 11, 2004. The Madrid attacks came just ahead of national elections that resulted in a dramatic shift in Spain's political landscape. (AP/Wide World Photos)

the electoral defeat, most experts agree that the PP government's clumsy handling of the aftermath of the attacks was the primary factor in the PSOE victory in the election. The PP had held only a narrow and shrinking lead in the polls prior to the attacks. The government's early declaration that the attacks were the work of the ETA had been seen by many as influenced by electoral considerations, and when the claim was quickly shown to be untrue, the government's credibility was badly damaged.

The PSOE had strongly opposed Spain's participation in the U.S.-led invasion of Iraq, which the PP had supported. Shortly after the elections the new government under Prime Minister José Luis Rodríguez Zapatero withdrew Spanish troops from the coalition in Iraq, adding some weight to the Al Qaeda assertion that its attacks had directly affected Spanish foreign policy. The precipitous Spanish troop withdrawal also led to considerable tension in U.S.-Spanish relations. As late as the 2008 U.S. presidential elections, Republican candidate John McCain said that he would not meet with Spanish prime minister Zapatero.

A few weeks after the attacks, on April 2, 2004, an additional explosive device was found on the tracks of a high-speed rail line. The explosives had been prepared for detonation but were not connected to any detonating device. Following this further discovery, new investigations were launched, and Spanish police tracked down suspects in an area south of Madrid. During the raid

to apprehend them an explosion, apparently caused by a suicide bomb, killed seven suspects. Security officials believe that between five and eight suspects managed to escape the police that day. They have not yet been apprehended.

In all, 29 suspects, 20 Moroccans, and 9 Spaniards were apprehended and charged for involvement in the attacks. Their trial began on February 15, 2007, and lasted four and a half months. The verdict, handed down on October 31, 2007, found 21 guilty of various crimes, ranging from forgery to murder. Two of the convicted terrorists were sentenced to prison terms that added up to 42,924 years, but Spanish law limits actual imprisonment to 40 years.

The court sentences did not mention any direct links between the convicted terrorists and Al Qaeda, however. While Al Qaeda may have inspired the Madrid terrorists and a connection cannot be ruled out, no irrefutable evidence has been found to connect it with the planning, financing, or execution of the Madrid attacks.

Nevertheless, the Madrid attacks may well have been the first major success for an Al Qaeda–type terrorist organization in Europe. The attacks did lead to greater cooperation between West European security services in an attempt to prevent further attacks. Yet on July 7, 2005, London suffered multiple terrorist bombings that also appear to have independent from but inspired by Al Qaeda.

Elliot P. Chodoff

**See also**

Al Qaeda; Global War on Terror; McCain, John Sidney, III; Spain, Role in Persian Gulf, Afghanistan, and Iraq Wars; Terrorism

**References**

*Jane's Intelligence Review, August 2004,* Vol. 16, No 8. Coulsdon, Surrey, UK: Janes, 2004.

Puniyani, Ram. *Terrorism: Facts versus Myths.* New Delhi: Pharos Media, 2007.

Von Hippel, Karin. *Europe Confronts Terrorism.* New York: Palgrave Macmillan, 2005.

# Mahdi Army

Paramilitary wing of the Iraqi political movement Tayyar al-Sadr (the Sadr Movement) led by Iraqi junior Shiite cleric Muqtada al-Sadr. Muqtada al-Sadr is the son of Ayatollah Muhammad Sadiq al-Sadr, a prominent and outspoken critic of the Iraqi Baath Party and of President Saddam Hussein's regime during the 1990s. The elder Sadr was assassinated along with two of his other sons, Mustafa and Muammal, on February 18, 1999. Sadiq al-Sadr was a cousin of both Grand Ayatollah Muhammad Baqir al-Sadr, a prominent Iraqi Shiite activist cleric in the 1960s and 1970s, and Musa al-Sadr, the prominent cleric who oversaw the political mobilization of Lebanese Shia from the late 1950s until his disappearance on a trip to Libya in 1978.

Sadiq al-Sadr received his religious education in the seminary of Najaf and studied with his cousin, Baqir al-Sadr, and Iranian Grand Ayatollah Ruhollah Khomeini, who lived in exile in Najaf from 1965 to 1978. Sadiq al-Sadr's popularity among Iraqi Shia began to grow beginning in the mid-1980s, and by the end of that decade, despite debates among clerical circles about his qualifications for the rank, he had come to be recognized by many to be an elevated religious leader known as a *marja' al-taqlid,* meaning a source of authority whom a follower might emulate.

Sadr was a rising star in the 1990s because of his vocal criticism of the Baathists and his belief in an active seminary, a dangerous position in Iraq. He challenged the silent seminary, which was represented by the politically quietist Grand Ayatollah Ali al-Husayn al-Sistani and the other members of the *marjaiyya,* the council of Iraq's resident grand ayatollahs that sits in Najaf. Sadr took advantage of government crackdowns on the traditional Shiite seminaries in southern Iraqi cities, such as Najaf, Karbala, and Kufa, following the suppression of the 1991 Shiite and Kurdish rebellions in Iraq.

While senior clerics such as Sistani came under increasing government scrutiny and were basically placed under house arrest, Hussein's regime initially tolerated Sadr because he was seen as a potential counterweight to Sistani. A divided Iraqi Shiite community was more advantageous to the ruling Baathists than a unified one. However, by the mid-1990s Sadr had begun to take more confrontational positions vis-à-vis the government, issuing a fatwa (juridical opinion) forbidding his followers from joining the Baath Party, holding Friday prayers in defiance of a government ban, and calling for the implementation of a clerically governed Islamic state in Iraq.

Sadr was also critical of Sistani and the *marjaiyya* for remaining politically disengaged in the face of government suppression. An Iraqi native and Arab, Sadr presented himself as the native alternative for Iraqi Shiites to follow in opposition to the Iranian-born Sistani and the other members of the *marjaiyya,* all of whom were foreign born. Sadr's speeches and sermons drew tens of thousands of people, and his representatives successfully took over thousands of mosques, local religious centers, and Husseiniyyas (buildings used to commemorate the lives and martyrdom of the Shiite imams, such as the third imam Hussein).

After the assassination of Sadr in February 1999, control of his grassroots movement in Iraq was assumed by his son Muqtada al-Sadr, a low-ranking seminary student, although most of his followers took as their *marja' al-taqlid* Ayatollah Kadhim Hairi, one of Sadiq al-Sadr's best students. Hairi, however, resided in Qum, where he remains today, and thus was not well placed to assume control of Sadiq al-Sadr's movement in Iraq. For a time Muqtada al-Sadr recognized Hairi as the spiritual guide of the Sadr Movement; however, the two had a falling out in late 2003 after Hairi declined to return to Iraq.

In early April 2003 following the March U.S.- and British-led invasion of Iraq, Muqtada al-Sadr's representatives and clerical allies reopened mosques and religious centers in Sadrist strongholds in places such as the southern city of Kufa and the sprawling Shiite district known as Sadr City in eastern Baghdad. These mosques and centers form the social support base for the Sadr Movement and remain as key elements of Sadr's influence and authority. Sadr City and large swaths of southern Iraq are Sadrist strongholds, giving the movement significant popular support among the Iraqi Shiite population, which makes up an estimated 60–65 percent of Iraq's 28 million people. Despite its continued prominence, the Sadr Movement began to splinter in 2005. Ayatollah Muhammad Yaqubi and Mahmoud Sarkhi al-Hassani, two former students of Sadiq al-Sadr, broke away from the movement and formed their own sociopolitical groups. Yaqubi created the Fadhila (Islamic Virtue) Party, and Hassani formed a smaller movement popular among more messianic Iraqi Shiites who await the return of the Twelfth Shia Imam, Muhammad al-Mahdi.

The Mahdi Army was formed soon after the collapse of the Iraqi government in the spring of 2003, and by the spring of 2004 its membership had swelled to an estimated 6,000–10,000 fighters, of whom a core group of 500–1,000 were highly trained. Muqtada al-Sadr has been blamed for ordering the murder of Hujjat al-Islam Abd al-Majid al-Khoi, a midlevel cleric and son of the late prominent Iraq-based grand ayatollah Abu al-Qasim al-Khoi, who was a U.S. ally; the younger Khoi was stabbed to death in a crowd in Najaf on April 10, 2003. Sadr has repeatedly denied that he was involved in the murder. Later that month Mahdi Army fighters

Members of the Mahdi Army, loyal to Shiite cleric Muqtada al-Sadr, guard a Shiite mosque in the Sadr City area of Baghdad, Iraq, on July 12, 2006. (AP/Wide World Photos)

surrounded the Najaf homes of Sistani and other members of the *marjaiyya,* demanding that they leave Iraq. The Mahdi Army was forced to stand down when several thousand Shiite Arab tribesmen loyal to the *marjaiyya* came to Najaf to protect the grand ayatollahs. Sadr has maintained a tenuous relationship with the grand ayatollahs and has publicly recognized their authority, although he may simply be paying them lip service.

Sadr ordered the Mahdi Army into the streets in April 2004 after the Coalition Provisional Authority (CPA), the U.S.-dominated governing body headed by L. Paul Bremer that ran Iraq from 2003 to June 28, 2005, closed the offices of the main Sadrist newspaper, *al-Hawza,* and pressured an Iraqi court to indict Sadr and several of his aides for the murder of Khoi. Fighting between the Mahdi Army and coalition forces continued until early June, when a tenuous cease-fire was negotiated.

Heavy fighting between the two sides began again on August 3, 2005, when U.S. and Iraqi forces tried to arrest Sadr. The fighting lasted until August 25, when Sistani, who had recently returned to Iraq after undergoing medical treatment in Great Britain, brokered a cease-fire. During the height of the fighting,

Sadr and several hundred of his supporters took over Najaf's Shrine of Imam Ali, a revered Shiite holy site where the first imam is buried. The old city of Najaf was heavily damaged in the fighting. After meeting with Sistani on August 25, Sadr and his armed supporters left the shrine compound and turned over its keys to Sistani's representatives.

Following the December 2005 national elections, the Sadr Movement gained control of four ministries and reportedly infiltrated branches of the security services with Mahdi Army militiamen, who were accused of carrying out attacks on Sadr's rivals and Sunni Arabs. Despite such allegations, Sadr remained the most popular Iraqi Shiite leader with Sunni Iraqis, many of whom respected and admired his resistance to continued U.S. and British occupation. His crossover popularity, however, was shattered following the February 22, 2006, bombing of the revered Shiite Askari shrine in Samarra. Mahdi Army militiamen and other rogue elements, some of them former members of his movement, ignored instructions from Sadr not to carry out random revenge attacks and instead attacked Sunni mosques and murdered Sunni religious leaders and random passersby in retaliation.

The ensuing descent of Iraq into a virtual civil war has made it more difficult to determine which elements are truly a part of the Sadr Movement and the Mahdi Army, whose membership reportedly has swelled to some 60,000 according to the Iraq Study Group report. Many groups that are carrying out sectarian killings are thought to be led by former Mahdi Army commanders who were expelled from the movement or even individuals who have never been Mahdi Army members but use its name to carry out extortion and kidnappings for ransom. The real Mahdi Army and the Sadr Movement, although initially supportive of Iraqi prime minister Nuri al-Maliki, began to face government-led attacks in April 2008 when Iraqi forces and U.S. aircraft attacked Mahdi Army positions in the southern port city of Basra. These assaults were reportedly spearheaded by Iraqi Army and police units dominated by the Supreme Islamic Iraqi Council, headed by Sadr's chief Shiite rival, Abd al-Aziz al-Hakim. The attacks are believed to have been an attempt to damage the Sadrists' political chances in provincial elections set for 2009.

The Mahdi Army and the Supreme Council's paramilitary wing, the Badr Corps, have engaged in running gun battles since 2005, with a large-scale battle between the two occurring in Karbala in January 2008 during Ashura religious processions. Despite these attacks, in early May 2008 Sadr announced the six-month renewal of a 2007 cease-fire agreement between the Sadr Movement and the Iraqi government. He ordered his supporters not to engage in violence and instead requested that they focus on grassroots nonviolent political protests against the continued occupation of Iraq.

Christopher Anzalone

**See also**

Baath Party; Badr Organization; Fadhila Party; Fayyad, Muhammad Ishaq al-; Hakim, Abd al-Aziz al-; Hakim, Muhammad Baqir al-; Iraq, History to 1990; Iraq, History of, 1990–Present; Maliki, Nuri

Muhammed Kamil Hasan al-; Sadr, Muqtada al-; Shia Islam; Sunni Islam; Supreme Iraqi Islamic Council

## References

Cockburn, Patrick. *Muqtada: Muqtada al-Sadr, the Shia Revival, and the Struggle for Iraq.* New York: Scribner, 2008.

Cole, Juan. "The United States and Shi'ite Religious Factions in Post-Ba'athist Iraq." *Middle East Journal* 57 (2003): 543–566.

Jabar, Faleh A. *The Shi'ite Movement in Iraq.* London: Saqi Books, 2003.

Nakash, Yitzhak. *Reaching for Power: The Shi'a in the Modern Arab World.* Princeton, NJ: Princeton University Press, 2006.

Visser, Reidar. *The Sadrists of Basra and the Far South of Iraq: The Most Unpredictable Political Force in the Gulf's Oil-Belt Region?* Oslo: Norwegian Institute of International Affairs, 2008.

# Mahmoud, Salah Aboud
## Birth Date: ca. 1950

Iraqi military officer who led the Khafji offensive during the 1991 Persian Gulf War and was part of the delegation that negotiated the end of the war with the Americans in February 1991. Salah Aboud Mahmoud was born in Baghdad, probably in 1950, to a Sunni Arab family. Like many Iraqis from modest background, he joined the army. He rose to prominence in the latter stages of the 1980–1988 Iran-Iraq War, when Iraq had begun to seize the initiative with offensive operations at Fao and other areas to solicit Iranian responses that were then successfully met with Iraqi infantry, artillery, and mechanized units. Mahmoud acquitted himself admirably in these operations and was promoted to brigadier general and then to major general. His military career was exceptional in a regime in which political ties based on family, tribe, and region were essential to advancement; instead, he rose on the basis of his achievements alone.

In 1990 Mahmoud, now a lieutenant general, commanded the Iraqi III Corps, a key part of the invasion force that stormed into Kuwait on August 2, 1990. Mahmoud was then charged with the attack at Khafji, near the border with Saudi Arabia. As it turned out, it was the only organized Iraq offensive of the entire Persian Gulf War. With recent Iraqi artillery shelling Khafji civilians had already evacuated, but a Saudi National Guard force remained. Iraqi president Saddam Hussein visited Basra to discuss the Khafji offensive with Mahmoud. The Khafji attack was part of a wider Iraqi offensive into Saudi Arabia designed to inflict casualties and encourage opposition to the war there.

On January 29, 1991, Mahmoud's forces, made up of two mechanized divisions and an armored division, successfully drove off Saudi forces, but American troops from the 1st Marine Division stopped the offensive cold, although Khafji remained in Iraqi hands. On January 31, 1991, Saudi and Qatari forces retook the town, aided substantially by coalition air strikes. Given the losses endured, Mahmoud asked several times for permission from Baghdad to withdraw but was refused. Despite his orders, he could

not achieve a victory, and on February 1, 12 hours from his first communication with Baghdad, he ended the putative offensive. The Iraqis suffered heavy casualties during their retreat when they came under heavy and prolonged air attack.

After the retreat from Khafji, Mahmoud was ordered to Baghdad to account for his failure. Meanwhile, what was left of his corps was assigned to protect an air force base at Jaber, Kuwait. When the allied ground offensive began, the 1st U.S. Marine Division was tasked with taking that base, and on February 25 Mahmoud employed two of his brigades to attack the flanks of the marine division as it approached. Although unsuccessful, the counterattacks marked Mahmoud as one of the more competent Iraqi military commanders in an officer corps awash with mediocrities.

Mahmoud ordered a withdrawal early on the morning of February 26, and until February 28 Iraqi troops were subjected to air attacks along Highway 6 to Basra, the so-called Highway of Death. Mahmoud's force, already reduced by the Khafji offensive, was further degraded during its rapid retreat from Kuwait. When Baghdad agreed to truce terms, Mahmoud, along with General Sultan Hashim Ahmad, the deputy chief of staff at the Defense Ministry, made up the Iraqi delegation that negotiated with coalition commander U.S. General H. Norman Schwarzkopf and Saudi Prince Khalid ibn Sultan al-Saud. Ahmad and Mahmoud ultimately agreed to terms that set conditions for the peace, allowed for prisoner transfers, and permitted the Iraqis to continue to fly helicopters in what were otherwise no-fly zones.

After the war Mahmoud was cycled out as commander of III Corps, a regular process in the Hussein regime to ensure that officers did not retain commands too long lest they pose a threat to the regime. Mahmoud was later made governor of Dhi Qar, a predominantly Shia province in southern Iraq, that in 1991 briefly fell to the Shiite insurgency before it was brutally suppressed. In December 1994 when Iraqi major general Wafiq as-Samarrai defected to Jordan and called on a number of officers to revolt, Mahmoud's name was listed among those being asked to defect. Still other officers, as well as Hussein's two sons-in-law, defected. Despite Mahmoud's connection to many of the purged and defected officers, he was not executed, although he was cycled out of his governorate and other positions, likely because of Samarrai's statements.

In 1998 Hussein created four administrative regions for Iraq and appointed naval commander Mizban Khidher Hadi as the governor of the Central Euphrates Region. In late March 2003 at the time of the Anglo-American–led invasion, many in the Iraqi leadership believed that Mahmoud would be recalled to duty and appointed to the Central Euphrates governorship after Mizban was dismissed, but Mizban was reinstated before this could occur. Mahmoud's fate and whereabouts after 2003 remain unknown.

MICHAEL K. BEAUCHAMP

**See also**

DESERT STORM, Operation, Ground Operations; Hussein, Saddam; Iran-Iraq War; Khafji, Battle of; Schwarzkopf, H. Norman, Jr.

**References**

Khalid ibn Sultan, Prince, with Patrick Seale. *Desert Warrior: A Personal View of the Gulf War by the Joint Forces Commander.* New York: HarperCollins, 1995.

Morris, David J. *Storm on the Horizon: Khafji, the Battle That Changed the Course of the Gulf War.* New York: Free Press, 2004.

Schwarzkopf, H. Norman, with Peter Petre. *It Doesn't Take a Hero: General H. Norman Schwarzkopf, the Autobiography.* New York: Bantam Books, 1993.

---

# Majid al Tikriti, Ali Hassan al-

**Birth Date: 1941**
**Death Date: January 25, 2010**

High-ranking Iraqi government official, minister of defense (1993–1995), cousin of Baath Party leader and Iraqi dictator Saddam Hussein, and known as "Chemical Ali" because of his role in the use of chemical weapons to suppress ethnic uprisings by the Kurds and Shiites. Ali Hassan al-Majid al Tikriti was born sometime in 1941 in Tikrit to a relatively modest family.

Majid, along with many others from Tikrit, joined the Baath Party in 1958 and enlisted in the Iraqi Army that same year. He was arrested during the 1963 coup when Colonel Abd al-Salam Arif seized power and moved against the Baathists. After the Baath Party seized power in 1968, Majid rose steadily within the party ranks, along with his cousin Saddam Hussein and many other men from Tikrit, a number of them interrelated. This cadre formed the base of Hussein's power, as all were family members or members of the same tribe, people whom he could trust. By 1978 Majid headed the Regional Secretariat Office of the Baath Party. That same year, after graduating from the National Defense Academy, he was appointed to the Military Bureau.

When Hussein became president of Iraq in 1979, replacing Ahmad al-Hassan Bakr, Majid's star continued to rise. In 1982 he became a member of the Regional Command. After an assassination attempt on Hussein in 1983, Majid was charged with punishing those connected—even tangentially—with the attempt. During 1984–1987 he was the director-general of internal security, making him a key part of Hussein's security apparatus that ensured the survival and continuation of the regime.

In 1987 Hussein appointed Majid governor of the northern bureau, which included Kurdistan in northern Iraq. By 1987, with the pressures of the Iran-Iraq War weighing heavily upon Baghdad, the security situation in northern Iraq was seen as very precarious, with a growing Kurdish resistance movement distracting the government from the war effort against Iran. To bring an end to the Kurdish insurgency, Majid ordered civilian Kurds to be attacked using chemical weapons, including mustard gas and sarin. One attack on Halabja resulted in more than 5,000 deaths, leading to the sobriquet of "Chemical Ali." Following the Halabja massacre, Majid oversaw an Arabization campaign in Anfal that involved the forced transfer of Kurdish populations and the continued use of chemical weapons to break the Kurdish resistance.

In 1989 Majid became minister of local administration, a position designed to oversee the repopulation with Arabs of the areas that he had depopulated in Kurdistan in his last posting. After the invasion of Kuwait in August 1990 Majid was made governor of Kuwait, in which position he oversaw the organized Iraqi looting and sacking of the nation and the elimination of opposition to Iraqi rule.

With the 1991 Persian Gulf War and the Shiite rebellion centered in Basra against the regime, Hussein placed Majid in charge of the southern forces to put down the insurgency, which he did with brute force. In 1991 Majid became a member of the Revolutionary Command Council. He served as minister of the interior during 1991–1993, and from 1993 to 1995 he headed the Ministry of Defense. These appointments to key security posts clearly illustrated Hussein's trust in Majid, but the constant shifts in assignments also revealed Hussein's paranoid nature. No official served in any key military or security post for long, lest he come to pose a threat to the regime. Rotation in office was a key element of Hussein's modus operandi, even if the rotation occurred among a limited elite.

In 1995 Majid was removed from office for allegedly having traded with Iran, but in 1998 he reemerged to govern the southern portion of Iraq, where government power was limited because of the no-fly zone established by the allies after the Persian Gulf War. Shortly before the Iraq War began in March 2003, Hussein divided the nation into four administrative areas, with Majid having charge of the southern portion. During the American-led invasion, Majid was reportedly killed in an air raid on Basra, but this proved false. Indeed, he was arrested on August 17, 2003, and handed over to Iraqi authorities to be put on trial on charges of crimes against humanity and genocide arising from his campaign against the Kurds. During the trial Majid was unapologetic, arguing that his actions had been approved by the legitimate Iraqi government and that he was simply carrying out orders. On June 24, 2007, an Iraqi court found Majid guilty. The court gave him five death sentences. A series of judicial and political hurdles delayed the sentence from being carried out until January 25, 2010, when Majid was executed by hanging.

MICHAEL K. BEAUCHAMP

**See also**

Baath Party; Chemical Weapons and Warfare; Hussein, Saddam; Iran-Iraq War; Iraq, History of, Pre-1990; Iraq, History of, 1990–Present; Kurds; Kurds, Massacres of

**References**

Aburish, Said K. *Saddam Hussein: The Politics of Revenge.* New York: Bloomsbury, 2000.

Cleveland, William L. *A History of the Modern Middle East.* 3rd ed. Boulder, CO: Westview, 2004.

Khalil, Samir al-. *Republic of Fear: The Politics of Modern Iraq.* Berkeley: University of California Press, 1989.

## Major, John Roy
### Birth Date: March 29, 1943

British Conservative Party politician and prime minister (1990–1997). Born in Carshalton, London, on March 29, 1943, John Major was christened John Roy Major. He used the middle name until the early 1980s, although his birth certificate does not include the name Roy. His father was a former circus performer who also ran a business selling garden gnomes, and in 1955 the family moved to Brixton where Major, after leaving school at age 16, managed to obtain a job as a clerk for an insurance broker. He then secured a position with the London Electricity Board and began a correspondence course to study banking, joining the Standard Chartered Bank in May 1965. Two years later he was sent to Nigeria for business, and by this time he had become active in politics as a supporter of the Conservative Party. He contested the two general elections in 1974, and in 1979 he won the seat for Huntingdonshire (later Huntingdon, after boundary changes) in Parliament. In that election Margaret Thatcher was elected prime minister, and the Conservatives began a long tenure in power.

Major held a number of minor positions in the government, entering the cabinet in 1987 as chief secretary to the Treasury. Two years later he became foreign secretary but was in the post for only three months before becoming chancellor of the Exchequer, presenting the budget in 1990.

When the Iraqi invasion of Kuwait occurred in August 1990, the British government under Thatcher was one of the strongest supporters of the deposed emir of Kuwait. Soon after the invasion but unconnected with events in the Middle East, Thatcher's leadership of the party was challenged by Michael Heseltine, a longtime rival. After she came just short of securing the party's leadership in the first ballot she withdrew, and Major stood in the second round, winning the top post easily and becoming leader of the Conservative Party on November 27, 1990. The following day he was appointed prime minister. The British were already closely involved in Operation DESERT SHIELD, the preparations that led to Operation DESERT STORM.

Major's humble origins, along with his quintessential Englishness, made him a popular figure in Britain, although this tended not to go over so well in Scotland and Wales. There was no doubt that Major would support the international coalition against Iraq, for which he had support from the opposition Labour Party, but in his memoirs he noted two serious reservations about the war. The first was the strength of Iraqi forces, and the second was whether the Iraqis would employ chemical and/or biological weapons. The British hoped that the Iraqis might withdraw from Kuwait without an armed confrontation and repeatedly urged them to do so.

Conservative Party politician John Major replaced Margaret Thatcher as British prime minister in the midst of the Persian Gulf crisis in 1990 and remained prime minister until 1997. (Corel)

After diplomacy failed and the war began in January 1991, Major and his war cabinet met regularly to discuss the nature of the war and the possible effects of it on Britain's relations with other countries. They also debated whether or not there would be an increase in terrorism after the war was won. Major always believed that the cease-fire signed on February 28, 1991, was a "frustrating conclusion" to the war, but over the succeeding years his government continued to enforce sanctions against Iraq. In spite of the successful conclusion to the war, Major and the Conservatives were expected to lose the general election in April 1992. Nevertheless, he managed to win a narrow victory, with a majority of 21 seats.

During Major's tenure there were numerous economic crises, and there was much discussion over the role Britain should or should not play in post–Cold War Europe. There were also a number of scandals, one of which involved Minister of State for Defence Procurement Jonathan Aitken, who was accused of being involved in secret business arrangements with Saudi princes and specifically allowing an Arab businessman to pay for Aitken's stay at the Ritz Hotel in Paris. In the court case that followed Aitken was found to have lied under oath and was jailed for perjury. The event not only reflected badly on the Major government but also associated it more clearly with negative events in the Middle East.

Major gradually lost his majority in parliament through by-election defeats, and in 1997 he lost the general election to Tony Blair's Labour Party. Major remained in Parliament until 2001. In 1998 he became a member of the European Advisory Board to the Carlyle Group, a major U.S.-based private equity investment firm, and he as well as former president George H. W. Bush, former secretary of state James A. Baker III, and others were at the Ritz-Carlton Hotel in Washington, D.C., in 2001 attending meetings of the Carlyle Group when the September 11 attacks on the World Trade Center and the Pentagon took place. Major is a sought-after speaker, and in December 2006 he called upon Parliament to launch an independent investigation of Prime Minister Blair's motives for participating in the March 2003 invasion of Iraq.

JUSTIN J. CORFIELD

**See also**

Blair, Tony; DESERT SHIELD, Operation; DESERT STORM, Operation; Thatcher, Margaret; United Kingdom, Middle East Policy

**References**

Dorey, Peter, ed. *The Major Premiership: Politics and Policies under John Major, 1990–97.* New York: St. Martin's, 1999.

Major, John. *The Autobiography.* London: HarperCollins, 1999.

Seldon, Anthony, and Lewis Baston. *Major: A Political Life.* London: Weidenfeld and Nicolson, 1997.

# Makiya, Kanan

*See* Khalil, Samir al-

# Makkawi, Muhammad Ibrahim

*See* Adl, Sayf al-

# Maliki, Nuri Muhammed Kamil Hasan al-
## Birth Date: June 20, 1950

Iraqi political leader and prime minister since May 20, 2006. For many years, Nuri Muhammed Kamil Hasan al-Maliki was a leader of the Islamic Dawa Party, an Islamist organization that was ruthlessly suppressed by former Iraqi president Saddam Hussein. He remains the secretary-general of the party. Until 2006, Maliki was known by the pseudonym "Jawad," which he adopted while in exile in Syria.

Maliki was born in Abi Gharq, Iraq, near Karbala, on June 20, 1950. He received a bachelor's degree at the Usul al-Din College in Baghdad and a master's degree in Arabic literature at Salahaddin University in Sulamaniyah. It was during his college years that he became politically active and joined the Islamic Dawa Party in 1968, steadily rising in the organization's hierarchy. Maliki represents the jihadist faction within the party.

When Iraqi president Saddam Hussein cracked down on the Dawa Party in the 1970s, its members were sentenced to death, even in absentia. Maliki was forced to flee Iraq in October 1979. Fleeing through Jordan, he first traveled to Syria and remained there until 1982, when he moved to Iran. He resided for a year in Ahwaz and then moved to Tehran. In September 1989, he returned to Damascus. He remained in Syria until the fall of Saddam's government in April 2003.

While in Syria, Maliki supervised the Dawa Party's publication, *Al-Mawqif,* and became the head of the organization in Damascus and in Lebanon, participating in the Iraqi opposition coalition known as the Joint Action Committee in 1990. He toured the Middle East and Europe to solicit support for the Iraqi opposition movement and convened an important conference representing the various Iraqi opposition groups held in Beirut in 1991.

On his return to Iraq in 2003, Maliki served in various positions in the new Iraqi interim government; he was named to the National Council, headed the security committee of the transitional Iraqi National Assembly, and was then elected to the new National Assembly, where he served on the National Sovereignty Committee. He also became the chief spokesperson and negotiator for the alliance of the various Shia parties and groups known as the United Islamic Alliance during the drafting of the new Iraqi constitution.

When Ibrahim al-Jafari, Iraq's first prime minister, was unable to obtain support from the United States and certain Iraqi groups, Maliki was nominated as prime minister. He took office on May 20, 2006; he also served as the acting minister of the interior until June 2006.

Iraq's prime minister–designate Nuri al-Maliki during a news conference in Baghdad on May 9, 2006. Maliki was officially sworn in as the country's new prime minister on May 20. (AP/Wide World Photos)

Maliki has been described by Iraq experts as a pragmatic individual who represents the Arab-Iraqi-centered orientation of the Dawa Party and is not overly influenced by Iran. However, it has been difficult for Iraqi officials to steer clear of pressure from the United States and to deal with sectarian and party loyalties in the context of intersectarian fighting, which has further delayed reestablishing stability in Iraq. U.S. senator Carl Levin (D-Mich.), chairman of the Senate Armed Services Committee, attacked the Maliki government in August 2007 for being "too beholden to religious and sectarian leaders." At the same time, Senator Hillary Clinton (D-N.Y.) charged that Maliki was too "divisive" a figure. Yet, his political skills have been demonstrated, certainly prior to his assuming the office of prime minister, in his generally good working relationships with various opposition parties. These relationships were strained later, in part because of the tension between Washington's and Baghdad's differing goals and priorities.

Under the Maliki government, the U.S. military has forged new alliances with Sunni tribal elements to defeat Al Qaeda in Iraq and other Sunni insurgency groups and has urged measures to reverse de-Baathification, causing concerns among Iraqi Shiites. A point of controversy has been legislation regarding the sharing of oil revenues, resisted by Sunni and Kurdish leaders. A major Maliki triumph, however, was passage of the Status of Forces Agreement of December 2008.

On these issues, Maliki has been responsive to Iraqi concerns and has consistently called for a definite time frame for a U.S. troop withdrawal, despite various American warnings that setting a withdrawal date is unwise. The United States has reportedly monitored all of Maliki's and other Iraqi government leaders' communications, perhaps because of these differences.

Maliki has also had to deal with inter-Shiite tensions, such as when the Fadhila Party withdrew its representatives from the Shiite coalition in 2007 and when he responded to pressures to counter the power of the Mahdi Army of Muqtada al-Sadr and the Badr organization/militia. Indeed, he moved against the latter two in 2008. In November 2008, tensions with the Kurds expressed itself in directives made to the Peshmerga forces.

SHERIFA ZUHUR

Badr Organization; Iraq, History of, 1990–Present; Islamic Dawa Party; Mahdi Army; Sadr, Muqtada al-; Status of Forces Agreement, U.S.-Iraqi

**References**

Raghvan, Sudarsan. "Maliki's Impact Blunted by Own Party's Fears: Hussein-Era Secrecy Persists, Analysts Say." *Washington Post*, August 3, 2007, A-01.

Shanahan, Rodger. "The Islamic Da'wa Party: Past Development and Future Prospects." *Middle East Review of International Affairs* 8(2) (June 2004): 112–125.

Woodward, Bob. *The War Within: A Secret White House History, 2006–2008.* New York: Simon and Schuster, 2008.

Zuhur, Sherifa. *Iran, Iraq and the United States: The New Triangle's Impact on Sectarianism and the Nuclear Threat.* Carlisle Barracks, PA: Strategic Studies Institute, 2006.

---

# Mandates

System of administration of the former German overseas colonies in Africa and Asia and territories of the Ottoman Empire in the Middle East after World War I (1914–1918). The mandates were established under the aegis of the League of Nations, the predecessor to the United Nations (UN). Early in the war, the Ottoman Empire joined the Central Powers. By the end of the war, British Empire forces had driven the Ottoman Army from Mesopotamia, Palestine, and Syria.

Following the war, the disposition of these occupied territories became an international issue. U.S. president Woodrow Wilson, who held a strong bargaining position at the 1919 Paris Peace Conference, refused to allow the distribution and outright annexation of colonial territory by the victorious powers. The peoples of the Middle East sought independence, but the leaders of Britain and France did not believe this was feasible.

To resolve the matter, the conferees at Paris created the mandate system in Article 22 of the Covenant of the League of Nations. Colonial areas acquired from Germany and the Ottoman Empire would thus be in a transitional status until the people of these territories "could stand by themselves." These territories were entrusted to certain victor states until such time as they were deemed ready for independence. Mandates were divided into three categories: Class-A mandates (the former Ottoman territories in the Middle East); Class-B mandates (mostly in Tropical Africa); and Class-C mandates (those territories of Southwest Africa and the Pacific). The local populations in Class-A mandates were to have a higher degree of autonomy, whereas those in Class-C would have the least autonomy. A Permanent Mandates Commission (PMC) was established within the League of Nations machinery to examine the annual administration reports submitted by the mandatory states and advise the League Council concerning them.

In the Class-A Middle East mandate system, France controlled Lebanon and Syria. Great Britain meanwhile took control of three mandated Class-A territories—Iraq, Transjordan (present-day Jordan), and Palestine. In Iraq and Transjordan, the British allowed some autonomy early on by placing on the throne in Iraq the Hashimite Amir Faisal, who became King Faisal I in 1921. In Transjordan, Prince Abdullah, also a son of the Sharif Hussein of Mecca and Medina, became King Abdullah I, also in 1921. The Palestine mandate was the most difficult to administer, not only because of conflicting claims of interest by both Arabs and Jews there but also because the British had sent conflicting signals to both groups over who would ultimately control the region. This tension continues to the present day. Between 1945 and 1955, the British had divested themselves of all their formal ties to the Middle East; France followed suit.

Some accused the victorious imperial powers of an overt attempt to annex the conquered territories. Others saw these developments as a denial of the right of conquest and the forerunner of decolonization. The truth probably lies somewhere in between.

The British mandate of Iraq was terminated in 1932, when Iraq became an independent state (it joined the League of Nations the same year). However, Great Britain remained influential in Iraq and intervened to crush a subsequent coup and shift of power there during World War II, in 1941. Outside of the formal mandate system and despite nominal independence granted in 1922, Britain maintained a military presence and administrative control in Egypt. Also outside the mandate system, France retained control over Algeria, Tunisia, and Morocco, where the Spanish also held a colony until the 1970s; Italy controlled Libya.

Independence that had been pledged to the Middle Eastern mandates was put off due to World War II. Early in that conflict, the Axis powers sought to stir up nationalist sentiment in

**Decolonization of the Middle East and North Africa**

| Country | Received Independence on | Received Independence from |
|---|---|---|
| Algeria | July 5, 1962 | France |
| Bahrain | August 15, 1971 | Britain |
| Egypt | February 28, 1922 | Britain |
| Iraq | October 3, 1932 | Britain (League of Nations mandate) |
| Israel | May 14, 1948 | Britain (League of Nations mandate) |
| Jordan | May 25, 1946 | Britain (League of Nations mandate) |
| Kuwait | June 19, 1961 | Britain |
| Lebanon | November 22, 1943 | France (League of Nations mandate) |
| Libya | December 24, 1951 | United Nations Trusteeship |
| Morocco | March 2, 1956 | France |
| Qatar | September 3, 1971 | Britain |
| Syria | April 17, 1946 | France (League of Nations mandate) |
| Tunisia | March 20, 1956 | France |
| United Arab Emirates | December 2, 1971 | Britain |

the region. Germany also supplied arms to Iraqi nationalists, the government of Vichy France having provided permission for their shipment through Lebanon and Syria. This led the British to intervene militarily in both Lebanon and Syria. At the end of the war there was some violence, as both Syria and Lebanon secured their independence.

Increased Jewish migration into Palestine, meanwhile, led to tensions and outright violence between Arabs and Jews in that British mandate in the 1930s. London soon found itself caught in a three-way war among the British Army, Arabs, and Jews. The inability to work out a political arrangement satisfactory to the two sides led to a precipitous British abandonment of their mandate in Palestine in 1948. This decision brought a declaration of independence by the Jews of Palestine and the first Arab-Israeli war.

TOHMATSU HARUO

**See also**

Article 22 of the League of Nations Covenant; France, Middle East Policy; Iraq, History to 1990; Jordan; Lebanon; Syria; United Kingdom, Middle East Policy

**References**

Crozier, Andrew J. *Appeasement and Germany's Last Bid for Colonies.* London: Macmillan, 1988.

Hall, H. Duncan. *Mandates, Dependencies, and Trusteeship.* New York: Carnegie Endowment for Peace, 1948.

Khoury, Philip S. *Syria and the French Mandate: The Politics of Arab Nationalism.* Princeton, NJ: Princeton University Press, 1989.

Smuts, Jan Christian. *The League of Nations: A Practical Suggestion.* London: Hodder and Stoughton, 1918.

Wright, Quincy. *Mandates under the League of Nations.* Chicago: Chicago University Press, 1930.

## Marsh Arabs

Indigenous people, known as the Madan (Ma'dan), who have traditionally inhabited the marshlands in southern Iraq (hence "Marsh Arabs"). The Marsh Arabs have a unique seminomadic 5,000-year-old waterborne culture, derived from the ancient Sumerians and Babylonians. They live in the marshy lowlands of southern Iraq in the disputed border area near the Iranian border (historically known as Persia), an area also known as the Tigris-Euphrates alluvial salt marsh and Hawizeh. They are ethnically Arab and are Shiite Muslim, the majority religious group in Iraq. Although the marshes provided a refuge from persecution by the Sunni Muslim Ottoman Turks, the Persians, and the British, the wetlands did not insulate the Marsh Arabs from the Iran-Iraq War (1980–1988), Iraqi president Saddam Hussein's wrath following

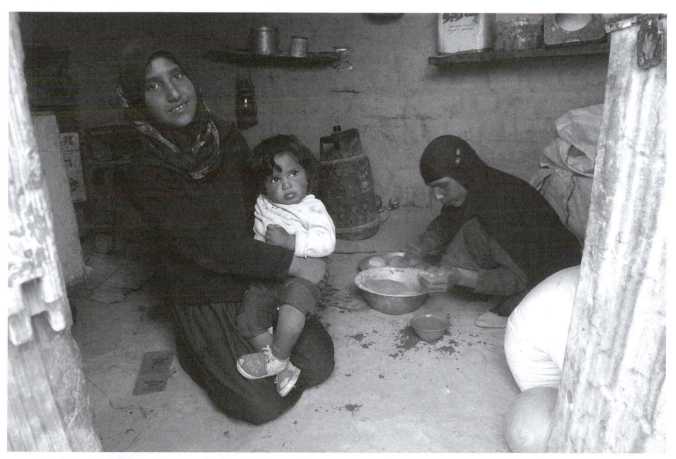

A Marsh Arab family inside their home in southern Iraq. Humanitarian groups characterized Iraqi president Saddam Hussein's repression of the Marsh Arabs as a crime against humanity. (AP/Wide World Photos)

his defeat in the 1991 Persian Gulf War, or the 10 years of United Nations (UN) economic sanctions that followed.

At the beginning of the Iran-Iraq War, there were 250,000–500,000 Marsh Arabs inhabiting approximately 7,700 square miles of wetlands. That conflict saw great pressure on the Marsh Arabs and their numbers plummeted. The subsequent Persian Gulf War had removed Hussein's forces from Kuwait, but U.S. president George H. W. Bush also encouraged an internal revolt against Hussein. The Marsh Arabs joined the resultant short-lived Shiite uprising in southern Iraq. It lasted for just a month, during March 1991.

Hussein brutally crushed the rebellion. Also, starting in the 1950s, British engineers working for the Iraqi government planned and began carrying out a project to build embanked canals that would concentrate the water of the Tigris and the Euphrates rivers and reclaim the water of the marshes, so as not to waste it. The project, which began in 1953, was reenergized during the Iran-Iraq War. The problems with the project are both ecological and social, since the Iraqi government was essentially forcing the Madan from their homelands, apparently for political purposes. The destruction of the wetlands' rich biodiversity drastically reduced the Marsh Arabs' primary food sources (rice, barley, wheat, pearl millet, fish, sheep, and cattle) as well as the reeds used to create their boats and homes. By 1993, about two-thirds of the rivers waters had been diverted from the marshes into the constructed Third Waterway. The Marsh Arabs' sources of income were sharply curtailed, and the desertification decimated the Marsh Arabs' commercial fisheries.

Between 1991 and 2000 or so, many Marsh Arabs were killed and many others fled to Iran or to other Shiite areas within Iraq, leaving approximately 40,000 of the original Marsh Arab population in their ancestral region. By 2001, the United Nations Environment Program (UNEP) estimated that Hussein's efforts had reduced the marshes to no more than 386 square miles. Hussein and his supporters asserted that the diversion was not intended to destroy the Madan people and culture. Rather, they argued that the draining of the marshes was intended to make rich oil reserves more accessible and to create new agricultural opportunities for an impoverished region.

The American- and British-led March 2003 invasion of Iraq that ousted Hussein and overthrew Iraq's Sunni-led Baathist government (Operation IRAQI FREEDOM) was followed by a planned restoration of the marshes. This was aided initially by the ending of a four-year drought in 2003 and the destruction of Hussein's diversion dams by the Marsh Arabs. By 2007, the marshes had been restored to approximately 50 percent of their area prior to the wars. The restoration of Madan culture and the resettlement of the region by the indigenous population has been slow and fitful, however, hindered by the continuing conflict in Iraq, growing tensions with Iran, and the vastly reduced number of Marsh Arabs.

RICHARD M. EDWARDS

**See also**

DESERT STORM, Operation; Hussein, Saddam; IRAQI FREEDOM, Operation; Shatt al-Arab Waterway; Shia Islam; Sunni Islam

**References**

Brown, Sarah Graham. *Sanctioning Saddam: The Politics of Intervention in Iraq.* London: I. B. Tauris, 1999.

Coughlin, Con. *Saddam: His Rise and Fall.* New York: Harper Perennial, 2005.

Hiro, Dilip. *The Longest War: The Iran-Iraq Military Conflict.* London: Routledge, 1991.

Ochsenschlager, Edward L. *Iraq's Marsh Arabs in the Garden of Eden.* Philadelphia: University of Pennsylvania Museum Publication, 2004.

Thesiger, Wilfred. *The Marsh Arabs.* 2nd rev. ed. London: HarperCollins, 1985.

# Martyrdom

The act of dying for principles or a particular cause, usually religious. The term is derived from the Greek *martys,* meaning "witness," and was first used in a religious context in reference to the apostles of Jesus Christ, who were "witnesses" of the life and deeds of Jesus, although the idea of death and suffering for religious beliefs appears earlier in Egyptian, Hindu, and Mesopotamian faiths.

Martyrdom acquired its current usage in the Western, Christian world in the early Christian period, when Christians were being persecuted by authorities of the Roman Empire. Those killed for upholding their beliefs were called martyrs, their acceptance of death being considered a testimony of their faith. Some Christian martyrs sought out and welcomed martyrdom as a means of emulating Jesus' willingness to be sacrificed on the cross. Judaism does not connect martyrdom to the idea of witnessing faith but rather refers to it as sanctification of the name of God, or *kiddush ha-Shem.* In both Christianity and Judaism, martyrdom refers to a case in which the believer accepts death rather than denies or changes his or her religious beliefs.

In Islam, martyrdom (*shuhada*) or becoming a martyr for the faith (*istishhad*) is connected to the concept of declaring or witnessing Islam and to struggle for the sake of Islam (*jihad*). The most important Qur'anic verse usually connected with martyrdom is 4:69: "Whosoever obeys Allah, and the Messenger—they are with those whom God has blessed, Prophets, just men, martyrs [*shuhada*], the righteous; the best of company are they!" According to Islam, martyrs are not questioned after death by the two angels Munkar and Nakir, bypass purgatory, and do not require the intercession of the Prophet to proceed to paradise, as they are free of sin. Martyrs can serve as intercessors for others and are buried in the clothes they die in and not washed after death.

In the early period of Islam, martyrdom referred to those Muslims killed in battle against the armies of Mecca, for example at the Battle of Uhud, and to 11 of the Shia imams. Today, the term also refers to suicide attackers who believe they are defending the cause of Islam. A true martyr (*shahid*) is, according to doctrine, one who does not seek his own death deliberately but accepts it and is granted religious legitimacy and assured a place in heaven. However, suicide committed for personal reasons is prohibited by

Islamic law and may be punished by an endless repetition of the same form of death in hell.

Present-day Islamic terrorist organizations alluded to the concept of martyrdom when they began using suicide attacks as a tactic. This was not a new phenomenon but both a revival of an ancient tradition dating back to the early wars of Islam and an adaptation of the discourse of radical Islamic leaders who believed that martyrdom was inevitable for those struggling in the Islamic cause.

Suicide attacks provide two significant advantages over standard attacks. First, if successful, they are tactically and logistically easier to execute, because no escape route or retreat is needed, and they are therefore more efficient. Second, they provide a shock to the enemy that goes beyond the actual casualty figure, as they suggest great vulnerability and further probable use of this tactic. Third, they provide a martyr symbol that makes recruiting new members for the organization an easier task by strengthening the ideology behind a group's agenda. The fact that the martyr is willing to commit suicide is used by the group as "testimony" and "evidence" of the worthiness of its cause.

Terrorist suicide attacks in contemporary times began outside the Middle East, in Sri Lanka by Tamil separatists. Much used there, it has no connection with Islamic ideology and demonstrated only the resolve of the attackers. Claims of martyrdom, however, were made for those killed in demonstrations against the Iranian government prior to the Islamic Revolution. Suicide attacks were not used in that revolution, however. Suicide attacks that involved claims of martyrdom did occur in Syria in the late 1970s and early 1980s in battles between Islamic groups and the Syrian government in Damascus, Hama, and Homs.

The term "martyr" was used in the Lebanese civil war by both Christians and Muslims. The connection between martyrdom and suicide attacks came with the Islamic resistance, which responded to the Israeli invasion and occupation of Lebanon in 1982. These actions were undertaken by only a few, but some of the large attacks launched in 1983, as by Islamic Jihad against the U.S. Marines and barracks and French forces, were truck bombings involving suicide.

Much of the present-day discussion of martyrdom comes out of the War on Terror. This depends on one's point of view. Thus Americans note suicide bomber attacks in Iraq, while some Iraqis style such events as martyrdom operations and part of the resistance against the occupation.

A long-standing discussion of martyrdom in acts of resistance also arose among Palestinians opposing Israeli occupation of what

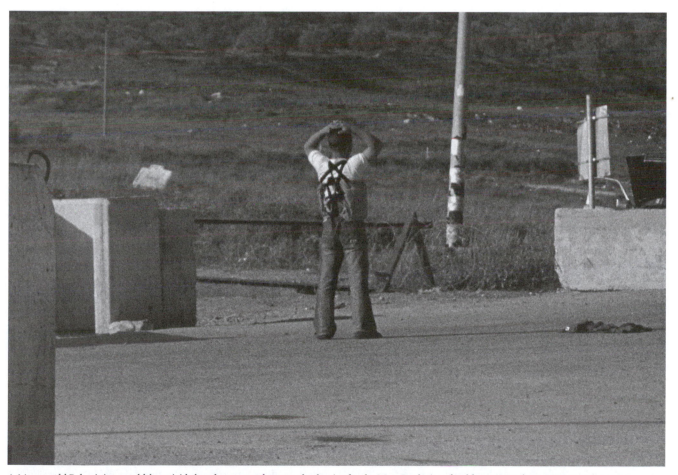

A 14-year-old Palestinian would-be suicide bomber surrenders at a checkpoint for the West Bank city of Nablus on March 24, 2004. Israeli troops arrested the boy before he could detonate his explosive belt. (FLASH 90/Reuters/Corbis)

they perceive to be their homeland. Those killed in all stages of the resistance to Israel—but particularly those active in political movements—have been referred to by most Palestinians as martyrs. Suicide attacks began to be employed in the Palestinian-Israeli struggle in 1994 and were at the time very controversial among Palestinians. Were these necessary acts of desperation or a bona fide tactic in a war of the weak? That question led to discussions among religious leaders that only expanded after the September 11 Al Qaeda terrorist attacks on the United States. Although these later were largely condemned by Muslim leaders, Palestinian suicide attacks were not, because of the conditions of the Israeli occupation and collective punishment and other tactics employed by the Israeli government. Sheikh Qaradawi, a popular Egyptian preacher who now lives in Qatar, has pronounced those who engage in such attacks in Palestine to be reacting under defensive jihad, justified by the Qur'an.

Some prominent Muslim religious leaders have given their public support for various types of martyrdom. Iranian leader Ayatollah Ruhollah Khomeini approved self-sacrifice by Iranian troops and citizens during the war against Iraq (1980–1988), when these forces, which included civilian volunteers, were forced to advance in human wave assaults against Iraqi defensive fire, in what would have to be classified as suicidal attacks. Other organizations that adopted the suicide/martyr method for attacks include Al Qaeda, Abu Sayyaf, and a Bedouin group called Tawhid wa-l Jihad by the Egyptian security services, as well as the non-Islamist al-Aqsa Martyrs Brigades. Even Al Qaeda leaders such as Sayf al-Adl indicate that they have sought to rein in the desire for suicide attacks by younger and less self-controlled members for, if such fervor were uncontrolled, there would be few operatives to run the movement.

Controversial aspects of the present-day link between jihad and martyrdom include the deaths of innocent civilian victims who are not the primary targets of such attacks. Extremist groups employing suicide attacks excuse these victims away as simply additional martyrs. There is also the issue of motivation—whether the suicide bombers are impelled to act by the wrong intent (*niyah*)—because if so, then they are not true martyrs. According to the companion of the Prophet and early caliph Umar, those waging jihad should not set out deliberately to die and become martyrs in an egotistical aim to be known as a hero. There is also a financial aspect to this, as those who engage in jihad (including those who are martyred) are enjoined not to leave their families without support or in debt. In contemporary times, would-be suicide martyrs sometimes ignore or reinterpret these rules or organizations promise to provide for their widows and families.

All of this has led to a serious effort to deradicalize by uncoupling the concepts as jihad and martyrdom within Muslim communities and by Muslim governments. While not uniform in approach and content, these attempts generally stress moderation and peaceful efforts rather than violence to change society. This task is extremely difficult where foreign occupation and military campaigns are ongoing, as in Pakistan, Afghanistan, and Iraq, but also in Saudi Arabia, where alliances with the United States are blamed for violence against Muslims.

ELLIOT P. CHODOFF AND SHERIFA ZUHUR

**See also**

Adl, Sayf al-; Al Qaeda; Fatah; Hamas; Hezbollah; Intifada, Second; Islamic Jihad, Palestinian; Jihad; Khomeini, Ruhollah; Suicide Bombings

**References**

Ayoub, Mahmoud M. *Redemptive Suffering in Islam: A Study of the Devotional Aspects of 'Ashura' in Twelver Shi'ism.* The Hague: Brill, 1978.

Gambetta, Diego, ed. *Making Sense of Suicide Missions.* Oxford: Oxford University Press, 2005.

Oliver, Anne Marie, and Paul Steinberg. *The Road to Martyrs' Square: A Journey into the World of the Suicide Bomber.* Oxford: Oxford University Press, 2005.

Shay, Shaul. *The Shahids: Islam and Suicide Attacks.* New Brunswick, NJ, and London: Transaction Publishers, 2004.

Smith, Jane I., and Yvonne Haddad. *The Islamic Understanding of Death and Resurrection.* Albany: State University of New York Press, 1981.

# Mashal, Khaled
## Birth Date: 1956

Leader of Hamas. Khaled Mashal (Mashaal, Meshal) was born in 1956 in the village of Silwad, north of Ramallah in the West Bank (then Jordan, now controlled by Israel). The son of a farmer, Mashal moved with his family to Jordan in 1967. He earned a BS degree in physics from Kuwait University. While a student there, Mashal challenged the leadership of Yasir Arafat's Fatah organization in the General Union of Palestinian Students and helped form the Islamic Haqq Bloc that competed with Fatah.

Mashal joined the Muslim Brotherhood in 1971. He taught school in Kuwait during 1978–1984. Mashal was one of the founders of the Palestinian Islamist organization known as Hamas in 1987 and has been a member of its political bureau from the beginning. He first headed its Kuwaiti branch. Mashal lived in Kuwait until 1990 when, due to the Iraqi invasion of that country, he moved to Jordan. He became the chairman of the political bureau, in effect head of Hamas, in 1996. Mashal survived an assassination attempt on September 25, 1997, carried out by the Israeli Mossad special operations service and ordered by Prime Minister Benjamin Netanyahu. He was poisoned, but the Israeli agents were caught and a furious King Hussein of Jordan demanded that Israel supply an antidote, which was done.

With the expulsion from Jordan of the leadership of Hamas by King Abdullah in August 1999, Mashal relocated first to Qatar and then to Syria. He has lived in Damascus since that time. Although he is not in the Palestinian territories, Marshal directs Hamas strategy. Free of restraints, he is also the chief fund-raiser for the organization, which has proved critical for Hamas after the United

States and Western European countries cut off aid to the Palestinian National Authority (PNA) in 2006. Described as charismatic with developed diplomatic skills, he has met with Western diplomats as well as Arab leaders.

In May 2009, shortly after his reelection to a fourth four-year term as the leader of Hamas, Mashal gave an extensive two-day interview in Damascus to correspondents of the *New York Times*. In what may have been a gesture toward the Barack Obama administration in the United States and other Western governments, Mashal announced that Hamas was for the time being suspending rocket attacks from the Gaza Strip against Israel and that the organization sought a Palestinian state only in the areas taken by Israel from Jordan in the 1967 war. Although he announced that Hamas sought to be "part of the solution," he stopped short of recognizing Israel. Indeed, Mashal noted, "There is only one enemy in the region, and that is Israel." Although he said he would not seek to amend it, he urged outsiders to ignore the provision in the Hamas charter that calls for the obliteration of Israel through jihad. "We are shaped by our experiences," Mashal said.

SPENCER C. TUCKER

**See also**

Abbas, Mahmoud; Arafat, Yasser; Hamas; Netanyahu, Benjamin

**References**

El-Khodary, Taghreed, and Ethan Bronner. "Addressing U.S., Hamas Says It Has Grounded Its Rockets to Israel." *New York Times,* May 5, 2009.

McGeough, Paul. *Kill Khalid: The Failed Mossad Assassination of Khalid Mishal and the Rise of Hamas.* New York: New Press, 2009.

# Mashhadani, Mahmud al-
## Birth Date: 1948

Iraqi politician and speaker of the Council of Representatives during 2006–2008. Born in 1948 in a Shiite district of Baghdad, Mahmud al-Mashhadani is a Sunni Muslim. He graduated from Baghdad Medical College in 1972. Commissioned in the Iraqi Army as a lieutenant, he rose to the rank of major but was imprisoned by the government owing to his opposition to the Iran-Iraq War (1980–1988). Subsequently tried, he was convicted and given a death sentence, which was commuted to 15 years in prison, reportedly on the payment of bribes. Following the U.S.-led invasion of Iraq in March 2003, Mashhadani was also briefly imprisoned by American authorities, allegedly for his association with Ansar al-Islam and Jaysh Ansar-al-Sunna.

Elected to the new Council of Representatives on the Sunni-Arab-led Iraqi Accord Front list, Mashhadani was selected its speaker on April 22, 2006, after the United Iraqi Alliance objected to the nomination of Tariq al-Hashimi. The vote was unanimous. Mashhadani received 159 affirmative votes, although there were also 97 spoiled ballots and 10 abstentions.

Mashhadani's tenure as speaker was marked both by sharp and abusive language, most often directed toward Kurdish and Shiite legislators, and by erratic personal behavior. He met with President George W. Bush during the latter's June 2006 visit to Baghdad, and the American leader later declared that he was much impressed with the speaker. That July, however, Mashhadani blamed the violence in Iraq on "Jews, Israelis, and Zionists" and charged that the perpetrators were directed by Israeli intelligence on orders from Tel Aviv. Later that same month, Mashhadani created considerable controversy in the United States when he also declared that while Saddam Hussein's regime was certainly corrupt, regimes should be changed by surgery and not by "butchery of the Iraqi people" under the "slogan" of democracy and human rights. In subsequent conversations with U.S. officials concerning his remarks, he was quoted as having said that he appreciated the sacrifice made by so many Americans on behalf of Iraq. However, Mashhadani also described suicide bombers who attacked and killed Americans as "heroes."

In June 2007, there was general agreement among deputies in the Council of Representatives to replace Mashhadani as a consequence of his repeated verbal clashes with both Kurdish and Shiite lawmakers and an altercation in which his bodyguards attacked and beat a Shiite legislator. He continued in his post, however.

Mashhadani expressed opposition to the 2008 conclusion of a Status of Forces Agreement with the United States and other nations that would allow U.S. forces to remain in Iraq into 2009, and he refused to allow debate on the matter of the detention of journalist Muntadhar al-Zaydi, who threw his shoes at President Bush during a press conference on December 14, 2008. This latter event led to a shouting match in the Council of Representatives. Mashhadani had called al-Zaydi "the pride" of Iraq; however the journalist was severely punished in court proceedings.

With Kurdish and Shiite representatives pressing for him to step down, Mashhadani threatened to resign. The legislators appeared to be determined to force him to make good on his threat by a boycott of parliament if necessary, and Mashhadani stepped aside on December 23, 2008, although he retained his seat in the parliament.

Within a half-hour of his resignation as speaker, the legislators approved on a voice vote a resolution that would allow British, Australian, and other nations to retain their troops in Iraq until July 31, 2009. This came only one week before the United Nations (UN) mandate authorizing foreign forces in the country was to expire.

Mashhadani said he feared for the future of his country. He also said he had "consulted" God on the matter of his resignation. The deeply religious Mashhadani adheres to salafism, as do many Sunni Iraqis today. Some members of the parliament expressed concerns that the way Mashhadani's departure was handled might encourage more sectarianism.

SPENCER C. TUCKER

**See also**

Ansar al-Islam; Bush, George Walker; Salafism; Status of Forces Agreement, U.S.-Iraqi; Zaydi, Muntadhar al-

**References**

Allawi, Ali A. *The Occupation of Iraq: Winning the War, Losing the Peace.* New Haven, CT: Yale University Press, 2007.

Woodward, Bob. *The War Within: A Secret White House History, 2006–2008.* New York: Simon and Schuster, 2008.

Zuhur, Sherifa. *Iran, Iraq and the United States: The New Triangle's Impact on Sectarianism and the Nuclear Threat.* Carlisle Barracks, PA: Strategic Studies Institute, 2006.

## Mauz, Henry H., Jr.
### Birth Date: May 4, 1936

U.S. Navy admiral who commanded naval forces during Operations EL DORADO CANYON (1986) and DESERT SHIELD (1990). Born in Lynchburg, Virginia, on May 4, 1936, Henry H. Mauz Jr. graduated from the U.S. Naval Academy at Annapolis in 1959. He then served on destroyers before graduating from the Naval Postgraduate School in 1965. During 1966–1967, Mauz commanded River Section 543, a flotilla of 10 river patrol boats that operated in the Mekong Delta during the Vietnam War. Returning to the United States, he then commanded the minesweeper *Prime* (1967–1969); studied at the Air Force Command and Staff College (1969–1970); earned an MBA from Auburn University (1970); and commanded the guided missile destroyer *Semmes* (1972–1973) and the guided missile cruiser *England* (CG-22) (1980–1982).

Promoted to rear admiral in 1983, Mauz served as chief of the Operations/Readiness Branch at Supreme Headquarters Allied Powers Europe in Belgium (1983–1985) and then commanded Cruiser Destroyer Group 12 (1985–1986). As commander of the aircraft carrier *America* battle group deployed to the Mediterranean, Mauz was the Battle Force Anti-air Warfare Commander during Operation ATTAIN DOCUMENT III against Libya, March 24–27, 1986; he then commanded the Battle Force Sixth Fleet during Operation EL DORADO CANYON when U.S. aircraft from the *America* and *Coral Sea* (CV-43) struck Libyan targets on April 15, 1986.

Mauz was promoted to vice admiral in 1988. He then commanded the U.S. Seventh Fleet (October 1988 to December 1990). In August 1990 he became commander, U.S. Naval Forces, Central Command (ComUSNavCent) in command of all U.S. naval forces in the Middle East during Operation DESERT SHIELD. Mauz exercised command not from Central Command (CENTCOM) headquarters in Riyadh, Saudi Arabia, but rather from command ships afloat, first the *La Salle,* a Raleigh-class amphibious transport dock, and then the command ship *Blue Ridge* (LCC-19). Mauz held that the two ships possessed better equipment for communicating with the multinational flotilla of warships assembled by the coalition forces.

Early in DESERT SHIELD, Mauz advocated implementing a system of "route packages" in which each service was assigned delineated geographical regions in which it would conduct autonomous air operations in the case of an Iraqi attack south from Kuwait into Saudi Arabia. He believed such a system would simplify planning and help prevent pilots from mistakenly firing on coalition aircraft.

Air force officials opposed the system, apparently based on experiences dating back to the Vietnam War. Mauz also believed that techniques developed by him and his staff to suppress Soviet air defenses in the Far East could be applied to planning the destruction of Iraqi radars, command and control centers, and missile batteries to pave the way for U.S. bombers. Air force leaders, however, resisted navy participation in planning the air campaign (at the end of September 1990 only 2 of 29 officers assigned air campaign planning in the Pentagon were from the navy), but Mauz's presentation of his views directly to air force lieutenant general Charles Horner, the Joint Force Air Component Commander (JFACC), led to a shift of focus to that of crippling Iraq's air-defense system at the start of Operation DESERT STORM, which occurred in January 1991, six weeks after Mauz had turned over control of CENTCOM naval forces to Vice Admiral Stanley Arthur on December 1, 1990.

Early in the summer of 1990, Mauz had been slated to succeed Vice Admiral William Smith as deputy chief of Naval Operations (DCNO) for Navy Program Planning, but the change in command of the Seventh Fleet was postponed when Mauz also became ComUSNavCent in August. By November, with no firm military operations against Iraq in sight, and Smith's departure for a North Atlantic Treaty Organization (NATO) position in Brussels, the rotation of officers could not be delayed longer, and Arthur relieved Mauz at Central Command. Moving to the Pentagon, Mauz served as DCNO from 1991 to 1992; he received a fourth star in July 1992 and took command of the Atlantic Fleet during 1992–1994.

Upon retirement in November 1994, Mauz moved to Pebble Beach, California. He served as president and chairman of the Naval Postgraduate School Foundation (1997–2008) and continued to serve on the board of directors of Texas Industries Con-way, Inc., and CoalStar Industries, Inc. He also serves on the Northrop Grumman Ship Systems Advisory Board.

JAMES C. BRADFORD

**See also**

Arthur, Stanley; DESERT SHIELD, Operation; DESERT STORM, Operation, Planning for; Horner, Charles; United States Navy, Persian Gulf War; Warden, John Ashley, III

**References**

Marolda, Edward, and Robert Schneller. *Shield and Sword: The United States Navy and the Persian Gulf War.* Annapolis, MD: U.S. Naval Institute Press, 2001.

Pokrant, Marvin. *Desert Shield at Sea: What the Navy Really Did.* Westport, CT: Greenwood, 1999.

Stanik, Joseph T. *El Dorado Canyon: Reagan's Undeclared War with Qaddafi.* Annapolis, MD: Naval Institute Press, 2003.

## Mawdudi, Sayyid Abu al-Aala
### Birth Date: September 25, 1903
### Death Date: September 22, 1979

Muslim scholar, author, journalist, political activist, and founder of the Jamaat-e Islami. Abu al-Aala Mawdudi, who occupies an important place in the Islamic revival movement of the 20th century, was born September 25, 1903, in the city of Aurangabad in central India. Mawdudi's father was a well-educated lawyer of the middle class. His education was a mix of home tutoring, education at a madrasah, self-learning, and study at Dar al-Ulum, which prepared him for the examinations required to become an Islamic teacher in India, known as a *maulvi.*

Mawdudi was also raised on the history of early Islam, which clearly affected his own views later in life. When civil disturbances grew in India over British rule in the 1920s, Mawdudi participated in the Khilafat movement, which called for the expulsion of the British and the creation of an Islamic state based on the rule of a caliph. He became a journalist, contributing to leading Urdu publications and then Islamic news sources.

Mawdudi founded the Jamaat-e Islami in 1941 to promote Islamic values, and throughout his life he contributed to scholarship and writing on Islam. He produced a serious interpretation, or *tafsir,* of the Qur'an in Urdu, which took 30 years, and he wrote many other works discussing the ideal Islamic society. Mawdudi originally opposed the idea of a separate state for Muslims in Pakistan, but he later accepted this course of action, arguing for Pakistan to be an Islamic state. Mawdudi's writings also promoted the Muslim practice of *dawa,* as missionaries spread Islam. He argued that they were not to assimilate into non-Muslim cultures, and that Muslims should be in control of governmental affairs. He called on non-Muslims to pay the historical *jizya* or poll tax. He believed an Islamic government could be a theo-democracy but should oppose conditions of nonbelief and underdevelopment. While it is generally believed that he promoted jihad as an effort for Islam's success, he also wrote that active combat was not always the proper method of jihad. Distressed over the lack of unity among Muslims in the region, Mawdudi worked to organize a united political front, via the Jamaat-e Islami.

Mawdudi's principal concern was that any separate state created for Muslims, such as Pakistan, should be based solely on Islamic law, and that the movement should eventually spread internationally. To aid in this process, Muslims were not only to convert non-Muslims but were to engage in a birth-rate revolution to increase their numbers. The creation of the Jamaat devoted itself to ensuring Islamic rule in what was soon to become Pakistan. Many supporters moved north into the Punjab region in anticipation of this event, and by 1947 Mawdudi had migrated to the newly created nation of Pakistan.

Mawdudi's conception of an Islamic state was one where life would be guided by Islamic law and where the sovereignty of God, *hakmiyya,* would be reflected in the political system. This last was among the most influential of his ideas in the Muslim world. Non-Muslims could continue to live in such a state, but could not attempt to convert Muslims, as Islam was a public affair, and such conversion was illegal under Islamic law, meriting the death penalty. He advocated a three-fold process for seizing power. Initially, an invitation to Islam would be made, followed by efforts to gain power through peaceful and legal means. If this second

stage failed, he discreetly advocated the use of revolutionary force to create the Islamic state. Criticized by some for this revolutionary approach, he was also rejected by salafists for noting that the Dajjal, or Antichrist, had not appeared in the time of Muhammad, Prophet of Islam, as predicted.

The establishment of Pakistan in 1947 did not lead to the Islamic state he so desired, so Mawdudi's political activism led to multiple arrests and the banning of some of his works by the Pakistani government. In the early 1950s he supported the violent Muslim suppression of the schismatic Qadianis, receiving a death sentence from the government, which was later commuted. His struggle for an Islamic constitution for Pakistan was largely fulfilled in 1956. Later rulers scrapped this document, however, and beginning in 1958 Mawdudi and his followers endured four years of martial law under which the Jamaat was banned. It was restored in 1962 under a new constitution, which was seen as a departure from the nation's initial Islamic foundation.

While continuing his political work, Mawdudi focused on writing his *tafsir,* or commentary, of the Qur'an, which he completed in 1972. Of particular importance were his introductions to each of its chapters, or *surahs.* Having traveled to the United States to seek medical treatment, Maudidi died on September 22, 1979, in Buffalo, New York, from complications arising from stomach, kidney, and heart problems. He was buried in Lahore, Pakistan. Mawdudi, who wrote more than 120 books and pamphlets and gave close to 1,000 speeches, is considered one of the most prominent and important advocates of the modern Islamic revival movement and of the social activism promoted by the Jamaat. His works are still widely read by Muslims around the world, especially his *tafsir* of the Qur'an and introductions to its *surahs.*

RUSSELL G. RODGERS AND SHERIFA ZUHUR

**See also**
Islamic Radicalism; Pakistan; Qur'an; Shia Islam; Sunni Islam

**References**
Hasan, Masudul. *Sayyid Abu al-Aala Maududi and His Thought.* Lahore, Pakistan: Islamic Publications, 1984.
Mawdudi, Sayyid Abu al-Aala. *First Principles of the Islamic State.* Lahore, Pakistan: Islamic Publications, 1983.
———. *Jihad in Islam.* Beirut, Lebanon: Holy Koran Publishing House, 1980.
———. *Political Theory of Islam.* Lahore, Pakistan: Islamic Publications, 1980.
Nasr, Seyyed Vali Reza. *Mawdudi and the Making of Islamic Revivalism.* New York: Oxford University Press, 1996.

## Mayville, William
Birth Date: April 15, 1960

U.S. Army officer and commander of the 173rd Airborne Brigade when it parachuted into northern Iraq at the beginning of Operation IRAQI FREEDOM in March 2003. William Mayville was born on April 15, 1960, in Springfield, Virginia, and graduated from the

U.S. Military Academy, West Point, in 1982. Commissioned a second lieutenant, his first command was as a platoon leader in the 1st Battalion of the 75th Infantry Battalion (Ranger). Mayville moved steadily up the command ladder, leading units at the company, battalion, and brigade level.

Mayville graduated from the Airborne, Ranger, Pathfinder, the Infantry Basic and Advanced courses, and the U.S. Army Command and General Staff course. He also holds an MS from Georgia Institute of Technology and an MA from the National War College.

Prior to IRAQI FREEDOM, Mayville had participated in two combat operations. He parachuted into Grenada during Operation URGENT FURY in 1983 and also parachuted into Panama during Operation JUST CAUSE in 1989. By 2003 Mayville, now a colonel, was commanding the 173rd Airborne Brigade. Located at Vicenza, Italy, it is the principal combat force of the U.S. Southern European Task Force. The brigade consisted of two airborne infantry battalions, a light reconnaissance unit, and a detachment of field artillery. In 2005, the army began converting the 173rd into a full six-battalion brigade combat team.

Initial planning for Operation IRAQI FREEDOM began in November 2001. The original operational plan called for a two-pronged attack. The first attack would be the main advance from the south, out of Kuwait toward Baghdad and on to Tikrit. The second, and secondary, attack would be from the north, out of Turkey toward Tikrit and on to Baghdad. This plan was foiled when the Turkish government refused to allow the staging of U.S. troops on its soil. Turkish officials did, however, allow the use of their airspace for the transit of American aircraft. With this accommodation, the 4th Infantry Division was no longer an option for the northern operation. The 173rd was chosen instead.

On March 26, 2003, the 173rd was moved by McDonnell Douglas Globemaster III C-17 cargo aircraft from Aviano Air Base (Italy) to its drop zone, where the brigade parachuted into Bashur Air Base (Iraq). Mayville was one of the first men of the brigade to jump. Within six hours, the 173rd had taken Bashur and was ready to receive follow-up forces. By March 30, 2003, the entire 173rd was in Iraq. Following the establishment of the airhead, troopers began operations against the local Iraqi military. The 173rd's mission was to keep these units in northern Iraq and prevent their use in the south to fight the main invasion.

In early April 2003, U.S. and allied Kurdish forces advanced south and liberated Kirkuk. This was important because that city is the hub of the northern oil region. Its possession would assist the Kurds and starve the Iraqi military of precious resources. The 173rd then carried out security and counterinsurgency operations in Kirkuk and the vicinity. Mayville saw this shift as the most important part of his mission. Without a stable Kirkuk, Iraq could possibly descend into civil war.

The 173rd was relieved in February 2004 and returned to its Italian base. Mayville was then promoted to brigadier general and assigned as the deputy director of the European Plans and Operations Center (EPOC), Headquarters, U.S. European Command,

Stuttgart, Germany, in 2006. In 2008, Mayville became deputy commanding general of the 82nd Airborne Division, at Fort Bragg, North Carolina.

Shawn Livingston

**See also**

IRAQI FREEDOM, Operation; United States Army, Iraq War

**References**

Hershman, M. Shane. "Employment of the C-17 in Airdrop and Airland Operations in Closing the Force." *USAWC Strategy Research Project.* Carlisle, PA: U.S. Army War College, 2005.

Tunnell, Harry D. "Red Devils' Tactical Perspectives from Iraq." Fort Leavenworth, KS: Combat Studies Institute Press, 2005.

---

# Mazar-e Sharif, Battle of
## Event Date: November 9, 2001

First major battle of Operation ENDURING FREEDOM. It occurred on November 8, 2001, between forces of the Northern Alliance, supported by American, British, and North Atlantic Treaty Organization (NATO) forces, and Taliban fighters. Lying astride the famous Silk Road, Mazar-e Sharif is located just 40 miles from Uzbekistan and is situated north of the Hindu Kush mountains. Mazar-e Sharif is held sacred by Afghans as the birthplace of the caliph Ali, who ruled during 656–661. It is the capital of Afghanistan's Balkh Province. Mazar-e Sharif has a mainly Uzbek population of nearly 250,000, but it also possesses a significant Pashtun minority.

In August 1998 after heavy fighting, Taliban forces captured Mazar-e Sharif from General Abd al-Rashid Dostum, an Uzbek warlord. Its military importance lay in the fact that it possessed an airstrip that could be used to supply troops and act as a springboard for the Taliban to capture Kabul, the Afghan capital.

Before the Americans and coalition forces entered Afghanistan in the autumn of 2001, the mainly Pashtun Islamist Taliban, which claimed to be the legitimate Afghan government, seemed to have an overwhelming advantage over their Tajik-led Northern Alliance opponents. The latter group was under the command of General Muhammad Fahim, who took over for Ahmed Shah Massoud, who was assassinated in an Al Qaeda–orchestrated bombing just two days before the September 11, 2001, Al Qaeda terrorist attacks on the United States. General Dostum, who had once been a Soviet ally but who had later joined forces with Massoud, led the coalition forces that advanced on Mazar-e Sharif. The Uzbek warlord was joined in the effort by Ustad Atta Mohammed, a Tajik commander and erstwhile foe.

At the time of the November 2001 battle, forces of the Northern Alliance controlled a mere 10 percent of Afghanistan and were outmanned, outgunned, and on the defensive. The Northern Alliance had an estimated 8,000 troops as opposed to the 40,000–50,000 that the Taliban allegedly mustered under the leadership of Mullah

Mohammed Omar. The latter included 8,000–12,000 foreign fighters, counting members of the Al Qaeda terrorist organization.

On October 7, 2001, the United States began a bombing campaign as part of what came to be called Operation ENDURING FREEDOM. At the same time, having to negotiate more than 100 miles of winding, mountainous roads with the constant danger of ambushes presented a daunting logistical problem for the anti-Taliban forces, which received supplies from across the border with Tajikistan. The United States provided food, supplies, and weapons for the Northern Alliance. An American air campaign employing bombers and cruise missiles preceded the move to capture Mazar-e Sharif. Small teams of U.S. Special Operations Forces (SOF) as well as Central Intelligence Agency (CIA) agents, who had been inserted into Afghanistan in mid-October aboard specially modified Boeing CH-47 Chinook helicopters, lent support to the Northern Alliance. These teams directed close air support (CAS) and offered tactical advice in the capture of Mazar-e Sharif.

Ground operations began just before Ramadan so as not to arouse Muslim sensibilities. The approach of winter added even more pressure to mount a quick and decisive military campaign. The Northern Alliance advance on Mazar-e Sharif was methodical and came along the axes of the Dar-i-Suf gorge and Balkh River valley. In the former, a SOF team located exposed Taliban positions close to Bishqab from a distance of five to six miles and called in precision air strikes. General Dostum took the village on October 21 and continued his push toward Mazar-e Sharif.

Over the next few days, Dostum's force pressed northwards and clashed with and defeated the Taliban and their allies along the way. In these engagements, American SOF teams played a vital role calling in strikes against enemy command posts, armor, antiaircraft guns, and troop concentrations when weather permitted aerial sorties. U.S.-directed CAS proved deadly for those Taliban and Al Qaeda fighters who did not learn from their mistakes and improve the concealment of their men and matériel. Unable to pinpoint the location of mainly Al Qaeda forces at Bai Beche, near a strategically situated mountain pass south of Mazar-e Sharif, Northern Alliance forces came under heavy rocket fire and found their advance obstructed. As a consequence, the coalition employed bombing to degrade well-prepared defenses and then overran the hamlet on November 5 with the aid of CAS in what proved to be a close victory. By that day, the Northern Alliance forces had moved to within 45 miles of Mazar-e Sharif. Although the Taliban had brought up some 400 reinforcements, they were under incessant U.S. air attack.

Meanwhile, General Atta Mohammed's men were advancing along the Balkh River to the east of Mazar-e Sharif. They encountered forces that had not learned the lessons of seeking cover from aerial attack, so American aircraft, directed by SOF observers, wiped out exposed targets with relative ease. Thus, the outlying village of Ac'capruk fell to the Northern Alliance, and the way was clear for a combined attack on Mazar-e Sharif. Reportedly a number of Taliban fighters switched sides and others simply took flight, allowing the Northern Alliance forces into their lines.

After a four-day push from the south, the combined Northern Alliance forces conducted the final assault of the city on November 9, 2001, using artillery, tanks, horse-mounted soldiers, and infantry. At 2:00 p.m., the attack began. U.S. aircraft once more provided invaluable CAS for opposition troops. SOF units joined in the remarkable, 21st-century cavalry charge of 2,000 Uzbeks on the Taliban stronghold. The application of combined arms proved devastating. The battle was bloody and intense but lasted less than four hours.

To begin the assault on the city, American planes dropped dozens of bombs on Taliban fighters who had concentrated to defend it at its southern approach at the Chesmay-i-Safa Gorge. Entering Mazar-e Sharif from both the south and the west, opposition forces managed quickly to capture the Pul-i Imam Bukhri Bridge and likewise overran the airport to the south of the city. Resistance quickly collapsed with the panicking Taliban fleeing Mazar-e Sharif en masse. As they withdrew, they torched homes, killing many ethnic Uzbeks, Tajiks, and Hazaras in the process.

Left behind in the melee, however, were hundreds of foreign fighters, many of whom took refuge at a military base and others at a girls' school. Northern Alliance forces lay siege to both of these pockets of resistance, used tanks and air strikes against those who continued fighting, and it took another 48 hours before the city had been entirely pacified. Unconfirmed reports of troop strengths indicated that as many as 8,000 men constituted the Northern Alliance force, while their opponents had perhaps 12,000 fighters in the battle. According to an estimate by the International Committee of the Red Cross and the Afghan Red Crescent, the Taliban and Al Qaeda lost 300–400, mostly non-Afghans killed in the fighting, and the Northern Alliance claimed to have captured another 500 men. The opposition's losses were fewer than 100 men.

The capture of Mazar-e Sharif proved a watershed event for ENDURING FREEDOM. Although some small pockets of resistance remained, for all intents and purposes the battle brought to an end the Taliban presence in northern Afghanistan. Besides its military significance, this first major victory of the war provided a boost to the George W. Bush administration, which was under heavy criticism concerning the wisdom of its strategy in Afghanistan. Able now to land planes and helicopters at a base in the north, the United States increased its operational capability and was able to fly far more sorties with heavier payloads and thus greatly intensify the air war in Afghanistan. The battle gave further credibility to the military capabilities of the Northern Alliance and accelerated defections from the Taliban, especially from ethnic groups other than the Pashtuns. The Taliban collapsed in the days immediately after the fall of Mazar-e Sharif, and Kabul soon fell into the hands of the Northern Alliance.

GEORGE L. SIMPSON

**See also**

Dostum, Abd al-Rashid; ENDURING FREEDOM, Operation; Northern Alliance

**References**

Biddle, Stephen. *Afghanistan and the Future of Warfare: Implications for Army and Defense Policy.* Carlisle, PA: Strategic Studies Institute, 2002.

Clements, Frank A. *Conflict in Afghanistan: A Historical Encyclopedia.* Santa Barbara, CA: ABC-CLIO, 2003.

Griffin, Michael. *Reaping the Whirlwind: Afghanistan, Al-Qa'ida, and the Holy War.* London: Pluto, 2001.

# McCaffrey, Barry Richard

### Birth Date: November 17, 1942

U.S. Army general. Barry Richard McCaffrey was born November 17, 1942, in Taunton, Massachusetts. A graduate of the Phillips Academy, he attended the U.S. Military Academy, West Point, graduating in 1964. McCaffrey served overseas for 13 years, 4 as a combat officer. These tours began in 1965 with duty in the Dominican Republic with the 82nd Airborne Division. He then served two tours in Vietnam as a rifle company command, receiving two Distinguished Service Crosses and three Purple Hearts for combat wounds, including a severe wound to his arm—his doctors initially wanted to amputate it—that nearly ended his military career.

McCaffrey advanced through the ranks and attended both military and civilian schools. He earned an MA in government from American University and completed the National Security Course at Harvard University's John F. Kennedy School of Government.

U.S. Army general Barry R. McCaffrey commanded the U.S. Southern Command during 1994–1996. He then directed the Office of National Drug Control Policy in the Bill Clinton administration during 1996–2001. McCaffrey is currently a business adviser and military commentator. (U.S. Department of Defense)

Military courses included the Armor Advanced Officer Course, Command and General Staff College, the Army War College, and the General Officer Strategic Course at the National Defense University.

As a major general, McCaffrey served in the Pentagon as a strategic planner for the deputy chief of staff for operations. In 1991, McCaffrey commanded the 24th Infantry Division at Fort Stewart, Georgia. On August 2, 1990, Iraqi forces invaded Kuwait and the United States began planning to counter this action. Planning included deployment of U.S. military forces to the Persian Gulf, including the XVIII Airborne Corps, consisting of the 24th Infantry Division, the 82nd Airborne Division, and the 101st Airborne Division (Air Assault). Within days, elements of McCaffrey's division were en route to the Persian Gulf as part of Operation DESERT SHIELD. McCaffrey was intimately involved in the planning for the expulsion of Iraqi forces from Kuwait, Operation DESERT STORM, in 1991.

In February 1991, McCaffrey held a key place on the assault line; his division began the ground attack on February 25, 1991, on the far right of XVIII Corps. McCaffrey's objective was to drive to and cross the Euphrates River near An Nasiriyah. To McCaffrey's right was the farthest left division of Lieutenant General Frederick M. Frank's VII Corps, the 1st Armored Division, moving toward the Euphrates, then turning east to isolate Iraqi forces. This offensive was an overwhelming success, resulting in a cease-fire in 100 hours and very few coalition casualties.

At the combat level, there were two controversial issues during the war, one now called the "Generals' War," in which General H. Norman Schwarzkopf, commanding coalition forces, criticized Frank for not advancing as quickly as desired. Others questioned whether McCaffrey continued his division's attack after the cease-fire, killing and wounding more Iraqi troops than necessary. Pulitzer Prize–winning author Seymour Hersh claimed in *New Yorker* magazine that McCaffrey ordered his division to fire on retreating Iraqi forces after the declaration of the cease-fire, a charge supported by some officers in McCaffrey's headquarters during the incident but which was later dismissed by an army investigation. The 24th Infantry Division was at a critical junction between the XVIII and VII Corps, and there is often a problem in coordinating the operations of units under different commands such as the two corps. Ending fire while still engaged is not an easy task after a cease-fire is declared by higher headquarters. Neither controversy ended these officers' careers. Both men advanced to the four-star rank before retiring.

McCaffrey was promoted to lieutenant general and served as the strategic planner for the Joint Chiefs of Staff (JCS) and special assistant to General Colin Powell from 1992 to 1994. He then commanded the U.S. Southern Command at four-star rank, responsible for U.S. forces defending Central and South America. These numbered some 84,000 personnel. The command devoted great effort to combating the drug trade in the region. This experience led to President Bill Clinton's selection of McCaffrey to be director of the White House National Drug Control Policy in 1996 when he retired from the army. McCaffrey held the post commonly referred to as the U.S. Drug Czar until 2001. There he supervised a federal budget of about $20 billion annually.

From 2001 to 2005, McCaffrey was the Bradley Professor of International Security Studies at the U.S. Military Academy, and he continues to be an adjunct professor of International Affairs there. The author of numerous articles, he has also served as national security and terrorism analyst for NBC News and is consulted widely by the media on national security affairs. He is president of BR McCaffrey Associates, a consulting firm based in Alexandria, Virginia.

Since the Anglo-American–led invasion of Iraq in 2003, McCaffrey has traveled to Iraq several times at the behest of the U.S. Central Command (CENTCOM). His first report on the situation there, released in the summer of 2005, was upbeat, predicting that the insurgency would peak in early 2006 and would thereafter subside, allowing some troop withdrawals by late summer 2006. His subsequent visits, however, resulted in sharply negative assessments of the Iraq War. In 2006, he asserted that "Iraq is abject misery." His third visit, in March 2007, echoed his summation from 2006 and also voiced his concern about the effects of the continuing war on U.S. military readiness. In a cautious conclusion, however, he did laud the apparent willingness of Iraqi moderates to stem the tide of violence and reassert control over their own affairs.

DANIEL E. SPECTOR

**See also**

Bush, George Herbert Walker; DESERT SHIELD, Operation; DESERT STORM, Operation; Franks, Frederick Melvin, Jr.; IRAQI FREEDOM, Operation; Powell, Colin Luther; Schwarzkopf, H. Norman, Jr.

**References**

Freedman, Lawrence, and Efraim Karsh. *The Gulf Conflict, 1990–1991: Diplomacy and War in the New World Order.* Princeton, NJ: Princeton University Press, 1993.

Gordon, Michael R., and General Bernard E. Trainor. *The Generals' War: The Inside Story of the Conflict in the Gulf.* New York: Little, Brown, 1995.

Newell, Clayton R. *The A to Z of the Persian Gulf War, 1990–1991.* Lanham, MD: Scarecrow, 2007.

# McCain, John Sidney, III
## Birth Date: August 29, 1936

U.S. Navy pilot, prisoner of war (POW) during the Vietnam War (1967–1973), U.S. Representative (1983–1987), U.S. Senator (1987–present), advocate of normalized U.S. relations with Vietnam, and Republican presidential nominee in 2008. Born on August 29, 1936, in the Panama Canal Zone, John Sidney McCain III came from a line of navy admirals. His father, Admiral John S. McCain Jr., was commander in chief, Pacific Command (CINCPAC) from 1968 to 1972; his grandfather John S. McCain Sr. was a four-star admiral who served in both World War I and World War II.

McCain was a rebel who graduated fifth from the bottom of his class at the U.S. Naval Academy, Annapolis, in 1958. He became a naval aviator and his devil-may-care attitude and leadership skills made him a highly effective pilot. On October 26, 1967, Lieutenant Commander McCain was piloting a Douglas A4 Skyhawk when he was shot down and he crashed in Western Lake in the middle of Hanoi in the Democratic Republic of Vietnam (North Vietnam). The Vietnamese made the site and plane into a military memorial, which McCain visited on his return to Hanoi in 1992.

With two broken arms, a broken leg, a broken shoulder, and a deep wound in his foot, McCain was probably the most seriously injured pilot to enter the Hoa Lo Prison (also known as the Hanoi Hilton). "The crown prince," as the Vietnamese guards called him because of his father's high position, was a tough and highly respected POW who, despite his serious condition and being subjected to torture by his captors, refused the opportunity to be sent home in June 1968.

Released at the end of the war on March 14, 1973, McCain retired from the Navy to enter politics. In 1980 he divorced his first

Sen. John McCain (R-Ariz.) ran for the Republican Party's presidential nomination in 2000. Although McCain was unsuccessful, his campaign raised important ethical questions about politics. McCain won his party's nomination in 2008, but lost the national election to Democrat Barack Obama. (Shutterstock)

wife and married Cindy Lou Hensley, the daughter of a wealthy beer distributor. For a time he worked in the family business, but he seemed destined for political office. In 1982 he was elected to the House of Representatives from Arizona's 1st District, and in 1986 he was elected a U.S. Senator from Arizona as a Republican, taking office in January 1987.

McCain had a generally distinguished record in the Senate, and on several occasions he was on the short list to be a vice-presidential candidate. In Congress, he naturally gravitated toward foreign, military, and national security matters. The only blight on his record was his involvement, in the mid-1980s, in a scandal involving Charles Keating and the Lincoln Savings and Loan Association, which had bilked depositors and investors out of millions of dollars. Although McCain had been involved with Keating without knowing of his nefarious dealings, he nonetheless admitted that he had used poor judgment in accepting contributions and other perks from him.

McCain made several trips to Vietnam after he reached Congress. The first visit was in 1985; the second one came in 1992, as part of his work on the Senate Select Committee on POW/MIA Affairs. McCain met with some of his former captors in 1992 during what was an emotion-filled visit. McCain, along with other committee members, concluded in 1993 that there were no known POWs or soldiers missing in action (MIA) still residing in Vietnam. He came under attack from some who strongly believed that Americans were indeed still being held by the Vietnamese. After his second visit, McCain became a strong supporter of normalized relations with Vietnam and an end to economic sanctions, which was realized beginning in 1995.

In 2000, McCain ran in the Republican presidential primary, ultimately losing to George W. Bush in a fairly close contest. McCain's allure was that he was not an ideologue and was not afraid to go against his own party. McCain generally backed the Bush administration's War on Terror after the September 11, 2001, terror attacks, but he parted company with Bush on several issues, including the use of torture against enemy combatants, tax cuts for the wealthy, gun legislation, and climate change.

McCain backed the Iraq War from the beginning, but by 2004 he had begun to question the prosecution of that conflict; he openly challenged Secretary of Defense Donald Rumsfeld to put more ground troops into the theater to deal with the mounting Iraqi insurgency. He traveled to Iraq numerous times to see for himself the situation on the ground, and what he saw did not impress him. In August 2006, McCain publicly charged the Bush administration with having constantly underestimated the Iraqi insurgency and took military commanders in Iraq to task for having provided unrealistic assessments of the ground situation. McCain repeatedly urged the Bush administration to prosecute the Iraq war with more zeal and greater commitment, and so it is no surprise that he strongly backed the troop surge strategy implemented in 2007.

In 2008, McCain sought and gained the Republican presidential nomination. From the start, however, he was hobbled by his relatively close association with President Bush, who by then was wildly unpopular; his stance toward the Iraq War; and a failing U.S. economy. His campaign began strongly but fell victim to repeated verbal and strategic gaffes. He shifted from one issue to another while his opponent, Senator Barack Obama, successfully portrayed McCain as Bush redux. McCain's charge that Obama's call for withdrawing U.S. troops from Iraq as quickly as possible was tantamount to defeat fell on deaf ears. McCain touted his role in the successful troop surge, but Obama stuck with his position that the Iraq War had been a mistake in the first place. McCain's choice of Sarah Palin as a running mate, the governor of Alaska who had little national recognition, may not have helped his candidacy. In the end, McCain lost by a large margin in both the popular and electoral vote, but he opted to remain in the Senate as one of its most senior—and seasoned—members.

PAUL G. PIERPAOLI JR.

**See also**

Bush, George Walker; Obama, Barack Hussein, II; Surge, U.S. Troop Deployment, Iraq War

**References**

Howes, Craig. *Voices of the Vietnam POWs: Witnesses to Their Fight*. New York: Oxford University Press, 1993.

McCain, John, with Mark Salter. *Faith of My Fathers*. New York: Random House, 1999.

———. *Worth the Fighting For: A Memoir*. New York: Random House, 2002.

---

# McChrystal, Stanley A.
## Birth Date: August 14, 1954

U.S. Army general and commander of U.S. forces in Afghanistan (2009–2010). Stanley McChrystal was born on August 14, 1954, and graduated from the U.S. Military Academy, West Point, in 1976. Commissioned a second lieutenant in the U.S. Army, his first assignment was with the 82nd Airborne Division. In 1978 he underwent Special Forces training at Fort Bragg, North Carolina. He commanded a detachment of the 7th Special Forces Group (Airborne) until 1980, when he attended the Infantry Officer Advanced Course at Fort Benning, Georgia.

McChrystal served a tour in the Republic of Korea before being assigned to Fort Stewart, Georgia. During 1989–1990, he completed the Command and Staff Course at the Naval War College, Newport, Rhode Island. Assigned to the Joint Special Operations Command during 1990–1993, he deployed to Saudi Arabia during Operations DESERT SHIELD and DESERT STORM. Promoted to lieutenant colonel, during 1993–1994 McChrystal commanded a battalion of the 82nd Airborne division. Following a year as a senior fellow at the John F. Kennedy School of Government at Harvard University and promotion to colonel in September 1996, he commanded the 75th Ranger Regiment during 1997–1999. He next spent a year as a fellow at the Council on Foreign Relations.

Promoted to brigadier general in January 2001, McChrystal was the assistant division commander for operations of the 82nd Airborne Division in 2000–2001. During 2001–2002, he was chief of staff of the XVIII Airborne Corps. This assignment included duty as chief of staff of Combined Joint Task Force 180, the headquarters formation charged with direction of Operation ENDURING FREEDOM, the U.S.-led invasion of Afghanistan. From July 2002, McChrystal was director of operations on the Joint Staff in Washington, D.C., where he delivered public briefings on the military situation during the U.S.-led invasion of Iraq.

In September 2003 McChrystal took command of the Joint Special Operations Command (JSOC), first as commanding general of JSOC from September 2003 to February 2006 and then as commander, JSOC/Commander, JSOC Forward, from February 2006 to August 2008. Although the command was situated at Fort Bragg, McChrystal spent most of his time in Afghanistan, in Qatar, and in Iraq.

McChrystal's Task Force 6-26 was subsequently accused of abuses in prisoner interrogations at Camp Nama in Baghdad, and five Rangers were ultimately convicted of prisoner abuses at the facility. McChrystal also came under criticism for his handling of details surrounding the death by friendly fire of Ranger and former professional football player Pat Tillman in Afghanistan in 2004. Although McChrystal was one of eight officers recommended for disciplinary action in the affair, the army declined to take action against him.

In February 2006, McChrystal was promoted to lieutenant general. His colleagues described him as a warrior-scholar. His JSOC was widely praised for its ability to find and kill Iraqi insurgents, and some observers have stated that it, rather than the so-called surge, was largely responsible for the decline in violence in Iraq during 2007–2008.

McChrystal was nominated to direct the Joint Staff in February 2008, but his confirmation was held up for a time in the Senate over charges of mistreatment of detainees by forces under his command in Afghanistan and in Iraq. He took up his new post in August 2008.

On May 11, 2009, Secretary of Defense Robert Gates announced that he was recalling General David McKiernan, the top U.S. commander in Afghanistan, and nominating McChrystal as his replacement. McKiernan had held the post for less than a year and been instrumental in securing additional U.S. forces for Afghanistan. Although Gates said that McKiernan had done nothing wrong, he also said that "new leadership and fresh eyes" were needed. The announcement came less than one week after President Barack Obama's meeting with the leaders of Afghanistan and Pakistan, during which he pledged a more coordinated effort to fight Taliban forces in both countries. It is believed that a planned shift in favor of counterinsurgency as opposed to conventional operations and the fact that McKiernan did not get on well with Central Command commander General David Petraeus was the principal reason for McKiernan's ouster and McChrystal's selection.

On June 24, 2010, following a brief meeting with McChrystal at the White House, President Obama removed him from command of U.S. and NATO forces in Afghanistan. McChrystal had been recalled to Washington following the release of the copy of an article to appear in *Rolling Stone* magazine with highly critical comments by McChrystal and his staff of Obama, Vice President Joseph Biden, and other key members of the administration. The last time a U.S. president stepped in to remove a commander in the middle of a war was in April 1951, when President Harry S. Truman removed United Nations Command (UNC) commander in Korea General Douglas MacArthur over the general's all-too-public criticisms of U.S. policy. Obama said there were no policy differences in this case, but that McChrystal's comments fell far short of the conduct expected of commanders and represented a clear violation of the military chain of command that could not be tolerated. Although there was shock at the decision, which reportedly went against appeals by Afghan president Hamid Karzai and U.S. secretary of defense Robert Gates, negative reaction was muted and passed quickly. McChrystal's replacement was Central Command commander General David H. Petraeus, whose appointment sent a clear signal that the current U.S. strategy in Afghanistan would continue.

SPENCER C. TUCKER

**See also**

ENDURING FREEDOM, Operation; Gates, Robert Michael; IRAQI FREEDOM, Operation; Iraqi Insurgency; McKiernan, David Deglan; Obama, Barack Hussein, II; Petraeus, David Howell; Taliban; Tillman, Patrick Daniel

**References**

Bumiller, Elisabeth, and Mark Massetti. "General Steps from Shadow." *New York Times*, May 13, 2009.

Bumiller, Elisabeth, and Thom Shanker. "Pentagon Ousts Top Commander in Afghan War." *New York Times*, May 12, 2009.

Schmitt, Eric, and Carolyn Marshall. "In Secret Unit's 'Black Room,' a Grim Portrait of U.S. Abuse." *New York Times*, March 19, 2006.

Woodward, Bob. "Why Did Violence Plummet? It Wasn't Just the Surge." *Washington Post*, September 8, 2008.

---

# McClellan, Scott
## Birth Date: February 14, 1968

Republican Party strategist, campaign official, and White House press secretary (2003–2006). Scott McClellan was born in Austin, Texas, on February 14, 1968, to a politically prominent family. His mother, Carole Keeton Strayhorn, a longtime politician in Texas, served as the state's comptroller for several terms and ran unsuccessfully for the governorship of Texas in 2006. His father, Bar McClellan, is a noted attorney and author, and his brother Mark was a former commissioner of the Food and Drug Administration (FDA) and later head of Medicaid and Medicare Services from 2004 to 2006.

McClellan graduated from the University of Texas at Austin and immediately went into politics. In addition to running three of his mother's electoral campaigns, he worked with several grass-roots political action committees and was, for a time, chief of staff to a Texas state senator.

While working for his mother, McClellan caught the eye of Karen Hughes, a close political confidante and adviser to then-Governor George W. Bush. Impressed by his performance and dedication, Hughes invited McClellan to join Bush's 2000 presidential election campaign team as a media analyst and traveling press agent. After being named deputy press secretary, he became press secretary on July 17, 2003, upon the resignation of Ari Fleischer. McClellan left his post on April 26, 2006, succeeded by Tony Snow.

McClellan's tenure coincided with the Valerie Plame Wilson debacle, which saw senior-level Bush administration officials leak classified information to the media that revealed Plame Wilson's identity as an operations officer for the Central Intelligence Agency (CIA). The revelation was purportedly in retaliation for a newspaper piece that was critical of the Bush administration's pre–Iraq War intelligence written by Plame Wilson's husband, former ambassador Joseph Wilson. At the time, McClellan was instructed to deny any connection between the White House and the Valerie Plame Wilson incident.

In May 2008, much to the surprise of the White House—for it was totally unexpected from its heretofore presumed entirely loyal staffer—McClellan published one of the most revealing and incendiary accounts of the Bush White House to date, which among other things accused the president and his inner circle of deception, hubris, and incompetence (*What Happened: Inside the Bush White House and Washington's Culture of Deception*). In his book, McClellan made it clear that he had unwittingly helped deceive the American public about the Valerie Plame Wilson incident and had falsely exonerated two top-level officials alleged to have been guilty of the leak—Karl Rove, senior adviser to the president, and I. Scooter Libby, chief of staff to Vice President Dick Cheney. He further alleges that the two men held a secret meeting as the federal prosecutor was investigating the case in an attempt to cover up their role in the affair. Libby was later found guilty of perjury, but Rove was never prosecuted. Bush, McClellan believes, was also misled about the affair, perhaps by his own vice president.

McClellan's tell-all book was derided for disloyalty and even retribution by Bush supporters, while others used the account to further attack the Bush administration and, in particular, its conduct of the war in Iraq. Among many assertions, McClellan charges the president and his advisers of self-deception, and he alleges that they manipulated public opinion to manufacture a cause for war against in Iraq in 2003, a war that he claims was entirely unnecessary. He wrote that the White House operated as if it were in a perpetual campaign mode, with key personnel unwilling to assert themselves when policies appeared misguided. McClellan also took to task the American media, which he claims allowed the Bush White House free rein in the early years of the war and was not sufficiently aggressive in its reporting.

PAUL G. PIERPAOLI JR.

**See also**

Bush, George Walker; Cheney, Richard Bruce; Libby, I. Lewis; Rice, Condoleezza; Rove, Karl; Wilson, Joseph Carter, IV; Wilson, Valerie Plame

**References**

McClellan, Scott. *What Happened: Inside the Bush White House and Washington's Culture of Deception.* New York: PublicAffairs, 2008.

Woodward, Bob. *State of Denial: Bush at War, Part III.* New York: Simon and Schuster, 2006.

---

# McGinnis, Ross Andrew
**Birth Date: June 14, 1987**
**Death Date: December 4, 2006**

U.S. soldier and posthumous Medal of Honor recipient. Born in Knox, Pennsylvania, on June 14, 1987, Ross Andrew McGinnis graduated from Keystone Junior-Senior High School in 2005 and enlisted in the army. Following basic training at Fort Benning, Georgia, he joined the 1st Battalion, 26th Infantry Regiment at Schweinfurt, Germany. In August 2006, the regiment deployed to Iraq. Private First Class McGinnis was assigned as an M2 .50-caliber machine gunner in a Humvee during operations against insurgent forces at Adhamiyah.

On December 4, 2006, in the course of a mounted patrol in Adhamiyah, an insurgent was able to throw a hand grenade into McGinnis's vehicle. Reacting quickly, McGinnis shouted "Grenade!" to alert the other occupants of the Humvee, then quickly threw his body against the grenade. McGinnis absorbed most of the explosion and, although he was mortally wounded, his action saved the other occupants of the Humvee from serious injury or death.

For his selfless action, McGinnis was posthumously promoted to specialist and awarded the Medal of Honor. President George W. Bush presented the award to his family in a White House ceremony on June 2, 2008. McGinnis was the second soldier to receive the Medal of Honor in the Iraq War and the fourth member of the U.S. armed forces to be so honored for heroism in Iraq.

SPENCER C. TUCKER

**See also**

Bush, George Walker

**References**

Shane, Leo, III. "19-year-old Who Died Protecting Others Will Be Awarded Medal of Honor." *Stars and Stripes,* May 24, 2008.

Tan, Michelle, "Medal of Honor Nominee McGinnis Laid to Rest." *Army Times,* March 26, 2007.

---

# McGonagle, William Loren
**Birth Date: November 19, 1925**
**Death Date: March 3, 1999**

U.S. Navy officer and commander of the electronic intelligence-gathering ship *Liberty* when it came under Israeli attack during the

June 1967 Six-Day War. William McGonagle was born in Wichita, Kansas, on November 19, 1925. He attended secondary school in California and joined the Naval Reserve Officers' Training Corps (NROTC) while a student at the University of Southern California. He was commissioned an ensign on graduation in June 1947.

During 1947–1950, McGonagle served in the destroyer *Frank Knox* and the minesweeper *Partridge*. During the Korean War (1950–1953), he was assigned to the minesweeper *Kite* and took part in its extensive minesweeping operations. From 1951 to 1966 he served in various postings ashore and afloat, including command of the fleet tug *Mataco* and the salvage ship *Reclaimer*.

In April 1966, with the rank of commander, McGonagle assumed command of the *Liberty* (AGTR-5), taking the ship on intelligence-gathering missions off the west coast of Africa. Ordered to gather intelligence during the war between Israel and Egypt, Syria, and Lebanon, McGonagle took his ship into the Mediterranean. On June 8, 1967, the *Liberty* was located in international waters 13 miles off the Egyptian port of El Arish when it came under attack from Israeli aircraft and torpedo boats. Messages from Washington ordering McGonagle to move 100 miles from the coast were not received in time by the *Liberty*.

McGonagle was badly wounded early in the Israeli strike but remained at his station on the bridge for the next 17 hours. Only when his ship rendezvoused with a U.S. Sixth Fleet destroyer did he relinquish command. He also refused medical treatment until the most seriously wounded had been cared for. The attack on the *Liberty* claimed 34 dead and 172 wounded among its crew. The survivors were able to keep the ship afloat, however, and it steamed to Malta for stopgap repairs. For his heroism and leadership on that occasion, McGonagle was awarded the Medal of Honor. His ship received the Presidential Unit Citation.

Promoted to captain in October 1967, McGonagle commanded the new ammunition ship *Kilauea* and led the NROTC unit at the University of Oklahoma. He retired from active duty in 1974. McGonagle died at Palm Springs, California, on March 3, 1999.

SPENCER C. TUCKER

**See also**

Arab-Israeli Conflict, Overview; *Liberty* Incident

**References**

Bamford, James. *Body of Secrets: Anatomy of the Ultra Secret National Security Agency*. New York: Anchor, 2002.

Cristol, A. Jay. *The Liberty Incident: The 1967 Israeli Attack on the US Navy Spy Ship*. Washington, DC: Brassey's, 2002.

Ennis, James M., Jr. *Assault on the Liberty: The True Story of the Israeli Attack on an American Intelligence Ship*. New York: Random House, 1979.

# McKiernan, David Deglan
## Birth Date: December 11, 1950

U.S. Army officer, commander of the Coalition Force Land Component Command (Middle East) during 2002–2004, and commander of the International Security Assistance Force–Afghanistan (ISAF) led by the North Atlantic Treaty Organization (NATO) during 2008–2009. As such, David Deglan McKiernan was the top military official in Afghanistan for all international military forces and commander of all U.S. armed forces in Afghanistan. McKiernan was born on December 11, 1950. He attended the College of William and Mary, where he was a member of the Reserve Officers' Training Corps (ROTC). Upon his graduation in 1972, he entered active service in the army as an armor officer. He later earned a master's degree in public administration from Shippensburg University and graduated from the U.S. Army Command and General Staff College and the Army War College. As an advancing career officer, McKiernan spent his years as a junior officer in the United States, South Korea, and Germany and held several staff positions in Germany and at the U.S. Army Training and Doctrine Command (TRADOC).

During Operation DESERT STORM in 1991, McKiernan ran the army's VII Corps mobile command post in Saudi Arabia as the assistant G-3 (operations). He was the G-3 for the 1st Cavalry Division, later becoming the division's 1st Brigade commander from 1993 to 1995. McKiernan was promoted to brigadier general in October 1996 when serving as the deputy chief of staff in the Allied Command Europe Rapid Reaction Corps, which was stationed in Germany and deployed in Sarajevo, Bosnia. After becoming the assistant division commander of the 1st Infantry Division in Germany, he served as the deputy chief of staff for operations for the U.S. Army Europe during military operations in Bosnia, Albania, and Kosovo in 1998 and 1999. Promoted to major general, he commanded the 1st Cavalry Division. McKiernan became a lieutenant general shortly after becoming the army's deputy chief of staff for plans and operations in October 2001.

As the United States prepared for an invasion of Iraq in 2002, McKiernan assumed command of the U.S. Third Army and U.S. Army Forces Central Command, known by the acronym ARCENT. He assisted with the plans for the initial Iraq invasion in March 2003, which embroiled him in a conflict between Secretary of Defense Donald Rumsfeld and other top army commanders about the appropriate number of troops to deploy. McKiernan was among those army officers who advocated that more troops be sent to the region. In interviews, McKiernan claimed that he had sufficient troops to accomplish his mission for the invasion. As the Coalition Forces Land Component Command (CFLCC) commander from 2002 to 2004, McKiernan directed all U.S. and coalition ground forces during the initial phases of the war. As such, he was also involved in the controversies surrounding the lack of clear postconflict plans and the slow recognition of the Iraqi insurgency. In October 2004, McKiernan served as the deputy commander and chief of staff at the U.S. Army Forces Command. Promoted to full general in December 2005, McKiernan became the commanding general of U.S. Army Europe and Seventh Army.

In June 2008, McKiernan assumed command of ISAF and called for additional troops to help contain the Taliban insurgency and prevent the resurgence of the Al Qaeda terrorists who had previously used Afghanistan as their base of operations. In February 2009, President Barack Obama authorized an additional force of 17,000 soldiers to deploy to Afghanistan, which would raise U.S. force levels to 50,000. Many of those troops were deployed to southern Afghanistan, where the fighting was fiercest. McKiernan believed that further resources, including the deployment of more civilians, had to be dedicated to Afghan police training, eliminating corruption, and combating the drug trade.

In May 2009 after only 11 months on the job, in a surprise announcement, Secretary of Defense Robert Gates said that he was replacing McKiernan with Lieutenant General Stanley A. McChrystal, a former commander of the Joint Special Operations Command. Gates said that McKiernan had done nothing wrong but that "new leadership and fresh eyes" were needed in a war that Washington has admitted is not being won. It was the first replacement of a field commander during combat operations since the dismissal of General Douglas MacArthur during the Korean War. Factors behind the dismissal of McKiernan were that he and Central Command (CENTCOM) commander General David Petraeus had not developed a close relationship and that leadership believed greater emphasis should be placed on counterinsurgency initiatives. Although McKiernan had an unblemished record, his expertise lay in conventional rather than insurgent warfare.

LISA MUNDEY

**See also**

Al Qaeda; Coalition Force Land Component Command; DESERT STORM, Operation; International Security Assistance Force Afghanistan; IRAQI FREEDOM, Operation; Iraqi Insurgency; North Atlantic Treaty Organization in Afghanistan; Obama, Barack Hussein, II; Rumsfeld, Donald Henry; Taliban; Taliban Insurgency, Afghanistan

**References**

Bumiller, Elisabeth, and Thom Shanker. "Pentagon Ousts Top Commander in Afghan War." *New York Times*, May 12, 2009.

Fontenot, Gregory, et al. *On Point: The United States Army in Iraqi Freedom*. Annapolis, MD: Naval Institute Press, 2005.

Metz, Steven. *Iraq & the Evolution of American Strategy*. Washington, DC: Potomac Books, 2008.

Ricks, Thomas E. *Fiasco: The American Military Adventure in Iraq*. New York: Penguin, 2006.

Woodward, Bob. *Plan of Attack*. New York: Simon and Schuster, 2004.

---

# McKnight, Daniel
## Birth Date: April 9, 1951

U.S. Army Ranger officer, who participated in the October 3–4, 1993, Battle of Mogadishu. Daniel "Danny" McKnight was born on April 9, 1951, in Columbus, Georgia. His family moved in 1959 to Rockledge, Florida, where he spent his formative years. McKnight graduated from high school in 1969 and spent two years at Brevard Community College. He continued his higher education at Florida State University, where he was a member of the army Reserve Officers' Training Corps (ROTC) unit. Upon graduation in 1973, McKnight was commissioned a second lieutenant in the U.S. Army.

McKnight completed the Infantry Officer Basic Course, Airborne School, and Ranger School. Among his early assignments were positions as a company executive officer and Ranger instructor. He also served as an aide to the commanding general at Fort Benning, Georgia, and as a company commander in the 58th Infantry Regiment (Mechanized). McKnight was then assigned to the ROTC Department at the University of Florida, and while there he also completed a master's degree. He then attended the Air Force Command and Staff College.

In 1989, McKnight was assigned as the executive officer of the 3rd Ranger Battalion, 75th Ranger Regiment. In this capacity he participated in Operation JUST CAUSE, the U.S. invasion of Panama in December 1989. In 1991 he commanded a battalion of the 27th Infantry Regiment garrisoned in Hawaii. In February 1993, Lieutenant Colonel McKnight returned to the Rangers as commander of his former unit of the 3rd Ranger Battalion.

In August 1993, McKnight deployed with his battalion to the Horn of Africa as part of the U.S. contingent in support of United Nations (UN) operations to ensure humanitarian aid to Somalia and to quell the Civil War there. The 3rd Battalion was part of Task Force Ranger. Among that unit's missions was the capture of the warlord Mohammed Farrah Aidid (Aideed), leader of the Somali National Alliance. Following two previous unsuccessful efforts, on October 3, 1993, Task Force Ranger received intelligence that Aidid and his aides were meeting in downtown Mogadishu. An attack plan was developed to include both helicopters and ground forces to take the men prisoner.

The plan went awry after Somali rocket-propelled grenades brought down two U.S. Sikorsky UH-60 Black Hawk helicopters, and a 15-hour firefight ensued between the lightly armed U.S. forces on the ground and Aidid's militia. McKnight's ground convoy was ordered to the first crash site but confusion in Mogadishu's streets and Somali armed resistance forced the convoy to return to base. In the fighting, McKnight was wounded in the neck. A Pakistani force with tanks was slow to arrive on the scene, and the October 3–4 battle claimed 18 U.S. dead and 79 wounded. The high U.S. death toll and images of the bodies of U.S. soldiers being dragged through the streets of Mogadishu led to a backlash in the United States against the mission and the subsequent withdrawal of all U.S. forces.

Upon redeployment to the United States, McKnight attended the Army War College. His last army assignment was as deputy chief of staff for training, First Army. He retired at the rank of colonel on January 1, 2002. After retirement, McKnight worked in the security field.

SHAWN LIVINGSTON

**See also**

Aidid, Mohammed Farrah; JUST CAUSE, Operation; Somalia, International Intervention in

**References**

Bowden, Mark. *Black Hawk Down: A Story of Modern War.* 1st ed. New York: Atlantic Monthly Press, 1999.

Clarke, Walter S., and Jeffrey Ira Herbst. *Learning from Somalia: The Lessons of Armed Humanitarian Intervention.* Boulder, CO: Westview, 1997.

---

# McNeill, Dan K.
## Birth Date: 1946

U.S. Army general. Dan K. McNeill was born in Warsaw, North Carolina, in 1946 and earned an undergraduate degree from North Carolina State University in 1968. A Reserve Officers' Training Corps (ROTC) student, he was commissioned a second lieutenant in November 1968 and saw duty in the Vietnam War. Returning stateside in 1969, he held a variety of posts in the United States, South Korea, and Italy. He attended the Army Command and General Staff College and graduated from the Army War College in 1989. McNeill also participated in the 1989 invasion of Panama and the 1991 Persian Gulf War.

Promoted to brigadier general in September 1995, McNeill assumed command of the 3rd Brigade, 82nd Airborne Division, at Fort Bragg, North Carolina; he held the command until July 1993, at which time he became assistant chief of staff, G-3 (Operations), XVIII Airborne Corps. McNeill left that post in March 1995 to serve as assistant division commander of the 2nd Infantry Division, a position that he retained until June 1996. Until August 1997, he was chief of staff, XVIII Airborne Corps, Fort Bragg. From August 1997 to July 1998 McNeill served as deputy commanding general, I Corps; from July 1998 to July 2000 he was the commanding general of the 82nd Airborne Division. McNeill was promoted to major general in October 1998 and lieutenant general in July 2000.

In July 2000, McNeill took command of XVIII Airborne Corps. After Operation ENDURING FREEDOM began in 2001, he also acted as commanding general, Combined Joint Task Force 180 in Afghanistan. He retained that command until August 2003, at which point he became deputy commanding general/chief of staff, U.S. Army Forces Command, Fort McPherson, Georgia. He was promoted to full general (four-stars) in July 2004. He held this command until February 2007, at which time he became commander of the International Security Assistance Force–Afghanistan; he held that position until June 2008.

During his first tour in Afghanistan, in an attempt to defeat the Taliban and allied insurgents, McNeill was a strong proponent of coalition air strikes. But these strikes killed many civilians, which outraged Afghanis and raised concerns in the international community. Afghani citizens became even more disgruntled when, following a July 2002 attack on Deh Rawood, a number of Afghan wedding participants and guests were killed during an American attack on a suspected Taliban stronghold. McNeill offered compensation and assistance to those innocents killed or wounded by U.S. strikes, but he made no apologies. Afghanis became even more alarmed when they began to hear rumors about torture and deaths in U.S. detainment camps, which they believed were being covered up by the American military.

While in command, McNeill also oversaw the prison at Bagram Air Force Base. In December 2002, two Afghani prisoners died while in custody at Bagram. McNeill maintained that the men had died of natural causes, but autopsy reports showed both had died from blunt-force injuries. As commander, McNeill should have known that prisoners were being treated harshly, but he insisted that no international laws of conduct had been broken. He also refused to acknowledge the autopsy reports of the dead prisoners.

On February 4, 2007, McNeill took command of the International Security Assistance Force–Afghanistan (ISAF). With this command, he became the highest-ranking U.S. general in the region, which many surmised to be a demonstration of the renewed U.S. commitment to Afghanistan. Many hoped that McNeill's appointment would witness a reinvigorated effort to pacify the troubled Afghani-Pakistani border areas, rife with insurgent activity. Others, however, citing McNeill's past performance in Afghanistan, wondered if he were the right man for the job. Certainly many Afghanis did not welcome his return. Nevertheless, all sides believed that McNeill would bring a more hard-line approach to the growing Taliban insurgency. At the same time, McNeill was expected to boost Afghani reconstruction efforts, which had lagged in recent years.

When McNeill departed Afghanistan in June 2008, he admitted that insurgency activity had increased substantially over the preceding year, up 50 percent in April 2008 alone. He stated clearly that the insurgency could not be contained or defeated without significantly more "boots on the ground," a stance that many American politicians had taken, including then presidential candidate Barack Obama. McNeill also voiced concern with the growing Taliban insurgency in the border areas of Pakistan. McNeill retired from the army at Fort Bragg, North Carolina, on June 20, 2008.

PAUL G. PIERPAOLI JR.

**See also**

Afghanistan; Afghanistan, Coalition Combat Operations in, 2002–Present; Combined Joint Task Force 180; ENDURING FREEDOM, Operation; International Security Assistance Force; Taliban Insurgency, Afghanistan

**References**

Mackay, Chris, and Greg Miller. *The Interrogators: Inside the Secret War Against Al Qaeda.* New York: Little, Brown, 2004.

Naylor, Sean. *Not a Good Day to Die: The Untold Story of Operation Anaconda.* New York: Berkley Trade, 2006.

---

# Meals, Ready to Eat

U.S. self-contained individual field rations issued to soldiers at the front. In 1981 the Meal, Ready to Eat (MRE) became the new standard food ration for U.S. soldiers in the field. The MREs were derived from Vietnam-era experiences with rations issued to long-range patrols, which operated far from base areas. Soldiers had to carry sufficient food to survive for an extended period of time, but traditional canned C Rations were too heavy. In response, the Department of Defense developed a special, dehydrated ration stored in waterproof canvas.

In 1975, the military began developing a new ration stored in a plastic retort. This became the MRE, which replaced both the traditional canned individual ration and the Long-Range Patrol ration. The modern MRE has a shelf life of about three years.

The first MRE came in a heavy plastic bag holding one entire meal. Inside the bag was an entrée. For example, an entrée labeled "Chicken in Thai Style Sauce" came in a box that was 8¼ inches by 4¾ inches by ¾ inch. Inside the box was a flexible pouch containing an eight-ounce serving of chicken and sauce. Officially labeled a "tri-laminate retort pouch," the pouch was basically a flexible can made up of layers of aluminum foil and plastic. Compared to a traditional metal can, the pouch was lighter, flexible (so that it could withstand rough handling), and flat (so that it fit well inside a soldier's backpack or pocket).

Also inside the plastic bag was a slightly smaller box labeled "Yellow and Wild Rice Pilaf," which contained a flexible pouch with a five-ounce serving of rice. A flameless heater using a simple chemical reaction allowed a soldier to warm the food. Additional contents included: one 1.4-ounce foil package of crackers; one 1.3-ounce Nutra Fruit cereal bar; one packet each of spiced cider drink mix, instant coffee, sugar, salt, pepper, and grape jelly; one piece of chewing gum; one moist towelette; one pack of matches; one packet toilet paper; and a plastic spoon. The entire meal provided 820 calories.

As time passed, soldiers requested more menu options with larger serving sizes. Accordingly, MREs expanded from an initial set of 12 to some 24 options. Chicken entrées included "Chicken with Salsa and Mexican Rice," "Country Captain Chicken with Buttered Noodles," and "Chicken Breast with Minestrone Stew." Other varieties of MREs provided beef, pork, and pasta entrées. There were even a few relatively exotic MREs, such as "Jambalaya" and "Black Bean and Rice Burrito" as well as old reliables, such as "Meat Loaf with Gravy" and "Turkey Breast with Gravy and Potatoes."

The food was not wonderful. According to the manufacturer, the food tasted like any canned food. For example, the "Chicken in Thai Style Sauce" tasted liked canned chop suey with its mix of chicken, celery, red pepper, and mushrooms in a slightly sweet, slightly salty sauce. The taste and texture were monotonous. But, if it was the only food available, hungry soldiers wolfed it down. Still, soldiers learned to call the rations "Meals Refused by Everyone."

Because of the development of microwave cooking, commercial food preservation technology made notable advances during the 1980s. Commercial products that resisted spoilage offered an alternative to the MREs. During the 1991 Persian Gulf War, the military supplemented the unpopular MREs with commercially packaged food. Before the war ended, the U.S. Army alone had purchased almost 24 million individual commercial meals. They proved a popular, tasty alternative to the MREs.

Based on combat experience in Kuwait, Iraq, and Afghanistan, the Department of Defense continued to improve and modify the MREs in an effort to provide more varied and nutritious food in lighter-weight, more durable packages. For example, in 2006 so-called beverage bags were added to the basic MRE.

JAMES ARNOLD

**See also**

Logistics, Persian Gulf War

**References**

Hutchison, Kevin Don. *Operation Desert Shield/Desert Storm: Chronology and Fact Book.* Westport, CT: Greenwood, 1995.

Matthews, James K., and Cora J. Holt. *So Many, So Much, So Far, So Fast: United States Transportation Command and Strategic Deployment for Operation Desert Shield/Desert Storm.* Washington, DC: Joint History Office, Office of the Chairman of the Joint Chiefs of Staff and Research Center, United States Transportation Command, 1996.

Scales, Robert H. *Certain Victory: The U.S. Army in the Gulf War.* Washington, DC: Brassey's, 1994.

## Media and Operation DESERT STORM

The media coverage of Operation DESERT STORM marked the beginning of a new era in war reporting and the way in which people receive information regarding war. Major news organizations from around the world spent millions of dollars to cover the crisis in the Persian Gulf region. What is more, they were subjected to the loss of millions of dollars in lost advertising revenue as broadcast networks switched from regularly scheduled programming to live, uninterrupted war programming. Beginning in January 1991, DESERT STORM unfolded on television screens across the world in real time. Coverage was also notable for the extensive efforts of leaders on both sides of the conflict to use the media as a vehicle by which to conduct foreign policy and shape public opinion.

Media coverage of war in the early 1990s had changed dramatically from the 1960s and 1970s coverage of the Vietnam War, the last significant U.S. conflict before 1991. By 1990, 65 percent of American adults had identified television as their primary source of news from around the world. In America, at the beginning of Operation DESERT STORM, the three major broadcast networks (ABC, CBS, and NBC) broke away from their regular schedules and offered hours of news coverage. On top of the coverage offered by the three major broadcast networks, other news outlets provided in-depth coverage. By early 1991, over 1,400 journalists were in the Persian Gulf region. During the first few hours of war, Cable News Network (CNN), a 24-hour cable news organization, provided eyewitness reports of the bombing with its live, electronic connection to Baghdad.

Besides television alone, several wire services, newspapers, and news organizations offered extensive coverage of DESERT STORM. Many American newspapers, and magazines like *Time, Newsweek,*

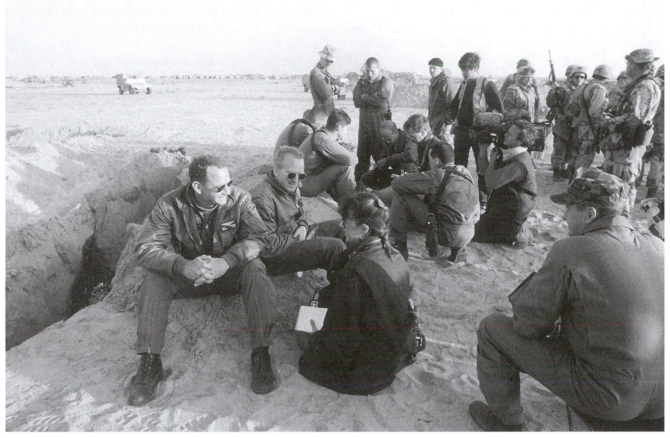

Journalists interview U.S. Marine Corps aviators at a desert landing strip following the withdrawal of Iraqi forces from Kuwait during Operation DESERT STORM. (U.S. Department of Defense)

and *U.S. News and World Report,* published special editions devoted to DESERT STORM. In newspaper issues the day after the air campaign began in January 1991, most headlines ran in gigantic typeface, the likes of which had not been seen since the assassination of President John F. Kennedy in 1963 or the Japanese bombing of Pearl Harbor in 1941.

Because the American public received information about war much faster than in any previous conflict, the U.S. government took great measures to make sure that the American media did not report information that would hamper the war effort or give the enemy any advantage. Because of the way in which many Americans had turned against the U.S. war effort in Vietnam after viewing repeated negative news reports about it, the George H. W. Bush administration was very sensitive to public opinion. As a result, the U.S. military imposed limits on the press, which restricted them from unfettered physical access to the troops or battle zones while at the same time limiting what they could report to the public. This was the first time that the U.S. military had placed restrictions on the media since the 1950–1953 Korean War. Because of such restrictions, many members of the media were unable to witness everything that they wished to see or report all that they may have known.

There were few so-called imbedded reporters in Iraq and Kuwait, and the few who were there had been vetted thoroughly by the U.S. military establishment. They were exhaustively briefed on what they could and could not report, and any interviews with troops were in the company of at least several officers. And the military had the option of censoring any portions of any interview when it deemed appropriate.

Portable satellite transmitters and cell phones, not available to reporters until at least the 1980s, undoubtedly lent to the war coverage an air of imminent danger and suspense. A number of television news reporters, for example, stayed in Baghdad even when war was just hours away. Their reporting, complete with ear-splitting explosions, fireballs, and tracers in the background, was riveting. While they were hunkered down in Baghdad's Al-Rashid Hotel, CNN's Peter Arnett, John Holliman, and Bernard Shaw became media stars when they began transmitting reports via cell phone as the first bombs of the war met their targets on the outskirts of Baghdad. Indeed, many media pundits credit the Persian Gulf War and its reporting for catapulting the fledgling network into the avant-garde of television journalism.

Both sides tried to use the media to their own advantage. Iraqi president Saddam Hussein willingly opened his country to media members and their cameras. Hussein wanted to use the media to disseminate images of coalition destruction in Iraq. In doing so, he hoped to build sympathy for his country and its citizens and force the citizens of coalition countries to question the actions of their governments. On January 20, 1991, photographs of a bombed "baby milk factory" with Iraqi employees wearing uniforms with "Baby Milk Factory" printed in English on their backs were taken and then disseminated to a worldwide audience the next day through CNN. On February 13, the bombing of a civilian bomb shelter at Amariyah produced images of civilian casualties that totaled 314.

The media reaction around the world to such attacks was varied. Many in Europe and the Muslim world deplored, in particular, the raid on the Amariyah bomb shelter. Others, however, saw such casualties as unavoidable and blamed Hussein for bringing them on his own people. The U.S. government combated negative press coverage by attempting to vilify Hussein. The government spread images of oil fires that Iraqi forces had set in Kuwait and oil dumps into the Persian Gulf. The U.S. essentially charged Hussein with environmental terrorism and used media images to back up its assertion. Some foreign papers, like the French paper *Paris Journal de Dimanche,* accused coalition forces of starting most of the fires, although there is no reliable evidence to back up this claim.

The media coverage of Operation DESERT STORM forever changed the way in which war was reported. Government attempts to manipulate media coverage in order to shape public opinion, while a major part of earlier wars, played a larger role during the Persian Gulf War because of the mass amount of information that could be distributed to news consumers around the world. Because technological advances allowed news organizations to provide real-time updates on the war instantaneously, governments had to ensure that information detrimental to their mission did not reach the enemy. During the Persian Gulf War, both sides attempted to use the media against one another and each side had its successes. However, by war's end, it was the coalition that had ultimately translated those media successes to victory on the battlefield.

GREGORY W. MORGAN

**See also**

DESERT STORM, Operation; National Media Pool

**References**

Greenberg, Bradley S., and Walter Gantz, eds. *Desert Storm and the Mass Media.* Cresskill, NJ: Hampton, 1993.
Mowlana, Hamid, George Gerbner, and Herbert I. Schiller, eds. *Triumph of the Image: The Media's War in the Persian Gulf—A Global Perspective.* Boulder, CO: Westview, 1992.
Smith, Hedrick, ed. *The Media and the Gulf War: The Press and Democracy in Wartime.* Washington, DC: Seven Locks, 1992.

---

# Medina Ridge, Battle of
## Event Date: February 27, 1991

The last major ground engagement of the 1991 Persian Gulf War and a decisive tank battle, which took place on February 27, 1991, near Basra, Iraq. The battle occurred when a brigade of the U.S. 1st Armored Division attacked and defeated the 2nd Brigade of the Iraqi Republican Guard (Medina Division). The battle demonstrated the superiority of American training and technology during the conflict.

The coalition's plan for the liberation of Kuwait called for two U.S. Marine Corps divisions to attack directly into Kuwait to pin the Iraqi Army to its defenses. The main attack would be carried out by the U.S. VII and XVIII Corps, which would execute a giant left hook through the western Iraqi desert before turning right and encircling Iraqi forces in Kuwait. These two corps would also engage the Republican Guard divisions of the Iraqi Army, which were stationed in reserve north of Kuwait.

The ground offensive began on February 24, 1991. On the morning of February 27, the U.S. VII Corps was preparing to complete the encirclement of Iraqi forces in Kuwait. The 2nd Brigade, 1st Armored Division, commanded by Colonel Montgomery Meigs, and consisting of 200 vehicles of all types, encountered an armored brigade of the Medina Republican Guard Division dug into the far side of a long, low ridge that ran north-south, known as the Medina Ridge. The Iraqi plan was to pick off American tanks and armored vehicles as they crested the ridge. The Iraqis were equipped with T-72 tanks mounting 125-millimeter main guns and with BMP-1 armored vehicles and backed by an assortment of older T-55 and T-62 tanks. The Iraqi deployment line stretched for a distance of about six miles.

Meigs's brigade massed 200 vehicles for the engagement. The Americans were equipped with M1A1 Abrams tanks and Bradley Fighting Vehicles. The 105-millimeter main gun on the Abrams tank had a range of 4,375 yards and fired armor-piercing discarding sabot (APDS) ammunition, with a core projectile made of depleted uranium. Abrams tanks were also equipped with thermal sights that enabled them to fight in conditions of poor visibility. In assault formation, Abrams tanks advanced ahead of the more vulnerable Bradleys. Iraqi tank guns had ranges of only about 2,000 yards, and the ammunition fired from Iraqi tanks could not penetrate the front armor of Abrams tanks. Only a very small proportion of Iraqi tanks, specifically the most advanced models of the T-72, had laser rangefinders, and these were still outranged by the Abrams. T-72 tanks weighed much less than the Abrams, reflecting the difference in armor protection and crew space. The BMP vehicles used by the Iraqis were obsolete in comparison to the Bradley.

Having arrived on the ridge, the tanks of the 2nd Brigade located Iraqi tanks by using thermal sights and then began destroying them at long range. The Bradleys fired antitank missiles and engaged lighter Iraqi vehicles with 25-millimeter cannon. The Iraqis aimed at the muzzle flashes of the Abrams tanks, but they were completely outranged and unable to respond adequately. Air support for the Americans was provided by Fairchild-Republic A-10 Thunderbolt (Warthog) aircraft. Additional air support came from six AH-64 Apache helicopters firing Hellfire missiles. One U.S. aircraft was shot down by Iraqis firing a ZSU-23/4 antiaircraft gun. Artillery support for the 2nd Brigade was provided by Multiple Launch Rocket System (MLRS) launchers.

Although the Iraqis knew the Americans were coming, they failed to deploy observation teams and left many vehicles unmanned while the crews ate lunch. They had also attempted to dig their tanks into hull-down positions, leaving only the turrets exposed, to provide more protection. However, the procedure was improperly carried out. Instead of digging their tanks into the ground, the Iraqis simply pushed sand up against the sides and front of the tanks, a technique that proved useless, because American tank rounds easily penetrated this makeshift defense. Iraqi artillery fired only at preregistered positions and could not adjust to new targets. The Iraqi tank crews that did fight back mostly stayed in position and failed to move effectively. The one group of Iraqi tanks that attempted a fighting withdrawal was promptly located and destroyed. The outcome of the battle, which lasted only about three hours, was never in doubt.

The Battle of Medina Ridge was the largest armored engagement of the war and ended in a lopsided American victory after only a few hours of combat. Medina Ridge also marked the last truly substantial attempt at opposition offered by the Iraqi Army in the Persian Gulf War. Superiority in American equipment and technology was an important factor in the victory, but training and discipline enabled U.S. tank crews to fight successfully in conditions of extreme duress. Estimates of Iraqi losses vary, but about 93 Iraqi tanks and 73 other vehicles were destroyed. The 2nd Brigade suffered 1 fatality, 30 wounded, and 4 Abrams tanks disabled but not destroyed. The Persian Gulf War ended in a cease-fire the following day.

PAUL W. DOERR

**See also**

Armored Warfare, Persian Gulf and Iraq Wars; BMP-1 Series Infantry Fighting Vehicles; Bradley Fighting Vehicle; DESERT STORM, Operation, Ground Operations; Infantry Fighting Vehicles, Iraqi; M1A1 and M1A2 Abrams Main Battle Tanks; Multiple Launch Rocket Systems; T-54/55 Series Main Battle Tank; T-62 Main Battle Tank; T-72 Main Battle Tank

**References**

Biddle, Stephen. "Victory Misunderstood: What the Gulf War Tells Us about the Future of Conflict." *International Security* 21(2) (Fall 1996): 139–179.

Gordon, Michael R., and General Bernard E. Trainor. *The Generals' War: The Inside Story of the Conflict in the Gulf.* New York: Little, Brown, 1995.

Pollack, Kenneth M. *Arabs at War: Military Effectiveness, 1948–1991.* Lincoln: University of Nebraska Press, 2002.

Scales, Robert H. *Certain Victory: The U.S. Army in the Gulf War.* Washington, DC: Brassey's, 1994.

# MEDUSA, **Operation**
## Start Date: September 2, 2006
## End Date: September 17, 2006

Military campaign undertaken by the International Security Assistance Force–Afghanistan (ISAF), which was led by the North Atlantic Treaty Organization (NATO), from September 2 to September 17, 2006, against the Taliban and Al Qaeda insurgents. Operation MEDUSA was in response to increased insurgent activity in an area west of Kandahar and was part of a broader ISAF effort to expand the regions under the authority of the Afghan national government.

The main area of operations of ISAF forces during the operation were the districts of Panjwali, Pashmul, and Zhari in Kandahar Province. ISAF forces numbered about 2,000 and included troops from Canada, Denmark, the Netherlands, the United Kingdom, and the United States, as well as soldiers from the Afghan National Army. The primary forces were elements of the Royal Canadian Regiment Battle Group, companies of the U.S. Army 10th Mountain Division and special operations forces, Dutch artillery units, and assorted Afghan infantry. U.S. aircraft from the aircraft carrier *Enterprise* provided air support and used precision-guided munitions against insurgent positions. The American planes flew more than 100 support sorties during MEDUSA. Brigadier David Fraser of the Canadian Army was the operational commander of the offensive.

The Taliban numbered between 1,000 and 1,500 men and were dug-in in caves and ground bunkers. The number of Al Qaeda fighters is unknown. Coalition forces used air power and artillery to suppress the insurgents as ground forces advanced from village to village and conducted search-and-destroy missions against Taliban and Al Qaeda positions. Meanwhile, other coalition forces blockaded the main roads and trails, cutting off the potential escape routes of the enemy. The Taliban and Al Qaeda employed a combination of hit-and-run tactics and defensive stands against the advancing ISAF forces; they also planted land mines and improvised explosive devices (IEDs).

On the first full day of combat, September 3, coalition forces killed about 200 insurgents, and 4 Canadians were killed. Afghan security forces also took part in the fighting and captured about 80 suspected Taliban insurgents. ISAF forces were subsequently able to capture three large insurgent bases and a dozen smaller compounds, including a weapons-manufacturing facility and weapons caches. On one of the most difficult days of fighting, September 10, the insurgents launched a counterattack in an unsuccessful effort to break through the ISAF lines and create an escape route. The attacking force suffered 92 dead; no coalition troops were killed.

One of the immediate successes of MEDUSA was that the majority of Taliban and Al Qaeda fighters were either killed or captured during the campaign, unlike previous operations in which large numbers of the rebels were able to escape. Only about 150 to 200 insurgents were able to flee the area. The ISAF estimated that more than 500 Taliban and Al Qaeda fighters were killed and more than 100 were captured. During the operation, a British reconnaissance aircraft crashed, killing all 14 on board. In addition, 12 Canadians and 1 American died. The combat operations of MEDUSA were followed by a series of ISAF-led reconstruction projects, including highway construction.

TOM LANSFORD

**See also**

Afghanistan, Coalition Combat Operations in, 2002–Present; Al Qaeda; Canada, Role in Persian Gulf and Afghanistan Wars; International Security Assistance Force; North Atlantic Treaty Organization in Afghanistan; Taliban; Taliban Insurgency, Afghanistan

**References**

Feickert, Andrew. *U.S. and Coalition Military Operations in Afghanistan: Issues for Congress.* Washington, DC: Congressional Research Service, 2006.

Guistozzi, Antonio. *Koran, Kalashnikov and Laptop: The Neo-Taliban Insurgency in Afghanistan.* New York: Columbia University Press, 2008.

Jones, Seth G. *Counterinsurgency in Afghanistan: RAND Counterinsurgency Study No. 4.* Santa Monica, CA: RAND Corporation, 2008.

---

# Meir, Golda Mabovitch

**Birth Date: May 3, 1898**
**Death Date: December 8, 1978**

Israeli politician and prime minister (1969–1974). Born in Kiev, Russia, on May 3, 1898, Golda Mabovitch was one of eight children. Her father immigrated to the United States in 1903, and the remainder of the family joined him in Milwaukee in 1906. Intent on becoming a teacher, she enrolled at the Wisconsin State Normal School in 1916 but never finished her degree. That same year she became an active member in the Zionist labor movement where she met Morris Meyerson, whom she married in 1917.

Golda Meyerson and her husband immigrated to Palestine in 1921. They worked on a kibbutz, and Golda became active in the Histadrut, Israel's labor movement. She joined its executive community in 1934, became the head of its political department in 1940, and helped raise funds for Jewish settlement in Palestine.

Shortly before the 1948–1949 Israeli War of Independence, Meyerson twice met secretly with Jordan's King Abdullah. While she was unsuccessful in averting a Jordanian invasion of the Jewish state, these secret contacts proved useful in limiting Jordanian participation in the war. Such secret meetings became the norm in Israeli-Jordanian relations. During the war Meyerson traveled to the United States, where she raised $50 million for Israel from private citizens. Following the war, Israel's first prime minister, David Ben-Gurion, sent her to Moscow as Israel's ambassador. On his urging, she adopted the Hebrew surname Meir, which means "to burn brightly."

Elected to the Knesset (Israeli parliament) in 1949 as a member of Mapai (the Israel Workers Party), Meir was immediately appointed minister of labor by Ben-Gurion. Her greatest task was the resettlement of hundreds of thousands of Jewish refugees who immigrated to Israel during these years. The new arrivals, 685,000 of whom arrived in her first two years in office, lived in large tent cities, while Meir marshaled the new state's scant resources to construct housing for them, instruct them in Hebrew, and integrate them into Israeli society. Over the next six years, she gained a reputation as an aggressive politician, a powerful speaker, and a decisive manager.

Ben-Gurion forced moderate Moshe Sharett to resign as foreign minister on June 18, 1956, and appointed Meir in his place. She held that post until 1965, gaining international fame as one of the few women to hold a prominent position in international affairs. Ben-Gurion, who expected Sharett to oppose war, believed that Meir would support his decision to go to war with Egypt in collusion with France and Britain in 1956, and this proved correct. While uninvolved in planning the war, Meir supported Ben-Gurion's decision to take military action to break Egypt's blockade of Eilat, Israel's Red Sea port.

As foreign minister, Meir worked to strengthen Israel's relationship with the new nations of Africa, to which she dispatched a series of aid missions. This was possible only because Israel's victory in the 1956 Sinai Campaign had secured Israel's right of transit through the Red Sea. Meir hoped to build bridges between Israel and other developing nations and share Israel's practical experience in agriculture and land reclamation. As with many Israeli leaders, she believed that trade with Africa would prove vital to Israel and help offset the Arab economic embargo. She

Golda Meir was a prominent Israeli political leader and the first woman to hold the office of prime minister of Israel (1969–1974). She was forced to resign in the aftermath of the 1973 Yom Kippur War, which had caught Israeli leaders by surprise. (Library of Congress)

was also acutely conscious of Israel's need for friendly nations that would support its policies.

Meir also worked to improve U.S.-Israeli relations damaged by the Sinai Campaign, but she met a generally cold reception from President Dwight D. Eisenhower's administration. President John F. Kennedy's administration proved different, and Meir developed a particularly good relationship with Kennedy. In a conversation with Meir in December 1962, Kennedy first referred to a "special relationship" between Israel and the United States that resembled the relationship between the United States and Great Britain.

Along with Israeli ambassador Abba Eban, Meir convinced Kennedy to sell sophisticated Hawk antiaircraft missiles to Israel. This sale ended the U.S. embargo on arms sales to Israel and opened the door to further arms transfers. Presidents Lyndon B. Johnson and Richard M. Nixon both increased arms sales to Israel, and after the 1967 Six-Day War and a French embargo on arms to the Jewish state, the United States replaced France as Israel's primary arms supplier.

Due to worsening health, Meir resigned as foreign minister in 1965 but continued to serve in the Knesset, and the members of Mapai elected her the party's secretary-general. In that capacity she helped orchestrate the merger of Mapai with several smaller parties that created the new Labor Party, which dominated Israeli politics for the next decade as Mapai had for the previous two decades.

On February 26, 1969, the ruling Labor Party elected Meir prime minister following the death of Levi Eshkol. Meir, the fourth prime minister in Israel's brief history, faced daunting challenges, including Israeli national security imperatives and Middle Eastern instability. Her efforts to trade recently conquered land for peace with Egypt, Syria, and Jordan failed, and terrorist attacks and cross-border raids into Israel increased.

Skirmishing with Egypt escalated into the War of Attrition, which lasted through August 1970 and caused the deaths of 700 Israelis. Meir insisted on Israeli retaliation for any attacks and apparently hoped that increasingly successful Israeli commando raids and air strikes would force Egyptian president Gamal Abdel Nasser into either peace negotiations or resignation. Meir insisted that peace precede withdrawal. Nasser, who had arranged the Arab League's September 1967 resolution that stated there would be no peace, no recognition, and no territorial negotiations with Israel, remained intransigent and insisted on the return of all occupied territory as a prelude to any peace negotiations. A U.S.-brokered cease-fire ended the skirmishing in August 1970, but tensions hardly lessened, and Soviet arms shipments to Egypt increased. The following month, Syria invaded Jordan to support a Palestinian rebellion but withdrew its forces after Meir, encouraged by the United States, threatened an attack on Syria.

Meir increasingly coordinated Israel's foreign policy with the United States, and during her tenure as prime minister the special relationship between Israel and the United States blossomed. U.S. arms sales to Israel increased, while Israel shared important intelligence information with the United States and allowed U.S.

technicians to examine sophisticated Soviet weapons systems captured by the Israeli Army during the War of Attrition. Meir developed a close relationship with President Nixon and Henry Kissinger, Nixon's key foreign policy adviser. Mired in Vietnam, Nixon and Kissinger both came to see Israel as a vital ally in the Cold War. Despite this increasingly close relationship with the United States, Meir managed to convince the Soviet Union to allow some Russian Jews to immigrate to Israel.

Anwar Sadat, who assumed power following Nasser's death on September 28, 1970, offered to reduce Egyptian troop strength west of the Suez Canal if Israel withdrew its forces 24 miles from the canal. This came on the heels of the War of Attrition, and few of Meir's advisers trusted the Egyptian proposal, which would allow Egypt to reopen the canal but give nothing except promises to Israel. Despite protests led by opposition leader Menachem Begin, Meir indicated her interest in returning most of the territory occupied by Israel in the 1967 war in exchange for peace and limited the establishment of Israeli settlements in the occupied territories to a mere handful. The main stumbling block remained her refusal to withdraw from occupied territory as a prelude to negotiating a peace settlement, although other factors, including the rivalry of Egypt's and Israel's superpower patrons, also hindered the negotiations, which ended without result.

Tensions with Egypt and Syria increased steadily until the morning of October 6, 1973, when Israel's director of intelligence warned of an imminent attack. Concerned about Israel's international reputation, Meir rejected proposals to launch a preemptive attack, as Israel had done in 1967. That afternoon, as Meir met with her cabinet, Egyptian and Syrian forces invaded Sinai and the Golan Heights, driving back the surprised and outnumbered Israeli Army units. While some leaders recommended deep retreats on both fronts, Meir overruled them. The Israeli Army held fast, retreating only when forced back by the furious Egyptian and Syrian assaults. The Soviet Union airlifted and shipped arms to sustain the Arab offensive, and the United States countered with an airlift that supplied vital equipment to Israel. Following a series of early defeats, Israeli counteroffensives finally contained both Arab forces and left Israel in possession of additional Arab territory on the Syrian front and in Egypt. Israeli forces crossed the canal and had almost cut off two Egyptian divisions east of the canal from their bases. Neither the Soviet Union nor the United States wished to see Egypt completely defeated, and under their pressure a cease-fire went into effect on October 24.

Although the war was won, the early setbacks, surprise of the invasion, heavy casualties, and rumors that Meir had considered using nuclear weapons during the first days of the war tarnished her administration. A special investigating committee cleared Meir of responsibility for the near disaster, blaming the head of military intelligence and the Israel Defense Forces (IDF) chief of staff, but she remained under constant attack from opposition politicians, particularly Likud leader Menachem Begin. Despite this, Meir led her party to another victory in the December 1973 elections and established a ruling coalition despite Labor's loss of six seats in the Knesset and the growing strength of the Likud Party.

In the following months, thanks to Kissinger's shuttle diplomacy, Meir negotiated cease-fire and disengagement agreements with Egypt and Syria. The complicated negotiations to extricate the trapped Egyptian Army paved the way for future negotiations that finally produced a lasting peace between Israel and Egypt. Meir resigned on June 3, 1974, and returned to private life, dying of leukemia in Jerusalem on December 8, 1978.

STEPHEN K. STEIN

**See also**

Arab-Israeli Conflict, Overview; Begin, Menachem; Kennedy, John Fitzgerald; Kissinger, Henry Alfred; Nasser, Gamal Abdel; Sadat, Muhammad Anwar; United States, Middle East Policy, 1945–Present

**References**

Martin, Ralph G. *Golda Meir: The Romantic Years.* New York: Scribner, 1988.

Meir, Golda. *My Life.* New York: Putnam, 1975.

---

# Mesopotamia

Middle Eastern region corresponding to the lands bordered by the Euphrates River to the west and the Tigris River to the east, in what is now Iraq. "Mesopotamia" is a Greek term meaning "lands between the two rivers" and was generally used as a reference to the actual region and at times as a generic term for various civilizations that arose from or controlled that region. Both rivers originate in eastern Turkey and flow through Iraq; the Euphrates also runs through eastern Syria. Although parts of Turkey and Syria have also been historically associated with Mesopotamia, the term has primarily focused on the territory running about 200 to 250 miles northwest of Baghdad and southward to where the Tigris and Euphrates merge at the Shatt al-Arab (River of the Arabs), about 100 miles north of the Persian Gulf in far southeastern Iraq.

Physically, Mesopotamia is in general divided into two regions: lands north of Baghdad, referred to as Assyria, and those to the south, known as Babylonia or Sumer. With only minor exceptions, most of Mesopotamia ranges in elevation from 0 to 1,500 feet in Iraq, with the highest area approximately 4,000 feet. Although some variations of climate exist between the north and the south, generally Mesopotamia's average temperatures, depending on the season, range from 68 to 95 degrees; however, during the hottest months (summer), temperatures can reach more than 120 degrees. Rainfall in northern Mesopotamia averages between 15.75 and 31.5 inches per year, while the south averages about 7.78 inches or less, primarily between December and February.

Mesopotamian land use in the northern area is somewhat varied, with arable land in the northeast, irrigated farming along the rivers and canals, and lands for grazing and pasturage. Although some wastelands, marshes, and swamps were in the southern region, irrigation allows areas along the rivers to be used for cultivation. Many of the marshes in the south were drained by order of Iraqi president Saddam Hussein during the early 1990s. Major crops include dates, cotton, barley, and rice. Although petroleum is a major natural resource in Mesopotamia, its importance was of limited value until the mid-1900s. In addition to being an important region on various trade routes for goods from Africa, Europe, and Asia, cities in Mesopotamia often served as important trading centers.

Mesopotamia demographics vary according to the particular era and/or particular area of Mesopotamia being discussed. Ethnically, several different groups have been represented in the region throughout history, including various Semitic groups, such as the Assyrians and Arabs; Aryan groups, such as the Kurds and Persians; and unknown ethnic groups, such as the Sumerians and Turks during the Ottoman era. Prior to the Persian Empire's conquest of Mesopotamia during the mid-sixth century CE, the vast majority of civilizations and empires practiced either polytheism or pantheism. The Persians and their successors, the Parthians and the Sassanians, all established Zoroastrianism as their empires' official religion, although other religions were tolerated. Although the exile of Jews after the Assyrian and Babylonian conquests of the Kingdom of Israel and Kingdom of Judah respectively introduced Judaism into parts of Mesopotamia, it was practiced exclusively by Jewish exiles.

Following the conquest of the region by the Arabs during the middle to late seventh century, Islam has been and remains the dominant religion in Mesopotamia. Although the majority of practitioners are Shia, a significant number of Sunnis are also in the region. Furthermore, a small remnant of Jewish practitioners remains in Mesopotamia, as well as a small Assyrian population in the north that practices Christianity.

The region may be broken into three major chronological divisions: ancient, Islamic, and modern. Although Mesopotamia has long been considered the "cradle of civilization," other cultures predating ancient Mesopotamia existed elsewhere. Permanent civilizations in Mesopotamia arose circa 3500 BCE. Irrigation techniques developed by inhabitants in the region were responsible for the creation of agricultural surpluses, which led to the development of urban centers referred to as city-states. Kings with religious support or priest-kings ruled the various city-states. Urban development had a significant impact on a number of areas. The Sumerians created cuneiform, the world's first writing system, as a means to maintain written records; it would also be used by a number of Mesopotamian civilizations even after Sumer no longer existed. The world's first major piece of literature, the *Epic of Gilgamesh,* was also written during the period of Sumer's prominence. Laws were codified for the first time in Mesopotamia. Hammurabi, an Amorite ruler, promulgated the most well-known early law code, Hammurabi's Code.

Sargon the Great, generally recognized as the first emperor in the world, ruled the Akkaddian Empire, which ran from the Persian Gulf through Mesopotamia and onward to the Mediterranean

Sea and the Taurus Mountains in Turkey. His grandson Naram-Sim also extended the empire. After the downfall of Akkad, the city-state Ur arose to prominence in the region, leading to the Ur III dynastic state, which established control over the region of Sumer. Amorites, a nomadic group, eventually conquered the region, leading to the establishment of several Amorite kingdoms, the most famous being the Amorite kingdom of Babylon, ruled by Hammurabi. The Amorite Kingdom, also known as the Old Babylonian Kingdom, lasted for slightly over 100 years, before the Hittite Empire defeated Babylonia. However, the Kassites occupied Babylonia for approximately 400 years, and other parts of Mesopotamia retained their independence.

In 934 BCE, the Neo-Assyrians, commonly referred to as Assyrians, began to arise as a major power in Mesopotamia. During the reign of Tiglath-Pileser III, the Assyrians began to conquer large parts of Mesopotamia, areas south of Babylon, parts of the Kingdom of Israel, Turkey, and the Caucasus regions. Assyria's empire was further expanded by the Sargonid dynasty, which included Sargon II, Sennacherib, Esarhaddon, and Ashurbanipal. By 627 BCE Assyria's control over Mesopotamia and other regions began to decline. The Neo-Babylonians, also known as Babylonians or Chaldeans, joined with the Medes to overthrow the Assyrian empire and reestablish control over Mesopotamia. Among them, Nabopolassar and his successor Nebuchadnezzar are the most well known. Both the Assyrians and the Chaldeans were responsible for deporting Jews from their homeland to Mesopotamia.

The Medes and Persians would dominate Mesopotamia for approximately 300 years. Cyrus the Great and his successors established and maintained the Persian Empire, which included Mesopotamia from 550 BCE through 330 BCE and was conquered by Alexander the Great's Macedonian armies. Seleucid rule in the region ran from 330 BCE to 238 BCE, followed by Parthian control from 238 BCE to 264 CE. Mesopotamia was then ruled by the Sassanid Empire from 265 CE to 651 CE when Arab armies under Khalid ibn al-Walid conquered Mesopotamia between April 633 and January 634. The region would thereafter remain as part of various Islamic empires, including the Umayyad and the Abbasid. Eventually, the Ottoman Empire, during the reigns of Selim I and Suleiman the Magnificent, conquered the region between 1512 and 1566. Mesopotamia was then divided into three provinces: Mosul, Baghdad, and Basra. Following World War I (1914–1918), Great Britain received the region as a League of Nations mandate. Eventually, the three provinces were merged into Mesopotamia, which eventually became the present-day nation of Iraq on October 3, 1932.

Some of the most important historical cities in or near the Mesopotamian region included Nineveh, Babylon, and Baghdad. The first was destroyed by the Babylonians and their allies in 612 BCE; the second was destroyed by Sennacherib in 689 BCE, rebuilt, and finally fell after 275 BCE when the people were deported from the city. Baghdad was destroyed by the Mongols in the Battle of Baghdad January 29–February 10, 1258 CE. Baghdad was rebuilt, only to be partially destroyed by Tamerlane in 1401, and then rebuilt

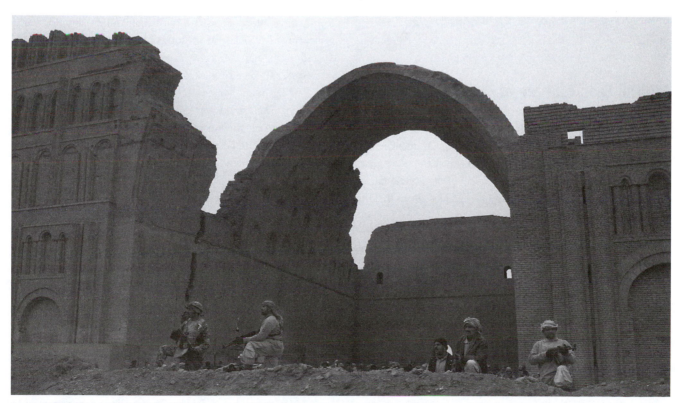

Iraqi police and Anbar Awakening militia members establish a position on the historical site of Ctesiphon, the capital of the Sassanid Empire, January 22, 2008. (AP/Wide World Photos)

to serve as a capital during the Ottoman Empire. Other cities of importance established during the Islamic period in the region include Nasiriyah, Najaf, Kut, Ar Ramadi, Karbala, Samarra, and Mosul. All were targeted during either the Persian Gulf War (1991) and/or Operation IRAQI FREEDOM.

Because of Mesopotamia's physical location between Asia and the West, along with the relatively flat terrain, it has often been the target of invasions from multiple civilizations. Persians, Macedonians, Arabs, Mongols, and the Ottomans are only some of the empires that have invaded the region over the centuries. In more recent times, Mesopotamia was invaded by the British in 1917, underwent missile attacks from Iran in 1987, during the Iran-Iraq War (1980–1988), and was attacked, invaded, and/or occupied in the 1990s and again after 2003 by U.S.-led coalition forces.

WYNDHAM WHYNOT

**See also**

Iraq, History of, Pre-1990; Iraq, History of, 1990–Present; Ottoman Empire

**References**

Bauer, Susan Wise. *The History of the Ancient World: From the Earliest Accounts to the Fall of Rome.* New York: Norton, 2007.

Bertman, Stephen. *Handbook to Life in Ancient Mesopotamia.* New York: Oxford University Press USA, 2005.

De Camp, L. Sprague. *The Ancient Engineers.* New York. Barnes and Noble Books, 1993.

Rawlinson, George. *The Five Great Monarchies of the Ancient Eastern World: Or, The History, Geography, and Antiquities of Chaldaea, Assyria, Babylon, Media, and Persia,* Vols. 1–3. Reprint ed. Elibron Classics series. Boston: Adamant Media Corporation, 2001.

Roux, George. *Ancient Iraq.* 3rd ed. New York: Penguin, 1992.

---

# Middle East, Climate of

The climate of the Middle East is surprisingly variable. This runs contrary to the popular misperception abroad that the region is a uniformly hot and dry desert environment. The Middle East is a region of great temperature extremes and considerable variances in precipitation. Nevertheless, a good deal of the Middle East is known for its blazing hot summers and great dust storms that can reduce visibility to less than one-quarter of a mile, making land travel difficult at best and air travel impossible. Except in mountainous regions and on high plains, the region's winters range from cool and rainy to mild and relatively dry.

Syria's climate is mostly characterized as that of a desert. There are three principal climate zones in Syria, however. They include a somewhat humid Mediterranean-style climate in the west, a semiarid central steppe, and a torrid desert environment in the east and southeast. The coastal climate experiences mild rainy winters from December to February and hot relatively dry summers. Because of the elevation, the highlands experience cold winters punctuated by occasional snow. Sometimes this weather affects areas as far south and west as Damascus. The eastern

deserts receive 10 inches or less of rainfall a year and are characterized by hot summers with temperatures as high as 120 degrees. High winds blowing from the south (from Arabia) can create dust storms, particularly in the desert.

Lebanon, with a long coastline along the Mediterranean Sea, enjoys a fairly typical Mediterranean climate, characterized by hot sunny summers and mild wet winters. Along the coast, which is warm and humid, there is rain but not snow. Heavy snow falls in Lebanon's mountain areas in the winter. Lebanon's climate may be the most moderate of the Middle East countries owing to its small size and proximity to the coast. Rainfall is greatest from December to April.

The climate of Israel is moderately temperate. It features very hot and dry summers in the southern and western deserts. Elsewhere the climate is similar to that of Lebanon, with long and dry hot summers and short and rainy cool winters. Some 70 percent of the nation's rain occurs from November to April, with rainfall slackening the farther south one goes. Only about one-third of the small country is capable of agricultural pursuits that do not require heavy irrigation. In the winter, light snow is not uncommon at higher elevations.

The climate of Jordan, like that of Syria, is largely desert. In the west, a rainy season from November to April brings most of an entire year's rainfall. Aside from that, the area is very dry. Jordan's summers are quite hot, with average high temperatures over 100 degrees and higher still in the desert. The winters are moderately cool with snow occasionally at higher elevations. In the late spring and early autumn, the country is subject to periodic hot dry winds from the south-southeast, which can drive relative humidity to 10 percent or less. These winds sometimes produce dust storms and sandstorms that can greatly impede transportation, pose health dangers, and force vehicles to halt.

The Egyptian climate is characteristic of a true desert environment. There are two seasons: a hot dry summer from May to October and a moderate winter from December to March. Most of the country's rain falls along and close to the northern coast, and owing to the moderating influence of the Mediterranean Sea, the northern part of Egypt is slightly cooler. For this reason, Alexandria on the Mediterranean coast used to be a popular tourist destination particularly in the summer months, although Egyptians now prefer instead to visit areas farther to the west on the north coast. There are, however, some weather variations. In the Delta and North Nile Valley, occasional winter cold snaps can bring light frosts. In the south, near Aswan, there are great temperature fluctuations in the summer. High temperatures can be as high as 126 degrees or more during the day and then dip as low as 48–50 degrees at night. From mid-March through May, howling dust storms sometimes occur, precipitated by southerly winds that can reach 90 miles per hour. These dust storms are known as the sirocco by Europeans and the khamsin by the Egyptians.

Saudi Arabia has a dry, hot, harsh climate characterized by great temperature extremes. Except for the Asir Province, which

A forest creek in northern Iran. (Oxine/Dreamstime.com)

is subject to monsoons from the Indian Ocean region and is more temperate, and the sometimes humid conditions of the coast of the Hejaz, the nation's climate is all desert. The desert areas experience dry cloudless summers with high temperatures of 120 degrees and higher. Temperatures of 125–130 degrees are not uncommon. During times of drought, which are not that infrequent, the southern two-thirds of Saudi Arabia can go for two years or more without measurable rainfall. In the late spring and summer, strong winds often create choking sandstorms and dust storms.

The climate of Iraq is similar to that of the southwestern United States. Iraq is mostly a semiarid desert that experiences hot dry summers and mild to cool winters with periodic rainfall. The mountainous regions along the Iranian and Turkish borders have cold winters with periodic heavy snowfalls. The great majority of Iraq's precipitation comes in the winter (December to April), while the northern areas receive more rainfall over a slightly longer time span. From June to September, winds from the north and northwest can whip up heavy dust storms (called *shamal* by Iraqis) that cause plummeting humidity and decreased visibilities. As in the American Southwest, the southern two-thirds of Iraq is prone to flash flooding.

Iran's climate may be the most varied of all the major nations in the Middle East. It has arid and semiarid climate zones and even a subtropical climate along the coast of the Caspian Sea. In the northwest, summers are hot and dry, the autumn and spring are mild, and the winters are cold and frequently snowy. Most of the country's rainfall occurs from October to April, with the most falling near the coast. In the south, particularly near the Persian Gulf, average high temperatures in the summer are 112 degrees. Tehran, shielded by the Alborz Mountains, is more temperate, with average high temperatures in the summer of 96 degrees.

The climate of Afghanistan, which borders Iran to the east, is also highly varied. Afghanistan's rugged mountains, which cover a significant portion of the country, offer great extremes in terms of both temperature and precipitation. The highlands and mountains of Afghanistan share a climate quite similar to that of the southern Himalayas. Winters are harsh, cold, and punctuated by frequent snows. At higher elevations, snow may be present all year long. Huge temperature variations can occur within hours, however, ranging from well below freezing to well above freezing. In the north of the country winters are uniformly cold and snowy, with snow covering the ground for two to three months per year.

## Average Temperature and Rainfall in Selected Middle Eastern and Southwest Asian Cities

| Location | Average Temperature, January | Average Temperature, July | Average Rainfall, January | Average Rainfall, July |
|----------|------------------------------|---------------------------|---------------------------|------------------------|
| Baghdad, Iraq | 48.9° | 94.3° | 1.1" | 0.0" |
| Beirut, Lebanon | 55.4° | 77.4° | 7.4" | 0.0" |
| Damascus, Syria | 43.9° | 80.1° | 1.5" | 0.0" |
| Jerusalem, Israel | 47.1° | 73.9° | 5.5" | 0.0" |
| Kabul, Afghanistan | 28.8° | 77.2° | 1.3" | 0.2" |
| Riyadh, Saudi Arabia | 57.7° | 94.3° | 0.5" | 0.0" |
| Tehran, Iran | 37.9° | 85.1° | 1.7" | 0.1" |

Summers, except in the highlands and mountains, can be brutally hot and dry. At Jalalabad, in the far eastern portion of Afghanistan, the climate is similar to that of India. Around Kandahar in the south, summers are usually torrid and dry with frequent dust storms. Although the nation is relatively sunny and rain-free the year round, some monsoonal moisture makes its way into the eastern half of Afghanistan, bringing much-needed rainfall.

Despite the many variations in the region's climate, almost all of the Middle East nations feature extremely hot summers, dust storms, and sandstorms. From a military perspective, the region can be daunting for troops as well as equipment. The searing heat of the summers is dangerous for troops, who can quickly succumb to heat exhaustion, heat stroke, and dehydration. For this reason, military action in the dead of summer is avoided, particularly on the Arabian Peninsula. The heat can also take a heavy toll on equipment, especially trucks, armored personnel carriers, and tanks.

Another perilous weather phenomenon is the region's frequent dust storms and sandstorms. These storms can reduce visibility to a quarter of a mile or less, thus grounding aircraft. Moving a large number of troops in the midst of one of these storms is ill-advised. Airborne sand and dust can also foul the engines of ground vehicles as well as aircraft. The difficulties of operating in such conditions were graphically illustrated in April 1980 when President Jimmy Carter's administration attempted to mount a clandestine rescue of American embassy workers being held hostage in Tehran, Iran. On their way toward Tehran, two of eight RH-53 U.S. helicopters broke down in a sandstorm. A third was damaged on landing, but when it attempted to take off after surveying the damage to the downed choppers, it clipped a U.S. Air Force C-130 transport airplane. The helicopter went down, resulting in the deaths of eight U.S. servicemen. The debacle was a major embarrassment for Carter.

The failed hostage mission serves as a stark example of the inherent dangers of military operations in the often inhospitable climate of the Middle East. And the lack of rainfall throughout much of the region may well serve as the flash point for a future Middle East conflict as nations there scramble for increasingly precious water supplies.

PAUL G. PIERPAOLI JR.

**See also**

Carter, James Earl, Jr.; EAGLE CLAW, Operation

**References**

Gleick, P. H. "Water, War and Peace in the Middle East." *Environment* 36(3) (1994): 6–11.

Gribbin, John. *Weather Force: Climate and Its Impact on Our World*. New York: Putnam, 1979.

Riley, Dennis, and Lewis Spolton. *World Weather and Climate*. New York: Cambridge University Press, 1982.

## Middle East, History of, 1918–1945

The history of the Middle East for four centuries prior to 1918 was greatly influenced by the fortunes of the Ottoman Empire, which controlled most of the Arab lands via a decentralized political system. Outside of Ottoman control lay Persia, the Arabian peninsula, and the interior of many provinces ostensibly under Ottoman control or by 1914 subject to European control. In November 1914, Ottoman leaders took their state into World War I on the side of the Central Powers against the Allied (Entente) Powers. This decision was of immense import for the course of the war. It not only opened a new front but it had profound impact on the Middle East and on Russia.

In 1915 the British and French attempted to drive the Ottoman Empire from the war and establish a southern supply route to Russia. The subsequent naval (Dardanelles) and land (Gallipoli) campaigns were failures. In June 1916, however, with British assistance, Sharif Hussein of Mecca led a revolt by Arab forces against Ottoman rule. Based on his negotiations with the British, Hussein was convinced that an Allied victory in the war would bring independence for much of the Middle East, to include the area occupied by present-day Israel, Jordan, Iraq, Lebanon, Syria, and the Arabian Peninsula. However, British and French leaders secretly contravened the agreement with Hussein in the 1916 Sykes-Picot Agreement, whereby they effectively divided control of the Middle East between their two countries. Britain and France also undertook to compensate both Russia and Italy. The British complicated matters in the Balfour Declaration, issued by Secretary of State for Foreign Affairs Arthur James Balfour on November 12, 1917. Intended to mobilize Jewish support behind the Allied war effort, it promised the creation of a Jewish "homeland" in Palestine following an Allied victory. Reconciling these various promises and claims would be virtually impossible. In any case, the Allies were victorious in the Middle East. Ottoman forces in

**Population Growth in Selected Middle Eastern and Southwest Asian Countries, 1925–2005**

| Country | 1925 | 1935 | 1945 | 1955 | 1965 | 1975 | 1985 | 1995 | 2005 |
|---|---|---|---|---|---|---|---|---|---|
| Afghanistan | 5,735,000 | 6,855,000 | 8,194,000 | 12,652,000 | 15,051,000 | 16,665,000 | 14,650,000 | 23,481,000 | 30,977,000 |
| Iran | 11,780,000 | 13,520,000 | 15,660,000 | 18,325,000 | 24,813,000 | 33,343,000 | 44,212,000 | 64,120,000 | 75,126,000 |
| Iraq | 3,111,000 | 3,560,500 | 4,611,400 | 5,961,000 | 8,047,000 | 11,124,000 | 15,319,000 | 20,097,000 | 28,422,000 |
| Israel | 805,000 | 963,000 | 1,834,900 | 1,748,000 | 2,563,000 | 3,455,000 | 4,296,000 | 5,521,000 | 6,465,000 |
| Jordan | 746,000 | 914,000 | 1,118,000 | 1,437,000 | 1,909,000 | 2,702,000 | 3,512,000 | 4,291,000 | 5,946,000 |
| Lebanon | 924,000 | 862,600 | 1,320,000 | 1,613,000 | 2,151,000 | 2,799,000 | 2,668,000 | 4,005,000 | 4,630,000 |
| Pakistan | 21,678,000 | 25,203,000 | 32,741,000 | 44,194,000 | 57,145,000 | 74,734,000 | 96,180,000 | 129,905,000 | 167,121,000 |
| Saudi Arabia | 2,194,000 | 2,552,000 | 2,968,000 | 4,305,000 | 5,405,000 | 7,180,000 | 11,595,000 | 18,979,000 | 25,812,000 |
| Syria | 1,828,000 | 2,035,400 | 2,926,000 | 3,967,000 | 5,325,000 | 7,380,000 | 10,267,000 | 14,153,000 | 19,948,000 |
| Yemen | 3,184,000 | 3,591,000 | 4,058,000 | 4,495,000 | 5,735,000 | 6,972,000 | 10,041,000 | 15,272,000 | 20,088,000 |

Jerusalem surrendered to British lieutenant general Sir Edmund Allenby in December 1917, and Allied troops occupied all Palestine in September 1918. The war ended two months later.

The disposition of territory belonging to the now defunct Ottoman Empire became a primary topic of discussion at the Paris Peace Conference following the war. Clearly, both Arabs and Jews expected to be rewarded for their support of the Allies in the war, yet the final postwar settlement saw the British and French controlling much of the modern Middle East under the oversight of the new League of Nations. The British dominated Iraq and Palestine, while the French controlled Syria and Lebanon. Supposedly French and British authorities were to oversee these "Mandates" until such time as the states could become fully independent. The Middle East did not long remain quiescent.

Following the armistice signed on October 30, 1918, at Mudros that ended fighting between the empire and the Entente (the United States never declared war on the Ottoman Empire), Allied troops occupied much of Ottoman territory. The empire ended on November 15 when Sultan Mehmed VI, who had succeeded to the throne in October on the death of Mehmed V, established a new government under the control of British and Greek troops. The punitive Allied peace terms of the Paris Peace Conference, whereby the Allies divided much of the territory of the former Ottoman Empire among themselves, spurred Turkish nationalism and led to a revolution under Mustafa Kemal. Under the terms of the punitive Treaty of Sèvres in 1920, Turkey was largely restricted to Anatolia and its economy was controlled by the Entente powers. There was widespread opposition in Turkey to this and, on August 10, 1920, Mustafa Kemal Ataturk, a former Ottoman Army officer who had distinguished himself in the war, led what came to be known in Turkey as the War of Liberation to reclaim lands ceded by the sultan. Ataturk and his followers forced the Greeks from western Anatolia and formally abolished the sultanate on November 1, 1922, ending forever the Ottoman Empire as a political entity and Islamic religious authority.

The Republic of Turkey was created on October 29, 1923. Ataturk won unanimous election as the first president of Turkey, and on March 3, 1924, he abolished the Islamic Caliphate held by the Ottomans since 1517. The Caliphate was the only unified legal, governmental, and clerical structure recognized by classical Islam. Its end eventually splintered Islam into over 50 constituent nations divided by race, language, geography, ethnicity, politics, understandings of the Qur'an, acceptance of different rightful successors to Muhammad, and divergent local histories. Ataturk also abolished the strict observance of Sharia and created new secularized educational and judicial systems. Turkey officially replaced religious law with secular law on February 17, 1926, making Turkey the most secular nation with a majority Muslim population in the Middle East.

In Egypt, anti-British riots erupted. In response to these, in February 1922 the British formally ended the protectorate that had been in effect since 1882 and declared Egypt a sovereign, independent kingdom. This was only rhetorical, however, for British authorities continued to exercise real authority and had military forces in the country to defend the Suez Canal, now Britain's lifeline to India.

British concerns over Italy's invasion of Ethiopia (Abyssinia) in September 1935 led to new British concessions in Egypt and a new treaty between London and Cairo in August 1936. Britain pledged to defend Egypt against external attack, while Egypt promised to place its facilities at Britain's disposal in case of war. Egypt also formally agreed to fixed numbers of British forces in the Canal Zone, but Britain agreed to evacuate all other bases, save the naval base at Alexandria, which it would have for eight additional years. The Egyptian military was also bound closely to Britain. Britain agreed to work for the removal of the capitulations, and its high commissioner was replaced by an ambassador. The treaty was to be of indefinite duration but with negotiations for any changes permitted after 20 years. The future of the Sudan was unresolved. Both the Egyptian government and Britain worked to break the power of the nationalist Wafd Party, which had been founded in 1919 and had dominated the parliament and was hostile to the Egyptian monarchy.

During World War II, there was some pro-Axis sentiment in Egypt, but the British did secure the cooperation of the Egyptian government in the war against the Axis powers. More than a half million British Empire troops were stationed in Egypt, which became the principal British and Allied base in the Middle East.

Allied forces under British lieutenant general Edmund Allenby enter Jerusalem on December 12, 1917. (Israeli Government Press Office)

Syrian nationalists declared their country an independent nation in 1920, but the French military intervened and crushed the nationalists in the Battle of Maysalun on July 23, 1920. On September 1, 1920, the French created out of what had been known as Greater Syria the state of Greater Lebanon, a largely Christian (mainly Maronite) enclave that nevertheless included many Muslims and Druze. The enclave proved unworkable, leading the French to create a smaller Christian enclave/protectorate in the coastal areas in 1923 and the Lebanese Republic on September 1, 1926, thereafter independent of Syria but nonetheless administrated under the French Mandate of Syria.

During World War II, the Vichy France government allowed the Germans to transit Syria in order to supply forces in Iraq against the British. The British, accompanied by Australian and some Free French forces, as well as the Transjordan Arab Legion, responded by invading Syria and Lebanon, where they defeated the Vichy French forces and secured control. Under considerable political pressure both from within Lebanon and from the Allied powers, on November 16, 1941, the government of Free France headed by Charles de Gaulle declared Lebanon independent under the Free French government. Formation of a workable government proved difficult. Elections were held in 1943, and on November 8 the new government unilaterally declared the mandate at an

end. Later that month, after first arresting the members of the new government, the French acceded to Lebanese independence. The 1943 National Pact distributed seats in the legislature of Lebanon according to population figures and required the president to be a Christian and the prime minister to be a Muslim, but an independent government was not created until January 1, 1944. French troops were not withdrawn until 1946.

Meanwhile, Syria remained under French rule. Following the 1941 British-led invasion of Syria and Lebanon, Syria was turned over to the Free French authorities. Although the French recognized Syrian independence, they continued to occupy the country and declared martial law, imposed strict press censorship, and arrested a number of individuals. In July 1943, under Allied pressure, the Free French authorities agreed to new elections. A nationalist government came to power that August under President Shukri al-Quwatli. France formally granted Syria independence on January 1, 1944, but the country remained under Allied occupation for the remainder of the war. In February 1945, Syria declared war on the Axis.

In early May 1945 anti-French demonstrations erupted throughout Syria, whereupon French forces bombarded Damascus. Some 400 people died before the British intervened. A United Nations (UN) resolution in February 1946 called on France to evacuate the country, and by mid-April all French and British forces had departed. Evacuation Day, April 17, is still celebrated in Syria as a national holiday.

World War I saw Great Britain as master of the former Ottoman provinces of Baghdad, Basra, and Mosul, which constitute modern Iraq. The first two were joined into a single country in 1921, while the third was added in 1926. Iraq was, however, sharply divided between Sunni and Shia, Arab and Kurd, urban and rural. In 1921, the British installed as a figurehead king of Iraq the Hashemite Faisal, whom the French had forced out of Syria. The British then established a temporary government for Iraq in October 1920 and made Prince Faisal king in 1921. Britain continued its mandatory governance of Iraq until 1932 when, on Faisal's urging, they granted what turned out to be only nominal independence. The British retained military bases and transit rights. Faisal died in 1933 and was succeeded by Ghazi I, who was followed in 1933 by King Faisal II. The Hashemite monarchy, which was overthrown in 1958, never was able to serve as a unifying force in Iraq. A succession of coups and coup attempts, meanwhile, kept Iraq in near constant turmoil.

Iraq was a major oil producer, and during World War II the British government feared that, if that nation were to side with Germany, its location on the Persian Gulf might enable the Germans to threaten Britain's lifeline with India. In April 1941, nationalist Rashid Ali al-Gaylani led a coup by the Iraqi military and became prime minister. Encouraged by the Axis powers, the new government refused Britain the rights of transit guaranteed under the earlier treaty and threatened British bases. The British responded with force and, despite Axis military aid channeled through Syria, crushed the nationalists and forced their leaders to flee. Nuri al-Said then again became prime minister with a pro-British administration, which in 1943 declared war on the Axis powers.

Palestine proved an intractable problem. Under agreements reached at the San Remo Conference in April 1920, Palestine became a British mandate. It proved impossible for Britain to honor the pledges it had made during the war to both the Jews (a homeland for Jews) and Arabs (an Arab state). With some 85–90 percent of the total population, the Arabs were unwilling to compromise on the issue of emigration and land sales to Jews. Increasingly they took out their anger against both the British administration and the Jews. In 1920 and 1921, there was widespread violence against Jews. In 1921, the Jewish community responded by forming the Haganah, a self-defense force that was the precursor to the Israeli Defense Forces (IDF).

Efforts by the British to establish a legislative council involving both groups failed on Arab opposition. Violence throughout 1929 led the British to halt Jewish settlement in Palestine, but they soon reversed this policy. By 1936 the Jewish population of Palestine numbered some 400,000 people, or 30 percent of the population. That same year, a full-fledged Arab revolt or rebellion began. Lasting until 1939, it obliged the British government to dispatch 20,000 troops to Palestine. By its end some 5,000 Arabs had been killed and thousands more were wounded.

At first the British government recommended partition of Palestine into separate Arab and Jewish states, but then it decided this was not feasible. In 1939, with a new war in Europe looming, the British government sought to shore up its position in the Middle East by favoring the Arabs. It severely limited future Jewish immigration and restricted land sales to Jews. In consequence, some Jews took up arms against the British.

The World War II Holocaust—the death of some 6 million Jews by the Germans—led to demands for resettlement of Jews in Palestine and establishment of a Jewish state. Jews worldwide believed that only a sovereign state could really protect them. Britain's rejection of such a course of action brought heightened Jewish terrorism and guerrilla warfare and was a major factor in Britain's decision to relinquish control of Palestine in 1948.

Palestine east of the Jordan River, known as Transjordan (today Jordan), was part of Britain's League of Nations mandate. In 1921, Abdullah ibn Hussein, a member of the Hashemite dynasty, became the de facto ruler of Transjordan, and in 1928 it became a constitutional monarchy under Abdullah, although it was still considered part of the British Mandate. Transjordan received its independence in 1946. On May 25, the parliament proclaimed Abdullah to be King Abdullah I. The same body also changed the name of the country to the Hashemite Kingdom of Jordan.

Ibn Saud ruled central Arabia. He had conquered various parts of the Saudi peninsula with his Ikhwan warriors early in the 20th century. When the Hashemites were forced out of the Hijaz, he was able to extend his control over this area. After World War I he consolidated his control, becoming king in 1925. Overcoming a revolt against his rule during 1927–1929 by the fundamentalist Wahhabi Ikhwan warriors who had fought for him for years, he exiled them to the oases of Burayda and areas of Najd. In 1932, the kingdom formally became Saudi Arabia.

Saudi Arabia's fortunes took a dramatic turn with the discovery of vast reserves of oil in the 1930s. American oil companies played the leading role in its exploitation—exploring, extracting, and shipping the oil. The importance of oil during World War II enhanced the Saudi-American relationship, leading to the formation in 1944 of ARAMCO, the Arab-American Oil Corporation.

In Persia on February 21, 1921, army officer Reza Khan overthrew the Qajar dynasty. He appointed himself shah (king), attempted to centralize authority, and changed the name of the state to Iran in 1935. He Persianized Iran and moved against the traditional clergy, seeking to modernize the country. During August–September 1941, Soviet and British forces occupied northern and southern Iran, respectively, to ensure the flow of Lend-Lease supplies to the Soviet Union. Shah Pahlavi abdicated to his son Mohammad Reza Shah Pahlavi on September 16, 1941. At the end of World War II, securing the removal of foreign forces was a major preoccupation of the government and, in the case of Soviet troops, became a test for the new UN.

The period 1918–1945 saw many changes in the Middle East, including the transition to independent states. It also witnessed

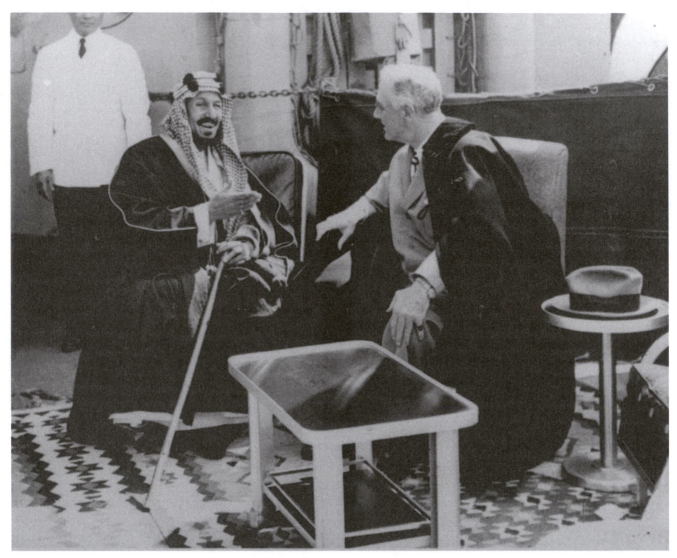

U.S. president Franklin D. Roosevelt and King Abdul Aziz Ibn Saud discuss Saudi-U.S. relations aboard the U.S. Navy cruiser *Quincy* on the Great Bitter Lake north of Suez, Egypt, February 14, 1945. (AP/Wide World Photos)

the beginnings of what would erupt after World War II in armed confrontation between Jews and Arabs over the new state of Israel. Unfortunately for the region, considerable violence lay ahead.

SPENCER C. TUCKER

**See also**

Egypt; Iran; Iraq, History of, Pre-1990; Jordan; Lebanon; Kuwait; Ottoman Empire; Saudi Arabia; Sudan; Syria; Turkey, Role in Persian Gulf and Afghanistan Wars; United Arab Emirates; Yemen

**References**

Cleveland, William L. *A History of the Modern Middle East.* 3rd ed. Boulder, CO: Westview, 2004.

Goldschmidt, Arthur, Jr., and Lawrence Davidson. *A Concise History of the Middle East.* 8th ed. Boulder, CO: Westview, 2005.

Kamrava, Mehran. *The Modern Middle East: A Political History since the First World War.* Berkeley: University of California Press, 2005.

Mansfield, Peter, and Nicolas Pelham, eds. *A History of the Middle East.* 2nd ed. New York: Penguin Group, 2005.

Ochsenwald, William, and Sydney Nettleton Fisher. *The Middle East: A History.* 6th ed. New York: McGraw-Hill, 2004.

# Middle East, History of, 1945–Present

The Middle East assumed increased importance with the end of World War II, and for a variety of reasons. The Suez Canal continued to be one of the world's most important strategic waterways, the West increasingly relied on the region's vast supplies of oil (estimated at two-thirds of the world's proven reserves), and the status of Palestine was unresolved but threatened full-scale regional war. The 65 years following World War II in the region have seen a rising tide of Arab nationalism; continuing Arab-Israeli confrontation that is frequently marked by terrorism; Arab oil as a global economic weapon wielded by the Organization of Petroleum Exporting Countries (OPEC); and national rivalries leading to wars, in part because of the lack of clear geographical boundaries in the region and the arbitrary nature of how the national borders were drawn by the former colonial powers. The Middle East also became a central focal point of the Cold War between the United States and the Soviet Union (1945–1992), as both the American and Soviet blocs sought to gain the upper hand in the region. That in turn led to significant arms transfers to powers in the region by both the United States and Soviet Union, which affected the regional balance of power.

The period is dominated by three major wars between Israel and the Arab states, which led to the threat of foreign intervention and confrontation between the Soviet Union and the United States. There were also Israeli invasions of Lebanon and other sporadic military clashes between the Jewish state and its individual neighbors. Iran and Iraq fought a protracted eight-year war (1980–1988), which may have claimed 1 million casualties, and the Soviet Union waged an even longer, although less bloody, unsuccessful struggle to maintain communism in Afghanistan (1979–1988). There have also been two wars between United States–led coalitions and Iraq, in 1991 and in 2003 (with insurgent actions in Iraq continuing to the present), not to mention an ongoing war in Afghanistan with Taliban and Al Qaeda insurgents since 2001. In addition, there have been numerous civil wars, such as in Yemen and Lebanon; coups d'état; and untold acts of terrorism. The Middle East continues to live up to its reputation as one of the most violent and volatile regions on earth.

Although some scholars identify the Middle East in cultural terms to include those countries embracing Islam, the region is more often delineated by geography, to consist of those countries of southwest Asia west of Afghanistan and Pakistan. Under this definition, the term Middle East embraces Turkey, Israel, Syria, Lebanon, Jordan, Iraq, Iran, Kuwait, Saudi Arabia, Bahrain, Qatar, the United Arab Emirates, Oman, Yemen, and Egypt.

The region was of immense importance to the Allies during World War II. In order to secure the Suez Canal—Britain's imperial lifeline to Asia—the British maintained in Egypt their largest overseas base. Persian Gulf oil was also of immense strategic importance to the Allied war effort, and Iran also became an important supply corridor for U.S. Lend-Lease aid shipped to the Soviet Union.

World War II brought a repudiation of colonialism driven by the United States and Soviet Union. The British and French, who had largely controlled the region since the end of World War I, now were forced to quit it. Economic factors as well as U.S. and Soviet pressure also played a role in their decisions. This did not come all at once (for example, it was only in 1956 that Britain surrendered its remaining military bases in Egypt). Syria, Lebanon, Jordan, and Iraq all achieved independence in the years immediately after World War II. In some parts of their empires there was considerable bloodshed. In North Africa, for example, France fought a prolonged struggle in Algeria during 1954–1962, which affected the Middle East and resulted in Algeria securing full independence.

Frustrated in its efforts to keep Jewish refugees out of Palestine and in its inability to secure Jewish and Arab agreement on a partition plan for Palestine—and finding itself at war with both—the British government unilaterally (and precipitously) terminated its Palestinian mandate, departing in 1948. This brought the Jewish proclamation of the State of Israel and immediate war between it and the neighboring Arab states. There was strong support for Israel from the United States, which has the world's largest Jewish population, but also from Western Europe. There was great sympathy for the Jews as a result of the death of some 6 million Jews in the Nazi-inspired Holocaust, as well as support for the Zionist position that only a Jewish national state could protect the Jewish people. Such a step was anathema to most Arabs. In large part because of the Cold War, the Soviet Union shifted from strong support of Israel (it had been the second state after the United States to recognize the Jewish state) to siding with the Arabs and becoming a major arms supplier to them. The United States and France assumed the same role for Israel.

At the same time, however, the United States and other Western powers sought to maintain close ties with the oil-producing Persian Gulf states. Despite being strongly anti-Israel, these states were tied to the United States financially through their exploitation of their oil riches. Influential Islamic clergy in these states also found Soviet policies toward religion distasteful.

The Soviets hoped to supplant British influence in the region. They had long sought to secure a port on the Mediterranean, and in the years immediately after World War II brought immense pressure on Turkey in an effort to control the straits connecting the Black Sea with the Mediterranean. They also sought to secure

Two members of the Palmach, the Jewish fighting force, take up position at a wall during training for city fighting, Jerusalem, March 1948. (Bettmann/Corbis)

## MIDDLE EAST, 1990

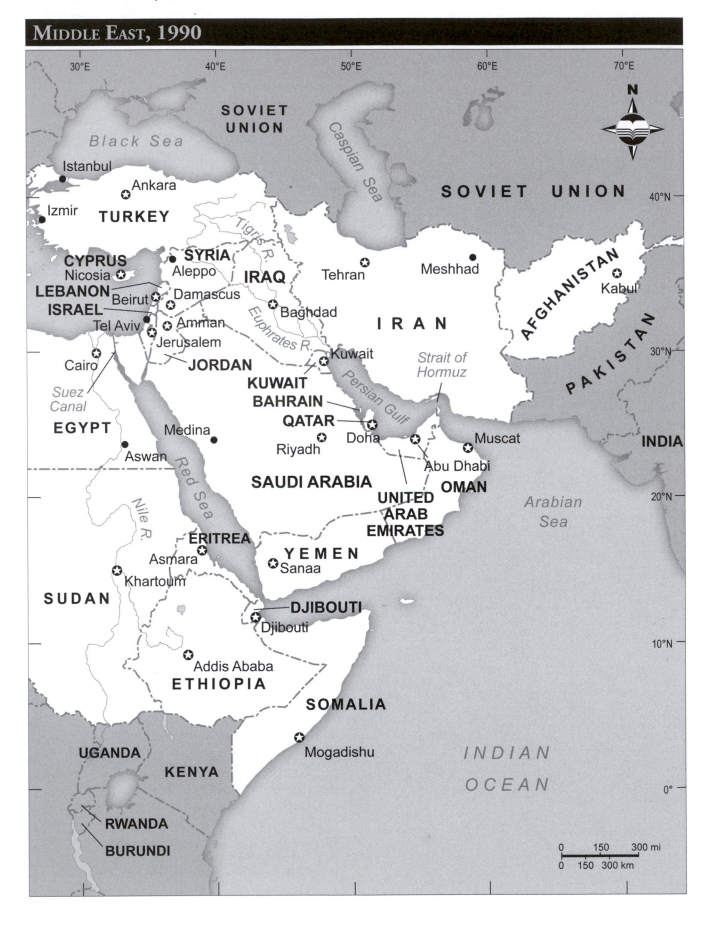

the province of Azerbaijan in northern Iran, which they had occupied during the war.

The United States sought to counter Soviet pressure in the region. When Britain announced in 1947 that it could no longer support the Greek government in its war with communist insurgents, the United States took up that role. In the 1947 Truman Doctrine, President Harry S. Truman proclaimed U.S. aid for both Greece and Turkey and pledged U.S. support for any nation fighting communist insurgents and outside pressures. The United States also maintained a strong naval presence in the region through its Sixth Fleet in the Mediterranean.

The Israeli declaration of independence was, in any case, immediately followed by the first Arab-Israeli War of 1948–1949. Although vastly outnumbered, the Israelis were much better disciplined and organized. They ultimately prevailed over their divided opponents, who in any case had conflicting war aims. At the end of the war, Israeli forces succeeded in driving back the armies of Egypt, Jordan, Iraq, and Syria. In the process, many tens of thousands of Palestinians fled, precipitating a massive refugee crisis, and the Israelis forced others to leave.

A revolution in Egypt in 1953 and the rise of Gamal Abdel Nasser dramatically changed the Middle East. Nasser was a committed Arab nationalist with Pan-Arab aspirations. His goals greatly alarmed Israeli leaders, for the security of the Israeli state rested in large part on Arab division. Among his accomplishments, Nasser secured a final British departure from Egypt. He also gained a pledge of U.S. financial support for construction of an immense dam on the Nile at Aswan. But when the West rejected Nasser's requests for modern weaponry, the Egyptian leader turned to the Soviet bloc for assistance. The United States feared this would upset the arms balance in the Middle East to the detriment of Israel, and Nasser's subsequent conclusion of an arms deal with Czechoslovakia led to the withdrawal of U.S. assistance for the Aswan Dam project. The Soviets stepped in to provide technical assistance, but to pay for the dam project Nasser nationalized the Suez Canal in 1956, which had been owned by a private company, in which the British government was the largest stockholder.

Nasser's decision to nationalize the canal had immense repercussions, ultimately bringing the British government into a secret arrangement developed by the French and Israeli governments to topple Nasser from power. The Israelis were convinced that as soon as Nasser had integrated modern Soviet weapons into its armed forces, Egyptian forces would invade Israel. Indeed, Nasser had already sponsored terrorist raids across the border into Israel, and he had closed the Strait of Tiran to Israeli shipping. The secret plan developed by the three powers called for Israel to invade Egypt and threaten the canal and also advance into the Sinai peninsula. The British and French would then demand that both sides pull back and allow their forces to occupy the canal zone. If, as expected, Egypt refused, British and French forces would invade.

The 1956 Suez Crisis was one of the major international events of the Cold War. Although Egypt did indeed reject the Franco-British ultimatum and British and French troops attacked Egypt, the three invading powers were soon forced to withdraw under heavy U.S. pressure and Soviet threats. An angry President Dwight D. Eisenhower, caught by surprise by the allied move, insisted on a unilateral withdrawal. Far from toppling Nasser, the Suez Crisis strengthened his position both in Egypt and throughout the Middle East. Indeed, in 1958 Egypt and Syria came together in the United Arab Republic, which however broke apart in 1961 following Egyptian domination of the new state. Britain emerged as the biggest loser in the Suez Crisis. Soviet prestige soared and the United States also gained credibility, although it continued to be hampered by its unqualified support of Israel, which was another winner, for the United Nations (UN) established observers along the Israeli-Egyptian border, and the blockade of the Strait of Tiran came to an end.

The Soviet Union, meanwhile, had now allied itself closely with Arab nationalism against the West and Israel. Thanks to expanded Soviet military assistance, by 1966 the Egyptian armed forces appeared to be sufficiently strong to threaten Israel. This fact, the signing of a defense pact between Egypt and Syria in 1966, and increasing Palestinian attacks on Israel from the neighboring Arab states all greatly alarmed Tel Aviv. Then in mid-May 1967 Nasser ordered Egyptian troops into the Sinai peninsula and demanded the concentration of UN observers there, leading to their withdrawal. Convinced that the Egyptians would soon attack, Israel struck first.

Securing the approval of the Lyndon Johnson administration in the United States, the Israelis launched a devastatingly effective air strike on June 5, 1967. It was carefully timed so as to destroy the bulk of the Egyptian Air Force on the ground. The Israelis also moved against the Syrians and reluctantly against Jordan, for King Hussein had decided to enter the war at the last moment. The resulting Six-Day War changed the map of the Middle East. Israel took the Sinai peninsula from Egypt, the Golan Heights from Syria, and the territory of the West Bank of the Jordan River and East Jerusalem from Jordan.

The Soviets threatened intervention, but in the end they did nothing, which greatly diminished their prestige in the Arab world. French president Charles de Gaulle, angered over the preemptive Israeli strike, ended French military assistance to Israel. The United States, which had done little to assist Israel in the war, nonetheless positioned the Sixth Fleet in the eastern Mediterranean as a warning to the Soviets, and shortly after the war, it substantially increased its military and economic assistance to Israel. The Soviets, meanwhile, made good the military losses sustained by the Arab states.

In 1964, meanwhile, Palestinian nationalist Yasser Arafat had formed the Palestine Liberation Organization (PLO) as an umbrella organization for disparate Palestinian groups fighting Israel. It began launching terrorist raids of its own with the aim of eliminating the Jewish state. The bulk of the PLO attacks came from Jordan, and soon the PLO there was virtually a state within a state. In September 1970, King Hussein moved to expel the PLO, prompting military intervention on the part of Syria, a staunch PLO supporter. Jordan secured pledges of support from Britain and the United States but was able both to expel the PLO and to hold off the Syrians without outside assistance.

Nasser died in September 1970 and was followed as president of Egypt by Anwar Sadat, who concluded that the United States was the only country capable of forcing Israel into a negotiated settlement. He therefore ordered Soviet military advisers to leave Egypt and Soviet bases there closed. When these moves failed to win concessions from the United States or Israel, Sadat concluded that only a renewal of the fighting could force a settlement. To enhance the possibility of success, Sadat concluded a secret understanding with Syria for a joint surprise attack on Israel.

As Sadat hoped, the Egyptian attack caught the Israelis completely by surprise. Their strike of October 6, 1973, occurred at the start of Yom Kippur. Elaborate deceptions masked the Egyptian preparations. What became known as the Yom Kippur War, the Ramadan War, or the War of Atonement began with an Egyptian crossing of the Suez Canal. The Egyptians then set up defensive positions. Their surface-to-air (SAM) missile sites on the other side of the canal devastated reacting Israeli aircraft and their new, handheld Soviet antitank missiles took a heavy toll of responding Israeli armor. In the north along the Golan Heights, Syrian forces almost overran severely outnumbered Israeli defenders. Israeli forces rallied on both fronts and by the time a cease-fire was declared, they had driven the Syrians back and penetrated Syria itself almost to Damascus. On the southern front against Egypt, Israeli forces crossed the Suez Canal and were threatening to sever the supply lines to the Egyptian Third Army. A complete victory by either side was not acceptable to the United States or Soviet Union, and under their joint pressure a cease-fire came into effect, followed by a military withdrawal.

One important side effect of the Yom Kippur (Ramadan) War was the Arab oil embargo of 1973–1974. The major Arab oil-producing states sided with Egypt and Syria, and cut off oil shipments to nations supporting Israel, including the United States. This action exposed the dependence of the Western nations, especially western Europe and Japan, on Arab oil and greatly strengthened the influence of OPEC over both the supply and pricing of petroleum. Huge increases in oil and energy prices, combined with shortages of each, badly crippled the West's already fragile economy, and not until the early 1980s would Western economies recover fully from the oil shocks of the 1970s. At the same time, increases in the price of oil gave the oil-producing states of the Persian Gulf vastly increased wealth as well as expanded influence. These states contributed considerable sums to support the Palestinians and also directly or indirectly supported Palestinian terrorist attacks on Israel. The oil embargo also increased the world influence of the Soviet Union, the world's largest oil-producing nation.

In November 1977, Anwar Sadat took a major step toward reaching a settlement with Tel Aviv by visiting Israel, the first Arab head of state to officially visit the nation. His initiative ultimately resulted in the 1978 Camp David Accords, which were followed the next year by a comprehensive Egyptian-Israeli Peace Treaty. The administration of President Jimmy Carter in the United States hoped that the Egyptian-Israeli treaty would lead to one between Israel and Jordan, but the ensuing widespread condemnation of Sadat in the Arab world and his assassination in 1981 largely prevented this. At the same time, increasing Palestinian terrorist attacks from Lebanon led Israel to invade southern Lebanon and to establish a defensive zone there. Syria, meanwhile, sent its forces into Lebanon at different points during the civil war there. The Syrians subsequently exerted extensive control over Lebanese politics and the economy. In effect they took control of that country, which was now sharply divided between Muslim and Christian populations.

The oil-producing states, although they provided financial support to the Palestinians and states opposing Israel, took no military action of their own. This enabled them to maintain friendly relations with the West, especially the United States. This situation was particularly true with Iran, ruled by pro-Western Mohammad Reza Shah Pahlavi. Soviet pressure on Iran following World War II and a close alliance between the Soviet Union and Iraq, Iran's regional rival, also served to cement a bond with the United States. Iran and Iraq were at loggerheads over the Shatt al-Arab waterway, which separated the two nations. The shah, however, was increasingly unpopular and out of touch with the aspirations of his people. Opposition to the shah was centered among Islamic fundamentalists opposed to his close ties with the United States and westernization efforts. In January 1979, the shah was forced to flee Iran, and the next month the Ayatollah Ruhollah Khomeini returned from exile to establish an Islamic fundamentalist state. The new regime was strongly anti-American. In November 1979, Iranian militants overran the U.S. embassy in Tehran and seized 160 Americans as hostages, precipitating a crisis that probably cost Carter reelection as president in 1980. The hostages would not be released until January 1981, at the precise moment that Carter's rival, Republican president Ronald Reagan, took the oath of office.

In late December 1979, Soviet forces invaded neighboring Afghanistan, in keeping with the doctrine of Leonid Brezhnev stipulating that the Soviet Union would ensure the continuation of communism where it was already established. It turned out to be a nightmare for the Soviets as mujahideen ("holy warriors," freedom fighters) took up arms against the occupiers and fought a nine-year struggle that saw the Soviets and their allied Afghan Army controlling the population centers while the mujahideen controlled much of the rural areas of Afghanistan.

The war attracted Muslim fundamentalists from around the Arab world who saw it as a new jihad (holy war). Afghanistan turned out to be a training ground for insurgent fighters elsewhere, particularly in the largely fundamentalist tribal regions of neighboring northwestern Pakistan. In the end, the Soviets were worn down, their technological edge in armed and armored helicopters offset by Western technology in the form of small but lethal U.S. Stinger and British Blowpipe surface-to-air missiles,

American drivers wait in line to purchase gasoline for their cars during the 1970s energy crisis. (Library of Congress)

which had been furnished to the mujahideen by the United States. The Soviets quit Afghanistan in 1988, with their last forces leaving in February 1989. Soon, Afghanistan descended into a virtual civil war and political chaos, allowing the Muslim fundamentalist group known as the Taliban to seize control there. The Soviets, meanwhile, had been practically bankrupted by their war, and less than three years after their troops quit Afghanistan, the Soviet Union broke apart peacefully, marking the end of the Cold War.

In 1980 Iraq invaded Iran, beginning an eight-year (1980–1988) immensely costly, and yet inconclusive conflict for regional dominance. The war was in many ways a continuation of the ancient Persian-Arab rivalry, fueled by border disputes, waterway rights, and competition for hegemony in the Persian Gulf and Middle East regions. The long-standing rivalry was also abetted by religion, a collision between the Pan-Islamism and revolutionary Shia Islamism of Iran and the Pan-Arab Sunni nationalism of Iraq.

The border between the two states had been contested for some time, and in 1969 Iran abrogated its treaty with Iraq on the navigation of the Shatt al-Arab waterway, Iraq's only outlet to the Persian Gulf. Two years later, Iran seized islands in the Gulf, and border clashes occurred. The rivalry was also complicated by minorities issues, as both states had large Kurdish populations in their northern regions, while an Arab minority inhabited the oil-rich Iranian province of Khuzestan.

Given the long-standing rivalry, thorny border and diplomatic issues, and personal ambitions, it was quite natural that the leaders of both states should seek to exploit any perceived weakness in the other. Thus Iraqi president Saddam Hussein sought to take advantage of the upheaval following the fall of Mohammad Reza Shah Pahlavi and the establishment of Ayatollah Ruhollah Khomeini's Islamic fundamentalist regime in 1979, during the Iranian Revolution. Iraq attacked Iran on September 22, 1980, beginning the war.

Although Iraq registered early gains, it was unable to capitalize on them and overcome the Iranian advantage in manpower and religious fanaticism. Stalemate eventually ensued. In many respects, the war came to resemble the position warfare of World War I. Attacks on cities by both sides failed to end the stalemate. War weariness finally led to a cease-fire in August 1988. The conflict may have claimed 1 million casualties, and it left both sides financially prostrate. Not until 1990, following two years of negotiations, was there a peace agreement that provided for the exchange of prisoners, the status quo antebellum, and the division of sovereignty over the Shatt al-Arab. The war helped unite the Iranian people behind the regime. Iran, meanwhile, remained the most diehard opponent of Israel and was committed to the spread of Islamic fundamentalism. It continued to stoke the fires of the region in Iraq, in Lebanon, and among the Palestinians.

Hussein emerged from the war with the strongest military in the Middle East, second only to Israel, but this came at great cost to his people. His power unchallenged in Iraq, he trumpeted a great national victory. The war had put Iraq deeply in debt to its Persian Gulf Arab neighbors, and this played a major role in the coming of the Persian Gulf War (the $14 billion debt owed to Kuwait was a key factor in Iraq's decision to invade that nation in 1990).

In December 1988, meanwhile, the PLO publicly accepted the existence of Israel, increasing pressure on both sides for a resolution of the Arab-Israeli conflict, which remains elusive. Meanwhile the Muslim Brotherhood organization in Gaza and other elements created the Hamas movement, which participated in the Palestinian Intifada, an uprising which lasted until the Oslo Accords of 1993. Hamas refused to treat with Israel and was responsible for a new wave of suicide attacks against Jews in Israel. In 2006, Hamas won the Palestinian elections in the Gaza Strip and subsequently took control of that area from the PLO, which however retained control over the more populous West Bank.

In August 1990, believing that the United States would not intervene, Iraqi president Saddam Hussein sent his forces into Kuwait and took over that state. Iraq had long claimed Kuwait as a province, and Hussein was angered over Kuwait's slant-drilling into a large Iraqi field, as well as over excessive Kuwaiti oil production, which tended to drive down the price of oil. Iraq wanted the price of oil as high as possible in order to pay off its massive debts from the Iran-Iraq War. U.S. president George H. W. Bush was convinced that Iraq would next pressure Saudi Arabia, and so he put together a broad international coalition of regional and global powers that ultimately drove Iraq from Kuwait. The ground phase of the Persian Gulf War lasted only 100 hours, ending in February 1991. Having expelled the Iraqis from Kuwait at little human cost, Bush was anxious to avoid further bloodshed on both sides and was reluctant to intervene in Iraq for fear that it might then break apart (the country was sharply divided between the ruling Sunnis, the more populous Shiites, and the Kurds) and thus serve to benefit Iran. Bush ended the war early, with the result that Hussein remained in power. From 1991 to 2001, the U.S. and global policy toward Iraq would be one of containment, attained through periodic low-scale military operations and economic sanctions. The 1991 Persian Gulf War was made possible, in large part, by the melting away of the Cold War, as the Soviets neither participated in nor strongly objected to the conflict.

Israel and Jordan finally reached a peace settlement in July 1994. A peace deal with Syria remains elusive, although there were hints at the end of 2008 that some sort of arrangement might be in the offing. This would have to include the return of the Golan Heights to Syria and agreement on the thorny issues of security and water rights.

The presence of U.S. troops in Saudi Arabia angered Saudi extremist Osama bin Laden, who had formed the Al Qaeda terrorist organization to wage jihad against the West and especially the United States. Expelled from Saudi Arabia and then Sudan, he settled in Afghanistan, where he established a partnership with the Taliban and from which he launched terrorist attacks, by far the most damaging of which occurred on September 11, 2001, when members of Al Qaeda seized control of four airliners in the United States and flew two of them into the twin towers of the World Trade Center and one of them into the Pentagon.

After the attacks, which completely destroyed the twin towers, killed more than 2,900 people, and injured 6,300 others, the United States demanded that the Taliban surrender bin Laden and, when it refused, undertook military action (Operation ENDURING FREEDOM) in October 2001 in concert with its North Atlantic Treaty Organization (NATO) allies in support of the forces of the Northern Alliance, which were then waging war against the Taliban. While the Taliban was quickly driven from power, the Afghanistan War continues, fueled by Islamic fundamentalism, especially from across the border in northwestern Pakistan.

Meanwhile, Iraqi leader Saddam Hussein, anxious to reassert his position in the Middle East, continued to defy the United Nations regarding provisions of the cease-fire agreement that had ended the Persian Gulf War, particularly those that concerned disarmament and the eradication of weapons of mass destruction (WMDs). Again, the United States took the lead. President George W. Bush and his neoconservative advisers believed that they saw an opportunity to transform the Middle East. Hussein would be toppled from power and Iraq made into a democracy. Its example would then force change elsewhere in the region. Operating on inadequate and incorrect intelligence information, Bush claimed that Iraq possessed WMDs. The fact that Hussein had repeatedly blocked UN inspections and defied the United States served to lend credence to Bush's claims of the need to destroy Iraqi WMDs. After securing approval from Congress in October 2002 (many members later claimed they had voted for the resolution in the belief that this would be used to bluff Hussein to back down), the Bush administration went to war in March 2003. This occurred in the teeth of opposition from the United Nations and without the support of traditional U.S. allies, with the notable exception of Great Britain. Although Hussein's regime was easily overthrown, the United States and its allies found themselves with a ground force inadequate to effectively occupy the country and deal with a growing insurgency. The decision to dissolve the Iraqi Army also proved unfortunate, as many of its former members joined the resistance against coalition forces.

Faced with a growing insurgency, mounting American casualties, high military spending, and considerable political pressure, even from his own party, in January 2007 Bush implemented a troop surge strategy, inserting as many as 30,000 more troops in Iraq by mid-2007. This squared with advice that had been ignored by the White House in 2003, which had called for far more troops to be deployed during and after an invasion of Iraq. By the end of 2007, the troop surge appeared to be paying dividends, as violence in Iraq began to fall off markedly. Still, however, the United States maintained as many as 150,000 military personnel in Iraq in early 2008, and the long-term results of the troop surge remained unclear.

Soldiers with the latest Stryker brigade to arrive in Iraq as part of the troop "surge" on patrol in Taji, May 15, 2007. (U.S. Department of Defense)

As of this writing, the war continues, although new U.S. President Barack Obama, who made as the centerpiece of his campaign a timetable for U.S. withdrawal from Iraq, was determined to bring U.S. involvement to a speedy end and shift resources to Afghanistan, where the lack of resources to fight had contributed to a growing insurgency there.

Intractable problems remain. As 2009 began, Israel responded to Hamas rockets being fired into its territory from the Gaza Strip by launching punishing air attacks on the Gaza Strip. Iran continued its defiance of the United Nations and bulk of world opinion as it strove to develop an atomic bomb. Russia, emboldened by a flow of petrodollars, once more pushed for involvement in the Middle East to include the sale of offensive weaponry to Lebanon, where Iran also sought to protect its own interests by developing nuclear weapons. It was also accused of supplying arms (to include missiles) to Hezbollah over a period of many years.

SPENCER C. TUCKER

**See also**

Afghanistan; Algerian War; Arab-Israeli Conflict, Overview; Arab Nationalism; DESERT STORM, Operation; Egypt; ENDURING FREEDOM, Operation; France, Middle East Policy; Germany, Federal Republic of, Middle East Policy; Global War on Terror; Hamas; Hezbollah; Hussein, Saddam; Iran; Iran-Iraq War; Iranian Revolution; Iraq, History of, Pre-1990; Iraq, History of, 1990–Present; IRAQI FREEDOM, Operation; Jordan; Khomeini, Ruhollah; Kuwait; Lebanon; Libya; Middle East Regional Defense Organizations; Morocco; Mubarak, Hosni; Nasser, Gamal Abdel; Oil; Organization of Petroleum Exporting Countries; Reza Pahlavi, Mohammad; Russia, Middle East Policy, 1991–Present; Sadat, Muhammad Anwar; Saudi Arabia; September 11 Attacks; September 11 Attacks, International Reactions to; Soviet-Afghanistan War; Soviet Union, Middle East Policy; Suez Crisis; Syria; Terrorism; United Kingdom, Middle East Policy; United States, Middle East Policy, 1917–1945; United States, Middle East Policy, 1945–Present

**References**

Cleveland, William L. *A History of the Modern Middle East.* 3rd ed. Boulder, CO: Westview, 2004.

Cohen, Michael J., and Martin Kolinsky, eds. *The Demise of the British Empire in the Middle East.* London: Frank Cass, 1998.

Cooley, John K. *Payback: America's Long War in the Middle East.* Washington, DC: Brassey's, 1991.

Efrat, Moshe, and Jacob Berkovitch, eds. *Superpowers and Client States in the Middle East: The Imbalance of Influence.* New York: Routledge, 1991.

Freedman, Lawrence. *A Choice of Enemies: America Confronts the Middle East.* New York: PublicAffairs, 2008.

Freedman, Robert Owen. *Moscow and the Middle East: Soviet Policy since the Invasion of Afghanistan.* New York: Cambridge University Press, 1991.

Knights, Michael. *Cradle of Conflict: Iraq and the Birth of Modern U.S. Military.* Annapolis, MD: Naval Institute Press, 2005.

Levgold, Robert, ed. *Russian Foreign Policy in the 21st Century and the Shadow of the Past.* New York: Columbia University Press, 2007.

Mansfield, Peter. *A History of the Middle East.* New York: Penguin, 1992.

Oren, Michael B. *Six Days of War: June 1967 and the Making of the Modern Middle East.* Novato, CA: Presidio, 2003.

Ovendale, Ritchie. *Britain, the United States, and the Transfer of Power in the Middle East, 1945–1962.* Leicester, UK: Leicester University Press, 1996.

Rumer, Eugene. *Dangerous Drift: Russia's Middle East Policy.* Washington, DC: Washington Institute for Near East Policy, 2000.

Salt, Jeremy. *The Unmaking of the Middle East: A History of Western Disorder in Arab Lands.* Berkeley: University of California Press, 2008.

Taylor, Alan R. *The Superpowers and the Middle East.* Syracuse, NY: Syracuse University Press, 1991.

Wall, Irwin M. *France, the United States, and the Algerian War.* Berkeley: University of California Press, 2001.

Watson, William E. *Tricolor and Crescent: France and the Islamic World.* Westport, CT: Praeger, 2003.

# Middle East Regional Defense Organizations

When the Clement Attlee government came to power in Great Britain in July 1945, British foreign minister Ernest Bevin moved to end British colonial rule in much of the Middle East. To that end, he hoped to replace older British protectorate agreements with Iraq, Jordan, and Egypt with bilateral treaties that would reduce British commitments without giving up influence in the region. Talks for new agreements were frustrating, however. The Iraqis backed out at the last minute and did not sign the 1947 Portsmouth Agreement. The Egyptians were also not ready to accept Britain's new terms and demanded the removal of British troops. While the Iraqi rejection did not pose any immediate difficulties for the British, Egypt's demand jeopardized Britain's main stronghold in the Middle East.

Great Britain's inability to reach a bilateral defense agreement with Egypt led Britain and the United States to promulgate regional defense organizations instead. The latter included the Middle East Command (MEC) in October 1951 and the Middle East Defense Organization (MEDO) in 1953. It was believed that the organizations would commit Egypt to regional defense without subjecting it to British dominance. Nevertheless, the Egyptian monarchy and successive revolutionary regimes rejected any formal military link with the West.

Efforts to create a regional defense structure with Egypt at its core ended in May 1953, following a visit by U.S. secretary of state John Foster Dulles to the Middle East. Discussions with regional leaders—mainly with Egyptian officials—convinced Dulles that there was no chance of including Egypt in a regional defense organization. He suggested that a different country should be the linchpin of the organization, and Iraq seemed a viable alternative.

At the time, Turkey and Iraq were negotiating a mutual defense agreement. Cultural ties between Iraq and Turkey made such a pact a natural union. With tacit encouragement from Washington and with the understanding that the parties to a regional defense organization would be rewarded with military aid, the two governments agreed to expand the treaty and to use it as a platform from which to launch a regional defense organization that would include Turkey, Pakistan, and Iraq. Turkey and Pakistan had signed a defense agreement earlier, so the proposed regional defense organization was a logical extension.

In February 1955 Iraq signed a defense agreement with Turkey, the initial step toward the establishment of what became known as the 1955 Baghdad Pact, which included Iraq, Turkey, Iran, Pakistan, and Great Britain. Washington thereupon announced that it would strengthen the Iraqi Army, which stood on the front line against the Soviet Union.

Iraq took a leading role in the initiative, and not simply from fear of the Soviets. It agreed to take part in a Western-oriented regional defense agreement so as to claim regional dominance over Egypt. At the time, Iraq was the only rival to Egypt's leadership in the Arab world. Indeed, the Iraqis deeply resented the establishment of the Arab League under Cairo's auspices and saw an Iraqi-based defense organization, the headquarters of which was to be located in Baghdad, as an effective counterbalance to Egypt's push for regional hegemony.

Egyptian president Gamal Abdel Nasser did perceive the pact as a challenge to Egypt's position in the Arab world and was still reeling from criticism over the "humiliating clause" in the October 1954 Anglo-Egyptian agreement that would allow British troops access to Egyptian bases in case of war. Thus, the Egyptian leader fought back by suppressing opponents and adopting a strong Pan-Arab line. He devoted considerable energy to preventing any expansion of the Baghdad Pact. Waving the banner of Pan-Arab nationalism and resorting to manipulation and even violence, Nasser spared no effort to ensure that other Arab states did not come under the Iraqi sphere of influence.

Nasser's struggle against the Baghdad Pact stirred trouble for the pro-Western Jordanian and Lebanese regimes. His agitation reached its zenith in July 1958 when the Iraqi regime was toppled by anti-Western elements, and the Jordanian and Lebanese regimes faced a similar danger. The United States and Britain were determined to prevent Jordan and Lebanon from falling under Nasser's influence, and American and British forces were sent to Beirut and Amman, respectively, in July 1958 to prop up the pro-Western governments. In March 1959 the new Iraqi republic withdrew from the Baghdad Pact, which then became known as the Central Treaty Organization (CENTO). In the end, however, Nasser had his way, as the Baghdad Pact lost its main pillar, Iraq, and never expanded in the way that the United States and Great Britain had envisioned.

DAVID TAL

**See also**

Arab Nationalism; Baghdad Pact; Egypt; Iraq, History of, Pre-1990; Middle East, History of, 1945–Present; Nasser, Gamal Abdel

**References**

Hahn, Peter L. *The United States, Great Britain, and Egypt, 1945–1956: Strategy and Diplomacy in the Early Cold War.* Chapel Hill: University of North Carolina Press, 1991.

Podeh, Elie. *The Quest for Hegemony in the Arab World: The Struggle over the Baghdad Pact.* New York: E. J. Brill, 2003.

---

# Middle East Treaty Organization

*See* Baghdad Pact

---

# Midhat Pasha, Ahmad
## Birth Date: October 1822
## Death Date: May 8, 1884

Key Ottoman reformer and statesman considered the force who centralized Iraq as a modern nation. Ahmet (Ahmad) Midhat was born at Istanbul, the son of a *qadi* (civil judge) in October 1822. Midhat spent his early years in religious schools, and his father trained him for a career in the Ottoman civil service. At 22 years old, Midhat became the secretary of Faiq Effendi and accompanied him to Syria for three years. In 1858, Midhat spent six months visiting several European capitals.

Upon his return to Istanbul, Midhat was appointed chief director of confidential reports and, after a new mission in Syria, became second secretary of the Grand Council. His enemies, however, succeeded in ousting him from this post. Soon thereafter, he was given the seemingly impossible task of settling the widespread revolt and violence in Rumelia (present-day Balkans). His drastic measures were successful in curtailing the violence there, and the Ottoman government restored him to a place on the Grand Council.

In a similar fashion Midhat helped restore order in Bulgaria in 1857. In 1860 he was made vizier, or minister, received the title of pasha, and made governor of Nis (present-day Serbia). As a result of his reforms at Nis, Sultan Abd al-Majid I charged him, along with Fuad Pasha, the Ottoman minister of foreign affairs, and Ali Pasha, the grand vizier, or prime minister, with adapting these reforms to the whole of the empire. The result of their efforts was the Law of the Vilayets, which the sultan proclaimed in 1864. The law provided for the popular election of some local officials in the *vilayets* (provinces) of the Ottoman Empire in an attempt to eliminate corruption and favoritism in local government.

Following further administrative work, in 1866 the new sultan, Abd al-Aziz, ordered Midhat to organize the Council of State, and he served as its president from 1868 to 1869. He was then made governor of Baghdad, and also commander of the VI Corps of the Ottoman Army. In Iraq, he had great success in implementing reforms. He improved transportation by promoting steam vessels on the Tigris and the establishment of a state steamship company.

He also organized shipping lines that linked Basra with Istanbul and London following the opening of the Suez Canal, and he expanded shipping further up the Tigris to Mosul and to Aleppo on the Euphrates. Under Midhat Pasha, the extraction of oil was begun; he built a refinery at Baquba, which, although it later closed, attracted the attention of Calouste Gulbenkian, the Armenian businessman who played a major role in making Middle East oil available for Western development. Midhat Pasha also promoted the Euphrates railway and carried out agricultural improvements.

Midhat Pasha applied the Vilayet Law in Iraq, creating new schools, municipal councils, and courts. He set about trying to eradicate tribal and feudal linkages in Iraq by expanding the central government and establishing national military conscription. He taxed the Arab tribes, forced them to send recruits to his army, and put down their uprising in 1869. However, as force was insufficient to win over the tribes, he instituted a new settlement policy and began selling state land usage rights at a low price to the tribal sheikhs. Midhat Pasha also seized Kuwait and Hasa in 1871, including them in an administrative unit governed from Iraq. Under Midhat Pasha, however, Arabs were not politically empowered; Turks held the higher positions in government.

In 1871, the sultan appointed Midhat Pasha as grand vizier to replace the antireformist Mahmud Nedim Pasha. However, Midhat was in this position for only three months as he proved too independent-minded. He stayed out of government affairs, except for a short tenure as the governor of Salonica, until 1875.

Beginning in 1875, Midhat's career took a series of strange twists. While he sympathized with the ideas and aims of the Young Ottomans, a secret Turkish nationalist society formed in 1865 that wanted to reform the empire, Midhat also wanted to restrain their impatience. The obstinacy of Abd al-Aziz in preventing governmental reforms led to a coalition between the grand vizier, the war minister, and Midhat Pasha, which deposed the sultan in May 1876. The sultan was murdered the following month. His nephew Murad V became sultan, but he was deposed in August and replaced by his brother, Abd al-Hamid II.

The new sultan appointed Midhat Pasha grand vizier, and the new government promised significant reforms, including an Ottoman parliament. Midhat and other reformers drafted the Ottoman Empire's first constitution, proclaimed in December 1876 by Abd al-Hamid II after he had made numerous changes that watered down its provisions. In February 1877, the sultan dismissed Midhat and banished him for alleged complicity in the murder of Abd al-Aziz. Midhat then toured several European capitals and remained for some time in London, where he carefully studied parliamentary procedures in the House of Commons.

In 1878, Sultan Abd al-Hamid II recalled Midhat to government service and appointed him governor of Syria. In August, he exchanged offices with the governor of Smyrna. However, in May 1879, the sultan had him rearrested. Midhat first managed to escape, but then surrendered himself after a promise of a fair trial. The three-day trial took place in the Yildiz Palace in Istanbul in June 1881. Midhat and the others were sentenced to death. Because the trial was generally regarded as a mockery, the sultan commuted the sentence to banishment upon the intercession of the British government.

Midhat spent the remaining three years of his life in exile at Taif on the Red Sea coast of Arabia, where he died on May 8, 1884. Various sources claim he was murdered at the orders of Sultan Abd al-Hamid or starved to death.

ROBERT B. KANE AND SHERIFA ZUHUR

**See also**
Ottoman Empire

**References**
Kinross, Lord John Patrick Balfour. *The Ottoman Centuries: The Rise and Fall of the Turkish Empire.* New York: Morrow, 1977.

Lewis, Bernard. *The Emergence of Modern Turkey.* 3rd ed. London: Oxford University Press, 2001.

Shaw, Stanford, and Shaw Ezel Kural. *History of the Ottoman Empire and Modern Turkey,* Vol. 2, *Reform, Revolution, and Republic: The Rise of Modern Turkey, 1808–1975.* Cambridge: Cambridge University Press, 1977.

---

# Mihdhar, Khalid al-
### Birth Date: May 16, 1975
### Death Date: September 11, 2001

One of the hijackers of American Airlines Flight 77, which crashed into the Pentagon on September 11, 2001. Born on May 16, 1975, in Mecca, Saudi Arabia, little is known about Khalid al-Mihdhar's background. He traveled to Afghanistan in 1993 and then to Bosnia, where he and his friend Nawaf al-Hazmi joined Muslim fighters in fighting against the Serbs there. In 1996 Mihdhar moved back to Afghanistan with Hazmi and Hazmi's brother in time to fight with the Taliban against the Afghan Northern Alliance. In 1997, he joined the Chechen rebels in Chechnya in their fight against the Russian Army.

By 1998, Mihdhar had become a part of the terrorist group Al Qaeda. He then returned to Afghanistan for training at a special Al Qaeda training camp at Mes Aynak. In early 1999 he traveled to Saudi Arabia, and on April 7, 1999, he obtained a U.S. visa through the U.S. Consulate in Jeddah.

In late 1999 the Saudi government placed Mihdhar on a Saudi terror watch list, and then-Saudi intelligence minister Prince Turki al Faisal warned the U.S. Central Intelligence Agency (CIA) about both Mihdhar and Hazmi. By that time, both were living in San Diego, California, where they had arrived in November 1999.

Sometime in early 1999, Mihdhar was recruited to join the September 11 plot by Muhammad Atta. On January 5, 2000, Mihdhar attended the three-day conference of Al Qaeda supporters in Kuala Lumpur, Malaysia, where the outline of the September 11 plot was discussed. He and Hazmi returned to the United States on January 15, 2000, arriving in Los Angeles, where they met Omar al-Bayoumi, a Saudi who directed them to the large Muslim community in San Diego, California. Bayoumi found them an apartment and helped them settle in. Because neither Mihdhar nor Hazmi spoke English, they made no attempt to make contact with anyone outside the Muslim community. Later, they moved to another apartment, in the home of a retired literature professor, Abdussattar Shaykh, who, unbeknownst to them, was an informer for the Federal Bureau of Investigation (FBI).

Mihdhar's role was to learn to become a pilot, and he tried to learn to fly small aircraft at San Diego's Montgomery Field. But both Mihdhar and Hazmi proved such poor students that their instructor told them to go to college and learn English. This meant that the organizers of the plot had to train other pilots. Mihdhar instead became the recruiter for the muscle part of the operation.

In June 2000, Mihdhar headed back to the Middle East for an extended stay. On June 10, 2001, he traveled to Saudi Arabia, where he finalized plans for the emigration of the final 12 members of the plot. To do this, he traveled extensively throughout the Middle East, Southeast Asia, and Afghanistan. Despite his suspicious activity, Mihdhar was able to return to the United States on July 4, 2001, on the Visa Express Program. That August he moved to Laurel, Maryland.

On September 10, 2001, Mihdhar and 2 associates traveled to Herndon, Virginia, where they stayed at a Marriott Residence Inn, preparing for the suicide mission the next day. Early on the morning of September 11, Mihdhar and 4 others boarded American Airlines Flight 77 at Washington-Dulles International Airport. Mihdhar provided much of the protection for the hijacking team's pilot until the airliner crashed into the west wing of the Pentagon at 9:37 a.m. Mihdhar and the 4 other hijackers were killed, as were all 64 passengers and crew. Another 125 people died on the ground.

STEPHEN A. ATKINS

**See also**
Al Qaeda; Atta, Muhammad; Hazmi, Nawaf al-; September 11 Attacks

**References**
Graham, Bob. *Intelligence Matters: The CIA, the FBI, Saudi Arabia, and the Failure of America's War on Terror.* New York: Random House, 2004.

McDermott, Terry. *Perfect Soldiers: The 9/11 Hijackers: Who They Were, Why They Did It.* New York: HarperCollins, 2005.

---

# Military Sealift Command

The U.S. Navy component of the United States Transportation Command (USTRANSCOM), responsible for the oceanic transport of supplies, equipment, and fuel to all branches of the U.S. armed forces. Initially formed in 1949 as the Military Sea Transportation Service (MSTS), the Military Sealift Command (MSC) has varied missions. Using a combination of civilian mariners, U.S. Navy personnel, and contractors, the MSC is organized around four programs. The first is the Naval Fleet Auxiliary Force (NFAF), which includes ships charged with delivering fuel, ammunition, and supplies to U.S. Navy forces at sea. This program began in 1973. The second is the Special Mission Ships, which is tasked with performing oceanographic research, missile tracking, submarine support, and other specialized missions. The third program, known as Prepositioning, involves the stocking of prepositioned fuel, ammunition, and equipment in dedicated vessels for U.S. military forces around the world. This program began in 1980. The fourth and final program is Sealift; this provides ocean transportation to the Department of Defense. The last two programs proved critical to U.S. military operations against Iraq in 1991 and 2003.

During the 1980s, the rising geostrategic importance of the Middle East and the U.S. loss of access to many land bases in the area led the United States to establish a force of prepositioning ships in various locations to partially mitigate the huge distances and times required to move supplies by sea from the United States to areas of conflict. Troops could then be flown to the area of operations and utilize this prepositioned equipment and supplies. The first test of the prepositioning ships in particular, and the modern MSC force as a whole in a major conflict, came in 1990, when Iraq invaded Kuwait and threatened to move into Saudi Arabia. At this time, the United States had no ground forces and little infrastructure in the area. Prepositioned equipment was hardly sufficient; in planning the defense of Saudi Arabia and the liberation of Kuwait, it became obvious that several hundred thousand troops would be required. More than 90 percent of their equipment, fuel, and supplies would have to be transported by sea.

The United States eventually deployed more than 500,000 troops to the Middle East in Operations DESERT SHIELD and DESERT STORM. Almost 200 MSC ships, prepositioned ships near the crisis area and sealift vessels coming from the continental United States, carried out the fastest, largest, and most distant sealift in the history of war in support of this force. Cargo moved by sea included more than 2,000 tanks, 2,200 other armored vehicles, 1,000 helicopters, 7 billion pounds of fuel, and 2.2 billion pounds of assorted cargo. The devastating air campaign and lightning ground actions that subsequently ejected Iraqi forces from Kuwait in early 1991 would not have been possible without the MSC's Herculean efforts.

Drawing on the lessons of this conflict, MSC continued to invest in new and improved cargo vessels in the 1990s. Most significant was the addition of a new class of 17 large roll on/roll off cargo ships specifically designed to carry large numbers of wheeled and tracked vehicles.

In the buildup to Operation IRAQI FREEDOM in late 2002 and early 2003, these ships were among 50 MSC vessels that once again proved critical to the logistics effort required to support over 100,000 U.S. troops in Iraq. Since 2003, MSC ships have continued to support troop rotations in and out of the theater.

The ships of MSC, particularly the prepositioning and fast sealift vessels, give the United States military a unique global power projection capability. In any future crisis in the Middle East or elsewhere, these assets will be indispensable to mission accomplishment.

ROBERT M. BROWN

**See also**

DESERT SHIELD, Operation; DESERT STORM, Operation; DESERT STORM, Operation, Planning for; IRAQI FREEDOM, Operation; Logistics, Persian Gulf War

**References**

Brewer, David L. *Military Sealift Command*. Alexandria, VA: Defense Transportation Journal, 2003.

Martin, James B. *Logistics: Desert Storm and into the 21st Century*. Fort Leavenworth, KS: U.S. Army Command and General Staff College, 1995.

Matthews, James K., and Cora J. Holt. *So Many, So Much, So Far, So Fast: United States Transportation Command and Strategic Deployment for Operation Desert Shield/Desert Storm*. Washington, DC: Joint History Office, Office of the Chairman of the Joint Chiefs of Staff and Research Center, United States Transportation Command, 1996.

# Military Strategic Tactical Relay Satellite Communications System

Joint service satellite communications system that provides secure, jam-resistant, worldwide communications to meet essential wartime needs for high-priority military users. The multisatellite constellation links command authorities with combat operations centers, ships, submarines, aircraft, and ground stations.

The operational Military Strategic Tactical Relay (MILSTAR) satellite communications system constellation consists of five satellites placed in geosynchronous orbits around the earth. Each satellite weighs approximately 10,000 pounds and has a design life of 10 years. Each MILSTAR satellite serves as a space-based "switchboard" by directing traffic from terminal to terminal anywhere on the earth. The need for ground-controlled switching is thus significantly reduced because MILSTAR satellites actually process the communications signal and can link with each other through crosslinks. MILSTAR terminals provide encrypted voice, data, teletype, or facsimile communications and interoperable communications among the users of U.S. Army, Navy, and Air Force MILSTAR terminals. Geographically dispersed mobile and fixed control stations provide survivable and enduring operational command and control for the MILSTAR constellation.

The first MILSTAR satellite was launched on February 7, 1994, by a Titan IV expendable launch vehicle. The second was launched on November 5, 1995. The third launch, on April 30, 1999, placed the satellite into an unusable orbit. The fourth, fifth, and sixth satellites have a greatly increased capacity because of an additional medium data rate payload and were launched on February 27, 2001; January 15, 2002; and April 8, 2003.

The MILSTAR system is composed of three segments: space (the satellites), terminal (the users), and mission control. The Air Force Space Command's Space and Missile Systems Center (SMC),

812   Miller, Geoffrey D.

Los Angeles Air Force Base, California, developed the space and mission control segments. The Electronics Systems Center, Hanscom Air Force Base, Massachusetts, developed the air force portion of the terminal segment. The 4th Space Operations Squadron, Schriever Air Force Base, Colorado, is the front-line organization providing real-time satellite platform control and communications payload management.

During Operation ALLIED FORCE, the North Atlantic Treaty Organization (NATO) bombing campaign against Yugoslavia, two first-generation MILSTAR satellites provided low data rate, extremely high frequency (EHF) communications support. Because of their onboard processing and crosslink capabilities, they served as a global space network without the need for ground relay stations. The U.S. Navy especially used MILSTAR's capabilities to link command authorities, ground stations, aircraft, and ships for the majority of its communications needs during this operation, including the transmission of air tasking orders and other tactical requirements. Unfortunately, a launch failure on April 9, 1999, left a damaged MILSTAR satellite in a useless orbit and limited MILSTAR support.

MILSTAR and Defense Satellite Communications System (DSCS) satellites continued to anchor the U.S. military's satellite communications network after the September 11, 2001, terrorist attacks. In October 2001, anti-Taliban forces of the Northern Alliance, supported by U.S. Special Operations Forces (SOF), launched Operation ENDURING FREEDOM (OEF) to oust the Taliban, which had supported Islamic terrorists and protected Al Qaeda training camps in Afghanistan. Because of the primitive nature of the in-theater communications system and the mountainous terrain of Afghanistan, satellite communications were the most viable means by which commanders, operations centers, strike aircraft, SOF ground controllers, and Northern Alliance forces could communicate among each other.

The successful launch of a second MILSTAR Block II satellite on January 5, 2002, allowed the four-satellite constellation to operate as a fully cross-linked network. The deployment of large numbers of EHF terminals provided badly needed capability for rising satellite communications (SATCOM) capability to support requirements, especially for precision-guided munitions strikes and mobile user communications. Unfortunately, Unmanned Aerial Vehicles (UAVs) could not link to either MILSTAR or DSCS satellites. As a result, military planners had to turn to civil and commercial satellite providers to supplement MILSAR and DSCS satellites for satellite communications.

Because of the limitations encountered in the first year of OEF combat operations, the Joint Staff appointed a team of experts to examine the OEF experience and propose options for increasing SATCOM capability for a possible conflict with Iraq. In the spring of 2003, war fighters had access to newer DSCS and MILSTAR satellites in orbit. As a result, when coalition forces invaded Iraq in March 2003, the MILSTAR constellation handled secure communications, UAV surveillance video feeds, and reach-back

intelligence routed from the United States to the Iraq theater. MILSTAR, acting as a spaced-based switchboard, served to enhance network-centric warfare by providing mobile forces with essential video, facsimile, and data messages. Additionally, the Combined Air Operations Center stayed informed of evolving combat conditions and provided airborne strike aircraft with up-to-date target coordinates. The U.S. Navy used MILSTAR to send current targeting coordinates to ships in the Persian Gulf region, which, in turn, updated Tomahawk attacks.

ROBERT B. KANE

**See also**

Defense Satellite Communications System; ENDURING FREEDOM, Operation; IRAQI FREEDOM, Operation; Network-Centric Warfare; Satellites, Use of by Coalition Forces; Unmanned Aerial Vehicles

**References**

Levis, Alexander H., John C. Bedford (Colonel, USAF), and Sandra Davis (Captain, USAF), eds. *The Limitless Sky: Air Force Science and Technology Contributions to the Nation.* Washington, DC: Air Force History and Museums Program, 2004.

Spires, David N. *Beyond Horizons: A Half Century of Air Force Space Leadership.* 2nd ed. Maxwell Air Force Base, AL: Air Force Space Command and Air University Press, 2007.

## Miller, Geoffrey D.
### Birth Date: 1949

U.S. Army general and commander of U.S. detention facilities at Guantánamo Bay, Cuba; and in Iraq. Born in Gallipolis, Ohio, Geoffrey D. Miller graduated from Ohio State University in 1971 with a BA degree in history.

Miller was commissioned in the army as a second lieutenant of field artillery through the Reserve Officers' Training Corps (ROTC) upon graduation at Ohio State. Miller went on to earn an MS degree in education from the University of Southern California. His military education included the army's Command and General Staff College and the National War College. He served tours in Germany and then, beginning in 1980, in Korea. He served with the 7th Infantry Division and the 101st Airborne Division (Air Assault) and was ultimately deputy commanding general of the Eighth U.S. Army in Korea. He was then assigned to the Pentagon as deputy chief of staff for personnel and installation management.

In November 2002, Miller, now a major general, assumed command of Joint Task Force Guantánamo Bay, Cuba, which ran the detention facilities for enemy combatants consisting of camps X-Ray, Delta, and Echo. Miller later claimed that two-thirds of the 600 prisoners held at these three facilities had confessed to terrorist activities and that they had provided U.S. authorities with "actionable intelligence." Nonetheless, there were charges that under Miller's administration flagrant violations of prisoner rights occurred, including beatings, sleep deprivation, solitary confinement, and threatening the prisoners by means of attack dogs. Also, on September 22, 2003, Miller ordered the arrest of army captain James Yee, who was serving as a chaplain for the prisoners on the base. Miller accused Yee of having stolen documents and of espionage, but these charges were subsequently dropped and it is believed that they were never substantiated.

Miller was, meanwhile, ordered to Iraq to command the detention facilities there, including Abu Ghraib prison, Camp Cropper, and Camp Bucca, reportedly having been charged to secure more information from the prisoners. Miller recommended that "Gitmo" (Guantánamo Bay) techniques be introduced at Abu Ghraib, in which the detention and interrogation units would be combined into the Theater Joint Interrogation and Detention Center. Miller specifically urged that the guards employ techniques that would prepare the prisoners for interrogation. Although Miller denied that he ordered the guards to employ anything that would humiliate or physically abuse the prisoners prior to their interrogation, Major General Antonio Taguba, who headed the army's subsequent investigation into the Abu Ghraib scandal, concluded otherwise and noted that using military police in intelligence interrogations constituted a major policy breach.

When the Abu Ghraib prisoner abuse scandal broke in March 2004, Brigadier General Janis Karpinski, who commanded Abu Ghraib, was suspended from her command and later reduced in rank to colonel. Karpinski has blamed Miller, charging that he told her to treat the prisoners "like dogs." Colonel Thomas Pappas, who headed the interrogation unit at Abu Ghraib, has made similar charges against Miller and said that the policy had been approved by Lieutenant General Ricardo S. Sanchez, then senior U.S. military official in Iraq. Miller has denied all these allegations and any wrongdoing.

Miller was then appointed the deputy commanding general for detainee operations for the Multi-National Force in Iraq. He soon announced his intention to reduce the number of prisoners at Abu Ghraib, to abide by the Geneva Convention regarding the treatment of prisoners, to improve conditions for the prisoners, and to end the practice of hooding prisoners during transfers. Miller was reassigned in November 2004.

Miller testified at the court martial proceedings of soldiers tried in the Abu Ghraib scandal during which he said dogs were to be used for guard purposes only and that his instructions had been misunderstood. Although investigators twice cleared Miller of any wrongdoing, he sought to retire in February 2006. Discrepancies between his testimony before the Senate Armed Services Committee in May 2004 and sworn statements made several months later led to his retirement being held up until July 31, 2006. He was allowed to leave the army only when he pledged in writing that he would appear before Congress and testify truthfully if called upon to do so. On his retirement, Miller was awarded the Distinguished Service Medal and praised as an "innovator."

SPENCER C. TUCKER

**See also**
Abu Ghraib; Karpinski, Janis; Sanchez, Ricardo S.

**References**
Danner, Mark. *Torture and Truth: America, Abu Ghraib, and the War on Terror.* New York: New York Review Books, 2004.
Greenberg, Karen J., and Joshua L. Dratel, eds. *The Torture Papers: The Road to Abu Ghraib.* Cambridge: Cambridge University Press, 2005.
Lewis, Neil A. "Court in Abuse Case Hears Testimony of General." *New York Times,* May 25, 2006.
Smith, R. Jeffrey. "General Is Said to Have Urged Use of Dogs." *Washington Post,* May 26, 2004.
Strasser, Steven, ed. *The Abu Ghraib Investigations: The Official Independent Panel and Pentagon Reports on the Shocking Prisoner Abuse in Iraq.* New York: PublicAffairs, 2004.
White, Josh. "General Who Ran Guantanamo Bay Retires." *Washington Post,* August 1, 2006.

# Mine Resistant Ambush Protected Vehicles

The mine resistant ambush protected (MRAP) vehicle is an armored truck developed by the U.S. military Operation IRAQI FREEDOM in Iraq and Operation ENDURING FREEDOM in Afghanistan to protect troops from improvised explosive devices (IEDs). IEDs are field-expedient explosives developed by insurgents or guerrillas from whatever material is available. (A better name might be "homemade bombs.") They can be simple artillery rounds rigged to a detonator that is set off remotely or by physical contact with vehicles or people, preferably enemies of those setting the mines. They can also be very sophisticated devices, with explosives designed to pierce armored vehicles. IEDs have been the cause of almost half the fatalities suffered by U.S. forces in Iraq, while about half the fatalities in Afghanistan have been from IEDs.

While IEDs can sometimes be effective against the Abrams tank and the Bradley Fighting Vehicle, they are very highly effective against unarmored transport vehicles. These include the High Mobility Multipurpose Wheeled Vehicle (Humvee), the modern equivalent of the World War II–era Jeep, and the 2.5- and 5-ton trucks and tanker trucks used to move personnel, ammunition, provisions, and fuel over the extensive roadways of Afghanistan and Iraq. These vehicles were not designed as armored combat vehicles; rather, they were specially designed and reinforced versions of commercial transports for military logistics purposes.

The threat from IEDs led to a program to armor Humvees and other transport vehicles, a program that continues. The basic problem of refitting such vehicles is how to cope with the added weight of the armor without making major modifications to engine power, transmissions, engine cooling, and suspension systems. This has to be balanced with the differences between up-armoring vehicles in the theater of war versus the extended choices of doing so at depots in the United States.

A parallel approach to retrofitting existing vehicles has been the development and fielding of MRAPs to provide better protection for vehicles and crews. MRAPs are wheeled vehicles with a "V" shaped hull and armored plating designed to deflect the impact of IEDs. They were used in small numbers in Iraq and Afghanistan in

A U.S. Marine Corps mine resistant ambush protected (MRAP) vehicle in Afghanistan, 2009. (U.S. Department of Defense)

2003 for route clearance and explosive ordnance disposal (EOD). The protection they provided led to the U.S. Department of Defense decision in 2007 to make deployment of MRAPs a high priority.

The resulting program involves three categories of MRAPs based on size and mission. Category I MRAPs are 7 to 15 tons, carrying a crew of two plus four passengers, mainly for urban transportation. Category II vehicles weigh between 15 and 25 tons, carry a crew of two and eight passengers, and are designed for road escort, ambulance, and EOD missions. Category III vehicles weigh 25 tons or more, carry a crew of two plus four passengers, and are designed for EOD missions that require more equipment than can be carried in Category II vehicles. The dimensions and missions have already changed, and will likely be further refined as testing and fielding proceeds.

Several companies, both domestic and foreign, have had various types of vehicles under development or in production, and as the U.S. military began to invest in armored vehicles, many companies competed for the new market, potentially worth several billion dollars. The vehicles are called Cougar, Buffalo, Maxx-Pro, Caiman, and Alpha. The Defense Department continues to prefer referencing the vehicles as Category I, II, and III MRAPs, but the commercial names have also remained, leading to some confusion, as the Cougar and Caiman come in both 4X4 and 6X6 versions. Domestic production companies have included Force

Protection Industries, BAE Systems of North America, Navistar subsidiary International Military and Government LLC, Armor Holdings LLC, Oshkosh Truck, General Dynamics, Textron, and Protected Vehicles. Companies in Canada, Germany, Israel, and South Africa have also been involved because they have also been developing new, armored wheeled vehicles.

The designs of the vehicles vary. Some have a one-piece hull and chassis. Others have the hull bolted to the chassis. Some have the "V" shaped armor covering the entire vehicle, while others have that protection only for the crew and passengers. There are variations in mobility both on and off the road, engine size, and dimensions. All have been through extensive tests at Aberdeen Proving Ground and elsewhere, and are being evaluated by in-field performance in Iraq and Afghanistan.

By the end of 2007, the Defense Department had placed orders for 7,774 MRAPs and projected a total requirement of 23,000 if troop levels remained steady in Iraq. By April 2008 there were about 5,000 MRAPs in Iraq, with projections of having about 6,000 by December 2008. Costs through fiscal year 2009 are estimated at $25 billion. Costs are based on the actual cost of the various vehicles, which vary widely even within category, and mode of shipment. The military prefers air transport to bring the vehicles into the war zone, but doing so costs $135,000 for each vehicle, compared with just $18,000 by ship.

Although several vehicle models are in Iraq and Afghanistan, there are three that represent the categories well. Their characteristics demonstrate the flux in the scope of the Defense Department categories in a very short time. For Category I, the Navistar MaxxPro, a model that dominates that category with $3.5 billion in orders, has an 8.7-liter six-cylinder diesel engine that produces 330 horsepower. It is 21 feet long, 8.5 feet wide, and 10 feet high. It weighs 40,000 pounds, has a ground clearance of 11 inches, and carries a 2-man crew and up to 10 passengers. The cost is $549,000.

For Category II, the Force Protection Cougar 6X6 has a 7.2 liter diesel engine that produces 330 horsepower. It is 23 feet long, 8.5 feet wide, and 8.8 feet high. Weighing in at 39,000 pounds, it has a 15-inch ground clearance. It carries a crew of two and eight passengers. Unit cost is $649,000.

The Force Protection Buffalo represents Category III. Its 12-liter six-cylinder diesel engine produces 400 horsepower. It is 27 feet long, 8.25 feet wide, and 13 feet high. The weight is 45,320 pounds, ground clearance is 16 inches, and it has a crew of two plus four passengers. The $855,000 cost includes a remote-controlled external arm to help with EOD. Its large size allows more EOD equipment.

The armored Humvee has a 6.5-liter diesel V-8 engine producing 190 horsepower. It is 16 feet long, 7.5 feet wide, and 6.25 feet high. It weighs 12,000 pounds and has a ground clearance of 16.8 inches. Carrying four people, its unit cost is $150,000.

It is impossible to determine what the U.S. military, both army and marines, will eventually choose for transport vehicles, both wheeled and tracked, armored or not. It is clear that the decisions will be based not only on testing in the United States but also on performance of the many versions of transport vehicles. They will be expected to perform in the varied terrain presented by Iraq and Afghanistan, which ranges from desert to densely populated urban areas and from sea level to mountain ranges higher than any in the continental United States, with climates of intense heat to below-zero temperatures and widely different challenges posed by rain, snow, drought, and blinding sandstorms. Ground clearance will be a critical factor for off-road travel. Size will be important not only for maneuverability in crowed urban areas but for transport to the field of battle, especially by air. The height of the vehicles will be important as bigger targets are more vulnerable to attack from armor-piercing rounds from rocket-propelled grenades (RPGs) and other weapons. If applied with thought, the lessons learned from actual combat in Iraq and Afghanistan should lead to a U.S. military equipped with the best possible range of transport vehicles for future challenges.

DANIEL E. SPECTOR

See also

BMP-1 Series Infantry Fighting Vehicles; Bradley Fighting Vehicle; High Mobility Multipurpose Wheeled Vehicle; Improvised Explosive Devices; M1A1 and M1A2 Abrams Main Battle Tanks; Rocket-Propelled Grenade; Vehicles, Unarmored

References

Dixon, Chris. "Blast Proof Wheels for the Mean Streets of War Zones." *New York Times,* February 24, 2008.

Feickert, Andrew. *Mine-Resistant, Ambush-Protected (MRAP) Vehicles: Background and Issues for Congress.* Washington, DC: Congressional Research Service, Library of Congress, 2007.

Schwartz, General Norton A. *Statement before the Senate Homeland Security and Government Affairs Committee.* Washington, DC: U.S. Government Printing Office, September 27, 2007.

---

# Mines, Sea, Clearing Operations, Persian Gulf and Iraq Wars

From its occupation of Kuwait in August 1990 to the January 1991 Persian Gulf War (Operation DESERT STORM), Iraq laid more then 1,200 Soviet-manufactured mines off the Iraqi and Kuwaiti coasts. These mines provided a cheap deterrent to coalition naval forces, limited movement by sea, and required time and specially equipped units to remove them. In January 1991, the U.S. military confirmed the presence of Iraqi mines and announced that recently planted mines had broken their moorings and drifted with the Persian Gulf current. By January 20, 1991, 29 mines had been destroyed in the northern Persian Gulf, and by March 1991, 250 additional mines had been destroyed by coalition forces.

Countermine warfare requires specialized ships that can detect and render mines inert. The U.S. Navy deployed four mine countermeasure ships to the Persian Gulf during the Gulf War. The MCM-1 *Avenger*, MSO-509 *Adroit*, MSO-449 *Impervious* and MOS-490 *Leader* were deployed along with the LPH-10 *Tripoli*, which was deployed to the Gulf to coordinate mine countermeasures. The *Tripoli* carried six MH-53 Sea Dragon helicopters that could participate in mine countermeasure work. The British Navy also provided mine countermeasure ships in the *Atherstone, Cattistock* and *Hurworth;* the *Herald* acted as a supply ship. This Royal Navy contingent was later reenforced by HMS *Ledbury* and *Dulverton.* The Belgians also contributed three mine countermeasure ships, while the Saudi Arabian Navy contributed four.

Two U.S. Navy vessels were damaged by mines in the course of operations in the Persian Gulf in 1991. The *Tripoli* was struck by a moored contact mine on February 18, 1991, in the northern Persian Gulf. The mine, packed with 300 pounds of explosives, blew a 16x20-foot hole 10 feet below the waterline on the ship's forward starboard side. Four crew members were injured in the blast, but none were killed. The *Tripoli* was repaired and eventually returned to countermine duties in the Persian Gulf. The second ship struck by mines in the Persian Gulf was the CG-59 *Princeton.* It was hit by two mines three hours after the *Tripoli* had been struck. The first mine exploded near the stern of the ship and lifted it 10 feet out of the water. The second mine exploded 300 yards off the starboard bow. Three crew members were injured in these blasts, and the *Princeton* was out of service for the remainder of the war. It eventually returned to duty after extensive repairs.

K-Dog, a bottlenose dolphin, leaps out of the water while training near USS *Gunston Hall* in the Persian Gulf on March 18, 2003. The specially trained dolphins are fitted with underwater cameras to locate mines. (U.S. Department of Defense)

During the 2003 invasion of Iraq (Operation IRAQI FREEDOM), U.S. and coalition navies provided aggressive mine countermeasure support and applied the valuable lessons of the 1991 Persian Gulf War to operations in Iraq. For mine countermeasures operations during the 2003 invasion of Iraq, coalition forces relied on Task Force 55 to clear mines from the northern Persian Gulf to allow humanitarian aid and military equipment to enter Iraq by sea.

U.S. countermine operations were coordinated from the landing transport dock ship *Ponce* (LPD-15), and the U.S. Navy countermine contingent included the *Ardent* (MCM-12), *Cardinal* (MCH-60), *Dexterous* (MCM-13) and *Raven* (MHC-61). Along with ships, countermine forces relied on specialized helicopters, such as the MH-53 *Sea Dragon*, which towed sleds with detection gear. The U.S. Navy's Marine Mammal System (MMS) was also used in detecting mines. The MMS utilizes specially trained bottlenose dolphins fitted with underwater cameras to locate mines. To date the coalition has not lost a single ship to Iraqi mines in Operation IRAQI FREEDOM.

STEVEN F. MARIN

**See also**

DESERT SHIELD, Operation; DESERT STORM, Operation; DESERT STORM, Operation, Coalition Naval Forces; IRAQI FREEDOM, Operation; IRAQI FREEDOM, Operation, Coalition Naval Forces; Iraq, Navy; United States Navy, Iraq War; United States Navy, Persian Gulf War

**References**

Hartmann, Gregory K., and Scott C. Truver. *Weapons That Wait: Mine Warfare in the U.S. Navy.* Updated ed. Annapolis, MD: Naval Institute Press, 1991.

Marolda, Edward, and Robert Schneller. *Shield and Sword: The United States Navy and the Persian Gulf War.* Annapolis, MD: U.S. Naval Institute Press, 2001.

Melia, Tamara Moser. *"Damn the Torpedoes": A Short History of U.S. Naval Mine Countermeasures, 1777–1991.* Washington, DC: Naval Historical Center, 1991.

## Mines, Sea, and Naval Mine Warfare, Persian Gulf and Iraq Wars

Sea mines are marine explosive devices designed to detonate underwater and sink or damage an enemy ship. Mines are exploded through direct contact or by means of various proximity-detecting triggering mechanisms. Long considered the most cost-effective means of inflicting great losses on an opponent's maritime forces, the sea mine—whether laid by ships, submarines, or aircraft—is a truly stealthy naval weapon, needing no tracking, supervision, or reloading, and maintaining its potential lethality for decades. An important book on the subject calls mines the "weapons that wait." Mine warfare encompasses the development and strategic placement of these weapons, and the corresponding need to develop countermeasures against them when they are employed by an opposing force.

The laying of mines in the Persian Gulf by Iran during the 1980–1988 Iran-Iraq War created a regional navigational peril, beginning with a spate of some 18 mine strikes on commercial ships from 15 countries passing through the Red Sea and Gulf of Suez in the summer of 1984 alone, and during the "Tanker War" in the Persian Gulf, most notably when the reflagged Kuwaiti tanker *Bridgeton* was damaged in July 1987, and the U.S. Navy frigate *Samuel B. Roberts* (FFG-58) nearly sank in April 1988, both as a consequence of Iranian mines. The 1991 Persian Gulf War and the Iraq War that began in 2003 saw renewed naval mine warfare in the region, engaging U.S. and coalition mine countermeasures (MCM) vessels and aircraft once again in hazardous detection and elimination duties.

Coalition minesweepers and mine hunters have had to contend with two basic types of mines in the period since early 1991: contact mines and influence mines. The contact mine has its roots in the late 18th century. American David Bushnell endeavored to sink British ships with primitive contact mines set adrift in the Delaware River during the American Revolutionary War. These contact mines were kegs of powder triggered by a flintlock arrangement inside the keg. The hammer was released by the shock of the mine striking an object, which in turn set off the mine. Contact mines were employed by the Russians in the Crimean War (1853–1856) and by the Confederates with considerable effect in the American Civil War (1861–1865). Both sides made extensive use of mines

## IRAQI LAND AND SEA MINEFIELDS, JANUARY 1991

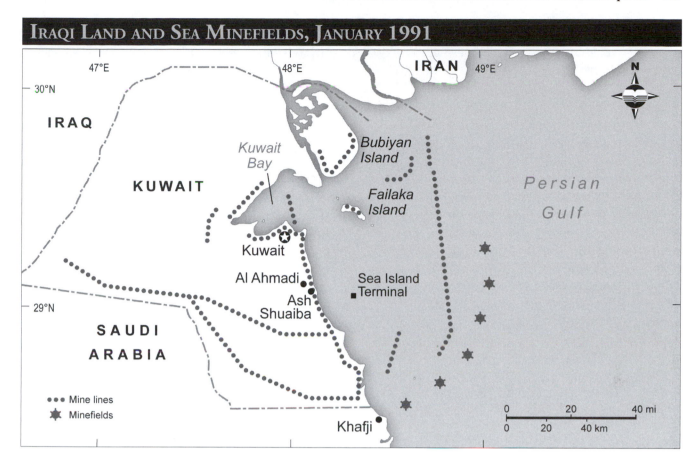

in World Wars I and II. Such mines consist of explosive charge encased in a metal sphere that is either moored by a tether to an anchor on the seabed or placed on the bottom in shallow water. The contact mine's positioning below the surface renders it invisible to oncoming shipping. Its protruding "Hertz horns" activate the sensitive triggers that release the mine's explosive power against any vessel that runs into it. To counter the effects of a suspected field of moored contact mines, a formation of minesweeping ships would stream a wide array of cables and floats equipped with powerful cutting devices to sever the mines from their moorings and bring them to the surface, where divers could then disarm them, or they could be destroyed at safe distance by gunfire.

While operating as a "mother ship" for coalition minesweepers and base for minesweeping helicopters during Operation DESERT STORM, in February 1991, the amphibious assault ship *Tripoli* (LPH-10) struck a moored contact mine, part of an undetected Iraqi minefield in the northern Persian Gulf. The *Tripoli* sustained severe damage.

A further danger from contact mines occurs when they break free of their anchor cables. They might then drift into shipping lanes. It is believed that some of the drifting mines culled by coalition forces during and after the Persian Gulf War had been deliberately and randomly released without anchors by Iraqi minelayers to confound their naval foes in the northern Gulf.

Influence mines, developed in the years between the two world wars, are magnetic, acoustic, and pressure mines, plus those mines that are triggered by combinations of these influences. Moored in deeper water, burrowed into or positioned on the sea floor, and not needing contact with a vessel to damage or destroy them, these mines—once identified and understood—brought about sweeping changes in MCM in all navies during World War II and in the years since.

The magnetic mine detects a significant change in the magnetic field around it, which usually signifies a steel-hulled ship passing overhead or nearby. The mine then reacts by detonating. The wooden or glass-reinforced plastic (GRP) hulls of many MCM vessels in service since the 1940s effectively "blind" a magnetic mine to their presence, and by trailing two long electrically charged cables and sending powerful jolts of current into the water from their large generators, MCM ships could mimic a significant magnetic anomaly and detonate magnetic mines far behind them. To defeat this sweep technique, those developing new mines created devices called ship-counters that could trigger mines to detonate only after a given number of ships (or minesweepers' electrical cables) had passed. This introduced a challenging element of randomness that thereafter required minesweepers to undertake repetitious but necessary "check sweeps" of previously swept channels.

The acoustic mine operates on the same principle as the magnetic mine, but instead "listens" for the appropriate constant intensity of sound generated by the cavitation of a ship's propellers and the frequency signature of its engines, and explodes when the noise peaks. To simulate the approach of a ship, devices such as the acoustic hammer box—a blunt, bomb-shaped noisemaker—were towed far behind a minesweeper, creating a varied intensity of shiplike sounds that would set off nearby acoustic mines. Soon thereafter, acoustic mines, like magnetic mines, came to be fitted with ship-counters, causing MCM experts, in turn, to introduce timing devices to acoustic hammer boxes and other sound-generating countermeasures, thereby fabricating imaginary distances between the equally imaginary ships these measures created.

Pressure mines, first encountered by Allied minesweepers during the 1944 Normandy campaign, are triggered by the sustained water pressure anomalies caused by passing ships, and have proven very vexing to counter effectively except by a "hunt to kill" approach, first used by divers in the Korean War (1950–1953) and continued up to the present day by mine-hunting forces in many navies. Most effective is the combination of sonar, closed-circuit television in remotely controlled robotic vehicles, and divers: the mine-hunter ship proceeds slowly over the seabed as it plots likely mine positions with its sonar, after which divers—or trained dolphins and sea lions, in some cases—carefully seek out the mines and attach remotely controlled charges that are detonated after their safe return to the ship. During the 1991 Persian Gulf War, the U.S. Navy cruiser *Princeton* (CG-59) was seriously damaged by two combination acoustic-magnetic Manta influence mines. The Italian-made Mantas had been purchased earlier on the international weapons market by Iraq, and were part of an extensive mine-laying effort in late 1990 around the approaches to Kuwait, undertaken by Iraq during the protracted period in which the U.S. and coalition forces were assembling in Operation DESERT SHIELD.

During the Persian Gulf War proper, minesweepers and mine hunters from the navies of the United States and the United Kingdom were active in MCM patrolling in the northern Gulf, as were six U.S. Navy Sikorsky MH-53 Sea Stallion MCM helicopters equipped with towed minesweeping arrays. After hostilities ended, a considerable but imperfectly coordinated multinational force coalesced, comprising additional ships and teams from Australia, Italy, France, Belgium, the Netherlands, Germany, and, eventually, Japan. This was the Japanese Navy's first combat zone deployment since assisting with minesweeping during the Korean War. Despite initial procedural uncertainties, effective clearance operations ensued, with two-dozen MCM vessels netting some 1,300 Iraqi mines. The German Navy's sophisticated use of remotely operated vehicles in performing sweeps for influence mines set a new standard for effectiveness and cooperative training among the participants, spurring the U.S. Navy once again to address deficiencies in its mine warfare capabilities and readiness, as it had in the 1950s as a result of Korean War experiences.

Operations ENDURING FREEDOM and IRAQI FREEDOM have involved the navies of the United States and some coalition nations, although with somewhat reduced MCM activities. Their refusal to support the U.S.-led invasion of Iraq in 2003 caused a number of North American Treaty Organization (NATO) allies to withhold MCM and other naval assets from deployment in the region, but a combined U.S., Australian, and British mine warfare force was able to locate and eradicate nearly 70 Iraqi mines in coastal waters of the northern Persian Gulf, and Australian warships prevented the mine-laying mission of an intercepted Iraqi ship carrying a large cargo of influence and contact mines.

In the years after Operation DESERT STORM, many advances and refinements in MCM were incorporated into coalition efforts, and their application during the initial phase of IRAQI FREEDOM proved the effectiveness of such new systems as autonomous underwater vehicles (AUV), unmanned underwater vehicles (UUV), and the Sea Fox, a German-developed "expendable destructor" that is essentially an exploding UUV that is remotely guided to a mine, much like a smart bomb. As Operation IRAQI FREEDOM continues, the U.S. Navy and its coalition partners maintain a regional MCM force in the region bolstered by technical and tactical developments from European military, industrial, and technological sources.

GORDON E. HOGG

**See also**

DESERT STORM, Operation, Coalition Naval Forces; IRAQI FREEDOM, Operation, Coalition Naval Forces; Minesweepers and Mine Hunters; United States Navy, Iraq War; United States Navy, Persian Gulf War

**References**

Hartmann, Gregory K., and Scott C. Truver. *Weapons That Wait: Mine Warfare in the U.S. Navy.* Updated ed. Annapolis, MD: Naval Institute Press, 1991.

Marolda, Edward, and Robert Schneller. *Shield and Sword: The United States Navy and the Persian Gulf War.* Annapolis, MD: U.S. Naval Institute Press, 2001.

Morison, Samuel L. *International Guide to Naval Mine Warfare.* 2nd ed. Washington, DC: King Communications Group, 2000.

Pokrant, Marvin. *Desert Storm at Sea: What the Navy Really Did.* Westport, CT: Greenwood, 1999.

Rios, John J. *Naval Mines in the 21st Century: Can NATO Navies Meet the Challenge?* Monterey, CA: Naval Postgraduate School, 2005.

## Mines and Mine Warfare, Land

Land mines are stationary explosive weapons planted in the path of an enemy to hinder his movement or to deny him access to certain territory. Mines may be considered both offensive and defensive weapons. Mines are generally concealed and rigged so that they will be initiated by the presence of either enemy troops or vehicles, save in instances where they are exploded by remote control. Land mines produce casualties by direct explosive force, fragmentation, shaped-charge effect, or the release of harassing agents or lethal gas. Land mines include improvised explosive devices (known today as IEDs).

There are two main types of land mines: antitank (AT) and antipersonnel (AP). Antitank mines are large and heavy. They are triggered when vehicles such as tanks drive over or near them. These mines contain sufficient explosives to destroy or damage the vehicle that runs over them. They also frequently kill people in or near the vehicle. Antitank mines are laid in locations where enemy vehicles are expected to travel: on roads, bridges, and tracks.

Antipersonnel mines are triggered much more easily and are designed to kill or wound people. They may be laid anywhere and can be triggered by stepping on them, pulling on a wire, or simply shaking them. Antipersonnel mines may also be rigged as booby traps to explode when an object placed over them is removed. Generally speaking, AP mines contain small amounts of explosives. They are therefore smaller and lighter than antitank mines. They may be as small as a pack of cigarettes. Antipersonnel mines come in all shapes and colors and are made from a variety of materials.

Mines are normally laid in groups to form minefields. There are several types of these fields. Defensively, the hasty protective minefield provides local, close-in security protection for small units. This minefield employs no standard pattern in laying the mines. An example of a hasty protective minefield would be placing mines to cover a likely avenue of approach by an enemy force. A second type is the point minefield. It is utilized primarily to reinforce other obstacles, such as road craters, abatis, or wire obstacles not associated with hasty protective minefields. A third type is the tactical minefield. Its primary use is to arrest, delay, and disrupt an enemy attack. The field may be employed to strengthen defensive positions and protect their flanks. A fourth type is the interdiction minefield. It is utilized to trap or harass an enemy deep in his own territory, assembly areas, or defensive positions. Artillery- or air-delivered scatterable mines are ideal for this type of minefield.

Modern land mines may be said to date from the Russo-Japanese War of 1904–1905, but World War I witnessed continuous use of land mines to protect trench lines. Land mines continued to play an important role during World War II. Two important developments took place in land-mine warfare during that conflict: the appearance of the antitank mine; and the introduction of antipersonnel mines employed against infantry and to protect antitank mines from detection and removal.

Many current antitank mines are derived from those of World War II. For example, the TMM1, produced in the former Yugoslavia, and the PT Mi-Ba, produced by the Czech Republic and Slovakia, are descendants of the German antitank Tellermine 43 and 42. The American designs are the M-15 and M-21 series; the Russians produce a similar mine, the TM-46, the Italians the M-80, and the Chinese the Type 72. These are canister-shaped mines that are buried using tilt rod fusing and pressure fusing. They range from 10 to 30 inches in diameter and 3 to 7 inches in height. They contain between 7 and 15 pounds of high explosives. Another popular design is the square AT mine, such as the American M-19, Italian VS-HCT2, or Belgian PRB-ATK M3. The square mine is approximately 10 inches square and 4 to 5 inches high with 5 to 25 pounds

of explosives. Many of these are magnetic-influence mines with pressure as a backup fusing system.

Antipersonnel mine models introduced during World War II are still in service with only minor modifications. Examples are the Russian antipersonnel mine POMZ (and the later model POMZ-2M, a stake mine consisting of a wooden stake with a cast-iron fragmentation body). The Russian PDM-6 APM is basically the wooden-cased mine used during the Russo-Finnish War of 1939–1940. Its successors, the PDM-7, PDM-7ts, and PDM-57, are employed worldwide. There are also bouncing mines similar to the U.S. M16 series or the Russian OMZ (fragmentation obstacle APM or "Bouncing Betty")—canister mines topped with a pressure fuse. Such mines stand five to seven inches tall (including the fuse) and are three to four inches in diameter, with approximately one pound of explosive. The improvised version of these APMs consists of an artillery shell or a mortar bomb buried nose down in the ground. It is similar to IEDs used in both the Vietnam and Iraq wars.

After World War II, the trend in land mines has been toward miniaturization and substitution of plastic parts for metal ones. For example, the American M14 series, first used in Vietnam, and the Russian APM PFM-1 and PFM-1S, first used during the Israeli-Syrian conflict of October 1973 and massively by Soviet troops in Afghanistan, are small air-delivered plastic weapons with a low metallic signature. Other common APMs with low metallic content are the Type-72 series (People's Republic of China), encountered throughout Southeast Asia; and the PMN (Russia) present in Asia (Afghanistan, China, Iraq, Vietnam) and in southern Africa, where it is known as the "Black Widow." These are all small canister-type mines 2.5 to 4 inches in diameter and 1.5 to 4.5 inches in height. They all use pressure fusing. They carry one to four ounces of explosive.

The Korean War (1950–1953) saw widespread use of mines, particularly in the intense, largely static warfare of the second half of the war following the entry of the PRC in the fighting. The demilitarized zone across Korea remains one of the most heavily mined areas in the world. The Vietnam War of the 1960s and 1970s saw an increase in the use of APMs offensively as part of ambushes, with the American M18 Claymore as well as its copies in the Soviet MON 50 and Chinese Type 66. These mines are generally command-detonated. All are of curved rectangular shape. The Claymore was about 1 inch thick, 3.5 inches tall, and 8 to 12 inches long, filled with 1.5 pounds of explosive with a layer of metal balls (similar to 00-Buck shotgun pellets) faced toward the target area. These mines are never buried but are positioned on bipod legs that allow aiming. These mines were employed in Vietnam offensively but were also defensively employed around fire bases (U.S. and allied forces) and sanctuaries (for communist forces).

The United Nations (UN) estimates that 24,000 people are killed and at least 10,000 are maimed each year as a result of active and inactive minefields. A high percentage of these casualties are children. The present method for clearing mines involves painstaking detection and careful destruction of the devices. In 2004 the UN listed 35 countries with minefields of more than 1,000 mines.

A soldier from the U.S. Army 41st Engineer Battalion uses a metal detector to mark land mines and unexploded ordnance near Bagram Air Base in Afghanistan, 2004. (U.S. Department of Defense)

Egypt leads the list with 23 million mines planted, followed by Iran with 16 million; Angola with 15 million; and Afghanistan, the PRC, and Iraq with an estimated 10 million each. It can take one person 80 days to clear 2.5 acres.

Those who clear the mines, known as de-miners, are at great risk of becoming victims themselves. More than 80 de-miners died in mine-clearing operations in Kuwait following the 1991 Gulf War. French de-miners still clear mines and unexploded artillery shells from World War I and as far back as the Franco-Prussian War of 1870–1871. It is estimated that worldwide up to 85 million antipersonnel mines await clearance. In 2004 the UN estimated the cost of laying a single mine at less than $10 but its removal at $1,800.

In 1991, nongovernmental organizations and individuals began discussions regarding a ban on antipersonnel land mines. In October 1992 the International Campaign to Ban Landmines (ICBL) was formed by founding organizations Handicap International, Human Rights Watch, Medico International, Mines Advisory Group, Physicians for Human Rights, and Vietnam Veterans of America Foundation. The ICBL called for an international ban on the production, stockpiling, transfer, and use of antipersonnel land mines, and for increased international resources for mine clearance and mine victim assistance programs.

An international treaty often referred to as the Ottawa Mine Ban Treaty was negotiated in 1997. It is formally named "The Convention on the Prohibition of the Use, Stockpiling, Production and Transfer of AntiPersonnel Mines and On Their Destruction." Among the first governments ratifying the treaty were Belgium, Canada, France, Germany, and the United Kingdom. The treaty went into effect in March 1999. In recognition of its achievements, the campaign was awarded the Nobel Peace Prize in 1997. Signatories to the treaty include all Western Hemisphere nations except the United States and Cuba, all NATO states except the United States and Turkey, all of the European Union except Finland, 42 African countries, and 17 nations in the Asia-Pacific region, including Japan. Important military powers not ratifying the treaty include the United States, Russia, China, India, Pakistan, and North and South Korea.

The treaty binds states to destroy their stockpiled antipersonnel mines within 4 years and those already in the ground must be removed within 10 years. In addition to comprehensively banning antipersonnel mines, the treaty requires signatories to perform mine clearance and urges mine victim assistance programs. Despite the treaty, mines continued to be laid in such nations as Angola, Cambodia, Senegal, and Sudan.

HERBERT MERRICK

**See also**
Artillery; Mines, Sea, Clearing Operations, Persian Gulf and Iraq Wars; Mines, Sea, and Naval Mine Warfare, Persian Gulf and Iraq Wars

References

Crol, Mike. *History of Landmines*. London: Pen and Sword Books, 1998.

Davies, Paul. *War of the Mines: Cambodia, Landmines and the Impoverishment of a Nation*. London: Pluto, 1994.

Heyman, C. *Trends in Land Mine Warfare: A Jane's Special Report*. London: Jane's Information Group, 1995.

Matthew, Richard, Bryan McDonald, and Ken Rutherford. eds. *Landmines and Human Security: International Politics and War's Hidden Legacy*. New York: SUNY Press, 2004.

McGrath, Rae. *Landmines: A Resource Book*. Milwaukee: University of Michigan Press, 2000.

# Minesweepers and Mine Hunters

Ships dedicated to mine countermeasures (MCM), specifically equipped to enter waters likely to have been sown with mines in order to clear them by means of various towed cable arrays, or to locate and eliminate mines with sonar, divers, or unmanned underwater vehicles (UUV).

Minesweepers as a ship type date to the early 20th century, particularly the World War I era, when the Allies and the Central Powers developed similar small vessels (displacing from 450 to 950 tons) to open channels through the minefields that menaced navies on both sides. Since late in World War II, minesweeper hulls have been constructed of wood, demagnetized steel, and composites such as glass-reinforced plastic (GRP) to allow safer navigation when sweeping or neutralizing magnetic mines. While moored contact mines were snagged and cut from their anchors by gear streamed astern from a minesweeper, mines sensitive to magnetic or acoustic influences required more specialized measures. Trailing electrically charged cables far behind the minesweeper mimicked the magnetic field of a large steel hull, detonating magnetic mines at a harmless distance. Acoustic mines, which responded to the sound signatures of an approaching ship's engines and propellers, exploding when the volume reached its apex, could be foiled by a minesweeper towing (again, at a safe distance) noise-generating devices that convincingly re-created the sounds of a large vessel nearby, causing the acoustic mine to detonate.

The greatest challenge was posed by the development of the pressure mine, first encountered by the Allies during the 1944 Normandy campaign. Sensitive to the low-water-pressure field caused by a passing ship, and difficult to distract or deceive plausibly by existing minesweeping technology, pressure mines—and newer mines that responded to combinations of influences such as magnetic-acoustic, pressure-magnetic, etc.—led directly to the new practice of mine hunting, pioneered during the Korean War (1950–1953).

As patrolling aircraft came to identify and dispatch moored mines in Korean waters, less visible bottom-placed mines of various types were increasingly detected by those U.S. Navy minesweepers mounting sonar. Divers trained in demolition then located the mines and attached remotely actuated charges to detonate them from a safe distance. This search-and-destroy model became increasingly sophisticated over the ensuing decades, and while the U.S. Navy's dedication to mine warfare ebbed and flowed, other, smaller navies—those of North Atlantic Treaty Organization (NATO) countries, especially—actively fostered improvements and innovations in the field, making use of transferred U.S. minesweepers, but also designing and building new minesweepers and mine hunters in their own shipyards. Some of the advanced features in recent mine-hunter construction include: very quiet engines made of nonmagnetic alloys, automatic radar navigation, auxiliary "hovering" and side-thrusting motors to maintain a position or to allow precise maneuvering at very slow speeds, and disposable remotely operated vehicles (ROV) that seek out and destroy bottom mines such as underwater smart bombs.

NATO and other affiliate navies provided the minesweepers and mine hunters that formed the core of the coalition mine warfare force during and after Operation DESERT STORM, and to a lesser extent during Operation IRAQI FREEDOM. During DESERT STORM, active MCM operations in the conflict zone were carried out by units of the U.S. Navy and the Royal Navy; other coalition members joined in postwar mine clearance.

In August 1990, the U.S. Navy contracted with the Netherlands to transport four of its MCM vessels from Norfolk Naval Station to the Persian Gulf aboard the semisubmersible heavy-lift ship *Super Servant 3: Avenger* (MCM-1), the navy's newest MCM ship, and the veteran ocean minesweepers *Impervious* (MSO-449), *Leader* (MSO-490), and *Adroit* (MSO-509). With the amphibious assault ship *Tripoli* (LPH-10) in the role of MCM support ship and platform for six minesweeping MH-53E helicopters, the U.S. ships joined with the Royal Navy's mine hunters *Atherstone* (M-38), *Cattistock* (M-31), *Hurworth* (M-39) and support ship *Herald* (A-138) as Operation DESERT STORM commenced. During the war phase, the force was augmented by the British mine hunters *Ledbury* (M-30) and *Dulverton* (M-35). In the early postwar period, three more British mine hunters arrived in the Persian Gulf: the *Brecon* (M-29), *Brocklesby* (M-33), and *Bicester* (M-36), followed in May 1991 by the U.S. MCM ship *Guardian* (MCM-5), which made a solo Atlantic crossing to relieve the *Avenger*. The combined effort of Royal Navy and U.S. MCM operations yielded the location and destruction of 107 bottom mines and 231 moored mines.

During DESERT STORM, a small Belgian force operated in the Gulf of Oman: the Tripartite (a joint Belgian-Dutch-French MCM design) mine hunters *Dianthus* (M-918), *Iris* (M-920), and *Myosotis* (M-922), with the support ship *Zinnia* (A-961). Credited with finding 64 bottom mines and 211 moored mines, the Belgian group departed the theater in July 1991. France contributed the Tripartite mine hunters *Orion* (M-645) and *Sagittaire* (M-650), along with the support ship *Loire* (A-615), which cleared 68 bottom mines and 134 moored mines.

Germany operated the mine hunters *Göttingen* (M-1070), *Koblenz* (M-1071), *Schleswig* (M-1073), *Paderborn* (M-1076), and *Marburg* (M-1080), accompanied by the depot ship *Donau* (A-69)

The U.S. Navy ocean minesweeper *Impervious* is moved to the pier after being unloaded from the Dutch heavy lift ship *Super Servant 4*. (U.S. Department of Defense)

and support ship *Freiburg* (M-1413). They were credited with dispatching 28 bottom mines and 64 moored mines. The *Schleswig* and *Paderborn* employed the German-developed Troika remote sweep unit. Italy employed the Lerici class of mine hunters: *Lerici* (M-5550), *Sapri* (M-5551), *Milazzo* (M-5552), and *Vieste* (M-5553). They contributed to the postwar mine clearance of the northern Persian Gulf. Accompanied by the support ship *Tremiti* (A-5348), the Italian mine hunters, each equipped with variable depth sonar (VDS), three station-holding thrusters, and the wire-guided Pluto mine destruction system, collectively accounted for 11 bottom mines and 60 moored mines.

Following intensive legislative debate on the constitutionality of Japanese participation in clearing a (postconflict) war zone of mines, the Japanese Maritime Self-Defense Force (JMSDF) received approval to dispatch the mine hunters/minesweepers *Yurishima* (MSC-668), *Hikoshima* (MSC-669), *Awashima* (MSC-670), and *Sakushima* (MSC-671) to the Persian Gulf, accompanied by the support ship *Hayase* (MST-462) and replenishment oiler *Tokiwa* (AOE-423). The Japanese MCM force was responsible for finding and eliminating 21 bottom mines and 10 moored mines. The Netherlands deployed the Tripartite mine hunters *Haarlem* (M-853), *Haarlingen* (M-854), and *Zierikzee* (M-862), which cleared 3 bottom mines and 35 moored mines in minefields off the Kuwaiti coast. A Saudi Arabian MCM force in early February 1991

was directed to patrol the northern Saudi waters for mines. The U.S.-built coastal mine hunters/minesweepers *Addriyah* (MSC-412), *Al Quysumah* (MSC-414), *Al Wadeeah* (M-416), and *Safwa* (M-418), judged unsuited for open sea operations, were confined to coastal operations.

Under the weight of sanctions since the 1991 war, and stymied by U.S. naval units operating in the Persian Gulf on the eve of Operation IRAQI FREEDOM, Iraq was unable to carry out any large-scale minelaying by the time IRAQI FREEDOM was under way. Disapproval of the U.S.-led 2003 invasion of Iraq by many of its allies resulted in a situation in which a smaller coalition of the United States, the United Kingdom, and Australia carried out initial MCM operations in the Persian Gulf. NATO did agree to dispatch an MCM task group to assist the United States. NATO MCM ships did patrol the approaches to the Suez Canal and other vital regional transit points during the war, but with the understanding that this deployment was in support of the still-acceptable Operation ENDURING FREEDOM. In their combined operations as the Iraq War got under way, the U.S.-British-Australian MCM force found and dispatched more than 68 mines, and Australian warships captured an Iraqi minelaying vessel laden with a variety of contact and influence mines; other smaller minelayers were prevented from deploying their cargo.

A number of MCM systems developed since the 1991 Persian Gulf War were employed in the combat zone to good effect, including new unmanned underwater vehicles (UUV), autonomous underwater vehicles (AUV), and the expendable UUV Sea Fox system. In addition to the U.S. and British MCM ships, a team of Australian underwater warfare experts joined with U.S. Navy and Royal Navy EOD (explosive ordnance disposal) divers to clear the important harbor of Umm Qasr.

The U.S. MCM vessels active in the Persian Gulf at the outset of Operation IRAQI FREEDOM were the *Ardent* (MCM-12), *Dextrous* (MCM-13), *Cardinal* (MHC-60), and *Raven* (MHC-61), all based in Bahrain. The Royal Navy MCM group consisted of the *Ledbury* (M-30), *Brocklesby* (M-33), *Sandown* (M-101), *Grimsby* (M-108), *Bangor* (M-109), *Blyth* (M-111), and their support ship *Sir Bedivere* (L-3004).

In the years since the cessation of major military operations in the Iraq War, units of the U.S. Navy and Royal Navy MCM force in the region have been relieved on a regular basis by counterparts from both navies, while NATO minesweepers and mine hunters of the Mediterranean-based Mine Counter Measures Group 2 (SNMCMG2) have also operated in the Middle East theater. Since May 2008, MCM vessels of the Royal Navy have joined with the U.S. Navy in an effort to locate and eliminate all remaining mines and other unexploded ordnance from both the 1991 and 2003 wars in the shallower waters off the Iraqi and Kuwaiti coasts. Newly developed MCM systems now allow these further investigations, which have as their goal the eventual safe access for all shipping, large and small, to commercial ports in the northern Persian Gulf.

GORDON E. HOGG

**See also**

DESERT STORM, Operation, Coalition Naval Forces; IRAQI FREEDOM, Operation, Coalition Naval Forces; Mines, Sea, and Naval Mine Warfare, Persian Gulf and Iraq Wars; United Kingdom, Navy, Persian Gulf War; United States Navy, Iraq War; United States Navy, Persian Gulf War

**References**

Busquets, Camil. *Minehunters, Patrol Boats, and Logistics*. Barcelona: Lema, 1999.

Marolda, Edward, and Robert Schneller. *Shield and Sword: The United States Navy and the Persian Gulf War*. Annapolis, MD: U.S. Naval Institute Press, 2001.

Saunders, Stephen, ed. *Jane's Fighting Ships, 2008–2009*. Coulsdon, Surrey, UK, and Alexandria, VA: Jane's Information Group, 2008.

Sharpe, Richard, ed. *Jane's Fighting Ships: 1991–1992*. London: Jane's Information Group, 1991.

---

# Missiles, Air-to-Ground

Air-to-ground missiles (AGMs) have been employed more often and in greater numbers in the Middle East than in all the world's other post-1945 conflicts combined. AGMs trace their origins back to World War I, during which the British tested a simple wire-guided rocket near the end of the conflict, but World War II saw the first introduction of AGMs in combat. The Germans developed them to enable aircraft to attack ships without facing the increasingly deadly fire of radar-guided antiaircraft guns firing shells with proximity (radio-activated) fuses. Both the United States and the Soviet Union captured the technology involved, but the weapons' progress languished in the first postwar decade as all the major powers pursued supersonic aircraft. However, the Korean War (1950–1953) demonstrated the deadliness of radar-directed air defenses and the relative fragility of jet aircraft. That and the introduction of surface-to-air missiles (SAMs) drove the world's air forces to develop guided AGMs so that their pilots would not have to enter the SAMs' range to attack their targets.

The early systems were too large to be carried on the tactical fighter aircraft employed in the Middle East's first post–World War II wars, but the lessons learned from those conflicts led the major powers to seek ever-lighter AGMs. None were in service during the first three Arab-Israeli conflicts, but the French decision to stop supplying Israel with arms forced Israel to shift its arms purchasing to the United States. That transition began in 1968, enabling Israel to enter the 1973 Yom Kippur (Ramadan) War with a stable of U.S.-supplied AGM systems.

The United States developed the first tactical AGM in 1959. Known as the Bullpup, it was initially designated the ASM-N-7 by its sponsoring service, the U.S. Navy, and became the AGM-12 under U.S. secretary of defense Robert McNamara's joint weapons designation system in 1962. Weighing in at just under 1,000 pounds, the Bullpup could be carried by the A-4 Skyhawks and F-4 Phantoms that entered Israeli service in late 1969. Designed to enable the attacking aircraft to make a precision attack from outside antiaircraft artillery range, the early Bullpup had a 250-pound warhead and was powered by a small solid-fuel rocket engine. The A-4 pilot or the F-4 weapons operator visually guided the missile to the target via a joystick control, not unlike that used by the German Fritz X guided bomb of World War II. As with the German weapon, the Bullpup had a burning tracer in the tail fin that enabled the operator to track the missile as it flew to the target. The Bullpup also came in a larger version with a 1,000-pound warhead and a more powerful rocket engine to increase its range and speed. Nevertheless, it lacked the range to conduct a standoff attack from beyond the reach of the SA-2 and SA-6 SAM systems then used by Egyptian and Syrian forces.

To deal with the SA-2 threat, the United States developed the AGM-45 Shrike antiradiation missile. Essentially an AIM-7 Sparrow air-to-air missile with its seeker modified to home in on missile fire-control and acquisition radars, the Shrike weighed less than 200 pounds and was carried by A-4 and F-4 aircraft. Although its range of 10–12 nautical miles placed the launch aircraft within the SA-2's maximum range, the Shrike's 44-pound warhead shredded the SAM's fire-control radar. More importantly, it was easy to modify in response to newly emerging threats. For example, the United States developed and supplied an improved version capable of engaging the Soviet-supplied SA-6 within two weeks of the SAM's initial employment in the Yom Kippur (Ramadan) War. Arab radar operators often shut down their systems if they thought they were facing a Shrike attack, effectively ending the SAM threat to incoming Israeli aircraft without a missile being fired. Phased out in the early 1990s, the Shrike has been replaced by the Harpy Drone–based SAM suppression system.

Israel acquired the AGM-114 Hellfire missile from the United States in the early 1990s. Fired from the AH-64 Apache attack helicopter, the 100-pound missile has a maximum range of 5 miles and an 18-pound warhead. The Israelis have used the Hellfire primarily for precision strikes against Palestinian and Hezbollah leaders and strong points. Most often employed against Hamas and Islamic Jihad leaders in Gaza, the Hellfire also saw extensive employment during Israel's 2006 conflict with Hezbollah in southern Lebanon.

Israel has also developed AGMs of its own. The 3,000-pound Popeye I Have Nap missile first entered service in 1985. Propelled by a solid-fuel rocket engine, it has a range of more than 45 nautical miles. Early Popeye I missiles used inertial guidance, but later variants employ either a new closed-loop imaging infrared and television guidance for the weapons officer to guide it into the target or other form of terminal or precision guidance. The later and lighter Popeye II Have Lite missile incorporates those improvements and has a greater range of 90 nautical miles. Both variants are carried by Israel's F-4 Phantom and F-15E Strike Fighter aircraft and were used against Hezbollah targets in Lebanon during the July–August 2006 Lebanon invasion.

The Soviet Union, the only major arms supplier to provide AGMs to the Arab countries, was slower than the United States in developing them. Instead, the Soviets had focused on developing heavy long-range strategic air-to-surface missiles (ASMs). These are basically aircraft-launched ICBMs, and because of the relatively small area of the Middle East they are largely unnecessary for regional conflicts.

The Soviet Union did not introduce its first tactical ASM, the AS-7 Kerry (NATO designation), until 1968 and did not supply them to its Arab clients—Egypt, Libya, Iraq, and Syria— until the mid-1980s. Carried on the MiG-23 and Su-24 aircraft, the AS-7 was a beam-riding missile. That is, the missile's guidance system was designed to keep the missile within the guidance beam, which the pilot or weapons operator kept centered on the target via a visual sighting system in the cockpit. The AS-7 had a range of 6.5 nautical miles and a 222-pound warhead. Iraq employed the AS-7 against Iranian targets during the 1980–1988 Iran-Iraq War.

Although Israel has the longest history of using AGMs in the region's conflicts, the United States holds the record for employing the largest variety and number of AGMs there. The first U.S. use of AGMs in the Middle East came in 1986, when U.S. forces conducted Operation EL DORADO CANYON, during which U.S. Navy and U.S. Air Force aircraft conducted retaliatory strikes against Libya for its support of terrorism. AGMs have figured prominently in all U.S. air strikes and campaigns conducted ever since. They not only ensured a high success rate, but their accuracy and reliability

ensured that American and later allied aircraft losses were the lowest of any major conflict of the last 60 years.

Operation EL DORADO CANYON saw the first employment of the AGM-88 high-speed antiradiation missile (HARM). Fully replacing the Shrike by 1988, the supersonic HARM has more than four times the range (57 nautical miles) and double the warhead of the Shrike (68 pounds versus only 28). Carried by both U.S. Navy (A-6, A-7, EA-6B, and F/A-18) and U.S. Air Force (F-4G and EF-111) aircraft, the HARM saw extensive use in the 1991 Persian Gulf War, the Iraq War, and in several retaliatory strikes conducted between those conflicts. The most commonly used American AGM in the wars with Iraq was the AGM-65 Maverick missile, a short-range (15 nautical miles) infrared electro-optical or laser-guided antitank/antivehicle/antibunker missile carried by both helicopters (AH-1 Cobra and AH-64 Apache) and fixed-wing aircraft (A-6, A-7, AV-8, A-10, F-4, F-15E, F-16, and F/A-18). American forces employed hundreds of AGM-65 Maverick missiles against Iraqi tanks in each of the conflicts with Iraq. The newer AGM-114 Hellfire was also employed in large numbers in those wars. Carried by AH-64 helicopters in both the Persian Gulf War and the Iraq War, by 2002 it was also fired from Predator unmanned aerial vehicles (UAVs) against terrorist targets in Yemen and Iraq. The Hellfire has a 5-mile range and an 18-pound warhead.

The oldest AGM used in the Persian Gulf wars was the AGM-62 Walleye. A 2,000-pound TV-guided glide bomb directed against hardened targets such as bunkers and heavy bridges, it was carried by U.S. Navy A-6, A-7, and F/A-18 aircraft. The U.S. Air Force's AGM-86C was the longest-range weapon of the Persian Gulf wars. A cruise missile launched from B-52Gs, the turbojet-powered air-launched cruise missile (ALCM) carried a 2,000-pound conventional warhead 640 nautical miles at low altitude to within one-tenth of a mile of the aim point. It incorporates a Global Positioning System (GPS) capability into its navigation system that makes it one of the most accurate missiles in the world. A deep-penetrating variant with a 3,000-pound warhead was introduced in 1998. In addition to their use in Operation DESERT STORM in 1991, the AGM-86C saw service in the 1996 and 1998 coalition strikes against Iraq for attacking the Kurds in northern Iraq and in Operation IRAQI FREEDOM in 2003.

Both the U.S. Navy and the U.S. Air Force employed kits that converted unguided bombs into rocket-propelled guided missiles. The navy was the first to develop such systems when it introduced the AGM-123 Skipper into service in 1982. Essentially a Mark 83 1,000-pound bomb with a rocket engine and laser-guidance system mounted on it, the AGM-123 has a range of about 15.5 nautical miles. First employed against Libya in 1986, it also saw extensive service against Iraq. It is carried by A-7E, A-6E, AV-8, and F/A-18 aircraft. The air force's AGM-130 is based on the same principle. Essentially a rocket-powered GBU-15 guided bomb, it uses a GPS-assisted inertial navigation system to deliver a 1,000-pound Mark 84 or 500-pound BLU-109 warhead within 5.5 yards of the aim point from a maximum range of 40 nautical miles. First deployed with the F-111 in 1994, today it is carried on the F-15E Strike Eagle aircraft.

The 1990s saw the United States aggressively pursuing newer and more flexible and accurate weapons based on the lessons learned from DESERT STORM. The only AGM to arise successfully from that effort so far was the AGM-154, a joint U.S. Navy–U.S. Air Force project. Entering production in 1999, it uses a GPS-assisted inertial guidance system with an infrared terminal seeker to provide a maximum miss distance of 1 yard from a range of up to 200 nautical miles. The first variant was intended as a combined effects weapon, delivering 100 guided bomblets into the target area, each equipped with a shaped charge to penetrate armor and utilizing zirconium ringlets for incendiary effect and a fragmentation casing for antipersonnel effect. The B-variant carried 6 BLU-108 infrared-guided antitank systems with four submunitions each, while the C-variant employs a 1,000-pound unitary warhead intended for taking out point targets. First employed against Yugoslavia in 1999, the AGM-154 was carried by the A-6E, F/A-18, F/A-14C, F-16, and F-15 aircraft and has been used in every bombing campaign conducted since.

Once considered too heavy for tactical aircraft, AGMs are now considered essential to any successful aerial campaign. Their precision has ensured the success of the aerial campaigns of the United States and its allies over the last decade, all but guaranteeing the destruction of military targets while minimizing—but not eliminating—loss of innocent lives. Equally important, by enabling pilots to conduct their attacks from outside the range of enemy air defenses, AGMs are responsible for the United States and its coalition partners enjoying the lowest aircraft loss rate of any sustained aerial bombing campaign since airpower was born.

CARL OTIS SCHUSTER

**See also**

DESERT STORM, Operation; ENDURING FREEDOM, Operation; Hamas; Hezbollah; Iran-Iraq War; IRAQI FREEDOM, Operation; Lebanon; Libya; Missiles, Cruise; Missiles, Surface-to-Air

**References**

Aloni, Shlomo. *Arab-Israeli Air Wars, 1947–1982.* London: Osprey Books, 2001.

Cohen, Eliezer. *Israel's Best Defense.* New York: Crown, 1993.

Cooper, Toni, and Farzad Bishop. *Iran-Iraq War in the Air: 1980–1988.* Atglen, PA: Schiffer Military History, 2000.

Cordesman, Anthony. *Iran's Military Forces in Transition: Conventional Threats and Weapons of Mass Destruction.* Westpoint, CT: Praeger, 1999.

Frieden, David R. *Principles of Naval Weapons Systems.* Annapolis, MD: Naval Institute Press, 1985.

Katz, Samuel. *The Shield of David: The Israeli Air Force into the 1990s.* Cape Girardeau, MO: Concord, 2003.

Lambeth, Benjamin. *Moscow's Lessons from the 1982 Lebanon Air War.* Washington, DC: RAND Corporation, 1985.

Nicolle, David, and Mark Styling. *Arab MiG-19 & MiG-21 Units in Combat.* Oxford, UK: Osprey, 2004.

Nordeen, Lon, and David Nicolle. *Phoenix over the Nile: A History of Egyptian Air Power, 1932–1994.* Washington, DC: Smithsonian Books, 1996.

# Missiles, Cruise

One of the most effective long-range weapons of modern warfare, cruise missiles essentially are unmanned aircraft that cruise at various altitudes until they dive or crash into their targets. Cruise missiles have also figured prominently in warfare in the Middle East wars. Conceptually, all cruise missiles trace their roots to the German World War II V-1 buzz bomb. The only real differences between today's cruise missiles and the V-1 are the improved propulsion and guidance systems, increased range, far better accuracy, and a much more powerful warhead. The V-1's pulse jet engine and simple gyro-timing guidance system have given way to highly efficient turbofans and a variety of guidance systems tailored to the missile's specific mission or target. With those improvements has come a significant increase in price ($5,000 for a V-1 and $500,000 for a modern U.S. Tomahawk) as well as in capabilities. Today's cruise missiles can fly a terrain-hugging deceptive flight route to a target 1,000 miles distant and have a 70 percent probability of a direct hit (99 percent chance of hitting within 30 feet).

The United States and the Soviet Union both exploited the German V-1 in trying to develop their own cruise missiles after World War II. By 1950, both countries had working prototypes of turbo-jet-powered flying bombs under development. The best known of the American cruise missile models were the U.S. Navy's Regulus and the U.S. Air Force's Hound Dog. Like the V-1, these missiles were seen as area attack weapons, but the American missiles carried nuclear instead of conventional warheads. The Regulus had a range of 600 miles and was designed to be launched from submarines, while the similarly ranged Hound Dog was air-launched from Boeing B-47 Stratojet and Boeing B-52 Stratofortress bombers. Neither American missile was particularly accurate, and both left service by the mid-1960s.

With more accurate and more powerful submarine-launched ballistic missiles entering service, the major Western naval powers dropped their cruise missile programs. Moreover, their possession of aircraft carriers obviated the need for their surface ships to have a long-range strike capability. However, the carrier-shy Soviet Union lacked the resources and experience to build aircraft carriers and therefore pursued a different path, developing in 1958 the SS-N-1, a cruise missile intended to attack ships. It was followed two years later by the SS-N-2. These missiles differed from their American counterparts primarily in having a radar-based terminal guidance system that took them into the targeted ship. France was the only country to see any value in developing its own antiship missiles, but the program enjoyed only a low priority.

All this changed with Egypt's sinking of the Israeli destroyer *Eilat* in 1967 with an SS-N-2 Styx ship-to-ship missile. Suddenly, all navies saw antiship cruise missiles (ASCMs) as the poor man's naval strike weapon. They also recognized the value of such weapons in situations where increasingly expensive aircraft carriers were not available. That led the United States and other powers to initiate accelerated cruise missile programs. ASCMs, such as the French Exocet and the American Harpoon and Tomahawk, were the first to enter service, but their relative light weight and expense, compared to that of an aircraft carrier and its air wing, led some to examine their use in the land-attack role. Meanwhile, the Soviets developed their own family of long-range ASCMs: the SS-N-3, SS-N-12, SS-N-19 and SS-N-22.

The Yom Kippur (Ramadan) War in October 1973 saw the first naval engagements fought entirely between ASCM-equipped patrol boats. Having been stung by these weapons in the 1967 Six-Day War, Israel had developed its own ASCM, the Gabriel missile, and installed it on a new class of small patrol boats and corvettes. More importantly, Israel had developed tactics and electronic countermeasures to defeat the Soviet-built ASCMs supplied to Egypt and Syria. The October 7, 1973, Battle of Latakia saw six Israeli patrol boats sink five Syrian naval units. During October 12–13, the Israelis sank three more Egyptian missile patrol boats in the Battle of Baltim. Superior electronic countermeasures and tactics enabled the Israelis to win those battles without suffering any losses or damage. The Syrian fleet and Egypt's Mediterranean-based fleets remained in port for the rest of the war. Unfortunately for Israel, it had not deployed missile patrol boats to its Red Sea port, Eilat, and Egypt's Red Sea blockade remained unbroken.

By the early 1980s, advances in microminiaturization, avionics, and navigation systems brought land-attack cruises back into vogue for both conventional and nuclear missions. The U.S. Land-Attack Tomahawk cruise missile initially was equipped with a Terrain Contour Matching guidance system, which enabled it to navigate over land by matching its onboard radar's picture of the terrain below against a computer-developed map of its flight route to the target. By the late 1990s, this system was replaced by a module that guided the missile by using the Global Positioning System (GPS), making the missile accurate to within three to six feet. Finally, a Digital Scene Matching Area (DSMA) correlation feature was added to ensure that the missile would select the right target as it entered the target area by matching a digital image of the target scene (radar, optical, or infrared, or a combination of them) against an onboard image database. DSMA is particularly useful against mobile targets.

By the end of the Cold War, treaties and other considerations had driven all of the nuclear cruise missiles out of service. Conventional cruise missiles were now so accurate that Western political and military leaders had come to see them as politically safe precision weapons that could be employed in an infinite variety of situations.

ASCMs figured prominently in the 1982 Falklands War, with Argentine naval air force units sinking two British warships and damaging four others with their French-supplied AM-39 Exocet missiles. Iraq employed the same weapon in larger numbers against Iranian shipping during the 1980–1988 Iran-Iraq War. Although the missiles failed to sink any tankers or merchant ships, they damaged more than 200, driving up insurance rates and forcing the United States to escort tankers through the Persian Gulf during the war's final year. More ominously, on March 17, 1987, the Iraqis hit the U.S. Navy frigate *Stark* (FFG-31) with two Exocets, killing 37 crew members and injuring 21 (the total casualties representing more than a third of the crew). The crew saved the ship, but it took more than 18 months to repair the damage and return it to service.

The 1991 Persian Gulf War saw the first major employment of land-attack cruise missiles. The anti-Iraq coalition opened Operation DESERT STORM by launching 122 of the U.S. Navy's Tomahawk land-attack missiles (TLAMs) against key Iraqi air defense posts, radar systems, and communications facilities. The TLAMs were employed almost entirely against targets considered too dangerous or risky for attack by aircraft. Typically, they preceded an air strike, taking out a key facility that was critical to the Iraqis' local or area air defense. The United States fired nearly 300 TLAMs during the war at a total cost of approximately $360 million.

The TLAMs then became the weapon of choice for U.S. retaliation against terrorist attacks, used to strike Al Qaeda and related camps in Afghanistan and the Sudan in the late 1990s. More than 250 were fired during Operation IRAQI FREEDOM in 2003, and America's 2001 invasion of Afghanistan was also preceded by a series of TLAM strikes against Taliban-related targets.

Cruise missiles are a relatively inexpensive, expendable alternative to expensive aircraft and ballistic missiles. Unlike bomber

The USS *Bunker Hill* fires the first Tomahawk missile to be launched at an Iraqi target, 5:25 a.m. on March 20, 2003, at the beginning of the Iraq War. (U.S. Department of Defense)

aircraft, they do not put crew members in harm's way. For nations not concerned with accuracy, cruise missiles remain a cheap solution to their long-range strike problem. However, for militaries seeking precision, for both antiship and land-attack missions, cruise missiles have become the complex weapons of choice for retaliatory strikes and the initial military operations conducted during a war. The newest have incorporated stealth technologies to make them more difficult to detect and engage. Others rely on supersonic dash speeds to defeat air defenses. In any case, cruise missiles are used to take out key enemy command centers, air defense sites, and airfields before manned aircraft are committed to the fight. In peacetime, cruise missiles are used for situations where a rapid and precise attack is required and the political-military leadership doesn't want to risk pilot losses.

China, France, India, Israel, Russia, Taiwan, and the United States produce ASCMs, but only two countries—the United States and Russia—manufacture land-attack cruise missiles. China, India, and Pakistan are developing indigenous cruise missiles that are expected to enter operational service. Undoubtedly, the 21st century will see a proliferation of cruise missiles. In combination with unmanned aerial vehicles, they will become an increasingly prominent element of modern warfare.

CARL OTIS SCHUSTER

**See also**

Al Qaeda; DESERT STORM, Operation, Coalition Air Campaign; ENDURING FREEDOM, Operation, U.S. Air Campaign; IRAQI FREEDOM, Operation, Air Campaign; Taliban

**References**

Finlan, Alastair. *The Gulf War, 1991*. Oxford, UK: Osprey, 2004.
Frieden, David R. *Principles of Naval Weapons Systems*. Annapolis, MD: Naval Institute Press, 1985.
Herzog, Chaim. *The Arab-Israeli Wars: War and Peace in the Middle East from the War of Independence to Lebanon*. Westminster, MD: Random House, 1984.
Hewson, Robert. *Jane's Air-Launched Weapons, 2001*. London: Jane's, 2002.
Hooten, Ted. Jane's Naval Weapons Systems, 2001–2002. London: Jane's, 2002.
Knight, Michael, ed. *Operation Iraqi Freedom and the New Iraq*. Washington, DC: Washington Institute for Near East Policy, 2004.
Tripp, Robert. *Lessons Learned from Operation Enduring Freedom*. Santa Monica, CA: RAND Corporation, 2004.

# Missiles, Intermediate-Range Ballistic

Ballistic missiles with a range of approximately 1,500–4,000 statute miles and capable of delivering conventional, biological, chemical, or nuclear payloads. The development of intermediate-range ballistic missiles (IRBMs) began in the early 1950s. They were derived from the successful German V-2 rockets of World War II. Both Cold War superpowers, the United States and the Soviet Union, initiated development of such missile systems in an effort to gain strategic advantage. For the Soviet Union, IRBMs offered a cheaper alternative to long-range bombers in order to attack America's forward-based strategic airpower. For the United States, IRBMs offered the ability to respond quickly to a Soviet attack. Moreover, IRBMs were simpler and easier to develop than longer-ranged intercontinental ballistic missiles (ICBMs).

By 1956, both the United States and the Soviet Union had significant IRBM programs under way. The resulting missiles figured prominently in the Cuban Missile Crisis of 1962 and the nuclear disarmament talks of the late 1980s. More recently, IRBMs have figured prominently in Asia and the Middle East, where several countries have developed or are developing nuclear-capable types. These nations include the Democratic People's Republic of Korea (DPRK, North Korea), India, Pakistan, Israel, and Iran.

In the United States, the U.S. Air Force had responsibility for the country's land-based IRBMs, while the U.S. Navy acquired control over sea-based missiles. The air force focused on liquid-fueled rockets because of the greater power they provided. The navy pursued such solid-fueled missiles as the Polaris and the Poseidon, which could be stored safely on submarines. The air force IRBM programs, which were conducted in collaboration with Britain's Royal Air Force, were designated Jupiter and Thor. President Dwight D. Eisenhower accorded the program the same high priority as the Atlas and Titan ICBM programs. The first four U.S. Thor IRBM squadrons deployed to England in late 1957, followed by two more to Italy the next year. They were operational two years after deployment. By 1959, however, the Atlas ICBM program's steady progress made many question the value of the IRBM and call for their decommissioning as the Atlas squadrons came on line. Nevertheless, by 1960 Jupiter squadrons were being deployed to Turkey, and the U.S. Air Force retained its IRBMs in service despite President John F. Kennedy's order to remove them shortly after he took office in January 1961.

In the Soviet Union, the Ministry of Armaments directed all strategic rocket research. As a result, all Soviet sea-based missiles were derived from land-based variants and were therefore liquid-fueled. As with their American counterparts, all Soviet ballistic missiles were derived from the initial work done by sequestered German engineers. The first Soviet IRBM to enter service, the R-12 (NATO designation SS-4) was based on the initial designs provided by the German engineers held on Gorodomlya Island during 1946–1950. Under development since 1953, the R-12 first entered testing in 1957. Unlike the American IRBMs, the R-12 and all later Soviet IRBMs were designed to be fired from mobile truck-drawn launchers. However, the R-12 was later modified for silo-based firing. The early model R-12s had a range of only 1,200 miles, and the first operational systems were deployed in late 1960. However, the R-12 is most famous for its September 1962 deployment in Cuba, which triggered the Cuban Missile Crisis. The withdrawal of the R-12s from Cuba, and the American agreement to pull its IRBMs from Turkey, effectively ended the crisis.

France was the only other country to build IRBMs during the Cold War. Its program began in the late 1960s as the third leg of France's nuclear deterrent force, which President Charles de Gaulle had decided to develop in 1958, separately from the United States. The S-2 IRBM was first test-fired in 1968 and entered service in 1971. France built a longer-ranged S-3D that entered service in 1980. Both were silo-based missiles that carried a single 120-kiloton nuclear warhead, but the S-3D had a range of 1,800 miles versus only 1,200 for the S-2. France maintained a force of 18 silo-based IRBMs as the missile element of its nuclear deterrent force until 1996.

The escalating presence of IRBMs in Europe during the early 1980s led to the first international agreement that eliminated a nuclear weapons system, the Intermediate Nuclear Force (INF) Treaty of 1989. That treaty called for the destruction of all U.S. and Soviet IRBMs. Missiles covered by the agreement included the Soviet SS-4 and SS-20 and the U.S. Pershing IIa and ground-launched cruise missile (GLCM) systems. France subsequently decommissioned and destroyed its IRBM force in 1996.

Since that time, however, several nations have initiated IRBM programs, including the People's Republic of China (PRC), India, Iran, Israel, North Korea, and Pakistan. Israel's nuclear-capable IRBM Jericho II was the first to enter service in 1984. Iraq pursued IRBM development, but its defeat in the Persian Gulf War of 1991 prevented the program from reaching fruition. However, Iraq's successful use of modified Scud missiles as medium-range ballistic missiles led Iran to develop its own IRBMs. Nearby Pakistan and India had nuclear-capable IRBMs programs well under way at the beginning of the 21st century. Iran's Shahab 3 and Pakistan's Gauri IRBMs are based on North Korea's No Dong missile, while India's Agni-III is a totally indigenous missile design that traces its initial development back to 1979. These nuclear-capable systems are the easiest and cheapest long-range missiles to build and, when equipped with a nuclear, biological, or chemical warhead, enable a country to threaten any potential opponent within a range of 2,000 to 3,000 nautical miles. As such, these weapons are considered to be the most threatening weapons in existence today. Except for Iraq's limited employment of Scud missiles during the 1991 Persian Gulf War, no IRBMs have been employed in the Middle East wars.

CARL OTIS SCHUSTER

**See also**

Biological Weapons and Warfare; Chemical Weapons and Warfare

**References**

Davis, Jacquelyn, Charles M. Perry, and Jamal S. Al-Suwaidi, eds. *Air/Missile Defense Counter-Proliferation.* London: British Academic Press, 1999.
Owen, Wyn Q. *The Politics of Ballistic Missile Non-Proliferation.* Hampshire, UK: Palgrave, 2000.
Sioris, George M. *Missile Guidance and Control Systems.* New York: Springer Verlag, 2004.
Spencer, Jack. *Ballistic Missile Threat Handbook.* Washington, DC: Heritage Foundation, 2002.

# Missiles, Surface-to-Air

Although ballistic-missile defense was the only significant role played by coalition air defense missiles, Iraq's surface-to-air missile (SAM) systems constituted the most significant component of that country's integrated air defense system during and after Operation DESERT STORM. Iraq used radar-guided SAMs for medium-to-high altitudes and area air defense, and man-portable infrared-guided SAMs for tactical air defense and to complement its antiaircraft artillery systems. Because the most common tactic to evade radar-guided SAMs involved a high-speed roll and dive to lower altitudes, the integration of guns, missiles, and fighter aircraft into a layered defense in depth theoretically provided an almost impenetrable barrier to air attack. Aircraft that successfully avoided radar-guided SAMs found themselves flying through a gauntlet of intense antiaircraft fire supplemented by infrared-guided SAMs, the intensity of which increased as the plane approached its target. Those that made it past the target pulled up into the sights of waiting fighter aircraft.

Fighters escorting the attack aircraft had to penetrate the same gauntlet to engage enemy interceptors. Although it did not lead to high scores among the defending pilots, it was a system that had inflicted heavy losses on American aircraft during the Vietnam War. Unfortunately for Iraq, the United States and its allies had learned from that conflict and had the electronic warfare equipment and weapons to defeat the Iraqi air defense system. The coalition's air defense problem was much simpler. Iraq neither challenged allied air supremacy nor conducted offensive air operations, which limited its aerial bombardment during Operation DESERT STORM to sporadic short-range ballistic missile strikes. Thus, most coalition air defense systems saw little action in that conflict or in the later Operation IRAQI FREEDOM.

As a result, the American-built Raytheon MIM-104 Patriot missile was the only coalition air defense missile system that saw combat. Iraq's ballistic missile force and air force were all but destroyed in Operation DESERT STORM and were therefore nearly nonexistent by Operation IRAQI FREEDOM's launch. Development of the Patriot began in 1961, when the U.S. Army initiated a program to replace the MIM-23 Hawk SAM. The Hawk was an outstanding mobile tactical SAM, but army planners believed it would be obsolete against the Soviet fighters expected to enter service after 1970. Electronic-warfare vulnerability and counter-countermeasures figured prominently in the new design. The resulting Patriot missile entered service in 1984. Its 90–nautical mile range and 79,000-foot engagement ceiling marked a major improvement over the earlier Hawk. Using the AN/MPQ-53 phased array radar for tracking and guidance, the Patriot has a track-via-missile system to reduce vulnerability to jamming and chaff, but more importantly its fire-control system includes features that give the Patriot an antiballistic missile capability. Like its predecessor, the Patriot is propelled by a single-stage, solid-fuel rocket engine, but it is launched from canisters instead of being loaded directly onto a launcher. Canisters can be loaded more quickly and protect the

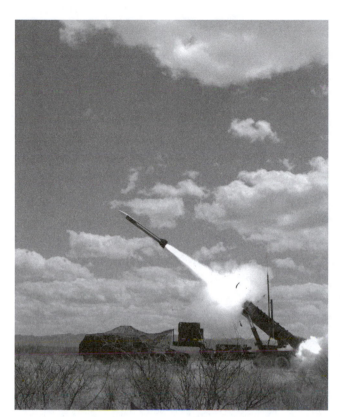

A MIM-104 Patriot antiaircraft missile is fired during a training exercise in 1990. (U.S. Department of Defense)

missiles from environmental and handling damage. The result is a more robust system with a faster firing and reload rate.

The U.S. Army deployed Patriot battalions to Saudi Arabia and Israel during Operation DESERT STORM, and they engaged 40 Iraqi-launched "Al Hussein" Scud SRBMs (short-range ballistic missiles), usually firing 2–3 Patriots at each SRBM. However, the actual success-downing rate remains controversial, with some evidence indicating that few or no SRBMs were actually hit. Although it is clear that the majority of the SRBMs were destroyed en route to their targets, there is as much evidence to suggest that missile design failures were involved as much as Patriot-inflicted damage. Based on lessons learned from DESERT STORM, the Patriot underwent extensive improvements in the 1990s and reportedly destroyed eight Iraqi SRBMs during Operation IRAQI FREEDOM in March 2003.

Other allied air defense missile systems included the British Rapier, French Crotale and Roland, and man-portable air defense (MANPAD) systems (e.g., RBS-70 and Stinger). Rapier and Roland were deployed for airfield defense in Saudi Arabia during DESERT STORM, while Saudi army forces used vehicle-mounted Crotale for tactical air defense. Of these, the British Aircraft Company–built Rapier was the oldest, having entered service in 1971.

Originally introduced with an optical-guidance system in which the gunner controlled the missile with a joystick, the Rapier (range of 4.1 nautical miles) also used a "Blindfire" tracking radar for all-weather guidance and infrared terminal guidance to increase effectiveness by 1991. The Euromissile-produced Roland (range of 3 nautical miles) entered service in 1977 and served both French and Iraqi forces during DESERT STORM. Like the Rapier, it used optical guidance. Saudi Arabia acquired its vehicle-mounted Crotale system in 1980. A radar-commanded guided missile with a maximum range of 3 nautical miles, Saudi Crotale units never engaged Iraqi aircraft, but they did accompany Saudi armored units into Kuwait, becoming some of the first units to enter that nation's capital in February 1991. The United Arab Emirates (UAE) used the laser-guided Bofors RBS-70 MANPAD for airfield defense. The tripod-mounted RBS-70 had a maximum range of 5.5 nautical miles. The Raytheon FIM-92 Stinger is a handheld infrared-guided MANPAD that entered service in 1984. It can intercept both incoming and outgoing targets. It has a maximum range of 3 nautical miles. As with most other coalition SAM systems, Stingers never had the opportunity to engage Iraqi aircraft.

On the other hand, Iraqi SAM systems saw extensive action and suffered accordingly. Most Iraqi air defense missiles were Soviet-built, with the venerable SA-2 Guideline and its supporting Fan Song radar being the oldest and longest-ranged weapon in service. Developed in the 1950s, the SA-2 (range of 27 nautical miles) had enjoyed great success during the Vietnam War but was at best obsolete by 1990. It could engage aircraft operating at altitudes of up to 89,000 feet, but its radar was easily defeated and only a highly trained crew could employ its electro-optical guidance and electronic counter-countermeasures features effectively. Also, its minimum range of 4–5 nautical miles and minimum 3,280-foot altitude made it all but useless against low-flying targets. The SA-3 Goa was newer and longer ranged. Brought into Soviet service in 1963, Goa (range of 22 nautical miles) used the Flat Face radar for guidance. It had an operational engagement ceiling of 59,000 feet and enjoyed better tactical mobility than the SA-2. The SA-2 and SA-3 were deployed around major cities.

Iraq also deployed a wide range of Soviet mobile SAM systems, including the SA-6 Gainful, SA-9 Gaskin, and SA-12. Of these, the Gainful was the best known, having inflicted heavy losses on the Israeli Air Force when first employed during the 1973 Yom Kippur (Ramadan) War. Mounted on a tracked chassis, the Gainful was a medium-ranged SAM supported by a robust Straight Flush fire-control radar that was difficult but not impossible to deceive. Introduced into Soviet service in 1970, the SA-6 deployed in four transporter-erector-launcher (TEL) batteries supported by a single fire-control radar. The missile has a maximum range of 13.2 nautical miles and operational engagement ceiling of 39,000 feet.

The SA-9 Gaskin was a much shorter-ranged SAM mounted on a wheeled vehicle that carried two pairs of ready-to-fire missiles. The Gaskin was infrared guided, but unlike most infrared-guided missiles, it could engage an incoming target, provided that the aircraft was not obscured by the sun. Normally deployed in proximity to the ZSU-23/4 mobile antiaircraft gun, the SA-9 dated from 1966 and had a maximum range of 4.4 nautical miles and ceiling of 20,000 ft. The SA-9 did not have a significant impact on allied air operations in either of the Persian Gulf conflicts.

Destroyed Iraqi SA-6 surface-to-air missiles (SAMs) atop a Soviet ZIL-131 6 × 6 truck after coalition forces had attacked the area during Operation DESERT STORM, 1991. (U.S. Department of Defense)

The newest mobile SAM in the Iraqi inventory was the short-ranged radar-guided SA-8 Gecko. Carried in six-missile canisters mounted atop a wheeled Transporter-Erector-Launcher-and-Radar (TELAR), the SA-8 was employed with Iraqi Army units in the field. Its six-wheeled TELAR was amphibious and equipped with a frequency agile fire-control radar and alternate electro-optical guidance that made it particularly difficult to defeat electronically. Its normal engagement range was 1.1 to 5 nautical miles against targets flying between 80 and 1,650 feet. The most common tactics employed against the SA-8 were to use antiradiation missiles against its radar or fly above its engagement envelope.

The remaining SAMs in Iraqi service were man-portable. Of these, the Soviet-built infrared-guided SA-7 Grail, SA-14 Gremlin, SA-16 Gimlet, and SA-18 Grouse were the most numerous. The SA-7 was the shortest ranged, reaching out only about 9,800 feet, and only effective against slow-moving targets flying away at altitudes below 4,000 feet. The SA-14 was an improvement on the SA-7, providing greater range (6 kilometers) and a limited capability for head-on engagements. The SA-16 incorporated an identification-friend-or-foe feature and more effective infrared-guided counter-countermeasures capability. The SA-18 was a simplified and more reliable improvement of the SA-16. The Gimlet and Grouse can engage a target from any aspect, and have a maximum

range of 3.1 miles and a ceiling of 15,700 feet. Their performance is comparable to the U.S. FIM-92A Stinger.

The last SAM in Iraqi service was the French-built Roland. The Iraqis used the Roland for airfield defense. The radar-guided Roland had a maximum operational range of 5 miles and an engagement ceiling of 17,100 feet. Its rapid acceleration and high speed make it an ideal air defense weapon. However, in the hands of inexperienced or poorly trained operators, it proved vulnerable to jamming and other electronic countermeasures. Also, the missile crews had to operate the system from exposed positions, making them vulnerable to bomb fragmentation and direct enemy attack, a factor that inhibited the weapon's employment and effectiveness.

Coalition numerical and electronic superiority and superior tactics all but negated Iraq's integrated air defense system. Its SAMs achieved only limited success in the few opportunities the air campaign presented to them. Allied air defense suppression systems, antiradiation missiles, and well-orchestrated electronic countermeasure operations blinded Iraqi radars, destroyed their command and control systems and communications networks, and inflicted heavy losses on any SAM battery that remained active long enough to attempt an engagement. Although Iraq nominally possessed a modern, integrated air defense system, its weapons, sensors, and communications networks were outdated and its operators poorly trained and ill prepared for war against a well-trained opponent equipped with third- and fourth-generation aircraft and precision-guided weapons.

CARL OTIS SCHUSTER

**See also**

Air Defenses in Iraq, Iraq War; Air Defenses in Iraq, Persian Gulf War; Aircraft, Attack; Aircraft, Electronic Warfare; Aircraft, Suppression of Enemy Air Defense; Antiaircraft Guns; Antiradiation Missiles, Coalition; Bombs, Precision-Guided

**References**

Blake, Bernard, ed. *Jane's Weapons Systems, 1988–89 (Jane's Land-Based Air Defence)*. London: Jane's, 1988.

Cooper, Toni, and Farzad Bishop. *Iran-Iraq War in the Air: 1980–1988*. Atglen, PA: Schiffer Military History, 2000.

General Accounting Office, U.S. *Operation Desert Storm Evaluation of the Air War: Report to Congress*. Washington, DC: U.S. Government Printing Office, 1996.

Hallion, Richard P. *Storm over Iraq: Air Power and the Gulf War*. Washington, DC: Smithsonian Institution Press, 1997.

Isby, David. *Weapons and Tactics of the Soviet Army*. London: Arms and Armour Books, 1984.

Lynch, Kristin. *Supporting Air and Space Expeditionary Forces: Lessons from Operation Iraqi Freedom*. Washington, DC: RAND Corporation, 2004.

# Missile Systems, Iraqi

Among weapons in the Iraqi missile arsenal, one system stood out: the Soviet-designed Scud B missile and its variants. Scud missiles were very much in the news during the 1991 Persian Gulf War. The Scud B carries a 1,000-pound warhead and has a range of 175 miles. Modified Iraqi models developed during the war against Iran (1980–1988), like the al-Hussein and al-Abbas missile, could strike up to 375 and 575 miles, respectively. The most modern of the Scud variants was the al-Hijarah, with a range of 466 miles. To obtain this longer range, Iraqi scientists had to reduce the missile's payload. The modified Scuds lacked a sophisticated guidance system, and an al-Abbas missile fired to maximum range could hit anywhere within about a 3-mile radius. The Iraqi leadership apparently chose not to use the al-Hussein and al-Abbas missiles during Operation DESERT STORM.

Before DESERT STORM began, U.S. intelligence had identified 64 fixed Scud missile sites in western Iraq, all aimed at Israel. Twenty-eight of those sites were complete, with the balance nearing completion. The fixed sites were easy targets to attack with the precision weapons systems available to the U.S. military at the time. Iraq also had an unknown number of mobile Scud launchers placed on Soviet-made tractors or locally manufactured tractors and trailers. Intelligence estimates held that Iraq possessed 48 such mobile launchers, but this was not certain.

Because of their potential to deliver chemical weapons and indiscriminately strike both civilian and military targets, the Scuds received the most attention of any Iraqi weapons during the Persian Gulf War. The threat posed by Iraq's surface-to-surface ballistic missiles greatly worried coalition military and political leaders. If Iraqi missiles were used to attack Israel, it seemed likely that Israel would retaliate and that this would cause the allied coalition, which included a number of Arab nations, to break apart.

During the Persian Gulf War, Iraq fired 91 Scuds. About half of them were directed at Saudi Arabia and 3 at Bahrain; the balance struck Israel. Although the missile strikes against Israel caused some public panic and caused 4 people to die from heart attacks, the missiles directly killed only 2 people while wounding another 200 Israelis.

The political impact of the missile attacks against Israel was nonetheless considerable. As expected, the Israeli public and some political leaders demanded retaliation. In response, the George H. W. Bush administration rushed Patriot antimissile missiles to Israel. Their presence helped calm the Israeli public and end the likelihood that Israel would enter the war.

Simultaneously, the United States devoted enormous effort to locating and destroying mobile Scud launchers. This proved to be the most difficult problem of the war. The Scud crew loaded and prepared the launcher in a hidden position, and then drove the vehicle to a separate launch site that the crew had already surveyed. Set up and launch occurred quickly. Essentially, the mobile launchers could fire from almost anywhere inside Iraq.

From January 18 to February 6, 1991, the Iraqis fired 29 Scuds from their western desert. Thereafter, the effect of the intense coalition anti-Scud efforts reduced the rate of fire. Iraqi launch teams had to fire blindly, making the already inaccurate Scud even less likely to hit its target. For three weeks following February 6, Iraq launched only 11 missiles, 2 of which fell harmlessly in the desert.

Iraq protected its forward troops in Kuwait from coalition air attack with a mixture of missiles and guns. The missile systems included short-range SA-9s and SA-13s as well as shoulder-fired SA-14s and SA-16s. Behind the front lines, the older SA-2 and SA-3 formed the backbone of the Iraqi air defense system. The SA-2 has a range of 31 miles. The SA-3, which has a range of 14 miles, was specifically designed to destroy aircraft flying at low and medium altitudes. The Iraqis positioned SA-6s in fixed sites to defend airfields, command and control centers, and important logistical centers. They composed the centerpiece of the Baghdad air defense system. A few SA-8s also were used to defend other strategically important areas.

At the time of the Persian Gulf War, most of the ships in the Iraqi Navy were obsolete. However, Iraq did possess 13 missile boats armed with the French-built Exocet but principally with the Soviet-designed Styx antiship missile. The Exocet had a range of more than 100 miles and warhead of 75 pounds. The larger Styx had a range of 16 to 45 miles and carried a far larger 1,100-pound warhead. The Persian Gulf War showed that coalition warships, with their overwhelming numerical and technological superiority, had little to fear from Iraqi naval missiles, however.

The Iraqi Air Force presented a potentially more serious threat to coalition forces. During the Persian Gulf War, the Iraqi Air Force possessed a small number of sophisticated missiles for attacks against land or sea targets. Iraq had purchased most of these missiles from France. In addition, Iraqi development programs had produced the Faw family of air-to-surface cruise missiles derived from the Soviet Styx. The threat posed by Iraqi air-launched missiles was demonstrated well prior to the Persian Gulf War. On March 17, 1987, the Iraqis mistakenly hit the U.S. Navy frigate *Stark* (FFG-31), which was operating in the Persian Gulf, with 2 air-launched AM-39 Exocet antiship missiles. The attack badly damaged the frigate and killed 37 crewmen. Nevertheless, during the Persian Gulf War the Iraqis achieved no hits with air-launched missiles.

Iraq also possessed about 50 land-based antiship missiles called Silkworms, derived from the Chinese design. The Silkworms had a range of about 70 miles. On February 25, 1991, the Iraqis fired two Silkworms at the U.S. battleship *Missouri*. A U.S. Navy radar warning system detected 1 incoming missile. The

British destroyer *Gloucester* then destroyed this Silkworm. The second Silkworm fell harmlessly into the Persian Gulf. A coalition air strike then destroyed the Iraqi missile site.

The Iraqi missile arsenal also included the Soviet-designed FROG-7 (Free Rocket Over Ground). The Frog-7 was able to deliver chemical and possibly nuclear weapons. The FROG-7 could propel a 990-pound chemical warhead about 37 miles from a mobile launcher. Because it was obsolete by 1991, its major threat was as a potential terror weapon. The Iraqi leadership apparently chose not to utilize this weapon during the Persian Gulf War.

The number of missiles Iraq retained after the Persian Gulf War was unclear. However, Iraq did still possess significant stocks of modern air-to-air missiles. Consequently, the Iraqi air defense system was considered to be among the world's most formidable. The Iraqi air defense arsenal included a heavy surface-to-air arsenal with an estimated 130 to 180 SA-2s, 100 to 125 SA-3 launchers, 100 to 125 SA-6s, 20 to 35 SA-8s, 30 to 45 SA-9s, some SA-13s, and about 30 Roland VII and 5 Crotale surface-to-air missiles. Republican Guard air defense units used the proven SA-6 mobile surface-to-air missile to protect high-value strategic targets. The Iraqi command also positioned SA-7 and SA-10 antiaircraft missiles near key buildings to provide a last line of defense. In addition,

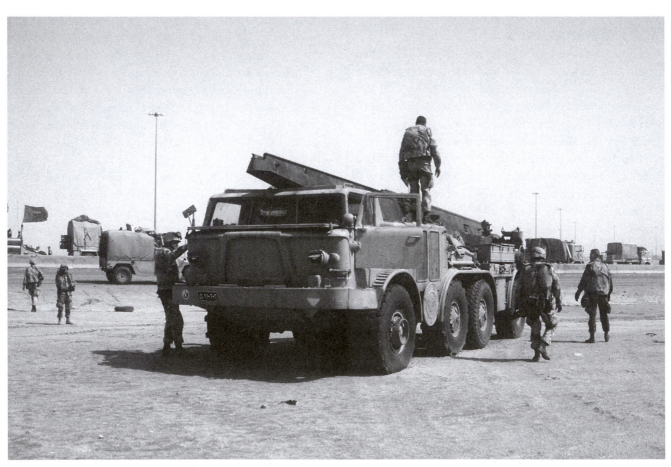

An Iraqi FROG artillery rocket system captured during Operation DESERT STORM in February 1991. (U.S. Department of Defense)

Iraqi ground units carried an estimated 2,000 man-portable SA-7s and SA-14 antiaircraft missiles along with a handful of SA-16s.

Under the allied aerial onslaught beginning during the Persian Gulf War, the Iraqis learned to rapidly move their missile and radar units to avoid allied retaliation. In addition, the Iraqis skillfully employed decoys. However, overall the Iraqi air defense system was completely overshadowed by the sophisticated, state-of-the-art, allied aerial attacks. During tens of thousands of allied aerial sorties over Iraqi territory between 1991 and 2003, the Iraqis never managed to shoot down an allied manned aircraft. This trend continued through the 2003 Iraq War. The Iraqis were unable to effectively engage high-altitude coalition aircraft. Although they tried to defend major strategic targets including the command posts of senior Iraqi leaders, they failed.

The Iraqi missile arsenal on the eve of the Iraq War (Operation IRAQI FREEDOM) included French-designed Matra 530, Matra 550, and Matra Super 530 air-to-air missiles. The only major improvement the Iraqi Air Force made between the Persian Gulf War and the Iraq War was the installation of French-designed Matra Magic 2 air-to-air missiles on the Dassault Mirage F-1, a French-built fighter/attack aircraft. This missile gave the Mirages a useful "dogfight" missile. However, the Iraqi Air Force never flew during IRAQI FREEDOM.

Iraq also retained a variety of air-to-surface missiles, such as the AM-39 Exocet and some surface-to-surface, long-range missiles including the Al-Samoud 2 and Ababil-100 missiles and an estimated 12 to 25 surviving Scuds dating from the early 1990s. However, these missiles lacked the range, accuracy, and destructive capacity to be a serious threat to allied aircraft.

On March 20, 2003, Iraq launched its first theater ballistic missile against Kuwait. Subsequently, Iraq fired such additional theater ballistic missiles as the Ababil-100 and such cruise missiles as the CSS-C-3 Seersucker. A typical Iraqi missile operation occurred on March 20–21, when the Iraqis fired seven missiles at Kuwait, four of which were intercepted by Patriot batteries and three of which were allowed to strike unpopulated areas.

JAMES ARNOLD

**See also**

Antiaircraft Missiles, Iraqi; DESERT STORM, Operation; IRAQI FREEDOM, Operation; Missiles, Air-to-Ground; Missiles, Cruise; Missiles, Intermediate-Range Ballistic; Patriot Missile System; Scud Missiles, U.S. Search for during the Persian Gulf War

**References**

Cordesman, Anthony H. *The Iraq War: Strategy, Tactics, and Military Lessons.* Westport, CT: Praeger, 2003.

Dunnigan, James F., and Austin Bay. *From Shield to Storm: High-Tech Weapons, Military Strategy, and Coalition Warfare in the Persian Gulf.* New York: William Morrow, 1992.

*Jane's Armour and Artillery, 1990–1991.* London: Jane's Information Group, 1990.

*Jane's Armour and Artillery, 2001–2002.* London: Jane's Information Group, 2001.

Spencer, Jack. *Ballistic Missile Threat Handbook.* Washington, DC: Heritage Foundation, 2002.

# Mitchell, George John
## Birth Date: August 20, 1933

Attorney, Democratic politician, U.S. senator (1980–1995), and special peace envoy for the William J. Clinton and Barack H. Obama administrations. George John Mitchell was born to a family of humble origins in Waterville, Maine, on August 20, 1933; his mother was an immigrant from Lebanon. Mitchell graduated from Bowdoin College in 1954 and earned a law degree from Georgetown University in 1961. He thereafter worked in the U.S. Department of Justice, was an aide to Senator Edmund S. Muskie (D-Maine) from 1962 to 1965, was in private law practice in Portland, Maine, from 1965 to 1977, and served as assistant county attorney in Maine in 1971.

In 1974, Mitchell ran unsuccessfully for the governorship of Maine; three years later, President Jimmy Carter appointed him U.S. attorney for the U.S. District Court, District of Maine. In 1979, he became a federal judge for the district, a post he held until 1980, when he was appointed a U.S. senator from Maine to replace Edmund Muskie, who had been tapped to be Carter's secretary of state.

Mitchell served in the Senate from 1980 until his retirement in January 1994. He was considered a loyal Democrat capable of reaching bipartisan consensus when necessary. His calm, amiable demeanor and ability to see both sides of an issue earned him a reputation as a Senate diplomat, and he played a prominent role in the 1987 Iran-Contra hearings. From 1989 to 1995, Mitchell served as Senate minority leader, another sign that he enjoyed broad-based respect among his peers. In 1994, President Clinton reportedly offered Mitchell a seat on the U.S. Supreme Court, but Mitchell demurred, instead choosing to focus on his legislative agenda.

After leaving the Senate in January 1995, Mitchell joined a prominent law firm based in Washington, D.C. That same year, President Clinton named him as a special envoy to Northern Ireland. Mitchell worked diligently and garnered much admiration for his ability to bring the long-standing violence and enmity in the region to an end. His work helped bring about the Belfast Peace Agreement (Good Friday Agreement) of 1998. He remained special envoy until 2000 and was awarded the Presidential Medal of Freedom (1999) for his efforts.

During 2000–2001, Mitchell participated in the Sharm al-Sheikh Fact-Finding Committee in the Middle East. During his sojourn to the Middle East, Mitchell highlighted the problems caused by Israel's settlements in the West Bank, and the Palestinians' inability to foil terrorist activity launched from their areas of control.

During 2006–2007, Mitchell served as head of an investigative committee that sought to evaluate the past and present use of performance-enhancing drugs by Major League Baseball (MLB) players. He had been handpicked by MLB commissioner Bud Selig. Mitchell conducted a methodical investigation that captured national headlines. The committee's December 2007 report, known as the Mitchell Report, named 89 players—both past and current MLB members—who were believed to have used steroids and other illegal drugs while they played. In the meantime, Mitchell served on numerous boards of directors and was named chief executive officer of the Walt Disney Company in 2004.

In January 2009, President Obama named Mitchell as his special envoy to the Middle East. He was charged with restarting the Israeli-Palestinian peace process and evaluating the results of Israel's incursion into Gaza, which had begun in December 2008. He reported directly to Secretary of State Hillary Rodham Clinton. Mitchell seemed well placed for the difficult task that lay ahead of him, given his past track record as an impartial arbiter and peacemaker. Indeed, his past criticisms of both Israel and the Palestinian National Authority (PNA) lent credence to the claim that he would bring a fresh and unbiased approach to the Middle East peace process.

PAUL G. PIERPAOLI JR.

**See also**

Clinton, Hillary Rodham; Iran-Contra Affair; Obama, Barack Hussein, II

**References**

Mitchell, George. *Making Peace.* New York: Knopf, 1999.

Mitchell, George, with William S. Cohen. *Men of Zeal: A Candid Inside Story of the Iran Contra Hearings.* New York: Viking, 1988.

---

# Mitterrand, François
## Birth Date: October 26, 1916
## Death Date: January 8, 1996

French political leader and president of France (1981–1995). Born in the town of Jarnac near Cognac (Charente), France, on October 26, 1916, François Mitterrand studied at the Sorbonne and the École Libre des Sciences Politiques in Paris, earning degrees in law and political science. Mitterrand began his military service in 1938 and was a sergeant when World War II began. Wounded in May 1940 during the Campaign for France, he was taken prisoner by the Germans, but after several attempts escaped at the end of 1941. He then made his way to Vichy, where he found a position on the Commission for War Prisoners. In 1943 he joined the Resistance, claiming that Vichy's anti-Semitism left him no choice. Under the nom de guerre of Morland, Mitterrand became a Resistance leader.

After the war Mitterrand founded and headed an organization of former prisoners and deportees. He also took up journalism and politics, joining the small centrist Democratic and Socialist Union of the Resistance (UDSR). Although he lost his first election attempt in 1946, shortly thereafter he won election to the Chamber of Deputies from Nièvre in Burgundy, holding that seat until 1958. In 1947 he became the youngest cabinet minister in a century as minister of veterans' affairs. He went on to serve in 11 different governments during the Fourth Republic as minister of overseas territories (1950–1951), of the interior (1954–1955), and of justice (1956–1957). After 1953 he also headed the UDSR.

Mitterrand's service in so many different cabinets earned him the reputation of a political opportunist, but he opposed the return to power of Charles de Gaulle in 1958. Mitterrand failed to win election in 1958, but the next year he was elected both to the Senate and as mayor of Château-Chinon in Burgundy. He won election to the National Assembly in 1962 and thereafter until 1981.

Mitterrand ran unsuccessfully for the French presidency in 1965 as the candidate of the moderate Left and secured communist support in the second round of balloting. He then capitalized on his strong election showing to organize the Federation of the Democratic and Socialist Left (FGDS) for the 1967 legislative elections. The FGDS included his new party, the Convention of Republican Institutions (CIR), which won 192 seats, reducing the Gaullist majority to 6 seats. However, the FGDS disintegrated in the Gaullist June 1968 landslide that followed the events of May 1968, and Mitterrand did not run for the presidency in 1969.

Mitterrand then merged his own CRI with the Socialist Party (PS) and, despite his own lack of socialist credentials, assumed the leadership of the PS in 1971. He again ran for the presidency in 1974 but lost by a single percentage point to Valéry Giscard d'Estaing. Meanwhile, in 1977 the socialists broke with the communists, enhancing Mitterrand's position as a moderate.

Mitterrand won the French presidential election of May 1981, ending 23 years of conservative rule. He then called a general election in which the PS won an absolute majority in the new assembly. As president, Mitterrand carried out a sweeping legislative agenda. He nationalized major industries and financial institutions; raised worker benefits and reduced the workweek to 36 hours; increased the minimum wage and benefits for single mothers, retirees, and the handicapped; established a ministry of women's rights; liberalized abortion rights; and abolished the death penalty. He also increased defense spending with the creation of a rapid reaction force and the modernization of the nation's nuclear strike force. France also continued nuclear testing. Sharply increased government spending, however, created great budget deficits and an economic turndown, forcing Mitterrand into an austerity program in 1982 and decreased social spending.

In foreign affairs, Mitterrand fully supported European integration. He also backed Britain in the 1982 Falklands War, and he established a close working relationship with U.S. president Ronald Reagan, despite Reagan's conservative agenda. Mitterrand's state visit to Israel in 1981 was the first by a French president.

The 1986 legislative elections produced a Gaullist majority and forced Mitterrand to name rightist Jacques Chirac as premier. The resulting cohabitation, as it came to be known for a socialist president and a Gaullist premier, worked surprisingly well and pleased the French electorate. Mitterrand concentrated on international affairs, only occasionally intervening in domestic issues. He defeated Chirac in the 1988 presidential elections, winning 54 percent of the vote.

Mitterrand concentrated on foreign policy issues, including the Maastricht Treaty, construction of the cross-channel tunnel with Britain, and full support for both the 1991 Persian Gulf War, in which French military forces participated, and the North Atlantic Treaty Organization (NATO) intervention in Bosnia. His second presidential term also brought scandal, including fresh controversies over his wartime record and revelations of a daughter by a longtime mistress. Consumed by cancer, Mitterrand resigned the presidency in May 1995. He died in Paris on January 8, 1996.

SPENCER C. TUCKER

**See also**

Chirac, Jacques René; France, Middle East Policy; France, Role in Persian Gulf and Iraq Wars; Reagan, Ronald Wilson

**References**

Friend, Julius. *The Long Presidency: France in the Mitterrand Years.* Boulder, CO: Westview, 1991.

Giesbert, F. O. *Le Président.* Paris: Seuil, 1990.

Mitterrand, François. *The Wheat and the Chaff.* New York: Seaver, 1982.

Northcutt, W. *Mitterrand: A Political Biography.* New York: Holmes and Meier, 1992.

Ross, George. *The Mitterrand Experiment: Continuity and Change in Modern France.* Oxford: Oxford University Press, 1987.

# Mohammed, Khalid Sheikh
## Birth Date: March 1, 1964, or April 14, 1965

Al Qaeda terrorist and operative who played a major role in the planning and execution of the September 11, 2001, terror attacks on the United States. Khalid Sheikh Mohammed was born either on March 1, 1964, or April 14, 1965, to a religious family in Kuwait, although he traces his ethnic origins to the Baluchistan region of Pakistan. He studied mechanical engineering in the United States at North Carolina Agricultural and Technological State University, from which he graduated in 1986. The next year, Mohammed joined his brother Zahid in Peshawar, Pakistan, where he took an assignment performing administrative tasks for Abdullah Azzam, the leader of the Maktab al-Khidimat (Jihad Service Bureau). There he became acquainted with Ayman al-Zawahiri and Azzam's protégé, Osama bin Laden, who financed the bureau's operations in Afghanistan.

Following the final Soviet withdrawal from Afghanistan in 1989, Mohammed's terrorist activities were limited until he learned of his nephew Ramzi Ahmed Yousef's plans to attack the United States. In the early 1990s Omar Abdel Rahman, known as the "blind Sheikh" and as a spiritual guide to the Islamic Jihad movement, settled in Brooklyn, New York, and became imam of three mosques in the New York City area. A follower of Rahman, Yousef was involved in the bombing of the World Trade Center in February 1993. Mohammed wired Yousef $600 for his role in the attack.

Following the 1993 bombing, Mohammed and Yousef traveled to the Philippines to collaborate on the so-called Bojinka Plot, in which Mohammed proposed hijacking twelve U.S. airliners and destroying them over the Pacific Ocean during a two-day period. Both Mohammed and Yousef secured and prepared the explosives to destroy the aircraft, and succeeded in blowing up a Philippine Airlines aircraft flying between Manila and Tokyo. Yousef was arrested by Pakistani authorities in an Al Qaeda safe house after Philippine military officials discovered his bomb-making facilities. Mohammed, however, eluded capture and fled to Afghanistan while Yousef was extradited to the United States. In 1997 Yousef was convicted for his role in the 1993 World Trade Center bombing and the Bojinka Plot.

In Afghanistan Mohammed met with bin Laden and outlined his plans for multiple terror attacks against the United States. According to Mohammed's testimony, bin Laden was initially unconvinced that such a plot would succeed. Following the 1998 attacks on the U.S. embassies in Nairobi, Kenya, and Dar es Salaam, Tanzania, Mohammed, bin Laden, and bin Laden's confidant Muhammad Atef began planning the September 11 attacks on New York City and Washington, D.C. Initially, Mohammed's plan called for attacks on both the Eastern and Western seaboards of the United States. He later stated, however, that he wanted to strike at the economic and political centers of the United States: New York and Washington. On September 11, 2001, 19 members of Al Qaeda hijacked four U.S. airliners and crashed two of them into the twin towers of the World Trade Center in New York; a third crashed into the Pentagon in Arlington, Virginia, while the fourth aircraft, the target of which was presumably either the White House or the Capitol building in Washington, D.C., crashed into a field in western Pennsylvania. In response, the United States went to war in October 2001 against the Taliban regime in Afghanistan, which had harbored bin Laden and Al Qaeda. Mohammed, like the other Al Qaeda principals, initially eluded capture by the United States.

On March 1, 2003, Mohammed was arrested in Pakistan and placed in the custody of the Central Intelligence Agency (CIA) until his transfer to Camp Justice at Guantamano Bay, Cuba, in September 2006. According to the U.S. Department of Defense, he confessed to masterminding the September 11 attacks in addition to other activities during his Combatant Status Review Tribunal in March 2007. During the proceedings, he also admitted to having beheaded *Wall Street Journal* reporter Daniel Pearl in Karachi, Pakistan, with "his own right hand." It seems that Mohammed admitted to more many actions than he could have committed, however. It is also unclear to what degree his admissions were compromised by torture. The March tribunal revealed that Mohammed had been subjected to enhanced interrogation techniques, including "waterboarding," a total of 183 times.

On June 5, 2008, Mohammed faced Colonel Ralph Kohlmann, the chief judge of the military tribunals at Guantánamo Bay during the initial tribunal proceedings and rejected his military- and civilian-appointed attorneys. He informed Kohlmann that he wished to represent himself during the war crimes trial. According to the Associated Press, the judge warned Mohammed that he faced execution if convicted, to which he responded that he wanted to "die as a martyr." The Military Commissions Act of 2006 requires that in order to be convicted and given a death sentence, a panel of at least 12 officers of the U.S. Armed Forces must unanimously concur on the death sentence and that the president of the United States must ultimately authorize it.

OJAN ARYANFARD

**See also**

Al Qaeda; Bin Laden, Osama; Coercive Interrogation; Dar es Salaam, Bombing of U.S. Embassy; Nairobi, Kenya, Bombing of U.S. Embassy; September 11 Attacks; September 11 Commission and Report; Terrorism

**References**

Gunaratna, Rohan. *Inside Al Qaeda: Global Network of Terror.* New York: Berkley Publishing Group, 2003.

Kepel, Gilles, and Jean-Pierre Milelli, eds. *Al Qaeda in Its Own Words.* Cambridge: Harvard University Press, 2008.

*The 9/11 Commission Report: Final Report of the National Commission on Terrorist Attacks upon the United States.* Authorized edition. New York: Norton, 2004.

Rabasa, Angel. *Beyond al-Qaeda: Part 1, The Global Jihadist Movement and Beyond al-Qaeda; Part 2, The Outer Rings of the Terrorist Universe.* Santa Monica, CA: RAND Corporation, 2006.

# Moldova, Role in Afghanistan and Iraq Wars

Former Soviet republic, independent since 1991, and now known as the Republic of Moldova. With a 2008 population of 4.342 million, Moldova covers 13,100 square miles and lies between Ukraine to the east and Romania to the west. Moldova's government is a parliamentary democracy with a president as head of state and a prime minister as head of government. The president is chosen by the legislature, and it is he who selects the prime minister, who in turn forms an executive cabinet. In recent years, two political entities have held sway in Moldova: the Party of Communists of the Republic of Moldova, by far the largest, and the Party Alliance–Our Moldova, a liberal political grouping.

Although closely tied to Russia in the postindependence era, Moldovan political leaders did endeavor to increase economic and security ties with the West, particularly the United States. Moldova also initiated steps to increase cooperation with the North Atlantic Treaty Organization (NATO), including joining the alliance's Partnership-for-Peace program in 1994 and launching a partnership action plan to better ensure interoperability between Moldovan forces and their NATO counterparts. One of the key components of the action plan has been increased training to develop a Moldovan battalion that could be used for international peacekeeping operations. In response, NATO and the United States have supported Moldovan efforts at a diplomatic solution that would lead to the withdrawal of Russian troops from the disputed Transdniestria region, where Russian forces have been stationed since a 1992 cease-fire agreement between that breakaway province and Moldova was brokered.

Moldova sharply condemned the September 11, 2001, terrorist attacks on the United States and supported United Nations (UN) Security Council Resolutions that called for member states to increase their counterterrorism efforts. Moldova's government offered the U.S.-led coalition use of the country's airspace and Chisinau Airport to conduct Operation ENDURING FREEDOM. Moldova also increased intelligence cooperation with NATO and the U.S.-led coalition.

Moldova also supported the U.S. effort to assemble an international coalition to overthrow the Iraqi regime of Saddam Hussein. At the beginning of September 2003, some six months after Operation IRAQI FREEDOM began, the Moldovan parliament approved the deployment of troops to support the U.S.-led forces in Iraq. The first Moldovan forces arrived in Iraq on September 8. The initial force included elements of an infantry platoon as well as medical and engineering personnel. Moldova maintained a small deployment of about 40 soldiers throughout its involvement in Iraq. The Moldovan troops were initially stationed with U.S. troops near Samarra, north of Baghdad. Later, units were stationed near Mosul. Moldovan soldiers typically served six-month deployments, and several units undertook multiple tours in Iraq.

Moldovan troops were sent first to Kuwait, where they underwent training and were acclimated to the conditions in the region. Subsequent deployments included ordnance disposal units and a staff contingent that was stationed in Baghdad as part of the headquarters unit of the Multi-National Force in Iraq. In addition, a Moldovan staff officer was stationed with U.S. Central Command (CENTCOM) to coordinate troop rotations and deployments with the coalition. The Moldovan ordnance disposal units were highly experienced as a result of domestic operations to remove land mines and destroy ordnance left over from the 1992 Transdniestria conflict. During one six-month tour in 2005, a Moldovan unit destroyed or otherwise disposed of more than 182,000 unexploded bombs, mines, and improvised explosive devices (IEDs). In total, and including joint operations with U.S. forces, the Moldovans disposed of more than 520,000 explosives.

Moldova's final rotation of troops began in August 2008. Instead of the full six-month deployment, however, in December 2008 the government announced that it would withdraw the forces because of the improving security conditions in Iraq. No Moldovan soldiers were killed during the country's five-year involvement in Iraq.

TOM LANSFORD

**See also**

IRAQI FREEDOM, Operation, Coalition Ground Forces; Multi-National Force–Iraq; North Atlantic Treaty Organization in Afghanistan

**References**

Cockburn, Patrick. *The Occupation: War and Resistance in Iraq.* New York: Verso, 2007.

Keegan, John. *The Iraq War: The Military Offensive, from Victory in 21 Days to the Insurgent Aftermath.* New York: Vintage, 2005.

# Mongolia, Role in Afghanistan and Iraq Wars

Central Asian nation covering 604,207 square miles. With a 2008 population of 2.996 million people, Mongolia is bordered by Russia to the north and the People's Republic of China to the south. Long a bastion of one-party communist rule, in 1990 an indigenous pro-democracy movement broke the back of the long-reigning Mongolian People's Revolutionary Party (MPRP), paving the way for a multiparty democracy. Mongolia's government is a parliamentary system in which the head of government is the prime minister. The presidency is largely symbolic, but the president does have the right to veto parliamentary legislation, which can then be overridden by a two-thirds majority in parliament. In recent years, the Mongolian political landscape has been dominated by the MPRP (socialist), the Democratic Party (social democratic), the Republican Party (centrist), and the Motherland Party (democratic-socialist).

Mongolia was able to successfully use participation in Operations ENDURING FREEDOM and IRAQI FREEDOM to obtain security and economic assistance from the United States. The United States formally recognized Mongolia in 1987 and provided a variety of economic aid through the 1990s. When the invasion of Afghanistan (Operation ENDURING FREEDOM) began in 2001, Mongolia became a member of the U.S.-led coalition in Afghanistan. After the fall of the Taliban in December 2001, Mongolia agreed to help train the new Afghan National Army. In October 2003, a 12-member Mongolian artillery crew and its support staff were dispatched to Afghanistan. The Mongolian forces had extensive experience with the Soviet-era military equipment used by the Afghan military. Mongolia has maintained 20 to 25 troops in Afghanistan, and the soldiers serve six-month deployments.

The Mongolian government also joined the U.S.-led coalition during the Iraq War (Operation IRAQI FREEDOM). In April 2003, Mongolia agreed to deploy forces to Iraq, and the first contingent arrived there in August in the military's first foreign mission since 1921. Mongolia initially dispatched 170 soldiers, including infantry and engineering units. The troops were part of the Polish-led Multi-National Force and were stationed in Al Hillah, in Babil Province, at one of the coalition's largest supply bases. The troops undertook general force protection missions as well as humanitarian and reconstruction projects. Subsequent deployments were mainly infantry troops that undertook security missions. In February 2004, Mongolian sergeant Garbold Azzaya intercepted and killed a suicide bomber who was attempting to drive a vehicle, laden with explosives, onto the coalition base.

Beginning in 2006, Mongolian forces were garrisoned in Diwaniya, in Qadisiya Province. Mongolia's peak deployment was about 180 soldiers. The Mongolian troops were withdrawn in September 2008. More than 990 Mongolians served in Iraq during the country's involvement in the coalition; none suffered serious injuries or wounds.

Participation in Afghanistan and Iraq was popular among the Mongolian population and the country's political leadership.

Following elections in 2006, which were won by the opposition MPRP, the new government maintained the country's commitment to the U.S.-led coalitions. In return for its alliance with the United States, Mongolia received a variety of direct and indirect benefits. For instance, prior to their deployment, some Mongolian units participated in military maneuvers and training exercises in the United States. Furthermore, during their service in Iraq, Mongolian troops were provided new military equipment by the United States, including uniforms, weaponry, and communications equipment. Mongolia also received $14.5 million from the United States to upgrade and modernize its small, 15,000-member military establishment. In addition, in 2007, under the Millennium Challenge Compact, the United States pledged $285 million in new economic assistance over a five-year period. Significantly, many of the units that were deployed in Iraq subsequently joined United Nations (UN) peacekeeping operations in Kosovo, Sierra Leone, and the Western Sahara. The UN also converted a former military base in Mongolia into a training center for multilateral peacekeeping missions in Asia.

TOM LANSFORD

**See also**

IRAQI FREEDOM, Operation, Coalition Ground Forces; Multi-National Force–Iraq; North Atlantic Treaty Organization in Afghanistan

**References**

Cockburn, Patrick. *The Occupation: War and Resistance in Iraq.* New York: Verso, 2007.

Keegan, John. *The Iraq War: The Military Offensive, from Victory in 21 Days to the Insurgent Aftermath.* New York: Vintage, 2005.

---

# Monsoor, Michael Anthony

Birth Date: April 5, 1981
Death Date: September 29, 2006

U.S. Navy SEAL and posthumous Medal of Honor recipient. Born in Long Beach, California, on April 5, 1981, Michael Anthony Monsoor graduated from Garden Grove High School, in Garden Grove, California, in 1999. Enlisting in the U.S. Navy in March 2001, Monsoor attended Basic Training at the Recruit Training Command, Great Lakes, Illinois. Forced to drop out of Basic Underwater Demolition/SEAL (BUD/S) training because of an injury, Monsoor reentered that program and in September 2004 graduated as one of the top members of his class. He then completed the Basic Airborne School; cold weather training in Kodiak, Alaska; and, in March 2004, SEAL Qualification Training at Coronado, California. Master-at-Arms Monsoor was then assigned to SEAL Team 3.

Seal Team 3 arrived in Ramadi, Iraq, in April 2006. There, Monsoor was regularly on patrol and involved in frequent clashes with Iraqi insurgents. Monsoor was awarded a Silver Star for an action on May 9, 2006, in which he braved insurgent fire to rescue a wounded comrade.

On September 29 Monsoor was manning a machine gun with three SEAL and several Iraqi Army snipers assigned to a rooftop sniper detail when they became engaged in a firefight with insurgents, killing several. Fighting continued, and the sniper element came under insurgent small-arms and rocket-propelled grenade attack. An insurgent from an unseen location then hurled a grenade on the roof. It bounced off Monsoor's body. As the only member of the detail to have easy access to an escape route, he might have saved himself but instead yelled "Grenade!" and covered the explosive device with his own body. Monsoor was badly wounded in the blast seconds later; although soon evacuated, he died 30 minutes later.

On March 31, 2008, Master-at-Arms Second Class Michael Monsoor was awarded the Medal of Honor for his selfless action in saving the lives of several of his colleagues. President George W. Bush presented the award to his family at the White House on April 8. Monsoor was the first navy recipient of the Medal of Honor for the Iraq War and the third member of the U.S. armed forces to receive the medal for Iraq. In October the Navy Department announced that the DDG-1001, the second ship in the Zumwalt-class of destroyers, would be named in Monsoor's honor.

Spencer C. Tucker

**See also**
Bush, George Walker

**References**
Abruzzese, Sarah. "Bush Gives Medal of Honor to Slain Navy SEALs Member." *New York Times,* April 9, 2008.
Perry, Tony. "Destroyer to Bear O.C. SEAL's Name." *Los Angeles Times,* October 30, 2008.

---

# Monti, Jared Christopher
## Birth Date: September 20, 1975
## Death Date: June 21, 2006

U.S. soldier and posthumous recipient of the Medal of Honor. Born in Abington, Massachusetts, on September 20, 1975, Jared Christopher Monti grew up in Raynham, Massachusetts. He enlisted in the army in March 1993 and graduated from Bridgewater-Raynham High School in 1994. Monti attended both basic and advanced training at Fort Sill, Oklahoma. He also received artillery observer training and earned the Parachutist Badge and Air Assault Badge. Monti saw overseas service in the Republic of Korea and in Kosovo. In February 2006, Monti was assigned to Afghanistan as a targeting noncommissioned officer in the 3rd Squadron, 71st Cavalry Regiment, 3rd Brigade Combat Team of the 10th Mountain Division (Light Infantry) stationed at Fort Drum, New York. On June 21, 2006, Staff Sergeant Monti was the assistant leader of a 16-man reconnaissance force that came under fire in the mountainous area near Gowardesh, Nuristan Province. In the ensuing firefight, two of the members of Monti's unit were

separated from the rest, and both were wounded. Monti dragged one to safety under fire. He returned to assist the other wounded soldier but was killed by a rocket-propelled grenade. Monti was posthumously promoted to sergeant first class.

Monti was the second U.S. service member to be awarded the Medal of Honor for actions in Afghanistan, and Monti's medal is the sixth for service in either Iraq or Afghanistan. All six Medals of Honor have been posthumous awards.

President Barack Obama signed the award in July 2009 and presented the Medal of Honor to Monti's parents in a White House ceremony on September 17, 2009.

Spencer C. Tucker

**See also**
Obama, Barack Hussein, II

**References**
Cavallaro, Gina. "Fallen Soldier to Receive Medal of Honor." *Army Times,* July 23, 2009.
Weinstein, Susan Parkou. "Raynham's Jarod C. Monti Posthumously Awarded Medal of Honor." *Daily News Tribune* (Waltham, MA), July 23, 2009.

---

# Moore, Michael
## Birth Date: April 23, 1954

Controversial American author, film director, and outspoken opponent of the Iraq War (Operation IRAQI FREEDOM). Born in Flint, Michigan, into a working-class family on April 23, 1954, Michael Moore briefly attended the University of Michigan–Flint. Moore founded the *Flint Voice,* a liberal weekly magazine, in 1976.

In 1986, Moore moved to California and became the editor of *Mother Jones,* a liberal political magazine with more than 250,000 paid subscribers. More worked for *Mother Jones* for just a few months. His personality and tactics clashed with many members of the magazine's staff, and he was fired in the autumn of 1986. Moore later sued the magazine for wrongful dismissal. He accepted a settlement of $58,000, which helped fund his first film, *Roger & Me* (1989). This film, which is critical of the neoliberal economic model of development, examines the impact of General Motors' decision to close its Flint, Michigan, plant, where many of Moore's family members had worked, and move its operations to Mexico. "Roger" was Roger Smith, chief operating officer of General Motors.

Moore also directed *Bowling for Columbine* (2002), which explores the culture of guns and violence in the United States, especially in the public school system. He is, however, best known for *Fahrenheit 9/11* (2004), a film that is sharply critical of the George W. Bush administration's war on terrorism and U.S. involvement in the Middle East, especially the March 2003 invasion of Iraq.

The film's title alludes to *Fahrenheit 451,* a science-fiction book by author Ray Bradbury, who objected to the hijacking of his book's title. The analogy between 451°F, the temperature at which paper

American filmmaker Michael Moore. An outspoken liberal political activist, Moore produced *Fahrenheit 9/11* (2004), a film that is sharply critical of the George W. Bush administration's war on terrorism and U.S. involvement in the Middle East. (Shutterstock)

combusts, and "Fahrenheit 9/11," the "temperature" at which, according to Moore, "freedom burns," is endemic of Moore's wit. For the first time since 1956, a documentary film, *Fahrenheit 9/11,* won the Palme d'Or, the main prize at the Cannes Film Festival in France. Moore had hoped that the release of the film prior to the 2004 presidential election would dissuade voters from reelecting President Bush to a second term in office. Although the film was much talked about and grossed more money than any other documentary in history, Moore failed in his aim of preventing Bush's reelection.

Moore's documentary style, which follows an involved, essayed format and frequently employs tinges of humor, often reveals as much about Moore and his opinions as about the subject of his film. Although many film critics have praised Moore's approach, traditional documentary directors, who prefer a more observational style of filmmaking, have criticized it. Perhaps most controversial is Moore's commentary on U.S. involvement in Iraq. In books, interviews, and films, he characterized Iraqi militant opponents of the U.S. military occupation as "freedom fighters" and predicted that they would eventually be successful. Whether one agrees with Moore or not, there can be little doubt that his

*Fahrenheit 9/11* documentary provoked much debate over decision-making that some would have preferred to keep under wraps.

In 2007, Moore continued his documentary-film career by producing *Sicko,* a film about the poor state of the American health care industry. Released at the Cannes Film Festival in May 2007, *Sicko* offered a stinging indictment of the U.S. pharmaceutical industry and managed care system, claiming that their quest for profits and political clout has made them unresponsive to the very public whom they are charged to serve. Moore later came under fire when it was discovered that a portion of the film had been shot in Cuba, which might have violated the long-standing trade embargo against that island nation.

MICHAEL R. HALL

### See also
Bush, George Walker; *Fahrenheit 9/11*; IRAQI FREEDOM, Operation; September 11 Attacks

### References
Hardy, David T., and Jason Clarke. *Michael Moore Is a Big Fat Stupid White Man.* New York: Regan Books/HarperCollins, 2004.

Moore, Michael. *Stupid White Men and Other Sorry Excuses for the State of Our Nation.* New York: Regan Books/HarperCollins, 2002.

Schultz, Emily. *Michael Moore: A Biography.* Toronto: ECW Press, 2005.

# Morocco

Northwest African nation. The Kingdom of Morocco borders on the Mediterranean Sea to the north, the Atlantic Ocean to the west, Western Sahara to the south, and Algeria to the east. Morocco has an area of 172,414 square miles, slightly larger than the U.S. state of California. The nation's current population is approximately 33 million people.

Morocco has been influenced by European, African, and Arab-Islamic influences in combination with its native Berber and Arab population. From 1912 to 1956, Morocco was both a French and Spanish protectorate. France granted independence to Morocco in 1956, although Spain continued to control the Western Sahara region until the mid-1970s and still retains the small enclaves of Cuenta and Melilla along the Mediterranean coast.

When the State of Israel was founded in May 1948, Morocco, like other countries in the Maghreb, was confronted with the considerable problem of Jewish emigration, which was to continue for the next several decades. From 1947 to 1960, approximately 50,000 Jews, or 25 percent of the Jewish population of Morocco, left the country, most to settle in Israel but some in Europe and the United States. Although most émigrés were poor or middle-class, Jews were an important part of the country's economy. Unlike many other Arab nations, the Moroccan government has maintained relatively amiable contacts with Israel since the early 1950s, although the Moroccan population is deeply opposed to Israeli policies. Neither the king, Mohammed V, nor the ruling Istiqlal Party were anti-Jewish, and many members of the country's elite were Jewish, including judges, government ministers, and university

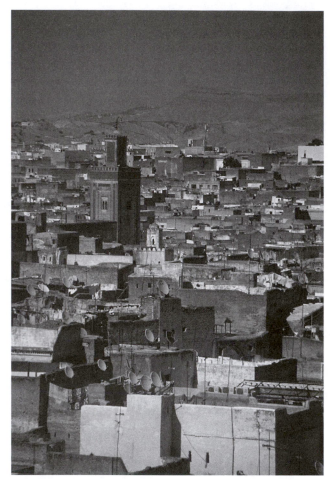

View of Fez (Fes), the third-largest city in Morocco, 2009. (Stephan Scherhag/Dreamstime.com)

administrators. While Morocco attempted to limit Jewish emigration in opposition to the desires of the United Nations (UN) and the United States, this process nevertheless continued, frequently with the covert involvement of Israeli military forces. In 2006 the Jewish population in Morocco was estimated to be only 5,000 people.

In March 1961, Crown Prince Moulay Hassan succeeded his father, Mohammed V, as King Hassan II. He ruled for the next four decades until his death in July 1999. The king was both the nation's spiritual leader, as a direct descendant of the Prophet Muhammad, and its political head of government. Hassan, while lacking the charisma and unifying ability of his father, was nonetheless an effective leader, able to balance relations with the West, whose economic and political aid helped modernize his country, and the Middle East, whose Islamic heritage was his basis for power.

Morocco was essentially kept isolated from the June 1967 Six-Day War, although the relationship between Israel and Morocco was tested when Morocco provided military support to Syria during the October 1973 Yom Kippur (Ramadan) War. In October 1976 Morocco hosted a meeting with Israeli prime minister Yitzhak Rabin. The following year Morocco hosted another meeting between Israeli foreign minister Moshe Dayan and Egyptian deputy prime minister Hasan Tuhami. To strengthen his position

in the wake of political and military opponents of his centralized authority, Hassan embarked on an effort to secure the Western Sahara, which he claimed had historically been part of Morocco, after its abandonment by Spain in 1975. To allay widespread international criticism, Moroccan officials and a delegation of Moroccan Jews visited the United States in 1978 to win support for the movement among allies of Israel in the U.S. Congress.

Domestically, efforts were made to improve the social and economic disparity between urban and rural populations, education, health care, and communications. Under Hassan's rule, however, the Moroccan countryside grew ever poorer and was depopulated of men who immigrated to Spain, Italy, and elsewhere. Extreme disparities in income and literacy remain.

In the 1980s Hassan worked to secure Arab recognition of Israel and an end to the Arab-Israeli conflict. In November 1981 and again in September 1982 he hosted an Arab summit to address conflicts in the region through a Saudi-sponsored peace plan. The plan called for the Israeli withdrawal from all occupied territories and the establishment of a Palestinian state. In July 1986 he held two days of talks on continued Palestinian issues with Israeli prime minister Shimon Peres. Hassan also sought to improve relationships among other Arab states. In 1984 he organized the Islamic Congress of Casablanca and created the Arabic-African Union with Libya. During the 1991 Persian Gulf War, Morocco aligned itself squarely with the United States and sent troops to defend Saudi Arabia.

Morocco expressed agreement with the principles of the 1993 Oslo Accords and received Israeli prime minister Rabin and Foreign Minister Peres in Casablanca following the signing ceremony in Washington, D.C. On September 1, 1994, Morocco and Israel established semiofficial diplomatic relations with the opening of liaison offices in Jerusalem and Rabat. These offices served to promote tourism and trade between the two countries, an issue of great economic importance to Morocco. They remained open for eight years but closed following the Palestinian uprising in 2002.

Rising extremist Islamist and salafist groups posed difficult challenges for Morocco in the late 1980s and early 1990s and continue under the leadership of Hassan's son and successor, King Mohammed VI. Severe government countermeasures including torture have not seriously weakened these movements, and indeed have spurred them to revenge. Mohammed VI voiced his firm support of the War on Terror following the September 11, 2001, terror attacks on the United States, and in 2004 his government signed free-trade pacts with both the European Union and the United States. On May 16, 2003, 12 suicide bombers of Salafiyya Jihadiyya, an offshoot of the Moroccan Islamic Combatant Group and similar to the Al Qaeda organization, killed 45 people in Casablanca in five separate bombings. Although the attack on the Jewish Sabbath ultimately killed no Jews, the targets included a Jewish social club and restaurant, a Jewish cemetery, and a Jewish-owned Italian restaurant. The Moroccan government subsequently passed a stringent antiterrorism law that saw the arrests of hundreds of suspected terrorists during 2004 and 2005. Some human rights groups have criticized the crackdown, however, as they point to human rights abuses and the problem of further radicalizing the movement.

For the immediate future, it appears that domestic issues, rather than foreign policy, will continue to be the focus of the Moroccan monarchy. Other challenges facing the nation include continued fighting in Western Sahara, reducing constraints on private activity and foreign trade, increasing democracy, and achieving sustainable economic growth. Recently, the Center for Strategic and International Studies in Washington, D.C., lauded Morocco's efforts to undertake important political and economic reforms, citing it as an example that other Middle Eastern nations should emulate.

MARK SANDERS

**See also**

Al Qaeda; Global War on Terror; Islamic Radicalism; Israel-Egypt Peace Treaty

**References**

Entelis, John P. *Culture and Counterculture in Moroccan Politics.* Boulder, CO: Westview, 1989.
Pennell, C. R. *Morocco since 1830: A History.* New York: New York University Press, 2000.

# Moseley, Teed Michael
## Birth Date: 1949

U.S. Air Force officer and chief of staff of the U.S. Air Force (2005–2008). Teed Michael Moseley (known as T. Michael Moseley) was born in 1949 in Grand Prairie, Texas. He graduated from Texas A&M University in 1971. He joined the air force that same year, and the following year earned a master's degree in political science, also from Texas A&M.

From 1973 to 1977, Moseley was stationed at Webb Air Force Base, Texas. From 1977 to 1979, he was an instructor for the McDonnell Douglas/Boeing F-15 Eagle. He accrued over 2,800 flight hours as a command pilot. Moseley subsequently held a series of command posts, including the 33rd Operations Group and the 57th Wing, the largest in the U.S. Air Force; and commander of the Ninth Air Force and then the U.S. Central Command Air Forces (the latter from November 2001 to August 2003).

Moseley's staff assignments included operational, joint, and personnel positions. Among them was service in Washington, D.C., as director for legislative liaison for the secretary of the air force; deputy director for politico-military affairs for Asia/Pacific and Middle East, in the office of the Joint Chiefs of Staff; chief of the Air Force General Officer Matters Office; chair and professor of joint and combined warfare at the National War College; chief of the tactical fighter branch, tactical forces division; and directorate of plans, Headquarters U.S. Air Force.

Moseley was promoted to brigadier general on December 1, 1996, and to major general on February 1, 2000. On November 7,

2001, he was promoted to lieutenant general. He was promoted to general (four stars) on October 1, 2003.

Beginning in August 2003, Moseley served as vice chief of staff of the air force. Two years later, in September 2005, he moved up to the position of chief of staff. Moseley's tenure as chief of staff engendered much controversy, which ultimately led to his resignation in July 2008.

Two incidents concerning the mishandling of nuclear weapons, which occurred on his watch, were the most serious issues. The first involved the mistaken shipment of nuclear warhead fuses to Taiwan in 2006. The mistake was never caught by the air force; instead, Taipei brought it to the U.S. government's attention and shipped the fuses back in early 2008. The revelation was a major embarrassment to the United States and caused consternation in Beijing.

In August 2007, six nuclear-tipped cruise missiles were unwittingly loaded onto a Boeing B-52 Stratofortress in North Dakota. The bomber was then flown across much of the continent to Barksdale Air Force Base, Louisiana. Compounding the miscue was the fact that the six nuclear missiles were not reported missing for almost 36 hours and remained mounted under the wing of the aircraft. The mistake raised serious issues of control of U.S. nuclear weapons, and while it was unlikely that the bombs would have detonated, the incident egregiously broke air force regulations, which forbid the overflight of the United States with any aircraft equipped with nuclear devices. A wide-ranging investigation followed, and Moseley was compelled to resign because the security breaches had occurred during his command tenure. The U.S. media reported that the August 2007 incident was among the worst breaches of security involving nuclear weapons in the 60-year history of the air force. Moseley retired from the air force on July 11, 2008.

PAUL G. PIERPAOLI JR.

**See also**

United States Air Force, Iraq War; United States Central Command

**References**

Boyne, Walter J. *Beyond the Wild Blue: A History of the U.S. Air Force, 1947–2007.* 2nd ed. New York: Thomas Dunne Books, 2007.
Vanden Brook, Tom. "Nuclear Mishaps Lead to Air Force Resignations." *USA Today,* June 6, 2008.

# Mosul

Iraq's third largest city, Mosul is located on the west bank of the Tigris River, some 250 miles north of Baghdad. Mosul's 2008 population was estimated at about 1.8 million; only Baghdad and Basra are larger. The city was the site of the Battle of Mosul (November 8–16, 2004). Muslin, a finely woven cotton fabric, was once produced in the city in great quantities, and it may have been named for Mawsil, the French version of the town's Arabic name.

This predominantly Kurdish city is the hub of both Iraq's oil and domestic electricity production and was the scene of ongoing

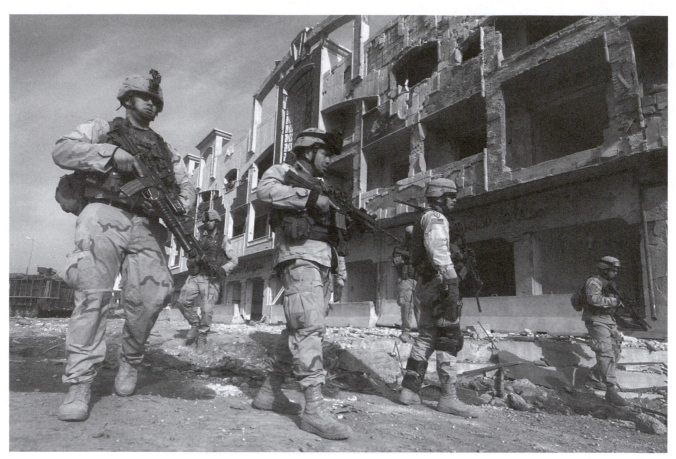

Soldiers of the U.S. Army's 1st Battalion of the 24th Infantry Division on patrol in Mosul, Iraq, January 15, 2005. (AP/Wide World Photos)

Arabization efforts by Iraqi president Saddam Hussein's Baath Party. Mosul's Kurdish majority proved to be the stumbling block in the U.S. and Turkish negotiations prior to the March 2003 invasion of Iraq. The Battle of Mosul in 2004 was one of the last steps in the Anglo-American–led fight for control of Iraq during Operation IRAQI FREEDOM.

Mosul is built on a site rich in Assyrian history. The city is located where, in 850 BCE, King Assurnasirpal II of Assyria chose to build Nineveh where the city of Nimrud had been located. Later, in 700 BCE, Sennacherib, king of Assyria, made Nineveh the capital of Assyria. After changing hands a number of times over the next few hundred years, the city remained a critical trade center because of its position on key trade routes. Mosul would remain a critical part of the trade route until the opening of the Suez Canal in 1869. The discovery of oil and the construction of the Qyurrah refinery in the 1920s led to Mosul's return to strategic and economic importance.

In 1958 Abd al-Karim Qasim, as a part of his plan to integrate non-Arab ethnic groups into Iraqi cities, began encouraging Kurds to relocate to Mosul. Hussein and his Baath Party undertook an aggressive plan to Arabize Mosul, however, and many of those Kurds who had survived the Arabization returned to traditionally Kurdish regions either by choice or by force. After the overthrow of Hussein in March 2003, some Iraqi Kurds have called for Mosul to be included in the Kurdish regional government. These displays of Kurdish nationalism have angered Sunni Arabs and certainly soured U.S.-Turkish relations.

In 2003 the United States had planned to launch an arm of its invasion into Iraq from bases in Turkey, with the goal of quickly securing the oil fields at Mosul. Because of questions about the disposition of the Kurds, however, the Turks refused to allow the Americans to stage any part of the invasion from Turkish soil. Therefore, instead of being secured in the initial hours of the war, Mosul was not taken until April 11, 2003, two days after the fall of Baghdad, when Kurdish fighters assumed control after Hussein's forces abandoned the town. After days of looting and fighting between Kurds and Arabs, the Kurds relinquished control of the city to U.S. troops.

Mosul was also the scene of the shoot-out between Hussein's sons Uday and Qusay and coalition troops on July 22, 2003, in which both men were killed. In November 2004, after insurgents conducted coordinated attacks on Iraqi police installations, the Mosul police fled the city. This precipitated the Battle of Mosul, in which U.S. and Iraqi forces together with Kurdish fighters retook the city on November 16.

Since the Battle of Mosul, the city has been plagued by violence and disorder. In December 2004 a suicide bomber killed scores of people, including 14 U.S. soldiers and 4 Halliburton employees.

In 2005 an Iraqi government official was assassinated in the city. Ethnic and sectarian violence in Mosul increased sharply between 2005 and 2007, and the city's buildings and infrastructure have been in increasingly poor repair. In January 2008 another suicide bombing leveled an apartment building in Mosul, killing 36 people; the following day, the city's police chief was assassinated. The continuing unrest has coincided with a large exodus of middle-class and professionals from the city, only complicating the situation in Mosul. In May 2008 the Iraqi army, with U.S. support, launched a major campaign to bring law and order back to Mosul. A 2009 investigation concluded that more than 2,500 Kurds had been killed in the city since 2003.

B. KEITH MURPHY

**See also**

Baath Party; Hussein, Qusay; Hussein, Saddam; Hussein, Uday; IRAQI FREEDOM, Operation; Kurds; Mosul, Battle of; Qasim, Abd al-Karim; Turkey, Role in Persian Gulf and Afghanistan Wars

**References**

Ricks, Thomas E. *Fiasco: The American Military Adventure in Iraq.* New York: Penguin, 2006.

Tucker, Mike. *Among Warriors in Iraq: True Grit, Special Ops, and Raiding in Mosul and Fallujah.* Guilford, CT: Lyons, 2005.

# Mosul, Battle of

**Start Date: November 8, 2004**
**End Date: November 16, 2004**

Pitched battle fought in the city of Mosul, located in northern Iraq some 250 miles northwest of Baghdad, during November 8–16, 2004. The battle involved the United States Army 1st Battalion, 24th Infantry Regiment, Iraqi Security Forces (Iraqi police, Iraqi Army, Iraqi National Guard, and Iraqi Border Patrol), and Kurdish Peshmerga fighting Iraqi insurgents (former Baath Party members, fundamentalist factions with ties to the Al Qaeda in Iraq organization, and fighters from other "extremist" groups). The Battle of Mosul was brought on as much by political expediency as it was by the need to protect civilians from harassment by the insurgents. It ended in a clear-cut victory for coalition forces.

The Battle of Mosul occurred simultaneously with another furious battle between coalition forces and insurgents in Fallujah. The Second Battle of Fallujah (November 7–23, 2004) drew insurgents and foreign fighters in droves. The coalition responded to the insurgent attacks with overwhelming force, which included recalling Lieutenant General David Petraeus and the 101st Airborne Division to Fallujah. The 101st had been maintaining a peaceful occupation of the primarily Sunni Mosul for the preceding year. Coalition troops took little time to rout the insurgency, and the surviving insurgents fled Fallujah. A number of them then went to Mosul.

The 25th Infantry Division was deployed to Mosul in mid-October 2004 to replace the 101st Airborne. This was approximately the same time that displaced insurgents began arriving from Fallujah. The insurgents announced their arrival with an enormous wave of kidnappings and beheadings that left more than 200 of Mosul's residents dead in the streets for resisting the insurgents.

On November 8, 2004, Iraqi insurgents began to carry out coordinated attacks within Mosul. It was on this day also that the 1st Battalion, 24th Infantry Regiment reported the first major engagement of what would become the Battle of Mosul, near the Yarmuk traffic circle in the western part of the city. Soldiers of the regiment were pinned down by coordinated mortar fire from the north and were being pounded from the other three directions by rocket-propelled grenades (RPG) and machine gun fire in a daylong firefight.

The insurgents also used this opening day of the battle to overrun two Iraqi police stations. The insurgents then cleaned out the station armories, taking weapons and flak jackets, and killed a dozen Iraqi policemen. The western media reported that the majority of the policemen had deserted their posts after reporting attacks by "hundreds" of insurgents against their stations. However, when the Americans retook the stations, they estimated that only 20–30 insurgents had taken each station.

On November 9, insurgents successfully attacked a Forward Operating Base in Mosul, killing two American army officers. By November 10, Iraqi insurgents were openly taking to the streets in defiance of coalition forces, and by November 11 they had taken another Iraqi police station and destroyed two others. The time had come for a coalition counteroffensive.

Members of the U.S. 24th Infantry Regiment were sent out in an effort to crush the insurgents between two companies. The blow was aimed, again, at the strategically critical Yarmuk traffic circle. The 24th encountered fierce resistance as it pushed from house to house in close-quarter urban fighting. Yet with air support, the 24th was able to regain control of four of the five bridges over the Tigris River.

In the meantime, the insurgents sacked nine more police stations, destroying eight and occupying the ninth. On November 12, additional insurgent reinforcements arrived and, despite U.S. Air Force bombing, by November 13 insurgent forces held as much as 70 percent of Mosul. The insurgents became so secure in their military superiority that they began seeking out members of the Iraqi Security Forces to behead.

Coalition reinforcements began to arrive by November 13, including a battalion of the U.S. 25th Infantry Regiment, a group of Kurdish Peshmerga fighters, and elements of the Iraqi Special Forces and National Guard. On November 16 U.S. forces retook the fifth insurgent-held bridge over the Tigris and began to sweep through all of Mosul except for the western sector. The Americans met little resistance, but the insurgents burned many of the police stations they had occupied. By November 16, the major fighting was over. The western sector of Mosul, however, would remain in insurgent hands until another coalition surge involving an influx of 12,000 troops arrived in December and January 2005. This was timed to secure Mosul for Iraq's first democratic elections in January.

The coalition official casualty report for the Battle of Mosul was 4 U.S. soldiers killed, 9 Peshmerga fighters killed, and 116 Iraqi Security Forces killed (as many as 5,000 are believed to have deserted). Total losses for insurgents are unknown, although 71 were confirmed killed. Also, 5 civilians were reported killed, as were 2 contractors (1 British and 1 Turkish). Precise casualty figures, including the number of wounded, remain unknown, and some estimates claim much higher death tolls for both the civilians and insurgents.

The importance of the battle could be measured by the fact that, although there were mass desertions of Iraqi police and security forces targeted by insurgents, a sense of esprit de corps and pride among Iraqi forces developed, which had been sorely lacking before the event. In turn, the police and the security forces became better equipped to handle the insurgency, and the Iraqi citizenry gained trust in them, which led to the citizenry providing more information to coalition forces regarding insurgent activity. The terrorist tactics employed by the insurgents in the battle backfired. However, Mosul remained one of the most violent places in Iraq as of the spring of 2009.

B. KEITH MURPHY

**See also**
Fallujah; Fallujah, Second Battle of; Iraqi Insurgency; Mosul; Petraeus, David Howell

**References**
Allawi, Ali A. *The Occupation of Iraq: Winning the War, Losing the Peace.* New Haven, CT: Yale University Press, 2007.
Tucker, Mike. *Among Warriors in Iraq: True Grit, Special Ops, and Raiding in Mosul and Fallujah.* Guilford, CT: Lyons, 2005.

# "Mother of All Battles"

Expression employed by Iraqi president Saddam Hussein to describe the impending 1991 Persian Gulf War (Operation DESERT STORM). As early as September 1990, just weeks after he sent his forces into Kuwait, Hussein began preparing his people for potential war with the United States, exhorting them that "this battle will become the mother of all battles." On January 17, 1991, as U.S. bombers were about to begin the air campaign against Iraq, Hussein calmly informed his people that the "mother of all battles has begun."

In resorting to such terminology, Hussein was simply using the forms of rhetoric important in Iraqi Arabic and that had been his stock and trade throughout his career. The Arabic expression *umm al-ma'arik* ("mother of all battles") is a metaphoric reference to the 636 CE Battle of al-Qadisiyyah (in present-day Iraq) in which Islamic Arabs united to win their first decisive battle against the Sassanian (Persian) Army. The phrase figuratively means "major" or "best." It is also important to note that the Qur'an is known as *umm al Kitab,* or "the mother of all books." Here, "mother" metaphorically means "origin."

Thus, Hussein's rallying cry called up powerful images from both religious and cultural history for the Iraqis. The term was quickly spread by the Iraqi government as a catchphrase in a grand propaganda scheme, which renamed the governmental-run radio station "the Mother of All Battles Radio."

After the rapid disintegration of the Iraqi military in February 1991, the United States was quick to turn the Iraqi ideological archetype into a symbol that served to reinforce the image of the overwhelming military might of the U.S.-led military coalition. In February 1991 Secretary of Defense Dick Cheney was quoted as saying, "It looks like what's happened is that the mother of all battles has turned into the mother of all retreats." The catchphrase entered American popular culture as well. U.S. general H. Norman Schwarzkopf's press conferences were known as "the mother of all press conferences," a 1991 war game based on the Persian Gulf War was titled "The Mother of All Battles," and in 2003, a three-quarter-ton bomb tested for the U.S. Air Force was nicknamed the "Mother of All Bombs," just in time for the Anglo-American–led war against Iraq.

Yet for Iraqis, the phrase continues to have meaning. In 2001, before his capture, Hussein unveiled the "Mother of All Battles" Mosque just outside Baghdad, which featured a Qur'an supposedly written with Hussein's own blood. *Umm al-ma'arik* is also said to be a battle cry among the Iraqi insurgents who continue to oppose the U.S. forces there. For some, the "mother of all battles" still rages.

B. KEITH MURPHY

**See also**
DESERT STORM, Operation; Hussein, Saddam; Iraq, History of, Pre-1990; Iraq, History of, 1990–Present; IRAQI FREEDOM, Operation

**References**
Bengio, Ofra. *Saddam's Word: Political Discourse in Iraq.* New York: Oxford University Press USA, 1998.
Bin, Alberto, Richard Hill, and Archer Jones. *Desert Storm: A Forgotten War.* Westport, CT: Praeger, 1998.
Kent, Zachary. *The Persian Gulf War: "The Mother of All Battles."* Berkeley Heights, NJ: Enslow Publishers, 2000.
Williams, Paul L. *Al Qaeda: Brotherhood of Terror.* Upper Saddle River, NJ: Alpha (Pearson), 2002.

# MOUNTAIN THRUST, Operation
**Start Date: June 14, 2006**
**End Date: July 31, 2006**

A multinational, U.S.-led coalition campaign against the Taliban and Al Qaeda in southern Afghanistan from June 14 to July 31, 2006. By the spring of 2006, the Taliban and allied foreign fighters had dramatically increased attacks against Afghan national targets and coalition forces in southern Afghanistan. Coalition military leaders thus decided to undertake a large offensive against the rebels to destroy their growing network of compounds and to disrupt supply routes from Pakistan. Operation MOUNTAIN THRUST was the largest coalition campaign in Afghanistan since the initial 2001 invasion and was centered on the provinces of Helmand and Uruzgan. The principal objective of MOUNTAIN THRUST was to pacify the provinces so that they might be turned over to the North Atlantic Treaty Organization (NATO)–led International Security Assistance Force (ISAF) to begin major reconstruction efforts.

Coalition forces included some 11,500 troops from the United States, Australia, Canada, the Netherlands, Romania, the United Kingdom, and the Afghan National Army. The largest contributors were the Afghans, with 3,500 troops; followed by the British, with 3,300; the United States, with 2,300; and Canada, with 2,200. Coalition forces ranged from special operations forces to mechanized units to infantry. The forces were initially brought into the country through Bagram Air Base and Kandahar and then moved south. Coordinating the movement was a monumental task as logistics planners had to integrate transport from several different nations. U.S. logistics transported food, medicine, and other supplies to allow individual national assets to concentrate on the supply of ammunition and troops. Opposing the coalition were an estimated 2,500 chiefly Taliban insurgents who had spent the previous winter and spring rearming and preparing defensive encampments.

Operation MOUNTAIN THRUST began on June 14 with the insertion of special operations forces and targeted air strikes. Ground operations on June 15 resulted in 40 Taliban killed and 12 captured. Three days later U.S. forces were inserted in the Baghran Valley in Helmand Province to disrupt a major Taliban supply route. The U.S. outpost faced a series of Taliban attacks but was able to repel the insurgents through concentrated fire and air support. Throughout the campaign, the Taliban repeatedly launched aggressive attacks and counterattacks on coalition forces. They also frequently conducted mortar and rocket attacks on coalition forces under the cover of darkness and began to use improvised explosive devices and land mines extensively on roadways and trails. In a major counterattack toward the end of the operation in July, Taliban forces were able to seize two towns in Helmand from Afghan forces. Both were subsequently recaptured by coalition forces.

During the operation, more than 1,100 insurgents were killed and 387 others captured. Coalition forces destroyed dozens of compounds and seized a range of weaponry. Among those killed on the allied side were 24 U.S. troops, 4 Canadians, and 107 soldiers of the Afghan National Army. Following MOUNTAIN THRUST, which officially ended on July 31, the United States transferred control of Helmand Province to the ISAF. However, the Taliban regrouped and launched a new round of attacks the following year.

TOM LANSFORD

See also

Afghanistan, Coalition Combat Operations in, 2002–Present; Al Qaeda; International Security Assistance Force; North Atlantic Treaty Organization in Afghanistan; Taliban; Taliban Insurgency, Afghanistan

References

Feickert, Andrew. *U.S. and Coalition Military Operations in Afghanistan: Issues for Congress.* Washington, DC: Congressional Research Service, 2006.

Guistozzi, Antonio. *Koran, Kalashnikov and Laptop: The Neo-Taliban Insurgency in Afghanistan.* New York: Columbia University Press, 2008.

Jones, Seth G. *Counterinsurgency in Afghanistan: RAND Counterinsurgency Study No. 4.* Santa Monica, CA: RAND Corporation, 2008.

# Moussaoui, Zacarias
## Birth Date: May 30, 1968

One of several individuals accused of being the "twentieth member" of the suicide hijacking mission of September 11, 2001, Zacarias Moussaoui (Zakariyya Musawwi) was born on May 30, 1968, in St. Jean-de-Luz, near Narbonne, France, to Moroccan parents. During Moussaoui's youth, his family moved around France before finally settling down in Narbonne. Moussaoui spent a year in an orphanage and had frequent and furious arguments with his mother, forcing him to leave home in 1986. A good student, he easily passed his vocational baccalaureate. After passing entrance exams, he opted to study mechanical and electrical engineering at a school in Perpignon. Moussaoui transferred to the University of Montpellier's Economic and Social Administration program, but he had begun to tire of school when the Persian Gulf War began in January 1991.

The plight of Iraqi civilians and Palestinians concerned Moussaoui, and he became increasingly politicized. He had experienced racism in France, and his sympathy for Muslim causes increased. While at the University of Montpellier, he came into contact with Muslim students advocating extremist Islamist views. He made a six-month visit to London in 1992, but his stay in England proved disillusioning when he claimed he found British society intolerant and class-ridden. This experience did not prevent him from returning to England, where he stayed for the next three years. He attended the South Bank University in London, studying international business. Moussaoui earned his degree in 1995 and moved back to Montpellier.

Some time during his stay in England, he was attracted to the salafi jihadist cause, perhaps by the militant Islamic teacher Abu Qatada in London. His behavior during visits to France and Morocco alarmed his family. Apparently Al Qaeda recruiters convinced him to join the terrorist group.

Between 1995 and 2001 Moussaoui's association with Al Qaeda became even closer. He received training in Afghanistan at Al Qaeda's Khaldan camp in 1998, at the same time as Muhammad Atta. Moussaoui's trainers found him enthusiastic but questioned his stability. He was finally recruited for a future suicide mission, but little evidence exists to show that it was the September 11, 2001, plot. The Al Qaeda leadership had other plans for him, and he wanted to work on a Boeing 747 simulator, unlike the hijackers of the September 11 bombings, who trained exclusively on 757 and 767 simulators.

In the hope of becoming a pilot Moussaoui entered the United States, arriving at Chicago's O'Hare Airport on February 23, 2001, with a 90-day visa. Within days of his arrival, he began learning to fly small aircraft at the Airman Flight School in Norman, Oklahoma, but he became frustrated by his lack of progress after failing the written examination. After looking at other pilot schools, Moussaoui contacted the Pan Am International Flight Academy in Eagan, Minnesota, near Minneapolis, hoping to learn how to fly the huge Boeing 747-400. After only a few days of training in mid-August, the school's instructors became suspicious of Moussaoui, who showed more interest in flying than in either taking off or landing. He also inquired about the protocols used for communicating with flight towers and asked about cockpit doors. After a meeting of Mousaaoui's instructors, one volunteered to contact a friend in the Minneapolis Federal Bureau of Investigation (FBI) field office. Instead, the call went to FBI Special Agent Harry Samit, a U.S. Navy aviation veteran and small-engine pilot who was immediately suspicious of Moussaoui.

The Minneapolis FBI field office was part of the Joint Terrorism Task Force (JTTF) system, and a brief investigation showed that Moussaoui's visa had expired on May 22, 2001. This led the Immigration and Naturalization Service (INS) agent in the JTTF to authorize the arrest of Moussaoui on August 16, 2001. Moussaoui refused to allow the FBI agents to search his belongings but agreed to allow them to be taken to the local INS building. Because of Moussaoui's French citizenship, the FBI requested information concerning him from French authorities, who deemed Moussaoui dangerous and conveyed this to the FBI office in Minneapolis.

The Minneapolis FBI agents sought a search warrant to examine Moussaoui's belongings—in particular, his laptop computer—but ran into difficulties at FBI headquarters in Washington, D.C. FBI headquarters found insufficient cause for a criminal warrant. The agents' request for a court-issued warrant was denied because Moussaoui was not affiliated with a recognized terrorist group, even though Moussaoui had contacts with Chechen rebels and close ties to Al Qaeda.

After the September 11 attacks, the political climate changed, and Moussaoui became a key target for retribution. U.S. federal prosecutors charged Moussaoui with capital crimes, accusing him of six acts: preparing acts of terrorism, conspiracy to hijack an aircraft, destruction of an aircraft, use of weapons of mass destruction, murder of American officials, and destruction of property, even though Moussaoui had been in jail for twenty-five days when the events of September 11 occurred. Moreover, doubt still lingered about Moussaoui's role in the September 11 plot. The FBI had difficulty in proving that had Moussaoui cooperated with authorities, the September 11 attacks could have been prevented.

Nevertheless, U.S. Attorney General John Ashcroft insisted that the Justice Department seek the death penalty. Opposition to this position arose within the Justice Department, because a death sentence would make plea-bargaining impossible. Although Moussaoui had information about Al Qaeda, no attempt was made to extract it from him.

Moussaoui's 2006 trial was a national event, and his irrational behavior and sudden guilty plea created even more controversy. It became apparent that Moussaoui *sought* martyrdom. During the sentencing, prosecutors argued for the death sentence, but in May 2006 a dubious jury handed him a life sentence without chance of parole instead, reflecting Moussaoui's alleged role as an Al Qaeda operative who intended to commit acts of terror rather than any action he might have taken. Moussaoui is now serving his sentence at a federal maximum-security prison.

STEPHEN A. ATKINS

**See also**

Al Qaeda; September 11 Attacks

**References**

Graham, Bob. *Intelligence Matters: The CIA, the FBI, Saudi Arabia, and the Failure of America's War on Terror.* New York: Random House, 2004.

Hersh, Seymour. *Chain of Command: The Road from 9/11 to Abu Ghraib.* New York: HarperCollins, 2004.

*Joint Inquiry into Intelligence Community Activities before and after the Terrorist Attacks of September 11, 2001, Hearings before the Select Committee on Intelligence U.S. Senate and the Permanent Select Committee on Intelligence House of Representatives,* Vol. 2. Washington, DC: U.S. Government Printing Office, 2004.

Moussaoui, Abd Samar, with Florence Bouquillat. *Zacarias, My Brother: The Making of a Terrorist.* New York: Seven Stories, 2003.

---

# Mubarak, Hosni
## Birth Date: May 4, 1928

Egyptian Air Force air marshal and since 1981 president of Egypt. Muhammad Hosni Said Mubarak was born on May 4, 1928, in Kafr al-Musayliha, a town in the Nile River delta Egyptian governorate of Minufiyyah, where his father was an inspector in the Ministry of Justice. Mubarak graduated from the Egyptian Military Academy in 1949 and the Egyptian Air Force Academy at Bilbeis in 1950, from which he earned a degree in aviation sciences. He briefly was a fighter pilot before teaching at the Air Force Academy during 1952–1959. He continued his military training at the Soviet General Staff Academy in Moscow during 1964–1965, followed by advanced flight training at the Soviet air base at Frunze Bishkek in what was then Soviet Kyrgyzstan.

Mubarak advanced steadily in the Egyptian Air Force from pilot to instructor, squadron leader, base commander (Western Air Force Base, Cairo West Airfield), head of the Egyptian Military Delegation to the Soviet Union (1964), commandant of the Egyptian Air Force Academy (1967–1969), chief of staff of the Egyptian Air Force (1969–1972) during the War of Attrition (1967–1970), and then deputy minister of war (1972–1975). The early success of the Egyptian Air Force in the October 1973 Yom Kippur (Ramadan) War with Israel was attributed in large part to Mubarak's leadership and led to his promotion to air marshal in 1974.

In April 1975 Egyptian president Anwar Sadat appointed Mubarak as vice president. Three years later Mubarak was chosen to serve as the vice chairman of the ruling National Democratic Party (NDP). In October 1981 Sadat was assassinated by Muslim extremists. Mubarak was injured, although not seriously, in the attack. He then succeeded Sadat as president and became the chairman of the NDP.

Since the Sadat assassination, Mubarak has been elected to four additional six-year terms as Egyptian president, 1987, 1993, 1999, and 2005. Only in the 2005 elections were any other candidates allowed to run for president, and they were severely hampered by election rules. As president, Mubarak has mediated the dispute among Morocco, Algeria, and Mauritania concerning the future of Western (Spanish) Sahara, and he has maintained sufficient neutrality in the Israeli-Palestinian conflict to mediate some of the elementary disputes of the Second Intifada that began in 2000. He also played a role in the bilateral agreement between Israel and the Palestine Liberation Organization (PLO) in 1993 that emerged from the Oslo Accords.

Although Mubarak supports Egypt's 1979 peace treaty with Israel under the Camp David Accords, Egypt's relations with other Arab countries nevertheless improved during his presidency. These ties had been badly strained by the 1979 peace accord. In 1989 Egypt was readmitted to the Arab League after being expelled for making peace with the Israelis. Its headquarters, originally in Cairo and then moved, were also relocated to the Egyptian capital. A nongovernmental boycott of cultural, educational, and political relations with Israel continued during his presidency.

Mubarak also played a key role in the 1991 Persian Gulf War. On August 2, 1990, Iraqi dictator Saddam Hussein sent his forces into Kuwait. The tiny nation was quickly overrun and occupied. After the 1990-imposed United Nations (UN) sanctions against Iraq—supported by Mubarak—failed to dislodge Iraq from Kuwait, Mubarak organized the Arab League's opposition to the invasion of Kuwait. Based largely on the Saudis' decision to allow the U.S.-led international military coalition to use their nation as a staging area, Mubarak decided to contribute approximately 38,500 troops to the coalition. Indeed, Egyptian infantry soldiers were among the first of the coalition to enter Kuwait. Mubarak certainly had no use for Hussein, whom he viewed as a threat and a potential source of regional destabilization, but he was also attracted to the Kuwaiti cause by Western incentives to join the fight. The West—with the United States in the lead—promised many coalition nations, including Egypt, significant economic assistance and debt forgiveness in return for their support and involvement in the war. After the war, Mubarak continued to support sanctions against the Hussein regime to force it to comply with UN mandates, including those relating to disarmament and weapons of mass destruction (WMD).

Egyptian president Muhammad Hosni Said Mubarak arrives in the United States at Andrews Air Force Base, Maryland, January 27, 1983. (U.S. Department of Defense)

But Mubarak dispatched no troops to the Anglo-American–led ouster of Hussein in the Iraq War that began in March 2003. Indeed, he spoke out against the war, arguing that it would complicate the War on Terror and create a "hundred Osamas." He held that resolution of the Arab-Israeli conflict should take precedence over the unseating of Hussein. Be that as it may, the United States continues to be Egypt's chief source of military equipment, also granting the country a smaller amount of economic aid. Since 2003, Egypt's relations with Russia have been strengthened, although Mubarak continues to forge a careful course of neutrality when dealing with the Americans and Russians.

Mubarak used the enormous power given to him under Egypt's 1971 constitution to continue the sweeping program of economic recovery instituted by Sadat and to implement privatization and rationalization policies pressed upon Egypt by the International Monetary Fund and the World Bank. But the large public sector is far from being dismantled. Mubarak's other major tasks have been to limit terrorism and control nonviolent opponents. In the late 1990s his government more directly confronted Islamic radicals, such as the Islamic Group and the Gamaat Islamiya. The latter was responsible for the killing of 60 foreign tourists at

Luxor in 1997. The more moderate Islamist group, the Muslim Brotherhood, along with many small secular parties, also oppose Mubarak and the present Egyptian state. Mubarak was unharmed in an assassination attempt by five assailants in June 1995 in Addis Ababa, Ethiopia, and was slightly wounded in a second assassination attempt in Port Said on September 6, 1999.

Mubarak's government has encouraged joint ventures and is generally supportive of big business, so much so that workers and segments of the military have periodically rioted and demonstrated their displeasure. In the 1980s and 1990s the Egyptian economy suffered from debt, lack of savings, a trade imbalance, and blows to the tourist industry. The government could not abandon the subsidies it provides to its large population with a very low per capita income, and unemployment only increased. Nonetheless, the economy offered a favorable opportunity for investors, especially in the construction sector. During 2004–2006 terrorist attacks again threatened the tourist industry. Since December 2006, labor protests, sit-ins, and strikes have occurred around the country, including a strike of 10,000 workers in the textile industry. Unemployment persists at high levels.

Mubarak has twice served as chairman of the Organization of African Unity (OAU), during 1989–1990 and again during 1993–1994. Although he remains dedicated to Arab unity, the peaceful resolution of Middle East conflicts, positive neutrality, Egyptian economic growth, and a secular non-Islamic Egyptian state, opposition to his rule in Egypt appears to be growing.

Much of the opposition stems from the almost complete power vested in the Egyptian executive branch, the lack of a pluralistic political process, and the repeated extensions of the Emergency Laws. In addition there is a great deal of opposition to the prospect of Mubarak's son Gamal succeeding him, yet Mubarak has never named a vice president. The Egyptian parliament is largely a pro forma body that merely rubber-stamps the wishes of the ruling party. Until 2005, presidential elections were seen as a sham. Vote rigging and election fraud was endemic until the judiciary was told to oversee the elections. When it did so and raised questions of fraud, some leading figures were punished. Corruption in general has been on the rise.

Until very recently, the media in Egypt has been one-dimensional and controlled by the state, which has further entrenched the political system. Although the state still controls the major networks and newspapers, a few independent media outlets have surfaced to offer mild criticism of the Mubarak government.

Mubarak has been able to retain a tight grip on power thanks to a large and loyal military and security establishment, which has responded to repeated assassination attempts against him, foiled coups, and faced a new set of Islamist radicals since 2003. In the past several years Mubarak has come under increasing international pressure to democratize Egypt. He made small steps in that direction and then reformed the constitution in the opposite direction. He jailed the leader of the tiny al-Ghad Party, Ayman Nur, for years, as well as the sociologist Sa'd Eddin Ibrahim. He

has also repeatedly arrested Muslim Brotherhood leaders prior to every election, and the police and security services have routinely employed torture or excessive force against demonstrators and prisoners.

Egypt lacks a pluralist system and, given Mubarak's long tenure, many Egyptians have known no other political leader. Egyptians do not therefore know what to expect, if he indeed steps down in 2011 as he has earlier stated to be his intention.

RICHARD EDWARDS, PAUL G. PIERPAOLI JR., AND SHERIFA ZUHUR

**See also**

Arab-Israeli Conflict, Overview; Arab League; Camp David Accords; DESERT STORM, Operation; Egypt; Egypt, Armed Forces; Islamic Radicalism; Israel-Egypt Peace Treaty; Muslim Brotherhood; Sadat, Muhammad Anwar

**References**

Cox, Viki. *Hosni Mubarak*. Philadelphia: Chelsea House, 2002.
Kassem, Maye. *Egyptian Politics: The Dynamics of Authoritarian Rule*. Boulder, CO: Lynne Rienner, 2004.
McDermott, Anthony. *Egypt from Nasser to Mubarak: A Flawed Revolution*. London: Routledge and Kegan Paul, 1998.
Tripp, Charles, and Roger Owen. *Egypt under Mubarak*. London: Routledge, 1990.

## Muhammad, Prophet of Islam
Birth Date: ca. 569
Death Date: 632

Prophet of Islam who established the first community of Muslims in the Arabian Peninsula in the seventh century. Muhammad ibn Abdullah ibn Abd al-Mutallib, born in 569 or 570 CE and always referred to by Muslims as the Prophet Muhammad, was at once a military, political, and religious leader who effectively united the disparate tribes of the region into a single empire. As a prophet of Allah (God), he received a series of orally transmitted revelations that were eventually transcribed as the Qur'an; therefore, the Qur'an is referred to as the Message, and he, the Messenger. The Prophet Muhammad is called the Seal of Prophecy, which means that he, following the earlier prophets of the Bible and Jesus, was the last and final prophet. Unlike Jesus, the Prophet Muhammad is not considered to be a divine figure, but he is revered by Muslims as the Beautiful Model because his Sunna, or Way, provided the example for future generations of Muslims.

Muhammad was born into a branch of an important clan, the Banu Hashim of the Quraysh tribe, in Mecca, located in the western Arabian Peninsula area of the Hejaz. Prior to his birth, his father died. Thus Muhammad was, in the status of that era, an orphan. As an infant, he was sent, as was the custom, to a wet nurse, Halima, a tribal woman. While in her care there were signs and portents of his future greatness. Muhammad's mother died when he was six years old, and his grandfather, Abd al-Mutallib, died just two years later. Muhammad then passed under the guardianship of his uncle, Abu Talib, who was an influential merchant. Muhammad soon began accompanying his uncle on trading journeys during the pilgrimage season. On one journey to Bosra, Syria, he was greeted by a monk named Buhaira, who hailed Muhammad as a future prophet.

As an adult, Muhammad entered the employ of Khadija (555–619), a wealthy 40-year-old widow, and managed her caravans, earning a reputation for honesty such that he was known as al-Amin ("the faithful one"). Khadija subsequently proposed to him. The two married in 595, and Muhammad remained devoted to her until her death in 619. The number of children born to the marriage remains in dispute. The pair had four daughters—Zaynab, Ruqayya, Umm Kulthum, and Fatima—and one or two sons who died. Only Fatima was still living after her father's death. Muhammad married other women after Khadija's death, and he had a son by one of these wives who also died before the son was 2 years old. Of Muhammad's other wives, Aisha was said to be his favorite.

According to Muslim tradition, Muhammad received his first revelation in the year 610 while fasting in the cave of Hira, near Mecca during the month of Ramadan. He heard the voice of the archangel Gabriel, who commanded him to recite verses of scripture, which Gabriel spoke to Muhammad. At first Muhammad did not know how to respond to his experience, but Khadija regarded his words as proof of a new revelation and thus became the first formal convert to Islam. For the remainder of his life, Muhammad continued to receive revelations. Within a few years of his initial revelations, he began to preach to any who would listen to his message about the One God, Creator and Judge of the World. As the Meccans then worshiped a pantheon of gods and goddesses, they were not very impressed with his message and later became increasingly hostile toward him.

As Muhammad's group of followers grew, the leadership of Mecca, including Muhammad's own tribe, perceived them as a threat. Some of the early converts to Islam came from the disaffected and disadvantaged segments of society. Most important, the Muslims' new set of beliefs implicitly challenged the Meccans' and the Quraysh tribe's guardianship over the Kaaba, the holy site dedicated to the gods and goddesses of the area, which hosted an annual pilgrimage. The city's leading merchants attempted to persuade Muhammad to cease his preaching, but he refused. In response, the city leadership persecuted Muhammad's followers, and many fled the city. One group of his followers immigrated to Abyssinia. In 619 Muhammad endured the loss of both Khadija and Abu Talib, while the mistreatment of his followers increased.

The following year Muhammad undertook two miraculous journeys with the archangel Gabriel. The first, called the Isra, took Muhammad from Mecca to Jerusalem, where he ascended to the site of today's Dome of the Rock in the al-Aqsa Compound in Jerusalem. The second, called the Miraj, included a visit to heaven and hell. During the Miraj, Muhammad also spoke with earlier monotheistic prophets, including Abraham, Moses, and Jesus, and saw Allah, "the Soul of Souls, the Face of Him who made the universe."

Muhammad asked Allah for forgiveness for his ummah, the Muslim community, and Allah accepted his intercession (shafa'). Allah assigned Muhammad with the task of 50 daily prayers for Muslims, and Moses advised Muhammad to return to Allah and request the number of prayers be reduced to 5, which he did. The Isra and Miraj were accomplished in a single night. Scholars have presented the travels as both a spiritual vision and an actual physical experience.

In 622 Muhammad decided to leave the city of his birth at the invitation of groups residing in the city of Yathrib. Yathrib was located at a major oasis, and there Muhammad hoped to firmly establish a new community of Muslims free from the persecution of the Meccans. The immigration to Yathrib, called the Hijra, marks the beginning of the Muslim calendar. When Muhammad arrived in Yathrib he found a city divided by competing tribes, the Aws and the Khazraj. Both soon converted to Islam, uniting under Muhammad after a century of fighting. Yathrib later took the name of Madinat al-Nabi, or City of the Prophet. With the exception of a sizable Jewish community divided into three clans, the city of Medina was entirely under Muhammad's control by 624. At Medina, the rituals of Islam were established.

After Muhammad and most of his followers departed Mecca for Yathrib, the Meccans confiscated all Muslim property that had been left behind. In 624 Muhammad led an abortive raid on a Meccan caravan. In retaliation, 1,000 Meccan warriors marched on Medina. Not content to await the attack, Muhammad led a force of approximately 300 warriors to meet the invading army. At Badr the armies collided, and Muhammad's followers achieved a decisive victory, inflicting more than 100 casualties at a cost of only 14 Muslims and driving off the Meccan army.

In 625 a Meccan army of 3,000 returned to menace Medina. Emboldened by the victory at Badr, Muhammad marched his army out of the city to face the enemy. At the Battle of Uhud the Muslims were defeated, but the Meccan leader, Abu Sufyan, chose to withdraw his army rather than raze Medina. Two years later Abu Sufyan again attacked Medina but failed to destroy Muhammad's army at the Battle of the Trench. In 628 Muhammad led a band of 1,400 followers to Mecca, ostensibly as a pilgrimage, or hajj. They were refused entry to the city, although the differences between the Meccans and the Muslims were formally abolished in the Treaty of Hudhaybiyya. The truce lasted only two years. Renewed skirmishing led Muhammad to attack Mecca directly.

Eight years of converting other client tribes on the Arabian Peninsula provided Muhammad with an army of more than 10,000 followers, far too numerous for the Meccans to withstand. The polytheistic statues at the Kaaba in Mecca were destroyed, and the majority of the populace converted to Islam. Following the conquest, Mecca became the heart of the Muslim empire, which rapidly unified the competing tribes of the region.

Muhammad did not live long after consolidating his power. In 632 he fell ill in Medina, and after several days of pain and weakness he died. He was buried in a plot adjacent to his house. His followers quickly moved to expand his legacy, moving out of the Arabian Peninsula to challenge the Sassanians and the client tribes of the Eastern Roman (Byzantine) Empire. Eventually they conquered lands stretching from Central Asia to the Iberian Peninsula. However, political divisions coupled with external threats created competing dynasties rather than a united Muslim empire and also led to the growth of religious sects and varying intellectual trends within the religion and Muslim culture.

In nearly all these sects the Prophet Muhammad is honored to this day. His birthday is celebrated, and he has been a favorite subject of Muslim poets. The stories of his deeds and words, collected into the Hadith, remain an important source of religious law and history.

Modern Islam is one of the largest religions in the world, with approximately 1.3 billion adherents spanning the globe.

PAUL J. SPRINGER AND SHERIFA ZUHUR

**See also**

Allah; Jihad; Qur'an; Shia Islam; Sunni Islam

**References**

Cook, M. A. *Muhammad.* New York: Oxford University Press, 1983.

Haykal, Muhammad Husayn. *The Life of Muhammad.* Translated by Isma'il R. al-Faruqi. Indianapolis: North American Trust Publications, 1976.

Schimmel, Annemarie. *And Muhammad Is His Messenger: The Veneration of the Prophet in Islamic Piety.* Chapel Hill: University of North Carolina Press, 1985.

Watt, W. Montgomery. *Muhammad at Mecca.* Oxford, UK: Clarendon, 1953.

———. *Muhammad at Medina.* Oxford, UK: Clarendon, 1962.

Weinberger, Eliot. *Muhammad.* New York: Verso, 2006.

# Muhammarah, Treaty of

Treaty signed on May 5, 1922, at Muhammarah (present-day Khorramshahr in southeastern Iran) that attempted to prevent war between Great Britain and the Kingdom of Najd (present-day Saudi Arabia) on the Arabian Peninsula and to establish arbitrary and informal boundaries between that kingdom and British-held Iraq. The Treaty of Muhammarah was quickly superseded by the Protocol (Treaty) of Uqair, signed in December 1922.

Prior to World War I, British Middle East foreign policy and military strategy focused on keeping their land and sea lines of communication open through Mesopotamia and the Suez Canal. In December 1915 Britain and Abdul Aziz ibn Abdul Rahman ibn Saud, of the Kingdom of Najd, signed a treaty of friendship, in which Britain recognized the independence of the Najd.

On May 16, 1916, without Arab knowledge, the British and French secretly concluded the Sykes-Picot Agreement, which divided the Ottoman Empire between them. This agreement conflicted with pledges given by the British government to Hussein Ibn Ali, leader of the Hashemite Kingdom and Sharif of Mecca. Because the Ottomans had sided with the Germans in World War I, the British induced Hussein, with promises of independence and

land grants, to lead the Arabs of the Hijaz against the Turks. This Arab Revolt began on June 5, 1916. In anticipation of independence, Hussein proclaimed himself King of the Arabs in November 1916. Britain and France recognized only his suzerainty over the Hijaz, however.

Ottoman rule over Muslim lands ended with the signing of the Mudros Armistice at the end of the war on October 30, 1918. Problems involving tribal and ethnic boundaries and migratory routes now came to the fore. Arab nationalists wanted one nation, and they requested Sir Percy Cox, the first British High Commissioner under the League of Nations Mandate, to legislate this Arab state into existence. Ibn Saud wanted a boundary reflecting tribal areas, but Cox demurred.

On April 24, 1920, the San Remo Conference formally designated Britain as exercising a mandate for Iraq, and on May 3, 1920, the British government formally accepted. Arab unrest over the solution was quickly suppressed, but Amir Faisal El-Hashemi was put forward as king of Iraq and was formally crowned on August 23, 1921.

Faisal immediately had to deal with the matter of boundaries, for there was no formal delineation between Mesopotamia, the Najd, and the Hijaz. Ibn Saud now sought to consolidate his own power by seizing and occupying lands in the Hijaz. His presumed intent included securing Mesopotamia as a step toward creating a unified Arab nation. The Treaty of Muhammarah of the spring of 1922 was an effort to frustrate his objectives. The treaty did not stipulate a boundary between Iraq and the Najd, but both sides agreed in principle to implement measures to prevent tribes from seizing and occupying Mesopotamian lands. Ibn Saud refused to ratify the treaty, however, over concerns involving both grazing rights and certain tribal allegiances.

The Treaty of Muhammarah never came into force. It was superseded by the Treaty of Uqair of December 2, 1922, which created the Iraqi–Kuwait Neutral Zone—the first such demarcation in the Middle East. Tribes could cross back and forth, but no military forces or fortifications could be built near any wells or oases.

The resulting boundary was 426 miles long. Surveys to demarcate the boundary on the ground have never been undertaken. One of Iraqi dictator Saddam Hussein's justifications for his August 1990 invasion of Kuwait was that Kuwait was historically part of Iraq. His assertion echoed the argument made by Iraqi nationalists from the mid-1920s: namely, that both Iraq and Kuwait were within the same administrative unit of the Ottoman Empire. Iraq has no legitimate claim to Kuwait, however, because the two nations officially and legally accepted the Iraq-Kuwait border when they signed the "Agreed Minutes between the State of Kuwait and the Republic of Iraq Regarding the Restoration of Friendly Relations, Recognition, and Related Matters" in 1932. In 1993 the United Nations (UN) Security Council unanimously approved a demarcation of an Iraq-Kuwait boundary. Saudi Arabia registered this boundary with the UN in 1995, even though Iraq refused to accept it.

Currently there are no active disputes between Saudi Arabia and Iraq over this boundary. Iraq's historical animosity toward

Kuwait over this matter and other border issues, as well as over certain access rights, could continue until a formal Iraq-Kuwait border is set by an actual survey on the ground.

DONALD R. DUNNE

**See also**

Iraq, History of, Pre-1990; Kuwait; Saudi Arabia; Uqair, Treaty of

**References**

Held, Colbert C. *Middle East Patterns: Places, Peoples, and Politics.* 4th ed. Boulder, CO: Westview, 2006.

Kemp, Geoffrey, and Robert E. Harkavy. *Strategic Geography and the Changing Middle East.* Washington, DC: Brookings Institution Press, 1997.

Mohd, El Ghoneimy Talaat. "The Legal Status of the Saudi-Kuwaiti Neutral Zone." *International and Comparative Law Quarterly* 15(3) (July 1966): 694–698.

## Mujahideen, Soviet-Afghanistan War

Afghan resistance fighters who fought against the Soviet-backed Kabul government and Soviet troops during the Soviet War in Afghanistan (1979–1989) were collectively known as the mujahideen. They were an alliance of seven Sunni political factions and eight Shiite organizations, as well as Muslim volunteers from various North African and Middle Eastern countries. Initially trained and funded by Pakistan's intelligence service, the Inter-Services Intelligence (ISI), and then later by the United States, the United Kingdom, Saudi Arabia, Iran, the People's Republic of China (PRC) as well as other Sunni Muslim nations, the mujahideen fought the Soviet Union to a bloody stalemate, forcing it to withdraw its troops from Afghanistan in 1989.

The Soviet invasion of Afghanistan on December 27, 1979, and subsequent intervention in Afghan domestic politics in support of the People's Democratic Party of Afghanistan (PDPA) had the unintended consequence of galvanizing a disparate Islamic opposition into a grassroots resistance movement. Indeed, the Soviet invasion triggered a backlash among Afghans that crossed kinship, tribal, ethnic, and geographic lines. It gave the conflict an ideological dimension by linking the Islamic insurgency with the goal of national liberation when mullahs issued declarations of jihad against the Soviet invaders. Islam and nationalism became interwoven as an Islamist ideology replaced tribal affiliations.

At the onset of the Soviet War in Afghanistan, the mujahideen were divided along regional, ethnic, tribal, and sectarian lines. Mobilization was linked to allegiances of the tribal *lashkar* (fighting force), as the mujahideen were loosely organized tribal militias under the command of traditional leaders at the local level. Membership was fluid, fluctuating by the season and family commitments, with no coordinated central command structure.

An Afghan mujahideen ("one engaged in struggle" jihad), demonstrates the firing technique for a surface-to-air Stinger missile in 1988, when the United States supported the mujahideen against Soviet forces in Afghanistan. The Soviets withdrew the next year. (U.S. Department of Defense)

Mujahideen commanders owed their position to social standing, education, leadership ability, and commitment to Islam.

Seven major Sunni mujahideen factions based in neighboring Peshawar, Pakistan, came to dominate the political and military landscape. These were Islamic Unity for the Liberation of Afghanistan (IULI), Hezb-i-Islami Afghanistan (HIA), Jamiat-i-Islami (IA), Hezb-i-Islami (HI), Harakat-i-Inquilabi Islami (IRM), Mahaz-ye Nijate Milli Afghanistan (NIFA), and the Jabhe-ye Nijate Milli Afghanistan (NLF). In addition to the Sunni mujahideen factions, there were Shia mujahideen organizations as well. These were Shura, Nasr, Harlat-eIslami, the Revolutionary Guards, and Hezbollah. The other organizations were either splinter factions or groups that joined larger movements. In March 1980 the Sunni mujahideen factions created an umbrella organization known as Islamic Alliance for the Liberation of Afghanistan to lobby for international recognition and support.

In the early days of the occupation, the Soviets waged classic large-scale armored warfare in Afghanistan. The mujahideen responded with traditional mass tribal charges. Disorganized, having limited military equipment and training, and facing overwhelming military superiority, the mujahideen were easily defeated in early skirmishes with the Soviet army in 1980 and 1981. As desertions and defections of Afghan army units began to increase, however, the mujahideen military capacity increased.

By 1982 the mujahideen began to counter Soviet offensives with a change in tactics and increased firepower. Unable to pacify the countryside, Soviet troops deployed in strategic areas, occupying cities and garrison towns and controlling supply routes. This allowed the mujahideen to roam freely throughout the countryside, launching raids and ambushes at will. Having an insufficient number of troops to pursue the mujahideen, the Soviets attempted to deprive them of their base support by depopulating the countryside. Villages, crops, and irrigation systems were destroyed, while fields and pastures were mined. Undeterred by the loss of their support, the mujahideen continued to sabotage power lines, pipelines, and government installations as well as knocking out bridges, assaulting supply convoys, disrupting the power supply and industrial production, and attacking Soviet military bases throughout 1982 and 1983.

As the war broadened, the mujahideen appealed for arms and ammunition to counter the overwhelming Soviet military superiority. In 1983 the United States, the United Kingdom, Saudi Arabia, and the PRC became major contributors to the mujahideen cause. Money and weapons were funneled through Pakistan for distribution to the various Sunni *mujahideen* factions. The mujahideen were now able to counter the Soviet military superiority with increased firepower.

The year 1985 proved an important one for the mujahideen. The mujahideen withstood the massive deployment of Soviet forces designed to impose a favorable outcome within a Moscow-set timeframe, and the seven Sunni mujahideen factions formed the Seven Party Mujahideen Alliance to coordinate their military operations against the Soviet Army. By late 1985 the mujahideen had closed in on Kabul, conducting operations against the Moscow-backed Kabul government.

In the spring of 1986, a combined Soviet-Afghan force captured a major mujahideen base in Zhawar, Pakistan, inflicting heavy losses. It was also about this time that the mujahideen acquired antiaircraft missiles as well as ground-to-ground rockets (the U.S. Stinger and the British Blowpipe) that altered the course of the war. The mujahideen were now able to take down Soviet helicopters, especially the heavily armored Mi-24 Hind attack helicopter, and airplanes. By the time Soviet leader Mikhail Gorbachev decided to withdraw Soviet forces from Afghanistan in the spring of 1989, the mujahideen were content to allow them an orderly retreat as they themselves readied to attack Kabul and replace the Soviet-backed government there. Many historians today credit the mujahideen, at least in part, for the fall of the Soviet Union in 1991. The war cost the Soviet state billions of dollars it did not have, and called into question the wisdom of the government.

KEITH A. LEITICH

**See also**

Afghanistan; Aircraft, Helicopters, Soviet-Afghanistan War; Soviet Union, Middle East Policy

**References**

Bradsher, Henry St. Amant. *Afghan Communism and Soviet Intervention.* Oxford: Oxford University Press, 1999.

Brigot, Andre, and Oliver Roy. *The War in Afghanistan: An Account and Analysis of the Country, Its People, Soviet Intervention and the Resistance.* Translated by Mary and Tom Bottomore. Brighton, UK: Wheatsheaf, 1988.

Farr, Grant M., and John G. Merriam, eds. *Afghan Resistance: The Politics of Survival.* Boulder, CO: Westview, 1987.

Hyman, Anthony. *Afghan Resistance: Danger from Disunity.* London: Institute for the Study of Conflict, 1984.

Kakar, M. Hasan. *Afghanistan: The Soviet Invasion and the Afghan Response, 1979–1982.* Berkeley: University of California Press, 1995.

Kaplan, Robert D. *Soldiers of God: With Islamic Warriors in Afghanistan and Pakistan.* Boston: Houghton Mifflin, 1990.

Tanner, Stephen. *Afghanistan: A Military History from Alexander the Great to the Fall of the Taliban.* New York: Da Capo, 2003.

# Mulholland, John
## Birth Date: September 1, 1957

U.S. Army officer who was particularly instrumental in combat operations during Operation ENDURING FREEDOM and the fall of the Taliban regime in Afghanistan in late 2001. John F. Mulholland was born on September 1, 1957, in Clovis, New Mexico, but spent his formative years in Bethesda, Maryland. He graduated from Furman University in South Carolina with a bachelor's degree in history in 1978, and received a commission in the U.S. Army as a second lieutenant in the infantry through its Reserve Officers' Training Program (ROTC).

Mulholland served at U.S. bases in the Panama Canal Zone during 1979–1982. He then entered the Special Forces. Upon graduation from the Qualification Course in 1983, he was assigned to the 5th Special Forces Group (Airborne) stationed at Fort Bragg, North Carolina, from 1983 to 1986. While with the group, he served as an Operational Detachment-A commander as a captain. He also served as a Special Forces company commander. In 1987 Mulholland returned to Panama attached to U.S. Southern Command. He returned to the United States in 1989.

Mulholland then attended both the Defense Language Institute and the Army Command and General Staff College (CGSC). While at the CGSC, he earned a master's degree in military arts and science.

In 1991 Mulholland was assigned to the 1st Battalion, 7th Special Forces Group (Airborne) as operations officer and later as executive officer. Following this tour of duty, in 1993 Mulholland was transferred to a staff position in the headquarters company of the U.S. Army Special Operations Command until 1996.

That same year, Mulholland was promoted to lieutenant colonel and given command of the 1st Battalion, 1st Special Forces Group (Airborne) stationed in Tori Station, Japan. He held that post during 1996–1998, then transferred to Washington, D.C., where he worked in the Office of Military Support until 2000. He attended the National War College and earned a Master of Science degree in national security strategy in 2001. In September 2001 he was promoted to colonel and assumed command of the 5th Special Forces Group (Airborne) at Fort Campbell, Kentucky.

In retaliation for the September 11, 2001, terrorist attacks the United States and its allies undertook Operation ENDURING FREEDOM against the Al Qaeda terrorist organization and the Taliban regime in Afghanistan. Unlike many previous combat operations, ENDURING FREEDOM was at first the domain of Special Forces. Fighting began on October 7, 2001. Members of 5th Special Forces Group worked closely with Northern Alliance Forces of Afghans already locked in combat against the Taliban.

After helping to equip and train Northern Alliance fighters, Special Forces operators began a ground offensive. The offensive involved the use of U.S. and allied air power to destroy enemy positions and indigenous forces to capture Taliban-held positions and towns. This pattern continued throughout the country, with the fall of Kabul, the Afghan capital, on November 12, 2001. Further actions continued as the allies attempted to capture Taliban and Al Qaeda leadership. Throughout these operations, Mulholland had command of the 5th Special Forces Group (Airborne) and all United States commando forces in theater.

In early 2003 Mulholland was named chief of the Office of Military Cooperation in Kuwait, as a brigadier general. In 2005, now a major general, Mulholland assumed command of Special Operations Command Central at MacDill Air Force Base, Florida. In November 2008 he was promoted to lieutenant general and became commander of the U.S. Army Special Operations Command.

SHAWN LIVINGSTON

See also

ENDURING FREEDOM, Operation

References

Briscoe, Charles H. *Weapon of Choice: U.S. Army Special Operations Forces in Afghanistan.* Washington, DC: U.S. Army, 2003.

MacPherson, Malcolm. *Roberts Ridge: A Story of Courage and Sacrifice on Takur Ghar Mountain, Afghanistan.* New York: Bantam Dell, 2008.

Moore, Robin. *The Hunt for Bin Laden: Task Force Dagger.* New York: Random House, 2003.

"Mulholland to Lead Army Sf Command." *Special Warfare: The Professional Bulletin of the John F. Kennedy Special Warfare Center & School* 18(3) (2005): 6–6.

# Mullen, Michael Glenn
Birth Date: October 4, 1946

U.S. Navy admiral and chairman of the Joint Chiefs of Staff since 2007, Michael Glenn Mullen was born in Los Angeles, California, on October 4, 1946. After graduation from the U.S. Naval Academy at Annapolis, he was commissioned in the navy in 1968. He first served in the waters off Vietnam in a variety of surface warfare positions. Additional deployments and exercises took him to the

Admiral Michael Mullen was chief of U.S. Naval Operations during 2005–2007. He assumed the position of chairman of the Joint Chiefs of Staff (JCS) in 2007. (U.S. Department of Defense)

Caribbean and the Mediterranean. In 1973 Mullen assumed command of his first ship, the gasoline tanker *Noxubee.*

Mullen next reported to the U.S. Naval Academy, where he served as a company tactical officer and later as executive assistant to the commandant of midshipmen. He then returned to sea duty, gaining further experience aboard the guided missile cruisers *Fox* and *Sterett.* These ships featured increasingly advanced naval weapons systems with vastly improved capabilities that transformed naval operations during the 1980s. Mullen gained operational experience in the Western Pacific, Indian Ocean, and Red Sea.

In 1985 Mullen graduated from the Naval Postgraduate School in Monterrey, California with a master's degree in operations research. He then assumed command of the guided missile destroyer *Goldsborough.* Deploying to the Persian Gulf, he participated in the maritime escort of Kuwaiti oil tankers during the 1980–1988 Iran-Iraq War.

Following command of the *Goldsborough,* Mullen served as director of the division officer course at the Navy Surface Warfare Officer School and, following promotion to captain on September 1, 1989, became a staff officer in the office of the Secretary of Defense for the director, Operational Test and Evaluation Force. He then assumed command of the Ticonderoga-class cruiser *Yorktown,* conducting a broad range of missions, from support of the United Nations (UN) embargo of Haiti to counter-drug operations and joint and multinational exercises in the North Atlantic. Mullen was then assigned to the Bureau of Naval Personnel, where he served as the director, Surface Officer Distribution; and later as director, Surface Warfare Plans, Programs and Requirements Division. Still later, following his promotion to rear admiral on April 1, 1996, he became the bureau's deputy director, affording him invaluable experience in manpower and resource management.

Later in 1996 Mullen was named commander of Cruiser-Destroyer Group 2, in command of the ships, submarines, and aircraft of the *George Washington* Battle Group. The battle group deployed to the Mediterranean, where it participated in peacekeeping operations. The following year, it served as the cornerstone of the U.S. military presence in the Persian Gulf, compelling Iraq to comply with UN disarmament inspections, as well as enforcing the no-fly zone over southern Iraq. Following promotion to rear admiral on October 1, 1998, Mullen was chosen to serve as the director, Surface Warfare Division, Office of the Chief of Naval Operations. Responsible for the direction of acquisition plans and programs for the navy surface force, Mullen gained vital understanding of resource management, planning, programming, and budgeting.

On November 1, 2000, Mullen was promoted to vice admiral and was named the combined commander, U.S. Second Fleet and North Atlantic Treaty Organization (NATO) Striking Fleet Atlantic. Mullen soon found himself back in Washington, D.C., however, assuming responsibility for the direction and management of all navy acquisition programs as the deputy chief of Naval Operations for Resources, Requirements and Assessments. He guided the navy's resource decisions during critical reevaluations in the aftermath of the September 11, 2001, terror attacks, directing such key programs as the Next Generation Destroyer, Littoral Combat Ship, and Theater Ballistic Missile Defense. After two years as the navy resource director, Mullen was promoted to full admiral on August 28, 2003, and named the 32nd vice chief of naval operations. He had served as vice chief for just over a year when he was reassigned as the commander of the NATO Allied Joint Force Command Naples and simultaneously commander of U.S. Naval Forces Europe. Mullen immediately established clear priorities for these separate but closely connected commands, but as quickly as they were on course, Mullen was recalled to Washington.

On July 22, 2005, Mullen became the 28th chief of naval operations. He assumed command of a service facing issues of relevance, an apparent loss of operational significance, and the profound cost of continuing war in the Middle East. In response, Mullen committed the navy to easing the strain on the nation's land forces by assigning naval personnel to serve in an unusually broad range of supporting roles. Faced with a tight fiscal environment, Mullen ensured that the navy's budget priorities were clearly aligned with the realities of the strategic environment. In regard to the navy crisis of mission, Mullen immediately directed that a new maritime strategy be developed to guide the efforts of the nation's maritime services. After nearly two years of study and collaboration, "Cooperative Strategy for 21st Century Seapower" was released. It was the nation's first maritime strategy document developed collaboratively and signed by all three of the nation's maritime services, the navy, marines, and coast guard.

On October 1, 2007, Admiral Mullen was appointed the 17th chairman of the Joint Chiefs of Staff. He assumed the post amid the most divisive and politically charged environment since the Vietnam War era. Almost immediately, he demonstrated a pragmatic, long-term view of U.S. military requirements by voicing concern over the broader effects of continuing U.S. military commitments in Afghanistan and Iraq, and campaigned for a broad, strategic reassessment.

Mullen explained that a rebalancing of global strategic risks was needed, and that a comprehensive, sustainable long-term Middle East security strategy was a vital priority. He also asserted the requirement for a more balanced, flexible, and ready force. Describing a future characterized by persistent conflict and irregular warfare, but simultaneously uncertain and unpredictable, Mullen argued that U.S. forces must not only possess the ability to conduct counterinsurgency operations but also remain unmatched in their ability to fight a conventional war. Mullen helped secure legislation passed by Congress to increase military strength by 100,000 personnel. He also instituted efforts to ease the tempo of operational deployments and began a measured troop redeployment from Iraq.

Kenneth A. Szmed Jr.

**See also**

United States Navy, Afghanistan War; United States Navy, Iraq War; United States Navy, Persian Gulf War

**References**

Baer, George W. *One Hundred Years of Sea Power: The U.S. Navy, 1890–1990.* Stanford, CA: Stanford University Press, 1994.

Love, Robert W. *History of the U.S. Navy, 1775–1991.* Mechanicsburg, PA: Stackpole Books, 1992.

Polmar, Norman. *The Naval Institute Guide to the Ships and Aircraft of the U.S. Fleet.* 18th ed. Annapolis, MD: Naval Institute Press, 2005.

# Multi-National Force–Iraq

U.S.-led military command of coalition forces in Iraq, established on May 15, 2004. The Multi-National Force–Iraq (MNF-I) was created ostensibly to combat the growing Iraqi insurgency, which began in earnest in late 2003 and early 2004; it replaced Combined Joint Task Force 7, which had been in operation from June 2003 to May 2004.

Commanders of the MNF-I have included lieutenant generals Ricardo Sanchez (May–June 2004), George W. Casey (June 2004–January 2007), David Petraeus (January 2007–September 2008), and Raymond Odierno (September 2008–). The MNF-I was tasked with bringing the growing Iraqi insurgency to an end but was largely unsuccessful in that effort until the George W. Bush administration placed General Petraeus in command and implemented a troop surge that placed as many as 30,000 additional U.S. troops on the ground in Iraq. The strategy seemed to have worked, for violence had fallen off markedly beginning by late 2007; Petraeus was given much of the credit for this development. At the same time, the so-called Anbar Awakening groups in Iraq also helped to curb sectarian and insurgent violence. The current MNF-I commander, General Odierno, while acknowledging that the surge has provided strengthened security forces, credits a change in counterinsurgency strategy more than the surge itself in reducing the level of violence. Referring to it as an "Anaconda strategy," Odierno has explained the strategy as a comprehensive approach that has shown success in, among other areas, cutting off insurgents from their support within the Iraqi population.

Since its inception, the MNF-I has overwhelmingly comprised U.S. troops; the second-largest deployment is from Great Britain. The size of the MNF-I has been fluid, but on average it has contained around 150,000 combat-ready personnel, the vast majority of whom have been American. The troop surge brought the total closer to 180,000, but that number has dwindled as troop withdrawals began in 2008. Working with the MNF-I, but not falling under its direct command, are the United Nations (UN) Assistance Mission–Iraq, which provides humanitarian aid and observation, and the North Atlantic Treaty Organization (NATO) Training Mission–Iraq, whose goal is to train Iraqi security, police, and military personnel. The major component parts of the MNF-I are Multi-National Security Transition Command; Gulf Region Division; U.S. Corps of Engineers; Joint Base Balad; Multi-National Corps–Iraq; Multi-National Division–Baghdad; Multi-National Division–North; Multi-National Force–West; Multi-National Division Center; Multi-National Division–Southeast.

**Peak Troop Deployment of Former Members of the Multi-National Force–Iraq as of May 2009**

| Country | Peak Troop Strength | Withdrawal Date |
| --- | --- | --- |
| Albania | 240 | December 2008 |
| Armenia | 46 | October 2008 |
| Azerbaijan | 250 | December 2008 |
| Bosnia and Herzegovina | 85 | November 2008 |
| Bulgaria | 485 | December 2008 |
| Czech Republic | 300 | December 2008 |
| Denmark | 545 | December 2008 |
| Dominican Republic | 302 | May 2004 |
| El Salvador | 380 | January 2009 |
| Estonia | 40 | January 2009 |
| Georgia | 2,000 | August 2008 |
| Honduras | 368 | May 2004 |
| Hungary | 300 | March 2005 |
| Iceland | 2 | Date unknown |
| Italy | 3,200 | November 2006 |
| Japan | 600 | December 2008 |
| Kazakhstan | 29 | October 2008 |
| Latvia | 136 | November 2008 |
| Lithuania | 120 | August 2007 |
| Macedonia | 77 | November 2008 |
| Moldova | 24 | December 2008 |
| Mongolia | 180 | September 2008 |
| Netherlands | 1,345 | March 2005 |
| New Zealand | 61 | September 2004 |
| Nicaragua | 230 | February 2004 |
| Norway | 150 | August 2006 |
| Philippines | 51 | July 2004 |
| Poland | 2,500 | October 2008 |
| Portugal | 128 | February 2005 |
| Singapore | 175 | December 2008 |
| Slovakia | 110 | December 2007 |
| South Korea | 3,600 | December 2008 |
| Spain | 1,300 | April 2004 |
| Thailand | 423 | August 2004 |
| Tonga | 55 | December 2008 |
| Ukraine | 1,650 | December 2008 |
| Total | 21,487 | |

In addition to battling the Iraqi insurgency and other indigenous violence, other goals of the MNF-I include support and aid to the Iraqi government, reconstruction efforts, specialized training of Iraqi military personnel, intelligence-gathering, and border patrols. When the MNF-I is withdrawn in its entirety, it is expected that Iraq will have been pacified; will have a stable, representative democratic government; and will be able to protect itself from internal pressures and foreign intrusions. The December 2008 Status of Forces Agreement between the U.S. and Iraqi governments stipulates that all U.S. troops be withdrawn by December 31, 2011. Under the terms of this arrangement, U.S. troops vacated Iraqi cities by July 31, 2009. The Iraqis concluded similar agreements with other coalition forces that still maintained a presence in Iraq.

Numerous nations supplied troops to the MNF-I, many of which were withdrawn by the end of December 2008. The participating members, along with the size of their deployments include: United States (145,000 troops as of December 2008), Great Britain

(4,000 as of December 2008), Romania (500 as of December 2008), Australia (350 as of December 2008), El Salvador (300 as of December 2008), and Estonia (40 as of December 2008).

Those nations that participated but were withdrawn by December 31, 2008, include (figures in parentheses represent peak deployments): South Korea (3,600), Italy (3,200), Poland (2,500), Georgia (2,000), Ukraine (1,650), Netherlands (1,345), Spain (1,300), Japan (600), Denmark (545), Bulgaria (458), Thailand (423), Honduras (368), Dominican Republic (302), Czech Republic (300), Hungary (300), Azerbaijan (250), Albania (240), Nicaragua (230), Mongolia (180), Singapore (175), Norway (150), Latvia (136), Portugal (128), Lithuania (120), Slovakia (110), Bosnia-Herzegovina (85), Macedonia (77), New Zealand (61), Tonga (55), Philippines (51), Armenia (46), Kazakhstan (29), Moldova (24), and Iceland (2).

To entice potential coalition partners to join the MNF-I effort, the U.S. government offered a plethora of financial aid and other incentives. Because the invasion of Iraq had not been sanctioned by the UN, the United States found it more difficult to convince other nations to become involved in the postwar stabilization effort in Iraq. Some nations, and previously close allies, however, refused to take part in the mission, despite U.S. promises of financial and other rewards. The United States reportedly offered Turkey up to $8.5 billion in loans if the country sent peacekeeping troops to Iraq; Turkey, which had forbade the use of its bases during the March 2003 invasion of Iraq, demurred. France and Germany refused any participation in Iraq. Some countries, such as Great Britain and Australia, were offered lucrative private-contractor business that would help fuel their economies. The Bush administration, however, refused to acknowledge that there were any quid pro quo arrangements in the assembling of international forces in Iraq.

PAUL G. PIERPAOLI JR.

**See also**

Casey, George William, Jr.; IRAQI FREEDOM, Operation, Coalition Ground Forces; Iraqi Insurgency; Odierno, Raymond; Petraeus, David Howell; Sanchez, Ricardo S.; Surge, U.S. Troop Deployment, Iraq War

**References**

Cockburn, Patrick. *The Occupation: War and Resistance in Iraq.* New York: Verso, 2007.

Keegan, John. *The Iraq War: The Military Offensive, from Victory in 21 Days to the Insurgent Aftermath.* New York: Vintage, 2005.

# Multiple Launch Rocket Systems

A mobile, automatic rocket system designed to extend the range of coverage of conventional cannon field artillery. Multiple launch rocket systems (MLRS) deliver high volumes of fire and employ a variety of warheads. Mobile rocket systems' firing of rockets that have a short burn time gives the target little warning, thus limiting the ability of the target to evade or seek shelter. The rocket's short range also precludes engagement by contemporary missile defense systems. This makes them ideal weapon systems for fire support missions on the battlefield. Typical multiple launch rocket systems include the Brazilian Astros, Soviet/Russian Smerch, and the U.S. Multiple Launch Rocket System.

During the 1991 Persian Gulf War, the U.S. version of the MLRS was a highly accurate, multiple rocket launcher carried on a stretched M2 Bradley Fighting Vehicle chassis. The rocket launcher itself was an automated system capable of firing either surface-to-surface rockets or the U.S. Army's tactical missile system (ATACMS). The United States, United Kingdom, Germany, and France jointly developed the MLRS. The first model entered service in the U.S. Army in 1983.

The self-propelled launcher is 22-and-one-half feet long and 9-and-three-quarters feet wide, and weighs 55,000 pounds. The MLRS was readily transported to areas of operations because it could be carried by the Lockheed C-5 Galaxy transport aircraft or by ship. After it is unloaded, it has excellent cross-country mobility, with a road speed of about 36 miles per hour (mph). The vehicle has a range of 300 miles. The three-man crew includes a driver, gunner, and section chief.

The MLRS has an automated self-loading and self-aiming system. It contains a fire-control computer that integrates the vehicle and rocket-launching operations.

The MLRS launcher unit comprises a launcher with two weapons pods. Each pod, or canister, carries either 6 rockets or one Army Tactical Missile (ATACMS). The rockets can be fired individually or in ripples of 2 to 12. Without leaving the cab, the crew can fire up to 12 rockets in less than 60 seconds. The system is so automated that a reduced crew, even a single crew member, could load and unload the launcher. Accuracy is maintained in all firing modes because the computer reaims the launcher between rounds. The launcher's very precise positioning system allows the rockets to travel over 30 miles (or the ATACMS to travel over 60 miles) before releasing their submunitions directly above the designated target.

In 1991, the MLRS was considered a new artillery technology. In times past, conventional artillery fired shells at a target. Typically, the shells arrived one after another over a period of time. The MLRS permitted the crew to fire all 12 rockets at nearly the same time. In contrast to conventional artillery fire, the simultaneous arrival of a rocket salvo on its target did not give an enemy time to seek cover. Consequently, in theory, accurate multiple rocket fire was both more deadly and more demoralizing to an enemy.

The Persian Gulf War marked the first time the MLRS was used in combat. Coalition forces had 140 MLRS available for that conflict. The United States fought the Persian Gulf War according to a war-fighting doctrine known as AirLand Battle. Formally introduced in 1982, AirLand Battle emphasizes four basic principles: initiative, depth, agility, and synchronization. As applied to Operation DESERT STORM, the AirLand Battle doctrine called for engaging the enemy at long range with all available weapons including air strikes, conventional artillery fire, and the MLRS. American

An artillery battery of the U.S. Army's 4th Infantry Division launches a multiple launch rocket system (MLRS) rocket from Forward Operating Base Q-West, Qayyarah Airfield West in Ninawa Province, Iraq, against Iraqi insurgents, January 2006. (U.S. Department of Defense)

planners intended this long-range bombardment to shatter Iraqi military organization. The bombardment would split large Iraqi units into small, uncoordinated subunits. Ground forces would then advance to engage and easily defeat these vulnerable subunits. The AirLand Battle required all weapon systems to work as a team to complement each other. For example, the MLRS targeted Iraqi air defenses to allow Fairchild-Republic A-10 Thunderbolt II aircraft to fly over enemy lines and attack without having to worry about Iraqi antiaircraft fire.

The MLRS first entered combat on the evening of February 13, 1991, somewhere near the Saudi Arabia, Iraq, Kuwait triborder area. The U.S. Army's Alpha Battery, 21st Field Artillery acted as a single firing unit, with all 10 of its MLRS launchers deployed along a two-mile line. In less than one minute, Alpha Battery fired more than 100 rockets.

During DESERT STORM, the MLRS fired two types of weapons. The most common was the M-26 tactical rocket. The warhead of each rocket containS 644 M77 dual-purpose improved conventional munitions, submunitions, or bomblets. The flashlight-battery-sized

submunitions are effective against personnel or lightly armored targets. The rocket released the bomblets when it was still in the air. A drag ribbon stabilized the bomblet so that it descended nose first. The bomblet exploded when it made contact with something hard, such as the ground, and the M77 could penetrate up to four inches of armor. Its steel case fragmented and produced antipersonnel effects within a radius of about four yards.

Prewar tests showed that a dozen rockets fired from a single launcher could kill or injure over half the troops in an area measuring about 100 yards by 700 yards. During the Persian Gulf War, the allies fired more than 17,000 M-26 rockets against Iraqi artillery and antiaircraft positions; troop and vehicle concentrations; headquarters and communications centers; and logistics facilities. The British were particularly pleased with the performance of the rockets.

The MLRS also fired Army Tactical Missile Systems (ATACMS). With a range of about 60 miles (exact range is classified), these missiles had three times the range of the M-26 rocket. They carried a much larger payload of 950 M-74 baseball-sized bomblets. The M-74 bomblets function in a similar manner as the M-77 bomblets delivered by the M-26 rocket. On January 18, 1991, the 1st Battalion, 27th Field Artillery fired the first precision tactical missile strike in history. Its target was an Iraqi surface-to-air missile site inside Kuwait. Two minutes after launch, the missile released its bomblets and destroyed its target. During the Gulf War, the MLRS fired 32 ATACMS.

The Iraqis learned to fear the rockets and missiles fired by the MLRS. When the first bomblet detonated, surviving Iraqi soldiers knew that they had only a few seconds to find protection before being torn to pieces. The Iraqis called the bomblets "steel rain." The allies used the MLRS at all hours in both daylight and at night to keep the Iraqis off balance. In addition, allied propaganda helped spread the word about this fearsome weapon among Iraqi soldiers. Consequently, many Iraqi soldiers, particularly those serving with artillery units that were the special target for the MLRS, chose to stay in the fortified bunkers rather than man their guns. This made it easy for allied ground forces to capture their positions and force the Iraqis to surrender. Other Iraqis abandoned their weapons and fled rather than face death from the "steel rain." The best Iraqi forces tried to fight artillery duels with the coalition, but the allies' bomblets wiped them out.

Long-range bombardment by the MLRS proved extremely successful during the Persian Gulf War. It contributed enormously to the Iraqi impression that they were badly outgunned by allied forces and helped precipitate widespread Iraqi demoralization.

By the time of the 2003 Iraq War (Operation IRAQI FREEDOM), the MLRS had gained widespread acceptance in the armies of both the United States and its allies, and the system continued to evolve. New and improved munitions were added to the inventory available for use by the MLRS. Another important change was a transition from unguided rockets to guided missiles. The use of guided missiles allowed the MLRS to fire with unprecedented accuracy.

For example, in September 2005 an MLRS fired at specific buildings in Tal Afar, west of the Iraqi city of Mosul. The missiles sped some 30 miles from the launch site to strike—without warning—two fortified complexes known to house enemy insurgents. The rockets destroyed their targets without harming nearby buildings, thus avoiding so-called collateral damage. The U.S. Army claimed that 48 insurgents died in the rocket attacks. As had been the case in the Persian Gulf War, the ability of the MLRS to strike without warning had valuable physical and psychological benefits.

The MLRS ended production in 2003, but upgrade work on existing models continued. The major updating effort sought to arm the system with guided munitions. Instead of releasing a bundle of unguided, or dumb, bomblets that drop to the ground, the more advanced rockets release guided bomblets. In 2007, the British government sent an MLRS unit to Afghanistan to support ground operations in that country. The British unit employed newly developed, guided munitions. That was the first time the system was deployed in that theater.

During DESERT STORM, Iraqi forces possessed multiple rocket launcher systems purchased from the Soviet Union, Egypt, and Brazil as well as locally manufactured variants of these systems. They included the 550-millimeter (mm) Laith 90 Artillery Rocket System based on the Soviet-designed Frog-7a and a 107-mm portable rocket launcher system mounted on a Soviet-designed GAZ-66 four-by-four truck. The Brazilian system was known as the Artillery Saturation Rocket System (ASTRO). During the 1980s, Brazil sold an estimated 66 ASTROs to Iraq. In addition, Iraq, acting under license from Brazil, manufactured its own variant of this system.

None of these systems could come close to matching the accuracy of the MLRS used by the allies. Iraqi systems lacked precise target-finding devices and sophisticated weather stations and computerized fire control. The warheads used on their MLRS were also less sophisticated.

Iraq apparently neither expanded nor improved its multiple rocket launcher capabilities after the Persian Gulf War. By 2003, its arsenal included some 200 multiple rocket launchers. Most of them were the nearly obsolete 122-mm and 127-mm systems, but some were the longer-range 400-mm Ababil-100 systems.

JAMES ARNOLD

**See also**

AirLand Battle Doctrine; Artillery; DESERT STORM, Operation; IRAQI FREEDOM, Operation

**References**

Cordesman, Anthony H. *The Iraq War: Strategy, Tactics, and Military Lessons.* Westport, CT: Praeger, 2003.

Dunnigan, James F., and Austin Bay. *From Shield to Storm: High-Tech Weapons, Military Strategy, and Coalition Warfare in the Persian Gulf.* New York: William Morrow, 1992.

*Jane's Armour and Artillery, 1990–1991.* London: Jane's Information Group, 1990.

*Jane's Armour and Artillery, 2001–2002.* London: Jane's Information Group, 2001.

Scales, Robert H. *Certain Victory: The U.S. Army in the Gulf War.* Washington, DC: Brassey's, 1994.

# Murphy, Michael Patrick

**Birth Date: May 7, 1976**
**Death Date: June 28, 2005**

U.S. Navy SEAL lieutenant and posthumous recipient of the Medal of Honor. Born in Smithtown, New York, on May 7, 1976, Michael Patrick Murphy grew up on Long Island. He graduated from Pennsylvania State University in 1998 with bachelor degrees in political science and psychology.

Although accepted to law schools, Murphy decided to enter the navy, and in December 2000 he graduated from the U.S. Navy's Officer Candidate School in Pensacola, Florida, and was commissioned an ensign. Following his graduation from Basic Underwater

Demolition/SEAL (BUD/S) training at Coronado, California, Murphy underwent further training at the U.S. Army Airborne School, SEAL Qualification Training, and SEAL Delivery Vehicle (SDV) School. He then served in Hawaii, Florida, Qatar, and Djibouti.

In early 2006 Murphy was assigned to Afghanistan as a member of SDV Team 1. On June 27, 2005, Murphy took part in Operation RED WING, leading a four-man reconnaissance unit that was inserted by helicopter east of Asadabad, in Kunar Province near the border with Pakistan, in an attempt to capture a top Taliban leader. Murphy and his men were discovered by Afghans cooperating with the insurgents, and on June 28 the reconnaissance unit was surrounded and came under attack by 30–40 insurgents. In the ensuing firefight, Murphy's team inflicted numerous casualties on the attackers, but all of his team were wounded. Disregarding his own wounds, Murphy knowingly left his relatively secure position and moved to an exposed area in order to get a clear signal to notify headquarters of events. He calmly continued to report his position while under fire and request assistance, then returned to his original position and continued to fight until mortally wounded. A helicopter dispatched to the scene with reinforcements was shot down with the loss of all 16 aboard. Two other members of Murphy's team, Gunner's Mate Second Class Danny Dietz and Sonar Technician (Surface) 2nd Class Matthew Axelson, also perished in the firefight. Only Hospital Corpsman First Class Marcus Luttrell survived. All members of the team were awarded the Navy Cross for their actions that day.

Murphy's actions were subsequently recognized by the award of the Medal of Honor. He was the first U.S. serviceman to be so honored in the Afghanistan War and the first member of the U.S. Navy to receive the award since the Vietnam War. On October 22, 2007, President George W. Bush presented the award to Murphy's family at the White House. On May 7, 2008, the Navy Department announced that DDG-112, the last planned ship in the Arleigh Burke-class of destroyers, would be named in Murphy's honor.

SPENCER C. TUCKER

**See also**
Bush, George Walker

**References**
Evans, Martin C. "Slain Patchogue Sailor to get Medal of Honor." *Newsday,* October 11, 2007.
Hernandez, Raymond. "A Protector as a Child, Honored as a Hero." *New York Times,* October 22, 2007.

# Murphy, Robert Daniel
## Birth Date: October 28, 1894
## Death Date: January 9, 1978

U.S. diplomat and State Department official. Born in Milwaukee, Wisconsin, on October 28, 1894, Robert Daniel Murphy attended Marquette University and George Washington University, where he earned a law degree in 1917. He joined the foreign service that same year, and his first postings were as a consul in various European cities. Beginning in 1930 he served in various capacities in Paris, leaving there as chargé d'affaires in 1941.

Murphy's hitherto typical career took a dramatic turn when he was asked by President Franklin D. Roosevelt to be his representative to French North Africa, with the purpose of obtaining the defection of French forces from the collaborationist Vichy regime. Following this mission, Murphy was involved in the planning for the Allied invasion of North Africa in 1942. Following the German defeat of May 1945, he became a political adviser in Germany and later director of the Office for German and Austrian Affairs.

During 1949–1952 Murphy served as U.S. ambassador to Belgium and then, in 1953, as ambassador to Japan. In 1953 Eisenhower sent Murphy to Seoul, in the Republic of Korea (ROK, South Korea), to convince President Syngman Rhee to sign the armistice ending the Korean War. The following year Murphy traveled to Belgrade, in the Federal Republic of Yugoslavia, to encourage Marshal Josip Broz Tito to reach an agreement with Italy over the territory of Trieste. During the 1956 Suez Crisis Murphy was dispatched to London to evaluate the position of the British government. He completed his government service as deputy undersecretary of state during 1954–1959. President Dwight D. Eisenhower called Murphy out of retirement in 1960 to assess the turbulent situation in the newly independent Congo, and during the Eisenhower era Murphy became a top diplomatic troubleshooter for the U.S. government.

Perhaps most significant, during the U.S. intervention in Lebanon in 1958, Murphy acted as a personal representative of the president. He established communications with all of the opposing factions in Lebanon, helped to ensure the safety of the 14,000 U.S. marines in Beirut, and promoted a peaceful handover of power from Lebanese president Camille Chamoun to end the crisis. Before returning to the United States, Murphy visited Baghdad and Cairo in an effort to calm the tensions that had erupted in the Middle East during the tumultuous summer of 1958.

Following his retirement from government, Murphy served as the director of several companies, including Morgan Guaranty Trust Company and Corning Glass Works. He died in New York City on January 9, 1978.

BRENT M. GEARY

**See also**
Chamoun, Camille Nimr; Lebanon; Lebanon, U.S. Intervention in (1958); United States, Middle East Policy, 1945–Present

**References**
Brands, H. W. *Cold Warriors: Eisenhower's Generation and American Foreign Policy.* New York: Columbia University Press, 1988.
Murphy, Robert D. *Diplomat among Warriors.* New York: Doubleday, 1964.

# Musharraf, Pervez
### Birth Date: August 11, 1943

Pakistani military officer and president of Pakistan from 1999 to 2008. Pervez Musharraf was born in Delhi, India, on August 11, 1943. Following the division of the Empire of India into separate Indian and Pakistan states in 1947, Musharraf moved with his family to Karachi, Pakistan. In 1961 he entered the Pakistan Military Academy at Kakul, graduating in 1964. He then attended the Command and Staff College at Queta and the National Defense College. In 1971 Musharraf commanded a company in the Indo-Pakistani War of that year. In 1987 Musharraf was based in Kashmir in command of a mountain warfare unit at Khapalu. He was promoted to major general in 1991.

Musharraf achieved the rank of lieutenant general in 1995 and took command of a corps. He became Pakistan Army chief of staff in 1998 and organized the Pakistani military strategy in the Kargil War against India. The success of this operation was limited, and Musharraf came under criticism for his failure to achieve any substantial gains, while at the same time antagonizing India. During the war, Musharraf encouraged what were essentially terrorist actions in Indian-held Kashmir, and the Pakistani Army consequently became closely linked with these activities.

In early 1999 Musharraf clashed with the civilian government of Prime Minister Nawaz Sharif over two main issues: relations

Pakistani general Pervez Musharraf overthrew the democratically elected government of Prime Minister Nawaz Sharif on October 12, 1999. Musharraf claimed he staged the coup only to prevent the country's economic and political demise. (AP/Wide World Photos)

with India and the high level of corruption within the government. In October 1999 Sharif sought to remove Musharraf as head of the army while he was out of the country. When Musharraf attempted to return to the country via a commercial jetliner, officials loyal to Sharif refused to allow the plane to land. Army officers supporting Musharraf then took over key government installations, including the airport, and Musharraf's plane landed.

Musharraf assumed control of the country, and Sharif was exiled. The October 12, 1999, coup had been a bloodless affair. Although many groups in Pakistan pressed for new elections, Musharraf refused to yield to the demands. President Rafiq Tarar remained as titular head of Pakistan, but Musharraf assumed this post as well on June 20, 2001.

Following the September 11, 2001, terrorist attacks on the United States, Musharraf allowed U.S. forces access to three Pakistani airbases to prosecute Operation ENDURING FREEDOM against the Taliban regime in Afghanistan. In public, Musharraf expressed support for and unity with the George W. Bush administration's Global War on Terror. There is evidence, however, that the Bush administration strong-armed Musharraf into supporting the U.S. action.

Following a terrorist attack against India's parliament building in December 2001 carried out by Pakistani militants, Musharraf distanced himself from Kashmiri separatists, who had previously enjoyed the support of the Pakistani government. He also launched an antiterrorist operation in the Wana region of Pakistan. On January 12, 2002, Musharraf made a pivotal speech in which he sharply criticized all acts of terrorism and explicitly withdrew support for any form of terrorist activity against India.

During the October 2002 Pakistani elections, Musharraf mobilized sufficient support to remain in power. Although he promised to relinquish his command of the army, this did not occur until November 2007. His position was legitimized by a bill passed by the Pakistani parliament in January 2004.

Musharraf remained a less than enthusiastic ally of the United States, in part because of threats against his own government from Pakistani Islamic militants based primarily in the tribal regions of the northwest. He refused to commit troops to the Anglo-American war in Iraq and stated that he would not do so unless there was a resolution from the United Nations (UN). In 2004 Musharraf began a series of talks with India to reduce tensions between the two states and to resolve the ongoing problem of Kashmir. This tension has been heightened by the development of nuclear weapons by both nations. Musharraf's government came in for considerable criticism from its citizens regarding its handling of relief operations following a large earthquake in northern Pakistan in October 2005.

In March 2007 Musharraf precipitated a major crisis when he suspended from office Pakistan's chief justice of the Supreme Court, Iftikhar Muhammad Chaudhry. Fearful that the court was going to successfully challenge his bid for reelection in the fall, Musharraf claimed that the suspension was in response to Chaudhry's "abuse of power." The action led to major demonstrations and a boycott by many of Pakistan's attorneys. Chaudhry was reinstated in July. In October the Pakistani legislature elected Musharraf to another term as president, even though 85 legislators had resigned in protest. The Supreme Court ruled that the results of the election could not be validated until it ruled on the legality of the election itself.

On November 3, 2007, Musharraf declared a state of emergency and fired Chaudhry. Under much domestic and international pressure to restore constitutional rule, Musharraf lifted the declaration on December 15 but had clearly been wounded politically. In the meantime, his political opponents were allowed to return to Pakistan, including former Prime Minister Benazir Bhutto, who would be running in the 2008 legislative elections, to which Musharraf was forced to accede. On November 28, 2007, he finally stepped down as chief of army staff and was replaced by General Ashfaq Kayani.

When Bhutto was assassinated on December 27, 2007, many blamed Musharraf for her murder; he has denied any involvement in the killing, however. The general elections were finally held on February 28, 2008, and the Pakistan People's Party won the majority of the votes. The party then formed a coalition with the Pakistan Muslim League. In spite of his efforts to cling to power, Musharraf resigned in August 2008, and was succeeded as Pakistani president by Asif Ali Zardari.

RALPH BAKER

### See also

Afghanistan; Bhutto, Benazir; ENDURING FREEDOM, Operation; Pakistan; Pakistan, Armed Forces; Taliban

### References

Kras, Sara L. *Pervez Musharraf.* New York: Chelsea House, 2004.

Mahmood, Sohail. *Musharraf Regime and the Governance Crisis: A Case Study of the Government of Pakistan.* Hauppauge, NY: Nova Science Publishers, 2002.

Mohan, Sulakshan. *Pakistan under Musharraf.* Delhi: Indian Publishers Distributor, 2001.

## Music, Middle East

The position of the Middle East at the crossroads of Africa, Europe, and Asia contributed to its unique cultural and musical makeup. Its musical production can be divided into art music, produced for the royal courts and the elites, such as classical Persian and Ottoman or Arabo-Ottoman music, some of which is still taught and performed today; folk or popular music; and modern musical forms that may combine indigenous and Western harmonies, instrumentation, or rhythms. Middle Eastern music has some overall unifying characteristics such as its instruments, which include the lute family, the *ud, saz, buzuq, nashat kar, tar, tanbura,* and *sarinda* from Afghanistan; the lyre family, the Sinai and Nile *tanbura* and the *simsimiyya;* the bowed instruments, the *kamanja, rebab,* and *sarang;* the horn and reed instruments, the *zurna, mijwiz,* and *mizmar;* the reed flute, or *nay;* the zither family,

including the *qanun* and *santur;* and the percussion family, clay and metal hand drums, larger drums (*tabl*) and tambourines with or without cymbals, finger cymbals, and spoons. Even the Arabic coffee grinder (a mortar and pestle) is used as an instrument in some folk music. These have been supplemented with such Western instruments as the violin, called *kamanja,* the same name as its Middle Eastern bowed predecessor; viola, cello, and bass; the electronic keyboard or piano; concert flute and brass; and the accordion. The most important and valued instrument is, however, the human voice. Other similarities are the avoidance of polyphony (one melodic line, no harmony); the use of microtones (usually quarter tones); melodic structures known as *maqam* (*maqamat*), which are modes rather than scales; the use of improvisation on the *maqamat,* which, when instrumental, is called *taqasim;* the use of ornamentation and call-and-response; the valuing of *tarab,* or emotional artistry rather than mere technique; and the dominance of percussion in many folk genres.

An early-20th-century ensemble performing classical or art music might have consisted of an *ud,* a *qanun,* a violin, a *nay* (reed flute), and the cymbaled tambourine (*riqq*) and was called a *takht* (meaning stage or platform). A pop musical group, or *firqa,* might consist of musicians playing the electronic keyboard, *tabla* or *darbakka* (the vase-shaped hand drum), and either violin, accordion, or possibly electrified bass. Musical performances are more interactive than in the West. If the music is considered excellent, the audience reacts emotionally and vocally.

Some religious music, such as the *sama'iat* (a composition in a 10/8 rhythm) of the Sufi orders, may be close to art music or played in a simpler style. Other Sufi celebrations feature *inshad,* or Sufi poetry sung with a full band playing a synthesis of Arab pop and folk melodies. Songs for the hajj and the *mulids* (days commemorating holy men and women) are also popular. The Coptic Church, like the Syriac and other Arab churches, has its own liturgy and sung music, but religion does not dominate the music of the region.

The great popularity of music and the oral tradition in the region benefited from nationally subsidized radio from the 1930s to the 1950s, when such singers or instrumentalists as Munira al-Mahdiyya, Umm Kulthum, Muhammad abd al-Wahhab, Asmahan, Farid al-Atrash, and others began their careers. Radio al-Quds, broadcast from Jerusalem, played a very important role in elevating music and musical figures as did radio stations in Lebanon, where the singer Fairuz began her career, and in Afghanistan, where Ferida Mahwash worked. Her career began in the 1960s, and she was given the title "Ustadha" to signify a master musician by the Afghan government in 1976. Sadly, the reclamation of music by women from respected families, such as Mahwash, from its dubious past associations was lost when the Taliban later banned music and musical recordings.

Musical plays, called *masrahiyyat,* also became popular, such as the extravaganzas performed and recorded by the Rahbani Brothers of Lebanon with the singer Fairuz. Nearly all countries of the region established national folk ensembles to preserve their local musical and dance traditions. Cinema was also a very important vehicle for music, and many musical stars made films. In the 1960s few were as popular as the Egyptian singer Abd al-Halim Hafiz. Television and most recently music videos allowed audiences to experience established and newer performers as well as Western performance styles and musical content.

Egyptian artist Umm Kulthum (1904–1975), known as Kawkab al-Sharq (Star of the East) or by Egyptians as simply al-Sitt (the Lady), began her career as a child singing in religious celebrations and weddings. Family members performed with her, and she wore a male head-covering to indicate her modesty. After reinventing herself as a modern singer in Cairo and hiring modern composers and lyricists, she became the most celebrated singer of the Arab world. At the height of her career, she gave Thursday evening concerts that were broadcast throughout the Arab world, typically featuring one lengthy composition displaying her vocal power, improvisational skill, and emotional interpretation. Like other singers, she sang such nationalist compositions as the anti-British "University Song" and supported the Arab and Palestinian cause in 1948. After the Arab defeat in the 1967 Six-Day War, she staged a series of concerts and donated $2 million for reconstruction projects.

Other examples of political music and music related to war could include male singer and *udist* Farid al-Atrash and his song celebrating the union of Egypt and Syria in 1958, the popular Lebanese performer Marcel Khalifa, and the Palestinian group Sabrin.

The cause of Iraq has also been memorialized in music in different ways. The maqam tradition in Iraq, a special type of music, instrumentation, and singing typified by the singer Salima Murad, nearly died out, but some of its musicians continue recording in Europe, like Farida Ali. Better known in the Arab world was the great *udist* (lutist), the late Munir Bachir. Nasir al-Shamma continues the renowned Iraqi tradition of the *ud* he performs and records in Cairo. He is best known for his song "It Happened at al-Amiriyya," in reference to the bombing of civilians during the Persian Gulf War.

Another Iraqi, Kadhim al-Sahir, has achieved pop-star status, having sold 30 million records. Part of his appeal is his Iraqi musical style. In his song "Beauty and His Love," a man's girlfriend fears he has a new flame, which turns out to be the city of Baghdad.

Popular music in Israel was largely state-controlled through media and cultural policies until the 1970s, when the Israel Defense Forces' (IDF) entertainment ensembles (known as the *lehakot tsva*) performed songs that combined indigenous elements with international popular influences. After the 1970s popular music became ethnic markers of different groups in Israel, such as the eastern Jewish communities whose members had emigrated from Arab countries. They consciously incorporated Arab and Yemenite musical characteristics, like the elongated melismatic embellishments or quarter tones, to signify their eastern Mediterranean style while voicing the political struggles of their particular group. A contemporary example of this is Ofra Haza and Dana International. Israeli and Palestinian songs allude frequently to the land itself and sometimes to various stages of their struggles with each other.

Palestinian musical performance suffered from the dispersion and refugee status of the population, as well as from Israeli censorship. The Israeli government created a radio orchestra for Arab music. The performers were from the Egyptian, Iraqi, and Syrian Jewish communities, however, and the orchestra's musical repertoire and apolitical content differed from the Palestinian music produced for such private settings as weddings. Traditional weddings featured a *zaffa,* a musical procession, and songs accompanied by the *dabka,* a line dance also found in Lebanon, Syria, and Jordan. Today, families bring in DJs and recorded music instead of musical ensembles. The Islamist movement has on the one hand discouraged music in some weddings, while on the other promoted songs with jihadist lyrics.

An exception to other Palestinian musicians of his time was Hikmat Shahin. He taught the traditional repertoire at the Arab conservatory at Haifa and led the Arabic Music Ensemble of Tarshiha, which reorganized after his death as the Tarshiha Ensemble. There is also the Sabrin ensemble in the West Bank that blends more contemporary elements into its music. The music conservatories at Ramallah and Amman are quite active in trying to preserve Arabic music, as are those in Cairo and Beirut.

Western classical music is also important in many countries of the Middle East. Some Israeli, Arab, and Turkish composers have experimented with Middle Eastern themes or inspirations that either juxtapose Middle Eastern and Western music or combine the two. Examples are the Egyptian composers Abu Bakr Khayrat, founder of the Cairo Conservatory; Jamal (Gamal) abd al-Rahim; Aziz al-Shawan, composer of the first Egyptian opera; and Sharif Muhiddin.

Many Palestinians migrated into surrounding countries and to the West, and they sometimes perform music with political themes—although in family and wedding settings more than commercial ones. Certain songs were composed and performed as a nationalist repertoire.

Fairuz (b. 1935) became known as the "Voice of Lebanon," although there were other singers, such as Sabah, who also popularized folk melodies. Fairuz produced an album, *Jerusalem in My Heart,* in 1966 that featured songs devoted to particular Palestinian sites, along with vocals by Joseph Azar and a chorus.

Afghanistan's music is a mix of traditional, folk, and beginning in the 1950s, modern-style popular music. Its music scene was influenced by the music of neighboring Pakistan, and also of India. Afghanistan's classical music genre, known as *klasik,* includes both vocal and instrumental music and borrows elements from Indian Hindu music. In the 1960s and 1970s some performers from aristocratic families, like Ahmad Zahir from the Mohammadzai family, gave such music more respectability. A singer, Zahir played the organ, along with other Western instruments. When the Taliban came to power in the mid-1990s, it banned

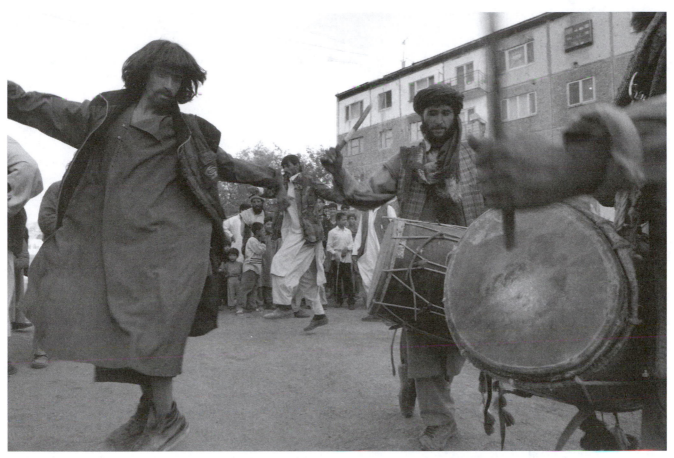

Afghan men play folk music and dance during a wedding party in Kabul, Afghanistan, on October 21, 2003. (AP/Wide World Photos)

virtually all public music and only now is Afghanistan beginning to redevelop its music industry.

The unique music of the Persian Gulf and North Africa is found in two forms, a folk format and more polished and larger orchestral arrangements with a greater number of non–folk instruments. Saudi performer Muhammad Abduh's songs were learned by other Arab performers, and today many from the Levant and North Africa include one or two Gulf-style compositions in their recordings. In North Africa a very specific classical tradition has been preserved. There is also lighter popular music. Rai music is a synthesis of Algerian folk tunes and irreverent, often countercultural, lyrics with Western-style accordion and guitar accompaniment. Some rai performers, such as Shab (Cheb) Khalid, became more widely known in Europe. Rai performers were attacked by radical Islamists during the civil war in Algeria. Middle Eastern music has also synthesized in the Jewish Diaspora, where musicians of various national origins learn the tastes of their local audiences. Music remains a vital connection, shaping the cultural, societal, and national identity of members living abroad.

CAROLYN RAMZY AND SHERIFA ZUHUR

**See also**

Afghanistan; Arab Nationalism; Casualties, Operation DESERT STORM; Egypt; Israel, Armed Forces; Taliban

**References**

Cohen, Dalia, and Ruth Katz. *Palestinian Arab Music: A Maqam Tradition in Practice.* Chicago: University of Chicago Press, 2004.

Danielson, Virginia. *The Voice of Egypt: Umm Kulthum, Arabic Song, and Egyptian Society in the Twentieth Century.* Chicago: University of Chicago Press, 1997.

Massad, Joseph. "Liberating Songs: Palestine Put to Music." *Journal of Palestine Studies* 127 (2003): 21–38.

Zuhur, Sherifa, ed. *Colors of Enchantment: Theater, Music, Dance, and Visual Arts of the Middle East.* Cairo: American University in Cairo Press, 2001.

---

# Muslim Brotherhood

Muslim fundamentalist (Islamist) organization founded in Egypt in 1928 that promotes the Islamic way of life and has been active in the political arena for many years. With separate and autonomous branches in many other countries, the Muslim Brotherhood (Jama'at al-Ikhwan al-Muslimin, or Society of Muslim Brothers) provides education, social services, and fellowship for religiously active Muslims. The secret military wing of the organization was involved in assassinations or attempted assassinations after being outlawed by the Egyptian government in the late 1940s and was also involved in an alleged assassination attempt on President Gamal

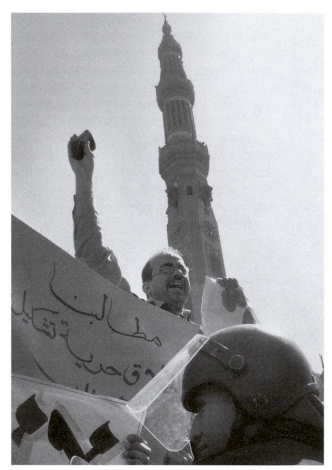

A member of the Muslim Brotherhood shouts antigovernment slogans during a demonstration in Cairo, Egypt, on March 27, 2005. (AP/Wide World Photos)

Abdel Nasser in 1954. The Muslim Brotherhood opposed the formation of Israel and the Israeli seizure of Palestinian lands. It is impossible to speak of the Muslim Brotherhood as a unified body, because its policies have necessarily varied in its various locations.

The Muslim Brotherhood was founded in March 1928 in Ismailiyya, Egypt, by Hassan al-Banna, a 22-year-old elementary school Arabic teacher and former leader of the Society for Moral Behavior and secretary to the Hasafiyya Sufi order. Banna was deeply troubled by the British presence in the Suez Canal Zone and the gap between the Egyptian wealthy and the poor. He adopted some of the ideas of Egyptian-Syrian salafism, which called for a reform of Islamic society through education. He also believed that communities and youths needed an Islamic organization. Soon he had established branches in Port Said and Suez City and contacts elsewhere in Egypt. The organization's motto was "Islam is the solution." Banna and his brother established the first Ikhwan branch in Cairo in 1932, and the organization expanded significantly in size over the next two decades, at least in part because of its nationalist stance and because the Wafd Party was somewhat discredited by its enforced cooperation with the British.

The Ikhwan established its own companies, schools, and hospitals and set up a secret military apparatus in the 1940s. It also carried out actions against British and Jewish interests in Egypt in the late 1940s.

Some members of the Muslim Brotherhood traveled to Syria in the 1930s, and Sudanese, Syrian, and Palestinian individuals either met with the Ikhwan in Egypt or became familiar with Banna's ideas. These individuals then formed their own associations. One example is Mustafa al-Siba'i, the Syrian Ikhwan's first general guide. A women's organization was established under Zaynab al-Ghazali and promoted political and charitable work as well as the wearing of the hijab, or Islamic dress. The Muslim Brotherhood, then as now, promoted *dawa* (its mission) and reform and later emphasized a shift to Islamic law.

On December 28, 1948, a member of the Muslim Brotherhood assassinated Egyptian prime minister Mahmud Fahmi Nuqrashi. Banna was assassinated in February 1949, most likely by the Egyptian security forces. The next leader of the organization, Hasan al-Hudhaybi, hoped for a better relationship with the new revolutionary government, since the Muslim Brotherhood supported the Free Officers Revolution in 1952. Anwar Sadat had been a liaison between the Free Officers and the Ikhwan, followed by Abd al-Munim Abd al-Rauf, a Brother and a Free Officer. General Muhammad Naguib was also linked to the Ikhwan. When Gamal Abdel Nasser succeeded Naguib and reined in political dissent, matters worsened for the Ikhwan. On October 26, 1954, an Ikhwan member attempted to assassinate Nasser, who responded by outlawing the Muslim Brotherhood, executing a few of its members, and imprisoning more than 4,000 of its members, some for as long as 17 years. Other members fled abroad. This confrontation led to the radicalism expressed by an Ikhwan member, Sayyid Qutb, and a bitterness on the part of the Ikhwan toward Nasser and his regime. Qutb had previously promoted societal change through education and reform, but he wrote of the necessity of jihad and martyrdom in his final book, *Ma'alim fi-l-Tariq* (*Milestones*) that was banned and for which he was executed in prison.

The first Jordanian branch of the Ikhwan was founded in Salt in 1946. Other centers formed and were led by a cleric, Haj Abd al-Latif al-Qurah. The group received informal approval from King Abdullah of Saudi Arabia to operate as a religious and not a political organization, and the organization grew in the West Bank and Jordan. In 1957 King Hussein of Jordan rescinded all political parties except for the Muslim Brotherhood. The group formed an Islamic Charitable Society by 1964. The Muslim Brotherhood supported the king to some degree against Palestinian guerrilla fights, but in the 1980s it openly criticized corruption and immorality in Jordan, and King Hussein moved against it. In 1989 the first Jordanian elections in 22 years were held; the Muslim Brotherhood won 22 of 80 seats, and its other Islamist allies won 12 additional seats.

In Syria a small society in Aleppo transferred to Damascus and became the Muslim Brotherhood in 1944. It soon grew in Syria's urban Sunni-dominated centers. Those in Hama and Aleppo opposed the Baathist Alawite regime of Hafiz al-Asad, but the Damascus wing supported it until a controversy over the secular character of the constitution occurred in 1973. The Muslim Brotherhood assassinated some Baath officials and attacked buildings associated with the Baath Party and the army. The organization killed 83 Alawi cadets in 1979 and mounted large-scale demonstrations in 1980, when the government outlawed the Muslim Brotherhood. It then joined the Syrian Islamic Front. In a showdown between the Syrian military and the Syrian Islamic Front in the city of Hama, somewhere between 10,000 and 30,000 inhabitants were killed. Some of the leadership went into exile, and others went underground. However, the Muslim Brotherhood has revived in Syria in recent years.

Contacts began with Sudan in the 1940s, and the Sudanese Muslim Brotherhood was formed in 1954. There, the organization advocated independence from Egypt. In 1964 Hasan al-Turabi became a leader of the Muslim Brotherhood in the Islamic Charter Front and much later in the National Islamic Front, founded in 1985. The National Islamic Front was associated with the military coup of 1989, and the succeeding regime implemented stricter Islamization practices.

Sadat, who became president of Egypt in September 1970 following Nasser's sudden death, released members of the Muslim Brotherhood from prison but refused to allow the organization to operate as a political party. He also encouraged Islamic student organizations. The Muslim Brotherhood operated within the regime's rules and argued for gradual change, in contrast with other extremist groups that emerged in the 1970s whose ideas were more similar to the later, more extreme ideas of Qutb. The Muslim Brotherhood attempted to forge an alliance with several of the small opposition parties, with the Wafd Party, and then with the Socialist Labor and the Liberal Party to promote itself in parliament. A younger segment of its leadership also split off from the Ikhwan to become the Wasit Party. Electoral rules and corruption prevented the Muslim Brotherhood from achieving larger political gains than it might have made, but the party is today larger and more popular than ever in Egypt.

The Muslim Brotherhood also had a following in Gaza, and Sheikh Ahmed Yassin ran a welfare and educational organization for Palestinian Muslims in the 1970s. He gave his approval when physician Abdel al-Aziz al-Rantissi, Salah Shihada, and Yahya al-Sinuwwar formed Hamas (Harakat al-Muqawama al-Islamiyya) in 1987. Sheikh Omar Abdel Rahman al-Khalifa of the Muslim Brotherhood of Jordan also gave his assent to the formation of the West Bank branch of Hamas the following year. The Muslim Brotherhood has additionally had a strong influence in Kuwait and has or had members in other countries, such as Iraq. This is in line with the Muslim Brotherhood's stance that it is a universal Islamic assembly and not a movement restricted to Arabs or to one country.

AMY HACKNEY BLACKWELL AND SHERIFA ZUHUR

**See also**

Asad, Hafiz al-; Egypt; Hamas; Hussein ibn Talal, King of Jordan; Jihad; Jordan; Nasser, Gamal Abdel; Sadat, Muhammad Anwar; Sudan; Syria

**References**

Ayubi, Nazih N. *Political Islam: Religion and Politics in the Arab World.* New York: Routledge, 1993.

Baker, Raymond William. *Islam without Fear: Egypt and the New Islamists.* Cambridge: Harvard University Press, 1993.

El-Ghobashy, Mona. "The Metamorphosis of the Egyptian Muslim Brothers." *International Journal of Middle East Studies* 37(3) (August 2005): 373–395.

Mitchell, Richard P. *The Society of Muslim Brothers.* Oxford: Oxford University Press, 1993.

# Mutla Ridge

Mutla Ridge is the highest point in Kuwait, located just north and west of the city of Kuwait. In February 1991, during Operation DESERT STORM, U.S. forces managed to capture Mutla Ridge in a lopsided battle and cut off Iraqi forces fleeing to Iraq. A massive convoy of Iraqi vehicles was trapped on the highway leading to Mutla Ridge and was devastated by coalition aircraft, as well as by U.S. ground forces. The scene of the destruction became known as the "Highway of Death."

The Jahrah Road crosses Mutla Ridge and is the major multi-lane highway from the city of Kuwait and southern Kuwait to the north. Steep ditches and slopes make the crossing at Mutla Ridge a natural choke point, where only a few vehicles at a time can pass. The sixth highway of the belt of roads circling the city of Kuwait also runs along the ridge and intersects the Jahrah Road near the Mutla police station.

Mutla Ridge caught the attention of war planners while they were deciding how to liberate Kuwait. They realized that if they could seize the ridge, they could trap Iraqi forces in southern Kuwait. The 2nd Marine Division was assigned Mutla Ridge as an objective in the campaign. To help them deal with the Iraqi armor they might encounter, the marines were supplemented with the Tiger Brigade from the U.S. Army's 2nd Armored Division.

The ground campaign began on February 24. The marines quickly breached the Iraqi defenses on the Kuwaiti–Saudi Arabian border and moved north. They captured an entire Iraqi tank battalion, along with more than 5,000 prisoners. By the end of the first day, the 2nd Marine Division was 20 miles into Kuwait. An Iraqi counterattack the next morning was quickly defeated, and the division continued to move north.

That night, marine aircraft reported a large convoy of vehicles leaving Kuwait on the Jahrah Road. The same situation was reported by air-ground radar from the Joint Surveillance and Target Reader System (JSTARS) aircraft that kept watch over the area. A flight of 12 Boeing F-15 Eagle attack aircraft was immediately dispatched to attack the convoy as it crossed Mutla Ridge. The aircraft managed to destroy the leading vehicles, using cluster bombs. Airdropped mines were also used to seal off the road, to prevent the following vehicles from continuing around the destroyed leaders. Other vehicles were destroyed at the rear of the convoy to bottle up the Iraqis. U.S. Navy and other air force planes continued to pound the Iraqis during the night. It was estimated that 1,400 to 1,500 vehicles were trapped there.

On the morning of February 26, the marines and the Tiger Brigade continued to advance toward Mutla Ridge. The area was defended by a minefield, through which the Americans had to clear lanes for their vehicles. They then encountered a number of Iraqi bunkers, which had to be cleared and destroyed. Dug-in Iraqi tanks were also defending the slopes of Mutla Ridge. Almost all of these were older T-55 models. During a three-hour battle, the Tiger Brigade destroyed 20 Iraqi tanks, and took several hundred prisoners.

When the Americans finally reached the crossroads on Mutla Ridge, the tankers saw 18 Iraqi tanks trying to pass through. They opened fire and destroyed 3, and the crews of the other 15 tanks quickly surrendered. The U.S. armored infantry then dismounted and began to clear the Mutla police station nearby. Fighting was fierce, as the Iraqis had to be cleared from each room. Forty Iraqis were killed. One American died when he was wounded and bled to death before he could be evacuated.

With the capture of Mutla Ridge, the Iraqi vehicles were completely trapped between the 2nd Marine Division and the 1st Marine Division approaching from the south. Coalition aircraft had bombed the convoy all day, and now marine and army tanks began to fire on the vehicles below. Witnesses said the vehicles completely filled all six lanes of the highway for more than two miles, as well as the available shoulders for several hundred yards on either side of the road. Most vehicles were civilian types taken from Kuwaiti citizens and were filled with goods stolen from Kuwaiti stores and homes. Most of the Iraqis now realized they would not be able to drive away, so they abandoned their cars and trucks, walking across the desert for home.

Television crews soon arrived on Mutla Ridge, and the images they took were flashed around the world. The stretch of highway below Mutla Ridge became known as the "Highway of Death." The carnage was more apparent than real, however. Tiger Brigade officers who were the first U.S. personnel on the scene said their troops found 200 Iraqi bodies among the vehicle wreckage while capturing 2,000 live Iraqis hiding nearby in the desert; but the burned-out and bombed vehicles, along with some charred bodies, made a gruesome spectacle. In Washington, D.C., President George W. Bush and his advisers feared that U.S. and world opinion would turn against the coalition forces, for it was patently obvious that the Iraqis had been defeated. The images from Mutla Ridge helped convinced the president to order a cease-fire after only four days of ground operations.

TIM J. WATTS

**See also**

Bombs, Cluster; DESERT STORM, Operation, Ground Operations; Kuwait; T-54/55 Series Main Battle Tank

**References**

Gordon, Michael R., and General Bernard E. Trainor. *The Generals' War: The Inside Story of the Conflict in the Gulf.* New York: Little, Brown, 1995.

Mroczkowski, Dennis P. *U.S. Marines in the Persian Gulf, 1990–1991: With the 2d Marine Division in Desert Shield and Desert Storm.* Washington, DC: History and Museums Division, U.S. Marine Corps, 1993.

---

# Myatt, James Michael
## Birth Date: 1941

A U.S. Marine Corps general who commanded the 1st Marine Division during the 1991 Persian Gulf War, James Michael (Mike) Myatt was born in 1941 in San Francisco, California. He enrolled at Sam Houston State University in the autumn of 1959 before enlisting in the Marine Corps Reserve in 1960. Upon graduation in 1963 with a degree in physics, Myatt was commissioned a second lieutenant. Myatt served two combat tours in Vietnam and had much experience in unconventional warfare.

Myatt rose steadily through the ranks and held posts of increasing responsibility. He attended the Naval Postgraduate School and earned a master's degree in engineering electronics. Other postings included a tour as a professor at the U.S. Naval Academy, service as operations officer for the 4th Marine Amphibious Brigade, and commanding a Marine Expeditionary Unit in the Mediterranean. In 1987 Myatt was promoted to brigadier general. His next posting was as director of Manpower Plans and Policy in Washington, D.C.

At the beginning of August 1990, Myatt was assigned to command the 1st Marine Division at Camp Pendleton, California. Within days, the division was alerted for deployment to Saudi Arabia as part of Operation DESERT SHIELD to protect that country from a potential Iraqi invasion. The division consisted of three infantry regiments, an artillery regiment, a light armored infantry battalion, and two tank battalions. Upon arrival, Myatt organized his division into five different task forces tailored to specific tasks, and organized his men more like army brigades than traditional marine units. One contingent was organized around lightly armored vehicles and assigned to screen the border. Two others were reinforced with M-60 tanks, while the remaining two were normal light infantry. Myatt continued to use this organizational structure for his division throughout the Persian Gulf War.

As more U.S. and coalition troops arrived in Saudi Arabia, the 1st Marine Division occupied the part of the border close to the Persian Gulf. On January 29, 1991, Iraqi forces crossed the border to attack the Saudi town of Khafji. Marine light armor, infantry, and attack helicopters from the 1st Division helped stop them. Two marine reconnaissance teams were trapped in Khafji, but they were relieved by Arab military forces supported by marine artillery and aircraft.

The Battle of Khafji convinced marine commanders that most Iraqis would not fight if pushed. The ground offensive plan was then modified, with the 1st and 2nd Marine Divisions assigned to breach the Iraqi defenses side-by-side. Their assignment was to divert Iraqi attention to southern Kuwait, so the main effort farther west could advance more easily. On February 22 Myatt ordered Task Forces Grizzly and Taro of two battalions each to cross into Kuwait and begin clearing lanes through the Iraqi mine-fields. When the main ground offensive began on February 24, lanes were quickly available for the mechanized forces to advance. They passed quickly through the Burgan Oil Field and bypassed the Ahmed Al Jaber Air Base. Follow-up infantry cleared the air-field, making it available for use by marine helicopters. By the end of February 24, the 1st Marine Division had taken thousands of Iraqi prisoners and advanced 20 miles into Kuwait. The advance was so successful that General H. Norman Schwarzkopf ordered the main attack in the west to begin earlier than scheduled.

The next morning, an Iraqi armored counterattack surprised the marines and came close to Myatt's forward command post. The marines drove back the Iraqis after a three-hour battle and destroyed some 30 tanks. They then advanced to within 10 miles of the city of Kuwait. On February 26 the marines attacked the Kuwait International Airport, supported by the 16-inch guns of the battleship USS *Wisconsin*. The defenders included 300 Iraqi tanks and armored personnel carriers. Fighting continued late into the night, but the marines destroyed most of the opposing Iraqi armor and secured the airport early on February 27. Later that day, the marines allowed Arab forces to pass through their lines and liberate the city of Kuwait.

Myatt returned with the 1st Marine Division to California after the war. He remained in command until the summer of 1992 and then served in South Korea until 1994, when he became director of Expeditionary Warfare at the Pentagon. In 1995 Myatt retired from the marines, at the rank of major general, and took a position with Bechtel Corporation. In 2001 he took a leave from Bechtel to serve as president of the Marines' Memorial Association, a position he continues to hold.

TIM J. WATTS

**See also**

DESERT STORM, Operation; Khafji, Battle of; United States Marine Corps, Persian Gulf War

**References**

Cureton, Charles H. *With the 1st Marine Division in Desert Shield and Desert Storm.* Washington, DC: History and Museums Division, Headquarters, U.S. Marine Corps, 1993.

Moore, Molly. *A Woman at War: Storming Kuwait with the U.S. Marines.* New York: Free Press, 1993.

---

# Myers, Richard Bowman
## Birth Date: March 1, 1942

A U.S. Air Force general and chairman of the Joint Chiefs of Staff (JCS) from 2001 to 2005, Richard Bowman Myers was born in Kansas City, Missouri, on March 1, 1942. He graduated from Kansas State University in 1965 and entered the air force through the Reserve Officers' Training Corps (ROTC) program. He served as

a fighter pilot during the Vietnam War, accumulating 600 combat flying hours. In 1977 he earned a master's degree in business administration from Auburn University.

Myers was promoted to brigadier general in April 1990 and was assigned as director of Fighter, Command and Control and Weapons Programs in the Office of the Assistant Secretary of the Air Force for Acquisition in Washington, D.C. In September 1992 he was promoted to major general, and in November 1993 he was promoted to lieutenant general. From July 1996 to July 1997 he was the assistant to the chairman of the JCS. He then commanded the Pacific Air Forces at Hickham Air Force Base, Hawaii, during July 1997 to July 1998. He was promoted to full general in September 1997.

From August 1998 to February 2000 Myers headed the North American Aerospace Defense Command and U.S. Space Command. He also commanded the Air Force Space Command and was the Department of Defense manager of the space transportation system contingency support at Peterson Air Force Base, Colorado.

Myers was vice chairman of the JCS from March 2000 to September 2001. As vice chairman, he served as chairman of the Joint Requirements Oversight Council, as vice chairman of the Defense Acquisition Board, and as a member of the National Security Council (NSC) Deputies Committee and the Nuclear Weapons

U.S. Air Force general Richard Myers was chairman of the Joint Chiefs of Staff (JCS) during 2001–2005. He has been criticized for underestimating the number of ground troops required in the invasion of Iraq in 2003 and ignoring the possibility of an Iraqi insurgency. (U.S. Department of Defense)

Council. In addition, Myers acted for the JCS chairman in most aspects of the planning, programming, and budgeting system, including participation in the Defense Resources Board.

In August 2001 President George W. Bush nominated Myers as chairman of the JCS. Myers thus had held his new position for only a few weeks—and had not yet been confirmed by the U.S. Senate—when the terrorist attacks of September 11 took place. After the second plane hit the World Trade Center during the attacks, Myers called the Pentagon's command center and ordered the military's alert status to defense condition (DEFCON) 3, the highest state of military readiness since the October 1973 Yom Kippur (Ramadan) War. Myers was confirmed to the chairman's position by the Senate and was sworn in on October 1, 2001.

Myers closely analyzed the status of both Afghanistan and Iraq prior to U.S. military involvement in those two countries in Operation ENDURING FREEDOM beginning in 2001 and Operation IRAQI FREEDOM beginning in 2003, respectively. While much of the blame for the debacle of the war in Iraq fell on Secretary of Defense Donald Rumsfeld, Myers has also been sharply criticized. Many argue that, among others things, he underestimated the potential likelihood of a postinvasion insurgency and failed to provide enough troops to secure the country from the very beginning.

Myers retired on September 30, 2005. Two months later he was awarded the Presidential Medal of Freedom. The following year he was named Foundation Professor of Military History at Kansas State University. Myers has also served on several boards, including those of Northrop Grumman and United Technologies Corporation. He holds the Colin L. Powell Chair for National Security, Leadership, Character and Ethics at the National Defense University, and in 2009 he published his memoirs, *Eyes on the Horizon*.

CHARLENE T. OVERTURF

**See also**

Bush, George Walker; ENDURING FREEDOM, Operation; IRAQI FREEDOM, Operation; Iraqi Insurgency; Nuclear Weapons, Iraq's Potential for Building; Rumsfeld, Donald Henry

**References**

Fawn, Rick, and Raymond A. Hinnebusch, eds. *The Iraq War: Causes and Consequence.* Boulder, CO: Lynne Rienner, 2006.

Lifton, Robert Jay, Richard Falk, and Irene Gendzier. *Crimes of War: Iraq.* New York: Nation Books, 2006.

Myers, Richard B., and Malcom McConnell. *Eyes on the Horizon: Serving on the Front Lines of National Security.* Riverside, NJ: Threshold Editions, 2009.

Woodward, Bob. *State of Denial: Bush at War, Part III.* New York: Simon and Schuster, 2006.

# N

## Nahyan, Zayid bin Sultan al-

**Birth Date:** 1922
**Death Date:** November 2, 2004

President of the United Arab Emirates (UAE) from 1971 to 2004, and emir of Abu Dhabi from 1966 to 2004. Sheikh Zayid bin Sultan al-Nahyan (al-Nuhayyan) was born in 1922 (exact date unknown) in the Ain region of Abu Dhabi. He spent his youth as a desert nomad and received no formal education. Under his brother's rule, Sheikh Zayid served as governor of Abu Dhabi's agricultural Eastern Province from 1946 to 1966. In 1966 he deposed his brother, Sheikh Shakbut al-Nahyan, to become emir of Abu Dhabi.

As emir, Sheikh Zayid was the principal architect behind the formation of the Trucial States, a group of Arab states or sheikhdoms that included Abu Dhabi. In December 1971 Sheikh Zayid became president of the Trucial States (soon renamed the United Arab Emirates). In 1973 he reorganized the UAE's political structure, bringing most of Abu Dhabi's ministries under central control. Under the direction of Sheikh Zayid, the UAE's provisional constitution (a document that essentially defined the federation of the seven states) was ratified on July 18, 1971, although the document did not become permanent until 1996.

In Sheikh Zayid's second term as president of the UAE, which began in 1976, he promulgated more political reforms, including the centralization of the government, integration of defense forces, and increased financial contributions from member states. One of his primary goals as emir of Abu Dhabi and president of the UAE was to use oil revenues to raise the standard of living in the region. To meet this goal, he shared Abu Dhabi's oil wealth with the poorer sheikhdoms, thereby reflecting his traditional tribal values. As such, it was no surprise that Sheikh Zayid was reelected president of the UAE in 1981, 1986, 1991, 1996, and 2001. Under his rule, the country became a prosperous nation and a leading financial center, and it adopted measures to advance women's rights.

Sheikh Zayid is also credited for his involvement in the creation of the Cooperation Council for the Arab States of the Gulf (also known as the Gulf Cooperation Council, or GCC). In terms of foreign relations, particularly with the West, Sheikh Zayid proved an able diplomat. During the 1991 Persian Gulf War, the UAE joined the United Nations (UN) coalition to force Iraq out of Kuwait. Furthermore, in 1992 heightened tensions with Iran induced the emir to expand the UAE's military cooperation with the United States. In June 2001, after facing increased international criticism of the UAE's poor record on human rights, Sheikh Zayid ordered the release of more than 6,000 prisoners on humanitarian grounds.

Sheikh Zayid supported the 2001 invasion of Afghanistan to topple the Taliban regime and also supported the 2003 Anglo-American–led invasion of Iraq. Indeed, U.S. and allied forces have used UAE facilities as staging areas for these conflicts. Sheikh Zayid died on November 2, 2004, in Abu Dhabi. His son, Sheikh Khalifa bin Zayid al-Nahyan, who had played an increasing role in government affairs since the 1990s, succeeded his father as emir.

KIRSTY MONTGOMERY

**See also**

Gulf Cooperation Council; United Arab Emirates

**References**

Countrywatch. *United Arab Emirates: 2003 Country Review.* Houston, TX: Countrywatch, 2003.

Davidson, Christopher M. *The United Arab Emirates: A Study in Survival.* Boulder, CO: Lynne Rienner, 2005.

Metz, Helen Chapin. *Persian Gulf States: Country Studies.* 3rd ed. Washington, DC: Federal Research Division, Library of Congress, 1994.

Zahlan, Rosemarie Said. *The Making of the Modern Gulf States: Kuwait, Bahrain, Qatar, The United Arab Emirates, and Oman.* London: Unwin Hyman, 1989.

---

# Nairobi, Kenya, Bombing of U.S. Embassy
## Event Date: August 7, 1998

Bombing of the U.S. embassy compound in Nairobi, Kenya, on August 7, 1998, by Al Qaeda terrorists. The bombing occurred almost simultaneously with an Al Qaeda terrorist bombing of the U.S. embassy in Dar es Salaam, Tanzania. The two bombings were among the largest terrorist attacks on U.S. interests to date, and precipitated a military response by the United States in the form of Operation INFINITE REACH, which took place on August 20, 1998. The retaliatory action featured cruise missile strikes on terrorist camps in Afghanistan and an attack on the El Shifa pharmaceutical factory in Khartoum, Sudan. In retrospect, the embassy bombings in Kenya and Tanzania were part of an escalating spiral of violence involving Al Qaeda terrorists. After President Bill Clinton's administration struck Sudan and Afghanistan with Tomahawk cruise missiles, Al Qaeda leader Osama bin Laden vowed revenge in the way of a spectacular attack on American interests. This came about on U.S. soil during the September 11, 2001, attacks that destroyed the World Trade Center in New York, damaged the Pentagon in Virginia, and forced the crash of another jetliner in rural Pennsylvania.

The destruction of the embassy in Nairobi was precipitated by a well-placed truck bomb and—it is believed—at least two determined suicide bombers. Timing their mission with the one occurring in Dar es Salaam, the suicide bombers struck at about 10:30 a.m. local time, or 3:30 a.m. Washington, D.C., time. The truck was apparently driven up to the rear entrance of the building. The detonation severely damaged the structure, which had to be torn down and rebuilt.

The death toll, which was staggering, included 200 Kenyans and 12 Americans. More than 4,000 people were injured, including 10 Americans and 12 foreign service nationals. The death toll was much higher in Nairobi than in Dar es Salaam for two principal reasons. First, the truck carrying the explosives to the Nairobi embassy was able to gain access to the inner embassy compound, which was

Rescue workers carry a woman pulled from the wreckage of the U.S. embassy in Nairobi, Kenya, on August 7, 1998, when a terrorist bomb killed more than 200 people. (AP/Wide World Photos)

not the case in Dar al-Salaam. Second, the Nairobi embassy was in a densely populated area close to the center of the city, so when the bomb detonated, there were far more collateral casualties.

The resultant investigation of the bombings, which included the Federal Bureau of Investigation (FBI), concluded that bin Laden had approved the attacks. The U.S. government subsequently issued indictments against him and offered a $5 million reward for his capture. For the first time he was also placed on the FBI's "Ten Most Wanted" list. In 2001 four men were convicted in a U.S. federal court in New York City, which heard impassioned testimony from the families of the victims. Two of the men, Khalfan Khamis Muhammad of Tanzania and Muhammad Rashid Daud al-Awhali of Saudi Arabia, had some direct role in the bombings and could have received the death penalty, but the jury could not reach a unanimous decision. The two others convicted were Muhammad Sadiq 'Awdeh, allegedly the adviser to the bombers, and Wadih al-Hage, an American who was convicted of being Al Qaeda's leader in Nairobi. Their pleas for reduced sentences were rejected. All four were ordered to pay $7 million to the victims and $26 million to the U.S. government.

In October 2008 charges were brought against a Guantánamo Bay, Cuba, detainee, Tanzanian Ahmad Khaffan Gailani, to be tried in a special military tribunal for his role in the attack in Dar es Salaam. Rashid Swailah Hemed was acquitted in 2004 after a several years' trial in Tanzania.

In response to the bombings, President Clinton pledged to wage a war on terrorism. On August 20, 1998, the United States launched cruise missiles (Operation INFINITE REACH) against terrorist camps in Afghanistan, where bin Laden was believed to reside, and the El Shifa pharmaceutical factory. The factory was a target because of allegations that bin Laden had some connection to it, which proved false, and because of allegations that the facility might have been producing nerve gas that was being shipped to Iraq. This latter claim was based on a soil sample; however pesticide decomposition can also produce the same trace chemical that was suspected.

The attacks in Afghanistan killed at least 20 people but failed to kill bin Laden. The attack on the plant in Sudan was severely criticized because it killed at least 20 people and because it had been producing pharmaceuticals necessary for Sudan to fight malaria and tuberculosis, among other diseases. These retaliatory U.S. strikes precipitated massive protests around the world, mostly in Muslim nations.

The U.S. State Department Bureau of Intelligence and Research had questioned the intelligence that linked El Shifa to bin Ladin in a report to Secretary of State Madeleine Albright prior to the attack, but it was disregarded. Some of Clinton's detractors charged that he ordered the strikes to take the public's attention off the Monica Lewinsky scandal. Just three days prior to the cruise missile strikes, Clinton had been forced to admit that he had had an affair with Lewinsky, a former White House intern.

PAUL G. PIERPAOLI JR.

**See also**
Al Qaeda; Bin Laden, Osama; Clinton, William Jefferson; Dar es Salaam, Bombing of U.S. Embassy; INFINITE REACH, Operation; September 11 Attacks; Terrorism

**References**
Ferguson, Amanda. *The Attack against the U.S. Embassies in Kenya and Tanzania.* New York: Rosen, 2003.
Labévière, Richard. *Dollars for Terror: The United States and Islam.* New York: Algora, 2000.
Obwogo, Subiri. *The Bombs That Shook Nairobi & Dar es Salaam: A Story of Pain and Betrayal.* Nairobi: Obwogo and Family, 1999.

## Najaf, First Battle of
Start Date: August 5, 2004
End Date: August 27, 2004

Iraq War battle between U.S. forces and the Islamist Mahdi Army militia, controlled by Muqtada al-Sadr, during August 5–27, 2004. The Iraqi city of Najaf is located about 100 miles south of Baghdad and had a prewar population estimated at 585,000 people. Najaf is one of the holy cities of Shia Islam and a major center for Shia religious pilgrimages, education, and political power.

In March 1991, following the Persian Gulf War, the residents of Najaf rebelled against the regime of Iraqi dictator Saddam Hussein as part of a larger Shiite uprising against the government. Hussein's forces suppressed the uprising in the city with great brutality. Early in the Iraq War (Operation IRAQI FREEDOM), following two days of heavy fighting, Najaf was assaulted and then captured on April 1, 2003, by units of the U.S. 101st Airborne (Air Assault) Division, commanded by Major General David Petraeus.

Following the overthrow of Hussein's regime later that same month, Najaf witnessed the gradual emergence of the powerful cleric Muqtada al-Sadr, whose Mahdi Army militia was based in the city, as were the Badr Brigades. In April and May 2004 Sadr's militia led an uprising in Najaf that largely usurped control of the city from U.S. forces. Sadr's militia also took on U.S. and coalition military forces across the Shia-controlled areas of southern Iraq. On May 27 Sadr reached a deal with the Americans by which both sides agreed to withdraw their forces from Najaf. The Mahdi militia soon began rebuilding their forces in the city, however.

On July 31, 2004, the 11th Marine Expeditionary Unit, commanded by Colonel Anthony Haslam, took up positions around Najaf, relieving the army's Task Force Dragon. The marines first clashed with the Mahdi militia on August 2, when a marine patrol approached a house believed to be occupied by Sadr. Major fighting erupted on August 5 when the Mahdi militia attacked an Iraqi government police station and the marines responded in force. On August 9 three additional battalions of troops from the 1st Cavalry Division were sent from Baghdad to Najaf to reinforce the marines. Combat took the form of street fighting with the Mahdi militia employing rocket-propelled grenades, mortars, and automatic rifles against U.S. Abrams tanks, Bradley Fighting Vehicles, attack helicopters, and infantry. A number of Abrams tanks and Bradley Fighting Vehicles were knocked out or heavily damaged by rocket-propelled grenades, and one U.S. helicopter was shot down.

After a few days, the scene of the fighting had approached the Imam Ali Mosque and a huge adjacent cemetery known as the Wadi of Peace. Because the mosque and cemetery represent some of the holiest sites in Shiite Islam, concerns were expressed throughout the Arab world for their safety, but the heavy fighting continued.

The turning point in the battle came on August 26, when two F-16s dropped four 2,000-pound Joint Direct Attack Munition (JDAM) bombs on hotels near the Imam Ali Mosque, then occupied by the Mahdi militia. The air strike prompted Sadr to negotiate a truce the next day. The Mahdi militia agreed to turn in its weapons and leave Najaf. In return, U.S. forces also left Najaf, and security was turned over to the Iraqi police. The Imam Ali Mosque did not suffer any significant damage during the Battle of Najaf.

Casualty figures remain in dispute. The Americans claim that several hundred members of the Madhi Army were killed in the fight, but militia spokesmen claim the toll was fewer than 30 dead. Eight U.S. service personnel were killed and 30 more were wounded. The Battle of Najaf showcased not only the rise to prominence of such radical extremists as Sadr but also the general elevation of tensions between Shia, Sunnis, and Kurds in Iraq. By the end of 2004 U.S. and coalition forces found themselves locked in a deadly struggle with all the signs of a civil war, despite protestations to the contrary by both U.S. president George W. Bush and British prime minister Tony Blair. Indeed, the situation in Iraq continued to deteriorate until the summer of 2008, when some signs indicated that the Iraq insurgency violence had subsided a bit, a development the British and Americans said was the result of the troop surge, implemented in 2007.

PAUL W. DOERR

**See also**

ENDURING FREEDOM, Operation; Hussein, Saddam; Iraqi Insurgency; Mahdi Army; Petraeus, David Howell; Sadr, Muqtada al-; Shia Islam

**References**

Bremer, L. Paul, with Malcolm McConnell. *My Year in Iraq: The Struggle to Build a Future of Hope.* New York: Simon and Schuster, 2006.
Ricks, Thomas E. *Fiasco: The American Military Adventure in Iraq.* New York: Penguin, 2006.
Woodward, Bob. *State of Denial: Bush at War, Part III.* New York: Simon and Schuster, 2006.

# Najaf, Second Battle of
## Event Date: January 28, 2007

Fierce battle between the Iraqi army and police, heavily aided by U.S. and British military units and air power, and hundreds of well-armed followers of Ahmad al-Hassan al-Basri. The battle occurred on January 28, 2007, in Zarqa, a town located 10 miles from the southern Iraqi Shia shrine city of Najaf. Details about Basri, his messianic religious movement known as the Soldiers of Heaven (Jund al-Samaa), and the battle itself are hotly debated.

According to some accounts, based on interviews with captured members of the group, Basri was the deputy to Dhia Abd al-Zahra Khadhim al-Krimawi (who died in 2007), a shadowy Iraqi Shia leader who claimed to be Imam Mahdi, the 12th in a line of religious and political leaders who Shias believe will return at a time decided by God to usher in a period of absolute justice that will precede the Day of Judgment. The fate of Basri remains unknown, with some sources in the Shia religious establishment in southern Iraq claiming that he survived the battle and is living in seclusion, possibly in the southern shrine city of Karbala.

Following the suppression of the group, the Iraqi government and military spokespeople claimed that Basri, Krimawi, and their followers were really Sunnis and not Shias, although evidence of this is sketchy at best. The Iranian government, Al Qaeda, and remnants of the Iraqi Baath Party have all been accused of supporting the group. Initial Iraqi government reports claimed that foreign Sunnis from countries as far as Pakistan and Afghanistan were killed or captured fighting against Iraqi security forces. These reports were challenged, however, when dead and captured Jund fighters were identified as Iraqis instead of foreigners.

Anonymous sources in the Hawza Ilmiyya, the Shia seminary system in Najaf, have stated that Basri was a former student who left because of disagreements over religious theology with the seminary's religious scholars. Shia clerics loyal to Mahmoud Sarkhi al-Hassani, who heads another Shia messianic party in southern Iraq, denied that Basri and Krimawi were associated with their group. Hassani is a former student of Grand Ayatollah Sayyid Muhammad Sadiq al-Sadr, the father of Muqtada al-Sadr, and claims to be the representative of Imam Mahdi. His group broke with the larger Sadr Movement (Tayyar al-Sadr) over theological and political disputes, including a disagreement about who should assume command of the movement, Muqtada or Hassani. The latter has a relatively small but devoted following in southern Iraq. According to other sources, Basri was also a former student of the late Sadiq al-Sadr, a popular Shia religious opposition leader who was assassinated with two of his sons in 1999, probably by Baath Party operatives. These sources claim that the two had a falling out when the Iraqi Baathists attempted to split Sadiq al-Sadr's increasingly powerful sociopolitical network by sponsoring a rival splinter group, the Mehwadiya led by Basri.

Fighting began on January 28, 2007, when Iraqi police and a battalion of soldiers from the Iraqi 8th Army Division attempted to carry out a morning raid on an alleged safe house used by the Jund. They were acting on information that the group planned to assassinate Grand Ayatollah Sayyid Ali Husayn al-Sistani, Iraq's senior resident Shia religious authority, and other grand ayatollahs and senior religious leaders in Najaf. The assassinations allegedly were to be carried out during Ashura, the Shia period of mourning

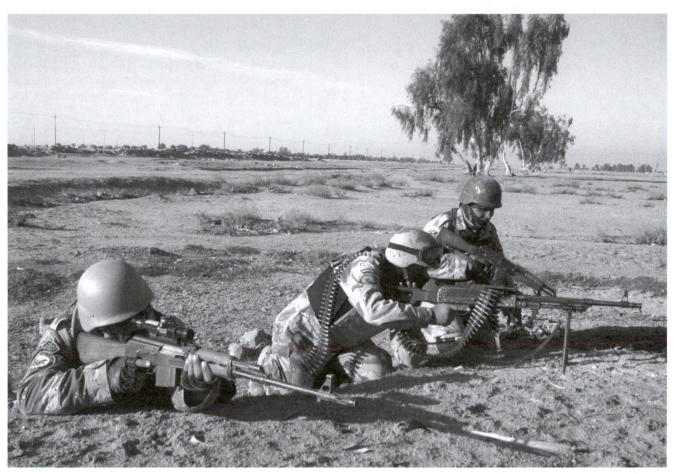

Iraqi soldiers take up positions at Zarqa, some 12 miles northeast of Najaf, Iraq, January 28, 2007. (AP/Wide World Photos)

in commemoration for the martyrdom of Imam Hussein bin Ali and dozens of his companions and family members at Karbala in 680 by soldiers sent by the Umayyad caliph Yazid I. The Jund were reportedly acting on the orders of Basri to prepare for the return of Imam Mahdi and the establishment of a religious state governed with absolute justice, as foretold in Shia religious sources and traditions. Reportedly, group members planned to hide their weapons and use the sheer number of people, millions of Iraqis and foreign Shia, who flood into the southern Iraqi shrine cities of Najaf, Karbala, and Kufa during Ashura, to their advantage, hiding in the crowds to get close to the grand ayatollahs' residences.

The Iraqi soldiers and police were soon overwhelmed by hundreds of armed Jund fighters and became pinned down by heavy gunfire, forcing them to call for U.S. and British air support, which came in the form of air strikes by Lockheed Martin F-16 Fighting Falcons and Hughes/McDonnell Douglas AH-64 Apache helicopter gunships along with a small contingent of British fighter jets. The aircraft dropped 500-pound bombs on Jund positions, including significant numbers of fighters in a grove of trees in Zarqa. In the early afternoon, the U.S. 25th Infantry Division and other units were sent from bases near Baghdad to aid the besieged Iraqi units.

During the 15 hours of fighting, one U.S. Apache helicopter was shot down, killing its 2 crew members, and 25 Iraqi soldiers

and police were also killed. Iraqi government and U.S. military estimates place the number of Jund casualties at somewhere between 250 and 400, although the number was probably closer to 250–263, among them Krimawi. More than 450 Jund fighters were captured alive and later tried by Iraqi courts. Millions of dollars and a large cache of weapons, including antiaircraft guns, rockets, and automatic rifles, were seized from the Jund's well-equipped compound.

In September 2007 an Iraqi court sentenced 10 Jund leaders to death and 384 fighters to prison terms ranging from 15 years to life. It freed 54. Despite the trial and the apparent decimation of the Jund, the group is but one of several messianic Mahdist Shia groups active in post-Hussein Iraq. The largest is the party led by Mahmoud al-Hassani, who claims the rank of grand ayatollah despite the fact that his religious scholarly credentials do not support his claims and he is not recognized as such by Iraq's Shia religious establishment, the *marjaiyya*. Hassani's popularity is reportedly growing in southern Iraq as a greater number of the country's Shias become disenchanted with the *marjaiyya* traditionalists and the ruling Shia political parties such as the Islamic Dawa Party, the Sadr Movement, and the Supreme Islamic Iraqi Council.

CHRISTOPHER ANZALONE

**See also**

Islamic Dawa Party; Najaf, First Battle of; Sadr, Muqtada al-; Sistani, Sayyid Ali Husayn al-

**References**

Cave, Damien. "Mystery Arises over Identity of Militia Chief in Najaf Fight." *New York Times,* February 1, 2007.

———. "250 Are Killed in Major Iraq Battle." *New York Times,* January 29, 2007.

Cockburn, Patrick. "US 'Victory' against Cult Leader Was 'Massacre.'" *Independent,* January 31, 2007.

Colvin, Ross. "US Military Still Probing Iraqi Cult Battle." *Reuters,* February 2, 2007.

Hardy, Roger. "Confusion Surrounds Najaf Battle." *BBC News,* January 31, 2007.

Jamail, Dahr, and Ali al-Fadhily. "Pilgrims Massacred in the 'Battle' of Najaf." *Asia Times,* February 2, 2007.

Santora, Marc. "Fierce Militia Fighters Catch Iraqi Army by Surprise." *International Herald Tribune,* January 30, 2007.

Visser, Reidar. *The Sadrists of Basra and the Far South of Iraq: The Most Unpredictable Political Force in the Gulf's Oil-Belt Region?* Oslo, Norway: Norwegian Institute of International Affairs, 2008.

# Najibullah, Mohammed

**Birth Date: February 1947**
**Death Date: September 28, 1996**

Afghan politician and last president of the Democratic Republic of Afghanistan. Mohammad Najibullah was born in Gardiz, Afghanistan, in February 1947 to parents of the Ahmadzai clan of the Ghilzai Pashtun tribe. In 1964 he undertook the study of medicine at Kabul University, finally earning a degree in 1975, although he never became a practicing physician.

In 1965 Najibullah began his political career by joining the People's Democratic Party of Afghanistan (PDPA), a communist organization supported by the Soviet government. He was jailed briefly on two separate occasions for his political activities, but by 1977 had become a member of his party's Central Committee. The following year the PDPA seized power in Afghanistan, and Najibullah became a member of the Revolutionary Council.

Soon after the PDPA took power, however, the Khalq faction of the party seized the majority of the power, pushing Najibullah's Parcham faction aside. For a very brief time Najibullah was the Afghan ambassador to Iran, but in a matter of months he had been dismissed from his post and was living in exile in Eastern Europe. After the 1979 Soviet invasion of Afghanistan, the Parcham faction was placed in power and Najibullah was named the head of the secret police in 1980, with the rank of major general. This made him one of the most powerful and feared men in Afghanistan, and also gave him direct access to Kremlin policymakers.

Najibullah proved to be utterly ruthless while running the secret police, reportedly ordering the arrest, torture, and execution of tens of thousands of Afghan citizens. Soviet leaders were pleased with his performance during the early years of the Soviet occupation, which helped keep radicals and other troublemakers in check. Indeed, for his efficient bloodletting he became a member of the Afghan Politburo. As the Soviet War in Afghanistan continued and mujahideen fighters began to gain the upper hand, Moscow forced Afghan president Babrak Karmal to resign in 1986, replacing him with the loyal Najibullah.

As president, Najibullah presided over the writing of a new constitution that gave Afghans more rights and more access to the political system, but he remained very much in charge and used his extensive police and military establishments to keep the country under his control. By 1987, however, the mujahideen were scoring victories. Despite an offer of reconciliation by Najibullah, they continued their struggle against the Soviet and Afghan government forces. Also by 1987, the Kremlin, beset by financial woes and a crumbling political structure, announced that it would withdraw its troops from Afghanistan by 1989. Najibullah was thus left alone to deal with the potent insurgency, which would stop at nothing less than the overthrow of his regime.

It soon became clear that Najibullah was waging a futile struggle, and in 1990 he narrowly averted a coup d'état fomented by his own defense minister. In the meantime, his government engaged in United Nations (UN)–sponsored talks with the warring parties, but the negotiations quickly broke down. In March 1992, with his government on the verge of collapse and the capital city of Kabul drastically short of food and fuel supplies, Najibullah agreed to resign. The next month, he was ousted from his own political party. On April 17, 1992, fearing for his life, he took refuge in a UN compound in Kabul. He remained in the compound as a virtual prisoner until September 28, 1996, when he and his brother, having been captured, were hanged and their bodies mutilated by Taliban fighters. The following day, his bodyguards and personal secretary were also hanged.

PAUL G. PIERPAOLI JR.

**See also**

Afghanistan; Mujahideen, Soviet-Afghanistan War; Soviet-Afghanistan War; Taliban

**References**

Corwin, Philip. *Doomed in Afghanistan: A UN Officer's Memoir of the Fall of Kabul and Najibullah's Failed Escape.* New Brunswick, NJ: Rutgers University Press, 2003.

Ewans, Martin. *Afghanistan: A Short History of Its History and Politics.* New York: Harper Perennial, 2002.

# Napalm

Although popular misconception has applied the term "napalm" to any fire-producing materials, strictly speaking it is an incendiary material made from thickened gasoline. Gasoline had been employed as an incendiary for some time, as in the case of flamethrowers in World War I. The brown, syrupy napalm mixture was far more effective than gasoline as an incendiary, as it stuck to the target area. Developed by American scientists at Harvard University early in World War II, napalm was available as a weapon in late 1942.

The name "napalm" comes from naphthene and palmitate, which when combined with gasoline create a gel-like mixture. Napalm is not only sticky but possesses improved burning characteristics compared to gasoline. Napalm is also relatively safe to handle.

Napalm was employed both in bombs and in flamethrowers. It was initially used in the U.S. 100-pound M47 chemical weapons bomb. The United States employed napalm bomb in its extensive fire-bombing campaign against Japanese cities at the close of World War II. The initial B-29 Pathfinder aircraft dropped the M47 to mark the targets, while following bombers dropped 6.2-pound M69 incendiary bombs with delayed-action fuses to allow the bombs to penetrate buildings before ignition. Napalm was also employed extensively in the Korean War and the Vietnam War. Often auxiliary fuel tanks were filled with the napalm mix and equipped with an igniter, and they were then dropped in areas where enemy forces were thought to be located.

Improved napalm, developed after the Korean War, was known as super napalm or napalm B. It employed benzene (21 percent), polystrene (46 percent), and gasoline (33 percent). Its great advantage was that it was less flammable, and thus less hazardous, than the original napalm. Normally, thermite is the igniter.

In the Middle East, Israel used napalm during the 1967 Six-Day War and in the 1980s in Lebanon. Egypt employed it in the 1973 Yom Kippur (Ramadan) War. Coalition forces also used napalm during the Persian Gulf War in 1991, delivered primarily from U.S. Marine Corps McDonnell Douglas AV-8 Harriers to ignite the oil-filled fire trenches that formed part of the Iraqi barrier in southern Kuwait. The Saddam Hussein regime also subsequently employed napalm and chemical attacks against the Kurdish population in northern Iraq. The U.S. Department of Defense denied the use of napalm during Operation IRAQI FREEDOM; however, incendiary weapons were apparently used against Iraqi troops in the course of the drive north to Baghdad, although these consisted primarily of kerosene-based jet fuel (which has a smaller concentration of benzene) rather than the traditional mixture of gasoline and benzene used for napalm.

Napalm is particularly effective against troops caught in the open, who have little defense against it. Death results not only from the burning but also from asphyxiation. Only those on the perimeter of the strike zone usually survive a napalm attack, although they may suffer severe burns.

SPENCER C. TUCKER

**See also**

Aircraft, Attack; DESERT STORM, Operation, Coalition Air Campaign

**References**

Bjornerstedt, Rolf, et al. *Napalm and Other Incendiary Weapons and All Aspects of Their Possible Use.* New York: United Nations, 1973.

Kerr, E. Bartlett. *Flames over Tokyo: The U.S. Army Air Forces' Incendiary Campaign against Japan, 1944–1945.* New York: Donald I. Fine, 1991.

Stockholm International Peace Research Institute. *Incendiary Weapons.* Cambridge, MA: MIT Press, 1975.

# Narcoterrorism

Term used to describe terrorist-like tactics employed by narcotic traffickers to intimidate local populations and exert influence on governmental antidrug policies. The term "narcoterrorism" is credited to Fernando Belaúnde Terry, former president of Peru, who used it in a speech in 1983. He employed the descriptive when referring to the aggressive tactics used by his nation's drug traffickers and the rebel group Sendero Luminoso (Shining Path) against Peruvian antinarcotic police squads. In its original connotation, narcoterrorism referred to the tactics used by drug traffickers and dealers that oftentimes resembled terrorism.

Narcoterrorism was designed to keep local populations in fear, thus reducing the chances that they will cooperate with police, and to influence government policy that might be detrimental to the drug trade. Perhaps the most infamous of all narcoterrorists was the late Pablo Escobar, leader of the Medellin drug cartel in Colombia and considered one of the most ruthless outlaws of modern times. His narcoterrorism included the murder of at least 30 judges, more than 450 policemen, and as many as 500 other people. In more recent years narcoterrorism has also been used to describe more traditional terror organizations that rely upon drug trafficking to fund their activities and recruit new members. Some of these include the Revolutionary Armed Forces of Colombia (FARC), the United Self-Defense Forces of Colombia (AUC), and the National Liberation Army of Colombia (ELN).

The U.S. government's War on Drugs, which has been ongoing for several decades, was given a large boost in 1988 with the formation of the Office of National Drug Control Policy, the director of which is commonly referred to as the U.S. drug czar. Through this office, the U.S. government has centralized its antidrug efforts, including those in the United States and abroad. Although little is said about such programs, the United States routinely cooperates with other nations in drug interdiction efforts, and some even include the limited use of U.S. military troops and specially trained antidrug units.

In 1998 the United States became involved in major paramilitary efforts in Colombia (referred to as Plan Colombia) to destroy drug crops there and to detain and arrest drug traffickers who were aiding rebel and terrorist groups within Colombia. Since the September 11, 2001, terror attacks in the United States, the federal government has stepped up its antidrug efforts overseas, fearing that terrorist groups of all stripes might be using the lucrative drug trafficking business to fund their activities and recruit members.

The opium trade in Afghanistan helped fuel rebel groups there well before the September 11 attacks, and as Afghanistan has grown more unstable in the years after the overthrow of the Taliban, opium production is again on the rise. The George W. Bush administration actually decreased its efforts to dissuade opium production. The crop is undoubtedly being exploited by elements in the Afghan government and also being employed by Afghan insurgents to secure funds with which to purchase arms and supplies, so the nation is becoming a part of narcoterrorism.

Drug trafficking certainly funds some Taliban activities. In addition, both the radical Hamas and Hezbollah organizations have been identified with drug smuggling activities. Programs aimed at curbing the international drug trade have become an integral part of the Global War on Terror.

PAUL G. PIERPAOLI JR.

**See also**

Afghanistan; Al Qaeda; Global War on Terror; Karzai, Hamid

**References**

Friman, H. Richard. *Narcodiplomacy: Exporting the U.S. War on Drugs.* Ithaca, NY: Cornell University Press, 1996.

Tarazona-Sevillano, Gabriela. *Sendero Luminoso and the Threat of Narcoterrorism.* New York: Praeger, 1990.

Valentine, Douglas. *The Strength of the Wolf: The Secret History of America's War on Drugs.* London: Verso, 2004.

---

# Nasar, Mustafa Sittmariam

*See* Suri, Abu Musab al-

---

# Nasiriyah, Battle of
**Start Date: March 23, 2003**
**End Date: March 29, 2003**

The Shiite-dominated town of Nasiriyah occupies an important location in southern Iraq. Situated some 225 miles southeast of the capital of Baghdad, Nasiriyah is the fourth most populous city of Iraq after Baghdad, Basra, and Mosul. In 2003 Nasiriyah had a population of some 560,000 people. It is also an important transportation hub, with key bridges spanning the Euphrates River on either side of the city. Located close to Tallil Airfield and the headquarters of the Iraqi Army III Corps of three divisions, Nasiriyah was thus a key objective in the first phases of the Iraq War. During the 1991 Persian Gulf War, Nasiriyah had been the most northerly point in Iraq for U.S. forces, with the 82nd Airborne having reached the city's outskirts.

In 2003 the task of taking Nasiriyah and the bridges over the Euphrates fell to U.S. Marine Corps Task Force Tarawa (TF Tarawa), commanded by Brigadier General Richard Natonski. TF Tarawa was the code name for the 2nd Marine Expeditionary Brigade, centered on the 2nd Marine Regiment, Marine Aircraft Group 29, Company A of the 8th Tank Battalion (with M-1 Abrams tanks), and Combat Service Support Battalion 22. TF Tarawa was the vanguard of the I Marine Expeditionary Force (I MEF), commanded by Lieutenant General James Conway, that was centered on the 1st Marine Division led by Major General James Mattis.

TF Tarawa's assignments were to first secure Jalibah Air Base and then secure the bridges across the Euphrates and the Saddam Canal. Taking and holding these crossing points were essential for enabling the 1st Marine Division to continue its drive northward on Highway 7 toward Kut. With this accomplished, TF Tarawa was to keep open the supply corridor that would enable the 1st Marine Division to continue north and engage and defeat the Republican Guard divisions defending the southern approaches to Baghdad.

In its drive north into Iraq from Kuwait, TF Tawara was obliged to move through the desert to get to Jalibah Air Base because the supply vehicles of the U.S. Army's 3rd Infantry Division, which had movement priority, occupied the roads. Meanwhile, the 3rd Infantry Division also advanced toward Baghdad, taking a crossing over the Euphrates west of Nasiriyah. As the 3rd Infantry Division defeated Iraqi forces in and around Tallil Airfield and bypassed Nasiriyah to the west, TF Tarawa moved on that city.

TF Tarawa departed Jalibah Air Base for Nasiriyah early on March 23, but taking the city did not go according to plan. Natonski had planned for the 1st Battalion, 2nd Marine Regiment, to move through the eastern part of Nasiriyah and seize one of the northern bridges, after which another battalion was to secure the city, thereby allowing the three regimental combat teams of the I MEF to continue the drive north on Route 7.

The marines had anticipated fighting at Nasiriyah but not the level of resistance encountered. One thing did go according to plan: much of the Iraqi 11th Division simply deserted. What the marines had also expected did not occur, however: an uprising by the population of Nasiriyah against the regime. The inhabitants had done so in 1991, and many had been massacred by the Saddam Hussein regime. The survivors had learned their lesson. Indeed, they now prepared to defend the city. The composition of those fighting is still disputed, with some of the fighters certainly being members of the Fedayeen Saddam who began arriving in the city on March 22 in private vehicles and commandeered buses. Although poorly trained, they were fanatical fighters and willing to die in a jihad. Under the command of ruthless Iraqi general Al Hassan al-Majid, a relative of Hussein who had charge of the south, the defenders of Nasiriyah prepared to do battle with the marines.

Fighting began as soon as the leading marine element, the 1st Battalion, 2nd Marine Regiment, supported by some armor, arrived at the city outskirts. The marines quickly destroyed nine stationary T-72 tanks—a number of them bereft of engines—that had been dug in to defend a railroad bridge south of the river.

At about 7:30 a.m., marines of A Company were startled to make contact with an American military truck belonging to the army's 507th Maintenance Company. The men in it informed the marines that their 18 trucks had been part of a 3rd Infantry Division supply column. The 507th Maintenance Company, which included female soldiers Jessica Lynch and Lori Piestewa, had taken a wrong turn on Route 7 and proceeded into Nasiriyah, where it had been ambushed. In the ensuing fighting, 11 American soldiers had been killed and 6 others, including Lynch and Piestewa, were taken prisoner. Piestewa died of her wounds shortly after capture, while the remaining 5 prisoners, including Lynch, were later rescued. Piestewa was a member of the Hopi tribe and is thus believed to

A U.S. marine assists displaced Iraqi civilians caught in a firefight north of Nasiriyah, Iraq, on March 26, 2003. (U.S. Department of Defense)

have been the first Native American woman killed in combat in a foreign war. On learning of the plight of the 507th Maintenance Company, the marines immediately headed north and rescued a dozen wounded members of that unit.

Unfortunately for the marines, the appearance of the 507th Maintenance Company trucks had alerted the defenders of Nasiriyah to the imminent arrival of other American forces. The ensuing firefight and the desperate effort of the members of the maintenance company to escape also served to give the defenders a false sense of their ability to stop the Americans.

After a pause to refuel, the marines then drove to the Euphrates. The Iraqis had not blown the bridge, but a major firefight soon erupted. One company took a wrong approach to another bridge over the Saddam Canal, and a number of its vehicles became bogged down in soft sand. The marines resumed their advance to the canal down the city's main road, which they soon dubbed "Ambush Alley."

Supported by tank fire, the marines succeeded in getting across the canal, but one of their amphibious assault vehicles (AAV) took a hit from a rocket-propelled grenade (RPG) on the bridge. Four marines were wounded, and the AAV barely made it across the span. Worse, a Fairchild-Republic A-10 Warthog aircraft, supporting the marines, attacked marines on the north side of the

bridge, mistaking them for Iraqis and killing six. Two other marine vehicles sent south of the river back down Ambush Alley as part of a convoy to remove wounded were struck and destroyed by RPG and small-arms fire that killed most of those inside. Heavy fighting for the bridgehead raged during the night, with the marines supported by Bell AH-1S Cobra attack helicopters. By the morning of March 24 the marines had control of both bridges and had suppressed some of the resistance along Ambush Alley. Determined to press on as quickly as possible in order to threaten Kut and thereby present the Iraqis with two threats to Baghdad, Conway, Mattis, and Natonski decided to push the 1st Marnie Regiment up Ambush Alley through Nasiriyah and up Highway 7. At the same time, the 5th and 7th Marine regiments were able to secure the bridge outside the urban area and reach Highway 1.

The 5th and 7th Marine regiments had a relatively easy time of it, but it was a different story for the members of the 1st Marine Regiment, pushing up Highway 8 on the evening of March 24. They came under heavy small-arms fire including RPGs and mortar fire. Sustaining relatively few casualties, however, the 1st Marine Regiment passed through the city on the night of March 24–25 and was soon on its way to Kut.

TF Tarawa now was faced with the difficult task of clearing Nasiriyah in order to protect the marine supply line north to Routes

1 and 7. These efforts were severely impacted by the arrival of a *shamal*. This fierce sandstorm lasted several days and not only reduced air support available to the marines but also made the efforts to clear out snipers and fighters more difficult, complicating fighting conditions. Artillery proved to be the only all-weather continuous fire support asset for TF Tarawa. On March 26 high-explosive (HE) rounds with concrete-piercing fuses were fired against a hospital that was serving as a paramilitary strong point and that was then seized by the marines. A concentrated artillery fire mission against an estimated 2,000 fedayeen at a railroad station in the southern part of the city reported to be preparing to launch a counterattack not only ended that threat but also killed some 200 of the fedayeen.

A number of marine vehicles were lost to RPGs, but the situation was eased by a cordon around the city that cut off resupply to the Iraqi fighters. With the end of the *shamal* and the arrival of unmanned aerial vehicles over Nasiriyah, more accurate targeting information was soon available. Marine aircraft also took part. Also, some residents began to come forward to identify Iraqi sniper nests and command centers, and Special Forces units also assisted in the targeting.

Intelligence provided by friendly Iraqis also enabled a team of marines, navy SEALs, and army Rangers to rescue Private Lynch and the other Americans who had been captured earlier. The fighting was largely over by March 29, but it was not until early April that Nasiriyah was completely secure. The fighting for the city had claimed 18 marines killed and more than 150 wounded.

SPENCER C. TUCKER

**See also**

"Ambush Alley"; Conway, James Terry; Fedayeen; IRAQI FREEDOM, Operation, Ground Campaign; Lynch, Jessica; Majid al Tikriti, Ali Hassan al-; *Shamal;* Tallil Airfield

**References**

Cordesman, Anthony H. *The Iraq War: Strategy, Tactics, and Military Lessons.* Westport, CT: Praeger, 2003.

Keegan, John. *The Iraq War: The Military Offensive, from Victory in 21 Days to the Insurgent Aftermath.* New York: Vintage, 2005.

Livingston, Gary. *An Nasiriyah: The Fight for the Bridges.* North Topsail Island, NC: Caisson, 2004.

Lowry, Richard S. *Marines in the Garden of Eden: The Battle for An Nasiriyah.* New York: Berkley, 2006.

Murray, Williamson, and Robert H. Scales Jr. *The Iraq War: A Military History.* Cambridge, MA: Belknap, 2005.

Pritchard, Tim. *Ambush Alley: The Most Extraordinary Battle of the Iraq War.* New York: Ballantine Books, 2007.

# Nasser, Gamal Abdel

**Birth Date: January 16, 1918**
**Death Date: September 28, 1970**

Egyptian nationalist leader, vice president (1953–1954), premier (1954–1956), and president (1956–1970). Born in Bani Mur, Egypt, on January 16, 1918, Gamal Abdel Nasser at an early age developed great antipathy toward Britain's rule over Egypt, setting the stage for his later championing of Arab nationalism and unity. Embarking on a military career, he graduated from the Egyptian Royal Military Academy in 1936. While stationed in the Sudan, he met and became friends with future Egyptian president Anwar Sadat.

In 1947 Nasser organized a secret nationalist and antigovernment organization among fellow officers, known as the Free Officers Association. Its members were primarily of lower- and lower-middle-class backgrounds unlike most Egyptian politicians of the time, who were from the upper classes. The officers sought to end both British influence in Egypt and the reign of King Farouk.

After months of painstaking planning, the organization staged a bloodless coup against Farouk's government on July 23, 1952. Three days later the king abdicated and fled abroad. Meanwhile, a Revolutionary Command Council (RCC) of 13 Free Officers assumed authority over Egypt. Major General Muhammad Naguib served as the spokesperson for the younger, junior, and more radical officers. He became commander of the Egyptian armed forces, while Ali Maher Pasha was made premier.

When the council declared Egypt a republic in June 1953, Naguib became its first president, and Nasser became vice president. Beginning in February 1954, a political power struggle ensued between Nasser and his faction of the RCC and Naguib's faction. By May, Nasser had taken de facto control as president of the RCC and premier of Egypt. Naguib was allowed to continue as president although as little more than a figurehead.

Nasser and his faction consolidated their hold on power, and after an October 1954 attempt on Nasser's life, in November he ordered Naguib arrested. Using the assassination attempt to solidify his power base, Nasser became premier of Egypt on February 25, 1955. Seven months later he also took the title of provisional president.

Nasser quickly moved to centralize his authority. The 1952 revolution was popular with the Egyptian public, but the power elite around Nasser contained opponents, first in the labor movement and communists and then in the Muslim Brotherhood. In June 1956 a national election occurred in which Nasser was the sole candidate for the presidency. Thus, he officially became Egypt's second president.

When the military junta came to power it decreed a series of reforms, including the abolition of honorary and hereditary titles as a means of addressing the feudal power system in Egypt where urban and rural *bashawat* (pashas) in effect controlled their poor subjects. Prior to the revolution, rural poverty and violence were rampant, with a small number of people owning much of the rural land. This situation had encouraged proposals for land reform in the Egyptian parliament, and discussion of the issue continued in the RCC. In 1952 Naguib then announced the first Agrarian Reform Law, which sparked many panicked land sales. Under the terms of the legislation, individual rural landholdings could be no more than 200 feddans (about 208 acres).

Nasser became even more popular when he nationalized the Suez Canal in 1956. He weathered the Suez War, which to

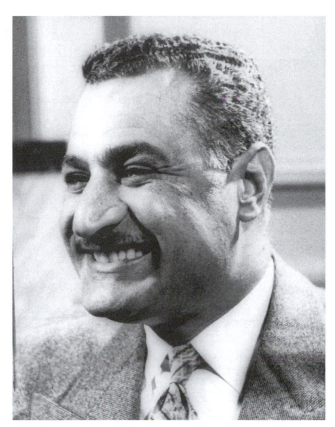

As premier (1954–1956) and then president (1956–1970) of Egypt, Gamal Abdel Nasser was a staunch nationalist and champion of Arab unity who led Egypt until his death. (AP/Wide World Photos)

Egyptians simply proved the enmity of the former colonial powers and Israel. In the wake of the Suez War, many minority groups left voluntarily or were forced out of Egypt.

Nasser's effort to join Egypt with Syria in the United Arab Republic (UAR) in 1958 ended unsuccessfully in 1961. In its wake, Nasser put more effort into social and economic reform, including an additional land reform measure that was supposed to limit individual holdings to no more than 100 feddans (about 104 acres) and provide for the distribution of the surplus land to needy peasants. However, this measure was never fully implemented.

The RCC government aimed to weaken the social class that had most benefitted under the previous regime by both land reform and the sequestration of foreign-owned or large businesses and property. In addition, Nasser announced plans to increase agricultural production by the reclamation of lands in the delta area and construction of a new high dam on the Nile south of Aswan.

Following an assassination attempt on him, Nasser outlawed the Muslim Brotherhood, arresting and imprisoning many of its members. He then banned the organization outright. The universities were purged of elements that supported the previous regime and those urging a return to parliamentary and constitutional life.

In foreign affairs, Nasser achieved several successes. On February 12, 1953, Egypt and Britain signed a treaty providing for the future of the Sudan. Over a three-year period the Sudan would

develop self-governing institutions, after which the Anglo-Egyptian occupation would end and a Sudanese Constituent Assembly would choose its future course. Egyptian leaders agreed to this because by November 1952 they had acknowledged the right of Sudanese self-determination themselves. Sudan's independence was announced in February 1955.

Egyptian nationalists had long worked for British withdrawal from the Suez Canal. On October 19, 1954, Nasser's government reached agreement with the British on the abrogation of the Anglo-Egyptian Treaty of 1936, the evacuation of all British troops from the Canal Zone within 20 months (the last troops departed in June 1956), maintenance of the canal base by British civilian technicians under the sovereign control of Egypt, and Britain's right to reenter Egyptian territory to protect the canal in the event of an attack "by an outside power on Egypt."

Nasser stated early that he was basically inclined toward the West, but he did not wish to see Egypt manipulated by outside powers, as had been the case in so much of the past. He made it clear that communism could not take root in Egypt. At the same time, he warned the Western powers to postpone implementing any security pacts in the Middle East. Washington rejected this call, and by the end of 1954 relations between the Western powers and Egypt had badly deteriorated over the impending conclusion of the Baghdad Pact. Nasser strongly criticized the pro-British Iraqi prime minister over the new Egyptian radio station, Voice of the Arabs, in an effort to discourage other Arab signatories to the treaty.

Nasser was one of the leaders of the neutralist bloc at the Bandung Conference in April 1955, thereby angering the United States, which viewed neutralism as a cover for pro-Soviet attitudes. Nasser's increasing opposition to Western security arrangements led him in October 1955 to conclude military agreements with Saudi Arabia and Syria. The leaders of both states agreed to a joint command arrangement headed by Egyptian generals.

Following a strong Israeli military strike into Gaza in February 1955, Nasser increasingly devoted attention to Egyptian military preparedness. To improve his armed forces, he approached the United States and Britain about purchasing arms, but after the failure of the Baghdad Pact, Washington refused. Nasser then turned to the communist bloc. In September 1955, with Soviet encouragement, he reached a barter arrangement with Czechoslovakia for substantial quantities of weapons, including jet aircraft and tanks, in return for Egyptian cotton.

The arms deal infuriated the United States and directly impacted the Aswan Dam construction project, which was the centerpiece of Nasser's plans to improve the quality of life for Egyptians. Nasser had sought Western financing, and in December 1955 Washington declared its willingness to lend $56 million for financing the Aswan Dam. Britain pledged $14 million, while the World Bank agreed to $200 million. The condition to the aid was that Egypt provide matching funds and that it not accept Soviet assistance.

Nasser was unhappy with the attached strings and in any case expected a Soviet offer of assistance. The tightly controlled

Egyptian press then launched an all-out propaganda offensive against the West, especially the United States. However, when no Soviet offer was forthcoming, Nasser finally accepted the Western aid package on July 17, 1956. Much to his chagrin, two days later the American government announced that the offer had been withdrawn. The official U.S. reasons were that Egypt had failed to reach agreement with the Sudan over the dam and that Egyptian financing for the project had become uncertain. The real reasons were objections from some U.S. congressmen, especially Southerners fearful of competition from Egyptian cotton, and Secretary of State John Foster Dulles's desire to teach Nasser and other neutralists a lesson. Dulles was especially upset over Egypt's recent recognition of the People's Republic of China (PRC).

A furious Nasser took immediate action. On July 26 he nationalized the Suez Canal Company, claiming that this revenue would pay for the construction of the cherished dam project. Seeing an opportunity to gain additional influence with the Egyptians and the Arab world in general, Moscow quickly offered to assist Nasser with the dam.

Nasser's action of nationalizing the canal and the failure of the United States and the United Nations (UN) to take a strong stand on the matter led to secret talks among the governments of France, Britain, and Israel. The leaders of these countries had the common aim of overthrowing Nasser. Their secret agreement culminated in the Suez Crisis, one of the major events of the Cold War.

On October 29, 1956, acting in accordance with a secret treaty with Britain and France, Israeli forces struck deep into Egyptian territory in the Sinai. The French and British governments then announced the existence of a threat to the security of the canal and demanded that both sides cease hostilities and withdraw from the canal area. When Egypt refused, French and British forces launched air attacks on Egypt on October 3. On November 5 French and British airborne forces landed in Egypt, and the next day they came ashore in an amphibious assault, the British at Port Said and the French at Port Fuad.

The United States, not privy to the secret discussions among France, Britain, and Israel, was taken by surprise and applied heavy pressure on the invaders, especially Britain. London caved under this pressure, and France and Israel were then forced to follow suit. The Soviet Union, distracted by the concurrent Hungarian Revolution, threatened intervention on the Egyptian side, but it was U.S. pressure that proved decisive in the outcome.

Far from being defeated, Nasser appeared vindicated by the Suez Crisis despite the fact that he had to surrender to Israeli navigation in the Gulf of Aqaba. The event elicited great sympathy in the Arab world for Egypt, from the masses if not the leaders, and Nasser shrewdly used this so-called victory to further consolidate his rule at home and to promote Pan-Arabism throughout the Middle East. Photographs of him could be seen in every small storefront in the region. Indeed, the Suez Crisis turned Nasser into the chief spokesperson for Arab nationalism and Arab unity.

Nasser relentlessly pursued his dream of Arab unity on a variety of fronts, employing diplomacy, oratory, and subversion. In January 1958 Shukri al-Qawatli, a Syrian nationalist leader who hoped to forestall a communist victory in Syria, pressured Nasser to join Egypt into a formal union with that country. Nasser agreed to the creation of the UAR and became its president. In early March, Yemen joined Egypt and Syria in a federal union, forming the United Arab States that existed alongside the unitary state of the UAR. Nasser traveled by train through Syria and was hailed by large crowds as the hero of Arabism.

The UAR did not last. The struggle between Syrian factions that had predated the union intensified during this period. The Syrian middle class had not been subjected to authoritarian rule as had the Egyptians, and insufficient attention had been given to the structures needed to share power. Moreover, the head of Syrian military intelligence, who was loyal to Nasser, was very unpopular in Syria. The UAR fell apart when Syria withdrew on September 28, 1961. Nevertheless, Nasser continued to promote Arab nationalism and his vision of Arab states joining together in political action, although the breakup of the UAR did cause him to place more emphasis on Arab socialism. These views and his attempts to topple the monarchies in the conservative Arab states, coupled with Western policies, brought about an Arab cold war.

Relations with the Soviet Union remained reasonably close, cemented by anti-imperialist rhetoric, Soviet support for the Arab position against Israel, and arms deals. The bulk of the Egyptian population disliked the presence of many Soviet advisers in the country. At the same time, however, Nasser was uncompromising in his repression of communism within Egypt. Under Nasser, relations with the United States fluctuated from good to poor.

Nationalizations that went beyond seizing properties belonging to the British and French went into effect after 1961 and included banks, insurance companies, and large enterprises. Businesses employing more than 4,000 people were taken over by the state, although some of these were later returned. These policies were not unpopular except among those directly affected. There were many economic problems, abetted by unrealistic state planning, poor management of industry, and the siphoning off of government revenues on defense spending. Nasser's government was state-capitalist in nature rather than truly socialist.

Nasser's nationalization program was unpopular in the West, but his attacks on the small rural and political elite who had run the country gained him the loyalty of the workers and peasants. Also, although the regime was quite repressive, it did produce a sense of pride in Egypt and things Egyptian that had not existed up to that time.

In September 1962 a military coup toppled the monarchy in Yemen. A civil war then ensued between supporters of the monarchy and the new republican government. The republican side sought help from Egypt, and Nasser eagerly responded, anxious to fulfill his commitment to Arab republicanism. Egypt supplied equipment and increasing numbers of men. The Saudis meanwhile provided aid to the monarchist side. Yemen became a quagmire for Nasser who, by the mid-1960s, had committed some 80,000 men there. The war dragged on until 1967, and it might have continued far longer without Israel's defeat of Egypt that same year.

In 1966 Nasser signed a defense pact with Syria, and in early 1967 he began provoking the Israelis by a number of different actions, including insisting on the departure of UN peacekeepers from the Egyptian-Israeli border, where they had been in place since the 1956 Suez Crisis. He also ordered a blockade of the Gulf of Aqaba and moved Egyptian troops into the Sinai.

In retaliation for these actions, on June 5, 1967, the Israelis launched a surprise attack, first on Egypt, then on Syria, and, when it entered the war, on Jordan. In a matter of a few hours, the Israelis all but eliminated their opponents' air forces. The resulting Six-Day War proved to be a humiliating defeat for Nasser in which the Israelis conquered the entire Sinai peninsula and entrenched themselves on the eastern bank of the Suez Canal. Nasser's belief that he could bluff his way through the crisis without fighting had cost 12,000 Egyptian dead and the loss of three-quarters of his air force. He took the blame himself and resigned, but mass public demonstrations in his support brought him back to power. He then blamed the army.

The cease-fire that halted the fighting steadily deteriorated into almost continuous firing across the canal and retaliatory Israeli air strikes deep into Egypt. Finally, in July 1970 Nasser agreed to a cease-fire arrangement put forward by U.S. secretary of state William Rogers, ending the so-called War of Attrition. Nasser's health may have deteriorated as a result of his efforts in 1970 to negotiate the crisis involving the Jordanian Army and the Jordanian regime on the one hand and the Palestinian militants known as Black September on the other. Now in deteriorating health, Nasser died of a heart attack in Cairo on September 28, 1970.

DALLACE W. UNGER JR., SPENCER C. TUCKER, AND SHERIFA ZUHUR

**See also**

Arab-Israeli Conflict, Overview; Arab Nationalism; Dulles, John Foster; Egypt; Muslim Brotherhood; Suez Crisis

**References**

DuBius, Shirley Graham. *Gamal Abdel Nasser, Son of the Nile.* New York: Third Press, 1972.

Kerr, Malcolm. *The Arab Cold War: Gamal Abd al-Nasir and His Rivals.* New York: Oxford University Press, 1971.

Lacouture, Jean. *Nasser: A Biography.* New York: Knopf, 1973.

# National Defense Authorization Act for Fiscal Years 1992 and 1993

Comprehensive legislation consisting of 35 titled provisions authorizing appropriations for Department of Defense operations and certain U.S. strategic initiatives during fiscal years 1992 and 1993.

The act was sponsored by Representative Les Aspin (D-Wis.) and was passed by Congress on November 22, 1991. President George H. W. Bush signed the act into law on December 5, 1991.

Appropriations legislation for Department of Defense operations for each governmental fiscal year necessarily mirrors the nuts-and-bolts needs of the department and the required funding for certain U.S. strategic initiatives evident at the time of approval. The National Defense Authorization Act for fiscal years 1992 and 1993 was no exception. Congress dealt with a vast array of programs and contractual arrangements to support Department of Defense operations across all of the military services as well as initiatives such as the strategic missile defense system. But coming on the heels of the Persian Gulf War, the act also addressed several unique issues stemming from both the troop buildup and combat phases of the conflict (Operations DESERT SHIELD and DESERT STORM). These included health concerns related to oil well fires set by Iraqi forces, the service of women during the war, and the relatively large complement of reservists and National Guard personnel called to active duty.

Concerns over the health effects of thick smoke from the more than 750 oil well fires set by Iraqi military personnel in Kuwait had steadily mounted since the cease-fire. Responding quickly, the Department of Veterans Affairs initially established its own registry list of concerned veterans in April 1991 and offered basic clinical examinations. Congress expanded this effort by mandating in the act the establishment of a Department of Defense registry to list all members of the armed services exposed to the fumes of burning oil wells. A pulmonary function examination and chest X-ray were also to be given to any registry member upon request. Congress went even further by mandating annual reports from the Department of Defense detailing the progress of studies related to the short-term and long-term effects of such exposure. A thorough review of the military medical system was also directed. Coupled with the Department of Defense Veterans Affairs' initial stop-gap measure, the act's Department of Defense registry provision served as a foundation for subsequent congressional actions.

Increasing health concerns over biological and chemical warfare vaccinations and other petroleum-based emissions from daily operations in the war zone resulted in expansion of the Department of Defense registry to cover all Persian Gulf War veterans. This occurred with the establishment of the 1992 Persian Gulf War Veterans Health Registry.

The service in the war of a higher percentage of women (7 percent) as compared to previous conflicts prompted Congress to also establish in the act the Commission on the Assignment of Women in the Armed Forces. A year-long mandate, the commission was tasked with exploring various matters relating to the military service of women, including the implications of appointing women to combat positions and requiring women to register for a future draft. Furthermore, in consultation with the commission, the secretary of defense was authorized in the interim to promote a pilot program to test the feasibility of assigning women to combat positions. Acknowledging the effectiveness of women pilots who had flown noncombat aircraft, Congress also repealed U.S. Air Force, U.S. Navy, and U.S. Marine Corps prohibitions on assigning women to combat aircraft positions.

Finally, Congress addressed the potential of a rapidly mobilized reservist complement once again serving on active duty in wartime. The Persian Gulf War witnessed the activation of a reserve and National Guard force comprised of 17 percent of the total force. To ensure a constant combat readiness of these components, the act increased the number of army officers assigned for full-time support of National Guard units, authorized a pilot program to provide active army advisers to reserve units with a high probability of deployment, and maintained the number of reserve and National Guard personnel in accordance with fiscal year 1991 levels. In concert with the health registry and women combatant provisions, the reserve support provisions foreshadowed far-reaching effects of the act on the U.S. military well beyond fiscal years 1992 and 1993.

MARK F. LEEP

**See also**

Gulf War Syndrome; Oil Well Fires, Persian Gulf War; Persian Gulf Conflict Supplemental Authorization and Personnel Benefits Act of 1991; Persian Gulf War Veterans Health Registry

**References**

Guzzardo, Joseph M., and Jennifer L. Monachino. "Gulf War Syndrome—Is Litigation the Answer? Learning Lessons from *In Re Agent Orange*." *St. John's Journal of Legal Commentary* 10 (1995): 673–696.

Institute of Medicine. *Health Consequences of Service during the Persian Gulf War: Recommendations for Research and Information Services.* Washington, DC: National Academy Press, 1996.

Knight, Amy W., and Robert L. Worden. *The Veterans Benefits Administration: An Organizational History, 1776–1994.* Collingdale, PA: Diane Publishing, 1995.

---

# National Geospatial-Intelligence Agency

The primary U.S. government agency responsible for mapmaking, imagery analysis, and geographic intelligence. The National Geospatial-Intelligence Agency (NGA), established in 2004, is the product of more than two centuries of U.S. government involvement in geography and cartography that may be said to have begun with the U.S. Army's Lewis and Clark Expedition of 1803.

In the 1800s the U.S. Army developed some of the country's first mapmaking capabilities, producing both large-scale and small-scale maps. The U.S. Navy developed a similar tradition for producing naval charts. Throughout the 1800s, maps and charts remained the principal focus of specialty units within these branches of the service, although some functions were gradually passed to civilian agencies, such as the U.S. Geological Survey (USGS), which was established in 1879.

The focus on maps and charts broadened during World War I, when the development of aerial photography led to the establishment of specialized photo interpretation units. During World War II the armed forces expanded production of maps and charts, refined techniques for converting aerial photographs to tactical maps, and developed increasingly sophisticated capabilities in imagery intelligence.

The onset of the Cold War ensured continued developments in these fields. Aerial photography advanced significantly with the development of the Lockheed U-2 and Lockheed SR-71 reconnaissance aircraft as well as better cameras and film. Likewise, the Corona Program inaugurated the modern era of satellite imagery. In one of the last official acts of his administration, President Dwight Eisenhower approved the formation of the National Photographic Interpretation Center (NPIC), which provided a joint structure for imagery intelligence units drawn from the U.S. Army, the U.S. Navy, the U.S. Air Force, and the Central Intelligence Agency (CIA). A decade later, military units responsible for producing maps and charts were also consolidated with the 1972 establishment of the Defense Mapping Agency (DMA).

During Operation DESERT STORM, the DMA produced more than 60 million maps. Although some were out of date and distribution problems arose, this marked a significant step forward. Likewise, imagery analysts processed unprecedented numbers of images, although delays in transmitting intelligence information to tactical units posed a problem. The development of smaller and lighter Global Positioning Systems (GPS) allowed troops to more accurately determine their locations. Cartographers developed sophisticated digital elevation models (DEMs), computer-generated 3-D terrain maps based on latitude, longitude, and elevation, that are critically important to the guidance systems of smart weapons such as the Tomahawk cruise missile. These geospatial developments enabled the U.S. Navy to fire cruise missiles from the Persian Gulf and hit specific windows in targeted buildings in Baghdad. In the years following DESERT STORM, the DMA systematically updated its regional maps for the Middle East and helped improve the distribution system, while other agencies refined the distribution process for imagery intelligence.

By the mid-1990s, the rapid pace of advances in technology was steadily eroding the distinction between mapmaking and imagery intelligence. Consequently, the two functions were merged in 1996 with the creation of the National Imagery and Mapping Agency (NIMA), which absorbed the DMA and related organizations. Within the NIMA, geographers, cartographers, imagery analysts, computer experts, and others continued working toward ever greater capabilities in geospatial intelligence (GEOINT). In 2004 the NIMA officially became the National Geospatial Intelligence Agency (NGA). Unlike the consolidation of agencies in 1996 resulting in the creation of the NIMA, this was essentially a name change only, albeit one that provided a title that more accurately reflects the expanding scope of its activities.

The September 11, 2001, terrorist attacks and subsequent combat in Afghanistan and Iraq provided the catalyst for further developments. The NGA continues to refine the technology that guided cruise missiles to Baghdad in 1991, making it increasingly available for frontline ground units. For instance, many units can now view DEMs of urban neighborhoods as they prepare and conduct combat operations. NGA personnel developed the Gridlock system to link intelligence, surveillance, and reconnaissance information to geospatial reference points, thus adding the capacity to provide tactical units with information that they can exploit on short notice. The NGA also assists in the development of precision-guided minimunitions. A 500-pound bomb may be appropriate for bunkers and armored vehicles but is not appropriate against a pickup truck driven by a terrorist, especially when civilians are in the vicinity. The development of minimunitions allows troops to destroy hostile targets while reducing the likelihood of killing innocent civilians. This reduces the number of people likely to join the insurgents in pursuit of revenge.

The National Security Agency (NSA), which engages in signals intelligence (SIGINT), describes itself as the "ears of the nation." Likewise, the NGA sees itself as the "eyes of the nation." Geography is a holistic discipline, so it is not surprising that NGA personnel actively promote interagency cooperation, perhaps realizing that eyes and ears work better when they work together.

CHUCK FAHRER

### See also

Aircraft, Reconnaissance; Bombs, Precision-Guided; Central Intelligence Agency; Defense Meteorological Satellite Program; Joint Surveillance and Target Radar System Aircraft; Land Remote-Sensing Satellite; National Reconnaissance Office; Navigation Satellite Timing and Ranging Global Positioning System; Reconnaissance Satellites

### References

Beck, Richard A. "Remote Sensing and GIS as Counterterrorism Tools in the Afghanistan War: A Case Study of the Zhawar Kili Region." *Professional Geographer* 55(2) (May 2003): 170–179.

DeMers, Michael. *Fundamentals of GIS.* 3rd ed. Hoboken, NJ: Wiley, 2004.

Doty, John M. "Geospatial Intelligence: An Emerging Discipline in National Intelligence with an Important Security Assistance Role." *DISAM Journal* 27(3) (Spring 2005): 1–14.

McGlone, Chris, ed. *Manual of Photogrammetry.* 5th ed. Bethesda, MD: ASPRS, 2004.

# National Intelligence Council

The center for midterm and long-term intelligence planning within the U.S. intelligence community. The National Intelligence Council (NIC) officially began operating in 1979. Its origins date back to 1947, when the U.S. government reorganized the nation's intelligence services via the National Security Act and created the Central Intelligence Agency (CIA). The director of central intelligence (DCI) had the responsibility of ensuring that all intelligence data was properly evaluated and shared among appropriate U.S. government organizations. Toward that end, Congress gave the DCI a permanent staff. However, intelligence estimates continued to be flawed. Consequently, acting in his capacity as DCI, in 1950 General Walter Bedell Smith created the Board of National Estimates. It was charged with preparing and disseminating assessments of both international trends and foreign threats to American interests. The Board of National Estimates operated as a council composed of experts in the various fields of intelligence and oversaw the production of National Intelligence Estimates.

In 1973 DCI William J. Colby reformed the way in which the board produced the National Intelligence Estimates. Colby was persuaded that the board had become too insular and out of touch. He thus eliminated the Board of National Estimates, replacing its council of experts with regional and functional specialists called national intelligence officers. These officers had the responsibility of drafting the National Intelligence Estimates. The CIA's Directorate of Intelligence and the analytical branches of the national intelligence community provided the national intelligence officers with staff and research support. In 1979 the national intelligence officers became the National Intelligence Council (NIC), with the mission of reporting directly to the DCI.

The NIC's mission is to serve as the intelligence community's center for midterm and long-term strategic thinking. The NIC's overall mission is to manage the intelligence community's estimative process, incorporating the best available expertise from inside and outside the government. It speaks authoritatively on substantive issues for the entire intelligence community. The NIC is charged with five formal functions: supporting the director of national intelligence in his role as head of the intelligence community, acting as a focal point for receiving and responding to queries from policy makers, broadening the intelligence community's perspective by reaching outside of the intelligence community to engage experts in academia and the private sector, assisting the intelligence community in responding to the changing requirements from policy makers, and leading the intelligence community in the production of National Intelligence Estimates and related products.

The NIC's National Intelligence Estimates are considered the most authoritative written judgments concerning national security issues. They contain comprehensive judgments regarding the likely course of future events of the entire intelligence community, an entity that after 2004 consists of the CIA; the Defense Intelligence Agency; the National Security Agency; the National Geospatial Intelligence Agency; the National Reconnaissance Office; the State Department's Bureau of Intelligence and Research; Air Force, Army, Coast Guard, Marine Corps and Navy Intelligence; the Federal Bureau of Investigation (FBI); the Department of Homeland Security; the Department of Energy; and the Treasury Department. The NIC's stated goal is "to provide policymakers with the best, unvarnished, and unbiased information—regardless of whether analytic judgments conform to U.S. policy."

The formal structure of the NIC has a chairman, a vice chairman, a counselor, and a director of strategic plans and outreach. There are seven national intelligence officers assigned to geographic regions: Africa, East Asia, Europe, the Near East, Russia and Eurasia, South Asia, and the Western Hemisphere. Six national intelligence officers deal with specific areas of concern: economics and global issues, military issues, science and technology, transnational threats, warnings, and weapons of mass destruction (WMDs) and proliferation. By the terms of the Intelligence Reform and Terrorism Prevention Act of 2004, the NIC reports directly to the director of national intelligence (DNI) and represents the coordinated views of the entire intelligence community.

Throughout its history, the NIC's process of creating National Intelligence Estimates has been fraught with uncertainty and subject to controversy. By definition, estimates are speculative. Estimates were performed when analysts often did not know something with precision or confidence. Effective estimates rely upon sound data—a problematic foundation given the active efforts of other nations to conceal their plans—and careful analysis. Because the estimates are used by the executive branch to craft policy and by political parties to evaluate presidential choices, the analysts who craft the National Intelligence Estimates have frequently been subject to political pressures.

In the aftermath of the September 11, 2001, terrorist attacks followed by the U.S. invasion of Afghanistan and the U.S. invasion of Iraq, two NIC publications represented the council's efforts to provide U.S. policy makers with an assessment of how the world would evolve and to identify opportunities and negative developments that might require policy actions. "Mapping the Global Future 2020" sought to depict what the world would look like in 2020. "Global Trends 2025: A World Transformed" sought to provide a fresh examination of how global trends would unfold. The NIC, like other organizations within the intelligence community, came under scrutiny for its perceived failings in providing actionable information that may have prevented the September 11 attacks. But in fairness, the failings pervaded the entire intelligence apparatus as well as the FBI. The NIC again came under scrutiny after it became apparent that prewar intelligence concerning Iraq's WMDs was either faulty or misrepresented. No WMDs were found after the 2003 invasion of Iraq, even after a 16-month search.

JAMES ARNOLD

**See also**

Central Intelligence Agency; Defense Intelligence Agency; September 11 Attacks; Weapons of Mass Destruction

**References**

Ford, Harold P. *Estimative Intelligence: The Purpose and Problems of National Intelligence Estimating.* Washington, DC: Defense Intelligence College, 1993.

Steury, Donald P., ed. *Sherman Kent and the Board of National Estimates: Collected Essays.* Washington, DC: History Staff, Center for the Study of Intelligence, Central Intelligence Agency, 1994.

Theoharis, Athan, ed. *The Central Intelligence Agency: Security under Scrutiny.* Westport, CT: Greenwood, 2006.

# National Liberation Front in Algeria

The primary insurgent movement opposing French colonial rule during the Algerian War of Independence (1954–1962) and the predominant political force in Algeria since 1962. The Front de Libération Nationale (FLN, National Liberation Front) has largely dominated the Algerian government since the end of the war.

In 1830 French troops landed at Algiers and then gradually expanded their holdings to create what would become the modern state of Algeria. The French ended up dominating the economic life of Algeria, and tens of thousands of French, Italian, and Spanish settlers (colons) came to Algeria to engage in agriculture and commerce there. Unlike Morocco and Tunisia, Algeria, which was divided into three departments, was considered to be an integral part of France. The reality was quite different, for the political structure, as with the economy, was rigged in favor of the Europeans. Moderate Arabs such as Ferhat Abbas, who spoke French and admired French institutions, found to their dismay that despite repeated promises, France was not willing to extend equal rights to the Muslim population, which came to outnumber the Europeans in Algeria about nine to one. The failure of the French government to understand the need for meaningful reform led to Muslim riots at the end of World War II and the growth of radical nationalism. Algerian nationalists formed the Comité Révolutionnaire d'Unité et d'Action (Revolutionary Committee of Unity and Action, CRUA), which became the FLN in 1954. Its military wing, the Armée de Libération Nationale (National Liberation Army, ALN), commenced guerrilla operations on November 1, 1954. This began the Algerian War of Independence.

During the Algerian War of Independence, French forces consistently defeated ALN insurgents in pitched battle, and French counterinsurgency efforts included construction of the 200-mile Morice Line of barbed wire, electric fences, sensors, minefields, and spotlights along the Tunisian border. The Pedron Line, along the Moroccan border, served the same purpose to the west. Nonetheless, the insurgency continued as more and more Muslim Algerians became radicalized. The war's costs and mounting French casualties also had their effect in metropolitan France.

Failure in rural operations prompted the FLN to launch major operation in Algiers, culminating in what became known as the Battle of Algiers in 1957. FLN terrorist tactics ultimately failed because of aggressive French search and interrogation techniques led by French brigadier general Jacques Massu. It was those very techniques, however, that alienated many citizens in France itself. Documented reports of atrocities perpetrated by French forces created outrage in France. Nonetheless, word that the French government was considering peace talks with the FLN led to rioting among the Europeans in Algeria, and the French Army stepped in. A threatened military takeover in May 1958 was averted only by the return to power of General Charles de Gaulle, who pledged to maintain French control over Algeria. De Gaulle attempted reform in Algeria, including the promise of a vast economic program known as the Constantine Plan, but it came too late. In April 1961 a group of disaffected

French generals in Algiers who opposed secret French government negotiations with the FLN attempted and failed to topple the government of President Charles de Gaulle. Having exhausted all other options, de Gaulle opened peace talks with the rebels in Evian, France, that finally led to Algerian independence on July 5, 1962, the 132nd anniversary of the French invasion of Algiers.

Soon after independence, fighting erupted among rival FLN factions. Eventually Ahmed Ben Bella displaced enough rivals to gain control of the country. In 1965 his continued efforts to outmaneuver rivals provoked a military coup d'état led by Houari Boumédienne, who ruled Algeria until his death in 1978.

Under Boumédienne, the FLN focused on expanding the capital-intensive oil industry but neglected the labor-intensive agricultural sector. The FLN also had to recruit foreign Arabic-speaking teachers for a school system in which French had been the language of instruction. Many of these teachers were Egyptian Islamists fleeing their government's crackdown on the Muslim Brotherhood. Their efforts to reintroduce Arabic ultimately produced a new generation of Algerian Islamists who spoke Arabic in preference to French.

Chadli Benjedid, another Algerian Army officer, assumed the presidency in 1979. Although he worked hard to improve the agricultural sector, high population growth, unemployment, and a growing rich-poor gap made food subsidies essential for many Algerians. In the early 1980s, however, high oil prices provided sufficient revenue to fund such subsidies. That changed when oil prices plunged in 1986. In 1988 the FLN announced austerity measures to a public already angry with food prices, unemployment, housing shortages, and corruption. The reaction on the street was swift and violent. Hundreds died in riots that even the army failed to quell. Although the riots took everyone by surprise, Islamists seized the opportunity to express the rage on the street within an Islamic context. As the protests grew, Benjedid capitulated and announced the advent of multiparty politics. Islamists formed the Front Islamique du Salut (Islamic Salvation Front, FIS), which scored major victories in December 1991 elections, with the FLN finishing third behind Berber nationalists. In January 1992, however, military officers quietly ordered President Benjedid to dissolve the legislature and then resign. Having created a power vacuum, the officers stepped forward to announce the formation of the Haut Conseil d'État (High Council of State, HCÉ), which seized power, nullified the elections, and began arresting Islamist leaders.

The move sparked an insurgency. FIS members joined other Islamists to form the Armée Islamique du Salut (Islamic Salvation Army, AIS). The Groupe Islamique Armeé (Armed Islamic Group, GIA), an extremist group formed from Algerian veterans of the anti-Soviet jihad in Afghanistan, also began attacks throughout Algeria. Atrocities committed by the GIA were so horrific that the populace resumed support for the FLN despite its many shortcomings. Ultimately, the conflict claimed more than 150,000 lives.

The terrorist threat in Algeria has subsided but not disappeared. Abdelaziz Bouteflika, who has ruled Algeria since 1999, granted amnesty to thousands of insurgents, but many reportedly rejoined militant groups, such as Al Qaeda in the Islamic Maghreb. Although the FLN now shares power, many smaller parties are dominated by former FLN members, with moderate Islamists playing a diminished role.

CHUCK FAHRER

**See also**
Al Qaeda; Algerian War; Terrorism

**References**
Bennoune, Mahfoud. *The Making of Contemporary Algeria, 1830–1987.* Cambridge: Cambridge University Press, 1988.
Horne, Alistair. *A Savage War of Peace: Algeria, 1954–1962.* New York: Viking, 1977.
Metz, Helen Chapin, ed. *Algeria: A Country Study.* Washington, DC: U.S. Government Printing Office, 1994.
Ruedy, John. *Modern Algeria: The Origins and Development of a Nation.* Bloomington: Indiana University Press, 1992.
U.S. State Department. *Background Note: Algeria.* Washington, DC: Bureau of Public Affairs, U.S. State Department, 2007.

# National Media Pool

Revolving pool of U.S. print and broadcast reporters chosen by the U.S. Department of Defense to cover U.S. military operations. The National Media Pool (NMP) was an attempt to ensure the American media's access to military operations while simultaneously controlling media coverage of certain events and providing for the safety of battlefield reporters. The NMP was first activated on July 19, 1987, a reaction to the media's vociferous complaints about the Defense Department's mishandling of reporters during the 1983 invasion of Grenada (Operation URGENT FURY). On July 19, 1987, 10 reporters were flown—in secrecy—to the Persian Gulf to report on the reflagging of Kuwaiti oil tankers by the U.S. government, a by-product of the ongoing Iran-Iraq War (1980–1988).

The NMP was comprised of reporters representing news wire services, television, magazines, newspapers, and radio. Membership in the NMP was rotated every three months by way of a lottery system. Normally, there were 16 media representatives in each rotation and a staff of 3 military escorts. At least one of the escorts had to be a lieutenant colonel, colonel, or equivalent rank (0-5 or 0-6).

The NMP was not designed to endure for the entirety of a military operation or campaign. Rather, media coverage was supposed to become more or less open once the Defense Department determined that the situation would be amenable to a larger media presence. The Defense Department, however, made this decision unilaterally and thus in theory could maintain an NMP for as long as it wished.

The Defense Department also determined the particular units in which reporters were placed (sometimes referred to as embedding reporters), and news reports had to be read and authorized by the top-ranking media escort before any information could be released to the public. It was understood that the NMP reporters would share their information and reporting with other news outlets. Typically, the Defense Department created an NMP for the beginning stages of an operation or conflict and then phased it out once battle lines had stabilized. In-theater commanders were sometimes able to requisition a particular reporter or group of reporters from the NMP to cover a specific military mission or situation.

The NMP was activated several times between 1987 and the 1991 Persian Gulf War, and in general reporters believed that they had been treated fairly and had not been subjected to undue or unnecessary censorship. Indeed, because many of the NMP members were serving alongside U.S. and coalition troops, they realized full well that some information could not be released for fear of compromising an operation or aiding the enemy. The NMP was activated on August 12, 1990, just 10 days after Iraqi forces invaded Kuwait. On August 26 it was disbanded when the Saudi government announced that it would allow international media reporters to cover the action from Saudi Arabia.

The NMP was activated a few more times in the 1990s, largely to cover military events in the Balkans. After the September 11, 2001, terror attacks on the United States, however, the Pentagon began to reconsider the use of the pool. Fearful that any media coverage might compromise the clandestine operations in Afghanistan (Operation ENDURING FREEDOM), in October 2001 the Defense Department chose not to activate the NMP, with one official stating that Afghanistan was not amenable to reporters. Furthermore, the irregular operations and remote battlegrounds made the conflict difficult to cover. The NMP was resurrected during the Anglo-American–led invasion of Iraq in March–April 2003 (Operation IRAQI FREEDOM). Pool reporters were once more embedded with U.S. and coalition units, but some reporters complained that military press officials pressured soldiers into remaining silent.

PAUL G. PIERPAOLI JR.

**See also**
Media and Operation DESERT STORM; Television, Middle Eastern

**References**
Greenberg, Bradley S., and Walter Gantz, eds. *Desert Storm and the Mass Media*. Cresskill, NJ: Hampton, 1993.
Katovsky, Bill, and Timothy Carlson. *Embedded: The Media at War in Iraq, an Oral History*. Guilford, CT: Lyons, 2003.
Massing, Michael. *Now They Tell Us: The American Press and Iraq*. New York: New York Review of Books, 2004.
Smith, Hedrick, ed. *The Media and the Gulf War: The Press and Democracy in Wartime*. Washington, DC: Seven Locks, 1992.

# National Reconnaissance Office

U.S. intelligence agency responsible for oversight of building, launching, and monitoring the nation's reconnaissance satellites. Established on the recommendation of two presidential scientific advisers, James Killian and Edwin Land, by President Dwight D. Eisenhower on August 25, 1960, the National Reconnaissance

Office (NRO) was conceived as a centralized agency that would coordinate and manage U.S. orbital missions and aerial reconnaissance. The NRO is part of the Department of Defense. One of 16 U.S. intelligence agencies, its mission is to secure the information superiority by means of satellites for the U.S. government and military.

The NRO director is appointed by the secretary of defense with the concurrence of the director of national intelligence but without congressional confirmation. The NRO's staff is comprised of both CIA and Defense Department personnel. The NRO is headquartered in Chantilly, Virginia.

In July 1961 Secretary of Defense Robert McNamara finalized the formation of the NRO. Its existence was kept secret for more than 30 years. Not until September 1992 did a Defense Department directive finally declassify the existence of the NRO.

The primary focus of the NRO has always been developing reconnaissance satellites for the U.S. government and military. Its Corona satellite project during 1960–1972 took more than 800,000 photographic reconnaissance images. At the conclusion of the Cold War in 1991, the NRO reoriented its mission to better meet the current demands of the U.S. government and military. The focus of the NRO shifted to gathering intelligence for regional conflicts instead of Cold War–era global war.

Information supplied by the NRO during Operation DESERT STORM (January–February 1991) proved immensely important in the war. Satellite imagery provided by the NRO provided targeting information and poststrike damage assessments. The conflict was proof positive of the value of satellite reconnaissance in war. NRO intelligence made possible the full exploitation of precision-guided weapons (smart bombs). However, one lesson learned from DESERT STORM was the need to improve the flow of information directly to the war fighters.

In response to DESERT STORM experiences, the NRO developed a new generation of satellites for collecting intelligence for the U.S. military and other intelligence agencies. In September 1995 an article in the *Washington Post* reported that the NRO had hoarded between $1 billion and $1.7 billion in unspent funds. In recent years, the NRO has played a significant role in the Global War of Terror. In both Operation ENDURING FREEDOM and Operation IRAQI FREEDOM, commanders relied daily on NRO-supplied intelligence. NRO personnel were deployed to the theaters of war to aid in providing new or updated NRO-developed equipment, systems, and applications. The improved real-time dimension provided by space satellites has contributed significantly to the success registered by coalition forces.

NRO systems also provide for global communications, precise navigation, early warning of missile launches, signals intelligence, and real-time imagery to U.S. forces no matter their deployment location. Satellite surveillance also contributes to planning programs for precision-guided weapons and identifying friendly troop locations. All information and intelligence collected receives careful evaluation, analysis, and interpretation of material collected through space surveillance. The NRO boasts the ability to gather intelligence from any location at any time of the day regardless of the weather.

To aid in its mission, the NRO operates ground stations located around the globe that collect and distribute reconnaissance information. The NRO also works closely with the National Intelligence Agency, the National Geospatial-Intelligence Agency, the Defense Intelligence Agency, and other government entities. NRO operations remain cloaked in secrecy for national security reasons.

TARA K. SIMPSON

**See also**

Bombs, Precision-Guided; Central Intelligence Agency; Defense Intelligence Agency; National Geospatial-Intelligence Agency; Reconnaissance Satellites

**References**

Richelson, Jeffrey T. *The U.S. Intelligence Community.* 4th ed. Boulder, CO: Westview, 1999.

Spires, David N. *Beyond Horizons: A Half Century of Air Force Space Leadership.* 2nd ed. Maxwell Air Force Base, AL: Air Force Space Command and Air University Press, 2007.

Temple, L. Parker. *Shades of Gray: National Security and the Evolution of Space Reconnaissance.* Reston, VA: American Institute of Aeronautics and Astronautics, 2005.

# National Security Agency

U.S. intelligence-gathering agency. Headquartered at Fort Meade, Maryland, the National Security Agency (NSA) is the component of the U.S. intelligence community that specializes in activities related to cryptography and signals intelligence (SIGINT). Established on November 4, 1952, by President Harry S. Truman in the wake of a series of intelligence failures regarding the Korean War, the NSA has served as the U.S. government's primary technical intelligence-collection organization since that time.

The United States was renowned for its success in the realm of SIGINT (the gathering and analysis of intercepted voice communications intelligence, or COMINT) and electromagnetic radiation (electronic intelligence, or ELINT) during World War II. Yet Americans entered the early years of the Cold War with a disorganized SIGINT apparatus loosely coordinated among the independent and oftentimes redundant cryptologic agencies of the U.S. Army, the U.S. Navy, and the U.S. Air Force. In line with the centralizing theme of the 1947 National Security Act, Secretary of Defense Louis A. Johnson established the Armed Forces Security Agency (AFSA) in 1949 to streamline SIGINT collection. Plagued by the weaknesses of limited jurisdiction and ill-defined authority, however, deficiencies in AFSA's relationship with the service agencies were made readily apparent prior to and during the outbreak of the Korean War in June 1950.

At the urging of President Truman, Secretary of State Dean Acheson appointed New York attorney George Abbott Brownell to head a probe investigating AFSA's failings. The resultant "Brownell Committee Report" advocated replacing AFSA with a centralized national agency capable of unifying all U.S. SIGINT efforts. Fully agreeing with this recommendation, within months President Truman had dissolved AFSA and quietly signed into law the NSA.

Throughout the 1950s and early 1960s the NSA established itself as a key intelligence player in virtually all major Cold War political and military conflicts. In 1953 the NSA began overflights of Soviet airspace using converted B-47 Stratojets equipped with various receivers capable of intercepting Soviet air defense radar signals. By intentionally triggering the activation of the Soviet air defense radar system, the B-47s could pinpoint and map the locations of Soviet systems on the ground, providing crucial information for U.S. pilots. By the late 1950s the Stratojets had been replaced by the high-flying U-2 reconnaissance jet, and overflights to collect Soviet SIGINT data continued, focusing on radar emissions and telemetry information related to intercontinental ballistic missile (ICBM) launches. The overflight program ended suddenly amid an international crisis. On May 1, 1960, U-2 pilot Francis Gary Powers was shot down over the central Soviet city of Sverdlovsk. Initially disavowing any knowledge of the overflight program, the Eisenhower administration, when faced with irrefutable evidence presented by Soviet premier Nikita Khrushchev, was forced to concede that it had ordered the flights.

Although direct flights over Soviet airspace were terminated in the wake of the Powers controversy, the NSA maintained a robust collection effort utilizing ground, air, sea, and space-based antennas and sensors to monitor the transmissions of the Eastern bloc as well as nonaligned and allied nations. In an often contentious relationship with the U.S. Navy, NSA listening posts were established on both adapted warships such as USS *Liberty* and on smaller dedicated collection platforms such as USS *Pueblo* to loiter in international waters collecting transmissions, while NSA-directed submarines tapped into undersea communication cables. Ground stations concentrating on intercepting shortwave and very high frequency (VHF) emissions were established in strategically important

**Directors of the National Security Agency, 1988–Present**

| Name | Rank | Branch | Dates of Service |
| --- | --- | --- | --- |
| William O. Studeman | Vice admiral | U.S. Navy | August 1988–May 1992 |
| John M. McConnell | Vice admiral | U.S. Navy | May 1992–February 1996 |
| Kenneth A. Minihan | Lieutenant general | U.S. Air Force | February 1996–March 1999 |
| Michael V. Hayden | Lieutenant general | U.S. Air Force | March 1999–April 2005 |
| Keith B. Alexander | Lieutenant general | U.S. Army | April 2005–present |

locations around the globe, including Ellesmere Island in the upper reaches of the Arctic Circle, Ayios Nikolaos in Cyprus, Field Station Berlin in West Berlin, and Misawa Air Force Base in Japan. After the undisclosed launch of the first SIGINT satellite in June 1960, the NSA also began to establish an array of ground-based relay centers in remote locations on the periphery of the Soviet Union.

By the late 1970s the NSA was enjoying great success in decoding the encrypted Soviet messages that had previously eluded the U.S. intelligence community. As the NSA's mission grew, its budget increased exponentially. Exact budgetary figures from the Cold War period continue to be withheld as classified information as is the current budget, but during that time the NSA established itself as the largest U.S. intelligence agency in terms of both manpower and financial resources.

The proliferation of consumer-oriented electronic communication devices that began in the 1980s proved a boon to the NSA. With the advent of fax machines, cell phones, personal computers, and handheld computers, the NSA has greatly increased its ability to monitor transmissions of all kinds and from all around the world. Because of this, the NSA has been central in U.S. antiterrorism efforts. It is believed that the NSA has the capability of intercepting and monitoring transmissions of most of the planet's electronic devices. This ability has come in handy since the Global War on Terror began in 2001, but it has also caused much consternation among those who fear further encroachments on privacy and civil liberties. In December 2005 the NSA came under great scrutiny when the *New York Times* published a story about the George W. Bush administration's order to tap telephone conversations of select Americans placing calls out of the country. The operation was carried out largely by the NSA and without the requisite court warrants. There have also been concerns that the NSA, working with Internet service providers, may be monitoring customers' Internet communications even between Americans, a situation with serious implications regarding U.S. civil liberties.

ROBERT G. BERSCHINSKI

**See also**

Central Intelligence Agency; Global War on Terror; National Intelligence Council

**References**

Bamford, James. *Body of Secrets: Anatomy of the Ultra Secret National Security Agency.* New York: Anchor, 2002.
———. *The Puzzle Palace: A Report on America's Most Secret Agency.* New York: Penguin, 1983.
Johnson, Chalmers. *The Sorrows of Empire: Militarism, Secrecy, and the End of the Republic.* New York: Metropolitan Books, 2004.

# National Security Council

U.S. agency utilized by the president of the United States and his chief military and political advisers to analyze and determine foreign (sometimes domestic) and military policy that will best protect the national security of the United States. The National Security Council (NSC) was established in 1947 under the auspices of the National Security Act of that year, which established the NSC as the central organization for coordinating foreign policy that would bring together all key national security policy makers. The act called for a small NSC staff and an executive secretary who would supervise the council's workings, resulting in a membership that was much smaller than today's NSC staff.

With the end of World War II, the United States became a global superpower. As the competition between the United States and the Soviet Union intensified into the Cold War, it was clear that a more centralized structure was necessary in order to discuss national security decisions. The resulting NSC has steadily grown in power since it was first convened by President Harry S. Truman, and today it is comparable to that of a cabinet-level agency.

The NSC is composed of the president (chair), vice president, secretary of state, secretary of the treasury, secretary of defense, and the national security adviser (assistant to the president for national security affairs). Serving as the military adviser to the NSC is the chairman of the Joint Chiefs of Staff (JCS). The director of national intelligence (a position established only in 2005) serves as the NSC's intelligence adviser. Other regular but nonpermanent attendees include the chief of staff to the president, the counsel to the president, the assistant to the president for economic policy, the U.S. attorney general, and the director of the Office of Management and Budget. Other officials and representatives are invited to attend meetings as required.

Since the NSC was established, it has continued to change and evolve with each presidential administration. Different events and situations have called for different processes and policies emanating from the NSC. Today the national security adviser is much more than an executive secretary who controls the flow of information. Instead, the national security adviser is a powerful adviser to the president. This has been accompanied by an exponential growth in the NSC staff. The NSC has also lost much of its earlier formality, and weekly meetings have not been common since the 1950s. More informal episodic meetings are the norm.

Despite the significant changes in the structure and operations of the NSC throughout the decades, its fundamental mission has not changed. The NSC continues to be used as a forum for discussion and debate before the president makes a final decision on matters relating to foreign, military, or national security policy. Since 1986, each president has been required to submit a National Security Strategy (NSS) annually. The NSS is a document that outlines the current threats to the national security of the United States and how the presidential administration plans to deal with these. Each administration chooses how best to use the NSC to create the NSS, but the process usually involves different committees, each drafting an NSS.

Since the 1991 Persian Gulf War, the NSC has been deeply involved in conflicts in the Middle East. President George H. W. Bush used the NSC to good effect before and during the Persian

Gulf War (Operation DESERT STORM). Brent Scowcroft, a former U.S. Air Force general, was perhaps one of the most effective NSC advisers in history, serving the George H. W. Bush administration from 1989 to 1993. Scowcroft's tenure was marked by unusually cordial relations with Secretary of State James A. Baker III, and the NSC dealt successfully with the end of the Cold War, the collapse of the Soviet Union, rocky relations with the People's Republic of China (PRC), the unification of Germany, and the invasion of Panama as well as DESERT STORM and its aftermath.

When President William J. Clinton took office in 1993, he greatly expanded NSC membership. Clinton used the NSC mainly to focus on using American power to create a safer world through humanitarian intervention, free trade, and the spread of democracy. His administration did, however, engage in military operations, with input from the NSC, including the bombardment of Iraq to punish it for failing to abide by United Nations (UN) sanctions, the bombing of suspected terrorist sites in Afghanistan and Sudan in retaliation for the U.S. embassy bombings in Kenya and Tanzania, and the North Atlantic Treaty Organization (NATO) bombing campaign against Serbia in 1999, designed to end the Kosovo War.

After President George W. Bush came into office in 2001, the terror attacks of September 11, 2001, greatly impacted the sessions of the NSC, which was headed by Condoleezza Rice until January 2005 and Stephen Hadley from January 2005 to January 2009. The president's 2002 NSS argued that while deterrence was a workable solution for the Cold War, such a policy could not effectively combat terrorism. This marked the implementation of the Bush Doctrine, which was shaped by Rice and other neoconservatives in the White House and argued for the use of preemptory force to foil terrorist acts before they could be perpetrated. This thinking led to the March 2003 invasion of Iraq. Rice went on to become secretary of state in Bush's second term, although she since seemed to moderate her position on the use of force. The Department of Homeland Security, created in 2002, also interacts with great frequency and on many issues with the NSC.

Following the election of President Barack Obama, in January 2009 retired U.S. Marine Corps general James L. Jones became national security adviser.

ARTHUR M. HOLST

**See also**

Baker, James Addison, III; Bush, George Herbert Walker; Bush, George Walker; Bush Doctrine; Clinton, William Jefferson; Neoconservatism; Rice, Condoleezza; Scowcroft, Brent; United States Department of Homeland Security

**References**

Doyle, Richard B. "The U.S. National Security Strategy: Policy, Process, Problems." *Public Administration Review* 67 (2007): 624–629.

Newmann, William W. "Reorganizing for National Security and Homeland Security." *Public Administration Review* 62 (2002): 126–137.

Zegart, Amy B. *Flawed by Design: The Evolution of the CIA, JCS, and NSC.* Stanford, CA: Stanford University Press, 1999.

# Navigation Satellite Timing and Ranging Global Positioning System

A constellation of 31 orbiting satellites, 6 in each of four orbital planes, that produce an extremely precise timing signal for use in determining accurate position information in three dimensions in all weather conditions on a receiver located on the earth's surface. A Global Positioning System (GPS) receiver picks up the signals from the 4 satellites with the strongest signal and then calculates its position by carefully timing the signals sent by the GPS satellites and using the arrival time of each message to measure the distance to each satellite. Using geometric and trigonometric calculations, it then determines the position (coordinates) of the receiver and converts them to longitude and latitude within yards of its real position relative to the satellites. Additionally, the GPS signal can provide velocity within 0.45 miles per hour, or better than 1 foot per second, and correct time to within 1 millionth of a second.

The U.S. Department of Defense initiated the Navigation Satellite Timing and Ranging (NAVSTAR) GPS in 1973 to reduce the proliferation of navigational aids and launched its first satellite in February 1978. After Soviet aircraft shot down Korean Air Lines Flight 007 in September 1983, the U.S. Air Force made the system available for civilian use at no charge. As the air force launched more satellites to provide the minimum number of satellites for the timing signals, the GPS quickly proved itself in providing positioning coordinates for typical navigation applications and fostered many new applications in mapmaking, land surveying, commerce, scientific uses, and hobbies. GPS also provides a precise time reference used in many applications, including scientific study of earthquakes and synchronization of telecommunications networks. The U.S. Air Force Space Command declared the GPS satellite system fully operational in April 1995.

The GPS signal is available in two basic forms: Standard Positioning Service (SPS) for general public users and Precise Positioning Service (PPS) for U.S. military and allied military users. The SPS provides a horizontal position that is accurate to 109 yards (100 meters), and the PPS horizontal accuracy is 22 yards (20 meters). The latter also provides greater resistance to jamming and greater immunity to deceptive signals.

The GPS includes a feature called Selective Availability (SA) that can introduce intentional, slowly changing random errors of up to 328 feet (100 meters) into the publicly available navigation signals to confound the use of the more accurate GPS signal by adversaries. When enabled during crises or war, the U.S. military forces, its allies, and other government users can access the more accurate signal in an encrypted form. However, even those who managed to acquire military GPS receivers would still need to obtain the daily key, the dissemination of which is tightly controlled by the U.S. government.

Delta rockets launch GPS satellites from Cape Canaveral, Florida, placing them in circular orbits 12,600 miles above the earth. The satellites continually orientate themselves to point their solar panels toward the sun and the antennas toward the earth. Each

Illustration of the NAVSTAR satellite. (U.S. Department of Defense)

satellite contains four atomic clocks that provide the highly accurate timing signals. The U.S. Air Force has several replenishment satellites ready for launch and has awarded contracts to provide satellites well into the 21st century.

The U.S. Air Force tracks the flight paths of the satellites via monitoring stations in Hawaii, Kwajalein Atoll in the Pacific, Ascension Island, Diego Garcia, and Colorado Springs, Colorado. The 50th Space Wing, Schriever Air Force Base, Colorado, controls the movement of the orbiting satellites and provides regular navigational updates, using the ground antennas at Ascension Island, Diego Garcia, Kwajalein, and Colorado Springs to synchronize the atomic clocks on board each satellite.

The user segment consists of vehicle-mounted and handheld military and commercial procured receivers. Millions of people worldwide have purchased relatively inexpensive small GPS receivers for accurate position information and travel directions. Surveyors use GPS receivers to accurately determine boundary lines in remote locations. Emerging GPS technologies include the determination of the attitude of a vehicle as well as its position.

In the lead-up to and during the Persian Gulf War, coalition military forces made the first extensive combat use of the GPS system. The U.S. Air Force moved several GPS satellites into orbits to give coalition forces in the Persian Gulf access to signals from four satellites. Forces could observe voice and radar radio silence during a rendezvous, and aircraft could link up for midair refueling without communications. Combat aircraft used the GPS signals to attack specified targets with bombs and guided weapons more accurately. The U.S. Navy employed GPS to provide position data for its cruise missiles to attack heavily defended high-priority targets, map minefields, and direct the rendezvous of supply ships. U.S. Army Apache helicopters, M60 tanks, and ground troops all used GPS receivers to maneuver across the featureless Saudi Arabian and Kuwait deserts. Forward air controllers, working with ground forces, used GPS receivers to direct artillery fire on Iraqi positions.

During the short conflict, the NAVSTAR GPS made the various night maneuvers possible. In the past, ground forces would have required numerous scouts and guides along the routes of advance. GPS allowed attacking coalition forces to shift their attack plans back and forth virtually up to the moment of attack because forces using GPS had no need for fixed markers on the ground. Additionally, in response to fresh intelligence, coalition forces could accurately maneuver in response to the movement of Iraqi forces. The drivers of meal trucks also used GPS receivers to find and feed widely dispersed frontline units.

During Operation RESTORE HOPE in Somalia in 1992–1993, U.S. Air Force and civilian cargo aircraft used GPS receivers to approach and land at makeshift airfields without the electronic aids found at larger airports. All military services employed GPS receivers during Operations ALLIED FORCE (1991) and DENY FLIGHT (1994–1995) in the Balkans. GPS receivers have also been extensively used in the fighting in Afghanistan since 2001 and during and after the invasion of Iraq since March 2003.

After the Persian Gulf War, U.S. Air Force chief of staff General Merrill A. McPeak directed the Air Force Materiel Command to develop a low-cost, highly accurate, all-weather air-to-ground weapon that would overcome the limitations of the laser-guided bombs used in the Vietnam War and the Persian Gulf War. By 1995 the air force had produced the Joint Direct Attack Munition (JDAM), a gravity bomb with a tail kit that picks up the GPS signal and uses that signal, along with the Inertial Navigation System (INS), to direct the weapon to within 10 feet of its target. During Operation ALLIED FORCE in 1999, the JDAM, carried by the B-2 Spirit bomber, proved highly successful in destroying discrete targets in Serbia.

Following the terrorist attacks on the United States on September 11, 2001, the United States initiated the Global War on Terror. During Operations ENDURING FREEDOM, which began in October 2001, and IRAQI FREEDOM, which commenced in March 2003, the JDAM has become the air-delivered weapon of choice for coalition air forces to attack enemy forces in close proximity to allied ground forces or near groups of noncombatants or sensitive structures, such as mosques or apartment buildings. The JDAM, using GPS technology, permits accurate bombing while reducing the likelihood of collateral damage and civilian casualties. By 2006, the U.S. Air Force had developed the Small Diameter Bomb (SDB), a 250-pound version of the JDAM that produces a smaller blast and fragmentation pattern than the JDAM. The SDB also uses the GPS signal and INS for precision targeting.

ROBERT B. KANE

**See also**

Bombs, Gravity; Bombs, Precision-Guided; DESERT STORM, Operation; ENDURING FREEDOM, Operation; IRAQI FREEDOM, Operation; Joint Direct Attack Munition and Small Diameter Bomb; Somalia, International Intervention in

**References**

History Office. *History of the Air Armament Center, 1 October 2005–30 September 2006,* Vol. 1. Eglin Air Force Base, FL: Air Armament Center, 2007.
History Office, Space and Missile Systems Center, Los Angeles Air Force Base. *Historical Overview of the Space and Missile Systems Center, 1954–2003.* Los Angeles: Missile Systems Center, 2003.
Levis, Alexander H., John C. Bedford, and Sandra Davis, eds. *The Limitless Sky: Air Force Science and Technology Contributions to the Nation.* Washington, DC: Air Force History and Museums Program, 2004.
Peeples, Curtis. *High Frontier: The United States Air Force and the Military Space Program.* Washington, DC: Air Force History and Museum Program, 1997.

# Negroponte, John Dimitri
## Birth Date: July 21, 1939

U.S. diplomat and the first director of national intelligence (2005–2007). John Dimitri Negroponte was born in London, England, on July 21, 1939. His father, Dimitri, was a Greek shipping tycoon. Negroponte attended elite schools in the United States, including Phillips Exeter Academy and Yale University from which he earned an undergraduate degree in 1960. Attending Harvard University Law School for only a brief time, he joined the Foreign Service in 1960 and stayed with the State Department until 1997. During his long career, Negroponte served in eight overseas posts, including those in Asia, Latin America, and Europe. He also held a series of increasingly important positions with the State Department in Washington, D.C. In 1981 he was appointed to his first ambassadorship, that to Honduras, a post he held until 1985. He subsequently served as ambassador to Mexico (1989–1993) and the Philippines (1993–1996). From 1987 to 1989 Negroponte was deputy assistant to the director of national security affairs in the Ronald Reagan administration.

Negroponte retired from the Foreign Service in 1997 and joined the publishing firm of McGraw-Hill as a senior executive. In 2001 President George W. Bush tapped him to become the U.S. ambassador to the United Nations (UN), a post he held until 2004. Negroponte worked at the UN to secure support for U.S. policies in the aftermath of the September 11, 2001, terror attacks and vowed not to bend to international pressure in the ensuing Global War on Terror. This stance did not always make him popular among his UN colleagues. In the run-up to the 2003 Iraq invasion, Negroponte was the Bush administration's reliable point man in dealing with the sometimes intransigent UN.

In April 2004 Negroponte was named ambassador to Iraq. He assumed his duties on June 30, when Anglo-American occupation forces turned sovereignty of Iraq over to the provisional government. Negroponte, who replaced L. Paul Bremer, was immediately faced with a rapidly expanding insurgency and the problems of stabilizing and rebuilding a war-torn nation.

A year later, in February 2005, President Bush named Negroponte as the first director of national intelligence, a new cabinet-level position. Negroponte was charged with coordinating the work of all of the nation's intelligence-gathering services. As such, he was largely responsible for establishing the budgetary requirements of the new intelligence apparatus, which approached $40

John Negroponte, national intelligence director during 2005–2007, shown here testifying before the Senate Armed Services Committee on February 28, 2006. Negroponte introduced much-needed reforms in the U.S. intelligence community. (AP/Wide World Photos)

billion by 2006. Negroponte's appointment was lauded by many who saw in him the required steadiness of a diplomat combined with the ability to organize and lead. Having worked under both Democratic and Republican administrations, he was seen as a relatively bipartisan public servant who could be counted on to do the right thing in the face of considerable political pressures.

Negroponte wasted no time in instituting needed reforms in the intelligence community and reorganizing the intelligence-gathering apparatus to make it far more efficient and less vulnerable to leaks and political infighting. Indeed, his policies earned high praise from both executive-branch and congressional officials. In January 2007 Negroponte left his post to become deputy secretary of state, a position that he had long coveted and held until January 2009.

PAUL G. PIERPAOLI JR.

**See also**

Bremer, Jerry; Bush, George Walker; Central Intelligence Agency; Iraq, History of, 1990–Present; United Nations

**References**

Draper, Robert. *Dead Certain: The Presidency of George W. Bush.* New York: Free Press, 2008.

U.S. Senate, Committee on Foreign Relations. *The Nomination of Hon. John D. Negroponte to be U.S. Ambassador to Iraq, April 27, 2004.* Washington, DC: U.S. Government Printing Office, 2004.

## Neoconservatism

A form of conservative political thought and also a political movement that had its genesis in the 1964 presidential campaign of Republican candidate Barry Goldwater. Neoconservatism is most prevalent among rightist Republicans and has steadily gained followers over the years. It was said to be the prevailing mind-set in the foreign policy of President George W. Bush and many of his senior officials, including Vice President Richard (Dick) Cheney, Secretary of State Condoleezza Rice, Secretary of Defense Donald Rumsfeld, and Deputy Secretary of Defense Paul Wolfowitz. Irving Kristol, William Kristol, Charles Krauthammer, Richard Perle, Robert Kagan, and William Bennett are also identified as prominent neoconservatives (neocons). The term "neoconservative" can be controversial, however, because it is said to be pejorative or a code word used by those espousing anti-Semitic and/

or anti-Israeli views. Many neoconservatives are either Jewish or strong supporters of Israel.

Neoconservatism rose to maturity in the 1970s as a reaction to the policies of détente pursued by presidents Richard Nixon, Gerald Ford, and Jimmy Carter in dealing with the Soviet Union. Some disenchanted liberals and conservatives favored confronting the Soviet Union rather than tolerating or seeking to accommodate its allegedly aggressive policies. The foreign policy of the Ronald Reagan administration largely embraced neoconservative principles, the first administration to do so. Reagan placed renewed emphasis on military force and deterrence and promoting democracy by supporting what he called "freedom fighters" battling communist regimes or insurgencies. Reagan's staunch anticommunism and controversial 1983 speech denouncing the Soviet Union as "an evil empire" and blaming it for the arms race was vintage neoconservative thought, even if the term itself was not yet in vogue. In the same speech, Reagan characterized the Cold War as a struggle between "right and wrong, good and evil," just as George W. Bush labeled Iraq, Iran, and North Korea an "axis of evil" and the Global War on Terror as a war of moral righteousness against the forces of evil and tyranny. Part of neoconservative rhetoric—if not philosophy—tends to view the world in stark contrasts of black and white, leaving few gray areas that might yield to diplomacy rather than force.

One of the earliest neoconservative statements by George W. Bush came in a speech he delivered at the U.S. Military Academy, West Point, on June 1, 2002. In this speech, formalized in a document three months later titled "The National Security Strategy of the United States of America," Bush indicated that the Cold War–era doctrines of deterrence and containment were now less relevant because the new threats posed by Al Qaeda and other nonstate terrorist groups required new thinking. According to Bush, deterrence could not succeed against terrorist groups because, unlike governments, they do not have a nation or citizens to defend. Containment could not work with dictators, he claimed, who could deliver weapons of mass destruction (WMDs) or secretly provide them to their terrorist allies.

Thus, Bush built the case for preemptive action to defend the United States. No longer would the United States wait for threats to materialize fully before taking action. Indeed, a central premise of the so-called Bush Doctrine and neoconservative thought is that the United States must take advantage of its military superiority and neutralize threats before they are capable of threatening American interests, even if this means acting unilaterally without the support of the international community. President Bush justified the invasion and overthrow of Iraqi dictator Saddam Hussein's regime in March 2003 by arguing that Hussein posed a growing threat to both American security and the stability of the Middle East. Therefore, Bush undertook military action before Hussein had rearmed with WMDs.

Another important neoconservative theme is the so-called democratic peace theory: that the United States should promote democracy and freedom around the world because, as Democratic president Woodrow Wilson believed, democracies do not wage war with each other. This line of reasoning holds that it is dictatorships that are responsible for causing wars and threatening peace.

Critics of the Bush Doctrine and neoconservatism in general object to its alleged aggressiveness and militarism and its de-emphasis on diplomacy and international law to promote peace. Instead, critics find the ever-present willingness to use force as a threat to peace and stability, which can lead to wars such as the one in Iraq, predicated on faulty intelligence that was never questioned by civilian leaders until it was too late.

In more recent years, neoconservatism has lost some of its former luster. The apparent lack of WMDs in Iraq, which had been a primary motivation for the March 2003 invasion of Iraq, led many to question the use of preemptive force in the absence of reliable intelligence. The Iraq insurgency, which has been raging since 2004, also gave pause to those who had previously believed that invading Iraq was a prudent course of action. Finally, the November 2006 midterm elections sent a powerful signal to the Bush administration and neoconservatives. The electorate apparently had not bought the precepts of the neocons, and this likely was a major factor in the Republicans losing control of both houses of Congress in the November 2006 congressional elections. Rumsfeld was forced out within days of the election, and others of like mind also left the administration. Vice President Cheney, perhaps the most militant of the neocons, kept an exceedingly low profile after the 2006 elections and was rarely in the public eye until after he left office in January 2009.

STEFAN M. BROOKS

**See also**

Al Qaeda; Bush, George Walker; Bush Doctrine; Carter, James Earl, Jr.; Cheney, Richard Bruce; Hussein, Saddam, IRAQI FREEDOM, Operation; Reagan Administration, Middle East Policy; Rice, Condoleezza; Rumsfeld, Donald Henry; Weapons of Mass Destruction; Wolfowitz, Paul Dundes

**References**

Bennett, William J. *Why We Fight: Moral Clarity and the War on Terrorism.* New York: Regnery, 2003.

Chernus, Ira. *Monsters to Destroy: The Neoconservative War on Terror and Sin.* Boulder, CO: Paradigm, 2006.

Dolan, Chris J. *In War We Trust: The Bush Doctrine and the Pursuit of Just War.* Burlington, VT: Ashgate, 2005.

Kaplan, Lawrence, and William Kristol. *The War over Iraq: Saddam's Tyranny and America's Mission.* San Francisco, CA: Encounter Books, 2003.

Murray, Douglas. *Neoconservatism: Why We Need It.* New York: Encounter Books, 2006.

---

# Netanyahu, Benjamin
## Birth Date: October 21, 1949

Israeli soldier, diplomat, politician, and prime minister (1996–1999 and March 2009–). Born in Tel Aviv, Israel, on October 21, 1949, Benjamin (Binyamin) "Bibi" Netanyahu moved with his

Benjamin Netanyahu was prime minister of Israel during 1996–1999. Seen as a hardliner regarding peace with the Palestinians, Netanyahu again became prime minister in 2009. (Israeli Government Press Office)

family from Jerusalem to Philadelphia, where his father, Benzion Netanyahu, taught history at the University of Pennsylvania. The younger Netanyahu returned to Israel in 1967 and entered the Israel Defense Forces (IDF) to serve as a soldier and officer in the antiterrorist Sayeret Matkal unit during 1967–1972. Netanyahu participated in the IDF's Operation GIFT during December 28–29, 1968, at Beirut Airport and was wounded during the rescue, led by Ehud Barak, of hijacked Sabena Airlines hostages at Ben-Gurion Airport on May 8, 1972.

Netanyahu's studies for a degree in architecture from the Massachusetts Institute of Technology (MIT) were interrupted by his service as a captain in the Yom Kippur (Ramadan) War of October 1973, but he returned to receive his bachelor's degree in 1974. He then earned a master's of science degree in management studies from MIT in 1976 and pursued studies in political science both at MIT and Harvard University. He joined the international business consulting firm of Boston Consulting Group in 1976, but in 1978 he accepted a position in senior management at Rim Industries in Jerusalem.

Netanyahu created the Jonathan Institute, dedicated to the study of terrorism, in Jerusalem. The institute was named in memory of his brother, who was the commander and the only IDF fatality of the successful raid to free the Jewish passengers and crew of an Air France commercial flight held captive at the airport in Entebbe, Uganda, in 1976. The institute sponsors international conferences and seminars on terrorism.

As the deputy chief of mission at the Israeli embassy in Washington during 1982–1984, Netanyahu participated in initial discussions on strategic cooperation between the United States and Israel. As Israeli ambassador to the United Nations (UN) during 1984–1988, he was instrumental in opening the UN Nazi War Crimes Archives in 1987. A member of the conservative Likud Party, he won election in 1988 to the Knesset (Israeli parliament) and served as deputy foreign minister during 1988–1991, as a coalition deputy minister to Prime Minister Yitzhak Rabin during 1991–1992, and as the Israeli spokesman during the Persian Gulf War (1991). Netanyahu also participated in the Madrid Peace Conference of October 1991 that saw the first direct negotiations among Israel, Syria, Lebanon, and a joint Jordanian-Palestinian delegation.

Following Likud's defeat in the 1992 elections, Yitzhak Shamir stepped down as party leader. Netanyahu won election as party leader in 1993, in part because of his opposition to the 1993 peace accords between Israel and the Palestine Liberation Organization (PLO) that led to Israeli withdrawals from the West Bank and the Gaza Strip.

In the May 1996 national elections, for the first time Israelis elected their prime minister directly. Netanyahu hired an American campaign adviser and narrowly defeated Shimon Peres of the Labor Party, who had succeeded as prime minister after the 1995 assassination of Yitzhak Rabin. The election took place following a wave of Muslim suicide bombings that killed 32 Israeli citizens and that Peres seemed powerless to halt. Netanyahu took office in June 1996, the youngest prime minister in Israeli history. He was also the first Israeli prime minister to be born after the establishment of Israel.

Netanyahu's tenure as prime minister was marked by worsening relations with Syria that led to the occupation of Lebanon by the posting of Syrian troops in Lebanon; the troops were not withdrawn until 2005. Relations with the Palestinians also deteriorated when Netanyahu and Jerusalem mayor Ehud Olmert in September 1996 opened ancient tunnels under the Western (Wailing) Wall and the al-Aqsa Mosque complex. Netanyahu's position weakened within Likud when he ceased to oppose the Oslo Peace Accords of 1993 and withdrew troops from Hebron in the West Bank in 1997. His attempt to restore that support by increasing Israeli settlements in the West Bank, promoting Jewish housing in predominantly Arab East Jerusalem in March 1997, and decreasing the amount of land to be ceded to the Palestinians only served to provoke Palestinian violence and impede the peace process.

Netanyahu again angered the conservative wing of Likud when he agreed in the 1998 Wye River Accords to relinquish control of as much as 40 percent of the West Bank to the Palestinians. He again reversed himself and suspended the accords in December

1999. He resigned from the Knesset and the chairmanship of Likud after he was defeated by Barak in his bid for reelection in May 1999, stepping down as prime minister that July.

Netanyahu accepted the position of minister of foreign affairs in November 2002, and after the 2003 elections he became the finance minister under Prime Minister Ariel Sharon until August 2005. Netanyahu resigned to protest the Israeli pullout from the Gaza Strip. Following Sharon's departure from the Likud Party, Netanyahu was one of several candidates to replace him. In December 2005 Netanyahu retook the leadership of Likud. He has written or edited a number of books, among them *International Terrorism: Challenge and Response* (1979), *Place among Nations: Israel and the World* (1992), *Fighting Terrorism: How Democracies Can Defeat Domestic and International Terrorists* (1995), and *A Durable Peace: Israel and Its Place among the Nations* (2000). Despite the fact that Netanyahu and his wife have been the subject of criminal investigations, he continued to lead Likud and again became Israeli prime minister on March 31, 2009. This followed an election in which his party had actually failed to win a majority, technically lost, but the opposing Labor Party was unable to build a coalition. The coalition that Netanyahu was able to form included Avigdor Lieberman in the government as foreign minister.

RICHARD EDWARDS

**See also**

Arab-Israeli Conflict, Overview; Israel; Palestine Liberation Organization; Rabin, Yitzhak; Sharon, Ariel

**References**

Caspit, Ben, and Ilan Kfir. *Netanyahu: The Road to Power.* Translated by Ora Cummings. New York: Birch Lane, 1998.

Shindler, Colin. *Israel, Likud and the Zionist Dream: Power, Politics, and Ideology from Begin to Netanyahu.* New York: I. B. Tauris, 1995.

# Network-Centric Warfare

A technological theory of warfare developed by the U.S. Department of Defense in the late 1990s that has matured during the Global War on Terror, which commenced in 2001. Network-centric warfare seeks to translate an information advantage, enabled in part by information technology, into a competitive war-fighting advantage through the robust networking of well-informed geographically dispersed forces. It is most widely embraced by the U.S. Air Force.

Throughout the history of warfare, most changes in the tactical level of warfare occurred through advancing weapons technology. For example, the development of gunpowder weapons brought about revolutionary changes in the organization of military forces and battlefield tactics and eventually affected Western governments, economies, and social organizations. Since the late 1980s, technological changes in the acquisition of information about an adversary's infrastructure and military forces and the ways in which this information is processed, disseminated, and utilized by the combatants have been changing the way the U.S. Air Force

conducts air warfare. Instead of changes in weapons technology, these current leaps in tactical warfare are being built upon a growing combination of sophisticated manned and unmanned aircraft, airborne sensors, data links, satellites, computers, and other elements through which information passes and is processed and forwarded to the war fighters for their utilization.

By the late 1990s the U.S. military began to realize a growing importance of command, control, communications, computers, intelligence, surveillance, and reconnaissance (C4ISR) through interoperability and systems integration. The North Atlantic Treaty Organization (NATO) Operation ALLIED FORCE against Serbia in 1999 provided the first signs of selective tactical uses of data links and collaborative analysis that provided a rough network between the Combined Air Operations Center (CAOC) in Italy and airborne command and control (C2) and strike aircraft over the Balkans. Later, Operation ENDURING FREEDOM in late 2001 brought together many new systems in joint operations and more extensive use of airborne networks to distribute sensor information, share tactical messages, and exert increased C2 over combat

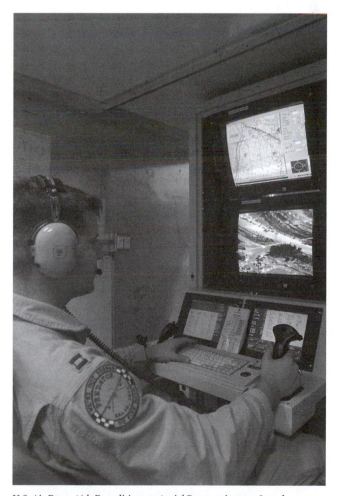

U.S. Air Force 46th Expeditionary Aerial Reconnaissance Squadron Predator pilot Captain John Songer operates an individual Predator unmanned aerial vehicle (UAV) using a remote control system at Balad Air Base, Iraq, in 2004. (U.S. Department of Defense)

forces. For example, after the first three weeks of ENDURING FREEDOM, coalition strike aircraft over Afghanistan ran out of preplanned targets, and ground controllers soon began talking directly to pilots above, a process dubbed immediate airborne close air support (XCAS), to request air strikes with precision-guided munitions against enemy targets in close proximity to coalition ground forces. Long-range bombers and carrier-based aircraft, tasked to strike preplanned targets in Afghanistan, began receiving updated targeting information through data links after they were en route and then reprogrammed their NAVSTAR Global Positioning System–guided weapons to strike new targets.

Additionally, digital networks, designed, developed, and tested in the years before ENDURING FREEDOM began, linked aircraft and ground forces with operations centers thousands of miles away. For example, U.S. Central Command's (CENTCOM) headquarters at MacDill Air Force Base, Florida, was successfully networked with the forward headquarters in Kuwait and a headquarters in Uzbekistan through satellites and related technologies to a degree not previously achieved. The growing use of surveillance unmanned aerial vehicles (UAVs) increased the quantity of battlefield surveillance and intelligence that was then passed to both ground forces and theater commanders, providing them with near–real-time and real-time battlefield situational awareness. For example, ground controllers and pilots above them could simultaneously view video streamed from a Predator UAV at a higher altitude through a satellite to the controller's computer and the pilot's cockpit and then talk to each other, using satellite communications, to identify in several minutes a prospective target from the video. Through networked communications, the CENTCOM commander directed the battle from his MacDill Air Force Base headquarters at an unprecedented level, especially compared to Operation DESERT STORM in 1991.

After the first stage of combat operations in Iraq (Operation IRAQI FREEDOM) ended in May 2003, U.S. Air Force chief of staff General John P. Jumper learned the value of networking. Although the experiences in the early phase of IRAQI FREEDOM were a good start, it was a patchwork approach. The ability to stream Predator video to orbiting AC-130 gunships and ground controllers with laptops putting coordinates up in the Boeing B-52 Stratofortresses to drop Joint Direct Attack Munitions (JDAMs) demonstrated networks with a limited number of platforms. Yet fresh intelligence-surveillance-reconnaissance (ISR) data or updated CAOC communications and tracking had multiplied the power of all major strike aircraft. About half of all 2006 air strikes in Iraq utilized equipment and nodes that allowed ground controllers and pilots to view Predator videos for real-time target identification.

The U.S. Air Force envisioned platforms and network elements that would be capable of transforming the tactics of aerial warfare. New aircraft, such as the Lockheed Martin/Boeing F/A-22 Raptor stealth fighter and the Lockheed Martin F-35 Lightening II strike fighter, and major upgrades on existing aircraft would lead the way. Lieutenant General William T. Hobbins has stated that the

F/A-22, with its computing power, data links, and sensor fusion, "will be the best sensor on the battlefield for net-centric operations." The F-35 will also have the capability to form its own networks once it is fielded in quantity after 2010. Both aircraft have advanced sensors that enhance the quality of targeting information through improved ranges and resolution. At the same time, with these advanced sensors these aircraft can survey and reconnoiter the battle space at great depth, allowing them to take on the role of highly survivable forward nodes of an airborne network.

Network-centric warfare is still very much theory in progress and far from the magic bullet that its proponents claim for it. Exercise Millennium Challenge 2002 was a $250 million Department of Defense exercise that was supposed to showcase the new way of war fighting. But retired U.S. Marine Corps lieutenant general Paul Van Riper, acting as the commander of the Red Force, completely crippled the high-tech Blue Force by employing low-tech methods, such as motorcycle couriers and small reconnaissance boats that neutralized almost all of the technological overmatch of the Blue Force. The exercise was such a complete disaster that Secretary of Defense Donald Rumsfeld peremptorily ordered it suspended. With the rules rewritten, the exercise was restarted, and the Red Force was ordered to stick to the script. Refusing to participate in the sham, Van Riper resigned in protest, but he had very dramatically managed to demonstrate the sort of threats that U.S. forces would face in both Iraq and Afghanistan in the coming years.

So far, network-centric warfare has failed to live up to the promises of its advocates in the insurgency warfare environments of both Iraq and Afghanistan. The entire concept has lost much of its former luster in recent years. There is no doubt that there is an upward and continuous technological trend in warfare, but the history of warfare is littered with high-tech innovations that have been neutralized or defeated by low-tech countermeasures. Improvised explosive devices (IEDs) are only the latest case in point. All the computers and communications connectivity in the world are not going to help a soldier caught in a kill zone when an IED goes off, nor will PowerPoint superiority or complete dominance of the air defeat determined insurgents.

ROBERT B. KANE

**See also**
Bombs, Precision-Guided; Joint Direct Attack Munition and Small Diameter Bomb; Navigation Satellite Timing and Ranging Global Positioning System; Rumsfeld, Donald Henry; Satellites, Use of by Coalition Forces; Unmanned Aerial Vehicles

**References**
"Air Force Developing Handheld Video Receiver." *Aviation Week* (May 7, 2007): 46–47.
Grant, Rebecca. "Air Warfare in Transition." *Air Force Magazine* 87(12) (December 2004): 120–132.
Lambeth, Benjamin S. *Air Power against Terror: America's Conduct of Operation Enduring Freedom.* Santa Monica, CA: RAND Corporation, 2005.
Tiboni, Frank. "Information Becomes Weapon." *Federal Computer Week,* February 13, 2006, 10–13.

Zabecki, David T. "Landpower in History: Strategists Must Regain an Understanding of the Role of Ground Forces." *Armed Forces Journal* (August 2002): 40–42.

## New Zealand, Role in Persian Gulf, Afghanistan, and Iraq Wars

Island nation located in the South Pacific Ocean about 1,000 miles to the southeast of Australia. New Zealand's landmass covers 104,454 square miles; its 2008 population was some 4.173 million people. New Zealand is a parliamentary democracy that still retains allegiance to the United Kingdom's Queen Elizabeth II, who is the titular head of state. She appoints a governor-general, who is chosen upon consultation with the prime minister, to represent her. The prime minister is the head of government. Modern New Zealand politics have been dominated by the National Party (center-right), the Labour Party (center-left), and the Green Party, which often form coalition governments with each other and other smaller political parties. Since 1990, New Zealand has had five prime ministers: Michael Moore, James Bolger, Jennifer Mary Shipley, Helen Clark, and, since November 2008, John Key.

New Zealand has participated as an ally of the United States in conflicts in the Middle East and Asia and has provided forces as part of United Nations (UN) peacekeeping missions. The United States and New Zealand have a long history of military cooperation and collaboration dating back to World War I. During the Cold War, the United States, New Zealand, and Australia signed a collective defense agreement, the Australia–New Zealand–United States (ANZUS) Treaty. ANZUS remained the cornerstone of the U.S.–New Zealand alliance through the superpower struggle, including the Vietnam War in which New Zealand contributed troops to support the U.S. operations in South Vietnam. In 1984 tensions emerged between the two countries when New Zealand banned warships with nuclear weapons from its waters. Because U.S. policy is not to declare which of its warships are carrying nuclear weapons, this effectively barred U.S. Navy ships from New Zealand territorial waters. In response, the United States suspended its obligations under the ANZUS accord. This eliminated most combined training exercises and undermined the ability of the two nations' militaries to work together. Meanwhile, a succession of New Zealander governments increasingly shifted the nation's security focus to the regional defense of its home territory and that of key allies such as Singapore. Overseas deployments were limited mainly to peacekeeping operations.

Through the 1980s and 1990s, New Zealand participated in a range of UN and other multilateral peacekeeping missions in the Middle East. Troops from New Zealand have been serving as part

A New Zealand Army medic gives directions to a clinic for Afghan men, Nayak, Afghanistan, March 2, 2006. (U.S. Department of Defense)

of the ongoing UN peacekeeping and observation mission in the Sinai since 1982. New Zealand has also deployed troops and military observers as part of the UN operations in Israel, Lebanon, and Syria. In addition, New Zealand contributed troops to the humanitarian mission in Somalia from 1992 to 1994 and to the UN mission in Sudan. When the Iran-Iraq War disrupted shipping in the Persian Gulf during the late 1980s, New Zealand dispatched two frigates as part of the multilateral coalition of forces that monitored the sea-lanes and escorted merchant ships and tankers. The ships then served in the British-led naval task force that helped enforce UN economic sanctions against Iraq following that country's invasion of Kuwait in August 1990.

During the 1991 Persian Gulf War, New Zealand supported the diplomatic efforts of U.S. president George H. W. Bush to develop an international coalition of countries to oppose the Iraqi occupation of Kuwait. New Zealand maintained its naval deployment during the conflict and also made a minor contribution to the military coalition that liberated Kuwait in the form of a 50-member medical unit and three transport aircraft. The New Zealand forces served in a support capacity rather than in a direct combat role. After the Persian Gulf War, New Zealand continued to deploy warships in support of Operation SOUTHERN WATCH, the UN-authorized operation to oversee the southern no-fly zone in Iraq, and to enforce international sanctions against Saddam Hussein's regime.

In the aftermath of the September 11, 2001, terrorist attacks on the United States, Australia and New Zealand invoked the collective defense clause of the ANZUS Treaty, and both Canberra and Auckland offered military, intelligence, and diplomatic support to the George W. Bush administration. In October the New Zealand Parliament voted overwhelmingly to authorize the deployment of air, naval, and ground units to participate in Operation ENDURING FREEDOM, the U.S.-led campaign against the Taliban and Al Qaeda in Afghanistan. New Zealand's participation in ENDURING FREEDOM was dubbed Operation ARIKI by the Defense Ministry. New Zealand dispatched an officer contingent for planning purposes within the U.S. Central Command (CENTCOM) in Tampa, Florida.

In November 2001 New Zealand sent one of its three operational frigates and an aerial surveillance aircraft to participate in the naval operations of ENDURING FREEDOM. New Zealand also stationed personnel at Bagram Air Base, Afghanistan, to coordinate air operations. In addition, New Zealand deployed 50 Special Air Service (SAS) troops to participate in ENDURING FREEDOM combat operations. They joined other coalition forces in Operation ANACONDA (March 2002), the assault on Al Qaeda and Taliban fighters in the Shahi-Kot Valley and Arma Mountains in southeastern Afghanistan. SAS forces remained in Afghanistan for subsequent missions through December 31, 2005. A member of the SAS became the first recipient of the New Zealand Victoria Cross since World War II for bravery in action on June 17, 2004. There were no deaths among New Zealand personnel during the deployment.

In addition to its presence as part of ENDURING FREEDOM, New Zealand also contributed forces to the International Security Assistance Force–Afghanistan (ISAF), the multilateral operation led by the UN and later the North Atlantic Treaty Organization (NATO) in support of the Afghan national government. In 2002 New Zealand became the first non-European country to contribute troops to ISAF. Its initial deployment of 25 soldiers and a transport aircraft supported the UN's World Food Program. In August 2003 New Zealand agreed to lead one of the ISAF-sponsored provincial reconstruction teams (PRTs). New Zealand's PRT was stationed in Bamyan Province, about 200 miles to the northwest of Kabul. The Taliban and other insurgents had only a minimal presence in the area, making it one of the more secure regions of Afghanistan. The PRT included soldiers and police officers from New Zealand as well as development officials from both New Zealand and the United States. At the core of the PRT were 120–130 military personnel, including infantry, as well as engineers, medics, and logistics personnel. In 2004 the PRT was reinforced to provide additional security for the presidential and legislative elections and provided $1 million in assistance for the balloting. The PRT was divided into five smaller teams, one for each of Bamyan's five regions. These groups were deployed to conduct specific missions, including school and clinic construction, road building and maintenance, and the delivery of medical aid and humanitarian supplies. PRT personnel serve six-month rotations, and the mission has been repeatedly reauthorized. As of the end of 2009, New Zealand maintained 220 military personnel in Afghanistan.

While New Zealand remained integrated into the ISAF mission in Afghanistan, differences quickly emerged between Auckland and Washington over the U.S.-led invasion of Iraq. New Zealand announced that it would supply noncombat military forces to support the U.S.-led coalition if the UN authorized military action. Meanwhile, New Zealand contributed inspectors to the UN weapons inspections effort prior to the war. When the Bush administration was unable to secure an explicit UN authorization for the invasion, New Zealand's government declined to provide personnel to the coalition during the major combat phases of Operation IRAQI FREEDOM. However, after the end of major combat operations on May 1, 2003, New Zealand contributed 60 military engineers to support the reconstruction of Iraq. The New Zealanders conducted minesweeping operations and undertook reconstruction projects and were part of the Multi-National Force, stationed in the southern areas of Iraq. New Zealand also provided humanitarian and reconstruction aid to the Iraqi government.

The decision to deploy the forces to Iraq reflected diplomatic pressure from the Bush administration. The decision also followed a 2003 incident in which New Zealand prime minister Helen Clark publicly declared that if Bush had lost the 2000 presidential election, the war would not have occurred. Clark later apologized for the remark, but the Bush administration threatened to block New Zealand's participation in trade talks and enact other tacit sanctions against the country. The Iraq mission proved highly unpopular among New Zealanders, however, and the government faced mounting pressure to withdraw the unit. Subsequently, New

Zealand withdrew its troops in September 2004. Some support for the U.S.-led effort continued. For example, Air New Zealand, the government-controlled national air carrier, flew some 600 Australian troops to Iraq.

TOM LANSFORD

**See also**

Afghanistan, Coalition Combat Operations in, 2002–Present; DESERT STORM, Operation; IRAQI FREEDOM, Operation, Coalition Ground Forces; Multi-National Force–Iraq; North Atlantic Treaty Organization in Afghanistan; United States

**References**

Cockburn, Patrick. *The Occupation: War and Resistance in Iraq.* New York: Verso, 2007.

Feickert, Andrew. *U.S. and Coalition Military Operations in Afghanistan: Issues for Congress.* Washington, DC: Congressional Research Service, 2006.

Keegan, John. *The Iraq War: The Military Offensive, from Victory in 21 Days to the Insurgent Aftermath.* New York: Vintage, 2005.

Murray, Williamson, and Robert H. Scales Jr. *The Iraq War: A Military History.* Cambridge, MA: Belknap, 2005.

Ryan, Mike. *Battlefield Afghanistan.* London: Spellmount, 2007.

Sinno, Abdulkader. *Organizations at War in Afghanistan and Beyond.* Ithaca, NY: Cornell University Press, 2008.

# Niger, Role in Origins of the Iraq War

A landlocked West African country with a population estimated at 13.2 million. About 80 percent of Niger lies in the Sahara desert. Niger's economy is based on subsistence agriculture and exports of uranium. In 2002 during the lead-up to the Iraq War, the George W. Bush administration alleged that Iraqi dictator Saddam Hussein had attempted to secure supplies of uranium oxide (yellowcake uranium) from Niger as part of a program to build a nuclear bomb. Disputes concerning the accuracy of Bush's allegations and U.S. intelligence flared into a major postwar controversy over whether or not the administration had misrepresented intelligence to gain support for the war.

On January 28, 2003, President Bush, in his State of the Union address, alleged that Iraq had built mobile biological weapons laboratories and amassed 25,000 liters of anthrax and 38,000 liters of botulinum toxin along with stockpiles of Sarin gas and nerve agents. He also claimed that the British government had learned that Iraq had obtained significant quantities of uranium from an unspecified country in Africa. Although Bush was not specific in his speech, the African country in question was Niger. Uranium oxide, a slightly processed form of uranium, is an essential ingredient in the uranium-enrichment process necessary to produce nuclear weapons.

Behind the scenes, U.S. government agencies had been debating the validity of the allegation for some time. A draft version of a speech given by Bush in Cincinnati on October 7, 2002, had said that Iraq had been caught attempting to procure up to 500 tons of uranium in Africa. However, the wording had been dropped at the urging of Central Intelligence Agency (CIA) director George Tenet and Deputy National Security Advisor Stephen Hadley. The CIA believed that the story was unsubstantiated.

Joseph C. Wilson IV, a former U.S. ambassador to the African state of Gabon, which also exported uranium, had traveled to Niger in February 2002, interviewed numerous officials there, and concluded that the allegation was unfounded. He had been dispatched by the CIA.

The yellowcake story had also been considered for inclusion in Secretary of State Colin L. Powell's dramatic PowerPoint presentation to the United Nations (UN) Security Council on February 5, 2003, a presentation that outlined the administration's case against Iraq. Objections from advisers in the State Department persuaded Powell to drop the allegation from his speech.

The issue next surfaced sometime after the March 2003 invasion of Iraq. In June 2003 reports appeared in the press casting doubt on the yellowcake allegation made by Bush. On June 8 National Security Advisor Condoleezza Rice appeared on *Meet the Press* to deny that anyone in her department knew that the uranium story was bogus.

On July 6 Wilson published an article in the *New York Times* providing details of his trip to Niger. He wrote that he had been asked to go to Niger by the CIA and officials in the office of Vice President Dick Cheney. Wilson was instructed to discover if there was any truth to reports that Iraq had purchased uranium oxide from Niger in the late 1990s. Wilson had been stationed in Niamey, Niger's capital, as a diplomat in the mid-1970s.

Wilson first met with the American ambassador to Niger, Barbro Owens-Kirkpatrick, who was fully aware of rumors that Niger had sold uranium oxide to Iraq. Wilson pointed out that the American embassy in Niger kept close tabs on Niger's uranium exports. Owens-Kirkpatrick told Wilson that she thought she had discredited the rumors in her reports to Washington.

Wilson spent eight days in Niamey interviewing government officials, former government officials, and businesspeople involved in Niger's uranium trade. He concluded that Niger had not sold uranium oxide to Iraq. Strict monitoring of Niger's exports by the International Atomic Energy Agency effectively made such a sale impossible.

Wilson revealed that the basis for the rumor about the uranium oxide sale was a memorandum of agreement that purportedly documented the sale to Iraq, a memorandum that he never saw. Other reporters, he noted, had shown the document to be a probable forgery because it contained numerous errors and was signed by individuals who were not in Niger's government at the time. The CIA later discovered that the document had been forged by a con man who passed it on to Italian journalists who, in turn, passed it on to a wider audience.

Wilson said that he returned to the United States and provided briefings to the CIA and the State Department's Africa Bureau. He was thus surprised when the allegation surfaced in the president's

State of the Union address, citing British sources. Because Niger had not been specifically mentioned in the president's speech, he assumed that the African uranium must be coming from Gabon or possibly Namibia or South Africa. However, the State Department had already issued a fact sheet naming Niger, despite what Wilson had said in his briefing. Wilson claimed that the administration had deliberately distorted the intelligence picture in order to drum up support for the war.

Following the publication of Wilson's incendiary article, a round of recriminations erupted in the government over who was responsible for allowing the now-discredited allegation to appear in Bush's State of the Union address, especially when it had been dropped from the Cincinnati speech in October 2002 and Powell's address to the UN in February 2003. Eventually, Tenet took responsibility for not properly vetting the president's speech. Hadley went before the press and admitted that he had simply forgotten that the story had been discredited. Critics of the administration claimed that Tenet was a scapegoat, while others thought that Hadley was protecting Cheney. The vice president had been the one administration official who had been the most insistent that Iraq was producing a nuclear weapon.

In 2004 Wilson published a book, *The Politics of Truth,* providing further details of his trip to Niger. He noted that in his initial meeting with Ambassador Owens-Kirkpatrick she had informed him that four-star U.S. Marine Corps general Carlton W. Fulford Jr., who supervised American military relations with African states, had already visited Niger. General Fulford had interviewed government officials and business contacts, concluded that the allegations were untrue, and sent his report to Washington. In 2006 a report in the *New York Times* revealed that a State Department memorandum written in late February 2002 had rejected claims that Niger had sold uranium to Hussein.

Bush's reference to Iraq's alleged uranium purchase accounted for only 16 words in his State of the Union address. He did not name Niger specifically and attributed the story to British, not American, sources. However, the 16 words became highly symbolic for critics of the war who argued that Bush had relied on selective and distorted intelligence to justify the invasion.

The Niger allegations had one last major repercussion. On July 14, 2003, eight days after the appearance of Wilson's article, syndicated columnist Robert Novak published an article claiming that two senior administration officials had told him that Wilson's wife, Valerie Plame, was a CIA expert on weapons of mass destruction (WMDs) and that she had used her influence to send her husband on a trip to Niger. Novak's article triggered a Justice Department criminal investigation into who was responsible for leaking Plame's identity as a CIA officer to Novak. Such a deliberate leak is unlawful. Eventually, I. Lewis "Scooter" Libby, Cheney's chief of staff, was indicted and convicted on charges of perjury, obstruction of justice, and making false statements for his part in the leak. Libby was convicted, sentenced to 30 months in jail, and ordered to pay a $250,000 fine. President Bush soon commuted his jail sentence,

saying that the punishment was excessive. However, the bogus Iraq-Niger connection proved to be a major embarrassment to the Bush administration and showcased the poor intelligence and judgments surrounding the decision to go to war in 2003.

PAUL W. DOERR

**See also**
Bush, George Walker; Central Intelligence Agency; Cheney, Richard Bruce; Libby, I. Lewis; Powell, Colin Luther; Rice, Condoleezza; Tenet, George John; Wilson, Joseph Carter, IV; Wilson, Valerie Plame

**References**
Gordon, Michael R., and General Bernard E. Trainor. *Cobra II: The Inside Story of the Invasion and Occupation of Iraq.* New York: Pantheon Books, 2006.
Lichtblau, Eric. "2002 Memo Doubted Uranium Sale Claim." *New York Times,* January 18, 2006.
Plame Wilson, Valerie. *Fair Game: My Life as a Spy, My Betrayal by the White House.* New York: Simon and Schuster, 2007.
Wilson, Joseph. *The Politics of Truth: Inside the Lies That Led to War and Betrayed My Wife's CIA Identity.* New York: Carroll and Graf, 2004.
———. "What I Didn't Find in Africa." *New York Times,* July 6, 2003.
Woodward, Bob. *Plan of Attack.* New York: Simon and Schuster, 2004.
———. *State of Denial: Bush at War, Part III.* New York: Simon and Schuster, 2006.

# Night-Vision Imaging Systems

Night-vision technology utilizes image intensification and infrared thermal imaging to provide soldiers the ability to engage in their mission in the darkness of night and at other times of restricted light and reduced visibility.

At present, engineers and scientists of the United States Army Research, Development and Engineering Command (RDECOM) at the Night Vision and Electronic Sensors Directorate (NVSED) are developing the military's night-vision devices (NVDs) in their directive to "Own the Night." NVDs intensify existing light, capturing ambient light from the moon, stars, and man-made sources. NVDs are sensitive to a broad segment of the spectrum of light, and therefore they intensify lights that are both visible and invisible to the human eye.

Light, a form of electromagnetic radiation, consists of extremely fast oscillations creating frequencies that define in which part of the spectrum individual types of light are found. The spectrum from the highest to lowest frequencies is defined as X-rays, ultraviolet, visible light (violet to red), infrared, and radio waves. NVDs collect light from the visible and infrared sections of the spectrum to form images.

Light enters the NVD through a lens and strikes a high-powered photo cathode located within a vacuum tube that emits free electrons when struck by light. These electrons then strike a phosphor screen, where the image is focused. A soldier views this picture through an eyepiece that also magnifies it.

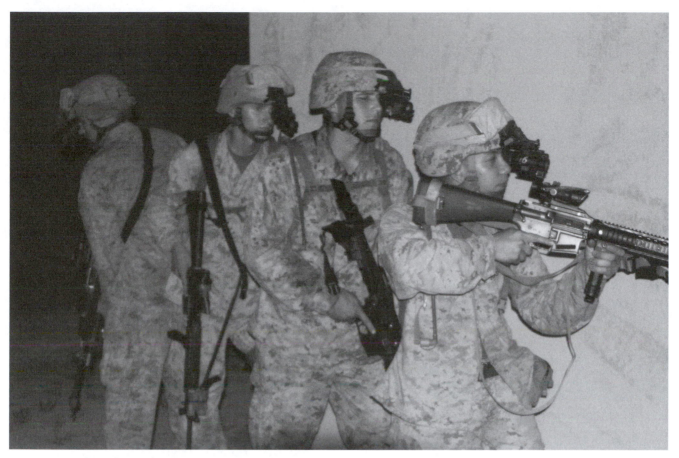

U.S. marines employ night-vision scopes to help them see in low-light situations while clearing and assessing objectives during training at Camp Lejeune, North Carolina, September 14, 2009. (U.S. Department of Defense)

Engineers designed the screen to display the image in green because the human eye can differentiate more shades of green than any other color produced by phosphor when chemically activated. In this way, NVDs enable soldiers to accomplish their objectives without activating their own light source, which could compromise mission stealth and expose troop positions and maneuvers.

Night-vision imaging systems had their genesis during World War II when the United States, Great Britain, and Germany experimented with development of the technology. Improving the German cascade image tube became the goal of night-vision engineers during the 1950s. About this time, the U.S. Army Corps of Engineers produced an infrared sniper scope, but the equipment required to use the scope proved too bulky and required infrared searchlights that gave away troop positions to anyone who also had an infrared detecting scope. Additionally, the Radio Corporation of America (RCA) developed a near-infrared two-stage cascade image tube that used a multialkali photocathode to intensify ambient light. However, this technology had its limitations: the output was inverted and provided minimal gain in imaging. RCA solved this problem by adding a third stage, which corrected the inversion and increased the image gain but also made the tube too large for military use.

NVSED continued its development of NVDs and in the 1960s manufactured the first personal devices for troops as part of the First Generation Image Intensifier Program. The primary first-generation NVD was a small starlight scope that could be mounted as a rifle sight or used as a handheld viewer. The Vietnam War marked the first war in which U.S. troops used NVDs when the U.S. Army issued soldiers the small starlight scope in 1964. These first-generation image intensifiers lasted about 2,000 operating hours and could amplify light only 1,000 times.

The second generation of image intensifiers came into production during the late 1960s and early 1970s. Engineers were able to compact more electron gains into a smaller tubes. Second-generation NVDs increased operating time from 2,500 to 4,000 hours. Equally important, these additions enhanced the amplification ability of these devices 20,000 times.

The development of linear scanning imagers in the 1970s offered a high-quality image by using multiple-element detector arrays and allowed for the creation of Forward Looking Infrared (FLIR) systems. FLIR provides an advantage over image intensification because it layers infrared scans to provide the final image. This enables FLIR to work in total darkness and produce images despite fog, smoke, dust storms, and other masking agents that would obscure image-intensification NVDs.

FLIR systems saw first combat use in Kuwait and Iraq in 1991 during Operation DESERT STORM and proved invaluable to American

902 Nixon, Richard Milhous

soldiers. Night-vision imaging systems using image intensification and FLIR were fitted on M-1A1 and M-1A2 Abrams and M-60 Patton tanks, helicopters, airplanes, and tube-launched optically tracked wire-guided (TOW I and TOW II) antitank missile systems. Additionally, ground troops received individual NVDs and outfitted Bradley infantry fighting vehicles (IFVs) with night-vision capabilities to aid in safely transporting infantrymen and firing TOW missiles to knock out Iraqi tanks. Targeting systems utilizing FLIR technology aided troops in hitting Iraqi armored vehicles and other targets through intense smoke, dust, fog, and haze.

Lockheed F117A Nighthawks, known as stealth fighters, also utilized night-vision imaging systems in their support of ground troops. The AH-64 Apache helicopter was created as an all-weather day-night military attack helicopter in large part because of the Target Acquisition and Designation System, Pilot Night Vision System (TADS/PNVS), which combines night-vision sensors and the targeting unit to enhance the ability of the pilot and the copilot/gunner to accurately engage enemy contacts. However, Operation DESERT STORM also revealed flaws in the individual systems and led to the integration of image intensification and FLIR technologies.

The third generation of image intensifiers combined light amplification technology with FLIR. These intensifiers multiply the light-gathering power up to 30,000 to 50,000 times. Additionally, these NVDs boost the tube life expectancy up to 10,000 hours, greatly improving their cost-effectiveness.

The third-generation NVDs were developed in time for use in Operation ENDURING FREEDOM (2001–) in Afghanistan and Operation IRAQI FREEDOM (2003–). These imaging systems, along with first- and second-generation NVDs, fulfilled the same role in Afghanistan and Iraq as they had in Kuwait a decade earlier. Third-generation devices provided upgrades to the troops' helmet units with the development of the AN/PVS-14 Monocular Night-Vision Device (MNVD), a lighter-weight and enhanced viewing piece. The AN/PVS-10 Night-Vision Sniper Night Sight connected to the M24 sniper rifle system for both day and night optical improvements. The night channel incorporates a third-generation image intensifier that aided snipers in both Iraq and Afghanistan after its implementation in 2002.

Fairchild Republic A10 Thunderbolt IIs, known as Warthogs, were workhorses for the U.S. Air Force in Kuwait and received NVDs shortly after Operation DESERT STORM to increase their support ability. The U.S. Army added second-generation FLIRs to the Abrams tanks' System Enhancement Package (SEP) tanks, Bradley A3 IFVs, LRAS3 Scout Humvees, and Stryker reconnaissance vehicle systems to increase their combat effectiveness prior to the wars in Afghanistan and Iraq. These enhancements not only increased the weapons capabilities of these vehicles but also improved survivability of troops.

By 2008, scientists had developed a new technology that could replace image-intensifier tubes in NVDs. The suggested alteration would replace image intensifiers with liquid crystal (LC) materials. Despite the combination of infrared sensors, FLIR, and image intensification in third-generation NVDs, these night-vision imaging systems are still affected by visible light, which can obscure images. Placing LC materials that are spectrally tunable with a semiconductor can produce an NVD that is unaffected by visible light and allows users the ability to see through other objects. Proponents claim that LC technology should revolutionize night-vision imaging systems because of its high sensitivity, spatial resolution, and contrast. Additionally, LC affords the possibility of much cheaper NVDs by cutting the expensive optics and high-voltage components.

ADAM P. WILSON

**See also**

Bradley Fighting Vehicle; M1A1 and M1A2 Abrams Main Battle Tanks

**References**

Erwin, Sandra I. "'Owning the Night' Means Fusing Sensors: Night-Vision Goggles Designed for Next-Generation Information-Centric Force." *National Defense* 87, 588 (November 2002): 32–35.

Youst, Gregory. *Desert Storm's Night Vision and Electro-optical Equipment Suitability Survey.* Fort Belvoir, VA: Night Vision and Electro-Optics Directorate, 1992.

---

# Nixon, Richard Milhous

**Birth Date: January 9, 1913**
**Death Date: April 22, 1994**

American politician and president of the United States (1969–1974). Richard Milhous Nixon was born on January 9, 1913, in Yorba Linda, California, the son of a modest grocer. Nixon graduated from Whittier College in 1934 and received his law degree in 1937 from Duke University Law School. That same year he passed the California bar exam, and he practiced law in Whittier until 1942. Following a brief stint in the Office of Price Administration, he spent four years in the U.S. Navy during World War II. In 1946 he was elected to Congress from California as a Republican, and in 1950 he won election to the Senate. Both races were notable for his use of anticommunist smear tactics.

In the 1952 presidential campaign, former U.S. Army general Dwight D. Eisenhower, the Republican nominee, selected Nixon as his running mate. With an election victory that November, Nixon spent eight years as vice president, demonstrating particular interest in foreign affairs. In 1960 he narrowly lost a presidential race to John F. Kennedy, and in 1962 Nixon was defeated in the California gubernatorial race. In a bitter and close election race in 1968, however, he was elected president on the Republican ticket and won a second term with a landslide victory in 1972.

In 1968 the inability of the United States to achieve victory in the Vietnam War dominated the political agenda. Nixon had won the presidency in part by giving the impression that he had a secret plan to end the war expeditiously. Instead, he fell back on the policies of President Lyndon Johnson's administration while embracing Vietnamization, or the gradual withdrawal of

Richard M. Nixon realized his dream of becoming president of the United States in 1969. A strong proponent of opening relations with the People's Republic of China (PRC) and of détente with the Soviet Union, Nixon was forced to resign the office in August 1974 as a result of the Watergate Scandal. (National Archives)

American troops from Vietnam and their replacement by units of the South Vietnamese military. In August 1969 Henry Kissinger, Nixon's national security adviser, embarked on protracted negotiations with the North Vietnamese that ultimately resulted in the accord signed in Paris in December 1972. After the South Vietnamese government balked at the terms and North Vietnam made them public, Nixon launched a renewed U.S. bombing campaign against North Vietnamese targets in December 1972, and the peace accords were finally signed in January 1973. The Vietnam War continued without the Americans, however, and in April 1975 North Vietnamese forces triumphed.

American withdrawal from Vietnam was only part of the broader strategic realignment that Nixon and Kissinger (secretary of state from 1973) envisaged, terming it the Grand Design. The Nixon (Guam) Doctrine, announced in July 1969, called upon American allies to bear the primary burden of their own defense. Meanwhile, new worldwide economic realities and a deteriorating U.S. economy led Nixon in 1971 to eliminate the direct American dollar convertibility to gold.

Conscious that growing economic difficulties mandated cuts in defense budgets, Nixon and Kissinger hoped to negotiate arms limitations agreements with the Soviet Union rather than unilaterally cutting U.S. military spending. To pressure the Soviets, Nixon began the process of reopening U.S. relations with the People's Republic of China (PRC). In 1972 he visited Beijing, where he had extended talks with Chinese officials. These tactics alarmed Soviet leaders, who facilitated a relaxation of Soviet-U.S. tensions, broadly termed détente, that led to the conclusion of a major nuclear arms control agreement.

Upon winning reelection in 1972, Nixon hoped to move toward full recognition of China and further arms control agreements. The outbreak of the Yom Kippur (Ramadan) War in October 1973, however, diverted his administration's attention from these plans, as it precipitated an Arab oil embargo that contributed to fuel shortages, an international spiral of inflation, and high unemployment. From then on, the U.S. economy would bedevil three U.S. presidents: Nixon, Gerald Ford, and Jimmy Carter.

Initially, Nixon and Kissinger had let Secretary of State William P. Rogers handle Middle Eastern policy. Seeking to resolve outstanding issues from the 1967 Six-Day War, in 1969 Rogers and Joseph Sisco, assistant secretary of state for Near Eastern and South Asian affairs, developed an Arab-Israeli peace plan envisaging Israeli withdrawal from occupied territories in return for a brokered peace settlement guaranteed by both the superpowers. Kissinger privately informed the Soviets that the White House had no interest in this scheme, effectively sabotaging the Rogers Plan, which the Soviet Union rejected in October 1969.

U.S. Middle Eastern policy thereafter remained largely static, utilizing what was known as Kissinger's Pillars Doctrine, the pillars of U.S. foreign policy resting on the shah of Iran, Israel, and to some degree Saudi Arabia until the October 1973 Yom Kippur (Ramadan) War, when Egypt and Syria launched a surprise attack on Israel to regain the territories they had lost in the previous 1967 war. When the Israelis rallied and then counterattacked, threatening to wipe out the Egyptian Third Army, President Anwar Sadat of Egypt, who had tilted toward the United States the previous year in the hope that this would enable Egypt to regain the Sinai, appealed for aid to the Soviet Union. To prevent Soviet intervention, Nixon ordered military forces to a DEFCON 3 military alert, two levels below outright war, while successfully pressuring the Israelis not to destroy the Egyptian Third Army.

The oil-producing Arab states reacted to events by imposing an oil embargo on the United States and other Western powers that had supported Israel. This greatly enhanced the international clout of the Organization of the Petroleum Exporting Countries (OPEC) in a quadrupling of oil prices. The European powers quickly responded by adopting more pro-Arab policies, a shift that Nixon and Kissinger strongly resented. Kissinger embarked on several months of high-profile shuttle diplomacy with Israel, Syria, and Egypt, eventually brokering an armistice. Under both Nixon and President Ford, for the next two years Kissinger continued to mediate among the contending Middle Eastern powers, eventually negotiating the Sinai Accords of September 1975 whereby Israel returned part of the Sinai to Egypt, a settlement that probably contributed to the more extensive Camp David Accords that President Carter negotiated in 1978.

His superpower juggling apart, Nixon's record in foreign affairs was decidedly mixed. Relations with European nations were somewhat strained, as leading allies resented the secrecy that characterized Nixon-Kissinger diplomacy. Japan particularly resented being left ignorant of U.S. intentions to reopen relations with China, an initiative that also horrified Jiang Jieshi's Guomindang regime in Taiwan. In 1973 the Nixon administration also sanctioned Central Intelligence Agency (CIA) involvement in a military coup against left-wing Chilean president Salvador Allende, in the course of which Allende died. Critics charged that Nixon and Kissinger showed little understanding of or empathy toward developing nations and were overly eager to support authoritarian regimes. Critics also attacked U.S. diplomacy for its insensitivity to human rights.

The Watergate political scandal, which embroiled the president and his closest advisers in a web of lies and cover-ups, not only led to Nixon's resignation in disgrace in August 1974 but also finally aborted all his ambitions for further progress in overseas affairs. After his resignation, Nixon devoted his final two decades to writing his memoirs and numerous other publications on international affairs, part of a broader and ultimately successful attempt to engineer his personal rehabilitation and win respect from contemporaries, not to mention a place in history. Nixon died from complications of a massive stroke in New York City on April 22, 1994.

PRISCILLA ROBERTS

**See also**

Arab-Israeli Conflict, Overview; Camp David Accords; Egypt; Israel; Kissinger, Henry Alfred; Organization of Petroleum Exporting Countries; Sadat, Muhammad Anwar; Soviet Union, Middle East Policy; Syria; United States, Middle East Policy, 1945–Present

**References**

Ambrose, Stephen E. *Nixon.* 3 vols. New York: Simon and Schuster, 1986–1991.

Bundy, William. *A Tangled Web: The Making of Foreign Policy in the Nixon Presidency.* New York: Hill and Wang, 1998.

Greene, John Robert. *The Limits of Power: The Nixon and Ford Administrations.* Bloomington: Indiana University Press, 1992.

Hoff, Joan. *Nixon Reconsidered.* New York: Basic Books, 1995.

Nixon, Richard M. *RN: The Memoirs of Richard Nixon.* New York: Grosset and Dunlap, 1978.

Small, Melvin. *The Presidency of Richard Nixon.* Lawrence: University Press of Kansas, 1999.

# Nixon Doctrine

Cold War foreign policy doctrine of President Richard M. Nixon first put forward in a press conference on Guam on July 25, 1969, and formally enunciated in an address to the nation on November 3. The Nixon Doctrine called for the United States to continue to meet all its current treaty commitments and to provide a nuclear shield for vital allies. But the doctrine backed away from the open-ended commitment that the United States had made to contain communism via the 1947 Truman Doctrine. As such, the United States promised only economic aid and military weaponry to allies in the developing world threatened by communist aggression, with the stipulation that such nations must enlist their own manpower to confront armed challenges to their security. In the wake of the politically unpopular deployment of hundreds of thousands of U.S. troops to Korea and then Vietnam, the Nixon Doctrine warned that the United States would no longer bear the burden of directly confronting communist threats in the developing world.

Criticized as a foreign policy retrenchment, the Nixon Doctrine grew out of a rapidly changing international strategic and economic environment. The doctrine signaled an end to the postwar bipolar era in which a nearly omnipotent United States rose to counter every perceived Soviet challenge. Nixon saw the world of the late 1960s as multipolar, a pentagonal world in which the United States, Western Europe, Japan, the Soviet bloc, and the People's Republic of China (PRC) all exerted powerful military and/or geopolitical influence. The Sino-Soviet rift, France's 1967 withdrawal from the North Atlantic Treaty Organization (NATO) military command, Britain's retreat from the Persian Gulf region, and the rise of the developing world all marked this sea change. The Nixon Doctrine also took into account the relative U.S. economic decline as Western Europe and Japan forged competitive economies. Indeed, rising budget deficits, increasing inflation, and slow economic growth were already plaguing the American economy by 1970. The high costs of the Vietnam War, in conjunction with other U.S. commitments, had clearly influenced Nixon's posture.

Nixon and his national security adviser, Henry Kissinger, realized that domestic resistance would preclude direct U.S. intervention in another bloody brushfire war like Vietnam. Indeed, Nixon alluded to his new strategic initiative on July 25, 1969, the very day he announced the first U.S. troop withdrawals from the Republic of Vietnam (ROV, South Vietnam). South Vietnam would serve as the first model for the Nixon Doctrine. Nixon's implementation of Vietnamization, the gradual replacement of U.S. troops with South Vietnamese forces, shaped U.S. policy in the later years of the war, although greater economic assistance and military equipment transfers to South Vietnam accompanied Vietnamization.

The United States employed the Nixon Doctrine in other key areas of the globe in the early to mid-1970s. Increasingly, the doctrine relied upon regional strong men assigned by Washington to guard U.S. interests. These U.S.-backed "deputy sheriffs" included Mohammad Reza Shah Pahlavi of Iran, Egyptian president Anwar Sadat, Filipino president Ferdinand Marcos, Nicaragua's Anastasio Somoza, Zaire's Mobutu Sese Seko, and King Faisal of Saudi Arabia, among others. All were to safeguard U.S. interests in their respective regions while the United States provided them with aid and arms. In the Middle East, Iran became the chief beneficiary of U.S. weaponry and military aid, as that nation became the linchpin of U.S. policy in the region.

Relying on the despotic rule of many of these so-called deputy sheriffs elicited sharp criticism, however. Opponents viewed the Nixon Doctrine as a stratagem for U.S. hegemony on the cheap. Indeed, when many of the rulers fell in the late 1970s and 1980s, there were costly negative consequences to U.S. strategic interests. The 1979 collapse of the shah's regime in Iran offered a prime example of the Nixon Doctrine's distinct limitations.

The Nixon Doctrine prompted the 1980 Carter Doctrine, promulgated by President Jimmy Carter, that was actually a turn away from the Nixon Doctrine's more hands-off approach to U.S. security in the Middle East. Carter promised direct military intervention in the region to protect vital U.S. interests in the Persian Gulf, namely oil supplies and shipping lanes. This set the stage for a much stronger U.S. presence in the Middle East, which would ultimately serve as a catalyst for American involvement in the 1991 Persian Gulf War and the 2003 Iraq War.

The Nixon Doctrine was born of the recognition that U.S. power had limits following the Vietnam War debacle. No longer could the nation afford to "pay any price" or "bear any burden," as President John F. Kennedy had promised in his 1961 inaugural address. The world had changed drastically since then. Nixon and Kissinger attempted to manage the U.S. retreat as cost-effectively as possible without undue loss of U.S. power and influence. In the economically troubled 1970s, the use of U.S. proxies and arms transfers, together with rapprochement with the PRC and détente with the Soviet Union, seemed the best solution to maintaining U.S. hegemony in a multipolar world. The Reagan administration's use of U.S. troops in Lebanon (1982–1984) and Grenada (1983) effectively ended the Nixon Doctrine for good, signaling the return of U.S. unilateralism and direct U.S. military interventions overseas, including the Middle East.

MICHAEL E. DONOGHUE

**See also**

Carter Doctrine; Containment Policy; Iran; Iranian Revolution; Kennedy, John Fitzgerald; Kissinger, Henry Alfred; Lebanon, U.S. Intervention in (1982–1984); Nixon, Richard Milhous; Reza Pahlavi, Mohammad; Truman, Harry S.; United States, Middle East Policy, 1945–Present

**References**

Hoff, Joan. *Nixon Reconsidered*. New York: Basic Books, 1995.

Kimball, J. "The Nixon Doctrine: A Saga of Misunderstanding." *Presidential Studies Quarterly* 36(1) (2006): 59–74.

Klare, Michael T. *Blood and Oil: The Dangers and Consequences of America's Growing Dependency on Imported Petroleum*. New York: Owl Books, 2005.

Litwak, Robert S. *Détente and the Nixon Doctrine: American Foreign Policy and the Pursuit of Stability, 1969–1976*. Cambridge: Cambridge University Press, 1984.

Schurmann, Franz. *The Foreign Politics of Richard Nixon: The Grand Design*. Berkeley: Institute of International Studies, University of California, 1987.

# No-Fly Zones

Restrictions imposed on the flight of Iraqi military aircraft following the 1991 Persian Gulf War (Operation DESERT STORM). As part of the March 3, 1991, cease-fire agreement ending the war, coalition forces insisted on a no-fly zone in the northern part of Iraq. Extending north from 36 degrees north latitude, it was designed to protect the Kurds from Iraqi government aircraft. In discussions with the Iraqis over the cease-fire agreement, coalition military commander General H. Norman Schwarzkopf allowed the Iraqis to continue to fly armed helicopters. Not until April 10 did the United States order Iraq to cease all military action in the northern zone.

No prohibition was imposed on the flight of military aviation in the southern part of the country. During the Persian Gulf War the Shiites in the south had answered the call of the George H. W. Bush administration to rebel, and after the war they had been abandoned by the United States. Iraqi dictator Saddam Hussein ordered a bloody repression in which as many as 50,000 Shiites died. Not until a year and a half later, on August 2, 1992, did the Bush administration proclaim a no-fly zone in the south that covered Iraqi territory south of the 32nd Parallel. On September 3, 1993, the William J. Clinton administration extended the southern no-fly zone north to reach to the 33rd Parallel and the suburbs of Baghdad. The northern and southern no-fly zones were designed to protect civilians in these areas from air attack and to demonstrate to the Iraqi people that their government would not have full sovereignty over these regions until Hussein was driven from power. In effect the

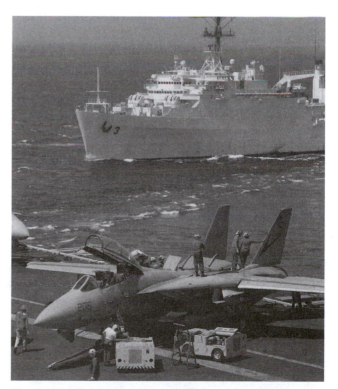

The U.S. Navy aircraft carrier *Nimitz* and the command ship *La Salle* patrol the Arabian Gulf on March 1, 1993, during Operation SOUTHERN WATCH. The operation served to enforce the no-fly zone in southern Iraq and lasted for more than a decade. (U.S. Navy)

no-fly zones led to a continuation of warfare, albeit at a low level, between the United States and Britain on the one hand and Iraq on the other extending from Operation DESERT STORM to the March 2003 invasion of Iraq in Operation IRAQI FREEDOM.

Initially American, British, and French pilots conducted the no-fly patrols, but the French withdrew from participation in 1996. Most patrols were fairly routine, but on December 29, 1992, a U.S. plane shot down an Iraqi MiG-25 when it entered the southern no-fly zone. To circumvent the southern no-fly ban, the Iraqi government used its ground forces to begin a program of draining the Euphrates River marshes inhabited by the rebellious Shiite Marsh Arabs.

The air patrols and air strikes against ground targets were controversial. The United States and Britain alone among United Nations (UN) Security Council members justified the no-fly zones as being in accordance with UN Security Council Resolution 688. This resolution of April 5, 1991, condemned the repression of the civilian population in many parts of Iraq but made no mention of no-fly zones. Other Security Council members, most notably the People's Republic of China (PRC) and Russia, sharply criticized the British and U.S. air actions.

In the last weeks of the Bush administration, Iraqi air defenses fired on British and U.S. aircraft patrolling the no-fly zones. In response, on January 13, 1993, the Bush administration ordered air attacks against Iraqi air defense sites. More than 100 sorties were flown against Iraqi radar and missile air defense sites near Nasiriyah, Samawah, Najaf, and Amarah. Then, in response to Hussein's noncompliance with UN inspectors searching for weapons of mass destruction (WMDs), on January 17, 1993, the Americans attacked the Zafraniyah nuclear weapons program factory on the outskirts of Baghdad. Fearful of the possible loss of pilots in the downing of aircraft, the Bush administration decided to carry out this attack with 42 Tomahawk cruise missiles alone.

President Clinton continued the retaliatory air strikes of his predecessor. These met increasing opposition from the governments of France, Russia, and Turkey. Tragedy struck in the northern no-fly zone in April 1994 when two U.S. F-15Cs mistakenly shot down two U.S. Army helicopters carrying allied officers to meet with Kurdish officials in northern Iraq.

The undeclared air war continued. Iraqi forces used their radar sites to target British and U.S. aircraft and occasionally to fire missiles at them. Under the rules of engagement, pilots were authorized to attack the ground targets in the event of a radar lock-on, which would be preparatory to a missile launch. In December 1998 in Operation DESERT FOX, U.S. and British aircraft carried out an extensive bombing campaign to destroy suspected Iraqi WMDs programs. By 1999 the United States maintained at considerable expense some 200 aircraft, 19 naval ships, and 22,000 American military personnel to enforce the no-fly zones.

The no-fly zones and the low-level warfare that ensued there reflected, at least as far as the United States and Great Britain were concerned, the lack of a satisfactory end to DESERT STORM in 1991.

At the time, Bush administration officials assumed that Hussein would soon be driven from power, but that proved incorrect. At least the northern no-fly zone provided de facto autonomy for a large portion of the Kurdish population. The no-fly zones ceased to exist with the beginning of the Iraq War (Operation IRAQI FREEDOM) on March 19, 2003.

SPENCER C. TUCKER

**See also**

Bush, George Herbert Walker; DESERT FOX, Operation; Hussein, Saddam; Marsh Arabs; Persian Gulf War, Cease-Fire Agreement

**References**

Byman, Daniel, and Matthew C. Waxman. *Confronting Iraq: U.S. Policy and the Use of Force since the Gulf War*. Santa Monica, CA: RAND Corporation, 2002.

Gordon, Michael R., and General Bernard E. Trainor. *The Generals' War: The Inside Story of the Conflict in the Gulf*. New York: Little, Brown, 1995.

U.S. Congress, House of Representatives, Committee on Armed Services. *United States Policy toward Iraq*. Hearing, 106th Congress, 1st Session. Washington, DC: U.S. Government Printing Office, 1999.

---

# Norfolk, Battle of
**Start Date: February 26, 1991**
**End Date: February 27, 1991**

One of four engagements during the 1991 Persian Gulf War (Operation DESERT STORM) fought by Lieutenant General Frederick M. Franks Jr.'s VII U.S. Corps against the Tawakalna Mechanized Division in southeast Iraq. These included the 2nd Armored Cavalry Regiment's engagement with the Iraqi division during the Battle of 73 Easting; the 3rd Brigade of the U.S. 1st Armored Division's envelopment of the northern portion of the Tawakalna's line; the 3rd Armored Division's attack toward Objective Dorset in the center; and Major General Thomas G. Rhame's 1st Infantry Division (Mechanized) seizure of Objective Norfolk.

The Iraqi 18th Mechanized Brigade and the 37th Armored Brigade from the Iraqi 12th Armored Division defended this area, which was the southern portion of the Tawakalna's defensive line. These Iraqi forces defended a large collection of supply dumps and logistics areas that branched off from a high-speed road that ran along the Iraqi-Saudi Arabia strategic pipeline (IPSA) west of the Kuwait border. These forces had the role of blocking the coalition attack from the west, allowing units in Kuwait to withdraw to Iraq.

At 2:00 p.m. on February 26, General Rhame ordered Lieutenant Colonel Robert Wilson's 1st Squadron, 4th Cavalry, to contact the 2nd Cavalry's staff and coordinate the 1st Infantry Division's forward passage through its units engaging the Iraqi units. Moving with two brigades forward and one trailing, the division arrived behind the cavalry shortly before 10:00 p.m. Soon after, the lead brigades passed through the passage lanes and into the battle. In the distance, AH-64 Apache attack helicopters attacked the Iraqi brigade's second tactical echelon. The helicopter attack continued the pressure on the Iraqi commander and his artillery, preventing him from interfering with the 1st Infantry Division's approach.

At 10:30 p.m. Colonel Lon E. Maggart's 1st Brigade attacked in the north through a single passage lane. The lead battalion ran into elements of the Iraqi 18th Mechanized Brigade. Iraqi gunners destroyed two Bradley M3 Cavalry Scout vehicles silhouetted against the fires of burning Iraqi vehicles. The commander immediately pulled his scouts back and moved his tank companies forward. Unlike the division's experience in the first battle of the war along the border, these Iraqis intended to fight. Two company teams of the 2nd Battalion of the 34th Armor Regiment strayed off their axis and began moving north rather than east. Lieutenant Colonel Gregory Fontenot, commander of the 2nd Battalion, realized the error and soon had them heading in the right direction.

At the same time, Colonel David Weisman's 3rd Brigade in the southern portion of the sector moved immediately into battle with his three battalions abreast, running into an Iraqi tank battalion equipped with T-55s. Although the American assault caught many Iraqi tank crews on the ground in their shelters taking cover from the air attack, their scattered deployments made the night battle difficult. All night, bypassed Iraqi infantry squads and tanks tried to engage the American vehicles as they crossed their sector. In one instance, an M1 Abrams tank platoon passed by several Iraqi positions that appeared to contain only burning or destroyed vehicles. Hidden in this array were at least five operational T-55 tanks behind revetments and masked from the American's thermal sights. Iraqi infantry units, ranging in size from platoons to companies, also hid among the tanks. A slightly disoriented Bradley fighting vehicle platoon, attempting to follow the M1 tanks, moved across the front of these Iraqi positions, illuminated by burning vehicles behind them. The Iraqis took advantage of this and opened fire from three directions. The initial volley hit a Bradley, killing three American soldiers.

An American tank company trailing the lead units saw the engagement to their front and joined the melee, quickly destroying three T-55s before they could get off another shot. At the same time, several antitank missiles hit the Bradley platoon. From the perspective of the tank gunners looking through the thermal sights of the approaching M1 tanks, these Bradleys appeared to be T-55 tanks shooting at them. The young and exhausted American gunners, convinced that they were fighting against a determined enemy, opened fire, hitting three more American vehicles. When the confusion in the 3rd Brigade's sector was over, 1st Infantry Division crews had destroyed five of their own tanks and four infantry fighting vehicles. Six American soldiers perished in these attacks, and 30 others were wounded.

By 12:30 a.m. on February 27, nine American battalions were on line and began methodically crossing the remaining six miles of Objective Norfolk. As they advanced, M1A1 Abrams tank commanders acquired the thermal images of the Iraqi tanks or infantry fighting vehicles long before they were themselves spotted. Platoon

leaders, team commanders, and even battalion commanders issued unit-wide fire commands. Before the defending Iraqis had any idea of what was happening, their entire line of vehicles exploded.

In the north of the 1st Infantry Division's sector, Colonel Wilson's 1st Squadron, 4th Cavalry, screened the division's flank with the 3rd Armored Division and bumped into an Iraqi unit. With a mixture of both T-55 and T-72 tanks as well as many dismounted infantry, it was probably not an organized battalion. After the initial engagement, Wilson pulled his screen line back and consolidated his force. Attacking at 6:15 a.m., the squadron destroyed another 11 tanks, many infantry vehicles, artillery batteries, and logistics bunkers.

By dawn on February 27 the 1st Infantry Division controlled Objective Norfolk. The attack of the division and the 2nd Armored Cavalry Regiment killed approximately 5,000 Iraqi soldiers and destroyed two brigades of armored equipment. American casualties were 6 killed and fewer than 70 wounded. The way was now set for the 1st Infantry Division to clear northern Kuwait of Iraqi troops.

STEPHEN A. BOURQUE

**See also**

DESERT STORM, Operation; DESERT STORM, Operation, Ground Operations; 73 Easting, Battle of

**References**

Bourque, Stephen A. "Correcting Myths about the Persian Gulf War: The Last Stand of the Tawakalna." *Middle East Journal* 51(4) (1997): 566–83.

———. *Jayhawk! The VII Corps in the Persian Gulf War.* Washington, DC: Department of the Army, 2002.

Bourque, Stephen A., and John W. Burdan III. *The Road to Safwan: The 1st Squadron, 4th Cavalry in the 1991 Persian Gulf War.* Denton: University of North Texas Press, 2007.

Fontenot, Gregory. "Fright Night: Task Force 2/34 Armor." *Military Review* 73(1) (1993): 38–52.

Scales, Robert H. *Certain Victory: The U.S. Army in the Gulf War.* Washington, DC: Brassey's, 1994.

Staff, 1st Squadron, 4th Cavalry, 1st Infantry Division. "Riders on the Storm: A Narrative History of the 1–4 Cav's Campaign in Iraq and Kuwait (24 January–March 1991)." *Armor* 100 (May–June 1991): 13–19.

Woods, Kevin M. *The Mother of All Battles: Saddam Hussein's Strategic Plan for the Persian Gulf War.* Annapolis, MD: Naval Institute Press, 2008.

# North Atlantic Treaty Organization

International organization created by 12 Western nations in April in 1949 to provide for their collective security against an attack by the Soviet Union or its client states. The North Atlantic Treaty Organization (NATO) was born amid the fears of the early Cold War. With the disintegration of the Soviet Union in December 1991, NATO's focus shifted from the Soviet threat to broader regional and international threats, including terrorism. NATO headquarters is located in Brussels, Belgium. NATO currently

Headquarters of the North Atlantic Treaty Organization (NATO) in Brussels, Belgium. (NATO)

has 28 member states, representing North America, Western and Eastern Europe, and the Middle East (Turkey).

NATO's primary 21st-century mission is to safeguard the freedom and security of its member countries by political and, if necessary, military means. This is to be achieved chiefly through Article V of the NATO Treaty, which stipulates that an armed attack against any one member shall be considered an attack against them all. As a collective security organization, NATO therefore obligates each member to come to the aid and defense of a fellow member that has been attacked to restore and maintain the security of the North Atlantic area. Article V was invoked for the first time in NATO's history in response to the September 11, 2001, terrorist attacks against the United States.

Invoking Article V less than 24 hours after the September 11 attacks, NATO embarked on Operation EAGLE ASSIST on October 9, 2001. It numbered 830 personnel from 13 NATO states. They assisted with the air defense and patrol of U.S. airspace with NATO Airborne Warning and Control System (AWACS) airplanes. This operation ended on May 16, 2002, after it had flown 360 sorties for a total of 4,300 hours.

On October 26, 2001, elements of NATO's naval forces were deployed to patrol the eastern Mediterranean Sea to monitor and protect shipping against terrorism there. On March 10, 2003, the operation was expanded to include escorting civilian shipping through the Strait of Gibraltar.

Since the September 11, 2001, attacks, Afghanistan has been the scene of NATO's greatest involvement in the Global War on Terror. Since August 2003 NATO has been directing the International Security Assistance Force (ISAF), defending the government of Afghanistan and seeking to secure that nation against terrorism. This occurred after the United States in Operation ENDURING FREEDOM had overthrown the Taliban regime in 2001. A number of NATO countries, especially Great Britain and Canada, maintain sizable forces in Afghanistan to carry out military operations against terrorists in Afghanistan.

Beginning in the summer of 2006, there was a sharp escalation in attacks in Afghanistan against NATO forces and the civilian population by remnants of the Taliban and the terrorist organization Al Qaeda. Most of the attacks were in the south and east, areas of the country that are still problematic. On October 5, 2006, NATO assumed full command of all ISAF forces, including 12,000 U.S. troops deployed in eastern Afghanistan. This brought the total of NATO-led forces in Afghanistan to 30,000 personnel from 37 countries, including Great Britain, Canada, Denmark, France, Germany, Iceland, Italy, Portugal, Poland, and Spain. By February 2010 this number had increased to 82,897 personnel, 47,085 from the United States. From 2001 through the end of 2009, 621 NATO and coalition personnel had been killed in Afghanistan, excluding 946 U.S. troops.

As violence has escalated especially in southern Afghanistan, there has been some concern that NATO nations are not providing adequate troop numbers to counter the insurgents. In many member nations, national legislatures and politicians have placed restrictions on the numbers of troops that can be sent to Afghanistan. However, in late 2007 France deployed a squadron of Mirage 2000 fighter-attack aircraft to Kandahar and its environs to cope with rising insurgent violence in that region. In addition to its mandate to stabilize Afghanistan and rid it of insurgents, NATO troops are also training the Afghan National Army.

STEFAN M. BROOKS

### See also

Afghanistan; Al Qaeda; ENDURING FREEDOM, Operation; Taliban; Taliban Insurgency, Afghanistan

### References

Asmus, Ronald. *Opening NATO's Door*. New York: Columbia University Press, 2002.

Dunigan, Peter. *NATO: Its Past, Present and Future*. Stanford, CA: Hoover Institution Press, 2001.

Kaplan, Lawrence. *The Long Entanglement: NATO's First Fifty Years*. Westport, CT: Praeger, 1999.

Rupp, Richard. *NATO after 9/11: An Alliance in Continuing Decline*. New York: Palgrave Macmillan, 2006.

Yost, David. *NATO Transformed: The Alliance's New Role in International Security*. Washington, DC: United States Institute of Peace, 1998.

## North Atlantic Treaty Organization in Afghanistan

As of February 2010, the North Atlantic Treaty Organization (NATO) had 82,897 troops (47,085 from the United States) in Afghanistan, operating under the International Security Assistance Force–Afghanistan (ISAF). NATO troops are assisting that country's government in providing security and stability, training the Afghan Army and police, reconstructing the economy, and promoting effective governance. NATO was established in 1949 chiefly to protect Western Europe from the Soviet Union, but after the terror attacks of September 11, 2001, for the first time in its history NATO undertook an operation outside the European theater to prevent Afghanistan from being used again as a sanctuary and base for Islamic terrorists. Indeed, immediately after the attacks NATO, for the first time in its existence, invoked Article 5, the collective security clause in its charter, as a show of solidarity in the Global War on Terror.

The NATO-led ISAF operates under a United Nations (UN) mandate and at the request of the government of Afghanistan. In 2003 NATO took formal command of the ISAF, a multinational force comprising troops from 40 countries, including all NATO member states. ISAF's ultimate goal is to enable Afghanistan to provide for its own security and stability. Helping Afghanistan recover from decades of civil war, the brutally repressive rule of the Taliban, and the aftermath of the U.S. war that overthrew the Taliban government in 2001 are difficult and long-term challenges for NATO, particularly because combat operations against the Taliban and Al Qaeda insurgents are ongoing, and since 2007 the country has witnessed a rise in violence and terrorist-related activities against ISAF troops.

ISAF security and stabilization operations are conducted in cooperation with Afghan security forces, and as these forces increase in strength and combat capacity, they will be able to assume primary responsibility for the country's security. In 2004 the Afghan National Army (ANA) barely existed, but by April 2008 it numbered at least 50,000 troops.

The ANA currently numbers about 100,000, and the United States aims to increase its size to 134,000. Major problems continue to plague American and allied efforts to train the ANA to assume primary responsibility for security so as to allow U.S. and allied forces to begin withdrawing from Afghanistan. Illiteracy among Afghans is the biggest problem in training Afghan soldiers, as only about 14 percent of army recruits are able to read and write. The United States is also committed to building an ethnically diverse Afghan Army, but the senior officer corps is still primarily drawn from the northern minority Tajiks, many of whom fought against the Taliban during the late 1990s. Furthermore, the Taliban pays Afghans about the same as the prevailing wage of joining the ANA. Until most Afghans trust their government and regard it as competent and effective, the ANA will struggle to be a self-sufficient and independent force.

The reason for the resurgence of the Taliban and Al Qaeda insurgency is disputed. Some proffered reasons include frustration with and opposition to the Afghan government of President Hamid Karzai, which is seen as corrupt and ineffective; a lack of progress in improving living standards and economic development; the Taliban's adaptation of tactics from the Iraqi insurgency, including suicide and roadside bombings; the reticence of some NATO countries to confront the insurgents in battle; Pakistan's failure to prevent insurgent infiltration into Afghanistan; and, owing to the Iraq War, the Americans' dilution of their war effort in Afghanistan. Regardless of the reasons, there is no disputing that the security situation in Afghanistan has deteriorated rapidly since 2007, a situation that the new Barack Obama administration faced in January 2009.

The largest troop deployments for the ISAF come from the United States, followed by Great Britain, Germany, France, Canada, Italy, the Netherlands, and Poland. Non-NATO troop contributors to the ISAF include those from NATO's Partnership for Peace: Albania, Austria, Azerbaijan, Croatia, Finland, Georgia, Ireland, Sweden, Macedonia, and Ukraine. Countries with no association with NATO but that have also contributed forces include Jordan, Australia, New Zealand, and Singapore. Since 2001, there have been

U.S. soldiers of the International Security Assistance Force, the NATO-led security and development force in Afghanistan, conduct a combined foot patrol with Afghan National Army soldiers at the bazaar in the Shajoy District of Zabul Province, November 20, 2009. (U.S. Department of Defense)

12 NATO commanders of the ISAF: General John McColl of the United Kingdom, Major General Hilmi Zorlu of Turkey, Lieutenant General Norbert Van Heyst of Holland, Lieutenant General Goetz Gliemeroth of Germany, Lieutenant General Rick Hillier of Canada, General Jean-Louis Py of France, General Ethem Erdagi of Turkey, General Mauro del Vecchio of Italy, General David Richards of the United Kingdom, General Dan K. McNeill of the U.S. Army, and from June 2, 2008, General David McKiernan of the U.S. Army. On June 15, 2009, General Stanley A. McChrystal assumed command.

NATO and the ISAF face many formidable challenges in Afghanistan, including supporting and strengthening a weak government; promoting security and stability in a country with rugged inhospitable terrain, including many mountains, against a determined and well-organized insurgency; and rebuilding a country devastated by war with a history of a strong narcotic (opium, heroin) trade estimated at $4 billion per year. The UN has reported that Taliban and Al Qaeda forces could make as much as $500 million in 2008 alone from the sale of opium. The corruption of the Afghan government under Karzai and its inability to improve living standards have led to a rise in international criticism and a decline in domestic political support. In addition, turmoil in neighboring Pakistan and the use of that country as a sanctuary for the Taliban and Al Qaeda have added to NATO's challenges.

Further complicating NATO-ISAF operations in Afghanistan are disagreements among its members on how to accomplish the ISAF's objectives given that many countries are unwilling or reluctant to authorize their forces to engage the Taliban and Al Qaeda in counterinsurgency combat operations. The United States, the primary contributor of troops in Afghanistan, has expressed displeasure with what it views as the weak and limited political and military support from many countries. Some NATO members have in turn questioned U.S. leadership, namely its alleged preoccupation with military and combat operations while ignoring or undervaluing economic and political objectives. An additional complication is that in Europe the overwhelming unpopularity of the Iraq War has led to a steep decline in American prestige and support for American leadership, and opposition to the Iraq War has spilled over into declining support for the ISAF. For all of these reasons, the most optimistic estimates are that it will take at least several more years for the ISAF to achieve its objectives. A successful exit strategy will require a combination of economic, military, and political successes; simply defeating the insurgents, while crucial, will not by itself bring security and stability to Afghanistan.

Currently, three-fifths of Afghanistan is considered relatively stable and secure: the north and west of Afghanistan along with the capital, Kabul. But the Taliban and Al Qaeda are very active in the eastern part of the country and in the southern provinces of Helmand, Uruzgan, and Kandahar. According to NATO, from October 2006 to the end of 2007, 70 percent of terrorist incidents occurred in 10 percent of Afghanistan's 398 districts, where less than 6 percent of the Afghan people live.

As an indication of the security challenges still facing NATO-ISAF, in 2009 coalition forces, including the United States, suffered 520 fatalities, nearly double those of 2008 (295). Through the end of 2009, excluding U.S. troops, 621 international troops have died in Afghanistan. As ISAF casualties mount, so do insurgent deaths (53 died on November 29, 2008, alone, including a Taliban commander disguised as a woman). Deaths among Afghan forces have also been on the rise. Because of the rise in insurgent attacks and violence in Afghanistan, in September 2008 President George W. Bush announced the deployment of an additional 4,500 U.S. troops to Afghanistan; that same month, Germany boosted its troop presence by 1,000 to 4,500 men. President Barack Obama had also pledged to wind down the U.S. troops strength in Iraq, refocus America's attention on Afghanistan, and deploy additional troops there. On February 17, 2009, he announced plans to increase U.S. forces in Afghanistan by 17,000 troops, and on December 1, 2009, he announced that he would add an additional 30,000 U.S. troops.

In November 2008 Taliban insurgents rejected an offer for peace talks from President Karzai, refusing to negotiate until all foreign troops leave Afghanistan. As Taliban attacks increase, so too have the number of civilian deaths, including allegedly several dozen following an August 22, 2008, raid by U.S. forces in Herat Province, prompting Karzai to publically demand that NATO end civilian deaths by air strikes and raids. Increasingly frustrated with the rising level of violence, facing growing domestic opposition, and gearing up for reelection in 2009, on November 26, 2008, Karzai publicly complained that NATO and the United States are not succeeding in his nation. Indeed, he went so far as ask NATO to set a time line for withdrawal. In response, U.S. secretary of state Condoleezza Rice noted that the Taliban not only lives and hides among civilians but launches attacks in civilian areas, making it difficult for ISAF forces to avoid killing civilians. Karzai also complained that NATO had not dealt with what he has termed the "sanctuaries and training centers" of the Taliban and Al Qaeda in Pakistan. However, in the last part of 2008, the United States stepped up attacks against insurgents in Pakistan, prompting the Pakistanis to protest what they call violations of their sovereignty. In May 2009 following a Taliban land grab in Pakistan, new U.S. president Barak Obama met with Karzai and Pakistan president Asif Ali Zadari, and the three pledged a cooperative effort against Al Qaeda and the Taliban in both Afghanistan and Pakistan.

Prompted by a deteriorating security situation in Afghanistan and the resurgence of the Taliban and Al Qaeda, on December 1, 2009, President Obama announced the deployment of an additional 30,000 U.S. troops to Afghanistan during the course of the next six months, with the United States to begin handing over

security arrangements to the Afghan government by the middle of 2011 to allow the beginning of a drawdown in U.S. forces. The cost of this deployment is projected to be $30 billion for the first year. In 2009 the Afghanistan War cost $51 billion, and President Obama has requested $95 billion for 2010. According to the Congressional Budget Office, since 2001 the United States has spent approximately $345 billion on the war in Afghanistan. Obama announced that these additional 30,000 troops would be deployed in areas that have witnessed the greatest violence by a resurgent Taliban and Al Qaeda: southern and southeastern Afghanistan, particularly Kunduz and Helmand provinces and also Kandahar Province, the birthplace of the Taliban. As of April 2010 about half of these additional 30,000 troops had arrived in Afghanistan, and the remaining troops would arrive by late spring. This marks the second time in Obama's presidency that he has increased troop levels in Afghanistan. On February 17, 2009, he announced the deployment of an additional 17,000 troops to "stabilize a deteriorating security situation." On June 15, 2009, he also replaced the commander of U.S. forces in Afghanistan, General David McKiernan, with General Stanley McChrystal, a former Special Forces commander.

When Obama first became president on January 20, 2009, the number of American forces in Afghanistan stood at 34,000; 11 months later the number had grown to 70,000. With his December 1, 2009, announcement, the total number of U.S. troops in Afghanistan will grow to about 100,000. Obama's December 1, 2009, announcement came after a three-month review of the deteriorating situation in Afghanistan and the request by General McChrystal for an additional 40,000 troops to stem the gains made by the Taliban and Al Qaeda. The deployment of these additional troops has since become known as the surge. By the summer of 2010, the number of U.S. troops being deployed to Afghanistan is expected to eclipse the number of U.S. troops in Iraq. Reflective of the deteriorating situation in Afghanistan and the resurgence of the Taliban and Al Qaeda, the number of U.S. casualties has also increased steadily since 2007, from 117 deaths that year to 155 in 2008, 316 in 2009, and 97 in the first four months of 2010, bringing to 1,020 the number of U.S. combat deaths in Afghanistan. The number of U.S. troops killed in the first three months of 2010 has been approximately double the same number of deaths in the same period in 2009, and almost 700 allied troops have died in Afghanistan since 2001, including 281 from Britain, 141 from Canada, 31 from Denmark, 41 from France, 36 from Germany, and 21 from the Netherlands.

The biggest challenge that U.S., NATO, and Afghan forces face is not securing territory and denying the Taliban and Al Qaeda sanctuary but building an effective local Afghan government that can not only win over the loyalty and support of the people but also protect them and deliver local services. This, however, has proven exceedingly difficult to accomplish owing to the weak, corrupt, and unpopular Afghan government of President Karzai. In addition to a resilient and now resurgent Taliban and Al Qaeda in Afghanistan, complicating American efforts in Afghanistan is the fact that 90 percent of the world's opium supply—the raw ingredient in heroin—comes from that country, and the booming opium drug trade is said to finance the Taliban insurgency, netting it more than $100 million annually.

STEFAN M. BROOKS

**See also**

Afghanistan; Al Qaeda; ENDURING FREEDOM, Operation; International Security Assistance Force; North Atlantic Treaty Organization; Taliban; Taliban Insurgency, Afghanistan

**References**

Moore, Rebecca R. *NATO's New Mission: Projecting Stability in a Post–Cold War Era.* Westport: Praeger Security International, 2007.

Sundquist, Leah R. *NATO in Afghanistan: A Progress Report.* Carlisle Barracks, PA: U.S. Army War College, 2008.

Williams, M. J. *NATO, Security and Risk Management, from Kosovo to Kandahar.* Milton Park, UK: Routledge, 2008.

---

# North Yemen Civil War

*See* Yemen, Civil War in

---

# Northern Alliance

League established by several predominantly non-Pashtun nationalities in northern Afghanistan to oppose the Pashtun-dominated Taliban movement in the mid-1990s. Also known as the United Islamic and National Front for the Salvation of Afghanistan (United Front), the Northern Alliance fought in tandem with U.S. and allied troops against the Taliban regime in the autumn of 2001, during Operation ENDURING FREEDOM.

Afghanistan is a multiethnic country. Pashtuns account for approximately 42 percent of the population and have traditionally held political power. Other groups include the Tajiks (25 percent), Hazaras (10 percent), Uzbeks (8 percent), and numerous smaller groups.

Four coups d'état and widespread unrest in the 1970s set the stage for the 1979 Soviet invasion of Afghanistan and a decade of subsequent resistance by mujahideen (warriors of God) groups. After a disastrous 10-year occupation, the Soviets departed in 1989 and Afghan communists were defeated in 1992. Instead of another Pashtun government, however, it was the Tajiks, commanded by Ahmed Shah Massoud, and the Uzbeks, led by Abdurrashid Dostum, who seized control of Kabul and established a government with Burhanuddin Rabbani, a Tajik Islamist, as president.

Fighting between Pashtuns and non-Pashtuns had begun before the communist defeat and escalated into a civil war in 1992, but Pashtuns under Gulbuddin Hekmatyar failed to capture Kabul. Hekmatyar was only one of many Pashtun warlords whose followers were too divided to succeed. Consequently, Massoud and other leaders were able to keep Pashtun forces at bay.

Leaders in neighboring Pakistan, however, distrusted the non-Pashtun government. They wanted a Pashtun-dominated group to control the country and provide stability along lucrative trade routes emerging between Pakistan and Central Asia. Consequently, they supported the Taliban (Islamic students) when they emerged in 1994. These students were Afghan and Pakistani Pashtuns from madrasahs (Islamic schools) in Pakistan. Led by Mullah Mohammed Omar, they sought to establish strict Islamic rule throughout Afghanistan. Many Pashtuns accepted the Taliban's harsh version of Islamic law, but that changed as the Taliban moved against non-Pashtun groups in the north. The Taliban were also offering aid and safe haven to terrorist groups, such as Al Qaeda.

The Northern Alliance evolved in the mid-1990s from the Tajik Islamist Rabbani-led government. Tajiks, Uzbeks, and Shia Hazaras provided more than 90 percent of the alliance's fighters. Although the Northern Alliance scored a number of early victories, ethnic diversity and rivalries worked to the advantage of the Taliban, which gradually seized control of most of central and northern Afghanistan. India, Iran, Russia, and the Central Asian

Northern Alliance fighters in Afghanistan listen to their commander, unseen, at the front-line position at a former Soviet Army Air Force base at Bagram, some 18 miles north of Kabul, the nation's capital, on September 25, 2001. (AP/Wide World Photos)

states provided assistance to the Northern Alliance, but Pakistan and Saudi Arabia matched that with support for the Taliban. Furthermore, the Taliban benefitted from a continuing supply of new recruits from the madrasahs and refugee camps located in Pakistan.

Although the international community continued to recognize the Rabbani government, by 2000 the Northern Alliance controlled less than 10 percent of the country. The Northern Alliance suffered one of its last setbacks on the eve of the September 11, 2001, terror attacks on the United States when two Al Qaeda suicide bombers posing as Belgian journalists assassinated Ahmed Shah Massoud.

The September 11 attacks changed everything, however, preventing the Taliban from capitalizing on Massoud's death. The United States quickly sent supplies and advisers to the Northern Alliance in preparation for its successful offensive against the Taliban and Al Qaeda during Operation ENDURING FREEDOM, which began on October 7, 2001. Members of the Northern Alliance, along with anti-Taliban Pashtuns, subsequently formed a transitional government in Afghanistan, although threats from the Taliban persist, and are growing stronger. ENDURING FREEDOM is still in progress, and U.S. and coalition/North Atlantic Treaty Organization (NATO) forces have stepped up their efforts to keep radical elements, particularly the Taliban, at bay in Afghanistan.

CHUCK FAHRER

**See also**

Afghanistan; Al Qaeda; ENDURING FREEDOM, Operation; Islamic Radicalism; Madrasahs; Mujahideen, Soviet-Afghanistan War; Omar, Mohammed; Pakistan; Soviet-Afghan War; Taliban; Taliban Insurgency, Afghanistan

**References**

Coll, Steve. *Ghost Wars: The Secret History of the CIA, Afghanistan, and bin Laden, from the Soviet Invasion to September 10, 2001.* New York: Penguin, 2004.

Goodson, Larry P. *Afghanistan's Endless War: State Failure, Regional Politics, and the Rise of the Taliban.* Seattle: University of Washington Press, 2001.

Rashid, Ahmed. *Taliban: Militant Islam, Oil, and Fundamentalism in Central Asia.* New Haven, CT: Yale University Press, 2001.

---

# NORTHERN WATCH, **Operation**
## Start Date: January 1, 1997
## End Date: May 1, 2003

Surveillance and air-policing operation of the U.S. European Command (EUCOM) that enforced the United Nations (UN) mandated no-fly zone above the 36th Parallel to prevent Iraqi attacks on the Kurds in northern Iraq and to enforce Iraqi compliance with UN Security Council resolutions. Operation NORTHERN WATCH, carried out by the United States, Great Britain, and Turkey, began on January 1, 1997, and ended unofficially on March 17, 2003, and officially on May 1, 2003.

With the 1991 Persian Gulf War, the United States encouraged the Kurds in northern Iraq to revolt against the regime of Iraqi

president Saddam Hussein. However, Hussein ordered devastating military attacks on the Kurds, and more than 1 million Kurds, remembering the Iraqi gas attacks on their settlements in 1988, fled northward toward Turkey. Turkey, which already had a substantial problem with its existing Kurdish population, would not allow the Iraqi Kurds to cross the border. As a result, the Kurds were left stranded in the mountains, starving, ill prepared for severe weather winter, and at the mercy of Iraqi forces.

Thus, on April 6, 1991, U.S. president George H. W. Bush directed EUCOM to form a joint task force to protect the Kurds of northern Iraq. For this mission, called Operation PROVIDE COMFORT, coalition air forces flew more than 40,000 sorties, relocated more than 700,000 refugees, rebuilt more than 70 percent of the Kurdish villages destroyed in northern Iraq, delivered more than 17,000 tons of supplies, and prevented new Iraqi attacks on the Kurds. U.S. Air Force fighters from Incirlik Air Base, Turkey, patrolled the northern no-fly zone until PROVIDE COMFORT officially ended on December 31, 1996.

To continue policing the northern no-fly zone and to ensure Iraqi compliance with UN resolutions calling for UN inspection of Iraqi nuclear, biological, and chemical weapons facilities, EUCOM began Operation NORTHERN WATCH on January 1, 1997. The three coalition partners for this mission collectively provided approximately 45 aircraft and more than 1,400 personnel. Headquartered at Incirlik Air Base, the joint U.S. force numbered some 1,100 personnel from the air force, army, navy, and marines. The air force contingent consisted of active-duty, air force reserve and air national-guard airmen on 14- to 180-day duty, depending on their status. With a 700 percent annual turnover rate in personnel, more than 9,000 personnel rotated through NORTHERN WATCH annually.

The Turkish government, which was opposed to a permanent U.S. military operation based in its territory, originally permitted operations for six months and subsequently approved additional extensions at six-month intervals. Turkish prime minister Bulent Ecevit, who was critical of American policy in Iraq, placed major operational restrictions on the activities of NORTHERN WATCH forces, including the size of the operation, hours of flight operations, the types of aircraft deployed, and the types of munitions used. As a result, U.S. forces had to closely link U.S. responses to Iraqi provocations, and the Turkish military monitored American operations to ensure that they adhered to restrictions. Turkish authorities also refused to allow coalition aircrews based at Incirlik Air Base to participate in Operation DESERT STRIKE in 1996 and in Operation DESERT FOX in 1998, effectively grounding NORTHERN WATCH aircraft during those operations.

The coalition used a variety of fighters, tankers, and intelligence, surveillance, and reconnaissance aircraft working together to enforce the no-fly zone. Typical missions required a mix of aircraft. Among the aircraft used—at one time or another—were the Grumman EA-6B Prowler; Boeing E-3 Sentry AWACS (Airborne Warning and Control System), McDonnell Douglas F-15 Eagle, Lockheed F-16 Fighting Falcon, Sikorsky HH-60 Jayhawk,

Armed with AIM-9 Sidewinder missiles, iron bombs, and air-to-air missiles, a U.S. Air Force F-16CJ Fighting Falcon fighter of the Ohio Air National Guard flies over northern Iraq during Operation NORTHERN WATCH, 2002. (U.S. Department of Defense)

Lockheed HC-130 Hercules, Boeing KC-135 Stratotanker, Sikorsky UH-60 Black Hawk, EP-3 Aries, Beechcraft C-12 Huron, Sepecat GR-3 Jaguar, Hawker Siddeley Nimrod, and Vickers VC10 tanker.

British and U.S. aircraft flew patrol missions over Iraq an average of 18 days per month. In 2000 they flew 164 days; in 2001, 146 days; and by late November 2002, 106 days. For the first year of the operation, northern Iraq was quiet, with no incidents between coalition aircraft and Iraqi forces. However, Iraqi ground-based antiaircraft defenses engaged patrolling coalition aircraft during every subsequent mission.

Despite the coalition's enforcement of the no-fly zone for almost two years, Iraq continued to avoid compliance with UN resolutions, especially Security Council Resolution 687, requiring Iraq to dispose of its weapons of mass destruction (WMDs), ballistic missiles with a range of more than 93 miles, and related production facilities and equipment. Iraq greatly interfered with the activities of the UN arms inspectors on three separate occasions. On November 13, 1997, Iraq expelled UN arms inspectors, who returned one week later. On January 13, 1998, Iraq banned UN arms inspectors, led by an American, and expelled the inspectors

three days later. Finally on October 31, 1998, Iraq stopped cooperating with UN inspectors, who were forced to withdraw on November 7, 1998.

These actions resulted in a flurry of diplomatic action by UN Secretary-General Kofi Annan and a buildup of coalition military forces. The U.S. military then prepared units in the United States for deployment under operations DESERT THUNDER I and II. However, Annan managed to convince Hussein to accept a tentative agreement that would allow UN arms inspectors full access to suspected Iraqi weapons sites. One month later, however, a report that summarized Iraq's continued history of uncooperative actions and violations of the WMD disposal requirements resulted in Operation DESERT FOX. During this operation (December 16–19, 1998) NORTHERN WATCH aircraft ceased operations for four days to allow aircraft designated for the contingency to reach their targets.

Shortly after DESERT FOX ended, Iraq announced that it would no longer recognize the northern and southern no-fly zones. When NORTHERN WATCH resumed, Iraqi air defenses shot at coalition aircraft with surface-to-air missiles (SAMs) on December 28, 1998. Up until March 1999 Iraqi SAM sites and antiaircraft guns, the most common threat, fired on U.S. and British aircraft over northern Iraq almost daily. Coalition forces retaliated by attacking Iraqi air defense systems, the first such action in northern Iraq since August 1993. Coalition aircraft used 485 weapons, including laser-guided bombs, the AGM-88 High-Speed Anti-Radiation Missile (HARM), and the AGM-130 long-range air-to-surface missiles, against 225 targets. NORTHERN WATCH saw the first combat use of the AGM-130.

From June 1998 to June 1999, coalition aircraft flew patrols an average of 18 days per month, accumulating more than 5,000 combat/combat-support sorties. These coalition air attacks severely degraded Iraq's integrated air defense systems without any loss of coalition aircraft, despite a $14,000 bounty Hussein promised to anyone who downed a coalition aircraft. During early 1999, coalition air activity over northern Iraq came to a temporary halt as aircraft transferred to Italy for Operation ALLIED FORCE.

The air policing and surveillance of northern Iraq had a number of critics. Some believed that coalition aircraft deliberately provoked Iraqi antiaircraft defenses to turn on their radars and/or fire SAMs or antiaircraft guns to draw a coalition attack. As this type of criticism mounted, Brigadier General Robert DuLaney, the American commander of Operation NORTHERN WATCH after October 1999, ordered coalition aircraft to be less confrontational and avoid known Iraqi air defense sites. Also, coalition planes stopped dropping cement-filled laser-guided bombs that had been used to attack SAM and radar sites located near sensitive buildings, such as mosques. Because of the length of the operation and the rules of engagement, some military strategists and even pilots who had flown missions for NORTHERN WATCH no longer saw any military objective in the ongoing operation.

The last flight for Operation NORTHERN WATCH occurred on March 17, 2003, two days before the start of Operation IRAQI FREEDOM. NORTHERN WATCH officially ended on May 1, 2003. Since its inception in 1997, more than 40,000 troops had rotated through Incirlik Air Base to support the mission, and assigned aircraft flew more than 36,000 sorties.

ROBERT B. KANE

**See also**

Annan, Kofi; DESERT FOX, Operation; DESERT THUNDER I, Operation; DESERT THUNDER II, Operation; Hussein, Saddam; Kurds; No-Fly Zones; PROVIDE COMFORT, Operation; SOUTHERN WATCH, Operation; United Nations Special Commission; United Nations Weapons Inspectors

**References**

Boyne, Walter J. *Beyond the Wild Blue: A History of the U.S. Air Force, 1947–2007.* 2nd ed. New York: Thomas Dunne Books, 2007.

Byman, Daniel, and Matthew C. Waxman. *Confronting Iraq: U.S. Policy and the Use of Force since the Gulf War.* Santa Monica, CA: RAND Corporation, 2002.

Knights, Michael. *Cradle of Conflict: Iraq and the Birth of Modern U.S. Military.* Annapolis, MD: Naval Institute Press, 2005.

RAND Corporation. *Interoperability of U.S. and NATO Allied Air Forces: Supporting Data and Case Studies: Project Air Force.* Santa Monica, CA: RAND Corporation, 2003.

# Norway, Role in Persian Gulf, Afghanistan, and Iraq Wars

Norway is a Scandinavian nation located on the western part of the Scandinavian Peninsula. The Kingdom of Norway borders the Norwegian Sea to the west, the North Sea to the south, Sweden to the east, and Finland and Russia to the north. With an estimated 2008 population of 4.644 million, the nation covers 125,181 square miles. A founding member of the North Atlantic Treaty Organization (NATO), Norway is a constitutional, parliamentary monarchy. Olav V reigned until January 17, 1991; since then, Harald V, Olav V's son, has reigned as Norwegian king. The monarchy is a chiefly ceremonial institution. Modern Norwegian politics have been dominated by a series of center, center-left, and center-right coalition governments. Since 1990 Norway has had seven different governments and five prime ministers.

Norway supported the U.S.-led military coalitions in the 1991 Persian Gulf War and the conflict in Afghanistan (Operation ENDURING FREEDOM), and it contributed troops to the postwar occupation of Iraq following the 2003 Iraq War. Norway has traditionally supported peaceful resolutions to conflicts and sought to advance diplomatic solutions to disputes in the Middle East. Norway has participated in a range of United Nations (UN) peacekeeping missions in the region, including those in Egypt, Lebanon, Somalia, and Yemen. During the Iran-Iraq War (1980–1988), Norway called for a peacekeeping mission to supervise a withdrawal of the forces of both countries, a suggestion rejected by Iran. After the end of that war, Norwegian troops took part in the UN monitoring mission between the two opponents.

In 1985 the Norwegian Parliament decreed that women should be allowed to undertake combat operations. Norway subsequently led the successful effort to ensure that women service personnel were permitted to participate in UN peacekeeping operations.

Norway has contributed significant monetary aid to the Middle East. The Palestinian National Authority (PNA) receives about $75 million in aid annually from Oslo and is the third largest recipient of Norwegian foreign assistance. Norway also has a history of making significant contributions directly to UN agencies and nongovernmental organizations that provide aid in the Middle East.

Norway strongly backed U.S. efforts to assemble an international military coalition to oppose Iraq in the run-up to the Persian Gulf War. During that conflict, Norway deployed approximately 350 military personnel, including a field hospital unit and the coast guard ship *Andenes*, which functioned as a support ship for the Danish corvette *Olfert Fischer* in the maritime mission to enforce the economic sanctions imposed on Iraq after its invasion of Kuwait. The 50-bed medical unit was attached to British forces, and it remained in Saudi Arabia, where it treated mainly wounded Iraqi prisoners of war. During the war, Norway also provided medical equipment and assistance to NATO ally Turkey. Also, 25 Norwegian merchant vessels were chartered by the government or coalition partners for service during Operations DESERT SHIELD and

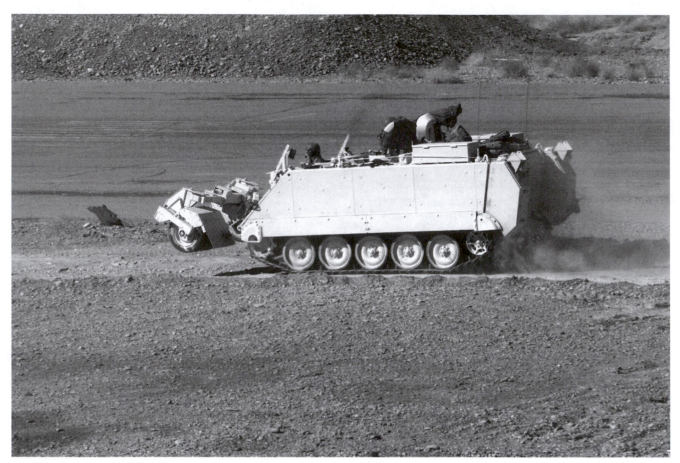

A Norwegian M-113 armored personnel carrier, equipped with a mine roller in front, drives along the runway at Kandahar International Airport, Kandahar, Afghanistan, during Operation ENDURING FREEDOM in 2002. (U.S. Department of Defense)

DESERT STORM. These included container vessels, tankers, and roll-on/roll-off vessels. Oslo also gave funds to assist Kuwaiti and Iraqi refugees displaced by the war, and it provided a Lockheed C-130 Hercules aircraft to transport humanitarian assistance. After the end of the conflict in February 1991, 169 Norwegian troops remained in the theater as part of the UN Iraq-Kuwait Monitoring Mission (UNIKOM) from 1991 until 1994.

In the aftermath of the September 11, 2001, Al Qaeda terrorist attacks on the United States, Norway, along with several other NATO countries, initially opposed the invocation of Article Five of the Washington Treaty, the alliance's collective defense clause. The Norwegian government had reservations over NATO assuming a counterterrorism role. Oslo did, however, join other NATO states in invoking Article Five in October 2001, after the United States pledged that military action would only be one component of a larger campaign that would also include intelligence and law-enforcement cooperation, as well as efforts to address the root causes of terrorism. Norway subsequently joined other NATO allies in offering the United States troops for military action in Operation ENDURING FREEDOM, the military campaign waged against the Taliban and Al Qaeda in Afghanistan.

Norway contributed one frigate to a NATO task force that was stationed in the eastern Mediterranean to support Operation ENDURING FREEDOM. Simultaneously, Oslo also assumed command of the NATO-led Kosovo peacekeeping mission and deployed an additional 200 troops in order to free up U.S. personnel. It participated in the deployment of NATO Boeing E-3 Sentry AWACS (Airborne Warning and Control System) aircraft to the United States, which allowed U.S. planes to be sent to Afghanistan.

Norway also provided a range of conventional ground troops, support units, and special operations forces for Operation ENDURING FREEDOM. Norwegian troops were valued by ENDURING FREEDOM commanders because of their training in mountainous terrain and cold climates. Oslo also deployed four Lockheed Martin F-16 Fighting Falcon fighters and several helicopters to support the NATO-led International Security Assistance Force–Afghanistan (ISAF). When the F-16s provided close air support for ENDURING FREEDOM ground units in 2002, it marked the first time that the Royal Norwegian Air Force had seen combat since World War II.

The country's contributions to ENDURING FREEDOM were especially noteworthy because Norway was in the midst of a decade-long series of defense reorganizations and military downsizing. By the early 2000s, Norway had reduced conscription so that it only affected about one-third of eligible youths and reduced its peacetime military to 21,000 troops and its home guard from 83,000 to 50,000. In addition, the country had consolidated its military facilities, eliminating one-third of them, including one of its two major headquarters, and eliminating some weapons programs.

Norwegian special operations forces known as the *Forsvarets Spesialkommando*, or FSK, took part in Operation ANACONDA in March 2002. The U.S.-led campaign targeted Al Qaeda and Taliban forces in the Shahi-Kot Valley and Arma Mountains. The valley was surrounded by the Turgal Gar Mountains, with peaks as high as 11,000 feet. The insurgents controlled some 100 caves along the eastern ridge of the slopes, and the mountainous conditions prevented the detection of the enemy sites by aerial reconnaissance. Consequently, coalition forces had to identify the Taliban caves by searching the slopes. The operation killed about 500 insurgents and dislodged their forces, but the majority of the Taliban and Al Qaeda forces were able to escape.

Since 2001 Norway has maintained between 450 and 700 troops in Afghanistan. The majority is attached to ISAF. Through 2008 three Norwegian soldiers had been killed in action in Afghanistan. Norway also leads a Provincial Reconstruction Team (PRT) in Meymaneh in Faryab Province, in the northwest of the country. The PRT contains both military personnel and civilians. The nonmilitary personnel include police trainers and political advisers for the local and regional government. Norway assumed command of the PRT from the British in 2005. In 2006 the PRT's headquarters was attacked. Although there were no fatalities, a number of Norwegian troops were injured and a new, more secure facility was constructed.

Norwegian forces also form part of the PRT under Swedish command in Mazar-e Sharif, where they operate a field hospital and are responsible for training Afghan security forces. There is also a Norwegian quick reaction force stationed at Mazar-e Sharif. Norway has continued to deploy FSK units for specific missions on short rotations. It has also deployed detachments to train Afghan security forces and undertaken de-mining operations. Furthermore, Oslo has supplied arms and military equipment for the new Afghan national army and has helped in the construction of new bases and police facilities. The government provides about $40 million per year in humanitarian and reconstruction assistance to Kabul.

Both the Norwegian government and public opposed the U.S.-led invasion of Iraq in March 2003 (Operation IRAQI FREEDOM). Kjell Magne Bondevik, the Norwegian prime minister at the time, strongly argued that UN weapons inspectors should be allowed to undertake a thorough investigation of Iraq's weapons of mass destruction (WMDs) programs before any military action was initiated. However, after the fall of the Saddam Hussein regime in April 2003, Norway offered to provide humanitarian and reconstruction assistance to the U.S.-led coalition, after the UN designated the coalition as the official occupying power. Norway also agreed to accept a substantial number of Iraqi refugees; at their peak in 2004, they numbered more than 13,300. In 2004 Norway sent a military engineer unit to Iraq with 150 personnel. The unit was withdrawn in 2005, but 10–15 soldiers remained in Iraq as part of the NATO mission to train Iraqi security forces. They were withdrawn in 2006. Oslo also conducted advanced training

courses for Iraqi security officials at the NATO Joint Warfare Center in Stavanger, Norway, beginning in 2004. Norway further pledged to support the political process in Iraq and donated more than $75 million to support elections and political reconciliation between 2003 and 2006.

The original deployment of engineers to Iraq was authorized by a center-right coalition government, led by the Christian People's Party, the Conservative Party, and the Liberal Party, but elections in 2005 brought a new coalition government to power. The resulting center-left government included the Labor Party, the Socialist Left Party, and the Center Party, all of which were opposed to Norway's participation in Iraq. Meanwhile, public and political support for Norway's participation in the Afghan War was mixed. The original deployment was authorized by the center-right government in 2001, but the deployment caused rifts in the center-left government because it was strongly opposed by the Socialist Left Party. However, the other two parties of the coalition have supported Norwegian participation in Afghanistan as part of the nation's commitment to NATO.

TOM LANSFORD

**See also**

Afghanistan, Coalition Combat Operations in, 2002–Present; IRAQI FREEDOM, Operation, Coalition Ground Forces; Multi-National Force–Iraq; North Atlantic Treaty Organization in Afghanistan

**References**

Cockburn, Patrick. *The Occupation: War and Resistance in Iraq*. New York: Verso, 2007.

Feickert, Andrew. *U.S. and Coalition Military Operations in Afghanistan: Issues for Congress*. Washington, DC: Congressional Research Service, 2006.

Keegan, John. *The Iraq War: The Military Offensive, from Victory in 21 Days to the Insurgent Aftermath*. New York: Vintage, 2005.

Murray, Williamson, and Robert H. Scales Jr. *The Iraq War: A Military History*. Cambridge, MA: Belknap, 2005.

Ryan, Mike. *Battlefield Afghanistan*. London: Spellmount, 2007.

Sinno, Abdulkader. *Organizations at War in Afghanistan and Beyond*. Ithaca, NY: Cornell University Press, 2008.

# Nuclear Weapons, Iraq's Potential for Building

From 1968 to 1991, Iraq sought to obtain uranium and create an industrial base for uranium enrichment and nuclear weapons production. Operation DESERT STORM and the resulting United Nations (UN) sanctions assured the destruction of Iraq's nuclear infrastructure in 1991. From 1991 to 2003, Iraq attempted to preserve the scientific talent needed to restart its nuclear program. American suspicions, based on faulty intelligence, that Iraq was secretly reconstituting its nuclear program, and Iraqi dictator Saddam Hussein's recalcitrance in cooperating with UN inspectors greatly influenced the George W. Bush administration's decision to invade Iraq in March 2003.

From 1968 to 1990 the Iraqis sought and received foreign assistance for nuclear weapons programs. In the late 1970s the French built a light water reactor at the Al Tuwaitha Nuclear Center, located some 11 miles southeast of Baghdad. This type of reactor was known as Osiris; the French named it Osiraq, for the reactor and Iraq. The Iraqis called it the *Tammuz I* for the month in the Babylonian calendar when the Baath party took power in Iraq in 1968. In June 1981, during Operation OPERA, Israeli aircraft largely destroyed Osiraq; it was entirely destroyed in the Persian Gulf War in 1991.

Thereafter, the United States claimed that Iraq pursued clandestine uranium enrichment. With German assistance, by 1990 Iraq was operating industrial-scale electromagnetic isotope separation facilities and had built prototype centrifuges. Iraq constructed a facility able to make 1,000 to 4,000 centrifuges annually (1,500 centrifuges can enrich sufficient uranium for one nuclear weapon a year). Iraq also began designing a first-generation nuclear weapon and a ballistic missile delivery vehicle. In 1992 some experts estimated that Iraq was six months to three years from completing a nuclear bomb in January 1991. However, the Persian Gulf War crippled Iraq's nuclear infrastructure, and it never recovered.

In April 1991 UN Security Council Resolution 687 required Iraq to abstain from the acquisition, research, development, and manufacture of nuclear weapons. To ensure compliance, the UN Special Commission (UNSCOM) conducted inspections in Iraq from 1991 to 1998. UNSCOM discovered and destroyed many Iraqi nuclear-related capabilities and facilities, despite determined Iraqi efforts to frustrate the inspectors. It was alleged that Hussein hoped to conceal key elements of his nuclear program and preserve its scientific potential until UN sanctions on Iraq were lifted. However, Hussein might also have been trying to demonstrate his sovereign rights, since it seemed to many in Iraq that the United States and some European nations were pressuring the International Atomic Energy Agency (IAEA) process. In 1995 General Hussein Kamil al-Majid, Hussein's son-in-law, defected from Iraq along with his brother. Majid subsequently revealed that he personally had ordered the destruction of all stockpiles of weapons of mass destruction (WMDs) in Iraq. He also divulged extensive information on Iraqi weapons programs and facilities, which greatly assisted UNSCOM. Majid and his brother and their wives, Hussein's daughters, were then tricked into returning to Iraq, where the two men were killed three days after they arrived.

In 1998 Hussein ended cooperation with UNSCOM and the IAEA. Britain and the United States launched a punitive air strike, and Iraq responded by renouncing compliance with all UN resolutions. From then on, many in the American intelligence community believed that Iraq had begun to reconstitute its nuclear program. To support this view, intelligence assessments cited Iraq's efforts to obtain equipment necessary for uranium enrichment, to enhance its cadre of weapons personnel, and to acquire yellow-cake uranium from Africa.

In 2001 U.S. intelligence learned that Iraq was trying to obtain high-strength, high-specification aluminum tubes. The Central Intelligence Agency (CIA) believed that Iraq would use these tubes for uranium-enrichment centrifuges. The Department of Energy, however, claimed that the tubes were unsuitable for centrifuge production and were probably intended for conventional 81-mm rocket production. Investigations conducted after the 2003 overthrow of Hussein showed that the latter assessment was correct.

U.S. intelligence also detected Iraqi efforts to obtain carbon filament winding machines, flow-forming machinery, magnets, and other "dual use" machine tools. Such machinery could support both nuclear research and nonnuclear programs. The Central Intelligence Agency (CIA) assumed the former, but postwar investigations revealed that the machinery actually supported conventional military programs.

U.S. intelligence discovered Hussein's direct personal interest in the Iraqi Atomic Energy Commission (IAEC) after 1999, when he provided IAEC scientists with increased security and funding. The CIA believed that this development indicated his intent to restart nuclear work immediately. In fact, Hussein did not order IAEC scientists to conduct nuclear work. Rather, he wanted to sustain their morale, keep Iraq's scientific base intact, and have them conduct nonnuclear research.

British and U.S. intelligence also learned that Iraqi officials had visited Niger in 1999, and they assumed that Iraq had sought to purchase yellow-cake uranium for a reconstituted nuclear program. Whether the Iraqis actually obtained an agreement was uncertain, and in 2002 the CIA sent Ambassador Joseph C. Wilson to Niger to investigate. He reported that Niger's government denied any deal with Iraq and that a forged document had been the evidence. The CIA leadership in Washington did not believe this denial, and did not change its assessment that Iraq had sought to purchase uranium from Africa. Indeed, this assessment was a major part of President Bush's justification for war. Yet the postinvasion investigations revealed that Iraq indeed did not seek any foreign uranium after 1991.

The final National Intelligence Estimate, published in October 2002, noted Iraq's efforts to acquire aluminum tubes. The estimate concluded that Iraq could make a nuclear weapon within a year if foreign states provided fissile material, but otherwise would not be able to make a weapon "until the last half of the decade." In order to justify U.S. military action against Iraq, President George W. Bush and Secretary of State Colin Powell issued public warnings that Iraq could soon make nuclear weapons. Following the U.S.-led invasion, former UNSCOM inspector Charles Duelfer led the Iraq Survey Group, a 1,400-member team that comprehensively studied Iraq's weapons programs. Duelfer determined that prewar warnings about Iraq's weapons were based on incorrect intelligence. In fact, Iraq had made no concerted effort to restart its nuclear program after 1991, and never intended to do so while UN sanctions were in force.

JAMES D. PERRY

**See also**
Bush, George Walker; DESERT STORM, Operation; Hussein, Saddam; International Atomic Energy Agency; Iraq, History of, Pre-1990; Iraq, History of, 1990–Present; IRAQI FREEDOM, Operation; Powell, Colin Luther; United Nations Security Council Resolution 687; United Nations Special Commission; Wilson, Joseph Carter, IV

**References**
Brockwell, The Lord Butler of. *The Review of Intelligence on Weapons of Mass Destruction.* London: Stationery Office, 2004.
Duelfer, Charles. *Comprehensive Report of the Special Advisor to the DCI on Iraq's WMD.* Washington, DC: U.S. Government Printing Office, 2004.
United States Senate, Select Committee on Intelligence. *Report on the U.S. Intelligence Community's Prewar Intelligence Assessments on Iraq.* Washington, DC: U.S. Government Printing Office, July 9, 2004.

# Nuri al-Said
Birth Date: 1888
Death Date: July 15, 1958

Prominent pro-British Iraqi politician who served as prime minister of Iraq 14 times between 1930 and 1958. Born in Baghdad in 1888, Nuri al-Said was the son of a minor Ottoman government official. Trained at the Staff College in Constantinople as an officer in the Ottoman Army, he was converted to the Arab nationalist cause and fought with British major T. E. Lawrence in the Arab Revolt (1916–1918) as an adviser to Emir Faisal of Hejaz, who would later reign briefly as the king of Syria before becoming King Faisal I of Iraq. In 1918 Nuri commanded the Arab troops who took Damascus for Faisal, and he accompanied Faisal to the Paris Peace Conference following World War I.

Nuri secured his first cabinet position, as director-general of the police in Iraq, in 1922. He used this post to staff the police with his own followers, a tactic he would repeat again and again. In 1924 he became deputy commander of the Iraqi Army, and in 1930 he became prime minister for the first time, signing the Anglo-Iraqi Treaty. The treaty provided for Iraqi independence in 1932 but was unpopular because it also provided for a 25-year alliance between Britain and Iraq that included the leasing of bases to Britain. Nuri held numerous cabinet positions and served many times as prime minister.

Although he was dismissed from office in 1932, Nuri, a trusted ally of the British, was never far from the seat of power. In early 1941 he denounced Prime Minister Rashid Ali al-Gaylani's anti-British,

pro-German policies, which were strongly influenced by Haj Amin al-Husseini, the mufti of Jerusalem. At the end of January 1941, Gaylani fled into exile, only to return to power in April. It was then Nuri's turn to flee, to Jordan. When Gaylani attempted to restrict British troop movements in Iraq, British forces, supported by Jordan's Arab Legion, deposed Gaylani and installed Nuri as the new Iraqi prime minister. This time he held office until June 1944.

Nuri was prime minister for the 9th through 14th times during the periods November 1946–March 1947, January–December 1949, September 1950–July 1952, August 1954–June 1957, and March–May 1958. In February 1954 he signed the Baghdad Pact with Iran, Turkey, Pakistan, and the United Kingdom. This treaty was intended to serve as a buffer against Soviet encroachments in the region.

Nuri's pro-Western position brought him into conflict with Egyptian leader Gamal Abdel Nasser, who opposed Western influence in the region. Nasser launched a media campaign that challenged the legitimacy of the Iraqi monarchy and called on the Iraqi military to overthrow it. In response to the Egyptian-Syrian union known as the United Arab Republic, on February 12, 1958, the Hashemite monarchies of Jordan and Iraq declared an Iraqi-Jordanian union known as the Arab Federation. In May 1958 Nuri resigned to become the first prime minister of the short-lived Arab Federation.

Nuri's pro-Western policies and his increasingly heavy-handed methods, from crushing a miners' strike in November 1946 to putting down demonstrations against the Baghdad Pact, made him very unpopular in Iraq. On July 14, 1958, a military coup led by Abd al-Karim Qasim ended the Arab Federation and the Iraqi monarchy. King Faisal II and other members of the royal family were executed. Nuri, disguised as a veiled woman, eluded capture for a day but was caught on July 15 and promptly put to death. His body was buried but then dug up and reportedly tied to the back of a car and paraded through the streets of Baghdad until nothing remained but a portion of one leg.

MICHAEL R. HALL

**See also**
Anglo-Iraqi Treaty; Baghdad Pact; Faisal II, King of Iraq; Iraq, History of 1990; Nasser, Gamal Abdel; United Arab Republic

**References**
Birdwood, Lord. *Nuri as-Said.* London: Cassell, 1959.
Dodge, Toby. *Inventing Iraq: The Failure of Nation-Building and a History Denied.* New York: Columbia University Press, 2003.
Gallman, Waldemar J. *Iraq under General Nuri: My Recollection of Nuri Al-Said, 1954–1958.* Baltimore, MD: Johns Hopkins University Press, 1964.

O

# Obaidullah, Akhund

**Birth Date:** ca. 1965
**Death Date:** Unknown

Former Taliban minister of defense and a leader in the neo-Taliban insurgency in Afghanistan since 2002. Believed to have been born in Kandahar, Afghanistan, perhaps in 1965, Mullah Akhund Obaidullah (also spelled Ubaidullah and Ubaydullah) emerged as the third most senior leader of the Taliban and a confidant to its spiritual leader, Mullah Mohammed Omar.

Having been educated in a Pakistani madrasah in the border town of Quetta, Obaidullah was a mujahideen fighter during the Soviet invasion and occupation (1979–1988). In 1996 Obaidullah was named minister of defense for the Taliban regime. He participated in the 1998 capture of Mazar-e Sharif and the subsequent massacre that followed. In addition to his ministerial position, Obaidullah acted as liaison with Pakistan's Inter-Service Intelligence Agency (ISI) and with Al Qaeda and its leader, Osama bin Laden.

The Taliban's refusal to surrender bin Laden in the wake of the September 11, 2001, terror attacks on the United States resulted in an invasion of Afghanistan by the United States and its allies in October 2001. By November 2001, with the fall of Kandahar inevitable, Mullah Mohammed Omar abandoned the capital and turned conduct of the war over to a council comprising senior Taliban leaders, led by Mullah Obaidullah. On December 6, 2001, Obaidullah agreed to transfer the leadership of Afghanistan to a Western-supported tribal council under the leadership of Hamid Karzai. Taliban fighters were subsequently ordered to cease combat and surrender their weapons. Karzai, on December 22, issued a general amnesty to Taliban fighters, including Taliban leaders captured during the fall of Kandahar. Obaidullah and other senior Taliban leaders, including former Minster of Justice Mullah Nuruddin Turabi, were then released from captivity.

Following his release, Obaidullah emerged as a leader among the numerous insurgencies that were developing in Afghanistan and the border areas in Pakistan. Unlike others, however, Obaidullah never wavered from his support of the Taliban and Mullah Omar. As one of the few with direct access to Mullah Omar, Obaidullah acted as a conduit, transferring orders from Omar to the Taliban insurgents in the field. In March 2002 he issued a call to arms against Western forces and for the establishment of support areas in the northwestern frontier between Pakistan and Afghanistan. In 2003 Mullah Omar appointed Obaidullah to the newly created Rahhari Shura (Leadership Council), which was responsible for furthering the jihad against the United States and its allies. During this time, Obaidullah traveled unimpeded between Pakistan and Afghanistan, and he is rumored to have traveled even further abroad to purchase antiaircraft weapons.

In March 2004 Mullah Omar issued orders for Obaidullah to organize former mujahideen fighters to continue the fight against both the Karzai government and the United States. Rather than remaining focused on regaining control of Afghanistan, this new organization was designed to carry the fight beyond Afghan borders. Obaidullah, Mullah Omar, and their followers now had adopted a more universalist Islamic outlook similar to that espoused by Al Qaeda. The use of suicide bombers was also adopted. In March 2005 Obaidullah personally ordered the killing of foreign aid workers in Kabul. He later led about 400 troops against North Atlantic Treaty Organization (NATO) forces in the Penjwayi district of Kandahar in 2006. As late as December 2006, Obaidullah bragged in interviews of the growing power of the Taliban insurgency and its increased use of suicide attacks.

Under increased pressure from the U.S. government and acting on a tip from American intelligence, Pakistani officials succeeded in capturing Obaidullah and a number of Taliban leaders during a raid in Quetta in March 2007. Rumors emerged that Obaidullah was among 50 Taliban leaders released in exchange for the Pakistani ambassador to Afghanistan, Tariq Azizuddin, who had been held hostage for three months. Pakistani officials denied this. His current whereabouts are unknown, but there are some reports that he was killed on May 11, 2007, in a shoot-out with Afghan/NATO forces in Helmand Province.

ROBERT W. MALICK

**See also**

Afghanistan; Al Qaeda; Bin Laden, Osama; Karzai, Hamid; Omar, Mohammed; Taliban Insurgency, Afghanistan

**References**

Crews, Robert D., and Amin Tarzi, eds. *The Taliban and the Crisis of Afghanistan.* Cambridge: Harvard University Press, 2008.

Gall, Carlotta. "Top Taliban Leader Is Arrested in Pakistan." *New York Times,* March 1, 2007.

Giustozzi, Antonio. *Koran, Kalashnikov, and Laptop. The Neo-Taliban Insurgency in Afghanistan.* New York: Columbia University Press, 2008.

Rashid, Ahmed. *Taliban: Militant Islam, Oil, and Fundamentalism in Central Asia.* New Haven, CT: Yale University Press, 2001.

Wikinson, Isambard. "First Senior Taliban Leader Arrested by Pakistan on its Own Soil." *Telegraph,* March 3, 2007.

# Obama, Barack Hussein, II
## Birth Date: August 4, 1961

Attorney, Democratic Party politician, U.S. senator from Illinois (2005–2008), and president of the United States (2009–). Barack Hussein Obama II was born on August 4, 1961, in Honolulu, Hawaii, the son of a white American woman and an African from Kenya. Obama's parents separated when he was just two years old, and they divorced in 1964. Obama's father returned to Kenya and had limited contact with his son after that time; Obama saw his father, who died in a car accident in 1982, only once after he left for Kenya. Obama's maternal grandparents were a major force in his life, and in many ways served as his surrogate parents.

Obama's mother subsequently married a man from Indonesia, and Obama moved to Jakarta, Indonesia, where he attended several schools until he returned to live with his grandparents in Hawaii in 1971. In 1979 Obama entered Occidental College before transferring to Columbia University, from which he graduated in 1983. From 1985 to 1988 he worked as a community organizer on the South Side of Chicago; his experiences there led to his adoption of Chicago as his home city.

In 1988 Obama entered Harvard Law School, where his keen intellect and engaging personality earned him the presidency of the *Harvard Law Review;* he was the first African American ever to

hold the position. In 1991 he secured his law degree and returned to Chicago; the following year he led a successful voter-registration drive in Illinois that registered as many as 150,000 previously unregistered African American voters. In 1992 Obama joined the faculty of the University of Chicago School of Law, serving in various teaching capacities until 2004. From 1993 to 2004 Obama was also a member of a small Chicago law firm that specialized in civil rights issues and local economic development. In 1997 Obama became an Illinois state senator, a post he held until 2004. As a state senator, Obama garnered much praise for his grasp of important issues and his ability to sponsor and guide bipartisan-backed legislation through the senate.

In 2004 Obama, a gifted orator, made a run for the U.S. Senate, winning by the largest landslide in Illinois electoral history. He campaigned on a platform that was sharply critical of the Iraq War and that promised to reorder America's social and economic priorities. He also vowed to help unite Americans and heal racial, social, and economic divisions.

In July 2004 Obama delivered the keynote address at the Democratic National Convention, as a result of which he became a national phenomenon. His electrifying speech caught the attention of many and helped prepare the way for his run for the White House in 2008. Obama was sworn in as a U.S. senator in January 2005. He worked closely with Republican senator Richard Lugar, chairman of the Senate Committee on Foreign Relations; the two visited nuclear missile launch sites in Russia in an effort to ensure the safety of the armaments. Obama also continued his criticism of the Iraq War, arguing that it had been an unnecessary operation and badly managed by the George W. Bush administration.

In February 2007 Obama announced his intention to run for the U.S. presidency on the Democratic ticket in 2008. At the time many dismissed his intentions, pointing to his relative inexperience and the likely candidacies of such heavy-hitters as senators Hillary Clinton, Joseph Biden, Christopher Dodd, and John Edwards, among others. But Obama ran an impressively earnest and well-executed primary campaign, and by the mid-winter of 2008 his many rivals had all dropped out of the race, except for Senator Clinton. Meanwhile, the Obama campaign's brilliant use of the Internet to raise money and get out his message began to tell, and in early June 2008 Obama became the presumptive Democratic nominee when Clinton conceded the race. From then on, Obama, who eschewed public funding of his campaign, continued to raise massive sums of money and garnered an impressive list of endorsements from both Democrats and Republicans, including former secretary of state and Republican Party stalwart Colin L. Powell. By the early fall, Obama had raised more money by far than any other presidential candidate in history.

In the general election Obama faced off against Republican senator John S. McCain, a war hero and prisoner of war during the Vietnam War, and the son and grandson of U.S. Navy admirals. Until September the tenor of the race focused chiefly on Obama's insistence that U.S. troops be withdrawn from Iraq as

Democrat Barack Obama became president of the United States in 2009. The first African American to hold that position, he promised a new era of engaging foreign governments and of multinationalism in U.S. foreign policy. (U.S. Department of Defense)

expeditiously as possible, his calls for energy independence, his desire to implement universal and affordable health care for all, and his hope to lessen the power of Washington lobbyists and special interests. He traveled to the Middle East and several European nations in July 2008 amidst much fanfare, in an attempt to bolster his foreign policy bona fides. The McCain camp sought to portray Obama as too inexperienced and naive to be president, and McCain argued that the troop surge in Iraq, begun in early 2007, had made a quantifiable difference in the course of the conflict. He suggested that Obama's plan for a specific timetable for the withdrawal of U.S. troops from Iraq represented a "cut and run" mentality that would play into the hands of the insurgents. Obama's suggested timetable ended up being embraced by the Iraqi government and became the basis for the U.S.-Iraq Status of Forces Agreement, finalized in late 2008.

Obama continued to argue that the Iraq War had been unnecessary from the start and based on flimsy intelligence and poor judgment on the part of the Bush administration. He also asserted that the conflict had caused the United States to dilute its efforts in the Afghanistan War, resulting in the increasingly deadly Taliban insurgency there. Obama promised to redouble U.S. efforts in Afghanistan and to dispatch significantly more troops there.

In August, Obama named Senator Joseph Biden, from Delaware, to be his vice presidential running mate. Biden added his years of governmental experience to the ticket, and the choice was generally hailed as a wise move. Just a few days later, McCain revealed his choice for a running mate: Governor Sarah Palin of Alaska, a 44-year-old with no experience in national politics. She had been governor for only 20 months and before that had been the mayor of a small town in Alaska. The choice proved controversial, although it energized media coverage of the McCain campaign that, until then, had largely been dominated by Obama. Meanwhile, Obama continued to run a highly disciplined campaign, which portrayed McCain as another version of George W. Bush, who by the autumn of 2008 had the lowest approval ratings in modern presidential history. McCain's not infrequent gaffes, mixed debate performances, and unfocused messages began to work against him, while Obama's tactics and campaign strategy aided his own campaign.

In September the focus of the campaign shifted dramatically as the U.S. economy plunged into a downward spiral. By mid-month, the Iraq War had taken a distant second place to the struggling economy. Each day brought more bad news: the financial system was paralyzed by a series of spectacular bank and investment house failures; the stock market gyrated wildly but in a persistently downward trajectory; unemployment rose dramatically; and the housing market was in full-fledged crisis. Obama made the most of the situation, asserting that a vote for McCain would be a vote for more economic chaos. By Election Day, Obama enjoyed a comfortable lead over McCain, and he went on to win the presidency, winning 52.9 percent of the popular vote and 365 electoral votes.

Obama's transition to power went smoothly, although Republicans, in the now well-established pattern of U.S. partisan politics, consistently challenged both his appointees and statements. His nomination of former rival Senator Hillary Clinton for secretary of state proved an adroit move, and she won easy confirmation in the Senate. Choosing stability over change, Obama chose to keep Robert M. Gates, a holdover from the Bush administration, in the key post of secretary of defense.

Obama's early efforts to solve the financial crisis through massive government bailouts to the financial and auto industries generated some opposition, but nothing like the opposition to his health care plan, which passed in March 2010 amid much acrimony among the Republicans, who rejected it en masse. Obama's public approval ratings began to sag late in 2009 and continued to fall into 2010. Internationally, Obama's taking over the reins of the U.S. government was generally well received, particularly his apparent willingness to reach out to European and other allies, "reset" deteriorating relations with Russia, and undertake new diplomatic initiatives and approaches to the Muslim world. In December 2009 after much study and internal debate, the Obama administration announced a troop surge in Afghanistan. The surge would deploy as many as 30,000 additional troops to deal with the worsening Taliban insurgency and would occur over a 6-month period, from January to June 2010. Obama, however, stipulated that troop withdrawals from Afghanistan would begin 18 months after the surge ended in June 2010. Obama's strategy met some opposition. Many Democrats disagreed with the surge, and many Republicans found a mandated timetable for troop withdrawals ill-advised.

PAUL G. PIERPAOLI JR.

**See also**

Biden, Joseph Robinette, Jr.; Bush, George Walker; Clinton, Hillary Rodham; Gates, Robert Michael; McCain, John Sidney, III

**References**

Life Magazine. *The American Journey of Barack Obama*. Boston: Little, Brown, 2008.

Obama, Barack. *The Audacity of Hope: Thoughts on Reclaiming the American Dream*. New York: Three Rivers, 2007.

———. *Dreams from My Father: A Story of Race and Inheritance*. New York: Three Rivers, 2004.

Obama for America. *Change We Can Believe In: Barack Obama's Plan to Renew America's Promise*. New York: Three Rivers, 2008.

---

# Odierno, Raymond
## Birth Date: September 8, 1954

U.S. Army general appointed commander of Multi-National Forces-Iraq (MNF-I) on September 16, 2008. Born in Rockaway, New Jersey, on September 8, 1954, Raymond Odierno graduated from the United States Military Academy, West Point, in 1976 and was commissioned in the field artillery. During his career, he earned a master's degree in nuclear effects engineering from North Carolina State University and another in national security and strategy from the Naval War College.

Odierno's initial tours of duty took him to the Federal Republic of Germany, where he served as platoon leader and survey officer of the 1st Battalion, 41st Field Artillery, 56th Field Artillery Brigade, as well as aide-de-camp to the brigade's commanding general. Following completion of the Field Artillery Officer Advanced Course at Fort Sill, Oklahoma, Odierno was assigned to the XVIII Airborne Corps Artillery at Fort Bragg, North Carolina, where he commanded a battery and served as S3 in the 1st Battalion, 73rd Field Artillery. Additionally, upon completion of his master's degree in nuclear effects engineering, he served as arms control officer for the Office of the Secretary of Defense. During operations DESERT SHIELD and DESERT STORM, Odierno was the executive officer of the 2nd Battalion, 3rd Field Artillery, and then held the same position in the Division Artillery of the 3rd Armored Division.

Following DESERT STORM, Odierno went on to command 2nd Battalion, 8th Field Artillery, 7th Infantry Division, during 1992–1994. After attending the Army War College and being promoted to colonel, he commanded the Division Artillery, 1st Cavalry Division, during 1995–1997. Following an assignment at the Army War College in Carlisle Barracks, Pennsylvania, he served as chief of staff, V Corps, U.S. Army Europe, and assistant division commander (support) of the 1st Armored Division, during which time he acted as deputy commanding general of Task Force Hawk, Albania. Upon promotion to brigadier general in July 1999, he became director of Force Management in the Office of the Deputy Chief of Staff for Operations and Plans in the Pentagon.

From October 2001 to June 2004, Odierno commanded the 4th Infantry Division (Mechanized) at Fort Hood, Texas. Promoted to major general in November 2002, he deployed with his division to participate in Operation IRAQI FREEDOM from March 2003 to April 2004. Originally, the division planned to enter Iraq from the north through Turkey; however, the Turkish government refused permission to move the unit through its territory, and the division deployed into Iraq through Kuwait. Subsequently, the 4th Infantry Division acted as a follow-on force and conducted operations in the Sunni Triangle north of Baghdad.

In December 2003 Odierno's troops captured deposed Iraqi dictator Saddam Hussein. Despite this success, Odierno's area of responsibility, which centered on Tikrit and Mosul, experienced ever-increasing insurgent violence. Subsequently, some critics characterized as overly heavy-handed Odierno's attempts to suppress the growing insurgency through confrontational armed measures, thereby driving some Iraqis into the insurgent fold. He has since argued that these measures were justified, as similar tactics had been successfully employed to suppress radical insurgents, notably Al Qaeda in Iraq, in 2007.

Upon his return to the United States in August 2004, Odierno served briefly as special assistant to the vice chief of staff of the army. From October 2004 until May 2006, he was the assistant to the chairman of the Joint Chiefs of Staff, serving as military adviser to Secretary of State Condoleezza Rice. He was promoted to lieutenant general in January 2005.

In May 2006 Odierno took command of III Corps at Fort Hood, Texas, assuming command of Multi-National Corps-Iraq (MNC-I) on December 14, 2006, the second-most senior command position in Operation IRAQI FREEDOM responsible for implementing the campaign plan of the MNF-I commanding general. Shortly thereafter, General David Petraeus assumed command of MNF-I and implemented a thorough revision of strategy emphasizing counterinsurgency operations in conjunction with his rewriting of army doctrine on counterinsurgency.

In February 2007 Odierno launched Operation ENFORCING THE LAW, also known as the Baghdad Security Plan. U.S. and Iraqi troops were dispersed throughout Baghdad and maintained a continual presence to establish security for its inhabitants through a system of joint security stations. His subsequent operations were aimed to deny Al Qaeda in Iraq its operational sanctuaries throughout the various provinces and to deny it an opportunity to regroup. The so-called Awakening Councils in Anbar Province aided these efforts.

Following rotation back to Fort Hood in February 2008, Odierno was selected to succeed Petraeus as commanding general of

MNF-I. He assumed that position on September 16, 2008, with promotion to full general.

KARL RUBIS

**See also**

Al Qaeda in Iraq; Anbar Awakening; Counterinsurgency; IRAQI FREEDOM, Operation; Iraqi Insurgency; Petraeus, David Howell; PHANTOM THUNDER, Operation; Sunni Triangle

**References**

Kagan, Frederick W., and Kimberly Kagan. "The Patton of Counterinsurgency." *Weekly Standard* 13 (2008): 27–33.

Ricks, Thomas E. *Fiasco: The American Military Adventure in Iraq.* New York: Penguin, 2006.

Woodward, Bob. *The War Within: A Secret White House History, 2006–2008.* New York: Simon and Schuster, 2008.

---

# Office of Military Cooperation Afghanistan

Agency formed by the U.S. Central Command (CENTCOM) in December 2002 to help rebuild the Afghan National Army (ANA) after a year of major fighting in Afghanistan against Al Qaeda and Taliban forces. The main purpose of the Office of Military Cooperation Afghanistan (OMCA) was to develop, train, field, and sustain the Afghan defense establishment from the Ministry of Defense down to combat battalions in the field. The agency consisted of more than 220 people from six coalition nations that oversaw the 1,800-person Coalition-Joint Task Force (JTF) Phoenix, comprising American National Guard units from more than 20 states, U.S. active duty and reserve units, and contingents from seven different countries, in a $7 billion security assistance program to re-create the Afghan military, which would serve the post-Taliban government in Kabul. The first chief of the OMCA was U.S. Army lieutenant general Karl W. Eikenberry, who served in 2002 and 2003. The second head was U.S. Air Force major general Craig P. Weston, who was also U.S. security sector coordinator in Afghanistan from December 2003 to February 2005.

In the first years of its existence, the OMCA completed the training, equipping, and garrison construction for the 10,000-man Central Corps of the ANA in Kabul. The Coalition-JTF Phoenix oversaw the construction of 14 brigade complexes, each costing about $75 million and capable of supporting 3,500 soldiers. Additionally, it oversaw the training of four additional corps in the four regions of the country as well as at field recruiting stations. The OMCA also assisted the Afghan Ministry of Defense in hiring and training more than 1,200 individuals of an eventual 3,000 people. Additionally, troop strength increased from two to five battalions in simultaneous training. The goal was to develop the ANA into a force that could defeat terrorists within Afghanistan by preventing them from threatening the Afghan people or using Afghanistan to launch their attacks.

Since late 2002, the ANA has received billions of U.S. dollars to rebuild and train its forces. The United States provided most of the weapons, which included 2,500 High Mobility Multipurpose Wheeled Vehicles (HMMWV, or Humvee), tens of thousands of M-16 assault rifles, body armor, and other types of vehicles and weapons. The aid also helped to construct a national military command center with training compounds in different parts of the country and housing for ANA members. Additionally, part of the aid went to cash incentives and vocational training to encourage Afghanis to join the ANA and to thwart and dissolve former militias or Taliban supporters. On September 18, 2005, the ANA and Afghan National Police ensured the security of the first free election in Afghanistan's history, and on December 19, 2005, the inauguration of the first parliament in Afghanistan in more than 35 years.

On July 12, 2005, the OMCA was redesignated as the Office of Security Cooperation Afghanistan (OSCA). U.S. Air Force major general John T. Brennan, who had been the OMCA's chief since February 2005, continued as the head of the renamed organization. The new organization's responsibilities included both national defense and internal security. In addition to rebuilding Afghanistan's national defense force, OSCA now also assisted German advisers and the Afghan Ministry of the Interior in developing the Afghan National Police. The creation of the OSCA emphasized the commitment of the United States to the continued development of a safe, secure, and prosperous Afghanistan. By this time, the ANA had steadily increased in capability, professionalism, and size, reaching a strength of more than 24,300 trained and equipped soldiers, with another 6,000 in training by the end of 2008. As of October 2008 the Afghan National Army comprised at least 80,000 active troops. The goal in early 2009 was to expand the ANA to about 134,000 troops.

The expanded role of the new OSCA was crucial to the future success of Afghanistan. The Afghanistan reconstruction effort and transfer to democracy was inextricably linked to security. The ability of the OSCA to further develop the ANA's capabilities and to train an effective, reliable police force would have a direct impact on democracy and reconstruction in Afghanistan. By 2006 the OSCA was renamed the Combined Security Transition Command–Afghanistan.

ROBERT B. KANE

**See also**

Afghan National Army; Combined Security Transition Command–Afghanistan; United States Central Command

**References**

Barnes, David W. "Fighting 'The Other War' Counterinsurgency Strategy in Afghanistan, 2003–2005." *Military Review* (September/October 2007): 32–44.

Dale, Catherine. *War in Afghanistan: Strategy, Military Operations, and Issues for Congress.* Washington, DC: Congressional Research Service, Library of Congress, 2009.

Katzman, Kenneth. *Afghanistan: Post-War Governance, Security, and U.S. Policy.* Washington, DC: Congressional Research Service, September 2008.

Levin, Lew. "Transformation: the Case of the Afghan National Police." *Warrior-Citizen* 53 (Summer 2008): 36.

U.S. Government Accountability Office. "Afghanistan: Security Efforts to Establish Army and Police Have Made Progress, but Future Plans Need to Be Better Defined." Report to the Committee on International Relations, U.S. House of Representatives, June 2005.

# Oil

A strategic, nonrenewable energy resource at the center of debates regarding the U.S. role in international politics and economics, particularly in the Middle East. Oil from the Middle East has long been an essential security priority of the United States and other industrialized nations, and a major source of energy for the world economy. Strategic concerns about access to petroleum reserves played a role in regional Middle East conflicts after World War II, including the Suez Crisis (1956), the Six-Day War (1967), the Yom Kippur (Ramadan) War (1973), the Iranian Revolution (1979–1980), the Iran-Iraq War (1980–1988), the Persian Gulf War (1991), and the Iraq War (2003–).

In Paris, at the end of 1968, the director of the U.S. State Department Office of Fuels and Energy informed delegates of the Oil Committee of the Organization of Economic Cooperation and Development that American oil production would soon reach capacity. Since then, growing oil demand has caused U.S. economic and military dependence on foreign petroleum production to be an important part of national and international political and economic debates.

The Persian Gulf basin is the source of approximately two-thirds of all known global petroleum reserves. Of the major oil producers, Saudi Arabia has the largest proven reserve, with 264 billion barrels. Iraq has the third largest reserve of conventional oil in the world, with a total of 115 billion barrels; Kuwait has the fifth position at 97 billion barrels. Middle East oil production played a central role in the 1991 Persian Gulf War, the War on Terror that began in 2001, and the Iraq War that began in 2003. The

geopolitical importance of oil is clear in the international dialogue regarding these conflicts.

After a decade of relative energy stability and steady oil prices, Kuwait increased its oil production in 1988, causing a decrease in world oil prices. This had a negative effect on the Iraqi economy, which relied heavily on income from oil exports. Iraq was also significantly in debt to Saudi Arabia and Kuwait, which meant that its ability to repay the loans was being undermined by falling oil prices. Iraqi president Saddam Hussein used the situation as a principal justification for his invasion of Kuwait in August 1990, arguing that the Kuwaiti production increases were tantamount to economic warfare against Iraq.

The Iraqi invasion of Kuwait placed a large proportion of Middle Eastern oil supplies under Iraqi control. The invasion also placed the Iraqi army adjacent to the vastly productive Hama oil fields of Saudi Arabia, a source of further international anxiety. Despite some domestic and international protest under the banner "No blood for oil," U.S. president George H. W. Bush invoked the (Jimmy) Carter Doctrine, which had identified the uninterrupted flow of Persian Gulf oil as a vital interest of the United States since 1980, and announced Operation DESERT SHIELD to protect Saudi Arabia from a potential Iraqi attack. As DESERT SHIELD grew, oil supplies to the West remained largely uninterrupted, but speculation in the commodities market and angst over the potential of more Iraqi aggression pushed world oil prices sharply higher. This in turn stoked fears of inflation and other economic difficulties usually associated with the 1970s.

After bringing together an international coalition through the United Nations (UN), the United States justified its support of Saudi Arabia and Kuwait based on the violation of the latter's territorial integrity and the former's geopolitical importance as a key supplier of oil. In early January 1991 the U.S. Congress authorized the use of military force to free Kuwait, and the coalition began Operation DESERT STORM on January 17. On January 23 media sources reported the dumping of more than 400 million gallons

**Crude Oil Production in Selected Middle Eastern and North African Countries, 1965–2005 (in barrels per day)**

| Country | OPEC Member | 1965 | 1975 | 1985 | 1995 | 2005 |
|---|---|---|---|---|---|---|
| Algeria | Yes | 577,000 | 1,003,000 | 1,151,000 | 1,327,000 | 2,015,000 |
| Bahrain | No | 58,000 | 60,000 | 41,000 | 38,000 | 188,000 |
| Egypt | No | 126,000 | 228,000 | 882,000 | 924,000 | 696,000 |
| Iran | Yes | 1,908,000 | 5,387,000 | 2,205,000 | 3,744,000 | 4,049,000 |
| Iraq | Yes | 1,313,000 | 2,271,000 | 1,425,000 | 530,000 | 1,820,000 |
| Israel | No | 4,000 | 101,000 | Negligible | Negligible | 4,000 |
| Kuwait | Yes | 2,371,000 | 2,132,000 | 1,127,000 | 2,130,000 | 2,643,000 |
| Libya | Yes | 1,220,000 | 1,514,000 | 1,025,000 | 1,439,000 | 1,702,000 |
| Oman | No | Unknown | 341,000 | 502,000 | 858,000 | 780,000 |
| Qatar | Yes | 233,000 | 437,000 | 315,000 | 461,000 | 1,097,000 |
| Saudi Arabia | Yes | 2,219,000 | 7,216,000 | 3,601,000 | 9,127,000 | 11,035,000 |
| Syria | No | Negligible | 192,000 | 159,000 | 596,000 | 459,000 |
| Tunisia | No | Negligible | 97,000 | 114,000 | 90,000 | 74,000 |
| United Arab Emirates | Yes | 282,000 | 1,696,000 | 1,260,000 | 2,362,000 | 2,751,000 |

Negligible = less than 1,000 barrels a day

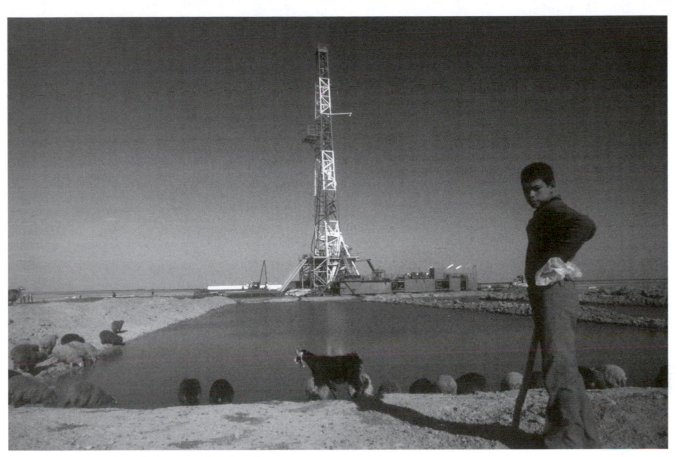

An Iranian shepherd tends his flock near an oil rig. (Corel)

of crude oil in the Persian Gulf as a purposeful Iraqi tactic to prevent the landing of coalition naval forces in Kuwait. The Iraqi government claimed that the spill, the largest in history to that time, resulted from the coalition bombing campaign, which was untrue.

While retreating from Kuwait in February, the Iraqi army set many Kuwaiti oil fields on fire, causing a significant short-term oil shortage in the world market and a major spike in oil prices. The shortage was quickly remedied by increased production within the Organization of Petroleum Exporting Countries (OPEC) and the utilization of U.S. and International Energy Agency strategic petroleum reserves. Despite these measures, the instability of the global oil supply caused the international price of oil to rise to a record of $40.42 per barrel in late winter of 1991. Following the war, Iraq received heavy economic sanctions but was later permitted by the UN to import certain products under the Oil-for-Food Programme.

Despite the fact that Iraqi oil output had been severely limited, world oil supplies became plentiful by the mid-1990s, and by 1999 an oil glut caused prices to drop to as low as $22 per barrel. In the United States, gasoline was selling in most places for less than 95 cents per gallon.

After the terrorist attacks of September 11, 2001, the fact that 15 of the 19 Islamist terrorists who hijacked the airliners used to carry out the attacks were Saudis initiated a close examination of the political and economic relationship between the United States and Saudi Arabia, the country's largest supplier of foreign oil.

The resultant War on Terror also sharply increased U.S. military involvement in the Middle East. The United States invaded Afghanistan in October 2001 (Operation ENDURING FREEDOM) with a considerable amount of world support. In March 2003 the United States, the United Kingdom, and a small international coalition extended the war by invading Iraq (Operation IRAQI FREEDOM) with the stated goal of ending the international threat posed by the regime of Saddam Hussein, which allegedly sponsored international terrorism and possessed weapons of mass destruction (WMDs). The coalition forces quickly defeated the Iraqi army, but they were unable to establish a stable government, and no WMDs were found.

The inability to achieve political stability had a profoundly negative effect on Iraqi oil production. In 2003 Iraqi production ceased, causing a loss of 2 million barrels a day. This affected the global oil market and sent prices higher. In 2006 Iraq's oil production was still down 600,000 barrels per day from prewar production levels. By the end of 2007, however, production had reached prewar levels.

The Iraqi production lapse had a profound impact on the international oil market. The lack of excess production capacity, refinery shortages, and individual production problems in the OPEC nations only exacerbated the effects of the Iraqi shortage on the global economy. The United States also decided not to tap oil from its strategic petroleum reserve. Because of continuing growth in world demand in a time of relative oil scarcity and instability, petroleum prices increased dramatically, reaching $80–90 per barrel at the beginning of 2007 and $140 per barrel by mid-2008. From that high, however, oil prices dropped substantially by the end of 2008 and early 2009.

The Iraq War effort has faced domestic and international criticism from both popular and official sources. Many of the protests against the war have centered around the themes of U.S. dependency on foreign oil, control of oil production, and rising oil prices. Among other nations, the war enhanced tensions among the United States, Iran, and Venezuela, also major international oil producers.

As early as 2003 international commentators alleged that the Bush administration had used military force in Iraq because the country had the potential to destabilize the international oil market. In 2003 the White House and the Department of Defense denied that oil was part of the motivation for the Iraq War. However, in the summer of 2005 President George W. Bush argued that U.S. troops needed to continue fighting in Iraq to prevent the country's oil fields from coming under the control of terrorist extremists. The Energy Task Force, headed by Vice President Richard Cheney, also noted the fundamental importance of the region, especially considering the dependence of the United States on oil imports. By 2008, thanks to the situation in Iraq, disruptions due to unrest in Nigeria, and growing demand in such nations as China and India, oil prices had reached historic highs, hitting more than $140 per barrel. In the United States, the surging fuel prices spiked inflation to its highest level in 17 years and, along with depreciating home prices, a major slump in homes sales, and the subprime mortgage crisis, threatened to tilt the economy into a full-blown recession. By the summer of 2008, gasoline prices were averaging more than $4 per gallon, drying up demand for large vehicles like sport utility vehicles and light trucks, and hammering the domestic car industry. Skyrocketing gas prices hit all sectors of the economy and reined in consumer spending as a whole. Despite substantially reduced oil prices and a corresponding reduction in gasoline prices in early 2009, U.S. consumer spending remains tentative, hampering recovery from the global economic crisis.

CHRISTOPHER R. W. DIETRICH

**See also**

Bush, George Herbert Walker; Bush, George Walker; Carter Doctrine; Cheney, Richard Bruce; DESERT SHIELD, Operation; DESERT STORM, Operation; ENDURING FREEDOM, Operation; Iran-Iraq War; Iranian Revolution; Iraq, History of, 1990–Present; IRAQI FREEDOM, Operation; Kuwait; Oil Well Fires, Persian Gulf War; Organization of Petroleum Exporting Countries; Saudi Arabia

**References**

Bush, George, and Brent Scowcroft. *A World Transformed.* New York: Knopf, 1998.

Klare, Michael T. *Blood and Oil: The Dangers and Consequences of America's Growing Dependency on Imported Petroleum.* New York: Owl Books, 2005.

Roberts, Paul. *The End of Oil: On the Edge of a Perilous New World.* Boston: Houghton Mifflin, 2004.

Yergin, Daniel. *The Prize: The Epic Quest for Oil, Money, and Power.* New York: Simon and Schuster, 1993.

## Oil Well Fires, Persian Gulf War

Fires that resulted from the deliberate torching of Kuwaiti oil wells by Iraqi military forces in late February 1991 at the beginning of the coalition's ground offensive (Operation DESERT STORM). On February 24, 1991, General H. Norman Schwarzkopf, commander of the U.S. Central Command (CENTCOM), launched the U.S.-led coalition ground offensive into western Kuwait to force the withdrawal of the Iraqi army, which had occupied Kuwait since August 2, 1990. At the start of the ground war, Iraqi president Saddam Hussein ordered his troops to set fire to oil wells and oil-related facilities in Kuwait. Iraqi forces set fire to 365 of some 700 wells in Kuwait's most productive oil reservoir, the greater Burgan Oil Field. The fires in this field accounted for the majority of the smoke and the greatest amount of burned oil. High pressures below the surface kept the fires burning despite firefighting efforts. The fires burned at temperatures as high as 2,000 degrees Fahrenheit and produced huge plumes of poisonous smoke that rose as high as 10,000 feet in places. The Burgan Oil Field fires presented the greatest risk to human health because of the field's proximity to Kuwait and to coastal towns where the great majority of Kuwaitis lived. As Hussein had hoped, the thick smoke inhibited coalition air and ground operations, although not decisively. The thick smoke hovering over the region prevented some pilots operating over northern Kuwait from seeing their targets. Other pilots had to deliver their weapons from higher altitudes because they could not get under the low overcast pall of smoke. The smoke from the oilfield fires became so thick that it blotted out the sun, and ground forces had to use flashlights to read maps during the day.

Imagery from the LANDSAT and SPOT satellites helped environmental experts locate the burning wellheads and oil spills and to assess the long-term environmental damage to the Persian Gulf region. A number of the fires burned out of control until November 1991. They caused the loss of about 6 million barrels of oil and 70 to 100 million cubic meters of natural gas per day. For these months, people in the Persian Gulf region had to contend with oil-thickened overcast skies.

The Kuwaiti government, through its Ministry of Oil, contracted with a number of professional oil firefighting companies, such as the Red Adair Company (later purchased by Global Industries of Louisiana), Boots and Coots (now Boots and Coots/IWC), Wild Well Control, Safety Boss, Cudd Well/Pressure Control, Neal Adams Firefighters, and Kuwait Wild Well Killers, to put out the fires. Those battling the blazes faced many of the previous obstacles

Smoke from oil well fires burning in the distance. The fires were intentionally set by Iraqi troops as they withdrew from Kuwait during Operation DESERT STORM in 1991. (U.S. Department of Defense)

in extinguishing and capping the wells. While many firefighting teams had previous experience in responding to accidental blazes, few had dealt with such widespread and deliberate arson. The oil-well firefighters developed a number of unique procedures, such as using large quantities of seawater pumped to the sites through a converted oil pipeline, liquid nitrogen, and dynamite charges.

In addition to the hazards involved in the firefighting effort, other obstacles posed serious challenges for the firefighters. The risks included large amounts of unexploded ordnance left over from the coalition bombing campaign and the ground offensives, and land mines placed around the burning oil wells by the retreating Iraqi soldiers. Before the firefighting teams could begin extinguishing the fires, coalition explosive ordnance disposal teams had to clear such munitions from each new work site or building where the firefighting teams planned to work. By November 1991, when the last of the fires had been extinguished, the total cost to Kuwait of putting out the fires had reached $1.5 billion.

The long-lasting oil fires caused significant widespread air and soil pollution. The smoke from the oil-well blazes adversely affected the weather pattern throughout the Persian Gulf region and beyond for most of 1991. The lower atmospheric wind blew the smoke along the eastern half of the Arabian Peninsula, and the uneven heating of the land and sea created local atmospheric

inversions during the summer months that trapped smoke in the lower atmosphere. Sandstorms, abetted by high winds, mixed sand and dust with the smoke. The gases and particulates in the dense black smoke caused respiratory problems for many Kuwaitis. The Kuwait Environment Protection Agency believes that the increasing number of cancer cases since 1991 is directly related to the oil fires. Many cities, such as Dhahran, Riyadh, and Bahrain, experienced many days with smoke-filled skies and carbon fallout. Some scientists have also linked the oil fires with what would later be called Gulf War Syndrome. Whether this amorphous collection of symptoms and illnesses was precipitated by the oil fires, chemical fallout and residue, or other causes has not been fully determined, and the long-term environmental effects of the fires still remain unclear.

The sabotage of the oil wells also impacted the desert environment, which has a limited natural ability to cleanse itself. In some cases, the oil from the wellheads did not ignite, but leaking oil formed some 300 oil lakes, contaminating about 40 million tons of sand and earth. Cleanup efforts led by the Kuwait Institute for Scientific Research and the Arab Oil Company, which have tested a number of technologies, including the use of petroleum-degrading bacteria, produced significant results. By 1995 vegetation in most of the contaminated areas next to the oil lakes began recovering, but the dry climate has also partially solidified some of the oil lakes. Over time, the oil has continued to sink into the sand, with as yet unknown consequences for Kuwait's precious and scarce groundwater resources.

ROBERT B. KANE

**See also**

DESERT STORM, Operation; Land Remote-Sensing Satellite

**References**

Hallion, Richard P. *Storm over Iraq: Air Power and the Gulf War.* Washington, DC: Smithsonian Institution Press, 1997.

Knights, Michael. *Cradle of Conflict: Iraq and the Birth of Modern U.S. Military.* Annapolis, MD: Naval Institute Press, 2005.

Jamieson, Perry D. *Lucrative Targets: The U.S. Air Force in the Kuwaiti Theater of Operations.* Washington, DC: U.S. Air Force History and Museums Program, 2001.

Rostker, Bernard. *Environmental Exposure Report: Oil Well Fires.* Washington, DC: U.S. Department of Defense, 2000.

---

# Oman, Role in Persian Gulf and Iraq Wars

Arab nation located along the southeastern coast of the Arabian Peninsula. With an estimated population of 3.312 million people, Oman covers 119,498 square miles. It is bordered by Yemen to the west; Saudi Arabia to the north; United Arab Emirates (UAE) to the northeast; the Arabian Sea to the south-southeast; and the Gulf of Oman to the east.

Oman is an absolute, hereditary monarchy governed by Sultan Qaboos bin Said al-Said, who has ruled since 1970. Although the sultan has enacted some political reforms that resulted in universal suffrage in 2003 and the election of an advisory council to the monarch, Said retains much control over the country and has solitary control over the armed forces. There are no political parties and there is no official opposition to the sitting government. Having enjoyed a long period of cordial relations with Great Britain, Oman entered into numerous military defense treaties with that nation. English is Oman's second language. In recent years, Oman has oriented its foreign and economic policies generally toward the West, and it has been a cooperative player with the United States and Britain in Middle East conflicts since 1991. The country enjoys a relatively high standard of living, primarily as a consequence of its petroleum revenues.

Oman's military consists of the Royal Army, Navy, and Air Force. Its military establishment is well equipped with modern hardware and weapons systems purchased chiefly from Great Britain, the United States, and France. The sultan has long worried about potential incursions from rival Arab nations and remains particularly concerned about Iran's foreign and military policies. As such, the nation spends a huge portion of its gross domestic product (GDP) on defense expenditures. These are currently estimated at about $2.1 billion a year, or 11.5 percent of GDP. In 2002, the last year for which reliable information was available, active military personnel numbered 41,750. That same year the army

was equipped with more than 100 main battle tanks, and the air force had approximately 40 combat aircraft.

In the years leading up to the Persian Gulf War of 1991, Sultan Said steadily increased the size and effectiveness of Oman's armed forces, especially during the Iran-Iraq War (1980–1988). During that conflict, Said deployed an infantry battalion to serve in the Peninsula Shield force, a military arm of the Gulf Cooperation Council (GCC) meant to deter aggression from either Iraq or Iran. Meanwhile, the British air force continued to use an air base on Masirah Island, off Oman's southern coast.

After Iraq invaded and occupied Kuwait in August 1990, Oman became a strong supporter of the international military coalition that would ultimately force Iraq to quit its occupation in 1991. Coalition forces used several of Oman's air bases as key staging areas for the conflict. The country also contributed 6,300 ground troops, who were deployed to Saudi Arabia. On the second day of the ground war in February 1991, Omani troops, along with the Saudi 10th Mechanized Brigade, entered Kuwait, helping to effect its liberation by February 28.

Although Oman's armed forces did not actively participate in the subsequent Afghanistan or Iraq wars, Oman has cooperated with coalition forces by permitting overflights of its air space and allowing some of its bases to be used as staging areas for coalition forces.

PAUL G. PIERPAOLI JR.

**See also**

DESERT STORM, Operation; DESERT STORM, Operation, Ground Operations; Gulf Cooperation Council; Iran-Iraq War

**References**

Kechichian, Joseph A. *Oman and the World: The Emergence of an Independent Foreign Policy.* Santa Monica, CA: RAND Corporation, 1995.

Owtram, Francis. *A Modern History of Oman: Formation of the State since 1920.* London: I. B. Tauris, 2004.

---

# Omar, Mohammed
## Birth Date: 1959

Radical Islamic cleric and a leader of the Taliban regime in Afghanistan from 1996 to 2001. Mohammed Omar (Umar), usually known to the West as Mullah Omar and in the region as Mullah Muhammed Omar Mujahid, was born near Kandahar, either just outside of Singesar or in Naduh, in Afghanistan sometime in 1959. He grew up in this impoverished area. His father died when he was young, leaving Omar as the primary breadwinner for his family, although some reports suggest that his mother remarried.

Mohammed Omar is a Pashtun from the Hotak tribe. The Pashtuns make up approximately 40 percent of the Afghan population and are concentrated in the southern portion of the country. Even before the withdrawal of Soviet troops in 1989, the Pashtuns expended considerable energy fighting one another. Eventually

An undated photograph reportedly of Taliban supreme leader Mullah Omar. (AP/Wide World Photos)

they split into pro- and anti-monarchical factions. They also engaged in fighting the northern Tajiks and Uzbeks.

With the Soviet invasion of Afghanistan in December 1979, Omar joined the mujahideen faction Harakat-i Inqilabi-i Islami (the Islamic Liberation Movement), guerrilla fighters opposing the Soviet forces and commanded by Muhammad Nek. The mujahideen received the support of much of the Islamic world and even some elements of the U.S. Central Intelligence Agency (CIA). Omar was wounded four times in actions against the Soviets, most famously from shrapnel that damaged his eye. Red Cross doctors surgically removed the eye, although the Taliban claim that Omar himself removed his damaged eye and sewed shut his eyelid.

Omar is a spiritual leader and not simply a commander of the Taliban, as indicated by the term "mullah," meaning a cleric or religious leader in the Dari and Farsi languages. Omar taught in madrasahs outside of Kandahar and in Quetta, was schooled in Arabic, and thought highly of Sheikh Abdullah Azzam, a founder of Al Qaeda. He was observed leading prayers at the Binoori Mosque in Karachi, where he met Osama bin Laden.

With the withdrawal of the Soviets from Afghanistan, the various tribes and factions there continued to be united in their opposition to the Afghan communist government in Kabul. With the collapse of that government in 1992, the country entered a state of civil war. Omar and others were outraged by public figures, including former mujahideen commanders who were sexually victimizing women and children, and otherwise engaged in corruption. Omar began the Taliban movement with about 50 followers from madrasahs and refugee camps. In early 1994 he led a small group of 30 Pashtun followers to rescue 2 kidnapped girls. This success led to more recruitment from Islamic religious schools and refugees in neighboring Pakistan. Omar and his followers considered themselves reformers trying to rid Afghanistan of the evils and corruption of the warlords. With the Taliban's growth through that year, Omar took control of Kandahar Province by September 1994 and Herat the following year.

In 1996 Omar publicly assumed the important title of *emir al-muminin* (commander of the faithful), the title accorded to the Prophet Muhammad and not used since the fourth caliph, indicating his military leadership of Muslims. He appeared wrapped in what was said to be the Prophet Muhammad's own cloak as a sign of that office. That same year the Taliban captured the Afghan capital city of Kabul and declared their intent to transform a secular nation into an Islamic emirate. Omar, however, remained in Kandahar, visiting Kabul in this period. From 1997 to 2001, Omar was recognized internationally as the Head of the Supreme Council of Afghanistan.

The Taliban strenuously enforced Sharia (Islamic law), which promotes moral behavior by heavily restricting the interaction of men and women, and limits all Islamically forbidden substances and actions. World human-rights groups were very critical of the new regime and especially its brutal treatment of women. One reporter sought in vain to persuade Omar against the destruction of the great Buddhas at Bamyan.

Omar had become acquainted with Al Qaeda leader Osama bin Laden when he was in Pakistan fighting against the Soviet occupation of Afghanistan. The two became close friends and associates and spoke often, perhaps daily, on satellite phones. Some reports claim that Omar married Osama bin Laden's eldest daughter and that one of Omar's daughters is bin Laden's fourth wife, although Taliban spokesmen deny this. Bin Laden was instrumental in financing the Taliban and thus made a significant contribution to its eventual takeover of Afghanistan. In turn, Omar allowed Al Qaeda operatives and terrorist training camps to operate within Taliban territory.

Following the terror attacks of September 11, 2001, Omar defended the Taliban as a moderate regime and argued that bin Laden had played no role in the 9/11 attacks. There is some evidence that a number of Taliban leaders had concerns about the presence of Al Qaeda and were dissatisfied with Omar's decision to allow the group to be located there in the first place. These individuals urged cooperation with the United States, but Omar remained firmly in control and refused to comply with U.S. demands. His refusal to hand bin Laden over to the U.S. government, a demand which would have violated Islamic and Pashtun tribal mores of politics and hospitality, led to the American military intervention Operation ENDURING FREEDOM, which drove the Taliban from power in the late autumn of 2001. In October Omar's home was bombed, killing his stepfather and 10-year-old son.

Since the Taliban's fall from power in Afghanistan in late 2001, Omar has eluded capture, although it is widely assumed that he is hiding in the Pashtun regions of Afghanistan or Pakistan. The U.S. government has offered a $10 million bounty for his capture. Omar retains the loyalty of many Taliban factions within Afghanistan. The Taliban deny that he is in hiding, but say that he is merely moving frequently for his own security. Omar has never met with a Western journalist and typically spoke through a Taliban governmental intermediary in the past. It is claimed that Omar remains active in directing the Taliban insurgency in Afghanistan, and numerous statements in his name have been released urging the Afghani and Iraqi insurgents to fight on in their struggle against "American imperialism." In January 2007 Omar exchanged emails and communications via courier with a journalist. He claimed that the Taliban had religious sanction for the many suicide attacks carried out in Afghanistan that year. He issued another statement via an intermediary in April 2007 encouraging more suicide attacks. On the occasion of Eid al-Fitr, the conclusion of Ramadan, on September 30, 2008, Omar's internationally circulated speech expressed sorrow at the loss of Afghan lives since 2001 and from the U.S. air attacks that season. He decried the corruption of the current Afghan government and American efforts to create *fitna* (division, loss of faith) in the region, setting Afghans against each other, as, according to Omar, U.S. authorities had done in Iraq and Palestine. He also called on the Afghan people not to cooperate with the National Army, Security Services, and police because these were "slave institutions." But he also called for them not to engage in such vicious actions as mosque bombings or summary punishments of brigandry, as had occurred in attacks blamed on the Taliban, which he attributed to the influence of anti-Islamic elements. These public statements rendered dubious a prior claim by Afghan president Hamid Karzai that Omar was in the custody of Pakistan's intelligence services.

MICHAEL BEAUCHAMP AND SHERIFA ZUHUR

**See also**

Afghanistan; Al Qaeda; Bin Laden, Osama; ENDURING FREEDOM, Operation; Karzai, Hamid; Mujahideen, Soviet-Afghanistan War; Taliban; Taliban Insurgency, Afghanistan

**References**

Coll, Steve. *Ghost Wars: The Secret History of the CIA, Afghanistan, and Bin Laden, from the Soviet Invasion to September 10, 2001.* New York: Penguin, 2004.
Goodson, Larry P. *Afghanistan's Endless War: State Failure, Regional Politics, and the Rise of the Taliban.* Seattle: University of Washington Press, 2001.
Rashid, Ahmed. *Taliban: Militant Islam, Oil, and Fundamentalism in Central Asia.* New Haven, CT: Yale University Press, 2001.
Woodward, Bob. *Bush at War.* New York: Simon and Schuster, 2002.

## Operational Art of War

*See* War, Operational Art of

## Organization of Petroleum Exporting Countries

Oil cartel founded on September 14, 1960, during the Baghdad Conference to give oil-exporting countries leverage in negotiations with foreign oil companies that, at the time, controlled production and dictated prices and the share of profits going to producing nations. In the late 1960s and early 1970s, the Arab member nations of the Organization of Petroleum Exporting Countries (OPEC) enacted embargoes against supporters of Israel during the 1967 Six-Day War and the 1973 Yom Kippur (Ramadan) War in an effort to influence Middle East policy. Since the 1980s, OPEC has acted largely apolitically, seeking to stabilize oil production and prices to maximize members' profits while guaranteeing a reliable oil supply to the world economy.

As early as 1945, oil-producing nations recognized that a unified stance on pricing and output would improve their effectiveness in bargaining with the major oil companies. In 1959 the U.S. government established a mandatory quota on all imported oil to the United States in an attempt to give preferential treatment to oil producers in Canada and Mexico. In so doing, the world's largest oil consumer effectively imposed a partial boycott on Middle East oil. The net result was depressed prices for Persian Gulf crude. To make matters worse, the oil companies enacted a series of unilateral price cuts in 1959 and 1960 that caused oil prices to fall even lower.

The severe impact that these policies had on Middle East oil provided the impetus for the world's five largest oil exporters—Saudi Arabia, Iran, Iraq, Kuwait, and Venezuela—to band together with the express purpose of reversing these price cuts. During its first two decades of operations, OPEC expanded its membership to include Qatar, Indonesia, Libya, United Arab Emirates (UAE), Algeria, Nigeria, Ecuador, and Gabon. During its first decade of operations, OPEC enjoyed little success. Prices continued to float lower well into 1971. In 1958 oil sold for $10.85 per barrel (in 1990 dollars). In 1971 it sold for just $7.46 per barrel. The cartel doggedly negotiated with oil companies but with little success in eroding the oil companies' power to set prices. Beginning in 1973, however, OPEC finally succeeded in wresting pricing power from the oil companies, which were increasingly vulnerable to political decisions made in the oil-producing states that housed their operations. On October 16, 1973, in reaction to the Yom Kippur (Ramadan) War, OPEC cut production, which ultimately quadrupled the price of oil and began a series of price hikes that effectively ended the companies' control over all but the technical side of oil production.

As Arab nations' production made up an increasing share of the world oil market, they began to use their power politically, applying oil embargoes against Britain and France during the 1956 Suez Crisis and against the United States, Britain, and West Germany during the 1967 Six-Day War. These embargoes failed, however, in large part because of U.S. willingness to make up the oil shortfalls to its allies. Also, because oil is a worldwide commodity, limited embargoes have little effect, as nations targeted by an embargo will usually find other ways to purchase petroleum.

A flag displaying the Organization of Petroleum Exporting Countries (OPEC) logo waves from the roof of OPEC headquarters in Vienna, Austria. OPEC regulates petroleum policies and production of member nations to protect their mutual interests. (AP/Wide World Photos)

Arab oil producers' attempts to use the oil weapon to influence the Arab-Israeli conflict enjoyed great success in October 1973 during the Yom Kippur (Ramadan) War, precipitated by Egypt and Syria's surprise attack on Israel. On October 17, one day after OPEC initiated production cuts that spiked sharp price increases, the Organization of Arab Petroleum Exporting Countries (OAPEC) decreased overall oil production and initiated a five-month oil embargo against the United States and the Netherlands to protest their support for Israel. The oil price shock, together with worldwide production cuts and the embargo, caused severe economic disruptions in much of the world. The impact on the United States was particularly severe. The nation's economy, which was already groaning under inflation, relatively high unemployment, low growth, and budget deficits, tilted into a serious recession. Government efforts to cap prices and control supplies only worsened the situation, as shortages and even limited rationing of gasoline became widespread. From 1973 to 1974, the price of oil catapulted from about $8 per barrel to more than $27 (1990 dollars). The American economy remained in a virtual recession into the mid-1980s.

The Soviet Union, an oil exporter, had little to lose from the Arab states' use of oil as a weapon. As such, it encouraged the oil embargo because it weakened the West economically and resulted in increased oil revenues for itself. At the same time, the Soviets took advantage of decreased Arab production and higher prices, significantly increasing its oil exports to the United States during the embargo, a fact that neither nation publicized at the time.

The oil embargo caught Americans largely unprepared. As a result, the U.S. government instituted gasoline rationing that resulted in long lines at gasoline stations and national anxiety over energy supplies. In response to the price increases and embargo, the United States sought to establish a cartel of oil-consuming nations to confront OPEC directly, but the major importers' diverse oil needs and political positions on the Arab-Israeli conflict stymied this plan. In 1975 the U.S. Congress did pass legislation to establish a Strategic Petroleum Reserve (SPR) to protect against future supply disruptions. Since then, the government has stored millions of barrels of oil in massive underground salt caverns along the Gulf Coast. The SPR may exist more for psychological reasons than anything else, however. The reserve would run out very quickly in the event of a partial or complete oil-supply shutdown, and there is not enough oil in the caverns to affect the worldwide price of oil.

Although the Arab states ended the oil embargo soon after hostilities ceased and without securing the desired Israeli withdrawal from territories occupied in 1967, this unprecedented attempt transformed the position of oil-producing states, gave OPEC major clout, and fueled Arab nationalism. Since 1973 both the United States and the Soviet Union devoted increasing attention to the Middle East as a strategic battleground. The Arab world, meanwhile, endeavored to exercise political influence independent of the superpowers.

OPEC's achievement of higher oil prices in 1973 and 1974 ultimately damaged the oil producers' economies by the late 1970s, when the resulting worldwide recession produced inflation and falling demand for oil. Two major crises in the Middle East during 1979–1980 resulted in yet another oil price spike. As a result of the 1979 Iranian Revolution, which saw the ousting of Mohammad Reza Shah Pahlavi, the imposition of an anti-Western Islamic fundamentalist government in his stead, and the taking of American embassy personnel by radical Iranian students, oil prices shot up from $24.46 per barrel (1990 dollars) to $49.52 by mid-1980. The effects on the world's economy were stunning. In the United States, inflation peaked at more than 13 percent, while interest rates approached 20 percent. The 1979–1980 oil shock was not part of OPEC's strategy, although it did benefit handsomely from it in the immediate term. Clearly, the markets were reacting to great regional instability in the Middle East, which began with the Iranian Revolution and was exacerbated by the start of the Iran-Iraq War (1980–1988).

Since the 1980s OPEC has pursued a policy of relatively prudent price control, ensuring substantial profits without adversely affecting the world economy. Beginning in the mid-1980s, the price of oil dropped and continued to drop until the Iraqi invasion of Kuwait in August 1990 precipitated more jolting price hikes. After mid-1991, however, when an international coalition reversed the Iraqi invasion and soundly defeated Iraqi dictator Saddam Hussein's army, oil prices fell again. They would continue to drift downward, reaching new inflation-adjusted lows by the late 1990s. Since 2002, however, OPEC again began to reap record revenues, as war and unrest in the Middle East and simple greed drove oil prices to record highs. This situation was reversed at the end of 2008 with the onset of the world economic crisis, when oil plunged to $38 a barrel, more than $100 less than it had been trading six months before.

Today, OPEC has 12 member states; Ecuador and Gabon left OPEC prior to the 1990s. Angola joined in 2007. Iraq remains a member although its oil production has not been a part of any OPEC quota agreements since March 1998. Having become a net importer of oil and unable to meet its production quota, Indonesia resigned at the end of 2008.

ELUN GABRIEL

**See also**

Arab-Israeli Conflict, Overview; DESERT STORM, Operation; Iran; Iraq, History of, 1990–Present; Kuwait; Russia, Middle East Policy, 1991–Present; Saudi Arabia; Soviet Union, Middle East Policy; United States, Middle East Policy, 1945–Present

**References**

Ahrari, Mohammed E. *OPEC: The Failing Giant.* Lexington: University Press of Kentucky, 1986.

Al-Sowayegh, Abdulaziz. *Arab Petro-Politics.* New York: St. Martin's, 1984.

Klinghoffer, Arthur Jay. *The Soviet Union & International Oil Politics.* New York: Columbia University Press, 1977.

Rustow, Dankwart A. *Oil and Turmoil: America Faces OPEC and the Middle East.* New York: Norton, 1982.

Skeet, Ian. *OPEC: Twenty-Five Years of Prices and Politics.* Cambridge: Cambridge University Press, 1988.

# Oslo Accords

The agreement commonly called the Oslo Accords and formally known as the Declaration of Principles on Interim Self-Government Arrangements was signed on September 13, 1993, in Washington, D.C., by Israeli prime minister Yitzhak Rabin, Palestine Liberation Organization (PLO) chairman Yasser Arafat, and U.S. president Bill Clinton. In the Oslo Accords, the PLO, the Palestinians' major representative party and de facto government-in-exile, formally recognized Israel's right to exist and Israel's sovereignty over 78 percent of historic Palestine and pledged to end military actions against Israel. Israel, while failing to recognize Palestinian statehood, did recognize Palestinian nationhood, including the right of self-determination, and the PLO's role as the Palestinians' legitimate representative body.

The document spelled out ways in which the Palestinians could achieve a degree of autonomy in parts of the West Bank and the Gaza Strip, which had been occupied by Israeli forces since the June 1967 Six-Day War. The hope was that by the PLO's demonstration of competent self-governance and control over anti-Israel violence, the Israelis would gain the confidence needed to make a phased withdrawal from the occupied territories and grant the Palestinians an independent state alongside Israel. Similarly, it was hoped that the removal of foreign occupation forces from certain areas, increasing levels of self-government, and the prospects of a viable independent state, would give the Palestinian population the incentive to end the violence against Israelis. The interim peace period was to be completed by 1998, at which time a permanent peace agreement would be signed.

Although the U.S. government became the guarantor of the Oslo Accords, Washington had little to do with the agreement itself. Soon after the election of a more moderate Israeli government in 1992, direct talks began in secret between representatives of Israel and the PLO. They were first facilitated by Norwegian nongovernmental organizations and later with the assistance of the foreign ministry. This apparently took place without the knowledge of American officials, who still took the position that the PLO should not be allowed to take part in the peace process, thereby excluding it from the stalled peace talks then going on in Washington. The secret talks occurred without the knowledge of such Arab states as Syria, then in negotiations with Israel, or the Palestinians, many of whom supported a comprehensive peace framework as established at the Madrid conference.

As the secret negotiations in Norway progressed during the summer of 1993, the Clinton administration put forward what it called a compromise proposal for Palestinian autonomy. This compromise was actually less favorable to the Palestinians than what was then being put forward by the Israelis.

The U.S. role in the Oslo process began with a historic signing ceremony on the White House lawn on September 13, 1993. The agreement had been finalized in Oslo on August 20. Given the ambiguities in the agreement, both parties agreed that the United States should be its guarantor. Indeed, the Israelis saw the U.S. government as the entity most likely to support its positions on outstanding issues, and the Palestinians saw the U.S. government as the only entity capable of forcing Israel to live up to its commitments and able to move the occupying power to compromise.

Peace talks resumed in Washington in the autumn of 1993 within the Oslo framework. Over the next seven years, the United States brokered a series of Israeli-Palestinian agreements that led to the withdrawal of Israeli forces from most of the Gaza Strip and parts of the West Bank. By the end of the decade, about 40 percent of the West Bank and the Gaza Strip, including most of its towns and cities, had been placed under the rule of the new Palestinian National Authority (PNA), headed by Arafat, and divided into dozens of noncontiguous zones wherein the Palestinians could, for the first time, exercise some limited autonomy within their sphere of control.

During this period, the Israeli government severely limited the mobility of Palestinians within and between the West Bank and the Gaza Strip, dramatically expanded its expropriation of land in the occupied territories for colonization by Jewish settlers, and refused to withdraw from as much territory as promised in the U.S.-brokered disengagement agreements. In addition, the United States tended to side with the Israelis on most issues during talks regarding the disengagement process, even after a right-wing coalition that had opposed the Oslo Accords came to power in Israel in 1996. This served to alienate many Palestinians who had been initially hopeful about the peace process and hardened anti-Israeli attitudes.

Meanwhile, much of the PNA proved itself to be rather inept, corrupt, and autocratic in its governance of those parts of the occupied territories under its control. The corruption alienated much of the Palestinian population, and the PNA's lack of control made it difficult to suppress the growth of radical Islamic groups. On more than two dozen occasions between 1994 and 2000, Islamic extremists from the occupied Palestinian territories engaged in terrorist attacks inside Israel, killing scores of Israeli civilians and thereby hardening anti-Palestinian attitudes.

The Palestinians had hoped that the United States would broker the negotiations based on international law that forbids the expansion of any country's territory by military force and prohibits occupying powers from transferring their civilian population into occupied land. The Palestinians also hoped that American officials would support a series of specific United Nations (UN) Security Council resolutions demanding that Israel honor these principles. From the Palestinians' perspective—as well as that of the UN, most U.S. allies, and most international legal experts—the onus of the burden was on Israel, as the occupying power, to make most of the compromises for peace. The Clinton administration, however, argued that the UN resolutions were no longer relevant and saw the West Bank and the Gaza Strip simply as disputed territories, thereby requiring both sides to compromise. This gave the Israelis a clear advantage in the peace process.

In signing the Oslo Accords, the Palestinians operated on the assumption that the agreement would result in concrete improvements in the lives of those in the occupied territories. They hoped that the interim period would be no more than five years and that the permanent settlement would be based on UN Security Council Resolutions 242 and 338, which called upon Israel to withdraw from the territories seized in the 1967 war. For their part, the Israelis had hoped that the Oslo Accords would lead to the emergence of a responsible Palestinian leadership and greater security. None of these wishes, however, came to pass, and negotiations continue—fitfully—between Israel and the PNA.

STEPHEN ZUNES

### See also
Arafat, Yasser; Clinton, William Jefferson; Palestine Liberation Organization; Rabin, Yitzhak

### References
Brown, Nathan J. *Palestinian Politics after the Oslo Accords: Resuming Arab Palestine.* Berkeley: University of California Press, 2003.
Freedman, Robert Owen, ed. *The Middle East and the Peace Process: The Impact of the Oslo Accords.* Gainesville: University Press of Florida, 1998.
Peres, Shimon. *The New Middle East.* New York: Henry Holt, 1993.
Weinberger, Peter. *Co-opting the PLO: A Critical Reconstruction of the Oslo Accords, 1993–1995.* New York: Rowman and Littlefield, 2006.

# Ottoman Empire

The current situation in the Middle East, including the Arab-Israeli conflict since 1948, is a product of the region's centuries of troubled history. That history witnessed the rise and fall of the Ottoman Empire and its partition by the Western powers in the post–World War I period. Until the beginning of the 20th century, the Ottoman Empire was the dominant political, economic, and military force in the Middle East. After centuries of expansion and conquest in the region, however, it underwent a decline during the 18th and 19th centuries and thereby became vulnerable to external pressures from the West. The European powers, taking advantage of the endless wars in the empire's various provinces, were able to penetrate Ottoman territory at the end of the 19th and beginning of the 20th centuries. This culminated in the occupation of much of the empire during World War I.

The Turkmen Oguz nomads from Central Asia invaded the Byzantine Empire from northeastern Anatolia in the 11th century, then occupied Eastern and Central Anatolia a century later. The ancestors of Osman, founder of the dynasty who declared his small principality independent of the Seljuk Turks in 1288, were members of the Kayi tribe, who entered Anatolia along with these nomads. One of the independent Turkic principalities established in Anatolia was that led by Osman. By 1300 Osman ruled an area stretching from Eskisehir to the plains of Iznik. His successor Orhan, by capturing Uskudar in 1338, brought the growing empire to the doorsteps of Constantinople, capital of the once mighty Byzantine Empire. From this point on, the Ottomans entered a long phase of territorial expansion in all directions.

Although it encountered numerous societies with different systems of production and exchange, the Ottoman Empire retained its despotic state structure for more than seven centuries. Interaction between Ottoman and Byzantine society developed after the conquest of Constantinople by Ottoman forces in 1453. This interaction, as well as interactions with other societies following Ottoman expansion into Europe in the 15th and 16th centuries and the institution of the state's land grant system (*timar*), led to the development of feudal forms in Ottoman agriculture and taxation (*iltizam*, or tax farming) whereby, over time, large-scale private property in land (*ciftlik*) acquired increasing importance, transferring a higher proportion of the land to a few owners. This system also consisted of the allocation of parcels of conquered lands to *sipahis* (rural cavalry with military and administrative functions in the provinces) and to the civilian sector of the *devshirmes* (top officials of the central bureaucracy) in the form of fiefs. The *sipahis* and civilian *devshirmes* were given these lands for the purpose of administering them in the name of the state. This system of land allocation was put into effect during the reign of Suleiman I.

The *timar* system remained in effect for quite some time. As the central state began to gradually lose its authority in the countryside, the *sipahis* and other fief holders increasingly evaded their obligations to the state and attempted to take the ownership of state lands. Realizing that the old rural military-administrative system had outlived its usefulness, the state moved against the *sipahis* and displaced them.

This transformation of the agrarian structure took place during the 17th and 18th centuries, and as a result a landed gentry (*ayan*) began to develop. This class displaced the *sipahis* as intermediaries between the state and the producers. Later, at the end of the 18th and the beginning of the 19th centuries, the *ayans* became a fully developed feudal landowning class and began to challenge the authority of the central state by equipping their own armies. Although they never became powerful enough to overthrow the political supremacy of the central state, they nonetheless came close to doing so.

In 1839 Mehmet Ali Pasha (Muhammad Ali Pasha), governor of Egypt, defeated the Ottoman armies in Kutahya, near the Ottoman capital of Istanbul. Mehmet Ali's forces were soon driven back, however, by those of Britain and France, who intervened on behalf of the Ottoman state. Ali was only able to obtain recognition as hereditary ruler of Egypt. While the *ayans* were thus defeated in their bid for state power, they nevertheless continued to exercise economic control over vast areas of the empire.

While the position of landlords was strengthened as a result of the introduction of tax farming initiated by the state, interaction with Europe also facilitated the expansion of European commercial capital into the empire, leading to the development of a merchant class tied to European capital. However, the development of feudalism in agriculture and, later, capitalism in commerce and industry all took place within the confines of a society dominated by the despotic state, which permitted the coexistence of these diverse systems until the very end.

While private property in land and feudal relations of production began to develop in the Ottoman Empire in the 17th century and privately held land rapidly surpassed that owned by the state in many parts of the empire by the 18th century, the feudal lords were never able to overthrow the central state. Thus, they continued to coexist with the developing merchant class under the political rule of the Ottoman state. State power remained in the hands of the despotic rulers and the palace bureaucracy until the collapse of the empire.

To gain greater insight into the nature and transformation of Ottoman society in the late 19th and early 20th centuries, it is necessary to take into account the structure of social forces dominating the empire's polity and economy during the final phase of its development. Political power in the empire rested in the throne of the central authority, the *padishah* (sultan) and his administrative deputy, called the *sadrazam* (grand vizier). Below this and under the direct control of the sultan there existed the large but carefully organized Ottoman palace bureaucracy. It was largely the corrupt practices of the sultan and the palace bureaucracy in the latter phase of the Ottomans' centuries-long imperial history that transformed the empire into a semicolony of the expanding European powers.

The dominant economic interests in the Ottoman Empire during this period were made up of powerful landowners (the *ayans*, *derebeys*, and *aghas*) in the countryside and commercial capitalists of mainly minority ethnic origin in major urban centers. In 1913 the top 1 percent of farming families owned 39 percent of the arable land. The traditional landed gentry (the *ayans* and *derebeys*), together with the *aghas*, comprising 5 percent of the farmer families, owned 65 percent of the arable land, while 87 percent of farming families, comprising broad segments of the peasantry, had access to just 35 percent of the arable land. As a result of their vast economic power in the countryside, the big landowners were able to monopolize local political power and, through links with the rural Islamic clergy, impose their social and cultural domination over the peasantry. The subjugation of the peasant masses by the landlord-clergy coalition (the *esraf* or *ashraf*) thus served the double function of exploitation and legitimization.

Largely involved in import-export trade and domestic marketing tied to European imports, the minority commercial

The first Ottoman attack on Constantinople in 1453. Painting by Palma Giovane (1548–1628). (Erich Lessing/Art Resource, NY)

interests—comprising Greek, Armenian, and Christian merchants and primarily concentrated in large urban centers—made up the basis of the empire's bourgeoisie, or urban middle class. The role of minority commercial interests was pivotal. Through their key position in the urban economy they were in effect the agency for external economic penetration and control, which contributed to the final demise of the empire's economy. Consequently, while their strategic role in accelerating contact with the West played a progressive role in the limited transformation of the despotic system in an earlier period, the continued existence of the minority commercial interests—as opposed to their transformation into industrial capitalists—perpetuated the backward and dependent structure of Ottoman industry. It also contributed to the further

dependence of the Ottoman economy on European capital, which assisted the development of capitalism in Western Europe. It was the antidevelopmental role of Greek, Armenian, and other non-Muslim agents of European capital that in good part gave rise to the nationalist movement of the Society of Union and Progress and to the Kemalist forces in the war of national liberation.

Closely linked with this minority commercial group and the palace bureaucracy was foreign finance capital. The penetration into Ottoman Turkey of foreign capital during this period was based on the empire's role as a raw materials–supplying semi-colony of the expanding European economy. Concentrated largely in the raw materials sector, foreign capital was also engaged in the construction of a network of railways in western and central

Anatolia, with the sole purpose of accelerating the process of extracting raw materials in Turkey. Hence, it was in this classic sense—as an exporter of raw materials and importer of finished goods—that the Ottoman Empire became, in essence, a dependent semicolony of Europe.

The dependent structure of the Ottoman economy during the 19th century, coupled with its tributary position in the Mediterranean basin, did not permit the development of large-scale local industry. However, smaller-scale industries, particularly in textiles, had developed in the Levant, Syria, Egypt, and Palestine. While a limited expansion did take place in small-scale manufacturing and processing industries, it was largely the minority urban bourgeoisie that, in addition to its traditional place in commerce, extended into the ownership and control of these industries. Although weak in numbers and economic strength, the political aspirations of Turkish industrialists coincided with and took expression in the leadership of the nationalist forces, as their economic position began to deteriorate with the further expansion into industry of foreign and minority interests. It was this deterioration in the position of the Turkish national bourgeoisie that would drive its members onto the side of the nationalist leadership.

Nor surprisingly, the size of the working class was also small. Moreover, the ethnic composition of the working class was highly fragmented and did not allow for the development of working class unity. This fragmentation within the working-class reached its peak during the liberation struggles, when non-Turkish workers joined the ranks of the forces of their own ethnic groups and fought against Turkish national liberation. Turkish workers were essentially cut off from Anatolia and could not contribute directly to or affect the outcome of the national liberation struggle.

In the countryside, the majority of the population consisted of peasants with small landholdings. Dispersed throughout the Anatolian interior and engaged in subsistence agriculture, the Ottoman peasantry was under the direct control of big landowners, who had connections to the rural Islamic clergy. Despite the enormous control exercised over them by the landlords and the clergy, the peasants took up arms in a number of mass peasant uprisings throughout Ottoman history.

Finally, in addition to the peasantry who had small landholdings, the rural areas of the empire also contained a class of small merchants and local artisans who, together with doctors, lawyers, teachers, and locally based government officials, made up the core of the Anatolian petit bourgeoisie. It was among this group that nationalist forces first found their crucial support. Dominated and controlled by imperialism and the minority urban bourgeoisie and oppressed under the *ayan, derebey,* and *esraf* rule in the countryside, the Ottoman petit bourgeoisie was fragmented, weak, and unorganized.

The centuries-old empire of the Ottomans began to face serious economic and political-military problems during the 18th and 19th centuries. The expanding power of local landowners and merchants, along with peasant uprisings and wars of national liberation, losses of territory, the decline of industry and increasing dependence on the West, and expanding public debt, were all major factors contributing to the disintegration of the Ottoman Empire.

The growth and expansion of tax farming and the development of Ottoman commerce, which acquired an intermediary function between local landowners and European commercial capital, contributed to two destructive trends. First, the authority of the central state in relation to the new propertied and moneyed classes in the countryside declined. Second, the direct economic ties with European capital, which became the basis of the expansion of Western capitalism into the empire's economy, also weakened the centralized state apparatus.

The growing power of local landowners on the one hand and increasing repression by the central state on the other did not go unchallenged. The oppressed peasants and minority nationalities in various parts of the empire soon rose up in arms. The peasant uprisings of the 17th century continued in various forms during the 18th and 19th centuries. Although these revolts did not yield substantial results, they did nevertheless create an unstable situation for both the peasantry's local exploiters and the central state.

National minorities, especially in the Balkans, battled against the repressive Ottoman state to gain their independence. As a result of the prolonged wars with the European powers, which extended from the second siege of Vienna (1683) to the Treaty of Jassy (1792), the Ottoman state became more and more vulnerable, leading to massive territorial losses that included Hungary, Greece, Transylvania, Bukovina, Crimea, the northern coasts of the Black Sea, and other regions. This in turn encouraged more indigenous nationalist forces to rise up and end Ottoman rule over their territories. By the 19th century, the Ottoman state faced serious challenges from every corner of the empire. By the end of the Balkan Wars (1912–1913), the Ottomans had lost almost all of their European possessions to Bulgaria, Serbia, Greece, Montenegro, and Albania. All in all, by mid-1913 the Ottomans had lost 83 percent of their territory and 69 percent of their population. The successful revolts of the colonized peoples reduced the area of plunder by the central state and the Ottoman lords. This contraction of the empire exacerbated the crises in the Ottoman economy and polity and further contributed to the empire's decline.

While the Ottoman state was becoming rapidly weaker, Europe had completed its transition from feudalism to capitalism. Thus, by the late 18th century Europe's feudal economy had been transformed into an expanding capitalist economy. Growing trade between Western Europe and the Ottoman Empire during this period began to have adverse effects on local Ottoman industry. Faced with rising costs and operating under strict price regulations, the Ottoman guilds were unable to provide goods at prices low enough to compete with the cheap European-manufactured goods. Consequently, traditional Ottoman industry entered a period of rapid decline, and the empire became more and more dependent on European economies.

A photograph of the battlefield during the Siege of Adrianople, November 3, 1912–March 26, 1913, in the Balkan Wars. (Library of Congress)

As European capital began to expand, there was no longer a need to depend on imports of manufactured goods from the East. In fact, the growing capitalist economy in Europe was in a position to bring about a complete reversal in international trade. Whereas Britain was previously an importer of textiles from the East, it now became an exporter of these. The process of European expansion into the Ottoman economy further accelerated following the Anglo-Turkish Commercial Convention of 1838, which extended extraterritorial privileges to all foreign traders and abolished the state's protective tariffs and monopolies. Consequently, whereas the Ottoman Empire had supplied almost all of Britain's cotton fabric imports in 1825, by 1855 this amount had fallen sharply to only a fraction of these imports. British textile exports to Turkey continued to expand in the postconvention period. This reversal in the import-export pattern of the empire led to the destruction of the textile industry in Ottoman Turkey. While the dismantling of native Ottoman industry by the British had begun in the textiles sector, all other branches of Ottoman industry were affected in a few short decades. Indeed, by the late 1800s the whole of Ottoman industry was on the verge of collapse.

These developments marked the end of industrialization through the manufacturing sector in Ottoman Turkey. Instead, the empire was relegated to increased raw materials production. Increases also occurred in such agricultural exports as raisins and dried figs, whose output nearly doubled from 1904 to 1913. Thus, the Ottoman Empire, with its native industry destroyed, was transformed into an agrarian reserve of the expanding European economies.

This process, coupled with continued territorial losses, frustrated the state's efforts to raise revenue for the public treasury. And this, in turn, greatly affected the empire's military power and jeopardized its political and military strength in the region. While increased taxation was seen as a short-term remedy to counteract these tendencies, the only long-term solution to the problem of revenue was seen to be foreign loans.

The first Ottoman foreign loan was in 1854, and by 1877 the nominal public debt was close to £191 million, or more than half the national revenue when interest was counted. Most of this debt was owed to two countries, with France accounting for 40 percent and England for 29 percent of the total in 1881. By 1877 the Ottoman state was no longer able to continue its loan repayments and, consequently, declared bankruptcy. A European-controlled organization, the Ottoman Public Debt Administration (OPDA), was set up in 1881 to collect payments on the loans. The OPDA subsequently acted as an intermediary with European countries seeking investment opportunities in Turkey and in this way was instrumental in facilitating the further penetration of European capital into the Ottoman economy.

By the 19th century, then, Ottoman Turkey had for all practical purposes become a semicolony of the expanding European powers. Widespread revolts throughout its conquered territories further weakened the rule of the sultanate and the palace bureaucracy and led to the emergence of nationalist forces destined to transform the collapsing Ottoman state.

In the early 1900s, a growing number of military students in Istanbul became discontented with the policies of the Ottoman state. Numerous intellectuals and journalists, the most prominent of whom was Namik Kemal, put forward nationalist ideas. Abdul Hamid II, the ruling sultan, tried to suppress the movement but without success. Secret societies were formed in army headquarters throughout the empire and in Paris, Geneva, and Cairo. The most effective of these was known as the Young Turks, which eventually became the Committee of Union and Progress.

Finally, in 1908, there was open discontent within the Third Army Corps in Macedonia. On July 4, 1908, the army, headed by Major Ahmed Niyazi, demanded from Salonika in Macedonia the restoration of the 1876 constitution and marched on Istanbul. The sultan's attempt to suppress the uprising failed, and rebellion spread rapidly. Unable to rely on other troops, Abdul Hamid II announced the restoration of the constitution on July 23. Elections were held, and a constitutional government was established. But in April 1909 the sultan struck back with a counterrevolution, and the army moved up again from Macedonia to depose Abdul Hamid II and install his brother, Mehmed V, as the constitutional monarch.

The Committee of Union and Progress, which led the 1908 Young Turk Revolution, declared itself to be a political party—the Party of Union and Progress (PUP)—in April 1909 and took power through the elections of April 1912. The top leadership of the party was composed mainly of Turkish intellectuals, who were to a great extent influenced by European progressive and nationalist thought. Their nationalist ideology brought them in line with their main class allies, namely the *esnaf* (artisans and self-employed) and the *tujjar* (merchants and commercial interests) of the towns, the sectors out of which the PUP sought to forge a future Turkish national bourgeoisie. Hence, it was in this context—and after the massive territorial losses following the two Balkan Wars and the failure of the ruling PUP clique to safeguard Turkey from the onslaught of foreign occupation forces during World War I—that the stage was set for the final downfall of the Ottoman Empire. By 1918, at the end of World War I, the Ottoman Empire ceased to exist in name as well as fact; most of its former territories in the Middle East were divided between France and Great Britain, to be administered as League of Nation Mandates. Only Turkey would survive, relatively whole and untouched, as a mere shadow of the once expansive Ottoman Empire.

BERCH BERBEROGLU

**See also**

France, Middle East Policy; Middle East, History of, 1918–1945; Turkey; Role in Persian Gulf and Afghanistan Wars; United Kingdom, Middle East Policy; World War I, Impact of

**References**

Berberoglu, Berch. *Power and Stability in the Middle East.* London: Zed, 1989.

———. *Turkey in Crisis.* London: Zed, 1982.

———. *Turmoil in the Middle East.* Albany, NY: SUNY Press, 1999.

Berkes, Niyazi. *The Development of Secularism in Turkey.* Montreal: McGill University Press, 1964.

Blaisdell, D. C. *European Financial Control in the Ottoman Empire.* New York: Columbia University Press, 1929.

Earle, Edward Mead. *Turkey, the Great Powers, and the Bagdad Railway: A Study in Imperialism.* New York: Russell and Russell, 1966.

Gibb, H. A. R., and H. Bowen. *Islamic Society and the West,* Vol. 1. London: Oxford University Press, 1957.

Lewis, Bernard. *The Emergence of Modern Turkey.* 3rd ed. London: Oxford University Press, 2001.

———. *What Went Wrong? The Clash between Islam and Modernity in the Middle East.* New York: Oxford University Press, 2002.

# Özal, Turgut

**Birth Date: October 13, 1927**
**Death Date: April 17, 1993**

Influential Turkish politician, premier, and president of the Turkish Republic (1989–1993). Born in Malatya, Turkey, on October 13, 1927, Turgut Özal received his bachelor's and master's degrees in electrical engineering from Istanbul Technical University and went on to study economics in the United States from 1952 to 1953. Upon his return to Turkey, he served as an adviser to the Defense Ministry, the State Planning Organization, the World Bank, and Premier Süleyman Demirel.

Following Turkey's 1980 military coup d'état, Özal was appointed deputy prime minister. He was forced to resign after a banking scandal in 1982, however. In 1983 his center-rightist Motherland Party garnered a majority of the votes in national elections, making him Turkey's prime minister. Although the party lost popular support as a result of its economic austerity program, it maintained its parliamentary majority in the 1987 elections, and Özal secured a second full term as prime minister. Two years later, the Turkish parliament elected him the first civilian president of the republic since 1960.

As premier, Özal implemented extensive economic liberalization reforms, including the lifting of exchange controls and privatization of state economic enterprises. His liberalism did not, however, extend equally to the political sphere. Özal campaigned for the ban on pre-1980 politicians' political rights, favored strict controls over the press, and turned a blind eye toward widespread human rights violations. He was at best a pragmatic democrat. He proposed greater rights for the Kurdish minorities, but mainly to curtail the military conflict in southeastern Anatolia.

In foreign affairs, Özal pursued pro-Western Turkish policies, including integration with the European Union (EU), active involvement in the North Atlantic Treaty Organization (NATO), and political partnership with the United States. He supported the international coalition arrayed against Iraq during the 1991 Persian Gulf War, and he allowed coalition air assets to use Turkish airfields. Prior to that, however, like his predecessors he attempted to maintain working relations with both Iraq and Iran. After the breakup of the Soviet Union in 1991, he began to establish cultural and economic ties with the new Central Asian republics. Özal died unexpectedly on April 17, 1993, in Ankara, Turkey.

BURCAK KESKIN-KOZAT

**See also**

DESERT STORM, Operation; North Atlantic Treaty Organization; Turkey, Role in Persian Gulf and Afghanistan Wars

**References**

Acar, Feride. "Turgut Özal: Pious Agent of Liberal Transformation." In *Political Leaders and Democracy in Turkey,* edited by Metin Heper and Sabri Sayari, 163–180. Lanham, MD: Lexington Books, 2002.

Aral, Berdal. "Dispensing with Tradition? Turkish Politics and International Society during the Özal Decade, 1983–93." *Middle Eastern Studies* 37(1) (2001): 72–88.

# P

## Pace, Peter
### Birth Date: November 5, 1945

U.S. Marine Corps general and chairman of the Joint Chiefs of Staff from 2005 to 2007. Peter Pace was born on November 5, 1945, in Brooklyn, New York, to Italian-American parents, and raised in Teaneck, New Jersey. He graduated from Teaneck High School in 1963. Pace secured an appointment to the U.S. Naval Academy at Annapolis and graduated in 1967, taking a commission in the Marine Corps. Following officer basic training at Quantico, Virginia, Pace was assigned in the summer of 1968 as a rifle platoon leader in Vietnam. He returned to the United States in March 1969 and subsequently held a series of posts both in the United States and abroad, advancing steadily through the ranks.

Pace received a master's of business administration from George Washington University in 1972 and completed advanced training at the Marine Corps Command and Staff College in Quantico, Virginia, in 1980. In 1986 he graduated from the National War College in Washington, D.C. Pace was promoted to brigadier general on April 6, 1992; major general on June 21, 1994; lieutenant general on August 5, 1996; and full general on September 8, 2000.

Pace served as president of the Marine Corps University during 1992–1994. In 1996, following his promotion to lieutenant general, he was assigned as director of operations, Joint Staff, in Washington, D.C. From 1997 to 2000 he served as commander, U.S. Marine Corps Forces, Atlantic/Europe/South. In 2000 he assumed the position of commander in chief, U.S. Southern Command, before returning to Washington in 2001 to serve as vice chairman of the Joint Chiefs of Staff. He became chairman of the Joint Chiefs of Staff, the highest-ranking U.S. military post, on September 30, 2005. He was the first marine officer to hold either the vice chairman or the chairman positions.

As vice chairman and then chairman of the Joint Chiefs of Staff, Pace was a key player in the planning and implementation of the War on Terror and the March 2003 invasion of Iraq. A loyal soldier to the end, he publicly supported the White House and his direct superiors, especially Secretary of Defense Donald H. Rumsfeld, as the invasion of Iraq was being formulated. Certainly, Rumsfeld relied heavily on Pace's support during the war planning. As the Iraq War lost public support because of the growing Iraqi insurgency, Pace saw his direct superior, chairman of the Joint Chiefs of Staff General Richard B. Myers, come under increased pressure to step aside. Upon the end of Myers's term in office, Pace became the 16th chairman of the Joint Chiefs of Staff on September 30, 2005.

In private Pace had questioned the planning, strategy, and implementation of many aspects of the Iraq War, although

### Chairmen of the Joint Chiefs of Staff, 1989–Present

| Name | Branch | Dates of Service |
| --- | --- | --- |
| Colin Powell | U.S. Army | October 1, 1989– September 30, 1993 |
| David Jeremiah (acting) | U.S. Navy | October 1–24, 1993 |
| John Shalikashvili | U.S. Army | October 25, 1993– September 30, 1997 |
| Hugh Shelton | U.S. Army | October 1, 1997– September 30, 2001 |
| Richard Myers | U.S. Air Force | October 1, 2001– September 30, 2005 |
| Peter Pace | U.S. Marine Corps | October 1, 2005– September 30, 2007 |
| Michael Mullen | U.S. Navy | October 1, 2007–present |

General Peter Pace, chairman of the Joint Chiefs of Staff (JCS) during 2005–2007, was the first Marine Corps officer to hold that position. (U.S. Department of Defense)

publicly he always loyally supported his superiors. Pace's position on the war was that U.S. troops were not in Iraq simply to eradicate insurgents and run up body counts. Rather, he was unwavering in his position that the military's job in Iraq was to provide a stable environment within which Iraqis could rebuild their infrastructure and society while humanitarian and development aid could flow into the war-torn nation. Remembering the consequences of the fixation with enemy body counts during the Vietnam War, Pace urged his superiors not to ask for or give these out, but rather to emphasize humanitarian successes and positive developments achieved by the new government in Iraq. His advice was mostly ignored.

Pace's public position against gays in the military and the fact that the American public saw the Iraq War in an increasingly negative light were key factors in the decision of newly appointed Secretary of Defense Robert Gates not to recommend Pace for a second term as chairman of the Joint Chiefs of Staff. Gates sought thereby to avoid a long, drawn-out confirmation hearing in Congress, now controlled by Democrats. Pace also had largely lost the confidence of many senior military leaders because of his failure to stand up to Rumsfeld's ideas about how wars should be fought. Gates asked Pace to step down, which he did on October 1, 2007, after serving only two years as chairman. Pace was succeeded by chief of naval operations Admiral Michael G. Mullen.

RANDY TAYLOR

**See also**

Gates, Robert Michael; Mullen, Michael Glenn; Myers, Richard Bowman; Rumsfeld, Donald Henry

**References**

Cloud, David S. "A Marine on Message." *New York Times,* April 23, 2005.

Keegan, John. *The Iraq War: The Military Offensive, from Victory in 21 Days to the Insurgent Aftermath.* New York: Vintage, 2005.

Woodward, Bob. *State of Denial: Bush at War, Part III.* New York: Simon and Schuster, 2006.

---

# Pagonis, William Gus
## Birth Date: 1942

U.S. army general who was the chief logistician responsible for the massive Operation DESERT SHIELD military buildup preceding Operation DESERT STORM. William Gus Pagonis was born in 1942 in Charleroi, Pennsylvania, of Greek-American heritage. He graduated from the Pennsylvania State University with a bachelor's degree in transportation and traffic management, and he subsequently earned a master's degree in business administration, also from Penn State. His 29-year U.S. Army career included service in the Vietnam and Persian Gulf wars, and a wide range of command and staff positions at virtually all levels.

Pagonis's most important military service occurred during operations DESERT SHIELD and DESERT STORM, for which he earned accolades as "the logistical wizard" of the coalition war effort. Indeed, U.S. Central Command (CENTCOM) commander General H. Norman Schwarzkopf termed the Persian Gulf War "a logistician's war," and pronounced Pagonis, who became his chief logistician, "an Einstein who could make anything happen."

As director of logistics for Lieutenant General John Yeosock's U.S. Army Central Command (ARCENT), the major subordinate command for American ground forces during the Persian Gulf War, then-Major General Pagonis faced the Herculean task of bringing order to the flood of troops, weapons, ammunition, and supplies that began to arrive in Saudi Arabia on August 7, 1990, only days after Iraqi president Saddam Hussein's army occupied neighboring Kuwait. Pagonis, one of the first Americans to arrive in the Kuwaiti theater of operations, immediately set about bringing necessary order to an otherwise chaotic situation, providing the vital key to the American-led coalition's victory in February 1991.

For six months (August 1990–February 1991), Pagonis's 22nd Support Command organized and supervised a methodical buildup of military might that included the gathering of 670,000 troops from 28 nations (500,000 were U.S. personnel), 150,000 wheeled vehicles, 40,000 containers, 2,000 helicopters, and 2,000 tanks into the Kuwaiti theater of operations. By the time the ground war began on February 24, 1991, Pagonis had amassed more than 7 million tons of supplies that arrived from halfway around the world.

Pagonis's prodigious logistical accomplishments did not end with the completion of the troop, equipment, and supply buildup of Operation DESERT SHIELD. His further efforts largely made possible the phenomenal success of Schwarzkopf's operational plan that won the ground war, Operation DESERT STORM, during the 100-hour ground-launched blitzkrieg. The tactical battle plan, which called for a giant left hook to be delivered against the Iraqi Army by the U.S. VII and XVII Airborne Corps, relied on secretly moving 150,000 American troops 150 miles westward across the desert wasteland. Thanks to an impressive effort led by Pagonis, the combat units' progress was facilitated by prepositioned advanced supply bases placed at key locations along the route of march. Mechanized forces, including swarms of fuel-guzzling tanks and armored fighting vehicles, found much-needed supplies and all necessary logistical support waiting for them when they arrived at Pagonis's desert bases. Pagonis later said, "I got the idea from a fellow Greek—Alexander the Great," citing Donald W. Engel's *Alexander the Great and the Logistics of the Macedonian Army* (1977) as his "logistical bible." Engel's work describes the sophisticated logistical effort, including the use of advanced logistical bases, that made Alexander's 4,000-mile march of conquest possible.

Equally as impressive as Pagonis's logistical efforts during the war were his no-less prodigious accomplishments in moving the masses of troops and supplies back from the war zone after the fighting had stopped. Perhaps no other major American military expedition has been followed up with the level of accountability (the meticulous tracking and accounting for individual items of equipment) that Pagonis ensured in the wake of DESERT STORM. His Persian Gulf War accomplishments were recognized by his promotion to lieutenant general soon after the war.

Pagonis retired from the army in 1993 and thereafter pursued a highly successful career in the business world and as a guest speaker on leadership and management topics. As executive vice president of logistics for Sears, Roebuck and Company, Pagonis was instrumental in revitalizing the giant retail chain. He retired from Sears in July 2004 and became chairman of the board of RailAmerica, Inc., the world's largest short-line railroad. He was also appointed chairman of the Defense Business Board in 2001 by Secretary of Defense Donald Rumsfeld, and serves as vice chairman of GENCO Supply Chain Solutions and CombineNet, Inc.

In addition to his successful business and speaking career, Pagonis is an author. His book, *Moving Mountains: Lessons in Leadership and Logistics from the Gulf War,* was published by Harvard Business School Press in 1992.

JERRY D. MORELOCK

**See also**

DESERT SHIELD, Operation; DESERT STORM, Operation; Schwarzkopf, H. Norman, Jr.; Yeosock, John J.

**References**

Pagonis, William G., and Jeffrey Cruikshank. *Moving Mountains: Lessons in Leadership and Logistics from the Gulf War.* Cambridge: Harvard Business School Press, 1992.

Schwarzkopf, H. Norman, with Peter Petre. *It Doesn't Take a Hero: General H. Norman Schwarzkopf, the Autobiography.* New York: Bantam Books, 1993.

# Pakistan

Largely Muslim nation that straddles the West Asian subcontinent and the Middle East. Encompassing some 310,500 square miles, Pakistan borders on Afghanistan and Iran to the west, the People's Republic of China (PRC) and India to the east, and the Arabian Sea to the south. The Islamic Republic of Pakistan's 2008 population was 172.8 million, making it the second most populous nation with a Muslim majority. Currently, it possesses the seventh-largest armed forces in the world. Moreover, as of 1998, Pakistan officially acknowledged being one of seven countries in the world to possess nuclear weapons, alongside its longtime enemy, India.

Pakistan has been occupied by a host of empires since ancient times. Situated along the famous "Silk Road" linking China and the West, it was a strategic crossroads for many peoples. Aryans, Persians, Macedonians, Greeks, Afghans, Arabs, Mongols, and Turkic groups at various stages made the region their home. Its modern history began in the early 17th century with the decline of the Mughal sultanates and the expansion of the British East India Company. In 1858 Pakistan (then part of India) fell under colonial rule as part of the British Raj until the partition and independence of the Indian subcontinent in 1947.

Decolonization, however, was a complicated affair. The population of the subcontinent was not only enormous, but it was also exceptionally diverse and divided by religion, ethnicity, and social caste. The independence movement spearheaded by the Indian National Congress (INC) and unofficially led after World War I by Mohandas Gandhi was a multifaith, multiethnic front, but it could not entirely bridge the gaps between the different groups. Formed in 1906, the All-India Muslim League (AIML) advocated the separation of British India into Muslim and Hindu states, and over the course of the 1930s support for the creation of an Islamic state grew. In March 1940 AIML leaders devised the Lahore Declaration, which called for the division of British India, with the majority Muslim areas of the northwest and northeast becoming independent states. Thereafter, the AIML's forceful leader, Muhammad Ali Jinnah, pushed the British for separate recognition.

Independence finally came on August 15, 1947, when Pakistan was officially created out of British India. Three provinces (the Northwest Frontier Province, West Punjab, and Sind) joined with Baluchistan States Union, an array of princely states, tribal areas, and the Federal Capital Territory around the city of Karachi to form the mainly Urdu-speaking West Pakistan. Separated by nearly 1,000 miles of India, Pakistan also included the province of East Bengal, with a predominantly Bengali-speaking Muslim population. The separation of West and East Pakistan from India ignited massive riots, rampant violence, and the migration of approximately 15 million people in the largest single movement of people in history. Some estimates put the death toll at as many as 1 million people, as both Hindus and Sikhs fled Muslim territories and Muslims evacuated the majority-Hindu India. While some blame Britain for passing the July 1947 Indian Independence Act prematurely, others note that without partition a much bloodier conflict would have ensued.

Indian refugees crowd onto trains following the creation of the two independent states of India and Pakistan. Muslims fled to Pakistan and Hindus fled to India in one of the largest transfers of population in history. This photograph was taken at Amritsar, India, on October 17, 1947. (Bettmann/Corbis)

Along with communal violence, Pakistan and India also confronted an immediate foreign policy crisis. Several princely states, notably Jammu and Kashmir, joined India after partition, angering Pakistan. Muslims comprised the largest single religious group in Jammu-Kashmir.

When local Hindu and Sikh forces clashed with Pakistani-backed Muslim militias, India entered the conflict. During 1948 regular Pakistani forces replaced the militias, and Indian involvement intensified. The First Kashmir War (or Indo-Pakistani War of 1947–1948) resulted in two-thirds of the state falling within Indian control.

Between April and September 1965, Pakistan and India again collided in the Second Kashmir War, with ultimately very little change to this division. However, the international implications of the conflict were considerable. Since partition, the United States had cultivated Pakistan as an ally in the region, drawing it into multilateral pacts like the Southeast Asian Treaty Organization (SEATO) in 1954 and the Central Treaty Organization (CENTO), or Baghdad Pact, in 1955. The United States also supplied substantial military aid to Pakistan. Simultaneously, however, the Americans wanted to cultivate better relations with nonaligned India, which courted both the United States and the Soviet Union for material assistance. The Indians attracted more Western support following the Sino-Indian War (1962), which

saw the Chinese invade and occupy their disputed border region. With no resolution to the conflict over Jammu-Kashmir by 1965, the United States feared renewed hostilities between what were ostensibly its two allies. Although the relationship with India improved after 1965, ties to Pakistan were undermined by what leaders there saw as American duplicity in providing aid to their enemy, especially given India's victory in the war. As a consequence, Pakistan pursued ties with China, America's major rival in the region.

Internal politics within Pakistan also significantly shaped its international relations. Between 1947 and 1958, the country had a succession of largely unstable civilian governments. A bloodless coup in 1958 led by General Ayub Khan brought the military to power. Along with Pakistan's strategic defeat in the 1965 war, rampant corruption and heavy-handed rule undermined Ayub Khan's popularity. In 1969 he was replaced by another general, Yahya Khan. When some questioned his ascension to power, Yahya Khan declared martial law and cracked down on all dissenters, including leaders in East Pakistan who pushed for separation. Although more populous than the West, the East received proportionally less of the national wealth, while Bengalis were marginalized in the government and the military. Compounding matters, one of the worst cyclones in history hit East Pakistan in November 1970, killing an estimated 500,000 people.

The response from West Pakistan to the disaster was slow and insufficient, adding to Bengali alienation. In the national elections of December 1970, voters in East Pakistan overwhelmingly supported Sheikh Mujibur Rahman and the separatist Awami League, in clear defiance of Yahya Khan. Negotiations between the two Pakistans followed but quickly fell apart. Rahman was arrested for treason and brought to trial in West Pakistan. Protests in East Pakistan were violently suppressed by the military, especially after Bengali officers within its ranks declared independence on behalf of Rahman on March 17, 1971. In fact, some argue that West Pakistan's actions constituted genocide. The number of dead is hotly disputed, with estimates ranging widely from 30,000 to 3 million. However, most experts agree that approximately 1 million Hindus and Muslims died because of West Pakistan's actions.

Ten million refugees now fled to India, which decided to intervene in the civil war in December 1971. The resulting Indo-Pakistani War (December 3–16, 1971) marked the third major war between the two nations since partition, and once again drew in world powers. For its support of Pakistan the United States was widely condemned, even by some of its allies like Britain and France. The war became a Cold War conflict when the Soviet Union and India concluded a series of diplomatic agreements, while Moscow openly supported Bengali independence. Consequently, U.S. president Richard M. Nixon continued to aid Pakistan. Against the U.S. Congress' wishes, he funneled aid via Iran to the Pakistanis, in part hoping to curry favor with China, another supporter of Pakistan with which he was beginning to move toward détente. American prestige in the region was seriously undermined when Pakistani forces surrendered to the Indians after only two weeks of war. India agreed to a cease-fire, thus avoiding a longer and wider conflict. However, the war led to the dissolution of the two Pakistans and the independence of Bangladesh.

The 1971 war also discredited the Pakistani military and Yahya Khan, who was replaced in December by Zulfikar Ali Bhutto. Bhutto quickly restored civilian rule and shifted the country's foreign policy away from dependence on the Americans. He built up the country's defenses, a decision that included development of nuclear weapons beginning in 1973. Bhutto also presided over the suppression of an independence movement in Baluchistan in 1973, and constitutional changes that made Pakistan an Islamic Republic later that same year. However, personal and political rivalries led to his downfall. He was overthrown in a military coup led by General Mohammed Zia al-Haq in July 1977. Found guilty of the murder of political rivals in what many still see as a political ploy by the military, Bhutto was executed in April 1979.

General Zia presided over considerable change within Pakistan, most notably the increasing Islamization of the country with the implementation in 1978 of Sharia (Islamic law), in which Sharia was intermingled with civil and secular law. He also facilitated an important reconciliation with the Americans predicated on the Soviet invasion of Afghanistan in December 1979. Almost immediately, Zia backed factions within the mujahideen, a loose federation of Afghan tribes opposed to the Soviet occupation. Having lost Iran as an ally following the Islamic revolution there earlier in the year, and fearing Soviet expansion in the Middle East, U.S. president Jimmy Carter offered Zia $400 million in aid to help fight in Afghanistan, which the general famously denounced as "peanuts."

It was not until President Ronald W. Reagan took office in January 1981 that the Americans and Pakistanis worked together, largely through their intelligence services, to supply and train mujahideen warriors. Thus, Pakistan once again became a major ally of the United States, in return receiving substantial military aid—approximately $1.36 billion between 1985 and 1991 alone. Worried about the Pakistani military buildup, in 1985 the U.S. Congress passed the Pressler Amendment, requiring the president to certify that Pakistan did not possess nuclear weapons before aid was approved. Zia's hard-line regime gradually became a liability for Washington, especially after the Soviets began withdrawing from Afghanistan in 1987.

Elements within the Pakistani military and particularly the intelligence services were opposed to the Islamization of the country, as were moderate, secular Pakistani politicians. Zia was also hated by the Soviets, while chieftains in Pakistan's tribal areas resented his suppression of their autonomy. Not surprisingly, Zia's days were numbered. In August 1988 he died in a plane crash, widely seen as an assassination carried out by at least one of these disaffected groups.

A caretaker government took control briefly before Benazir Bhutto—the daughter of Zulfikar Ali Bhutto—was elected in December 1988 as the first female prime minister of an Islamic country. Almost immediately her government battled charges of corruption, ultimately resulting in its collapse in August 1990. She was replaced by Nawaz Sharif between November 1990 and July 1993, before elections returned Bhutto as prime minister. During Bhutto's second term, Pakistan was once again active in Afghanistan, supporting the Taliban, a Sunni Muslim fundamentalist group formed from segments of the mujahideen. The Taliban came to power in September 1996, shortly before Bhutto's government was again dismissed amidst accusations of corruption. Sharif returned to power, but had a difficult time managing the Pakistani military, especially after yet another border conflict with India between May and July 1999 in the Kargil district of Kashmir.

In May 1998 Pakistan successfully exploded six nuclear weapons. These tests, despite the threat of sanctions by the United States and other Western powers, were in response to nuclear tests conducted by India less than a month before.

Following Pakistan's defeat in the brief fighting with India, Sharif tried to court-marshal senior military officials, but an October 1999 coup led by General Pervez Musharraf ousted him before he could do so. Musharraf's regime, which was widely viewed as oppressive and corrupt, was largely condemned by the Western world. In addition to the coup, he continued to support the fundamentalist Taliban regime in Afghanistan, while some members of

Soldiers of the Pakistani Army shut down state-run television in Islamabad on October 12, 1999. The soldiers were acting in support of dismissed Pakistani Army chief General Pèrvez Musharraf, who overthrew the government of Prime Minister Nawaz Sharif. (AP/Wide World Photos)

the Pakistani intelligence services were rumored to have ties with international terrorist organizations, including Al Qaeda.

Following the September 11, 2001, terror attacks on the United States, carried out by Al Qaeda, Musharraf declared his country an ally of the West in the U.S.-defined Global War on Terror. Given a choice between continuing support for the Taliban and incurring the wrath of the Americans, or facing a possible alliance between the United States and India, Musharraf decided to assist North American Treaty Organization (NATO) forces in their October 2001 invasion of Afghanistan to destroy Al Qaeda bases (Operation ENDURING FREEDOM).

Musharraf also denounced militants in Kashmir whom he had previously supported, and then condemned all forms of Islamic extremism. This provoked public anger within Pakistan, especially in the tribal areas where Al Qaeda and Taliban forces were receiving refuge. Having survived several attempts on his life, Musharraf also faced challenges from within his own government, especially by prodemocracy elements and those who supported a return of Benazir Bhutto. As the War on Terror progressed, Musharraf's commitment to fighting Islamic radicals was called into

question by many in Washington. Since 2005 remnants of the Taliban and Al Qaeda operatives have been operating with renewed vigor along the long, desolate, and porous border between Pakistan and Afghanistan, but also within the Punjab. The Musharraf government claimed that it was diligently pursuing these groups, but there was little evidence that its efforts were working. Indeed, by mid-2006 the Taliban was well established in some parts of Afghanistan, which triggered renewed NATO military operations against them beginning in late 2006 and into 2007. Despite Washington's doubts, it continued to court Pakistan as an ally, for to have turned its back on Musharraf would have been tantamount to opening the way for a radical, anti-American government to take hold in Karachi. Since 2001 the United States has relied on Pakistan as its most important regional ally.

As it turned out, Musharraf sewed the seeds of his own downfall. In the autumn of 2007 he precipitated a full-blown political crisis when he sacked most of the Supreme Court, suspended the constitution, ordered the mass arrests of dissidents and regime opponents, and declared a state of emergency on November 3, 2007. His actions provoked mass protests, sporadic violence, and much criticism from the international community, including the United States. Musharraf lifted the state of emergency on December 15, but Benazir Bhutto had returned to Pakistan. Both she and Nawaz Sharif, who had been disallowed from returning to the country, were outspoken critics of Musharraf. The crisis grew worse when Benazir Bhutto was assassinated on December 27 in Rawalpindi and her supporters alleged some involvement of either the government or Musharraf. After that, Musharraf's hold on power grew ever more tenuous, and he finally resigned in August 2008. He was succeeded by Benazir Bhutto's widower, Asif Ali Zardari, who assumed the presidency in September.

Zardari's government cooperated with the United States, although it protested air strikes against the Taliban and Al Qaeda by unmanned U.S. drones from Afghanistan into northwestern Pakistan. The new Pakistani government faced great challenges at home, not the least of which was Islamic radicalism. Ongoing tensions with India—especially following the December 2008 terrorist attacks in Mumbai, which were carried out by extremists based in Pakistan—raised for a time the specter of nuclear war in the subcontinent.

Zardari's government also set off alarm bells in Washington when it concluded a truce with the Taliban in northwestern Pakistan that allowed the imposition of Sharia, or law based on the Qur'an, in effect conceding rule of the Swat Valley to the Taliban. However, when Taliban forces broke the truce by also moving into the Buner District only some 60 miles north of the capital of Islamabad, Zardari responded with force. Under heavy pressure from the U.S. government and from moderate elements within Pakistan itself, he sent the army into Buner but also into the Swat Valley in late April 2009, declaring the truce with the Taliban to be at an end. After two weeks of heavy fighting, the government claimed that it had killed some 1,000 Taliban and Al Qaeda extremists, but the fighting also created the greatest refugee crisis in recent years, displacing as many as 1.5 million people.

The United States has promised additional financial and military aid to Pakistan. Zardari has also pledged cooperation with Afghan president Hamid Karzai in fighting the Taliban and Al Qaeda. Nonetheless, with continuing political instability, economic difficulties, and ever-present tensions with its nuclear-armed rival India, Pakistan's future remains clouded at best.

ARNE KISLENKO

**See also**

Afghanistan; Al Qaeda; Bhutto, Benazir; ENDURING FREEDOM, Operation; Mujahideen, Soviet-Afghanistan War; Musharraf, Pervez; Taliban

**References**

Hussain, Rizwan. *Pakistan and the Emergence of Islamic Militancy in Afghanistan.* Aldershot, UK: Ashgate, 2005.
Jones, Owen Bennett. *Pakistan: Eye of the Storm.* New Haven, CT: Yale University Press, 2002.
Kux, Dennis. *The United States and Pakistan, 1947–2000: Disenchanted Allies.* Washington, DC: Woodrow Wilson Center Press, 2001.
Sathasivam, Kanishkan. *Uneasy Neighbors: India, Pakistan, and U.S. Foreign Policy.* Aldershot, UK: Ashgate, 2005.
Weaver, Mary Anne. *Pakistan: In the Shadow of Jihad and Afghanistan.* New York: Farrar, Straus and Giroux, 2003.

# Pakistan, Armed Forces

The state of Pakistan, established in 1947, has spent more than half of its existence under military rule, and struggles have taken place during that time between civilian and military leadership. Periods of direct military rule (usually under the presidential title) occurred under General (later Field Marshal) Ayub Khan (1958–1968), General Yahya Khan (1968–1971), General Zia al-Haq (1977–1988), and General (later President) Pervez Musharraf (1999–2008). The army's incessant political intervention—including significant political alliances with Islamist parties—has eroded civilian authority and weakened democratic elements within the state, and thus the armed forces retain extraordinary influence over foreign and national security policy. The military has also directed, with decidedly mixed success, Pakistan's wars and irregular conflicts, and it remains a key decision-maker in Pakistan's recently tested nuclear arsenal. As a result, the Pakistani Army remains the most important institution in Pakistan and is of critical importance to both domestic and international political stability.

On June 3, 1947, the British announced a partition plan for the Indian subcontinent that established the independent states of India and Pakistan, the latter of which incorporated two widely separated entities known as West Pakistan and East Pakistan (now Bangladesh). The Indian Army was dissolved, and Indian and Pakistani authorities took operational control of their own national armed forces on August 15, 1947. Military assets were eventually divided in a 64:36 ratio, favoring the much larger Indian state. The Pakistani Army began with just 3 officers with the rank of brigadier or major general and 53 colonels to command a planned force structure of 150,000 men. As a result, British officers continued to play a crucial role in Pakistan until the 1950s, and the first 2 Pakistani Army chiefs of staff were British officers.

Partition led almost immediately to war, as India and Pakistan clashed over the Muslim-majority princely states of Jammu and Kashmir, which lay between the two new nations. Fighting began in October 1947 and was resolved in early 1949 by a United Nations (UN) cease-fire. The full conditions of the cease-fire have never been met, and the province remains divided along what is now referred to as the "Line of Control," with Pakistan governing approximately one-third, and India approximately two-thirds, of the territory in dispute. Kashmir remains a key obstacle to Indo-Pakistani relations and was the cause of later wars in 1965 and 1999.

Pakistan's army was instrumental in consolidating a political alliance with the United States in 1954, which secured both military and economic assistance. Pakistan entered into both the Central Treaty Organization (CENTO) and the South East Asian Treaty Organization (SEATO) with the understanding that U.S.-supplied military equipment would be used to contain international communist aggression, and not to fight neighboring India. Despite this commitment, bitterness remains from the partition, and each country considers the other to be its most serious threat. Pakistan reopened hostilities against India in 1965, infiltrating irregular forces into Kashmir in hopes of stirring up a popular uprising. This engagement escalated into a conventional war in September, when the Pakistani army began Operation GRAND SLAM, aimed at cutting Indian lines of communication to Kashmir. The United States and Britain immediately stopped military shipments to both sides, and after three weeks of indecisive fighting, Pakistan accepted a cease-fire that largely validated the prewar status quo.

In December 1971 Pakistan suffered a crushing military defeat at the hands of India. After elections in which the ethnic Bengali Awami League (based almost entirely in East Pakistan) won a majority of seats in Pakistan's parliament, the Pakistani Army responded by arresting and slaughtering vast numbers of Bengalis and forcing millions of others to flee to India, where the survivors organized a nationalist resistance. By late November 1971 Indian and Pakistani forces were fighting in East Pakistan, and an attempted preemptive strike by the Pakistani Air Force in the west achieved little except to provide India with an excuse to widen the conflict. Within two weeks, East Pakistan had been liberated by Indian forces, and the new state of Bangladesh was born. This defeat cemented in the minds of the military and political elites Pakistan's vulnerability to ethnic division, and proved a crucial motivation for Pakistan's pursuit of nuclear weapons. The Simla Accord that formally ended the conflict stated that India and Pakistan would resolve existing issues bilaterally, which further complicated solutions to Kashmir.

The Soviet invasion of Afghanistan in 1979 renewed the U.S.-Pakistan alliance, but also contributed to a marked increase in Indo-Pakistani tensions. From 1986 to 2008, the neighbors had no fewer than five potential nuclear crises involving large mobilizations of conventional forces. Pakistan's nuclear weapons program received significant assistance from the Chinese, and its decision to weaponize its nuclear capability triggered a cutoff of U.S. aid in 1990. India and Pakistan both tested nuclear weapons for the first time in 1998, and Pakistan's infiltration of irregular forces across the Line of Control the following year led to a significant military confrontation and nuclear threats by both sides. A terrorist attack by Pakistan-based militants against the Indian parliament in New Delhi on December 13, 2001, led to a 10-month-long crisis with both sides highly mobilized along their border. Most recently, the brutal November 2008 terrorist attacks in Mumbai, India, staged by Pakistan-backed militant groups, have again led to fears of war in the region. Both India and Pakistan probably each currently possess several dozen nuclear weapons of Hiroshima size (i.e., a blast equivalent to about 12.5 kilotons of TNT).

Since the mid-1970s the Pakistani Army, through its Inter-Service Intelligence (ISI) Directorate, has utilized religiously motivated militant groups as an important element of the nation's foreign, domestic, and national security policies. Many of these groups have emerged from intra-Pakistani divisions over its identity: whether it is merely a nation of Muslims, or an Islamic state. Some in the United States accuse Pakistan of being a state sponsor of terrorism, based on the ISI's relationship with various Taliban groups and the Al Qaeda network; however, this relationship evolved from Pakistan's role in the mujahideen versus Soviet conflict in Afghanistan.

Pakistan also supported groups opposing Indian rule in the states of Jammu and Kashmir (since 1989) and Punjab (late 1980s and early 1990s). Some elements in the ISI have also been charged with having connections to violent extremist groups carrying out actions inside Pakistan itself. The linkages between these groups, Pakistani official policy, and broader transnational movements such as Al Qaeda remain poorly understood by international analysts. Pakistanis point to the government's need for alliances of convenience, the spectrum of political behavior, and the deep poverty in the densely populated country. It is clear, however, that the West, particularly, the U.S. government, considers the Taliban and other extremist Islamist groups to be a threat to Pakistani political stability, and to political authority in peripheral areas along the Afghan border. Pakistan's army has played an important role overseas. It has participated in many different UN peacekeeping operations, including the ill-fated intervention in Somalia in the early 1990s, and deployed roughly 10,000 troops on behalf of UN operations in late 2008. Pakistani forces have provided training and support for the smaller countries on the southern side of the Persian Gulf, and the Pakistani military maintains a close relationship with Saudi Arabia.

Pakistan's army has generally performed well at the tactical level. Its troops are tough and determined, and they earned the respect of their Indian adversaries in 1965 and, more recently, in the Kargil conflict in 1999. The army has performed less effectively at the operational level, although this has not been tested in major combat since 1971. Key weaknesses have been performance at the strategic level and counterinsurgency efforts. At the strategic level, Pakistan's military has shown a consistent preference for risky offensive operations with inadequate logistic support, grossly over-optimistic planning, and a lack of consideration of consequences, branches, and sequels. In each of Pakistan's major wars (1947, 1965, 1971), as well as the Kargil crisis, Pakistan found itself unable to convert initial tactical surprise into significant military success, unable to end the conflict while in a position of tactical advantage, and incapable of securing meaningful international support. These difficulties allowed a numerically superior Indian force to protract the conflict until it could force Pakistan to negotiate from an inferior position.

The U.S. government has provided the Pakistani military with more than $1 billion a year in assistance, but the army had not been able to prevent the Talibanization of parts of Pakistan through counterinsurgency operations. Since 2004 the Pakistani Army had engaged in significant counterinsurgency operations in the Federally Administered Tribal Areas (FATA), where Al Qaeda,

Taliban, and other extremist terrorists are known to be hiding. In these operations, more than 1,000 members of Pakistan's army and paramilitary forces (primarily the Frontier Corps) have been killed. Press reports note that the operations had been marked by reliance on aerial bombing, helicopter gunships, and artillery fire; this has routinely resulted in massive devastation to local villages and created massive numbers of internal refugees (hundreds of thousands in Waziristan in early 2008). In addition, U.S. attacks on Taliban and Al Qaeda targets by unmanned drone aircraft have been roundly criticized by the Pakistani government, which considers such attacks to be in violation of its national sovereignty.

Counterinsurgency sweep operations have been marked by little provision for long-term security after the operation is complete. There has been some damage to militant forces, particularly during operations in South Waziristan in March 2007 and especially in October 2009, which combined local tribal *lashkars* (militia forces) with army heavy weapons support. Yet the northwestern frontier area remains a long-term problem for Pakistan, as it has been for years.

Today the Pakistani Army is one of the largest professional military forces in the world. It numbers approximately 520,000 active-duty soldiers and 500,000 reservists. The army is organized into 20 infantry division-strength formations (including Force Command Northern Areas); 2 mechanized, 2 artillery, and 2 armored divisions; and an additional 13 independent infantry and armored brigades. Operationally, it is divided into 9 corps, 7 of which directly face India. Two corps (XI Corps in Peshawar and XII Corps in Quetta) garrison western Pakistan but can move east rapidly in a crisis. The army as an institution focuses on the threat of war with India, but also must react to an increasing Islamist militant threat in the western provinces, as well as episodic terrorism in the major cities.

The army fields a mix of Chinese, American, and European equipment. The top-of-the-line main battle tanks are the Al-Khalid—a cooperative venture with Ukraine—and the T-80D. The rest of the tank force is a mixture of Chinese models—T-59s, T-69s, and T-85s. The army also fields 2,000 M-113 derivative armored personnel carriers and a largely American-derived artillery arsenal, including 105-mm and 155-mm towed howitzers and more than 250 M109 self-propelled 155-mm howitzers. The army also possesses 122-mm and 130-mm Chinese howitzers. Helicopters include U.S. Bell AH-1 Cobras and French, Pakistani, and U.S. utility helicopters of varying ages and effectiveness. Pakistan's ordnance factories produce a range of relatively unsophisticated light arms, missiles, and artillery systems, but most major weapons must still be purchased abroad.

The air force also employs a mix of Chinese, U.S., and European equipment, totaling 350–400 combat aircraft. It has roughly 45,000 personnel (less than 10 percent of the size of the army). The most modern aircraft are U.S.-made Lockheed Martin F-16 Fighting Falcons, which have been provided in sporadic fashion and have suffered maintenance problems because of periodic U.S.

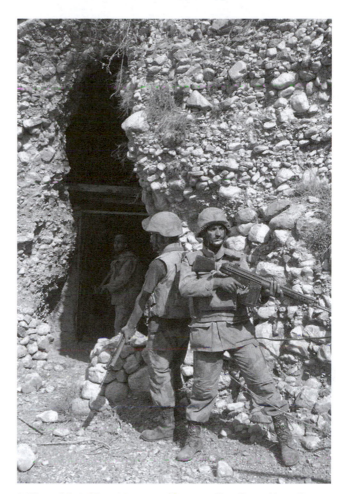

Soldiers of the Pakistani Army outside a cave allegedly used by militants in the Taliban stronghold of Kot Kai in the tribal area of Waziristan along the Afghan border, November 26, 2009. (AP/Wide World Photos)

sanctions, and Chinese-made JF-17s, which have only recently entered the Pakistani inventory. The Pakistani air force also relies heavily on Chinese F-7 and French Dassault Mirage III/V variants for a variety of roles, and it maintains a small force of obsolete Chinese A-5 strike aircraft. Pakistani pilots are well trained, but the air force is increasingly being outpaced by the rapid growth of the Indian Air Force in both quantity and quality of aircraft.

Pakistan's navy is the smallest and least influential of the armed services. It numbers just 25,000 personnel, including 5,000 reservists and almost 2,500 marines, special forces, and security personnel. This gives it less than 5 percent of the manpower of the army. Despite its small size, the Pakistani Navy has an important role in the region and has twice commanded Combined Task Force 150, a multinational naval coalition that patrols the North Arabian Sea and the Horn of Africa as part of the Global War on Terror. Because of resource limitations, the navy remains small and poorly equipped. However, it possesses small numbers of very effective units, including a squadron of American-supplied Lockheed P-3 Orion reconnaissance/ASW aircraft and 3 French Agosta diesel submarines equipped with an air-independent propulsion system. It possesses 2 other fairly modern submarines,

The surface fleet is essentially obsolete, relying on 6 aging British Amazon-class frigates and several fast-attack craft ships—4 small ships and 8 larger ones, of Pakistani, Chinese, Thai, and Turkish designs. There are also about 11 patrol craft of various sizes. The naval air arm (all shore based) has 52 aircraft and helicopters, and a squadron of PAF Mirage III aircraft is dedicated to the maritime strike role. The Pakistani Navy is upgrading to Chinese F-22 "Sword-class" missile frigates, at least one of which will be assembled at Karachi, but it still pales in comparison to the larger and more robust Indian Navy.

In late April 2009, after the Taliban broke a truce agreement with the Pakistani government that had given them effective control of the Swat Valley by also seizing control of Buner District, only 60 miles north of the capital of Islamabad, the Pakistani government declared the truce at an end and sent in the army. This decision followed heavy pressure from the U.S. government and moderate elements in Pakistan itself. After two weeks of operations, the government announced that its forces had killed some 1,000 Taliban and Al Qaeda fighters. The heavy fighting led to a major refugee crisis, in which as many as 2 million Pakistani citizens fled the region.

Because of its internal militant threats, proximity to Afghanistan, and knowledge of and familiarity with major militant groups in South and Central Asia, Pakistan remains a vital ally in the Global War on Terror, even though doubts exist about its commitment to and wholehearted cooperation with U.S. objectives in the region.

TIMOTHY D. HOYT

**See also**

Afghanistan; Al Qaeda; Global War on Terror; Pakistan; Taliban

**References**

Cheema, Pervaiz Iqbal. *The Armed Forces of Pakistan.* New York: New York University Press, 2002.

Cloughley, Brian. *A History of the Pakistan Army: Wars and Insurrections.* 2nd ed. Oxford: Oxford University Press, 2000.

Cohen, Stephen P. *The Pakistan Army.* Karachi: Oxford University Press, 1998.

Haqqani, Husain. *Pakistan: Between Mosque and Military.* Washington, DC: Carnegie Endowment for International Peace, 2005.

Hoyt, Timothy D. "Pakistani Nuclear Doctrine and the Dangers of Strategic Myopia." *Asian Survey* 41(6) (November/December 2001): 956–977.

Siddiqa, Ayesha. *Military Inc.: Inside Pakistan's Military Economy.* London: Pluto, 2007.

---

# Palestine Liberation Organization

A political and military organization founded in 1964 and dedicated to protecting the human and legal rights of Palestinians and creating an independent state for Palestinian Arabs in Palestine. Since the 1960s, the Munazzamat al-Tahrir al-Filastiniyyah (Palestine Liberation Organization, PLO) has functioned as the official mouthpiece for the Palestinian people. The PLO served as a coordinating council for the military, social, and political groups that were part of the Palestinian movement. In addition to Fatah, which is the largest of the political and military groups in the PLO, were the Popular Front for the Liberation of Palestine (PFLP), the Democratic Front for the Liberation of Palestine (DFLP), and the Communist Party. Also represented were guerrilla groups (in the past), Palestinian independents, and such "mass organizations" as the General Union of Palestinian Workers (GUPW), the General Union of Palestinian Students (GUPS), and the General Union of Palestinian Women, as well as social organizations like the Red Crescent.

Various other Palestinian groups have also been a part of the Palestinian liberation movement, including the Palestinian People's Party and umbrella groups such as the Palestine Liberation Front (PLF), or the military group funded by Syria, al-Saiqa. The Popular Front for the Liberation of Palestine–General Command (PFLP-GC) was formerly associated with the PLO, but did not accept the Oslo Accords. Hamas, now the largest Palestinian movement, has never been a part of the PLO.

The PLO's military wing was, by 1980, organized in the Palestinian Liberation Army. It also had a police organization, founded in Jordan, the Palestinian Armed Struggle Command, which functioned in Lebanon as a civilian police group.

Comprising centrist-nationalist groups (such as Fatah), leftist groups (including communists), and militant groups and nonmilitant groups, the PLO was intended to be as inclusive as possible; however, beginning in 1988, in contrast to other groups, it supported political negotiations and a two-state solution. The PLO has been enormously successful in attracting funding over the years. Indeed, a 1993 survey estimated the PLO's total assets at between $8 billion and $10 billion and its average yearly income at $1.5 billion to $2 billion.

The PLO was founded in 1964, and many of its leaders were also the founders of Fatah, which took the largest share of its budget. Its first president was Ahmad Shuqairi. The stated purpose of the PLO was the liberation of Palestine, condemnation of Zionist imperialism, and the dissolution of Israel through the use of armed force. From 1969 to 1973, various Palestinian organizations engaged in violent actions against Israel to draw attention to their cause. The extent of coordination between such groups as the Black September Organization (BSO) and Fatah is not clear, but many of the groups within the PLO were also part of its guerrilla wing. The Israelis labeled the PLO a terrorist organization for many years, although Palestinians and many international observers dispute that characterization. In 1988 PLO leader Yasser Arafat—the chairman of the organization since 1969 and then first president of the Palestinian National Authority (PNA)—renounced violence as a means to achieve Palestinian goals. This decision was binding on the member groups in the PLO. However, various intra-Palestinian battles were fought within the PLO, including the Rejection Front's struggle with Fatah. In addition, some other non-PLO groups, such as Islamic Jihad, were not in favor of the

Oslo Accords and continued to support Palestinian resistance in the form of violent jihad. During the Second (al-Aqsa) Intifada, groups that were originally a part of the PLO broke away from their leadership and formed the al-Aqsa Martyrs Brigades.

Although the PLO has been reorganized many times since its inception, its leading governing bodies have been the Palestinian National Council (PNC), the Central Council, and the Executive Committee. The PNC has 300 members and functions as a nominal legislature. The Executive Committee has 15 members elected by the PNC and holds the PLO's real political and executive power. The Palestinian Revolutionary Forces are the PLO's military arm.

On February 3, 1969, the PNC in Cairo officially appointed Arafat chairman of the PLO. Over the next four years, Arafat became the commander in chief of the PLO's military branch, the Palestinian Revolutionary Forces, and the political leader of the organization.

In 1968 and 1969 part of the PLO functioned as a well-organized unofficial state within Jordan, with its uniformed soldiers acting as a police force and collecting their own taxes. In 1968 King Hussein of Jordan and the PLO signed an agreement by which the PLO agreed that its fighters would stop patrolling in uniform with guns, and stop searching civilian vehicles. The PLO did not comply with this agreement, however, and both attacks on civilians and clashes between Palestinians and Jordanian soldiers increased. By 1970 Hussein decided that the Palestinians threatened national security and ordered his army to evict them. This led to several months of violence, during which Syria aided the Palestinians and the United States aided Jordan. The events of BSO (including an attempt on Hussein's life), several airliner hijackings by the PFLP, and a declaration of martial law in Jordan culminated with the PLO agreeing to a cease-fire on September 24 and promising to leave the country.

The PLO fighters left for refugee camps in southern Lebanon and those in Beirut. However, the PLO continued nonmilitary activities in Jordan, as it did throughout the Palestinian diaspora. The Lebanese government had already struggled with the Palestinian fighters in Lebanon, and it continued to restrict the PLO's movements, which led to tensions. Palestinians nevertheless launched periodic attacks across the Israeli border. Lebanese Muslims and members of Kamal Jumblatt's progressive coalition supported the Palestinian cause, seeing the Palestinians as allies in their struggle against nonprogressive factions who dominated the government and the Lebanese Forces (Maronite militias). The latter were opposed to the PLO presence and wanted to drive the Palestinians out by force.

During the 1970s and 1980s Fatah and the other various groups that comprised the PLO often came into conflict over the proper means of achieving the organization's goals. Fatah agreed on a policy of noninterference in host countries, but other groups like the PFLP did not always accept this. Likewise, the leadership of the PLO, including Arafat, had in the past recognized the need for armed struggle, but now believed that diplomacy and compromise

were also key to gaining international support. It seemed, however, apparent that the Arab countries could not defeat Israel militarily.

The commercial airliner hijackings carried out by radical Palestinian groups in the late 1960s and early 1970s in Europe and the Middle East were detrimental to PLO operations. Arafat himself condemned overseas attacks because he believed that they hurt the PLO's international image. When the radical BSO killed several Israeli athletes at the Olympic Games in Munich in 1972, Arafat promptly stated that the PLO was not responsible for the attacks. Arafat closed down the BSO in 1973, and in 1974 he ordered the PLO to restrict its violent attacks to Israel, the Gaza Strip, and the West Bank.

In 1974 the Arab Summit recognized the PLO as the sole representative of the Palestinian people. Arafat then appeared before the United Nations (UN) that same year as the official representative of the Palestinians. Speaking before the UN General Assembly, he condemned Zionism and said that the PLO would continue to operate as freedom fighters but also said that he wanted peace. This was the first time the international community had heard directly from the PLO, and many international observers praised Arafat and came to support the Palestinian cause. The UN granted the PLO observer status on November 22, 1974.

Also in 1974, the leaders of Fatah created a plan, known as the Ten-Point Program, that set forth the PLO's goals. This program called for a secular state in Israel and Palestine that would welcome both Jews and Arabs and provide all citizens equal rights regardless of religion, race, or gender. It also called for the creation of a Palestinian National Authority (PNA) on free Palestinian territory. Israel rejected the Ten-Point Program. Meanwhile, the radical guerrilla groups PFLP and PFLP-GC, which had earlier split from the PFLP, departed from the PLO in protest of its attempt to negotiate with Israel.

In 1975 the Lebanese Civil War broke out. Israel pursued a strategy of supporting the Lebanese Forces, the Maronite militia that opposed the Palestinians. The PLO and Fatah joined forces with the National Front, a more left-wing coalition of Muslims, Druze, and Christians. On January 12, 1976, the UN Security Council voted to grant the PLO the right to participate in Security Council debates. The PLO became a full member of the Arab League that same year.

During the late 1970s, members of the Palestinian Resistance continued to operate from Lebanon and engaged in attacks on Israel, which in turn attacked them in southern Lebanon. On July 24, 1981, the PLO and Israel agreed to a cease-fire within Lebanon and on the border between Lebanon and Israel. The Israelis violated the cease-fire numerous times, bombing PLO targets in Beirut. That autumn, Israeli prime minister Menachem Begin and defense minister Ariel Sharon planned an invasion into Lebanon to occupy southern Lebanon and territory all the way up to Beirut, where it planned to destroy the PLO. Israeli troops invaded, occupied much of southern Lebanon, and rounded up much of the male population of the area. The UN passed one resolution demanding that Israel withdraw its troops, but the United States

Palestine Liberation Organization (PLO) leader Yasser Arafat talks with his supporters in Beirut, Lebanon, on July 10, 1982, following a night of fighting between the PLO and Israeli troops. (AP/Wide World Photos)

vetoed another resolution repeating this demand. The United States demanded that the PLO withdraw from Lebanon. Sharon ordered the bombing of West Beirut beginning on June 15. The UN once again demanded that Israel withdraw, but the United States again vetoed the resolution.

On August 12, 1982, the two sides agreed to another cease-fire in which both the PLO and Israel would leave Lebanon. As a result, about 15,000 Palestinian militants left Lebanon by September 1. The Israelis, however, claimed that PLO members were still hiding in Beirut and returned to the city on September 16, killing several hundred Palestinians, none of whom were known to be PLO members. Sharon resigned as defense minister after the Sabra and Shatila massacres, which were carried out by Lebanese Christian militias with Israeli foreknowledge and approval.

Arafat and many surviving PLO members had always regarded Lebanon as a vulnerable location, and the organization was not destroyed by its forced removal because other operations continued outside that country. Arafat spent most of the 1980s in Tunisia. During this time, Iraq and Saudi Arabia donated substantial sums of money to the organization. But the Israeli government was determined to resist negotiations with the PLO, which also operated within the West Bank and Gaza. The Israel Defense Forces (IDF) bombed the PLO headquarters in Tunis in 1985, an attack that killed 73 people.

In December 1987 the First Intifada broke out spontaneously in the West Bank and Gaza, surprising Israelis with its intensity. On November 15, 1988, the PLO officially declared the formation of the State of Palestine. The PLO claimed all of Palestine as defined by the former British Mandate. However, the PLO had decided to seek a two-state solution. That December Arafat spoke before the UN, promising to end terrorism and to recognize Israel in exchange for the Israeli withdrawal from the occupied territories, according to UN Security Council Resolution 242. This was a distinct change from the PLO's previous position of insisting on the destruction of Israel. The PNC symbolically elected Arafat president of the new Palestinian state on April 2, 1989.

Arafat and the Israelis began conducting peace negotiations at the Madrid Conference in 1991. Although the talks were temporarily set back when Arafat and the PLO supported Iraq in the 1991 Persian Gulf War, over the next two years the two parties held a number of secret discussions. These negotiations led to the 1993 Oslo Accords, in which Israel agreed to Palestinian self-rule in the Gaza Strip and the West Bank, and Arafat officially recognized the existence of the State of Israel. Despite the condemnation of many Palestinian nationalists, the peace process appeared to be progressing apace. Israeli troops withdrew from the Gaza Strip and Jericho in May 1994.

In 1994 the PLO established the Negotiations Affairs Department (NAD) in Gaza to implement the Interim Agreement.

Mahmoud Abbas, then secretary-general of the PLO Executive Committee, headed the NAD until April 2003, when the Palestinian Legislative Council chose him as the first prime minister of the PNA. He was quickly replaced by Saeb Erakat. The Gaza office of NAD handled Israeli affairs, agreements between Israel and Palestine, colonization, and refugees. It also kept careful track of Israeli expansion into Palestinian territory. The NAD also opened an office in Ramallah to handle the implementation of the Interim Agreement and prepare the Palestinian position for negotiations toward permanent status. The government of the United Kingdom began assisting the NAD with its preparation for permanent status talks in 1998.

In 1996 the PNC agreed to remove from the PLO charter all language calling for armed violence aimed at destroying Israel, and Arafat sent U.S. president Bill Clinton a letter listing language to be removed. The organization announced that it was waiting for the establishment of the Palestinian state, when it would replace the charter with a constitution.

Arafat was elected leader of the new PNA in January 1996. The peace process began unraveling later that year, however, after rightist hard-liner Benjamin Netanyahu was elected prime minister of Israel. Netanyahu distrusted Arafat and condemned the PLO as a terrorist organization responsible for numerous suicide bombings on Israeli citizens. The accord collapsed completely in 2000 after Arafat and Israeli prime minister Ehud Barak failed to come to an agreement at a Camp David meeting facilitated by Clinton. After that, the Second (al-Aqsa) Intifada began when Palestinians, already experiencing the intractability of the Israeli government, saw Ariel Sharon lead security forces onto the Haram al-Sharif. During that period, suicide bombings increased. These attacks were in some instances claimed by Islamic Jihad of Palestine (PIJ), Hamas sympathizers, and other groups. Arafat and the PLO disavowed any support for such attacks. But whether right or wrong, the Israeli media continued to state or suggest that Arafat clandestinely supported the work of the terrorists.

Arafat died on November 11, 2004. There was much dissension over the succession, but Abbas eventually came to head the PLO's largest faction, Fatah. In December 2004 he called for an end to the violence associated with the Second Intifada that had begun in September 2000. In January 2005 he was elected president of the PNA, but Abbas has struggled to keep the PLO together and Fatah from losing its political and financial clout. In the January 2006 PNA parliamentary elections, Abbas and Fatah were dealt a serious blow when Hamas captured a significant majority of seats. The Israelis adamantly refused to recognize the Hamas government, declaring it an unfit "partner to peace," just as they had previously described Arafat himself. Israel refused to allow PNA funds to be transferred into the territories and cut off vital services as well as shipments of goods. The United States and its European allies also cut off funding to the PNA.

An even greater blow came in June 2007, when Hamas forcibly took control of Gaza. Abbas denounced Hamas and secured the restoration of funding to the Fatah-dominated section of the PNA. The Gazan Palestinians were left without salaries, food, gasoline, medicine, and services. The United States proposed that Israel commence negotiations with Abbas, who, however, did not completely control his part of the Palestinian National Authority (PNA).

The PNA found itself caught in an intractable predicament when Israel launched a major military operation against Hamas in Gaza beginning in December 2008. Although the PLO condemned the Israeli military action, it was forced to remain a bystander in a conflict that killed more than 1,100 Palestinians and inflicted some $2 billion in damage.

AMY HACKNEY BLACKWELL AND SHERIFA ZUHUR

**See also**

Abbas, Mahmoud; Arafat, Yasser; Fatah; Hamas; Israel; Jordan; Lebanon; Lebanon, Civil War in; Lebanon, Israeli Invasion of; Terrorism

**References**

Abbas, Mahmud. *Through Secret Channels: The Road to Oslo: Senior PLO Leader Abu Mazen's Revealing Story of the Negotiations with Israel.* Reading, UK: Garnet, 1997.

Aburish, Said K. *Arafat: From Defender to Dictator.* New York: Bloomsbury, 1998.

Cobban, Helena. *The Palestinian Liberation Organization.* Cambridge: Cambridge University Press, 1984.

Gabriel, Richard. *Operation Peace for Galilee: The Israeli-PLO War in Lebanon.* New York: Farrar, Straus and Giroux, 1985.

Hart, Alan. *Arafat: A Political Biography.* Rev. ed. London: Sidgwick and Jackson, 1994.

Kushner, Arlene. *Disclosed: Inside the Palestinian Authority and the PLO.* Philadelphia: Pavilion, 2004.

Livingstone, Neil C., and David Haley. *Inside the PLO.* New York: William Morrow, 1990.

Rubin, Barry. *Revolution until Victory? The Politics and History of the PLO.* Cambridge: Harvard University Press, 1996.

# Pan-Arabism and Pan-Arabist Thought

Philosophical and political movements based on the need to reinvest pride in Arab identity after centuries of dominance by the Ottoman Empire. Beyond this basic "Arabism" were versions of Arab nationalism that called for the solidarity of Arab peoples and movements for Arab unity, implying a political union of Arab governments. Pan-Turkism had arisen at the end of the 19th century and early 20th century, and the revival of Arab identity came in response to it. Other responses to Western encroachments were Pan-Islamist in orientation. Arab nationalism, sometimes with a Pan-Arab program, contrasted with such movements in calling for the appropriate response of Arab nations against increased Western imperial expansion. Pan-Arabism ultimately developed into such political doctrines in the region as Baathism, Nasserism, and more generally, Arab nationalism. The application of these doctrines was to have far-reaching consequences for power relations in the Middle East and beyond.

In the second half of the 19th century, a variety of Middle Eastern intellectuals began to theorize about the future of the Islamic world in relation to the increasingly powerful imperial nations of Europe. One influential movement was that of Pan-Islamism. Led by Jamal ad-Din al-Afghani, early Pan-Islamists were fiercely anti-imperialist and framed their desires for parity with the West along religious lines. Afghani did not believe that the West was superior to the Muslim East. Rather, he believed that over time Middle Eastern governments and religion had become corrupt and lost touch with the true message of Islam.

For Afghani, there were two major Islamic tenets that needed to be revised in order for the Muslim world to become as powerful as the West: unity and action. Unity of the Muslim world was crucial in the eyes of Afghani. He looked back to the early Muslim kingdoms and the success of early Islam as something that could be achieved anew in the Middle East. Muslims need only unify behind a progressive Islam, which would encourage its followers throughout the world to forget their ethnic and national differences and see themselves as part of one supernation of believers. In doing so, Muslims would actively unite against European expansionism and economic exploitation.

One of Afghani's most influential students was Muhammad Abduh, a well-respected theologian who ultimately became the mufti of Egypt in 1899. Abduh formulated one of the most influential modern interpretations of Islam in a book titled *Risalah al-Tawhid* (A Treatise on the Oneness of God), published in 1897. It asserted not only that Islam and modernity were compatible but also that modernity complemented Islam rather than restricted it. Abduh founded the Salafiyya movement, which called for the reintroduction into Sunni Islam of a legal principle of Islamic law allowing for more reinterpretation (*ijtihad*). As Pan-Islamists, both Afghani (who was not an Arab) and Abduh were concerned about Islamic affairs more than Arab affairs; however Abduh was also involved in an Egyptian uprising against the British. Punished for his views, he took up the reform of al-Azhar University, which has also fostered Pan-Islamism.

Abd al-Rahman al-Kawakibi (1849–1903), a journalist from Aleppo, was of Kurdish descent. He spent the last three years of his life in Cairo and published two key books in which he voices disgust toward the corruption of the Ottoman Empire, which ruled large segments of the Arab world. He blamed the decline of Muslim rule on the fact that non-Arabs had taken control of the Middle East. He looked at Islam as the greatest achievement of the Arabs, and because God had chosen to reveal Islamic teachings to an Arab prophet in Arabic, the Arabs were an ideal people for leadership. He wanted to see the restoration of an Arab caliphate, which, he believed, would hasten a revival in the region as well as in the religion. Kawakibi's ideology gave some Arabs a framework for opposing the Ottomans, which eventually took on nationalist tones.

Arab nationalism also evolved from Syrian nationalism and a movement of revival for the Arabic language called the *nahda*, or renaissance. Many of these Arab nationalists were Christians, including Jurji Zaydan, who wrote histories and novels; Ibrahim al-Yaziji, who established a secret society in 1875 that focused on Arab pride and rejected the Ottoman claim to the caliphate; and Najib Azury, who founded the Ligue de la Patrie Arabe (League of the Arab Fatherland) in 1903 in Cairo and wrote *The Awakening of the Arab Nation* in 1905. By 1913 other secret nationalist societies had formed and survived rounds of suppression from the Ottoman government.

As the Ottoman Empire collapsed at the end of World War I, and Britain and France secured control over much of the Middle East, other Arab intellectuals challenged European expansionism. It is in the ideas of these thinkers that the foundations of Pan-Arabism were laid.

One of the most noted individuals who focused his efforts on Arab nationalism was a Syrian Arab named Sati al-Husri, who had become known during the Ottoman era as a bureaucrat committed to educational reform. After the collapse of Ottoman rule in 1918, Husri introduced Arabist or Arab nationalist values into the Iraqi educational curriculum in the interwar years, when he headed the Ministry of Education in King Faisal I's Iraqi government. In the 1920s and 1930s, Husri wrote a series of pamphlets—*Arabism First, On Arab Nationalism,* and *What Is Nationalism?*—in which he calls for the creation of a single, united, and independent Arab state. He believed that the Arab people constituted one nation and that the Arabic language was the primary marker of that fact, as all who spoke Arabic shared other cultural attributes. Because the Arabic-speakers existed before Islam, both Muslim and Christian Arabs should be united under this nation. Husri hoped that the common language, shared culture, and shared history would inspire Arabs to found a modern nation-state and successfully combat the external, Western forces then dominating the region.

Another pair of influential thinkers who helped to establish the Baath Party along with Zaki al-Arsuzi and others were the Syrian intellectuals Michel Aflaq and Salah al-Din al-Bitar. Both had studied at the Sorbonne in Paris in the 1930s. Like many of their era, they were attracted to socialist ideology, particularly its anti-imperialism and messages of social justice. They called their new movement the Baath (Arabic for "resurrection"). Its principles were socialism, unity, and freedom. They expressed an Arab nationalist agenda in the context of social restructuring to build a powerful and independent Arab society. In part, their movement was a reaction to the pro-French attitudes of other elites, and the identification with a past Phoenician identity by some Lebanese at the time. Members of the Baath movement believed that the Arabs could regain their confidence only with unity. That unity would hearken back to Arab greatness under the conquering caliphs of early Islam and would put the Arab world on par with the West. In that way, Aflaq and Bitar were influenced by Kawakibi. Indeed, the Baath movement, although a secular philosophy inclusive of Muslims and Christians, idealized Islam as a cultural system and a symbol of what the Arab world was capable of producing. The Baaths' inclusive rhetoric also appealed to non-Muslim Arabs who wished to see their nation resurrected as well. The ideology of the Baath movement was coupled with two other powerful political developments in the Arab world: the dispossession of the Palestinians from their homeland and the emergence of Nasserism in Egypt during the rule of President Gamal Abdel Nasser.

Many Pan-Arab thinkers called on Egypt to take the lead in promoting the Arabist cause, and such ideas took hold during the 1930s and 1940s. In 1945 the Arab League was formed in Cairo, in the hopes of forging greater cooperation between Arab nations in the postwar period. The league was a coalition of Egypt, Syria, Lebanon, Iraq, and Transjordan (later Jordan). The leaders of these states pledged to support one another in building economic, political, and cultural strength and cooperation.

In May 1948, during the Israeli War of Independence, the member nations of the Arab League invaded Palestine to halt the formation of the State of Israel, but they were defeated by the Israelis in December. The defeat of Arab armies was a turning point for the Arab nationalist movement. The loss of Palestine to the Israelis was made more bitter by the humiliating crisis of the Palestinian refugees, who had fled and for several years lived only on Palestinian and Arab aid until the refugee camps were organized. For Arabs throughout the world, the shared rhetoric and considerable efforts taken to restore the Palestinians to their homeland and defeat the Israeli state became a powerful tool of political unification.

Nasser ultimately became the most well-known spokesperson for Arab nationalism. During his period in power (1952–1970), he promoted Arab unity and pride in the Arab nation to rally Egyptian resistance to the Western powers and Israel in the 1956 Suez War, and to oppose what he regarded as British and U.S. plans to divide the region. He convinced Jordan and Syria not to join the British-sponsored Baghdad Pact of 1954, and in 1956 he successfully faced off against the Western powers and nationalized the Suez Canal. Nasser, a brilliant orator, proclaimed the Arab nation to be one nation, and that "the Arab people are one people," in a speech following the failure of the British, French, and Israelis in the Suez Crisis to force a popular coup against his government. Later, he defined Egypt's embrace of Arabism to be a progressive and populist cause, in contrast to the Arabism espoused by traditional monarchies, such as Saudi Arabia.

Egyptian president Gamal Abdel Nasser acknowledges the acclaim of his supporters as he drives through Port Said, Egypt, on his way to the Navy House, where he will hoist the Egyptian flag, June 18, 1956. (AP/Wide World Photos)

As the propaganda war grew between Egypt and Saudi Arabia, because of their conflict in Yemen and efforts to be the dominant influence in the region, Nasser utilized the Voice of Cairo, a powerful radio network broadcast throughout the Arab world and beyond, to spread the doctrines of Arab unity and Arab socialism.

In late 1957 Syrian politicians turned to Nasser and asked him to join a union of the two countries, since they were at that time under threat by a rival faction. In February 1958 the United Arab Republic (UAR), the political unification of Syria and Egypt, was founded. Baath leaders believed that the union would assure their control over Syria, while the Egyptians saw the move as the first of several possible unions. Millions of Arabs saw the unification of Syria and Egypt as a dream combination; they ardently hoped that the UAR was the beginning of a new Arab superstate that could challenge Western hegemony.

It was not to be. It soon became clear that resentment existed among the Syrian bourgeoisie, who could justifiably claim that the administrative arrangements based on Egypt's demographic preponderance did not grant Syria an equal voice. Some of the Egyptian bureaucrats and officials who went to Syria were highly unpopular there. The unification also demonstrated that stated resistance to the programs of land reform and industrialization in Syria were politically destabilizing. The UAR was not a well thought-out formation but rather a hasty attempt by the Syrian opposition to capitalize on Nasser's power in a way that he could not refuse. In September 1961 Syrian military units staged an insurrection against the Egyptian commanders, and the UAR came to an end. Nasser accepted this defeat, but his subsequent statements were bitter and dwelt on the issues of class struggle that led to the union's failure, thus contributing to the discourse on Arab socialism at that time.

The failure of the UAR was followed by a lengthy Egyptian military involvement in Yemen and then in 1967 by the humiliating defeat of Egypt, Syria, and Jordan by the Israelis in the Six-Day War. The war brought great territorial losses for the Arab side and dramatic increases in the number of Palestinian refugees. For the Arab world, it appeared that Arab unity was now more necessary than ever. Yet the governments of the Arab nations were further divided by the 1967 defeat. Moreover, with the 1967 defeat it was clear to Palestinians that their cause could not be left in the hands of the Arab states. Although the Palestinian cause remained a symbol for Arab unity, real action for change was moved away from the Arab League and concentrated in the Palestine Liberation Organization (PLO) and other Palestinian movements.

In the 1970s and 1980s, Arab leaders employed the rhetoric of Arab nationalism or Baathism to rally their populations behind a number of issues, particularly the struggle against Israel. Saddam Hussein of Iraq, in particular, used the Arab cause as a rationale for his policies. But in 1990 an event occurred that spelled increasing factionalism in the Arab world. When Iraq invaded Kuwait in August 1990, the Western powers, led by the United States working through the United Nations (UN), convinced a number of other Arab nations to join their alliance against Iraq. Egypt and Syria committed troops to the Persian Gulf War in exchange for debt cancellation and other economic rewards, while Saudi Arabia agreed to host coalition forces. The punishing defeat of Iraq in February 1991 dimmed hopes for a unified approach by Arab nations.

Today, a significant number of people, parties, and governments still employ Arab nationalism and Arab unity as the framework for their policies, even though a larger segment of the population is searching for other alternatives to political, social, and economic problems. Many have turned instead to Islamist or Muslim fundamentalist movements.

NANCY STOCKDALE AND SHERIFA ZUHUR

**See also**

Arab-Israeli Conflict, Overview; Arab League; Baath Party; DESERT STORM, Operation; Egypt; Hussein, Saddam; Iraq, History of, Pre-1990; Iraq, History of, 1990–Present; Nasser, Gamal Abdel; Palestine Liberation Organization; Syria; United Arab Republic

**References**

Hourani, Albert. *Arabic Thought in the Liberal Age, 1798–1939*. New York: Cambridge University Press, 1983.
Khalidi, Rashid, et al., eds. *The Origins of Arab Nationalism*. New York: Columbia University Press, 1993.
Tibi, Bassam. *Arab Nationalism: Between Islam and the Nation-State*. New York: St. Martin's, 1997.

# Paris Peace Conference
## Start Date: January 12, 1919
## End Date: January 20, 1920

Conference convened by the victorious Allies in Paris to negotiate peace terms with the Central Powers at the end of World War I. The main sessions of the Paris Peace Conference debated the terms of peace with Germany between January 19 and June 28, 1919. The conference climaxed in an elaborate signing ceremony of the Treaty of Versailles on June 28, 1919. Lower-level diplomats continued the conference, leading to subsequent treaties with Austria, Bulgaria, Hungary, and the Ottoman Empire. Although the conference opened with much high-minded idealism, it ended with many dashed hopes and great disillusionment.

The conference brought together official and unofficial representatives from around the world. Thirty-two countries were officially represented. Germany and the other defeated Central powers were not invited to the conference. Russia, then in the midst of civil war, was the most notable absentee among the victorious powers. Initially, the key players were the Big Ten: the chiefs of delegation and the foreign ministers from France, Britain, the United States, Italy, and Japan. Conference deliberations then were dominated by the Big Eight, which devolved into the delegation heads alone, or the Big Four of French premier Georges Clemenceau, British prime minister David Lloyd George, U.S. president Woodrow Wilson, and Italian premier Vittorio Orlando. Orlando's position was

Allied leaders at the Paris Peace Conference on May 27, 1919. Pictured (from left) are British prime minister David Lloyd George, Italian prime minister Vittorio Emanuele Orlando, French premier Georges Clemenceau, and U.S. president Woodrow Wilson. The Paris Peace Conference resulted in treaties that ended World War I and in the formation of the League of Nations. It also made major decisions regarding the Middle East. (National Archives)

by far the weakest, and on April 24 he and the Italian delegation left the negotiations after it became obvious that Italy would not receive the city of Fiume. The Big Four thus became the Big Three.

In many ways, Wilson was the key figure of the conference. His knowledge of Europe was scant. This was also the first time that a sitting U.S. president had traveled to Europe. As the conference got under way, Wilson had tremendous popular support in Europe, but both Lloyd George and Clemenceau viewed him as meddling, naive, and inexperienced in European affairs. Still, Wilson was crucial to the settlement because of the vital contributions of American troops and U.S. finances to the Allied victory and because of the leading role that the United States was expected to play in enforcing the peace settlement and in the postwar world.

All three of the key leaders largely ignored their own staffs and made most of the critical decisions themselves, turning the deliberations into a clash of personalities and wills. This concentration of decision making also rendered almost impossible the resolution of the immensely complicated conference issues. Complicating matters further, the three leaders mistrusted the advice provided by their military advisers and kept them as far from the deliberations

as possible. The absence of a military voice at the conference both deprived the politicians of critical advice on security matters and undermined the legitimacy of the peace process, especially among veterans and conservatives.

Rather than confining themselves to the question of Germany, the conferees attempted to remake the entire global security system. For this task they were immensely unqualified. Lurking in the shadows were many non-German issues, such as the secret French and British accord (the Sykes-Picot Agreement) to divide the former Middle Eastern territories of the Ottoman Empire and the conflict between China and Japan over the latter's claim to the Shandong (Shantung) Peninsula. Issues such as these widened the scope of the conference significantly.

The conferees and their staffs had to resolve more than the dislocations of the war. The issues that had caused the conflict long predated the 1914 assassination of Archduke Franz Ferdinand. The basis for any lasting peace would likewise have to confront three specters of modern European history. The first was unfulfilled nationalism, represented by the Concert of Europe system that had dominated European diplomacy from 1815 to 1870. This haunted Wilson most of all. He believed that the Concert system had prevented the peoples of Europe from realizing their nationalist sentiments and had led directly to the outbreak of World War I. He argued that the postwar settlement must therefore address the question of unfulfilled national ambitions. Yet Wilson's goal of national self-determination, even restricted as it was to Europe, faced insurmountable problems. National lines were too blurred to permit the establishment of clear-cut borders. Drawing a tidy border between Russia and the new state of Poland, for example, proved impossible. The settlement was therefore bound to disappoint millions no matter what the conferees decided.

The second specter, that of the failed revolutions of 1848, haunted all the Big Three, most especially Lloyd George. Made tangible by the triumph of Bolshevism in Russia, political and social unrest threatened the postwar stability and economic growth of the Western powers. The new leaders of Russia preached international revolution, threatening to engulf Europe in war again. Attempted communist revolutions in Germany and Hungary made this all the more terrifying. The disappearance of the Austro-Hungarian Empire and the weakening of Germany left a political vacuum in Central Europe. With there thus being no obvious bulwark against Bolshevik expansion, the containment of Bolshevism came to occupy a larger role at the conference than had originally been foreseen.

The final specter, unfulfilled German militarism, particularly haunted Clemenceau. France had been invaded twice by the Germans in his lifetime, and he believed that World War I, which had brought the Germans tantalizingly close to victory, had only increased German acquisitiveness and antipathy toward France. Germany and Austria, he argued, might have been defeated, but they still had 75 million inhabitants compared to 45 million in France and Belgium. The war had been largely fought outside German borders, so Germany's industrial infrastructure remained largely intact. Thanks to the Bolshevik Revolution, Russia no longer served France as an Eastern ally and a counterweight to Germany. Thus, French leaders backed a strong Poland. Clemenceau was intent on using the conference to ensure that Germany could not pose a future threat to France.

The contradictions in the Allied aims created an untenable situation. Every solution posed a new problem: reducing Germany's army would lessen the menace of Prussian militarism but enhance the possibility of a Bolshevik revolution in Germany; separating the Rhineland from Germany would give France and Belgium security but ran the risk of creating an Alsace-Lorraine in reverse; giving Fiume to the Italians would reward them for their wartime sacrifices but it would also weaken the newly created state of Yugoslavia, whose Serbian leadership had also been a member of the alliance; and the creation of independent Arab states would fulfill British promises made during the war to Arab leaders but undermine Lloyd George's own desire for a greater British presence in the Middle East and promises made to Zionists in the Balfour Declaration.

Wilson's January 1918 pronouncement of the Fourteen Points further complicated matters by creating a pathway to peace that was at once unworkable and immensely popular. Several influential participants (and many Germans) quickly recognized the dilemma that the Fourteen Points created for the conference. If the conferees accepted them as the basis for negotiation, this would heighten the sharp points of disagreement among the victorious powers and enact measures antithetical to the interests of Britain and France. Such a peace would probably be more lenient than most French and British citizens found acceptable. If, on the other hand, the peace conference did not follow the spirit of the Fourteen Points, Germany could claim (as did leaders of the Weimar Republic) that it had been unfairly treated.

Despite their tremendous popular appeal, the Fourteen Points did not guide the conference as the U.S. president had anticipated and as the people of the Middle East had hoped. Although the people of Europe may have initially welcomed Wilson and his vision of the postwar world, desires for security soon overrode appeals to idealism. The November 1918 British elections, the first in eight years, returned a majority dedicated to a punitive treatment of Germany.

A similar situation existed in France, where bitter anger over Germany's invasion, wartime atrocities, and scorched-earth policies prevailed. All French parties except the socialists, who were divided on the issue, supported either outright annexation of the Rhineland or its separation from Germany. Clemenceau, for his part, had little sympathy for Wilsonian idealism.

Although many Europeans continued to cling to the idealism that the Fourteen Points represented, resentment toward Germany dominated. Germany's imposition of harsh terms on Russia at Brest Litovsk just two months after the announcement of the Fourteen Points seemed, even to Wilson, to demonstrate that Germany had no right to demand or expect leniency.

Unlike their counterparts at the Congress of Vienna a century earlier, the negotiators at Paris were all responsible to electorates. The conferees therefore worked largely behind closed doors but under tremendous scrutiny from the media and their own constituencies. The back-room bargaining that characterized so much of the conference violated Wilson's first point that "diplomacy shall always proceed frankly and in the public view." The Big Three failed to appreciate fully that a people's war could not be followed by a cabinet peace.

Lloyd George and Clemenceau found themselves in the awkward position of speaking favorably about the Fourteen Points in public while undermining many of Wilson's principles behind closed doors. This contradiction helped to discredit the final settlement in the eyes of those European voters who expected a peace based on the Fourteen Points.

Aware that the conference could not please all parties, the conferees agreed on the necessity of implementing Wilson's idea for the League of Nations. Wilson hoped that it would resolve problems emerging from the dissatisfactions, contradictions, and unanticipated problems of any treaty the conference produced. Clemenceau viewed the proposed League of Nations as a threat to the peace because it would cause people in the democracies to believe that it would actually resolve major disputes and would thus wean the Western democracies away from military preparedness.

Because of these contradictions, the most important product of the Paris Peace Conference, the Treaty of Versailles with Germany, embodied a series of uncomfortable and untenable compromises that gave all victorious parties only part of what they wanted and thus inevitably also left all parties frustrated. Worse, it did not significantly diminish German power, permitting a German nationalist resurgence a generation later. The other treaties were also inadequate. The settlements were compromises, their continued survival having been heavily dependent on wise, careful, and farsighted postwar diplomacy, which was not forthcoming.

All parties were frustrated by the peace conference's many compromises. Liberals and the Left found the conference's outcome particularly disillusioning, and in their disappointment many turned on Wilson as a failed messiah. In many ways, the conference created fertile ground for a far more deadly global conflagration less than a generation later.

MICHAEL NEIBERG

**See also**

Balfour Declaration; Ottoman Empire; Sèvres, Treaty of; Sykes-Picot Agreement; World War I, Impact of

**References**

Henning, Ruth. *Versailles and After*. London: Routledge, 1984.

Howard, Michael. *The Invention of Peace*. New Haven, CT: Yale University Press, 2001.

MacMillan, Margaret. *Paris, 1919: Six Months That Changed the World*. New York: Random House, 2002.

Mayer, Arno. *Politics and Diplomacy of Peacemaking: Containment and Counter-Revolution at Versailles*. New York: Knopf, 1967.

Watt, Richard. *The Kings Depart*. New York: Simon and Schuster, 1968.

# Pasha

A nonhereditary official title conferred upon wealthy landowners, government administrators, and senior military officers in the Ottoman Empire (1299–1918). Pashas (pasas) formed an important part of the Iraqi administrative structure under King Faisal I after 1921. Today, the term "pasha" is a social term of respect or endearment and is no longer applied to a group or class of individuals, but the lineal heirs of the pashas, those not forced out by political changes, remain an integral part of Iraqi society.

Three Ottoman provinces—Mosul, Baghdad, and Basra—constituted the territory that later became Iraq. Because of the many political, legal, religious, and ethnic disputes among the various tribes in the provinces, the sultans in Constantinople sought leaders who could effectively subdue all threats to Ottoman rule. Such leaders were the appointed pashas, who governed by a tribute system of taxation that separated the wealthy urban families from the agrarian tribes. The governing system also pitted competing tribes against each other.

In 1858 Constantinople implemented a new land law. The law increased the power of the Baghdad government and weakened the autonomy of tribal sheikhs by sending them to Constantinople for education. Graduates were offered titles to land, the only source of wealth available to them. Through this method, some sheikhs became pashas and adopted Ottoman social, political, and economic positions as their own. The followers of these sheikhs, many of whom were well-armed, did the same.

Significant reforms in the Ottoman Army also occurred in the second half of the 19th century. Arab subjects were allowed to attend military schools and academies to become commissioned officers. The army became their profession, and some would become pashas with the Ottoman VI Corps and the Ottoman Sixteenth Army in Iraq.

The origins of the Iraqi Army date to 1869, when Ottoman governor Ahmed Midhat Pasha established a military school in Baghdad, providing three years of military instruction to middle-school children. In 1914 two more military schools were opened in Baghdad and one in Sulamaniyah. Middle-school graduates entered the military high school in Baghdad, and the most promising graduates from that school entered the Ottoman Military Academy in Constantinople, which admitted 60–70 Arabs each year. Graduates were commissioned lieutenants in the Ottoman Army, and as such they were afforded opportunities for social and political advancement unavailable to other Arabs.

Many Iraqi officers in the Ottoman Army participated in the Arab Revolt (1916–1918), which had resulted from British promises that an Arab homeland would be created. They fought under Faisal, the sharif of Mecca and later the king of Iraq. They were known as Sharifian officers and formed the core of officers loyal to Faisal. They created a security force that maintained internal order and suppressed any objections to Faisal's rule. To expand this group of loyal officers, military training slots were allocated for sons of tribal chieftains as a means of guaranteeing their loyalty. This was a direct continuance of Ottoman military training policies. It also allowed King Faisal to counter officers less loyal to him.

When the Ottoman Empire fell in the aftermath of World War I, the Sharifians came along with Faisal to Iraq. As they had no local basis of power, the Sharifians sought to expand their status. Just as the tribes had consolidated and expanded their status on behalf of the sultans, King Faisal's Sharifian officers sought to do the same. Soon, the interests of the Sharifians and the sheikhs conjoined in parliament.

Sharifian officers wanted the Iraqi government to adopt conscription, for they had learned how valuable a tool it could be from their European-focused Ottoman military training. They also knew that it would dilute the loyalties of individual tribesmen, who were far better armed than the Iraqi Army. And an Iraqi military education would provide the same opportunities for social and political advancement as an Ottoman military education had done for the

Sharifians and some of the pashas. This new cadre would form a social class whose service was to the nation, not to a tribe. What evolved under the monarchy was an officer corps dominated by a limited number of perhaps 20 to 30 families, primarily Sunni. Most of the Iraqi military leadership in this period came from these families: Askari, Ayubi, Bajaje, Daftari, Gaylani, Hashimi, Jaderji, Saddoun, Sahrurdi, Said, Shabandar, and Suvveidi. These historically military families had originally been the product of Ottoman military training. They later intermarried and promoted their interests within the Iraqi armed forces. In 1958, however, these individuals were eclipsed by the Baathist military officers who came to power in 1958 and ousted King Faisal II. Some of these individuals were murdered by Iraqi dictator Saddam Hussein, who accused them of being elitists; others died in the wars against Iran, Kuwait, and the United States. But their descendants continue to protect their interests in Iraq today.

DONALD R. DUNNE

**See also**

Faisal II, King of Iraq; Iraq, Army; Iraq, History of, Pre-1990; Iraq, History of, 1990–Present; Midhat Pasha, Ahmad; Ottoman Empire

**References**

Batatu, Hanna. *The Old Social Classes and the Revolutionary Movement of Iraq: A Study of Iraq's Old Landed and Commercial Classes and of Its Communists, Ba'athists, and Free Officers.* Princeton, NJ: Princeton University Press, 1978.

Cetinsaya, Gokhan. *Ottoman Administration of Iraq, 1890–1908.* New York: Routledge, 2006.

Eppel, Michael. "The Elite, the Effendiyya, and the Growth of Nationalism and Pan-Arabism in Hashemite Iraq, 1921–1958." *International Journal of Middle East Studies* 30(2) (1998): 227–250.

Pool, David. "From Elite to Class: The Transformation of Iraqi Leadership, 1920–1939." *International Journal of Middle East Studies* 12(3) (1980): 331–350.

# Patriot Act

Legislation passed by the U.S. Congress and signed into law by President George W. Bush on October 26, 2001. It was prompted by the September 11, 2001, terrorist attacks on the United States. The Patriot Act greatly expanded U.S. government intelligence and law enforcement powers, thereby intended to boost the government's ability to combat terrorism. The legislation was renewed on March 9, 2006. Critics of the Patriot Act assert that it threatens and violates civil liberties. Supporters of the bill insist that it is vital to protecting America from terrorism.

The Patriot Act of 2001 amended federal criminal, banking, money-laundering, and immigration laws. For example, it authorizes roving wiretap authorization of a suspect rather than of a particular communication device. Two sections of the law amend immigration laws dealing with excludable aliens from entering the United States and allow the government to deport or detain aliens for associating with terrorists. Section 802 of the act created the

new category of the crime of domestic terrorism, while Sections 803 and 805, respectively, punish people who either harbor or provide material support for or conspire with terrorists and terrorist organizations.

Most of the criticism of the Patriot Act has been directed at Section 2 of the law. For example, by authorizing so-called sneak-and-peak warrants without having to immediately notify the suspect that their home or property has been searched, the act is said to violate the Fourth Amendment to the U.S. Constitution, which prohibits illegal search and seizure without probable cause. According to the Department of Justice, however, such warrants have been used for decades against organized crime and drug dealers, and the U.S. Supreme Court has ruled that in some circumstances the Fourth Amendment to the Constitution does not require immediate notification that a search warrant has been conducted.

Section 215 allows the Federal Bureau of Investigation (FBI) to order any person or entity to turn over "any tangible things" for an authorized investigation to protect against international terrorism or clandestine intelligence activities. Besides allegedly violating the Fourth Amendment, this section is also said to violate freedom of speech, according to the America Civil Liberties Union (ACLU). It is in use now by the Transportation Security Administration (TSA) when passengers, American and non-American, are required to open password-protected computers and surrender them to authorities.

Defenders of the Patriot Act note that Section 215 can only be used with the approval of one of three high-ranking FBI officials to obtain foreign intelligence information "not concerning a United States person" or "to protect against international terrorism or clandestine intelligence activities." It prohibits investigations based solely on activities protected by the First Amendment and requires the FBI to notify Congress every year of all investigations it has conducted. In addition, those served with a 215 order can challenge its legality.

Critics of the Patriot Act also object to Section 218 because it expands the authority of a secret federal court, the Foreign Intelligence Surveillance Court (FISC), to approve searches and wiretaps if foreign intelligence is a "significant purpose" of the investigation. This is counter to the 1978 Foreign Intelligence Surveillance Act (FISA) standard of "primary purpose." The ACLU argues that Section 218 violates the Fourth Amendment because it extends the FBI's authority to spy on Americans for "intelligence purposes" without having to prove that a crime has been or will be committed. Because those targeted for surveillance under Section 218 are never notified that they are under investigation and cannot challenge the warrant because the proceedings of the FISC are secret, the ACLU warns that the potential for abuse of power is immense.

Under the FISA, foreign intelligence had to be the primary purpose of wiretaps and searches; the new standard of significant purpose is defended to overcome a wall that prohibited information sharing and cooperation between intelligence and criminal investigations. Because of this wall, in August 2001 the FBI refused

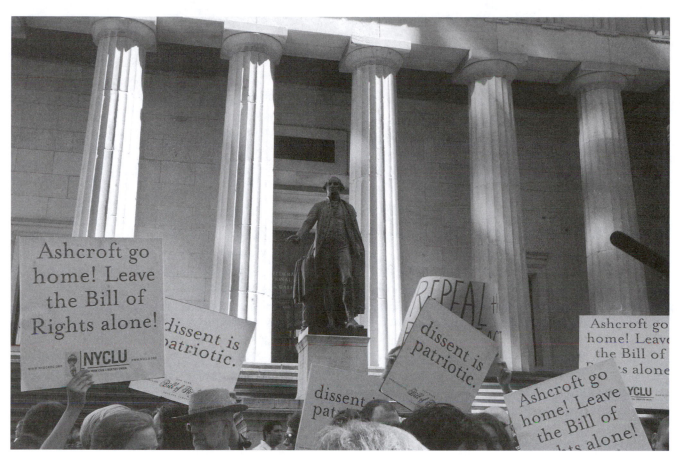

A statue of George Washington on the steps of Federal Hall looms over protesters holding up signs critical of the Patriot Act (2001) during a demonstration near the New York Stock Exchange in New York City on September 9, 2003. The protesters gathered within distant earshot of Attorney General John Ashcroft as he delivered a speech defending the legislation. (AP/Wide World Photos)

to allow criminal investigators to assist an intelligence investigation to locate two terrorists—Khalid al-Mihdhar and Nawaf al-Hazmi—who a month later piloted the plane into the Pentagon on September 11.

For all the claims of alleged abuse and violations to civil liberties by the Patriot Act, *USA Today* reported on March 1, 2006, that according to the chairman of the House Judiciary Committee (and sponsor of the Patriot Act), Representative James Sensenbrenner Jr. (R-Wis.), Congress had found no violations of civil liberties. Yet the ACLU points out that on January 23, 2004, a U.S. federal judge ruled Section 805 of the Patriot Act—which prohibits providing "expert advice or assistance" to designated international terrorist organizations—unconstitutional because it is vague. And on April 9, 2004, another federal judge ruled that Section 505, which allows the FBI to issue a "National Security Letter" demanding information about customers and subscribers from email and Internet service providers without any court review or approval, was also unconstitutional.

On December 16, 2005, the *New York Times* revealed that following the September 11 attacks, President Bush authorized the National Security Agency (NSA) to eavesdrop on international phone calls without a warrant, sparking a heated legal controversy. Bush maintained that his position as commander in chief

gave him the authority to protect the U.S. from terrorist threats and that on September 18, 2001, Congress recognized this when it authorized the president to use all necessary means to apprehend terrorists. By not seeking a warrant from the FISC, however, the ACLU maintains that this program is illegal and violates both the Fourth Amendment and the 1978 FISA. The Department of Justice, however, notes that the NSA program is "narrowly focused, aimed only at international calls targeted at Al Qaeda and related groups, and only applies to communications where one party is outside the U.S."

Furthermore, leaders from both parties along with the leaders of the House and Senate Intelligence Committees were briefed about the phone-tapping program a dozen or more times since 2001. Director of the Central Intelligence Agency (CIA) Michael Hayden stated on December 19, 2005, that this program "has been successful in detecting and preventing attacks inside the U.S." Nevertheless, the battle continues to rage over the extent and appropriateness of the Patriot Act, with many critics arguing that the law violates basic constitutional rights and has the potential to turn the nation into a secretive police state. Supporters, on the other hand, claim that the Patriot Act has made America safer and is a small price to pay to ensure that there is not another September 11.

STEFAN M. BROOKS

**References**
Bake, Stewart A. *Patriot Debates: Experts Debate the USA Patriot Act.* Chicago: American Bar Association, 2005.
Ball, Howard, and Mildred Vasan, eds. *The USA Patriot Act: A Reference Handbook.* Santa Barbara, CA: ABC-CLIO, 2004.
Gerdes, Louise I., ed. *The Patriot Act: Opposing Viewpoints.* Farmington Hills, MI: Greenhaven, 2005.
Schulhofer, Stephen. *Rethinking the Patriot Act: Keeping America Safe and Free.* Washington, DC: Brookings Institution, 2005.

# Patriotic Union of Kurdistan

Kurdish nationalist party in northern Iraq founded and led by Jalal Talabani. The Patriotic Union of Kurdistan (PUK) split from the Kurdistan Democratic Party (KDP) during the early 1960s and existed as a coalition of several Kurdish political groups before it was officially founded in June 1975, following the collapse of the Kurdish revolt against the Iraqi government. Talabani is currently the president of Iraq, having assumed the office on April 7, 2005. The PUK's base of support is principally in southern Kurdistan (i.e., in Sulamaniyah), and since the 1980s it has courted rural Kurds to broaden its appeal. Most of its adherents speak the Sorani dialect and some belong to the Qadiri Sufi order.

Talabani broke with the KDP chiefly over his refusal to serve under Massoud Barzani, son of the founder of the KDP and current head of the party. Talabani tried to consolidate his control of the entire Kurdish movement by marginalizing Barzani. Over the next several decades, the PUK and KDP fought for control of the Kurdish nationalist movement. But they also fought for and against the Iraqi and Iranian governments. The Peshmerga also included other Kurdish nationalist groups, including the KDP.

Because of the KDP's increasing support from Iran, in 1979 Talabani made overtures to Iraqi president Saddam Hussein, indicating that the PUK would cease its antigovernment activity for certain concessions. Hussein, however, was unwilling to meet these, which included giving the PUK control of the Kirkuk oil fields, allowing Kurdish forces to provide local security, and the development of independent financial systems. During the 1980–1988 Iran-Iraq War, the PUK formed guerrilla units and established links with Iran to obtain financial and military support. During that war, Hussein tried to eradicate the Kurds in the 1986–1988 Anfal Campaign, which involved chemical attacks on Halabja and other Kurdish strongholds. Some 4,000 villages were destroyed and more than 100,000 Kurds were killed. This campaign caused the Kurds to change their strategy prior to Operation DESERT STORM (1991) by temporarily laying aside their differences and uniting in order to resist the Iraqi government.

In 1988, the KDP, PUK, as well as other Kurdish groups formed the Iraqi Kurdistan Front (IKF), combining forces to fight Hussein's government. Once the DESERT STORM air war began in January 1991, 50 percent of the Kurdish soldiers in the Iraqi Army deserted and many of them joined the Peshmerga. After Hussein's defeat in the Persian Gulf War, Kurds of all political stripes joined the IKF. Meanwhile, Barzani and Talabani jointly directed IKF attacks on Iraqi government forces in the immediate aftermath of the war. In so doing, they seized Kirkuk, took 75 percent of Kurdistan, and added more Iraqi deserters to their ranks, thereby obtaining large numbers of weapons. However, the Iraqi Republican Guards destroyed many Kurdish irregular units, stopping the Kurdish rebellion. By March 1991, as many as 1.5 million Kurds had become refugees.

On April 5, 1991, the United Nations (UN) passed Resolution 688, which allowed for the air-dropping of food and medicine to the Kurds. Operation PROVIDE COMFORT, an American humanitarian mission, also began in April. On April 10, 1991, the United States established the northern no-fly zone at the 36th Parallel, and on April 18 the UN created a Kurdish-controlled enclave in northern Iraq. Because there was no widespread political support for a long-term occupation in northern Iraq, the UN withdrew all forces on July 5, 1991.

After that, the KDP and PUK established a de facto autonomous polity by taking control of the former UN zone. In May 1992, the Kurds founded the Kurdistan Regional Government (KRG), which is composed of, among other groups, the KDP, PUK, and the Iraqi Communist Party. The Kurds held elections and established a joint legislative assembly with a cabinet. However, the KDP and PUK each tried to seize control of the autonomous region, and a civil war ensued. Amnesty International reported that in 1994 and 1995, both groups had committed scores of killings in their efforts to gain power.

In August 1996, 2,000 Iranian Revolutionary Guards Corps (IRGC) soldiers entered Iraq and attacked the KDP on behalf of the PUK. Barzani now turned to Hussein for help. Hussein dispatched a force of as many as 60,000 Republican Guards to the autonomous region and drove the PUK from Irbil. The KDP then pushed the remnants of the PUK to the Iranian border.

On February 5, 1999, President Clinton issued Presidential Decision Directive 99-13. It authorized U.S. military assistance through the Iraq Liberation Act (ILA; Public Law 105-338) to both the KDP and PUK. It came as no surprise when the PUK and KDP cooperated with the U.S.-led coalition that drove Hussein from power in 2003. Most recently, the Kurdistan Brigades, led by Dilshad Kalari (Dilshad Garmyani), have begun publicly calling for jihad against the KDP and PUK, because Talabani and Barzani are viewed as apostate politicians because of their cooperation with the Nuri al-Maliki administration.

Many Iraqi Kurds, however, believe that they may be better off building their region and do not support any immediate Kurdish separatism. The Kurds want control of the Kirkuk oil fields, as control over this resource is essential to northern economy. Also the Arabization of Kirkuk under the Baath government was bitterly opposed by the Kurds.

The PUK is expected to continue demanding progress on autonomy for its continued support for all the KRG initiatives. Therefore, the prospect of a truly unified administration within the KRG seems remote.

The PUK is organized into eight bureaus, each designed to administer to a particular need of the party and of Kurds more generally. They include the Bureau of Organization; Bureau of Information; Bureau for Culture and Democratic Organization; Bureau of Finance and Management; Bureau for Human Rights; Bureau for Social Affairs; Bureau for Martyrs and Veterans' Affairs; and the Bureau for International Relations. The party is divided into 36 branches, each with its own head and 2 deputies. Depending on the number of PUK members in each branch, the number of assistant deputies ranges from 4 to 8. There are also 2 party branches that include Peshmerga.

DONALD R. DUNNE

**See also**

Kurdistan Democratic Party; Kurds; Kurds, Massacres of; Peshmerga; PROVIDE COMFORT, Operation

**References**

Batatu, Hanna. *The Old Social Classes and the Revolutionary Movement of Iraq: A Study of Iraq's Old Landed and Commercial Classes and of Its Communists, Ba'athists, and Free Officers.* Princeton, NJ: Princeton University Press, 1978.

Bengio, Ofra. *Saddam's Word: Political Discourse in Iraq.* New York: Oxford University Press USA, 1998.

Marcus, Aliza. *Blood and Belief: The PKK and the Kurdish Fight for Independence.* New York: New York University Press, 2007.

Natali, Denise. *International Aid, Regional Politics, and the Kurdish Issue in Iraq after the Gulf War.* Abu Dhabi: Emirates Center for Strategic Studies and Research, 1999.

O'Leary, Brendan, John McGarry, and Khaled Smith. *The Future of Kurdistan in Iraq.* Philadelphia: University of Pennsylvania Press, 2005.

Stansfield, Gareth R. V. *Iraqi Kurdistan: Political Development and Emergent Democracy.* New York: Routledge, 2003.

# Patriot Missile System

Defensive antiaircraft and antiballistic missile system. The U.S. Patriot missile system was untested in combat until the 1991 Persian Gulf War, when it was used to shoot down Iraqi Al Hussein short-range theater ballistic missiles, locally built versions of the Soviet Scud missile. Iraq launched Scud missiles at Israel and Saudi Arabia after the start of the war in January 1991. The Patriot was developed at the Redstone Arsenal in Huntsville, Alabama, in the late 1970s as an antiaircraft weapon and was modified in the 1980s as an antitheater ballistic missile weapon. U.S. Patriot units based in Germany were also deployed to Israel during the 2003 Iraq War. During the summer 2006 Israel-Hezbollah War, three Israel Defense Forces (IDF) Patriot batteries were deployed around Haifa in August 2006 and tasked with intercepting various types of missiles launched at the area from Lebanon by Hezbollah.

The Patriot is a long-range, high-altitude, all-weather missile defense system designed to defeat aircraft, theater ballistic missiles, and cruise missiles. The Patriot's multifunction phased array radar and track-by-missile guidance systems can simultaneously detect and engage multiple targets, despite electronic countermeasures. The Patriot missile is a single-stage, solid-fuel, 7.4-foot-long, 2,200-pound projectile operating at Mach 3 speed with an effective range of 43 miles.

The missile is armed with a proximity-fused 200-pound high-explosive warhead designed to disable or destroy an inbound target by detonating and dispersing fragmentation in a fanlike pattern immediately ahead of the threat. The Patriot is deployed as a Patriot Fire Unit, having 32 missiles loaded (4 each) in 8 M-901 storage and transportation canister launchers. Each launcher is arrayed atop an M-860 semitrailer launch platform. The Patriot Fire Unit also includes a 5-ton M-818 tractor truck variant mounted with a MSQ-104 engagement-control station, which houses the fire-control, radar, and computer engagement systems.

The Patriot is a three-phase intercept system that uses its engagement-control radar to detect an inbound target. The engagement-control computer plots an intercept trajectory and programs the intercept data into the missile's guidance system, elevates and trains the launcher, and then fires the missile. The missile's onboard radar then guides the missile to the optimal intercept point.

The Patriot missile was first launched in combat on January 18, 1991, when it mistakenly fired at a computer glitch misinterpreted as a Scud fired at Saudi Arabia. The Patriot engaged more than 40 theater ballistic missiles during the Persian Gulf War, but its intercept rate was well below the 97 percent claimed by U.S. officials at the time. The U.S. Army eventually claimed a 70 percent effective intercept rate for the Saudi Arabian theater of operations and a 40 percent effective intercept rate in Israel. The IDF, however, estimated the effective intercept rate at 10 percent or less. This substantially lower estimate may have been a function of the IDF's definition of success and effectiveness that counted any ground warhead detonation as a failure regardless of whether the incoming missile had been hit, disabled, or deflected.

Because the Patriot missile systems in both theaters of operation were manned by U.S. Army crews, there was much speculation concerning the higher reported effective intercept rate in Saudi Arabia. One reason may have been that the Saudi government simply lied, because all Saudi press reports on Scud strikes were censored. The Israeli targets were heavily populated areas where any debris or detonation could be reported by the uncensored Israeli press. The Saudi targets, on the other hand, were primarily desert military installations far from Saudi population centers.

Regardless of the reasoning used to explain the theater effective intercept rate differential, the success rate for the Patriot was not what had been anticipated, especially in Israel. One reason may simply have been that Iraqi modifications to the Soviet-built Scud made to increase the range and speed of the Al Hussein variant structurally weakened the missile. Many of the Al Husseins broke up as they reentered Earth's atmosphere, and those multiple pieces stretched the target so that the Patriot engagement-control radar and onboard missile radar could not differentiate between general debris and the warhead.

The Patriot was originally designed to intercept and destroy or disable aircraft, but when it was modified to defend against theater ballistic missiles, the targeting protocols were not sufficiently modified to compensate for the faster speed of the missile or the detonation point at the target's center of mass. Thus, the Patriot tended to spray its fragmentation at the tail of the Al Hussein, leaving the warhead in the nose intact.

A software error that was subsequently corrected caused a one-third of a second drift in the system's internal clock that translated into a one-third of a mile error in the targeting trajectory. The more time the system remained in use before a shutdown reset the clock, the greater the error. On February 25, 1991, that error caused a Patriot to miss the inbound Scud that hit the billets of the U.S. Army's 14th Quartermaster Detachment in Dharan, Saudi Arabia, killing 28 American soldiers.

The Patriot continues to be used by the United States, the Netherlands, Germany, Japan, Israel, Saudi Arabia, Kuwait, Taiwan, and Greece. The IDF continues joint development with the United States of the Arrow 2 antimissile system that was also deployed by Israel in the 2006 Israel-Lebanon War.

RICHARD EDWARDS

**See also**

Dhahran, Scud Missile Attack on; Hezbollah; Iraq, Air Force; Iraq, Army; Saudi Arabia; Saudi Arabia, Armed Forces

**References**

Atkinson, Rick. *Crusade: The Untold Story of the Persian Gulf War.* New York: Mariner Books, 1994.

Clancy, Tom, and Chuck Horner. *Every Man a Tiger: The Gulf War Air Campaign.* Rev. ed. New York: Berkley Publishing, 2005.

Dinackus, Thomas D. *Order of Battle: Allied Ground Forces of Operation Desert Storm.* Central Point, OR: Hellgate/PSI Research, 1999.

Hildreth, Steven A. *Evaluation of U.S. Army Assessment of Patriot Antitactical Missile Effectiveness in the War against Iraq.* Washington, DC: Congressional Research Service, 1992.

---

# Pearlman, Adam

*See* Gadahn, Adam Yahya

---

# Peay, Binford James Henry, III
## Birth Date: May 10, 1940

U.S. Army general, commander of the 101st Airborne Division during the 1991 Persian Gulf War, and then vice chief of staff for the U.S. Army and commander of United States Central Command (CENTCOM). Binford James Henry Peay III was born on May 10,

1940, in Richmond, Virginia. He graduated from the Virginia Military Institute (VMI) in 1962 and was commissioned from the Reserve Officers' Training Corps (ROTC) as a second lieutenant in the artillery. Peay subsequently earned a master's degree from George Washington University.

Peay served two tours in Vietnam, during 1967–1968 and 1971–1972, and rotated through a series of field and staff positions. He was senior aide to the chairman of the Joint Chiefs of Staff (JCS) and later chief of the Army Initiatives Group in the deputy chief of staff's office for operations and plans.

Peay was assigned to the 101st Airborne Division in July 1987 as a brigadier general and its assistant division commander for maneuver. After a one-year assignment as deputy commandant of the Command and General Staff College at Fort Leavenworth, Kansas, Peay returned to the 101st Airborne as its commander in August 1989. The 101st Airborne was one of the army's immediate reaction divisions, intended to respond rapidly to a crisis anywhere in the world.

When Iraqi dictator Saddam Hussein invaded Kuwait on August 2, 1990, the 101st was alerted for deployment to Saudi Arabia. At the time the division was in the middle of a training cycle, and its three brigades were scattered among Fort Campbell, Kentucky; Honduras; Panama; and West Point, New York. Peay immediately began reassembling the division at Fort Campbell and organizing a task force to fly to Saudi Arabia. Beginning on August 17, 1990, 117 helicopters, 487 vehicles, and 2,742 troops from the 101st Airborne deployed to Saudi Arabia. With elements of the division in place, by September 1 American planners had established a razor-thin screen of security for the Saudi oil fields.

During the course of the next five months, the remainder of Peay's troops and equipment arrived in Saudi Arabia. Planning then changed from defending that country to forcing the Iraqis to leave Kuwait. Peay was a leading advocate of using the division's air mobility capabilities to cut off the Iraqi divisions in Kuwait and destroy them as they retreated. The plan that was developed was anchored firmly in the U.S. Army's AirLand Battle Doctrine. To establish the conditions for success prior to the start of operations on February 24, coalition forces conducted a series of limited objective raids across the border into Iraq and Kuwait. One such raid occurred on February 21 when AH-64 Apache attack helicopters from the 101st Airborne took fire from an Iraqi bunker. Peay ordered an airmobile assault, which quickly overran the Iraqi positions. More than 400 Iraqis surrendered.

On February 24, 1991, coalition ground forces began the ground offensive. Peay's division was airlifted 93 miles into Iraq to establish firebase Cobra. With the base established in one day, Peay prepared to jump units farther forward to cut off Iraqi communications with Baghdad. Ground units soon linked up with the 101st and pushed east to engage Iraqi Republican Guard divisions.

Peay had placed forward units astride Highway 8, the roadway that paralleled the Euphrates River. These included only limited antiarmor units and field artillery and numbered no more than

1,000 troops. A few light Iraqi vehicles were destroyed, but the Iraqis made no serious attempts against Peay's blocking units. Peay realized that Iraqi units from Kuwait could still retreat through Basra and reach the north. He thus proposed to use his helicopters to move three battalions over the Euphrates and place them on the highway running north from Basra. With artillery and Apache gunship support, he believed that the force could prevent the Iraqis from escaping. The plan was not approved, and the war ended before Peay's division could move farther east and north.

Peay was promoted to lieutenant general in June 1991 and assigned as U.S. Army deputy chief of staff for operations and plans. He received his fourth star in March 1993, serving as vice chief of staff for the army. His last assignment was commander of the CENTCOM, with responsibility for the Middle East, South Asia, and Northeast Africa, from August 1994 to his retirement on August 13, 1997. Peay then served on the boards of several defense-related corporations before assuming the position of superintendent (president) of VMI in 2003.

TIM J. WATTS

**See also**

DESERT STORM, Operation; DESERT STORM, Operation, Planning for

**References**

Atkinson, Rick. *Crusade: The Untold Story of the Persian Gulf War.* New York: Mariner Books, 1994.

Gordon, Michael R., and General Bernard E. Trainor. *The Generals' War: The Inside Story of the Conflict in the Gulf.* New York: Little, Brown, 1995.

# Peel Commission

**Start Date: August 1936**
**End Date: July 7, 1937**

Commission tasked with studying the British-held mandate in Palestine. In August 1936 the British government appointed a Royal Commission of Inquiry headed by Lord Robert Peel to examine the effectiveness of the mandate system and to make proposals concerning future British policy in Palestine. Peel was the former secretary of state for British-held India. Members of the Royal Commission arrived in Jerusalem on November 11, 1936. While all of the committee's members were experienced in foreign affairs, none had any particular connection to either the Arab cause or the Jewish cause.

The Peel Commission, as it came to be called, was established at a time of increasing violence in Palestine. Indeed, serious clashes between Arabs and Jews broke out in 1936 and were to last three years. The commission was charged with determining the cause of the unrest and judging the merits of grievances on both sides. Chaim Weizmann gave a memorable speech on behalf of the Zionist cause. However, the mufti of Jerusalem, Hajj Amin al-Husayni, refused to testify in front of the commission. Instead, he demanded complete cessation of Jewish immigration into Palestine. Although the Arabs continued to boycott the commission officially, there was a sense of urgency to respond to Weizmann's speech. The former mayor of Jerusalem, Raghib Bey al-Nashashibi, was thus sent to explain the Arab perspective through unofficial channels.

The commission returned to Britain on January 18, 1937, and published its report on July 7, 1937. The Peel Commission attributed the underlying cause of the Arab Revolt of 1936–1939 to the Arabs' desire for independence and their hatred and fear of the establishment of a Jewish homeland in Palestine. Therefore, the commission recommended freezing Jewish immigration to Palestine at 12,000 people per year for five years. It also urged that a plan be developed for formal partition of the territory.

With regard to partition, the commission recommended that the mandate be eventually abolished except for a corridor surrounding Jerusalem and stretching to the Mediterranean coast just south of Jaffa and that the land under its authority be apportioned between an Arab state and an Israeli state. The Jewish side was to receive a territorially smaller portion in the midwest and the north, from Mount Carmel to south of Beer Tuvia, as well as the Jezreel Valley and the Galilee, while the Arab state was to receive territory in the south and mideast, which included Judea, Samaria, and the Negev desert.

The Peel Commission recommended that until the establishment of the two states, Jews should be prohibited from purchasing land in the area allocated to the Arab state. To overcome demarcation problems, the commissioners proposed that land exchanges be carried out concurrently with the transfer of population from one area to the other. Demarcation of the precise borders of the two states would be entrusted to a specialized partition committee.

These recommendations marked the beginning of the end of British rule in Palestine. The British government accepted the recommendations of the Peel Commission regarding the partition of Palestine, and Parliament announced its endorsement of the commission's findings. Among Jews, bitter disagreements erupted between supporters and opponents of the partition proposal, while the Arabs rejected it outright. Ultimately the plan was shelved. A new commission, the Woodhead Commission, was subsequently established to determine borders for the proposed states.

MOSHE TERDIMAN

**See also**

Arab Nationalism; Balfour Declaration; Mandates; United Kingdom, Middle East Policy

**References**

Ayaad, Abdelaziz A. *Arab Nationalism and the Palestinians, 1850–1939.* Jerusalem: Passia, 1999.

Cohen, Aharon. *Israel and the Arab World.* New York: Funk and Wagnalls, 1970.

*Palestine Royal Commission Report Presented by the Secretary of State for the Colonies to Parliament by Command of His Majesty, July 1937.* London: His Majesty's Stationery Office, 1937.

Swedenburg, Ted. *Memories of Revolt: The 1936–1939 Rebellion and the Palestinian National Past.* Minneapolis: University of Minnesota Press, 1995.

# Pérez de Cuéllar, Javier
Birth Date: January 19, 1920

Peruvian diplomat and United Nations (UN) secretary-general (1982–1991). Javier Pérez de Cuéllar was born in Lima, Peru, on January 19, 1920, into a Roman Catholic family of aristocratic Spanish descent. He studied law at Catholic University, Lima, and entered his country's diplomatic service in 1940, serving in France, the United Kingdom, Bolivia, and Brazil and attending the first UN General Assembly session in New York in 1946.

From 1964 to 1966 Pérez de Cuéllar was Peruvian ambassador to Switzerland, and in 1969 he became his country's first ambassador to the Soviet Union. From 1971 to 1977 he was Peru's permanent representative to the UN. He chaired the UN Security Council in 1974, where he helped to mediate the protracted dispute over Cyprus between Greece and Turkey. After two years as ambassador to Venezuela, in 1979 he became UN undersecretary-general for special political affairs. As Secretary-General Kurt Waldheim's special representative, from April 1981 Pérez de Cuéllar attempted to defuse tensions between Afghanistan and Pakistan.

Peruvian diplomat Javier Pérez de Cuéllar was secretary-general of the United Nations (UN) during 1982–1991. He played a significant role during the Persian Gulf crisis of 1990–1991 following Iraq's seizure of Kuwait. (Corel)

Elected secretary-general in December 1981 as a candidate acceptable to both the Western and Soviet blocs, Pérez de Cuéllar served two five-year terms, which coincided neatly with the ending of the Cold War. He encouraged the relaxation of Soviet-American tensions that began once Mikhail Gorbachev became Soviet general secretary in 1985. Pérez de Cuéllar believed that the new international climate gave new scope for the expansion of UN activities, ambitions largely stymied by the determination of the United States, under conservative Republican president Ronald Reagan, to cut rather than expand American contributions and dues to the UN on the grounds that the organization was plagued by waste, inefficiency, and a bloated bureaucracy.

Early in his tenure, Pérez de Cuéllar's efforts to mediate disputes between Argentina and Great Britain failed to prevent the 1982 Falklands (Malvinas) War. A staunch and widely respected advocate of negotiation, conciliation, and peacekeeping, he launched personal and ultimately successful initiatives, which Cold War de-escalation facilitated, to alleviate and end hostilities in Afghanistan, Namibia, and Lebanon and to relieve famine in Ethiopia. He also consistently emphasized refugee resettlement and human rights.

During 1987–1988 Pérez de Cuéllar took the lead in obtaining and implementing UN Resolution 598, which called for the cessation of hostilities in the lengthy and brutal Iran-Iraq War. Iraq's invasion of Kuwait in August 1990 brought new challenges, and UN Security Council Resolution 678 provided the legal basis for the international coalition that ultimately drove Iraqi president Saddam Hussein's forces from Kuwait in February 1991. Under Pérez de Cuéllar's leadership, the UN condemned Iraq's subsequent spring 1991 attacks on Kurdish rebels in northern Iraq, established a protective no-fly zone in that area, and ultimately took over control of Kurdish refugee camps there. Throughout his tenure as secretary-general, Pérez de Cuéllar displayed deft diplomatic skills and exhibited well-honed leadership in international crises.

Leaving office at the end of 1991, Pérez de Cuéllar accepted a visiting appointment at Yale University, where he wrote his memoirs. Looking ahead to the post–Cold War era, he urged the UN to move beyond international mediation and peacekeeping and focus on addressing social and economic problems and human rights abuses. In 1995 he ran unsuccessfully for president of Peru, losing to Alberto Fujimori. After Fujimori resigned on corruption charges, Pérez de Cuéllar served from November 2000 to July 2001 as foreign minister and president of Peru's Council of Ministers. He then became Peru's ambassador to France, where he remained after his final retirement in September 2004.

PRISCILLA ROBERTS

**See also**

DESERT STORM, Operation; Gorbachev, Mikhail; Kurds; Kurds, Massacres of; Iran-Iraq War; Iraq, History of Pre-1990; Iraq, History of, 1990–Present; Kuwait; Reagan, Ronald Wilson; United Nations

References

Forsyth, Harold. *Conversaciones con Javier Pérez de Cuéllar: Testimonio de un peruano* [Conversations with Javier Pérez de Cuéllar: Testimony of a Peruvian]. Lima, Peru: Noceda Editores, 2001.

Lankevich, George J. *The United Nations under Javier Pérez de Cuéllar, 1982–1991*. Lanham, MD: Scarecrow, 2001.

Pérez de Cuéllar, Javier. *Pilgrimage for Peace: A Secretary-General's Memoir*. New York: St. Martin's, 1997.

---

# Perle, Richard
## Birth Date: September 16, 1941

Highly influential lobbyist, political adviser and pundit, and vocal leader of the neoconservative movement. Richard Perle was born in New York City on September 16, 1941, but moved to southern California with his family as a youth. He graduated from the University of Southern California in 1964, studied in Copenhagen and at the London School of Economics, and earned a master's degree in political science from Princeton University in 1967. Perle entered the public arena in 1969, when he took a job on Senator Henry M. "Scoop" Jackson's staff. As a Senate staffer from 1969 to 1980, Perle gained considerable political insight and expertise and soon became known as an expert on arms control and national security issues.

Despite his considerable reputation, Perle preferred to work behind the scenes and was not a well-know figure outside the halls of Congress. By the late 1970s he had become an anti-Soviet hardliner and derided the Jimmy Carter administration's attempts to engage in arms control agreements with the Kremlin, which Perle believed were detrimental to U.S. defense and global security. During this time he also forged lucrative contacts with the private sector, which caused some to question his motives.

In 1981 the incoming Ronald Reagan administration named Perle assistant secretary of defense for international security policy, a post he held until 1987. Perle was predictably a champion of Reagan's get-tough approach with the Soviets and endorsed efforts to fight communism in Central America and the arming of the mujahideen in Afghanistan, who were waging an anti-Soviet insurgency. His tenure in office was not without controversy, however. In 1983 he was accused of conflict of interest after recommending that the Pentagon purchase an Israeli-made weapons system. The company that made the system had recently paid Perle a $50,000 consulting fee. Perle pointed out that the payment was for work done prior to his joining the Reagan administration, but his detractors used the incident to tarnish his image.

When not employed in the public sector, Perle busied himself with lucrative consulting jobs, served as an informal political adviser, wrote several books, composed myriad essays and op-ed pieces for foreign and domestic newspapers and magazines, and often appeared on television as a political commentator. He has subscribed to numerous conservative and neoconservative causes and think tanks, including the Jewish Institute for National Jewish Affairs, the Center for Security Policy, the Hudson Institute, and the American Enterprise Institute for Near East Policy, among others. He was one of the signatories to the Project for the New American Century's open letter to President Bill Clinton in 1998 that advocated the overthrow of Iraqi dictator Saddam Hussein. Perle cultivated close ties to fellow neoconservative Paul Wolfowitz, deputy secretary of defense from 2001 to 2005 and a key architect of the Iraq War, as well as Secretary of State Donald Rumsfeld.

During 2001–2003 Perle was well placed to advocate for his neoconservative outlook as chairman of the Defense Policy Board Advisory Committee, which was charged with advising the Pentagon on matters of defense and national security issues. As such, he was an early and vocal proponent of war with Iraq, and within days of the September 11, 2001, terror attacks was on record as having linked Hussein to Al Qaeda, ties that have never been proven. Perle was also on record as having proposed to invade Iraq with as few as 40,000 ground troops and was dismissive of U.S. Army chief of staff General Eric Shinseki's call for more than 600,000 troops to attack Iraq. Perle envisioned a scenario in Iraq similar to that which had unfolded in Afghanistan during Operation ENDURING FREEDOM, which had left most of the ground fighting to indigenous forces.

After leaving the chairmanship of the Defense Policy Board Advisory Committee in 2003, Perle continued writing and consulting. He has served as the chief executive officer of Hollinger International (a newspaper holding corporation) and is the director of the *Jerusalem Post*, a subsidiary of Hollinger. Because of his close ties to Israel (especially the rightist Likud Party, for which he has served as an adviser), Perle's advocacy of the Iraq War had been linked—rightly or wrongly—to his coziness with Israeli leaders. Indeed, in the 1990s he wrote a position paper for Likud that included the overthrow of Hussein as a tenet of Israeli policy. Perle has vigorously denied any connection between his war stance and past dealings with Israel, and in recent years he has downplayed his role in the run-up to the Iraq War, claiming that his influence had been greatly exaggerated. Perle has also attacked the efficacy of the United Nations (UN), arguing that it is essentially an ineffective organization that is incapable of policing the world in any meaningful way.

After the Iraqi insurgency began in earnest in 2004, Perle made a concerted attempt to distance himself from some of the George W. Bush administration's policies in Iraq. While Perle has yet to call his Iraq War advocacy a mistake, he has expressed regret about the way in which the war was waged and blamed "dysfunction" in the Bush administration for the failings of U.S. occupation and pacification policies. David Brooks, a conservative columnist, wrote in the *New York Times* in 2004 that Perle had "no noteworthy meetings with either Bush or [Vice President Dick] Cheney" since 2001 and intimated that Perle's influence over official policy was entirely overblown.

In 2004 Perle and other Hollinger executives were accused of fiduciary manipulation after they allegedly funneled company funds from stockholders' accounts into compensation packages for top company executives. Perle's compensation, at some $5.4 million, was questioned, but as of this writing, no judgments against Perle have been made in this case. Perle continues to write and consult.

PAUL G. PIERPAOLI JR.

### See also

Bush, George Walker; Cheney, Richard Bruce; ENDURING FREEDOM, Operation; IRAQI FREEDOM, Operation; Mujahideen, Soviet-Afghanistan War; Neoconservatism; Rumsfeld, Donald Henry; September 11 Attacks; Shinseki, Eric Ken; Wolfowitz, Paul Dundes

### References

Frum, David, and Richard Perle. *An End to Evil: How to Win the War on Terror.* New York: Random House, 2003.

Ricks, Thomas E. *Fiasco: The American Military Adventure in Iraq.* New York: Penguin, 2006.

---

# Perry, William James
## Birth Date: October 11, 1927

Engineer, businessman, secretary of defense under President William J. Clinton (1994–1997), and widely recognized authority on military technology and arms control. William James Perry was born October 11, 1927, in Vandergrift, Pennsylvania. After graduating from high school in 1945, he enlisted in the U.S. Army, where he surveyed tracts for the Corps of Engineers as a member of U.S.

William J. Perry, U.S. secretary of defense during 1994–1997. (Library of Congress)

occupation forces in Japan. In 1948 he joined the Reserve Officers' Training Corps (ROTC), and the next year he received his BS degree in mathematics from Stanford University. Perry was commissioned a second lieutenant in the Army Reserve in 1950, the same year he received an MA degree in mathematics from Stanford. From 1951 to 1954 he was a math instructor at Pennsylvania State University and a senior mathematician at the HRB-Singer Company in State College, Pennsylvania.

In 1954 Perry began his extensive defense industry career when he became laboratory director of GTE Sylvania Company in Mountain View, California. He received a PhD in mathematics from Pennsylvania State University in 1957. He left GTE in 1964 and cofounded Electromagnetic Systems Laboratory (ESL), Inc., in Sunnyvale, California, a military electronics company that made devices for code breaking and surveillance for the Pentagon. He served as the first president of the company.

In 1977 after Perry sold his holdings in ESL, a move that made him a multimillionaire, he was nominated by President Jimmy Carter to the third-highest position in the Pentagon, undersecretary of defense for research and engineering. As undersecretary, Perry advised the secretary of defense on the development of military technology, communications, intelligence, and atomic energy. He was also responsible for procuring new weapons systems and was at the forefront of developing the radar-evading Stealth aircraft and creating laser-guided missiles that later were used in the 1991 Persian Gulf War.

In 1981 after Carter left office, Perry left government service and returned to the private sector, serving as executive vice president of the research department at Hambrecht & Quist, Inc., a San Francisco venture-capital banking firm specializing in high technology. In 1985 Perry founded Technology Strategies and Alliances, an investment and consulting firm in Menlo Park, California; the firm helped large defense firms such as Lockheed, Chrysler, and Boeing secure smaller up-and-coming technology companies.

From 1989 to 1993 Perry directed Stanford University's Center for International Security and Arms Control, a think tank, and in this capacity consulted with East European governments on converting their post–Cold War military industries. On March 5, 1993, Perry was named deputy secretary of defense, and in this position his skills as a manager and technocrat in the private sector proved to be invaluable. As such, he supervised the day-to-day operations of the Pentagon, oversaw the annual weapons budget, and met with foreign dignitaries.

On February 3, 1994, after a unanimous U.S. Senate vote to confirm him, Perry was sworn in as the 19th secretary of defense, replacing the embattled Leslie (Les) Aspin Jr. Perry served the remainder of Clinton's first term but was replaced by Senator William Cohen in January 1997. During Perry's tenure as secretary, he reorganized the department, opposed the Senate's efforts to buy additional Northrop Grumman B-2 Spirit bombers, and supported the expansion of the North Atlantic Treaty Organization

(NATO). Perhaps his greatest challenge was the U.S. intervention in Bosnia-Herzegovina, which he initially opposed, and the military junta's refusal to reinstate deposed president Jean Bertrand Aristide in Haiti. To boost low morale in the military, Perry sought pay increases and more on-base housing for service personnel. Overall Perry's tenure was a success, and he managed to streamline and strengthen the U.S. armed forces. Citing the increasingly shrill partisan warfare on Capitol Hill, Perry made known to Clinton his desire to resign at the end of the president's first term.

Perry is currently a senior fellow with the Hoover Institution and a professor at Stanford University's School of Engineering and the Institute of International Studies.

GARY KERLEY

#### See also
Aspin, Leslie, Jr.; Clinton, William Jefferson; Cohen, William Sebastian; United States Department of Defense

#### References
Perry, William J. *Defense Investment: A Strategy for the 1990s.* Stanford, CA: Center for International and Arms Control, Stanford University, 1989.
Perry, William J., and Ashton B. Carter. *Preventive Defense: A New Security Strategy for America.* Washington, DC: Brookings Institution Press, 1999.
Warshaw, Shirley Anne. *Presidential Profiles: The Clinton Years.* New York: Facts on File, 2004.

---

## Persian Gulf

Inland sea located in the Middle East, considered by most geographers to be a part of the Indian Ocean. The Persian Gulf, also referred to as the Arabian Gulf by Arab countries, encompasses an area of some 96,525 square miles and connects to the Gulf of Oman and the Arabian Sea via the Strait of Hormuz to the east. To the west, the Persian Gulf is fed by the confluence of the Tigris and Euphrates rivers via the Shatt al-Arab waterway.

Nations bordering the Persian Gulf include Iran, Oman, the United Arab Emirates, Saudi Arabia, Qatar, Bahrain, Kuwait, and Iraq. Iraq's only access to the Gulf is through the Shatt al-Arab waterway, wide in some areas but in other areas a marshy delta that can be easily blocked in time of war. The eastern portion

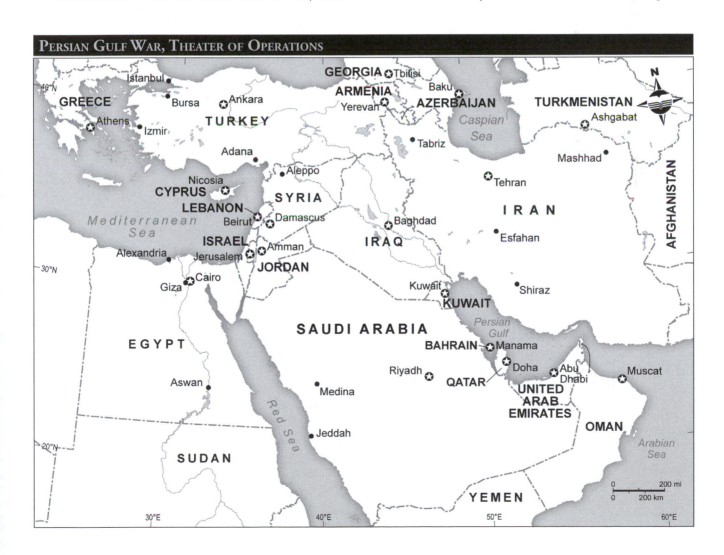

PERSIAN GULF WAR, THEATER OF OPERATIONS

of the Shatt al-Arab is controlled by Iran, a bitter and longtime rival of Iraq.

The Persian Gulf also contains a number of small islands, mostly all considered offshore or barrier islands. The Gulf is quite shallow, with an average depth of just 160 feet. Its deepest portion is approximately 300 feet deep. Because of the climate of the region, which is hot and very dry, high evaporation rates render the Persian Gulf quite salty; parts of the Gulf contain up to 40 percent salt. The southern coastline is rather flat, while the Iranian coastline is mountainous. Over the past 6,000 years, the size of the Persian Gulf has steadily decreased, and silt and sediment draining from the Shatt al-Arab waterway continue to slowly reduce the amount of water area.

The Persian Gulf is strategically significant not only because of its location and connection to the Arabian Sea but also because of its rich petroleum and natural gas resources. There are many oil fields and wells located in the Gulf including Al-Safaniya, the world's largest-producing oil field. Also, the Gulf is used to transport oil via large oceangoing tankers, and nations such as Kuwait, Bahrain, Qatar, and others operate major oil port facilities and refineries on or near the coast. In addition to petrochemical resources, the Persian Gulf has historically been quite rich in wildlife, including fish and major coral reefs. For many years Persian Gulf pearl-producing oysters were highly prized, but their numbers have been drastically reduced in the last 75 years or so.

The Persian Gulf's natural resources have come under enormous pressure since the discovery of oil in the region in the 1920s and 1930s and with the rapid industrialization of the region. Pollution, overharvesting of fish and other wildlife, and a lack of concern—until fairly recently—about what gets put into the Gulf have all imperiled its delicate ecosystem. The Gulf has been the scene of numerous large oil spills, including one in 1983, several large spills during the 1980–1988 Iran-Iraq War, and additional large spills in 1991 when the Iraqis dumped as many as 6 million barrels of oil into the water during the Persian Gulf War, precipitating an ecological catastrophe. The results of that conflict are still impacting Gulf waters and beaches.

In the late 1980s the Persian Gulf was also the scene of a series of tanker battles precipitated by Iraq and Iran during their eight-year-long war. The conflict led the United States to implement Operation EARNEST WILL during 1987–1988 in order to protect Kuwaiti and other neutral oil tankers plying the Gulf from attack. It was the largest naval convoy program since World War II.

PAUL G. PIERPAOLI JR.

**See also**

EARNEST WILL, Operation; Iran-Iraq War; Shatt al-Arab Waterway

**References**

Palmer, Michael A. *Guardians of the Gulf: A History of America's Expanding Role in the Persian Gulf, 1833–1992.* New York: Free Press, 1992.

Waterlow, Julia. *The Red Sea and the Arabian Gulf.* Orlando: Steck-Vaughan, 1997.

# Persian Gulf Conflict Supplemental Authorization and Personnel Benefits Act of 1991

Comprehensive Persian Gulf War veterans' benefits cost coverage legislation sponsored by Senator George J. Mitchell (D-Maine) and passed by Congress on March 25, 1991. President George H. W. Bush signed the act, popularly known as the Gulf Act, into law on April 6, 1991. The Gulf Act consisted of eight titles authorizing $655 million in appropriations for an increase in selective benefits for veterans of Operations DESERT SHIELD and DESERT STORM and $15 billion in appropriations to cover costs of the war not met by contributions from allied countries.

Triggered by patriotic fervor throughout the country and the rapid military success in Iraq, the flood of legislative proposals introduced in the 102nd Congress to address benefits for the 697,000 veterans of the Persian Gulf War and their families culminated in the passage of the far-reaching Gulf Act. The Gulf Act first addressed the practical cost concerns of operating military forces on foreign soil. Flexibility was provided to the Department of Defense to transfer funds among appropriate accounts to cover incremental costs associated with Operation DESERT STORM. In addition, military personnel strength limitations authorized by the National Defense Authorization Act for Fiscal Year 1991, enacted before the war, were waived to allow for needed strength upgrades.

The Gulf Act further defined the conflict to ensure the eligibility of veterans of both DESERT SHIELD and DESERT STORM in receiving general veterans' benefits, such as home loan eligibility, dental benefits, veterans' pensions, and survivors' benefits for veterans' spouses and dependents. This recognition was critical given the composition of the U.S. armed forces participating in the conflict. Reflecting a rapidly emergent national defense need, 17 percent of the troops involved in both operations of the war consisted of reservists and National Guard personnel recently called to active duty. This percentage was comparably higher than in previous American wars. The percentage of women involved in the war (7 percent) also rose comparably. In addition, more than 90 percent of all Persian Gulf War veterans experienced duty in a combat zone for the first time, further requiring the need for immediate benefit coverage expansion.

Beyond basic benefit coverage, the Gulf Act also provided all active duty personnel temporary increases in imminent danger pay, family separation allowances, and death gratuity payments for dependent survivors. A significant provision included the doubling of life insurance coverage from $50,000 to $100,000. Congress also increased monthly educational benefits under the Montgomery GI Bill program and authorized the secretary of education the discretion to waive educational loan repayment requirements if they adversely affected veterans.

The most important provisions, however, reflected Congress's sensitivity to the stresses imposed on a combat force composed of a relatively high proportion of reservists and National Guard troops. Many of these citizen-soldiers had abruptly left jobs and families when called to active duty. Accordingly, issues such as reemployment subsequent to active duty service and family support highlighted veterans' concerns. Congress addressed these concerns by amending the Veterans' Reemployment Rights Law to require employers to make reasonable accommodations for returning disabled veterans and reasonable efforts to reemploy veterans who could qualify for employment positions occupied prior to active duty service. Families of veterans also were provided relief in the form of appropriations for child care assistance, general education and family support services, education, eligibility to participate in the Food Stamp Program, and variable housing allowance payments to take into account cost-of-housing differences across the country.

Additional benefits included loan relief for farmer reservists activated for duty in the war, basic allowances for quarters for unmarried activated reservists so as to continue loan or rent payments on their civilian residences, special pay allowances for reservist and National Guard health care providers, and health care coverage for reservists transitioning to civilian life upon service deactivation.

MARK F. LEEP

### See also
National Defense Authorization Act for Fiscal Years 1992 and 1993; Veterans Health Care Act of 1992

### References
Knight, Amy W., and Robert L. Worden. *The Veterans Benefits Administration: An Organizational History, 1776–1994.* Collingdale, PA: Diane Publishing, 1995.
"Veterans' Benefits Notes: Congress Passes Persian Gulf Benefits Act." *Army Lawyer* 222 (June 1991): 37–39.

---

# Persian Gulf War, Cease-Fire Agreement
## Event Date: April 6, 1991

Agreement signed on April 6, 1991, under which U.S.-led coalition forces formally suspended hostilities against Iraq in the Persian Gulf War, terminating Operation DESERT STORM. The ground assault phase of DESERT STORM commenced on February 24, 1991, and quickly routed the Iraqi military. Three days later Iraqi foreign minister Tariq Aziz notified the United Nations (UN) that his country would comply with three of the 12 UN resolutions concerning a cessation of hostilities if the UN Security Council brokered a cease-fire. The council rejected the proposal that same day and asserted that Iraq must unconditionally agree to all 12 resolutions.

Meanwhile, chairman of the Joint Chiefs of Staff (JCS) General Colin L. Powell briefed President George H. W. Bush that the coalition had liberated Kuwait and eliminated Iraq's ability to threaten its neighbors. This assessment, combined with the desire to avoid the impression that the United States was employing excessive force, prompted Bush to unilaterally announce that the coalition's

forces would suspend operations at 8:00 a.m. the following day, February 28, 100 hours after the ground campaign began. Bush stressed that the suspension of hostilities would be temporary unless Iraq met certain conditions, including the release of prisoners of war, the revelation of the location of mines, and compliance with all UN Security Council resolutions.

Isolated fighting occurred during the next two days, but on March 3, 1991, Iraqi president Saddam Hussein dispatched the deputy chief of staff of the Ministry of Defense and the commander of his army's III Corps to discuss terms of a permanent cease-fire. They were to meet with American and coalition military leaders at Safwan Airfield in southern Iraq. U.S. General H. Norman Schwarzkopf, who had been chiefly responsible for prosecuting the war as head of U.S. Central Command (CENTCOM), represented the coalition and addressed issues such as a prohibition on Iraq's use of fixed-wing aircraft and the return of captured Iraqi territory. Unfortunately, the decision not to include helicopters in the no-fly prohibition allowed Iraq to employ them against the Shia uprising in southern Iraq.

UN Security Council Resolution 686, passed on March 2, created the framework for the subsequent formal cease-fire. Among other provisions, it required Iraq to renounce its claims on Kuwait, return all seized Kuwaiti property, return all prisoners of war, and pay war damages. On April 3 the Security Council passed the most complete list of 34 mandates in Resolution 687. The resolution reiterated earlier provisions and added additional measures, such as requirements that Iraq abandon weapons of mass destruction (WMDs) programs, faithfully pay its international debts, affirm that it would not aid international terrorists, and recognize Kuwaiti sovereignty. The official cease-fire was signed on April 6, 1991.

The cease-fire certainly did not end conflict between Iraq and the international community. In subsequent years, the Hussein regime employed helicopters to punish ethnic groups inside its borders in violation of UN mandates and threatened air patrols over northern and southern Iraq in the no-fly zones. Iraq's eventual refusal to cooperate with weapons inspectors from the United Nations Special Commission on Iraq (UNSCOM) largely contributed to the American-Anglo decision to invade the country and topple Hussein in March 2003

MATTHEW J. KROGMAN

### See also
Aziz, Tariq; Bush, George Herbert Walker; DESERT STORM, Operation; Hussein, Saddam; Schwarzkopf, H. Norman, Jr.; United Nations; United Nations Security Council Resolution 687; United Nations Special Commission; United Nations Weapons Inspectors; Weapons of Mass Destruction

### References
Bacevich, Andrew J., and Efraim Inbar, eds. *The Gulf War of 1991 Reconsidered.* Portland, OR: Frank Cass, 2003.
Gow, James, ed. *Iraq, the Gulf Conflict and the World Community.* London: Brassey's, 1993.
Yetiv, Steve A. *Explaining Foreign Policy: U.S. Decision-Making and the Persian Gulf War.* Baltimore, MD: Johns Hopkins University Press, 2004.

## Persian Gulf War Syndrome

*See* Gulf War Syndrome

---

## Persian Gulf War Veterans Health Registry

A major provision of Title VII of the Veterans Health Care Act of 1992 (P.L. 102-585; 106 Stat. 4943), passed by the U.S. Congress on October 6, 1992, and signed into law by President George H. W. Bush on November 4, 1992. Title VII established a comprehensive clinical health evaluation and registry program within the Department of Veterans Affairs to address the health care concerns and illnesses of veterans of the 1991 Persian Gulf War.

Both the Veterans Health Care Act of 1992 and the Persian Gulf War Veterans Health Registry reflected growing governmental concerns with health issues and health benefit needs of American veterans who served in Operations DESERT SHIELD and DESERT STORM. Initial specific concerns revolved around the environmental and chemical exposure of veterans to the smoke of more than 750 oil well fires set by Iraqi forces in the theater of operations in February 1991 and other petroleum-based emissions from everyday troop operations. Health concerns over the impact of troop chemical and biological warfare vaccinations also arose. In response, the Department of Veterans Affairs quickly established a registry soon after the war's April 1991 cease-fire to begin clinical examinations of Persian Gulf War veterans concerned with war-related illnesses.

The Department of Defense followed in December 1991 with its own registry of troops exposed to oil well fire smoke who desired examinations. During this time and into 1992, however, media outlets began reporting stories of Persian Gulf War veterans experiencing inexplicable symptoms of fatigue, joint pain, skin rashes, headaches, chronic sleeplessness, and cognitive problems. Initial investigations by researchers from the Walter Reed Institute of Research found no specific cause. The media reports, however, raised public concerns and the specter of a mystery illness, commonly labeled "Gulf War Syndrome."

Congress responded to these specific health issues and public concerns with inclusion of the registry under Title VII of the Veterans Health Care Act of 1992. A reinforcement and expansion of the Department of Veterans Affairs' initial 1991 program, Title VII and the registry also increased the outreach of the Defense Department's limited registry beyond veterans affected by oil well fire smoke and established cross-reference procedures between both departmental registries to enhance information sharing. Designed more as a descriptive informational database than a research program, the registry provided for the listing of the names of every Persian Gulf War veteran who either applied for Department of Veterans Affairs services, filed a disability claim associated with military service, requested a Department of Veterans Affairs health examination, or received such an examination from the Defense Department and asked to be included in the registry.

Deceased veterans whose dependents filed certain dependency and indemnity claims could also have their names listed. Title VII also provided for the inclusion of health information for a listed veteran who granted permission for such data to be included in the registry or the health information of a veteran who was deceased at the time his or her name was listed. Aware of veterans' ongoing health concerns, Congress required the Department of Veterans Affairs to periodically contact registry veterans as to the status of health research reviews conducted under other Title VII provisions.

Linked to the registry, other critical provisions under the title included health examinations, consultations, and counseling services requested by veterans and a mandated agreement with the National Academy of Sciences to review medical and scientific information on the health consequences of Persian Gulf War service. Medical information reviewed pursuant to this provision further included the medical records of registry veterans who granted permission for such a review as well as the records of Defense Department registry participants. Finally, as a capstone to the legislation, Title VII authorized the president to transfer government-directed Persian Gulf War health research and provide annual reports to Congress.

The registry's list has now grown to include the names of more than 50,000 veterans. Implementation of the registry and the research review provisions of Title VII also spawned numerous government-funded health studies and additional congressional legislation to enhance research efforts. The Institute of Medicine within the National Academy of Sciences has since explored potential health effects stemming from the use of insecticides, vaccines, nerve agents, depleted uranium, and fuels used or emitted during the war. Although research continues and much has been learned, specific or unusual causes of many veteran symptoms and illnesses have yet to be determined because of the lack of objective and timely predeployment and postdeployment health-screening information and exposure-monitoring measures.

MARK F. LEEP

**See also**

Gulf War Syndrome; Veterans Health Care Act of 1992

**References**

Barrett, Drue H., Gregory C. Gray, Bradley H. Doebbeling, et al. "Prevalence of Symptoms and Symptom-based Conditions among Gulf War Veterans: Current Status of Research Findings." *Epidemiologic Reviews* 24 (2002): 218–227.

Guzzardo, Joseph M., and Jennifer L. Monachino. "Gulf War Syndrome—Is Litigation the Answer? Learning Lessons from *In Re Agent Orange*." *St. John's Journal of Legal Commentary* 10 (1995): 673–696.

Institute of Medicine. *Gulf War and Health,* Vol. 4, *Health Effects of Serving in the Gulf War.* Washington, DC: National Academies Press, 2006.

———. *Health Consequences of Service during the Persian Gulf War: Recommendations for Research and Information Services.* Washington, DC: National Academy Press, 1996.

# Peshmerga

Armed Kurdish insurgents operating chiefly in Kurdistan (northern Iraq, Turkey and Iran). Peshmerga (meaning those facing death) are Kurdish irregular fighters whose origins predate the 20th century. Although primarily Kurdish men, their demographic composition has come to include women and non-Kurds. The fighters' chains of command were the successive leaders of the Kurdistan Democratic Party (KDP), namely Mullah Mustafa Barzani and, following his death, his successor and son Masoud Barzani, currently the president of the Kurdistan Regional Government (KRG), as well as the Patriotic Union of Kurdistan (PUK) led by Jalal Talabani. The Peshmerga in Turkey fall under the auspices of the Kurdistan Workers' Party (PKK).

In Iraq, the KDP and PUK comprise the current government of the KRG, by which the Peshmerga are largely governed. Historically, they have played a pivotal role in shaping Kurdish nationalist aspirations for independence since the early 1920s, particularly as a result of the dissolution of the Ottoman Empire after World War I and the quest for a Kurdish homeland.

The historical development of the Peshmerga was concurrent with the rise and fall of various Kurdish rebellions following the collapse of the Ottoman Empire. Failed promises by the Allied powers after World War I to grant Kurds local autonomy and possible independence as suggested in the Treaty of Sèvres (1920) helped solidify the Kurds' quest for independence thereafter. The 1920s witnessed various Kurdish uprisings led by Sheikh Mahmud Barzinji of Sulamaniyah, all of which were promptly quashed by the Iraqi government and the British Royal Air Force. In 1931 Sheikh Barzinji died in one such uprising. This critical juncture witnessed the rise of Mullah Mustafa Barzani as the leader of the Kurdish movement in Iraq and the first solidification of the Peshmerga as a united force.

Throughout the 1930s and 1940s the Kurdish nationalist movement remained largely dormant, as Barzani was forced into exile first in the Soviet Union, then Iran, and finally Western Europe. However, the ouster of Reza Shah's dictatorship in Iran enabled Kurdish intellectuals along with various Barzani followers to declare an independent Kurdistan in the Mahabad region, in northwestern Iran. This saw the swift dissolution of the Imperial Iranian Army there, which was replaced by the National Army comprised of Peshmerga. However, Mahabad, or the Republic of Kurdistan, succumbed to an Iranian invasion in 1946 during which both external influences and internal divisions, primarily between Iranian

A Peshmerga fighter of the Kurdistan Democratic Party (KDP) mans a position near Degala, the KDP's last checkpoint, October 16, 1996. An armored personnel carrier is in the background. (AP/Wide World Photos)

and Iraqi Kurds, shifted the power of the Peshmerga. In exile, Mustafa Barzani, greatly influenced by Marxist-Leninist ideals, solidified the Kurdish movement by the creation of the KDP, the political arm of which provided for the support of the Peshmerga. Instability in Iraq fueled by the decline of the Hashemite monarchy throughout the 1940s and 1950s created an opportunity for the KDP and the Peshmerga to affirm their position as a force to be reckoned with during the 1958 revolution in Iraq.

The 1958 coup witnessed the overthrow of the Iraqi monarchy by General Abd al-Karim Qasim. At the onset, Qasim favored the integration of Barzani and the KDP into the Iraqi political fabric; Qasim also legalized the KDP and the Peshmerga as political entities while recognizing Kurds as distinct but integral people of Iraq under Article 23 of the newly drafted constitution. This ephemeral success was short-lived, however, as Qasim's Pan-Arabist ideology blunted any demands for Kurdish autonomy within Iraq.

Under the leadership of Barzani, the Peshmerga occupied the northern region of Zakho stretching to the Iranian border as a result of the Kurdish revolt of 1962. The revolt had brought an unrelenting bombardment of Kurdish villages and towns across the northeastern frontier. Soon thereafter, Qasim's regime was quickly overthrown by the Baathist rise to power in 1963. The Baathists would prove steadfastly intolerant of Kurdish demands and would quickly increase their military campaign against the Peshmerga and the KDP. The Peshmerga launched counterattacks, which sustained their position and demands for autonomy by controlling much of the northern frontier by 1968.

The growing strength of the KDP and Peshmerga led to the 1970 Manifesto on Kurdish Autonomy, a proposal drafted by the Baath Party to dilute the rise of Kurdish power, particularly in the north. The ultimate futility of the manifesto led to the 1974 uprising headed by Barzani along with an estimated 50,000 trained Peshmerga. Geopolitical events forced Barzani to abandon the struggle and seek refuge in Iran along with thousands of trained fighters and civilians.

The 1988 Iraqi offensive against Kurds in northern Iraq saw the destruction of hundreds of Kurdish and non-Kurdish villages perceived as being in support of Peshmerga. Labeling the Peshmerga as traitors, the Saddam Hussein regime engineered the 1988 chemical weapons offensive against the town of Halabja, a PUK and Peshmerga stronghold. Kurdish leaders, along with thousands of Peshmerga and civilians, sought refuge in nearby countries. Estimates place the total number of militant and civilian deaths at 100,000.

After the 1991 Persian Gulf War, the Peshmerga became an even more vital military force. The creation of the northern no-fly zone by the United Nations (UN) in 1991 provided an opportunity for Kurdish parties to regroup and form the National Front of Kurdistan, which unified the Peshmerga as a force. In doing so, the Peshmerga, aided by Western powers, were able to secure key Iraqi government strongholds, namely Kirkuk, Arbil, and Sulamaniyah, during 1991–1992. Although friction between Kurds

and the Iraqi Army continued, the creation of the no-fly zone enabled leaders of the KPD and the PUK to establish the Kurdish National Assembly, which sought to unite the two major factions of the Peshmerga.

Currently, the Peshmerga are part of the official military force of the KRG, established in 2006. Its mandate seeks the implementation of law and order in the KRG and throughout Iraq and has been instrumental in sustaining security both inside and outside Kurdish-controlled territories in coordination with the Iraqi, U.S., and coalition militaries. Since 2003 the two parties comprising the KRG signed the Kurdistan Regional Government Unification Agreement, which oversees the administration of various governmental departments, most specifically the Department of Peshmerga Affairs, all in an effort to bolster Kurdish self-rule. Because of Kurdish unity and the presence of the Peshmerga, northern Iraq has been relatively free of the fighting that has plagued the rest of Iraq since 2004 with the exception of the campaigns against Ansar al-Islam and the Turcomen and Arab conflicts with the Kurds. It should be noted, however, that in the past the Peshmerga have battled each other in tribal and intra-Kurdish conflicts. The classification of the Peshmerga as an irregular force is rather disingenuous, given its current position within the Iraqi Army. The Peshmerga also remains a tenacious force in the geopolitical compositions of northern Iraq as well as neighboring Turkey, Iran, and Syria.

SHAMIRAN MAKO

**See also**

Baath Party; Hussein, Saddam; Iraq, History of, Pre-1990; Iraq, History of, 1990–Present; Kurdistan Democratic Party; Kurdistan Workers' Party; Kurds; Kurds, Massacres of; Patriotic Union of Kurdistan; Qasim, Abd al-Karim

**References**
Barkey, J. Henri, and Ellen Laipson. "Iraqi Kurds and Iraq's Future." *Middle East Policy* 12(4) (Winter 2005): 66–76.
Chaliand, Gerard, ed. *People without a Country*. London: Zed, 1980.
Gunter, M. Michael. *The Kurds of Iraq*. New York: St. Martin's, 1992.
Lawrence, Quil. *Invisible Nation: How the Kurds' Quest for Statehood Is Shaping Iraq and the Middle East*. New York: Walker, 2008.
McDowall, David. *A Modern History of the Kurds*. New York: I. B. Tauris, 2000.
O'Balance, Edgar. *The Kurdish Struggle, 1920–94*. London: Macmillan, 1996.
O'Leary, Brendan, John McGarry, and Khaled Salih, eds. *The Future of Kurdistan in Iraq*. Philadelphia: University of Pennsylvania Press, 2005.
Yildiz, Kerim, and Tom Blass. *The Kurds in Iraq: The Past, Present and Future*. London: Pluto, 2004.

# Petraeus, David Howell
## Birth Date: November 7, 1952

U.S. Army officer, commander of the Multi-National Force–Iraq (2007–2008), and commander the U.S. Central Command (CENTCOM) (2008–). Born on November 7, 1952, David Howell Petraeus

U.S. Army general David Petraeus commanded the Multi-National Force–Iraq during 2007–2008. He then assumed command of the U.S. Central Command (CENTCOM). (U.S. Army)

grew up and graduated from high school in Cornwall, New York. Petraeus graduated 10th in his class from the United States Military Academy, West Point, in 1974. Commissioned a second lieutenant of infantry, he graduated from Ranger School and served as a platoon leader in the 1st Battalion, 509th Airborne Infantry, in Italy. As a first lieutenant he served as assistant battalion operations officer, and as captain he served as company commander, battalion operations officer, and then commanding general's aide-de-camp, all in the 24th Infantry Division (Mechanized).

From 1982 to 1995 Petraeus served in a progression of command and staff assignments, with alternating assignments for both professional military and civilian academic education. He graduated from the Army Command and General Staff College in 1983 after which he attended Princeton University's Woodrow Wilson School of Public Affairs, where he earned a master's degree in public administration in 1985 and a doctorate in international relations in 1987. His doctoral dissertation dealt with the U.S. Army in Vietnam and the lessons learned there.

Petraeus returned to West Point as an assistant professor of international relations and then was a military fellow at Georgetown University's School of Foreign Service. In 1995 he was assigned as the chief operations officer of the United Nations (UN) mission during Operation UPHOLD DEMOCRACY in Haiti.

Petraeus's commanded assignments included the 3rd Battalion, 187th Infantry Regiment, 101st Airborne Division, during 1991–1993 and the 1st Brigade, 82nd Airborne Division, from 1995 to 1997. He was promoted to brigadier general in 1999.

Petraeus's first combat assignment, now at the rank of major general, came as commander of the 101st Airborne Division (Air Assault) in Operation IRAQI FREEDOM in March 2003. The division engaged in the Battle of Karbala and the Battle of Najar as well as the feint at Hilla. Petraeus later oversaw the administration and rebuilding of Mosul and Niveveh provinces. Subsequently, Petraeus commanded the Multinational Security Transition Command–Iraq and North Atlantic Treaty Organization (NATO) Training Mission–Iraq between June 2004 and September 2005. Petraeus's next assignment was as commanding general of Fort Leavenworth, Kansas, and the U.S. Army Combined Arms Center, where he exercised direct responsibility for the doctrinal changes to prepare the army for its continued efforts in Afghanistan and Iraq. He also coauthored *Field Manual 3-24, Counterinsurgency.*

On January 5, 2007, Petraeus, now a lieutenant general, was selected by President George W. Bush and later unanimously confirmed by the U.S. Senate to command the Multi-National Force–Iraq. Petraeus took formal command on February 10, 2007, replacing Lieutenant General George Casey. The Petraeus appointment was the keystone in Bush's troop surge strategy in Iraq designed to bring an end to the mounting violence there and to bring about peace in Iraq. Many welcomed the change in command but also remained skeptical that Petraeus could reverse the violence in Iraq.

In April 2007 Petraeus was tasked with reporting to Congress the progress of the Bush administration's surge strategy, begun that January, and met stiff and sometimes combative resistance. To his credit, however, Petraeus deftly handled the pressure and stated confidently that the strategy, given time, would show positive results. At the same time, he firmly argued against setting a timetable for the withdrawal of ground troops from Iraq. In July he submitted to Congress his first progress report, which was positive and upbeat. It met with derision, however, because it did not appear that Iraq was any more secure than it had been in January. His September 2007 report cited progress on the military and security fronts but admitted that the political climate in Iraq remained troubled. The September report drew sharp criticism from some Democrats and the antiwar lobby, compelling a bipartisan group of congressional representatives and senators to sponsor resolutions—which eventually passed—that condemned the recent attacks on Petraeus. Petraeus was promoted to four-star rank in December 2007.

By early 2008, defying high odds and most critics of the war, the surge strategy appeared to be paying off, as violence had fallen off markedly in the last quarter of 2007. Talk of troop drawdowns, however, were still subject to interpretation, as the possible numbers being cited would account mainly for the surge, meaning that troop strength in Iraq would remain unchanged from January 2007, even after troop reductions.

## Commanding Generals of the Multi-National Force–Iraq, 2003–Present

| Name | Dates of Command |
| --- | --- |
| Ricardo S. Sanchez | June 14, 2003–June 30, 2004 |
| George W. Casey Jr. | July 1, 2004–February 10, 2007 |
| David H. Petraeus | February 10, 2007–September 16, 2008 |
| Raymond T. Odierno | September 16, 2008–present |

By the spring of 2008, however, Petraeus could point to a significant reduction in sectarian and insurgency-based violence in Iraq. In addition, the Iraqis themselves seemed increasingly willing and able to take over security and police tasks. As a result, U.S. and coalition troop withdrawals accelerated throughout 2008, and violence in Iraq hit four-year lows. Petraeus was largely hailed in the United States for his efforts at undermining the Iraqi insurgency, and because of this President Bush tapped him to command CENTCOM. Petraeus took command on October 1, 2008; General Raymond Odierno succeeded him as commander of the Multi-National Force–Iraq.

During congressional hearings, Petraeus was careful to point out that talk of victory in Iraq was still premature; instead, he viewed the situation with a great deal of realism, suggesting that an Iraq that is "at peace with itself, at peace with its neighbors, and has a government that is representative of—and responsive to—its citizens" might be considered a victory. As the head of CENTCOM, Petraeus became responsible for U.S. military operations in 20 nations from Egypt to Pakistan as well as the ongoing conflicts in Afghanistan and Iraq.

On June 24, 2010, the same day that he removed General Stanley A. McChrystal as commander of U.S. and NATO forces in Afghanistan, President Barack Obama tapped Petraeus as McChrystal's successor, thereby sending a signal that there was no change in U.S. Afghanistan policy.

MARCEL A. DEROSIER

**See also**

IRAQI FREEDOM, Operation; McChrystal, Stanley A.; Multi-National Force–Iraq; North Atlantic Treaty Organization in Afghanistan; Odierno, Raymond; Surge, U.S. Troop Deployment, Iraq War; United States Central Command

**References**

Atkinson, Rick. *In the Company of Soldiers: A Chronicle of Combat.* New York: Henry Holt, 2005.

Day, Thomas L. *Along the Tigris: The 101st Airborne Division in Operation Iraqi Freedom: February 2003–March 2004.* Atglen, PA: Schiffer, 2007.

Fontenot, Gregory, et al. *On Point: The United States Army in Iraqi Freedom.* Annapolis, MD: Naval Institute Press, 2005.

## PHANTOM FURY/AL-FAJR, Operation

*See* Fallujah, Second Battle of

## PHANTOM STRIKE, Operation

Event Date: August 13, 2007

A Multi-National Force–Iraqi Army offensive launched on August 13, 2007. The force included 28,000 troops, many of whom were present as a result of the George W. Bush administration's troop surge, which had begun earlier in the year. Following on the heels of recent coalition offensive operations, which began in June 2007, including FARDH AL-QANOON (Baghdad Security Plan) and PHANTOM THUNDER (a nationwide counteroffensive), Operation PHANTOM STRIKE was designed to root out remaining Al Qaeda in Iraq terrorists and Iranian-backed extremist elements (including the Mahdi Army) and to reduce sectarian violence, with the goals of restoring law and order for the Iraqi people. PHANTOM STRIKE was led by U.S. Army lieutenant general Ray Odierno, then commander of the Multi-National Corps–Iraq. It was a joint mission conducted with the Iraqi Security Force. Opposing them were Abu Omar al-Baghdadi and Abu Ayyub al-Masri, leaders of Al Qaeda in Iraq. PHANTOM STRIKE was begun one month before General David Petraeus, commander of all coalition forces in Iraq, was to report to the U.S. Congress on progress in Iraq.

During the operation, coalition and Iraqi security forces went into previously unsecured regions and attempted to eliminate terrorist groups from safe havens in the capital city of Baghdad and the provinces of northern Babil, eastern Anbar, Salahuddin, and Diyala. Considerable emphasis was placed on destroying the terror cells in Baghdad, Diyala, and central and northern Iraq. Largely an intelligence-driven operation, PHANTOM STRIKE had coalition forces move into previous no-go zones and establish local security forces and intelligence networks designed to pinpoint the exact makeup and location of Sunni and Shia extremist groups while also rooting out Al Qaeda operatives in outlying regions of Baghdad and the more violent provinces. Both the Baghdad Security Plan and PHANTOM THUNDER shaped the culminating operations for PHANTOM STRIKE.

Coalition and Iraqi security forces launched dozens of raids in and around Baghdad. These included units of varying sizes and composition. Among those American and Iraqi units participating in the total operation were troops of the 3rd Stryker Brigade Combat Team, the 2nd Infantry Division, the 3rd Brigade Combat Team, the 1st Cavalry Division, the 25th Combat Aviation Brigade, and the 1st and 4th Iraqi Army divisions. Strike forces went into action by land and air. In some of the attacks, it was a matter of getting in and out quickly. In others, the forces remained for an extended period in order to keep the insurgents on the defensive and thus turn former "safe" insurgent areas into places too risky for them to return. Commanders of the surge forces were told only to take territory they could hold. As part of General Petraeus's new counterinsurgency strategy, PHANTOM STRIKE resulted in coalition forces moving out of their bases and into neighborhoods all across Baghdad and other major urban centers in the country in order to establish a security area based on the doctrine of clear, control, and retain (CCR).

PHANTOM STRIKE marked the last military offensive of Operation PHANTOM THUNDER and lasted until January 2008. From June 16 to August 19, 2007, alone, some 1,196 insurgents were killed and 6,702 captured. The precise number of killed or captured during the entire effort is uncertain. Eleven U.S. military personnel died during the operation; the number of Iraqi government casualties is unknown. The operation was termed a success in that insurgent groups were ejected from their strongholds in northern Babil, eastern Anbar, and Diyala provinces and the southern outskirts of Baghdad. Furthermore, the raids conducted during PHANTOM STRIKE gathered valuable information on Al Qaeda and Iranian-backed terror cells countrywide.

CHARLES F. HOWLETT

**See also**

Odierno, Raymond; Petraeus, David Howell

**References**

Filkins, Dexter. *The Forever War.* New York: Knopf, 2008.
Roggio, Bill. "Coalition, Iraqi Forces Launch Operation Phantom Strike." *Long War Journal,* August 13, 2007, http://longwarjournal.org/archives.
West, Bing. *The Strongest Tribe: War, Politics, and the Endgame in Iraq.* New York: Random House, 2008.

---

# PHANTOM THUNDER, **Operation**
## Start Date: June 16, 2007
## End Date: August 14, 2007

A corps-size operation carried out by coalition forces in Iraq (American and Iraq Security Forces) that commenced on June 16, 2007, under the command of General David Petraeus (Multi-National Force–Iraq, overall headquarters) and Lieutenant General Raymond Odierno (Multi-National Corps–Iraq, major troop force). Operation PHANTOM THUNDER was part of the U.S. troop surge strategy implemented in January 2007 and was designed to root out extremist groups, including Al Qaeda, from Iraq. PHANTOM THUNDER was comprised of several subordinate operations, including Operations ARROWHEAD RIPPER in Diyala Province, MARNE TORCH and COMMANDO EAGLE in Babil Province, FARDH AL-QANOON in Baghdad, ALLJAH in Anbar Province, and special forces attacks against the Mahdi Army in southern Iraq. In preparation for this campaign against the so-called Baghdad Belt, an additional five American brigades were deployed to Iraq between January and June 2007.

As the buildup began, Operation LAW AND ORDER began on February 14, 2007, in an effort to resecure Baghdad, with estimates running as high as almost 70 percent of the city under insurgent control. It became part of Operation PHANTOM THUNDER when American and Iraqi forces moved to clear Sunni insurgents, Al Qaeda fighters, and Shiite militiamen from Baghdad's northern and southern flanks. The United States wanted to take quick advantage of the arrival of 30,000 additional troops, so the offensive was begun as soon as possible. During LAW AND ORDER, 311 insurgents were killed.

Operation MARNE TORCH began on June 16 in Arab Jabour and Salman Pak, major transit points for insurgent forces in and out of Baghdad. By August 14, some 2,500 allied troops had killed 88 insurgents, captured more than 60 suspected terrorists, destroyed 51 boats, and destroyed 51 weapons caches.

On June 18, Operation ARROWHEAD RIPPER commenced when multinational troops assaulted Al Qaeda forces in the city of Baquba in Diyala Province with nighttime air strikes. As the ground forces moved in, intense street fighting engulfed the center of the city near the main market. By August 19, U.S. and Iraqi forces had killed 227 insurgents.

Multinational forces began Operation COMMANDO EAGLE on June 21 in the Mahmudiyyah region southwest of Baghdad. The area was known as the "Triangle of Death" because three U.S. soldiers had been kidnapped and killed there in mid-May 2007. Employing Humvee-based attacks supported by helicopter gunships, the operation resulted in roughly 100 insurgents killed and more than 50 captured.

Operations FARDH AL-QUANOON and ALLJAH were also conducted by multinational forces, this time west of Baghdad. The primary targets were Fallujah (Alljah), Karma, and Thar Thar. Allied planners developed a concept of attack similar to the one that took Ramadi in 2003. On June 17 a raid near Karma killed a known Libyan Al Qaeda fighter and six of his aides. Four days later, six Al Qaeda leaders were killed and five were captured near Karma. By the end of July, ground commanders reported that Karma and Thar Thar had been secured.

Throughout the summer, U.S. air strikes also proved effective against insurgents in Fallujah. However, on June 22 insurgents retaliated with two suicide bombing attacks on off-duty police officers that left four dead. On June 29 U.S. forces killed Abu Abd al-Rahman al-Masri, a senior Egyptian Al Qaeda leader east of Fallujah. They also captured and killed many others in the ensuing weeks. Fallujah proved hard to secure, and while officials declared it secure in late August, periodic incidents continued to occur well into 2008.

The final part of PHANTOM THUNDER was the action against the Mahdi Army. In June, Iraqi Special Forces, the core of the joint Iraqi-American operation, killed and captured dozens of troops belonging to the Mahdi Army.

Several lesser operations were also conducted against retreating insurgent forces in which an additional 234 were killed by August 14, when the Operation officially came to an end, and Operation PHANTOM STRIKE began. Operation ARROWHEAD RIPPER continued for another five days until street fighting in Baquba ended. This action blended into Operation PHANTOM STRIKE.

Official reports of the action stated that coalition and Iraqi security forces had pushed into areas previously not under their control and had killed or expelled insurgent forces from northern Babil, eastern Anbar, and Diyala provinces as well as from the southern outskirts of Baghdad. During the operation, Iraqi and coalition forces conducted intelligence raids against Al Qaeda in Iraq and the Iranian-backed cells nationwide.

Iraqi and coalition forces conducted 142 battalion-level joint operations, detaining 6,702 insurgents, killing 1,196, and wounding 419. Of this number, 382 were high-value targets. They captured 1,113 weapons caches and neutralized more than 2,000 improvised explosive devices (IEDs) and vehicle-borne IEDs. Of the approximately 28,000 U.S. and Iraqi military personnel who took part in PHANTOM THUNDER, 140 American soldiers died; the number of wounded has not been determined. Of the Iraqi security forces who fought with the Americans, 220 died; the number of wounded is not known. An additional 20 Iraqis died fighting in U.S.-allied militia units.

WILLIAM P. HEAD

**See also**

Al Qaeda in Iraq; ARROWHEAD RIPPER, Operation; Baghdad; Iraqi Insurgency; Mahdi Army; PHANTOM STRIKE, Operation; Surge, U.S. Troop Deployment, Iraq War

**References**

Institute for the Study of War Military Analysis and Education for Civilian Leaders. "Operation Phantom Thunder." http://www.understandingwar.org/operation/operation-phantom-thunder.

Roggio, Bill. "Operation Phantom Thunder: The Battle of Iraq." *Long War Journal,* June 21, 2007, http://www.longwarjournal.org/archives/2007/06/operation_phantom_fu.php.

---

# Phase Line Bullet, Battle of
## Event Date: February 26, 1991

A battle during the 1991 Persian Gulf War that led to the destruction of the 9th Mechanized Brigade of the Iraqi Republican Guard Tawakalna Division. The battle occurred on February 26, 1991, in southern Iraq. The engagement involved units of Major General Paul E. Funk's 3rd Armored Division and the 9th Armored Brigade of the Iraqi Tawakalna Republican Guard Division commanded by General Ayad Futayh al-Rawi. The battle was one of the very few examples during the Persian Gulf War in which entrenched and prepared Iraqi infantry were able to repulse American armor. It was also notable for the adverse weather conditions in which it was fought and for the American friendly fire casualties.

The Iraqi Republican Guard had proven itself during the 1980–1988 Iran-Iraq War. By early 1991 the Republican Guard numbered eight armored and mechanized divisions. Equipment was Soviet-made, including T-72 tanks and the latest infantry fighting vehicles. While some Republican Guard units remained in Baghdad to protect the regime, most divisions were in Kuwait or southern Iraq to defend against the anticipated coalition ground attack. One of the divisions was the Tawakalna Division (also known as the 3rd Mechanized Division). It had distinguished itself during the war with Iran and was regarded as one of the best units in the Iraqi Army. The

division had led the invasion of Kuwait in August 1990 and then assumed a defensive position near the western Kuwaiti border.

The Tawakalna Division included two mechanized brigades and one armored brigade, all organized and equipped according to Soviet doctrine. At the beginning of the war, the division was near full strength and was equipped with 220 T-72 tanks and 278 infantry fighting vehicles. Because the Tawakalna Division had taken up its position before the air campaign began, it was largely intact by the time the ground campaign began on February 24.

The coalition battle plan included a turning movement by forces in western Saudi Arabia. The American XVIII Corps on the far left flank would move north and east through largely unprotected deserts in southern Iraq to cut off escape routes to Baghdad. The American VII Corps to its right under Lieutenant General Frederick Franks Jr. would also move north and then wheel east in a more shallow movement to roll up the Iraqi forces in southern Iraq and Kuwait and destroy them before they could withdraw. Funk's 3rd Armored Division was part of VII Corps.

By February 26 the coalition plan was unfolding as expected, although VII Corps was somewhat behind schedule. Thousands of Iraqi soldiers had surrendered, most without a fight, and many coalition soldiers believed that the rest of the campaign would see little action. That morning, the divisions of the corps turned east and headed toward Kuwait City. As VII Corps moved east, it encountered and defeated Iraqi units, with the 2nd Armored Cavalry Regiment destroying two Iraqi armored brigades. The 3rd Armored Division headed for Phase Line Bullet, one of the lines drawn to mark the allied advance. The weather turned poor, with a sandstorm reducing visibility. The smoke from hundreds of oil well fires set by the Iraqis also helped to bring visibility near zero, forcing the advancing U.S. units to employ thermal lights.

Around 3:00 p.m. an advance unit of the 3rd Armored Division encountered heavy Iraqi resistance near Phase Line Bullet, about 80 miles from Kuwait City. This unit was Alpha Troop, 4th Squadron, 7th Cavalry Regiment, commanded by Captain Gerald Davie. It numbered 14 M3 Bradley armored fighting vehicles. Iraqi surprise was nearly complete because the unit had just received word from division headquarters that no Iraqi units remained between it and the Kuwaiti border to the east. The first indication that something was amiss was when the Americans saw a line of Iraqi armored personnel carriers only some 325 yards ahead. As Davie later admitted that was about one-tenth the preferred range. Iraqi small-arms and heavy machine-gun fire, along with rocket-propelled grenades (RPGs) and Sagger antitank missiles, raked the American formation. Fortunately, the accuracy of the Saggers was adversely affected by the weather conditions. Alpha Troop responded with 25-millimeter fire from their turret guns, machine-gun fire, and TOW antitank missiles.

The U.S. fire had little effect, as many of the Iraqis were dug into fighting positions along the line. They were supported by a dozen field artillery batteries to the rear along with mortars in position near the line. The engagement lasted about two hours.

Realizing that his unit was also receiving main gun tank rounds and running out of ammunition, Davie ordered a withdrawal.

Before they were able to withdraw, a majority of the Bradleys had been damaged by Iraqi fire to varying degrees. U.S. M-1 Abrams tanks positioned to the rear fired in support of A Troop and destroyed at least one Iraqi T-72 tank and several armored personnel carriers (APCs), but at least one Abrams mistook the Bradleys for Iraqi vehicles and fired on them. Two Bradleys were hit by Abrams tank fire, with two American soldiers killed.

General Funk recognized that a hasty assault on the entrenched Iraqi position could be costly. He ordered his screening forces to probe the position, identify weak points, and push through if possible. The 1st Brigade, on the right, sent a company from the 3rd Battalion, 5th Cavalry, forward. They were joined by two other companies in Bradleys. Because the visibility was so poor, the battalion was much closer to the Iraqis than normal. The thermal sights used in poor visibility were not working as well as expected because of the weather and the oil smoke. Even so, the battalion was able to call in artillery support as it identified Iraqi tanks and other vehicles. Iraqi field artillery that fired on American forces was quickly silenced. Despite the support, the Americans in this part of the field were unable to advance.

On the left, scouts from the 4th Battalion, 32nd Armor, identified Iraqi T-72 tanks advancing. They managed to destroy the leading tank, but the Americans were unable to advance any farther. The action was confused, and the Americans were unable to break through until early on the morning of February 27.

The Battle of Phase Line Bullet was an unexpected setback for the Americans. Four Bradleys were destroyed, and 10 others were damaged. Two Americans had been killed by friendly fire, and another 12 were wounded by both Iraqi and American fire. More importantly, the 3rd Armored Division's advance was held up by at least 12 hours while attempts were made to wear down the Republican Guard and force a breach in the line. When the American forces moved forward after the battle, they found 6 Iraqi T-72 tanks either destroyed or disabled by their crews. Eighteen Iraqi APCs were also destroyed or abandoned, along with some field artillery and other weapons. An unknown number of Iraqi soldiers died in the fighting.

In the end, the Battle of Phase Line Bullet did not change the course of the Persian Gulf War. It did, however, demonstrate that the Iraqis were capable of putting up a good fight against an American advance when the troops had the equipment and training to do so and when weather and terrain forced the Americans to fight in close proximity to Iraqi forces, thereby negating the overwhelming U.S. advantage in stand-off firepower.

TIM J. WATTS

**See also**

Armored Warfare, Persian Gulf and Iraq Wars; Bradley Fighting Vehicle; DESERT STORM, Operation, Ground Operations; Franks, Frederick Melvin, Jr.; Funk, Paul Edward; M1A1 and M1A2 Abrams Main Battle Tanks; Republican Guard; T-72 Main Battle Tank

**References**

Atkinson, Rick. *Crusade: The Untold Story of the Persian Gulf War.* New York: Mariner Books, 1994.

Bin, Alberto, Richard Hill, and Archer Jones. *Desert Storm: A Forgotten War.* Westport, CT: Praeger, 1998.

# Piracy

Piracy is the seizure of a ship or property on the high seas in an action without commission from a sovereign nation and under conditions that make it unfair to hold any state responsible. Piracy was endemic in the ancient world and continued to be widespread until the establishment of powerful national navies. From the Middle Ages to the first decades of the 19th century, piracy was concentrated largely in the Mediterranean off North Africa. Indeed, actions by the Barbary pirates (Barbary Wars of 1801–1805 and 1815) prompted the newly established United States to undertake its first military interventions in the region. It has not been unknown in the contemporary world, especially in Southeast Asia, but in recent years piracy has become a major problem in the busy shipping lanes of the Gulf of Aden and off the Horn of Africa.

Following the beginning of civil war in Somalia in the 1990s, acts of piracy increased off the 1,800-mile-long Somali coast. These have become especially pronounced since 2005. In late 2008, moreover, the pirates expanded their zone of operations south to intercept ships bound for Mombasa, Kenya. The incentive in these operations is entirely financial. Although there has been a general arms embargo on Somalia in effect since 1992, small bands of highly organized Somali pirates armed only with automatic weapons and rocket-propelled grenades and traveling in fast motorized skiffs have boarded and seized control of merchant ships plying the busy waterways. The ships and their crews are then held for ransom.

Piracy led to the establishment of Combined Task Force 150, a multinational coalition force that established a Maritime Security Patrol Area (MSPA) in the Gulf of Aden. This did not prevent two of the most brazen acts of piracy from occurring, however. On September 21, 2008, pirates in three speedboats seized an underway Ukrainian container ship off the Somali coast, hijacking it and taking its 19 crew members hostage. The pirates demanded $35 million in ransom. Among the ship's cargo were 35 T-72 tanks, considerable quantities of ammunition, and grenade launchers.

Both the United States and Russia dispatched warships to join a coalition of ships from eight European states. The Indian Navy joined the patrols in October. Yet on November 17 off the coast of Kenya, Somali pirates seized the 1,800-foot-long Saudi Arabian supertanker *Sirius Star* transporting 2 million barrels of oil worth an estimated $100 million.

The difficulty of bringing the pirates to justice can be seen in two examples. On November 18, 2008, the Indian Navy frigate *Tabar* engaged and sank what it claimed at the time to be a pirate

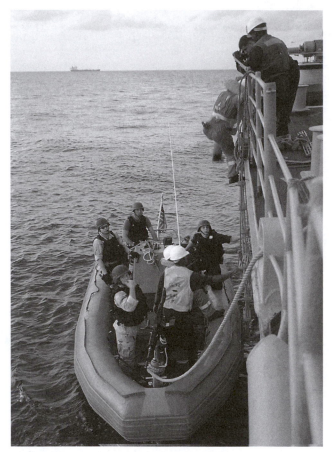

Crew members from the cargo ship Motor Vessel *Polaris* board the U.S. guided-missile cruiser *Vella Gulf* in the Gulf of Aden to identify suspected pirates apprehended by the *Vella Gulf*, on February 11, 2009. The American cruiser was the flagship of Combined Task Force 151, a multinational force conducting counterpiracy operations in and around the Gulf of Aden, Persian Gulf, Indian Ocean, and Red Sea. (U.S. Navy)

mother vessel with two speedboats in tow. The ship in question turned out to be the Thai cargo ship *Ekawat Nava 5,* with a crew of 16, that had put out a distress call when it was in the process of being seized by the pirates. The Thai ship was apparently under pirate control when the captain of the *Tabar* claimed that men on the deck had opened fire on the Indian warship with rocket-propelled grenades. The *Tabar* then returned fire, resulting in explosions about the Thai ship. Only 1 crew member was recovered alive after drifting nearly a week in the Gulf of Aden.

The second encounter occurred on December 25 and involved the German frigate *Karlsruhe.* Responding to a distress call from the Egyptian merchant ship *Wabi Al Arab,* which had come under attack, the *Karlsruhe* dispatched helicopters, causing the pirates to break off their attack. The pirates were subsequently captured and their weapons destroyed, but because the ship that had been the object of the attack was not German, the German government ordered the pirates released.

Although the pirates are totally outgunned by the patrolling warships, the hijackings have continued. In 2008 there were an estimated 124 attempted and actual hijackings of ships by Somali

pirates in the Gulf of Aden. Several dozen ships were taken, and at the end of the year pirate groups were holding some 200 crewmen seized with 14 ships. The pirates are difficult to apprehend and can easily flee to land, where it is nearly impossible to catch them. With the rewards high and risks of capture and punishment slim, it is no wonder that the attacks have continued. According to one source, Somali pirates collected some $150 million in ransoms in 2008 alone.

The situation was sufficiently serious for the United Nations (UN) Security Council to unanimously pass a resolution authorizing hot pursuit in the Gulf of Aden. The resolution allows forces of the North Atlantic Treaty Organization (NATO) and the Russian and Indian governments involved in antipiracy activities in the Gulf of Aden to pursue attacking pirates onto land.

With its own ships among those being captured and with it now importing 60 percent of its oil from the Middle East, the People's Republic of China (PRC) at the end of December 2008 dispatched a naval task force of two destroyers and a supply ship to the Gulf of Aden. It was the first modern deployment of Chinese warships beyond the Pacific.

The actions by the Somali pirates have driven up the price of food and shipping costs. The piracy has also greatly impacted the shipment of humanitarian aid. For example, some 90 percent of World Food Programme relief shipments to the region are by sea. By 2009 a number of states, including the United States, West European nations, Japan, and the PRC had sent naval units to the region in a cooperative effort to fight against this threat to world trade.

SPENCER C. TUCKER

**See also**
Somalia, International Intervention in

**References**
Burnett, John S. *Dangerous Waters: Modern Piracy and Terror on the High Seas.* New York: E. P. Dutton, 2002.
Gosse, Philip. *The History of Piracy.* Whitefish, MT: Kessenger, 2002.
Botting, Douglas. *The Pirates.* Alexandria, VA: Time-Life Books, 1978.

## Plame, Valerie

*See* Wilson, Valerie Plame

## Poland, Forces in Iraq

Poland is a nation of Central Europe bordered on the north by the Baltic Sea, to the northeast by Russia and Lithuania, to the east by Belarus and Ukraine, to the South by the Czech Republic and Slovakia, and to the west by Germany. With a land area of 121,196 square miles, Poland's current population is approximately 38.5 million people. A former communist bloc nation, Poland is a rising regional economic power and had been integrated fully into the Western-capitalist orbit; it has been a member of the North

Atlantic Treaty Organization (NATO) since 1999. Poland's government is a representative democratic republic, led by a prime minister and a president.

Poland was one of the few nations to assist the United States and Great Britain with troops in the March 2003 invasion of Iraq to overthrow Iraqi dictator Saddam Hussein; over the succeeding five years Poland maintained 2,500 troops in Iraq. On March 17, 2003, Polish prime minister Leszek Miller requested that President Aleksander Kwaśniewski authorize the deployment of Polish troops "as part of an international coalition to contribute to enforcing Iraq's compliance with United Nations Security Council Resolution 1441." Prime Minister Miller's request was approved the next day. In approving the request, President Kwaśniewski noted in a statement "the threat posed by weapons of mass destruction (WMDs)" and that "the Iraqi authorities have never demonstrated a will to disarm." He also linked Hussein with international terrorism, declaring that "we should all take measures against terrorism." Announcing as a "fact" that Hussein possessed WMDs, the Polish president concluded that "Iraq's willingness to disarm will not materialize other than by force." Kwaśniewski concluded by declaring that "we are part of a grand antiterrorist coalition formed in the aftermath of the events of September 11, 2001" and warned against "indifference" in the face of threats to peace,

recalling the events of 1939 when, owing to indifference by other countries, Nazi Germany invaded and occupied Poland that year.

During the invasion of Iraq, fearing the deliberate destruction of Iraqi oil wells as had occurred during the 1991 Persian Gulf War and an ensuing environmental catastrophe, some 200 Polish Operational Mobile Reconnaissance Group (GROM) commandos, along with U.S. and British Special Forces, took control of Iraqi oil platforms and oil tanker docking facilities in the Persian Gulf along with the southern Iraqi port city of Umm Qasr. They then participated in operations there. As the only Iraqi port city, Umm Qasr was a strategic military asset, and securing it was crucial to delivering humanitarian supplies to the rest of Iraq. British and U.S. Special Forces were highly complimentary of the skill of Poland's GROM's forces and their operations. Although GROM forces had performed peacekeeping operations in Haiti and the Balkans (including successfully capturing in 1997 Slavko Dokmanovic, "the Butcher of Vukovar," who had been held responsible for the murder of 260 Croats in 1991), this was their first wartime deployment.

After the successful invasion of Iraq, Poland maintained a contingent of 2,500 troops as of August 1, 2003. Polish forces operated out of Camp Echo in Qadisiya Province in south-central Iraq and in August were given command by the United States of a multinational force, which at its peak included troops from more than

Polish soldiers perform a mortar team demonstration for soldiers of the Iraqi 8th Army Division on May 13, 2008, during training at Camp Echo, Iraq. (U.S. Department of Defense)

20 other countries, including a number from Central and Eastern Europe. This Polish-commanded multinational force, initially led by General Andrzej Tyszkiewicz, was responsible for the security of five provinces south of Baghdad totaling approximately 31,000 square miles of land with a population of around 5 million, mostly Shia. The four provinces under Polish control were Qadisiya, Karbala, Babil, and Wasit, which also included the holy Shiite cities of Najaf and Karbala. A total of nine different Polish generals commanded the Polish-led multinational force from 2003 to 2008, no doubt to afford its previously combat-inexperienced officer corps combat experience.

The risks to Polish forces were immediately demonstrated on August 1, 2003—the same day Poland announced that it was expanding its presence in Iraq by deploying 2,500 additional troops to Iraq—when Polish troops already stationed in Iraq were attacked at their base by mortars. Over the next five years, Poland rotated a total of approximately 15,000 troops in and out of Iraq.

After five years of operations in Iraq, Poland's military mission in Iraq was ceremonially ended on October 4, 2008, although it is worth noting that Poland withdrew its forces only after violence in Iraq had declined significantly rather than during the height of the Iraqi insurgency. In the course of its five years of operations in Iraq, Poland lost 25 men killed and some 70 wounded.

Initially, Poland's participation in the Iraq War and subsequent occupation of the country was popular at home, but support began to erode quickly as the insurgency against U.S. and coalition forces developed in the summer and autumn of 2003 and Saddam Hussein's stockpiles of WMDs failed to materialize. In addition, when the expected economic benefits of the country's sacrifice in terms of access to Iraqi oil and lucrative contracts for Polish companies failed to materialize, public support for Poland's military role in Iraq declined further. Poland, heavily dependent on Russia for much of its energy needs, sought access to Iraqi oil to achieve greater energy independence. Indeed, according to the BBC, on July 3, 2003, Polish foreign minister Wlodzimierz Cimoszewicz admitted that "we have never hidden our desire for Polish oil companies to finally have access to sources of commodities," adding that access to Iraq oil was his country's "ultimate objective."

In spite of disappointment among the Polish public regarding their country's participation in Iraq, Polish-U.S. ties increased significantly, so much so that in 2008, over the strenuous objections of Russia, Poland agreed to allow the United States to place a missile defense base on its territory, part of a European missile defense shield against what the United States fears might be possible future missile attacks from rogue states such as Iran. Poland proudly views the defense shield as reflective of its stronger influence and role in NATO and also as a means to ensure its security against a resurgent Russia. Fearing what it sees as Russia's renewed ambitions to dominate Eastern Europe, in addition to economic and energy considerations, Poland almost certainly participated in the Iraq War and subsequent occupation to enhance the military prestige of its untested military and, equally importantly, to earn the goodwill and gratitude of the United States, which Poland sees as indispensable to its security. In so doing, Poland expected that it would be rewarded with stronger ties with the Americans and would gain additional security guarantees because this missile defense shield also has the ability to undermine, if not neutralize, Russia's missile arsenal.

Indeed, commenting on the effect of Poland's participation in Iraq, Stanislaw Koziej, a retired general and former deputy defense minister, acknowledged the increase in military prestige and power that Poland has gained: "the skills that Polish generals and officers, the experience, makes the army far more efficient than before. . . . [U]p until 2003, Poland was treated more like a third- or fourth-tier country [but now] its voice is listened to more seriously" in both NATO and the European Union (EU). There can be no doubt that Poland's military has gained invaluable combat experience that has helped transform its military into a modern professional force that thus serves as a greater asset to NATO, something the U.S. has duly noted.

Although Poland has since withdrawn all of its troops from Iraq, it has sent additional troops to Afghanistan, where it trains Afghan soldiers and provides security along a dangerous 180-mile stretch of road between the capital of Kabul and the Taliban-infested city of Kandahar.

STEFAN M. BROOKS

**See also**

IRAQI FREEDOM, Operation; Iraqi Insurgency; North Atlantic Treaty Organization; Umm Qasr, Battle of

**References**

Couch, Dick. *Down Range: Navy SEALs in the War on Terrorism*. New York: Three Rivers, 2006.

Donnelly, Thomas. *Operation Iraqi Freedom: A Strategic Assessment*. Washington, DC: American Enterprise Institute Press, 2004.

Keegan, John. *The Iraq War: The Military Offensive, from Victory in 21 Days to the Insurgent Aftermath*. New York: Vintage, 2005.

U.S. Department of Defense. *21st Century Complete Guide to Operation Iraqi Freedom, through 2006*. Washington, DC: Progressive Management, 2006.

# Pollard, Jonathan
## Birth Date: August 7, 1954

American spy for Israel and one of the most notorious spies in American history. Born in Galveston, Texas, into an affluent family on August 7, 1954, Jonathan Pollard graduated from Stanford University. He then attended the Fletcher School of Law and Diplomacy in Boston for two years but did not graduate. In 1977 he applied for a position at the Central Intelligence Agency (CIA) but apparently failed a polygraph test. Two years later, however, he secured a position with U.S. Naval Intelligence as a research specialist, working in the Field Operational Intelligence Office in

Suitland, Maryland. Unmasked as a spy and arrested in November 1985, he confessed and entered into a plea bargain by which he would agree to be interviewed, submit to polygraph examination, and provide damage assessment information. In return the government extended a plea bargain to Pollard's wife, Anne, and promised Pollard that he would be charged with only one count of conspiracy to deliver national intelligence information to a foreign government, which carried a maximum sentence of life in prison.

In 1986 Pollard was sentenced to life in prison. Before sentencing, U.S. secretary of defense Caspar Weinberger delivered a lengthy classified memorandum to the sentencing judge, the contents of which were not made available to Pollard's attorneys. Jonathan Pollard began his sentence in 1987. Anne Pollard was sentenced to five years in prison but was released after three and a half years for health reasons.

In the years since Pollard's sentencing many books and articles have appeared on the case, a number of them claiming that Pollard is either innocent or that his sentence was unjust, either because Israel is a U.S. ally or because Pollard had entered into a plea bargain agreement (which, however, did not detail sentencing). Because Pollard was never actually brought to trial and because of the classified nature of his crimes, a great many questions about the case remain. Certainly, Pollard's behavior was bizarre and should have alerted his superiors much earlier in his espionage career.

Extraordinarily costly to the United States in terms of sensitive information lost, by his own admission Pollard gathered and transferred to Israeli intelligence an astonishing 1 million pages of classified material occupying about 360 cubic feet. Although the exact information passed to the Israelis by Pollard remains classified, investigative reporters have charged that it included information on the U.S. global electronic surveillance network, the names of American agents in the Soviet Union (information that some say Israel may have traded to the Soviet Union in return for a continued flow of Jewish immigrants to Israel), and U.S. Navy techniques for tracking Soviet submarines.

Pollard first approached four other nations about selling the information to them. Although the Israeli government refused Pollard asylum in 1985, it also initially denied that he had spied for Israel. Nonetheless, the Israeli government continues to make efforts to secure Pollard's release. Not until 1998 did Israeli prime minister Benjamin Netanyahu admit that Pollard had spied for the Jewish state. That same year the Israeli government declared Pollard to be an Israeli citizen. Thus far, all appeals for Pollard's release have gone unanswered. The U.S. courts have also repeatedly rejected Pollard's appeals for a new trial on the grounds of ineffective assistance by counsel. In January 2008 while President George W. Bush held talks with Israeli prime minister Ehud Olmert during a state visit to Israel, the issue of Pollard's release was once more a topic of discussion. Bush refused to consider the request.

SPENCER C. TUCKER

**See also**

Israel; Netanyahu, Benjamin; Weinberger, Caspar Willard

**References**

Goldenberg, Elliot, and Alan M. Dershowitz. *The Hunting Horse: The Truth behind the Jonathan Pollard Spy Case.* Amherst, NY: Prometheus, 2000.

Olive, Ronald J. *Capturing Jonathan Pollard: How One of the Most Notorious Spies in American History Was Brought to Justice.* Annapolis, MD: Naval Institute Press, 2006.

# Portugal, Role in Persian Gulf, Afghanistan, and Iraq Wars

Nation located on the western portion of the Iberian Peninsula in Southwestern Europe, bordered to the south and west by the Atlantic Ocean and to the north and east by Spain. Officially known as the Portugal Republic, the country covers 35,645 square miles and is divided into three major landmasses: continental Portugal, the Azores, and the Madeira Islands. Portugal's 2008 population was estimated at 10.667 million people.

Portuguese political systems have varied widely throughout Portugal's existence. Initially a monarchy and under various dynasties, the country has also had several authoritarian and republican governments, although only one republic became a true dictatorship, led by António de Oliveira Salazar from 1933 to 1970. From 1970 to 1974 his successor continued his autocratic regime until a liberal-minded military revolution overthrew the old order and created a liberal-style democracy beginning in 1976. Presently, Portugal is a parliamentary democratic republic led by a prime minister and is a member of multiple international organizations, including the North Atlantic Treaty Organization (NATO), the United Nations (UN), the European Union (EU), and the Organization for Economic Cooperation and Development (OECD). As such, Portugal has strong ties to other Western industrial democracies, including the United States. Portugal's political landscape is dominated by two political groups: the Socialist Party and the Social Democratic Party. Both parties have held power in Portugal with considerable frequency since 1990.

Portugal's military forces currently consist of an army, air force, and navy. Additionally, the National Republican Guard is a military police force whose members serve as civil and military police officials in Portugal and are under the authority of the military. In recent years, Portugal has rarely deployed its military forces unilaterally overseas, but it has been willing to actively support NATO- and UN-sanctioned operations. Between 1990 and 2007 Portugal sent troops to internationally sanctioned military operations in Bosnia, Serbia, Lebanon, and throughout Southwest Asia, although its participation in military operations in Southwest Asia has been somewhat limited. During the 1991 Persian Gulf War, Portugal limited its military participation to the dispatch of one support ship to assist coalition forces.

Portuguese participation in Operation IRAQI FREEDOM occurred after major combat operations had been completed on April 30,

2003. Portugal deployed 128 military police officers to assist in peacekeeping operations who worked alongside those of Italy in the Nasiriyah region in southern Iraq. The last of these troops were removed by February 10, 2005. The NATO Training Implementation Mission–Iraq (NTIM-I) was responsible for training the new Iraqi military and police forces. Portugal provided four officers and two sergeants from the Independent Air Transport Brigade to train Iraqi military forces. Despite fairly strong support from the Portuguese government, a number of antiwar protesters actively opposed Portuguese participation in Iraq and sought to prohibit U.S. forces from using Portuguese facilities, and they also called for Portugal's withdrawal from NATO. Portuguese labor unions and the Portuguese Communist Party have demonstrated their opposition to Portuguese involvement in Iraq.

Portugal has actively supported NATO's International Security Assistance Force–Afghanistan (ISAF). Since the Portuguese began participating in the ISAF in January 2002, their units usually deployed for six months before being replaced by another unit. Portuguese combat units and forces in Afghanistan have primarily been parachute infantry troops, infantry troops, and commandos, which form a rapid reaction force that averages about 150 men. The Portuguese Air Force has provided a 7-man tactical air control party, assigned to Camp Warehouse in Kabul, to provide airport security. Portuguese forces were later deployed to Kandahar Province to provide additional support to ISAF operations. Portugal also sent one Lockheed C-130 Hercules aircraft plus a crew and support staff of 42 persons from the 501st Transportation Squadron in 2002 for three months. Since 2002, the 501st Transportation Squadron has deployed additional times, with a support staff ranging from 37 to 42 personnel. One deployment lasted for approximately a year, from July 2004 through July 2005. Portugal also provided an air force unit responsible for running Kabul International Airport between August and December 2005.

By 2007, ISAF commanders had shifted most Portuguese troops to Kandahar, Farah, and Herat provinces to provide additional combat support. Portugal's rapid reaction forces were used in actual combat operations and to provide support during other operations. Approximately 100 Portuguese commandos from the 2nd Commando Company (Scorpions) participated in Operation HOOVER (May 24–25, 2007) in Kandahar Province. During Operation MEDUSA (September 2–17, 2007) in the same region, Portugal's forces provided security for the regional airport. In addition to the 2nd Commando Company, Portugal's 1st and 2nd Parachute Infantry battalions have both provided companies for operation in Afghanistan.

In 2008 Portugal agreed to provide an operational mentoring and liaison team (OMLT) to help train the Afghan Army. Its OMLT includes members from their various military services, including four members of its naval forces. Although the Portuguese people have generally accepted their nation's participation in the ISAF, a small antiwar movement continues to protest Portugal's involvement in Afghanistan. In August 2008 the Portuguese government announced its plans to cut its contributions to the ISAF by 90 percent, leaving just a CH-130, its crew, and 15 soldiers to continue training the Afghan Army. By the end of 2009 Portugal had 110 troops in Afghanistan.

WYNDHAM WHYNOT

**See also**

Afghanistan; ENDURING FREEDOM, Operation; International Security Assistance Force; IRAQI FREEDOM, Operation; North Atlantic Treaty Organization; North Atlantic Treaty Organization in Afghanistan

**References**

Anderson, James. *The History of Portugal.* Westport, CT: Greenwood, 2000.
Manuel, Paul Christopher. *The Challenges of Democratic Consolidation in Portugal: Political, Economic, and Military Issues, 1976–1991.* Westport, CT: Praeger, 1996.
Ortiz-Griffin, Julia L., and William D. Griffin. *Spain and Portugal Today.* New York: Peter Lang, 2003.

# Post-Traumatic Stress Disorder

Medical and psychological condition that may be caused by exposure to hostile combat situations and other traumatic events. Post-traumatic stress disorder (PTSD) may be temporary or long lasting. In earlier wars, particularly beginning with the American Civil War, symptoms of combat trauma were not medically recognized. In some instances, soldiers executed for cowardice during the American Civil War may likely have suffered from combat-induced trauma. Prior to the Vietnam War the condition was well known, yet it was not uncommon for military doctors to diagnose PTSD as malingering, since PTSD sufferers typically lack physical wounds. Many officers viewed combat trauma as a threat to discipline and military readiness. The most notorious incident in this regard occurred during World War II in Sicily in 1943 when U.S. Army lieutenant general George S. Patton Jr. slapped two hospitalized soldiers who were likely suffering PTSD. Patton was forced to apologize publicly and was sidelined from high command for some time.

Various characterizations have been used to describe combat trauma over the years, including shell shock, war neurosis, and battle fatigue. "Shell shock" was the most common term during World War I, while the term "battle fatigue" replaced it in World War II (although the term "combat exhaustion" was often preferred in the U.S. Army). Symptoms associated with combat-induced trauma can include involuntary trembling, outbursts of uncontrollable anger, nightmares, flashbacks, restlessness, depression, alcoholism, drug addiction or dependency, and an inability to focus. Such conditions may last for days, months, or even a lifetime.

It was not until the 1980s that the U.S. government recognized psychic injury due to combat as a legitimate service-related disability. At the same time, such medical diagnoses became popularly known as PTSD. The outcome of successful lobbying of Congress and the Veterans Administration (VA) by veterans' interest groups led to a two-year study (1986–1988), known as the National Vietnam Veterans Readjustment Study. The study examined the psychological effects on veterans who had performed hazardous duty in Southeast Asia. The study revealed that 15.2 percent of all male veterans (497,000 out of 3.14 million who served in Vietnam) and 8.1 percent of women (610 out of 7,200), many nurses, were diagnosed with PTSD. In 2004 VA statistics noted that almost 161,000 Vietnam War veterans were still receiving disability compensation for PTSD. By then, combat trauma was no longer cast in a negative light or lightly dismissed, as in previous conflicts.

Although the short duration of the 1991 Persian Gulf War and lower levels of combat exposure in that conflict meant less psychological trauma, a 1999 study revealed that rates of PTSD among the approximately 697,000 deployed service members had increased significantly over time. A rate of 3 percent for men and 8 percent for women was detected immediately upon returning from the war. This rate rose to 7 percent for men and 16 percent for women within 18 to 24 months.

The Iraq War and the Afghanistan War are ongoing, and the full impact of these conflicts on the mental health of those fighting is not yet known. Certainly, suicide bombers, constant fear of improvised explosive devices (IEDs), multiple redeployments, and extended deployments have increased the risk factors associated with PTSD. A recent study for Afghanistan War veterans shows that 183 veterans out of 45,880 have been diagnosed with PTSD. A 2008 VA study noted that almost 12,500 of nearly 245,000 Iraq War veterans have visited VA counseling centers for readjustment problems related to PTSD symptoms. Almost all have been soldiers and marines because they have withstood the worst of the fighting, as opposed to air force and navy personnel. In addition, 8–10 percent of active-duty women and retired military women who served in Iraq beginning in 2003 suffer from PTSD. The high percentage of women PTSD sufferers clearly reflects the increasing number of females who have participated in combat as part of the All Volunteer Forces.

A 2005 study examining PTSD in one U.S. Marine Corps and three U.S. Army infantry units that fought in Iraq and Afghanistan pointed out the type and percentage of soldiers and marines who were exposed to some type of traumatic combat-related situation: those being attacked or ambushed, 92 percent; those located near dead bodies, 94.5 percent; those being shot at, 95 percent; and those knowing someone seriously wounded or killed, 86.5 percent. Currently, almost 1 in 8 Iraq War and Afghanistan War combat veterans has sought help for PTSD.

Within the psychiatric profession, treatment for combat trauma or PTSD has moved from psychodynamic psychotherapy to biopsychiatric pharmacological application (i.e., the use of drugs). Yet such treatment has not been matched by increased effectiveness capable of reducing the degree and length of time of this disorder. More troubling to the medical profession is the fact that almost 6 in 10 combat veterans remain unlikely to seek treatment out of fear that their commanders and fellow soldiers and marines will lose confidence in them.

CHARLES F. HOWLETT

**See also**
Veterans Health Care Act of 1992

**References**
Ensign, Tod. *America's Military Today: Challenges for the Armed Forces in a Time of War.* New York: Free Press, 2004.
Grossman, David. *On Killing: The High Cost of Learning to Kill in War and Society.* Boston: Little, Brown, 1995.
Keane, T. M., and D. H. Barlow. "Posttraumatic Stress Disorder." In *Anxiety and Its Disorders,* 2nd ed., edited by D. H. Barlow, 418–453. New York: Guildford, 2002.
Pierce, P. F. "Physical and Emotional Health of Gulf War Veteran Women." *Aviation, Space, and Environmental Medicine* 68 (1997): 317–321.
Stretch, R. H., D. H. Marlowe, K. M. Wright, P. D. Bliese, K. H. Knudson, and C. H. Hoover. "Post-Traumatic Stress Disorder Symptoms among Gulf War Veterans." *Military Medicine* 161 (1996): 407–410.

---

# Powell, Colin Luther
## Birth Date: April 5, 1937

U.S. Army officer, national security adviser during 1987–1989, chairman of the Joint Chiefs of Staff (JCS) during 1989–1993, and secretary of state during 2001–2005. Colin Luther Powell was born in New York City on April 5, 1937, the child of Jamaican immigrants. While pursuing a geology degree at the City College of New York, he joined the Reserve Officers' Training Corps (ROTC) and earned his commission as a second lieutenant in 1958. After paratrooper and Ranger training, Powell was deployed as a military adviser to Vietnam. Even though he was wounded and received a Purple Heart during his first tour, he chose to volunteer for a second tour before earning a master's degree in business administration at George Washington University in 1971. He was a White House fellow in 1972, followed by command assignments at the battalion, brigade, and division levels.

Powell served in executive assistant positions in the Energy Department and the Defense Department during the administration of President Jimmy Carter. Under President Ronald Reagan, Powell quickly moved up the ranks from senior military assistant to Secretary of Defense Casper Weinberger, whom Powell assisted during both the 1983 invasion of Grenada and the 1986 air strike on Libya. In 1986 Powell, now a lieutenant general, assumed command of the U.S. Army's V Corps in Germany. The following year he became Reagan's national security adviser. In 1989 Powell was promoted to full general (four stars) and assumed command of Forces Command. Later that year be became the youngest officer and the first African American to serve as chairman of the JCS.

As JCS chairman, Powell was responsible for developing the strategy that would allow a coalition of nations to push Iraqi president Saddam Hussein's invasion force out of Kuwait. Powell's

As chairman of the Joint Chiefs of Staff (JCS) during 1989–1993, General Colin Powell played a key role in the Persian Gulf War. As secretary of state during 2001–2005, he opposed an invasion of Iraq but loyally presented the U.S. case for war before the United Nations (UN). (U.S. Department of State)

strategy for dealing with the Iraqi Army was a simple one: "First we're going to cut it off, then we're going to kill it." Decisive force was the central tenet for the coalition strategy: overwhelming force should be brought to bear against the enemy. This approach led to a rapid and decisive victory over Iraqi forces in Operation DESERT STORM. The victory came so quickly that some argued that it left the job unfinished, as Hussein remained in power. However, neither President George H. W. Bush nor Powell was eager to prosecute the war beyond the coalition's mandate or to make it appear as if the West was intent on punishing the Iraqi people.

The use of overwhelming force was one of the three tenets of the Powell Doctrine, which guided U.S. military strategy in the immediate aftermath of the Cold War. The doctrine also held that the United States should use its military only when the country's vital interests were at stake, only when there was a clear goal, and only when there was a clearly defined exit strategy. Unfortunately, as soon as Powell left the JCS in 1993, the Powell Doctrine began to be diluted.

Powell served as secretary of state under President George W. Bush beginning in 2001. It was clear from the start, however, that Powell would play a rather subordinate role to Vice President Richard Cheney, Secretary of Defense Donald Rumsfeld, Deputy Secretary of Defense Paul Wolfowitz, and National Security Advisor Condoleezza Rice. Except perhaps for Rice, all were considered neoconservatives, particularly in matters of national security and warfare. Powell, who did not subscribe to the rigid ideology of neoconservativism and was also the only senior civilian member of the administration with any practical experience in fighting wars, found himself in the difficult position of having to rally the

international community around the Global War on Terror after the September 11 terrorist attacks. His job was not an easy one, as he walked a diplomatic tightrope between the Bush administration neoconservatives and the exigencies of the post-9/11 environment. Powell traveled less than any secretary of state in 30 years, demonstrating the demands that the Global War on Terror and the Iraq War exacted on his time.

Soon after September 11, 2001, Powell was given the responsibility for building the case for a second invasion of Iraq to topple the Hussein regime and ensure that the nation did not harbor or use weapons of mass destruction (WMDs). Powell was generally opposed to the forcible overthrow of Hussein, arguing that it was better to contain him, which the international community had effectively done since 1991. Nevertheless, Powell agreed to work with the administration if it sought an international coalition to effect regime change in Iraq. Powell did convince Bush to take the case for war before the United Nations (UN); however, Powell had to serve as the point man for these actions.

As the United States moved toward war with Iraq, Powell addressed a plenary session of the UN on February 5, 2003, carefully building a case for international military action. Powell emphatically stated that the Iraqis had biological weapons in hand and that Hussein had many of the key components for the construction of a nuclear weapon. Powell's speech was immediately controversial, as many claimed even then that Powell's statements concerning Iraqi WMDs were unsubstantiated. Powell was himself skeptical about some of the intelligence presented to him but nevertheless presented it as irrefutable. He would later refer to his UN speech as a blot on his record.

Powell must have been disappointed when the Iraq War was waged with insufficient numbers of troops to secure the peace in Iraq (a cardinal violation of the Powell Doctrine). The coalition that did invade Iraq in 2003 was not nearly as large, diverse, or unified as the 1991 coalition, another disappointment for Powell. Once Hussein had been toppled, Powell had the unenviable task of building international support for the rebuilding of Iraq, which was made far more difficult when a nearly two-year search found none of the WMDs that Powell and others had claimed were in Iraq.

As the war in Iraq began to deteriorate, Powell became even more marginalized with the administration. Realizing that his voice had been muted, he announced his intention to resign only days after Bush's November 2004 reelection. Powell left office in January 2005. He has since joined the venture capital firm of Kleiner, Perkins, Caulfield & Byers; embarked on an extended speaking tour; and has stayed active in moderate Republican political circles. In the summer of 2007 Powell revealed that he had spent much time attempting to persuade George W. Bush not to invade Iraq. Powell also stated that he believed that Iraq had descended into a civil war, the outcome of which could not be determined by the United States.

In 2007 Powell made a significant monetary contribution to Republican senator John McCain's presidential bid and has reportedly advised McCain on both military and foreign policy matters. However, in the run-up to the 2008 election, Powell publicly endorsed the candidacy of McCain's Democratic Party opponent, Barack Obama.

B. KEITH MURPHY AND PAUL G. PIERPAOLI JR.

**See also**

Bush, George Walker; Cheney, Richard Bruce; DESERT STORM, Operation; Global War on Terror; IRAQI FREEDOM, Operation; Neoconservatism; Powell Doctrine; Rice, Condoleezza; Rumsfeld, Donald Henry; Weapons of Mass Destruction; Wolfowitz, Paul Dundes

**References**

DeYoung, Karen. *Soldier: The Life of Colin Powell.* New York: Knopf, 2006.

Powell, Colin, and Joseph E. Persico. *My American Journey.* New York: Ballantine, 2003.

Roth, David. *Sacred Honor: Colin Powell: The Inside Account of His Life and Triumphs.* New York: HarperCollins, 1995.

---

# Powell Doctrine

A broad statement of the necessary conditions for determining when U.S. armed forces should be used and how military force should be applied, as defined by General Colin L. Powell during his service as chairman of the Joint Chiefs of Staff (JCS) from October 1, 1989, to September 30, 1993. Powell would later go on to be secretary of state from 2001 to 2005. Powell's concept complemented the six criteria for the use of military power as formulated by Secretary of Defense Caspar W. Weinberger in 1984. The two sets of criteria combined are commonly known as the Weinberger-Powell Doctrine, which constitutes a cautious approach to the employment of U.S. military power.

This policy construct reflected concerns with the effects of the Vietnam War and subsequent ineffective uses of American military power as well as the resulting desire to avoid similar circumstances in the future. Weinberger, for whom Powell served as senior military assistant in the 1980s, argued that U.S. armed forces should not be used in combat unless the security situation involved a specific threat to a vital national interest; the government was clearly committed to victory; political and military objectives were clearly defined; adequately sized and composed forces were committed, with the objectives and forces continuously assessed and adjusted; the commitment of forces has some reasonable assurance of support from the American people and from Congress; and force is used only as a last resort.

In Senate committee hearings before and during his confirmation process as JCS chairman, Powell indicated a general agreement with the Weinberger criteria but also noted that national decision makers should not use them as an ironclad checklist. Powell's perspective on the use of force embraced the cautious approach advocated by Weinberger but also emphasized the use of all instruments of national power, especially economic and political capabilities, along with the military. When military force was employed, Powell argued, the nation should use overwhelming force in pursuit of clearly defined political and military objectives. Additionally, military plans should emphasize a quick and decisive victory and, whenever possible, a rapid withdrawal of forces.

As a corollary to his primary concepts, Powell also noted that war was a complex activity that included a high probability of unintended consequences, especially if combat operations continued over an extended period of time. He also warned about overreliance on technology to provide an easy solution to complex problems. His emphasis on the use of overwhelming force was intended to overcome unforeseen difficulties that can emerge in conflict and also to minimize American casualties.

Critics charged that the criteria of both Weinberger and Powell make it extremely difficult for the United States to employ military power and limit the potential deterrent effects of standing military forces. Powell conceded that flexibility was required in the decisions to use force, and he recognized that some security situations would fall outside any rigid structures. Additionally, he noted that in some circumstances it was useful for national leaders to have some ambiguity concerning intentions and courses of action.

Nonetheless, in the response to the Iraqi invasion of Kuwait in August 1991, Powell clearly applied his cautious approach to the use of military force. During Operation DESERT SHIELD, which provided for the defense of Saudi Arabia and the buildup of forces in the theater, he was an advocate of economic sanctions and political pressure for an extended period of time, using the military first as a complementary deterrent threat and only employing the military option after the other instruments had failed.

Powell also helped shape the plan and force structure for Operation DESERT STORM, emphasizing clear and focused objectives and the use of overwhelming force to achieve a rapid and decisive victory. Although the William J. Clinton administration moved toward a more flexible position on the use of force, the Powell Doctrine continued to have an influence on decisions involving the commitment of U.S. forces overseas.

The U.S.-led invasion of Iraq (Operation IRAQI FREEDOM) violated a number of points within the Powell Doctrine while simultaneously showcasing the new Bush Doctrine, which relied on preemptive military force with or without an international mandate. Indeed, the United States did not have broad international support as it did during Operation DESERT STORM. While the assault began with what the Pentagon termed "shock and awe," American troops were too few to bring postwar order to Iraq. Instead, that nation slipped toward civil war and brutal sectarian violence.

In retrospect, the objectives of the war, other than the ouster of the Saddam Hussein regime, were hazy and not well explained. Beginning in 2005 and as casualties in Iraq skyrocketed, public support for the war began to plummet, even among some in the Republican ranks. In the U.S. 2006 national elections the Republicans lost control of Congress, in large part because of the perceived failures in Iraq. Finally, efforts to bring democracy to Iraq were also a blatant violation of the Powell Doctrine, which warns against the vicissitudes of nation building. After the Bush administration's early 2007 troop deployment surge, violence in Iraq finally began to abate, which may have vindicated the surge strategy but simultaneously indicted the original war strategy that clearly had not provided for adequate troop strength to secure the nation. It is widely believed that Powell resigned as secretary of state because his view of the war did not jibe with the hawkish components in the Bush administration, including Secretary of Defense Donald Rumsfeld and National Security Advisor Condoleezza Rice.

JEROME V. MARTIN

**See also**

Bush, George Walker; Bush Doctrine; DESERT SHIELD, Operation; DESERT STORM, Operation; IRAQI FREEDOM, Operation; Powell, Colin Luther

**References**

Gordon, Michael R., and General Bernard E. Trainor. *The Generals' War: The Inside Story of the Conflict in the Gulf.* New York: Little, Brown, 1995.

Powell, Colin L. "U.S. Forces: Challenges Ahead." *Foreign Affairs* 71(5) (Winter 1992): 32–45.

Powell, Colin, and Joseph E. Persico. *My American Journey.* New York: Ballantine, 2003.

Woodward, Bob. *The Commanders.* New York: Simon and Schuster, 1991.

———. *State of Denial: Bush at War, Part III.* New York: Simon and Schuster, 2006.

# PRAYING MANTIS, **Operation**
## Event Date: April 18, 1988

Retaliatory strike against Iranian targets carried out by the U.S. Navy that resulted in a major naval action. On April 14, 1988, the U.S. Navy guided-missile frigate *Samuel B. Roberts* struck a mine in the central Persian Gulf. The warship was involved in Operation EARNEST WILL, the 1987–1988 operation in which U.S. Navy warships provided escorts to tankers in the Persian Gulf during the 1980–1988 Iran-Iraq War. The *Roberts* was badly damaged in the blast, which blew a 15-foot hole in the ship's hull. Although no crewmen were killed, 10 were badly wounded and had to be medevaced. After a five-hour struggle, the crew of the *Roberts* managed to save its ship.

U.S. Navy divers subsequently recovered other mines in the area. These were identified as having the same identification numbers as Iranian mines seized the previous September from the Iranian Navy minelayer *Iran Ajr.* The United States had previously warned Iran not to lay mines in the Gulf, and four days later the U.S. Navy responded with Operation PRAYING MANTIS.

In the operation, the U.S. Navy committed the aircraft carrier *Enterprise,* one amphibious transport dock ship, one guided

U.S. marines inspect a ZU-23 23-mm antiaircraft gun on the Iranian Sassan oil platform in the Persian Gulf, April 18, 1988. The U.S. Navy attacked the platform as part of Operation PRAYING MANTIS, after Iranian mines were discovered in the Gulf. Earlier, the U.S. guided-missile frigate *Samuel B. Roberts* had been damaged by a similar mine while on patrol. (U.S. Marine Corps)

missile cruiser, four destroyers, and three frigates. The punitive operation was directed at the Sassan and Sirri inoperable oil platforms in the Gulf, which the Iranians had armed. Iranian personnel on the Sassan platform were given the chance to abandon it for a tugboat there, but they chose instead to open fire on the American ships. The destroyer *Merrill* immediately used its own five-inch gun to neutralize the Iranian fire. U.S. marines then went aboard the platform, collected intelligence data, and left explosive charges that damaged it. The American ships then attacked the Sirri platform.

In response, the Iranians sent a half dozen Boghammar speedboats to attack various targets in the Gulf, including an American supply ship and a Panamanian ship. Two U.S. Navy Grumman A-6E Intruder aircraft from the *Enterprise* were then directed to the speedboats and brought them under attack. Employing cluster munitions, the aircraft sank one of the speedboats and damaged several others. The surviving speedboats then fled to Iranian-controlled Abu Musa Island. The *Joshan,* an Iranian Combattante II Kasman-class fast-attack gunboat, then moved against the guided-missile cruiser *Wainwright* and its accompanying frigates *Simpson* and *Bagley,* firing a Harpoon missile at them. The American warships returned fire with Standard and Harpoon missiles, which destroyed the Iranian ship's superstructure but did not sink it; this was subsequently accomplished by naval gunfire. Although two Iranian U.S.-built McDonnell Douglas F-4 Phantom aircraft approached the *Wainwright,* they were driven off.

The Iranian frigate *Sahand* then departed Bundar Abbas in another effort to attack the American ships. It soon came under attack from two A-6Es on combat air patrol that used missiles and laser-guided bombs to set the ship afire. The fire soon reached the ship's magazines, and the resulting explosions sent it to the bottom. A sister ship to the *Sahand,* the *Sabaland,* also sortied. An A-6E dropped a laser-guided bomb on it, severely damaging the frigate and leaving it dead in the water. An Iranian tug appeared and soon took the frigate in tow. Pursuant to orders, the A-6Es did not continue the attack.

The daylong battle was the U.S. Navy's largest engagement involving surface warships since World War II. It also saw the first surface-to-surface missile engagement in the U.S. Navy's history. The battle was entirely one-sided. In it, the U.S. forces had damaged the two Iranian offshore oil platforms, sank one of the Iranian frigates and the gunboat, damaged the other frigate, and sank as many as three of the speedboats. U.S. losses were one helicopter to an accident and its two marine crewmen killed. Iranian personnel losses are unknown.

Shortly after PRAYING MANTIS, the United States extended its naval protection to all non-Iranian shipping in the Persian Gulf. The engagement probably helped push Iran into agreeing to a cease-fire with Iraq to end its eight-year-long war, convincing the Iranian leadership that the United States was now firmly on the side of Iraq in the conflict.

SPENCER C. TUCKER

**See also**

EARNEST WILL, Operation; Iran-Iraq War; Oil; Persian Gulf

**References**

Palmer, Michael A. *Guardians of the Gulf: A History of America's Expanding Role in the Persian Gulf, 1833–1992.* New York: Free Press, 1992.

Peniston, Bradley. *No Higher Honor: Saving the USS Samuel B. Roberts in the Persian Gulf.* Annapolis: Naval Institute Press, 2006.

Wise, Harold L. *Inside the Danger Zone: The U.S. Military in the Persian Gulf, 1987–1988.* Annapolis, MD: Naval Institute Press, 2007.

# Prepositioning Program, Military Sealift Command

A major component of the U.S. Navy's Military Sealift Command (MSC), the Prepositioning Program maintains a network of very large, forward-based supply ships providing matériel to ensure the effective and rapid response of U.S. armed forces engaging in combat or disaster relief operations around the world.

Maritime prepositioning ships are deployed in support of the U.S. Army, Navy, Air Force, Marine Corps, and the Defense Logistics Agency. The types of ships employed include chartered commercial ships, MSC Ready Reserve Force ships, container ships, vehicle/cargo ships, aviation logistics ships, and large, medium-speed, roll-on/roll-off ships (LMSR). Many of these ships were originally built in specialized non-U.S. shipyards and subsequently modified to U.S. armed forces prepositioning standards.

Their strategic forward positioning in appropriate seaways guarantees that the prepositioning ships can effect the efficient and rapid delivery of combat or humanitarian supplies to an incoming U.S. force that is poised to "marry up" with the necessary vehicles, ordnance, and stores. Operating without the uncertainty of dependence on another country's transportation routes or equipment is a key precept of the Prepositioning Program, and most of the MSC ships assigned to this force are capable of independently off-loading their own cargo onto a pier or onto barges (or lighters) carried specifically for the purpose of cargo delivery from an offshore anchorage. MSC maintains a number of dedicated crane ships to ensure quick deliveries from the more traditionally equipped cargo vessels in the force, as well as an array of tankers furnished with the means of pumping fuel ashore from a distance of eight miles.

The MSC Prepositioning Program serves the U.S. armed forces by means of the following distribution: The U.S. Marine Corps has 15 Maritime Prepositioning Ships (MPS), the U.S. Army possesses 9 Army Prepositioned Stocks, the U.S. Navy has 3 ships (APS-3), and the Defense Logistics Agency and U.S. Air Force have 8 NDAF (Navy, Defense Logistics Agency and Air Force) ships, which also supply the U.S. Army and the U.S. Marine Corps.

MSC Prepositioning ships are distributed geographically into three squadrons: MPS Squadron One in the Eastern Atlantic and the Mediterranean; MPS Squadron Two in the Indian Ocean at Diego Garcia; and MPS Squadron Three in the Western Pacific at Guam and Saipan. Since supporting Operation DESERT STORM, the three squadrons have also deployed in support of Operation IRAQI FREEDOM and several regional humanitarian initiatives. The ships of each squadron can be mobilized within 24 hours for deployment anywhere around the globe where U.S. forces might be dispatched.

GORDON E. HOGG

**See also**

Logistics, Persian Gulf War; Military Sealift Command; Support and Supply Ships, Strategic

**References**

Marolda, Edward, and Robert Schneller. *Shield and Sword: The United States Navy and the Persian Gulf War.* Annapolis, MD: U.S. Naval Institute Press, 2001.

Polmar, Norman. *The Naval Institute Guide to the Ships and Aircraft of the U.S. Fleet.* 18th ed. Annapolis, MD: Naval Institute Press, 2005.

Saunders, Stephen, ed. *Jane's Fighting Ships, 2008–2009.* Coulsdon, Surrey, UK, and Alexandria, VA: Jane's Information Group, 2008.

Sharpe, Richard, ed. *Jane's Fighting Ships: 1991–1992.* London: Jane's Information Group, 1991.

---

# Primakov, Yevgeni Maksimovich
## Birth Date: October 29, 1929

Soviet/Russian economist, journalist, and politician who served as a special envoy to Iraq for Soviet leader Mikhail S. Gorbachev prior to the 1991 Persian Gulf War and as a special representative for Russian president Vladimir V. Putin prior to the 2003 Iraq War. Yevgeni Maksimovich Primakov was born on October 29, 1929, in Kiev, Ukraine, and graduated in 1953 from the Moscow State Institute for Oriental Studies. He also pursued graduate studies at Moscow State University. His first job was as a Middle East correspondent for the Soviet newspaper *Pravda* from 1956 to 1970. During this time, he also participated in intelligence gathering for the Komitet Gosudarstvennoi Bezopasnosti (KGB, Committee for State Security). As a journalist, Primakov met the young Saddam Hussein, a member of the Iraqi Baath Party who would later become the president of Iraq. The two men formed a friendship, which later allowed Primakov to speak more freely than most other diplomats to the Iraqi president.

After leaving journalism, Primakov held other jobs, all in academia before he became involved in politics in 1989, when he became chairman of the Union Soviet, one of the two Soviet houses of parliament. In 1990, Gorbachev sent Primakov, now a member of the Presidential Council, to negotiate with Hussein and American officials in the hopes of averting a war in the Persian Gulf. Arriving in Baghdad on October 4, 1990, Primakov urged the Iraqi president to withdraw his forces from Kuwait. On October 18, Primakov met with U.S. president George H. W. Bush to talk about his plan for a conference to resolve the situation peacefully.

At the end of October, Primakov returned to Baghdad, at which time the Iraqi president agreed to withdraw his forces from Kuwait on two conditions: that the United Nations (UN) forces withdraw from the region and that an international coalition be assembled to solve all of the major conflicts in the Middle East at the time, including the intractable Israeli-Palestinian conflict. The United States refused the conditions and thus did not pursue either proposal. Primakov then concluded that both Prime Minister Margaret Thatcher of Great Britain and President Bush were not interested in further negotiations and were in fact intent on going to war with Iraq.

In 1991, Primakov was named first deputy chairman of the KGB, which became the foreign intelligence service after 1992. He retained this post until 1996. From January 1996 until September 1998, Primakov served as Russian foreign minister under President Boris Yeltsin. A proponent of multilateralism and a wary observer of American hegemony and the expansion of the North Atlantic Treaty Organization (NATO), Primakov was primarily responsible for the harder line that the Kremlin took against Washington in the mid- to late 1990s. In September 1998, Yeltsin named Primakov Russian prime minister. After Primikov had implemented a series of needed—but nonetheless unpopular—reforms and taken a

Yevgeni Primakov served as a special Soviet envoy to Iraq prior to the 1991 Persian Gulf War and as a special representative for Russian president Vladimir V. Putin prior to the 2003 Iraq War. (AP/Wide World Photos)

tough stance against NATO's Kosovo air campaign, Yeltsin sacked Primakov in May 1999. After an unsuccessful bid to win a seat in the Duma in 1999, he challenged Vladimir Putin for the presidency but lost. Primakov ultimately became a close adviser to Putin.

In the meantime, tensions continued to mount between Iraq and the West following the Persian Gulf War. In late 2002, Primakov styled Operation DESERT FOX, a 1998 joint British-American bombing campaign in response to Hussein's refusal to comply with UN resolutions regarding disarmament, as "outrageous," especially since the UN Security Council was still discussing the issue when the bombing began. In early 2003, Primakov, acting as Putin's special representative, tried to prevent another war. Primakov believed that the best way to avoid war was for Hussein to hand over all of his weapons of mass destruction (WMDs) to the UN, and he bluntly advised Hussein to do so. Hussein, however, stated that Iraq had destroyed all of its WMDs. Washington refused to accept Hussein's assertion, and once again Primakov's diplomatic attempts to avert war proved unsuccessful. The invasion of Iraq began in March 2003. No WMDs were found in Iraq, even after exhaustive searches.

Although now mostly retired from the political spotlight, Primakov continues to provide informal counsel to Putin and other Russian politicians. He also heads the Russian Chamber of Commerce and Industry.

GREGORY W. MORGAN AND PAUL G. PIERPAOLI JR.

**See also**

DESERT FOX, Operation; DESERT STORM, Operation; ENDURING FREEDOM, Operation; Gorbachev, Mikhail; Hussein, Saddam; Putin, Vladimir Vladimirovich; Russia, Middle East Policy, 1991–Present; Soviet Union, Middle East Policy; Yeltsin, Boris Nikolayevich

**References**

Freedman, Lawrence, and Efraim Karsh. *The Gulf Conflict, 1990–1991: Diplomacy and War in the New World Order.* Princeton, NJ: Princeton University Press, 1993.

Polk, William R. *Understanding Iraq: The Whole Sweep of Iraqi History, from Genghis Khan's Mongols to the Ottoman Turks to the British Mandate to the American Occupation.* New York: Harper Perennial, 2006.

Simes, Dimitri K. *After the Collapse: Russia Seeks Its Place as a Great Power.* New York: Simon and Schuster, 1999.

---

# PRIME CHANCE, **Operation**
## Start Date: August 1987
## End Date: June 1989

An American special forces operation in the Persian Gulf that occurred between August 1987 and June 1989. Operation PRIME CHANCE was intended to prevent Iranian Revolutionary Guards from mining the shipping lanes used by international oil tankers. PRIME CHANCE coincided with Operation EARNEST WILL, an effort by the U.S. Navy to escort unarmed tankers through the Persian Gulf.

PRIME CHANCE was the first operation in which helicopter pilots used night-vision goggles and forward-looking infrared vision devices in combat. It was also significant for the high degree of interoperability displayed by the special forces from different services.

Between 1980 and 1988, Iran and Iraq waged a brutal war of attrition. Unable to force a decision on land, the Iranian Revolutionary Guards began to attack international oil tankers carrying oil from Iraq and countries friendly to Iraq (including Kuwait) as they traversed the Persian Gulf. In December 1986, Kuwait requested that 11 of its tankers be reflagged as American ships, so they would receive protection from the U.S. Navy. After President Ronald Reagan approved the request on March 10, 1987, the Navy began preparing for Operation EARNEST WILL. After the tanker *Bridgeton* hit a mine laid by Iranians on July 24, 1987, during the first convoy, a secret operation was put in place to bring a halt to the Iranian mining.

Code-named PRIME CHANCE, the operation included helicopters and pilots from the Army's 160th Special Operations Aviation Regiment (Airborne) (SOAR[A]). SOAR pilots were trained to fly and fight at night, when the Iranian minelayers were most active. The operation's forces also included Navy SEALs and Mark III patrol boats. U.S. Marines guarded PRIME CHANCE's floating bases, and Air Force flight controllers monitored airborne operations.

The first PRIME CHANCE components arrived in the Persian Gulf on August 5, 1987. Two detachments of helicopters were formed, each with an MD Helicopters MH-6 Little Bird light transport helicopter and two McDonnell Douglas/Boeing AH-6 Little Bird attack helicopters along with crew and support personnel. The first operations were flown from the decks of navy frigates and the command ship *La Salle*. On August 8, 1987, the detachments flew their first missions escorting convoys and guarding minesweeping detachments. Soon afterward, operations were transferred to two large oil-servicing barges, *Hercules* and *Wimbrown VII,* which were converted into floating mobile sea bases.

The barges allowed PRIME CHANCE to be independent of land bases and released navy ships for other operations. Each barge was converted by erecting hangars for the 3 helicopters of each detachment, 10 small boats, ammunition and fuel, workshops, and accommodations for more than 150 men. The *Hercules* was manned by naval special warfare units from the East Coast of the United States, while the *Wimbrown VII* was manned by units from the West Coast. The mobile sea bases became operational in October 1987.

Typically, missions took place after sunset. The helicopters usually flew only 30 feet above the water, with the pilots relying on night-vision goggles. The MH-6s were used to spot Iranian boats and ships in the shipping lanes. Once they located Iranian targets, the MH-6 crews would call in the AH-6 gunships, which would attack the Iranians. When operating with conventional naval forces, the AH-6s would rely on information from the warships' radar and that of their Sikorsky SH-60 Seahawk helicopters. The patrol boats began operating on September 9, 1987, and were in close contact with the helicopters as well.

On September 21, the special forces enjoyed their first success. One helicopter detachment took off from the frigate *Jairett* and soon spotted the Iranian ship *Iran Ajr*. As the Americans watched, the ship extinguished its lights and began laying mines in the shipping lanes used by tankers. After receiving permission, the helicopters attacked the *Iran Ajr* with miniguns and high-explosive and fletchette anti-personnel rockets. The attack continued until the ship stopped and the crew abandoned it. The next morning, a SEAL team boarded the *Iran Ajr* while two patrol boats stood by. The SEALs found nine mines on board, along with documents showing where the Iranians had dropped other mines and papers implicating Iran in mining international waters. Twenty-three Iranians were rescued and taken prisoner. The *Iran Ajr* was scuttled by American forces on September 26.

The American forces quickly realized that the Iranians spent their daylight hours near the oil and gas separation platforms in Iranian waters, then moved into international waters after dark. The Iranians usually used the Middle Shoals Buoy, a navigation aid used by tankers, as their assembly point before laying mines. On October 8, PRIME CHANCE elements laid an ambush for the Iranians. The attack helicopters found three Iranian boats at the buoy and exchanged fire with them until all three were sunk. Patrol boats picked up five survivors.

Forces from PRIME CHANCE also took part in Operations NIMBLE ARCHER (October 1987) and PRAYING MANTIS (April 1988). In both operations, conventional forces destroyed Iranian oil platforms in response to attacks on American ships. After PRAYING MANTIS, Iranian interference with neutral shipping dropped dramatically. PRIME CHANCE patrols continued after the Iran-Iraqi cease-fire of July 1988. The last forces returned to the United States in June 1989. Between June 1987 and June 1989, 259 ships were escorted in 127 convoys.

TIM J. WATTS

**See also**

EARNEST WILL, Operation; Iran-Iraq War; PRAYING MANTIS, Operation

**References**

Partin, John W. *Special Operations Forces in Operation Earnest Will/ Prime Chance I*. MacDill Air Force Base, FL: U.S. Special Operations Command, History and Research Office, 1998.

Stubblefield, Gary. *Inside the Navy Seals*. Osceola, WI: Motorbooks International, 1995.

Wise, Harold Lee. *Inside the Danger Zone: The U.S. Military in the Persian Gulf, 1987–88*. Annapolis, MD: Naval Institute Press, 2007.

---

# Prince, Eric
## Birth Date: June 6, 1969

Wealthy Republican Party operative and chairman and chief executive officer of Blackwater, USA, a private military security company that received large U.S. government contracts for work in Afghanistan, Iraq, and poststorm operations after Hurricane Katrina hit Louisiana and Mississippi in August 2005. Blackwater has engendered much controversy for its role in Iraq, and Prince has been termed by detractors as an opportunistic insider of the George W. Bush administration. Eric Prince was born in Holland, Michigan, on June 6, 1969. Prince's father, Eric Prince Sr., was chairman of the Prince Corporation, a major auto-parts supplier, and a major donor to the Republican Party. When he died suddenly in 1995, his widow sold the company to Johnson Controls, Inc., for a reported $1.3 billion, making the Princes one of the wealthiest families in the United States.

Prince spent three semesters at the U.S. Naval Academy at Annapolis before finishing his studies at Hillsdale College (Michigan), from which he graduated in 1992. He also served as a White House intern in the last year of the George H. W. Bush administration. Later, he criticized the Bush White House in a local Michigan paper, intimating that its policies were too liberal. From 1993 to 1996, Prince took a commission in the U.S. Navy and served as a Navy SEAL officer, seeing duty in Haiti, the Middle East, the Mediterranean, and in Bosnia. Upon his father's unexpected death, he left the Navy in 1996 and, using some of his share from the sale of his father's company, bought 6,000 acres of land in North Carolina's dismal swamp, where he established a private, paramilitary, special operations school. In 1997, Prince created Blackwater, USA, so-named because of the black swamp waters that surrounded the instruction area. By now he had firmly established his Far Right Republican bona fides, having campaigned for Republican presidential candidate Pat Buchanan and contributed thousands of dollars to Far Right causes and organizations.

Until very recently, Prince kept an exceedingly low profile. Those who worked with him characterized him as intensely private and secretive. He rarely ever granted interviews and even disliked having his picture taken. However, he allegedly used his powerful connections with the George W. Bush administration and Republican Party to land lucrative government contracts to provide private security forces to American-led operations in Afghanistan beginning in 2002 and in Iraq after the fall of Iraqi President Saddam Hussein in March 2003. In the autumn of 2005, Blackwater, USA, garnered more contracts to help deal with the cleanup and restoration of public services after Hurricane Katrina ravaged the Gulf Coast. Prior to 2007, few Americans knew of Blackwater or its involvement in U.S. government and security work. While the company has not been specifically blamed for the inefficient Katrina clean-up operations, in which it is estimated that hundreds of millions of dollars were squandered or misappropriated, some detractors have charged the company with complicity in what had become a classic government boondoggle.

Because of the covert nature of many of Blackwater's enterprises, its operations and employee roster have been shrouded in mystery. Not until the company came under intense congressional scrutiny in the autumn of 2007 was it made known that many of its employees were neither U.S. citizens nor U.S. nationals. This revelation led some to describe Blackwater as a "mercenary" firm, something that Prince vigorously denied during testimony to Congress in October 2007.

Blackwater was in Iraq under a contract with the U.S. State Department. In September 2007, Blackwater guards in Baghdad tasked with escorting a convoy of State Department officials through the city killed 17 innocent Iraqi civilians. The killings provoked instant outrage, and Iraqi prime minister Nuri al-Maliki demanded that the perpetrators be brought to justice. This was not the first time that Blackwater employees were involved in controversy; numerous incidents of unnecessary violence against civilians had taken place. The U.S. government immediately suspended Blackwater's Iraq contract. Because the Blackwater employees involved were neither Iraqi nor American, they were not subject to immediate arrest, although the U.S. Federal Bureau of Investigation (FBI) began an extensive probe into the incident. To make matters worse, just a few days later, federal prosecutors announced that they were investigating allegations that some Blackwater personnel had illegally imported weapons into Iraq that were then being supplied to the Kurdistan Workers' Party, which has been designated by the United States as a terrorist organization.

These incendiary allegations prompted a congressional inquiry, and in October 2007 Prince was compelled to testify in front of the House Committee on Oversight and Government Reform. Prince did neither himself nor his company much good when he stonewalled the committee and told them that Blackwater's financial information was beyond the purview of the government. He later retracted this statement, saying such information would be provided upon a "written request." Blackwater now struggles under a pall of suspicion, and multiple investigations are underway involving the incident in Iraq, incidents in Afghanistan, and the allegations of illegal weapons smuggling by company employees. Prince continues to donate large sums of money to the Republican Party and right-wing organizations. In the meantime, Congress is considering legislation that would significantly tighten government control over private contractors, especially those involved in sensitive areas like military security. The Blackwater case has also provoked concerns about the outsourcing of military conflicts in the future.

In February 2009, Blackwater officials announced that the company would operate under the name Xe, which reflected a "change in company focus away from the business of providing private security."

PAUL G. PIERPAOLI JR.

**See also**
Blackwater; Bush, George Herbert Walker; Private Security Firms

**References**
Buzzell, Colby. *My War: Killing Time in Iraq.* New York: Putnam, 2005.
U.S. Congress. *Private Security Firms: Standards, Cooperation, and Coordination on the Battlefield: Congressional Hearing.* Darby, PA: Diane Publishing, 2007.

# Prisoners of War, Persian Gulf War

During their August 1990 invasion of Kuwait, Iraqi forces captured some 22,000 Kuwaitis, and during the 1991 Persian Gulf War (Operation DESERT STORM), they captured 46 coalition military personnel. In the Persian Gulf War, coalition forces captured 86,743 Iraqis. Of the estimated 22,000 Kuwaiti military personnel and civilians captured or taken hostage during Iraq's invasion and occupation of Kuwait, more than 1,000 were killed during the occupation. Most of the remaining were released or escaped during the Iraqi withdrawal from Kuwait in February 1991. At the end of the conflict, Iraq released 5,722 Kuwaiti prisoners of war (POWs) and freed 500 Kuwaitis held by rebels in southern Iraq. Kuwait subsequently claimed that 605 Kuwaitis and foreigners were missing after being taken to Iraq. Some of their bodies were later found in a mass grave near Samawah, Iraq. Most remain unaccounted for, however.

Of the 46 coalition military personnel taken prisoner by the Iraqis during DESERT STORM, 22 were Americans. All of the captured coalition personnel were subsequently repatriated, except for U.S. Navy pilot Captain Michael Scott Speicher, who remains missing. Captured coalition personnel also included 12 British, 2 Italians, 9 Saudis, and 1 Kuwaiti. Most of these POWs were airmen, although 4 survivors of a controversial British Army reconnaissance patrol with radio call sign Bravo Two Zero were also captured.

American POWs were driven to Baghdad and interrogated at an intelligence facility known as the "Bunker." They were then taken to an intelligence headquarters nicknamed the "Biltmore." The prisoners were later transferred to either Abu Ghraib prison or Al-Rashid Military Prison, where they were held until repatriation. All coalition prisoners were subjected to physical abuse and most were tortured, deprived of food, and subjected to cold temperatures. Both American women POWs were sexually abused. Some POWs were forced to make propaganda statements.

Prior to the commencement of DESERT STORM, coalition forces established a three-stage system of POW camps in Saudi Arabia through which war prisoners would be processed. Most prisoners would be sent to forward holding camps administered by the United States, Britain, and France. They were then transferred to U.S.-administered theater level camps and lastly transferred to Saudi camps. POWs captured by coalition Arab states were taken directly to the Saudi camps.

### Prisoners of War during the Persian Gulf War

| Nationality | Number of Prisoners |
| --- | --- |
| American | 22 |
| British | 12 |
| Iraqi | 86,743 |
| Italian | 2 |
| Kuwaiti (during Iraqi invasion) | 22,000 |
| Kuwaiti (during Operation DESERT STORM) | 1 |
| Saudi | 9 |

Temporary POW camps included one constructed by U.S. Navy Seabees at Kibrit, which could hold 40,000 prisoners. Similar facilities were established by XVII Airborne Corps and VII Corps, as well as by the British and French. The British camp near Qaysumah, known as "Maryhill," could hold 5,000 prisoners, and the French "Clemence" camp near Rafha could hold 500 POWs.

The four theater-level camps were designed to hold a total of 100,000 prisoners. Two of the camps, collectively known as "Bronx," were constructed to the southwest of Mishab. The other two camps, known as "Brooklyn," were constructed north of King Khalid Military City. The Saudi Arabia National Guard also maintained four camps: No. 1 at Hafr al-Batin, No. 2 near Nuariyah, No. 3 near Artawiyah, and No. 4 near Tabuk. These camps could hold a combined total of 41,000 Iraqis.

POW camps constructed by U.S. forces each covered nearly 1.5 square miles. Materials used to construct and maintain the camps included 35,000 rolls of concertina wire, 450 miles of chain-link fence, 296 guard towers, 10,000 tents, 1,500 latrines, 5,000 wash basins, as well as 100,000 towels, 300,000 meals, and 1.5 million gallons of water per day. A field medical hospital and an interrogation facility were located at each major camp.

During interrogations, American forces determined that 1,492 prisoners appeared to be displaced civilians, some of whom had surrendered seeking food and shelter. To determine their status, 1,196 tribunal hearings were held. Subsequently, 310 people were subsequently classed as enemy POWs, while the rest were classified as displaced civilians—none was found to have been an unlawful combatant. Among the Iraqi POWs were an American citizen and an Iraqi whose mother was an American. Both had been impressed into the Iraqi Army. They were released and allowed to join their families in the United States.

By war's end, coalition forces had captured 86,743 Iraqis: 63,948 were captured by the United States; 5,005 by the British; 869 by the French; and 16,921 by Arab forces. Over 13,000 Iraqis refused repatriation to Iraq and were reclassified as refugees.

GLENN E. HELM

**See also**
Abu Ghraib; DESERT STORM, Operation; Torture of Prisoners

**References**
Department of Defense. *Conduct of the Persian Gulf War: Final Report to Congress.* Washington, DC: U.S. Government Printing Office, 1992.

Marolda, Edward, and Robert Schneller. *Shield and Sword: The United States Navy and the Persian Gulf War.* Annapolis, MD: U.S. Naval Institute Press, 2001.

Yarsinske, Amy Waters. *No One Left Behind: The Lieutenant Commander Michael Scott Speicher Story.* New York: Dutton, 2002.

# Private Security Firms

Legally established for-profit enterprises contracted by government agencies to provide the contracting agency with armed security or to engage in security assistance aid—advisers, training, equipment and weapons procurement, etc.—to foreign military forces. Although broadly falling into the category of "government contractors," private security firms performing protective functions—providing armed guards whose duties may involve the use of deadly force—are set apart from the vast majority of government contractors, who provide only logistical, communications, administrative, and other service support. Indeed, the use of deadly force by some U.S.-contracted private security firms in Afghanistan and Iraq in recent years has generated significant controversy.

The use of private contractors by governments to provide military support dates back to at least the 18th century, when armies hired civilian drivers and teams to move artillery cannon around the battlefield. During the American Civil War (1861–1865), civilian teamsters were hired to drive army supply wagons, and "sutlers" (businessmen selling to soldiers food, drink, and other items not available in the military supply system) contracted with the army for the privilege of accompanying units in the field. During the Vietnam War, U.S. military forces hired commercial firms such as Pacific Architects and Engineers (PA&E) to provide construction and other services that were beyond the military's capability to accomplish. Widespread contracting of services previously performed by military personnel (such as dining hall workers) began in earnest in the U.S. armed forces during the Jimmy Carter administration and has increased since the military drawdown that began with the end of the Cold War (1991). Government contractors were employed during Operations DESERT SHIELD and DESERT STORM (1990–1991), and private security firms providing military assistance (advising, training, etc.) have been used extensively in support of several Balkan nations since the collapse of Yugoslavia. Since 2001, the Department of Defense has employed private security firms to provide military training assistance and advisers to the Afghan and Iraqi military and security forces.

However, the Defense Department is only one U.S. government agency employing civilian contractors in general, and private security firms providing armed guards in particular are most often contracted by non–Defense Department agencies, such as the State Department. Private armed security guards contracted by the State Department normally work for the Regional Security Officer (a career U.S. Foreign Service Officer) who is responsible for the security of a U.S. mission in a foreign country. Well-established American firms such as Halliburton, Blackwater, DynCorp, Kroll, Triple Canopy, Custer Battles, Military Professional Resources, Inc. (MPRI) have all competed and won U.S. government contracts from various government agencies and for a wide range of services in Iraq and Afghanistan (although most are in Iraq). In Iraq, Blackwater Worldwide Security Consulting provided security guards and helicopters for the now-defunct Coalition Provisional Authority. Similarly, British firms such as ArmorGroup, Global Risk Strategies, and Aegis have also won contracts to operate in these areas. Many private security firms recruit not only retired military and police personnel from their home country, but also people with similar skills from all over the world. Many of these companies are also currently recruiting Iraqis or joining with upstart security companies in Iraq.

In Afghanistan, the United States employs some 29,000 private contractor employees who provide a variety of services, but only about 1,000 of those likely are security contractors. The largest companies in Afghanistan are either U.S.- or British-based, and include DynCorp, USPI, ArmorGroup, Saladin, and Global Risk Strategies.

Critics of the use of private security firms claim they have eroded national sovereignty by diminishing the nation's monopoly on the use of force and point to alleged instances of abuse of local nationals by private security firm personnel. Proponents of private security firms counter that the firms perform vital functions that would otherwise be difficult to accomplish given scarce personnel resources.

The lack of clarity surrounding the legal status of contractors also poses concerns about their employees' accountability. Unlike military personnel, private security personnel working for the U.S. government are not subject to the Uniform Code of Military Justice (UCMJ)—indeed, they are security guards, not soldiers, and most do not even work for the Defense Department—and those who are not nationals of the hiring nation often are not subject to that nation's laws. In Iraq, for example, until the U.S.-Iraq security agreement signed in January 2009 stated that civilian contractors may face criminal charges in Iraqi courts, private security contractors were immune from legal prosecution under Coalition Provisional Authority Order 17, which effectively barred the Iraqi government from prosecuting contractor crimes in its own courts. There also have been several reported incidences in which armed guard security contractors working for the U.S. State Department have killed Iraqi civilians through the apparent use of excessive force. Such overly aggressive behavior is counterproductive as it undermines U.S. efforts at nation-building by alienating the Iraqi population in general. Indeed, the prevailing attitude among most U.S. military personnel toward private security guard contractors is overwhelmingly negative—a reaction that cannot simply be explained away by envy over the fact that private security firm employees may earn up to four times what uniformed military personnel are paid. U.S. military personnel tend to believe that those carrying weapons and authorized to exercise deadly force in the name of the United States should be limited to: uniformed military personnel subject to the UCMJ; sworn and commissioned law enforcement officers; and designated and trained operations officers of official government intelligence agencies.

Yet, despite the problems posed by the increasing use of private security firms, there is no indication that their influence seems likely to decrease. As yet, there has been no public commitment by the Barack Obama administration to change current U.S. policy regarding the use of private security firms.

Kristian P. Alexander, Jerry D. Morelock, and David T. Zabecki

**See also**
Abu Ghraib; Blackwater; Prince, Eric

**References**
Avant, Deborah D. *The Market for Force: The Consequences of Privatizing Security.* Cambridge: Cambridge University Press, 2005.

Caparini, Marina, ed. *Private Military and Security Companies: Ethics, Policies and Civil-Military Relations.* New York: Taylor and Francis, 2008.

Chesterman, Simon, and Chia Lehnardt, eds. *From Mercenaries to Markets: The Rise and Regulation of Private Military Companies.* New York: Oxford University Press, 2007.

Engbrecht, Shawn. *America's Covert Warriors: Inside the World of Private Military Contractors.* Dulles, VA: Potomac Books, 2010.

Mandel, Robert. *Armies without States: The Privatization of Security.* Boulder, CO: Lynne Rienner, 2002.

Scahill, Jeremy. *Blackwater: The Rise of the World's Most Powerful Mercenary Army.* Saddle Brook, NJ: Avalon, 2007.

Singer, Peter W. *Corporate Warriors: The Rise of the Privatized Military Industry.* Ithaca, NY: Cornell University Press, 2003.

## Project Babylon
### Event Date: 1960s

Iraqi attempt to develop a "supergun" capable of launching a small satellite into Earth's orbit or firing a weapon of mass destruction against Israel. The director of Project Babylon was Dr. Gerald V. Bull, a Canadian aerophysical engineer who believed that specially designed guns could launch small payloads into orbit at a fraction of the cost of missile launches. In the early 1960s Bull was the director of the joint Canadian-American High Altitude Research Project (HARP). Based on the island of Barbados, he and his team managed to fire projectiles from a 7-inch gun to as high as 60 miles. By 1966 the HARP team working in Arizona had fired a 185-pound projectile to an altitude of 108 miles using two welded-together tubes from 16-inch naval guns to form a barrel 30 meters long.

Despite the HARP team's impressive progress, funding for the project was cancelled in 1967. Frustrated at what he regarded as the Canadian-American small-minded bureaucracy, Bull turned his impressive engineering talents to the design of conventional field artillery. In the 1970s he introduced the GC-45 howitzer. One of the most revolutionary artillery designs ever produced, the GC-45 was capable of accurately firing a 155-millimeter (mm) projectile to ranges of some 42,700 yards, almost double the maximum range of the American M-109 howitzer that was the standard of most Western armies of the time.

Reportedly with CIA funding, Bull sold a version of the gun, designated the G-5, to South Africa, which was then involved in a war with Angola. The G-5 vastly outranged and quickly defeated almost all of the Cuban artillery in Angola. By 1980, however, a change in the U.S. administration and increasing world opposition to South Africa's apartheid regime eroded Bull's political

United Nations (UN) weapons inspectors stand at the base of Iraq's "supergun" in 1991. Under the terms ending the Persian Gulf War, Iraqi president Saddam Hussein agreed to allow UN inspection of facilities and the dismantling of weapons of mass destruction (WMDs). By 1998, the Iraqi leader had expelled the inspectors. (Corel)

protection. He was convicted of illegal arms sales and imprisoned in America for six months.

Upon his release, Bull established a company in Brussels and began to work with Iran, Chile, the Republic of China (Taiwan), the People's Republic of China, and other countries. In the early 1980s he sold 200 of his GC-45 howitzers to Iraq. Designated the GHN-45 in Iraqi service, the guns quickly gave Iraq a significant tactical advantage in its war with Iran, which was armed primarily with aging American-built guns. Bull also helped modify the warheads of Iraq's Scud missiles to extend their range. Despite his previous conviction for illegal arms sales to South Africa, Bull's work for Iraq had the covert support of many Western governments that saw that nation as a far lesser evil than Iran. Following the Iran-Iraq War, when Iraqi dictator Saddam Hussein assumed an increasingly aggressive posture in the region, that support evaporated.

Still trying to revive his old dream of launching satellites from large guns, Bull argued to Saddam that Iraq would never become a major power unless it could launch its own satellites, a capability already possessed by Israel. A supergun would be a relatively inexpensive and fast way for Iraq to achieve this. Such a gun also could be used to launch an antisatellite weapon designed to explode in the proximity of its target, either destroying it or at least neutralizing it. Saddam also might have believed that such a gun could be used

to fire chemical or nuclear projectiles against Israel, although it is questionable whether Bull himself was thinking along those lines.

Bull started working on Project Babylon in March 1988. The initial prototype, dubbed Baby Babylon, was completed in May 1989 at Jabal Hamrayn, about 100 miles north of Baghdad. The barrel was 45 meters long with a 350-mm bore. The entire gun weighed close to 110 tons. Not designed to be mobile, it was emplaced on a hillside at a fixed elevation of 45 degrees. That, of course, was too low an elevation to achieve the altitude necessary for an orbital shot, but it was the optimal elevation for maximum horizontal range, which has been estimated at some 450 miles.

Bull contracted with the Iraqis to build two full-size Babylon guns. With a bore of 1000 mm, the barrel would be assembled from 26 sections, each 6 meters in length, for a total barrel length of 156 meters. The completed barrel would weigh 1,655 tons and the entire gun 2,100 tons. With a specially designed propellant charge that weighed almost 10 tons, the gun was designed to fire a 1,320-pound projectile to a range of some 600 miles, or a 4,400-pound rocket-assisted projectile with a 440-pound payload into orbit. The launch cost would be less than $300 per pound.

Neither of the Babylon guns was ever completed. Bull was assassinated in Brussels on March 22, 1990. Although it is widely assumed that he was killed by operatives of the Mossad, the Israeli agency responsible for intelligence and special operations outside Israel, the Israeli government has neither confirmed nor denied it. If the Mossad did do it, it is far more likely the reason was the work Bull was doing on extending the Iraqi Scuds, rather than Project Babylon. As the Babylon guns were incapable of being elevated or traversed, the Israelis did not see them as a significant military threat. Their immobility also made them very vulnerable to air attack.

Project Babylon effectively died with Bull. In November 1990, British customs agents seized the final eight sections of the Babylon barrel that had been manufactured in the United Kingdom. At the end of the Persian Gulf War of 1991, the Iraqis admitted the existence of Project Babylon. United Nations teams destroyed the 350-mm Baby Babylon, the existing components of the 1000-mm Babylon, and a quantity of supergun propellant. Some of the 1000-mm barrel sections are on display at the Royal Armouries Fort Nelson museum in Portsmouth, England.

DAVID T. ZABECKI

**See also**

Artillery; Bull, Gerald Vincent; Hussein, Saddam; Iraq, History of, Pre-1990

**References**

Adams, James. *Bull's Eye: The Assassination and Life of Supergun Inventor Gerald Bull.* New York: Times Books, 1992.

Lowther, William. *Arms and the Man: Dr. Gerald Bull, Iraq, and the Supergun.* Novato, CA: Presidio, 1991.

---

# PROVIDE COMFORT, **Operation**
## Start Date: April 1991
## End Date: July 1991

A 1991 humanitarian relief mission carried out in northern Iraq by the United States and several of its military allies. Following the coalition victory over Iraq in Operation DESERT STORM, in March 1991 Kurds living in northern Iraq revolted against the rule of Iraqi president Saddam Hussein. The Kurds composed about one-fifth of Iraq's population and had long claimed northern Iraq (Kurdistan) as their ancestral home.

Initially, the rebellion went well, and demoralized Iraqi soldiers fled from Kurdish fighters called Peshmerga ("those who face death"). However, after dealing with a similar Shiite revolt in southern Iraq, Saddam Hussein sent his reconstructed military north to fight the Peshmerga. The lightly armed Kurdish fighters could not contend with Iraqi tanks, artillery, and helicopter gunships. The Iraqis also used chemical weapons against the Kurds. The Iraqis recaptured Kurdish cities one by one until only the city of Zakho, near the Turkish border, remained. On March 31, 1991, an Iraqi offensive against Zakho began. Fearing another chemical attack, most of the city's Kurds fled into the nearby mountains, where they joined a growing stream of Kurdish refugees.

Because of Turkish concerns about absorbing thousands of stateless Kurds, Turkish forces prevented the refugees from entering Turkey. Consequently, Kurdish refugees were caught in a vice between the Iraqi military and the Turkish border. Here the Kurds lived without shelter on cold mountain slopes where they suffered from hunger, exposure, and disease. The international aid group Doctors without Borders reported no health care while diseases like measles, cholera, typhus, and dysentery raged through refugee camps. A humanitarian disaster loomed with an estimated 750,000 people in danger of imminent death. Aid workers reported that about 1,500 Kurds were dying each day.

President George H. W. Bush did not want American forces to become involved in what he viewed as an Iraqi civil war, so he resisted calls for American intervention. However, on April 5, 1991, the United Nations Security Council passed Resolution 688 condemning the repression of Iraqi Kurds. Resolution 688 provided the legal basis for responding to the crisis.

President Bush then bowed to public pressure as well as requests from the United Kingdom and France and committed American resources to a relief effort. This decision marked the beginning of what became Operation PROVIDE COMFORT. On April 5, 1991, U.S. Air Force major general James L. Jamerson assumed command of a joint task force whose goal was to assist dislocated civilians living in northern Iraq. Jamerson's first task was to organize and manage the delivery of emergency relief. The second objective was to create a sustained relief effort.

Operation PROVIDE COMFORT was a particular challenge for Turkey. That country has had a long and uneasy history with the Kurds, who live along the Iraq-Turkey border. A Kurdish guerrilla group used bases inside Iraq to launch raids against Turkey. Inside Turkey itself, a sizable and restive Kurdish minority presented a challenge to the central government. However, by mid-April 1991, fleeing refugees had overwhelmed Turkey's capacity to provide assistance. Turkish president Turgut Özal accepted a United Nations (UN) plan to move refugees back into northern Iraq. Thereafter, Turkey offered vital logistical support to the mission.

On April 6, 1991, Joint Task Force Provide Comfort deployed to Incirlik Air Base at Adna, Turkey. American fighter aircraft provided aerial security. Two days later, six Lockheed C-130 Hercules cargo aircraft delivered 27 tons of supplies, including dehydrated combat rations, blankets, and water. The next day, a growing international force that included units from Denmark, Spain, Japan, New Zealand, and Australia joined the effort. From start to finish four countries—the United States, the United Kingdom, France, and Turkey—were the major contributors to the mission.

On April 16, 1991, President Bush expanded PROVIDE COMFORT to include multinational forces with the additional mission of establishing temporary refugee camps in northern Iraq. This was first labeled "Express Care." On April 17, when it had become apparent that a ground presence in northern Iraq was also necessary, Lieutenant General John M. D. Shalikashvili (who later succeeded General Colin Powell as Chairman of the Joint Chiefs of Staff)

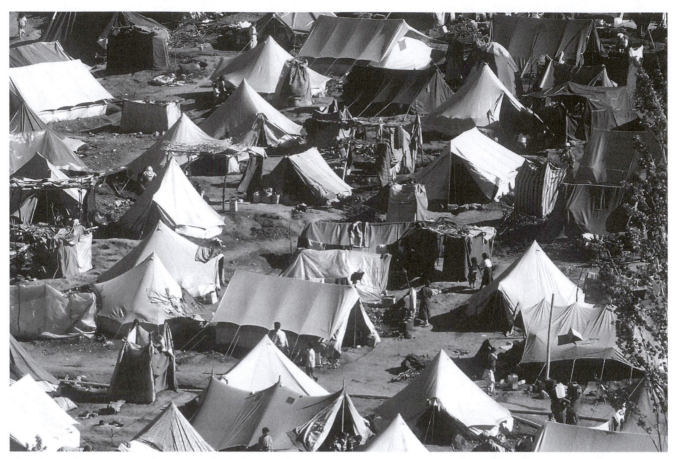

The Yekmel refugee camp in northern Iraq, established as part of Operation PROVIDE COMFORT, a coalition effort to aid Kurds fleeing retribution by Iraqi government forces following the Persian Gulf War. (U.S. Department of Defense)

replaced Jamerson as commander. Jamerson served as his deputy commander, and Marine brigadier general Anthony Zinni became chief of staff. Two subordinate joint task forces (JTFs) also formed (Alpha and Bravo).

JTF Alpha entered the mountains of southeast Turkey with the goal of alleviating the dying and suffering while stabilizing the situation. Commanded by Army brigadier general Richard Potter, JTF Alpha was composed primarily of the 10th Special Forces Group (10th SF). A special subunit began organizing to provide the first phase of emergency relief, Express Care. Some 200 U.S. Army Special Forces provided the ground component of Express Care. On April 13, only six days after the decision to commit American resources, the first Special Forces teams entered the refugee camps inside northern Iraq. Their mission was to help organize the camps while receiving and distributing supplies. Initially, planners thought that this first phase would last 10 days.

It soon became clear that relief efforts were inadequate to meet the crisis. Participants in the relief effort found 12 major refugee camps along the Iraq border. Each camp had an estimated 40,000 refugees, all of whom lacked food, clean water, and medical care. The initial phase of emergency aid expanded to first 30 days and then 90 days.

The second component, JTF Bravo, centered on the 24th Marine Expeditionary Unit under Major General Jay Garner. Its mission was to prepare the town of Zakho, in northern Iraq, as a transit point for the Kurdish refugees and to facilitate their eventual return home. An important part of this mission was to transfer responsibility over to nongovernment organizations. Task Force Encourage Hope (later renamed Joint Task Force Bravo) was formed to construct a series of resettlement camps where dislocated civilians could find food and shelter and security.

The formal decision to expand PROVIDE COMFORT's mission from emergency relief to comprehensive sustainment required organization changes. More then just U.S. Army and Marine forces were involved, and 12 countries sent military forces. Thirty-six sent financial assistance or supplies. Thirty-nine civilian relief agencies cooperated in PROVIDE COMFORT. Accordingly, in recognition of the international character of the operation, on April 9, 1991, JTF Provide Comfort became Combined Task Force Provide Comfort.

The emergency phase of Operation PROVIDE COMFORT stabilized the situation. Attention then turned to building temporary camps in the lowlands so refugees could move to a more accessible location. Coalition forces established a demilitarized zone inside northern Iraq to protect the Kurds. Air units operating from Incirlik enforced a no-fly zone above the 36th Parallel to prevent Iraqi interference. Within this zone, JTF Bravo established transit camps where refugees could live in safety until they returned home. The refugees enjoyed better sanitation facilities at these lowland camps. Here Kurdish officials could also assume administrative tasks. This was in keeping with the operational plan to transition rapidly from military to civilian control.

The city of Dohuk proved a major obstacle to the successful return of Kurdish refugees. Located near the Turkish border, this former Kurdish stronghold was a powerful symbol to thousands of refugees, but they refused to leave their camps until coalition forces had secured Dohuk. The Iraqis, in turn, refused to leave Dohuk. Several armed encounters took place between Iraqi and coalition forces. Exasperated by Iraqi harassment, General Shalikashvili ordered an American military response. Before this took place, however, the situation changed dramatically.

After meeting with Saddam Hussein, on May 18, 1991, the leader of the Kurdish Democratic Party, Masoud Barzani, announced a tentative agreement concerning Kurdish autonomy. It established a Kurdish Autonomous Zone in northern Iraq. The next day, Shalikashvili met with an Iraqi general to forge an agreement regarding the city of Dohuk. Dohuk became an "open" city where the Iraqis would allow limited humanitarian and related groups to operate. Turkey agreed to allow a multinational force to remain on Turkish soil along the Turkish border with Kurdistan. These events eased tensions and encouraged hundreds of thousands of refugees to leave the mountains and return home. The last refugee camp closed on June 7, 1991.

By mid-July, military forces assigned to Operation PROVIDE COMFORT had pulled out of Iraq; a residual force in southeastern Turkey was left to keep the Iraqis in check. A military coordination center remained in Iraq to link the armed forces and civilian relief workers, and the UN assumed responsibility for the refugee camps.

Operation PROVIDE COMFORT was the first post–Cold War humanitarian intervention conducted principally by the United States. During the operation, from April to July, 12,316 American and 10,926 coalition military personnel served. It was fundamentally a military operation, implemented and managed by military officers. In conjunction with civilian relief agencies, they met the operational objectives of stopping the suffering and resettling the refugees, first in transit camps and then back in their homes.

In late July 1991, after coalition military forces departed northern Iraq, Operation PROVIDE COMFORT II began. It was essentially a show of force designed to deter Saddam Hussein from launching further attacks against the Kurds and had a limited humanitarian component. PROVIDE COMFORT II ended on December 31, 1996.

JAMES ARNOLD

**See also**
Hussein, Saddam; Kurds; Kurds, Massacres of; No-Fly Zones; Peshmerga; Shalikashvili, John Malchese David; Zinni, Anthony Charles

**References**
Brown, Ronald J. *Humanitarian Operations in Northern Iraq, 1991, with Marines in Operation Provide Comfort.* Washington, DC: History and Museums Division Headquarters, U.S. Marine Corps, 1995.
Cuny, Frederick C. *Northern Iraq: One Year Later.* Washington, DC: Carnegie Endowment for International Peace, 1992.
Rudd, Gordon W. *Humanitarian Intervention: Assisting the Iraqi Kurds in Operation Provide Comfort, 1991.* Washington, DC: Department of the Army, 2004.
Seiple, Chris. *The U.S. Military/NGO Relationship in Humanitarian Intervention.* Carlisle Barracks, PA: Peacekeeping Institute, Center for Strategic Leadership, U.S. Army War College, 1996.

# Provincial Reconstruction Teams, Afghanistan

Teams composed of military and civilian personnel from the United States or coalition nations whose mission is to extend the authority of the Afghan central government, promote security, provide humanitarian relief, and sponsor reconstruction projects. Provincial Reconstruction Teams (PRTs), begun in late 2002 in the wake of Operation ENDURING FREEDOM, support provincial and district-level governments in Afghanistan and assist with national elections, both by explaining the process to local Afghans and providing security for polling areas. Teams monitor the disarming of local militias and illegally armed groups and provide training, support, and supplies to local police units. PRTs also provide humanitarian assistance and building projects in dangerous outlying areas where nongovernmental agencies cannot operate in safety.

Beginning in late 2001, U.S. Army Civil Affairs teams supplied some of the first humanitarian relief in Afghanistan. Civil Affairs teams created Coalition Humanitarian Liaison Cells (CHLCs), which provided humanitarian aid and assessed reconstruction needs. Established in January 2002, the Coalition Joint Civil-Military Operations Task Force (CJCMOTF) oversaw CHLC activities. It is unclear who initiated the idea to expand and reconfigure CHLCs into Provincial Reconstruction Teams. The U.S. Central Command (CENTCOM) developed the first version of the teams, initially designated "Joint Regional Teams," in December 2002. The mission of these teams was to extend the authority of the Afghan central government, enhance security, provide humanitarian relief, and support reconstruction efforts. The interim president of the Afghan Transitional Authority, Hamid Karzai, approved the plan and requested the name be changed to Provincial Reconstruction Teams. Karzai wanted to emphasize support for the central government and the mission of reconstruction rather than imply a tie to regional warlords. In 2005, the PRT mission expanded to incorporate reform of local security forces, such as the police, and support for governors and other provincial authorities.

Each PRT is a unique team with different-sized staffs, a variety of skills, and a structure to meet local political, economic, and

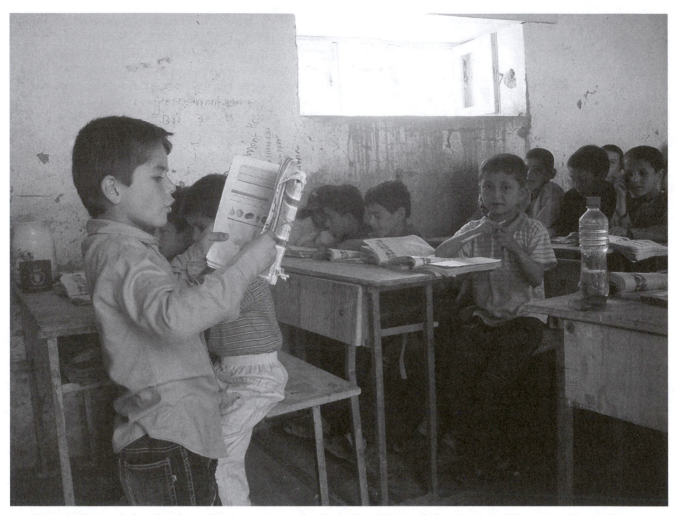

An Afghan schoolboy reads aloud from his workbook at a primary school in the Shutol District of Afghanistan's Panjshir Province. The Panjshir Provincial Reconstruction Team (PRT) is facilitating 12 education projects in Panjshir worth $2.8 million, including 9 schools, 2 dormitories, and 1 multipurpose building. June 30, 2009. (U.S. Department of Defense)

security conditions. A model American PRT has from 80 to 100 personnel and includes two army civil affairs teams, a military police unit, a psychological operations unit, an explosive ordnance/demining unit, an intelligence team, medics, a security force of about 40 soldiers, additional support personnel, as well as a representative from the U.S. State Department, U.S. Agency for International Development (USAID), the Afghan Ministry of the Interior, the U.S. Department of Agriculture, and a local interpreter. Quite often American PRTs cannot follow the standardized model, which depends on availability of units and personnel. American civilian agencies rely on volunteers to serve in PRTs and have limited funding to support them once in Afghanistan.

Military and civilian personnel have different responsibilities within the PRT. A military officer commands the team. Initially, American PRTs were led by army colonels or lieutenant colonels, male or female. Subsequently, equivalent officers from the other U.S. military services have commanded them. The military provides security and logistical support for the PRT. The State Department representative's role includes political oversight,

coordination, and reporting to the U.S. embassy in Kabul. USAID heads the reconstruction projects. The PRT's military commander, the State Department representative, and the USAID agent jointly approve all reconstruction projects, coordinating their activities with the central government and local authorities.

While these roles appear distinct on paper, the smooth functioning of the team often relies on the personalities, leadership styles, and individual experiences and skills of the key leaders. Some teams work well together, sharing a common vision, while others operate less effectively. The rotation of personnel sometimes limits the effectiveness of PRTs, as a new commander might have different priorities than the previous one. Skill sets for personnel do not remain consistent either, as a veterinarian could be replaced by an agricultural specialist, for example. Rotations of personnel also have a negative effect on the relationships with the local Afghan population if promises for reconstruction projects from one commander do not continue under the next one.

The first PRT opened in Gardez in January 2003, followed by ones in Kunduz, Mazar-e Sharif, and Bamyan. When Lieutenant

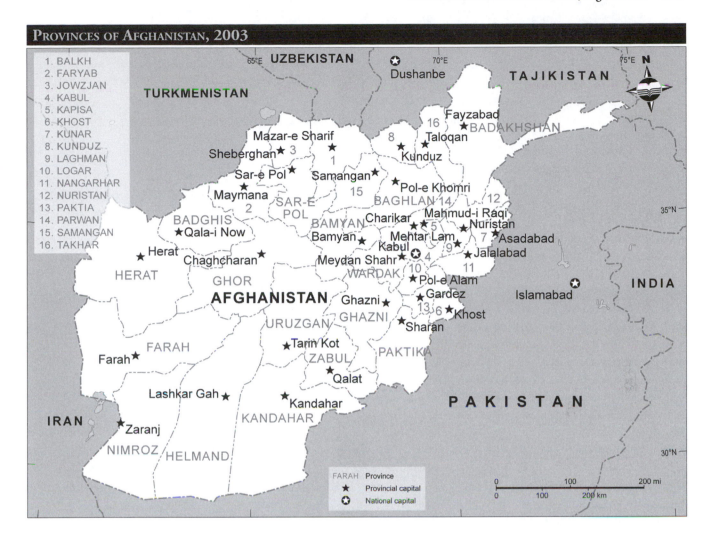

PROVINCES OF AFGHANISTAN, 2003

1. BALKH
2. FARYAB
3. JOWZJAN
4. KABUL
5. KAPISA
6. KHOST
7. KUNAR
8. KUNDUZ
9. LAGHMAN
10. LOGAR
11. NANGARHAR
12. NURISTAN
13. PAKTIA
14. PARWAN
15. SAMANGAN
16. TAKHAR

General David W. Barno assumed command in Afghanistan in October 2003, he expanded the PRTs as one component of a new counterinsurgency strategy to reach the Afghan people and to alleviate some of the causes of instability, such as poverty and the activities of local warlords. The Afghan central government controlled the capital in Kabul and surrounding areas but had limited influence in the provinces. Violence, corruption by local officials, and the activities of warlords limited the reach of the central government. Barno deactivated the CJCMOTF, and its personnel formed the military component of eight new PRTs in Asadabad, Fara, Ghazni, Herat, Jalalabad, Kandahar, Lashkar Gah, and Tarin Kot, all hot spots where it was too dangerous for civilian nongovernmental agencies to operate safely.

A PRT executive steering committee in Kabul creates guiding principles for the PRTs but does not oversee them directly. Members of the steering committee include the highest-ranking American military commander in Afghanistan, the commander of coalition forces, the Afghan minister of the interior, representatives from every contributing country, a representative from the United Nations (UN), and other key leaders. Initially, American PRTs reported to Combined Forces Command–Afghanistan, the highest

military headquarters in Afghanistan at the time. In 2004, regional commanders assumed control of areas in the east, south, and west. Thereafter, PRTs reported to the commander in their region.

It costs about $6 million to establish a single PRT and an additional $5 million to maintain it. The U.S. Department of Defense contributes between $10 and $20 million for commanders to use on quick-impact projects through a program called the Commander's Emergency Relief Program. Other agencies contribute funding, particularly USAID.

PRTs became a way to expand the reach of the International Security Assistance Force–Afghanistan (ISAF), the coalition force's command. In 2003, ISAF's responsibilities were limited to Kabul, so PRTs offered a way for the coalition to become active in other areas of Afghanistan. The United Kingdom took over operations of the PRT in Mazar-e Sharif, while New Zealand assumed control of the Bamyan PRT and Germany accepted responsibility for the Kunduz PRT. In each case, the areas were secure and relatively peaceful. The international effort expanded to include Canada, Italy, Lithuania, the Netherlands, and Spain, among other nations, and into more volatile areas in the east and south of Afghanistan. As of April 2008, American and ISAF nations run 26 PRTs across Afghanistan, including British and Canadian PRTs in Helmand and Kandahar provinces, the center of the Taliban resurgence.

While coalition PRTs share a common set of goals, the North Atlantic Treaty Organization (NATO), which commands ISAF, does not dictate how individual nations respond to them. Each nation shapes the focus and effort of its team with respect to reconstruction projects, extending the reach of the central government, working to reform local police forces, and supporting efforts to decrease the population's dependence on the cultivation of poppies, the plant from which opium and heroin originate. PRTs run by the coalition also have joint civilian-military teams, although the configuration varies. German PRTs, for example, have about 400 personnel. Civilian aid agencies of the various nations also play a role in ISAF teams, such as the Canadian International Development Agency or the British Department for International Development.

Given the unique organization and mission of PRTs, there has been confusion about their role, limits, and relationship to nongovernmental aid organizations. PRTs do not provide security for the local population, but their presence is meant to deter enemy forces and criminal elements because of their ability to call for quick military reinforcements. Reconstruction efforts focus on projects that can be quickly accomplished to win the trust of the local population and include building schools, clinics, water wells, roads, and other infrastructure. Sometimes these efforts conflict with similar projects run by nongovernmental agencies or were created in places where the local government could not provide teachers, doctors, or school or medical supplies. Nongovernmental agencies fear that the role of military personnel in reconstruction efforts jeopardizes their ability to work with the population as neutral actors in the conflict.

PRTs have provided some stability and infrastructure in Afghanistan. Between 2003 and 2006, USAID completed over 450 projects, such as buildings, irrigation systems, and road improvements. PRTs are limited in size, so they cannot replace an effectively centralized government, police force, or national army. The successes of PRTs in Afghanistan have led to the establishment of a similar program in Iraq. Some studies of PRTs in Afghanistan have shown that they have not demonstrated any quantifiable or proven effect in quelling the insurgency, but that they are thought to inhibit recruitment from the areas they serve.

LISA M. MUNDEY

**See also**

Afghanistan; Barno, David William; ENDURING FREEDOM, Operation; International Security Assistance Force; North Atlantic Treaty Organization; United States Agency for International Development, Afghanistan; United States Central Command

**References**

Barno, David W. "Fighting 'The Other War': Counterinsurgency Strategy in Afghanistan, 2003–2005." *Military Review* (September–October 2007): 32–44.
Jalali, Ali A. "The Future of Afghanistan." *Parameters* (Spring 2006): 4–19.
Maloney, Sean M. "Afghanistan Four Years On: An Assessment." *Parameters* (Autumn 2005): 21–32.
McNerney, Michael J. "Stabilization and Reconstruction in Afghanistan: Are PRTs a Model or a Muddle?" *Parameters* (Winter 2005–2006): 32–46.
Williams, Garland H. *Engineering Peace: The Military Role in Postconflict Reconstruction.* Washington, DC: United States Institute of Peace, 2005.

---

# Provisional Free Government of Kuwait

*See* Kuwait, Provisional Free Government of

---

# Public Shelter No. 25, Bombing of

*See* Amariyah Bunker or Shelter Bombing

---

# Putin, Vladimir Vladimirovich
## Birth Date: October 7, 1952

Prime minister of the Russian Federation (1999–2000 and 2008–present), acting president (December 1999–March 2000), and second president of the Russian Federation (2000–2008). Vladimir Vladimirovich Putin was born on October 7, 1952, in the city of Leningrad (present-day St. Petersburg). He graduated with a law degree from Leningrad State University in 1975 and then joined the foreign intelligence directorate of the Komitet Gosudarstvennoi Bezopasnosti (KGB), with which he served until 1990. For obvious reasons, little information has been made public regarding the details of Putin's KGB career other than that he spent some time during the Cold War in the German Democratic Republic (East Germany). However, since he became president, speculation about his intelligence career has flourished, with claims that he was involved in economic espionage in Western Europe; others allege that he was little more than a low-level domestic spy. Although international sources have raised concerns over Putin's background as an officer of one of history's most brutal internal police organizations, his KGB career has done little to detract from his growing popularity among Russians since his rise to power.

Returning to St. Petersburg after retiring from the KGB with the rank of colonel in 1990, Putin began his political career in the early 1990s under the tutelage of Anatoly Sobchak, who was then the mayor of St. Petersburg. Because Sobchak was known as a liberal democrat, Putin's role in his administration provides some of the few clues to his political orientation, which at the time of his later appointment to the federal government was not at all evident. Putin became deputy mayor of St. Petersburg in 1994 and proved himself a capable administrator. With just two years of political experience, he was brought to the Kremlin in 1996 to serve on President Boris Yeltsin's presidential staff. In 1998, Yeltsin appointed him to head the KGB's main successor organization, the Federal Security Service (FSB), where Putin managed all of Russia's intelligence agencies and ministries; on August 9, 1999, Yeltsin appointed Putin prime minister and indicated publicly that he favored him as his presidential successor.

As Yeltsin's fifth prime minister in less than two years, Putin quickly accomplished the improbable task of gaining the confidence of a wary Russian public that had grown tired and frustrated with government corruption and a flagging economy. He was swift and firm in his response to an Islamic insurgency in Dagestan that was threatening to erupt into war with Chechnya by the time of his confirmation as premier. This earned him a reputation among Russians as a pragmatist for his tough-minded conduct of a government invasion of Dagestan in the wake of a string of terrorist bombings that struck large apartment complexes in Moscow in September 1999.

Although Yeltsin's surprise resignation from the Russian presidency on New Year's Eve 1999 came as a shock to many, his appointment of Putin as acting president was not a surprise. Drawing speculation that a deal had been struck between the two, Putin, in his first official move as acting president, signed a decree granting Yeltsin, among other perks, full immunity from criminal prosecution as well as a lifetime pension.

While Putin did not win the March 2000 presidential elections by as large a margin as analysts had predicted, he nevertheless easily defeated his closest challenger, Communist Party leader Gennady Zyuganov, by some 20 percentage points. The vote demonstrated what experts and pollsters described as a profound shift in Russian public opinion, which for the first time in a decade rallied around one candidate—a newcomer to politics—who had amassed a significant support base from formerly split constituencies and disparate parties. Putin was inaugurated in May 2000 in the first democratic transfer of power in Russia's 1,100-year history.

Putin moved quickly to solidify his power base, and he acted aggressively to curb corruption in government and in Russia's large industries. His detractors claimed that he sometimes subverted democratic ideals in doing so. His administration also struggled to jump-start Russia's troubled economy, a task that was made considerably easier after 2001, when the soaring price of oil brought an economic windfall to the world's second largest oil producer.

Putin's relations with Western leaders, particularly with President George W. Bush, began on a cordial and cooperative note. He voiced full support for the War on Terror after the September 11, 2001, terror attacks, and supported Operation ENDURING FREEDOM in Afghanistan. Those relations suffered dramatically after the 2003 Iraq War, however, which Putin refused to endorse without a full United Nations (UN) authorization. He has also been angered over the expansion of the North Atlantic Treaty Organization (NATO) and is vehemently opposed to a U.S.-built missile defense system that would be deployed in Central and Eastern Europe. In December 2007, Putin pulled Russia out of the 1990 Treaty on

Vladimir Putin became president of the Russian Federation in 2000 on the resignation of Boris Yeltsin and held that office until 2008. He is currently prime minister. (President of Russia)

Conventional Armed Forces in Europe (CFE), a move that was likely a show of Russian disdain for the missile defense plans. By now, many in the West began to talk about a renewed Cold War. Russia has also refused to ratify tougher sanctions against Iran and began to move closer to the People's Republic of China in an attempt to check U.S. hegemony. Meanwhile, Putin's government was compelled to fight against a guerrilla insurgency in Chechnya from 2000 to 2004.

Putin came under fire by many in the West and in his own country for what were perceived as harsh crackdowns on the media and critics of his government. Nevertheless, Putin was reelected in March 2004 with over 70 percent of the vote. The result was never truly in doubt, as few sought to oppose him and those that did were unable to pierce the media blockade imposed on his critics. European and American election observers criticized both the media coverage and polling irregularities. In response, Putin said, "In many so-called developed democracies there are also many problems with their own democratic and voting procedures," a not so veiled reference to U.S. president George W. Bush's controversial victory over Vice President Al

Gore in 2000. By the time he reluctantly gave up the presidency on May 7, 2008, the Russian economy was faring very well, and the Russian government was already making plans to augment its military capabilities. Putin's handpicked successor, Dmitry Medvedev, easily won the May 2008 election, although most believe that Putin, who is now prime minister, continues to hold the majority of power in the Kremlin. He is also head of the powerful United Russia Party, which currently exercises sweeping power within the Russian political arena.

PAUL G. PIERPAOLI JR.

**See also**

Global War on Terror; Iran; Russia, Middle East Policy, 1991–Present; Yeltsin, Boris Nikolayevich

**References**

Kampfner, John. *Inside Yeltsin's Russia: Corruption, Conflict, Capitalism.* London: Cassell, 1994.

Politkovskaya, Anna. *Putin's Russia: Life in a Failing Democracy.* New York: Holt, 2007.

Sakwa, Richard. *Putin: Russia's Choice.* 2nd ed. London: Routledge, 2007.

# Q

## Qaddafi, Muammar
### Birth Date: June 1942

Libyan military officer and head of state (1970–present). Born the youngest child of a nomadic Bedouin family in the al-Nanja community in Fezzan in June 1942, Muammar Qaddafi attended the Sebha preparatory school from 1956 to 1961. He subsequently graduated from the University of Libya in 1963, the same year he entered the Military Academy at Benghazi, where he became part of a cabal of young military officers whose plans included the overthrow of Libya's pro-Western monarchy.

Qaddafi and the secret corps of militant, Arab nationalist officers seized power in Libya on September 1, 1969, following a bloodless coup that overthrew King Idris. After a brief internal power struggle that consolidated his rule, Qaddafi renamed the country the Libyan Arab Republic and officially ruled as president of the Revolutionary Command Council from 1970 to 1977. He then switched his title to president of the People's General Congress during 1977–1979. In 1979 he renounced all official titles but remained the unrivaled head of Libya.

Domestically, Qaddafi's reign was based on Libyan nationalism and Islamic socialism. Loosely following the model of his hero Egyptian president Gamal Abdel Nasser, Qaddafi believed in the cause of Arab unity. He also sought to promote his own developmental and economic policy, a middle path that was neither communist nor Western. He sought the privatization of major corporations, the creation of a social welfare system, and the establishment of state-sponsored education and health care systems. He also outlawed alcohol and gambling. His political and economic ideas are included within his Green Book. Qaddafi's regime encompassed a dark side, however, including the sometimes violent suppression of Libyan dissidents and the sanctioning of state-sponsored assassinations.

In foreign policy, Qaddafi promoted the ideals of Third Worldism, anti-imperialism, and solidarity between Arab and African nations. He was a major proponent of the Organization for African Unity (OAU) and supported various anticolonial liberation struggles in sub-Saharan Africa, including those in Mozambique and Angola. He also supported Zimbabwe's Robert Mugabe and was a staunch ally of Nelson Mandela and the African National Congress (ANC) in South Africa, stances that annoyed the United States, which had maintained a certain loyalty to European interests in Africa and viewed the South African apartheid regime as a bulwark against communism.

Qaddafi's national and Middle East policies further alienated him from the West. Libya had been deeply impacted by Italian colonization and, later, by European interests in its oil production. Qaddafi wanted no return of Western control. He viewed himself as heir to Nasser, who had, even with the failure of the United Arab Republic, continued to believe that Arab nations should cooperate politically.

In 1972 Qaddafi proposed a union of Libya, Egypt, and Syria, and in 1974 he signed a tentative alliance agreement with Tunisia, although neither scheme worked out. At the same time, he became a strong supporter of the Palestinian liberation movements and is rumored to have been a chief financier of the radical Islamic Black September Organization, which most notoriously engineered the killing of Israeli athletes at the 1972 Munich Olympics. He was also linked to other non-Arab movements such as the Irish Republican Army (IRA) and terrorist attacks including the December 1988 bombing of a Pan Am 747 airline jet over Lockerbie, Scotland.

As with many other Arab nationalists, Qaddafi generally held a visceral hatred for the State of Israel, which he viewed as a tool of

Western imperial domination. He made frequent threats of engaging Israel militarily and expressed public hope that the nation could be wiped off the map. He also urged several African states to withdraw support for Israel as a precondition for receiving foreign aid.

Qaddafi's ties to terrorism drove a deep wedge in Libyan-U.S. relations. By the early 1980s, he had marginally allied himself with and received significant weapons supplies from the Soviet Union. Meanwhile, tensions between Libya and the United States reached fever pitch during the presidency of Ronald Reagan. In 1986 Reagan authorized the U.S. bombing of Tripoli in retaliation for the bombing of a West Berlin discotheque, which had been tied directly to Qaddafi. The bombing raid, designed to kill Qaddafi, instead killed his infant adopted daughter and scores of civilians.

The end of the Cold War witnessed an easing of tensions in U.S.-Libyan relations as Qaddafi took a more conciliatory stance toward the West. He publicly apologized for the Lockerbie bombing and offered compensation to victims' families. He also openly condemned the September 11, 2001, terrorist attacks in the United States and has taken a more moderate line in the Palestinian-Israeli conflict. In February 2004, Libya publicly renounced its weapons of mass destruction (WMDs) program, and in May 2006 the United States and Libya resumed formal and full diplomatic relations. Most economic sanctions against Libya have now been lifted, and the U.S. State Department has removed Libya from its list of nations supporting terrorism.

Qaddafi continues to provide a radical, if unique, commentary in Arab affairs. In 2008, he called for a one-state solution to the Arab-Israeli issue. Qaddafi has not demonstrated any intention to ease his dictatorial grip on his country, and in 2006 he exhorted his supporters to kill those who sought political change.

JEREMY KUZMAROV

**See also**

Libya; Nasser, Gamal Abdel; Palestine Liberation Organization; Pan-Arabism and Pan-Arabist Thought

**References**

Davis, Brian L. *Qaddafi, Terrorism and the Origins of the U.S. Attack on Libya*. New York: Praeger, 1990.
Lemarchand, Rene. *The Green and the Black: Qadhafi Policies in Africa*. Bloomington: Indiana University Press, 1988.
Sicker, Martin. *The Making of a Pariah State*. New York: Westport, 1987.
Vanderwalle, Dirk, ed. *Qadhafi's Libya, 1969–1994*. New York: St. Martin's, 1995.

---

# Qala-i-Jangi Uprising
## Start Date: November 25, 2001
## End Date: December 1, 2001

Uprising by Taliban prisoners that resulted in a fierce battle between the Taliban and the Northern Alliance, which was being assisted by American and British forces. The Uprising of Qala-i-Jangi unfolded from November 25 to December 1, 2001.

Qala-i-Jangi, meaning "house of war" in Farsi, is a sprawling, 19th-century fortress surrounded by massive mud-baked, crenellated walls nearly 100 feet high. It is located just west of Mazar-e Sharif in northern Afghanistan and served as the personal headquarters of Northern Alliance commander General Abd al-Rashid Dostum. The compound contained stables and an armory and ultimately became a prison for hundreds of Taliban and Al Qaeda fighters after coalition forces captured Mazar-e Sharif in November 2001 as part of Operation ENDURING FREEDOM. The resulting clash was one of the bloodiest episodes of the Afghan War.

To understand the reasons for the uprising, it is important to understand how the fortress's prisoners had been captured. On the previous day, November 24, a substantial number of Taliban fighters had surrendered to Northern Alliance forces under General Dostum following air strikes and a coalition assault on the northern city of Kunduz. Dostum negotiated a deal whereby most Afghan prisoners were to go free and the 300 foreign fighters were to be handed over to Dostum. Nobody informed the foreign fighters of the arrangement, however, and these men had surrendered expecting to be released. Now they found themselves betrayed and transported by flat-bed trucks to Qala-i-Jangi, where they now expected to be tortured and murdered. Significantly, their captors had failed to conduct thorough body searches, and some of the prisoners had managed to conceal weapons.

In two incidents that occurred shortly after the detainees arrived at the fort, prisoners detonated grenades and killed themselves as well as two Northern Alliance officers, Nadir Ali Khan, who had recently become chief of police in Balkh Province, and Saeed Asad, a senior Hazara commander. The angry Uzbek captors in the meantime herded the prisoners into overcrowded cells in the basement of the stables in the fortress compound without food, water, or sanitary facilities, there to join other Taliban prisoners who had been taken earlier. Despite the above incidents, security was not increased.

The next morning a full-scale battle broke out. The exact circumstances of how the fighting began late the next morning remain unclear. As the detainees filed out of the building, the handful of Uzbeks who served as their guards made them sit on the ground in rows and began to bind their hands behind their backs. Meanwhile, other guards took the prisoners in small groups to the courtyard before two Central Intelligence Agency (CIA) agents: Johnny "Mike" Spann, a former U.S. Marine Corps captain, and Dave Tyson. The two Americans were conducting interrogations to gather intelligence on Al Qaeda and the whereabouts of the organization's leader, Osama bin Laden. Suddenly, some of the prisoners made use of what concealed weapons they had and rushed and overcame the guards. While Tyson managed to escape the onslaught, Spann fell to his attackers and was kicked, beaten, and shot to death. He thus became the first American to die in combat in Operation ENDURING FREEDOM.

Intense firefights followed, as some of the foreign fighters used arms taken from their captors to try to take control of the fort, while others remained bound in the courtyard. Foreign fighters remaining in the cells were released. Three tried to escape through a drain underneath a wall, only to be shot by Northern Alliance guards outside the fort. Others stormed a small armory and there seized mortars, rocket-propelled grenade launchers, AK-47 assault rifles, and other weapons and ammunition.

Northern Alliance forces then reorganized and mounted a counterattack, which killed many of the Taliban. Two Northern Alliance tanks, which were outside the fort, began to pound the prisoners' positions. In the meantime, Tyson, who had joined with a trapped German film crew in another part of Qala-i-Jangi, managed to contact the American embassy in Tashkent with a plea for help. Early in the afternoon, a Quick Reaction Force (QRF) team of British Special Boat Service (SBS) and American Special Operations Forces (SOF) arrived at the fortress in a pair of Land Rovers and engaged the Taliban fighters. One SOF team member directed air support in the form of McDonnell Douglas (Boeing) F-18 Hornet aircraft, which dropped several 500-pound bombs that missed the armory but forced the Taliban fighters to take refuge in the stable's cellar. At dusk on that first day of fighting, Tyson and members of the film crew managed to escape by climbing over one of the fortress walls. Because the QRF team did not know of their escape, the SBS team leader organized a rescue force, which braved Taliban fire only to find that Tyson was gone.

Over the next days, coalition forces attempted to subdue the stubborn Taliban fighters. Northern Alliance forces directed fire from tanks as well as mortars at the besieged, who continued a tenacious resistance. During the melee, a misdirected 2,000-pound bomb dropped by an American aircraft destroyed a tank and killed or injured several coalition soldiers. This was followed by another strike and an air-to-ground attack conducted by a Lockheed AC-130 Spectre gunship. Finally, with the surviving prisoners running out of ammunition and having nothing to eat but horseflesh, about 100 Northern Alliance troops, joined by SBS and SOF teams, mounted an assault on what remained of the Taliban defenses. With resistance apparently over, some of the Afghan soldiers reportedly looted the bodies of the fallen prisoners, only to discover them booby trapped.

There were still Taliban fighters who had been driven underground beneath the rubble of the ruined stables. These were dispatched with rifle fire, rockets, and grenades. Northern Alliance fighters also poured oil into the basement and lit it. Ultimately, Dostum's men flooded the underground hiding places with ice-cold water, finally forcing the surrender of those who remained alive. Some 86 prisoners were taken, including the so-called American Talib, John Walker Lindh.

For his activity, Lindh was later tried, convicted, and assessed a 20-year prison sentence. Many of his comrades were later transferred to Camp X-Ray at the American detention facility at Guantánamo Bay, Cuba. Besides Spann, the only American to die in the uprising, the coalition suffered 40 to 50 combat deaths with a similar number wounded. The Taliban death toll has been variously estimated at 200 to 500, many of these being foreign fighters determined to fight to the death.

The action at Qala-i-Jangi has been the subject of some controversy. Some critics charged that a massacre took place; others, such as Amnesty International, questioned the proportionality of the force employed against the revolting prisoners and demanded an investigation. The U.S. and British governments refused, claiming that their forces had acted according to the rules of engagement and international law.

GEORGE L. SIMPSON

**See also**

Al Qaeda; Bin Laden, Osama; Dostum, Abd al-Rashid; ENDURING FREEDOM, Operation; Mazar-e Sharif, Battle of; Northern Alliance; Taliban

**References**

Clements, Frank A. *Conflict in Afghanistan: A Historical Encyclopedia.* Santa Barbara, CA: ABC-CLIO, 2003.

Griffin, Michael. *Reaping the Whirlwind: Afghanistan, Al-Qa'ida, and the Holy War.* London: Pluto, 2001.

Maloney, Sean M. *Enduring the Freedom: A Rogue Historian in Afghanistan.* Washington, DC: Potomac Books, 2007.

Perry, Alex. "Inside the Battle at Qala-i-Jangi." *Time,* December 10, 2001.

---

# Qasim, Abd al-Karim

**Birth Date: November 21, 1914**
**Death Date: February 8, 1963**

Iraqi general and leader of the 1958 coup that overthrew the British-imposed monarch King Faisal II, sweeping away the last vestiges of colonial rule in Iraq. Abd al-Karim Qasim, son of a Sunni Arab and a Shia Kurdish mother, was born in a poor section of Baghdad on November 21, 1914. His father raised corn along the Tigris River, and as a young boy Qasim experienced poverty, which influenced his later efforts at social reform. He attended school in Baghdad, and at age 17, following a brief period teaching elementary school (1931–1932), he enrolled in the Iraqi Military College. Two years later, in 1934, he graduated as a second lieutenant. In 1935 he took part in suppressing unrest in the middle Euphrates region of Iraq.

In December 1941 Qasim graduated with honors from the al-Arkan (General Staff) College and became a staff officer. In 1942 while stationed in Basra near the Persian Gulf, he struck up a friendship with Abd al-Salam Arif. The two men shared a desire to overthrow the Iraqi monarchy. In 1945 Qasim commanded a battalion against rebellious Kurdish tribesmen in northern Iraq, a campaign that earned him the highest Iraqi military decoration.

In 1948, during the Israeli War of Independence (1948–1949), Qasim commanded a battalion of the Iraqi 1st Brigade in Palestine. Following the Arab defeat, he attended a senior officers' school in Britain for six months. Upon his return to Iraq, he was promoted to colonel and a year later attained the rank of brigadier general. During the Suez Crisis of 1956, he commanded Iraqi troops in Jordan, where his schooling and his combat experience earned him respect and prominence.

In 1956 Qasim helped organize and then headed the central organization of the Free Officers, a clandestine association working to overthrow the Iraqi monarchy. He worked closely with Arif, waiting for the right moment to stage a coup. That time came in 1958 when a revolt broke out in Jordan followed by a crisis in Lebanon, and the Iraqi monarchy ordered troops into Jordan.

Arif's battalion entered Baghdad on July 13 en route to Jordan, but on the next day his troops occupied the central radio studio and proclaimed the overthrow of the king. The following day, the king, the crown prince, some other members of the royal family, and Prime Minister Nuri al-Said Pasha were all assassinated. Qasim arrived in Baghdad with his troops after the assassinations. Some historians attribute the apparent delay in his arrival to a calculated decision to allow Arif to take the initial risk. Regardless, Qasim became prime minister and minister of defense, with Arif as deputy prime minister and interior minister.

Disputes soon arose between Qasim and Arif over the direction of the revolutionary government. Arif was more popular with the crowds than Qasim, and this also led to tension. Arif favored the unionist wing of the Baathists, who first argued for unity with Egypt and later Syria, while Qasim was attempting to balance the Baath Party with its several factions against the Arab nationalists and the communists. These tensions eventually resulted in a showdown with Arif and his imprisonment on charges of conspiracy.

Qasim allowed the Communist Party to operate, and he embarked on serious land reform to address rural poverty. The new government launched a series of attacks on opponents that prompted a public outcry. Two incidents in particular inspired revulsion. The first occurred in March 1959 when Qasim's communist allies, after crushing a revolt by army units in Mosul, went on a rampage, killing anticommunist supporters of the rebellion. The second incident occurred later that summer when Kurdish communists were involved in massacres, particularly of Turkomen in Kirkuk.

Meanwhile, Qasim launched several important domestic and foreign policy reforms. First, he addressed the maldistribution of land by limiting the size of holdings. Second, he expanded women's rights in the areas of marriage, divorce, and inheritance. Third, in a highly successful move, he reduced the influence of oil companies by confiscating large amounts of land held by the foreign-owned Iraq Petroleum Company. This step prepared the way for full nationalization in 1973.

In foreign affairs Qasim followed a policy of nonalignment, but his actions, including substantial arms purchases from communist-bloc nations, tilted Iraq toward the Soviet Union. Relations with Egypt deteriorated, encouraging unionists to contemplate Qasim's overthrow. In October 1959 the Iraqi branch of the Arab Baath Socialist Party concluded that Qasim's policies, particularly his antagonism toward Egypt and alliance with the communists, necessitated his removal. The Baathists plotted to kill Qasim in the streets of Baghdad, and on October 7 they attacked but only succeeded in wounding him. Several of the conspirators fled Iraq, including the young Saddam Hussein.

Following this attempt on his life, Qasim permitted the free organization of political parties, but only if they did not threaten national unity. In practice, this meant that no independent party could exist, a fact confirmed in late 1960 when Qasim suppressed all parties. His increasingly narrow support became restricted to segments of the military, and he lived an increasingly isolated existence, barricaded in the office of the Ministry of Defense.

Qasim's growing unpopularity was exacerbated by two military failures. One was the inability to quell a Kurdish rebellion in northern Iraq. The second was his bungled attempt to absorb Kuwait in 1961, when he announced that the small Persian Gulf nation was in reality a renegade Iraqi province. When British and later Arab League troops moved to protect Kuwait, Qasim was forced to back down. Another blow came in the form of an economic slump. All these factors led to growing disaffection in the army, Qasim's last bastion of support. On February 8, 1963, a military coup led by Arif Baathists toppled Qasim. Following a bloody street battle, he was captured and executed. Qasim achieved much in societal reform, health, education, housing for the poor, and agriculture, but perhaps his greatest accomplishment was the establishment of a truly independent Iraq.

NEIL HAMILTON AND SPENCER C. TUCKER

**See also**

Arab-Israeli Conflict, Overview; Arif, Abd al-Salam; Baath Party; Egypt; Faisal II, King of Iraq; Iraq, History of, Pre-1990; Nasser, Gamal Abdel; Nuri al-Said; Suez Crisis; United Arab Republic

**References**

Batatu, Hanna. *The Old Social Classes and the Revolutionary Movement of Iraq: A Study of Iraq's Old Landed and Commercial Classes and of Its Communists, Ba'athists, and Free Officers.* Princeton, NJ: Princeton University Press, 1978.
Dann, Uriel. *Iraq under Qassem: A Political History, 1958–1963.* New York: Praeger, 1969.
Makiya, Kanan. *Republic of Fear: The Politics of Modern Iraq.* Berkeley: University of California Press, 1998.
Marr, Phebe. *The Modern History of Iraq.* 2nd ed. Boulder, CO: Westview, 2003.

# Qatar

Independent Arab nation encompassing 4,416 square miles, a bit smaller than the size of the state of Connecticut, located in the northeastern part of the Arabian Peninsula. Qatar is itself a peninsula, as most of it fronts the Persian Gulf, but it does share a border to the south with Saudi Arabia. Qatar's current population is about 1.25 million people. Nearly 80 percent of Qatar's inhabitants live in the capital city of Doha and surrounding suburbs. Islam is the official religion of the country, although in the last decade several Christian churches have been established, which is reflective of the

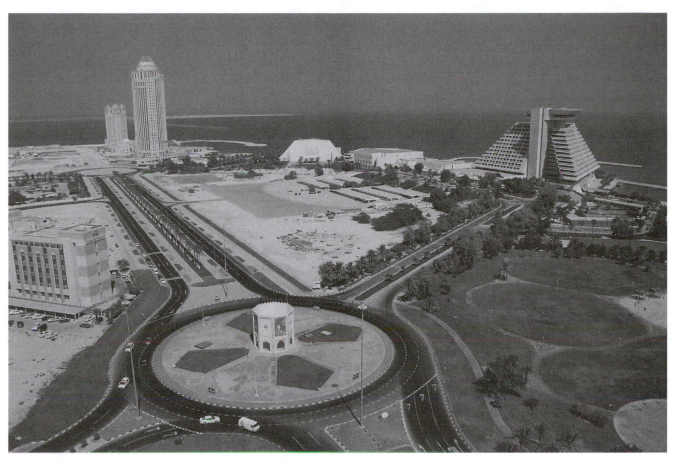

View of Doha, Qatar. Doha is the chief port and capital of Qatar. (iStockPhoto)

reformist impulses of the current ruler or emir, Sheikh Hamad bin Khalifa al-Thani.

Qatar was part of the Ottoman Empire for several centuries and was home to a large number of nomadic tribes until several sheikhs began to assert their authority in the 19th century. Qatar became a British protectorate following World War I and gained its independence on September 3, 1971.

The United States established diplomatic relations with Qatar in March 1973 and relations since then have been cordial. The era since the end of the 1990–1991 Persian Gulf War has been marked by greater political, economic, and military cooperation with the West (and the United States in particular) as the Iraqi invasion of Kuwait and the resulting threat to other small Gulf states forced Qatar to significantly alter its defense and foreign policy priorities. Qatar boasts a modern and impressive infrastructure and is a wealthy nation, owing in large part to its sizable oil reserves.

Qatar has a small military establishment, consisting of approximately 11,000 troops, 34 tanks, and about a dozen aircraft. Its most extensive role in combat operations came during Operation DESERT STORM. Between January 29, 1991, and February 1, 1991, a Qatari tank battalion participated with Saudi troops, backed by American artillery and air support, in repulsing an Iraqi cross-border assault on the Saudi city of Khafji. Qatari troops were officially part of the multinational coalition authorized by the United

Nations (UN) and led by the United States that expelled Iraq from Kuwait in February 1991.

Strains with Saudi Arabia and Bahrain and aspirations for a more assertive and influential position in foreign affairs explain Qatar's recent foreign policy, which has become more Western-oriented. On June 23, 1992, Qatar and the United States signed a bilateral defense cooperation agreement that provided the United States access to Qatari bases, the prepositioning of U.S. military equipment in the nation, and future joint military exercises. Since the Persian Gulf War, Qatar has also aligned itself more closely with the United States by allowing the construction of an extensive American military air base—Al Udeid—in the country, which served as the command center for the Anglo-American invasion of Iraq in March 2003. Presumably for this reason, Iraq launched Scud missiles at Qatar upon the commencement of the conflict. It is worth noting that Al Udeid boasts the longest runway (15,000 feet) in the Persian Gulf region and currently houses some 5,000 U.S. troops. It is equipped to accommodate as many as 10,000 troops and 40 aircraft in a 76,000-square-foot hangar. Qatar has also allowed the construction of the As-Sayliyah Army base, the largest prepositioning facility for U.S. equipment in the world.

Shortly after the terror attacks against the United States on September 11, 2001, Qatar granted the Americans permission to deploy warplanes to Al Udeid, and these flew missions in

Afghanistan during Operation ENDURING FREEDOM in the autumn of 2001 to overthrow the Taliban government there, which had given sanctuary to Osama bin Laden and his Al Qaeda terrorist organization.

In the months leading up to Operation IRAQI FREEDOM, the United States moved significant troops, weapons, and equipment, along with its Air Operations Command Center, from Prince Sultan Air Base in Saudi Arabia to Qatar, the consequence of Saudi Arabia's opposition to the invasion of Iraq. Indeed, during IRAQI FREEDOM, Saudi Arabia forbade the United States from using its territory to launch attacks against Iraq.

Unlike Saudi Arabia, Qatar has imposed far fewer restrictions on American operations launched from Al Udeid airbase. However, Qatar more recently announced that it would not participate in any American military attack on Iran, but it nevertheless objected to Iran's development of nuclear weapons and indicated that it was opposed to a nuclear arms race in the region.

STEFAN M. BROOKS

**See also**

DESERT STORM, Operation; ENDURING FREEDOM, Operation; Global War on Terror; IRAQI FREEDOM, Operation; Saudi Arabia

**References**

Blanchard, Christopher. *Qatar: Background and U.S. Relations.* Washington, DC: Congressional Research Service, the Library of Congress, December 21, 2005.

Cleveland, William L. *A History of the Modern Middle East.* 3rd ed. Boulder, CO: Westview, 2004.

Potter, Lawrence, and Gary Sick. *Security in the Persian Gulf: Origins, Obstacles, and the Search for Consensus.* New York: Palgrave Macmillan, 2002.

# Quayle, James Danforth
## Birth Date: February 4, 1947

Republican attorney, politician, and vice president of the United States (1989–1993). James Danforth Quayle was born in Indianapolis, Indiana, on February 4, 1947, into a politically prominent and well-to-do family. His mother's father, Eugene C. Pulliam, was a newspaper publishing scion, having created Central Newspapers, Inc., which included ownership of the *Indianapolis Star* and Phoenix's *Arizona Republic.* Quayle spent a good portion of his youth in Arizona before moving back to Indiana, where he completed high school. In 1969, he received a bachelor's degree from DePauw University (Indiana); that same year, he secured a position in the Indiana Army National Guard, thereby making it very likely that he would not be sent to Vietnam. He then attended law school at the Indiana University School of Law–Indianapolis, from which he earned a law degree in 1974.

In 1975, Quayle completed his last year of service in the National Guard and went to work for the *Huntington Herald-Press* as associate publisher. The paper was part of his family's

publishing empire. At the same time, he practiced law with his wife, Marilyn, who was also an attorney.

Quayle began his career in electoral politics in 1976, when he successfully ran for a seat in the U.S. House of Representatives on the Republican ticket. He took office in January 1977. He won reelection by a huge margin in 1978 and made a name for himself as an earnest young congressman. In 1980, at age 33, he ran for a seat in the U.S. Senate. Capitalizing on his family's name recognition and resources, he won the election, becoming the youngest Indiana senator ever seated when he was sworn into office in January 1981. His political ascendancy coincided with the beginning of the Ronald Reagan administration and the rise of the Republican Party in national politics. Quayle's success in the 1980 election was all the more miraculous considering he unseated three-term Democratic Senator Birch Bayh, who by then was a household name in the Senate.

In the Senate, Quayle had an undistinguished career but was reelected by a wide margin in 1986. That same year, he came under heavy criticism for supporting a U.S. Court of Appeals nominee whose credentials were unimpressive and whose judicial track record was seen as divisive. The nominee, who was eventually confirmed, had been an old law-school friend of Quayle's, bringing charges of cronyism.

In 1988, Vice President George H. W. Bush, the Republican nominee for president that year, selected Quayle to be his running mate. The decision seemed a bolt out of the blue, as Quayle was entirely unknown outside Indiana. His congressional record was uninspiring, and at age 41 his maturity and experience were questioned. Nevertheless, the Bush campaign claimed that Quayle would bring youth and vigor to the ticket and would appeal to younger voters. Almost immediately, the press and the Democrats sharply criticized Bush's selection, and Quayle's Vietnam-era service in the Indiana National Guard elicited a brief storm of controversy. His detractors alleged that he had used his family connections to avoid active military service.

Quayle's frequent verbal gaffes and malapropisms during the campaign were skewered by the Democratic vice-presidential nominee, Senator Lloyd Bentsen. In one of their most famous exchanges, when Quayle compared his own youth and inexperience to the late President John Kennedy during a televised debate, Bentsen shot back that he had known Kennedy and that Quayle was "no Jack Kennedy."

Nevertheless, Quayle had the last laugh when the Bush-Quayle ticket went on to victory, and he took office as vice president in January 1989. President Bush did not involve his vice president in most policy decisions. In fact, compared to his immediate predecessors and successors, Quayle appeared to be disengaged. His continued gaffes and often inane statements proved to be a boon to his detractors and fodder for comedians' jokes. Many had believed that Bush would dump Quayle from the 1992 reelection ticket, but he stood by his vice president. In an election that featured a strong showing by third-party candidate Ross Perot, the Clinton-Gore ticket won with a plurality of the popular vote (43 percent—four years earlier, Democrat Michael Dukakis had lost while receiving 45 percent of the popular vote). Quayle left office in January 1993.

In 1994, Quayle considered a run for the governorship of Indiana but demurred. Although he was perhaps unjustly criticized for his verbal and syntax miscues, Quayle had a difficult time appealing to voters after the 1992 defeat. He briefly sought the Republican nomination for president in 1996 but withdrew because of health problems. In 1999, he announced his intention to run for president in 2000, criticizing the presumptive front-runner George W. Bush for his inexperience. His campaign fizzled early, however, and he dropped out of the race. In the meantime, Quayle has practiced law, written his memoirs, sat on corporate boards, and been involved in political action committees and other political outlets. He has also had a syndicated newspaper column. Quayle and his wife now live in Paradise Valley, Arizona. He has kept a relatively low profile politically and neither strongly endorsed nor criticized President Bush's policies since 2001.

PAUL G. PIERPAOLI JR.

**See also**
Bush, George Herbert Walker; Bush, George Walker

**References**
Broder, David S., and Bob Woodward. *The Man Who Would be President: Dan Quayle.* New York: Simon and Schuster, 1992.
Quayle, Dan. *Standing Firm: A Vice-Presidential Memoir.* New York: HarperCollins, 1994.

---

# Qur'an

The principal religious and sacred text of Islam. The name Qur'an al-karim (the noble Qur'an) derives from the Arabic verb *qa-ra-'a* ("to declaim or recite"). This text is so-named because the Qur'an comprises divine revelations spoken to the Prophet Muhammad by the angel Gabriel from about 610 CE until Muhammad's death in 632. Muslims hold that the Qur'an in the holy original Arabic is the literal word of Allah transmitted to the Prophet Muhammad (the Messenger) for humanity. Reading of the Qur'an is a duty for every Muslim. Specially trained reciters or readers (*qariun* or *muqriun*) present the Qur'an in a format called *tajwid*, a chanting in the modal musical system (like the *maqamat*) and set to the natural rhythm of the Arabic words, with their longer or shorter syllables. The *tajwid*, which today may be enjoyed in audio recordings or over the radio, allows the listener to hear the voice of the sacred text.

Epic poetry and other forms of oral literature were especially prized in pre-Islamic Arabian society. Hence, Qur'anic recitation provided Muslims a literary as well as a religious experience and an opportunity to reflect on the meaning of the text as well.

According to tradition, the Prophet Muhammad was illiterate. Like the other men of Mecca with sufficient means for leisure time, he used to retreat to the hills beyond the city to spend time reflecting or meditating. When in retreat in a cave on Mount Hira he heard a voice commanding him to "recite," Muhammad protested that he did not know what to recite. The mysterious voice was that of the archangel Gabriel, and his words are the first of the Qur'an:

> Recite [*Iqra*]: In the name of thy Lord who created, Created a man from *Alaq* [a "clinging" clot, or small amount of fetal material].
> Recite: And thy Lord is the Most Generous, Who taught [the use of] the pen, Taught man that which he knew not.

This verse has been interpreted to mean that the omnipotent Allah (God) has the ability to bring and teach his message even to an illiterate man. This passage, from the Surat al-Alaq (96:1–5), was revealed to Muhammad in Mecca, and it is the first of many to be given to the Prophet over the next 23 years, signaling the beginning of the divine revelation that became the Qur'an and the message of Islam.

The Qur'an is not a story of the Prophet's life, but some understanding of his experience is helpful to the outsider seeking to comprehend the text. The ruling elite in Mecca were threatened by the growing crowds of followers and the messages of monotheism and strict moral codes that Muhammad was spreading. After about a decade, they increasingly threatened the Prophet because of his proselytizing. In 622 after their pressure increased and his vulnerability increased due to the deaths of his wife Khadija and his uncle Abu Talib, Muhammad fled with his followers to the town of Yathrib, later renamed Madinat al-Nabi (City of the Prophet), on a journey now known as the *hijra*. While the Muslims were living in Medina, the early and basic concepts and practices of the faith were defined, although some changed after Mecca was reconquered. Also, the Kaaba, or holy site where the Black Rock is located, was cleansed of its idols.

Early on, some of the Prophet's companions and his wives had partial collections of the Qur'an, and other collections were written down. These were different in the ordering of the *surahs*, which are chapters with titles that concern particular themes, and in the number of verses they contained. Many Qur'an reciters worked from memory and not written texts. There were different versions, including variant spellings, and even more important differences. Some Sunni sources claim that following the wars of Ridda when many Qur'anic reciters were killed, Umar asked the caliph Abu Bakr to assemble a written version of the Qur'an, which he then did. Up until that time various versions had been recited due to the variations on the Arabic dialect of that period. Most sources agree that it was the caliph Uthman who recensed the Qur'an, creating a committee that met and approved one version based on the members' understanding of the text and their agreement given the various versions then recited. Uthman burned all the other versions of the Qur'an that he could find and distributed this official version 23 years after the Prophet's death. The recension was controversial to different parties, especially the Shia Muslims. By the ninth century, Uthman's form, or codex, was vocalized, meaning that the normally unwritten Arabic vowels were included to stabilize its meaning. Some authorities suggest that, because of an inability

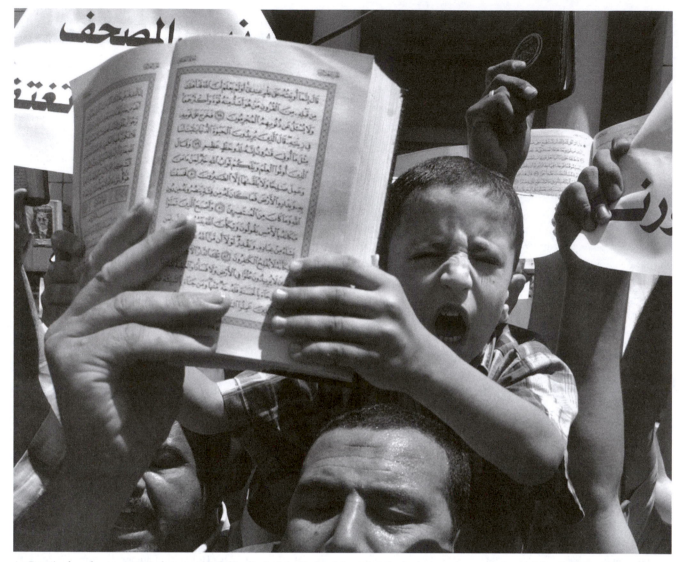

An Egyptian boy shouts anti-U.S. slogans as his father displays the Qur'an, Islam's holy book, during a demonstration in Cairo, Egypt, on May 27, 2005. The protest followed reports that the Qur'an had been desecrated at the U.S. base at Guantánamo Bay, Cuba, by U.S. military personnel. Similar protests took place across the Muslim world. (AP/Wide World Photos)

to destroy all variant versions, the Prophet Muhammad approved seven valid readings of this text. More than seven exist, however.

The Qur'an is organized into the basic divisions of *ayat*, or verses; surahs; and the *juz*, which is simply a section that is 1/30 of the entire Qur'an. Muslims use this 1/30 division to read the Qur'an over a one-month period, or they might divide it into 7 sections. There are 114 surahs in the Qur'an, each of a different length, from just 3 to 286 phrases, or *ayat*. Many of the shorter, more dramatic surahs were revealed at Mecca, while the longer, more legalistic surahs were revealed at Medina. The Qur'an is arranged so that following the first surah, the longest surah, the second one al-Baqarah, is at the beginning of the text, and the surahs decrease in length.

Exegesis, or the explanation of the Qur'an, is an area of Islamic studies. These explanations are called *tafsir* and are used as a basis for Sharia (Islamic law). The Qur'an is most important as the ultimate authority in Sharia. The Qur'an is used as liturgy, that is, in prayer. The first verse of the Qur'an is repeated before each

bowing and prostration, and devout Muslims recite a portion of the Qur'an each night (or more often).

The Qur'an has also served as a basis for education. The goal of learning to read in Arabic is the memorization of the Qur'an, often at a young age. The *kuttab,* or Qur'anic school, is found throughout the Muslim world. The Qur'an also serves various social purposes. It is read in funeral sittings and recited at public events or conferences. Contests in Qur'an reading are held, and calligraphy is based on the Qur'an.

The most basic aspect of the Qur'an is that it is proof of Allah's existence and gives information about His nature, which is at once powerful, tender, and mystical: "He is the First and the Last, the Outward and the Inward; and He is the Knower of every thing" (37:3). This is based on the notion of *tawhid,* the unicity of God, which is demonstrated in a multiplicity of ways.

Theology as expressed in the Qur'an begins with monotheism. The unity of Allah, his attributes, and the descriptions of heaven, hell, and the angels are all supported by the Qur'an. Another basic message in the Qur'an concerns the nature of humans, who have been warned through the revelations to follow the Straight Path, or divine law, and must also overcome their tendencies toward insecurity, haste, and panic. If humans honor their pact with Allah, maintaining their trust in Him and living according to his rules, they will be rewarded. If not, they will be grievously punished.

During the seventh century, the Arabs at Mecca were polytheistic. Moreover, their society benefited the wealthy and the powerful. According to the Qur'an, however, the disenfranchised, orphans, and the poor are the responsibility of the Muslim community, for wealth comes from Allah and must be used for the good of his community. Another important message of the Qur'an has to do with living in accordance with Allah's will and avoiding sin, for the Day of Judgment and the Resurrection will come, when all shall be reckoned with.

Islam means "submission," or "surrender to Allah," while Muslim means "one who submits." This does not, as in English, have any tinge of self-abasement. Rather, it implies one who trusts completely in God and thus in His revelation, the Qur'an. The Qur'an describes the Muslim community, or *ummah,* in its covenant with Allah, as a "community in a state of surrender" (*ummah muslimah*), in which Muslims are accountable and responsible for their actions. The opposite of Islam is *kufr,* which means that one covers up, obscures, or denies Islam and all of its requirements.

The Qur'an is seen as the final of a series of revelations that begins with the book of Genesis and the story of Adam and Eve, as revealed to Moses, continues through the Gospels of Christ, and ends with the revelations given to Muhammad. The Qur'an describes prophets and their messages to mankind from Abraham to Muhammad, mentioning some included and others excluded from the Bible. The Qur'an refers to Jews and Christians (as well as Zoroastrians) as "Peoples of the Book," meaning that they and their scripture are to be respected and that they are not infidels or polytheists. However, in places the Qur'an also criticizes Christians and Jews for failing to follow the dictates of their own Holy Scriptures and not heeding the teachings of their prophets. The Qur'an also commands its followers to "struggle in the way of Allah," meaning to engage in jihad. This is interpreted to mean an armed struggle in battle, as well as the struggle to fulfill all the elements of faith (*iman*) in Islam.

Muslims recite and learn the Qur'an in Arabic, because in that form it is considered to be the literal word of Allah. Muslim clerics long maintained that any translation of the words of the Qur'an is not divine speech, but today even translations are treated as holy texts. Incidents involving insults to the Qur'an, such as those at Guantánamo, Cuba, or when a U.S. soldier used it for target practice in Iraq in May 2008, outrage Muslims. As the majority of Muslims are non-Arabic speakers, the requirement to learn and study the Qur'an in Arabic means study of the Arabic language in Islamic studies, since many historic texts and commentaries that pertain to the Qur'an are also in Arabic. The book itself is treated with reverence. Some translations, such as that by Abdullah Yusuf Ali in English, contain a great deal of commentary in notes, and others less. These have helped to create and sustain Muslim scholarship and discussion about the Qur'an in other languages. Meanwhile, works of analysis and commentary on the Qur'an have led to discussions that are relevant to the political and social challenges facing Muslims today.

B. KEITH MURPHY AND SHERIFA ZUHUR

**See also**

Allah; Bible; Gog and Magog; Guantánamo Bay Detainment Camp; Jihad; Khomeini, Ruhollah; Mawdudi, Sayyid Abu al-Aala; Shia Islam; Sunni Islam

**References**

'Ali, Abdullah Yusuf. *The Meaning of the Holy Qur'an.* Beltsville, MD: Amana, 2001.

Ayoub, Mahmoud. *The Qur'an and Its Interpreters.* 2 vols. Albany, NY: SUNY Press, 1984, 1992.

Nelson, Kristina. *The Art of Reciting the Quran.* Austin: University of Texas Press, 1985.

Rahman, Fazlur. *Major Themes of the Qur'an.* Minneapolis: Biblioteca Islamica, 1980.

# Qutb, Sayyid
## Birth Date: October 9, 1906
## Death Date: August 29, 1966

Islamist theorist, educator, and Muslim Brotherhood leader incarcerated and executed by the Egyptian government. Sayyid Ibrahim Husayn Shadhili Qutb received considerable attention when, in the wake of the September 11, 2001, attacks, Westerners researched the older literature on Islamic revivalism and extremism in an effort to understand the roots of Al Qaeda. Sayyid Qutb was born on October 9, 1906. His father came from a family of landowners in the village of Musha, in Asyut Province in Upper Egypt, several hundred miles south of Cairo. His father was politically active and his mother was deeply religious.

Qutb had a traditional Islamic education alongside a modern education in the national education system. Around 1921, Qutb left Musha and moved to Cairo, where he trained to become a teacher of Arabic language and literature. At this time the Wafd Party and other groups were promoting Egyptian nationalism and, ever since the revolution of 1919, had demanded the expulsion of Britain from the country. Britain finally granted Egypt nominal independence and a degree of self-government. Qutb was influenced by key members of the Wafd Party, and during this period in his life he worked for the Egyptian Ministry of Education, taught, published poetry, and wrote works of literary criticism. In 1945 he was appointed director general of culture. As part of his work, and also to remove him from the limelight because of controversial statements he made opposing the government, Qutb was sent to the United States from 1948 to 1950 to study and report on its educational system. He was briefly in Washington, D.C., and also studied for several months at Colorado State in Greeley, Colorado.

While he was in the United States one of Qutb's most important books, *al-'Adala al-ijtima'iyya fi-l-Islam* (*Social Justice in Islam*), was published in 1949. This book thoughtfully analyzes the failure of Muslim-led governments to uphold the need for social justice and recommends a major shift in order to secure an Islamic system that would bring about this condition. The Muslim Brotherhood of Egypt's commitment to social justice is one of its continuous planks. In recent accounts of Qutb's life, it is claimed that he became anti-Western as a result of allegedly morally licentious behavior he observed. It is true that Qutb did not like the aura of certain mixed-sex events he saw, but his more significant criticisms of American life centered on the lack of true spirituality and the racism he observed in this period prior to the civil rights movement.

Qutb was already familiar with the Muslim Brotherhood movement in Egypt. In the late 1940s the secret militant wing of the organization battled with the Egyptian government, and Egyptian government agents assassinated the leader of the Brotherhood, Hassan al-Banna, in 1949.

Qutb returned to Egypt, resigned his government position, and joined the Muslim Brotherhood in 1951, declaring that he was "born" in that year. He became the editor-in-chief of *al-Ikhwan al-Muslimin,* the organization's weekly publication, and then the head of its Propaganda Department and a member of the Working Committee. In 1952, Qutb published his monumental work on the Qur'an, *Fi Dhilal al-Quran,* which is simultaneously exegesis (a *tafsir,* or interpretation) and an examination of the aesthetics of the Qur'an.

When the revolution of 1952 occurred, members of the Muslim Brotherhood had hopes that they would be able to operate legally. Some of the members of the Free Officers Movement who had overthrown the previous regime were allied with the Muslim Brotherhood. However, the organization clashed with the leader of the Muslim Brotherhood in 1949, and Qutb aligned himself with that organization. Many members of the Muslim Brotherhood were jailed in 1951 when the movement was banned in Egypt, and Qutb himself was arrested in 1954. He was held in prison until 1964 on charges of promoting antigovernment activities, and copies of his books were destroyed. Indeed, much of the recent characterization of him as a mastermind of radicalism springs from his struggle with the regime of Gamal Abdel Nasser.

In Qutb's book *Ma'alim fi Tariq* (*Milestones on the Road*), of 1964, he outlines the inevitability of conflict with an oppressive state that does not operate under Islamic principles and oppresses those supporting an Islamic society, equating it to the suppression of early Muslims. Qutb charged that the oppressors were, in essence, no longer Muslims, as they embraced the world of *jahiliyyah* (the term for the pre-Islamic environment), or "barbarism." He tells those struggling for Islam that they must embrace martyrdom, not by choice but because it is a matter of conflict between the forces that support Islam and those that oppose it. While this argument did not explicitly identify the rulers as nonbelievers as later radicals did in the 1970s, it paved the way for that interpretation. Death by martyrdom or death in revolutionary jihad is the fate of those locked in the struggle.

The book was banned, and in 1965, Egyptian authorities rearrested Qutb, along with other leaders of the Muslim Brotherhood. Qutb was brought to trial, found guilty, and executed by hanging in Cairo on August 29, 1966.

Some of the many Islamists jailed in the 1960s became more radical, but when most were released in 1971 by the Egyptian government of Anwar Sadat, they forswore violence and agreed to operate as a movement and were not a legalized political party. However, other more radical groups began to organize. Qutb's ideas are similar to some of those espoused by the radical Takfir wa-l Higrah and the Gamaat Islamiya, which arose in the 1970s. More recently, those dedicated to jihad in contemporary extremist organizations such as Al Qaeda make use of the same ideological constructs of jihad, which are part of Islamic history. What radicalizes them and causes them to pursue radical means is identical to that which confronted Qutb—a state power intent on their eradication.

RUSSELL G. RODGERS AND SHERIFA ZUHUR

**See also**
Islamic Radicalism; Muslim Brotherhood; Nasser, Gamal Abdel

**References**
Binder, Leonard. *Islamic Liberalism: A Critique of Development Ideologies.* Chicago: University of Chicago Press, 1988.
Moussalli, Ahmad. *Moderate and Radical Islamic Fundamentalism: The Quest for Modernity, Legitimacy and the Islamic State.* Gainesville: University of Florida Press, 1999
Qaradawi, Yusuf al-. *The Eye of the Beholder: The Muslim Brotherhood over the Past 70 Years.* Cairo, Egypt: Al-Falah Foundation, 2003.

# R

## Rabin, Yitzhak

**Birth Date: March 1, 1922**
**Death Date: November 4, 1995**

Israeli Army general, diplomat, leader of the Labor Party, and prime minister of Israel (1974–1977 and 1992–1995). Born in Jerusalem on March 1, 1922, Yitzhak Rabin moved with his family to Tel Aviv the following year. He attended the Kadoori Agricultural High School, graduating in 1940. He then went to work at the Kibbutz Ramat Yochanan, where he joined the Palmach, an elite fighting unit of Haganah, the Jewish self-defense organization that ultimately became the Israel Defense Forces (IDF).

In 1944 Rabin was second-in-command of a Palmach battalion and fought against the British Mandate authorities. He was arrested by the British in June 1946 and spent six months in prison. He became chief operations officer of the Palmach in 1947.

Rabin spent the next 20 years fighting for Israel as a member of the IDF. During the 1948–1949 Israeli War of Independence he commanded the Harel Brigade and fought for Jerusalem. He participated in the armistice talks and served as a deputy to Yigal Allon. During 1956–1959 Rabin headed the Northern Command. During 1959–1961 he was chief of operations, and during 1961–1964 he was deputy chief of staff of the IDF. On January 1, 1964, he became IDF chief of staff and held this position during the Six-Day War in 1967. Following the Israeli capture of the Old City of Jerusalem in the war, he was one of the first to visit the city, delivering what became a famous speech on the top of Mount Scopus at the Hebrew University.

On January 1, 1968, Rabin retired from the army and shortly thereafter was named Israeli ambassador to the United States. He held this position until the spring of 1973, when he returned to

Yitzhak Rabin, Israeli Army general, diplomat, leader of the Labor Party, and prime minister of Israel (1974–1977 and 1992–1995). Rabin's assassination in 1995 by a Jewish right-wing extremist was a major blow to the peace process. (Israeli Government Press Office)

Israel and joined the Labor Party. He was elected to the Knesset (Israeli parliament) in December 1973. Prime Minister Golda Meir appointed Rabin to her cabinet as minister of labor in April 1974. Meir retired as prime minister in May 1974, and Rabin took her place on June 2.

As prime minister, Rabin concentrated on improving the economy, solving social problems, and strengthening the IDF. He also sought to improve relations with the United States, which played a key role in mediating disengagement agreements with Israel, Egypt, and Syria in 1974. Egypt and Israel signed an interim agreement in 1975. That same year Israel and the United States signed their first Memorandum of Understanding. The best-known event of Rabin's first term as prime minister was the July 3–4, 1976, rescue of hostages of Air France Flight 139 held at Entebbe, Uganda.

In March 1977 Rabin was forced to resign as prime minister following the revelation that his wife, Leah, held bank accounts in the United States, which was at that time against Israeli law. Menachem Begin replaced him, and Rabin was praised for his integrity and honesty in resigning.

Between 1977 and 1984 Rabin served in the Knesset as a member of the Labor Party and sat on the Foreign Affairs and Defense Committee. He published his memoirs, *Service Notebook,* in 1979 and served as minister of defense in the national unity governments between 1984 and 1990. In 1985 he proposed that IDF forces withdraw from Lebanon and establish a security zone to protect the settlements along the northern border of Israel.

In February 1992 Rabin was elected chairman of the Labor Party in its first nationwide primary. He led the party to victory in the June elections. He became prime minister for the second time that July. In an effort to achieve peace in the Middle East, he signed a joint Declaration of Principles with Palestine Liberation Organization (PLO) chairman Yasser Arafat, shaking hands with him on September 13, 1993, during the Oslo Peace Accords. This agreement created the Palestinian National Authority (PNA) and gave it some control over the West Bank and the Gaza Strip. Rabin, Arafat, and Shimon Peres shared the 1994 Nobel Peace Prize for their efforts to achieve peace. In 1995 Rabin continued his negotiations, signing an agreement with Arafat expanding Palestinian autonomy in the West Bank.

A number of ultraconservative Israelis believed that Rabin had betrayed the nation by negotiating with the Palestinians and giving away land they considered rightfully theirs. On November 4, 1995, right-wing extremist Yigal Amir shot Rabin after a peace rally in Kings of Israel Square, afterward renamed Yitzhak Rabin Square. Rabin died of his wounds soon afterward in Ichilov Hospital in Tel Aviv. November 4 has since become a national memorial day for Israelis. Numerous squares, streets, and public foundations have been named for Rabin, who is revered by many for his efforts on behalf of peace.

AMY HACKNEY BLACKWELL

**See also**

Arab-Israeli Conflict, Overview; Arafat, Yasser; Begin, Menachem; Meir, Golda Mabovitch; Palestine Liberation Organization

**References**

Freedman, Robert Owen, ed. *Israel under Rabin.* Boulder, CO: Westview, 1995.

Kurzman, Dan. *Soldier of Peace: The Life of Yitzak Rabin, 1922–1995.* New York: HarperCollins, 1998.

Slater, Robert. *Rabin of Israel.* Rev. ed. New York: St. Martin's, 1993.

# Radio Baghdad

U.S.-funded radio station begun in March 2002 designed to penetrate Arab nations, particularly Iraq, with the aim of disseminating pro-American news and information. Radio Baghdad is one station in an umbrella broadcast organization known as Radio Sawa.

An Arabic-language station, Radio Baghdad is an outgrowth of the Voice of America (VOA) used during the Cold War to reach behind the Iron Curtain and into Eastern Europe. The VOA, along with the British Broadcasting Company's (BBC) World Service and the Federal Republic of Germany's Deutsche Welle, served to send Western news and propaganda into the communist nations of Eastern Europe. They proved effective enough that the Soviet Union referred to these stations as "The Voices" and attempted to block them. Hoping to build on this success in Europe, the United States in 1955 created Radio Swan, later called Radio Marti, to broadcast into Cuba.

Far from falling out of favor after the fall of the Soviet Union in 1991, the United States continued to use radio as a tool to complement foreign policy objectives and enhance its propaganda campaigns. Radio Rajo, or "hope," was set up to spread the American message in Somalia as well as to alert citizens to the location of relief stations after the U.S. humanitarian mission there in 1993. Prior to U.S. troops moving into Haiti in 1994, Radio Democracy was created to help instruct Haitians how to interact with American troops. And the VOA did not simply expand its number of stations, but it continued to broadcast into Eastern Europe in an attempt to solidify Western values and capitalist principles in those nations.

With the start of the so-called War on Terror after the September 11, 2001, terror attacks, radio appeared to be a perfect tool in the U.S. attempt to wage and win a highly ideological war. In 2002, the George W. Bush administration established the Office of Global Communications in the White House to oversee this global propaganda effort. Specifically, the number and type of Arabic broadcasts have increased and greater funding is available for cultural exchange programs.

Because Arabic culture is centered on oral and linguistic histories, radio could be an important tool in U.S. propaganda efforts. In the Arab world, radio has been a social instrument around which people often gather to listen in concert to news and music. Indeed, prior to the 1991 Persian Gulf War, Iraq possessed the largest broadcasting network in the Arab world and one of the strongest in the entire world.

Radio Sawa produced its first broadcast on March 23, 2002. It records its broadcasts in Washington, D.C., and Dubai in the

United Arab Emirates. Radio Sawa has also extended itself onto the Internet with a Web site in Arabic, appropriately named www.radiosawa.com. These broadcasts continue to send out American news and music, as well as Arabic and Spanish-language music. The exact impact of this effort is unknown.

ROBERT H. CLEMM

**See also**

Global War on Terror; Iraq, History of, Pre-1990; Iraq, History of, 1990–Present; IRAQI FREEDOM, Operation

**References**

Taylor, Philip M. *Munitions of the Mind: A History of Propaganda from the Ancient World to the Present Day.* Manchester, UK: Manchester University Press, 2003.

Wood, James. *History of International Broadcasting.* London: Peter Pereginus, 1992.

---

# Ramadi, First Battle of
## Start Date: April 6, 2004
## End Date: April 10, 2004

Military engagement between U.S. forces and Iraqi insurgents (mainly Sunnis) on April 6–10, 2004, in Ramadi in central Iraq. Ramadi is the capital of Anbar Province, with a population of some 450,000, and lies along the Euphrates River 70 miles west of Baghdad along a main highway that continues eastward to the Iraqi capital and to the west across the Syrian desert to Jordan. Most of the city's inhabitants are Sunni Muslims. The battle was precipitated when Sunni forces in Ramadi arose in rebellion against U.S. forces garrisoned there.

Situated in the western part of the so-called Sunni Triangle, Ramadi's population had long been a center of support for the government of deposed dictator Saddam Hussein, and as such became a focal point for anticoalition forces after the March 2003 invasion of Iraq. After the days immediately after the fall of Baghdad in April 2003, the *muqawama* (resistance), including those who supported the former regime as well as Sunni Iraqis opposed to the invasion and Iraqi and foreign jihadists, began to fight coalition forces. The insurgents routinely ambushed lightly armored coalition vehicles and attacked convoys with small-arms and rockets, set off bombs in public places and near police stations, and planted improvised explosive devices (IEDs), which they detonated by remote control to destroy or disable coalition vehicles. While U.S. forces sought to maintain a low-profile presence in the city and engaged in efforts to win the support of the city's population through constructive projects, they found that many of the Sunnis held them in contempt.

U.S. troops were blamed when a bomb-making group accidentally set off a charge in a local mosque and when another explosive device exploded in the city's marketplace. By September 2003, the U.S. camp at Ramadi was coming under nightly mortar and artillery fire, with 19 soldiers killed with more than 100 wounded. The Americans sought to turn the town over to Iraqi officials, but insurgents also targeted these alleged collaborators. The resistance also became increasingly brazen; there were even large, noisy pro-Saddam public demonstrations in the city's streets.

Thus, 13 months after the invasion, Ramadi had become one of the most perilous places in all of Iraq. When members of the Iraqi Governing Council agreed on a new constitution in March 2004 and drafted plans for elections the following January, an upsurge in violence occurred in Anbar Province. The most dramatic incident in this escalation occurred in Fallujah, which was another epicenter of the insurgency located just 30 miles east of Ramadi. There a mob lynched four civilian contractors who had been dragged from an ambushed convoy, desecrated their burned bodies, and hanged the corpses on a bridge over the Euphrates on March 31, 2004. As coalition forces moved to pacify Fallujah, insurgents in Ramadi confronted U.S. Marines at a level of intensity not seen since the early days of the Iraq War.

The worst of the Battle of Ramadi, from the American perspective, occurred on April 6, the first day of pitched battle. On that day, the 2nd Battalion, 4th Marine Regiment, 1st Marine Division, which was charged with maintaining order in the city, received intelligence that insurgents intended to seize a government building. Marine patrols entered the city to carry out a sweep in support of loyalist Iraqis to prevent the takeover and to disperse antigovernment elements. On their way, they fell into well-laid ambushes set up by scores of fighters who were thought to be former members of the Special Republican Guards. Thus the marines of Golf Company, who were carrying out the foot patrols, came under sniper fire, ran into insurgent ambushes, and spent much of the day pinned down and taking casualties. As other units moved to relieve the beleaguered marines, they, too, were ambushed. Several platoons engaged in firefights before they could extricate themselves with the help of other marines as well as members of the U.S. Army's 1st Brigade, 1st Infantry Division, which committed M1 Abrams tanks and Bradley fighting vehicles to the fight.

The deadliest of the attacks that day took place in the city's marketplace, where a group of perhaps 50 anticoalition fighters set up a .50-caliber machine gun on a rooftop and took positions atop other buildings or in nearby shops and behind trees with AK-47s, rocket-propelled grenade launchers, and other small arms. There they waylaid a group of some 20 marines from Echo Company as they entered the marketplace in 3 Humvees followed by 2 trucks. The hard-pressed marines were unable to call in helicopter air support, which was then committed elsewhere, and the heavy machine-gun fire ripped apart the lead vehicle with all but one of its occupants trapped inside. By the time reinforcements arrived and the marines were able to move forward again, they found that many of their Iraqi opponents had fled. Ten marines were killed and many others were wounded in this action.

Heavy fighting occurred in Ramadi over the next few days. On April 7, the marines returned in force to take the fight to the enemy and complete their original mission. They came under similar ambushes and sustained additional casualties, but no combat deaths in a series of firefights, which occurred throughout the city all that day. The marines also inflicted heavy losses on the insurgents. Ultimately, the marines conducted street-by-street and house-by-house raids that led to the capture and interrogation of dozens of suspects and the seizure of arms caches. Altogether before the battle ended on April 10, the marines suffered 16 killed-in-action and 25 wounded. Insurgent losses remain unclear, as many of those killed and wounded were removed before U.S. forces regained the upper hand; however, most estimates put insurgent casualties at around 250 killed and hundreds more wounded.

The insurgency swung into high gear with the fighting in Ramadi and elsewhere in March and April 2004. Heretofore, coalition leaders continued to hope that they would win the battle for the "hearts and minds" of Iraqi civilians. Now, many wondered whether this was possible. Others questioned whether there were sufficient numbers of "boots on the ground" to quell a growing resistance that was developing new and more lethal tactics. Rather than the desultory, hit-and-run efforts mounted by the insurgents in the past, the marines at Ramadi encountered well-coordinated attacks, with their opponents proving themselves adept at ambushes, laying down suppression fire, and making effective use of cover and concealment. Although the marines had won this battle, they and other forces in Iraq still faced a stiff resistance in many other towns and districts of Iraq that would not easily be extinguished.

GEORGE L. SIMPSON

**See also**

Fallujah, First Battle of; IRAQI FREEDOM, Operation; Iraqi Insurgency; Sunni Triangle; United States Marine Corps, Iraq War

**References**

Fitzgerald, Cpl. Paula M. "Marines Recall Ar Ramadi Battle." *Marine Corps News*, April 19, 2004.
Negus, Steve. "The Insurgency Intensifies." *Middle East Report* (Fall 2004): 22–27.
Swanson, David, with Joseph L. Galloway. "Battle at Ramadi." *Philadelphia Inquirer*, August 15, 2004, A-4.

# Ramadi, Second Battle of
**Start Date: June 17, 2006**
**End Date: November 15, 2006**

Military engagement in which U.S. Army and Marine forces, along with elements of the Iraqi Army, fought for control of Ramadi, the capital of Anbar Province in western Iraq. After U.S.-led forces took Fallujah for the first time during November–December 2004, Ramadi became the center of the growing insurgency in Iraq. In this city of some 400,000 people, about 80 miles west of Baghdad, insurgent leaders created the Islamic State of Iraq, a coalition of Islamist fighting groups that included al-Qa'ida fi Bilad al-Rafhidayn ("Al Qaeda in the Land of the Two Rivers," meaning Iraq). At the time, marine leaders believed that if Ramadi remained in insurgent hands, all of Anbar Province would be insecure.

In June 2006, with the situation worsening, the U.S. command dispatched the 1st Brigade Combat Team of the 1st U.S. Armored Division to the Ramadi area to initiate plans to attack the insurgents. Many feared another full-scale Fallujah-style assault that might kill dozens of noncombatants and level the city. However, U.S. commanders were determined to proceed with caution and they carefully planned their operation, which involved some 5,500 U.S. soldiers and marines and 2,000 Iraqi Army troops.

By June 10, the U.S. and Iraqi troops had cordoned off the city, and a growing number of air strikes were mounted on specific targets. U.S. forces, using loudspeakers, warned residents to evacuate before the impending attack. The main goal of the operation was to sever insurgent supply and reinforcement lines into Ramadi. The Americans also planned to set up locations outside Ramadi where noninsurgent Iraqis from the city could find safe haven.

On June 18, operations began in earnest when two U.S. mechanized columns and an Iraqi Army unit of some 2,000 men entered the city's suburbs from the south and cut off two access routes into the city. Concurrently, marine units captured and held the western portion of the city center, controlling the river and its two main bridges. While armored forces controlled the city's eastern exits, marine units established outposts east of Ramadi along the main road between Baghdad and Syria.

With these key points secured, several hundred coalition forces, supported by Lockheed AC-130 gunships, moved into eastern Ramadi. The gunships killed several insurgents as coalition troops established an outpost in Ramadi's Mulab neighborhood to allow U.S. and Iraqi troops to better patrol this problem area. There they discovered numerous weapons caches and improvised explosive device (IED) components in many homes.

While this part of the operation met with some success, the Americans soon found themselves in intense street fighting throughout the city. Insurgents would mount widely scattered points simultaneously and then vanish. On July 24, the jihadist forces launched a major attack and, while they suffered heavy casualties, they continued to press toward their main objective, the Ramadi Government Center, in which dozens of marines were barricaded.

To meet the threat, U.S. troops demolished several smaller surrounding structures, with the plan to turn the area into a park later. Still, all the coalition troops who ventured into the city faced IEDs, suicide attacks, and patrol ambushes. Sniper fire was a near constant.

In early July, U.S. troops captured the Ramadi General Hospital, which had been used as an insurgent barracks. Coalition wounded who had been taken to the hospital were found beheaded, and nearly every room on every floor of the seven-story building was rigged with explosive devices.

On August 21, the insurgents killed and defiled the body of Sunni Sheikh Abu Ali Jassim, who had encouraged many of his tribesmen to join the Iraqi police in their efforts to root out the insurgents. In response, with funding and organizational efforts coming from the coalition, on September 9, 2006, 50 sheikhs from 20 tribes from across Anbar Province formally organized an anti-insurgent council, named Anbar Awakening. Some of its members had been fighters with Al Qaeda in Iraq. However, as the council gained strength, its tribal members began attacking Al Qaeda fighters in the suburbs of Ramadi. By October, representatives from many tribes in northern and western Ramadi had joined the Awakening.

In mid-September 2006, new marine units relieved those holding western Ramadi. Throughout the next three months, truck bombs as well as suicide and sniper attacks continued as part of the daily routine for the occupying forces. U.S. Navy SEAL Michael A. Monsoor was posthumously awarded the Medal of Honor for having thrown himself on a grenade that threatened the lives of the other members of his team on September 29, 2006.

One of the more tragic events in the battle occurred in mid-November when, during a firefight, an air attack in central Ramadi inadvertently killed more than 30 civilians, many of them women and children. The Battle of Ramadi also marked the first time insurgents employed chlorine bombs. On October 21, 2006, they detonated a car bomb of two 100-pound chlorine tanks, injuring three Iraqi policemen and a civilian.

The battle formally ended on November 15. It had claimed the lives of 75 American soldiers and marines and more than 200 were wounded. U.S. officials estimated insurgent dead at 750. The number of Iraqi Army deaths were not known. Coalition forces claimed to have secured 70 percent of the city by the end of November.

On December 1, 2006, with insurgents still entrenched in parts of Ramadi, the United States launched Operation SQUEEZE PLAY. Supported by Anbar Awakening tribal fighters, by January 14, 2007, coalition forces had secured a much larger portion of the city and killed or captured roughly 200 additional insurgents.

By the spring of 2007, U.S. officials believed that they had finally gained control over all of Ramadi. On June 30, 2007, a group of 64 insurgents attempted to infiltrate the city but were wiped out by U.S. marines, who had been alerted by Iraqi police.

WILLIAM P. HEAD

**See also**

Al Qaeda in Iraq; Anbar Awakening; Fallujah, Second Battle of; Iraqi Insurgency

**References**

Barnes, Julian E. "In Ramadi, the Battle Is Ever Changing." *Los Angeles Times,* August 6, 2006, A5.

Campbell, Donovan. *Joker One: A Marine Platoon; Story of Courage, Sacrifice, and Brotherhood.* New York: Random House, 2008.

---

# Ratzinger, Joseph Alois

*See* Benedict XVI, Pope

# Reagan, Ronald Wilson
## Birth Date: February 11, 1911
## Death Date: June 5, 2004

U.S. politician and president of the United States (1981–1989). Born on February 11, 1911, in Tampico, Illinois, Ronald Reagan graduated from Eureka College, worked as a sports announcer, and in 1937 won a Hollywood contract with Warner Brothers, eventually appearing in 53 movies. Once a New Deal Democrat, his politics grew increasingly conservative in the late 1950s and early 1960s.

In 1966, Reagan won the first of two terms as the Republican governor of California. During his campaign he supported U.S. intervention in Vietnam and condemned student antiwar protestors. He soon became one of the leading figures of the increasingly powerful Republican Right, supporting high defense budgets, a strong anticommunist international posture, and deep cuts in taxes and domestic expenditures. These positions he affirmed while seeking the Republican presidential nomination in 1976 and 1980.

In November 1980, when Reagan defeated Democratic incumbent Jimmy Carter for the presidency, the United States was

Ronald W. Reagan was president of the United States during 1981–1989. A staunch anticommunist, he carried out the largest peacetime defense buildup in U.S. history and worked to reverse the liberal tradition that had dominated U.S. politics since the Great Depression. (Library of Congress)

suffering from spiraling inflation and high unemployment. In Iran, radical Muslims had overthrown Mohammad Reza Shah Pahlavi in 1979, sending oil prices soaring. For more than a year radical Iranian students held U.S. diplomatic personnel hostage in Tehran. An almost simultaneous Soviet-backed coup in Afghanistan intensified a sense of American impotence, as did communist insurgencies in Central America and Africa. Reagan opposed compromise with communism. Believing firmly that a U.S. victory in the Cold War was attainable, the ever-optimistic Reagan used blatantly triumphalist, anti-Soviet rhetoric, famously terming the Soviet Union "the Evil Empire."

Reagan purposefully engaged the Soviet Union in an arms race whereby he and his advisers hoped that American technological and economic superiority would strain the Soviet economy. The Reagan administration hiked the defense budget from $171 billion to $376 billion between 1981 and 1986 in the hopes of helping the United States to combat communism around the world.

Breaking with Carter's foreign policies, Reagan also deliberately supported dictatorships, provided they were pro-American, while at the same time assailing human rights abuses within the Soviet sphere. Covert operations intensified as the United States offered support to anticommunist forces around the world, providing economic aid to the dissident Polish Solidarity trade union movement and military and economic assistance to antigovernment rebels in Angola, mujahideen guerrillas in Afghanistan and the anti-Sandinista Contras in Nicaragua. Aid to the Contras included covert support. When Congress responded by passing the Boland Amendments (1982–1984), forbidding funding for Nicaraguan covert actions, the Reagan administration embroiled itself in an ill-fated secret enterprise to sell arms to Iran—thereby evading its own embargo but, officials suggested, enhancing the political standing of Iranian moderate elements—and using the proceeds to aid the Nicaraguan Contras. Revelations of these illegal activities embarrassed Reagan during his second term.

Notwithstanding his bellicose rhetoric, in practice Reagan was surprisingly pragmatic and cautious. In potentially difficult guerrilla settings, his administration favored covert operations, preferably undertaken by surrogates, such as the Afghan mujahideen or the Nicaraguan Contras, over outright military intervention. Wars were kept short and easily winnable, as in the small Caribbean island of Grenada in 1983 when American troops liberated the island from Marxist rule. When radical pro-Syrian Druze Muslims bombed the Beirut barracks of an American peacekeeping force in Lebanon that same year, killing 241 American soldiers, the United States quickly withdrew. In 1986, suspected Libyan involvement in terrorist incidents provoked retaliatory American surgical air strikes on Tripoli, but no war.

The Reagan administration's Middle East policies were characteristic of its approach toward other regions of the world. Anticommunism—laced with anti-Soviet rhetoric—was buffered by pragmatism and caution. U.S. officials took a hard line against

regional terrorist organizations, including Lebanon's Hezbollah, which was routinely taking Americans hostage and assaulting civilian targets. This became particularly acute after the June 1982 Israeli invasion of Lebanon. When radical Palestinians began a major terror campaign in the Gaza Strip and on the West Bank, Reagan administration officials sharply denounced the activity and made veiled hints of retaliation. In 1982 when the United Nations (UN) called for a limited peacekeeping force in Lebanon, Reagan sent U.S. Marines. Their job was not an easy one, given that Israel completely occupied Beirut and was attempting to flush out Palestine Liberation Organization (PLO) members. In September 1982, the massacre of Palestinian civilians in Lebanon's Sabra and Shatila refugee camps by Maronite Christian militias shocked and embarrassed the Reagan administration. As a result, Reagan helped form a new multinational peacekeeping force. The intensive U.S. diplomatic efforts to broker a peace deal between Israel and Lebanon ultimately bore fruit, although the October 1983 bombing of the U.S. Marine barracks in Beirut put an effective end to the American military presence there. In an attempt to keep American ties with Saudi Arabia on track, in 1981 Reagan pushed through the controversial sale of American-made Airborne Warning and Control System (AWACS) planes to the kingdom. Israel fiercely denounced the move.

Reagan had become president only months after the outbreak of the Iran-Iraq War (1980–1988). At first, the United States attempted to stay neutral. As time went on, the administration attempted to help both sides. However, Reagan administration officials began tilting toward Iraq as the war dragged on. A clear consensus had emerged that Iraqi dictator Saddam Hussein was the lesser of two evils. Indeed, the United States had more to fear from a triumphant Iran, which might foment fundamentalist revolutions in neighboring Arab states, than it did from a secular, albeit autocratic, Iraq. By 1982, when an Iranian victory looked likely, the Reagan administration launched Operation STAUNCH, an effort to prevent arms from making their way to Iran. The United States also began to provide financial and intelligence assistance to Hussein. At the same time, however, Reagan administration officials were secretly selling arms to Iran to fund its covert aid to the Nicaraguan Contras. It is also believed that the administration shipped so-called dual-purpose materials (such as biological and chemical agents) to Iraq, which was supposed to use them for civilian purposes. It is highly likely that they were used in Iraq's secret programs to manufacture chemical and biological weapons. The longer-term implications of these policies are now manifest. The United States has since been compelled to wage two separate wars against Iraq, the first one in 1991 and the second one in 2003, which is far from resolved.

Despite campaign pledges to the contrary, Reagan did not shun mainland China or restore U.S. relations with Taiwan. Sino-American trade increased, and Reagan made a 1984 state visit to Beijing. By 1984, international and domestic politics suggested that the president moderate his anti-Soviet line. In September 1984, Reagan proposed combining all major ongoing nuclear weapons talks into one package, and Soviet leaders soon agreed.

Reagan's mellowing coincided with the culmination of long-standing Soviet economic problems as military spending rose, diverting funds from domestic programs. The Solidarity Movement in Poland proved remarkably persistent, undercutting Soviet control. Assertive Soviet policies in Africa and Latin America carried a high price tag too, while the decade-long Afghan intervention had embroiled Soviet troops in a costly and unwinnable guerrilla war.

In 1985 the young and energetic Mikhail Gorbachev became the general secretary of the Communist Party of the Soviet Union (CPSU). He thought the only way to save communism was to immediately address Russia's problems and reform the Soviet Union's crumbling economic and social systems. American and European leaders were initially wary of Gorbachev's overtures, although he quickly won great popularity. After British prime minister Margaret Thatcher urged Reagan—her ideological soul mate—to work with Gorbachev, the president did just that. Domestic economic factors may have also impelled Reagan toward rapprochement. Deep tax cuts meant that heavy government budget deficits financed the 1980s defense buildup, and in November 1987 an unexpected Wall Street stock market crash suggested that American economic fundamentals might be undesirably weak. Reagan had several summit meetings with Gorbachev, and in 1987 the superpowers signed the Intermediate Nuclear Forces (INF) Treaty, eliminating all medium-range missiles in Europe. This marked the beginning of a series of arms reduction agreements, continued under Reagan's successor George H. W. Bush, and of measures whereby the Soviet Union withdrew from its East European empire and, by 1991, allowed it to collapse.

Reagan left office in 1989. After a decade-long battle with Alzheimer's disease, he died of pneumonia at his home in Los Angeles, California, on June 5, 2004.

PRISCILLA ROBERTS

**See also**

Carter, James Earl, Jr.; Iran; Iran-Contra Affair; Iran-Iraq War; Iranian Revolution; Iraq, History of, Pre-1990; Lebanon, Israeli Invasion of; Lebanon, U.S. Intervention in (1982–1984); Mujahideen, Soviet-Afghanistan War; Qaddafi, Muammar; Reza Pahlavi, Mohammad; Shultz, George Pratt; Soviet-Afghanistan War; Weinberger, Caspar Willard

**References**

Cannon, Lou. *President Reagan: The Role of a Lifetime.* New York: Simon and Schuster, 1991.

Fischer, Beth A. *The Reagan Reversal: Foreign Policy and the End of the Cold War.* Columbia: University of Missouri Press, 1997.

Matlock, Jack F., Jr. *Reagan and Gorbachev: How the Cold War Ended.* New York: Random House, 2004.

Pemberton, William E. *Exit with Honor: The Life and Presidency of Ronald Reagan.* Armonk, NY: M. E. Sharpe, 1997.

# Reagan Administration, Middle East Policy

Although the Cold War with the Soviet Union remained the primary focus of the Ronald Reagan administration's foreign policy, the Middle East became an increasing concern. Reagan administration policies were less a consistent approach than a series of reactions to events that were often manipulated by adversaries and allies alike. Harried by the complexities of the region, the Reagan White House pursued a number of different strategies, some of them dubious. Among the latter was the 1987 Iran-Contra Affair, which involved the illegal and covert sale of weapons to Iran, the resulting funds from which were used to support rightist Nicaraguan freedom fighters (Contras).

When Reagan took office in January 1981, the most important goal was securing the release of the Iranian hostages. Thereafter, his administration entered Middle East politics with the notion that it could use the Soviet threat as a basis for cooperation between Israel and moderate Arab states. Instead, the competing territorial claims of Israel, the Palestinians, and hostile Arab state neighbors superseded all other issues. American challenges were compounded by three wars in progress when Reagan took office: the Soviet-Afghanistan War (1979–1989), the Iran-Iraq War (1980–1988), and an ongoing civil war in Lebanon.

The Reagan administration proved to be a staunch supporter of Israel in almost all cases and sharply denounced Palestinian terrorism in the Gaza Strip and West Bank. At the same time, it allowed Israel a free hand to operate in Lebanon, despite the significantly destabilizing consequences of these actions. In June 1982, Israeli forces invaded southern Lebanon, recapturing the buffer zone it had already claimed in 1978. The Israelis hoped to eliminate the Palestinian resistance there. Given that the Israelis were also engaging Syrian forces deployed in Lebanon to maintain a sphere of influence, considerable potential existed for a wider war.

The U.S. response to the Israeli incursion was tepid; indeed, the White House had provided an implicit green light to such a move on the part of Israel. But as casualties and international outrage mounted, Reagan sought a diplomatic solution to the crisis. With a temporary cease-fire in place, a multinational force, including 800 U.S. Marines, facilitated an evacuation of PLO fighters in August 1982.

The following month, however, hundreds of Palestinians in the Sabra and Shatila refugee camps near Beirut were massacred by Christian militia units with the apparent knowledge of the Israelis. Reagan then dispatched 1,800 U.S. Marines to the vicinity of Beirut's airport to act as a buffer between the Israelis and their enemies. Meanwhile, the White House was gravitating toward the Christian Maronite faction in the civil war, which compromised the U.S. position as a peacekeeper. Further complicating matters, the Iranian theocratic government was also active in Lebanon, promoting terrorism among Shiite Muslims there.

In April 1983, a truck bomb destroyed the U.S. embassy in Beirut, taking 46 lives. The Israelis retreated to a more defensible

U.S. Marine Corps amphibious vehicles come ashore in Lebanon on September 29, 1982. In response to growing violence in Lebanon and a request by that country's president, U.S. president Ronald Reagan ordered the marines into Lebanon as part of an international peacekeeping force. (Marine Corps Historical Center)

position, which left the U.S. Marines even more dangerously exposed. On October 23, 1983, the marines suffered their worst day of combat deaths since the Battle of Iwo Jima of World War II. A truck loaded with explosives leveled their barracks, resulting in 241 fatalities, prompting Reagan to say later that this was the saddest day of his eight-year presidency. The Reagan administration withdrew the U.S. peacekeeping force early the following year with little to show for its efforts or the sacrifice by American servicemen. By 1983, the White House had unintentionally fostered the impression that it was complicit in all facets of Israeli policy.

In accordance with the Reagan Doctrine of supporting insurgencies against communist regimes around the world, in 1985 the White House began funding Afghan freedom fighters (mujahideen). The mujahideen were engaged in a long and bloody insurgency against Soviet occupation forces in Afghanistan. This policy aimed not only at augmenting the traditional containment doctrine but also at reducing U.S. casualties through the use of covert operations and client resources. The mujahideen had already been receiving U.S. military hardware of increasing sophistication since 1982, most notably Stinger surface-to-air missiles, which proved highly lethal to Soviet forces. In 1988, General Secretary Mikhail Gorbachev, the Soviet Union's new leader, announced that Soviet forces would begin a phased withdrawal from their quagmire in Afghanistan, although suspicions lingered in the White House that Moscow might continue to prop up a friendly regime in Kabul.

In the long term, American funding of the mujahideen and the rapid Soviet departure from Afghanistan left that nation highly unstable and susceptible to radicalized elements. By the mid-1990s, the Taliban, a radical fundamentalist theocracy took over there, which aided and abetted terrorists—most notoriously Osama bin Laden, the head of the Al Qaeda organization and mastermind of the September 11, 2001, terror attacks against the United States.

In 1986, the Reagan administration struck back against state-sponsored terrorism when it ordered a punitive air strike against the headquarters of Libyan president Muammar Qaddafi. Libya had been sponsoring terrorists and terrorist organizations for a number of years, the targets of which were invariably Western interests. Although the United States had been involved in low-level hostilities with the Libyans for years, the catalyst for the air strikes came in the April 5, 1986, bombing of a discotheque in West Berlin, Germany, in which two American servicemen were killed. When evidence for the deed pointed to Tripoli, Reagan ordered a punitive air strike against various Libyan targets, including some in the capital city of Tripoli. On April 15, 18 F-111F bombers carried out their mission. Although Qaddafi's home was targeted, he escaped injury, but an infant girl, said to be his adopted daughter, died in the raid. Two U.S. Air Force captains were also killed when their plane was shot down over the Gulf of Sidra. The bold attack provoked both shock and consternation internationally, but after the raid Libyan-sponsored terrorism dropped off precipitously.

In 1980, territorial, ethnic, and, religious disputes between Iran and Iraq, and Iran's seeming distraction following its 1979 Revolution, led Iraqi dictator Saddam Hussein to go to war with his neighbor. The result was an eight-year conflict that brought massive casualties on both sides and even the use of chemical and biological weapons. Although publicly calling on the international community to remain neutral in the Iran-Iraq War, the Reagan White House secretly provided arms and satellite intelligence to the Iraqis in response to America's recent anguish over the protracted hostage crisis with Iran.

Meanwhile, terrorist organizations with ties to Iran, such as Hezbollah and Islamic Jihad, had kidnapped seven U.S. citizens from Lebanon, most of whom had no connection to U.S. governmental policymaking. Agonizing over how to retrieve the hostages when the U.S. intelligence presence in the region was scant at best, the White House, though deeply divided, decided to cultivate relations with Iranian moderates. By 1985, negotiations were underway for the Central Intelligence Agency (CIA) to sell U.S. antitank (TOW) missiles to Iran (with Israelis acting as go-betweens) in exchange for Tehran's favorable influence on the hostage dilemma.

President Reagan approved the plan with the stipulations that the arms transfers would not alter the balance of power in the Iran-Iraq War and that no quid pro quo existed to obtain the captured Americans. By 1986 the weapons flow had increased dramatically (more than 1,500 total missiles changed hands) without much progress with the hostage negotiations. Only two of the original seven hostages had been returned by July 1986, and later that year three more Americans were taken from Beirut.

In a bizarre twist, the proceeds from the Iranian arms sales were funneled through secret Swiss bank accounts to fund clandestine aid to Nicaraguan Contras battling against the left-wing, Sandinista regime. During 1982–1984, a Democratic-controlled House of Representatives had passed the Boland Amendments, specifically barring any U.S. governmental agencies from providing military aid to influence events in Nicaragua. In November 1986, however, a Lebanese magazine broke the story of the Middle Eastern dimension of what ultimately became known as the Iran-Contra Affair. U.S. credibility in the region suffered as moderate Arab states lost faith in Washington's resolve against terrorism.

A congressional investigation soon centered around national security advisers Robert McFarlane and Vice Admiral John Poindexter as well as Oliver North, a marine lieutenant colonel on staff assignment to the National Security Council. Some 190 Reagan officials were indicted or convicted in relation to this conspiracy, which was a significant blight on Reagan's second term. Reagan himself was not implicated in the scheme.

When Reagan left office in January 1989, he bequeathed to his successor a Middle East still in turmoil and with no significant breakthrough in the enduring Palestinian-Israeli conflict. Less than two years later, the formerly U.S.-backed Iraq preemptively struck at Kuwait and occupied it, setting off the 1991 Persian Gulf War.

JEFFREY D. BASS

**See also**

Afghanistan; Al Qaeda; Bin Laden, Osama; Hezbollah; Hussein, Saddam; Iran-Contra Affair; Iran-Iraq War; Iranian Revolution; Iraq, History of, Pre-1990; Islamic Jihad, Palestinian; Lebanon; Lebanon, U.S. Intervention in (1982–1984); Libya; Mujahideen, Soviet-Afghanistan War; Reagan, Ronald Wilson; Taliban; Terrorism

**References**

Diggins, John Patrick. *Ronald Reagan: Fate, Freedom and the Making of History.* New York: Norton, 2006.

Laham, Nicholas. *Crossing the Rubicon: Ronald Reagan and U.S. Policy in the Middle East.* Aldershot, Hampshire, UK: Ashgate, 2004.

Lenczowski, George. *American Presidents and the Middle East.* Durham, NC: Duke University Press, 1990.

Reeves, Richard. *President Reagan: The Triumph of Imagination.* New York: Simon and Schuster, 2005.

---

# Reconnaissance Aircraft

*See* Aircraft, Reconnaissance

---

# Reconnaissance Satellites

Intelligence-gathering satellites, usually known as spy satellites, launched into Earth orbit to gather information about other nations' military capabilities. The Cold War between the United States and the Soviet Union in the years following World War II and the refusal of the Soviets to allow on-site weapons inspections as a condition of disarmament agreements led the United States to attempt to monitor Soviet military capabilities through specially designed high-flying reconnaissance aircraft. Although these aircraft—most notably the Lockheed U-2—carried out overflights of the Soviet Union, Eastern Europe, and China, the information they collected was rather limited, and the aircraft could be shot down. Indeed, a number of the aircraft were downed, most notably a U-2 on an overflight of the Soviet Union on May 1, 1960.

The U.S. Air Force ordered development of the first reconnaissance satellite on March 16, 1955, with the stated goal to "determine the status of a potential enemy's war-making ability." The first satellite in space, however, was the Soviet Sputnik on October 4, 1957. The U.S. Army launched the first American satellite, Explorer I, on October 1, 1958. Other launches by both powers followed in rapid succession, and both nations were soon using satellites equipped with specially designed cameras for intelligence collection. Now nearly a dozen nations utilize satellite technology for spying on foreign nations and their military dispositions. Satellites, of course, have the great advantage of not requiring overflight rights.

The first spy satellites were equipped with a single panoramic camera, the photographs from which were returned to Earth through ejected canisters of film on parachutes, which were then retrieved in midair. Currently intelligence satellites record digital images, which are then downloaded by means of encrypted radio links.

Established in 1960, the National Reconnaissance Office (NRO) had responsibility for the secret Corona project, the first and longest-running U.S. satellite program. For 12 years, until 1972,

Corona yielded invaluable information about the Soviet Union. While the NRO continues to create and build reconnaissance satellites for military and Central Intelligence Agency (CIA) use, in 1982 the Air Force Space Command was created to manage operational control of space systems. It has charge of all launch operations.

The NRO operates satellites for the U.S. military and other intelligence agencies. Reconnaissance satellite programs are among the most classified of a nation's intelligence operations. Five primary surveillance systems are in use, including optical satellites, which use a large mirror to collect light for photography; radar-imaging satellites that rely on microwave signals to see through cloud cover (radar-imaging and optical satellites are also able to view wider areas of the earth's surface); signals satellites, which monitor and intercept radio, telephone, and data transmissions; and ocean observation satellites, which help to locate and ascertain the positions and headings of ships at sea.

Not wishing to see Iran triumph during the Iran-Iraq War of 1980–1988, the United States shared information gathered by reconnaissance satellites with the Iraqi military. Intelligence information acquired from satellites provided valuable information to coalition military planning during Operation DESERT STORM (January–February 1991). Two Key Hole–class KH-11 satellites (N-7 and N-8) and a Lacrosse-1 satellite provided visual reconnaissance. Key Hole–class satellites return images to Earth through an electronic link. The KH-11–class satellites have infrared imagery, including a thermal infrared capability that allows images to be captured in darkness. The Lacrosse radar-imaging system is a satellite utilized for identifying tactical and strategic military targets. The system employs Synthetic Aperture Radar (SAR), which allows it to resolve images to within one meter. Also, Lacrosse satellites are all-weather, day-night satellites.

In addition to the military space systems, images were also secured from commercial satellites for surveillance of natural resources, including the LANDSAT-4 and LANDSAT-5 (U.S.), and the Spot-1 and Spot-2 (France). Intelligence information collected from these sources was combined with data collected from human and other sources. Information gleaned from the satellites was especially useful in targeting air strikes by cruise missiles and aircraft.

One of the important lessons learned by the NRO from the Persian Gulf War was the need for increased area surveillance. In the decade following Operation DESERT STORM, reconnaissance satellites were improved to meet the evolving tactical intelligence needs of the military community. These improvements were tested in the U.S.-led invasion of Afghanistan in Operation ENDURING FREEDOM in 2001.

In 2001 the United States had 10 times the satellite capacity of the Persian Gulf War. Satellite imagery was a central component of targeting Al Qaeda and the Taliban during the autumn of 2001, and it played a key role in the rapid defeat of the Taliban by the U.S.-backed Northern Alliance. Reconnaissance satellites also proved invaluable in Operation IRAQI FREEDOM, the U.S.-led invasion of Iraq in 2003. In March 2003 there were no less than six NRO high-resolution imaging satellites providing around-the-clock

intelligence coverage of Iraq. The KH-11 and Lacrosse radar satellites were able to monitor at night and in bad weather. Today, the U.S. military and those of other nations rely heavily on the surveillance capabilities of space satellite systems to provide timely, detailed information on enemy capabilities and dispositions.

TARA K. SIMPSON AND SPENCER C. TUCKER

**See also**

Aircraft, Reconnaissance; Land Remote-Sensing Satellite; National Reconnaissance Office

**References**

Norris, Pat. *Spies in the Sky: Surveillance Satellites in War and Peace.* Chichester, UK: Praxis, 2008.

Richelson, Jeffrey T. *A Century of Spies.* New York: Oxford University Press, 1995.

Richelson, Jeffrey T. *The U.S. Intelligence Community.* 4th ed. Boulder, CO: Westview, 1999.

Spires, David N. *Beyond Horizons: A Half Century of Air Force Space Leadership.* 2nd ed. Maxwell Air Force Base, AL: Air Force Space Command and Air University Press, 2007.

Temple, L. Parker. *Shades of Gray: National Security and the Evolution of Space Reconnaissance.* Reston, VA: American Institute of Aeronautics and Astronautics, 2005.

# Regime Change

A phrase that first appeared in American vocabulary in the early 2000s, in the aftermath of the September 11, 2001, terror attacks. Generally, the term refers to action taken by external actors to replace another state's government. In its contemporary American usage, "regime change" refers specifically to President George W. Bush's policy goal of removing Iraqi dictator Saddam Hussein from power. The stated belief that Iraq had weapons of mass destruction (WMDs) was the chief reason advanced by the Bush administration for the U.S.-led invasion of Iraq in March 2003 (Operation IRAQI FREEDOM). As a side issue, the poor human rights record and repression of Hussein's dictatorship were given as additional reasons for advocating a democratic Iraq. The neoconservatives believed that a democratic Iraq would help to transform the Middle East. When no WMDs were found in Iraq, "regime change" became the Bush administration's chief justification for the war.

Although the descriptor "regime change" is relatively new, the ideas behind it are not. Indeed, the United States has been involved in a number of military and diplomatic conflicts with similar goals. The United States has explicitly stated a policy of encouraging "regime change" in Iran for some years, although not by military means. Combined action by the United States and Britain indeed brought regime change to Iran in 1953, and covert U.S. actions fostered regime change in Latin America, specifically in Chile and Nicaragua. Operation ENDURING FREEDOM, the U.S.-led effort to topple the Taliban government in Afghanistan in late 2001, was clearly an effort to effect regime change there.

The origins of the U.S. aspiration for regime change in Iraq lie in the 1991 Persian Gulf War, in which the United States, under the leadership of President George H. W. Bush and within a broad international coalition, went to war with Iraq, then led by Saddam Hussein, to expel the Iraqis from Kuwait. In November 1998 President Bill Clinton signed the Iraq Liberation Act, which refers specifically to the "regime" of Saddam Hussein and the importance of ousting it.

In President George W. Bush's estimation, in the post–September 11 environment, the goal of regime change, along with the presumed threat of WMDs and the assumption that Hussein had ties to terrorist networks, necessitated military action. In his State of the Union Address on January 29, 2002, Bush identified Iraq as part of a global "Axis of Evil," which also included Iran and North Korea. This speech presaged his new foreign/military policy strategy of preemption, known as the Bush Doctrine, and was a break with past policy toward Iraq, which emphasized sanctions, containment, and localized bombing operations. Colin Powell, then secretary of state, made the case for an invasion of Iraq before the United Nations (UN) Security Council in February 2003, based partly on faulty intelligence. He later regretted his actions.

Operation IRAQI FREEDOM, which began in March 2003, has had various outcomes. To date, no WMDs have been found, and the Central Intelligence Agency (CIA) has established that there were no clear links between Hussein's government and Al Qaeda operatives from Afghanistan, in contrast with the Bush administration's claims that such links existed. President Bush and other administration officials also confused many Americans when they subsequently portrayed Al Qaeda in Iraq as being essentially the same as Al Qaeda in Afghanistan.

The goal of regime change was realized, although the Iraqi government still remains unstable and insurgents continue to clash with coalition and Iraqi troops. After the collapse of his government, Hussein was captured on December 13, 2004, tried before an Iraqi court, and executed by Iraqi authorities on December 30, 2006. In the meantime, the Iraqi government and military have been restructured. Democratic elections were held in January 2005, and constitutional negotiations are ongoing. Furthermore, U.S. troops are training Iraqi military and police personnel so that they can take charge of their nation's defense.

Although there was widespread recognition of the dictatorial nature of Hussein's regime, which held many political prisoners and was guilty of major human rights abuses against the Kurds and Shia Iraqis, significant portions of the international community remained unconvinced that regime change in Iraq was a goal worth pursuing. This was especially true given the skepticism over Iraqi WMDs or ties to Al Qaeda, as evidenced by the failure of the UN Security Council to support military action against Iraq when permanent members France and Russia exercised their veto power. Regime change by an international power without an additional casus belli is considered illegal under international law. Thus other American actions in this regard, such as the CIA's participation in the 1953 coup in Iran, had been covert, and underlying reasons, such as securing access to oil, were not discussed widely. Furthermore, many scholars, activists, and world leaders expressed concern that "regime change" was simply American imperialism by another name.

Regime change as foreign policy remained controversial within the United States as well. Although there was widespread popular dislike and fear of Hussein and his regime, only a slim majority of the country supported taking military action to remove him from power. Furthermore, as fighting persisted well beyond Bush's declaration of the end of major combat operations in May 2003, the war became increasingly unpopular, and a counterdiscourse of domestic regime change emerged. Democratic candidate John Kerry, in his failed 2004 presidential bid, called for regime change in the United States.

With Hussein removed from power, the Bush administration backed off the language of regime change and switched its emphasis to the rhetoric of spreading freedom and democracy in the Middle East. Popular support for the war continues to wane, however, and many critics wonder whether the removal of a dictatorial government justifies the continuing loss of American lives in Iraq. Although Hussein was eventually found guilty of war crimes and executed in December 2006, the debate over the wisdom of regime change in Iraq has continued, especially in the political realm. In the 2008 presidential race, the rhetoric of regime change was downplayed, especially among the Republicans, but the Democrats continued to assert that the invasion of Iraq should not have taken place.

REBECCA ADELMAN

**See also**

Bush Doctrine; Bush, George Herbert Walker; Bush, George Walker; Clinton, William Jefferson; Hussein, Saddam; IRAQI FREEDOM, Operation; Powell, Colin Luther; Weapons of Mass Destruction

**References**

Bolton, M. Kent. *U.S. Foreign Policy and International Politics: George W. Bush, 9/11, and the Global Terrorist Hydra.* Upper Saddle River, NJ: Pearson/Prentice Hall, 2005.

Dodge, Toby. *Iraq's Future: The Aftermath of Regime Change.* Adelphi Paper #372. New York: Routledge for the International Institute for Strategic Studies, 2005.

Everest, Larry. *Oil, Power, and Empire: Iraq and the U.S. Global Agenda.* Monroe, ME: Common Courage, 2004.

Lennon, Alexander T. J., and Camille Eiss, eds. *Reshaping Rogue States: Preemption, Regime Change, and U.S. Policy towards Iran, Iraq, and North Korea.* Cambridge, MA: MIT Press, 2004.

# Rendition

A legal term meaning "handing over." As applied by the U.S. government, rendition has been a controversial method to fight terrorism. Overseen by the Central Intelligence Agency (CIA), its use was approved by both President William J. Clinton and President George W. Bush.

There are two forms of rendition: ordinary rendition and extraordinary rendition. Ordinary rendition occurs when a terrorist suspect is captured in a foreign country and then turned over to the United States. The individual is then transported to the United States or held at a foreign site for interrogation. Extraordinary rendition is the turning over of a suspected terrorist to a third-party country for detainment and questioning. Often, the suspect is wanted by the third-party country as well, for past offenses or crimes.

The first use of ordinary rendition occurred in 1986, during the Ronald Reagan administration, in regard to a suicide bombing in Beirut, Lebanon, the previous year. Fawaz Yunis had participated in the 1985 hijacking of a Jordanian aircraft, during which three Americans were killed. Federal Bureau of Investigation (FBI) agents and U.S. Navy SEALs seized him in a boat off the Lebanese coast.

Rendition as a policy lay largely dormant until the rise of more terrorism in the early 1990s. One such rendition involved the capture of Ramzi Yusif and his transportation to the United States. Yusif had been implicated in the 1993 World Trade Center bombing.

By the mid-1990s, there was a need for rules to standardize rendition. Michael Scheuer, then the head of the Bin Ladin Issue Station (code-named Alex, or Alec Station) in the Central Intelligence Agency (CIA), drew up the guidelines for a new rendition program in 1996. He ultimately ran the rendition program for 40 months.

The intent of the rendition program was to dismantle and disrupt the Al Qaeda terrorist network and detain Islamic terrorists. Because the Clinton administration and the FBI did not want the captives brought to the United States, where the legal process gave them significant protection, the CIA focused on Al Qaeda suspects who were wanted in a third country. In the early years, most of the extraordinary renditions were to Egypt, where torture and other illegal methods of interrogation were, and remain, in use.

The CIA has always been ambivalent about rendition. It has justified the practice with the contention that when allied governments had intelligence on terrorists that could not be used in a court of law, rendition was sometimes the only way to neutralize the terrorists. For renditions, the CIA has frequently used paramilitaries organized into teams and operating under the supervision of a CIA officer.

The rendition program has been effective, but it includes the danger that the information gathered is tainted by torture. Moreover, international law prohibits the forced return of any person, regardless of the crime, to a foreign location where that person would be subject to torture or mistreatment. Michael Scheuer has maintained that he warned the lawyers and policymakers about the dangers of turning over Al Qaeda suspects to foreign countries.

In the George W. Bush administration, the CIA continued to handle rendition cases. Whereas rendition cases were infrequent in the Clinton administration, they became numerous during the Bush administration, especially after the September 11, 2001, terror attacks. Approximately 100 suspected Al Qaeda operatives were captured and turned over to foreign governments for interrogation from 1996 to 2008. In recent years, a white Gulfstream V jet has been used to move prisoners around to various countries.

Egypt, Afghanistan, and Syria have been principal destinations, but at least 14 European states have knowingly cooperated with the United States. Several Eastern European states are thought to have housed CIA detention centers.

In one case, two Egyptians were seized in Sweden and sent to Egypt. Ahmed Agiza and Muhammed al-Zery were radical Islamists, and they had sought political asylum in Sweden. On December 18, 2001, American agents seized both of them and placed them on a Gulfstream jet bound for Cairo, Egypt. The Swedish government cooperated after its representatives were assured that Agiza and Zery would not be tortured.

Once it was learned that both Agiza and Zery had indeed been tortured, there was a major political outcry in Sweden against the Swedish government and the United States. Egyptian authorities determined that Zery had no contacts with terrorists, and he was released from prison in October 2003. Agiza was less fortunate because he had been a member of Egyptian Islamic Jihad and close to its leader, Ayman al-Zawahiri. An Egyptian court subsequently sentenced Agiza to 25 years in prison.

Rendition has become more controversial after public revelations regarding several cases. The first such case was that of the radical Islamist cleric Abu Omar (full name Hassan Osama Nasr), who lived in Milan, Italy, under political refugee status. Omar had been under investigation for terrorist-related activities and support of Al Qaeda when the CIA, with the assistance of Italian security personnel, seized him on the streets of Milan on February 17, 2002. He was taken to a North Atlantic Treaty Organization (NATO) base near Aviano, Italy, and then flown to Egypt on February 18. There, Omar was offered a deal to be an informant. After he refused, he was sent to a prison where he was tortured. Italian authorities became incensed over this rendition, and a judge charged 25 American CIA operatives and two Italian security officers with abduction. The Italian government requested extradition of the CIA operatives, and initiated court proceedings in 2008. The trial has coincided with continuing popular Italian opposition to the Iraq War.

Two other cases of rendition also caused unease among U.S. allies. One was that of Maher Arar, a Canadian citizen from Ottawa and a software engineer. Arar arrived at JFK Airport in New York on an American Airlines flight from Zurich, Switzerland, on September 26, 2002, when U.S. authorities detained him. They were acting on inaccurate information given to them by the Royal Mounted Canadian Police (RMCP) that Arar was a member of Al Qaeda. After interrogation and a stay at the Metropolitan Detention Center, he was flown to Jordan on October 8, 2002. CIA operatives then transferred him to Syria. In Syria, he was imprisoned and intensively interrogated for nearly a year. It took intervention by the Canadian government to win Arar's release in October 2003, after more than 10 months in captivity. Since then, Arar has been seeking to sue both the U.S. and Canadian governments.

Another noteworthy case was the December 2003 rendition of Khalid al-Masri, a German citizen. Masri was born in Kuwait

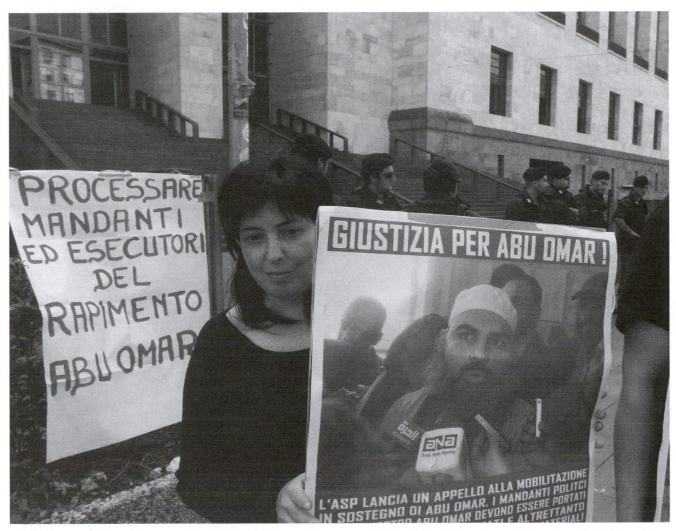

An Italian protester holds up a poster reading "Justice for Abu Omar" above a picture of Muslim cleric Hassan Mustaffa Osama Nasr, also known as Abu Omar. The protesters were demonstrating on September 23, 2009, outside Milan's courthouse during the trial of 26 Americans and 7 Italians accused of orchestrating a CIA-led kidnapping of the Egyptian terrorist suspect from Milan. (AP/Wide World Photos)

but raised in Lebanon. In 1985 he immigrated to Germany, where he became a German citizen in 1994. He took a vacation in Skopje, Macedonia, but was arrested at the Macedonian border on December 31, 2003, because his name resembled that of Khalid al-Masri, the mentor of the Al Qaeda Hamburg cell. CIA agents took him into custody on January 23, 2004, shortly after Macedonian officials had released him. He was sent to Afghanistan, where he was tortured during lengthy interrogations. Masri went on a hunger strike for 27 days in the confinement camp. American officials determined that he had been wrongfully detained, and he was released on May 28, 2004. He was dumped on a desolate road in Albania without an apology or funds to return home. German authorities have initiated legal proceedings against CIA officials for their handling of Masri.

Numerous cases of torture have been verified, and they have made rendition a difficult policy to justify. Most of the rendition cases came during the first two years following September 11; there have been fewer of them after that time. Political fallout regarding rendition cases, however, continues both in the United States and among its allies.

STEPHEN A. ATKINS

### See also

Alec Station; Bush, George Walker; Central Intelligence Agency; Clinton, William Jefferson; Global War on Terror

### References

Drumheller, Tyler, and Elaine Monaghan. *On the Brink: An Insider's Account of How the White House Compromised American Intelligence.* New York: Carroll and Graf, 2006.

Eccleston, Ron. "CIA 'Renditions' in Tune with Habib Claim of Abuse in Egypt." *Australian,* February 14, 2005, 17.

Grey, Stephen, and Ian Cobain. "From Secret Prisons to Turning a Blind Eye: Europe's Role in Rendition." *Guardian* [London], June 7, 2006, 1.

Scheuer, Michael. "A Fine Rendition." *New York Times,* March 11, 2005.

Whitlock, Craig. "In Letter, Radical Cleric Details CIA Abduction, Egyptian Torture." *Washington Post,* November 10, 2006.

Wilkinson, Tracy. "Details Emerge in Cleric's Abduction." *Los Angeles Times,* January 10, 2007.

# Repair Ships, U.S.

Large auxiliary ships equipped to effect heavy repairs on naval vessels far from port facilities. The last purpose-built repair ships delivered to the U.S. Navy were the four long-serving vessels of the Vulcan class. The lead ship, the AR-5 *Vulcan,* was launched in 1940 and commissioned in 1941. The other three were the AR-6 *Ajax,* AR-7 *Hector,* and AR-8 *Jason* (commissioned in 1944). The ships were 529.5 feet in length, with a beam of 73.33 feet and draft of 23.33 feet. They displaced 9,325 tons (light) and 16,245 tons (full load). Powered by two steam turbines, they had a top speed of 19.2 knots and range of 18,000 nautical miles at 12 knots. Their crew complement was 842 (29 officers; 813 enlisted). The ships were armed with 4 20-mm guns.

Outfitted with a pair of heavy-duty 20-ton capacity cranes, machine and electrical shops, foundries, and redundant tool sets of all kinds, the Vulcan-class ships carried abundant materials that their highly trained crews employed in damage control, repair or overhaul, and modifications aboard combat vessels of all sizes. Decks or hulls with gaping holes from bomb and torpedo strikes were routinely plated over, rewelded, and strengthened to nearly original configurations, and other repairs ranged from reoutfitting a battle-damaged crew's mess area to replacing a propeller shaft far below decks. During World War II, the repair ship operated nearly in the midst of conflict, sometimes tending to its own damage as it simultaneously assisted several alongside customers. In some cases, despite all its resources, the repair ship might only manage to render a severely disabled ship seaworthy enough to reach a harbor, where dry-docking and extensive reconstruction facilities could make permanent repairs.

In 1978 USS *Vulcan* was chosen by the U.S. Navy for its first implementation of a mixed male/female crew aboard an active-duty ship with the potential of experiencing combat; such crews are, by now, commonplace, and frequently are commanded by female officers. After long years of service to the Pacific fleet, two repair ships left U.S. naval service: *Ajax* was decommissioned in 1986, and *Hector,* decommissioned in 1987, was transferred to Pakistan (as PNS *Moawin*) in 1989, serving that navy until 1994. As no replacements for this class were forthcoming, *Vulcan* and *Jason* remained active fleet units in the Atlantic and Pacific, respectively, and eventually served in Operation DESERT STORM.

*Vulcan*'s final career deployment was to the Mediterranean and the Red seas, where the destroyer tender *Yellowstone* (AD-41) contributed its capabilities to the repair of coalition naval units as the two ships operated near the Suez Canal, and then from the harbor at Jeddah, Saudi Arabia, during DESERT SHIELD and DESERT STORM in January and February 1991. Returning to home port at Norfolk Naval Station, *Vulcan* was decommissioned there on September 27, 1991, after 50 years of active service. *Jason* had been on station since early January 1991 in the Persian Gulf when the amphibious assault ship *Tripoli* (LPH-10), maneuvering off Kuwait as flagship of the U.S. Mine Countermeasures Group (USMCMG), sustained massive hull and internal damage from an Iraqi mine on February

18, 1991. When the *Tripoli* reached dry-dock facilities at Bahrain after transferring USMCMG flag duties to USS *La Salle* (AGF-3, the U.S. Middle East Force flagship), repair and reconstruction crews aboard *Jason* began working on a 24-hour basis to return the assault ship (ahead of schedule) to service in the northern Persian Gulf by early April 1991.

After the *Vulcan*'s decommissioning in 1991, *Jason* became the sole active U.S. Navy repair ship. Navy plans initiated as far back as the late 1980s targeted the 1994 fiscal year for commencing a replacement class of repair ships, but these were deferred. The shipbuilding program for fiscal 1998 made provisions for a new design to replace both the Vulcan class and the destroyer tenders of the Dixie class, which also dated from the early 1940s. By the early 1990s these plans were cancelled, and disposal was recommended for the older submarine tenders of the Fulton class, the remaining Dixie-class ships, and *Jason,* which was decommissioned in June 1995.

Shipboard-based repair of all forward-deployed ship types shifted to the newer, more versatile destroyer tenders of the Samuel Gompers and Yellowstone classes, which are fully equipped to support nuclear-powered cruisers, gas-turbine-powered missile destroyers, and frigates. Where practicable, less heavily damaged ships might also be tended to by matériel and special teams flown to a nearby staging point to undertake repairs and reduce a vessel's off-station time. Seriously damaged ships, such as the Exocet-stricken frigate USS *Stark* (FFG-31) in 1987, mine victims USS *Samuel B. Roberts* (FFG-58) in 1988 and the cruiser *Princeton* (CG-59) and the *Tripoli* in 1991, and the suicide-bombed destroyer *Cole* (DDG-67) in 2000, all required greater repair measures. The *Stark* was repaired by destroyer tender USS *Acadia* (AD-42) at Bahrain before returning to the United States for permanent repairs. The *Tripoli* and *Princeton* both received initial ministrations from Royal Fleet Auxiliary *Diligence* (A-132) at Jabal Ali before the *Princeton* was docked at Dubai and more comprehensively repaired by the *Acadia* to ensure a safe passage home, where it received another two months of further shipyard attention. Quick-witted and persistent damage control had saved both the *Roberts* and *Cole,* but in each case the hull's condition was so precarious that the United States opted to contract for heavy-lift ship transport (by Dutch and Norwegian providers, respectively) to carry the vessels across the Atlantic for complete repairs, and the eventual return of each warship to the fleet. No major repairs were needed to U.S. warships during Operation IRAQI FREEDOM.

GORDON E. HOGG

## See also

*Cole,* USS, Attack on; DESERT STORM, Operation, Coalition Naval Forces; Destroyer Tenders, U.S.; Mines, Sea, and Naval Mine Warfare, Persian Gulf and Iraq Wars; *Stark* Incident; Support and Supply Ships, Strategic; United States Navy, Persian Gulf War

## References
Marolda, Edward, and Robert Schneller. *Shield and Sword: The United States Navy and the Persian Gulf War.* Annapolis, MD: U.S. Naval Institute Press, 2001.

Polmar, Norman. *The Naval Institute Guide to the Ships and Aircraft of the U.S. Fleet.* 18th ed. Annapolis, MD: Naval Institute Press, 2005.
Saunders, Stephen, ed. *Jane's Fighting Ships, 2002–2003.* Coulsdon, Surrey, UK, and Alexandria, VA: Jane's Information Group, 2002.
Sharpe, Richard, ed. *Jane's Fighting Ships, 1992–1993.* Coulsdon, Surrey, UK, and Alexandria, VA: Jane's Information Group, 1992.

## Republican Guard

Iraqi army formation created in 1978 that served as the elite force of Iraqi dictator Saddam Hussein's army. The Republican Guard was permanently disbanded after the 2003 Iraq War (Operation IRAQI FREEDOM). Throughout its existence, the Republican Guard was one of the mainstays of Hussein's regime and received the best equipment, training, and personnel. When first constituted, the Republican Guard was a palace guard of one brigade. At the outbreak of the Iran-Iraq War in 1980, the Guard was expanded to take on the role of an elite offensive force, and by 1988 it numbered seven divisions and had been redesignated as the Republican Guard Forces Command (RGFC). The total strength of this force was estimated at 50,000 men and 400 tanks in seven divisions. There were an additional 10,000 troops in the Special Republican Guard, which was composed of the most loyal troops, usually stationed close to Baghdad.

The names of the seven divisions reflected either past military victories or past monarchs, such as the 6th Nebuchadnezzar Division named after the 6th-century BCE king of Babylon. Republican Guard divisions were organized similarly to those of the regular army, apart from the fact that the tank battalions had more tanks. However, soldiers in the Republican Guard were volunteers rather than conscripts and received subsidized housing and new cars as incentives. These incentives were to help ensure the loyalty of the Guard to Hussein and his regime. Many members of the Republican Guard were either from the Tikrit area or from other bases of support for the regime. In terms of equipment, much of the armored forces of the Guard were equipped with Soviet-produced T-72 tanks, and training in their use was more thorough than in the regular army.

The Republican Guard was not under the control of the defense ministry, but rather served as Iraq's special security apparatus. By 1990 the RGFC was officially under the command of Saddam Hussein's son Qusay, although it is possible that he directed only the Special Republican Guard, which guarded the palaces and important headquarters of the regime.

The Republican Guard was the main strike force in the Iraqi invasion of Kuwait in August 1990. In response to the deployment of coalition forces in operations DESERT SHIELD and DESERT STORM, the majority of the Republican Guard was held in reserve. For the U.S.-led coalition against Iraq, destruction of the Republican Guard was a high priority. This was largely achieved by the 1st and 3rd U.S. Armored divisions. Following the end of the Persian Gulf War on February 28, 1991, Hussein rebuilt the Republican Guard, although, as with the rest of the Iraqi army, it was not to pre-1990 standards.

In 1995 an attempted military coup against Hussein led a battalion of the Guard from the al-Dulaymi tribe to rebel as well. They were subsequently defeated by two loyal brigades, and the clans of the al-Dulaymi tribe were severely punished. In July 1995 the Republican Guard was purged of all officers whom Hussein suspected of disloyalty. In 2002 there were reports that the Guard was being trained in urban warfare and guerrilla tactics. The U.S. military claimed that former Guardsmen constituted many of the insurgent forces in Iraq that fought the coalition and new Iraqi government after 2003; however these assertions have never been proven.

Before the March 2003 Anglo-American invasion of Iraq (Operation IRAQI FREEDOM), the Republican Guard was dug in along the Tigris River close to Baghdad. The Republican Guard was then thought to number between 55,000 and 60,000 troops; some estimates placed the number as high as 75,000–80,000 (including some 7,000–12,000 Special Republican Guards). The force had at its disposal between 350 and 450 Soviet-made T-62 and T-72 tanks and various other armored and unarmored mechanized vehicles. When some of these units advanced to meet the U.S. drive on the capital, they were largely destroyed by U.S. air strikes. Those that escaped the aerial bombardment were annihilated during the Battle for Baghdad, which took place April 3–12, 2003; particularly hard hit during that engagement was the Special Republican Guard. Following the end of official hostilities in May 2003, coalition forces broke up any remaining Republican Guard formations. Some of its personnel, however, were subsequently recruited into internal security formations because of their comparatively high level of training.

RALPH MARTIN BAKER

**See also**
Baghdad, Battle for; DESERT SHIELD, Operation; DESERT STORM, Operation; Hussein, Saddam; Iraq, Army; IRAQI FREEDOM, Operation; Special Republican Guards; T-62 Main Battle Tank; T-72 Main Battle Tank

**References**
Carhart, Tom. *Iron Soldiers: How America's 1st Armored Division Crushed Iraq's Elite Republican Guard.* New York: Pocket Books, 1994.
Ripley, Tom. *Desert Storm Land Power: The Coalition and Iraqi Armies.* London: Osprey, 1991.
Xenos, Nicolas. *Republican Guard: Leo Strauss, Foreign Policy, and the American Regime.* Oxford, UK: Routledge, 2006.

## Revolutionary Command Council

Supreme government entity in Iraq from 1968 to 2003. The Revolutionary Command Council (RCC) came into being in July 1968 after the Baath Party coup ousted Iraqi strongman Abd al-Rahman Arif. Between 1968 and 2003, the RCC was controlled exclusively by the Baath Party and retained both de facto legislative and executive powers. The chairman of the RCC, elected by RCC representatives (whose numbers varied over the years; by the late 1980s there were 10 members), was the president of Iraq.

Iraqi president Saddam Hussein chairs a joint meeting of the Revolutionary Command Council on March 26, 1999. That body was the most powerful decision-making body in Iraq. (AP/Wide World Photos)

The chairman was elected by a two-thirds majority vote; the vice chairman was similarly elected by RCC members and was the second-highest-ranking Iraqi government official. The vice chairman was to act as president upon the absence or death of the chairman, until such time that a new chairman could be elected. Once elected, the chairman was permitted to select his own vice president, who was not necessarily the vice chairman of the council.

The first RCC chairman was Ahmad Hassan al-Bakr, who led the government until his forced retirement in July 1979, at which time Saddam Hussein became chairman, a post he held until the U.S.-led invasion in 2003. Hussein had also served as vice chairman of the RCC before his rise to the chairmanship. Deputy chairmen of the RCC under Hussein included Izzat Ibrahim al-Douri, Tariq Aziz, and Taha Yasin Ramadan.

The RCC essentially acted as the policymaking tool of the Baath Party, which controlled all aspects of Iraq's government, politics, and economy. Its members were all high-ranking party members, many of whom were allies or loyalists to the RCC's chairman. In certain aspects, the RCC functioned similarly to a politburo in communist nations. The chairman, vice chairman, and other RCC members were answerable only to the RCC itself, which could dismiss members by a two-thirds vote and vote by the same margin to try any RCC official, cabinet member, or other high government official for wrongdoing.

After a government restructuring in 1977, the RCC's de facto membership included the Baath Party's regional chiefs. This change helped solidify the party's grip on political power throughout Iraq. RCC members were also members of the Iraqi legislature, the National Assembly.

The Iraqi constitution endowed the RCC with sweeping powers, not only in the executive realm, but also in legislative affairs. It was empowered to enact legislative initiatives with or without the National Assembly's involvement, establish internal security and military policies, declare war, negotiate treaties with other nations, establish and approve of governmental budgets, set parameters for the impeachment and removal from office of government officials, create an ad hoc court for such proceedings, and provide guidelines for its own functioning. The chairman, particularly Hussein, exercised dictatorial powers over both the RCC and Iraq itself. Although the Iraqi constitution had created a de jure separation of governmental powers, to be divided among the executive, legislative, and judicial branches, in reality the RCC acted with supreme impunity, dominating the legislative and judicial processes at will. After the Anglo-American–led invasion of Iraq in March 2003, L. Paul Bremer, head of the Coalition Provisional Authority, abolished the RCC by Order Number Two, on May 23, 2003.

PAUL G. PIERPAOLI JR.

See also

Aziz, Tariq; Baath Party; Bakr, Ahmad Hassan al-; Bremer, Jerry; Hussein, Saddam; Iraq, History of, Pre-1990; Iraq, History of, 1990–Present

References

Aburish, Said K. *Saddam Hussein: The Politics of Revenge.* New York: Bloomsbury, 2000.

Tripp, Charles. *A History of Iraq.* Cambridge: Cambridge University Press, 2007.

---

# Reza Pahlavi, Mohammad
Birth Date: October 26, 1919
Death Date: July 27, 1980

Ruler of Iran from 1941 to 1979. Mohammad Reza Shah Pahlavi, who was also known by the deferential title Aryamehr, which means "Light of the Aryans," was the second monarch of the Pahlavi dynasty and the last shah of Iran. He was born in Tehran on October 26, 1919, the son of Shah Reza Pahlavi, who ruled Iran from 1925 to 1941. Shah Reza Pahlavi's father was a military leader, Reza Khan, who had overthrown the Qajar dynasty and established the Pahlavi dynasty in 1925.

During the last decades of the Qajar dynasty, the British and Russians established spheres of influence in Iran. At the beginning of the 20th century, the Qajar shah granted a concession to the British government, which resulted in British domination of the lucrative Iranian oil industry. Reza Pahlavi sought to decrease British and Russian influence in Iran by forging closer ties with the Axis powers of Germany and Italy. The shah's policy had the opposite effect, resulting in the occupation of Iran by British and Soviet forces in 1941 during World War II. Meanwhile, Mohammad Reza Pahlavi completed his education at a Swiss boarding school in 1935 and, upon returning to Iran, attended a military academy in Tehran, graduating in 1938. Two brief marriages had ended in divorce by 1948. Concerned that Reza Pahlavi was planning to ally his nation with Nazi Germany, the British forced him to abdicate in favor of Mohammad Reza Pahlavi on September 16, 1941, shortly before the latter's 22nd birthday.

Unlike his father, Mohammad Reza Pahlavi was willing to cooperate with the Allied war effort, and the British and Americans used Iran as a conduit to ferry supplies to the Soviet Union during the war. For many Iranians, the new shah's legitimacy was in question because he was viewed as a puppet of the Western powers.

After World War II, Iran was plagued by economic problems, including a large and impoverished peasantry, little foreign capital

Mohammad Reza Pahlavi, shah of Iran, shown here as he prepares to depart following a visit to the United States on November 16, 1977. (U.S. Department of Defense)

and investment, and high unemployment. Although tremendous wealth was being generated by Iranian oil production, most of the profits were going to the British-owned Anglo-Iranian Oil Company (AIOC).

In 1951 the Iranian parliament nationalized the AIOC, and Dr. Mohammad Mosaddeq, a nationalist who was a member of the Qajar family, became prime minister of Iran. Mosaddeq and his political party had advocated for the nationalization of the AIOC. The British subsequently imposed a naval blockade on Iran and refused to allow Iran to export any of its oil. On April 4, 1953, U.S. president Dwight D. Eisenhower's administration approved $1 million in funding for the overthrow of Mosaddeq, who was being supported by radical Islamic clerics and the Tudeh Party, which was nationalist and prosocialist. The plan called for the shah to dismiss Mosaddeq. Although this initially failed and the shah was forced to flee Iran, within a few days a military coup, with support from the Central Intelligence Agency (CIA), restored the shah to his throne. Mosaddeq was placed under house arrest and then tried and imprisoned.

After being restored to power, the shah imposed an authoritarian regime funded by an increased profit-sharing plan negotiated with the foreign oil companies. By the early 1960s, the Iranian treasury was awash in money. The shah's secret police, however, the Sazeman-e Ettelaat va Amniyat-e Keshvar (SAVAK, National Information and Security Organization), crushed all politically and religiously based resistance in Iran. SAVAK was especially notorious for its brutal persecutions and torturing of prisoners. During the White Revolution of 1963, the shah nationalized large estates and distributed the land to 4 million landless peasants. And influenced by his third wife, Farah Diba, whom he married in 1959, the shah also granted women the right to vote. The move was fiercely unpopular among traditional Muslims and conservative clerics.

In 1975, citing security reasons, the shah effectively banned the multiparty system in Iran and ruled with even greater authority through his Rastakhiz (Resurrection) Party. These moves toward increased autocracy angered not only Islamic fundamentalists but also growing numbers of the middle class and intelligentsia. In 1976 the shah replaced the Islamic calendar, which begins in 622 when the Prophet Muhammad led his followers to Medina, with the Persian calendar, which begins more than 25 centuries earlier. The move outraged many conservative Muslims.

In foreign affairs, the shah was decidedly pro-Western. Under President Richard Nixon's administration, which came to view the shah's Iran as the central, pro-Western citadel in the Middle East, sales of U.S. arms and weaponry to Iran increased dramatically. Not surprisingly, the shah's pro-Western orientation did not sit well with Iran's Islamic clerics and other traditionalists. Although the shah never restored formal recognition to Israel, his government had various military and defense exchanges with the country. Because the shah also sponsored various opposition movements in the countries of such Arab neighbors as Iraq and Oman, there were other tensions with the Arab world.

The shah managed to straddle the fence during the 1967 Six-Day War and 1973 Yom Kippur (Ramadan) War by maintaining reasonably cordial relations with the Persian Gulf nations. He also enjoyed generally good relations with Jordan and Egypt. Relations with Iraq remained strained until the 1975 Algiers Accord brought a thaw. With vast revenues from the petroleum industry, the shah had built the largest military force in the Persian Gulf by the late 1970s.

By the end of the 1970s, however, the shah's strong-arm tactics, brutal suppression of dissidents, economic shortages and inflation, and increasing secularization had begun to take their toll. Following a year of intense political protests against the monarchy from students, Islamic traditionalists, and the middle class, a revolution occurred on January 16, 1979, and the shah and his family were forced to flee Iran. In February 1979, on his return from exile in France, the Ayatollah Ruhollah Khomeini was hailed by millions of Iranians as the father of the Iranian Revolution. He and his supporters quickly consolidated their political control over the country by eliminating opposing factions and clerics and establishing an Islamic-based government.

Mohammad Reza Pahlavi first went into exile in Egypt. Although President Jimmy Carter allowed the shah to seek treatment for lymphatic cancer in New York City, considerable political pressure was brought to bear on the U.S. government to expel the shah, and he was compelled to leave the United States after his treatment. His opponents charged him with pillaging the country and taking considerable sums of money when he fled Iran. The shah lived for a few months in Panama before returning to Cairo, Egypt, where he died on July 27, 1980, and was buried. The shah's oldest son, Reza Pahlavi II, who lives in the United States, is heir to the Pahlavi dynasty.

MICHAEL R. HALL

**See also**

Iran; Iran, Armed Forces; Iranian Revolution; Khomeini, Ruhollah

**References**

Barth, Linda. *Mohammed Reza Pahlavi*. New York: Chelsea House, 2002.

Farmanfarmaian, Manucher, and Roxane Farmanfarmaian. *Blood and Oil: A Prince's Memoir of Iran, from the Shah to the Ayatollah*. New York: Random House, 2005.

Gasiorowski, Mark. *U.S. Foreign Policy and the Shah: Building a Client State in Iran*. Ithaca, NY: Cornell University Press, 1991.

Ghani, Cyprus. *Iran and the Rise of the Reza Shah: From Qajar Collapse to Pahlavi Power*. London: I. B. Tauris, 2001.

# Rice, Condoleezza
## Birth Date: November 14, 1954

U.S. national security adviser (2001–2005) and secretary of state (2005–2009). Condoleeza Rice was born on November 14, 1954, in Birmingham, Alabama, to a prominent African American family. She graduated in 1973 from the University of Denver at age

19, then earned a master's degree from Notre Dame University in 1975. After working in the State Department during the Jimmy Carter administration, Rice returned to the University of Denver and received a doctorate in international studies in 1981. She joined the faculty at Stanford University as a professor of political science and fellow at the Hoover Institute.

In 1989 Rice joined the administration of George H. W. Bush, where she worked closely with Secretary of State James Baker. She was the director of Soviet and East European affairs on the National Security Council (NSC) and a special assistant to the president on national security affairs. She impressed the elder Bush, who subsequently recommended her to George W. Bush when the Texas governor began to prepare for his 2000 presidential campaign. From 1993 to 2000 Rice was the provost of Stanford University.

Rice served as a foreign policy adviser to George W. Bush in the 2000 presidential campaign, and on assuming the presidency Bush appointed her in January 2001 as the nation's first female and second African American national security adviser. Following the September 11, 2001, terrorist attacks on the United States, Rice emerged as a central figure in crafting the U.S. military and diplomatic response and in advocating war with Iraq. She played a central role in the successful implementation of Operation ENDURING FREEDOM in Afghanistan in late 2001.

In 2002 Rice helped to develop the U.S. national security strategy commonly referred to as the "Bush Doctrine," which emphasized the use of preemptive military strikes to prevent the use of weapons of mass destruction (WMDs) and acts of terrorism, although many associate this policy more with Vice President Dick Cheney, Paul Wolfowitz, and other individuals, such as Douglas Feith. She was also instrumental in the administration's hard-line policy toward the Iraqi regime of Saddam Hussein, including the effort to isolate Iraq and formulate an international coalition against it. Rice was one of the main proponents of the 2003 U.S.-led invasion of Iraq, Operation IRAQI FREEDOM.

During the 2004 presidential campaign, Rice became the first national security adviser to openly campaign on behalf of a candidate. She faced criticism by Democrats for her hard-line security policies and for her advocacy against affirmative action policies. After the election, upon the resignation of Colin Powell, Rice was appointed secretary of state.

Once in office in 2005, Rice worked to repair relations with such U.S. allies as France and Germany, the governments of which

U.S. secretary of state Condoleezza Rice addresses the media following a meeting at the U.S. embassy in Baghdad, Iraq, April 2006. Rice was secretary of state in the George W. Bush administration during 2005–2009. (U.S. Department of Defense)

opposed the U.S.-led invasion of Iraq. She also endeavored to increase international support for the continuing U.S. efforts in Iraq. Rice's closeness with Bush provided her with greater access, and therefore more influence, than Powell had enjoyed. Following Rumsfeld's replacement as secretary of defense, Rice's influence may have increased.

In 2005 Rice led the U.S. effort to develop a multilateral approach toward Iran in light of that country's refusal to suspend its nuclear program. In June 2006 the permanent members of the United Nations (UN) developed a plan to offer incentives in exchange for the cessation of Iran's nuclear program. Rice supported European Union (EU) high commissioner for foreign policy Javier Solana's efforts to negotiate with Iran after Tehran refused to meet an August 2006 deadline to suspend its nuclear enrichment.

Rice has been a staunch supporter of Israel. She endeavored to gain support for the Road Map to Peace, which endorsed the creation of a Palestinian state in exchange for democratic reforms and the renunciation of terrorism by the Palestinians. Rice supported the 2006 Israeli unilateral withdrawal from the Gaza Strip. When Israel began bombarding Lebanon in July 2006, following the kidnapping of Israeli soldiers by members of Hezbollah in the border town of Ghajar, Rice supported the Israeli action. She enraged the Lebanese by initially opposing a cease-fire in the hopes that Hezbollah would be destroyed. It was only after weeks of destruction that she supported a UN-brokered cease-fire based on UN Security Council Resolution 1701. In her last year of office, Rice

## U.S. National Security Advisers, 1987–Present

| Name | Dates of Service |
| --- | --- |
| Colin Powell | November 23, 1987–January 20, 1989 |
| Brent Scowcroft | January 20, 1989–January 20, 1993 |
| W. Anthony Lake | January 20, 1993–March 14, 1997 |
| Samuel R. Berger | March 14, 1997–January 20, 2001 |
| Condoleezza Rice | January 22, 2001–January 25, 2005 |
| Stephen Hadley | January 26, 2005–January 20, 2009 |
| James L. Jones | January 20, 2009–present |

was unsuccessful in moving forward the Palestinian-Israeli peace process of Israeli soldiers. She took a hard-line stance against the Russian incursion into South Ossetia and invasion of Georgia in the summer of 2008.

Rice left office with the end of the Bush administration in January 2009. She is currently the Thomas and Barbara Stephenson Senior Fellow on Public Policy at the Hoover Institution and professor of political science at Stanford University. She also serves on a number of boards, including the board of trustees of the Kennedy Center for the Performing Arts.

TOM LANSFORD

**See also**

Bush, George Herbert Walker; Bush, George Walker; Hezbollah; Hussein, Saddam; Iran; IRAQI FREEDOM, Operation; Israel; Nuclear Weapons, Iraq's Potential for Building; Terrorism

**References**

Felix, Antonia. *Condi: The Condoleezza Rice Story*. New York: Newmarket, 2002.
Lusane, Clarence. *Colin Powell and Condoleezza Rice: Foreign Policy, Race, and the New American Century*. Westport, CT: Praeger, 2006.
Morris, Dick, and Eillen McGann. *Condi vs. Hillary: The Next Great Presidential Race*. New York: Regan Books, 2005.

# Rice, Donald Blessing
## Birth Date: June 4, 1939

U.S. career government official who served as secretary of the U.S. Air Force (1989–1993). Donald Blessing Rice was born on June 4, 1939, in Frederick, Maryland. He earned a degree in chemical engineering from the University of Notre Dame in 1961 and was commissioned as a second lieutenant in the U.S. Army Ordnance Corps through the Reserve Officers' Training Corps (ROTC) upon graduation. In 1962 he earned a master's degree in industrial management from Purdue University. He went on to complete a PhD in economics from Purdue in 1965. From 1965 to 1967, Rice was assistant professor of management and acting deputy director for academics at the Navy Management Systems Center at the Naval Postgraduate School in Monterey, California. Rice left the army as a captain in 1967.

Rice then joined the Department of Defense as director of cost analysis. In 1969 he was appointed deputy assistant to the secretary of defense for resource analysis. In this position, he was responsible for cost analysis, manpower and logistics requirements, and budget planning for all defense programs. Rice was assistant director of the Office of Management and Budget from 1970 to 1972.

Rice left government service in 1972, when he became president and chief executive officer of the RAND Corporation, the independent, nonprofit think tank in Santa Monica, California. While at RAND, Rice also served as chair of the National Commission on Supplies and Shortages and served two terms

on the National Science Board. He also directed a study on resource management for the Department of Defense at the request of President Ronald Reagan. Rice left RAND in May 1989 when President George H. W. Bush appointed him secretary of the air force.

As secretary, Rice was faced with several important challenges, the majority of which involved the procurement budget, including that for the Northrop Grumman B-2 Spirit (stealth bomber) program. The top-secret aircraft was plagued by cost overruns and failed performance expectations. Rice reduced the order for B-2s from 132 to 75. The McDonnell Douglas C-17 Globemaster transport was another troubled program. It too suffered from budgetary problems and performance failures, but Rice was able to make the necessary changes and bring the program to fruition. Other programs done away with during Rice's tenure were the MX and Midgetman missiles.

Rice's tenure saw the successful employment of the Lockheed Martin F-117A Nighthawk in Operation JUST CAUSE, the U.S. invasion of Panama in 1989. Another success was the deactivation of the Looking Glass aircraft and of Strategic Air Command; both ended because of the conclusion of the Cold War. Perhaps Rice's greatest success was the air force's participation in Operation DESERT SHIELD, during which it assisted with the movement of men and supplies to the theater of operations; and in Operation DESERT STORM, when it achieved total air superiority and assisted ground forces in the liberation of Kuwait.

Leaving government service in 1993, Rice headed Teledyne Technologies. In 1996 he joined the Agensys Corporation, a biotechnology company.

SHAWN LIVINGSTON

**See also**

DESERT STORM, Operation; DESERT STORM, Operation, Coalition Air Campaign; DESERT STORM, Operation, Coalition Air Forces; JUST CAUSE, Operation

**References**

Nalty, Bernard C., ed. *Winged Shield, Winged Sword: A History of the United States Air Force*. 2 vols. Washington, DC: Air Force History and Museums Program, United States Air Force, 1997.
Winnefeld, James A., Preston Niblack, and Dana J. Johnson. *A League of Airmen: U.S. Air Power in the Gulf War*. Santa Monica, CA: RAND Corporation, 1994.

# Rifles

Shoulder-fired weapons that are soldiers' primary firearm. Although a soldier may be assigned to crew-served weapons, such as a machine gun, an artillery piece, or an air-defense missile system, or may serve in a support role, such as a truck driver or a cook, the rifle remains his or her basic weapon for self-defense, position defense, and general security duties. For the infantry soldier, survival and success on the battlefield depend on his or her skill with a rifle.

The carbine is a more compact version of a standard rifle, usually with a shorter barrel and sometimes chambered for a smaller caliber. Carbines were first developed for cavalry and mounted troops, and during World War II and the Korean War were issued as substitutes for pistols.

In the years following 1945, most of the world's major armies moved away from the standard battle rifle that characterized both world wars, widely adopting lighter and more rapidly firing shoulder weapons that came to be classified as assault rifles. The battle rifles, however, remained in limited numbers, serving in special functions as sniper or designated marksman rifles or antimatériel rifles.

The U.S. wars in the Middle East were typical of all modern wars, with the vast majority of the combatants on all sides carrying rifles into combat. Officers, section leaders, and certain crews operating in restricted spaces, like tanks and aircraft, frequently carried pistols, carbines, or submachine guns instead of rifles. The infantry squad is usually equipped with a light machine gun or a heavy-barrel automatic rifle, but the rifle remains the primary infantry tool.

The United States ended World War II with the world's best battle rifle, the .30-caliber, semiautomatic M-1 Garand. In the early 1950s, efforts to improve the M-1 rifle resulted in the M-14 rifle. Unlike the M-1, the M-14 was capable of both semiautomatic and full-automatic fire, and was fed by a more efficient 20-round detachable box magazine, a distinct improvement over the M-1's internal magazine system, which had to be reloaded from an 8-round clip inserted through the breech of the weapon. The M-14 was also chambered for what became the North Atlantic Treaty Organization (NATO) standard rifle round, the 7.62x51-millimeter (mm). Essentially the same round as the commercial .308 Winchester, the bullet was the same diameter as that of the M-1's .30–06 Springfield round, but the overall cartridge was 12 mm shorter.

The M-14 was adopted in 1957 and first issued to units in the field in 1959. It weighed 11.5 pounds and was 46.5 inches long. It had a cyclic rate of fire of 700 to 750 rounds per minute and a maximum effective range of 460 meters (500 yards) with iron sights, and 800 meters (875 yards) with optical sights. But the M-14 remained the U.S. Army's standard rifle only until January 1968, when it was replaced by the M-16. The M-14 continued in service in limited numbers as several variations of sniper rifles. In the Iraq and Afghanistan wars, M-14s also have been assigned to army and marine corps units, carried by selected individuals known as designated marksmen—not to be confused with snipers—whose mission is to engage special targets that require a rifle with the accuracy, long range, and stopping power that are not characteristic of modern assault rifles. U.S. Navy ships also still carry a number of M-14s in their armories, primarily for close-in defense while in port.

Immediately following World War II, the U.S. Army's Operations Research Office conducted an extensive analysis of the existing combat after-action reports from both world wars and reached the conclusion that the trend in mobile warfare was for

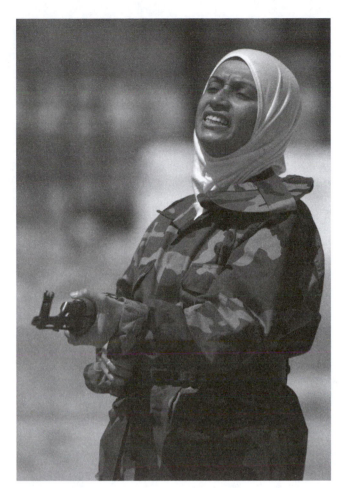

An Iraqi Army trainee with her AK-47 assault rifle at the Jordanian Royal Military Academy on June 22, 2004. She was one of 38 women in the second class of recruits undergoing basic training. (U.S. Department of Defense)

engagements that took place at shorter ranges and were initiated as surprise-meeting engagements. Under such conditions, the volume of fire, rather than accurate, aimed fire, was more important in determining the outcome. This led to the conclusion that the average soldier should be armed with an automatic-firing weapon. But the increased rate of ammunition consumption also meant additional weight for the already overloaded foot soldier to carry. That problem could be offset partially by decreasing the weight of the weapon as well as the size of the ammunition. Several other major armies, especially the Germans in the last years of World War II and the Soviets immediately after the war, reached the same conclusion. The result was the development of the assault rifle.

The M-16 rifle evolved through a series of innovative designs first introduced in the mid-1950s by armament designer Eugene Stoner and the ArmaLite Cooperation. Using milled aluminum, fiberglass, and emerging composite materials, Stoner's designs were significantly lighter than all other military weapons in service. Designed in 1957, Stoner's AR-15 weighed just 5.5 pounds and fired a 5.56x45-mm cartridge. In 1959 ArmaLite sold the rights to the AR-15 to Colt Industries.

In 1960 U.S. Air Force general Curtis LeMay ordered 8,500 AR-15s as a defense weapon for Strategic Air Command (SAC) bases. In air force service it was designated the M-16. Although there were still strong advocates for the M-14 in the army, Secretary of Defense Robert S. McNamara was pushing for large-scale consolidations of all Pentagon procurement programs, including the adoption of a single standard weapon for all the armed services. In November 1963 the army also ordered 85,000 AR-15s, but insisted on the addition of an external bolt assist, thought necessary to ram the bolt into the battery physically in the event that it failed to lock into the chamber because of fouling or corrosion. While the air force version, without the external bolt assist, remained designated the M-16, the army version was designated the XM-16E1. In February 1968 it was standardized as the M-16A1.

The M-16A1 had substantial "teething" problems when first introduced. Some experts maintain that, although it is now highly improved, it is still inferior to the Soviet-designed AK-47. Touted by Colt as a "self-cleaning" design requiring little maintenance, it originally was issued without adequate numbers of cleaning kits. Furthermore, the army made some modifications to the propellant used in the 5.56-mm ammunition without sufficient field-testing. After a rash of reports of the M-16 jamming and failing to fire during combat in Vietnam, the ammunition problem was corrected, adequate cleaning supplies reached the field, and the rifle itself received a chrome-plated chamber—and later fully chromed bores—that better withstood the still corrosive effects of the ammunition.

When the U.S. Army in March 1970 began to issue the M-16 to its troops stationed in Europe, it caused a great deal of turmoil in NATO circles, because the NATO standard rifle round was supposed to be the 7.62x51-mm. By the late 1970s, the U.S. was pushing its 5.56x43-mm M-193 cartridge as the new standard NATO round. The Europeans instead adopted the Belgian-designed SS-109 round, which was similar to the American M-193 but had a steel-tipped bullet to improve penetration. The SS-109 round eventually was standardized as the M-855, and the M-856 in its tracer version.

The M-16A2 was introduced by the U.S. Marine Corps in 1982 and adopted by the U.S. Army by the end of the decade. The M-16A2 had a thicker barrel, improved adjustable-dial rear sights, a stronger buttstock, and symmetrical cylindrical front grips, as opposed to the triangular grips of the M-16A1. The M-16A2 also fired the M-855 NATO standard 5.56x43-mm round. Most significantly, the new design also eliminated the full-automatic fire option, replacing it with a three-round burst mode, which conserved ammunition and improved fire discipline. The M-16A2 weighs 8.5 pounds, is 39.5 inches long, and has a 20-inch barrel. It has a cyclic rate of fire of 800 to 900 rounds per minute, and a maximum effective range of 550 meters (600 yards).

The M-16A3 is essentially the same weapon as the M-16A2, except that it retains the full-automatic fire capability. The M-16A3 is used primarily by the U.S. Navy and issued to SEAL, Seabee, and security units. The M-16A4, introduced by the marine corps

prior to Operation IRAQI FREEDOM, is now the standard-issue rifle for front-line marine and army units. It is essentially the same as the M-16A2, except that the fixed carrying handle and rear iron sights have been replaced with an integral rail-mounting system—called a Picatinny Rail for the Picatinny Arsenal—upon which can be mounted a detachable carrying handle and a variety of optical or infrared sights and auxiliary systems.

The carbine version of the M-16 first appeared in Vietnam in 1968 as the XM-177. A modification of the M-16A1, it had a 10-inch barrel and a telescoping stock. The current standard M-4 is the carbine version of the M-16A4. Adopted in 1994, the M-4 carbine has a 15.5-inch barrel and weighs 6.9 pounds.

In early 1967 the army field-tested the XM-148 grenade launcher as a potential replacement for the M-79 grenade launcher. One of the best weapons ever put in the hands of American soldiers, the M-79 was a single-shot weapon that reloaded like a break-open shotgun. A well-trained grenadier could reload in a matter of seconds and fire a 40-mm high-explosive grenade with great accuracy out to a range of 350 meters (380 yards). For close-in defense the grenadier carried a .45-caliber pistol. The XM-148 mounted underneath the barrel of the M-16A1. The combination was heavy, and the grenade launcher was cumbersome to use and slow to reload. The XM-148 was a complete failure and was withdrawn from Vietnam in a matter of months. In the early 1970s the army introduced an improved, but still cumbersome and slow, 40-mm grenade launcher, designated the M-203, and mounted under the barrel of the M-16A2, and later the M-16A4 and M-4 carbine. Although still not as capable or flexible as the original M-79, the M-203 mounted on the shorter M-4 carbine is a bit more maneuverable than one mounted on an M-16 rifle. The M-203's maximum effective range is only 150 meters (165 yards).

The U.S. military has used a number of different sniper rifles in the Middle East Wars. Introduced in 1969, the M-21 sniper rifle was a National Match grade M-14 rifle converted by the Rock Island Arsenal. Mounted with a 3x to 9x telescopic sight, the M-21 had a maximum effective range of 690 meters (755 yards) when fired from a bipod or a supported position. The M-25 sniper rifle also is based on the M-14, but has a different sight and a different stock. Specifically designed for U.S. Army Special Forces and U.S. Navy SEAL units, the M-25 was used during the 1991 Persian Gulf War. In 1988 the M-21 was officially superseded by the bolt action M-24 Sniper Rifle, but the M-21 nonetheless remained in active service through both wars in Iraq and in Afghanistan.

The U.S. Army's M-24 sniper rifle is a single-shot, bolt-action military version of the Remington 700 sporting rifle. Introduced in 1988, it has served in both Iraq wars and in Afghanistan. It is chambered for either the 7.65x51-mm NATO round, or the .300 Winchester Magnum round. The M-24 weighs 12.3 pounds, is 43 inches long, and has a maximum effective range of 800 meters (875 yards). The U.S. Marine Corps' M-40 sniper rifle is also based on the Remington 700, but after extensive modifications by marine armorers it has a maximum effective range of 1,000 meters (1,100 yards).

The M-82 was specifically designed as a sniper/antimatériel rifle. Introduced in 1989, it fires a massive 12.7x99-mm NATO round, the exact same ammunition as the venerable M-2 .50-caliber machine gun. The M-82 weighs 29.7 pounds, is either 48 or 57 inches long, depending on its configuration, and fires out to a maximum effective range of 1,850 meters (2,025 yards). It has been used extensively in both Iraq wars and in Afghanistan. As a captured weapon, it is highly prized by insurgent forces, and there have been several instances of captured M-82s being used against American troops. Although it has been used against individual human targets, the M-82 is principally designed for use against hardened point targets at far ranges. The M-82 was recently redesignated the M-107.

The ubiquitous Soviet-designed AK-47 is arguably the world's finest assault rifle. First designed in 1944 by Mikhail Kalashinikov while he was recovering from war wounds, the weapon was derived from the hard lessons of combat that the Soviets learned at the hands of the Germans. The AK-47 combined characteristics of both the rifle and the submachine gun, most significantly the high rate of fire of the latter. The result became known in the West as an assault rifle.

With a design based heavily on the German World War II *Sturmgewehr* 44 (which literally translates to "Assault Rifle 44"), the AK-47 was standardized in 1947 and adopted for general issue by the Soviet Army in 1949. Chambered for the 7.62x39-mm round (which is not compatible with the 7.62x51-mm NATO round), the basic version of the AK-47 weighs 9.5 pounds and had a cyclic rate of fire of 600 rounds per minute and a maximum effective range of 400 meters (435 yards). It is 37.1 inches long, with a barrel length of 16.3 inches. All of the AK-series weapons are known for their rugged reliability, ease of maintenance, and moderate accuracy. They almost never jam.

Early versions of the AK-47 went through a number of design variations, starting with a stamped receiver, switching to a heavier milled receiver, and finally reverting back to a stamped receiver. The final variant appeared in 1959 and was standardized as the AK-M, which was simpler than the original version and weighed only 6.8 pounds. The AK-47 was quickly adopted and manufactured under license by many other countries, including China, Iraq, Egypt, and most of the Warsaw Pact nations. More than 55 armies worldwide have issued the AK-47 to their troops. More than 11 major AK-47 variants exist, including models with fixed stocks of wood or polymers and the more popular folding-stock models for paratroopers. More than 100 million copies of all versions have been manufactured over the years.

Introduced in 1974, the AK-74 variant of the AK-47 is chambered for the lighter 5.45x39-mm round. Weighing 6.7 pounds, it has a cyclic rate of fire of 650 rounds per minute and a maximum effective range of 500 meters (550 yards). The AKS-74U is a shortened, or carbine, version of the AK-74, in much the same manner of the M-16A4 and the M-4. The AKS-74U has a folding stock and a short 8.3-inch barrel, giving it an overall length of 27.6 inches. It weighs only 5.5 pounds and was designed for airborne and special forces troops and tank crews.

The AK-47's very shape has become an iconic symbol of liberation movements and wars of resistance. After the falls of the Taliban regime in Afghanistan in 2002 and Iraqi dictator Saddam Hussein in 2003, the units of the new Afghan and Iraqi armies being trained by the Americans still insisted on carrying the AK-47 rather than the M-16. Beyond the symbolism, however, there is a solid tactical basis for that preference. The AK-47 family of assault rifles remains superior to the M-16 family by almost every measure.

DAVID T. ZABECKI

**See also**

Rocket-Propelled Grenade

**References**

Bishop, Chris, and Ian Drury, eds. *Combat Guns: An Illustrated History of Twentieth Century Firearms.* Secaucus, NJ: Chartwell, 1987.

Poyer, Joe. *The AK-47 and AK-74 Kalashnikov Rifles and Their Variants.* Tustin, CA: North Cape Publications, 2006.

Smith, W. H. B., and Edward C. Ezell. *Small Arms of the World.* New York: Barnes and Noble, 1992.

---

# Robertson, Pat
## Birth Date: March 22, 1930

Influential Christian televangelist, right-wing political activist, and entrepreneur whose conservative views often provoke great controversy. Marion Gordon "Pat" Robertson was born on March 22, 1930, in Lexington, Virginia. His father, Absalom Willis Robertson, was a conservative Democrat and served 34 years in the U.S. Congress, including 20 years in the Senate. Majoring in history, Robertson graduated magna cum laude from Washington and Lee University in 1950. He then served with the U.S. Marine Corps in Korea, although he did not see active combat.

Robertson earned a doctorate from Yale University's law school in 1955. In 1956, after meeting Dutch missionary Cornelius Vanderbreggen, Robertson experienced a renewal of his Christian faith. Failing the bar exam, he went on to earn a divinity degree from New York Theological Seminary in 1959.

In late 1959 Robertson and his family left New York for Tidewater, Virginia, where he purchased a bankrupt UHF television station in Portsmouth, Virginia. In 1960 Robertson founded the Christian Broadcasting Network (CBN), which went on the air for the first time on October 1, 1961. He was also ordained a minister of the Southern Baptist Convention that same year. As his broadcasting empire expanded, Robertson founded the CBN Cable Network in 1977; the network was renamed the CBN Family Channel in 1988. In 1990, to maintain the nonprofit status of CBN, Robertson created International Family Entertainment, Inc., with the Family Channel as its main subsidiary.

Pat Robertson is an evangelical religious broadcaster and television executive. The founder of the Christian Coalition, Robertson is one of the leaders of the conservative Republican movement in politics and a staunch defender of Israel. (AP/Wide World Photos)

The Family Channel was subsequently sold to the Fox Network, with the stipulation that Fox broadcast Robertson's television show *The 700 Club* twice daily in perpetuity. *The 700 Club* supports conservative and fundamentalist Christian views. The news and information show is seen in more than 175 countries and broadcast in approximately 70 languages. The news segments frequently emphasize Christian eschatology, particularly as it relates to Israel and the Arab-Israeli conflict.

In 1987 Robertson ran for president on a very conservative platform. When it was apparent that he would not secure the Republican Party nomination, he urged his followers to support the candidacy of George H. W. Bush. After his unsuccessful bid for the presidency, Robertson formed the Christian Coalition, an organization that campaigns for conservative political candidates. Robertson has repeatedly condemned feminism, Islam and the Prophet Muhammad, barriers between church and state, homosexuals, liberalism, and communists. Robertson has also been a staunch defender of Israel, and an opponent of many in the Muslim world. In the aftermath of the September 11, 2001, terror attacks, Robertson agreed with his guest, the Reverend Jerry Falwell, on a broadcast of *The 700 Club,* that the tragedy occurred

in retribution for the activities of gays, feminists, abortionists, and the American Civil Liberties Union (ACLU) in the United States. He later apologized, asserting that he had not meant to blame the attacks on these groups.

MICHAEL R. HALL

**See also**

Bush, George Herbert Walker; Falwell, Jerry; Rumsfeld, Donald Henry

**References**

Boston, Rob. *The Most Dangerous Man in America? Pat Robertson and the Rise of the Christian Coalition.* Amherst, NY: Prometheus Books, 1996.

Robertson, Pat. *The New World Order.* Nashville, TN: W. Publishing Group, 1992.

## Rocket-Propelled Grenade

A short-range, shoulder-fired, infantry antitank and antimatériel weapon. Rocket-propelled grenades (RPGs) have also been used from time to time against aircraft, especially helicopters. RPG has been popularly translated as "rocket-propelled grenade," but the acronym actually stands for *ruchnoy protivotankovy granatomyot,* Russian for "handheld antitank grenade launcher." In the 1950s the production of RPGs was taken over by the Bazalt State Research and Production Enterprise, which continues to produce the Russian-made RPG today. The RPG fires a fin-stabilized, oversized explosive charge to penetrate armored vehicles. RPG warheads, ranging from 70 mm to 85 mm in diameter, come in thermobaric (fuel-air explosive), fragmentation, HEAT (high-explosive antitank), and high-explosive configurations. The most successful and commonly used RPG version today is the RPG-7 and its variants. It has been in service since 1961, when it replaced the earlier RPG-2 that had been introduced in 1949.

The RPG is a single-shot weapon, requiring reloading after each firing. In its regular military deployment, the RPG is used by a two-man team, with the gunner carrying the weapon and two additional rounds of ammunition. The assistant gunner carries an additional three rounds of ammunition, and is also trained to fire the weapon if the gunner is incapacitated. A well-trained RPG team can fire four to six rounds per minute.

The weapon comprises a reusable smooth-bore 40-mm tube that fires a front-loaded projectile. The tube is 37.4 inches long and weighs 17.4 pounds, unloaded. With the grenade loaded, it weighs 22 pounds. The weapon is controlled by two pistol-grip handles with an unusual configuration, which has the trigger mechanism located in the forward handle, with the rear grip used for additional stability. The projectile itself is made up of two parts, the warhead with a sustainer motor and the booster charge. These parts must be screwed together before loading and firing.

The RPG is recoilless, with the recoil of the rocket exiting through the breech exhaust opening. The projectile is rocket-propelled and is fired from the launcher tube by a small strip-powder

U.S. Army private first class Jennifer McDonald of the 55th Signal Company, holds a rocket-propelled grenade launcher while waiting for Canadian infantry to enter a simulated Afghan village during a training exercise at Fort Pickett, Virginia, on February 19, 2009. (U.S. Department of Defense)

charge at a velocity of about 380 feet per second. After traveling about 36 feet, a sustainer rocket ignites and increases the projectile's velocity to a maximum 960 feet per second. As the projectile leaves the launch tube, a set of stabilizing fins opens in the tail section of the projectile.

Firing the new PG-7VR tandem-charge ammunition, the RPG-7 can penetrate nearly 2 feet of steel with explosive reactive armor, 5 feet of reinforced concrete, 6.5 feet of brickwork, or 12 feet of log or sand. The RPG round can put a 2-inch hole in walls, but does not knock down the entire wall. It is highly effective in urban warfare against troops inside buildings. In this manner, it was used to great effect against American forces during the Vietnam War at the Battle of Hue in 1968.

The RPG-7 has two standard sights, a primary 2.5 power optical telescopic sight, and a permanently attached iron sight as a backup. In addition, night-vision sights may be attached in place of the optical sight. Two factors make accurate firing difficult, particularly at longer ranges, even in ideal weather conditions. First, the gunner must estimate range with a high degree of precision. This is facilitated to some degree by the optical sight, but remains a crucial factor in achieving a hit. Second, the weight of the warhead at the forward end of the projectile makes it difficult to hold the weapon steady for any length of time. This means that the gunner must line up his sights and fire quickly. Without practice, a

gunner can hit a vehicle-sized target most of the time at ranges of 150–300 feet. With training, the RPG has an effective range of 1,000 feet against moving targets and about 1,600 feet against stationary targets.

Firing the RPG into a crosswind is difficult, as is the case with all unguided projectiles. In a crosswind of seven miles per hour (mph), a first round hit at 600 feet may be expected about 50 percent of the time. Insurgents have often compensated for poor accuracy by firing large numbers of RPGs at a single target. This technique was employed against the Soviets in Afghanistan in the 1980s, during the Afghanistan-Soviet War, and against the Israelis by Hezbollah in Lebanon in the summer of 2006.

The short effective range of the RPG forces the shooter to get close to the target, either by advancing or allowing the target to approach until within effective range. Rapid firing is critical, and the launcher is carried loaded to speed the firing procedure. When fired, the RPG emits a telltale puff of exhaust smoke. This factor, combined with the short range, necessitates evasive action by the gunner immediately after firing, unless the action is meant to be a suicide mission.

The RPG can be fired from the standing, crouching, or prone positions. Relatively low "back-blast" from the rocket's exhaust also allows the use of the RPG from enclosed spaces, such as rooms in fortified positions, making the RPG particularly useful in the covered, short-range combat environment of urban operations. This feature has been used to considerable advantage in Northern Ireland, Lebanon, Gaza, and Iraq since 2003.

Originally designed as an antitank weapon, the RPG was copied from the World War II–era German Panzerfaust. Improvements in armor technology, particularly the incorporation of gapped and reactive armor in main battle tanks in the 1970s and 1980s, reduced the effectiveness of RPGs as antitank weapons. However, an advanced grenade, the PG-7BR, featuring a tandem two-stage warhead designed to defeat reactive armor, was introduced in 1988.

Nonetheless, with the development of precision antitank guided missiles, such as the Russian AT-3 Sagger, deployed in 1963, and the American BGM-71 tube-launched, optically tracked, wire-guided missile, deployed in 1971, use of RPGs against tanks declined considerably, and they were adapted thereafter mainly for use against personnel, fixed positions, and light vehicles. In addition, the fact that the RPG round self-detonates after a range of about 3,000 feet allows it to be used as a form of light artillery, spraying the target area with fragmentation.

In Mogadishu, Somalia, in 1993, RPGs shot down two American UH-60 Black Hawk helicopters. This triggered an extensive battle between U.S. forces and local militiamen, resulting in the deaths of 17 Americans. That in turn ultimately led to the withdrawal of American forces from Somalia in March 1994. Specially modified RPGs were also used by the mujahideen against Soviet helicopters in Afghanistan during the 1980s, to great effect.

In its antipersonnel role, the RPG fires two different grenades. One, a thermobaric, air-fuel explosive round, TBG-7VR, has the blast equivalent of an artillery projectile or a 120-mm mortar shell. The second, a fragmentation round, OG-7V, is particularly effective against troop emplacements. In addition, the HEAT round sprays lethal metal fragments as far as 500 feet from the point of impact.

The RPG, while originally Russian and still produced in that country, is also produced in more than a dozen other countries, and is in use in some 40 countries worldwide. In addition to regular armed forces, RPGs can be found in the arsenals of almost every nonstate military organization in the world, including terrorist groups.

RPGs are easy to use and maintain, are relatively inexpensive to manufacture, and, like the AK-47 assault rifle, are readily available on the black market at low cost. These factors, coupled with low training requirements and ease of use, have made it a chosen weapon of insurgents, terrorist groups, and other nonstate militias around the world.

The RPG has been used extensively in Vietnam, Afghanistan (both during the Afghanistan-Soviet War and in the ongoing Operation ENDURING FREEDOM since 2001), Chechnya, the Middle East, and Africa. The Provisional Irish Republican Army (PIRA) also used it against British troops in Northern Ireland during the 1970s.

In Iraq, during Operation IRAQI FREEDOM, RPGs have been the favored weapon of various insurgent forces. While they are not capable of penetrating the M-1 Abrams tank, they have been successfully used against light-armored vehicles and U.S. and coalition infantry forces. Nevertheless, a perfectly aimed RPG-7 can disable tanks, which can cause problems of a different sort. In August 2006 and again in January 2008, an RPG-29, the most potent RPG to date, did partially penetrate the FV4034 Challenger 2 tank, which is the United Kingdom's main battle tank.

Additional versions, the RPG-26 and RPG-27, are single-shot, disposable antitank rocket launchers, similar to the American M-72 light antitank weapon entered into service in 1989. Firing a variant of the tandem two-stage warhead developed for the RPG-7, these are for use only against armored vehicles.

ELLIOT P. CHODOFF

**See also**

Aircraft, Helicopters; Aircraft, Helicopters, Soviet-Afghanistan War; Antitank Weapons; ENDURING FREEDOM, Operation; IRAQI FREEDOM, Operation; Iraqi Insurgency; Somalia, International Intervention in; Soviet-Afghanistan War

**References**

*Brassey's Infantry Weapons of the World.* New York: Crane Russak, 1979.

*Jane's Infantry Weapons, 2008–2009.* Coulsdon, Surrey, UK: Jane's Information Group, 2008.

U.S. Army. *Soviet RPG-7 Antitank Grenade Launcher.* Bulletin No. 3. Fort Monroe, VA: United States Army Training and Doctrine Command, 1976.

# Romania, Role in Afghanistan and Iraq Wars

Southeast European nation with an area of 91,699 square miles and a 2008 population of 22.247 million. Romania borders Ukraine and Moldova to the north, the Black Sea to the east, Bulgaria and Serbia to the south, and Hungary to the west. A communist country from the end of World War II to 1989, Romania was a member of the Warsaw Pact, although in the last years of the Cold War its leader, Nicolae Ceauşescu, pursued a foreign policy often at variance with that of the Soviet Union. With the crumbling of the Berlin Wall in 1989 and the dissolution of communism in Eastern Europe, Romanians overthrew Ceauşescu and his personal rule that had pushed Romania to the brink of ruin, and established a multiparty democracy modeled after that of the Fifth French Republic. The Romanian constitution provides for a popularly elected president and a prime minister selected by parliament; the two share executive powers. The prime minister, who is head of government, appoints the Council of Ministers, or cabinet. The president is head of state.

Following a somewhat rocky transition to free-market democracy, Romania aligned itself squarely with the West. It joined the North Atlantic Treaty Organization (NATO) in 2004 and the European Union (EU) in 2007. Since 2000 Romania's political landscape has been dominated by the National Union (a coalition comprising the Romanian Social Democratic Party and Humanist

Party); the Justice and Truth Alliance (a coalition comprising the National Liberal Party and the Democratic Liberal Party); the Greater Romania Party; and the Hungarian Democratic Union of Romania. There were five prime ministers between December 2000 and December 2008 representing several parties and coalitions, and three presidents.

Since January 2002 Romania has deployed troops to Afghanistan as one of 10 countries providing most of the support for NATO's International Security Assistance Force–Afghanistan (ISAF) and the U.S. military campaign dubbed Operation ENDURING FREEDOM against the Taliban and its Al Qaeda allies. A total of 8 Romanian soldiers died in Afghanistan between 2002 and the end of 2008. In early 2009 Romania had approximately 800 military personnel in Afghanistan (500 of whom serve with ISAF). As recently as April 4, 2008, at the annual NATO summit held in Bucharest, Romania, Romanian president Traian Basecu reconfirmed his country's "firm" commitment to operations in Afghanistan, adding that NATO success is "crucial for the future of that country, for the war against terrorism and, consequently, for our security." After announcing the deployment of an additional 280 troops to Afghanistan in the second half of the year, however, the president expressed displeasure that other coalition nations had withdrawn their troops or relocated them to less dangerous areas—a major source of tension among countries participating in NATO's ISAF.

The 500 or so Romanian forces assigned to ISAF include: a military police platoon; soldiers posted to the ISAF command headquarters; an intelligence and counterintelligence unit; and an air unit consisting of one Lockheed C-130 Hercules transport plane—all based in Afghanistan's capital, Kabul. Since 2003 an additional unit, also based in Kabul, has assisted in training the Afghan National Army. Small teams of Romanian soldiers also serve with ISAF Provincial Reconstruction Teams, which are charged with assisting in economic development and local governance throughout the country.

Romania also deployed a battalion consisting of between 300 and 400 troops as part of Operation ENDURING FREEDOM. According to the Romanian Defense Ministry, this battalion, based in southern Zabul Province, performs such tasks as surveillance, searching locations for Taliban insurgents, supporting humanitarian activities, escorting supply convoys, providing security for other coalition forces, and blocking insurgent communication and supply lines. In Zabul Province, these Romanian troops are responsible for safeguarding about 95 miles of Highway 1, a key 600-mile-long highway linking Kabul to the southern city of Kandahar and the city of Herat to the west.

As this road is a link between three major Afghan cities, Taliban insurgents and their Al Qaeda allies have sought to gain control of the roadway, particularly in Zabul Province, which has a common border with neighboring Pakistan. Insurgents and terrorists operate from bases in Pakistan against coalition forces in Afghanistan. These insurgents have attacked and ambushed road traffic, often not distinguishing between civilian and military targets, and they have also planted roadside bombs and mines. On June 16, 2008, one Romanian soldier was killed and three wounded when their patrol convoy was ambushed and attacked by Taliban insurgents armed with rocket-propelled grenades (RPGs). The commander of Romanian forces in Zabul Province, Lieutenant Colonel Adrian Soci, summed up his mission as that of denying the Taliban control of the 95-mile stretch of highway.

Romania also supported the U.S.-led 2003 invasion of Iraq (Operation IRAQI FREEDOM), and it has cooperated closely with the United States and its partners in Iraq. Just a few days before the invasion, Romanian president Ion Iliescu declared his country's full support for all United Nations (UN) resolutions calling for Iraq's dismantlement of weapons of mass destruction (WMDs) and "the need for the international community to act against the threat of WMD posed by a regime that endangers international peace and security." Seeking closer ties with the United States and admission into NATO, Romanian leaders defended the Anglo-American–led invasion. It also allowed the United States to use one of its air bases during the 2003 invasion—including the stationing of up to 3,500 troops. A year later, the Americans announced that they would establish four military bases in Romania, and that same year Romania was rewarded for its support by being admitted into NATO. By permanently hosting American forces, Romania clearly seeks close ties with the United States, but some Romanians view this as a dangerous development, making their country a potential front-line combatant in the Global War on Terror and raising its exposure to terrorist attacks.

In July 2003 Romania deployed about 800 troops to Iraq at a reported cost of $38 million, or 3.5 percent of the country's defense budget. In 2003 the country received $25 million in military aid from the United States, $15 million of which was related to Romania's troop deployment in Iraq. Over the last five years, more than 5,300 Romanian troops have been deployed to Iraq. At the end of 2008 there were about 500 Romanian troops in the country. Romania's total troop complement in Iraq includes infantry, military policeman, and civil engineers. These forces have performed intelligence and interrogation missions, provided base security, manned a hospital, provided medical treatment for detainees and military personnel at camps Cropper and Bucca, and trained Iraqi Army units. Romania has rotated its forces every February and August. Romanian troops in Iraq have served under British and Italian command. Most of Romania's troops are stationed in southern Iraq, in the cities of Basra and Nasiriyah. Prominent among Romanian forces was the Neagoe Basarab 26th Infantry Battalion of some 400 men, based in Craiova, southern Romania, which in 2003 was deployed to the Nassiyah area of Iraq. Its task was to conduct patrols in the area, monitor traffic, perform escort missions in urban areas, support humanitarian missions, and guard fixed and mobile checkpoints. This battalion had previously taken part in peacekeeping missions in Angola, Albania, Afghanistan, and the Balkans. By the end of 2008 Romania was reportedly spending $90 million a year on troop deployments to Iraq.

In 2006, at the height of the insurgency in Iraq and after the April 26 death of a Romanian soldier in Iraq from a roadside bomb, growing opposition to Romania's presence in Iraq prompted Prime Minister Calin Tariceanu to call for the withdrawal of troops from Iraq, but President Traian Basecu dismissed such calls, claiming that it was "a dishonor to leave your allies." The president also stated that withdrawing troops could mean that Iraq would sink into civil war. On September 21, 2007, another Romanian soldier was killed and five others were wounded by the explosion of a bomb while they were on a patrol mission outside the Tallil military air base, near Nasiriyah. Another five Romanian troops were wounded in a blast when traveling in an armored personnel carrier, and earlier that month, on September 11, two Romanian officers were wounded in a missile attack on the base Camp Victory near Baghdad. Through 2008 Romania had suffered two deaths in Iraq.

On December 2, 2008, President Traian Basecu pledged that Romania would keep its troops in Iraq until the Iraqi government asked that they leave; that same day, Basecu reported that the Iraq government had requested that Romania continue its mission in Iraq until at least 2011.

STEFAN M. BROOKS

**See also**

ENDURING FREEDOM, Operation; International Security Assistance Force; IRAQI FREEDOM, Operation; North Atlantic Treaty Organization in Afghanistan

**References**

Fawn, Rick, and Raymond A. Hinnebusch, eds. *The Iraq War: Causes and Consequence.* Boulder, CO: Lynne Rienner, 2006.

Murray, Williamson, and Robert H. Scales Jr. *The Iraq War: A Military History.* Cambridge, MA: Belknap, 2005.

Ryan, Mike. *Battlefield Afghanistan.* London: Spellmount, 2007.

---

# Rove, Karl
## Birth Date: December 25, 1950

Chief political consultant to President George W. Bush whose guidance led Bush to victory in the 2000 presidential race and whose influence continued in the White House well into Bush's second term. Karl Rove was born on December 25, 1950, in Denver, Colorado. While Rove was still in high school, his parents moved to Salt Lake City, Utah. Rove attended the University of Utah from 1969 to 1971 but dropped out of school to accept a position as the

Republican Party strategist Karl Rove, shown here addressing the Jackson County Lincoln Day dinner in Jackson, Michigan, on March 24, 2007. (AP/Wide World Photos)

executive director of the College Republican National Committee. After a contentious 1973 campaign, Rove was elected to serve as national chairman of the College Republicans.

Rove moved to Texas in 1977, advising William Clements in his successful 1978 gubernatorial campaign. Clements became the first Republican governor of Texas in more than 100 years, and Rove served as his deputy executive assistant from 1980 to 1981. Rove also established a direct-mail consulting firm, Karl Rove & Associates, which was involved in hundreds of Republican campaigns on both the state and national levels between 1981 and 1999.

Although Rove was removed from the 1992 presidential reelection campaign of George H. W. Bush for allegedly leaking criticism of the campaign to journalists, the consultant nevertheless advised George W. Bush in his successful 1994 and 1998 Texas gubernatorial bids. Despite having failed to earn a college degree, from 1981 to 1999 Rove taught graduate students at the University of Texas, Austin, in the LBJ School of Public Affairs and Department of Journalism.

In 1999 Rove sold his direct-mail business and assumed the position of chief strategist for George W. Bush's 2000 presidential campaign. As a senior adviser to the president, Rove played a key role in formulating the administration's response to the terrorist attacks of September 11, 2001 (Operation ENDURING FREEDOM) and the March 2003 invasion of Iraq (Operation IRAQI FREEDOM). Rove was also credited with targeting Christian evangelicals as a crucial constituency for Bush's 2004 reelection. Although Bush's political opponents questioned Rove's campaign ethics, the political consultant accepted a position in 2005 as the president's deputy chief of staff, heading the Office of Political Affairs, the Office of Public Liaison, and the Office of Strategic Initiatives. Because of his political skills and service as the president's top adviser, Rove came to be known as "Bush's Brain."

Rove retained the president's confidence, despite a grand jury investigation into his role in the White House's unauthorized disclosure in 2003 of Iraq War critic Ambassador Joseph C. Wilson's wife, Valerie Plame, as a CIA agent. In October 2005 Lewis "Scooter" Libby, chief of staff to Vice President Dick Cheney, was indicted for perjury in the case, while Rove remained a person of interest in the investigation. After participating in closed discussions with Special Counsel Patrick Fitzgerald, who was investigating the case, Fitzgerald informed Rove in June 2006 that he would not be indicted. Rove remained in Bush's inner circle, perhaps more a sign of the president's loyalty to his staff than anything else.

With Bush's poll numbers plummeting in late 2005 and into 2006, Rove was relieved of some of his policy tasks to concentrate on Republican strategy for the 2006 congressional elections. The combative Rove remained a political lightning rod, however, and the Republicans lost badly in 2006, relinquishing control of both houses of Congress. In 2005 he asserted that after September 11 Republicans prepared for war, while liberals were more interested in offering understanding to those who had attacked America, which outraged Democrats. In August 2007 Rove resigned from the Bush administration, citing personal reasons for his departure. Since then, Rove has been on an extended speaking tour and has served as a political analyst for Fox News Network, the *Wall Street Journal,* and *Newsweek* magazine. In July 2008 Rove refused to answer a summons to testify before a committee of Congress regarding the dismissal of U.S. attorneys by the Justice Department and was held in contempt of Congress.

RON BRILEY

**See also**

Bush, George Herbert Walker; Bush, George Walker; Cheney, Richard Bruce; ENDURING FREEDOM, Operation; IRAQI FREEDOM, Operation; Wilson, Valerie Plame

**References**

Dubose, Lou, Jan Reid, and Carl Cannon. *Boy Genius: Karl Rove, the Brains behind the Remarkable Political Triumph of George W. Bush.* Washington, DC: PublicAffairs, 2003.

Moore, John C., and Wayne Slater. *Bush's Brain: How Carl Rove Made George W. Bush President.* Hoboken, NJ: Wiley, 2003.

# Rumaila Oil Field

Strategic oil field on the Iraq-Kuwait border. A source of great wealth but also great controversy, the Rumaila Oil Field has been a focus of economic and military contest in the modern Middle East for years. Straddling the borders of Iraq and Kuwait, the oil field brought both countries great wealth, yet also helped to bring them to war in 1990. Indeed, the Rumaila field is estimated to contain 14 percent of the world's known oil reserves, a staggering figure that has made controlling it a central goal of all forces with an interest in the region.

Situated mainly in southern Iraq, the Rumaila Oil Field also lies under Kuwait. As one of the most productive and lucrative oil fields in the Persian Gulf region, Rumaila provides 60 percent of Iraq's oil output, making it the most important natural resource for that nation's economy. More than 30 miles long, the Rumaila field is capable of producing an astonishing 1.6 million barrels of oil per day. More than 1,000 wells, which constantly work to bring oil to the surface, sit atop the Rumaila field.

The Rumaila field attracted international attention in August 1990 when the Iraqi military invaded Kuwait. One of the reasons cited for Iraq's annexation of the small Persian Gulf nation was the belief that Kuwait had been using transverse, or slant, drilling to extract, and then sell, oil from the Iraqi side of the Rumaila field since 1980. This oil was estimated to have been worth at least $2.4 billion on the world market, an amount greater than the war debt Iraq owed Kuwait in loans racked up during the Iran-Iraq War (1980–1988). When Kuwait refused to forgive the loan, coupled with the historic dispute over Kuwait's status and other border issues, as well as differences over oil pricing, Iraqi leader Saddam Hussein claimed that taking control of Kuwait, along with all of Rumaila's riches, was justified.

Kuwaiti oil well control specialists direct a fire control rig over a raging oil well fire at the Rumaila Oil Field in southern Iraq on March 27, 2003. (U.S. Department of Defense)

The Rumaila field gained attention yet again in February 1991 when retreating Iraqi troops, fleeing Kuwait following Operation DESERT STORM, set on fire many of the field's wells on the Kuwaiti side of the border. The burning oil wells of Rumaila, along with 85 percent of the rest of Kuwait's oil wells, became one of the most devastating ecological disasters in history, polluting not only the Persian Gulf region but sending toxic clouds thousands of miles east of Rumaila. Indeed, since the fires at Rumaila, physicians have seen rates of various cancers and other fatal diseases skyrocket in the region, causing many to question the relationship between the toxins and these illnesses.

In March 2003, at the beginning of Operation IRAQI FREEDOM, nine of Rumaila's oil wells were set alight yet again by Iraqi troops retreating from advancing Anglo-American–led coalition forces. Nevertheless, keeping the oil pumping from Rumaila was a vital goal of the occupiers, and was met only with the work of a legion of skilled engineers supported by many troops. Within a few weeks of the invasion, Rumaila was pumping at near-normal capacity, securing the maintenance of its contribution to the world's oil needs.

NANCY STOCKDALE

**See also**

DESERT SHIELD, Operation; DESERT STORM, Operation; Hussein, Saddam; Iran-Iraq War; Iraq, History of, Pre-1990; Iraq, History of, 1990–Present; IRAQI FREEDOM, Operation; Kuwait; Oil; Oil Well Fires, Persian Gulf War

**References**

Klare, Michael T. *Blood and Oil: The Dangers and Consequences of America's Growing Dependency on Imported Petroleum.* New York: Owl Books, 2005.

Randall, Stephen J. *The United States Foreign Oil Policy since World War I.* 2nd ed. Montreal: McGill-Queens University Press, 2005.

Yergin, Daniel. *The Prize: The Epic Quest for Oil, Money, and Power.* New York: Simon and Schuster, 1993.

# Rumsfeld, Donald Henry
### Birth Date: July 9, 1932

Congressman, government official, ambassador, and U.S. secretary of defense (1975–1977, 2001–2006). Born in Chicago, Illinois, on July 9, 1932, Donald Rumsfeld graduated from Princeton University in 1954. He was commissioned in the navy through the Naval Reserve Officers' Training Corps (NROTC) and served during 1954–1957 as a pilot and flight instructor. Rumsfeld remained in the reserves, retiring as a navy captain in 1989.

Rumsfeld began his long association with Washington as an administrative assistant to Representative David S. Dennison Jr. of Ohio during 1957–1959, then joined the staff of Representative Robert Griffen of Michigan. During 1960–1962 he worked for an investment-banking firm. In 1962 Rumsfeld was elected to the U.S. House of Representatives as a Republican from Illinois and served until 1969, when he resigned to accept appointment as director of the Office of Economic Opportunity and assistant to President Richard M. Nixon (1969–1970). He was then counselor to the president and director of the Economic Stabilization Program (1971–1973). During 1973–1974 he was U.S. ambassador to the North Atlantic Treaty Organization (NATO) and thus avoided any involvement with the Watergate scandal.

When Nixon resigned and was succeeded by Gerald Ford, Rumsfeld returned to Washington in August 1974 to serve as chair of the new president's transition team. He was then Ford's chief of staff. During 1975–1977 Rumsfeld served as secretary of defense. At age 43, he was the youngest person to hold that position. During Rumsfeld's 14 months in office, he oversaw the transformation of the military to an all-volunteer force, as well as post–Vietnam War reforms. He also actively campaigned for additional defense appropriations and to develop weapons systems, such as the B-1 bomber, the Trident missile system, and the MX missile. Ford honored Rumsfeld for his government service in 1977 with the Presidential Medal of Freedom, the nation's highest civilian award.

Rumsfeld left government service when President James (Jimmy) E. Carter took office in January 1977. Following a brief period as a university lecturer, Rumsfeld entered private business. He was chief executive officer, then chairman, of G. D. Searle, the pharmaceutical company, from 1977 to 1985. From 1990 until 1993 Rumsfeld served as chairman and chief executive officer of General Instrument Corporation. During 1997–2001, Rumsfeld was chairman of Gilead Sciences, Inc. Concurrent with his work in the private sector, Rumsfeld served on numerous federal boards. He also served in the Ronald Reagan administration as special presidential envoy to the Middle East during 1983–1984.

In January 2001 newly elected President George W. Bush appointed Rumsfeld to be secretary of defense for a second time. Rumsfeld then became the oldest individual to hold the post. Bush charged him with transforming the military from its Cold War emphasis on major conventional warfare into a lighter, more efficient force capable of rapid deployment around the world. Rumsfeld worked to develop network-centric warfare, an approach to military operations that relies on technological innovation and integration of weapons and information systems to produce more firepower with fewer personnel. In addition, Rumsfeld initiated the restructuring of the U.S. military presence throughout the world and the closure and consolidation of bases. Rumsfeld also refocused the strategic forces of the United States by emphasizing missile defense and space systems following the 2002 U.S. withdrawal from the Anti-ballistic Missile Treaty. He made certain of the loyalty of top officers by personally reviewing all higher promotion decisions at the three-star level and above. He angered a number of congressmen when he canceled such weapons programs as the Comanche helicopter and Crusader self-propelled artillery system.

Donald Rumsfeld was U.S. secretary of defense during 1975–1977 and again during 2001–2006. The confrontational Rumsfeld was one of the strongest proponents of a U.S. invasion of Iraq but has been roundly criticized for his failure to provide adequate ground forces for the invasion and recognize the potential for insurgency operations. (U.S. Department of Defense)

Rumsfeld's reform efforts and his restructuring of the military were overshadowed by his role in the post–September 11, 2001, Global War on Terror. As secretary of defense and a proponent of neoconservatism, Rumsfeld oversaw the military operation that overthrew the Taliban regime in Afghanistan (Operation ENDURING FREEDOM), although the failure to capture Osama bin Laden tarnished the otherwise successful military campaign.

Rumsfeld was one of the foremost proponents of military action against Iraq, teaming up with President Bush and Vice President Richard Cheney to overcome opposition from within the cabinet by Secretary of State Colin Powell. Indeed, Rumsfeld was a major architect of the Bush Doctrine, which called for preemptive military action against potential adversaries. Rumsfeld then directed the 2003 invasion of Iraq (Operation IRAQI FREEDOM). In the campaign, Rumsfeld employed a strategy that relied on firepower and smaller numbers of "boots on the ground."

While the overthrow of the Iraqi regime of Saddam Hussein was highly successful, the subsequent occupation of Iraq did not go well. Within the Pentagon, there were complaints of Rumsfeld running roughshod over those who disagreed with him. Certainly he was much criticized for his outspoken, combative management style, as when he pointedly referred to the French and German governments, which had opposed the war, as "Old Europe." But there was good reason to criticize his military decisions and specifically his overly optimistic assessment of the situation that would follow the overthrow of Hussein. Disbanding the Iraqi Army to rebuild it from scratch came to be seen in retrospect as a major blunder. Rumsfeld had also ignored previous recommendations that 400,000 U.S. troops would be required for any occupation of Iraq. The actual number of troops involved was only about one-third that number. As a consequence, Iraqi arms depots, oil-production facilities, and even the national museum were looted in the immediate aftermath of the invasion.

Occupation troops were unable to halt a growing insurgency. As U.S. casualties escalated and Iraq descended into sectarian violence, calls for Rumsfeld's ouster came from Republicans as well as Democrats, and even a number of prominent retired generals. Just prior to the 2006 midterm elections, an editorial in all the *Military Times* newspapers demanded his removal.

Rumsfeld resigned on November 8, 2006. This came a week after President Bush had expressed confidence in his defense secretary and said that he would remain until the end of his term, but it was also one day after the midterm elections, in which the Republican Party lost its majorities in both the House of Representatives and the Senate. The election was widely seen as a referendum on the Iraq War and, by extension, Rumsfeld's leadership of it. President Bush named former Central Intelligence Agency (CIA) director Robert Gates to succeed Rumsfeld. Rumsfeld is reportedly seeking a publishing contract for his memoirs, which are likely to be a spirited defense of his policies in the George W. Bush administration.

TOM LANSFORD AND SPENCER C. TUCKER

**See also**

Bush, George Walker; Bush Doctrine; Cheney, Richard Bruce; ENDURING FREEDOM, Operation; IRAQI FREEDOM, Operation; Neoconservatism; Powell, Colin Luther

**References**

Graham, Bradley. *By His Own Rules: The Ambitions, Successes, and Ultimate Failures of Donald Rumsfeld.* New York: PublicAffairs, 2009.

Scarborough, Rowan. *Rumsfeld's War: The Untold Story of America's Anti-Terrorist Commander.* Washington, DC: Regnery, 2004.

Woodward, Bob. *Bush at War.* New York: Simon and Schuster, 2002.

———. *Plan of Attack.* New York: Simon and Schuster, 2004.

———. *State of Denial: Bush at War, Part III.* New York: Simon and Schuster, 2006.

# Russia, Middle East Policy, 1991–Present

Geography, oil, and economic imperatives have made the Middle East an area of considerable strategic interest for the Russian Federation since its beginnings in December 1991, although not until very recently has the nation possessed the economic and military means with which to flex its muscle in the region. Nevertheless, its actions in the Middle East have been fairly limited, especially when compared to its predecessor state, the Soviet Union, which made the region a pivotal Cold War battleground for some 40 years. From 1991 to 2003 or so, Russia, a state hobbled by financial crises and political turmoil, took a far more pragmatic and reactive stand in the Middle East. This does not mean, however, that the Soviet successor state abdicated its strategic or economic interests and commitments in the region. Since the late 1990s, in fact, the Kremlin has showed a renewed interest in the region. But this has not been driven by the old Soviet ideologies. Rather, it is based upon economic imperatives, traditional Russian conceptions of security and international power, and concerns about American hegemony in the Middle East.

As Soviet leader Mikhail Gorbachev's attempts to reform the Soviet Union (glasnost and perestroika) in the mid- and late 1980s morphed into a political sea change that witnessed the dissolution of the Soviet Empire in Eastern Europe, Soviet troops were also being withdrawn from the disastrous Afghanistan-Soviet War. By 1989, when the last Soviet troops left Afghanistan, the Soviet Union was reeling from a stagnant economy and a considerable loss of international prestige. By the time the Persian Gulf War began in January 1991, the Soviets, who did not participate in that conflict, had essentially given a green light to the international coalition designed to oust Iraqi forces from Kuwait. While the Kremlin did engage in some last-minute (and unsuccessful) diplomacy to avoid military confrontation, it did not stand in the way of either the United Nations (UN) or the American-led coalition that was about to invade Iraq. It had neither the economic nor political will to do so, even if it had objected to the operation. Such a scenario would have been virtually unthinkable during the Cold War. By the time the Persian Gulf War ended in February, the dissolution of the Soviet Union was but 10 months away. With the familiar bipolarity of the Cold War gone following the collapse of the Soviet Union, many in the Middle East worried about U.S. hegemony and unilateralism, especially following the September 11, 2001, terror attacks.

Under Russian presidents Boris Yeltsin, Vladimir Putin, and Dmitry Medvedev (Putin's handpicked successor), Russian policy in the Middle East has largely eschewed the ideologically oriented prescriptions of the communist era. Russian policies now tend to be grounded in pragmatism and economic opportunism. And while these administrations in theory have supported democracy in the region, they were (and are) more concerned with political and economic stability. Another change from the Soviet era is the role of private enterprise in the direction and creation of foreign policies. In the pre-1991 era, the state controlled Soviet industry. In addition to promoting economic autarky, the government largely dictated the policies and direction of industry. Thus, there was no process of push-pull in foreign policymaking. The state dictated industrial policies that were at all times consonant with its foreign policies, and vice versa. In the post-1991 era of emerging free market capitalism, however, Russian industrial concerns in the Middle East have begun to play a more central role in overall Russian policy in the region. To spur and protect Russian private

A Russian technician rides his bicycle in front of the main reactor of the nuclear power plant in Bushehr, Iran, February 26, 2006. (AP/Wide World Photos)

investments in the Middle East, for example, the Kremlin has had to cleave to policies that are economically and politically advantageous to Russian industry, and some of those may not necessarily be consonant with Russian foreign policy objectives.

Much to the annoyance and occasional chagrin of the West, the Russians continued to play a role in the Middle East, the natural consequence of long-standing ties to the region. The Soviet Union had supplied weapons, technology, and advisers to Iran for decades. From the 1990s, the United States government sought to press Russia into ending its support for Iran's nuclear program.

Russia also inherited long-standing ties with both Iraq and Syria. Russian diplomats have so far played a masterful juggling act by maintaining relations with Syria and Iran while at the same time keeping relations with Washington and London on a relatively even keel. In 2005 Putin visited Israel, Egypt, and the Palestinian National Authority (PNA). In January 2005 Syrian president Bashar al-Assad traveled to Moscow on an official state visit. Clearly, the Kremlin had to balance its policies in the Middle East with its relations with the United States.

Some of the Kremlin's caution in the region is derived from its long-standing struggle with Chechnya, the renegade Russian Republic territory that is peopled largely by Sunni Muslims. From 1994 to 1996 Yeltsin fought a bloody—and unsuccessful—war

with Chechnya, which desired to be completely independent. In 1999 military conflict between Russia and Chechnya inaugurated the Second Chechen War, which is still technically being fought. Hoping to quell Chechen rebels and court Chechen moderates, Putin has tried to cultivate positive relations with Islamic states to demonstrate Moscow's presumption of being an honest broker. Interestingly, in their immediate aftermath Putin was quick to decry the September 11 attacks, showing great sympathy for the United States. At the same time, however, he linked Moscow's war in Chechyna with the larger Global War on Terror, as if to justify Russian actions there.

Russia has been supportive of the Israeli-Palestinian peace process since 1993 and has courted positive relations with Tel Aviv. In the 1980s and 1990s millions of Jews, most of them emigrating to Israel and the United States, left the Soviet Union and its successor states. Russian businesses have also benefited from economic ties with Israel. Relations between Moscow and Tel Aviv have not been without tension, however, as the Kremlin's support of Iran and Syria has at times caused much dismay among Israeli policymakers.

Since the 1990s the Kremlin has engaged in major economic and technology deals with Iran, as Russian-Iranian ties owe much to the two nations' proximity and shared geopolitical interests.

Indeed, Iran concluded a major arms agreement and became Russia's third-largest arms client (after China and India) in the 1990s. Iran purchased advanced weapons, including Russian-made Kilo-class submarines, T-72 tanks, S-300 surface-to-air missiles (SAMs), and Su-24 and MiG-29 aircraft. Iran also acquired the rights to produce Russian weapons on its own soil. Iranian officers have attended Russian military schools, and Russian advisers are training Iranian forces in the use of Russian weapons. In 1995, under American pressure, Russia agreed not to conclude any new arms deals with Iran, but Putin abrogated this agreement in 2000. A particular U.S. concern has been the transfer of nuclear and missile technology. Russia sold Iran important missile components and manufacturing technologies in the 1990s and trained Iranian scientists in ballistics, aeronautic design, booster design, and missile guidance. Indeed, Iranian Shahab ballistic missiles were derived from Soviet SS-4 and SS-5 designs. In 1995 Russia obtained a contract to build a nuclear power plant at Bushehr, and despite U.S. protests remained determined to finish the project. Russia subsequently agreed to provide fuel for Bushehr and to build additional reactors in Iran.

The Russians notably abstained from voting when the International Atomic Energy Agency (IAEA) found Iran in noncompliance with Nuclear Non-Proliferation Treaty safeguards on uranium enrichment and reprocessing in September 2005, and opposed referring the issue to the UN Security Council. Russia has consistently opposed the imposition of sanctions on Iran and has sought to protract negotiations for as long as possible. Moreover, in late 2006 Russia began delivering advanced Tor-M1 air-defense missiles to Iran that would seriously complicate any preemptive military action to destroy Iran's nuclear facilities. In 2007 and again in 2008, Russia steadfastly refused to consider invoking tougher sanctions against Iran, even in the face of growing evidence that the Iranians were engaging in prohibited uranium-enrichment efforts and were stonewalling the UN and the IAEA.

In recent years Russia has, on occasion, expressed its support of Syria, and in 2005 President Putin defended the position of Hezbollah in Lebanon, which used to be funded by the Syrians and Iranians (who in turn have received weapons systems and armaments from Russia). Moscow's links with Iran, Syria, and Hezbollah have strained relations with Washington over the last several years, and Moscow's repeated dilution of U.S. efforts to enact UN sanctions against Iran for its nuclear program has only added to the tension.

In March 2003, as the Anglo-American invasion of Iraq commenced, Putin issued an unequivocal if not prescient statement labeling the endeavor a grave political miscalculation. Unlike the 1991 war against Iraq, the Russians refused to endorse in any way the 2003 invasion. While Putin stopped short of warning Washington and London of any Russian countermeasures, he made it clear that the move was not in the best interests of Moscow or the Middle East as a whole. The ongoing war in Iraq therefore continues to strain Russia's relations with the West.

During the Israeli War with Lebanon in 2006, the Putin government did not openly oppose the Israeli incursion into southern Lebanon. Nevertheless, it was a well-known fact that Hezbollah had obtained Russian-made Spandrel, Kornet, and Vampir anti-tank missiles from Syria and Iran. These missiles played a major role in blunting Israel's armored offensive. Once more, the Kremlin was attempting to hedge its bets by staying out of any direct conflict in the region. But behind the scenes, it played an important role while attempting to appear neutral.

Very recently, some in the United States have begun to assert that Russia is seeking to revive the Soviet Union's hegemonic foreign policies. Both U.S. presidential candidates in 2008, for instance, decried the Russian incursion into Georgia in August of that year, a conflict revolving around the breakaway province of South Ossetia. Republican nominee John McCain was particularly bellicose toward the Kremlin, and he suggested that Russia be evicted from both the G8 and World Trade Organization (WTO).

While McCain may well be overstating the Kremlin's intentions and capabilities in the Middle East, there can be no doubt that Russia's improving economic situation and military readiness over the past few years will pose a challenge for Western leaders, especially in their Middle East policies. Skyrocketing oil and natural gas prices since 2005 have resulted in a windfall for the Kremlin's coffers. This in turn has allowed the Russians to begin rebuilding their armed forces and has given them more clout on the world stage. While it is difficult to envision a Russian Middle East policy that is entirely at odds with that of the United States and other Western powers, rising Russian economic and political influence will certainly be a force to be reckoned with in the years to come.

JAMES D. PERRY AND PAUL G. PIERPAOLI JR.

**See also**

DESERT STORM, Operation; Global War on Terror; Hezbollah; Iran; IRAQI FREEDOM, Operation; Israel; Lebanon; Syria; United Kingdom, Middle East Policy; United States, Middle East Policy, 1945–Present

**References**

Levgold, Robert, ed. *Russian Foreign Policy in the 21st Century and the Shadow of the Past*. New York: Columbia University Press, 2007.

Mandelbaum, Michael, ed. *The New Russian Foreign Policy*. New York: Council on Foreign Relations, 1998.

Nizameddin, Talal. *Russia and the Middle East: Toward a New Foreign Policy*. New York: Palgrave Macmillan, 2000.

Rumer, Eugene. *Dangerous Drift: Russia's Middle East Policy*. Washington, DC: Washington Institute for Near East Policy, 2000.

# Rwanda

Nation located in East Africa, historically known as Ruanda or Ruanda-Urundi. Rwanda is bordered on the west by the Democratic Republic of Congo, on the south by Burundi, on the east by Tanzania, and on the north by Uganda. Most of the country lies between 1,600 and 6,500 feet above sea level, with some mountain ranges soaring above 13,000 feet. Its climate is primarily mountain highland, with a small tropical savannah region on the eastern side.

Officially called the Republic of Rwanda, its capital city is Kigali. Rwanda is 10,169 square miles in area, slightly smaller than the state of Massachusetts, with a current population of approximately 8 million people. The population comprises about 85 percent Hutu, 14 percent Tutsi, and 1 percent Twa. Christianity is the prevailing religion (including Roman Catholicism and Protestantism); only a small percentage of Rwandans practice Islam.

During the 1880s Rwanda was part of German East Africa and included parts of present-day Tanzania, Burundi, and Rwanda. Germany primarily ruled through local native leaders. During World War I, Belgian troops seized Rwanda on June 6, 1916. After the war, the League of Nations and then the United Nations (UN) granted Belgium the responsibility of preparing Rwanda for independence. Belgium's decision to grant the Tutsis a greater role in the early colonial government created animosity among the Hutus, which would have far-reaching repercussions. Prior to Rwandan independence, which took effect on July 1, 1962, Belgium shifted its support toward the Hutus during the latter part of colonial rule.

The years between 1959 and 1962 saw an increase in ethnic violence directed against the Tutsis, resulting in numerous deaths among them. Other Tutsis fled to bordering countries, many of them to Uganda. Under UN oversight, Rwanda became an independent nation on July 1, 1962, and was governed by the majority Hutus. Following a 1963 anti-Tutsi campaign launched by the Hutus that resulted in as many as 14,000 deaths, the country became a one-party dictatorship under Hutu control. For the next several decades, Rwanda suffered under the yoke of dictatorship in which Tutsis and their Hutu supporters were brutally suppressed. Its economy barely functioned, and its government was rife with cronyism and corruption.

In 1987 the Rwandan expatriate Tutsis residing in Uganda formed the Rwandese Patriotic Front (RPF) to overthrow the Hutu government in Rwanda. The ensuing years saw sporadic ethnic conflicts within Rwanda, which continued on a small scale until 1993, when the Rwandan genocide began.

The death in a plane crash in 1994 of Rwanda president Juvénal Habyarimana, a moderate Hutu, marked the beginning of systematic attacks against Tutsis. Although it is virtually impossible to get an accurate count of the resulting deaths, it is estimated that some 800,000 Tutsis were killed during the genocide, while many others fled Rwanda into neighboring countries. Except to rescue their own citizens, the Western powers, including the United States, were unwilling to intervene in Rwanda to stop the horrific bloodshed. Furthermore, the UN was powerless to act in the face of Western indifference.

In the aftermath of the genocide, the RPF continued fighting against the Hutu government, eventually taking over the country. Paul Kagame became president in 2000 and led Rwanda into an unsuccessful and bloody conflict with the Democratic Republic of Congo, which ended in 2002. During Kagame's administration, however, Rwanda slowly became safer and more stable.

The failure of the United States to intervene in Rwanda, its quick exit from Somalia (Operation RESTORE HOPE) in 1995, and its limited responses to terrorist attacks against American interests in Yemen and Africa in the late 1990s seemed to demonstrate Americans' unwillingness to risk U.S. lives for a greater cause. Some have speculated that this may have played a part in the decision of the Al Qaeda terrorist organization to attack the United States on September 11, 2001, believing it could do so with relative impunity. However, these attacks initiated the U.S. Global War on Terror, which then focused on the Middle East.

Since the early 2000s, Rwanda has slowly and steadily rebuilt its economy and infrastructure, and has voiced a keen interest in transforming its economy from one that is based largely on subsistence agriculture to one that is knowledge based. Such a transformation, however, will be slow going. Nevertheless, Kagame had made a concerted effort to attract outside investment and boost economic activity. By 2007 the nation was deemed safe for tourists, and only one mortar attack, in a rural area, was launched during that entire year.

WYNDHAM WHYNOT

**See also**

Al Qaeda; Global War on Terror; Somalia, International Intervention in

**References**

Nugent, Paul. *Africa since Independence: A Comparative History*. New York: Palgrave Macmillan, 2004.

Schwab, Peter. *Africa: A Continent Self-Destructs*. New York: Palgrave Macmillan, 2001.

# S

## Sabah, Jabir al-Ahmad al-Jabir al-
Birth Date: June 29, 1926
Death Date: January 15, 2006

Thirteenth emir of Kuwait (1977–2006) and a member of the ruling family of al-Sabah. Born in Kuwait on June 29, 1926, Sheikh Jabir al-Ahmad al-Jabir al-Sabah was the third son of the late Sheikh Ahmad al-Jabir al-Sabah, who was emir and head of state in Kuwait from 1921 to 1950. Sources report that Sheikh Jabir was educated at the al-Mubarakiyya School, al-Ahmadiyya School, and al-Sharqiyya School, and was further tutored privately in Arabic, English, religion, and science.

In 1949 Sheikh Jabir served as chief of public security in the Ahmadi oil fields. In 1962 he was appointed minister of finance, and under his direction Kuwait was transformed into a prosperous state with one of the world's highest per capita incomes. In 1965 he was appointed prime minister of Kuwait, and was subsequently named crown prince in 1966. He was thereby officially recognized as the heir apparent to the throne of Kuwait. In December 1977 Sheikh Jabir succeeded Sheikh Sabah al-Salim al-Sabah, his uncle, as emir.

A confluence of external and internal events dominated Sheikh Jabir's rule. During the 1980s a marked increase in political violence in Kuwait disturbed this historically peaceful country. This violence included the bombing of the U.S. and French embassies in December 1983, and an assassination attempt on the emir by a suicide bomber in 1985. In 1986, prompted by such events, Sheikh Jabir dissolved the National Assembly, exercising his powers as stipulated in Kuwait's constitution. Almost immediately, he took measures to curb civil and political rights. In 1991, however,

Sheikh Jabir al-Ahmad al-Jabir al-Sabah was head of the ruling 1,200-member Sabah clan and emir of Kuwait from 1977 until his death in January 2006. (AP/Wide World Photos)

after the Persian Gulf War, Sheikh Jabir reinstated the National Assembly; by 1992 many press and civil restrictions were lifted.

On August 2, 1990, following a long-running border dispute between Kuwait and Iraq, Iraq invaded and occupied Kuwait with the stated intent of annexing it. This was the first time in Kuwait's history that it had been placed under direct foreign rule. During and after the occupation, Sheikh Jabir was subjected to severe criticism for immediately fleeing to Saudi Arabia and for setting up a government-in-exile there. In March 1991, after the conclusion of the Persian Gulf War, the emir returned to Kuwait. He assumed his former role as head of state, in spite of the fact that he had all but removed himself from the struggle to liberate Kuwait from Iraqi occupation.

In 1999, despite opposition from tribal and Islamist factions in parliament, Sheikh Jabir approved an amendment allowing women the right to vote and run for office; the bill was rejected by a 41–21 vote in the National Assembly. The bill was reintroduced and approved in June 2005, however, when parliament finally granted Kuwait's women political rights.

Sheikh Jabir also helped found the Cooperation Council for the Arab States of the Gulf, or Gulf Cooperation Council (GCC), in 1981, an organization comprising Kuwait, Saudi Arabia, Bahrain, Qatar, Oman, and the United Arab Emirates (UAE). The GCC provided vital support during the Iraqi occupation of Kuwait. In September 2000 Sheikh Jabir suffered a stroke and traveled to the United Kingdom for medical treatment, returning four months later. Under Sheikh Jabir's watch, Kuwait remained a staunch ally of the United States and the West. His government fully supported the invasion of Afghanistan after the September 11, 2001, terror attacks and also supported the Anglo-American–led invasion of Iraq in 2003. Indeed, Kuwait continued to serve as a major staging area for coalition troops in the Middle East.

In July 2003 Sheikh Jabir announced that his brother—Prime Minister Sheikh Sabah al-Ahmad al-Jabir al-Sabah—would lead the formation of a new government. Sheikh Sabah was already the country's de facto leader because of the emir's failing health. Sheikh Jabir al-Ahmad died on January 15, 2006, in Kuwait. He was automatically succeeded by Crown Prince Saad Abdullah al-Salim al-Sabah, who resigned within nine days. On January 29, 2006, Sheikh Sabah al-Ahmed al-Jabir al-Sabah was confirmed as the new emir of Kuwait.

KIRSTY MONTGOMERY

**See also**
Gulf Cooperation Council; Kuwait

**References**
Casey, Michael. *The History of Kuwait*. Westport, CT: Greenwood, 2007.
Countrywatch. *Kuwait: 2006 Country Review*. Houston, TX: Countrywatch, 2006.
Mansfield, Peter. *Kuwait: Vanguard of the Gulf*. London and Sydney: Hutchinson, 1990.
Metz, Helen Chapin. *Persian Gulf States: Country Studies*. 3rd ed. Washington, DC: Federal Research Division, Library of Congress, 1994.
Zahlan, Rosemarie Said. *The Making of the Modern Gulf States: Kuwait, Bahrain, Qatar, The United Arab Emirates, and Oman*. London: Unwin Hyman, 1989.

# Sabkha

A relatively flat area of salty soil that is often found on or near the coast in arid regions of the world, especially in the vicinity of North Africa and the Persian Gulf. Sabkhas can be divided into two major types: coastal and inland. Both forms occur where the water table periodically reaches the surface. A coastal sabkha is found along tidal flats or in adjacent low-lying areas where tidal actions contribute to fluctuations in the water table. Inland sabkhas are typically found in low-lying areas, often between sand dunes, where water collects and later evaporates. In some cases, strong winds remove enough surface material to leave what remains in contact with the water table. Some sabkhas develop a thick salt crust over a bog that may have the consistency of quicksand. The variety in types of sabkhas as well as seasonal variations in their moisture content make them potential barriers to travel, especially by heavy vehicles.

The high temperatures and low humidity of Middle East and North African deserts cause water to evaporate rapidly. Freshwater runoff typically picks up minute amounts of salt. In other parts of the world, these salts are carried to the oceans. In arid regions, however, limited rainfall often prevents formation of perennial streams that could flush these salts into the sea. Instead, water may collect and evaporate in depressions, leaving the salts behind.

Although often lumped together, a sabkha does differ from a playa or kavir. A kavir, such as the Dasht-e Kavir (Salt Desert) in Iran, is a salt flat that may contain a shallow lake after rainfall, but is normally dry. Indeed, the Bonneville Salt Flats in Utah is renowned as a favored location for testing high-speed vehicles. In contrast, sabkhas are continuously wet, marshy, or water-filled, and they constitute formidable barriers for vehicular traffic, particularly military units with tanks, armored personnel carriers, and other heavy vehicles. In Iraq, the marsh areas are part of the Shatt al-Arab, the waterway that forms after the conjoining of the Tigris and Euphrates rivers.

During World War II, sabkhas in the Qattara Depression in northwestern Egypt formed a barrier that confined most military operations to the relatively narrow coastal strip. Although generally regarded as impassable, British Commonwealth units of the Long Range Desert Group traversed it during some of their operations against Nazi Germany's Afrika Korps. When the Germans retreated through south-central Tunisia, they found that the Shatt al-Djerid offered natural protection from flanking attacks.

In southern Iraq, the Tigris and Euphrates rivers converge at Basra to form the Shatt al-Arab waterway, which continues to the Persian Gulf. Numerous sabkhas, as well as extensive marshes, are found in this region, especially along the Faw (Fao) peninsula. During the Iran-Iraq War of 1980–1988, Iranian forces seized the Faw peninsula in a surprise offensive in 1986. Despite the Iraqis' advantages in armor, the sabkhas and marshes kept most of their armored units confined to main roads, where they were more vulnerable to Iranian antitank units. It was not until 1988 that the Iraqis recaptured the peninsula, conducting a number of amphibious operations in their own surprise offensive. During the early stages of Operation IRAQI FREEDOM, British forces reportedly had similar difficulties in the region.

Farther to the south are examples of inland sabkhas, which posed a significant obstacle during Operation DESERT STORM. February 1991 was unusually cold, with rain and snow falling throughout the region. When the ground war began, 60,000 American and French troops with XVIII Airborne Corps drove into southern Iraq to cut the main highway along the Euphrates River connecting Baghdad with Basra and Kuwait. The 24th Infantry had to cross the "Great Dismal Bog," a series of sabkhas approximately 45 miles southwest of Nasiriyah. Recent storms had turned them into bogs, slowing the advance considerably. Nevertheless, the 24th Cavalry found a passable, albeit circuitous, route through the sabkhas, allowing the 24th Infantry to seize its objectives. But the twisting course led to greater fuel consumption, which added to the logistical burden of supply units.

Immediately after Iraq invaded Kuwait in August 1990, speculation abounded regarding the possibility that Iraqi forces would invade Saudi Arabia and other Persian Gulf states. Had that occurred, Iraqi armored units would have encountered sabkhas blocking off-road approaches to Jubail, Dhahran, and other towns in Saudi Arabia, as well as the highway leading into Qatar. And Sabkhat Matti would have proven an even more formidable barrier to off-road movement in Abu Dhabi. Throughout the Middle East and North Africa, sabkhas represent a category of seasonally changing obstacles to the movement of civilian or military vehicles.

CHUCK FAHRER

**See also**

DESERT STORM, Operation; Faw Peninsula; IRAQI FREEDOM, Operation; Shatt al-Arab Waterway; Topography, Kuwait and Iraq; Umm Qasr, Battle of

**References**

Cordesman, Anthony H., and Abraham R. Wagner. *The Lessons of Modern War,* Vol. 4, *The Gulf War.* Boulder, CO: Westview, 1996.

Director of Military Survey. *Operational Navigation Chart, H-6.* London: HMSO, 1986.

Held, Colbert C. *Middle East Patterns: Places, Peoples, and Politics.* 4th ed. Boulder, CO: Westview, 2006.

Scales, Robert H. *Certain Victory: The U.S. Army in the Gulf War.* Washington, DC: Brassey's, 1994.

Underwood, James R., and Peter L. Guth, eds. *Military Geology in War and Peace.* Boulder, CO: Geological Society of America, 1998.

# Sadat, Muhammad Anwar
**Birth Date: December 25, 1918**
**Death Date: October 6, 1981**

Egyptian nationalist, vice president (1966–1970), and third president of Egypt (1970–1981). Born on December 25, 1918, in Mit Abu al-Kum, near Tala in the Minufiyya Province of Egypt, to an Egyptian father and a Sudanese mother, Muhammad Anwar Sadat attended the Royal Egyptian Military Academy, from which he graduated in 1938 as a second lieutenant. Early on he supported the Misr al-Fatat (an Islamist youth party) and the Muslim Brotherhood. His first posting was in the Sudan, where he met fellow nationalist and future Egyptian president Gamal Abdel Nasser. Sadat joined with Nasser in forming the secret organization that would eventually be called the Free Officers Movement, comprising young Egyptian military officers dedicated to ousting the British and replacing the government of King Farouk (Faruq).

In May 1941 Sadat took part in a plot led by ex-chief of staff General Aziz al-Masri and a group referred to as the Ring of Iron to aid the Axis powers in expelling the British from Egypt. British authorities foiled the plot, and Sadat was among those jailed in 1942. Escaping from prison in 1944, he was arrested again in 1946 and tried in the planning of the assassination of Amin Uthman. Released in 1948, Sadat regained his commission in 1950.

Anwar Sadat, president of Egypt from 1970 until his assassination in 1981. Sadat is remembered for his part in concluding the 1979 Camp David Peace Treaty between Egypt and Israel. (U.S. Department of Defense)

A group of reformist army officers known as the Free Officers Movement carried out the July 23, 1952, bloodless coup against King Farouk. Thereafter, Sadat served loyally under Nasser. He edited the newspapers *al-Jumhuriyya* and *al-Tahrir* from 1953 to 1956, when he became a minister of state and chaired the United Arab Republic (UAR) National Assembly during 1960–1968. He was general secretary of the Egyptian National Union from 1957 to 1961.

In 1969 Sadat became vice president of Egypt, and on Nasser's death in September 1970, he became temporary president. Sadat was elected president by the National Assembly on October 7, and in November he was elected president of the Arab Socialist Union.

In domestic affairs Sadat soon began to move away from Nasser's positions, introducing the Corrective Revolution, which ousted Nasser's supporters. In the 1970s the regime announced its intent to introduce political reforms, but other than allowing a tiny, insignificant, and divided opposition, this promise went unfulfilled. Egyptians were granted easier access to foreign travel, but by the end of the 1970s censorship had been extended even to verbal discussion of Sadat's policies. However, earlier, as a means of defeating his leftist opponents, journalists with pro-Islamist and anti-Nasserist views were allowed to publish. In 1976 Sadat ran unopposed for a second six-year term as president and was confirmed.

In 1974 Sadat began a new economic policy, called the Open Door policy (*infitah*), which encouraged foreign investment, not only from oil-rich Arab states but also from the West, and was intended to privatize industries. The government encouraged expansion of the private sector, although tax and other regulation structures inhibited this. This economic liberalization was slow to bring tangible benefits to the Egyptian people, however. After several decades of socialism and expropriation of properties, foreign governments were wary of investing in Egypt, while many Egyptians disapproved of the reforms.

Nasser's prêt project, the Aswan High Dam that provided electricity and controlled the yearly flooding of the Nile and was therefore of benefit to agriculture and the economy, also proved a mixed blessing. While it provided much more electricity, it prevented the annual silting that had enriched the soil and also adversely affected aquatic life in the Nile. Given an increase in population, the bulk of which required assistance, and a jump in imports, Egypt experienced a growing trade imbalance. This meant that the Sadat government was continually forced to seek new foreign loans and refinancing of existing loans, while the national debt continued to increase. At the same time, the World Bank and other granting agencies demanded massive changes, including privatization and an end to subsidies. This prospect threatened Egypt's many poor.

In foreign affairs, Sadat severed ties with the Soviets and then improved ties with the West, particularly the United States. Sadat also improved relations with Persian Gulf states, which had been tense in certain periods under Nasser. Many wealthy Gulf Arabs preferred to vacation in Egypt, and some of the banking and services sector in Beirut had shifted there.

The Camp David Accords between Egypt and Israel were so unpopular in the Arab world that relations with other Arab nations suffered for a few years, during which time Egypt was ousted from the Arab League. However, Egypt was brought back into the Arab fold by Sadat's successor, Hosni Mubarak.

Libyan strongman Muammar Qaddafi, a great admirer of Nasser, earnestly sought an Egyptian-Syrian-Libyan federation, which was signed in Damascus in August 1971. This arrangement was never enacted, however, and soon after, in April 1974, Cairo announced that it had discovered a plot to overthrow the Egyptian government and pointed to Qaddafi as being behind it.

When Sadat became president, Egypt had already experienced some years of tensions with military and technical advisers from the Soviet Union; these advisers were soon asked to leave the country. Indeed, Nasser had been moving away from the Soviet Union at the time of his death. Part of the reason for this may have been the refusal of the Soviet Union to sell advanced weapons systems to Egypt. On July 18, 1972, Sadat ordered the expulsion of all Soviet military advisers and experts from Egypt and placed all of their bases in the country under Egyptian control.

Meanwhile, Sadat did all he could to prepare Egypt for war, especially by increasing military training. He privately expressed the view to United Nations (UN) envoy Gunnar Jarring that he was willing to recognize the State of Israel and even to sign a peace treaty with the Jewish state but that the precondition for this was the return to Egypt and the Palestinians of all territory conquered by Israel. Sadat feared that the present situation of no war and no peace might go on indefinitely and that the world would ultimately come to accept this as a permanent situation, giving Israel de facto control over the annexed territories. Sadat believed that the only way to change this was for him to initiate a new war, which in turn would produce an international crisis that would force the world to deal with the situation once and for all.

Over a protracted period, Egyptian forces engaged the Israelis in low-level skirmishing across the Suez Canal. Then, on October 6, 1973 (Yom Kippur, the Jewish Day of Atonement), Sadat launched a massive cross-canal attack that caught the Israeli government and military completely by surprise, partly because of its timing. He had carefully coordinated his plans with Syria in order to oblige the Israelis to fight a two-front war. In the Yom Kippur (Ramadan) War, Syrian forces simultaneously struck Israel in the north along the Golan Heights. The war ended with Israeli forces poised to achieve total victory. On the Golan Heights front, Israeli forces held during desperate fighting and then counterattacked deep into Syria. Against Egypt, the Israelis had rallied from early setbacks, crossed the canal, and were in position to drive on Cairo. However, the Egyptians had achieved a psychological victory with their initial crossing of the canal. This and the relatively satisfactory cease-fire brokered by the United States and the Soviet Union earned Sadat great respect among his people and in the Arab world.

Painfully aware that only the United States could elicit any substantive concessions from Israel and seeking to orient Egypt to the West and overcome his leftist opponents, Sadat completely severed relations with the Soviet Union in March 1976 and began working with the Americans toward a peace settlement with the Israelis. In a courageous move, on November 19, 1977, Sadat traveled to Jerusalem on a two-day visit, becoming the first Arab leader to make an official trip to the Jewish state. There he met with Prime Minister Menachem Begin and even addressed the Israeli Knesset. In September 1978 Sadat signed the Camp David Accords. This agreement and the peace treaty of March 1979 produced a comprehensive peace agreement with Israel. Sadat's journey to Jerusalem and the accords were highly unpopular in the Arab world. While many of his countrymen realized that Egypt could not tolerate the cost of future wars with Israel, Sadat was nevertheless criticized by highly respected politicians and large sectors of the population for what they saw as a dishonorable arrangement with the Jewish state.

Although the Camp David Accords and the peace treaty of March 1979 were, in the long run, beneficial for Egypt, which with its larger army had borne the brunt of much of the previous three wars, many in the Arab world saw them as a great betrayal and Sadat as a traitor.

Throughout the late 1970s, several extremist Islamist groups had been operating in Egypt. One attempted to assassinate Sadat at the Egyptian Military Academy in 1976 (the Military Academy Group). Another, the Takfir wa al-Higrah, went underground and kidnapped the former minister of Awqaf before massive arrests. Students and militants in the Gamaat Islamiya and the Islamic Jihad movement were also organizing against the government and carrying out attacks in certain parts of the country. In September 1981 the Sadat government simultaneously cracked down on extremist Muslim organizations and many other non-Islamist and liberal opponents of the president, arresting more than 1,600 people in the process. Among them was the brother of Sadat's future assassin, Khalid al-Islambuli. Sadat's strong-arm tactics angered many in the Arab community and only exacerbated his problems, which included an increasing gap between the wealthy and new middle classes and the poor, and charges that he had quashed critical voices through force.

On October 6, 1981, Sadat was assassinated in Cairo while reviewing a military parade commemorating the Yom Kippur (Ramadan) War. The assassins were radical Islamist army officers who belonged to the Islamic Jihad organization, which hoped to overthrow the government and had bitterly denounced Sadat's un-Islamic rule and failure to implement Islamic law, his peace overtures with Israel, and the politically ruthless tactics of the state. Sadat was succeeded in office by Hosni Mubarak.

SPENCER C. TUCKER, DALLACE W. UNGER JR., AND SHERIFA ZUHUR

**See also**
Arab-Israeli Conflict, Overview; Begin, Menachem; Camp David Accords; Carter, James Earl, Jr.; Egypt; Nasser, Gamal Abdel

**References**
Beattie, Kirk J. *Egypt during the Sadat Years.* New York: Palgrave, 2000.
Finklestone, Joseph. *Anwar Sadat: Visionary Who Dared.* Portland, OR: Frank Cass, 1996.
Hirst, David, and Irene Beeson. *Sadat.* London: Faber and Faber, 1981.
Sadat, Anwar. *In Search of Identity: An Autobiography.* New York: Harper and Row, 1978.

# Saddam Line, Persian Gulf War

Following the Iraqi invasion and occupation of Kuwait on August 2, 1990, the Iraqi army constructed a network of fortifications along Kuwait's southern border with Saudi Arabia. These fortifications came to be known as the Saddam Line. The Iraqi invasion of Kuwait led to widespread international protest and the subsequent formation of an international military coalition to liberate Kuwait.

The Iraqi plan for defending Kuwait from a coalition attack was quite straightforward. Just inside Kuwait's border with Saudi Arabia, Iraqi army engineers constructed a network of fortifications designed to inflict casualties and slow down any enemy advance into Kuwait. This line of defense became known to the Americans as the Saddam Line. Next, the Iraqis massed infantry and mechanized divisions in a second line designed to contain and counterattack any enemy breakthroughs of the first line. Finally, the Iraqis held elite Republican Guard divisions in reserve for a strategic counteroffensive. The Iraqi intention was to contain any coalition advance, inflict heavy casualties, and force the enemy to the negotiating table.

The Saddam Line itself consisted of two belts of mines, sand berms, and concrete bunkers. The Iraqis also constructed a network of ditches that could be flooded with oil from Kuwaiti wells, then set afire to turn the battlefield into a smoky inferno. Farther north, the Iraqis had sited 800 South African–manufactured 155-mm long-range artillery pieces. The Iraqi artillery was preregistered to concentrate fire on likely invasion routes from Saudi Arabia.

Breaking the Saddam Line posed challenges for coalition planners. However, the coalition's relentless six-week aerial bombing campaign significantly reduced the combat capability of Iraqi troops manning the Saddam Line, many of whom were Shiite conscripts who had little enthusiasm for the war. Indeed, many of these troops had deserted or surrendered even before the coalition ground offensive began on February 24, 1991.

Coalition forces attacking into southern Kuwait, primarily the U.S. 1st and 2nd Marine divisions, used line charges fired from Amtrack armored personnel carriers to blast a narrow path through the Saddam Line's minefield. The line charges, propelled by rockets, consisted of heavy cords with attached explosives that detonated when the rope had fallen to the ground. M-60 and M-1 tanks equipped with steel plows then widened the pathway, along with conventional mine-detecting equipment, so that follow-on tanks could pass through.

Clearing and widening the minefields proved a laborious task, especially because the Iraqis had used British-manufactured L-9

Bar mines captured from Kuwaiti stockpiles. Made of plastic, the Bar mines could not be located by American mine detectors, which detected only metal mines. Some of the line charges also failed to detonate properly. The mine-clearing process took so long that some marine tanks ran out of gas and had to be refueled between the first and second Iraqi lines, a highly dangerous procedure. As a result, several marine tanks and vehicles were disabled or destroyed by Iraqi mines. Had Iraqi artillery been more competent and not suffered such serious losses from the air campaign, the marines might well have taken heavy casualties. Regardless, the marines were able to force a number of passages through the Saddam Line on February 24. Surviving Iraqi defenders in the Saddam Line were not inclined to put up much of a resistance, and the road into Kuwait was soon open.

PAUL W. DOERR

**See also**

DESERT STORM, Operation; DESERT STORM, Operation, Coalition Ground Forces; DESERT STORM, Operation, Ground Operations

**References**

Gordon, Michael R., and General Bernard E. Trainor. *The Generals' War: The Inside Story of the Conflict in the Gulf.* New York: Little, Brown, 1995.

Pollack, Kenneth M. *Arabs at War: Military Effectiveness, 1948–1991.* Lincoln: University of Nebraska Press, 2002.

# Sadr, Muqtada al-
## Birth Date: August 12, 1973

Influential religious figure in the Iraqi Shia community, leader of the Sadriyun that included the Mahdi Army militias, and considered by many to be the most populist of Iraqi Shiite leaders. The fourth son of the famous Iraqi cleric Muhammad Sadiq al-Sadr, Muqtada al-Sadr was born on August 12, 1973, in Baghdad. Sadr became a political leader with an enhanced following as a consequence of his nationalist stance against the coalition presence in Iraq, beginning in 2003. In Shia Islam in Iraq, believers follow a living cleric, but since Sadr had not attained the rank of his illustrious father in scholarly training or publications, he did not inherit the loyalty of many in his father's network of mosques who preferred a more senior cleric. Yet Sadr acquired a loyal following of his own and, during a period of political truce with the Iraqi government, sought to enhance his standing by continuing his own religious training. Like his father and Iraq's highest Shiite religious authority, Grand Ayatollah Sayyid Ali Husayn al-Sistani, Sadr drew support from a network of mosques but also from extensive charitable and social services provided to impoverished Shia communities in various areas of Baghdad. He also has followers in many other cities and areas of southern and central Iraq. Sadr became especially popular in the large slum areas in Baghdad, including the Thawra area, which became known as Sadr City from the strength of his followers there.

The elder Sadr was a revered member of the Iraqi Shiite clergy who was assassinated, along with his two elder sons, in 1999. It is widely believed that the assassination was ordered by Iraqi leader Saddam Hussein. Muqtada al-Sadr is also related to the late highly respected leader Imam Musa al-Sadr, who created a popular movement among the Shia of Lebanon.

Muqtada al-Sadr spoke out fiercely against the actions of the U.S.-led coalition in Iraq despite his opposition, and that of his followers, to Saddam Hussein's dictatorial government. Sadr's opposition to the coalition presence was based on both political and religious considerations. After the U.S. Coalition Provisional Authority (CPA) closed Sadr's newspaper *al-Hawza* on March 28, 2004, and there had been numerous attacks against him in the American-funded Iraqi press, Sadr mobilized his militia, known as the Mahdi Army. This was to protest what he perceived as the CPA's attempt to eliminate his organization prior to the transfer of authority to Iraqi officials, scheduled for June 30, 2004. The subsequent protests turned violent when a key Sadr aide was arrested on April 3, 2004. The situation was further enflamed two days later when CPA administrator L. Paul Bremer issued a warrant for Sadr's arrest and essentially declared him an outlaw. Sadr's Mahdi Army subsequently seized control of several cities in southern Iraq, provoking the worst crisis for the U.S.-led occupation since the spring of 2003, especially as the Mahdi Army held the loyalty of the most fiercely anti-Baathist groups in the country.

During the ensuing week of violence, Sadr sought refuge in the Imam Ali Mosque in Najaf, the holiest shrine in Shia Islam. Sadr's popularity soared during this period because he appeared to be the only Iraqi leader willing to actively resist the occupation. All others, even Ayatollah Sistani, appeared to be passively silent or even acquiescent to the Western authorities. Sadr declared a cease-fire on April 10, 2004, ostensibly to observe a three-day religious holiday, but momentum had also shifted as the CPA retook certain key bases in southern cities. In subsequent negotiations, the CPA called for Sadr to surrender but refrained from overt attempts to arrest him.

In late August 2004, following more than three weeks of renewed fighting between Mahdi Army fighters and U.S. forces, Sadr's forces withdrew from the Imam Ali Mosque. Sadr issued a statement urging his fighters to lay down their arms in line with an agreement he had reached with Ayatollah Sistani. On August 27, 2004, members of the Mahdi Army began surrendering their arms to Iraqi police. But Iraqi prime minister Iyad Allawi renewed the violence when he refused to honor the tenuous truce; fighting ensued, especially in Sadr City. Sadr, in an attempt to distance himself from the acrimony, was thereafter careful not to involve himself directly in Iraqi politics.

In October 2006 the Mahdi Army seized control of Amarah in southern Iraq. A pitched battle ensued between Iraqi security forces and the militiamen. Sadr implored the Mahdi soldiers to lay down their arms, and some have speculated that he had not authorized the Amarah offensive and had lost control over Mahdi Army

Muqtada al-Sadr, center, during prayers at the Al-Kufa Mosque in Najaf on July 18, 2003. Thousands gathered to listen to his speech opposing the new U.S.-appointed government. (AP/Wide World Photos)

groups in that area. Sadr's plea was largely ignored. In February 2007 the U.S. media reported that Sadr had fled to Iran in anticipation of the security crackdown attendant with the U.S. troop-surge strategy. Sadr, however, had merely gone into seclusion in Iraq, and during his two-month hiatus he sharply condemned the U.S.-led occupation and called for Iraqi security forces not to cooperate with occupation forces. In 2008 Sadr called for a truce and implored the Mahdi Army to lay down its arms, in response to myriad negotiations with Iranian and Iraqi leaders following several months of brutal fighting between the Mahdi Army and Iraqi government forces. Sadr continued to condemn the U.S. government and coalition forces' occupation in Iraq, as that was the primary concern of his followers. In late 2008 he called for attacks against U.S. troops in Iraq in retaliation for the Israeli incursion into the Gaza Strip seeking to defeat the radical Palestinian group Hamas. However, this was largely a rhetorical gesture, as his followers continued to observe the truce in place.

PAUL G. PIERPAOLI JR. AND SHERIFA ZUHUR

**See also**

Allawi, Iyad; Bremer, Jerry; Hussein, Saddam; Khomeini, Ruhollah; Mahdi Army; Shia Islam; Sistani, Sayyid Ali Husayn al-

**References**

Cockburn, Patrick. *Muqtada: Muqtada al-Sadr, the Shia Revival, and the Struggle for Iraq.* New York: Scribner, 2008.

Diamond, Larry. *Squandered Victory: The American Occupation and the Bungled Effort to Bring Democracy to Iraq.* New York: Times Book, 2005.

Nasr, Vali. *The Shia Revival: How Conflicts within Islam Will Shape the Future.* New York: Norton, 2006.

---

# Sadr City, Battle of
## Start Date: March 26, 2008
## End Date: May 11, 2008

A battle during the Iraq War that occurred March 26–May 11, 2008. In the Battle of Sadr City, coalition forces principally fought elements of the Mahdi Army. Sadr City is one of nine administrative districts of Baghdad, built in 1959 to ease a housing shortage in the capital city. It is home to more than 1 million Shia Muslims, many of them poor. Part of the district had been known as Thawra and was termed Saddam City by the Americans in 2003. American forces in the coalition then began to call the area "Sadr City" from the strength there of Muqtada al-Sadr's followers, known as the Sadriyun. The coalition forces in Iraq had long sought permission from Iraqi prime minister Nuri al-Maliki to subdue the Jaysh al-Mahdi (JAM) militias, which they called the Mahdi Army. The Sadriyun, or Sadrists, possessed militias just as did the Dawa Party and the Supreme Council of the Islamic Revolution in Iran (SCIRI). However, these militias also clashed with them, and therefore the coalition had to some degree been influenced by the competition of the various Shia political forces. The Americans claimed that certain elements from the Jaysh al-Mahdi were obtaining arms from Iran, although their competitors, such as the Badr Brigades, were more clearly linked with Iranian support, or at least had been in the past. Maliki was reluctant to approve coalition operations against fellow Shiites, particularly as he might not have been elected had it not been for his good relations with Muqtada al-Sadr and his followers. Also, the largest Shia party in the country had been even closer to Iran than the Sadriyun, who were seen as an Iraqi-based party. Another concern was the vulnerability of the poor civilian population of Sadr City. However, under pressure from Washington, when 12 rockets were launched from the Sadr City area into the Green Zone on March 25, 2008, Maliki approved a joint Iraqi-American response.

Forces of the Iraqi Army 11th Division entered Sadr City on March 26, supported by the U.S. Army 3rd Brigade Combat Team, 4th Infantry Division, commanded by Colonel John Hort. As the Iraqis moved in, American combat engineers began construction of a concrete barrier across the southern one-third of Sadr City in order to push insurgent forces back beyond rocket range of the coalition-controlled Green Zone. An American Stryker brigade and other supporting coalition units, including troops from the 2nd Stryker Cavalry Regiment, succeeded over the course of a month in building a three-mile-long wall across the southern third of the neighborhood. The concrete "Gold Wall" was constructed from sections 12 feet high by 5 feet wide, placed individually by crane. The "Gold Wall" and the construction of barriers has been highly criticized by Iraqis and others who believe that defense of perimeters or erection of "sanitized zones" is untenable in the long run.

The fighting in Sadr City was some of the heaviest in the Iraq War. Significantly, for the first time, an unmanned aerial vehicle (UAV), or drone, was placed under the direct control of a battlefield commander. Utilizing helicopters and armed and unarmed UAVs, and leveraging the persistent surveillance ability of the surveillance drones—which could follow a target on the ground for hours—American forces were able to strike insurgent targets deep within Sadr City. Precision attacks directed or conducted by UAVs killed numerous insurgent mortar and rocket teams.

The heaviest fighting took place on April 28 as militia forces, emboldened by the lack of American air support during a heavy sandstorm, attacked along the heavily contested area of al-Quds Street, known to allied forces as Route Gold. Dozens of militia fighters were killed in ensuing firefights. Mahdi Army forces marshaled heavy firepower to oppose the construction of the concrete wall. Although they employed .50-caliber sniper rifles and RPG-29 rockets, and detonated more than 120 Iranian-made mines with explosively forged projectiles against coalition forces, the militias nevertheless failed to prevent construction of the wall.

Of the some 2,000 American troops in the battle, 6 were killed. Some 5,000 men of the Iraqi Army took part in the battle; their casualty figures were not reported. The Mahdi militia numbered perhaps between 2,000 and 4,000 members; they are believed to have suffered some 700–1,000 casualties.

The forces of the Supreme Islamic Iraqi Council (Majlis al-'A'la al-Islami al-'Iraqu, or SIIC), formerly known as the SCIRI, are heavily represented in the new Iraqi Army; consequently the action was understood as one of intrasectarian and political warfare. Muqtada al-Sadr took refuge in Iran but called for his fighters to adhere to a truce, or this campaign could have led to a much wider popular rebellion against the new Iraqi government. Unfortunately, violence continued in Baghdad with numerous large-scale suicide bombings there and in other cities in the spring of 2009. These, however, were primarily Sunni attacks on Shia or Iraqi and coalition forces, or against the Awakening Shaykhs.

The Battle of Sadr City was seen as a significant victory for coalition forces; however, it came at the expense of Prime Minister Maliki's impartiality and credibility to some degree, making him appear to be a creature of the coalition. Sadrist forces and Maliki reached a cease-fire agreement on May 11, 2008, bringing an end to the major fighting in Sadr City.

SHAWN FISHER AND SHERIFA ZUHUR

**See also**

Iraqi Insurgency; Mahdi Army; Maliki, Nuri Muhammed Kamil Hasan al-; Sadr, Muqtada al-; Stryker Brigades

**References**

Gordon, Michael R., and Stephen Farrell. "Iraqi Troops Take Charge of Sadr City in Swift Push." *New York Times,* May 21, 2008.

Gordon, Michael R., and Alissa J. Rubin. "Operation in Sadr City is an Iraqi Success, So Far." *New York Times,* May 22, 2008.

Paley, Amit R. "U.S. Role Deepens in Sadr City." *Washington Post,* April 21, 2008.

# Said, Edward
## Birth Date: November 1, 1935
## Death Date: September 23, 2003

Literary theorist, writer, critic, pianist, and pro-Palestinian activist. The son of Wadie Said of Jerusalem and Hilda Musa of Nazareth, Edward Said was born on November 1, 1935, in Jerusalem, then part of the British Mandate for Palestine. He spent his early years living in Cairo and Jerusalem and visiting Lebanon every year. When he was 12 years old and attending St. George's School in Jerusalem, his immediate family left for Egypt. Then, his remaining relatives and neighbors in West Jerusalem were forced out.

At age 16 he attended the Mount Hermon School in Massachusetts before attending college. He received his bachelor's degree from Princeton University in 1957 and his master's degree from Harvard University in 1960. During these years, his family and many friends would be forced to leave Egypt as a consequence of arrests and sequestrations under Gamal Abdel Nasser's Arab socialist policies. Said's parents urged him to avoid politics, and they sent his four younger sisters to college in the United States as well.

In 1963 Said joined the faculty at Columbia University as a professor of English and comparative literature studies. A year later he earned his PhD from Harvard. Said spoke Arabic, English, and French fluently, and he was proficient in Latin, Spanish, Italian, and German. He remained on the Columbia faculty for several decades, ultimately becoming the Old Dominion Foundation Professor of Humanities in 1977. He also taught at Harvard, Johns Hopkins, and Yale universities.

Said's early work focused on the novelist Joseph Conrad. Perhaps Said's greatest intellectual contribution was his critique of orientalism that in turn spawned postcolonialist theory in political, literary, and historical forms. In his seminal book *Orientalism* (1978), he examined the prejudices and presumptions of the major European scholars of the Middle East. He argued that the European interest in the Middle East was rooted in a political agenda of domination and served as the justification for imperialist, colonial policies in the region. Said believed that these scholars and other writers had created a false, romantic, and exotic sense of the region, thus rendering it an "Other" and an enemy. He claimed that these counterproductive stereotypes still held sway in Western culture, and he worked to shape the study of and policy toward the Middle Eastern, African, and Asian worlds. In essence, he broke new ground in both cultural studies and literary theory. He also profoundly shook the academic establishment, opening the door to new Middle Eastern scholars and interpretations.

Said is also identified with postmodernism and discursive theory, which was perhaps best illustrated by the work of French philosopher Michel Foucault. The deconstructionist theory as propounded by the French literary theorist Jacques Derrida can also be found in Said's work. Said's critics claimed, however, that he had merely helped to create another type of academic dogma in place of orientalism. In another important work, *Culture and Imperialism* (1993), Said showed the breadth of imperial vision and how it deals with resistance. He also opened the door in the 1980s to the hiring of other Arab academics, who with the exception of language specialists or Israeli Arabs, had been mostly excluded from academic institutions.

As a Palestinian activist, Said initially supported the creation of a single, independent Palestinian state. He later lobbied for the establishment of a single Jewish-Arab state. He was an independent member of the Palestinian National Council (PNC), the Palestinian parliament in exile, during 1977–1991. He left the organization because of Palestine Liberation Organization (PLO) chairman Yasser Arafat's decision to support Iraq in the 1991 Persian Gulf War. Afterward, Said became an outspoken opponent of Arafat. For different reasons, he denounced the 1993 Oslo Accords as counterproductive to Palestinian interests. In 1995 an infuriated Arafat banned the sale of Said's books to Palestinians.

In 2000, however, Said softened his position toward Arafat when the PLO leader turned down Israeli peace offers at the Camp David Summit in 2000.

Said also wrote against the cultural boycott of Israeli Jews. His love of music and friendship with conductor-musician Daniel Barenboim led to the founding of a unique workshop in Europe for young Palestinian, Arab, and Israeli musicians to study with such figures as Barenboim and cellist Yo-Yo Ma. Said died on September 23, 2003, in New York City after a decade-long struggle with leukemia.

DANIEL KUTHY AND SHERIFA ZUHUR

**See also**

Arafat, Yasser; DESERT STORM, Operation; Nasser, Gamal Abdel; Palestine Liberation Organization

**References**

Hussein, Abdirahman. *Edward Said: Criticism and Society.* London: Verso, 2004.
Said, Edward. *Culture and Imperialism.* New York: Knopf, 1999.
———. *The End of the Peace Process: Oslo and After.* New York: Vintage Books, 2001.
———. *Orientalism.* New York: Pantheon, 1978.
———. *The Question of Palestine.* New York: Vintage Books, 1992.

# Said, Qaboos bin Said al-
## Birth Date: November 18, 1940

The sultan of Oman since 1970, Qaboos bin Said al-Said was born on November 18, 1940, in Salalah, Province of Dhofar, the son of Sultan Said ibn Tamir. He spent seven years in Great Britain during his youth and attended the Royal Military Academy at Sandhurst. He returned to Oman in 1965, much influenced by Western ideas; as a result, his conservative father placed him under virtual house arrest.

In 1970 Said, with the aid of military forces loyal to him, staged a coup d'état and deposed his father, who then went into exile in Great Britain. Said set about trying to modernize his country and bring it into the international political mainstream. As such, he built new roads, extended educational opportunities, and greatly improved medical care. He also fought off a guerrilla movement, known as the Dhofar Rebellion, in the early years of his rule that had been supported by the Soviet Union and its allies in South Yemen. That conflict finally ended in 1975.

During the first 15 or so years of his rule, Sultan Said maintained strong ties with the United States, sometimes alienating other Arab countries in the process. Indeed, he was one of only two Arab leaders to support the 1978 Camp David Accords signed by Israel and Egypt and brokered by the United States. In 1985 Said began to cultivate relations with the Soviet Union. He also attempted to assume a stronger stance in regional politics during the 1980s. In 1981 he brought Oman into the Gulf Cooperation Council and several years later tried to bring an isolated Iran into

The sultan of Oman since 1970, Qaboos bin Said al-Said has led his country into the modern era and maintained close ties with the United States, though he has taken an independent path in foreign affairs in recent years. (Embassy of the Sultanate of Oman Information Attache)

the organization. He also worked hard to stabilize the region in the wake of the 1991 Persian Gulf War, which he strongly supported and to which he dispatched 6,300 troops.

In 1996 the sultan issued a decree promulgating a new basic law that clarified royal succession, provided for a legislative council and a prime minister, and guaranteed basic civil liberties for Omani citizens. Said, who still rules with an iron hand, holds the positions of prime minister, minister of foreign affairs, defense, and finance. His rule has been fairly progressive, however, especially vis à vis Persian Gulf standards, and since 1994 he has appointed numerous women to government posts. Said has also been a cooperative partner in the U.S.-led war on terrorism since September 2001, allowing coalition forces overflight and basing rights. He was less supportive of the Iraq War, which commenced in 2003.

In October 2004, as a result of many of Said's reforms, which included the institution of universal suffrage in 2003, Oman held its first free elections for the economic advisory council, known as the Shura Majlis Council. Still, however, the sultan continues to exercise absolute power, and government institutions operate in a merely advisory capacity.

PAUL G. PIERPAOLI JR.

**See also**

Gulf Cooperation Council; Oman, Role in Persian Gulf and Iraq Wars

**References**

Kechichian, Joseph A. *Oman and the World: The Emergence of an Independent Foreign Policy.* Santa Monica, CA: RAND Corporation, 1995.

Owtram, Francis. *A Modern History of Oman: Formation of the State since 1920.* London: I. B. Tauris, 2004.

# Salafism

Term describing branches of reformist Islam as well as a widespread contemporary purist movement, an attempt to return to traditional Islamic roots and practices. Salafism (*salafiyya* in Arabic) is derived from the Arabic *salaf,* and means "(righteous) predecessors" or "(righteous) ancestors" in reference to the first three generations of Muslims. Some adherents seek a return to the spirit of that period.

Modernist reformers in the late 19th and early 20th centuries have been considered salafists. The name also applies to fervently observant or activist Sunni Muslims who follow the teachings of Muhammad abd al-Wahhab in the 18th century and other scholars. These latter are sometimes called the neo-salafis.

A key concept undergirding salafism is that the first several generations of Muslims were intent on following the Sunnah, or tradition of the Prophet, and sincere in their efforts to live according to Islamic teaching. One common thread in the different branches of salafism is that Islam must be cleansed of illicit innovations, known as *bid'ah.* The modernist school argued that tradition had rendered various principles rigid and imitative and that a return to previous creative principles would be of benefit. This school implicitly supported some innovations.

Both the modernist and purist strands of salafism have impacted such organizations as the Muslim Brotherhood. The purist trend of salafism has informed the worldviews of such organizations as Al Qaeda in Mesopotamia or Al Qaeda in Afghanistan and Pakistan. However, most Muslims who abide by the precepts of salafism and who may be found in many countries are neither violent nor radical.

The term "salafiyya" or "salafism" dates back hundreds of years and was applied to movements like the Ikhwan al-Safa arising in previous centuries. The term "salaf" appears in a number of early *hadith,* or sayings of the Prophet and his companions, as well as other writings, such as the *tafsirs* of al-Tabari and Ibn Kathir.

The title was applied in the late 19th century to various Muslim thinkers, including Jamal ad-Din al-Afghani and his disciple Muhammad Abduh, mainly in response to British colonialism in the Middle East.

Jamal ad-Din al-Afghani was born and raised in eastern Iran and was probably Shiite by doctrinal association. Nevertheless, in his effort to see the revival of Islam as a counter to British colonial policy, he strove to hide his doctrinal sympathies, focusing instead on building a philosophical opposition movement to oppose British occupation of Muslim lands. He traveled extensively and typically portrayed himself in ways that were not consistent with his background and training. In each instance when his benefactors, whether in Great Britain, Egypt, or Istanbul, became suspicious of him and his motives, Afghani would depart to another area of the world to continue his self-appointed mission to throw off the British yoke. Wherever he went he continued to preach the revival of the Islamic community, or *ummah,* as based on the lives of the Prophet and his early companions.

In his desire to defeat British colonialism, Afghani was willing to engage in a wide range of political and insurgency-type activities, ranging from simple fund-raising to endorsing assassination attempts against those Middle Eastern rulers he considered to be British puppets. He spoke openly of killing the leader of Persia, Nasir ad-Din Shah, and one of his disciples eventually carried out the deed in 1896. Although supportive of the Ottoman Empire as the current seat of the Islamic caliphate, Afghani spent his last years in Istanbul virtually as a political prisoner of the empire's sultan, and died of cancer in 1897.

Afghani's influence almost vanished after his death, but later his name would be resurrected as a folk hero to the revived Islamic movement in the Middle East. The principles of salafism would be pushed eloquently by one of his main disciples, Muhammad Abduh. Abduh collaborated with Afghani on a number of publishing projects and helped to popularize salafist ideas through what became known as "the Islamic League." He was savvy politically, and was able to secure the position as Grand Mufti of Egypt in 1899, a post he held until his death.

In some ways Abduh's influence was greater than Afghani's because Abduh was seen by many as more moderate and mainstream, even though his ideas were essentially no different than his mentor's. His writings were more readily accepted, and included a *tafsir* of the Qur'an along with other works defending the unity of Allah from Christian influences stemming from British colonial policy.

Abduh's ideas would have a tremendous impact on the thinking of Hassan al-Banna and the founding of the Muslim Brotherhood in Egypt in 1928. The focus of the brotherhood as well as other revivalist Muslim societies was initially based on personal piety and raising money through the imposition of *zakat,* or the charitable tax. Soon these activities turned to political activism and the brotherhood surged to the forefront of political thought in the struggle against British colonial occupation of the country. Although Banna was assassinated in 1949, the ideas of the brotherhood spread throughout the Middle East and into the rest of the Islamic world, especially through the work of such apologists as Sayyid Qutb and Yusuf al-Qaradawi, and have in large measure become the foundation of the Islamic revival movement.

The principles of salafism revolve around several key issues that involve the literal interpretation of the Qur'an and adopting certain aspects of the lifestyle of the Prophet and his companions. Shunning Western dress and grooming became important outward displays of this movement, although this was not always consistently done for political reasons. Coupled with this was a revival of interest in the writings of the Hanbalite jurist Ibn Taymiyyah, who discussed the conflict inherent between the *salaf* and the *khalaf,* or the authentic believers of the Prophet with those who are merely substitutes of the real thing.

This led to sporadic conflict in the Muslim world between the members of the salafist movement and the governments of the region. Efforts by Arabic governments to suppress salafism culminated in the judicial execution of Sayyid Qutb by the Egyptian government of Gamal Abdel Nasser in 1966, and the destruction of the town of Hama, which had become the base of the movement in Syria, by the government of Hafiz al-Asadin 1982 in which close to 30,000 people died. These attempts to destroy the movement were only temporary, however. Rebounding from these setbacks, the brotherhood continued its political activities throughout the Islamic world, spreading even into Europe and the United States.

Another important aspect of the salafist movement is the rejection in general of the concept of *taqlid,* and the call to revive *ijtihad. Taqlid,* often incorrectly labeled as "blind following," stresses the need for a Muslim to simply follow the rulings of a particular *madhhab,* or school of law, without doing the necessary research themselves. This is a convenient approach for it does not require an inordinate amount of time and energy to be expended on learning the fundamentals of Islam, particularly those considered well-established a few hundred years after the death of the Prophet Muhammad. Taking a ruling on faith, a Muslim can practice his religion on the basis of these early rulings by those much more learned than they.

The weakness of *taqlid,* however, is obvious, as for one to be a truly devoted follower it is best to learn the foundational material for oneself. This requires long hours of study and sometimes even formal training to become well versed in the early writings of Islam. This approach reopened the door to *ijtihad,* being the revival of personal interpretation of Qur'anic texts as well as other early writings. For many centuries the learned within Islam had considered *ijtihad* closed because of the solidification and codification of Islamic practice through the *madhhabs.* Salafism called for the return of *ijtihad* to allow the typical believer to make up his mind for himself, and this led to a massive revival in interest in the classical and medieval works of Islam. Translations of the *hadith* and *sunnah* writings flourished, and the works of medieval scholars such as Qadi Iyad, Ibn Taymiyyah, and Ibn Qayyim were resurrected. Even the writings of some early Sufi scholars such as Imam Ghazzali became popular, even though the salafist movement by and large considers Sufism a heretical interpretation of Islam.

The return of *ijtihad* meant that many devout Muslims began to question some aspects of the juristic rulings from later scholars of the *madhhabs,* while still retaining interest in the rulings of the founders of those schools. This revival of personal interpretation had significant influence on bringing back the earliest teachings regarding *zakat,* the proper forms of prayer, and the need to engage in jihad. *Zakat* became the means for the salafists to influence local politics through provision of welfare and family support, while jihad became more than an inward struggle, returning to the Prophet's own conception that jihad was a form of warfare to make Islam supreme. This revival not only spawned such groups as the Muslim Brotherhood but also led to a whole series of other lesser groups generally striving for the same goals, being the imposition of Islamic Sharia in the Muslim world, and a return to evangelistic operations to spread Islam throughout the non-Muslim world. The salafist movement's teachings can be found in virtually every Islamic revival today, largely because those teachings were built upon the earliest ideas and writings of the Prophet and his companions.

RUSSELL G. RODGERS

**See also**

Al Qaeda; Allah; Islamic Radicalism; Muslim Brotherhood; Qur'an; Sharia; Shia Islam; Sunni Islam

**References**

'Abduh, Muhammad. *Risalat al-Tauhid.* [The Theology of Unit]. Translated by Ishaq Musa'ad and Kenneth Craig. Kuala Lumpur, Malaysia: Islamic Book Trust, 2004.

Al-Hashimi, Muhammad Ali. *The Ideal Muslim Society: As Defined in the Qur'an and Sunnah.* Riyadh, Saudi Arabia: International Islamic Publishing House, 2007.

Al-Qaradawi, Yusuf. *The Eye of the Beholder: The Muslim Brotherhood over the Past 70 Years.* Cairo: Al-Falah Foundation, 2003.

Keddie, Nikki. *An Islamic Response to Imperialism: Political and Religious Writings of Sayyid Jamal ad-Din "al-Afghani."* Translated by Nikki Keddie and Hamid Algar. Berkeley: University of California Press, 1968.

Philips, Abu Ameenah Bilal. *The Evolution of Fiqh: Islamic Law & the Madh-habs.* Kuala Lumpur, Malaysia: A. S. Noordeen, 2005.

# Samawah, Battle of

**Start Date: March 30, 2003**
**End Date: April 4, 2003**

Battle fought during the 2003 Anglo-American–led invasion of Iraq (Operation IRAQI FREEDOM) involving U.S. and Iraqi troops. The fighting took place in Samawah, about 170 miles to the southeast of Baghdad. Beginning in late March, the U.S. Army's 2nd Brigade, 82nd Airborne Division swept through Samawah to rid it of Iraqi resistance. From March 22 to 25, on its way to Baghdad, the U.S. 3rd Infantry Division had encountered some hostile fire from Iraqi troops in Samawah. Although U.S. artillery and air strikes hammered Iraqi positions within the city, the decision was then made to skirt the city so that the 3rd Infantry Division could move directly on to Baghdad. At the same time, on March 25, the 2nd Brigade, 82nd Airborne Division received orders to assault Samawah and clear it of hostile forces.

On March 30 at approximately 3:00 a.m. the 2nd Brigade had reached the outskirts of Samawah. Inside the city were elements from the Iraqi Republican Guard, Fedayeen Saddam, and regular Iraqi army. Toward daybreak, U.S. forces began to advance into the city, expecting to meet stiff resistance on the city's perimeter; they encountered no such resistance and no organized defenses there. However, U.S. troops began to encounter heavy Iraqi small-arms fire and assaults by rocket-propelled grenades (RPGs) as they neared a concrete factory just inside the city's perimeter. At about 3:00 p.m. that same day, U.S. commanders called in air strikes, conducted by U.S. Navy McDonnell Douglas Boeing/Northrop F-18 Hornets, which leveled a warehouse next to the plant, temporarily neutralizing resistance there.

That evening, the 2nd Battalion, 325th Infantry Regiment began a feint on the bridges spanning the Euphrates River. The hope was to draw in Iraqi Republican Guard units so that they would be distracted and thus be unable to conduct a rear-guard maneuver against American forces. At the same time, U.S. aerial bombardment of the north bank of the river took place, allowing the 2nd Brigade to capture the bridges, cross them, and dig in north of the river. At around dawn the next day, American troops pulled back, having accomplished their objective. The remainder of that day, fighting was light and sporadic.

Iraqi resistance inside Samawah, meanwhile, was concentrated in and near the concrete factory. On April 2, U.S. forces (mainly from the 1st Battalion, 325th Infantry Regiment) finally took the entire factory complex, with the help of Lockheed/Boeing AC-130 Spectre gunships. This action permitted other forces to move into the city and take control. The operation culminated in an attack on the headquarters of an Iraqi paramilitary group on April 4. The U.S. strategy in taking the city was designed to demoralize the enemy while keeping American casualties to a minimum; much of the fighting involved concentrated, short attacks into the city followed by carefully staged withdrawals. Meanwhile, U.S. air strikes were called in against entrenched Iraqi positions, such as the local Baath Party headquarters, a school building being used as a shelter, and even a soccer field. By nightfall on April 4, Samawah had been secured, with just one U.S. combat death and 6 wounded. The Iraqis suffered at least 50 dead and 23 taken prisoner.

PAUL G. PIERPAOLI JR.

**See also**

IRAQI FREEDOM, Operation; IRAQI FREEDOM, Operation, Coalition Ground Forces; IRAQI FREEDOM, Operation, Ground Campaign; Republican Guard

**References**

Boyne, Walter J. *Operation Iraqi Freedom: What Went Right, What Went Wrong and Why.* New York: Forge Books, 2003.

Keegan, John. *The Iraq War: The Military Offensive, from Victory in 21 Days to the Insurgent Aftermath.* New York: Vintage, 2005.

Murray, Williamson, and Robert H. Scales Jr. *The Iraq War: A Military History.* Cambridge, MA: Belknap, 2005.

# Samita Incident
## Event Date: March 20, 1973

An attempt by the Iraqi government to chip away at the sovereignty of Kuwait by occupying a portion of territory disputed between the two countries. The Samita Incident was an armed confrontation between Kuwaiti and Iraqi troops on March 20, 1973, at Samita, several miles south of Umm Qasr. It was only one of a number of attempts by Iraq to lay claim to some or all of Kuwait. Both countries agreed to arbitration brokered by the Arab League before the crisis escalated into a more serious situation. The results, however, may have encouraged Iraqi leader Saddam Hussein and others of his countrymen to believe that a move against Kuwait would have only limited international impact.

After Iraq became independent from the Ottoman Empire, a major goal of Iraqi leaders was the acquisition of Kuwait. Even before oil was discovered in Kuwait in 1937, King Ghazi of Iraq made public statements about annexing it, and encouraged the Kuwaiti people to overthrow the al-Sabah family that ruled the emirate. The strong British presence in both countries limited the amount of direct pressure the Iraqis could put on the Kuwaitis. The situation changed after World War II, however. In 1958, the Iraqi monarchy strongly encouraged Kuwait to join a union of Jordan and Iraq to form a single state. The concept of Arab unity was very popular at the time, and Egypt and Syria had just formed the United Arab Republic.

The 1958 revolution that brought down the Iraqi monarchy put an end to the movement to unify Jordan, Iraq, and Kuwait, but it did not end Iraqi interests in Kuwaiti territory. In June 1961 a treaty between Great Britain and Kuwait that gave Britain control over the emirate was replaced by a treaty of friendship that acknowledged Kuwaiti's independence. Iraqi prime minister Abd al-Karim Qasim condemned the new treaty as illegal because Iraq held that the original treaty that had ended Kuwait's association with the Ottoman Empire was also illegal. His threats to Kuwaiti independence prompted the emirate to ask for help from Great Britain, which responded by stationing some 8,000 troops, along with supporting air units, in or near Kuwait. This was sufficient force to deter Iraqi leaders, who also faced a rebellion by Kurds in northern Iraq at the time.

Kuwaiti leaders were uncomfortable with having to rely on British armed forces, however, because it seemed to negate their independence and keep them in colonial status. Thus they turned to the Arab League for assistance. Thanks to an Iraqi boycott, Kuwait was accepted for membership in the league on July 20, 1961. Kuwait then requested Arab forces to protect it from Iraq, and Arab League members eventually sent 3,300 troops. Although they did not actually replace British troops already in place, the Arab forces were politically more acceptable.

After Qasim was overthrown in February 1963, a government apparently friendly to Kuwait replaced him, and Arab forces were gradually withdrawn as the threat to Kuwaiti independence seemed to recede. The Kuwaiti government tried to establish friendly relations with Iraq by making a number of long-term financial loans to that nation, and on October 4, 1963, an agreement was signed between the two countries that appeared to guarantee Kuwaiti independence. The government of Kuwait was so encouraged by developments that it terminated its treaty with Great Britain that guaranteed British military aid.

The Iraqi government, however, continued to try to impinge on Kuwait's sovereignty. At different times, it demanded ownership or occupation of the Bubiyan and Warba islands, off the narrow tip of Iraq that borders the Persian Gulf. Kuwaiti financial aid kept the Iraqis from pressing the issue too hard, however.

In April 1969 the Iraqi government tried another tack. It requested permission to station troops on Kuwaiti soil to protect the newly built port of Umm Qasr from Iranian attack. Kuwaiti defense minister Sheikh Saad al-Sabah gave his verbal consent, under pressure. Iraqi troops were to be allowed to occupy two square kilometers of land on the Kuwaiti side of the border, just south of Umm Qasr, near Samita. In fact, Iraqi troops had already begun crossing the border before Shaikh Saad had given his assent to what became the "unwritten agreement."

Even after relations between Iraq and Iran had cooled, Iraqi troops remained in Kuwait near Umm Qasr. In December 1972 an Iraqi construction crew began to build a paved road to Samita, under the cover of armed Iraqi soldiers. When Kuwait protested this step, the Iraqi government presented a draft treaty in March 1973 that would give Iraq virtual sovereignty over the area, including oil drilling and exporting rights. The Kuwaiti government rejected the treaty out of hand. Iraq responded by reinforcing its garrison in Kuwait and by establishing a new post at Samita. A Kuwaiti outpost was already in Samita, however, and tensions immediately rose.

On March 20, 1973, Kuwaiti soldiers approached the Iraqi troops and road construction crew with orders to eject them from what Kuwait considered its territory. The Iraqi commander warned the Kuwaitis to withdraw. When they refused, Iraqi troops opened fire. After a brief firefight, two Kuwaitis and one Iraqi were killed.

Two days later, the Kuwaiti government lodged a formal protest with the Iraqis. The secretary general of the Arab League and representatives from Syria and Saudi Arabia visited both capitals in an effort to mediate the situation. Nineteen truckloads of Iraqi soldiers subsequently withdrew to the old borders on April 5, but the Iraqi government refused to accept the borders that Kuwait claimed. It continued to claim parts of Kuwait, including the Bubiyan and Warba islands.

The Samita Incident attracted little attention in the West because it was quickly resolved, but it had long-term significance. Indeed, this was Kuwait's first test of protecting its sovereignty without British aid. Furthermore, the incident revealed to the world that the Kuwaiti government had tacitly allowed Iraqi troops to occupy part of Kuwait for years. This helped undercut Kuwait's claims for its existing borders. Finally, the crisis was settled by the Arab League, much as the 1961 crisis had been. This fact may have encouraged Saddam, 17 years later, to believe that another crisis with Kuwait might lead to a peaceful compromise brokered by other Arab states.

TIM J. WATTS

**See also**

Iraq, History of, Pre-1990; Iraq, History of, 1990–Present; Kuwait; Umm Qasr

**References**

Finnie, David H. *Shifting Lines in the Sand: Kuwait's Elusive Frontier with Iraq.* Cambridge: Harvard University Press, 1992.

"Iraq and Kuwait Clash at Border." *New York Times,* March 21, 1973, 6.

Terrill, W. Andrew. *Kuwaiti National Security and the U.S.-Kuwaiti Strategic Relationship after Saddam.* Carlisle, PA: Strategic Studies Institute, U.S. Army, September 2007.

---

# Sanchez, Ricardo S.
## Birth Date: May 17, 1951

U.S. Army officer best known for his command of coalition forces in Iraq from June 2003 to June 2004 (Operation IRAQI FREEDOM). Born on May 17, 1951, in Rio Grande City, Texas, Ricardo S. Sanchez began his military career in the Reserve Officers' Training Corps (ROTC) program at the University of Texas at Austin and Texas A&I University (now Texas A&M–Kingsville). A 1973 graduate of the latter institution, Sanchez was commissioned in the U.S. Army as a second lieutenant that same year. He served in both infantry and armor units early in his career. He was a platoon leader, an executive officer, an assistant logistics officer, and an operations officer. Sanchez's military education included both the Command and General Staff College and the U.S. Army War College. He also earned a master's degree in operations research and systems analysis engineering from the Naval Postgraduate School.

As a lieutenant colonel, Sanchez served in Operation DESERT STORM in 1991 as commander of the 2nd Battalion, 69th Armor, 197th Infantry Brigade. His performance in the Persian Gulf War contributed to his early promotion to colonel in September 1994. During July 1994 to June 1996 he commanded the 2nd Brigade of the 1st Infantry Division (Mechanized) at Fort Riley, Kansas.

Sanchez then served as an investigator in the Office of the U.S. Army Inspector General Agency and in various roles at U.S. Southern Command. After promotion to brigadier general in November 1998, Sanchez served as assistant division commander (support) of the 1st Infantry Division during 1999–2000. From July 2000 to June 2001 he was deputy chief of staff for operations, U.S. Army Europe and Seventh Army, Germany. During July 2001–June 2003 he commanded the 1st Armored Division, being promoted to major general in July 2002. Promoted to lieutenant general in August 2003, from July 2003 to June 2004 he was the commanding general of V Corps, U.S. Army Europe and Seventh Army, Germany, to include duty as commanding general, Combined Joint Task Force 7, Operation IRAQI FREEDOM.

With the rapid withdrawal of U.S. Central Command (CENT-COM) and its Combined Forces Land Component Command (CFLCC), Sanchez by default became the commander of Coalition Ground Forces in Iraq, the top military position in Iraq. This critical period after the end of major hostilities saw the emergence of the Iraqi insurgency, the deaths of Uday and Qusay Hussein, and the capture of deposed Iraqi president Saddam Hussein. The major challenges facing Sanchez were the reestablishment of essential services and basic security and ending the counterinsurgency. According to multiple sources, communications between Sanchez and L. Paul Bremer, head of the Coalition Provisional Authority, were strained and often nonexistent. This poor communication and lack of unified leadership is often cited as one of the contributors to the turmoil that followed the end of major conflict in Iraq. Compounding Sanchez's problems during this period was the fact that he was essentially a corps commander with little more than a corps staff yet was responsible for commanding an entire theater. With the vacuum created by the rapid withdrawal of the CFLCC, Sanchez was left with a staff that was nowhere near large enough for his responsible span of control or trained and experienced at the higher level of theater operations.

Despite progress in certain areas, this period of IRAQI FREEDOM was marked by a burgeoning insurgency, widespread lawlessness, and the challenge of detaining thousands of prisoners. The most glaring controversy during Sanchez's tenure was the prisoner abuse at Abu Ghraib Prison. In September 2003 Sanchez approved in writing 29 interrogation methods authorized for use with Iraqi detainees. At the direction of CENTCOM, 10 of those methods were later repealed after having been deemed unacceptably aggressive. However, the actual methods employed at Abu Ghraib went beyond even what Sanchez had authorized, as evidenced by the graphic photographs that were ultimately seen on worldwide media. On January 16, 2004, Sanchez issued a press release announcing the investigation of "detainee abuse at a Coalition Forces detention facility."

Sanchez left his post in June 2004. Ultimately several low-ranking military members were court-martialed over the abuse scandal, and Sanchez believed that he was denied his fourth star and was forced into retirement on November 1, 2006, because of it.

In 2008 Sanchez published his autobiography, *Wiser in Battle: A Soldier's Story,* a sweeping indictment of the handling of the Iraq War by Defense Secretary Donald Rumsefeld and the George W. Bush administration. Sanchez now lives in Texas.

BENJAMIN D. FOREST

**See also**

Abu Ghraib; Bremer, Jerry; Iraq, History of, 1990–Present; IRAQI FREEDOM, Operation; Iraqi Insurgency; Rumsfeld, Donald Henry

**References**

Gordon, Michael R., and General Bernard E. Trainor. *Cobra II: The Inside Story of the Invasion and Occupation of Iraq.* New York: Pantheon Books, 2006.

Ricks, Thomas E. *Fiasco: The American Military Adventure in Iraq.* New York: Penguin, 2006.

Sanchez, Ricardo S., and Donald T. Phillips. *Wiser in Battle: A Soldier's Story*. New York: Harper, 2008.

Woodward, Bob. *State of Denial: Bush at War, Part III*. New York: Simon and Schuster, 2006.

# San Remo Conference
## Start Date: April 19, 1920
## End Date: April 26, 1920

Conference held in San Remo, Italy, from April 19–26, 1920, that determined the allocation of various League of Nations mandates, regions that would come under the command of a colonial administration, among the principal Allied powers of World War I. The territory divided among the powers was land once ruled by the former Ottoman Empire, which had ceased to exist following World War I. The Middle Eastern mandates, known as Class A mandates, were Iraq, Palestine, and Syria. The Allied powers deemed that Class A mandated regions had developed to the point where they were nearly ready for independence, subject to the assistance of the mandatory power. Great Britain gained control of Iraq and Palestine as part of the conference, while France gained Syria (later to include Lebanon).

Well before the end of World War I, Great Britain and France had discussed how to divide Southwestern Asia after the war. Indeed, a secret deal between the two nations was concluded on May 16, 1916. Known as the Sykes-Picot Agreement after the two diplomats who negotiated the deal, Sir Mark Sykes of Great Britain and François Georges Picot of France, the agreement stated that the region would be broken up into two zones, with France getting access to the northern zone, which would be comprised of what is today southeastern Turkey, northern Iraq, Syria, and Lebanon. Great Britain would control the southern zone, which consisted of what is today Jordan, central and southern Iraq, and Haifa, a town in present-day Israel. The Sykes-Picot Agreement would be largely reaffirmed at the San Remo Conference.

The conference also confirmed the British support of a homeland for the Jewish people in Palestine. Many British leaders had been influenced by Zionism, an international movement whose goal was to reestablish a homeland for the Jewish people in Palestine, an area with much religious significance. In a classified formal statement dated November 2, 1917, the British foreign secretary, Sir Arthur James Balfour, declared that the British sympathized with Zionist aspirations. The Balfour Declaration was later incorporated into the Mandate for Palestine.

Delegates attending the conference held in San Remo, Italy, during April 19–26, 1920. The conference decided the allocation of mandated territory taken from the defeated Central Powers as a consequence of the Allied victory in World War I. (Underwood & Underwood/Corbis)

The Armistice of Moudros, signed on October 30, 1918, ended fighting in the Middle Eastern theater and was followed by the Allied occupation of Istanbul, the capital of the Ottoman Empire. At the London Conference in February 1920, the European Allied powers began the process of partitioning lands formerly held by the Ottoman Empire.

Attending the San Remo Conference were the prime ministers of Italy, Great Britain, and France as well as top-level representatives from Belgium, Greece, and Japan. Francesco Nitti, the Italian prime minister, was largely ineffectual at the conference, and discussions regarding the Middle East were dominated by British prime minister David Lloyd George and French prime minister Alexandre Millerand. France and England seemed to be most interested in Syria and Iraq. The controversy regarding Syria revolved around whether France should have all of what is geographically outlined in Syria or just certain parts. In respect to Iraq, oil was an issue with which both France and Great Britain were concerned. On April 24, 1920, Frenchman Philippe Berthelot, secretary to the Ministry of Foreign Affairs, and John Cadman, a British petroleum technologist, agreed secretly to divide up the oil of Europe, Asia Minor, North Africa, and Iraq.

The San Remo Resolution was adopted on April 25, 1920, and was binding among the Allied powers. The exact boundaries of the territories in question were left unspecified and were to be determined by the Allied powers at a later date. It was also announced that the creation of Palestine would not affect the nationality of Jews in other countries. A Jew of American, French, British, or other nationality could thus maintain her or his nationality while also being a citizen of Palestine. Nor was the creation of Palestine supposed to change the status of the 600,000 Arabs already living there. Also, the property and legal rights of the Arabs were not to be disturbed.

The British and French mandates led to many serious problems in the Middle East. On July 23, 1920, the Battle of Maysalun occurred between Syrian and French forces. The Syrians had recently claimed independence under King Faisal. French forces easily overran the Syrians. Despite their victory, the French continued to face uprisings in the Syrian mandate. French troops did not leave Syria until April 17, 1946.

The British faced numerous uprisings in Iraq and Palestine. Many nationalists in Iraq were upset when Iraq was accorded mandate status. The British faced major resistance there, and the country was in a state of anarchy following uprisings in July 1920. Iraqi independence was finally achieved on October 3, 1932, when the British mandate ended and Iraq was officially admitted to the League of Nations. The British retained bases and influence, however.

Violence also broke out in Palestine against the British presence and also because of the immigration of thousands of Jews into the mandated region. Violence in the region continued to take place throughout the mandatory period, including the bloody Palestinian Arab Uprising of 1936–1939. Finally, on May 14, 1948,

the British, not able to find a way to bring peace to Palestine, left the future of the mandate in the hands of the newly formed United Nations (UN).

GREGORY W. MORGAN

**See also**

Balfour Declaration; France, Middle East Policy; Mandates; Ottoman Empire; Sykes-Picot Agreement; United Kingdom, Middle East Policy; World War I, Impact of

**References**

Fromkin, David. *A Peace to End All Peace: The Fall of the Ottoman Empire and the Creation of the Modern Middle East.* New York: Henry Holt, 1989.

Hitti, Phillip Khuri. *History of Syria: Including Lebanon and Palestine.* London: Macmillan, 1951.

Méouchy, Nadine, and Peter Sluglett, eds. *The British and French Mandates in Comparative Perspectives,* Vol. 93. Leiden, UK: Brill Academic, 2004.

Stein, Leonard. *The Balfour Declaration.* New York: Simon and Schuster, 1961.

# Satellites, Use of by Coalition Forces

Some military leaders and analysts have dubbed the 1991 Persian Gulf War the "first space war" because of the extensive use of satellite systems during that conflict. Although the U.S. military had used satellite systems to some degree in prior conflicts, it utilized every type of satellite system during Operations DESERT SHIELD and DESERT STORM. The use of satellite systems became even more prominent in the years since the end of that war.

When Iraqi troops invaded Kuwait in August 1990, the U.S. Central Command (CENTCOM) had begun updating its war plans, an indication of CENTCOM's intent to fully use space systems in a future Middle Eastern conflict. When hostilities by a U.S.-led coalition to drive Iraq from Kuwait began in January 1991, most of the satellites eventually used in the conflict were already in orbit and available. The Department of Defense eventually launched additional satellites to provide increased theater coverage and deployed more than 7,000 terminals and receivers so that the military could readily access and use the satellite data and imagery.

With the initial deployment to Saudi Arabia, CENTCOM contacted numerous space organizations, such as the Defense Communications Agency, Joint Chiefs of Staff (JCS), the Defense Mapping Agency (DMA), the U.S. Space Command, the Space and Missile Systems Center, the Strategic Air Command, the U.S. Navy's Space Command, and the U.S. Army's Space Command, to secure access to satellites, resolve technical issues, and arrange for data and imagery dissemination. The time it took to mobilize these capabilities depended upon ground equipment and satellite availability, launch windows, processing actions required to launch a spacecraft into orbit, time required to check out newly launched satellites or to reposition a satellite for better coverage, and the placement of trained personnel where needed. CENTCOM eventually received the use of 51 military and 12 commercial satellites by February 1991.

Perhaps the most important system of the Persian Gulf War was the Navigation Satellite Timing and Ranging (NAVSTAR) Global Positioning System (GPS) satellite constellation. Coalition forces used GPS signals for numerous logistical, planning, and warfighting applications. With GPS receivers, ground troops could readily navigate the nearly featureless desert, especially in the frequent sandstorms, and supply trucks were able to locate dispersed frontline units. Units conducted large-scale night maneuvers that in the past would have required numerous scouts and guides along the routes of advance. GPS allowed coalition forces to shift their attack plans back and forth virtually up to the moment of attack, since they did not need fixed ground markers.

The Defense Meteorological Satellite Program (DMSP) satellites provided weather and climatic data and imagery directly to theater commanders in near real time. Commanders could now select targets and munitions for accurate targeting, plan and redirect aerial and ground missions, optimize night-vision equipment and night-capable targeting systems, and plan movement routes into Kuwait. DMSP satellites also provided information to alert troops to sandstorms, predict the possible spread of chemical agents, and monitor the extensive smoke plumes from the oil fires, ignited by the Iraqi Army as it fled Kuwait in February 1991.

Satellite communications (SATCOM) provided essential command and control (C2) of deployed coalition forces. Within the first 90 days of deployment, U.S. military forces established more military communications connectivity to the Persian Gulf than had existed in Europe over the previous 40 years. Theater commanders communicated through a U.S. Navy Fleet Satellite Communications (FLTSATCOM) satellite, a Leased Satellite (LEASAT) program satellite, and two Defense Satellite Communications System (DSCS) satellites over the Indian Ocean. In addition, the Defense Department used FLTSATCOM satellites over the Atlantic and DSCS satellites over the Eastern Atlantic to communicate between CENTCOM headquarters in Saudi Arabia and various headquarters in the United States.

CENTCOM also used three early warning satellites of the Defense Support Program (DSP), normally used to provide ballistic missile early launch warning and other surveillance information. The DSP satellites detected Iraqi Scud missile launches, especially against targets in Israel, to provide timely warning to military forces and civilians.

Before the Persian Gulf War, the Defense Department used LANDSAT, the longest-running satellite program for space-based imagery of Earth, to image the Persian Gulf region and identify areas of contention during the 1980–1988 Iran-Iraq War and areas of economic contention during the tanker wars of the late 1980s. During DESERT SHIELD, LANDSAT satellites provided multispectral imagery (MSI) of the Persian Gulf region that the DMA used to create detailed maps and that the U.S. Air Force used to produce engineering drawings for the construction of airfields in Saudi

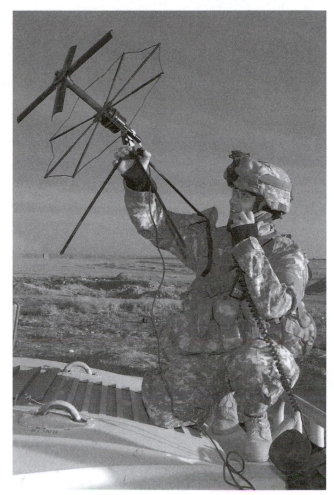

U.S. Army specialist Kerry Lampkin sets up a SATCOM antenna during Operation EAGLE CLAW VIII, carried out to find weapons caches and terrorist suspects in the village of Malhah in Kirkuk Province, Iraq, December 22, 2006. (U.S. Department of Defense)

Arabia. Coalition forces also used LANDSAT's MSI of the Saudi-Kuwaiti border to determine changes in Iraqi emplacements and significant military movements. Additionally, during and after the war, LANDSAT, along with Satellite Pour l'Observation de la Terre (SPOT) satellites, a French system similar to LANDSAT, helped evaluate the environmental damage to Kuwaiti and the Persian Gulf from oil spills and fires, most intentionally created by Iraqi forces.

During the course of the 1990s, the use of satellites by U.S. military forces grew as individual satellite systems, the integration of air and space elements to support joint war fighting, the development of digital data links, and increasing electronic airborne sensors to process information and deliver that information to field forces developed into network-centric warfare. More than 50 American and European satellites supported Operation ALLIED FORCE in March–June 1999 to force Yugoslavian president Slobodan Milosevic to end atrocities in Kosovo. Satellites connected the Combined Air Operations Center (CAOC) in Italy and other C2 centers to each other and to improved satellite sensors and other intelligence, surveillance, and reconnaissance (ISR) assets, such as the Predator unmanned aerial vehicles (UAV) and high-altitude U-2 reconnaissance aircraft. The Predators picked up ground imagery and relayed it through satellites to various C2 centers in real time, allowing commanders to calculate precise coordinates for the newly operational Joint Direct Attack Munition (JDAM), which used the NAVSTAR GPS signal to provide precise guidance to within 10 feet of its intended target and to improve timely battle damage assessment.

This short conflict made huge demands on SATCOM systems, especially the DSCS III satellites. After DESERT STORM, the U.S. Air Force had contracted with Lockheed Martin to upgrade the last four DSCS satellites to provide greater tactical capability. DSCS satellites, the U.S. Navy's Ultra-High Frequency Follow-on satellites, and the newly operational Military Strategic and Tactical Relay (MILSTAR) satellite constellation provided bandwidth not only for voice and message communications but also for video-conferencing among the leaders of the coalition nations and coalition military leaders. Additionally, these satellites relayed video imagery from Predator and other airborne ISR platforms to dispersed C2 centers and linked command authorities, ground stations, and aircraft and ships during the conflict. Although SAT-COM capability had risen by more than 100 percent since DESERT STORM, the unprecedented demand during Operation ALLIED FORCE forced the Defense Department and North Atlantic Treaty Organization (NATO) to lease commercial satellites to supply almost 75 percent of SATCOM's needs.

After the September 11, 2001, terrorist attacks on the United States, the Defense Department launched Operation NOBLE EAGLE to deter a future air attack on the United States. Military, civil, and commercial space capabilities played an important part during this operation. SATCOM provided immediate communications to New York City and Washington, D.C., when they lost cell service from very high postattack use. Weather satellites provided weather data for decision makers involved in protection, response, and recovery actions. GPS provided precise data for search and rescue work and vehicle surveillance and tracking. Intelligence-gathering satellites helped monitor, locate, and intercept terror communications and networks.

In October 2001 U.S. military forces, assisting indigenous anti-Taliban forces in Afghanistan, launched Operation ENDURING FREE-DOM to destroy the Al Qaeda terrorist infrastructure and overthrow the Taliban government. CENTCOM conducted an air campaign, relying on precision-guided weapons and U.S. Special Operations Forces (SOF) operating with the anti-Taliban forces. CENTCOM's newly operational CAOC at Prince Sultan Air Base, Saudi Arabia, served as the linchpin for the campaign's network-centric operations. Decision makers and planners could track every aircraft over Afghanistan, receive real-time video and data links from UAVs and other ISR platforms, and develop a common operating picture through global communications connectivity.

Coalition forces for this conflict utilized nearly 100 satellites of all types. Through a daily Space Tasking Order that paralleled the CAOC's Air Tasking Order, the Air and Space Operations Center of Fourteenth Air Force, the key provider of space support, could optimize coalition space capabilities by directing the appropriate space system to support a particular operational requirement and apportion space assets to meet both theater and global requirements. Because of greatly increased communications requirements, the military planners maximized the use of DSCS and MILSTAR satellites. Expanding use of UAV streaming-video imagery in real time to some strike aircraft and numerous worldwide C2 centers drove the need to obtain additional bandwidth and channels from civil and commercial communications satellites as the UAVs could not link through the military communications satellites. The widely dispersed and remote locations of coalition ground forces in Afghanistan increased the use of SATCOM between fielded forces and higher headquarters on the one hand and various control centers on the other hand.

Military and commercial weather and environmental satellites also made significant contributions to ENDURING FREEDOM operations. This variety of satellites provided imagery and data on surface wind speed and direction, fog and cloud conditions, and dust storms.

The GPS satellites have been the great enabler of network-centric and precision warfare in Operation ENDURING FREEDOM. SOF controllers with the ground forces used laser-designator binoculars to determine the exact range of enemy ground forces, fed this data into a GPS receiver to produce accurate target coordinates, and then relayed these coordinates to airborne warning and control (AWAC) aircraft, the CAOC, or strike aircraft that released laser-guided bombs (LGBs) or GPS-guided munitions against the designated targets. Additionally, some strike aircraft obtained the capability to directly receive Predator video imagery through SATCOM links to actually see the targets on the ground and resolve any questions about target identification directly with the ground controllers.

Additionally, the use of the JDAM in Operation ENDURING FREEDOM rose by almost 45 percent, while the use of LGBs dropped by nearly 32 percent. The U.S. Air Force increased its use of Boeing B-52 Stratofortress and North American/Rockwell/Boeing B-1B Lancer strategic bombers, which released 46 percent of the total number of JDAMs in precision attacks on hostile ground forces. Increasingly, land- and carrier-based fighter aircraft handled most of the LGB missions. The larger bombers could carry up to 80 of the smaller, more accurate JDAMs and, more recently, the Small Diameter Bombs (SDB) that enabled them to strike more targets in a single mission with greater accuracy and less collateral damage. Data links allowed pilots to change preprogrammed target coordinates in flight to meet current needs of the ground forces.

Because the larger percentage of coalition forces in Afghanistan consisted of small parties of tactical air controllers with the anti-Taliban forces, the CAOC and other headquarters and control centers needed a means to track and locate these widely dispersed units in remote locations of Afghanistan. The U.S. Army had initiated a digital battle command system, called Force XXI Battle Command Brigade and Below (FBCB2). In this system, ground vehicles equipped with GPS transponders reported their location to a host vehicle, which in turn retransmitted its position to all networked units. Computer screens in these vehicles then displayed the locations of all networked vehicles as blue icons. Operational and intelligence personnel could then input data on enemy forces, which showed up as red icons.

Because of the limited range of line-of-sight radios, the Army attached SATCOM receivers onto the roofs of the vehicles of two 4th Infantry Division brigades. These receivers allowed the operators to receive an aggregated picture of the blue (friendly) force from a satellite ground station. This system, known as FBCB2-Blue Force Tracking (FBCB2-BFT), provided commanders with a tactical internet that allowed them to control more decisive operations over vast distances more rapidly with greater force protection capability and allowed them to conduct operations in bad weather or at night in difficult terrain.

Space support for Operation IRAQI FREEDOM, which began in March 2003, was prominent, pervasive, and effectively more integrated than in previous operations. It produced a far greater level of coordination among air and space elements to support the fielded forces. As in Operation ENDURING FREEDOM, the Space Cell in the CAOC worked even closer with the mission planners to integrate space assets into the operational plan and then work with space operations organizations in the United States to provide tailored space systems for particular combat requirements.

DSP satellites detected and tracked Iraqi tactical ballistic missiles that resulted in the issuance of warning notices to targeted forces. Military, civil, and commercial satellites provided weather and environmental data and imagery to headquarters, C2 centers, mission planners, and fielded forces in virtually real time.

The use of GPS timing and ranging proved vital to IRAQI FREEDOM operations. With a full constellation, the GPS satellites provided unprecedented precise tracking, location, and targeting coordinates. The ENDURING FREEDOM experience with FBCB2-BFT resulted in the expansion of the program as U.S. Army, U.S. Marine Corps, and British forces in Iraq received more than 1,200 BFT systems. The use of GPS-guided air-delivered munitions increased to about 68 percent of all munitions expended, almost 8 percent above the ENDURING FREEDOM figure of 60 percent by late 2006.

SATCOM was another indispensable element in network-centric expeditionary warfare. The Defense Department increased available bandwidth capacity, especially from commercial satellites, by a factor of three to accommodate the growing requirements. Operation ENDURING FREEDOM saw an increase in the use and quantity of satellite phones for communications and blue force situational awareness. The CAOC increased its use of MILSTAR satellites for secure communications, UAV surveillance video feeds, reach-back intelligence data, and facsimile and data message transmission among multiple users, such as the CAOC, headquarters, C2 centers, and deployed air, ground, and naval forces.

Satellites will continue to take on even greater importance as technology continues to advance at a rapid pace.

ROBERT B. KANE

**See also**
Bombs, Precision-Guided; Defense Meteorological Satellite Program; Defense Satellite Communications System; Joint Direct Attack Munition and Small Diameter Bomb; Land Remote-Sensing Satellite; Navigation Satellite Timing and Ranging Global Positioning System; Network-Centric Warfare; United States Central Command; Unmanned Aerial Vehicles

**References**
El-Baz, Farouk, and R. M. Makharita, eds. *Gulf War and the Environment.* London: Taylor and Francis, 1994.
Keaney, Thomas A., and Eliot A. Cohen. *Gulf Air Power Survey Summary Report.* Washington, DC: Department of the Air Force, 1993.
Levis, Alexander H., John C. Bedford, and Sandra Davis, eds. *The Limitless Sky: Air Force Science and Technology Contributions to the Nation.* Washington, DC: Air Force History and Museums Program, 2004.
Mack, Pamela Etter. *Viewing the Earth: The Social Construction of the Landsat Satellite System.* Cambridge, MA: MIT Press, 1990.
Peeples, Curtis. *High Frontier: The United States Air Force and the Military Space Program.* Washington, DC: Air Force History and Museum Program, 1997.
Spires, David N. *Beyond Horizons: A Half Century of Air Force Space Leadership.* 2nd ed. Maxwell Air Force Base, AL: Air Force Space Command and Air University Press, 2007.

## Saud, Abdullah ibn Abd al-Aziz al

*See* Abdullah, King of Saudi Arabia

## Saud, Khalid ibn Sultan ibn Abd al-Aziz al-
**Birth Date: September 23, 1949**

Saudi prince, military officer, assistant minister of defense and aviation, and inspector general for military affairs for the Kingdom of Saudi Arabia. He also served as a lieutenant general and commander of Joint Forces and Theater of Operations during the 1991 Persian Gulf War.

Prince Khalid bin Sultan ibn Abd al-Aziz al-Saud was born on September 23, 1949, in Makkah, Saudi Arabia. He is the eldest son of the first crown prince and minister of defense, Prince Sultan, and the grandson of the kingdom's modern founder, King Abd al-Aziz, known as Ibn Saud. He studied at the Princes' School in Riyadh and attended the British Royal Military Academy at Sandhurst, graduating in 1967. He continued his advanced military training in the United States, at the Army Command and General Staff School and the Naval Postgraduate School, and he obtained his Air War Certification at the U.S. Air War College at Maxwell Air Force Base. He also earned a master's degree in political science at Auburn University.

With a reputation as an air defense expert, Khalid moved up rapidly in the military, holding the positions of air squadron chief, training officer and assistant staff officer for operations, army inspectorate chief, director of the administration of air defense projects, deputy chief of the air force, chief of air defense, and chief of the strategic missiles force.

Saudi air and air defense forces have played a special role in the kingdom's defense planning. One reason for this is its vast open spaces, most of which are inaccessible except from the air. Another reason is that with the deliberate decision to keep the military establishment quite small (an idea that Khalid later challenged), air defense became more crucial, and the kingdom traditionally relied on the West—first on Great Britain, and later the United States—for military support. Over the years, Saudi Arabia has spent billions on the acquisition of advanced weaponry, aircraft, and missiles.

Khalid was involved in numerous arms deals, certainly with the purchase of the medium-range surface-to-surface CSS-2 East Wind missiles from China. He has written that he and his half-brother, Bandar, formerly ambassador to the United States, negotiated the acquisition of these missiles for an estimated $3.5 billion.

On the eve of Operation DESERT STORM in 1991, Khalid was named commander of the Joint Forces and Theater of Operations at the rank of lieutenant general. The Joint Force Command allowed countries, in particular Arab and Muslim nations, to place their troops under Saudi leadership rather than that of the United States. In all, the Joint Forces included personnel from 24 nations. Saudi Arabia provided up to 100,000 personnel for the conflict. Prince Khalid's position in the war demonstrated Saudi Arabia's political leadership, not to mention its military capabilities. At the same time, however, the large wave of opposition within Saudi Arabia to military participation with the United States and the presence of Western troops in the kingdom unleashed strong reactions in the form of religiously based protests against the al-Saud family and the government as a whole.

Following the Persian Gulf War, Khalid was promoted to the rank of field marshal. He left government service in 1991. In 2001 he was called back to become the assistant minister of defense and inspector general for military affairs, posts he continues to hold. In the interceding years he was involved in private business and published his account of Operation DESERT STORM and Saudi Arabia's history in *Desert Warrior: A Personal View of the Gulf War* (1995), written with Patrick Seale. In the book Khalid disagrees with certain statements and assessments made by General H. Norman Schwarzkopf in his 1992 book *It Doesn't Take a Hero*.

An avid scuba diver, Khalid has involved himself in marine ecology, which he supports through the Living Oceans Foundation, and he has funded a multinational team of scientists called Scientists without Borders who will assess the health of coral reefs and marine life in the Caribbean beginning in 2010. He has also created a chair for environmental research at King Saud University.

SHERIFA ZUHUR

**See also**

DESERT STORM, Operation; Saudi Arabia; Saudi Arabia, Armed Forces; Schwarzkopf, H. Norman, Jr.

**References**

Gause, F. Gregory. *Oil Monarchies: Domestic and Security Challenges in the Arab Gulf States.* New York: Council on Foreign Relations Press, 1994.

Khalid ibn Sultan, Prince, with Patrick Seale. *Desert Warrior: A Personal View of the Gulf War by the Joint Forces Commander.* New York: HarperCollins, 1995.

Munro, Alan. *Arabian Affair: The Gulf War from Saudi Arabia.* Washington, DC: Potomac Books, 1996.

# Saudi Arabia

Middle Eastern nation located on the Arabian Peninsula and having a current population of approximately 28.2 million. The Kingdom of Saudi Arabia, founded in 1932, covers 756,981 square miles, nearly three times the area of the U.S. state of Texas. Saudi Arabia borders on Jordan, Iraq, and Kuwait to the north; the Persian Gulf, Qatar, and the United Arab Emirates to the east; Oman and Yemen to the south; and the Red Sea to the west.

Saudi Arabia has been dominated by its ruling family, the House of Saud, for all of its modern history. King Abd al-Aziz al-Saud, known as Ibn Saud, the founding monarch, ruled until his death in 1953. All succeeding kings have been his sons, of which he had 48. The House of Saud has a historical alliance with the Shaykh family, the descendants of Muhammad abd al-Wahhab, founder of Wahhabism (an interpretation of Islam). Saudi Arabia's legal system is based on the Hanbali school of Islamic law. Indeed, the Qur'an serves as the basic governing principles for Saudi Arabia.

The role of Ibn Saud in Saudi Arabia cannot be overstated. The state grew inexorably as a result of his increasing domination of the Arabian Peninsula in the early 20th century as the Ottoman Empire declined. After the end of World War I and the collapse of the Ottoman Empire, he consolidated his position and became king in 1925. The realm was renamed the Kingdom of Saudi Arabia seven years later and included the Hijaz region, which had been governed by the Sharifians who, unable to hold their territory, now headed the countries of Jordan and Iraq. The fortunes of the kingdom were transformed with the discovery of vast petroleum reserves in the 1930s. The nation's oil reserves would bring with them trillions of dollars of revenue and turn the kingdom into one of the world's wealthiest nations. After the 1960s, at which point the influence of foreign oil companies was on the wane, Saudi Arabia's oil assets gave the kingdom a great deal of geopolitical clout as well.

Initially, American oil companies (Chevron in particular) played the leading role in oil exploration and formed a partnership with the Saudi monarchy, paying royalties for the right to extract and ship Saudi oil. The importance of oil during World War II enhanced the U.S.-Saudi relationship, and in 1944 the Arab-American Oil Corporation (ARAMCO) was formed. President Franklin D. Roosevelt

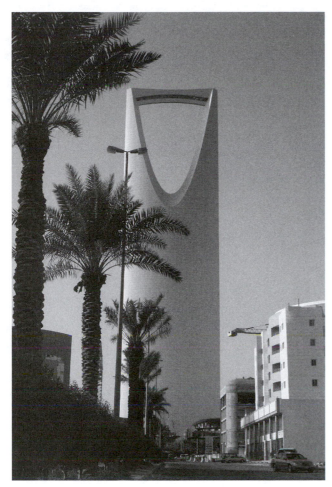

The Kingdom Center tower in the Saudi Arabian capital city of Riyadh. (iStockPhoto)

helped to cement the growing relationship when he met with Ibn Saud on February 14, 1945, aboard the heavy cruiser USS *Quincy*. The Saudi monarchy maintained close economic and strategic ties to the United States throughout the remainder of the century.

Nevertheless, the Israeli issue greatly complicated U.S.-Saudi relations. The Saudis firmly objected to the 1948 formation of the State of Israel, opposed the displacement of Palestinian Arabs, and played a minor military role in the Israeli War of Independence (1948–1949). Support of Palestinian rights and opposition to Israel became a central theme of Saudi foreign policy, and as with other Arab nations, the Saudis refused to recognize Israel. Nevertheless, strong American ties led Saudi diplomacy to depart significantly from that of the frontline republican Arab states such as Syria and Egypt. Because of the growing strategic importance of the Middle East and its oil reserves to Cold War geopolitics, the United States, the Soviet Union, and even the People's Republic of China (PRC) sought increased influence in the region. The Soviets pursued political relationships with secular, socialist Arab nationalist regimes in Egypt, Iraq, and Syria, and Soviet military assistance was crucial to these nations in their ongoing struggle with Israel. The United States countered these Soviet overtures by

tightening its links to the royal regimes in Iran and Saudi Arabia, which included vast arms sales.

In 1962 civil war broke out in Yemen when a republican faction broke with the traditional Zaydi rulers in northern Yemen. The war reflected political, sectarian, and geographic divisions. Egyptian president Gamal Abdel Nasser supported the republicans. Despite previous rivalries with the ruling house of Yemen, the Saudis gave financial support and military assistance to the Zaydi leadership. Egypt and Saudi Arabia thus confronted each other indirectly in the conflict while carrying out a wider propaganda war against each other. The House of Saud refused to tolerate the spread of Nasserists who might challenge royalism in the kingdom even as they supported Arab unity as a general principle. In addition, the respective affiliations of Egypt and Saudi Arabia with the Soviet Union and the United States turned the North Yemen Civil War into a regional theater of confrontation.

Israel's seizure of the West Bank, the Gaza Strip, the Sinai peninsula, and the Golan Heights in the June 1967 Six-Day War deeply concerned Saudis, as it did all Arab states. In the wake of Nasser's death, Saudi concerns over regional policy multiplied. As U.S. support for Israel increased, the Saudis sought to influence U.S. policy in favor of the Arabs. This resolve was also seen in the 1973 oil embargo. Saudi oil was largely controlled by American-owned oil companies until the early 1970s. At that point, the House of Saud negotiated the gradual transformation of ARAMCO into Saudi ARAMCO. By 1973 the transfer of control had begun. When Egypt and Syria attacked Israel in October 1973, prompting the Yom Kippur (Ramadan) War, Saudi Arabia's King Faisal obtained U.S. president Richard M. Nixon's assurances of American nonintervention.

The Israelis suffered severe reversals in the opening stages of the conflict, however, prompting Nixon to send U.S. military aid to Israel on October 19. The next day the Organization of Petroleum Exporting Countries (OPEC), to which Saudi Arabia belongs, implemented an oil embargo directed at the United States and other Western oil-importing states that supported Israel. The embargo hobbled the already weak U.S. economy and created inflationary pressures. American fuel prices rose 40 percent during the five months of the crisis. The boycott ended without securing any resolution of the Palestinian issue, yet afterward oil prices remained volatile and high, in part due to distributors and middlemen who benefited from this.

Saudi Arabia benefited immensely from this crisis, experiencing an economic boom. Massive increases in oil revenues (from $5 billion per year in 1972 to $119 billion per year in 1981) led to the kingdom's transformation of its urban centers from dusty provincial towns to modern cites. Generous government subsidies and programs were also extended to Saudi citizens, many of whom were poor and still remain so. However, the House of Saud maintained strict control over Saudi society, politics, and law. Religious conservatives strongly influenced local culture and social practices.

Opposition emerged to King Faisal, particularly from conservatives. On March 25, 1975, Faisal was assassinated by his nephew, the stated reason being revenge for the death of his brother who had been killed by Saudi Defense Force members during a demonstration in 1965.

Faisal was followed by his half brother, Khalid. In 1979 Juhayman al-Utaybi took hostages at the Grand Mosque in Mecca, triggering a full-scale political crisis, and foreign troops had to be brought in to deal with the rebels.

Saudi Arabia remained an absolute monarchy until 1992, when the royal family promulgated the nation's Basic Law following the 1991 Persian Gulf War.

The U.S.-Saudi relationship eventually recovered and remained close. Indeed, Saudi Arabia often used its influence in OPEC to keep oil prices artificially low from the mid-1980s to the late 1990s. However, the Saudis continued to oppose Israel's treatment of the Palestinians and its continued presence in the occupied territories. Saudi relations with Egypt declined precipitously after the signing of the Camp David Accords between Israel and Egypt in 1978. The Saudis objected to any individual peace deals with Israel that did not settle the entire Arab-Israeli conflict and address the plight of the Palestinian Arabs and the refugees of the 1948–1949 war. In 1981 Crown Prince Fahd (who ruled as king during 1982–2005) proposed a peace plan based on a Palestinian state in the West Bank and the Gaza Strip, removal of Israeli settlements in those areas, and a plan to address the needs of Palestinian refugees. Indeed, Saudi Arabia became a primary source of economic aid for the Palestine Liberation Organization (PLO) after the Camp David Accords. While the PLO's support for Iraqi dictator Saddam Hussein during the Persian Gulf War of 1991 effectively curtailed Saudi financial support for Fatah, then the PLO's principal political faction, the regime in Riyadh did not change its position on a comprehensive peace. In 2002 Crown Prince Abdullah of Saudi Arabia proposed another comprehensive peace plan to which the Israeli government did not respond.

During Operation DESERT SHIELD, which began in August 1990 after the Iraqi invasion of Kuwait, the Saudis took the highly unusual step of allowing some 500,000 foreign troops—most of them American—to use its territory as the main staging area for a potential strike against Iraq. Initially the buildup in Saudi Arabia was billed as a protective measure to keep Iraq from broadening its offensive into Saudi Arabia. The decision caused a negative reaction among the ultraconservatives and morals police in Saudi Arabia, and consequently the king had to rein them in. The conservatives argued that the foreigners were defiling Islamic traditions and law. But the troop deployment was seen in Riyadh as a necessary evil of sorts, as Iraqi dictator Hussein could not be trusted to end his land grab in Kuwait. Saudi troops subsequently joined the 34-nation international coalition that forced Iraq from Kuwait in February 1991 during Operation DESERT STORM.

After the September 11, 2001, terrorist attacks on the United States, which involved 15 Saudi Arabian nationals or citizens,

U.S.-Saudi relations suffered even though Riyadh decried the terrorist actions. The Saudis strongly disapproved of Operation IRAQI FREEDOM, which commenced in March 2003, and they refused to allow use of their territory as a base of operations for the invasion. The Saudis disapproved because of the likelihood of Iraqi fratricide following regime change and the boon that a destabilized Iraq would create for Iran. However, many Saudis were also concerned that if the coalition forces pulled out too soon, Iraq would degenerate into full-scale civil war. Also, the U.S. engagement in Iraq provided a rationale for Saudis who opposed their own government's alliance with America. Some went to join the insurgents in Iraq.

At the same time, an ongoing effort to close down U.S. military operations in the kingdom had been in progress for some time. In August 2003 all remaining U.S. troops were withdrawn.

During 2003–2005 a series of attacks by a hitherto unknown group calling itself al-Qa'ida fi Jazirat al-Arabiyya killed Saudis and Westerners. These included the bombing in May and November 2003 of two housing compounds for foreign workers in Saudi Arabia that resulted in many deaths (including Americans) and an attack on the American consulate in Jeddah. Attacks and attempted sabotage by this group continued into 2009 despite a strong counterterrorism effort carried out by the Saudi authorities and a thorough reeducation program designed by the Saudi Ministry of the Interior. The Saudis also cooperated with numerous American requirements such as exerting control over Islamic charitable groups, addressing extremism in parts of the Islamic educational system, cutting off funding to the *mutawa'in* (morals police), and providing information to the international counterintelligence effort. Still, the United States media and government remain highly critical of Saudi Arabia, in part because of increases in the price of oil, owing to political volatility in the region; threats in Nigeria, another oil producer; and Saudi efforts to more prudently manage its current economic boom. In 2007–2008 a sharp increase in oil prices created some panic in the United States. The George W. Bush administration asked Riyadh to increase oil output to ease prices, and the Saudis agreed in 2008.

ROBERT S. KIELY AND SHERIFA ZUHUR

**See also**

Al Qaeda; Arab-Israeli Conflict, Overview; Arab Nationalism; DESERT SHIELD, Operation; DESERT STORM, Operation; Faisal, King of Saudi Arabia; Global War on Terror; Nasser, Gamal Abdel; Oil; Organization of Petroleum Exporting Countries; Pan-Arabism and Pan-Arabist Thought; Saudi Arabia, Armed Forces; September 11 Attacks, International Reactions to; Wahhabism

**References**

Lacey, Robert. *The Kingdom.* London: Hutchinson, 1981.
Wynbrandt, James. *A Brief History of Saudi Arabia.* New York: Checkmark, 2004.
Zuhur, Sherifa. *Saudi Arabia: Islamic Threat, Political Reform and the Global War on Terror.* Carlisle Barracks, PA: Strategic Studies Institute, 2005.

# Saudi Arabia, Armed Forces

Saudi Arabia's military forces are currently divided into five major branches: the Saudi Arabian National Guard (SANG), the Royal Saudi Land Forces (RSLF), the Royal Saudi Air Defense Forces (RSADF), the Royal Saudi Air Force (RSAF), the Royal Saudi Naval Force (RSNF), and the Saudi Coast Guard (SCG). Operational control of these forces rests with the minister of defense and aviation in Riyadh. The head of the SANG is the first deputy prime minister and answers directly to the king.

SANG evolved from Ikhwan (the Brotherhood), the *muwahhadin,* or Wahhabi, warriors who fought in the establishment of the Saudi Arabian state. The Ikhwan were sometimes called the White Army for the traditional Arab robes rather than uniforms worn by its members. King Abd al-Aziz, known as Ibn Saud, the first king of Saudi Arabia, organized and led the White Army in the early decades of the 20th century to subdue tribal resistance and unify the tribes of the Arabian Peninsula into what is now the Kingdom of Saudi Arabia. From this origin, SANG has a long-honored tradition of bravery and loyalty to the nation and its ruling family.

Existing parallel to but separate from the regular Saudi military forces, SANG is a full-time standing, land-based, defensive force of approximately 75,000 regulars and 25,000 militia. It is headquartered in the capital city of Riyadh and has two regional headquarters at Dammam in the east and Jeddah in the west.

SANG is a mechanized infantry and light infantry force that relies on rapid mobility and firepower to defeat its adversaries. Armed with eight-wheeled light armored vehicles and towed artillery, SANG complements the heavier armor of the RSLF and is fully capable of conducting integrated operations. However, it primarily acts a very effective internal security force that can provide rear-area security for the army and help defend Riyadh.

The RSLF is headquartered in Riyadh and has field commands organized into eight zones under military zone commanders. The RSLF consists of armored, mechanized, and airborne forces with associated support elements. The RSLF has about 75,000 troops and an inventory of 1,000 tanks, 3,000 other armored vehicles, and 500 major artillery pieces. These forces are normally dispersed over much of the kingdom and focus on territorial defense.

The RSLF Aviation Branch employs a mix of Sikorsky UH-60 Blackhawk utility and support helicopters, Boeing-Vertol CH-47 Chinook transport helicopters, and Bell AH-64 Apache attack helicopters. The RSLF has its own tactical air defense resources designed to protect its maneuver forces in combat. These forces

A Royal Saudi Air Force F-15 Eagle fighter aircraft approaches a KC-135 Stratotanker for refueling during Operation DESERT SHIELD, May 1990. (U.S. Department of Defense)

**Military Expenditures of Selected Nations during the Persian Gulf War (in millions of dollars)**

| Country | 1990 | 1991 |
|---|---|---|
| Iraq | $14,110 | $8,776 |
| Kuwait | $13,170 | $15,950 |
| Saudi Arabia | $23,160 | $35,510 |
| United Kingdom | $37,090 | $39,620 |
| United States | $306,200 | $280,300 |

are armed with Mistral, Stinger, and Redeye surface-to-air missiles (SAMs). In addition, they employ a number of different antiaircraft gun systems, including the Vulcan, Bofors, and Oerlikon guns.

In 1984 the kingdom established the Royal Saudi Air Defense Force, a separate professional service dedicated to the territorial air defense mission. This separate force controls Saudi Arabia's heavy SAMs and fixed air defenses, including a mix of Crotale, Shahine, and I-Hawk surface-to-air missiles. It is a relatively static force of about 16,000 men designed for point defense that cannot easily support the army in mobile operations.

Saudi Arabia has given the modernization and expansion of the RSAF a higher priority than that of the land forces, navy, and air defense force. This is primarily because the RSAF is the only service that can cover Saudi Arabia's 888,035 sqaure miles (2.3 million square kilometers) of territory. The RSAF is headquartered at Riyadh and has a total strength of about 20,000 men. Its operational command is structured around its air command and operations center and base operations. The main air command and operations center is near Riyadh, and there are ancillary sector operating centers at Tabuk, Khamis Mushayt, Riyadh, Dhahran, and Kharj that control fighter aircraft, SAMs, and air defense artillery.

The RSAF has operational command facilities at a number of air bases located throughout the kingdom. According to one source, the RSAF's combat forces are organized into six wings with a total of 15 combat squadrons and more than 400 fixed-wing combat and training aircraft. The RSAF flies a mix of aircraft to include various models of the McDonnell Douglas F-15 Eagle, the Northrop F-5 Freedom Fighter and Tiger, and the Panavia Interdictor Tornado.

The RSNF is headquartered in Riyadh and has east and west fleets for its Persian Gulf and Red Sea coasts. It has a total strength of 13,500 to 15,500 men. The combat strength of the RSNF includes 7 frigates, 4 missile corvettes, and 9 guided missile ships. It also includes 3 torpedo boats, 20 inshore fast craft, 17 coastal patrol craft, 3 mine warfare ships, and a number of support and auxiliary craft. The RSNF also includes the Royal Saudi Marine Division. This 3,000-man force is organized into one regiment with two battalions.

The SCG is part of the Frontier Force, has a separate command chain, and maintains its primary base at Aziziah. The SCG contains up to 4,500 men who man a variety of coastal patrol craft.

Its primary mission is antismuggling activity, but it does have an internal security mission as well.

Saudi Arabia emerged as a significant regional military force during the 1991 Persian Gulf War. Two Arab task forces were organized under the command of Prince Khalid ibn Sultan al-Saud. By the time the land phase of the war began in February 1991, the Saudi ground forces in theater totaled nearly 50,000 men, some 270 main battle tanks, 930 other armored fighting vehicles, 115 artillery weapons, and more than 400 antitank weapons. The RSAF flew a total of 6,852 sorties between January 17 and February 28, 1991, second only to the United States in total air activity. In the four-day ground war that began on February 24, Saudi troops, including the SANG, helped defeat the Iraqis and drive them out of Kuwait. Saudi forces did not participate in the Iraq War that began in 2003, however. The military remains a significant employer of Saudi citizens, and despite rocky relations with the United States after the September 11, 2001, terror attacks, Riyadh remains the primary purchaser of U.S. armaments, with contracts exceeding $1.1 billion in 2005.

JAMES H. WILLBANKS

**See also**

Arms Sales, International; DESERT SHIELD, Operation; DESERT STORM, Operation; Saud, Khalid ibn Sultan ibn Abd al-Aziz al-; Saudi Arabia

**References**

Cordesman, Anthony H. *Saudi Arabia: Guarding the Desert Kingdom.* Boulder, CO: Westview, 1997.

———. *Saudi Arabia Enters the Twenty-First Century: The Military and International Security Dimensions.* New York: Praeger, 2003.

Khalid ibn Sultan, Prince, with Patrick Seale. *Desert Warrior: A Personal View of the Gulf War by the Joint Forces Commander.* New York: HarperCollins, 1995.

Pollack, Kenneth M. *Arabs at War: Military Effectiveness, 1948–1991.* Lincoln: University of Nebraska Press, 2002.

## SCATHE MEAN, Operation
### Event Date: January 17, 1991

Part of the air operations at the beginning of Operation DESERT STORM in 1991 intended to force the Iraqis to turn on their radars and track large numbers of decoys that would confuse and overwhelm their tracking systems. Operation SCATHE MEAN was to follow initial air strikes by conventionally armed cruise missiles and Lockheed F-117 stealth fighters that would target the major Iraqi air defense control centers. Coalition planners hoped that the Iraqis would also fire some of their surface-to-air missiles (SAMs) at the decoys. In any event, coalition aircraft armed with high-speed antiradiation missiles (HARMs) would attack the radars, helping to blind Iraqi air defenses. The operation went perfectly, leaving the Iraqis unable to seriously challenge coalition strike aircraft.

In 1981 Israel launched a surprise attack on Iraq's Osiraq nuclear reactor. The raid was a complete success, prompting Iraqi president Saddam Hussein to order the construction of a new air defense system. Companies from several countries provided parts for the new system. It was named Kari (Iraq spelled backwards in French) by the French engineers who oversaw the creation of the Iraqi defensive system. Although Kari used various radars from numerous countries, including China and Italy, the heart of the system was a centralized command structure employing mainframe computers to collect data from different sources and provide a clear picture to controllers in Baghdad. The central authorities could then decide how best to deal with an incoming threat.

Kari was based upon the Soviets' air defense system. By integrating radars, SAMs, and antiaircraft artillery, Kari was expected to make air strikes by coalition aircraft very costly. The weakness turned out to be the highly centralized control. Dictatorship generally seeks to have centralized control over different systems and disapproves of initiatives taken by local commanders.

Under Kari, intercept-operations centers fed information to sector operations centers, which in turn sent information to Air Defense Headquarters in Baghdad. The coalition air plan concentrated the first strikes against the command facilities in Baghdad, including the communications and power nodes. Essentially, the coalition plan was to break the Iraqi air defense system into component parts and then destroy each. Because Baghdad was so heavily defended, only stealth fighters and cruise missiles were assigned to the initial attacks.

Although U.S. war planners believed that they could disable the Iraqi central command structure, they recognized that the Iraqi air defenses remained dangerous. The navy's Strike Projection Evaluation and Anti-Air Research (SPEAR) study group had studied how to overcome antiaircraft defenses since 1983, when the navy lost two aircraft against relatively weak Syrian air defenses. SPEAR passed along what it learned about Iraqi defenses to the group in Saudi Arabia preparing the air campaign. The air force had a similar study group known as Checkmate. One of the plans to come out of Checkmate was to use decoys to fool the Iraqi defenses. The idea was based on the success enjoyed by the Israelis against Syrian air defenses in 1982.

One of the problems that planners faced was obtaining a sufficient number of decoys to fool the Iraqi defenses. The U.S. Navy had purchased more than 1,000 tactical air-launched decoys (TALDs) that were based on decoys used by the Israelis in 1982. They weighed between 400 and 450 pounds each, and up to six could be carried on a single wing pylon of a naval aircraft. The TALDs were unpowered gliders, but they had a glide ratio of 10:1, so they could fly more than 60 miles after being released. With an ability to reach speeds up to 460 miles per hour (mph) and the capability to return radar signatures similar to any military aircraft, the TALDs were able to fool the Iraqis into thinking that a major air attack was being launched.

The U.S. Air Force's part in Operation SCATHE MEAN was somewhat different because the air force had no decoys or drones that were suitable to the operation. Instead, it managed to obtain 44 BQM-74 Chukar drones from the U.S. Navy. The navy typically used the Chukars as targets. They were powered by a turbojet producing 240 pounds of thrust, giving the drone a top speed of nearly 600 mph. The gyroscopes used to control the Chukars' flight path were not as accurate as hoped, but the planners believed that they would work. Brigadier General Larry Henry, known as "Poobah," headed the air force operation, which became known as "Poobah's Party."

To launch the Chukars, the air force had to assemble the equipment and a team. Because the drones were not standard air force equipment, expertise regarding them was in short supply. Ordinarily the Chukars would be launched from a Lockheed DC-130 Hercules director aircraft, but none was available for duty in the Persian Gulf. Instead, Henry made the decision to use ground launchers. A dozen launchers were found in the navy's stockpiles and made available. Rocket-assisted takeoff packs were found in Belgium and flown to Saudi Arabia. Trucks were purchased from a California commercial trucking firm, and tool kits were bought at Sears. Field gear for the personnel was purchased at military surplus stores.

The only air force personnel with experience in ground-launched missiles were those who had been trained to launch nuclear-tipped cruise missiles. Those weapons had been eliminated in the 1987 Intermediate-Range Nuclear Forces Treaty, but a training unit was still operational in Arizona. Personnel from the unit were then formed into the 4468th Tactical Reconnaissance Group and sent to Saudi Arabia. They arrived in two six-launcher teams near the Iraqi border on October 15, 1990. One team was based near King Khalid Military City near Kuwait, while the other was near Arar, a town in western Saudi Arabia that was a base for U.S. Special Forces.

On January 17, 1991, the air campaign began. After F-117s and cruise missiles had hit targets in and around Baghdad, Operation SCATHE MEAN began. Twenty-five TLADs were launched by navy Grumman A-6 Intruders, apparently heading toward Iraqi targets. At 3:48 a.m. (local time), the Chukars were launched from Saudi Arabia. Although 38 decoys were supposed to be launched in groups of three, only 37 were actually sent on their way. The Iraqi defenders, deprived of central control and determined to prevent more strikes on the capital, lit up their radars and began tracking the decoys. As they identified targets, they began launching their Soviet-made SAMs. The Iraqis thought that they were scoring many successes. As the TALDs reached the end of their range they descended off the radar scopes, like so many aircraft being shot down. As the Chukars approached targets from Saudi Arabia, the Iraqis launched interceptor aircraft. One group of three was intercepted, while the others made it to their targets in and around Baghdad.

As the Iraqis turned on radars to track the decoys, U.S. Marine Corps and U.S. Navy McDonnell Douglas (now Boeing) F/A-18

Hornets and U.S. Air Force McDonnell Douglas F-4G Phantom II/Weasel aircraft launched more than 200 HARMs. Many Iraqi radars were destroyed, creating huge holes in their defenses for later air strikes. The loss of radars and the wasting of many SAMs on decoys were severe blows from which the Iraqi air defenses never recovered. Although coalition aircraft continued to be lost until the end of the war, the numbers were quite low. Indeed, most fell to unguided antiaircraft artillery or individually launched missiles.

The 4468th Group was disbanded after the Persian Gulf War, and a single BQM-74C was donated to the U.S. Air Force Museum at Wright-Patterson Air Force Base (Ohio) to commemorate the success of Operation SCATHE MEAN.

TIM J. WATTS

**See also**

Air Defenses in Iraq, Persian Gulf War; Antiradiation Missiles, Coalition; DESERT STORM, Operation, Coalition Air Campaign; Kari Air Defense System; Tactical Air-Launched Decoys; United States Air Force, Persian Gulf War; United States Navy, Persian Gulf War

**References**

Gordon, Michael R., and General Bernard E. Trainor. *The Generals' War: The Inside Story of the Conflict in the Gulf.* New York: Little, Brown, 1995.

Murray, Williamson. *Air War in the Persian Gulf.* Baltimore: Nautical and Aviation Publishing Company of America, 1995.

Olsen, John. *Strategic Air Power in Desert Storm.* London: Frank Cass, 2003.

---

# Schoomaker, Peter Jan
## Birth Date: February 12, 1946

U.S. Army general and the army's 35th chief of staff (2003–2007). Peter Jan Schoomaker was born on February 12, 1946, in Detroit, Michigan. He entered the army as a second lieutenant in June 1969 through the Reserve Officers' Training Corps (ROTC) upon graduation from the University of Wyoming. Following the Officer Basic Course, he graduated from both the Airborne and Ranger training programs. His first field assignment came in January 1970 as a reconnaissance platoon leader.

Thereafter, Schoomaker's military career involved a wide variety of command and staff assignments with both conventional and special operations forces. His military education included the Marine Corps Amphibious Warfare School, the U.S. Army Command and General Staff College, and the John F. Kennedy School of Government Program for Senior Executives in National and International Security Management. Schoomaker also earned a master's degree in management from Central Michigan University.

From 1978 to 1981 Schoomaker commanded a squadron of the 1st Special Forces Operational Detachment D. He led a Delta Force team during Operation EAGLE CLAW, the ill-fated 1980 attempt to rescue Americans being held hostage in Iran. This experience led to Schoomaker's conviction that proper training and proper equipment were vital to operational success. After attending the Army Command and General Staff College, he served as executive officer in an armored cavalry squadron based in West Germany from June 1982 to August 1983. During most of the period from August 1983 to August 1988, he served in command and staff positions with the Joint Special Operations Command and 1st Special Forces Operational Detachment D (popularly called the Delta Force) based at Fort Bragg. From October 1983 to February 1984 he was assigned temporary duty with the Department of Defense Commission on United States Marine Corps Terrorist Incident in Beirut, Lebanon.

After attending the National War College, Schoomaker returned to Fort Bragg in 1989 to serve as commander of the Combat Applications Group (Airborne) until July 1992. Promoted to colonel on June 1, 1990, he was the 1st Cavalry Division's assistant division commander from July 1992 to July 1993. He was promoted to brigadier general on January 1, 1993. In July 1993 Schoomaker became the deputy director of operations, readiness, and mobilization, Office of the Deputy Chief of Staff for Operations and Plans. From July 1994 to August 1996 Schoomaker served as the commanding general of the Joint Special Operations Command. Having been promoted to major general on March 1, 1996, and then to lieutenant general on August 1, 1996, he was the commander of the U.S. Army Special Operations Command at Fort Bragg through October 1997. Promoted to full (four-star) general in October 1997, Schoomaker served as the commander in chief, U.S. Special Operations Command, at MacDill Air Force Base, Florida, from November 1997 to November 2000, when he retired from the military.

When several activte duty generals declined to serve as chief of staff under him, Secretary of Defense Donald Rumsfeld recalled Schoomaker from retirement to become the army's 35th chief of staff on August 1, 2003. This appointment was particularly controversial because Schoomaker's predecessor, General Eric Shinseki, had fallen out of favor with many influential members of the George W. Bush administration. Schoomaker was the first U.S. Army chief of staff to possess wide experience with the Special Forces. In his first remarks after being sworn in, Schoomaker announced that he would focus on army training methods and leadership development. He also planned to evaluate the mix between active and reserve components. Schoomaker was most concerned with the soldiers, emphasizing that their capabilities were fundamental to creating a flexible, adaptable force.

Much of Schoomaker's time was devoted to supporting ongoing operations in Iraq and Afghanistan while implementing what some called the greatest reorganization of the U.S. Army since World War II. This also involved the most extensive modernization plan in three decades, the so-called Future Combat System. Under Schoomaker's guidance, the army transformation concept was updated with a stated goal of providing "relevant and ready current forces and future forces organized, trained, and equipped

General Peter J. Schoomaker, U.S. Army chief of staff during 2003–2007, center, is shown here in Iraq with 101st Airborne Division commander Major General David Petraeus, right, in 2003. (U.S. Army)

for joint, interagency, and multinational full spectrum operations." Simultaneously, Schoomaker worked to instill a warrior ethos throughout all levels of the military. Having completed his four-year term on April 10, 2007, Schoomaker retired for a second time. General George W. Casey Jr. succeeded him.

JAMES ARNOLD

**See also**

Rumsfeld, Donald Henry; United States Army, Afghanistan War; United States Army, Iraq War

**References**

Fontenot, Gregory, et al. *On Point: The United States Army in Iraqi Freedom.* Annapolis, MD: Naval Institute Press, 2005.

Parsi, Trita. *Treacherous Alliance: The Secret Dealings of Israel, Iran, and the United States.* New Haven, CT: Yale University Press, 2007.

Scales, Robert H. *Certain Victory: The U.S. Army in the Gulf War.* Washington, DC: Brassey's, 1994.

U.S. Congress. *Assessing U.S. Special Operations Command's Missions and Roles: Hearing before the Terrorism, Unconventional Threats and Capabilities Subcommittee of the Committee on Armed Services, House of Representatives.* 109th Congress, 2nd Session, June 29, 2006. Washington, DC: U.S. Government Printing Office, 2008.

Vandenbroucke, Lucien S. *Perilous Option: Special Operations as an Instrument of U.S. Foreign Policy.* New York: Oxford University Press, 1993.

# Schröder, Gerhard Fritz Kurt
## Birth Date: April 7, 1944

German attorney, politician, and chancellor of the Federal Republic of Germany (FRG) during 1998–2005. Gerhard Fritz Kurtz Schröder was born on April 7, 1944, in Mossenberg, Lower Saxony, just months before his father was killed in action in World War II. Schröder worked various unskilled jobs while studying at night to gain a high school diploma. He went on to study law at the University of Göttingen, graduating in 1971, and became active in the Social Democratic Party of Germany (SPD) from 1963 onward.

From 1972 to 1976 Schröder served as an assistant at the University of Göttingen, and from 1976 to 1990 he practiced law. Elected to the Bundestag (parliament) in 1980, he soon gained a reputation for his charisma. In 1990 he became the minister-president of Lower Saxony, where he served as the head of a coalition between the SPD and the Green Party, a relationship that he had conceptualized in the early 1980s. On October 27, 1998, he became the head of that same coalition, this time at the federal level as chancellor of Germany.

Economic and domestic issues dominated the first half of Schröder's chancellorship, but the terrorist attacks against the

United States on September 11, 2001, shifted his attention to terrorism and the Middle East. September 11 provided an opportunity for Germany to move its foreign policy away from its general post–World War II diffidence. As such, Schröder promised a 3,900-man force for the ensuing military action in Afghanistan (Operation ENDURING FREEDOM). This move served as both an important gesture of solidarity with the United States and a sign of Germany's willingness to project force abroad. Schröder now publicly asserted that Germany's responsibility to the world went beyond its economic strength and that it would have to exert political power as well. Thus, he pushed for the first ever FRG military action outside Europe, in Afghanistan. Because of the controversy surrounding this decision, Schröder insisted on a vote of confidence in the Bundestag. He secured a favorable vote, although this led to strained relations with the Green Party elements of his coalition.

As American rhetoric against Iraq intensified in 2002, Germany was one of many nations in the United Nations (UN) to argue for nonmilitary alternatives to enforce previous UN resolutions regarding Iraqi disarmament. Schröder went further, however, joining France in declaring unequivocally that his nation would not send military support of any kind to wage a war in Iraq even if a UN resolution authorized the use of force. Not surprisingly, Schröder's opposition to the Iraq War (2003–) caused a significant breach in German-American relations, which had heretofore been strong.

This situation was exacerbated when Schröder used the looming conflict in Iraq as a major campaign issue when he was lagging in the polls during the 2002 federal election process. Politically, the exposure of Al Qaeda cells operating in Hamburg undermined SPD control there and elsewhere, opening the door for more conservative movements to gain a foothold. Emerging information during the campaign only highlighted Germany's poor record of tracking Islamic groups with potential terrorist links. However, two-thirds of Germans remained opposed to war in Iraq, so this issue bore electoral fruit. Critics, however, accused Schröder of, at best, exploiting anti-American sentiments in his country and, at worst, intentionally cultivating them to gain reelection. Schröder's coalition won another four-year hold on power in the September 22, 2002, federal elections.

Both Chancellor Schröder and his American counterparts tried to put the best face on their now-rocky relationship, particularly considering the importance of the ongoing German presence in Afghanistan. Schröder also sent nonmilitary assistance for the reconstruction of Iraq after the Anglo-American–led March 2003 invasion and reinforced the consensus between the United States and Europe that Iran should be prevented from developing nuclear weapons capabilities. However, tensions in the U.S.-German relationship reemerged when Schröder warned the United States in August 2005 to back away from military threats against Iran. He tried to use Iran as a campaign issue that autumn, but this time the tactic failed, and he was forced from office in November 2005, replaced by Angela Merkel, a Christian Democrat who is more conservative than Schröder and far less anti-American.

Schröder had found a partner for his Middle East policy in the Russian Federation, while the U.S.-Russian relationship became strained. In his last weeks in office he signed a deal to build a natural gas pipeline under the Baltic Sea to supply Germany directly. After leaving office he became chairman of the North European Gas Pipeline, a project majority-owned by the Russian state-controlled natural gas giant, Gazprom, the primary beneficiary of the Baltic Sea pipeline. Critics on both sides of the Atlantic were outraged, asserting that Schröder had pursued policies in office that ultimately brought him private gain. Many critics in Germany accused Schröder of simply selling Germany and Western Europe to Russia. The affair cast a dark shadow on the legacy of his Middle East policy. Since leaving office, Schröder has continued to be an outspoken apologist for Russian policies, especially during the Russian attack on Georgia in 2008 and Russia's long-running campaign of seeking to assert its authority over Ukraine and the Baltic Republics.

STEPHANIE TROMBLEY

**See also**

ENDURING FREEDOM, Operation; Germany, Federal Republic of, Middle East Policy; IRAQI FREEDOM, Operation

**References**

Acker, Kerry. *Gerhard Schroeder*. New York: Chelsea House, 2003.

Conradt, David P., Gerald R, Kleinfeld, and Christian Soe, eds. *A Precarious Victory: Schroeder and the German Elections of 2002*. New York: Berghahn Books, 2004.

Serfaty, Simon. *Architects of Delusion: Europe, America, and the Iraq War*. Philadelphia: University of Pennsylvania Press, 2008.

---

# Schwarzkopf, H. Norman, Jr.
## Birth Date: August 22, 1934

U.S. Army officer, commander in chief of the U.S. Central Command (CENTCOM) from 1988 to 1991, and commander of coalition forces during Operations DESERT SHIELD and DESERT STORM. H. Norman Schwarzkopf Jr. (sometimes referred to as "Stormin' Norman") was born on August 22, 1934, in Trenton, New Jersey. His father, Herbert Norman Schwarzkopf, disliked his own first name and gave his son only its first letter. The elder Schwarzkopf had graduated from the United States Military Academy, West Point, and, following his military career, headed the New Jersey State Police. In the late 1940s the younger Schwarzkopf accompanied his father to Iran, where the elder Schwarzkopf helped establish and train that country's national police. This experience gave the young Schwarzkopf a lasting interest in Islamic culture and history.

Schwarzkopf followed his father in attending West Point, graduating in 1956. His first assignment was at Fort Benning, Georgia, where he received advanced infantry and airborne training. Schwarzkopf later served with the 101st Airborne Division in Kentucky and the 6th Infantry Division in Germany. He was in

As commander of the U.S. Central Command (CENTCOM) during 1988–1991, U.S. Army general H. Norman Schwarzkopf directed the highly successful international military coalition that drove Iraqi forces from Kuwait during the Persian Gulf War in 1991. (U.S. Department of Defense)

Berlin during the crises there in 1960 and 1961. In 1964 Schwarzkopf earned a master's degree in mechanical engineering from the University of Southern California, specializing in the development of precision-guided missiles, and in 1965 he began a three-year teaching assignment at West Point.

The Vietnam War cut short Schwarzkopf's West Point assignment, however, and at the rank of captain he served a tour as an adviser to the Republic of Vietnam Airborne Division before returning to the academy. Promoted to lieutenant colonel in 1968, Schwarzkopf attended the U.S. Army Command and General Staff College, and in 1969 he returned to Vietnam as a battalion commander, where he earned a Silver Star and was twice wounded. There he also acquired his reputation as a tough no-nonsense commander who was willing to risk his own life for his men. In 1970 Schwarzkopf, now a colonel, returned to the United States in a body cast. On his recovery he studied internal defense and national security issues at the Army War College. He then served in Alaska, Washington state, Hawaii, Germany, and Washington, D.C.

Schwarzkopf was promoted to brigadier general in 1978 and assigned at the assistant division commander of the 8th Infantry Division (Mechanized) in the Federal Republic of Germany. Promoted to major general in 1982, he assumed command of the 24th Infantry Division (Mechanized) at Fort Stewart, Georgia. A year

later he served as an adviser to the U.S. Navy in Operation URGENT FURY, the U.S. invasion of Grenada. Earning the confidence of the naval commanders, he was appointed deputy commander of the joint task force. He also learned valuable lessons from the experience, especially the need for more effective coordination and control in joint operations.

In 1984 Schwarzkopf returned to the Pentagon to serve in the Office of Deputy Chief of Staff for Operations. In 1986 he was promoted to lieutenant general and assigned as commander of I Corps at Fort Lewis, Washington. After only serving one year in that assignment, he returned to the Pentagon as the army's deputy chief of staff for operations.

Promoted to full (four-star) general in 1988, Schwarzkopf was assigned as commander of the U.S. Central Command (CENT-COM), headquartered at Tampa, Florida. CENTCOM was tasked primarily with potential U.S. operations in the Middle East and Southwest Asia. Although at the time Schwarzkopf assumed CENTOM command the possibility of U.S. military action in those regions seemed remote to American military planners, the situation changed dramatically in August 1990.

Following the Iraqi invasion of Kuwait on August 2, 1990, Schwarzkopf established a forward headquarters in Riyadh, Saudi Arabia, and played a key role in building the international coalition that carried out the United Nations (UN) mandate to restore the independence of Kuwait. Schwarzkopf doubted the ability of airpower alone to cause Iraqi leader Saddam Hussein to withdraw his forces from Kuwait and thus insisted on a large buildup of ground forces to do the job. Operations DESERT SHIELD and DESERT STORM proved highly successful, with coalition forces winning the ground war within only 100 hours in February 1991. Despite the overwhelming success of DESERT STORM, during the war Schwarzkopf's relations with his subordinates—and his superiors in Washington, D.C.—were often rocky. Many subordinates resented his bullying, confrontational manner of command, and his interaction with the Joint Staff and the U.S. Army Staff was often difficult. Although he was immensely popular with the American public, those who worked with him did not share the public's positive perception.

Reportedly, Schwarzkopf opposed the George H. W. Bush administration's decision to end the war without the destruction of the Iraqi Republican Guard. Yet Schwarzkopf himself made the decision in the cease-fire agreement that allowed the Iraqis to continue to fly helicopters, which very much surprised the Iraqi delegates. This decision greatly aided the Iraqi government in crushing insurrections against the Hussein regime.

Schwarzkopf returned to the United States a national hero, aided considerably by his ability to deal quite effectively with the press. He retired from the army in August 1991 and published his best-selling memoir, *It Doesn't Take a Hero,* in 1992. He currently resides in Florida and sits on several corporate boards, including that of Remington. Schwarzkopf was sharply critical of Secretary of Defense Donald Rumsfeld's management of the Iraq War but supported President George W. Bush's reelection bid in 2004 and Republican senator John McCain's presidential bid in 2008. Among Schwarzkopf's many decorations are three Silver Stars and the Presidential Medal of Freedom.

DEBORAH KIDWELL, PAUL G. PIERPAOLI JR.,
AND SPENCER C. TUCKER

**See also**

DESERT SHIELD, Operation; DESERT STORM, Operation; IRAQI FREEDOM, Operation; Rumsfeld, Donald Henry; United States Central Command

**References**

Cohen, Roger, and Claudio Gatti. *In the Eye of the Storm: The Life of General H. Norman Schwarzkopf.* New York: Farrar, Straus and Giroux, 1992.

Morris, M. E. *H. Norman Schwarzkopf: Road to Triumph.* New York: St. Martin's, 1993.

Schubert, Frank N., and Theresa L. Kraus, eds. *The Whirlwind War: The United States Army in Operations Desert Shield and Desert Storm.* Washington, DC: U.S. Government Printing Office, 1995.

Schwarzkopf, H. Norman, with Peter Petre. *It Doesn't Take a Hero: General H. Norman Schwarzkopf, the Autobiography.* New York: Bantam Books, 1993.

Woodward, Bob. *The Commanders.* New York: Simon and Schuster, 1991.

# SCORPION, **Operation**
## Event Date: Late 1990

A plan for ground operations during the 1991 Persian Gulf War to occupy western Iraq; the operation was never implemented. Supporters believed that Operation SCORPION, also known as "the Western Excursion," would prevent Iraqi Scud missiles from being fired at Israel, which might have threatened to break up the military coalition against Iraq. They also believed that it offered an opportunity to destabilize the regime of President Saddam Hussein and force a change in the Iraqi government. The cost to American personnel would be minimal, it was hoped, while Iraqi ground forces that moved to oust the Americans could be devastated by American airpower. The chief supporter of Operation SCORPION was U.S. secretary of defense Richard (Dick) Cheney.

When Hussein ordered his forces to occupy Kuwait in August 1990, the first American objective was to prevent the Iraqis from moving on and occupying the Saudi Arabia oil fields. When sufficient forces had been assembled to prevent this, under the code name DESERT SHIELD, planners then began to plan how to force the Iraqis to leave Kuwait. The United Nations (UN) had authorized tough economic sanctions against Iraq, and many members of the George H. W. Bush administration hoped that sanctions would force Hussein to quit Kuwait. Even so, military commanders began to plan how to use force if necessary to accomplish American goals.

By October 1990 the American XVIII Airborne Corps was fully in place in Saudi Arabia. With supporting units, including marines on amphibious assault ships in the Persian Gulf, it was a powerful force, but planners knew that it was outnumbered by Iraqi forces defending Kuwait. The coalition theater commander, General H. Norman Schwarzkopf, had organized a planning group to develop the options to drive the Iraqis out of Kuwait with the forces at hand. All plans recognized that the coalition organized to liberate Kuwait could quickly obtain air supremacy, and they proceeded from that assumption.

On October 10 and 11 military planners from Schwarzkopf's command presented their preliminary plans to the secretary of defense, President Bush, and his national security team. The original plan consisted mainly of a direct attack on Iraqi defenses in Kuwait. Planners estimated that American forces could suffer up to 10,000 casualties, with 1,500 killed in action. Because one important domestic political consideration was to limit American casualties, the plan was deemed unacceptable. One concrete result of the October conferences was to confirm that Bush expected to use a military solution for the problem. By that point he did not believe that sanctions would force the Iraqis out of Kuwait, and he was prepared to use whatever force was necessary. He then approved the transfer of another corps to Saudi Arabia, along with a large number of other military units. American ground, naval, and air forces in the theater were to be doubled by the beginning of 1991.

Rejection of Schwarzkopf's original plan encouraged others to develop their own. As chairman of the Joint Chiefs of Staff (JCS), General Colin L. Powell organized a planning staff at the Pentagon to develop alternatives. Because attacking directly into Kuwait had been implicitly rejected, the planners looked to a left-hook scenario to move American forces farther west and curve around behind the Iraqis in Kuwait.

By the late autumn of 1990 a certain amount of friction had developed between Powell and Cheney. Cheney favored a more immediate military solution than Powell and kept prodding his military commanders to prepare for war. Cheney had his own staff develop a plan intended to force the Iraqis out of Kuwait as well as to meet other political objectives. The genesis of what became Operation SCORPION came from former Stanford University professor Henry Rowen, who was the assistant defense secretary for international security affairs. The region of the world assigned to Rowen included Southwest Asia and the Middle East. Rowen had no higher political ambitions and was looking forward to returning to Stanford. Even after the invasion of Kuwait, he found time to take a vacation to France in September. While there he read *The History of the Arab Peoples* by Sir John Bagot Glubb. Also known as Pasha Glubb, the author had commanded the British Arab Legion during the 1930s and 1940s. Glubb recorded how he had led the legion from Transjordan across western Iraq in 1941, when Iraq revolted against British domination. The information was eye-opening for Rowen. He realized that Arab armies had maneuvered across the desert for centuries. Surely the U.S. Army, with its far greater logistic capabilities, could do the same. Rowen found that a two-lane asphalt highway, known as the Tapline Road, ran from western Iraq into Saudi Arabia and paralleled the border with Iraq. He believed that it could be used by U.S. forces for supply purposes.

When Rowen returned to the United States, he took his idea to Paul Wolfowitz, a key Cheney aide. Wolfowitz saw potential in the plan and took it to Cheney. Cheney liked the idea and had Wolfowitz set up a secret planning team in the Pentagon to flesh out the possibilities. To head the team, Wolfowitz picked retired U.S. Army lieutenant general Dale Vesser, who had been planning officer for the JCS. Cheney recognized that a plan that had been developed by a retired officer was more likely to be accepted by military commanders than one seen as coming strictly from civilians. Vesser and his team were told to discuss their work with no one else, including Powell.

Vesser was initially skeptical of the plan but liked it the more he studied it. Basically, the plan called for American airborne forces, including the 82nd and 101st Airborne divisions, to be moved by air into western Iraq. Presumably they would be able to occupy most of the region with little difficulty because only one low-grade Iraqi division was based in the area. The region was also sparsely populated, which lowered the possibilities of civilian casualties. The airborne units were to be supported by mechanized forces that would move up the Tapline Road with supplies and armor support.

Cheney and his team expected a number of results from this operation. They saw it as making the best use of American advantages in airpower and mobility, similar to the Inchon landings that turned the tide during the Korean War in 1950. They expected that the first result would be the destruction or capture of the Scud missiles located in western Iraq. Air force planners believed that coalition aircraft could knock out the Scuds before they could be launched.

Another benefit from Operation SCORPION was that road communications between Baghdad and Jordan would be cut. Intelligence reported that supplies were flowing through Jordan to Iraqi troops, a significant hole in the blockade authorized by the UN sanctions.

Cheney also expected that Iraqi Republican Guards, the most effective Iraqi troops, would be called upon to drive the Americans out of western Iraq. As they moved along the roads, coalition aircraft would be able to attack and significantly degrade them. The weakened divisions could then be defeated by American ground forces with fewer American casualties.

Finally, some planners believed that having U.S. forces within 60 miles of Baghdad would bring the overthrow of Hussein. Baghdad itself could be cut off from outside aid, and dissidents could be encouraged to rise up and revolt. While Cheney discounted this possibility, it remained attractive to some planners.

Cheney had Powell and the JCS briefed on Operation SCORPION. The JCS quickly dismissed it as failing to meet American objectives and having logistical problems. Nonetheless, when Powell was in Saudi Arabia in late October, Cheney took the plan to President Bush and briefed him on it. It was an unprecedented event for the civilian secretary of defense to go around his military commanders to present a plan directly to the president. Powell was furious, as were most other military leaders. They viewed it as a signal that Cheney had lost faith in their abilities. It also highlighted the tension that often exists between civilian and military leaders in wartime.

Although Operation SCORPION was not accepted, it did help convince Pentagon planners to move the American main effort farther west. The final plan for DESERT STORM had the main U.S. effort west of the Wadi al-Batin, much farther west than had been originally planned.

TIM J. WATTS

**See also**
Bush, George Herbert Walker; Cheney, Richard Bruce; DESERT SHIELD, Operation; DESERT STORM, Operation; Powell, Colin Luther; Schwarzkopf, H. Norman, Jr.

**References**
Gordon, Michael R., and General Bernard E. Trainor. *The Generals' War: The Inside Story of the Conflict in the Gulf.* New York: Little, Brown, 1995.
Rowen, Henry S. "Inchon in the Desert: My Rejected Plan." *National Interest* 40 (Summer 1995): 34–39.

# Scowcroft, Brent
## Birth Date: March 19, 1925

U.S. Air Force officer and national security adviser for presidents Gerald R. Ford (1974–1977) and George H. W. Bush (1989–1993). Born in Ogden, Utah, on March 19, 1925, Brent Scowcroft graduated from the U.S. Military Academy, West Point, in 1947 and was commissioned a second lieutenant in the newly formed U.S. Air Force that same year. His hopes of a career as a military pilot were dashed by injuries suffered in a plane crash. He then assumed operational and administrative positions within the air force. His military career, which included teaching posts at West Point, the U.S. Air Force Academy, and the National War College, ended with his retirement on December 1, 1975, as a lieutenant general.

Scowcroft received an MA degree in international relations from Columbia University in 1953. From 1953 to 1957 he taught Russian history at the U.S. Military Academy. In 1957 he received his PhD, also in international relations, from Columbia. From 1959 to 1961 Scowcroft was assigned to the U.S. embassy in Belgrade, Yugoslavia. He then attended the Armed Forces Staff College. In 1962 Scowcroft chaired the Department of Political Science at the Air Force Academy. He taught there until 1964.

In 1964 Scowcroft began a seven-year assignment at the Pentagon. From 1964 to 1967 he served in the planning division of the Office of Deputy Staff for Plans and Operations. From 1968 to 1969, he worked for the assistant secretary of defense on international security affairs, and from 1969 to 1971 he was a staff member on the Joint Chiefs of Staff (JCS). In November 1971 Scowcroft was named chief military aide to President Richard M. Nixon and accompanied him on his historic trip to the People's Republic of China (PRC) in 1972. Promoted to brigadier general upon his return, in May 1972 Scowcroft led an advance team to Moscow to prepare for Nixon's visit to the Soviet Union.

In 1973 Scowcroft was chosen by Henry Kissinger, then national security adviser, to be his deputy. Scowcroft continued in that post until 1974 in President Gerald Ford's administration. That same year Ford promoted Scowcroft to national security adviser. As Ford's chief adviser on national security issues, Scowcroft coordinated the April 1975 evacuation of Americans and foreign nationals from Saigon and headed the decision-making process that led to the freeing of U.S. hostages taken from the American merchant ship *Mayaguez* in May 1975.

When Jimmy Carter became president Scowcroft left the National Security Council in January 1977, although he served on a presidential committee that helped to formulate the SALT II Treaty. From 1982 to 1989 Scowcroft was vice chairman of Kissinger Associates, Inc., an international consulting firm. In 1983, President Ronald Reagan named Scowcroft to head the Commission on Strategic Forces, which helped to secure funding for the MX missile program.

In 1988 president-elect George H. W. Bush offered Scowcroft his second appointment as national security adviser and sent him

Former national security adviser Brent Scowcroft, shown here on September 27, 2006, served as chairman of President George W. Bush's Foreign Intelligence Advisory Board during 2001–2005. (Gerald R. Ford Presidential Library)

on two secret missions to China following the 1989 Tiananmen Square Massacre in Beijing. Scowcroft was integral to the planning and decision-making process involving Operation DESERT STORM, and he is credited for having reached the conclusion that Iraqi president Saddam Hussein should not have been removed from power in 1991 out of fear that Iraq would disintegrate into civil unrest and instability. Scowcroft presciently forecast that if that had happened, the United States would have become bogged down in a lengthy and expensive occupation. He was critical of President George W. Bush's Iraq policies after 2001.

Scowcroft left the White House in 1993 and founded the Scowcroft Group, an international business consulting firm. In 1998 Scowcroft coauthored a book of memoirs, *A World Transformed*, with former president George H. W. Bush. From 2001 to 2005 Scowcroft served as chairman of the President's Foreign Intelligence Advisory Board under President George W. Bush. Scowcroft is also the founder and president of the Forum for International Policy, a nonpartisan organization that promotes opinions and perspectives on issues of foreign policy. He is known as a behind-the-scenes presence and a trustworthy loyalist, and his habit of engaging in prolonged academic discussions is a hallmark of his approach to security issues. He continues to serve on numerous corporate, nonprofit, and university boards and on various presidential commissions, including the Center for Strategic and International Studies, the Gerald R. Ford Foundation, the George C. Marshall Foundation, and, in 1986, the President's Special Review Board (Tower Board) investigating the Iran-Contra Affair. Scowcroft is chairman of the American-Turkish Council and president of the George Bush Presidential Library Foundation and the International Advisory Board of the Atlantic Council. Named for him, is the Scowcroft Institute of International Affairs at the Bush School of Government and Public Service at Texas A&M University. Scowcroft, a devout Mormon and a moderate Republican who shuns the Washington social scene, currently resides in Bethesda, Maryland.

GARY KERLEY

**See also**

Bush, George Herbert Walker; Bush, George Walker; DESERT STORM, Operation; Iran-Contra Affair; IRAQI FREEDOM, Operation; Kissinger, Henry Alfred; Reagan, Ronald Wilson

**References**

Bush, George, and Brent Scowcroft. *A World Transformed.* New York: Knopf, 1998.

Prados, John. *Keepers of the Keys: A History of the National Security Council from Truman to Bush.* New York: Morrow, 1991.

Scowcroft, Brent. *Current Problems in Nuclear Strategy and Arms Control.* Claremont, CA: Center for International Strategic Studies, 1984.

Woodward, Bob. *The Commanders.* New York: Simon and Schuster, 1991.

## Scud Missiles, U.S. Search for during the Persian Gulf War

Coalition effort to locate Iraqi Scud missiles during Operation DESERT STORM. By January 16, 1991, when Operation DESERT STORM began with widespread air strikes against Iraqi targets, Secretary of State James A. Baker and President George H. W. Bush had put together an international military coalition that included such members of the Arab League as Saudi Arabia, Kuwait, Egypt, Syria, the United Arab Emirates, Qatar, Oman, and Bahrain. Beginning on January 18, Iraqi president Saddam Hussein, in an attempt to break up this coalition, launched seven al-Hussein missiles, a variant

of the Soviet Scud-B intermediate-range ballistic missile, at Haifa and Tel Aviv in Israel. U.S. officials feared that if Israel launched a counterstrike, America's Arab allies might abandon the coalition and might possibly side with Iraq in a wider Middle East war.

Iraqi Scud missile attacks imperiled not just Israel and the coalition but also Saudi Arabia and the U.S. troops stationed there. In all, the Iraqis launched a total of 40 Scud missiles against Israel and 46 against Saudi Arabia. One such attack killed 28 U.S. servicemen when a missile hit a U.S. Army barracks in Dhahran, Saudi Arabia, on February 25, 1991. Coalition policy makers were also concerned that Iraq might arm its Scud missiles with chemical or biological weapons, such as thickened VX gas, which would have wrought havoc and caused many deaths.

In addition to deploying advanced U.S. air and missile defense batteries with the Patriot missile to Israel and Saudi Arabia, the destruction of Iraq's Scud missile launch sites became a top priority for U.S.-led forces. To do so, U.S. Special Operations Command created a special task force that, together with British special operations, hunted for Iraqi Scuds in western Iraq. Intelligence and special operations teams worked closely with coalition air forces to destroy scores of Scud launchers and their support vehicles. Over a six-week period, from January 18 to February 27, Scud attacks against Israel dropped by more than half, from 29 launches in the first three weeks to 11 launches in the subsequent period. They also became less accurate. Scud missile attacks continued, however, and the air strikes against the Scuds were not as effective as claimed at the time. Indeed, so much airpower—40 percent of coalition air assets—was diverted to search for and destroy Scud missiles that the overall air campaign had to be extended for an additional week, and targeting goals could not be fully attained before the ground war began on February 24, 1991.

JASON N. PALMER

**See also**

Arab League; DESERT STORM, Operation; DESERT STORM, Operation, Coalition Air Campaign; DESERT STORM, Operation, Coalition Air Forces; Dhahran, Scud Missile Attack on

**References**

Rosenau, William. *Special Operations Forces and Elusive Ground Targets: Lessons from Vietnam and the Persian Gulf War.* Santa Monica, CA: RAND Corporation, 2001.

Scales, Robert H. *Certain Victory: The U.S. Army in the Gulf War.* Washington, DC: Brassey's, 1994.

### Scud Missile Specifications

| NATO Designation | U.S. Defense Intelligence Agency Designation | Date of Deployment | Length (feet) | Width (feet) | Launch Weight (pounds) | Payload | Range (miles) | Accuracy (feet) |
|---|---|---|---|---|---|---|---|---|
| Scud A | SS-1b | 1957 | 35.1 | 2.9 | 9,700.3 | 2,094.4 | 93.2 | 13,123.4 |
| Scud B | SS-1c | 1964 | 36.9 | 2.9 | 13,007.3 | 2,171.6 | 186.4 | 2,952.8 |
| Scud C | SS-1d | 1965 | 36.9 | 2.9 | 14,109.6 | 1,322.8 | 357.3 | 2,952.8 |
| Scud D | SS-1e | 1989 | 40.3 | 2.9 | 14,330.0 | 2,171.6 | 435.0 | 164.0 |

# Sealift Ships

Sealift refers to the movement of vehicles, equipment, sustainment supplies, and personnel by oceangoing ships. Although the U.S. military usually transports its personnel by air (as well as approximately 5 percent of its equipment, vehicles, and sustainment supplies), the remaining 95 percent of American military cargo is transported by ships because of their far superior carrying capacity. The Military Sealift Command (MSC) manages American sealift ships, which are normally manned through contracts with civilian industry. The MSC also charters American-flagged ships, contracts with civilian shipping companies for space on regular commercial routes known as liner service, and secures foreign-flagged charters during short periods of high-intensity (surge) operations related to movement for combat operations when other assets are not available to meet the shipping needs of the military.

The U.S. Army and the U.S. Marine Corps conduct the loading and offloading of most MSC-managed or MSC-chartered ships in American and foreign ports. The U.S. Army's Surface Deployment and Distribution Command (SDDC), a subordinate command of the Department of Defense's Transportation Command (TRANSCOM), oversees and manages the stevedore contracts associated with the loading and offloading of most MSC ships around the globe.

Sealift ships can be categorized by at least two methods: their design for loading cargo and their operational readiness status. First, ships can be distinguished by their loading methods. Military cargo is moved onto and off of a vessel via lift-on/lift-off (LO/LO) or roll-on/roll-off (RO/RO) operations. LO/LO is conducted by utilizing a crane to lift vehicles or containers, and RO/RO refers to the ability to actually drive a vehicle onto and off a vessel. Fuel and other liquid products are pumped directly into holding tanks on special tanker ships. Second, ships can be categorized by their readiness status. Prepositioned ships are loaded with the vehicles, equipment, and sustainment supplies required for a deployed military unit and then dispatched to areas around the world, where they await a situation requiring the introduction of U.S. military forces. Army or marine personnel are flown to an area, where they meet the ships carrying their equipment. Prepositioning reduces the amount of time required to load and transport the equipment and permits an American military unit with heavy equipment to hit the ground and be combat ready up to two weeks faster than shipping everything from the United States. Thirty-four ships are part of this program, and the number can fluctuate based on need. Normally, 10 ships are dedicated to the U.S. Army, 16 are dedicated to the U.S. Marine Corps, and 8 total are dedicated to the U.S. Navy and the U.S. Air Force.

The three prepositioned ship squadrons are located in the Mediterranean Sea, the Indian Ocean, and the western Pacific Ocean. The MSC also operates a small fleet of cargo ships utilized to conduct regular sustainment support and the movement of vehicles and equipment for American military personnel and facilities around the world. The number of ships in this second category fluctuates based on current needs. The Maritime Administration manages the Ready Reserve Force (RRF), a third type of ship available for transport operations. The organization bases these 44 ships at ports across the United States and minimally maintains them with small contract crews. Depending upon the contract, each vessel can be placed into active service within a period of 4, 5, 10, or 20 days. The MSC assumes control of the ships upon activation. The fourth group of ships comprises those of the Reserve Fleet. These older ships are mothballed and moored together in case of need by the U.S. military. The ships are not maintained by their own crews but can be placed back into active service within two weeks or less.

## Persian Gulf War

The Persian Gulf War proved to be the first major test of American sealift since the Vietnam War. The MSC placed a number of assets into service by transporting American military equipment and vehicles to the Middle East for the 1991 Persian Gulf War. Prepositioned ships were the first ships to arrive in Saudi Arabia after August 1990 with American military equipment. Most of these ships remained in service to haul more equipment between the United States and the Middle East and carried approximately 19 percent of all American equipment, including their prepositioned loads.

The MSC's eight-ship Fast Sealift Fleet (FSF) played a significant role in the Persian Gulf War. However, one vessel, the *Antares*, developed boiler problems in midocean and had to be towed to Rota, Spain, and then Gibraltar. The *Antares* remained out of commission for the rest of the conflict. FSF ships are the fastest cargo ships afloat and can exceed 30 knots. Although they were built in 1972 and 1973 as SeaLand Corporation container carriers, the U.S. military acquired the ships in 1982 and 1983 and converted them to their current configuration. Each of the eight FSF ships has RO/RO-capable decks in the middle of the vessel as well as cargo holds for LO/LO operations in the forward and aft sections. Vehicles can be loaded by either RO/RO or LO/LO, and these operations occur simultaneously. Seven of the eight FSF ships sailed in support of the Persian Gulf War deployment and retrograde following the conflict, moving approximately 13 percent of all military cargo transported from the United States.

The Maritime Administration activated all 17 of its RO/RO ships in the RRF as well as 55 other RRF ships in support of the Persian Gulf War. The RO/RO ships were of the Cape class of ships, all with names beginning with the word "Cape" and ending in a word with a common first letter. For example, Cape D–class ships include the *Cape Decision, Cape Diamond, Cape Domingo, Cape Douglas,* and *Cape Ducato* ships. Cape D ships vary slightly from other RO/RO ships, such as the Cape H and other classes. Although slightly different, each Cape ship is an RO/RO vessel that has been converted from civilian service to meet the needs of the military and can reach a speed of approximately 16 knots. The 55 RRF ships carried approximately 29 percent of all Persian Gulf War cargo for the American military.

The Military Sealift Command–chartered freighter *Cape Ducato* (T-AKR-5051) enters port during Operation DESERT SHIELD, 1990. (U.S. Department of Defense)

The MSC also chartered American-civilian and foreign-flagged ships to assist with the sealift of equipment bound for the Middle East. American-flagged ships carried approximately 13 percent of the total cargo, while foreign-flagged ships hauled approximately 26 percent. The heavy utilization of foreign-flagged ships was the result of a lack of available American-owned ships.

## Operations NORTHERN WATCH and SOUTHERN WATCH

The heavy reliance on foreign-flagged ships and delays in activating RRF ships served as important sealift lessons from the Persian Gulf War. In response, the 1992 Mobility Requirements Study recommended the acquisition of a new class of sealift ships—known as Large, Medium Speed, Roll-On/Roll-Off (LMSR)—for utilization in surge periods. The MSC acquired 19 of the new ships between 1996 and 2003. Four of the ships are container ship conversions, and the other 15 ships are new constructions. An LMSR, second in size only to an aircraft carrier when comparing military ships, is an RO/RO vessel but is also capable of LO/LO operations into some holds. Each vessel is capable of carrying up to 380,000 square feet of combat cargo. For comparison, FSF ships have 185,000 square feet of cargo space, and Cape-class ships vary in size. For example, Cape D–class ships have 178,000 square feet, and Cape H–class ships have 187,000 square feet. An LMSR can reach a speed of 24 knots.

As the military accepted the new LMSRs, they were placed into service supporting American forces in Operations NORTHERN WATCH and SOUTHERN WATCH or in the Prepositioning Program. LMSRs were not kept in constant service, and many reverted to the RRF for various periods of time. The MSC also continued to rely on FSF ships and other RRF ships in support of American forces deployed for Operations NORTHERN WATCH and SOUTHERN WATCH. The number and type of ships varied depending upon the needs of the military.

## Operation ENDURING FREEDOM

The initial cargo for Operation ENDURING FREEDOM arrived in Afghanistan by air. Subsequent equipment and sustainment supplies have been dispatched via sealift. MSC ships transport equipment and supplies that are then transloaded onto civilian ships for final delivery to ports and overland transportation, as Afghanistan is a landlocked country with no port facilities.

## Operation IRAQI FREEDOM

LMSR ships in the Prepositioning Program were the first ships to arrive in the Middle East with cargo to support Operation IRAQI FREEDOM in the spring of 2003. The MSC utilized ships from all of its programs during the buildup and opening of the conflict. Between January and May 2003 MSC ships delivered approximately 20.5

million square feet of vehicles, equipment, and supplies to Kuwait and other locations for the war effort in what is known as a surge operation. These ships included LMSRs, FSFs, and Cape-class ships as well as additional RRF assets and, later, civilian charters. After the fall of Saddam Hussein's government, the U.S. military settled into a long period of occupation, stabilization, pacification, and state building in Iraq.

The nature of the MSC sealift changed with the new military mission once Hussein's government was toppled. Sealift shifted into two components: force sustainment and cargo movement, the latter to support the arrival and departure of combat units. Sustainment operations involve the ongoing efforts to provide for the basic needs of military personnel including food, clothing, and personal goods bound for post exchanges. The military tends to send these items via commercial container ships. Equipment belonging to arriving and departing combat units is transported by MSC ships, commercial charter, and/or existing civilian liner service. The number and type of ships varies based on the requirements of combat units.

TERRY M. MAYS

**See also**

Aircraft, Transport; Fast Combat Support Ships; Logistics, Persian Gulf War; Military Sealift Command; Support and Supply Ships, Strategic

**References**

Fuchs, William. M. "Sealift Ships Play Major Role in Desert Storm." *Defense Transportation Journal* 47(2) (April 1991): 10–12.

Lowrey, Jon K. "High Speed Sealift." *Marine Corps Gazette* 86(3) (March 2002): 62–67.

Massimo, Annati. "Strategic Force Projection and Sealift Ships: The New Generation." *Military Technology* 29(8) (2005): 83–91.

Matthews, James K., and Cora J. Holt. *So Many, So Much, So Far, So Fast: United States Transportation Command and Strategic Deployment for Operation Desert Shield/Desert Storm.* Washington, DC: Joint History Office, Office of the Chairman of the Joint Chiefs of Staff and Research Center, United States Transportation Command, 1996.

"Military Sealift Command Ships." *Sea Power* 50(1) (January 2007): 50–61.

Mulcahy, Frank S. "High-Speed Sealift Is a Joint Mission." *U.S. Naval Institute Proceedings* 131(1) (January 2005): 34–37.

Pagonis, William G., and Jeffrey Cruikshank. *Moving Mountains: Lessons in Leadership and Logistics from the Gulf War.* Cambridge: Harvard Business School Press, 1992.

## SEAL Teams, U.S. Navy

The U.S. Navy SEALs (Sea, Air, and Land) are part of the U.S. Navy Special Warfare Command, which in turn is a unit of the U.S. Special Operations Command (SOCOM). SOCOM was formed in 1987 to better coordinate military special operations, including the U.S. Army Delta Force, the U.S. Army Special Forces, and U.S. Air Force and U.S. Marine Corps special operations elements. U.S. Navy SEALs have played important roles in Operations DESERT STORM, ENDURING FREEDOM, and IRAQI FREEDOM.

With nearly 2,500 members, SEALs have a distinguished tradition to draw upon. Tracing their heritage to the World War II navy frogmen who cleared underwater obstacles on Japanese-held islands in the Pacific prior to amphibious landings, SEAL Teams were officially formed by order of President John F. Kennedy on January 1, 1962. From the Vietnam War in the 1960s to the invasion of Grenada in 1983 and the 1989 invasion of Panama, SEALs played an important role in American covert and special operations missions.

While SEALs operate in small units from two to eight members, the organizational structure of the SEAL Teams is larger. There are eight SEAL Teams (four on the West Coast and four on the East Coast). Each team is subdivided into six platoons, with supporting units that make up a Naval Special Warfare Squadron.

SEALs have become a lead element in executing the Global War on Terror. From 2002 to the end of 2008 SEALS were undermanned by about 12 percent, but a mandate to remedy the shortfall has resulted in a slow expansion in their numbers. Since augmentation efforts began in 2005, the rate of completion for the Basic Underwater Demolition/SEAL Course has risen from 26 percent to about 32 percent. Training, at a cost of around $350,000 per individual, takes on average about 30 months before a SEAL candidate is ready to deploy to a team.

The international response to the Iraqi invasion of Kuwait in August 1990 led to Operation DESERT SHIELD and then to Operation DESERT STORM. Beginning in August 1990, SEAL Teams 1, 3, and 5 were in country and served in various missions. Prior to combat they operated on the Kuwait-Iraq border, gathering intelligence on Iraqi dispositions and helping to train Kuwaiti and Saudi sailors. SEAL Teams were the first U.S. combat forces to face Iraqi forces. When the war began in January 1991, SEALs performed maritime missions such as inspecting ships and capturing oil platforms. This included the first nonaerial combat of the war when SEALs assaulted Iraqis firing from a platform on U.S. helicopters. This SEAL operation killed 5 Iraqis and captured 23 others with no American casualties. Other tasks performed included combat search-and-rescue missions (including securing an American pilot who had ejected into the sea off Kuwait) and conducting beach reconnaissance to determine potential landing areas in Kuwait. Additionally, SEALs performed mine-clearing operations. During a 16-day period in January 1991, SEALs destroyed or rendered harmless 25 maritime mines. This activity went undetected by the Iraqis.

One SEAL mission during DESERT STORM was diversionary in nature and was designed to convince the Iraqi leadership that an amphibious assault was in the offing, fixing Iraqi coast defense units in place when the ground offensive began. SEALs planted explosive charges in Iraqi-held Kuwaiti beaches. These were later detonated remotely, part of a major deception operation involving more than 17,000 U.S. marines on landing ships off the coast.

The wars in Afghanistan and Iraq found the SEALs operating inland. During these conflicts they have performed various missions including covert combat action, escorting VIPs in Iraq and

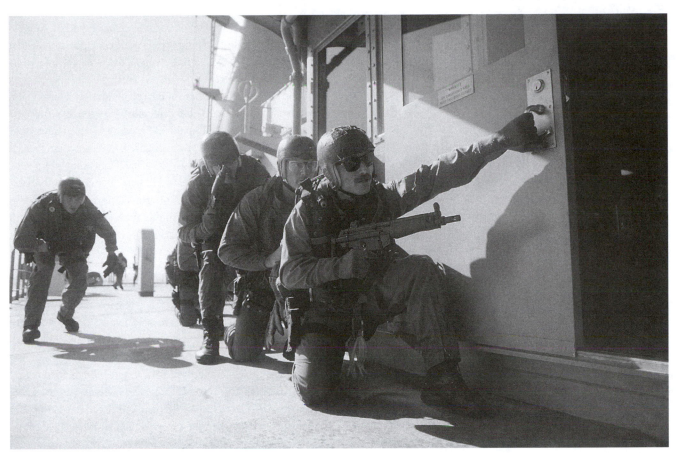

Members of Sea, Air, and Land (SEAL) Team 8 prepare to enter the bridge of the fleet oiler USNS *Joshua Humphreys* during a boarding exercise. SEAL Team 8 provided boarding teams to assist ships of the Maritime Interdiction Force in its enforcement of United Nations (UN) sanctions against Iraq during Operation DESERT STORM. (U.S. Department of Defense)

Afghanistan, the rescue of American and allied prisoners of war (including the April 2003 rescue of U.S. Army private Jessica Lynch in Nasiriyah, Iraq), search and rescue of downed pilots, and the capture or apprehension of high-value targets. Some examples in Afghanistan include the search for Al Qaeda organization leader Osama bin Laden and Taliban Mullah Khairulla Kahirkhawa in February 2002 and stability operations performed with indigenous forces. In January 2002 Seal Team 3 searched for weapons being smuggled into Afghanistan. In the Iraq War, SEAL operations have included safeguarding offshore oil platforms and dams (the latter included the April 2003 capture of Dam 57 in conjunction with Polish Special Operations forces before Saddam Hussein loyalists could destroy it) and reconnaissance and intelligence gathering.

Operations in conjunction with both conventional forces and special operations units of the other armed services have expanded the SEAL missions as well. A major strength of the SEAL Teams continues to be their great flexibility, which gives them tremendous force-multiplying capability. They tie up more enemy troops defending against their real or perceived threats than their actual numbers would seem to dictate.

The conflicts in Afghanistan and Iraq have taken a toll on the SEAL Teams. Between October 2001 and November 2008 SEAL deaths were estimated to exceed 25, a fairly large number for this small organization. By April 2010, that number had risen to 30. Decorations include a posthumous Medal of Honor to Master-at-Arms Second Class Michael A. Monsoor, a 25-year-old member of SEAL Team 3 who fell onto a grenade on September 26, 2006, in Ramadi, Iraq, to save the lives of his teammates. Another posthumous Medal of Honor was awarded to Lieutenant Michael P. Murphy for heroic actions in Afghanistan on June 27–28, 2005.

SCOTT R. DIMARCO

### See also

United States Navy, Afghanistan War; United States Navy, Iraq War; United States Navy, Persian Gulf War

### References

Couch, Dick. *Down Range: Navy SEALs in the War on Terrorism.* New York: Three Rivers, 2006.

Dockery, Kevin. *Navy SEALs: A Complete History from World War II to the Present.* New York: Berkley Books, 2004.

Fuentes, Gidget. "The Search for SEALs—Changes to Special-Warfare Recruiting, Training, Practices Shows Promise to Growing Unit." *Navy Times* (April 26, 2007): 18.

Luttrell, Marcus, with Patrick Robinson. *Lone Survivor: The Eyewitness Account of Operation Redwing and the Lost Heroes of SEAL-10.* Boston: Little, Brown, 2007.

Roth, Margaret. "Recent Conflicts Mark Turning Point for SEALS, Other Special Ops Forces." *Seapower* (February 2005): 14–16.

# Senate Select Committee on Intelligence and the House Permanent Select Committee on Intelligence Joint Inquiry into the Terrorist Attacks of September 11

Start Date: February 14, 2002
End Date: December 10, 2002

The first in-depth U.S. government attempt to study the intelligence failures leading up to the September 11, 2001, terror attacks. Senator Robert (Bob) Graham (D-Fla.), chair of the Senate Select Committee on Intelligence, and Representative Porter J. Goss (R-Fla.), chair of the House Permanent Select Committee on Intelligence, agreed on the need for a joint committee of the two houses to study intelligence gathering before September 11, which became the genesis of the Senate Select Committee on Intelligence and the House Permanent Select Committee on Intelligence Joint Inquiry into the Terrorist Attacks of September 11. The Joint Inquiry committee was convened during February 14–December 10, 2002. For the inquiry to be successful, Graham and Goss agreed that it had to be bipartisan and would need to have the full support of the congressional leadership and the George W. Bush administration.

Despite assurances of support, however, the committee ran into opposition from the Central Intelligence Agency (CIA), the Federal Bureau of Investigation (FBI), and the White House. There was also little enthusiasm in Congress for the probe. It took Congress five months to announce the inquiry and another four months before the committee began to function.

The Joint Inquiry committee finally received its mandate in early 2002, and the cochairmen, Robert Graham and Porter Goss, announced its beginning on February 14, 2002. The committee had a 10-month deadline to accomplish its task of evaluating the intelligence record prior to September 11, 2001. In the first months, investigators for the Joint Inquiry began to compile evidence. Hearings began in June 2002. Those hearings in June, July, and the first half of September were held in closed sessions. In the second half of September, there were open hearings. Hearings in October alternated between open and closed. A final report of the Joint Inquiry appeared on December 10, 2002, but only 24 of the more than 800 pages were released to the public.

Eleanor Hill, a lawyer and former Pentagon inspector general, was the staff director for the committee. She had not been the first choice of the committee, but its first choice, L. Britt Snider, had run into difficulty because of his friendship with George Tenet, the director of the CIA. Hill was recommended by Sam Nunn, a former U.S. senator from Georgia, to Senator Richard Shelby (R-Ala.). Hill was a partner in the law firm of King and Spalding when she was offered the job working with the Joint Inquiry committee.

Hill's job was to supervise the creation of a variety of staff reports that pointed out intelligence-gathering deficiencies. Her crew had to comb through the 150,000 pages of documents from the CIA and a like number of documents from the FBI. Most of the difficulty was in obtaining access to the documents in the first place. Members of the staff also conducted intensive interviews and attended briefings.

Hill reported to the Joint Inquiry committee on all aspects of the intelligence picture before September 11. Among her reports to the committee was one on the FBI's failure to react to the Phoenix Memo (a memo sent from an FBI agent in Phoenix, Arizona, in July 2001 warning about the use of civilian flight schools by potential terrorists) and the refusal of FBI headquarters to authorize a search warrant for Zacarias Moussaoui's possessions. She also reported that the intelligence community had received at least 12 reports of possible terrorist attacks before September 11 but that nothing had been done about them.

A controversy developed when there was a leak of closed-session testimony from General Michael V. Hayden, director of the National Security Agency (NSA). The testimony was about the fact that the NSA had intercepted two Al Qaeda messages on September 10, 2001, indicating that something would happen on September 11, but these fragmentary messages were not translated until September 12, 2001. Despite the classified nature of this material, first the *Washington Times* and then the Cable News Network (CNN) learned of it and publicized it widely. Other newspapers also picked up the story. This leak led Vice President Richard Cheney to attack the Joint Inquiry committee as the source of the leak; he also reprimanded both Goss and Graham by telephone. This incident produced negative publicity for the committee and led Goss and Graham to invite the FBI to investigate the leak. Nothing came of the investigation, but it gave critics of the committee more ammunition. It also further clouded an already tense relationship between the inquiry and the Bush administration.

Cooperation from the CIA and the FBI was minimal. Only four CIA witnesses testified, including George Tenet. None of the key FBI agents appeared before the committee. Not surprisingly, Senator Shelby complained about the lack of cooperation.

The Bush administration had doubts about the Joint Inquiry committee from the beginning but was more than unhappy about the final report. The administration wanted the final report to be a validation of its position that there was no way September 11 could have been avoided, meaning that no one was responsible. As soon as the White House realized that the Joint Inquiry committee did not subscribe to this view, all cooperation ceased.

Officials in the White House worked to block the release of the full report, wanting instead to classify parts of the material retroactively. Consequently, the issuance of the full report was delayed, and significant parts of it were classified as secret. Most notable of the blacked-out sections was the section concerning Saudi citizens on American soil on September 11. Even the September 11 Commission had difficulty gaining access to the full report, but in the end it did come out.

In the final analysis, the failure to obtain key documents negatively impacted the 37-member Joint Inquiry committee. The staff had reviewed almost 500,000 pages of documents from intelligence agencies and other sources. Approximately 300 interviews had been conducted, and 600 people had briefed them about intelligence matters. There had been 13 closed sessions and 9 public hearings.

Once the classified report was rendered on December 20, 2002, the battle began over the classified parts of the report. The first agency to look at it was the CIA. The CIA classified whole sections of the report, including material that had already appeared in the media. This wholesale reclassification proved too much for the Joint Inquiry committee's staff. In a meeting with representatives from the CIA, the FBI, and the NSA, the staff went over the report page by page, reclaiming much of the material. The final obstacle was the White House, whose representatives wanted large parts of the report classified. The most notable section blacked out by the White House consisted of 27 pages that dealt with the relationship of the Saudi government to the September 11 conspirators. White House representatives wanted the changes to the report to be hidden, but the final unclassified version of the report has those areas shaded in black. On July 24, 2003, the final unclassified report appeared.

Although there were gaps in the report because of documents that were never produced, the Joint Inquiry committee did document the failures of U.S. intelligence agencies. Both the CIA and the FBI received specific criticism. The staff did uncover new information, including the Phoenix Memo, the Moussaoui debacle, warnings about possible use of aircraft as weapons, failures to monitor known Al Qaeda operatives, and lack of coordination between CIA and FBI, to name only some of the new information. The Joint Inquiry committee's most important recommendation was for the creation of a cabinet-level position, a director of national intelligence, to coordinate all American intelligence agencies and their activities, a post that was formed in 2005.

Stephen A. Atkins

**See also**

Bush, George Walker; Central Intelligence Agency; Cheney, Richard Bruce; Goss, Porter Johnston; Moussaoui, Zacarias; September 11 Attacks; September 11 Commission and Report; Tenet, George John

**References**

Allen, Mike. "Bush Seeks to Restrict Hill Probes of Sept. 11." *Washington Post,* January 30, 2002, A4.

Gertz, Bill. *Breakdown: The Failure of American Intelligence to Defeat Global Terror.* Rev. ed. New York: Plume Books, 2003.

Lichtblau, Eric. "Report Details F.B.I.'s Failure on 2 Hijackers." *New York Times,* June 10, 2005, A1.

Prados, John. "Slow-Walked and Stonewalled." *Bulletin of the Atomic Scientists* 59(2) (March/April 2003): 28–37.

Priest, Dana. "FBI Leak Probe Irks Lawmakers." *Washington Post,* August 2, 2002, A1.

Risen, James. "White House Drags Its Feet on Testifying at 9/11 Panel." *New York Times,* September 13, 2002, A12.

# Senegal and Sierra Leone

Two independent sub-Saharan nations located in West Africa. Senegal is bordered by the Atlantic Ocean to the west, Mauritania to the north and northeast, Mali to the east, and Guinea-Bissau and Guinea to the south. Senegal also surrounds Gambia on three sides. Sierra Leone is bordered by the Atlantic Ocean to the west, Guinea to the north and east, and Liberia to the southeast.

Senegal, officially known as the Republic of Senegal, has its capital at Dakar. The country's territory encompasses 75,749 square miles, with 318 miles of coastline, and the majority of the land consists of either flatlands or rolling hills. Senegal's altitude ranges from sea level to 1,906 feet at its highest point in the east. Sierra Leone, officially known as the Republic of Sierra Leone, has its capital in Freetown. The country's total area encompasses 27,698 square miles, with 241 miles of coastline. Sierra Leone's terrain includes mountains in the east as high as 6,391 feet, rolling hill country and mangrove swamps in the center and west.

Both countries have a similar tropical climate, varying between rainy and dry seasons that run between May and December and December and April, respectively. The population of each country consists of multiple ethnic groups. Senegal, with approximately 12.5 million people, has three major groups: the Wolof (43 percent); the Pular (24 percent); and the Serar (15 percent). The remaining peoples include the Diola, the Mandinke, the Sonnike and other African groups as well as Lebanese and various Europeans. Sierra Leone has about 6.1 million people, with 90 percent of the population belonging to African ethnic groups (30 percent Temne, 30 percent Mende, and 30 percent all others). The remaining 10 percent consists primarily of the Creole (Krio), the descendants of freed slaves, and a very limited number of Europeans and South/Southwest Asians.

Both countries feature a variety of native languages spoken by the various groups in each country. In addition to the official native languages, French is an official language in Senegal, and English is an official language in Sierra Leone. Islam is the dominant religion in both countries, practiced by 94 percent of Senegalese and 60 percent of Sierra Leoneans. Indigenous religions are more prevalent in Sierra Leone, with approximately 30 percent in Sierra Leone compared to just 1 percent in Senegal. Christianity is practiced by about 5 percent of the Senegalese and 10 percent of Sierra Leoneans. Both countries are members of the United Nations (UN), the African Union, the Organization of Islamic Conference, and the Economic Community of West African States.

Senegal's territory during its precolonial history was either completely controlled or partially controlled by three of the great West African civilizations: the Ghana Empire, the Malian Empire, and the Songhai Empire. During the latter two empires Islam gained strong footholds in West Africa. Under the Songhai Empire, Islam was established as the official religion of the empire, which encouraged the expansion of Islam in the region.

During the age of exploration Portugal initially claimed a sphere of influence over West Africa's coastline, including Senegal and Sierra Leone. The Portuguese primarily focused on trading for natural resources and slaves rather than attempting to establish an inland colony. Dutch and French colonies were established at Goree Island and Saint Louis, respectively. During the Seven Years' War (1756–1763), Great Britain acquired control over the region but agreed to return it to France as part of the terms of the 1763 Treaty of Paris. France directly ruled Senegal from 1763 until 1960, when the latter acquired its independence.

Throughout its colonial period, France pushed farther inland, acquiring land that would be part of present-day Senegal. Senegalese soldiers served alongside French forces attempting to expand French control in Africa as well as in France's military during World War I (1914–1919) and World War II (1939–1945). Although Senegal temporarily joined with the Sudan Republic in 1960 to form the Mali Confederation, Senegal decided to become completely independent in August of that same year. Upon independence in 1960, Leopold Sedar Senghor of the Socialist Party of Senegal was chosen as the nation's first president. He served as the country's leader for the next 20 years, stepping down in 1980. His successor, Abdou Diouf, temporarily united Senegal with Gambia between 1982 and 1989, forming the Senegambia Confederation that eventually separated in 1989.

Senegal has remained relatively stable for much of its postcolonial history, with the major exception being a rebellion in southern Senengal's Casamance region, where rebels have opposed the government since 1983. President Abdoulaye Wade, elected in 2000 and reelected in 2007, is the first president from the Senegalese Democratic Party.

Sierra Leone fell within Portugal's sphere of influence during the 1500s and was called Serra Lyoa. By 1684 English traders established a presence within the country, which would allow the United Kingdom to dominate Sierra Leone until April 27, 1961, when Sierra Leone became independent. Freetown, founded in 1787, and the surrounding area served as a trading post for English traders, a naval base for English ships involved in operations to eliminate the transatlantic slave trade, and a court of admiralty to deal with ships captured by the British Royal Navy. In 1787 Sierra Leone also served as a colony for a small number of Africans living in England. Future settlement of Africans in the colony included free blacks from Nova Scotia, Canada, and Jamaica as well as the resettlement of slaves liberated by the Royal Navy's antislavery patrols. Sierra Leone eventually became a British protectorate in 1896.

From the 1780s through the present day, Sierra Leone has suffered much unrest. Neither British officials nor British trading company personnel were able to control or stabilize the protectorate. The reasons for this included ongoing conflicts among the

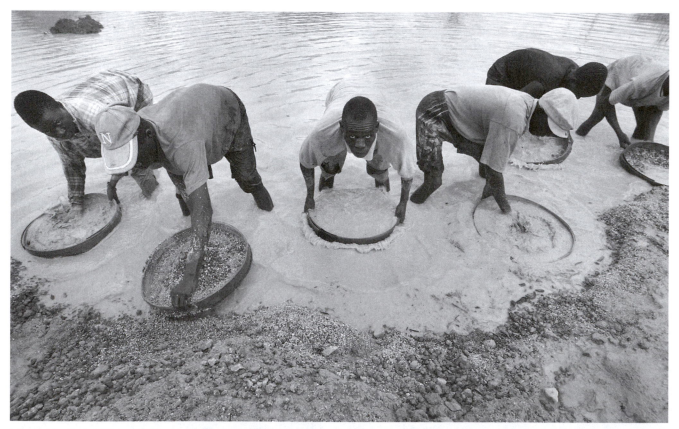

Men pan for diamonds near Koidu in northeastern Sierra Leone in 2004. During that country's 1991–2001 civil war, civilians were used as slaves to mine the diamonds that funded the rebels' war efforts. Even with the end of the civil war, the diamond industry struggles to reduce the number of "conflict diamonds" that enter the foreign market. (AP/Wide World Photos)

large number of ethnic groups in Sierra Leone as well as the various native systems of governance and landownership that were in use. After independence some of the same problems continued, and there were always questions as to who should rule the country. Initially the Sierra Leone People's Party (SLPP) ruled the nation, but in the 1967 elections the All-People's Congress (APC) won but was almost immediately overthrown in a military coup. Within one year the APC returned to power, eventually establishing one-party rule. Corrupt leadership within the APC, however, eventually resulted in another coup.

Between 1991 and 2002 Sierra Leone suffered gravely as the Revolutionary United Front (RUF) caused enormous disruptions in an attempt to overthrow the government and gain control over the diamond-rich regions of the country. The government initially signed agreements with Executive Outcomes, a private military contractor (PMC), to defeat the RUF and restore peace and stability to the country. But the Sierra Leonean government, despite the PMC's success, was forced by the World Bank to terminate the contract. Executive Outcomes left and the government was overthrown, resulting in other PMCs and Nigerian forces restoring the legitimate government. However, permanent peace was not achieved. Eventually military forces from the Economic Community of West African States Monitoring Group (ECOMOG) and British troops stabilized the country long enough to hold elections. In 2002 the SLPP won the elections; the RUF's political party failed to win any seats in the government. Although the political climate remains restless, relatively fair elections held in 2007 resulted in a victory for APC candidate Ernest Bai Koroma.

During the 1990–1991 Persian Gulf War, Senegal actively supported coalition forces in Operations DESERT SHIELD and DESERT STORM by sending 500 troops to Saudi Arabia. Senegalese personnel were also assigned to the Joint Forces Command East (JFCE), which included Morocco and the military forces of various countries of the eastern Arabian Peninsula, and were deployed south of the Kuwaiti border at the beginning of the ground invasion in February 1991. During the early 2000s the terrorist organization Al Qaeda issued threats against French interests in Senegal.

Sierra Leone's political instability prevented it from participating in international peacekeeping or other military operations in Southwest Asia or the Middle East. However, Al Qaeda has established a presence in Sierra Leone and is primarily involved in the illegal diamond trade whereby money and/or guns are often traded for diamonds. It is believed that at least one Al Qaeda cell continues operating within Sierra Leone's borders. In the past Sierra Leone's Lebanese population served as a potential financing source for the government, and because many of the Lebanese immigrants to Sierra Leone are Shia, the United States has claimed that they are connected with or are members of Hezbollah.

Neither Senegal nor Sierra Leone have been involved in military operations after Al Qaeda's September 11, 2001, attacks sparked the Global War on Terror and Operations ENDURING FREEDOM and IRAQI FREEDOM. However, the alleged presence of Al Qaeda operatives in both countries, especially in the volatile and unstable Sierra Leone, has been a source of concern for the United States and other Western governments.

WYNDHAM WHYNOT

### See also
Al Qaeda; DESERT SHIELD, Operation; DESERT STORM, Operation; Hezbollah

### References
Boone, Catherine. *Merchant Capital and the Roots of State Power in Senegal, 1930–1985.* New York: Cambridge University Press, 1992.

Chafer, Tony. *The End of the Empire in French West Africa: France's Successful Decolonization?* Oxford, UK: Berg, 2002.

Kargbo, Michael. *British Foreign Policy and the Conflict in Sierra Leone, 1991–2001.* New York: Peter Lang, 2006.

Khapoya, Vincent. *The African Experience: An Introduction.* 2nd ed. Upper Saddle River, NJ: Prentice Hall, 1998

Krup, A. P. *Sierra Leone: A Concise History.* New York: St. Martin's, 1975.

Nugent, Paul. *Africa since Independence: A Comparative History.* New York: Palgrave Macmillan, 2004.

Schwab, Peter. *Africa: A Continent Self-Destructs.* New York: Palgrave Macmillan, 2001.

## Sensor Fuzed Weapon

Laser-guided (smart) air-to-ground area weapon that can accurately detect and attack multiple ground targets, such as armored columns, antiaircraft batteries, and motorized supply and personnel convoys. Designated as Cluster Bomb Unit 97 (CBU-97), the Sensor Fuzed Weapon (SFW) manufactured by Textron Defense Systems weighs 1,000 pounds and consists of the Suspended Utility Unit 66 (SUU-66)/B Tactical Munitions Dispenser (TMD) with 10 Bomb Live Unit 108 (BLU-108)/B submunitions inside. Attached to each BLU-108 submunition are four Smart Skeet infrared sensing projectiles that resemble hockey pucks. Each Smart Skeet warhead has a dual passive infrared and active laser sensor to detect and then engage a target within a 30-acre area. BLU-108 can be integrated into several American weapon systems and foreign dispenser systems.

U.S. Air Force combat aircraft deploy the weapon from altitudes between 200 feet to 20,000 feet at speeds between 250 to 650 knots. After the delivery aircraft releases the TMD, the TMD opens at a set altitude and dispenses the parachute-stabilized submunitions. At a preset altitude sensed by a radar altimeter, a rocket motor fires to spin the submunition and initiate an ascent. The submunition then releases its four projectiles, which are lofted over the target area. The projectile's sensor detects a vehicle's heat signature, and an explosively formed penetrator fires at the heat source. If each Smart Skeet projectiles does not detect and engage a target after a preset time period, it will self-destruct to leave the battlefield clean of unexploded warheads that could endanger innocent civilians, a serious problem with earlier cluster bomblets.

The weapon is most effective when employed at low altitudes from level flight attitudes in an environment void of

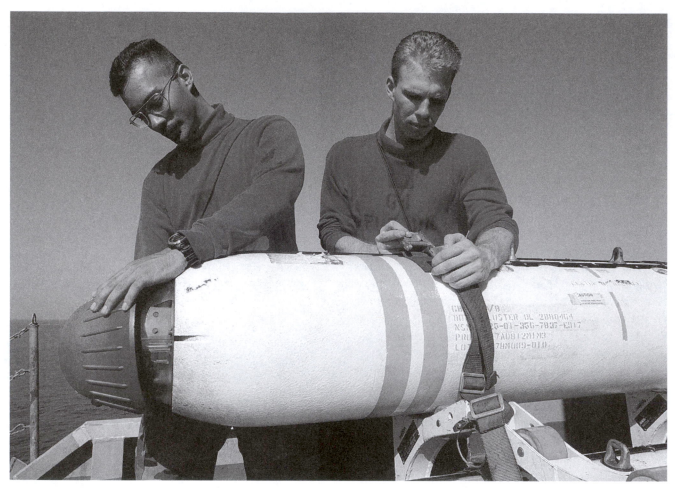

Two aviation ordnanceman airmen inspect a cluster bomb on the flight deck of the U.S. Navy aircraft carrier *Abraham Lincoln* (CVN-72) in 1998 during Operation SOUTHERN WATCH. (U.S. Department of Defense)

countermeasures. However, during the 1991 Persian Gulf War air campaign (January 17–27, 1991), most U.S. Air Force pilots had to deploy their air-to-ground weapons from medium to high altitudes to avoid enemy surface-to-air defenses. As a result, because the effectiveness of the weapon decreases as release altitude, dive angle, and/or time of flight increases from adverse effects of wind conditions, weapon dispersion, and aim point uncertainties, the Air Combat Command added the Wind Corrected Munitions Dispenser (WCMD) tail kit to the SFW. The WCMD tail kit uses the Navigation Satellite Timing and Ranging (NAVSTAR) Global Positioning System (GPS) signal to guide the weapon to a precise impact. The modification, designated the CBU-105, will expand the delivery envelope of the SFW to strategic aircraft and higher altitudes and will give the delivery aircraft some standoff capability.

Textron (then Avco) began concept development with the U.S. Army and the U.S. Air Force in the late 1970s for a weapon that could help North Atlantic Treaty Organization (NATO) forces overcome the numerical superiority of Soviet armored and artillery formations in Central Europe. The original mission requirements called for a weapon that would provide multiple kills per pass of an enemy's armored force over a wide area in any weather. The air

force began engineering and manufacturing development of the SFW in 1985. Over the late 1980s and the 1990s, the program office, contractor, and vendors overcame numerous technical and engineering challenges to produce the desired weapon. The end of the Cold War removed the original purpose for the SFW but opened the way to utilize the air force's strategic bombers to deliver large numbers of the SFW to the battlefield. The air force had the SFW system available for Operation ALLIED FORCE in 1999 against Serbian forces in the Kosovo War, but the Serbian Army never deployed its tanks in a sufficient concentration to warrant its use.

The SFW made its combat debut during Operation IRAQI FREEDOM. On April 2, 2003, a Boeing B-52 Stratofortress, assigned to the 20th Bomb Squadron, Barksdale Air Force Base, Louisiana, took off for a typical 17-hour-plus combat mission. After striking an Iraqi ammunition dump in northeastern Baghdad, the crew received a call for help from a U.S. Marine Corps division being threatened by an Iraqi tank column. The B-52 crew maneuvered their aircraft to attack the enemy tanks, received the coordinates of the target from a marine ground controller, programmed its SFWs for release against the target, and released two of these weapons against the Iraqi tank column. The weapons destroyed the Iraqi tanks from the first one-third to one-half of the column. Then, as the smoke from the attack cleared, the remaining Iraqi tank crews quickly exited their tanks and surrendered. Battlefield Damage Assessment reports from IRAQI FREEDOM indicate that the BLU-108 performed well against various armored threats. The Iraq experience with the SFW demonstrated the robustness of the weapon and has garnered it great respect for its capabilities.

ROBERT B. KANE

**See also**

Bombs, Precision-Guided; IRAQI FREEDOM, Operation, Air Campaign; Navigation Satellite Timing and Ranging Global Positioning System

**References**

Hansen, Ryan. "SFW Combat Debut Forces Troops to Surrender in Droves." *Eglin Eagle,* August 15, 2003, 1, 6.

Knights, Michael. *Cradle of Conflict: Iraq and the Birth of Modern U.S. Military.* Annapolis, MD: Naval Institute Press, 2005.

# September 11 Attacks

On September 11, 2001, the United States suffered a series of coordinated suicide attacks perpetrated by members of the Islamic terrorist group Al Qaeda, which was then based in Afghanistan and led by Osama bin Laden. On that day, 19 Al Qaeda terrorists hijacked four commercial American jetliners and crashed them into prearranged targets. Two of the airplanes crashed into the Twin Towers of the World Trade Center in New York City. Another plane crashed into the Pentagon, the headquarters of the Department of Defense, in northern Virginia. A fourth plane crashed into a field near Shanksville in rural Somerset County, Pennsylvania, after some passengers, having been informed of the other suicide airplane attacks from cellular phone communications with family members, attempted to storm the cockpit and regain control of the plane from the hijackers. The White House or the Capitol were the most likely suspected targets of this plane. Excluding the hijackers, a total of 2,974 died in the attacks, including 246 from all four planes in which there were no survivors. The attacks crippled not only the city and economy of New York City but also sectors of the U.S. economy. Particularly hard hit were the airline and insurance industries, which suffered billions of dollars of losses. The September 11 attacks were the worst terrorist attacks ever committed against the United States, and the resulting death toll surpassed that of the December 7, 1941, Japanese attack on Pearl Harbor.

The George W. Bush administration responded to the attacks by declaring a Global War on Terror. The next month the United States invaded Afghanistan, toppling the Taliban government that

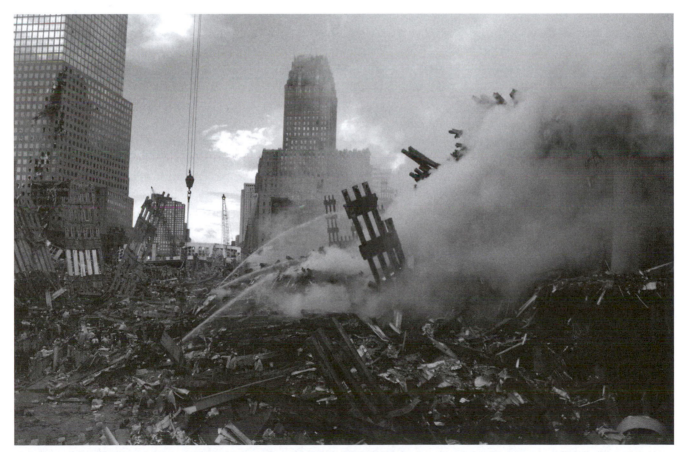

Fires burn amid the rubble and debris of the World Trade Center in New York City in the area known as Ground Zero two days after the September 11 terrorist attacks. (U.S. Department of Defense)

## Selected Terrorist Attacks Perpetrated by Al Qaeda

| Date | Location | Deaths |
| --- | --- | --- |
| February 26, 1993 | World Trade Center in New York City | 6 |
| September 10, 1997 | Tourist bus in Cairo, Egypt | 10 |
| November 17, 1997 | Tourists in Luxor, Egypt | 70 |
| August 7, 1998 | U.S. embassies in Nairobi, Kenya, and Dar es Salaam, Tanzania | 200+ |
| October 12, 2000 | USS *Cole* in the port of Aden, Yemen | 17 |
| September 11, 2001 | World Trade Center in New York City; Pentagon in Washington, D.C.; Pennsylvania | approximately 3,000 |
| April 11, 2002 | Synagogue in Dyerba, Tunisia | 21 |
| June 14, 2002 | U.S. consulate in Karachi, Pakistan | 12 |
| October 12, 2002 | U.S. consulate, Sari Club, and Paddy's Bar in Bali, Indonesia | 202 |
| May 12, 2003 | Compounds in Riyadh, Saudi Arabia | 30+ |
| May 16, 2003 | Spanish club, hotel, and sites in Casablanca, Morocco | 45 |
| November 8, 2003 | Residential compound in Riyadh, Saudi Arabia | 17 |
| March 11, 2004 | Trains in Madrid, Spain | 199 |
| September 9, 2004 | Australian embassy in Jakarta, Indonesia | 9 |
| July 7, 2005 | Subways and busses in London, England | 52 |
| April 11, 2007 | Prime minister's office and police station in Algiers, Algeria | 33 |
| February 1, 2008 | Pet markets in Baghdad, Iraq | 73 |
| June 2, 2008 | Danish embassy in Islamabad, Pakistan | 6 |

had given sanctuary and support to bin Laden and Al Qaeda. The U.S. government also enacted the Patriot Act in October 2001, a sweeping law designed to protect the country against terrorism by enhancing the power of the federal government to conduct criminal and intelligence investigations, engage in espionage, and conduct searches for communications records.

The four airliners hijacked—American Airlines Flight 11 (Boston to Los Angeles), American Airlines Flight 77 (Dulles, Virginia, to Los Angeles), United Airlines Flight 175 (Boston to Los Angeles), and United Airlines Flight 93 (Newark to San Francisco)—were all bound for the West Coast from the East Coast. Al Qaeda deliberately chose the flights because of their long distance, which meant that the large airplanes (Boeing 757s and 767s) would be carrying large amounts of jet fuel, thereby intensifying the destruction and explosions once the planes crashed. It is suspected that at least some of the hijackers had previously flown on some of the same flights from the East Coast in preparation for their suicide operations.

It is not entirely clear how exactly the hijackers gained control of the cockpits of each of the four planes, as federal aviation rules mandated that cockpit doors remain closed and locked during flight. The hijackers were armed with box cutters, however, and also mace or pepper spray. According to some passengers on some of the planes, the terrorists claimed to have bombs as well, although this was probably a ruse to control the passengers. According to the September 11 Commission Report, the hijackers probably opened the then-unreinforced cockpit doors by forcing a flight attendant to open them. Other theories hold that they may have stabbed the flight attendants to obtain a cockpit door key or somehow lured the captain or first officer out of the cockpit. During cell phone conversations as the attacks unfolded, some passengers on American Airlines Flight 11 reported that two flight attendants had been stabbed; passengers on United Airlines Flight 175 revealed that both pilots had been killed and that a flight

attendant had been stabbed. However, passengers on American Airlines Flight 77 and United Airlines Flight 93 reported no in-air injuries or deaths, but the cockpit voice recorder of United Airlines Flight 93 indicated that a woman, most likely a flight attendant, was being held in the cockpit and that she struggled with one of the hijackers, who either killed or otherwise silenced her.

None of the airport security checkpoint supervisors recalled the 19 hijackers or reported anything suspicious regarding their screening. The hijackers were apparently allowed to clear security unimpeded. The September 11 Commission, however, concluded that the quality of the screening was "marginal at best," particularly given the fact that two of the hijackers had set off metal detectors and were then hand-wanded and allowed to proceed. The security screeners never resolved what had set off the metal detector in the first place, and airport video footage showed that one of the hijackers was carrying an unidentified item clipped to his back pocket, which escaped any scrutiny. In addition, although some of the hijackers were selected by a computerized prescreening program known as Computer Assisted Prescreening Passenger System (CAPPS) to identify passengers who should be subjected to special security measures, this only meant that the hijackers' checked bags were held off the plane until it was confirmed that they were aboard the aircraft. CAPPS did not trigger any further scrutiny of what they carried on the planes with them.

American Airlines Flight 11 and United Airlines Flight 175 crashed into the 110-story North Tower and South Tower of the World Trade Center at 8:48 a.m. and 9:30 a.m. local time, respectively. Due to massive structural failure, the South Tower collapsed at 9:59 a.m., and the North Tower collapsed at 10:26 a.m., killing a total of 2,603 in both buildings (including 341 New York firefighters and two paramedics, 23 New York City police officers, and 37 Port Authority police officers); another 24 people remain listed as missing. The collapse of the two huge buildings also brought down

A view of the Pentagon in Washington, D.C., one day after the terrorist attack on September 11, 2001. (U.S. Air Force)

neighboring office towers and badly damaged others, all of which occurred in a densely populated part of the city.

According to a 2005 report by the National Institute of Standards and Technology of the U.S. Department of Commerce titled "Final Report on the Collapse of the World Trade Center Towers," the impact of both planes as they crashed ignited thousands of gallons of jet fuel, which melted the thermal insulation, or fireproofing, on the interior core steel-support columns of the World Trade Center. That caused the floors to sag and then collapse. In so doing, they pulled and collapsed the exterior, or perimeter columns, of the buildings, reducing their ability to support the floors above. This explains why neither tower collapsed immediately upon impact with the aircraft. The aircraft impacts did not cause the towers to collapse; instead, it was the ensuing fires from the exploding jet fuel that ultimately brought the buildings down. The South Tower collapsed more quickly than the North Tower because there was more aircraft damage to the central core of the South Tower, which then collapsed the exterior or perimeter support structure of that building. The report also found no evidence to substantiate some of the principal conspiracy theories alleging that the World Trade Center was destroyed by some elements of the U.S. government by means of a controlled implosion using explosives.

Meanwhile, American Airlines Flight 77 crashed at 9:37 a.m. local time into the Pentagon, killing 125 people, while United Airlines Flight 93 plowed into a field in Shanksville, Pennsylvania, at 10:03 a.m., killing all 40 passengers and crew aboard. It is clear from the cockpit voice recorder that the hijackers, who had gained access to the plane's controls, were aware of the passengers' assault against the cockpit and pitched the plane so that it crashed into an empty field.

The motives for the attacks of September 11, 2001, date from Al Qaeda's declaration of jihad (holy war) against the United States in February 1998. Bin Laden decried American foreign policy in the Middle East including America's military presence in Saudi Arabia, the site of Islam's two holiest shrines. According to bin Laden, American support for Israel and dictatorial Arab states such as Egypt and Saudi Arabia allegedly constituted proof of anti-Islamic U.S. policies. Sadly, the attacks of September 11, 2001, were but a tragic and devastating culmination of escalating attacks by Al Qaeda against U.S. targets around the world, including the August 1998 U.S. embassy bombings in Kenya and Tanzania and the October 2000 attack on USS *Cole* in a Yemeni port.

The fallout from the attacks was both long lasting and far reaching. No commercial air traffic was allowed for several days after the attacks, the stock market was closed for nearly a week, and the U.S. economy tilted toward recession as consumer spending plummeted in the weeks and months after the disaster. The attacks helped shape the Bush Doctrine, which would seek to prevent further attacks by launching preemptory strikes against nations or regimes likely to launch terrorist assaults on the United States. The 2003 invasion of Iraq was a case in point. The Iraq War and the Afghanistan War have both dragged on, without resolution. Finally, the September 11 attacks shattered Americans' sense of invulnerability, which has helped the federal government erect a pervasive and powerful internal security state to complement the broader national security state.

STEFAN M. BROOKS

**See also**

Al Qaeda; Bin Laden, Osama; Bush, George Walker; Bush Doctrine; *Cole*, USS, Attack on; Dar es Salaam, Bombing of U.S. Embassy; Global War on Terror; Nairobi, Kenya, Bombing of U.S. Embassy; September 11 Commission and Report; Terrorism

**References**

Bernstein, Richard. *Out of the Blue: The Story of September 11, 2001, from Jihad to Ground Zero.* New York: Times Books, 2002.

New York Magazine Editors. *September 11, 2001: A Record of Tragedy, Heroism and Hope.* New York: Harry N. Abrams, 2001.

*The 9/11 Commission Report: The Final Report of the National Commission on Terrorist Attacks upon the United States.* New York: Norton, 2004.

Talbot, Strobe, and Nayan Chanda, eds. *The Age of Terror: America and the World after September 11.* New Bork: Basic Books, 2002.

# September 11 Attacks, International Reactions to

Although the terrorist attacks on September 11, 2001, targeted the United States, many other countries throughout the world were also affected. In addition to the 2,657 Americans killed, 316 foreign nationals from 84 different countries also died in the attacks, including 67 Britons, 28 South Koreans, 26 Japanese, and 25 Canadians. The shock and horror engendered by the attacks were truly international in scope.

Most public reaction and media coverage outside the United States was extremely sympathetic. The French national newspaper, *Le Monde,* declared "*Nous sommes tous Américains*" ("We are all Americans"). The British *Mirror* labeled the attacks a "War on the World." The Spanish paper *El Correo* ran a single-word headline: "Muerte" ("Murder"). Most world leaders were also quick to condemn the terrorists. Russian president Vladimir Putin urged that "the entire international community should unite in the struggle against terrorism," adding that the attacks were "a blatant challenge to humanity." Japanese prime minister Junichiro Koizumi said that "this outrageous and vicious act of violence against the United States is unforgivable." German chancellor Gerhard Schröder told reporters that "they were not only attacks on the people in the United States, our friends in America, but also against the entire civilized world, against our own freedom, against our own values, values which we share with the American people."

Perhaps even more moving was the spontaneous outpouring of sympathy from average people around the globe. Tens of thousands of people left flowers, cards, and other personal mementos at U.S. consulates and embassies in many countries. Vigils and prayers were held throughout the world in a wide range of faiths. Thousands turned out in the streets of major capitals to protest the attacks, nearly 200,000 in Berlin alone. Ireland proclaimed a day of national mourning, while in Britain the American national anthem played at the changing of the guard in front of Buckingham Palace. With many international flights grounded for days after September 11, volunteers in 15 Canadian cities took care of 33,000 stranded passengers—mostly Americans—who had been aboard 255 planes diverted from U.S. airports.

Sympathy came from unlikely places. Libyan leader Muammar Qaddafi, himself linked to terrorism, called the attacks

A mourner weeps as she holds up the American flag during a special changing of the guard ordered by Britain's Queen Elizabeth II at London's Buckingham Palace to honor victims of the terrorist attacks in the United States on September 11, 2001. (AP/Wide World Photos)

"horrifying" and counselled Muslims that "irrespective of the conflict with America it is a human duty to show sympathy with the American people." Iranian president Mohammed Khatami expressed his "deep regret and sympathy with the victims," while a visibly shocked Palestinian president Yasser Arafat denounced the attacks, repeating how "unbelievable" they were. Even the Democratic People's Republic of Korea (DPRK, North Korea), a rogue nation considered by many a sponsor of international terrorism, offered Americans sympathy following such a great "tragedy." In fact, few people demonstrated anything but sympathy for those who suffered in the attacks.

Sympathy for the United States and the victims of September 11 continued when in October 2001 the United States led an invasion of Afghanistan to destroy Al Qaeda training camps, hunt its elusive leader Osama bin Laden, and overthrow the oppressive Taliban regime that had given refuge to the organization responsible for the carnage. On September 12 the North Atlantic Treaty Organization (NATO) had invoked Article 5 of its charter, which pledged mutual assistance in the war against Al Qaeda. This was the first time in NATO's 52-year history that Article 5 was invoked.

Pakistan offered bases from which to plan operations in Afghanistan and support in tracking down Al Qaeda and Taliban fighters. Simultaneously, British prime minister Tony Blair pursued multilateral antiterrorist planning within the European Union (EU). French president Jacques Chirac promised to stand with the United States, "fighting shoulder to shoulder" against terrorism. Many governments quickly arrested suspected terrorists operating in their countries. They also developed and implemented legislation aimed at combating terrorist organizations. While such measures were not without their critics, much of the world adopted more stringent security measures in the first few months after September 11.

This general outpouring of sympathy did not, however, translate into open-ended support for American foreign policy of its Global War on Terror. Many criticized U.S. president George W. Bush's worldview when he said a few days after September 11 that "you're either with us or with the terrorists." Some saw the Global War on Terror as a cover for extending U.S. power abroad, particularly when the Bush administration erroneously began to link September 11 terrorists with Iraq. Bush's controversial "Axis of Evil" reference, in which he grouped Iraq, Iran, and North Korea in his State of the Union address on January 29, 2002, struck many listeners as inflammatory and off the mark.

Reports by organizations such as Amnesty International would condemn the United States for the treatment of suspected terrorist prisoners in camps at Guantánamo Bay, Cuba, where detainees from the conflict in Afghanistan were held. More than anything, international sympathy for the United States was largely undermined by Bush's decision to invade Iraq in March 2003 despite the fact that its major allies and the United Nations (UN) refused to support such action. Thus, the legacy of September 11 turned from one of sympathy and commonality to one of suspicion and condemnation.

ARNE KISLENKO

**See also**

Al Qaeda; Bin Laden, Osama; Bush, George Walker; ENDURING FREEDOM, Operation; Global War on Terror; IRAQI FREEDOM, Operation; September 11 Attacks; Taliban

**References**

Goh, Evelyn. "Hegemonic Constraints: The Implications of 11 September for American Power." *Australian Journal of International Affairs* 57(1) (April 2003): 77–97.

Hirsh, Michael. "Bush and the World." *Foreign Affairs* 82(5) (September–October 2002): 18–43.

Scheuer, Michael. *Imperial Hubris: Why the West Is Losing the War on Terror.* Washington, DC: Potomac Books, 2004.

# September 11 Commission and Report

Commission and report on the September 11, 2001, terrorist attacks on the United States. Members of the Al Qaeda terrorist organization hijacked commercial jetliners and used them to destroy the World Trade Center towers in New York City and to damage a portion of the Pentagon in northern Virginia. Another simultaneous hijacking resulted in the downing of a jetliner in western Pennsylvania, killing all on board. Some 3,000 people died as a result of the attacks. The National Commission on Terrorist Attacks upon the United States, better known as the 9/11 Commission, was created by congressional legislation and signed into law by President George W. Bush on November 27, 2002.

Tomas H. Kearn was chairman of the commission, and Lee H. Hamilton was vice chairman. Other members of the commission were Richard Ben-Veniste, Fred F. Fielding, Jamie S. Gorelick, Senator Slade Gorton, Senator Bob Kerrey, John F. Lehman, Timothy J. Roemer, and James R. Thompson.

The commission's bipartisan membership and independence from the authority of any individual branch of the U.S. government was designed to ensure that political bias did not enter into its deliberations. Its charter enabled it to produce a full and complete account of the circumstances surrounding the September 11 terrorist attacks. The commission was also mandated to investigate and report on America's preparedness for and immediate response to the attacks and to make recommendations to guard against future attacks.

The commission examined documents dating back to three presidential administrations, including intelligence reporting and National Security Council staff minutes. The commission also interviewed hundreds of witnesses from midlevel to senior-level federal, state, and municipal officials and conducted interviews with some of the victims of the attacks. Although some commission critics have pointed to the vested interest of some of its members (e.g., Gorelick because of her authorship of one of the pre-9/11 government guidance documents that affected information exchanges among government agencies), few dispute that the commission's investigation and report were as thorough and balanced as could be achieved.

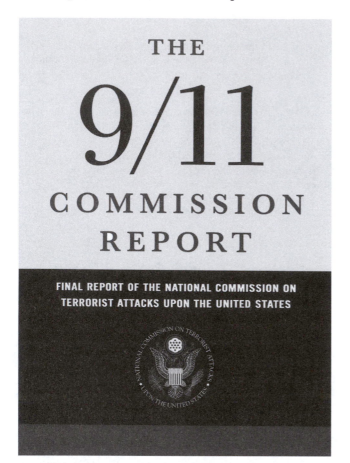

## THE 9/11 COMMISSION REPORT

**FINAL REPORT OF THE NATIONAL COMMISSION ON TERRORIST ATTACKS UPON THE UNITED STATES**

Cover of *The 9/11 Commission Report: Final Report of the National Commission on Terrorist Attacks upon the United States.* The report, issued on July 22, 2004, provides the findings and recommendations of the 9/11 Commission in its investigation into the terrorist attacks on the World Trade Center and Pentagon on September 11, 2001. (National Commission on Terrorist Attacks)

The 9/11 Commission's establishment and charter initially proved controversial, and the early debates over its formation were politically charged and passionate. Some government officials were afraid that the commission's deliberations and acquisition of intelligence reports would compromise sensitive sources at a time of war. Others saw it as a distraction from the war effort. Some Republicans viewed the call for an investigation as a Democratic effort to exploit the country's passions politically. Some Democrats believed that Republican calls for the commission to examine the evidence dating back a decade was an attempt to shift blame to President Bill Clinton, whose efforts to fight terrorism prior to the end of his term of office in January 2001 were largely ineffective.

In the end, the country's need to understand what went wrong and what was needed to face future terrorist threats won out. The commission's membership was divided equally between Democratic Party and Republican Party officials. Its membership included two former senators, an ex-congressman, a former White House counsel, a former secretary of the navy, two former governors, and three former Justice Department officials.

Former New Jersey governor Thomas H. Kearn accepted the position of chairman, and former Indiana congressman Lee H. Hamilton served as vice chairman. More than 100 staffers, drawn from federal agencies and Congress, were assigned to support the commission in its work.

The commission's first challenge was to gain access to intelligence documents and the Bush administration's National Security Council (NSC) records. As other administrations have done in the past when dealing with congressionally mandated commissions, the Bush administration claimed executive privilege. The resulting legal battle led to several months of negotiations before an agreement was reached governing the handling of sensitive materials, including NSC materials. Once the majority of the government documents had been examined, the commission began to hold public hearings to gather witness testimony. Most of the commission hearings were public and were held in locations that facilitated access to the potential witnesses and officials. The first set of public hearings was conducted from March to April 2003 in New York City. The remaining ones were held in Washington, D.C.

The 9/11 Commission's classified report was presented to Congress and the White House in June 2004. The public report was released one month later. The findings contained some key judgments about America's warning of and preparations for the 9/11 attacks. The most significant conclusion was that it was a "lack of imagination, not lack of intelligence information," that prevented the intelligence agencies from predicting 9/11. Moreover, the U.S. government had sufficient indications of a terrorist attack using commercial airliners. Had it taken some key precautions, these might have inhibited, if not prevented, the 9/11 hijackers from succeeding. Several of the hijackers had overstayed their visas or were on terrorist watch lists, and a few of them had even been involved in suspicious activities involving aircraft (such as taking flying lessons without concern about landings or takeoffs). Reports of these activities, however, never reached the appropriate officials because of the lack of information sharing and cooperation among the nation's intelligence, security, and law enforcement agencies.

The 9/11 Commission strongly recommended that the federal government restructure its domestic security efforts to ensure unity of purpose. The commission also recommended the unification of the country's intelligence community under a central authority that would report directly to the president. Finally, the commission recommended Congress's inclusion in that effort. Perhaps even more importantly, the commission identified several shortcomings in U.S. capacity and equipment for responding to the catastrophic effects of a major terrorist attack and identified several areas for improvement. These included compatible communications and data-processing systems among state, regional, and federal civilian and military agencies. Those recommendations ultimately led to the establishment of the Department of Homeland Security and the Office of the Director of National Intelligence.

CARL OTIS SCHUSTER

**See also**
September 11 Attacks; Terrorism; United States Department of Homeland Security

**References**
Griffin, David R. *The 9/11 Commission Report: Distortions and Omissions.* Northampton, MA: Arris Books, 2005.
Thompson, Paul. *The Terror Timeline: Year by Year, Day by Day, Minute by Minute.* New York: HarperCollins, 2004.
U.S. Government. *The 9/11 Commission Report.* Washington, DC: U.S. Government Printing Office, July 2004.

# 73 Easting, Battle of
## Event Date: February 26, 1991

Battle during Operation DESERT STORM fought on February 26, 1991, between elements of the U.S. Army VII Corps and the Tawakalnah Division of the Iraqi Army Republican Guard. The battle, which was part of the larger Battle of Wadi al-Batin, ended in a decisive American success and questions about how the outnumbered U.S. force was able to win such a lopsided victory.

During the ground phase of Operation DESERT STORM the U.S. VII and XVIII Airborne Corps undertook a left hook into the western Iraqi desert in which they skirted the western limit of Iraqi frontier defenses, the so-called Saddam Line. Both corps then made a great right turn with the intention of cutting off Iraqi forces remaining in Kuwait. On February 26 VII Corps came into contact with the Iraqi Republican Guard's Tawakalnah Division. The Iraqi division had been hastily redeployed to take up improvised defensive positions along the western side of the Wadi al-Batin, which marked the Kuwaiti-Iraqi border. The Iraqis hoped to delay VII Corps long enough to allow their forces in Kuwait to escape. The Battle of Wadi al-Batin refers to the VII Corps' attack on the Tawakalnah Division, while the Battle of 73 Easting was a part of the larger overall Battle of Wadi al-Batin. The term "73 Easting" simply refers to a Global Positioning System (GPS) coordinate. The Battle of 73 Easting was notable also for the fact that it was one of the few engagements during the war in which an outnumbered American force faced a larger Iraqi force in a stationary defensive position.

The main American force involved in the battle was the 2nd Armored Cavalry Regiment, consisting of eight troops each of about 120 soldiers in 20–30 armored vehicles. Three troops of the 2nd Armored Cavalry Regiment were most involved in the 73 Easting actions. Eagle Troop, commanded by Captain H. R. McMaster, took the lead and did most of the fighting, followed by Ghost Troop and Iron Troop.

Eagle Troop was acting as a reconnaissance unit for VII Corps when it ran into the 18th Brigade of the Tawakalnah Division late in the afternoon on February 26. The Iraqis had deployed T-72M-1 tanks supported by BMP infantry fighting vehicles, while the Americans had M1-A1 Abrams tanks and M-3 Bradley armored fighting vehicles. Weather conditions at the time were poor with a heavy storm limiting visibility, and the Americans could not call in air strikes because of the weather. However, the Abrams tanks and Bradley vehicles had the advantage of thermal sights, while the Abrams guns far outranged those of the T-72s. American tanks could also fire on the move, while the Iraqis could not. Eagle Troop found itself in a seam between the Iraqi 18th Brigade and the adjacent Iraqi 12th Armored Division. The surprised Iraqis quickly opened fire. Normal procedure called for the reconnaissance units to wait for heavier supporting units to catch up, but Iraqi fire was so intense that McMaster had no choice but to engage. At the start of the fighting, Eagle Troop consisted of just 9 Abrams tanks and 12 Bradleys.

The tank-versus-tank battle was over quickly, with 37 T-72s and 32 other vehicles destroyed in just 40 minutes. Ghost Troop and Iron Troop moved up to join in the battle. However, Iraqi resistance at 73 Easting proved to be unexpectedly determined. Iraqi tanks made attempts to maneuver and outflank American tanks, rather than remaining in stationary defensive positions, as was their normal operating procedure. Iraqi troops typically surrendered or broke and fled when their tanks were knocked out, but the infantry of the Tawakalnah Division continued to resist, employing rocket-propelled grenades. Ghost Troop was heavily counterattacked after nightfall and had to call in an artillery bombardment of 2,000 howitzer rounds and 12 rockets. Iraqi opposition finally ended about six hours after the battle first began.

The U.S. 1st Infantry Division arrived later that night to pass through the battle scene and continue the unrelenting U.S. advance. American losses in the battle were minimal, with the Iraqis destroying only one Bradley. A second Bradley was hit by friendly fire. Despite the ferocity of their resistance, the Iraqis proved ultimately ineffective in countering the American advance. Altogether, the Iraqis lost 113 armored vehicles and suffered 600 casualties.

The Battle of 73 Easting generated controversy after the war as commentators tried to explain how three troops of an armored cavalry regiment could destroy an entire Iraqi brigade. Some stressed the superiority of American technology and the woeful state of the Iraqi Army in which even the elite Republican Guard units fought unsuccessfully. Others pointed to the skill level of the American soldiers, arguing that their proficiency rather than the disparity in technology explained the battle's one-sided outcome. Still others thought that the air campaign that had preceded the ground phase of Operation DESERT STORM had been decisive in disorganizing the Iraqis' defense and their will to fight.

PAUL W. DOERR

**See also**
DESERT STORM, Operation, Ground Operations; M1A1 and M1A2 Abrams Main Battle Tanks; Republican Guard; Wadi al-Batin, Battle of

**References**
Biddle, Stephen. "Victory Misunderstood: What the Gulf War Tells Us about the Future of Conflict." *International Security* 21(2) (Fall 1996): 139–179.

Gordon, Michael R., and General Bernard E. Trainor. *The Generals' War: The Inside Story of the Conflict in the Gulf.* New York: Little, Brown, 1995.

Keaney, Thomas A. "The Linkage of Air and Ground Power in the Future on Conflict." *International Security* 27 (Autumn 1997): 147–150.

Pollack, Kenneth M. *Arabs at War: Military Effectiveness, 1948–1991.* Lincoln: University of Nebraska Press, 2002.

Scales, Robert H. *Certain Victory: The U.S. Army in the Gulf War.* Washington, DC: Brassey's, 1994.

---

# Sèvres, Treaty of

Peace treaty between 13 World War I Allied powers (most notably France, Great Britain, and Italy) and Turkey signed on August 10, 1920, at Sèvres, France. Although the Armistice of Mudros had ended World War I hostilities with the Ottoman Empire in October 1918, the Treaty of Sèvres took another 20 months to conclude. As with many other treaties that ended the war, its terms were presented by the winners to the losers without negotiation. Unlike many other treaties, few of its terms were ever implemented. In 1923 the Treaty of Lausanne superseded most of the terms of the Treaty of Sèvres. It was thus the shortest-lived of the treaties ending the war.

Although the Allies (specifically France and Great Britain) did not envision the destruction of the Ottoman Empire in 1914, the Treaty of Sèvres confirmed what had become an established fact. The Ottoman Empire was officially dissolved, and the new state of Turkey appeared in its place. Consistent with realities on the ground, Sèvres removed all predominantly Arabic-speaking regions from Turkish control. The region of the Hijaz (in what is now Saudi Arabia) was made an independent kingdom and named a signatory to the treaty.

The creation of an Arabian state notwithstanding, the treaty denied independence to much of the Middle East, which passed under French and British control as mandates. While nominally free of foreign rule, Arabia was in reality under British suzerainty. Palestine and Mesopotamia became British mandates, while Syria and Lebanon became French mandates. The mandates were supposed to lead to eventual independence under the supervision of the League of Nations. The United States, displeased at what it saw as the furtherance of European imperialism in the region and never itself at war with the Ottoman Empire, declined to participate in the treaty negotiations. Nevertheless, U.S. president Woodrow Wilson secured the right to determine the borders of the new state of Armenia.

The treaty was an immediate disappointment to Arab leaders. The British had made grandiose promises of independence during the war to Arab leaders such as Sharif Hussein. In return for staging rebellions in the Arab parts of the Ottoman Empire, the British had promised Hussein and other Arab leaders that Britain would support the creation of independent Arab states.

The Treaty of Sèvres fell far short of those guarantees. Instead, it upheld the secret Sykes-Picot Agreement of 1916 wherein Britain and France agreed to divide former Ottoman territories among themselves, although the treaty added the cloak of the mandate system. The treaty also reaffirmed the Balfour Declaration of 1917 in which Great Britain stated that it viewed with favor the creation of a Jewish homeland in Palestine. Nevertheless, the Great Powers took no definitive steps in that direction.

The treaty did not deal with the humiliations of the Capitulations, which had been solidified between the states of Western Europe and the Ottoman Empire since the 16th century. These involved unequal trade terms between the Great Powers and the Ottoman Empire and granted the right of extraterritoriality to foreign nationals. Under the terms of the Treaty of Sèvres, the Capitulations were effectively continued in relation to the new state of Turkey.

In addition, the treaty made the Bosporus and the Dardanelles international waterways. This provision existed mostly to prevent the Russian Bolshevik regime from claiming ownership of the straits. Armenia, the scene of a genocide during the war, was made independent, and Kurdistan received significant autonomy within the new Turkish state. Great Britain landed a force under General George Milne to guarantee the neutrality of the straits and ensure control of Constantinople.

The real humiliation for Turkey lay in the settlement of its European and Anatolian boundaries. Greece acquired all of European Turkey except the immediate area around Constantinople, which came under international control. The Greeks were also awarded the city of Smyrna, several Aegean islands, and large parts of western Anatolia. These areas were to remain under Greek control for five years, after which the Greeks were to conduct a plebiscite. Britain and France presumed that this vote would result in the annexation of these areas to the Kingdom of Greece. Finally, Ottoman finances were placed not in Turkish hands but instead under the supervision of British, French, and Italian financiers.

The principal architect of the treaty, British prime minister David Lloyd George, regarded it as the triumph of Romantic Hellenism and Christendom. He seems to have immediately recognized, however, that Great Britain could not enforce these terms. The Greeks were already showing an appetite for more of Anatolia than the treaty permitted, and Britain was facing intense domestic pressures to demobilize.

Most importantly, Turkish nationalists were showing determination to resist many of the terms laid out in the treaty. Brilliantly led by Mustafa Kemal, the hero of Gallipoli, the nationalists planned to overturn Sèvres. Most nationalists understood that reviving the Ottoman Empire and recapturing the lost Arab lands could not and should not be accomplished. They bristled, however, at any ethnically Turkish lands falling under foreign control. Kemal set out to regain all Anatolian and Armenian lands for Turkey.

Only Greece decided to meet Kemal with military force. The Greeks had 150,000 troops in Turkey, and Greek premier

Eleuthérios Venizélos was determined to use them to crush Kemal's nationalists. Kemal, however, carried out a brilliant military campaign in the Greco-Turkish War of 1920–1922. He recaptured Smyrna and its hinterland and then turned north to move on Constantinople. The Italians, who had come to view Greece as a more immediate rival than Turkey, agreed to withdraw their occupation troops after a defeat at Kemal's hands in Central Anatolia. The Italian decision led the British and French to also quit Turkey. Within only two years, the Treaty of Sèvres had been superseded by the Treaty of Lausanne, signed on July 24, 1923.

MICHAEL S. NEIBERG

#### See also

Balfour Declaration; France, Middle East Policy; Lausanne, Treaty of; Mandates; Ottoman Empire; Paris Peace Conference; Sykes-Picot Agreement; Turkey, Role in Persian Gulf and Afghanistan Wars; United Kingdom, Middle East Policy; World War I, Impact of

#### References

Fromkin, David. *A Peace to End All Peace: The Fall of the Ottoman Empire and the Creation of the Modern Middle East.* New York: Henry Holt, 1989.

Helmreich, Paul. *From Paris to Sèvres: The Partition of the Ottoman Empire at the Peace Conference of 1919–1920.* Columbus: Ohio State University Press, 1974.

Macfie, A. L. *The End of the Ottoman Empire, 1918–1923.* London: Longman, 1998.

MacMillan, Margaret. *Paris, 1919: Six Months That Changed the World.* New York: Random House, 2002.

## Shalikashvili, John Malchase David
### Birth Date: June 27, 1936

U.S. Army officer and chairman of the Joint Chiefs of Staff (JCS) from 1993 to 1997. John Malchase David Shalikashvili was born on June 27, 1936, in Warsaw, Poland, to parents of Georgian descent. His father, Dimitri, had been an army officer in the Democratic Republic of Georgia until that nation was overrun and occupied by the Soviets in 1921. Both his parents fled the Soviet occupation and settled in Warsaw, where the couple first met and later married. Dimitri later joined the Georgian Legion, one of the many ethnic units raised by the Germans during the war. Although the Georgian Legion was anticommunist and opposed to the Russian occupation of Georgia, it fought in Normandy against the Western Allies in 1944.

The Shalikashvili family survived the devastation of the Warsaw Uprising of August 1944. The future American general was only 8 years old and had already experienced war at its most brutal. After the uprising was crushed, the Shalikashvilis were evacuated to Germany. In 1952, when Shalikashvili was 16 years old, the family immigrated to the United States. They settled in Peoria, Illinois, and Shalikashvili taught himself English in part by watching old John Wayne movies on television.

Shalikashvili attended Bradley University and majored in mechanical engineering. In May 1958 he became an American citizen. The following month he graduated from Bradley, and the month after that he was drafted into the army. After attending officer candidate school at Fort Sill, Oklahoma, Shalikashvili was commissioned a second lieutenant of artillery in 1959.

Shalikashvili rose steadily through the ranks, serving in a variety of assignments in field artillery and air defense artillery units. He served in Germany, Italy, Korea, and various places in the United States. In 1968 and 1969 he served as a senior district adviser in Vietnam. He also attended the Naval Command and Staff College (Newport, Rhode Island), the U.S. Army War College (Carlisle, Pennsylvania), and George Washington University, from which he earned a master's degree in international affairs. In 1979 he was posted to the Federal Republic of Germany (FRG, West Germany) as the divisional artillery commander of the 1st Armored Division. He later served as the assistant division commander and was promoted to brigadier general in 1982. In 1986 he was promoted to major general and assigned to the Pentagon as assistant deputy chief of staff and later as deputy chief of staff of the army for operations and plans. From June 1987 to August 1989, Shalikashvili commanded the 9th Infantry Division (Motorized). Promoted to

Polish-born U.S. Army general John Shalikashvili was chairman of the Joint Chiefs of Staff (JCS) under President Bill Clinton from 1993 to 1997. (U.S. Army)

lieutenant general in August 1989, he became deputy commanding general of the U.S. Army, Europe, as well as the Seventh Army.

Shalikashvili received wide recognition for his highly effective command of Operation PROVIDE COMFORT, the major humanitarian relief effort carried out in northern Iraq in the immediate aftermath of Operation DESERT STORM. Starting in April 1991, PROVIDE COMFORT was designed to protect, feed, and house several hundred thousand Iraqi Kurds who had been forced to leave their homes. In August 1991 Shalikashvili was reassigned to Washington, D.C., as assistant to the chairman of the JCS, General Colin L. Powell.

In 1992 Shalikashvili became supreme allied commander, Europe, and served simultaneously as the commanding general of the U.S. European Command. After being nominated for the position of chairman of the JCS by President Bill Clinton, Shalikashvili, now a four-star general, began his four-year tour as JCS chairman on October 25, 1993. Just prior to his confirmation by the Senate, the *New York Times* broke the story that his father not only had been a German officer in World War II but was also suspected of having ties to the Waffen SS. Although the Georgian Legion was not technically part of the SS, Hitler had placed the legion under the operational control of the Waffen SS after Wehrmacht officers made an attempt on his life in July 1944. While some critics of the Clinton administration tried to make an issue of Shalikashvili's father's past, Secretary of Defense Les Aspin defended him strongly by saying, "Allegations about his father's history are not relevant to General Shalikashvili's nomination to be the next Chairman of the Joint Chiefs of Staff."

Shalikashvili faced several thorny issues in his new role. After the flap over gays in the military and the promulgation of the don't ask–don't tell policy, which seemed to have pleased no one, Shalikashvili worked hard to bolster morale in the armed forces and smooth over the dissension in the ranks. He also presided over the scaling back of the defense budget, which led to charges by some—especially on the Right—that he was complicit in the gutting of the American military establishment. The reductions in defense spending, however, were largely driven by politics, including the end of the Cold War and the so-called peace dividend, and the Clinton administration's desire to wipe out decades of budget deficits and national debt. Shalikashvili was well respected and well liked, and his steady leadership was crucial for Clinton, who did not enjoy harmonious relations with the armed services.

Shalikashvili stepped down in September 1997 at the conclusion of his term. He also retired from the army at that time, ending an impressive 38-year career. Upon his retirement he was awarded the Presidential Medal of Freedom, a rare honor for a military officer. Despite suffering a severe stroke in August 2004, he has been active in politics since retirement, having served as an adviser to Democratic senator John Kerry's failed 2004 presidential campaign and having publicly endorsed Democratic senator Hillary Rodham Clinton's 2008 presidential bid. Shalikashvili has served on a number of corporate boards, including that of United

Defense Industries, and holds a visiting professorship at Stanford University's Center for International Security and Cooperation.

PAUL G. PIERPAOLI JR.

**See also**

Clinton, William Jefferson; Kurds; Powell, Colin Luther; PROVIDE COMFORT, Operation

**References**

Clinton, Bill. *My Life*. New York: Knopf, 2004.

Halberstam, David. *War in a Time of Peace: Bush, Clinton, and the Generals*. New York: Scribner, 2001.

Woodward, Bob. *The Agenda: Inside the Clinton White House*. New York: Pocket Books, 1995.

---

# Shamal

A *shamal* is a prevailing northerly and northwesterly wind that typically occurs in summer and winter throughout Iraq and neighboring countries. Winds are named for the direction from which they blow. Thus, Iraq's *shamal* (meaning "north" in Arabic) blows from its northern highlands toward Arabia and the Persian Gulf. These winds are capable of producing fierce sandstorms. *Shamals* are not restricted to Iraq, so *shamal* can refer to different weather events, as in the *shamal* in northern Egypt. Latitudinal variations in solar radiation produce world wind patterns. Near the equator, intense solar radiation draws substantial amounts of water vapor into the atmosphere. This creates the intertropical convergence zone (ITCZ), a belt of equatorial low-pressure systems that shifts north and south of the equator with the changing seasons. As warm moist air rises above these systems, the process of cooling and condensation produces precipitation. With its moisture wrung out, the drier air flows north and south beneath the tropopause, a ceiling of sorts separating the stratosphere from the troposphere. Dry air is heavier than moist air, causing it to descend north and south of the ITCZ to create high-pressure systems and desert regions.

Just as water flows downhill, winds blow from high pressure to low pressure regions. The Coriolis force causes winds blowing toward the poles to veer to the east, producing westerly winds, while winds blowing toward the equator veer westward to produce easterly winds. In the summer, high pressure dominates much of North Africa, but the ITCZ shifts northward over Southern Asia. A low-pressure system forms over India, bringing rain as part of the summer monsoon (Arabic for season). This leaves Iraq between low pressure to its east and high pressure to its west. Thus, rotational patterns cause *shamal* winds to prevail in summer on the Iraqi side of both systems.

During spring and autumn, *sharq* (Arabic for "east") winds take precedence, although these are normally southeasterly rather than easterly winds. Winter marks a return of *shamal* winds, which vary in duration. The most common of these lasts a day or so and may occur a few times per month. These *shamals* are associated with the passage of storm fronts to the north. As the ITCZ moves south, so too does the belt of prevailing westerly winds, which periodically propels storms through Turkey. As the trailing edge of a storm passes through eastern Turkey, the low-pressure system generates strong *shamal* winds in Iraq. Longer winter *shamals* may last for several days or even for weeks in some areas.

*Shamal* winds can have a significant effect on military campaigns. During World War I, British Army lieutenant colonel T. E. Lawrence (aka Lawrence of Arabia) vividly recounted bone-chilling winds that made life miserable for Arab forces covering Lieutenant General Edmund Allenby's eastern flank during their winter offensive against Ottoman Turkish forces. Lacking highlands or forests to deflect or slow the wind, *shamals* in central and southern Iraq can easily achieve sufficient velocity to create blinding sandstorms or dust storms. Although desert soils are frequently sandy, those of Iraq contain substantial amounts of clay. When dry, the soil becomes like talcum powder. Besides making life miserable for troops, the dust can make weapons, vehicles, communications gear, and other equipment inoperable by clogging all accessible ports. *Shamal* winds that might not pick up as much sand can easily create dust storms from these finer aridisols (arid soils). Movement through these areas is made all the more difficult by the presence of sabkhas, or areas that may feature brittle, salty soil atop marshes. Winter *shamals,* which may bring rain or snow, can turn these regions into veritable mud baths.

A particularly strong *shamal* struck just as ground operations commenced during Operation DESERT STORM in February 1991, with rain making the sabkhas especially difficult to traverse. Although troops were forced to take fuel-consuming circuitous routes to cross the sabkhas, the *shamal* ultimately placed many coalition units upwind of Iraqi defenders, decreasing the likelihood of Iraqi chemical attacks.

*Shamals* are especially dangerous for aircrews flying at low altitudes. The hazards of flying across a featureless landscape are compounded by rain, sand, and dust. Air operations were repeatedly interrupted during Operation DESERT STORM by the severity of the *shamal.* This forced many American ground commanders to do without air support and destroy Iraqi units with armored forces.

Twelve years later, desert weather forecasting was much improved for Operation IRAQI FREEDOM. Forecasters provided early warning of the *shamal* that occurred on March 25–27, 2003. Although some air missions were cancelled, others succeeded because forewarned units prepared additional munitions, guided by the Global Positioning System (GPS), to compensate for poor visibility. Indeed, Iraqi units seeking to use the sandstorm as cover were devastated by these attacks. The predictability of *shamals* has not lessened their impact on military operations, however. Although the nature of combat changed with the advent of the Iraqi insurgency, *shamals* continue to make military operations more difficult to conduct in Iraq.

CHUCK FAHRER

**See also**
Defense Meteorological Satellite Program; Middle East, Climate of; National Geospatial-Intelligence Agency; Sabkha

**References**
Ahrens, C. Donald. *Meteorology Today.* 6th ed. Minneapolis: West Publishing, 2000.
Held, Colbert C. *Middle East Patterns: Places, Peoples, and Politics.* 4th ed. Boulder, CO: Westview, 2006.
Pannell, Richard P. "Climatology." In *Iraq: Geographic Perspectives,* edited by Jon C. Malinowski. New York: McGraw-Hill, 2004.
Scales, Robert H. *Certain Victory: The U.S. Army in the Gulf War.* Washington, DC: Brassey's, 1994.

## Shamir, Yitzhak
### Birth Date: October 15, 1915

Israeli politician and prime minister (1983–1984, 1986–1992). Yitzhak Shamir was born Yitzhak Jaziernicki on October 15, 1915, in Ruzinoy, Poland (now in Belarus). While a young man, he joined the Polish Betar Zionist youth movement. His law studies in Warsaw ended when he immigrated in 1935 to the British Mandate for Palestine (Eretz Israel), where he ultimately enrolled in Jerusalem's Hebrew University.

That same year Jaziernicki formally changed his name to Shamir. He then joined the Irgun Tsvai Leumi (National Military Organization), a right-wing paramilitary Zionist underground movement in Palestine. Irgun was known for its immediate and harsh retaliation for Arab attacks on the Jewish community in Palestine and its advocacy of military action against the British mandatory government.

When Irgun split into right-wing and left-wing factions in 1940, Shamir affiliated himself with the more militant Lohamei Herut Israel (Israel Freedom Fighters), a group that was classified by the British as a terrorist organization and later became known as the Stern Gang (after its founder, Avraham Stern). Shamir was arrested by the British in 1941 and escaped from their custody in 1943 following the death of Stern in 1942. Shamir now became one of those who led the organization and who reformed it and renamed it Lehi. It was under Shamir's leadership that in 1944 Lehi assassinated Walter Edward Guinness, Lord Moyne, the British minister resident in the Middle East and heir to the Guinness fortune.

Shamir served as Lehi's principal director of operations until he again was arrested by the British in 1946 and exiled to a British prison camp in Eritrea. Shamir escaped from there in 1947 to the neighboring French colony of Djibouti and, although granted political asylum by France, returned to Israel in 1948 to command Lehi until it was disbanded in 1949. Shamir directed the 1948 assassination of Count Folke Bernadotte, the United Nations (UN) representative in the Middle East, whom Shamir and his collaborators saw as an anti-Zionist and in league with the British.

Israeli prime minister Yitzhak Shamir, shown here in 1991. (AP/Wide World Photos)

Shamir served as a Mossad (Israeli intelligence service) operative from 1955 to 1965 and then engaged in business until he joined Menachem Begin's Herut movement (which became the Likud Party) in 1973. Shamir was elected to the Knesset (Israeli parliament) in 1973 and two years later became Herut's chairman. In the Knesset, Shamir served on the Foreign Affairs and Defense Committee as well as on the State Comptroller's Committee. The Likud Party's victory in the national elections for the ninth Knesset in May 1977 saw Begin become Israel's first non-Labor prime minister and Shamir become the Speaker of the Knesset. Begin immediately challenged King Hussein of Jordan, President Hafiz al-Asad of Syria, and President Anwar Sadat of Egypt to meet to negotiate a peace treaty. Sadat subsequently agreed to the Camp David Accords and the Israel-Egypt Peace Treaty that extended full Egyptian diplomatic recognition to Israel in exchange for the return of the Sinai peninsula, which Israel had seized in the Six-Day War in 1967. Shamir presided over the ratification of the treaty in the Knesset.

Following the resignation of Moshe Dayan, Shamir served as Israel's foreign minister during 1980–1983. In that capacity he oversaw the posttreaty normalization process with Egypt, reestablished diplomatic contacts with African countries severed during the Yom Kippur (Ramadan) War in 1973, and negotiated a postoperation peace agreement for Galilee with Lebanon. This treaty was later revoked by the Lebanese under Syrian pressure soon after

Begin's resignation as prime minister in October 1983. Shamir succeeded Begin both as leader of Likud and as prime minister.

Shamir's failure to decrease the inflation that racked Israel's economy led to an indecisive national election in July 1984 and the formation of a government of national unity that allied Likud with the Labor Party headed by Shimon Peres. Peres served as prime minister, with Shamir serving as vice premier until October 1986, when Shamir and Peres rotated positions and Shamir again became prime minister. While serving in these capacities, Shamir and Defense Minister Moshe Arens collaborated with U.S. president Ronald Reagan and Defense Secretary Caspar Weinberger to advance U.S.-Israeli strategic cooperation and free trade.

Following another indecisive election in 1988, Likud and Labor formed a new coalition government that retained Shamir as prime minister but did not have the rotation arrangement of its predecessor agreement. When this coalition government failed in 1990, Shamir formed a new government that included members of some ultraconservative parties and excluded Labor.

In 1991 Shamir's government ordered the rescue of thousands of Ethiopian Jews in Operation SOLOMON. At Washington's urging, Shamir did not retaliate in 1991 for unprovoked Iraqi Scud missile attacks during the Persian Gulf War that were designed to bring Israel into the conflict and break up the allied coalition. In September 1991 Shamir's government participated in the Madrid Peace Conference, which led to the 1993 peace accords between Israel and the Palestine Liberation Organization (PLO) that began Israel's withdrawal from the West Bank and the Gaza Strip.

Shamir's premiership ended in 1992 with the defeat of Likud in general elections. He resigned from the leadership of Likud in March 1993, although he retained his seat in the Knesset until 1996. Since that time, he has largely withdrawn from public scrutiny. In recent years he has reportedly been in failing health.

RICHARD EDWARDS

**See also**

Begin, Menachem; Camp David Accords; DESERT STORM, Operation; Israel; Reagan, Ronald Wilson; Weinberger, Caspar Willard

**References**

Brinkley, Joel. *The Stubborn Strength of Yitzhak Shamir*. New York: New York Times, 1988.
Enderlin, Charles. *Shamir*. Paris: O. Orban, 1991.
Shamir, Yitzhak. *Summing Up: An Autobiography*. London: Orion, 1994.

---

# Sham'un, Kamil

*See* Chamoun, Camille Nimr

---

# Sharia

Sharia is Islamic law, which Muslims regard as divine and a guide to an Islamic lifestyle. Islamic law is not monolithic; many differences in its principles and positions have occurred, and it is continually evolving. Sharia guides the believer's relationship with God (theology) as well as human relationships (ethics). Moreover, there are traces of tribal or customary law (*urf*) within the criminal principles of jurisprudence and penalties of Sharia. Especially since the terrorist attacks on the United States of September 11, 2001, but also earlier, some non-Muslims have attacked Muslims seeking to live under Sharia and have described Sharia in pejorative terms.

The term "Sharia" (Shari'ah) means the "straight path" or "the way." In the Qur'an (surah 1), which is part of daily prayers, Muslims ask to be guided on the straight path (*sirat al-mustaqim*) and not the path of those who have gone astray. Sharia provides that guidance. Reference to Sharia is found in the Qur'an in surah 45:18, where the Prophet is told that Allah (God) has "set Thee on the Way of our religion; so follow it, and follow not the desires of those who know not."

Sharia developed gradually over a considerable period and is based on the roots of jurisprudence (*usul al-fiqh*) as interpreted by Muslim scholars. The actual literature on Sharia deals with either the roots of Islamic jurisprudence, which differ slightly in each of the formal schools of Islamic law, or with *furu' al-fiqh*, the branches of Islamic law. The works on *usul al-fiqh* discuss the Qur'an as well as the hadith, the collections of the sayings and deeds of the Prophet Muhammad and in some cases those of his Companions or wives. The hadith are intended to illustrate the Sunnah, or tradition of the Prophet.

Islamic legal experts and scholars use the hadith, the Qur'an, and other legal principles of Sharia in order to determine the correctness of any action. The works that explain the *usul al-fiqh* acknowledge differences between scholars and discuss methodology. The *furu'* literature, on the other hand, concerns the ritual of Islam (*ibadat*) and social relations (*mu'amalat*). The first branch considers ritual purity, prayer, *zakat* (almsgiving), pilgrimage, fasting, and jihad, whereas the second might consider divorce; marriage; inheritance; the rules of buying, selling, lending, bequests, deposits, crimes, torts, *dhiyya* (compensatory payment to the family of the dead, or to the injured), or *talion* (retaliatory injury for injury); judicial procedure; contracts; rules about slaves; land ownership; the slaughter of animals for licit (*halal*) food; oaths; and many other topics, as virtually all aspects of life should be governed by Islamic law. Each action considered under the *furu'* is graded into one of five categories—neutral, reprehensible, forbidden, allowed, or recommended in Islam—and there may be further refinements of these gradations. In this literature, there are both expansive works with many subdivisions called *mahsus* and concise works called *mukhtasars*.

In Islam, the ultimate source of law is Allah. The Prophet Muhammad arbitrated disputes in Medina during his lifetime. After his death, lawmaking was carried out by secular rulers but also increasingly by scholars trained to be jurists. The Shia Muslims considered all the executive legislative functions of the ruler to be rightfully those of the Hidden Imam, so their scholars, *fuqaha* (those who make *fiqh*), were responsible for them.

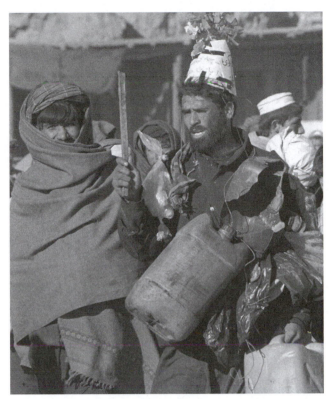

An unidentified man, his face blackened, covered with cans and scrap, is paraded around Kabul on February 5, 1997, after being convicted of stealing 10 liters of diesel fuel. As part of its strict interpretation of Islamic Sharia, the Taliban normally chops off the hands of thieves. However, those convicted of minor theft are subjected to public humiliation. (AP/Wide World Photos)

During their lifetimes, the first four caliphs (*khulafa*) were considered the *rashidun* (rightly guided). They had an input into lawmaking as well as the arbitration of disputes. However, as the Muslim empire expanded, the need arose for a more formalized methodology to deal with the myriad of cases.

The first step to this formalization was the compilation and recension of the Qur'an. Next came the systematization of the hadith literature in the period between 800 and 960 CE. Some of these individual hadiths were considered sound, or *sahih,* while others were considered weak (available only from single sources or possibly incorrect). The collections considered to be sound or most accurate included those by Muhammad ibn Ismail ibn Ibrahim ibn al-Mughirah al-Bukhari, Abu al-Husayn Muslim ibn al-Hajjaj Qushayri al-Nishapuri (simply referred to as Muslim), Abu Issa Muhammad ibn Issa al-Tirmidhi, Abu Abdullah ibn Yazid ibn Majah al-Rabiah al-Qazwini (Ibn Majah), Abu Dawud Sulayman ibn Ashath al-Azadi al-Sijistani, Abu Abdullah Malik ibn Anas ibn Malik ibn Amr al-Asbahi (Ibn Malik), and Ahmad ibn Shuayb ibn Ali ibn Sinan Abu Abd al-Rahman al-Nasai. The most widely used today are those by Muslim and Bukhari.

The earliest collection of hadith was the *Muwatta* of Ibn Malik. He interviewed numerous individuals whose early family relatives knew the Prophet and heard key sayings from him. Ibn Malik was also the founder of the Maliki *madhhab* (school of law). Bukhari then developed a list of more than 600,000 oral traditions, but he only accepted 7,000 as sufficiently authentic to be followed. This systematic approach to the collection of hadith literature was soon followed by the development of the *madhahib* (sing., *madhhab*), or schools of law.

The early *madhahib* were quite numerous, being developed by those who were disciples of scholars of the Qur'an and hadith. In addition to these sources of law, the jurists exercised opinion (*ra'y*) and used analogy (*qiyas*) and also consensus (*ijma'*), which could refer to scholarly agreement, or what scholars believed the consensus of the Muslim community at Medina to have been.

Another method was known as *ijtihad*, a form of creative inference and interpretation in making legal judgments. This process, coupled with practical application, led to a series of digests of legal rulings. From 800 to 1300 CE, these schools of law developed, matured, and consolidated until five Sunni schools had emerged as well as several Shiite schools. Today four Sunni and three Shiite legal traditions exist as well as the Ibadi tradition. The major Sunni *madhahib* differ in methodology and rulings, but they agree on the basic commonalities of Muslim practice, such as the need for prayer or *zakat*. The basic process that each school follows was generally the same, starting with the Qur'an and then working through hadith literature, followed by the consensus opinions of the Prophet's Companions and then their individual opinions. Failing this, solutions to problems could be derived through *ijtihad* at least until the 10th century or with reference to other principles such as *istislah* (consideration of the common good). Certain Sunni *madhahib* had put more emphasis on aspects of law other than the use of *ijtihad*; however, the tradition continued on in the Jafari *madhhab* followed by the Twelver Shiite Muslims.

The Hanafi *madhhab* was based on the teachings and writings of Abu Hanifa (703–767). He had the opportunity during his lifetime to meet some of those who actually saw and heard the Prophet speak and was thus able to ascertain some hadith from them. The *Kitab al-Athar* of Ibn Hanafi, compiled circa 750, serves as a key digest of hadith collections for this *madhhab*, while a number of other digests of legal rulings have come forth from its early days. Another important early writing of this school was the *Siyar* of Shaybani, written circa 800 and called the "law of nations," while another was *al-Hidayah* (*The Guidance*) of Marghinani, which was penned circa 1190. The Hanafi *madhhab* was the official school of the Ottoman Empire, so it is followed by the Sunni Muslims of Iraq and Syria and is one of the two schools followed in Egypt.

The Maliki *madhhab* was established by Malik Ibn Anas (717–801), sometimes called Imam Dar al-Hijra, or the Imam of the House of the Migration. A later Maliki work of Qadi Iyad ibn Musa al-Yahsubi called *al-Shifa*, written circa 1140, was an important collection of material on the life of the Prophet and its impact on the life of the Muslim. Maliki law prevails in North Africa and is characterized as being moderate; however, Maliki jurists, like others, are often influenced by the salafist movement.

The Shafii *madhhab* was founded by Muhammad bin Idris al-Shafi (769–820). Shafi was born in Gaza and belonged to the legal school of Medina, but developed his own legal school. The *Risala al-Fiqh of al-Shafi*, written circa 800, is extremely important in that Shafi created a conservative methodology different from the Hanafiyya use of private judgment and also distinct from the Traditionists of the Maliki and Hanbali schools. Shafi's method is rigorous hierarchy of the use of Qur'an, hadith, *ijma'*, and then *qiyas* (analogy). His other great work of jurisprudence was *Kitab al-Umm*. Another important source text is the *Umdat al-Salik wa Uddat al-Nasik* (*Reliance of the Traveller and the Tools of the Worshipper*) by Ahmad ibn Naqib al-Misri, which was written circa 1050 and contains the rulings and concepts of Imam Nawawi regarding Islamic public and foreign policy. Among many great Shafi scholars were Imam Ghazali and Abu al-Hasan Ashari. The Shafi legal school is found in Kurdistan, India, Sri Lanka, Ethiopia, Somalia, the Hijaz, Palestine, and throughout Southeast Asia and in some Egyptian and Chechen communities.

The Hanbali *madhhab* was developed by the disciples of Ahmad ibn Hanbal al-Shaybani (778–855). This school is considered by some scholars today to be more restrictive or purist than others. Hanbal's method of instruction revolved around a collection of 30,000 hadiths called the *Musnad*, and it was said that he knew 100,000 traditions by heart. Solutions to legal problems were sought first in the Qur'an and then in this collection, followed by recourse to the other sources of *fiqh* (*usul al-fiqh*) specified by Hanbal. Hanbal adamantly refused to allow his students to record his decisions. Hanbali law is not codified, and our knowledge of his own fatawa (response) comes from his disciples, including the two greatest hadith collectors Bukhari and Imam Muslim. Two of Hanbal's other followers were the distinguished jurists Ibn Taymiyyah (1263–1328) and his disciple Ibn Qayyim (1292–1350). Some of Ibn Taymiyyah's writings and ideas—for instance, some parts of his questions about the rightful authority of the Mongol rulers—have been instrumental in much of the salafist revival movement of the 19th and 20th centuries. The best collection of early Hanbali juristic decisions is found in Khiraqi's *al-Mukhtasar*, compiled circa 940. Ibn Hamid, Ibn al-Jawzi, Shams al-Din ibn Muflih, Sharaf al-Din al-Hajjawi, Muhammad al-Saffarini, and Muhammad ibn Abd al-Wahhab are among the many Hanbali jurists. The Hanbali *madhhab* was followed in Jerusalem, Greater Syria, and Saudi Arabia.

Applying Sharia principles in the modern world is complex. Sharia is considered immutable, but in fact scholars created jurisprudence (*fiqh*) in response to the questions that arose. Although every aspect or action in life is to be considered on the basis of Sharia, investigation into questions of jurisprudence and responses by Muslim jurists is deeply shaped by precedent and the way that the question (fatwa) is formulated.

In the 19th century, the Ottomans partially codified their use of Hanafi law, to some degree in response to the thinking that Sharia ought to be more systemized as was Western law. Important arguments were made during this century by Egyptian jurist Muhammad Abduh about the use of *ijtihad,* disregarding the strict traditions of the *madhahib* and instead using a kind of patchwork approach called *talfiq,* whereby a jurist could borrow from different legal schools.

As modern states subsumed or limited the activities of the traditional *ulama* (scholars), civil laws began to adjudicate individual activities, particularly in commercial, civil, and penal law. In certain countries, scholars only retained power over family law, sometimes called personal status law, and Islamic education.

This shift in legal authority has been contested by some in the Muslim world. The development of civil legal systems has certainly complicated the application of Sharia, as have developing civil legal systems that incorporate aspects of Sharia. This has led to advocacy by some to Islamize civil codes partially based on Sharia or to oppose further changes in them in the form of many proposed legal reforms. Still other groups have sought to establish an Islamic government based upon Sharia. This occurred in Iran, where the laws of the Pahlavi era were completely reworked.

Currently, many Muslim countries still include aspects of Sharia in family courts, maintain dual legal systems, or still incorporate Sharia in other areas of law. The use of Sharia impacts all areas of law in Iran, Sudan, Saudi Arabia, and parts of Malaysia and also in the criminal codes of Libya, Pakistan (now partially reformed), and parts of Nigeria. In the case of Kelantan in Malaysia, there is an effort to eventually impose Sharia on all aspects of life, as the Sharia law courts in that country have been gradually assuming many of the functions of the state-supported civil courts.

In Iraq there is today a dual legal system administering family law. Many elements of family law under Sharia have been classified as statutory discrimination against women by the Convention on the Elimination of All Forms of Discrimination against Women (CEDAW), adopted by the General Assembly of the United Nations (UN). These also impact civil laws that were partially based on Ottoman law and included exemptions for those who carried out murder in the name of family honor and for rapists who married their victims. Supporters of Sharia have argued that incorrect interpretations of Sharia might have prevailed but that Western-style reforms will destroy the morals of their societies.

Much criticism has come from the West and the UN against penal codes that utilize the severe *hadd* punishments, as in Iran, Libya, and Saudi Arabia; in the revised penal code adopted in Pakistan; and in areas controlled by the Taliban. These included capital punishment, amputations of hands or feet, and lashings. Some Muslim leaders, such as Tariq Ramadan in Switzerland, have called for a moratorium on such penalties on the grounds that true Sharia is not actually being applied today and requires revision and discussion, but other Muslim authorities oppose his idea of a moratorium.

The major reason for considering Sharia in a study of modern U.S. wars in the Middle East is the disagreements about its role either in violent extremism or in political opposition to regimes backed by or in conflict with the United States, such as the Taliban in Afghanistan. Images of corporal punishment being meted out in public by the Taliban in Pakistan prior to reconquest of the Swat Valley evoked widespread criticism in the United States of the Pakistani government's decision to conclude a truce there with the Taliban.

RUSSELL RODGERS AND SHERIFA ZUHUR

**See also**

Allah; Muhammad, Prophet of Islam; Qur'an; Salafism; Shia Islam; Sunni Islam

**References**

Al-Hashimi, Muhammad Ali. *The Ideal Muslim Society: As Defined in the Qur'an and Sunnah.* Riyadh, Saudi Arabia: International Islamic Publishing House, 2007.

Doi, 'Abdur Rahman. *Shari'ah: The Islamic Law.* London: TaHa Publishers, 1997.

Dutton, Yasin. *The Origins of Islamic Law: The Qur'an, the Muwatta, and Madinan 'Amal.* London: RoutledgeCurzon, 2002.

Gibb, H. A. R. *Mohammedanism.* London: Oxford University Press, 1970.

Hughes, Thomas Patrick. *Dictionary of Islam.* Reprint ed. Chicago: Kazi Publications, 1994.

Philips, Abu Ameenah Bilal. *The Evolution of Fiqh: Islamic Law & the Madh-habs.* Kuala Lumpur, Malaysia: A. S. Noordeen, 2005.

---

# Sharon, Ariel
## Birth Date: February 27, 1928

Israeli Army general, politician, and prime minister (2001–2006). Born Ariel Scheinermann on February 27, 1928, in Kfar Malal, Palestine, to Russian immigrants, at age 14 Ariel Sharon joined the Gadna, the paramilitary youth organization of the Haganah, the Jewish defense force that protected kibbutzim (collective-farming settlements) from Arab attacks.

Sharon commanded an infantry company in the Alexandroni Brigade during the Israeli War of Independence (1948–1949) and was severely wounded by Jordanian forces in an effort to relieve the besieged Jewish population of Jerusalem during the Second Battle of Latrun. Following the war he founded and commanded a special commando unit (Unit 101) that specialized in reconnaissance, intelligence gathering, and retaliatory raids designed to punish and deter Palestinian and Arab protagonists while enhancing Israeli morale.

Sharon was criticized for targeting both Arab soldiers and noncombatants and was condemned for the killing of 69 civilians, half of whom were women and children, during a raid on the West Bank village of Qibya in the autumn of 1953. In an effort to end the criticism, in 1954 Unit 101 was folded into the 202nd Paratroop Brigade. However, it continued to attack military and civilian targets, including the Kalkiliya police station raid in October 1956.

During the 1956 Suez Crisis, Sharon commanded the 202nd Brigade in the Israeli invasion of the Sinai peninsula, capturing the strategically important Mitla Pass at the onset. Later he received

Israeli prime minister Ariel Sharon speaks during a press conference at his office in Jerusalem in May 2001. (Ya'cov Sa'ar/Israeli Government Press Office)

heavy criticism for taking the pass rather than merely holding the ground east of it. Taking the pass claimed 38 Israeli dead. This incident hindered Sharon's military advancement during the next several years.

After studying at the British Staff College in 1957, Sharon commanded an infantry brigade and then the Israeli Army Infantry School. In 1962 he earned his bachelor of law degree from the Hebrew University of Jerusalem. He was appointed chief of staff of the Northern Command in 1964 and then in 1966 headed the Israel Defense Forces (IDF) Training Department.

Sharon was promoted to major general just before the 1967 Six-Day War, when forces under his command again took the Mitla Pass. He assumed leadership of the Southern Command in 1969. He retired from the IDF in June 1972 but was recalled to command the armored division that crossed the Suez Canal into Egypt at the end of the 1973 Yom Kippur (Ramadan) War. His direction of that crossing and the subsequent encirclement of Egyptian forces is widely considered one of the masterpieces of tactical command in modern mobile warfare.

Sharon helped found the Likud Party in September 1973 and was elected to the Knesset (Israeli parliament) in December 1973. He resigned in 1975 to serve as security adviser to Prime Minister Yitzhak Rabin until 1977 and then became minister of agriculture in Likud prime minister Menachem Begin's first government

(1977–1981). In this position Sharon actively promoted the construction of Jewish settlements in the occupied Arab territories. In June 1981 he became Begin's minister of defense, and in this position Sharon designed and prosecuted Israel's 1982 invasion of Lebanon, known as Operation PEACE FOR GALILEE. Sharon and Begin deliberately expanded the invasion to include a drive against Beirut. Although the Palestinians were driven from Lebanon, the invasion intensified the Lebanese Civil War, allowing Syria to become entrenched in the politics of that country. The Israeli presence in force lasted three years (a limited Israeli force remained until 2000) and resulted in such a high number of Palestinian civilian deaths that worldwide public opinion turned against Israel. Following the September 1982 massacre of Palestinians at the Sabra and Shatila refugee camps by Israel's Lebanese Christian Phalangist allies, Sharon was found to be indirectly responsible for failing to provide adequate protection for the refugees and thus resigned as Begin's minister of defense. This event overshadowed Sharon's diplomatic rapprochement with a number of African nations and his role in developing the first strategic cooperation agreement with the United States (1981), Operation MOSES (1984), and a free trade agreement with the United States (1985).

Sharon served in various Israeli governments as a minister-without-portfolio (1983–1984), minister of industry and trade (1984–1990), and minister of construction and housing and chairman of the ministerial committee on immigration and absorption (1990–1992). The latter post allowed him to double the number of Jewish settlements throughout the West Bank and the Gaza Strip during his tenure in office. He hoped that these settlements would not only provide a strategic buffer for Israel proper but also reduce the possibility of the return of these territories to Palestinian Arabs.

Sharon then served on the Knesset's Foreign Affairs and Defense Committee (1992–1996) and as minister of national infrastructure (1996–1998) under Likud prime minister Benjamin Netanyahu. As foreign minister (1998–1999), Sharon led Israel's permanent status negotiations with the Palestinian National Authority (PNA) and sought to promote long-term solutions to the region's water disputes and inadequacies.

Sharon assumed the leadership of the Likud Party after Ehud Barak's Labor Party victory in the elections of May 1999 led to Netanyahu's resignation. The failure of Barak's land for peace initiative at the 2000 Camp David Summit coupled with the collapse of his governing coalition and the eruption of Palestinian violence led to Barak's defeat by Sharon in the general election of February 2001, even though much of the civil violence was precipitated by Sharon's visit to the Temple Mount on September 28, 2000. The ensuing violence was known as the Second (al-Aqsa) Intifada (2000–2004).

Palestinians charged that as prime minister, Sharon pursued a policy of confrontation and nonnegotiation. On July 2004, he also angered the French government when he called for French Jews to immigrate to Israel following an upswing in anti-Semitic incidents in France. With 600,000 Jews, France had the largest Jewish population after the United States and Israel.

In 2004 Sharon began a bold policy of disengagement, or unilateral withdrawal, from the Gaza Strip, a policy opposed by his own Likud Party but supported by the Labor Party, the U.S. government, and many European nations. In January 2005 Labor Party leader Shimon Peres accepted the position of vice premier in Sharon's unity government that included members of Likud, Labor, Meimad, and United Torah Judaism. Sharon completed the withdrawal from Gaza of all Israeli settlers on August 30, 2005, and the destruction of all Israeli settlements and the complete withdrawal of the Israeli military on September 11, 2005.

Sharon narrowly defeated a challenge to his leadership of Likud by Netanyahu on September 27, 2005, and then on November 21, 2005, resigned his Likud position, dissolved parliament, formed a new center-right party known as Kadima (Forward), and set new elections for March 2006. On December 18, 2005, Sharon was hospitalized for what was thought to be a minor stroke and released. However, he suffered a massive cerebral hemorrhage at his Sycamore Ranch in the Negev region on January 4, 2006. He remains in a persistent vegetative state with little potential for recovery. On April 11, 2006, the Israeli cabinet declared Sharon incapacitated and ended his prime ministership three days later, naming Ehud Olmert as interim prime minister, a position made official after Kadima won the most Knesset seats in the national

election. Perhaps the most controversial of Sharon's projects as prime minister was a security wall designed to separate and secure Israel proper from territory to be ceded to the Palestinians.

RICHARD EDWARDS

**See also**

Arab-Israeli Conflict, Overview; Arafat, Yasser; Begin, Menachem; Intifada, Second; Katyusha Rocket; Lebanon; Netanyahu, Benjamin; Palestine Liberation Organization; Rabin, Yitzhak; Suez Crisis

**References**

Finkelstein, Norman H. *Ariel Sharon.* Minneapolis: First Avenue Editions, 2005.
Miller, Anita, Jordan Miller, and Sigalit Zetouni. *Sharon: Israel's Warrior-Politician.* Chicago: Academy Chicago Publishers, 2002.
Sharon, Ariel, and David Chanoff. *Warrior: An Autobiography.* 2nd ed. New York: Simon and Schuster, 2001.

## SHARP EDGE, **Operation**
**Start Date: June 2, 1990**
**End Date: January 9, 1991**

Evacuation of noncombatant personnel from the U.S. embassy in Liberia. By mid-1990 increasing internal unrest threatened U.S. diplomats and civilians living and working in Liberia; the situation in Liberia had been steadily deteriorating for a decade. On April 12, 1980, army master sergeant Samuel K. Doe led a coup that overthrew the government in Monrovia. Doe suspended the constitution and imposed martial law. A new constitution was drafted, and on October 15, 1985, elections were held. Doe was elected president and was inaugurated on January 16, 1986.

In December 1989 Charles Taylor began an insurgency against the Doe government. Taylor's insurgent organization became known as the National Patriotic Front of Liberia (NPFL). The organization grew in strength as dissatisfaction with Doe increased. As the NPFL gained strength it mounted military operations against the Doe government, and a civil war ensued. As the fighting spread from the interior toward the Liberian capital of Monrovia, President George H. W. Bush ordered an amphibious ready group consisting of four U.S. warships and 2,300 U.S. marines to proceed to the vicinity of Monrovia and be prepared to evacuate noncombatants and protect key U.S. installations there (which included a number of sensitive communications sites).

Amphibious Squadron Four, which had been undergoing an upkeep period in Toulon, France, included the *Saipan* (LHA-2), a Tarawa-class amphibious assault ship; the *Ponce* (LPD-15), an Austin-class amphibious transport dock; the *Sumter* (LST-1181), a Newport-class tank landing ship; the Spruance-class destroyer *Peterson* (DD-969); and Fleet Surgical Team Two. The amphibious ready group embarked elements of the 22nd Marine Expeditionary Unit (MEU), including Battalion Landing Team (BLT) 2/4, and departed on May 27, 1990, for the coast of Liberia. Additional units supporting the mission included Marine Medium Helicopter

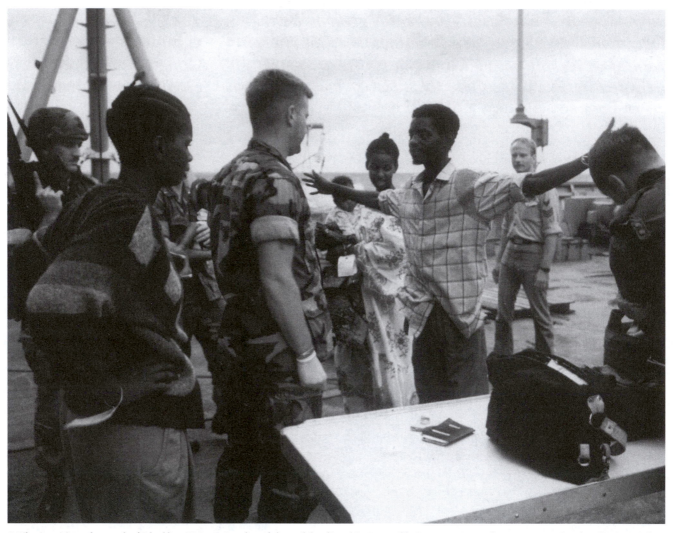

A Liberian citizen about to be frisked by a U.S. marine aboard the tank landing ship *Barnstable County* on September 6, 1990. During the Liberian Civil War, Operation SHARP EDGE evacuated citizens from the war-torn country in U.S. Navy ships. (U.S. Navy)

Squadron (HMM) 261 (Reinforced) and MEU Service Support Group (MSSG) 22.

As the amphibious ready group made its way toward Liberia, the situation there grew more perilous, particularly in Monrovia. The navy decided that it needed to get a helicopter-borne force within range of Monrovia as quickly as possible. The *Saipan* group could not close this distance until June 3, however, so the decision was made to put a Boeing CH-46 Sea Knight helicopter and a 75-man security force composed of a reinforced marine rifle platoon and a SEAL detachment on the *Peterson* to sprint ahead of the *Saipan* group. The *Peterson* arrived off Monrovia on June 2, but the situation in the capital had changed somewhat for the better, and it was deemed not necessary to deploy the security force to Monrovia at that point.

During June and July and into the first days of August, the NPFL and a splinter group, the Independent National Patriotic Front of Liberia (INPFL) under Prince Johnson, slowly tightened a noose around Monrovia. At the end of July the fighting intensified and threatened the U.S. embassy; subsequently the amphibious

ready group and the marines afloat were put on alert. The killing of approximately 200 civilians at the Lutheran Church of Monrovia added a new sense of urgency to the situation.

On August 4 Prince Johnson began rounding up foreigners and threatened to take U.S. hostages. That evening the U.S. ambassador advised the forces afloat that he was requesting assistance from the president. Shortly thereafter the amphibious ready group was given the order to secure the U.S. embassy and evacuate embassy personnel, U.S. citizens, and designated foreign nationals. Additionally, they were to evacuate U.S. workers at the telecommunication and receiver sites.

At 9:00 a.m. on August 5, 1990, marines from Echo Company, 2nd Battalion, 4th Marines, boarded helicopters and flew to the American communications sites. There they rescued 21 U.S. citizens. Simultaneously, a mix of CH-46s and Sikorsky Ch-53s Sea Stallion landed 234 marines from Hotel Company, 2nd Battalion, 4th Marines, at the U.S. embassy compound in Monrovia. Once on the ground, they evacuated not only 330 Americans but also Canadian, French, Italian, and some Liberian nationals. By the time the noncombatant operation was over on August 21, the marines had rescued 1,600 people.

On August 21 the original four-ship amphibious ready group was relieved by a two-ship amphibious force, which remained until November to assist the U.S. embassy and continue the evacuation of noncombatants. The 22nd MEU was relieved by the 26th MEU embarked on the *Inchon* (LPH-12), an Iwo Jima–class amphibious assault ship. The last amphibious ship, the *Nashville,* an Austin-class amphibious transport dock, left the coast of Liberia on January 9, 1991, ending the operation. A total of 2,609 people were evacuated from Liberia between August 5 and the departure of the *Nashville.* Additionally, sailors and marines from the task force provided humanitarian assistance, airlifting food, water, fuel, and medical supplies to the ravaged capital city.

Little has been written about this operation because it was overshadowed by Iraq's seizure of Kuwait on August 2, 1990, and the subsequent U.S. and coalition troop buildup in the Middle East (Operation DESERT SHIELD). However, at the time, SHARP EDGE was the longest-running noncombatant evacuation operation in recent naval history.

JAMES H. WILLBANKS

**See also**

DESERT SHIELD, Operation

**References**

Kennedy, Floyd D., Jr. "Operation Sharp Edge: Low End of the Spectrum." *National Defense* 75(463) (December 1990): 80–88.

Park, T. W. "Operation Sharp Edge." *Naval Institute Proceedings/Naval Review* 117 (May 1991): 102–106.

# Shatt al-Arab Waterway

A 120-mile waterway formed by the confluence of the Tigris and Euphrates rivers at Qurnah in the Basra governorate in southern Iraq and fed by a number of Iranian tributaries, of which the Karun River is the largest. The waterway traverses the eastern edge of the Faw (Fao) peninsula and empties into the Persian Gulf near Kuwait. Its southern half delineates the border between Iraq and Iran. Shatt al-Arab is Arabic for the "coast/shore of the Arabs." The Shatt al-Arab is Iraq's only access to the sea and is thus essential to Iraq's oil exportation and the importation of goods and commodities. Iran uses the waterway for the same purposes.

Alluvial deposits from the waterway's feeder rivers created an expansive marsh that remains the home of the 5,000-year-old Marsh Arab culture and people. These deposits continue to expand the delta at the mouth of the waterway on the Persian Gulf. The Shatt al-Arab shrinks from a width of one-half mile at its mouth to 120 feet at the Iraqi port city of Basra. Constant dredging is necessary to keep the waterway open to Basra and the Iranian port cities of Abadan and Khorramshahr. The legal course of the waterway is disputed between Iraq and Iran, because in the distant past the Tigris and Euphrates rivers flowed into the Persian Gulf more to the west than they do today and because the shifting delta now separates Abadan from the Gulf by 30 miles. About 1,000 years ago the city was situated at the head of the Gulf.

The earliest-known dispute over the waterway was resolved by the 1639 CE Treaty of Zohab between the Turkish Ottoman Empire, whose territory included current-day Iraq, and Persia, renamed Iran in 1935. A later dispute was resolved by the 1847 Second Treaty of Erzurum, with the British supporting the Ottomans' claim to both banks of the waterway and the Russians supporting the Persian claim to the eastern bank, which granted Persia rights of navigation on the waterway. The dispute continued, and a 1913 protocol signed in Constantinople gave Persia control of the eastern bank with expanded control to the middle of the waterway at Abadan and Khorramshahr, allowing easier navigation into and out of Iranian ports. World War I, however, halted implementation of this protocol. A 1935 British-led international commission gave Iran control of the approaches to Abadan and Khorramshahr while granting Iraq (renamed by the League of Nations in 1920 after the post–World War I division of the Ottoman Empire) complete control of the rest of the Shatt al-Arab and its delta.

As the economic importance of oil exportation to Iraq and Iran increased in the 1960s and 1970s, so did tensions and disputes over the Shatt al-Arab waterway. The 1975 Iran-Iraq Algiers Accord divided sovereignty using straight lines connecting at the waterway's deepest points (the thalweg principle), with Iraq controlling the waterway westward of the line and Iran controlling the waterway eastward of the line.

Believing that Iraq's greatest weakness was the Shatt al-Arab, the artery through which Iraq's oil passed, Iraqi president Saddam Hussein in 1980 verbally abrogated the 1975 accord, claimed sovereignty over both banks, and invaded Iran, sparking the Iran-Iraq War. Iraq initially took control of the waterway in the Iran-Iraq War. Iraqi fears about the waterway were realized when in 1987 Iran captured Iraq's Faw peninsula, blocking most of Iraq's export-import activities. The original pre-1980 accord boundaries were restored when the war ended in 1988. Hussein renounced his stated abrogation of the Algiers Accord in 1990, mollifying Iran prior to Iraq's 1990 invasion and occupation of Kuwait.

Although the 1991 Persian Gulf War removed Hussein's forces from Kuwait, the cessation of the war before Hussein was ousted led President George H. W. Bush to urge an internal revolt against Hussein. Responding to this call, the Marsh Arabs joined a short-lived (March 1991) Shiite uprising in southern Iraq. Hussein brutally crushed the rebellion and began draining the marshes by channeling the Tigris and Euphrates rivers directly into the Shatt al-Arab, essentially converting the wetlands into a desert. This decimated and dispersed the Marsh Arab population.

The waterway was an initial target in the Anglo-American–led 2003 Iraq invasion that ousted Hussein and overthrew Iraq's Sunni-led Baathist government. British Royal Marines employed the 1987 Iranian tactic and captured the Faw peninsula, severing Iraq's main economic artery. Restoration of the marshlands began in 2003 following the end of organized Iraqi military resistance, and by 2007 the marsh had been restored to approximately 50 percent of the area it comprised prior to the Iran-Iraq War.

In June 2004 the Iranians seized British Royal Marines patrolling the waterway and released them a few days later. United Nations (UN) Security Council Resolution 1723, passed in 2006, mandated that the British patrol, interdict contraband on, and keep the waterway open from Basra to the Persian Gulf. On May 23, 2007, the Iranians seized 15 British Royal Navy personnel patrolling the waterway and released them 13 days later. The incident increased the already strained relations between Iran and the West.

RICHARD EDWARDS

**See also**

DESERT STORM, Operation; Faw Peninsula; Hussein, Saddam; Iran; Iran-Iraq War; Iraq, History of, Pre-1990; Iraq, History of, 1990–Present; IRAQI FREEDOM, Operation; Marsh Arabs; Persian Gulf; Persian Gulf War, Cease-Fire Agreement

**References**

Brown, Sarah Graham. *Sanctioning Saddam: The Politics of Intervention in Iraq*. London: I. B. Tauris, 1999.

Coughlin, Con. *Saddam: His Rise and Fall*. New York: Harper Perennial, 2005.

Karsh, Efraim. *The Iran-Iraq War, 1980–1988*. Oxford, UK: Osprey, 2002.

Keegan, John. *The Iraq War: The Military Offensive, from Victory in 21 Days to the Insurgent Aftermath*. New York: Vintage, 2005.

Ochsenschlager, Edward L. *Iraq's Marsh Arabs in the Garden of Eden*. Philadelphia: University of Pennsylvania Museum Publications, 2004.

Schofield, R. N. *Evolution of the Shatt al Arab Boundary Dispute*. Middlesex, UK: Kingston, 1986.

Tripp, Charles. *A History of Iraq*. Cambridge: Cambridge University Press, 2007.

---

# Sheehan, Cindy Lee Miller
## Birth Date: July 10, 1957

Prominent antiwar activist made famous by her outspoken opposition to the Iraq War and to the George W. Bush administration in general. Born on July 10, 1957, in Los Angeles, California, Cindy Lee Miller Sheehan was a Catholic youth pastor and mother of four in suburban California but entered the national spotlight in 2005 as an audacious and outspoken critic of Operation IRAQI FREEDOM. Her activism was motivated by the April 2004 death in Iraq of her son, 24-year-old Army Specialist Casey Sheehan. Citing his memory, she became a key organizer of Gold Star Families for Peace and founded the Camp Casey installation in August 2005 near President Bush's ranch in Crawford, Texas.

Sheehan has stated that she had been a tepid critic of President Bush all along and was immediately skeptical of the invasion of Iraq in March 2003. She claimed that she had been surprised when her son enlisted in the army in 2000, but it was her grief over his death that galvanized her public dissension. Unable to recover from her loss, Sheehan embarked on a public campaign to challenge the war, demanding more information from Bush and other officials about the cause for which her son had died.

In August 2005 Sheehan began a three-week vigil outside the president's Crawford, Texas, ranch, vowing not to move until he granted her a meeting and an explanation for the war and its aftermath. According to Sheehan, she and her immediate family had met with the president in a condolence visit shortly after Casey's death; Bush did not, however, agree to meet again. Although her stint at Camp Casey failed to achieve the intended results, it did channel an unprecedented level of media attention onto the antiwar movement. Many argue that Sheehan's actions reinvigorated opposition to the war, which had flagged after its failure to prevent the initial invasion of Iraq.

Camp Casey transformed Sheehan into a highly visible public figure and an internationally recognized speaker and activist. She became a fixture at antiwar demonstrations and secured audiences with a number of celebrities and politicians, including controversial Venezuelan leader Hugo Chavez. Additionally, Sheehan has published two books, *Peace Mom* (2006), an autobiographical account of her development as an activist, and *Dear President Bush* (2006), a collection of essays. Through her work, she has promoted a platform of "matriotism," an antiwar perspective that she deemed the opposite of militaristic patriotism. Matriotism, as Sheehan has articulated it, eschews all war (except for explicitly defensive purposes) on the grounds that it kills other mothers' children. Because everyone has or had a mother and because

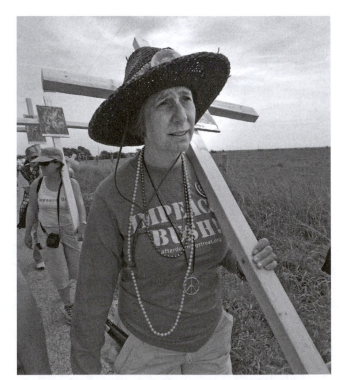

War protestor Cindy Sheehan carries a cross on the road leading to President George W. Bush's ranch in Crawford, Texas, April 14, 2006. (AP/Wide World Photos)

motherhood is the essence of caring, Sheehan reasons, all mothers should oppose war on ethical grounds.

Predictably, Sheehan's philosophy and actions have drawn a great deal of controversy. She has been the subject of multiple arrests, and her husband, who disagreed with activism, filed for divorce while she was entrenched at Camp Casey. Many of the criticisms of Sheehan's work are deeply personal, in large part because her efforts are often couched in and motivated explicitly by her own loss. Some question whether her project is as altruistic as it might appear, while others resent the way in which her actions monopolized the attention of the media and came to represent the entirety of the otherwise diverse peace movement. Perhaps the greatest debate over Sheehan's message is whether or not it has dishonored the war dead; many have argued that describing the war as senseless is disrespectful not only to her son but also to all the others who have died in the conflict. Consequently, other Gold Star families have undertaken a media campaign proclaiming that Sheehan does not speak for them because they support the cause for which their loved ones had died.

Despite her early tenacity, Sheehan publicly resigned from the peace movement in May 2007. Citing a need to return to mothering her surviving children and the ineffectiveness of antiwar organizing, she posted an open letter announcing her departure on the liberal Web site DailyKos and has largely disappeared from the public scene. Although she has formally renounced antiwar activism, Sheehan remains a sharply polarizing figure, a target of criticism for some and a source of inspiration for others.

REBECCA A. ADELMAN

**See also**

Antiwar Movements, Persian Gulf and Iraq Wars; Bush, George Walker; Casualties, Operation IRAQI FREEDOM

**References**

Abrams, Kathryn. "Women and Antiwar Protest: Rearticulating Gender and Citizenship." *Boston Law Review* 87 (2005): 849–882.

Cockburn, Cynthia. *From Where We Stand: War, Women's Activism, & Feminist Analysis.* London: Zed Books, 2007.

Houppert, Karen. "Cindy Sheehan: Mother of a Movement?" *Nation* 282 (June 12, 2006): 11–16.

Sheehan, Cindy. *Dear President Bush.* San Francisco: City Lights, 2006.

———. *Peace Mom: A Mother's Journey through Heartache to Activism.* New York: Atria, 2006.

# Shehhi, Marwan al-
**Birth Date: May 9, 1978**
**Death Date: September 11, 2001**

One of the key figures in the hijacking of American jetliners on September 11, 2001, who was the hijackers' pilot for United Airlines Flight 175 that crashed into the South Tower of the World Trade Center complex on September 11. Marwan Yousef Muhammed Rashid Lekrab al-Shehhi was born on May 9, 1978, and raised in Ras al-Khaiymah in the United Arab Emirates (UAE). Ras al-Khaymah was one of the poorest and most conservative of the emirates. The family, which was quite religious, was a member of the Shooh Bedouin tribe. His father served as the 'adhan (muezzin), the person who chants the daily calls to prayer at the mosques in Ras al-Khaymah.

Good grades allowed Shehhi to attend the Emirates al-Ain University. After finishing his schooling he joined the UAE Army. Soon after he entered the military and reached the rank of sergeant, the army awarded him a paid scholarship to further his education in Germany. His goal was to study marine engineering.

Shehhi entered into a German-language preparatory course in Bonn, which he passed in 1996. Next he enrolled at the University of Bonn, but his father's death in 1997 caused him to neglect his course work when he took an unofficial leave to return to the UAE. Returning to Germany some months later, Shehhi passed the next course in 1997. He proved to be an average student with little ambition. Also, by the time he returned to Germany, he was increasingly militant in his religious views. Unhappy with the environment in Bonn, he petitioned the UAE Army to allow him to transfer his studies to the Technical University of Hamburg-Harburg. The strict religious environment at the al-Quds Mosque in Hamburg satisfied his new religiosity, and his friendship with Muhammad Atta only increased this religious fervor.

Soon Shehhi's relationship with Atta had solidified, with Atta as the leader and Shehhi as a faithful follower. Shehhi was the acknowledged expert on Islamic scripture. Together with Ramzi Bin al-Shibh, the three are alleged to have made up the Hamburg Cell.

The friends constantly debated how they could make a contribution to the Muslim cause. At first they wanted to fight on the side of the Chechen rebels in Chechnya, then fighting Russian forces, but Shehhi then traveled with his friends to Afghanistan to train at Al Qaeda training camps.

Shehhi left for Afghanistan in the autumn of 1998 for training at the Al Qaeda Khalden camp. While in Kandahar he, along with Atta and Ziyad Jarrah, met and talked with Al Qaeda leader Osama bin Laden. Shehhi, Atta, and Jarrah were recruited at this conversation for a special future martyrdom mission. Once they had accepted the mission, Muhammad Atef, Al Qaeda's military strategist, outlined the basics of the September 11 plot. Returning to Germany, Shehhi joined with Atta and Shibh in working at a warehouse, packing computers for shipping. Never excited about his education, Shehhi stopped attending class, and he was dropped as a student in December 2000.

Shehhi became the number two man behind Atta in the September 11 plot. Shehhi arrived in the United States separately from Atta, but they kept in touch and trained together in Florida to pilot commercial jetliners. Although Shehhi was never a skilled pilot, he was nonetheless able to pilot United Airlines Flight 175 into the South Tower on September 11, 2001. Shehhi died when the Boeing 767 slammed into the World Trade Center at 9:03 a.m. All others on board, 64 people in all, also perished.

STEPHEN E. ATKINS

See also

Al Qaeda; Atta, Muhammad; Bin Laden, Osama; Hamburg Cell; September 11 Attacks; Shibh, Ramzi Muhammad Abdallah ibn al-

References

Corbin, Jane. *Al-Qaeda: The Terror Network That Threatens the World.* New York: Thunder's Mouth, 2002.

*Der Spiegel* Magazine, ed. *Inside 9-11: What Really Happened.* New York: St. Martin's, 2001.

McDermott, Terry. *Perfect Soldiers: The 9/11 Hijackers: Who They Were, Why They Did It.* New York: HarperCollins, 2005.

# Shevardnádze, Eduard
## Birth Date: January 28, 1928

Soviet foreign minister (1985–1990, 1991), chairman of the Georgian State Council (1992–1995), and president of Georgia (1995–2003). Born on January 28, 1928, in the Georgian village of Mamati, Eduard Shevardnádze graduated from the Party School of the Communist Party Central Committee in 1951 and from the Kutaisi Pedagogical Institute in 1959. He then became an instructor for the Komsomol (Communist Union of Youth). Joining the Communist Party in 1948, he rose quickly through its ranks and became a member of the Georgian Supreme Soviet in 1959.

During 1961–1964 Shevardnádze served as a party regional secretary, and during 1964–1965 he was deputy minister of internal affairs for Georgia. He became minister of internal affairs of Georgia in 1965, a post he held until 1972. During this period he reformed Georgian agriculture, creating new incentives for farmers and boosting production. He was also responsible for firing and imprisoning hundreds of officials in his fight against bureaucratic corruption, earning him the reputation of a merciless opponent of corruption and inefficiency. He also forced government officials to give up properties that they had attained through bribery and other illegal means. Shevardnádze stated that the Soviet economy would never move forward if corruption continued to plague the system.

In 1972 Shevardnádze was appointed first secretary of the Georgian Communist Party, a post he occupied until 1985. There too he continued his fight against corruption. He became a member of the Central Committee of the Communist Party of the Soviet Union (CPSU) in 1976. In 1977 Soviet authorities conducted a series of crackdowns against human rights activists, jailing many of the movement's top figures. Shevardnádze's Georgian government participated in the crackdowns, and among those jailed was Zviad Gamsakhurdia, who in May 1991 would become the first democratically elected president of the independent Republic of Georgia. In 1978 Shevardnádze was promoted to candidate member status of the Soviet Politburo, which functioned as the central policy-making and governing body of the CPSU. That same year he was awarded the Order of Lenin.

In 1985 the new reform-minded Soviet leader Mikhail Gorbachev appointed Shevardnádze minister of foreign affairs after

As foreign minister of the Soviet Union from 1985 to 1990, Eduard Shevardnádze pursued liberal policies designed to improve the Soviet Union's relationship with the West. Shevardnádze was president of the Republic of Georgia from 1995 to 2003. (U.S. Department of Defense)

the resignation of Andrei Gromyko. Shevardnádze also became a full member of the CPSU Politburo. As foreign minister, he played an important role in ending the Cold War. He reformed Soviet foreign policy making, implementing Gorbachev's policies. These included withdrawing all Soviet troops from Afghanistan, developing new arms control and Middle East peace strategies, establishing ties with Israel, negotiating German reunification, and allowing for the democratization of Eastern Europe. Shevardnádze rejected all aid requests by communist leaders in Eastern Europe when revolutions and democratization swept their countries, allowing for a smooth and relatively bloodless transition to democracy in the region.

These actions, however, made Shevardnádze many enemies in Moscow. Nevertheless, he adhered to a strict policy of liberalization, which gradually separated him from Gorbachev's incrementalist policy of preserving a socialist system. Because of these differences and growing criticism from Communist Party hard-liners, Shevardnádze resigned his post in December 1990 and warned that the nation was headed toward dictatorship. Following his resignation, an unsuccessful coup against Gorbachev by communist hard-liners in August 1991 seemed to prove that Shevardnádze's prediction was correct. He returned to the post of foreign minister in November 1991 but resigned together with Gorbachev in December when the Soviet Union was officially dissolved.

In March 1992 Shevardnádze became head of an interim Georgian government following the ouster of President Zviad Gamsakhurdia. In 1995 Shevardnádze survived an assassination attempt and that same year was elected president of the Republic of Georgia by a comfortable margin. He survived a second assassination attempt in 1998. In 2000 he won a controversial presidential election that was immediately followed by accusations of vote rigging. In November 2003 Shevardnádze was forced to resign the presidency after huge demonstrations showed that he had lost much of his political support. He was succeeded by the ardently pro-Western Mikheil Saakashvili. In 2006 Shevardnádze published his memoirs, titled *Thoughts about the Past and the Future*.

ARTHUR M. HOLST

**See also**

Gorbachev, Mikhail; Soviet Union, Middle East Policy

**References**

Ekedahl, Carolyn McGiffert, and Melvin A. Goodman. *The Wars of Eduard Shevardnadze*. University Park: Pennsylvania State University Press, 1997.

Shevardnadze, Eduard. *The Future Belongs to Freedom*. New York: Free Press, 1991.

# Shia Islam

The smaller of the two predominant branches of Islam, the larger being Sunni Islam. The name "Shia" derives from the Arabic term "Shiat Ali" (Party of Ali), whereas the name "Sunni" derives from the term "Ahl al-Sunnah wa al-Jama'ah" (People of the Prophet's Practice and Unified Community). Adherents to Shia Islam account for 12–15 percent of all Muslims worldwide. The Sunni sects or schools of Islam account for approximately 85 percent.

Shia Islam grew out of political struggles against the Umayyad caliphs. As a result of its political and theological evolution, it came to incorporate the descendents of several different trends: activists, moderates, and extremists. In addition, Shiite leadership is divided into different positions and differs in the degree of approved activism by clerics. The Ithna Ashariyya, called Twelvers by Westerners and Jafariyya by adherents for their school of Islamic law, were historically moderates; the Ismailiyya (Seveners) were labeled extremists, or *ghulat,* by their enemies; and the Zaydiyya (Fivers) were activists (in their support of Zayd in his jihad against the caliph). The three groups are named according to the prominent figures in the chain of religious leaders (*a'imah,* or imams) whom each recognizes as constituting the proper line of religious authority passed down to them from the Prophet Muhammad.

Shiism is the dominant branch of Islam in Iran (90 percent of the population), Iraq, Lebanon, Bahrain, and Azerbaijan. Shiism also has adherents in Syria, Yemen, East Africa, India, Pakistan, Afghanistan, Tajikistan, Turkey, Qatar, Kuwait, the United Arab Emirates, the Eastern Province of Saudi Arabia, and many areas outside the Middle East, such as the United States, Canada, South Asia, the United Kingdom, Europe, Australia, and East Africa. In the United States, Dearborn, Michigan, has a very large Shiite population.

The Shiat Ali (Party of Ali) were those who preferred the succession of Ali ibn Abu Talib as *khalifa* (caliph) when the Prophet Muhammad died. Ali ibn Abu Talib was the son-in-law of Muhammad by marriage to Muhammad's only surviving daughter, Fatima. Some suggest that in the mixture of southern and northern Arab Muslim tribes, it was the southerners, Aws and Khazraj of Medina, who most strongly supported hereditary rights in leadership rather than a leader chosen on a different basis.

Ali accepted Abu Bakr as caliph, or political leader of the Muslims, even though Ali's supporters preferred Ali, and he also accepted the caliph Umar. The caliphate was then offered to him, but he was told he would have to follow the precedents of Abu Bakr and Umar, and Ali refused to do this. His supporters agitated again when Uthman became the third caliph. Uthman was so disliked for nepotism and the enrichment of his Umayyad relatives that a revolt occurred in which he was killed. Ali's followers recognized him as the fourth caliph in 656 CE. However, the Umayyads claimed the caliphate for Muawiya, and this led to two civil wars in Islam and Ali's assassination in 661. Following Ali's death, his son Hasan was forced to abdicate, and his other son Husayn fought the Umayyads and was killed at Karbala. These events are commemorated in Shiism and given a deeply symbolic meaning.

While all Muslims revere the Prophet and his family (known as Ahl al-Bayt, or People of the House), Sunni Muslims recognize a large number of the Prophet's early companions at Medina as transmitters of hadith, the short texts relating Muhammad's words, actions, or preferences. In contrast, the Shia do not recognize the authority of certain Companions and teach the traditions (hadith) transmitted by others or the Ahl al-Bayt from the Prophet, his daughter Fatima, and Ali on to Ali's sons Hasan and Husayn and also the succession of imams who followed them. More importantly, because Ali had rejected the injunction to follow the precedents of the first two caliphs rather than the *sunnah* (traditions or practices) of the Prophet, the foundational logic for Shiism to develop its own *fiqh,* or legal school, was set.

In the Umayyad period, the followers of Ali began to develop their own attitudes and worldview in contrast to other Muslims. The Battle of Karbala in October 680 between the supporters and relatives of Muhammad's grandson Husayn ibn Ali and forces of Yazid I, the Umayyad caliph, reinforced the Shia belief in *walaya,* or devotion to the Prophet's family, and also provided a reason for rebellion. A movement called the *tawabbun* (penitents) rose up to fight the Umayyads a year after the Battle of Karbala because they had not defended Husayn then, and 3,000 of them were killed.

Shiites believe that Ali was the first imam, thereby inheriting the *nass,* or spiritual legitimacy, of the Prophet. The imam is the

Shiite Muslim women walk past the shrine of Imam Ali in Najaf, Iraq, in April 2003. The site honors Abu ibn Abi Talib, the cousin and son-in-law of the Prophet Muhammad, considered by Shiites to be the rightful successor of Muhammad. (AFP/Getty Images)

sole legitimate religious successor of the Prophet, and each imam designates his own successor. In Shia Islam, each imam is held to have special knowledge of the inner truth of the Qur'an, Muhammad's *sunnah,* and Islam. This institution is called the imamate in English (*a'imah*). The *a'imah,* or chain of imams, are believed to be infallible, sinless, and personally guided by Allah (God) and are also believed to possess the divine authority over Islam and humanity granted to Ali by the Prophet Muhammad.

Shiites and Sunnis have the same beliefs about Allah, who has omnipotence over all beings and is also perceived as Merciful and Beneficent, closer to man than his own jugular vein and one who cares deeply about his creation. In both branches of Islam there is also a dynamic between faith and the acceptance of divine will along with the responsibility of the human believer. Indeed, apart from the differences in the Shia view of leadership, the two sects are very similar in many aspects. They diverge, however, in their legal systems.

The Shia recognize all the same religious duties as the Sunnis, which are described in the study of Islam in the West as the Five Pillars with two additional duties. However, the Ismailiyya sect and its subsects also stress the inner truths, or esoteric knowledge of Islamic principles. Therefore, to their spiritual elite simply reading the Qur'an is inadequate; one must understand its hidden meaning.

The Shia stress the unicity or oneness (*tawhid*) of Allah, a strict monotheism, and the avoidance of any trace of polytheism. They support social justice (*'adalah*), which means equity within society, and aid to the oppressed and the needy. As with Sunni Muslims, the Shia adhere to the principle of the *hisba,* or commanding the good and forbidding the reprehensible. This refers to all that is licit or recommended in Islamic law as opposed to sins that are forbidden. Entrance into Paradise is based on doing more good than evil or upon martyrdom. All Muslims, Shia as well as Sunni, respect the prophets, including Abraham, Moses, Jesus, and Muhammad, whom they believe revealed to humans the true religion of Allah.

The concept of the *a'imah* (imamate)—that specific leaders are appointed by Allah and then designated by other imams (*nass*)—grew in strength thanks to the sixth imam, Jafar al-Sadiq. His followers developed the Twelver legal and theological tradition. The last of these 12 imams, Muhammad al-Mahdi, did not make himself known at the death of the 11th imam, al-Hasan al-Askari; however, texts revealed his presence. Mahdi is believed to be hiding on Earth, neither alive nor dead but in a state of occultation, and will return at the Day of Judgment and the Resurrection (*qiyamah*) when Allah will decide the fate of all humanity, Muslim and non-Muslim alike.

The Twelvers believe that Mahdi, born in 689, was the son of Hasan. The Shia believe that Mahdi was in hiding from the caliph and that between the years 874 and 941 he communicated by letters with his people. During this period, called the Lesser Occultation, the community recognized four regents for Mahdi. In his last letter, he wrote that he would no longer communicate with humanity. Thus, the period from 941 to the present is known as the Greater Occultation.

In Islam, every human is held accountable for his or her deeds. The deeds of each individual are judged by Allah and weighed on a scale. If the good outweighs the evil, then the individual gains entrance into Paradise. If the evil outweighs the good, the individual spends eternity in Hell. The Shia, like the Sunni, also believe that the prophets, imams, and martyrs can intercede with Allah for a soul on the Day of Judgment and may seek this intercession (*shafa'a*) if possible through prayer, religious rituals, or appeals to the Fourteen Infallibles: the Prophet Muhammad, his daughter Fatima, the Twelve Imams, or martyrs. They also seek redemption through the ritual of repentance performed on the Day of Ashura, the commemoration of Imam Husayn's death.

Shiism's Twelvers, the largest Shia group, proclaim the necessity of obligatory religious duties or acts of outward worship. The first is the *shahada,* or testimony that there is no God but God and that Muhammad is his prophet and Ali his imam. The next is prayer (*salat*), recited five or more times a day. The third is fasting (*sawm*) during the daylight hours for all of the month of Ramadan, the ninth month of the Islamic calendar. The fourth religious practice is the pilgrimage (*hajj*), a journey to the holy city of Mecca that should be made at least once during a person's life if he or she is physically and financially able to undertake it. The fifth religious practice is the paying of *zakat*, a voluntary tax that is used to support the poor, to spread Islam, or sometimes for other purposes such as aid to travelers and the funding of jihad. The assessment of *zakat* should be 2.5 percent of one's income and assets in any given year. (All Muslims also give gifts of money during and at the end of Ramadan and the Id al-Adha, but these are in addition to *zakat*.) Another form of tithing, the *khums,* is a 20 percent tax on all annual profits from any source levied on all adult males and is used to support the mosque and the clerics. Jihad is also a commanded duty in Shiism and refers to the struggle of the faithful to please Allah as well as to defend Islam by waging war against those who attack Muslims. The idea of the *walaya* is important in Shiism (but also in Sufi Islam), as is the *tabarra*. These mean a special reverence for all members, past and descended, of the Ahl al-Bayt; the guardianship of the imamate; and the disassociation from all enemies of the Ahl al-Bayt.

In addition to the Shia groups mentioned above, there are others. The Shaykhiyya of Basra and Bahrain are a subsect of the Twelver Shia, influenced by Akhbari thought. The Druze (who call themselves *muwahiddun,* or unitarians) are an offshoot of the Ismailiyya sect, and the Alawites found in Syria and Turkey are a distinct subsect of Shiism. Sunni Muslims and some Shia, however, consider the Alawi sect extreme because of some of its syncretic practices. Nonetheless, it was declared a licit school of Islam in a fatwa issued by Imam Musa al-Sadr in order to legitimate the rule of President Hafiz al-Asad, an Alawi, in Syria. Although all branches of Islam believe in a divine savior, the Mahdi (the Guided One) who will come at the Day of Judgment, the Twelver branch of Shiism holds that the Twelfth Imam, or Hidden Imam since he is in occultation, is the Mahdi and call him the Imam Mahdi.

Mahmoud Ahmadinejad, president of Iran, and his cabinet have pledged to work to make the conditions right for the return of the Imam Mahdi, a return that Shia Muslims believe will lead Islam to world domination. In Iran, many believe that the Imam Mahdi will reappear from a well at the mosque in Jamkaran just outside of the holy city of Qum, Iran. The site is frequently visited by Shiite pilgrims who drop messages into the well hoping that the Hidden Imam will hear them and grant their requests. Along with the Imam Mahdi's return at the Day of Judgment, there are various beliefs about other millenarian events and wars that will occur before this period.

Since the disappearance of the Twelfth Imam, the Shia *ulama* (clerics) have served as his deputies, interpreting the law and leading the Shiite faithful under the authority of the Hidden Imam. In Twelver Shiism it is believed that four persons acted as the deputies or special vice-regents (*wakala al-khassa*) of the Hidden Imam during the Lesser Occultation. These persons were called the *bab* (gate) or *na'ib* (deputy) for the imam. From 941 there have been no overt claims of a *bab* except for Sayyid Ali Muhammad (known as "The Bab"), who established Babism in the 19th century, and the Shaykhi Shia, who put forth the idea of the perfect Shia who lives in each age. Generally in this period, the idea is that there is a *wakala al-'amma*, or a general vice-regency, that has been delegated to the Shia clerics. When Iran's Ayatollah Ruhollah Khomeini and his government established the system of rule of the cleric (*vilayat-e faqih*) in Iran, there were disputes about whether he was to be considered the *na'ib* al-Imam, or deputy of the Hidden Imam. The idea of rule of the cleric, developed from the increasingly activist opinions of one branch of Shiism—the Usulis (*usuliyya*)—opposed the Akhbaris, a different intellectual tradition. This notion that clerics should rule, therefore becoming a part of the political system, is still controversial even among many Usulis.

Khomeini's official title became "Supreme Faqih" (Jurist), and he governed the Council of Guardians as its supreme religio-political authority. There had been several clerics more senior to Khomeini who were, however, marginalized or even assassinated after the Islamic Revolution. Khomeini's successor, Ali Husayni Khamenei, was not the most senior of the clerics who might potentially have followed Khomeini in power. Khamenei was granted the title of ayatollah to ensure his authority. Some described him as a political appointee.

Iranian president Mahmoud Ahmadinejad speaks during a gathering in Kalat, Iran, on April, 11, 2006. A picture of Iran's late leader Ayatollah Ruhollah Khomeini is at left. (AP/Wide World Photos)

Ismaili Shiites, also known as Ismailiyya, or the Seveners, are followers of the living Agha Khan and constitute the second-largest branch of Shia Islam. Ismailis believe that the imamate is a position that continues unbroken since the caliphate of Ali, although the living imams since the Seventh Imam serve as regents awaiting the return of the Hidden Imam. Ismailis acknowledge only six of the Twelve Imams and assert that the real Seventh Imam was Ismail Ibn Jafar. Other Muslims assert that Ismail's son Muhammad was the Seventh Imam and that he is presently occulted awaiting the end of time to reveal himself as the last imam. The Ismaili movement spread through missionary activity as a secret organization beginning in the later ninth century. It split in a factional dispute about leadership in 899. Ismaili Shia are found primarily in South Asia, Syria, Saudi Arabia, Yemen, China, Tajikistan, Afghanistan, and East Africa but have also, in recent years, immigrated to Europe and North America.

Ismailis mandate the same religious practices as the Twelvers, but their emphasis is on esoteric teachings and thus on an inner or deeper interpretation of each that can make them distinct. As with the Twelvers, the Ismailis evince love and devotion (*walayah*) for Allah, the prophets, the Ahl al-Bayt, the imam, and the Ismaili *da'i* (preacher) and also believe in personal purity and cleanliness (*taharah*). As with all other Muslims, they must also practice prayer and *zakat*, or almsgiving. In addition, they fast during Ramadan, carry out the *hajj*, and believe in jihad.

Zaydis, also known as Zaydiyya or the Fivers, are theologically and in the view of Islamic law closer to a Sunni school of the law. There are Zaydi communities in India, Pakistan, and Yemen.

Zaydis derive their name from Zayd ibn Ali ibn Abi Talib, the son of Husayn ibn Ali ibn Abi Talib (626–ca. 680), the grandson of the Prophet Muhammad. Most Zaydis regard Husayn as the third rightful imam. After Ali, Hasan, and Husayn, the followers of Zayd had asserted that the succession of the imamate would be determined after engaging in armed rebellion against the Umayyad caliphs. Zayd's followers did not want a Hidden Imam, but a living one who would rule instead of the Umayyads, and so the Zaydiyya are considered activists. Although Zayd's rebellion against the corrupt Umayyad caliph Hisham ibn Abd al-Malik (691–743) in 740 was unsuccessful, his followers thereafter recognized Zayd as the fourth Zaydi imam.

Zaydism does not support the infallibility of the imams and asserts that no imam after Husayn received any divine guidance. Zaydis reject the Hidden Imam and the idea that the imamate must be passed from father to son, although they do believe that the living imam must be a descendant of Ali, and some of their own leaders passed on their leadership to their sons. Zaydi Islamic law (*fiqh*) is most like the Sunni Hanafi school.

While there was never a concept of Sunni Islam as a sect as it is described today, the non-Alid Muslims (those who did not insist on Ali gaining political leadership) accepted the institution of the caliphate even though the caliph was not a spiritual descendant of the Prophet. Still, the caliph received an oath of allegiance from his people and had to be pious and promote and protect Islam. Alids (supporters of Ali), later called the Shia, accepted their temporal rulers but did not regard them as being spiritually legitimate in the manner of the imams. For purposes of survival, they could deny their Shia beliefs if need be in the practice known as *taqqiya* (dissimulation). There are major legal and philosophical differences in Shia Islam, such as the theme of the oppressed Muslims who act out their penitence for their inability to defend Husayn at Karbala, the imamate, the concept of the Occultation and the Return, and the concept of *marjaiyya,* the idea that a believer should follow a particular cleric as a guide. Minor differences pertain to aspects of daily prayer and the commencement of holidays, which often begin on one day in Iran and, typically, a day earlier in Saudi Arabia and other Sunni centers.

Shiite Islamic education is centered in Najaf and Karbala in Iraq and in Qum and Mashhad in Iran, with other religious authorities in Tehran and additional centers of learning elsewhere. Shia clerics from Lebanon typically studied in Iraq or in Iran. One of the most influential Shia theorists in Iran following the Islamic Revolution was probably Abd al-Karim Sorush, who is famous for his idea of the expansion and contraction of Islamic law (*qabz va baste shari'at*). The most senior cleric in Iraq today is the Shia Grand Ayatollah Sistani. The clerical establishment in Iraq is referred to as the *hawzah,* and its duty is to train the future clerics of Shiism, provide judgments, and officiate over pilgrimages and those who wish to be buried at the holy sites. Other important cities of Shia learning are Qum, Mashhad, and Tehran, all in Iran.

In Iran the great leaders of Tehran, Ayatollah Sayyid Muhammad Tabatabai (1841–1920) and Sayyid Abd Allah Bahbahani (d. 1871), were part of the revolutionary organization of the constitutional movement early in the 20th century, but other clerics opposed that movement. Shiite authorities also resisted British colonialism and encroachments on their power by Reza Shah Pahlavi in Iran.

The last great single *marja' al-mutlaq* (the absolute source of emulation), Ayatollah Burujerdi, died in 1961. Debate then began between different reformist leaders and the degree of activism in which clerics should engage. In the 1960s a more radical, or activist, Shiism began to develop. Informal gatherings and new publications began to spread new radical Shiite thought. Ayatollah Khomeini's resistance to Mohammad Reza Shah Pahlavi was significant, but so too was the work of Dr. Ali Shariati (1933–1977).

Educated in Mashhad and Paris, Shariati challenged the quietism of many religious scholars, writing essays and giving lectures to galvanize a new activism in Shiism that combined with existentialism and Third Worldist views. Another major influence on radical Shiism in this period was Murtaza Mutahari (1920–1979).

Sunnis and Shiites have different approaches to jurisprudence, or the making of Islamic law, and therefore also in the issuance of fatawa to broader religious questions of Muslims. The different Sunni schools of law use as sources (*usul al-fiqh*) the Qur'an, the hadith, analogy (*qiyas*), and *ijma,* or the consensus of the community at Medina or of the jurists. In earlier periods, these legal schools also used *ray* (opinion of the jurist) or *ijtihad,* a particular technique of intellectual problem solving. In the 10th century, the Sunni jurists decided to stop using *ijtihad* so as to avoid the introduction of too many innovations into Sharia (Islamic law). However, the Shia legal school of the Twelvers retained this principle. Consequently, Shia cleric-jurists who train in this technique and qualify receive the title of *mujtahid,* or one who can enact *ijtihad.*

*Ijtihad* has come to mean more than a principle of Islamic jurisprudence. As contemporary activist Shiism was developing, Ali Shariati began to apply *ijtihad* to Muslim life, including a vibrant definition of monotheism and the application of Muslim principles.

There are various ranks of clerics in Shia Islam in addition to the *mujtahid,* such as the elevated designations of ayatollah and grand ayatollah that other clerics should agree on. In addition, the Shia may follow his or her own preferred *marja' al-taqlid* (source of emulation). Above all of these clerics, there may be one agreed-upon *marja' al-mutlaq,* or source of emulation of the age.

These are not the only differences between Sunni and Shia Islam. Shia constituted minorities in such countries as Lebanon and Saudi Arabia, where they were an underclass socially and economically. In the modern period, leaders such as Ali Shariati and Imam Musa Sadr in Lebanon supported populism and addressed the discrimination against and suffering of the Shiite masses.

While at times some Sunni groups have expressed both discrimination and hatred toward Shia Muslims, there have also been efforts at ecumenism and more cooperation between the sects. Al-Azhar University in Egypt teaches about the Jafariyya (Twelver) *madhhab,* or legal school of Islam, in spite of the government of Egypt having outlawed Shiism. It should also be noted that Shia and Sunni Muslims had coexisted peacefully and have frequently intermarried in Iraq. Shia Muslims were often members of the Communist Party or the Baath Party, and just like the Iranian clerics responding to the inroads made by secular ideologies in that country, the clerics in Iraq began an Islamic movement in part to encourage youths to reengage with Islamic education. When this movement developed from a clerical organization into an activist one, Iraqi president Saddam Hussein ruthlessly suppressed it. Sadly, the end of Hussein's rule brought Shia-Sunni sectarian conflict to Iraq, fueled in part by Sunni Islamists and nationalists who viewed the new Shia-dominated majority as conspirators with the Americans and who call the Shia apostates or renegades.

RICHARD EDWARDS AND SHERIFA ZUHUR

**See also**

Iraq, History of, Pre-1990; Iraq, History of, 1990–Present; Iraqi Insurgency; Islamic Dawa Party; Jihad; Khomeini, Ruhollah; Martyrdom; Qur'an; Sunni Islam; Syria

**References**

Ajami, Fouad. *The Vanished Imam: Musa al-Sadr and the Shia of Lebanon.* Ithaca, NY: Cornell University Press, 1986.

Daftari, Farhad. *The Isma'ilis: Their History and Doctrines.* Cambridge: Cambridge University Press, 1990.

Fuller, Graham E., and Rend Rahim Francke. *The Arab Shi'a: The Forgotten Muslims.* Hampshire, UK: Palgrave Macmillan, 2001.

Gregorian, Vartan. *Islam: A Mosaic, Not a Monolith.* Baltimore: Brookings Institute Press, 2004.

Halm, Heinz. *Shi'a Islam: From Religion to Revolution.* Princeton, NJ: Markus Wiener, 1997.

Momen, Moojan. *An Introduction to Shi'i Islam: The History and Doctrines of Twelver Shi'ism.* New Haven, CT: Yale University Press, 1987.

Nasr, Seyyed Hossein. *Islam: Religion, History, and Civilization.* New York: HarperCollins, 2003.

Sobhani, Ayatollah Jafar, and Reza Shah Kazemi. *Doctrines of Shi'i Islam: A Compendium of Imami Beliefs and Practices.* London: I. B. Tauris, 2001.

# Shibh, Ramzi Muhammad Abdallah ibn al-
## Birth Date: May 1, 1972

One of the chief planners of the September 11, 2001, terror attacks against the United States and an active member of the Hamburg Cell. Ramzi Muhammad Abdallah ibn al-Shibh was born on May 1, 1972, in Ghayl Ba Wazir (al-Ghayl) in the province of Hadramawt, Yemen. His father was a merchant. The family moved to Sanaa, the capital of Yemen, when ibn al-Shibh (known in colloquial Arabic and FBI sources as bin al-Shibh) was a small boy.

Bin al-Shibh was more religious than some of his family members. After finishing his schooling, he began working as a messenger boy at the International Bank of Yemen. For a time he studied at a business school before deciding to leave Yemen. In 1995, he applied for a U.S. visa, but his application was turned down.

Determined to leave Yemen, bin al-Shibh then traveled to Germany, where he claimed to be a Sudanese citizen seeking political asylum under the name Ramzi Omar. German authorities were suspicious of his claim, and it was initially turned down. Germany then received more than 100,000 political asylum seekers annually. Bin al-Shibh spent two years at the so-called Container Camp, awaiting his appeal.

During the period pending the appeal of his asylum claim, bin al-Shibh attended the al-Quds mosque in Hamburg. There he met Mohammed Atta and other Islamist militants. After his appeal was denied by the German government, bin al-Shibh returned to Yemen in 1997. Shortly thereafter, he returned to Germany, this time using his true name. Bin al-Shibh subsequently enrolled in a school in Hamburg, although academic problems led to his expulsion in September 1998.

Bin al-Shibh was alleged to have been an active member of the so-called Hamburg Cell. There he was known by associates as Omar. He roomed with Atta and Marwan Yufif Muhammed Rashid Lekrab al-Shehhi beginning in 1998. In summer 1998, bin al-Shibh traveled to Afghanistan for special training at one of Al Qaeda's training camps. He was obviously valued because Al Qaeda leaders selected him for a special mission. A fellow recruit later testified that bin al-Shibh had extensive contact with Al Qaeda leader Osama bin Laden while in Afghanistan. Officials believe that along with Atta, Ziyad al-Jarrah, and Shehhi, he was recruited by bin Laden for a special martyrdom mission. Muhammad Atef, the military commander of Al Qaeda, gave them a briefing on the outlines of the September 11 plot. Returning to Germany, bin al-Shibh joined with Atta and Shehhi in working at a warehouse packing computers for shipping.

Bin al-Shibh is believed to have recruited Zacarias Moussaoui (Zakarias Mussawi) into Al Qaeda and to have given him funds for pilot training in the United States. Although Moussaoui was not a part of the Hamburg Cell and the September 11 plot, he was being considered for a future martyrdom mission.

Bin al-Shibh gathered cassette tapes of Muslim jihadist activities in Chechnya, Bosnia, and Kosovo and played them to various Muslim audiences in Hamburg. Bin al-Shibh was the only member of the Hamburg Cell to attend the January 2000 Kuala Lumpur meeting where Al Qaeda midlevel operatives discussed future operations.

Bin al-Shibh's inability to obtain a U.S. visa prevented him from joining Mohammed Atta's suicide team on September 11. He is called the 20th hijacker, and his slot went unfilled. Instead, bin al-Shibh provided logistical support and money from Germany and kept in close contact with Atta, serving as his banker. He also protected the men of the Hamburg Cell by keeping them registered

Ramzi ibn al-Shibh, shown here in an undated photograph, is believed to be one of the chief planners of the September 11, 2001, terrorist attacks against the United States. Captured in Pakistan a year later, he is currently in U.S. custody. (AP/Wide World Photos)

as students. When bin al-Shibh finally learned in late August 2001 of the date of the planned Al Qaeda attack on the World Trade Center complex, the Pentagon, and the U.S. Capitol or White House in late August 2001, he began to shut down operations in Germany, as he was well aware that all members and anyone affiliated with the Hamburg Cell would be subject to arrest. In early September, he fled to Pakistan, where he apparently believed he would be safe from American reprisal.

In Karachi, bin al-Shibh gave a key interview to an Al Jazeera journalist who also interviewed Khalid Sheikh Mohammed. This interview, and not subsequent interrogation or torture sessions, provided information concerning Al Qaeda's activities and planning. Although the reporter was blindfolded, he passed on information about his location to his supervisor, who in turn gave it to Qatari authorities, who then provided it to the U.S. Central Intelligence Agency (CIA). This led to bin al-Shibh's capture in the same apartment complex in Karachi, Pakistan, on September 11, 2002, following a gunfight with Pakistani security forces.

On September 16, 2002, the Pakistani government turned bin al-Shibh over to U.S. security officials, who moved him out of Pakistan to a secret interrogation site. Bin al-Shibh has expressed no regrets about his involvement with Al Qaeda; had he not been captured, he would still be an active participant. Under interrogation, bin al-Shibh revealed some information about organizational aspects of Al Qaeda, verifying the participation of particular individuals, such as Sayf al-Adl. In August 2006, bin al-Shibh was transferred to the Guantánamo Bay Detainment Camp with 13 other high-profile terrorist suspects.

Bin al-Shibh and four other Guantánamo detainees were charged in military commissions in the spring of 2008. All said they refused U.S.-appointed attorneys and would boycott their proceedings, but only bin al-Shibh has held out, refusing to meet an attorney and saying he wanted to plead guilty. The court pressured his codefendants to persuade him to appear. It has been suggested that bin al-Shibh is psychotic, and his attorneys have charged that his mental condition is the result of torture since his incarceration.

STEPHEN A. ATKINS

**See also**

Al Qaeda; Atta, Muhammad; Bin Laden, Osama; Guantánamo Bay Detainment Camp; Hamburg Cell; Jarrah, Ziyad al-; September 11 Attacks; Shehhi, Marwan al-

**References**

Fouda, Yosri, and Nick Fielding. *Masterminds of Terror: The Truth behind the Most Devastating Terrorist Attack the World Has Ever Seen.* New York: Arcade, 2003.

Griffin, David Ray. *Dubunking 9/11 Debunking: An Answer to Popular Mechanics and Other Defenders of the Official Conspiracy Theory.* Northampton, MA: Olive Branch, 2007.

McDermott, Terry. *Perfect Soldiers: The 9/11 Hijackers: Who They Were, Why They Did It.* New York: HarperCollins, 2005.

Posner, Gerald. *Why America Slept: The Failure to Prevent 9/11.* New York: Ballantine Books, 2003.

# Shinseki, Eric Ken
## Birth Date: November 28, 1942

U.S. Army general and chief of staff of the army (1999–2003). Born in Lihue on the island of Kauai, Hawaii, on November 28, 1942, Eric Shinseki graduated from the United States Military Academy, West Point, in 1965 and was commissioned a second lieutenant. His military education included the Armor Officer Advanced Course from 1968 to 1969, the United States Army Command and General Staff College in 1979, and the National War College in 1986. Shinseki also earned a master's degree in English literature from Duke University in 1976.

Shinseki served two combat tours in Vietnam with the 9th and 25th Infantry divisions. He was wounded during each of those tours, the second time by a land mine that took off most of his right foot. After recovering, he had to fight the military personnel system to stay in the army with his handicap.

Shinseki's subsequent command and staff assignments included more than 10 years in Europe, with assignments in command and staff at Schweinfurt, Kitzingen, Würzburg, and Stuttgart in the Federal Republic of Germany. Promoted to brigadier general (July 1991), Shinseki served in Verona, Italy, as deputy chief of staff of Allied Land Forces Southern Europe, a component

U.S. Army general Eric Shinseki was chief of staff of the U.S. Army during 1999–2003. He became secretary of veterans affairs in 2009. Shinseki sharply disagreed with Secretary of Defense Donald Rumsfeld on the number of troops that would be required in an invasion of Iraq. (U.S. Department of Defense)

of Allied Command Europe, and later as the assistant division commander for maneuver of the 3rd Infantry Division in Würzberg. Promoted to major general in June 1994, he commanded the 1st Cavalry Division at Fort Hood, Texas. Promoted to lieutenant general (August 1996), Shinseki became U.S. Army deputy chief of staff for operations and plans. Promoted to full general in August 1997, he commanded United States Army Europe and Seventh Army. In that capacity, he was directly responsible for the peacekeeping and stabilization operations, led by the North Atlantic Treaty Organization (NATO), in Croatia and Bosnia.

From June 22, 1999, to June 11, 2003, General Shinseki was the U.S. Army's chief of staff. He was both the first four-star Asian American general in U.S. history and the first Asian American to head one of the armed services. As chief of staff he initiated the controversial Army Transformation Campaign, by which the army was to be transformed into a lighter, more mobile force to address contemporary emerging strategic challenges. These included antiterror operations such as the invasion of Afghanistan (Operation ENDURING FREEDOM) in 2001 and the more conventional campaign against Iraq (Operation IRAQI FREEDOM) in 2003. Shinseki launched his Army Transformation Campaign well before Donald Rumsfeld became secretary of defense and announced his own strategic vision of smaller and more flexible forces. Nonetheless, Shinseki found himself constantly at loggerheads with the brusque and imperious defense secretary. In 2001 Shinseki resisted Rumsfeld's call for additional reductions in army strength. Some insiders suggest that Shinseki's opposition to Rumsfeld's overzealous force reductions bordered on insubordination. Others considered Shinseki to be one of the few senior military leaders willing to challenge Rumsfeld's far-fetched and unfounded notions about fighting modern wars, which almost all proved failures.

In February 2003, just one month prior to the launching of Operation IRAQI FREEDOM, Shinseki testified before the Senate Armed Service Committee that "something on the order of several hundred thousand soldiers" would be needed for the pacification and occupation of Iraq. Shinseki's estimate was based on his own experience with such operations in the Balkans, but his troop estimate for Iraq was immediately dismissed by Rumsfeld and others because it directly contradicted their theories about high-technology military operations on the cheap. If Shinseki's recommendations had been followed, there can be no doubt that the Iraq War would have played out much differently.

In what was considered by many to be an unbelieveably shabby and small-minded bureaucratic maneuver, Rumsfeld undercut Shinseki's authority by selecting his successor more than a year before Shinseki was due to step down as chief of staff. Shinseki retired from active duty in August 2003. Despite his disagreements with Rumsfeld and the Pentagon's planning for Iraq, Shinseki has kept silent on the issue, choosing not to engage in any public discussions or castigations concerning the defense secretary or the ongoing war in Iraq. Nevertheless, the apparent success of the Bush administration's troop surge—accompanied by a revitalized counterinsurgency strategy—seems to have vindicated Shinseki's view that more troops were required in Iraq. When Barack Obama became president in 2009, he selected Shinseki as his administration's secretary of veterans affairs. Shinseki's appointment was greeted enthusiastically by both members of the military and veterans' groups.

MICHAEL DOIDGE

**See also**

ENDURING FREEDOM, Operation; IRAQI FREEDOM, Operation; Iraqi Insurgency; Rumsfeld, Donald Henry; Surge, U.S. Troop Deployment, Iraq War

**References**

Bell, William. *Commanding Generals and Chiefs of Staff, 1775–2005: Portraits and Biographical Sketches of the United States Army's Senior Officer.* Washington, DC: Center of Military History, 2005.

Fontenot, Gregory, et al. *On Point: The United States Army in Iraqi Freedom.* Annapolis, MD: Naval Institute Press, 2005.

---

# Shughart, Randall David
**Birth Date: August 13, 1958**
**Death Date: October 3, 1993**

U.S. Army soldier who received the Medal of Honor (posthumously) after giving his life to defend fellow U.S. soldiers during the Battle of Mogadishu in Somalia on October 3, 1993. His story was told in the popular book and movie *Black Hawk Down*. Randall (Randy) David Shughart was born on August 13, 1958, in Lincoln, Nebraska. While still in high school he enlisted in the U.S. Army and then entered active duty upon graduation in 1976.

Shughart subsequently graduated from Ranger School and was assigned to the 2nd Ranger Battalion, 75th Infantry (Airborne) at Fort Lewis, Washington. After briefly leaving the army, Shughart reenlisted and qualified for Special Forces. He was then assigned to the premier army Special Forces unit, the 1st Special Forces Operational Detachment–Delta, better known as Delta Force.

Shughart served in Operation JUST CAUSE, the invasion of Panama, in 1989. In the summer of 1993 Sergeant First Class Shughart was ordered to Somalia with other Delta Force members to participate in Operation RESTORE HOPE, designed to help bring stability to the troubled country. As part of Task Force Ranger, Shughart was assigned to a three-man sniper team. His teammates were Sergeant First Class Brad Hallings and Master Sergeant Gary Gordon, the team leader. On October 3, 1993, they were part of Operation GOTHIC SERPENT, an assault mission designed to capture key advisers to Somali warlord Mohammed Farrah Aidid (Aideed) in the part of Mogadishu still controlled by Aidid.

During the operation, one of the Sikorsky UH-60 Black Hawk helicopters transporting the assault teams was shot down and crashed into Aidid-held territory. The Combat Search and Rescue (CSAR) team on standby was dispatched to secure the crash site and to rescue any survivors. While they were fighting their way through to the crash site, a second Black Hawk was shot down. The crew of four survived, but they were soon threatened by Aidid's militia and civilian supporters. The CSAR was still engaged in trying to reach the first crash site. Shughart's team was aboard another Black Hawk, and they were attempting to cover the second crashed helicopter. Gordon requested permission to land so his team could take position to protect the injured crew. Their field commander twice refused permission, believing that their position in the air would better allow them to target hostile Somalis. On Gordon's third request, the field commander gave in and allowed the sniper team to land.

Before landing, the minigun operator on the Black Hawk was wounded, so Hallings was assigned to man it and provide cover. Shughart and Gordon then landed alone. Debris and ground fire prevented their Black Hawk from landing at the crash site, so they found an open area some 100 yards away. The pair made their way through buildings to the crash site, taking Somali fire along the way. When they arrived at the downed helicopter, Gordon and Shughart managed to remove the crew, including Chief Warrant Officer Mike Durant and three others. Shughart and Gordon established a perimeter around the helicopter, moving from place to place to keep the attacking Somalis away. Armed only with their personal weapons, the pair managed to kill or disable numerous attackers. Finally, their ammunition ran low, and the Somali attackers were able to move closer.

Accounts vary about whether Gordon or Shughart was killed first by Somali gunfire. Shughart's citation for the Medal of Honor indicates that he was killed first, but some authorities believe that he was the last to die. Durant survived, and he testified that after one Ranger had been killed, the other gave him the extra weapon. Durant could not identify if it was Shughart or Gordon, but the weapon he had was not Shughart's distinctive M14 but rather Gordon's weapon. Other Rangers did not believe that Gordon would have given another soldier his own weapon, indicating that it was Shughart's. In any event, after Shughart and Gordon were killed, Durant was captured by the Somalis. The other three members of the crew died, making Durant the only American survivor. In all, 18 American servicemen died in Operation GOTHIC SERPENT. The failure led to a loss of public support for operations in Somalia, eventually causing the William J. Clinton administration to withdraw American troops from that country.

On May 23, 1994, Shughart and Gordon were decorated posthumously with Medals of Honor for their sacrifice in attempting to save fellow Americans. They were the only soldiers in Operation GOTHIC SERPENT to receive the medal and its first recipients since the Vietnam War. Shughart was further honored by having a U.S. Navy ship named after him. The ship, USNS *Shughart,* was the navy's first large medium-speed roll-on/roll-off ship, intended to hasten the rapid deployment of forces overseas.

TIM J. WATTS

**See also**
Delta Force; Somalia, International Intervention in

**References**
Bowden, Mark. *Black Hawk Down: A Story of Modern War.* 1st ed. New York: Atlantic Monthly Press, 1999.
DeLong, Kent, and Steven Tuckey. *Mogadishu! Heroism and Tragedy.* Westport, CT: Praeger, 1994.

---

# Shultz, George Pratt
## Birth Date: December 13, 1920

U.S. secretary of labor (1969–1970), secretary of the treasury (1972–1974), and secretary of state (1982–1989). Born in Englewood, New Jersey, on December 13, 1920, George Pratt Shultz graduated from Princeton University, majoring in economics, in 1942 and then joined the U.S. Marine Corps, serving in the Pacific theater as an artillery officer and ending World War II as a captain. After demobilization, in 1949 he obtained a doctorate in industrial economics from the Massachusetts Institute of Technology, where he subsequently taught industrial relations, moving to the University of Chicago in 1957.

Under Republican president Richard Nixon, Shultz served successively as secretary of labor (1969–1970), the first director of the Office of Management and Budget (1970–1972), and secretary of the treasury (1972–1974). He resigned in March 1974 to become

George Shultz held three cabinet-level posts under five U.S. presidents. A trained economist and specialist in labor relations, Shultz put his negotiating skills to use in service to presidents Dwight D. Eisenhower, John F. Kennedy, Lyndon B. Johnson, Richard M. Nixon, and Ronald W. Reagan. (U.S. Department of Defense)

vice president of Bechtel Corporation, an international construction company, where he remained until 1982.

In June 1982 Shultz became Republican president Ronald Reagan's second and last secretary of state, replacing the forceful but overbearing Alexander M. Haig and adopting a low-key nonconfrontational style. Even so, Shultz's cautious readiness to negotiate arms control agreements with the Soviet Union brought repeated clashes with the more hawkish secretary of defense, Caspar Weinberger, who favored major increases in weapons systems.

Shultz's tenure of office saw the emergence in 1985 of Mikhail Gorbachev as general secretary of the Communist Party of the Soviet Union. Gorbachev was a conciliatory leader who became increasingly committed to reducing his country's international military commitments and improving Soviet-American relations. Shultz, initially somewhat skeptical and inclined to discountenance the more optimistic Reagan's readiness in his 1986 Reykjavik meeting with Gorbachev to consider abolishing all nuclear weapons, nonetheless negotiated the 1987 Intermediate Nuclear Force (INF) Treaty that removed all such weapons from Europe. In 1988 the Soviets also concluded an agreement to withdraw all their forces from Afghanistan, where since 1979 they had been at war with U.S.-backed mujahideen guerrillas.

From the time Shultz took office, one of his major preoccupations was with initiatives to resolve or at least ease the entrenched disputes dividing Israel and its Arab opponents after Israel's June 1982 invasion of Lebanon. Except in Afghanistan, the warming in Soviet-American relations had relatively little impact on the nearly intractable Middle Eastern situation. Shultz drafted the September 1982 Reagan Plan envisaging partial Israeli withdrawal from occupied territory in return for Arab acceptance and respect for Israeli security interests, proposals that the Israeli government strongly rejected. Throughout his years in office, Shultz repeatedly but unsuccessfully tried to broker similar schemes. In December 1988 he prevailed upon Palestine Liberation Organization (PLO) leader Yasser Arafat to renounce the use of terrorism, a stance enabling the United States to open direct talks with the PLO, but Arafat failed to force his more radical followers to respect this stance, and within a year the U.S.-PLO talks broke down.

Shultz was a determined opponent of international terrorism and of governments such as those of Libya and Iran, which sponsored such tactics. After powerful bombs from Imad Mughniya's radical Shiite group destroyed the barracks of the U.S. Marine Corps peacekeeping force in Beirut, Lebanon, in October 1983, killing 241 American servicemen, Shultz began to press Reagan to respond forcefully to such attacks on Americans. Shultz supported the use of force as well as military and economic sanctions, not just against individual terrorists but also against states that sponsored terrorism. He applauded Reagan's readiness in 1985 to employ military personnel to capture Palestinian hijackers of the American cruise ship *Achille Lauro* and to mount bombing raids on Libya in April 1986 in retaliation for a discotheque bombing in West Germany that killed U.S. servicemen.

Shultz opposed and was therefore deliberately left in ignorance of efforts by National Security Advisor Robert McFarlane and others based in the Reagan White House to sell arms to the fundamentalist Islamic regime in Iran and surreptitiously use the proceeds to fund the activities of anticommunist Contra guerrillas in Nicaragua. The Iran-Contra Scandal, which broke in 1986, damaged but did not destroy Reagan's presidency, and his final years in office saw further incremental warming in Soviet-American relations that came to full fruition under his successor, George H. W. Bush.

Shultz retired at the end of Reagan's presidency and became a senior fellow at the conservative Hoover Institution in Palo Alto, California. In retirement Shultz has written lengthy memoirs. In January 2006 he joined other former secretaries of state and defense for a White House summit to debate the current and future course of American foreign policy.

PRISCILLA ROBERTS

**See also**

Arafat, Yasser; Bush, George Herbert Walker; Iran; Lebanon, U.S. Intervention in (1982–1984); Libya; Nixon, Richard Milhous; Palestine Liberation Organization; Reagan, Ronald Wilson; Reagan Administration, Middle East Policy; Terrorism; Weinberger, Caspar Willard

**References**

FitzGerald, Frances. *Way Out There in the Blue: Reagan, Star Wars, and the End of the Cold War.* New York: Simon and Schuster, 2000.

Laham, Nicholas. *Crossing the Rubicon: Ronald Reagan and U.S. Policy in the Middle East.* Aldershot, UK: Ashgate, 2004.

Martin, David C., and John Walcott. *Best Laid Plans: The Inside Story of Americas War against Terrorism.* New York: Harper and Row, 1988.

Matlock, Jack F., Jr. *Reagan and Gorbachev: How the Cold War Ended.* New York: Random House, 2004.

Quandt, William B. *The Peace Process: American Diplomacy and the Arab-Israeli Conflict since 1967.* Washington, DC: Brookings Institution Press, 1993.

Shultz, George P. *Turmoil and Triumph: My Years as Secretary of State.* New York: Scribner, 1993.

Woodward, Bob. *Veil: The Secret Wars of the CIA, 1981–1987.* New York: Simon and Schuster, 1987.

# Sierra Leone

*See* Senegal and Sierra Leone

# Singapore, Role in Persian Gulf and Iraq Wars

A small island nation in Southeast Asia encompassing just 272 square miles, the Republic of Singapore had a 2007 population of approximately 4.7 million people. Located some 85 miles north of the equator, Singapore is located south of the Malaysian state of Johor and north of the Riau Islands of Indonesia. One of the last remaining city-states in the world, Singapore was a British colony until 1963, when it became a part of the Federation of Malaysia.

In 1965 it became a fully independent country. Since its independence, the government of Singapore has been a strong supporter of the United Kingdom, and also of the United States. A parliamentary democracy, the tiny nation is very Westernized in terms of culture and politics, and enjoys a relatively high standard of living. National service is compulsory, and although the Singaporean Armed Forces are very small, they are among the best equipped in the region, with a heavy reliance on high-tech equipment.

With the Iraqi invasion of Kuwait in August 1990, Singapore's government was keen to participate in the multilateral force to liberate Kuwait, although it did not send any combat troops to fight in the subsequent war. As a member of the United Nations (UN) and as an ally of the United Kingdom and the United States, Singapore fully supported UN sanctions against Iraq.

In late 1990 with war in the Persian Gulf imminent, the British government made a formal request for medical support from Singapore. In response, on January 7, 1991, on orders from the Singaporean government, the Headquarters Medical Services was activated and began preparing for a medical mission to the Gulf. Using the code name Operation NIGHTINGALE, the mission consisted of 30 men led by Major Tan Chi Chiu, a physician. It deployed to the Persian Gulf on January 20, 1991.

The Singaporean medical team included 2 physicians, 2 surgeons, 1 flight surgeon, 1 anesthetist, 1 sports medicine specialist, 1 ophthalmologist, 3 general practitioners, 2 nursing officers, 12 medical orderlies, and a number of communications specialists in a signals detachment that included 1 officer, 2 noncommissioned officers (NCOs), 1 administrative officer, and 1 mechanic. They were attached to the British 205th General Hospital, and during their 54 days in the Gulf they treated some 200 casualties. In fact, the Singaporean medical team was the first to perform surgery during the existence of that hospital group. During this time, the Singaporeans helped develop and improve nursing procedures for injured personnel and gained much experience in the operating theaters. They were also able to take part in a series of in-house lectures that focused on the care of postoperative patients, treatment of victims of chemical and biological weapons, management of ocular trauma, aeromedical evacuation procedures, and the diagnosis and treatment of respiratory problems.

Singapore's medical team was based at a hospital that had been established in Terminal 4 of the King Khalid International Airport near Riyadh, the Saudi Arabian capital. On many occasions coalition forces, concerned about the possible use of nerve gas and chemical or biological attacks, worked wearing gas masks and chemical suits. The team worked in 12-hour shifts from noon until midnight. Operationally, the 205th General Hospital had a total of 80 doctors and 20 dental surgeons.

The arrival of the Singaporean medical team in Saudi Arabia coincided with former Singaporean prime minister Lee Kuan Yew's visit on January 21, 1991, to Washington, D.C., where he met with President George H. W. Bush at the White House. Lee spent the evening meeting with Bush in his private quarters along with Brent Scowcroft, the national security adviser. Lee congratulated Bush on waging the war in the Gulf using a broad coalition, but stated that he believed that victory in the war should lead to a broader Middle East peace settlement that was fair to both the Israelis and the Palestinians. On their return to Singapore on March 7, 1991, the members of the Singaporean medical mission were awarded Singapore Armed Forces Overseas Service Medals (Operational Service).

Subsequently, Singapore's government was involved in monitoring UN sanctions against Iraq and contributed to the United Nations Iraq-Kuwait Observer Mission (UNIKOM). Singapore did not participate militarily in the war in Afghanistan or the 2003 invasion of Iraq but did assist with humanitarian and reconstruction assistance in both Afghanistan and Iraq. Singapore provided a landing ship tank and a C-130 transport aircraft and later deployed a Republic of Singapore Air Force KC-135 tanker aircraft in the Gulf region. Singapore was also involved in sending a police training team to the International Police Training Center in Jordan, where it helped with the training of Iraqi police officers.

On March 21, 2003, less than a day after the invasion of Iraq began, Deputy Prime Minister Tony Tan stated that Singapore was a member of the "coalition for the immediate disarmament of Iraq." In May 2003 the United States signed a free trade agreement with Singapore, and President George W. Bush hailed Singapore as "a strong partner in the war on terrorism and a member of the coalition on Iraq." In December 2003 Singapore dispatched one soldier to serve with the Multi-National Force in Iraq as a gesture of support and solidarity. In June 2005 the inaugural Asia–Middle East Dialogue was held in Singapore, and the Singaporean government pledged to continue its contributions to reconstruction in the Middle East.

JUSTIN J. CORFIELD

### See also
DESERT STORM, Operation; IRAQI FREEDOM, Operation

### References
Chong, Alan. *Goh Chok Tong: Singapore's New Premier.* Petaling Jaya, Malaysia: Pelanduk, 1991.
Huxley, Tim. *Defending the Lion City: The Armed Forces of Singapore.* North Sydney: Allen and Unwin, 2001.
Lee Kuan Yew. *From Third World to First: The Singapore Story.* New York: HarperCollins, 2000.

## Sistani, Sayyid Ali Husayn al-
### Birth Date: August 4, 1930

Islamic cleric and the most imposing traditional religious authority in Iraq, a prolific author (38 books), and a key presence in post-2003 Iraq. Grand Ayatollah Sayyid Ali Husayn al-Sistani was born in Mashhad, Iran, on August 4, 1930, into a *sayyid* family that traced its lineage to the Prophet Muhammad. The family has produced scholars since the 17th century. Sistani began his

Grand Ayatollah Sayyid al-Sistani is the leading Shiite cleric in Iraq and one of the most revered religious leaders in Shia Islam. (EPA/Corbis)

religious training in Mashhad and then moved to Qum, Iran, to study Islamic jurisprudence and theory when the supreme and only *marja'-e mutlaq* (source of emulation) of his time, Muhammad Husayn Burujerdi, taught there.

Sistani moved to Najaf, Iraq, in 1951. There he attended lectures by grand ayatollahs Abu al-Qassim Khoi and Sheikh Hussayn Hilli. Upon his return to Mashhad, Sistani received the certificate of *ijtihad* by both Khoi and Hilli. *Ijtihad* is a source of law in Jafari jurisprudence involving independent deductive and creative reasoning attainable only after sufficient study and with acknowledgment by certain clerics.

Sistani later returned to Najaf to teach, remaining a quietist during the Islamic revival and rise of activist parties, such as the Islamic Dawa Party, and surviving when other Shiite clerics were persecuted by the Baathist government. Sistani served as the prayer imam in Khoi's own mosque from 1987 to 1993 and announced his status as a *marja' al-taqlid* (religious source of emulation) after Khoi's death. This led to challenges to his authority by clerics in Qum, but Sistani shrugged them off thanks largely to responses of his *wakil* (agent) and son-in-law Javad Shahrastani. Sistani's mosque was closed in 1994, and he was placed under

house arrest. Sistani rarely traveled except for pilgrimages, but he went to London in 2004 to be treated for a heart condition.

Grand Ayatollah Sistani and his *wakils,* including Shahrastani, built and continue to maintain a vast network of adherents and centers of learning and charity. This includes a main office in Qum, which manages his mosques, scholarly libraries, charities, schools, hospitals, seminaries, the publishing of Islamic legal codes, and the distribution of preachers' and students' salaries. The main office also manages the transfers to other agents of his international network, which consists of mosques, charitable organizations, Internet sites, and seminaries, all of which operate on a multimillion-dollar budget. Sistani's activities in Najaf further the *hawzah* (scholarly establishment) there, shaping the future role of clerics, supporting pilgrims and other religious traffic to Iraq's holy cities, and managing educational, Internet, and publishing outlets.

Beyond his religious reach, since 2003 Sistani has significantly impacted the political life of Iraqis, facilitating the integration of clerical influence in the country with government agencies, for the dominant political parties are Islamist and extremely powerful within the various ministries. He has helped move the Iraqi polity more toward an Islamic democratic system than the secular, liberal democracy envisioned by American administrators.

From the beginning of the Iraqi occupation, the Americans realized that Sistani was an important contact point for them in postinvasion Iraq, but they did not fully understand his beliefs or stances vis-à-vis Islamic life and government, Iraqi sovereignty, Iran's role in the country, or Shiism. He refused to meet with them, as he did not support a lengthy occupation of Iraq and did not wish to be compromised. Communications were thus carried on through intermediaries.

With his thick Iranian accent and his image as a cleric steeped in the Iranian tradition, Sistani has garnered ire from those who oppose Islamic clerics, the Shia, and Iran in general. He could have initially more forcefully opposed the American occupation, but he instead urged Iraqi cooperation to build stability and independence. However, on June 26, 2003, Sistani's office called for an immediate general election instead of the formation by the Coalition Provisional Authority (CPA) of a transitional government. He then opposed the CPA-supported plan for caucuses that would precede an election. His followers staged protests throughout Iraq and ultimately defeated the plan. Sistani, however, was sustaining his legacy as a quietist scholar who had to preserve clerical independence from politicians and the media. At the same time, he had to oppose undue Western interference in Iraqi affairs.

Sistani nevertheless encouraged all Iraqis to participate in the 2005 elections as their Islamic duty. The result was the emergence of a democratically elected coalition of Shiite parties with an Islamist agenda. One may conclude that Sistani's interpretation of the role of the cleric (*ulama*) differs from that of the late Ayatollah Ruhollah Khomeini's in that Sistani does not argue for *vilayat al-faqih* (rule of the cleric) and opposes authoritarianism. Instead, he holds that the cleric's role in Muslim society is a holistic defense of Islam.

Sistani decried the civil and sectarian violence that has raged in Iraq since 2005, calling for restraint in revenge attacks against Sunni Iraqis, although his ability to moderate these conflicts, or inter-Shiite conflict, in central and southern Iraq is limited. He opposed the Iraqi government's 2008 attacks on the Mahdi Army, the militia controlled by cleric Muqtada al-Sadr, because of the need for Iraqi unity. Sistani has not favored the proposed mutual security agreement between Iraq and the United States, intended to become operational after the United Nations (UN) Security Council's authorization of U.S. troop presence in Iraq ends in December 2008.

SHERIFA ZUHUR

### See also
Iraq, History of, 1990–Present; Islamic Dawa Party; Khomeini, Ruhollah; Mahdi Army; Sadr, Muqtada al-; Shia Islam

### References
Khalaji, Mehdi. *The Last Marja: Sistani and the End of Traditional Religious Authority in Shiism.* Policy Focus #59. Washington, DC: Washington Institute for Middle Eastern Affairs, September 2006.

Nasr, Vali. *The Shia Revival: How Conflicts within Islam Will Shape the Future.* New York: Norton, 2006.

Rahimi, Babak. *Ayatollah Sistani and the Democratization of Post-Ba'thist Iraq.* Special Report No. 187. Washington, DC: U.S. Institute of Peace, June 2007.

Visser, Rieder. *Sistani, the United States and Politics in Iraq: From Quietism to Machiavellianism?* No. 700. Oslo: Norwegian Institute of International Affairs, 2006.

# Slovakia, Role in Afghanistan and Iraq Wars

Landlocked East European nation encompassing some 18,725 square miles of territory. With a 2008 population of approximately 5.455 million people, Slovakia is bordered by the Czech Republic and Austria to the west, Poland to the north, Ukraine to the east, and Hungary to the south. Slovakia, formerly a part of Czechoslovakia until it became an independent nation in 1993, has oriented itself squarely with the West and is a member of the European Union (EU) and the North Atlantic Treaty Organization (NATO). Slovakia has a democratic parliamentary-style political system and multiple political parties. The popularly elected president is head of state, while the prime minister, who is head of government, is appointed by the president. The largest and most influential parties include the Direction-Social Democracy, the Slovak Democratic and Christian Union, the Slovak National Party, the People's Party/Movement for a Democratic Slovakia, and the Christian Democratic Movement. Slovakia enjoyed a booming economy after 1993 and by 2007 had attained the fastest growth rate of any EU nation.

Slovakia joined other East European states in supporting the U.S.-led campaigns in Afghanistan and Iraq. After its former partner in Czechoslovakia, the Czech Republic, joined NATO in 1999, Slovakia initiated a sustained wider campaign to also become part of the alliance. As part of its effort to increase security cooperation with the United States and the West, Slovakia deployed peacekeeping forces in a range of missions in the Balkans during the late 1990s. When terrorists struck the United States on September 11, 2001, the Slovak government pledged diplomatic and security support for the U.S.-led coalition that invaded Afghanistan.

In August 2002 Slovakia deployed an engineer company of 40 soldiers to Bagram Air Field in Afghanistan. The troops helped rebuild and expand the air base for coalition operations based there. In December, Slovak forces were moved to Kabul, where they joined the NATO-led International Security Assistance Force (ISAF). Slovakia subsequently dispatched other engineering forces that undertook ordnance disposal missions and reconstruction projects. In addition to service in and around Kabul, elements of the Slovak contingent were stationed in Kandahar, where they worked to expand the air facilities. Slovak troops worked mainly with national units from the Netherlands and the Czech Republic. The peak Slovak deployment in Afghanistan was 115 soldiers in 2008, but the government announced in early 2009 plans to increase its number of troops to more than 250. The country also dispatched civilian advisers to serve as part of the NATO provincial reconstruction teams throughout Afghanistan.

Slovakia also donated a significant amount of military equipment to the Afghan National Army. The Slovak aid included small arms and ammunition, rocket launchers, and artillery. In 2005 Slovakia wrote off Afghanistan's debt of approximately $3 million. During its involvement in Afghanistan, Slovakia funded eight reconstruction and infrastructure projects totaling more than $1 million.

Slovakia also supported the effort by the George W. Bush administration to assemble a coalition to invade Iraq and oust Saddam Hussein from power. The Slovak government's main interests in backing the United States were a concern over the proliferation of weapons of mass destruction (WMDs), support for the Global War on Terror, and the country's continuing effort to join NATO (Slovakia was admitted to membership in the alliance in 2004). In July 2003 Slovakia sent an engineering company to Iraq as part of the U.S.-led coalition. The Slovaks were deployed as part of the Multi-National Force in the southern area of Iraq. They engaged in demining and ordnance disposal missions. Slovakia rotated seven deployments through Iraq (each lasing six months). Slovakia withdrew the bulk of its forces, which peaked at 110 personnel, from Iraq in February 2007 but continued to participate in the NATO-led training mission for Iraqi security forces. The country maintained a small contingent of six officers and soldiers as part of the NATO operation until July 2007. The government also provided training for Iraqi police officers in Slovakia and donated surplus military equipment, including small arms and ammunition to the Iraqi security forces. During the country's involvement in Iraq, four Slovakian soldiers were killed.

TOM LANSFORD

**See also**

Afghanistan, Coalition Combat Operations in, 2002–Present; IRAQI FREEDOM, Operation, Coalition Ground Forces; Multi-National Force–Iraq; North Atlantic Treaty Organization in Afghanistan; Provincial Reconstruction Teams, Afghanistan

**References**

Cockburn, Patrick. *The Occupation: War and Resistance in Iraq.* New York: Verso, 2007.
Keegan, John. *The Iraq War: The Military Offensive, from Victory in 21 Days to the Insurgent Aftermath.* New York: Vintage, 2005.

# Small Diameter Bomb

*See* Joint Direct Attack Munition and Small Diameter Bomb

# Smart Bombs

*See* Bombs, Precision-Guided

# Smith, Paul Ray

Birth Date: September 24, 1969
Death Date: April 4, 2003

U.S. Army sergeant and posthumous recipient of the Medal of Honor for service in Operation IRAQI FREEDOM, the first U.S. soldier in the Iraq War to be so recognized. Paul Ray Smith was born in El Paso, Texas, on September 24, 1969, but grew up primarily in Tampa, Florida. After graduating from Tampa Bay Technical High School in 1989, he joined the army. He completed basic training and advanced individual training at Fort Leonard Wood, Missouri, and became a combat engineer. Before his death in 2003, Smith had some 14 years of service and had risen to the rank of sergeant first class. He served in both Germany and the United States in the 82nd Engineer Battalion in Bamberg, Germany; in the 1st Engineer Battalion at Fort Riley, Kansas; in the 317th Engineer Battalion at Fort Benning, Georgia; and in the 9th Engineer Battalion in Schweinfurt, Germany. Smith served in the Persian Gulf War and in Bosnia. In 1999 he joined the 11th Engineer Battalion based at Fort Stewart, Georgia, which was deployed to Kosovo in 2001.

During the invasion of Iraq in March 2003, Smith was a member of Bravo Company, 11th Engineer Battalion, of the 3rd Infantry Division. His company was assigned to support the 2nd Battalion, 7th Infantry Regiment, which was advancing toward Saddam International Airport in Baghdad. To reach that objective, the battalion had to pass through the Karbala Gap, across the Euphrates River. The battalion encountered some resistance on its way to the airport on April 4, 2003, and fighting ensued that led to the taking of a number of Iraqi prisoners.

To hold these prisoners, Smith and his unit had to establish a makeshift holding pen. He and his men used an earthmover to make a hole in a nearby enclosed courtyard with a tower. At this point Smith discovered that 50–100 Iraqi troops had taken up position near its gate. Smith called up an M-3 Bradley fighting vehicle in order to attack the position, which was supported by three M-113 armored personnel carriers (APCs). One of the M-113s was hit, possibly by a mortar round, and all three crewmen were wounded. Smith aided in their evacuation but then discovered that there was an aid station in the area with a number of combat casualties. In order to protect the aid station, Smith elected not to withdraw but instead to stand and fight. Now under intense Iraqi cross fire, Smith took command of the M-113 and organized a counterattack, which was successful. At the end of the firefight, however, his comrades found Smith slumped over the Bradley's M-2 .50-caliber machine gun. His body armor had been pierced 13 times, but he had been killed by a shot to the neck and head. Smith is credited with having killed as many as 50 of the enemy and saving the lives of a number of his own men.

President George W. Bush presented the Medal of Honor to Smith's 11-year-old son David during a White House ceremony on April 4, 2005. Smith was the first Medal of Honor recipient of the Iraq War. Several months after the award of Smith's Medal of Honor, his German-born wife Brigit became an American citizen.

MICHAEL K. BEAUCHAMP

**See also**

Bush, George Walker

**References**

Collier, Peter. *Medal of Honor: Portraits of Valor Beyond the Call of Duty.* New York: Artisan, 2006.
Leary, Alex. "Iraq Hero Joins Hallowed Group." *St. Petersburg Times,* February 2, 2005.
Myers, Steven Lee. "Medals for His Valor, Ashes for His Wife." *New York Times,* September 23, 2003.

# Somalia

East African nation covering 246,199 square miles with a 1945 population of approximately 9.56 million people. Somalia is bordered by the Gulf of Aden to the north, the Indian Ocean to the east, Djibouti to the northwest, Ethiopia to the west, and Kenya to the southwest. On July 1, 1960, the former colony of British Somaliland and the United Nations (UN) trusteeship of Italian Somaliland merged to form Somalia. Clan loyalties divided the population and formed the basis of the political parties that continually vied for power. During 1960–1967, Aden Abdulla Osman served as president and was succeeded by Abdirashid Ali Shermarke (1967–1969).

In 1960, recognizing Somalia's potential as a counterbalance to the American presence in neighboring Ethiopia, Soviet leader Nikita Khrushchev established relations with the nation and offered economic aid and expanded the port facilities at Berbera. In October 1969 following President Shermarke's assassination, General Mohamed Siad Barre, commander in chief of the armed forces, seized power. He dismissed the elected government and proclaimed Somali socialism. Siad's attempts to improve conditions within Somalia included the adoption of an official script for the Somali language, improved education and health care facilities, and large-scale agricultural projects. He also granted the Soviets access to military facilities and received military aid sufficient to make Somalia one of the most heavily armed states in Africa. The Soviet-Somali Treaty of Friendship and Cooperation was signed in July 1974, the same year that Somalia joined the Arab League. In 1976 the Somali Revolutionary Socialist Party was founded.

Nationalism and irredentism—not communism—motivated Siad. He believed that the European scramble for Africa in the 19th century had destroyed his nation by dividing land inhabited by the Somali people among the colonial powers. Siad wanted to reunite ethnic Somalis in neighboring Ethiopia, Kenya, and Djibouti with the rest of the Somali nation but was constrained by the 1964 Cairo Resolution that pledged African states to maintain existing borders. With diplomatic backing unlikely, Siad resorted to military conquest to implement his plans whereby chances of victory would be improved by external support. Hence, he tightened relations with the Soviet Union.

Siad began his campaign in July 1977 when, supported by Soviet arms and advisers, he attempted to seize the Ogaden region of Ethiopia. However, his fears that the Soviets had developed relations with Somalia only because they could not control Ethiopia were soon realized. Although Ethiopia and Somalia had both received military aid from the Soviet Union since 1974, the onset of the Ogaden War forced the Soviet Union to choose sides; in October 1977 Moscow halted military aid to Somalia.

In November 1977 Siad broke ties with the communist bloc and turned instead to the United States, hoping that the Americans would appreciate Somalia's value as a Cold War counterbalance. However, newly elected president Jimmy Carter refused to aid Siad's regime. With no external support and with the might of the communist bloc aiding Ethiopia, the war reached an inevitable conclusion. On March 9, 1978, Siad announced the withdrawal of all Somali forces from Ethiopia.

By 1980, however, the changing international environment, particularly the 1979 Soviet invasion of Afghanistan and the 1979 Iranian Revolution, compelled Carter to steer U.S. foreign policy toward a more traditional Cold War orientation. In August 1980 an agreement was reached that granted the Americans access to military facilities in Somalia in return for military aid, thus countering the Soviet presence in Ethiopia and facilitating American military operations in the Indian Ocean. Siad's dictatorial reputation prevented a closer relationship, and in 1989 his continued human rights violations prompted the U.S. Congress to halt military assistance.

As conditions in Somalia deteriorated, the misgivings felt by the Americans were progressively shared by the Somali people. During the 1980s the economy declined steadily, and periodic droughts aggravated food shortages caused by poor agricultural policies and government price controls. Siad's persistence in awarding key positions to members of his own Marehan clan and other subclans of the Darod clan exacerbated clan rivalries and government corruption. Dissent increasingly manifested itself through violence, and the country entered a state of virtual civil war following an uprising that began in the north in May 1988, then consolidated under the leadership of the Issaq-led Somali National Movement (SNM). Siad provided the Darod clan with arms with which to oppose the SNM, but Darod loyalty to Siad was diminishing. In April 1988 he lost support of the Ogadeeni subclan when Somalia and Ethiopia signed a peace treaty in which Siad renounced all claims to the Ogaden.

Opposition from the Hawiye clan led to the formation of the United Somali Congress (USC), which concentrated on efforts to take control of Mogadishu, prompting Siad to withdraw those troops still loyal to him to defend the capital. By December 1990 much of Mogadishu had been destroyed, and thousands had been killed in the fighting. On January 27, 1991, Siad fled Mogadishu, and the USC took control of the city. With the common enemy gone, however, clan rivalries exploded once more, and civil war resumed.

In 1992 the USC split when the Haber-Gedir subclan formed the United Somali Congress/Somali National Alliance (USC/SNA), which came to be headed by General Mohammed Farrah Aidid (Aideed). Meanwhile civil warfare continued unabated, and a humanitarian catastrophe loomed. Beginning in April 1992, the UN attempted to broker a peace in Somalia and dispatched a small number of troops to distribute aid, which did little to alleviate the suffering of the Somali people. In December 1992 the United Task Force (UNITAF), led by the United States, commenced Operation RESTORE HOPE. UNITAF included some 30,000 troops, mostly American. By the spring of 1993 it had helped alleviate the worst of the living conditions in Somalia, and in March 1993 the UN took over all operations in Somalia. Further attempts to broker a peace, however, were unsuccessful. In March 1993, the UN created the United Nations Operation in Somalia II (UNOSCOM II), which sought to disarm the warring factions of their heavy weapons and to broker a lasting peace. The United States opted to keep many of its troops in Somalia operating within the framework of UNOSCOM II, which numbered about 28,000 military and support personnel.

The UN peacekeeping force soon encountered resistance from Aidid's USC/SNA, which believed that UNOSCOM II had undermined its gains made in the civil war. Fighting now broke out between Aidid's faction and UNOSCOM in June 1993. Between June and October, UN forces attempted to defeat the USC/SNA and capture Aidid. In the process several thousand more Somalis perished, and Aidid remained at large. By the autumn of 1993 many Somalis had turned against UNOSCOM II and began supporting

Two soldiers of the U.S. Army 10th Mountain Division conduct a nighttime sweep for weapons in the small Somali village of Afgooye in January 1993. (U.S. Department of Defense)

Aidid. During October 3–4, 1993, in the Battle of Mogadishu, 18 U.S. soldiers died; there were many other casualties. President Bill Clinton, his administration deeply embarrassed by the debacle, announced that U.S. troops would be withdrawn from Somalia by March 31, 1994. Meanwhile, Aidid announced a cease-fire.

After the Battle of Mogadishu there was some stability in south-central Somalia, but no peace had been brokered. UN peacekeeping and humanitarian workers remained in Somalia until March 1995, but any gains made during the UN intervention were quickly erased by renewed fighting. In August 1996 Aidid was killed, but this did little to quell the civil violence. Al Qaeda sent exploratory groups into Somalia in this period, and these linked up with the local militias and activists. Some U.S. government experts believed that the cells that attacked the U.S. embassies in Nairobi and Dar es Salaam, carried out the attacks on an Israeli-owned hotel in Mombasa, and attempted to down an Israeli airplane in 2002 were based in Somalia. In 2002 the United States established the Combined Joint Task Force–Horn of Africa in Djibouti, with some 2,000 troops, to confront the threat in Somalia.

Several subsequent attempts to reach a peace settlement in Somalia and to create a central government failed, although in 2004 the UN helped some Somali factions establish the Transitional Federal Government (TFG), but it proved unable to assert control over the country.

In May–June 2006 a coalition of Islamic fundamentalist courts, known as the Union of Islamic Courts, and their militias asserted authority over most of south-central Somalia. Its forces were successful in defeating clan militias. The Islamists now invoked Islamic law in Mogadishu and surrounding areas. The neighboring Ethiopians, however, were threatened by the hard-line Islamists and sent forces into Somalia in December 2006, allying with the TFG. The Islamists were temporarily defeated, allowing the TFG to finally assert a semblance of control in south-central Somalia. The TFG, however, was not able retain control and has been forced to deal from Djibouti with an insurgency mounted by the Islamists. Meanwhile, in the northwest (Somaliland) relative peace and stability were achieved beginning in 1991. In the northeast (Puntland) relative stability was achieved by 1998, but this area remains desperately poor.

In 2007 fighting among TFG, Ethiopian, and Islamist forces resulted in scores of deaths and created another humanitarian crisis, as more than 300,000 residents of Mogadishu were forced to flee their homes. In January 2007 the United States launched air strikes against retreating Islamist militants, claiming that Al Qaeda members were among them. The move angered many in the Muslim world because numerous civilian died in the attacks. In June 2008 the TFG brokered a truce with moderate Islamist groups and agreed to the withdrawal of Ethiopian troops, which would be replaced by UN peacekeeping troops. In January 2009 Ethiopia began removing its 3,000 troops; 4,500 Ugandan and Burundian peacekeeping troops from the African National Union replaced them. However, the TFG's hold in Somalia collapsed at the end of that month, and the TGF then attempted to rule from Djibouti. A growing insurgency by Islamic extremists continued, and by June 2009 they even held parts of Mogadishu. The government-in-exile has included Islamists in its ranks.

One of the Islamist extremist groups, al-Shabab, expanded through central and southern Somalia, capturing some towns near Mogadishu. In May 2009 al-Shabab took the strategic town of Jowhar, some 50 miles northeast of the capital, forcing some 40,000 civilians from their homes.

Meanwhile, a growing threat of piracy from Somali warlords operating in the Indian Ocean and Gulf of Aden has showcased the inherent dangers of an unstable and anarchic Somalia. Most of the pirates operate from Puntland, which has been relatively stable, but the grinding poverty there has encouraged many to resort to illegal means by which to earn a living.

The TFG formed a coalition with its two principal Islamic opposition parties in June 2009 that proceeded to announce that Sharia law would govern the nation's judiciary. This was not well received among Western nations. Nevertheless, fighting continues in the central and southern parts of Somalia between government forces and Islamic extremists groups, many of which have ties to Al Qaeda. In September 2009 U.S. Special Forces conducted a daring helicopter commando raid in Somalia that killed an Al Qaeda operative who was believed to have been involved with the bombings of U.S. embassies in Kenya and Tanzania in 1998.

DONNA R. JACKSON AND PAUL G. PIERPAOLI JR.

**See also**

Aidid, Mohammed Farrah; Somalia, International Intervention in

**References**

Henze, Paul B. *The Horn of Africa: From War to Peace.* London: Macmillan, 1991.

Menkhaus, Kenneth. *Somalia: State Collapse and the Threat of Terrorism.* Oxford: Oxford University Press, 2004.

Oakley, Robert B., and John I. Hirsch. *Somalia and Operation Restore Hope: Reflections on Peacemaking and Peacekeeping.* Washington, DC: United States Institute of Peace Press, 1995.

Schraeder, Peter J. *United States Foreign Policy toward Africa: Incrementalism, Crisis and Change.* Cambridge: Cambridge University Press, 1994.

# Somalia, International Intervention in
## Start Date: April 1992
## End Date: March 1995

Intervention in Somalia that lasted from April 1992 to March 1995 and was an international response to deteriorating humanitarian conditions in the war-torn nation. By 1992, continuing civil unrest in Somalia had rendered the government unable to react to a rising humanitarian crisis among its people, which threatened to bring wholesale starvation to millions of people. The intervention was made possible due largely to a consensus among the United Nations (UN) Security Council members to take action in a country where the central government had essentially ceased to exist. A major relief and humanitarian effort on the part of the United States, code-named Operation RESTORE HOPE, became the backbone of the intervention. It began on December 9, 1993.

Modern Somali history has been repeatedly punctuated by international involvement and interventions. Somalia was forced into the European colonial system at the end of the 19th century. Italy ruled its southern, central, and northeastern regions, while Great Britain ruled the northwestern region. During World War II, Great Britain conquered the entire country; after the war ended, Somalia was incorporated into the international mandate system. On July 1, 1960, all regions of Somalia were united to form one independent state.

Because Somalia had long been dominated by clan politics, forming a stable regime there proved to be impossible. In 1969 General Mohamed Siad Barre formed a dictatorship. In May 1988 the Somali National Movement (SNM), which represented the northwestern clan, the Isaaq, openly challenged Siad's rule. In the years that followed, a full-scale civil war unfolded in Somalia. Other clans joined the SNM's struggle against Siad, such as the Majerteen/Darod from the northeast and the Hawiye from the central region. Each clan formed its own political faction. When the clans' coalition finally defeated Siad's forces in early 1991, they turned against each other.

By 1992 the state was divided among the various warring factions. In the northwest, the Isaaq clan declared independence from Somalia and formed Somaliland. The Majerteen declared autonomy in the northeast of Somalia. The south-central region, which was the most populous, was dominated by the Hawiye, who formed the United Somali Congress (USC). The Haber-Gedir, a subclan of the Hawiye, split from the USC and formed the most powerful faction, the USC/SNA (United Somali Congress/Somali National Alliance). This faction was headed by General Mohammed Farrah Aidid (Aideed). The continuous fighting among the factions crushed whatever remained of Somalia's state authorities and infrastructure, threatening the well-being of millions of Somalis who were suffering from starvation, disease, and daily violence.

The first phase of the international intervention in Somalia lasted from April 1992 to December 1992. During this period, UN representatives tried to broker a peace deal among warring factions in Somalia while deploying a small peacekeeping force, called the United Nations Operation in Somalia I (UNOSOM I). The UN military contingent numbered approximately 500 soldiers from Pakistan stationed in the country's capital, Mogadishu. Another objective of the intervention was to deliver humanitarian aid to the country. But UN efforts failed to bring about change on the political, security, or humanitarian levels. The situation

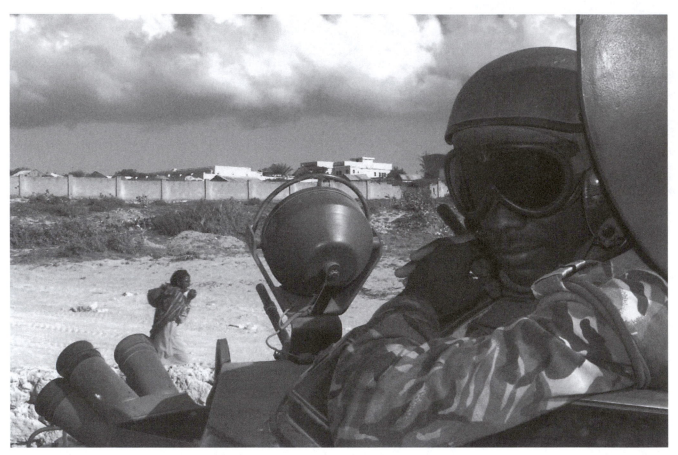

A Botswana member of the United Task Force (UNITAF) in an armored personnel carrier provides security at Mogadishu Airport in support of Operation RESTORE HOPE, 1993. (U.S. Department of Defense)

remained unchanged until the George H. W. Bush administration in the United States took the decision to lead a United Task Force (UNITAF) comprised of multinational forces to help deliver humanitarian aid to approximately 2 million Somalis.

UN Security Council Resolution 794 of December 3, 1992, marked the beginning of the second phase of the international intervention in Somalia and began Operation RESTORE HOPE, which commenced on December 9, 1992, when the first contingent of U.S. forces landed on Somali shores. This phase lasted until March 1993, when UN forces took over responsibility for all international operations in the country. For the first time in UN history, the Security Council had now confirmed the fact that obstacles to humanitarian aid are to be considered a threat to international peace and security.

UNITAF numbered more than 30,000 men at its peak, with the United States contributing approximately two-thirds of this manpower. UNITAF troops were deployed solely in the south-central region of the country, encompassing some 40 percent of the country's territory, in the areas that had experienced the worst warfare and famine in the early 1990s. The international force took control of all ports, airfields, and main roads within its deployment areas.

Massive aid operations soon began reaching the needy, and within a few months UNITAF had succeeded in ameliorating the humanitarian conditions. All local Somali factions cooperated

with the multinational forces and in January and March 1993 signed the Addis Ababa Peace Agreements, calling for the establishment of a Transitional National Council, a political body that was to include all Somali factions and work as an interim government for the country.

During the intervention, a controversy developed between the U.S. government and the UN Secretariat concerning the disarming of the Somali factions. The UN Secretariat wanted UNITAF to disarm all Somalis, whereas the United States refused to do so, claiming that it had led UNITAF for strictly humanitarian reasons, not to impose peace. The Americans claimed that once the humanitarian crisis was over, it would be time for the UN to lead the international force. As a compromise, instead of disarming the population, the international force concentrated its efforts on supervising the storage of the factions' heavy weapons under international supervision.

Security Council Resolution 814 of March 26, 1993, established the United Nations Operation in Somalia II (UNOSOM II), which replaced the American-led UNITAF. For the first time in history, UN forces were authorized under Chapter VII of the UN Charter to use force. This authorization marked the third phase of the intervention in Somalia.

During the third phase, which lasted from March 1993 to February 1994, UNOSOM II numbered approximately 28,000 soldiers,

## OPERATIONS IN SOMALIA, 1992–1994

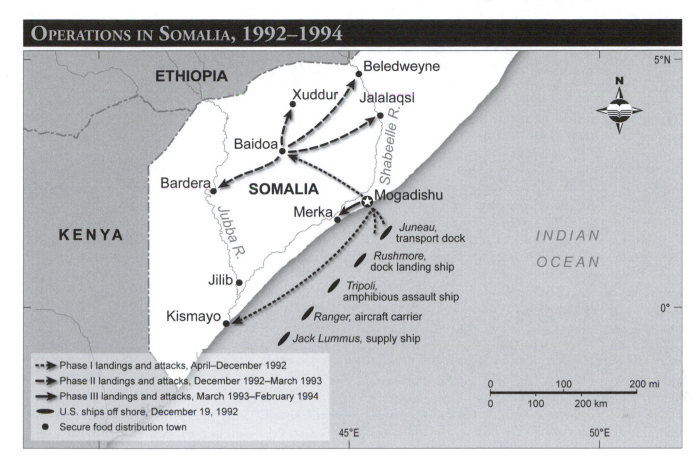

ETHIOPIA

Beledweyne

Xuddur  Jalalaqsi

Baidoa

Bardera  SOMALIA

KENYA

Merka  Mogadishu

*Juneau,* transport dock

*Rushmore,* dock landing ship

*Tripoli,* amphibious assault ship

Jilib

Kismayo  *Ranger,* aircraft carrier

*Jack Lummus,* supply ship

INDIAN OCEAN

5°N

N

*Shabeelle R.*

*Jubba R.*

0°

- ➤ Phase I landings and attacks, April–December 1992
- ➤ Phase II landings and attacks, December 1992–March 1993
- ➤ Phase III landings and attacks, March 1993–February 1994
- U.S. ships off shore, December 19, 1992
- ● Secure food distribution town

| 0 | 100 | 200 mi |
| 0 | 100 | 200 km |

45°E  50°E

---

civil police, and civilian personnel. These forces were supposed to assist the local Somali factions in implementing the Addis Ababa Peace Agreements. The UN forces had many objectives resulting from the agreements, such as establishing civilian institutions in Somalia, continuing the humanitarian aid, and instituting various development projects.

Instead of conciliation, however, UN actions strained the multinational force's relations with the most powerful Somali faction in the south-central region of the country, the USC/SNA. Aidid, the faction's leader, perceived the UN actions as efforts to undermine his faction's achievements from the civil war. He then encouraged his supporters to attack the UN forces.

Tension between the UN and the USC/SNA reached a climax on June 5, 1993. Fighting erupted that day between Pakistani peacekeeping contingents and armed locals who were probably connected to the USC/SNA. The Pakistani soldiers were supposed to inspect a USC/SNA arms depot and to assist in the delivering of humanitarian aid. When the fighting ended, 24 Pakistani soldiers and approximately 50 Somalis were dead.

This fighting marked the beginning of a four-month war between the UN forces and Aidid and his allies. Between June and October 1993 the UN launched numerous operations to capture Aidid and his faction's coleaders. Most of the operations were led by U.S. Special Forces units in the streets of southern Mogadishu, but these operations yielded bad results. Thousands of Somalis

died, and Aidid was not caught. As a result of the high number of Somali casualties, many Somalis began to support Aidid against the international intervention.

The deadliest engagement occurred during October 3–4, 1993. A raid by U.S. Rangers and Delta Force troops on a USC/SNA house on Mogadishu was upset when, because of street fighting, the American force became disoriented and two U.S. Sikorsky MH-60 Black Hawk helicopters were shot down. Pakistani armor failed to arrive as intense fighting took place in southern Mogadishu between the American forces and hundreds of Somalis. At the end of battle there were many casualties, including 18 American soldiers. After the battle, Aidid declared a unilateral cease-fire.

Outraged and embarrassed by the turn of events, on October 7 President Bill Clinton declared his intention to withdraw all American forces from Somalia by March 31, 1994. After the Battle of Mogadishu, relative political and military stability prevailed in south-central Somalia until February 1994 but with no progress made regarding the core problems that had led to the intervention in the first place. The Somali factions retained their armaments, and the UN continued the rebuilding of civilian institutions under its auspices.

The beginning of the final phase of the intervention was defined by UN Security Council Resolution 897 of February 4, 1994. This phase lasted until the evacuation of the last UN contingent in March 1995. In March 1994 the last Western soldiers (including

U.S.) were withdrawn from the country. Other countries withdrew their forces as well. After its forces were reduced to less than 20,000 soldiers, the UN changed its focus to that of the original mandate in 1992. The forces' operations would now emphasize reconciliation efforts among the local factions and the development of civilian institutions and infrastructure. In total, all forces under the UN suffered 147 casualties between 1992 and 1995.

Most of the UN's achievements were temporary. Even before the last UN forces were evacuated, the Somali factions renewed their fighting. Most of the civilian institutions that the UN helped to establish, such as a force of approximately 8,000 civil police and local authorities, disintegrated after the end of the intervention.

Aidid died on August 1, 1996, after being mortally wounded a week earlier. During the late 1990s the international community tried to broker a national peace agreement. In 2000 an attempt to create a Transitional National Government was undermined by the clans' mistrust of each other. This was encouraged by the fact that various African and Arab countries supported different clan coalitions. In 2004 another international effort created the Transitional Federal Government (TFG), which included all Somali clans. However, the TFG failed to establish authority in Somalia.

During 2006 a union of fundamentalist Islamic courts took hold of most of south-central Somalia. Their base of power was in Mogadishu, and they succeeded in defeating the clans' militias. The Islamists were able to restore law and order to the areas under their control by invoking Islamic laws. However, their hard-line calls for religious war (jihad) put them at odds with Ethiopia. On December 24, 2006, Ethiopian military forces, aided by the TFG's forces, invaded the Islamist-held territories, defeating the Islamists in a series of battles. The Ethiopian victories paved the way for the TFG to finally take root in Mogadishu. However, the TFG faces continued insurgencies by Islamists and supporters of the various clans. In contrast to the turbulent history of south-central Somalia, relative political stability has prevailed in the northwestern self-declared state of Somaliland since 1991 and in the northeastern self-declared autonomy of Puntland since 1998.

CHEN KERTCHER

**See also**

Bush, George Herbert Walker; Clinton, William Jefferson; Durant, Michael

**References**

Clarke, Walter S., and Herbst Jeffrey Ira. *Learning from Somalia: The Lessons of Armed Humanitarian Intervention.* Boulder, CO: Westview, 1997.

Kertcher, Chen. *The Search for Peace—Or for a State: UN Intervention in Somalia, 1992–95.* Jerusalem: Harry S. Truman Research Institute for the Advancement of Peace, 2003.

Lewis, Ioan M. *A Modern History of Somalia Nation and State in the Horn of Africa.* Boulder, CO: Westview, 1988.

Menkhaus, Kenneth. *Somalia: State Collapse and the Threat of Terrorism.* Oxford: Oxford University Press, 2004.

Oakley, Robert B., and John I. Hirsch. *Somalia and Operation Restore Hope: Reflections on Peacemaking and Peacekeeping.* Washington, DC: United States Institute of Peace Press, 1995.

# SOUTHERN WATCH, Operation
**Start Date: August 26, 1992**
**End Date: March 19, 2003**

Coalition surveillance and air policing operation of southern Iraq from August 26, 1992, to March 19, 2003. Operation SOUTHERN WATCH was implemented to prevent Iraqi fixed- and rotary-wing military aircraft from flying in Iraqi airspace south of the 32nd Parallel (33rd Parallel after 1996). The operation effectively established a southern no-fly zone to enforce United Nations (UN) Security Council Resolution 688, passed on April 5, 1991.

Following the end of the Persian Gulf War in February 1991, Iraqi leader Saddam Hussein ordered his military forces to repress Shia Muslims in southern Iraq who had revolted against his rule. In April, UN Security Council Resolution 688 demanded that Hussein end attacks on Iraqi Shiites, but the Iraqi dictator refused.

On August 26, 1992, U.S. president George H. W. Bush announced that a coalition of UN-member military forces would begin air policing operations of Iraq below the 32nd Parallel to ensure Iraq's compliance with Resolution 688. The coalition barred all Iraqi fixed- and rotary-wing aircraft from flying in the designated area. The U.S. Central Command (CENTCOM) activated Joint Task Force Southwest Asia (JTF-SWA) as the command and control organization for coalition forces monitoring the southern no-fly zone, and the mission was dubbed Operation SOUTHERN WATCH. Lieutenant General Michael A. Nelson, then commander of CENTCOM air forces, became the first commander of JTF-SWA, headquartered in Riyadh, Saudi Arabia. Besides the United States, the other coalition partners were Great Britain, France, Russia, and Saudi Arabia.

Coalition air forces flew the first SOUTHERN WATCH sortie on August 27, 1992. At first Iraq complied with the no-fly restrictions, but Hussein soon began challenging SOUTHERN WATCH operations after the UN decision of November 24, 1992, to retain sanctions against Iraq. On December 27, 1992, a U.S. Air Force Lockheed Martin F-16 Fighting Falcon patrolling the no-fly zone encountered an Iraqi MiG-25 Foxbat. After the Iraqi pilot locked his air-to-air radar onto the F-16, the American pilot destroyed the Foxbat with an air-to-air missile. Shortly afterward, Hussein moved surface-to-air missiles (SAMs) into southern Iraq below the 32nd Parallel. Because of the threat this posed to coalition pilots flying SOUTHERN WATCH missions, the coalition ordered Hussein to remove them. He ignored the demand.

On January 6, 1993, the United States, Russia, France, and the United Kingdom agreed to work together to enforce Resolution 688. A week later, coalition aircraft destroyed Iraqi SAM sites and their command and control units in southern Iraq, and on January 17, 1994, coalition naval forces disabled an Iraqi nuclear facility with Tomahawk cruise missiles to emphasize the need for Iraq to comply with UN Security Council Resolution 687, which had demanded the destruction of all Iraqi weapons of mass destruction (WMDs).

On April 18, 1993, a McDonnell Douglas F-4G Phantom II fired a missile into an Iraqi antiaircraft position after its radar

An F-14 Tomcat lands on the U.S. aircraft carrier *Independence* (CV-62). The carrier was taking part in Operation SOUTHERN WATCH, a multinational effort establishing a no-fly zone for Iraqi aircraft south of the 32nd Parallel in Iraq. (U.S. Department of Defense)

had illuminated the aircraft. On June 26, 1993, the United States launched Tomahawk missiles against targets in Iraq in retaliation for an April 1992 Iraqi government plan to assassinate former President George H. W. Bush during a visit to Kuwait.

Because the first nine months of 1994 passed without any Iraqi challenges in the SOUTHERN WATCH area, JTF-SWA began to withdraw forces in February 1994. By late spring almost 20 aircraft, about 300 personnel, and almost 1,000 tons of equipment had redeployed to their home stations in the United States. However, in October 1994 Iraq began to move troops toward Kuwait after the coalition refused to set a date to end sanctions against Iraq.

Coalition forces then deployed additional forces into the theater in Operation VIGILANT WARRIOR. In response the UN Security Council passed Resolution 949, which prohibited Iraq from using its forces to threaten neighboring countries or UN operations in Iraq, deploying units south of the 32nd Parallel, and enhancing its military capabilities in southern Iraq.

After another Iraqi confrontation in September 1996, JTF-SWA continued to monitor the airspace south of the 32nd Parallel in southern Iraq with aircraft from the American, British, French, and Saudi Arabian air forces from land bases in the region and from U.S. Navy carrier groups in the Persian Gulf and the Red Sea. Coalition naval forces also provided maritime intercept operations in the northern Red Sea and the Persian Gulf in support of UN sanctions against Iraq. By this time, the U.S. Air Force had deployed more than 6,000 personnel to support Operation SOUTHERN WATCH air operations over southern Iraq. Aircraft included the F-4 Phantom II, the McDonnell Douglas F-15 Eagle, and the F-16 Fighting Falcon and, for refueling coalition strike aircraft, the Boeing KC-135R Stratotanker. Between August 1992, when SOUTHERN WATCH began, and the end of January 1997, U.S. Air Force aircraft and crews had flown more than 28,800 sorties (68 percent of the total sorties) in support of the coalition operation.

After the June 1996 bombing of the Khobar Towers in Saudi Arabia, the U.S. Air Force relocated the majority of its SOUTHERN WATCH forces from Prince Sultan Air Base to Kharj, Saudi Arabia, located to the southeast of Riyadh, and instituted additional force protection measures throughout the CENTCOM's area of responsibility.

In November 1998 U.S. president William J. Clinton warned Hussein that the coalition would use force if he continued to hamper UN weapons inspectors looking for Iraqi WMDs. When Hussein continued to do so, the coalition conducted Operation DESERT FOX during December 16–19 to show its resolve in supporting the UN's weapons inspections. Coalition air forces attacked installations associated with Iraq's development of WMDs, national command and control systems, air defense facilities, Republican Guard facilities, airfields, and the Basra oil refinery, which was involved in the illegal production of petroleum products for export.

After DESERT FOX began, France ended its participation in SOUTHERN WATCH air operations on December 16, 1998, contending that the United States and British air forces had conducted attacks against Iraqi targets for more than a year, contributing to the continuing tensions. France, however, still retained men and equipment in the region.

By early 2001, coalition pilots had entered the southern no-fly zone 153,000 times since the start of SOUTHERN WATCH without losing any pilots. Since December 1998 the Iraqis had illuminated coalition aircraft with their radar or attacked them with antiaircraft weapons on 500 occasions. In the same period, CENTCOM reported that Iraqi aircraft violated the southern no-fly zone more than 150 times, often trying to lure coalition aircraft north of the 33rd Parallel into so-called SAM-bushes. Although some published reports indicated that coalition air operations had caused the deaths of 175 civilians and wounded nearly 500 others between January 1999 and April 2000, coalition aircraft did not target civilian populations or infrastructure and sought to avoid injury to civilians and damage to civilian facilities.

During 2001 and into 2002, U.S. and British aircraft launched sporadic attacks against Iraqi command centers, radars, and communications centers in southern Iraq. Coalition aircraft hit only about 40 percent of the targets, but these attacks sparked adverse opinion in the foreign press, reflecting growing world skepticism about U.S.-British policy toward Iraq. Then, attacks by Iraqi antiaircraft defenses on coalition aircraft, followed by retaliatory air strikes, began to occur almost weekly.

In June 2002 American and British forces stepped up their attacks to degrade Iraqi air defense and communication targets all over southern Iraq to soften them up in preparation for a future invasion of Iraq. Lieutenant General Michael Mosley revealed the existence of this operation, called SOUTHERN FOCUS, in mid-2003. Later revelations discovered that these attacks were part of a preplanned operation to degrade the Iraqi air-defense system in preparation for the planned invasion of Iraq. This operation continued until the beginning of the invasion of Iraq during Operation IRAQI FREEDOM in March 2003. By that time, coalition air forces had flown nearly 300,000 sorties in support of Operation SOUTHERN WATCH and related operations.

In December 2002 the U.S. Air Force sent an RQ-1 Predator unmanned reconnaissance aircraft, armed with infrared AIM-92 Stinger air-to-air missiles, to patrol the no-fly zone in an attempt to bait Iraqi fighters into a fight. An Iraqi MiG-25 spotted the unmanned aerial vehicle and attacked. Both aircraft fired missiles at each other, but the Iraqi aircraft was outside the range of the Stinger. While the U.S. missile fell short, the Iraqi missile hit the Predator, destroying it. This mission was the first time an unmanned aircraft had been used in air-to-air combat.

During the 10 years of its duration, Operation SOUTHERN WATCH sparked a number of both good and bad results. First, it provided a major impetus for the U.S. Air Force to reorganize itself into 10 Aerospace Expeditionary Forces (AEFs) that could handle regular, extended, or temporary deployments. Additionally, the need for combat-ready forces produced equipment upgrades and modernization for Air National Guard and Air Force Reserve units, which provided 10 percent of the U.S. Air Force's deployed aerospace expeditionary forces. On the down side, the operation contributed significantly to very fast-paced operations that caused major readiness problems throughout the air force. In May 2000, for example, one-third of the air force's combat units were not fully ready for war, largely because manning and spare parts shortages had reduced its readiness level to the lowest point in 15 years. Many believed that the long-term sustained air operations of SOUTHERN WATCH contributed significantly to this problem.

ROBERT B. KANE

**See also**

DESERT FOX, Operation; Missiles, Surface-to-Air; No-Fly Zones; United Nations; United Nations Security Council Resolution 687; United Nations Special Commission; United Nations Weapons Inspectors; United States Central Command; VIGILANT WARRIOR, Operation

**References**

Boyne, Walter J. *Beyond the Wild Blue: A History of the U.S. Air Force, 1947–2007*. 2nd ed. New York: Thomas Dunne Books, 2007.
Byman, Daniel, and Matthew C. Waxman. *Confronting Iraq: U.S. Policy and the Use of Force since the Gulf War*. Santa Monica, CA: RAND Corporation, 2002.
Hines, Jay E. "From Desert One to Southern Watch: The Evolution of the U.S. Central Command." *Joint Forces Quarterly* (Spring 2000): 42–48.
Kitfield, James. "The Long Deployment." *Air Force Magazine* 83 (July 2000): 31–36.
Knights, Michael. *Cradle of Conflict: Iraq and the Birth of Modern U.S. Military*. Annapolis, MD: Naval Institute Press, 2005.

# Soviet-Afghanistan War
**Start Date: 1979**
**End Date: 1989**

War that destroyed the U.S.-Soviet détente of the 1970s; inaugurated a new, dangerous stage in the Cold War; destabilized Afghanistan; and badly weakened the Soviet military and economic establishments. The Soviet-Afghanistan War represented the culmination of events dating to April 1978, when Afghan communists, supported by left-wing army leaders, overthrew the unpopular, authoritarian government of Mohammad Daoud Khan and proclaimed the People's Democratic Republic of Afghanistan. Although the extent of Soviet involvement in the coup remains unclear, Moscow certainly welcomed it and quickly established close relations with the new regime, which was headed by Nur Muhammad Taraki. He was committed to bringing socialism to Afghanistan.

With the ambitious, extremely militant foreign minister Hafizullah Amin as its driving force, the Taraki regime quickly alienated much of Afghanistan's population by conducting a terror campaign against its opponents and introducing a series of social and economic reforms at odds with the religious and cultural norms of the country's highly conservative, Muslim, tribal society. Afghanistan's Muslim leaders soon declared a jihad (holy war) against "godless communism," and by August 1978 the Taraki regime faced an open revolt, a situation made especially dangerous by the defection of a portion of the army to the rebel cause.

As Afghanistan descended into civil war, Moscow grew increasingly concerned. Committed by the Brezhnev Doctrine to preventing the overthrow of a friendly, neighboring communist government and fearful of the effects that a potential Islamic fundamentalist regime might have on the Muslim population of Soviet Central Asia, specifically those in the republics bordering Afghanistan, the Soviets moved toward military intervention. During the last months of 1979, the Leonid Brezhnev government dispatched approximately 4,500 combat advisers to assist the Afghan communist regime while simultaneously allowing Soviet aircraft to conduct bombing raids against rebel positions. Although Soviet deputy defense minister Ivan G. Pavlovski, who had played an important role in the 1968 Soviet invasion of Czechoslovakia, counseled against full-scale intervention in Afghanistan, his superior, Defense Minister Dmitry Ustinov, convinced Brezhnev to undertake an invasion, arguing that only such action could preserve the Afghan communist regime. He also promised that the Soviet presence there would be short.

Brezhnev ultimately decided in favor of war, the pivotal factor arguably being the September 1979 seizure of power by Hafizullah Amin, who had ordered Taraki arrested and murdered. Apparently shocked by Amin's act of supreme betrayal and inclined to believe that only a massive intervention could save the situation, Brezhnev gave approval for the invasion. Beginning in late November 1979 and continuing during the first weeks of December, the Soviet military concentrated the Fortieth Army, composed primarily of Central Asian troops, along the Afghan border. On December 24, Soviet forces crossed the frontier, while Moscow claimed that the Afghan government had requested help against an unnamed outside threat.

Relying on mechanized tactics and close air support, Soviet units quickly seized the Afghan capital of Kabul. In the process, a special assault force stormed the presidential palace and killed Amin, replacing him with the more moderate Babrak Karmal, who attempted, unsuccessfully, to win popular support by portraying

Soviet soldiers ride aboard an airborne combat vehicle in Kabul, Afghanistan, in March 1986. (U.S. Department of Defense)

### Soviet Military Expenditures during the Occupation of Afghanistan (1979–1989)

| Year | Military Expenditures (in millions of 1989 dollars) | Military Expenditures as % of Total Government Spending |
|---|---|---|
| 1979 | $284,400 | 56.8% |
| 1980 | $292,000 | 53.4% |
| 1981 | $295,200 | 51.7% |
| 1982 | $300,500 | 48.8% |
| 1983 | $304,900 | 50.2% |
| 1984 | $309,200 | 50.2% |
| 1985 | $315,600 | 50.0% |
| 1986 | $319,200 | 46.9% |
| 1987 | $325,900 | 45.9% |
| 1988 | $330,900 | 46.4% |
| 1989 | $311,000 | 45.7% |

himself as a devoted Muslim and Afghan nationalist. Soviet forces, numbering at least 50,000 troops by the end of January 1980, went on to occupy the other major Afghan cities and secured major highways. In response, rebel mujahideen forces resorted to guerrilla warfare, their primary goal being to avoid defeat in the hopes of outlasting Soviet intervention.

Moscow's invasion of Afghanistan had immediate and adverse international consequences, effectively wrecking détente that was already in dire straits by December 1979 thanks to recent increases in missile deployments in Europe. Having devoted much effort to improving relations with Moscow, U.S. president Jimmy Carter believed that he had been betrayed. He reacted swiftly and strongly to the Afghan invasion.

On December 28, 1979, Carter publicly denounced the Soviet action as a "blatant violation of accepted international rules of behavior." Three days later, he accused Moscow of lying about its motives for intervening and declared that the invasion had dramatically altered his view of the Soviet Union's foreign policy goals. On January 3, 1980, the president asked the U.S. Senate to delay consideration of the Strategic Arms Limitations Talks II (SALT II) treaty. Finally, on January 23, in his State of the Union Address, Carter warned that the Soviet action in Afghanistan posed a potentially serious threat to world peace because control of Afghanistan would put Moscow in a position to dominate the strategic Persian Gulf and thus interdict at will the flow of Middle East oil.

The president followed these pronouncements by enunciating what soon became known as the Carter Doctrine, declaring that any effort to dominate the Persian Gulf would be interpreted as an attack on U.S. interests that would be rebuffed by force if necessary. Carter also announced his intention to limit the sale of technology and agricultural products to the Soviet Union, and he imposed restrictions on Soviet fishing privileges in U.S. waters. In addition, he notified the International Olympic Committee that in light of the Soviet invasion of Afghanistan, neither he nor the U.S. public would support sending a U.S. team to the 1980 Moscow Summer Games. The president called upon U.S. allies to follow suit.

Carter also asked Congress to support increased defense spending and registration for the draft, pushed for the creation of a Rapid Deployment Force that could intervene in the Persian Gulf or other areas threatened by Soviet expansionism, offered increased military aid to Pakistan, moved to enhance ties with the People's Republic of China (PRC), approved covert CIA assistance to the mujahideen, and signed a presidential directive on July 25, 1980, providing for increased targeting of Soviet nuclear forces.

Carter's sharp response was undercut to a certain extent by several developments. First, key U.S. allies rejected both economic sanctions against the Kremlin and an Olympic boycott. Second, Argentina and several other states actually increased their grain sales to Moscow. Third, a somewhat jaded U.S. public tended to doubt the president's assertions about Soviet motives and believed that he had needlessly reenergized the Cold War.

Ronald Reagan, who defeated Carter in the November 1980 presidential election, took an even harder stand with the Soviets. Describing the Soviet Union as an "evil empire" that had used détente for its own nefarious purposes, the Reagan administration poured vast sums of money into a massive military buildup that even saw the president push the development of the Strategic Defense Initiative (SDI)—labeled "Star Wars" by its critics—a missile defense system dependent on satellites to destroy enemy missiles with lasers or particle beams before armed warheads separated and headed for their targets. The Soviet response was to build additional missiles and warheads, further straining the Soviet Union's already heavily militarized economy.

Meanwhile, confronted with guerrilla warfare in Afghanistan, the Soviets remained committed to waging a limited war and found itself drawn, inexorably, into an ever-deeper bloody quagmire against a determined opponent whose confidence and morale grew with each passing month. To make matters worse for Moscow, domestic criticism of the war by such prominent dissidents as Andrei Sakharov appeared early on, while foreign assistance in the form of food, transport vehicles, and weaponry (especially the FIM-92 "Stinger" man-portable antiaircraft missile launchers) from the United States began reaching the mujahideen as the fighting dragged on.

Neither the commitment of more troops, the use of chemical weapons, nor the replacement of the unpopular Karmal could bring Moscow any closer to victory. Accordingly, by 1986 the Soviet leadership, now headed by the reformist General Secretary Mikhail Gorbachev, began contemplating ways of extricating itself from what many observers characterized as the "Soviet Union's Vietnam."

In April 1988, Gorbachev agreed to a United Nations mediation proposal providing for the withdrawal of Soviet troops over a 10-month period. One month later, the departure of Soviet military forces, which had grown to an estimated 115,000 troops, commenced—a process that was finally completed in February 1989.

Although the Soviets left Afghanistan with a procommunist regime, a team of military advisers, and substantial quantities of

# AFGHAN REFUGEE FLOW DURING THE SOVIET-AFGHANISTAN WAR, 1979–1990

60°E    65°E    70°E

40°N

**Soviet Union**

Osh

Samarkand

Turkmenabat

Ashkhabad    Dushanbe

Mary    Khorugh

Termiz

Kunduz

Mazar-e
Sharif    Baghlan

Mashhad

35°N

Maymana

Herat    Chaghcharan    Kabul

**AFGHANISTAN**    Jalalabad    Islamabad

Khost    Peshawar

Kandahar

**IRAN**

Farah    Zhob

Zaranj    **PAKISTAN**

3.25 million refugees

30°N

Zahedan    Quetta

Sibi

Surab

3 million refugees
(mostly located in
urban areas)

Sukkur

**INDIA**

Bela

Turbat

25°N

☐ Main refugee camp/settlement
➜ Refugee movement    Arabian Sea

CHINA

Amu R.    Indus R.

Lahore

Indus R.

0    100    200 mi
0    100    200 km

Members of the Afghan resistance return to a village that has been destroyed by Soviet forces, March 25, 1986. (U.S. Department of Defense)

equipment, the nine-year-long war had exacted a high toll, costing the Soviets an estimated 50,000 casualties. It seriously damaged the Red Army's military reputation, further undermining the legitimacy of the Soviet system, and nearly bankrupted the Kremlin. For the Afghans, the war proved equally costly. An estimated 1 million civilians were dead, and another 5 million were refugees. Much of the country was devastated. The social and political chaos in postwar Afghanistan paved the way for more civil war there, fostered the rise of the Taliban, and, ultimately, embroiled the country in the Global War on Terror after the September 11, 2001, terror attacks prompted the United States to topple the Taliban regime during Operation ENDURING FREEDOM.

BRUCE J. DEHART

**See also**

Abu Daoud; Afghanistan; Afghanistan, Economic Cost of Soviet Invasion and Occupation of; Carter, James Earl, Jr.; Carter Doctrine; ENDURING FREEDOM, Operation; Gorbachev, Mikhail; Jihad; Mujahideen, Soviet-Afghanistan War; Reagan, Ronald Wilson; Reagan Administration, Middle East Policy; Soviet Union, Middle East Policy; Taliban

**References**

Goodson, Larry. *Afghanistan's Endless War: State Failure, Regional Politics and the Rise of the Taliban.* Seattle: University of Washington Press, 2001.
Grau, Lester W., ed. *The Bear Went over the Mountain: Soviet Combat Tactics in Afghanistan.* London: Frank Cass, 1998.
Hauner, Milan. *The Soviet War in Afghanistan: Patterns of Russian Imperialism.* Lanham, MD: University Press of America, 1991.
MacKenzie, David. *From Messianism to Collapse: Soviet Foreign Policy, 1917–1991.* Fort Worth, TX: Harcourt Brace, 1994.
Russian General Staff. *The Soviet-Afghan War: How a Superpower Fought and Lost.* Lawrence: University of Kansas Press, 2002.

## Soviet Union, Middle East Policy

Geography and oil made the Middle East a crucial arena of Cold War competition, and the foreign policy of the Soviet Union in the region sought to counteract British, French, and other European influences there, as well as American involvement, and to create allies for itself and markets for its weapons and wheat. In general, the Soviet Union realized that it could not gain dominance in the region, although it had special and historic interests in Iran and some parts of the former Ottoman Empire, and had to keep in mind the allegiances of its significant Muslim population.

The Soviets supported some of the Arab states for geopolitical reasons, such as access to the Mediterranean Sea, the Suez Canal, and the Indian Ocean, just as its policies toward Iran and Turkey concerned access to the Black Sea. The Soviets generally backed the Arab states during the various Arab-Israeli wars; however, it also benefited from the regional arms race that was a part of those conflicts. Much earlier in the 20th century, the Soviet Union hoped to expand its alliances for ideological reasons, but later pragmatism took center stage. It would have been foolish for the Soviets to attempt anything like overt efforts to dominate the Middle East, given the region's deep religiosity and antipathy to atheism. However, leftist, nationalist, and semisocialist groups were less opposed to the Soviet Union and sought to employ it as a counterweight to the West. However, there were some exceptions to this pattern, as when governments in Afghanistan, Azerbaijan, and Pakistan were identified more directly with the Soviets and especially with the long war in Afghanistan.

The primary vehicle of Soviet influence in the Middle East was military aid, often offered from East European satellite countries. Soviet arms were available in large quantities, at low prices, and on favorable credit terms. The Soviet Union was the chief military patron of Egypt (1955–1973), Syria (after 1958), Iraq (after 1958), Libya (after 1974), Algeria (after 1962), Somalia (1962–1977), Ethiopia (after 1977), South Yemen (1960s), and Afghanistan (after 1973). During the Iran-Iraq War (1980–1988), the Soviets supplied both Iraq and Iran via intermediaries. The Soviets provided advisers to their clients, obtained air and naval basing rights in the region, and deployed combat forces in Afghanistan (1979–1989).

The Soviets had negligible influence in the Middle East before World War II. This was the period when communist parties in the Middle East were at their most robust; their political fortunes in most countries turned later, with the exception of the Sudan, where the Communist Party remained strong through the 1970s.

After World War I the Soviet Union assumed power over many former khanates and areas, including Georgia, Armenia, and northern Azerbaijan, which assured it access to Caspian Sea oil and trade. A Soviet republic was briefly established in Gilan, Iran, and then again during World War II, in Iranian or southern Azerbaijan. After World War II had decisively weakened Britain and France, Soviet interest in the northern Middle Eastern states, Pakistan, and Afghanistan altered.

The Soviets also hoped to gain influence in other parts of the Middle East. They decided to support the Zionist movement in order to weaken British power and create tensions between the United States and Britain, and because of the common suffering of the war that had claimed up to 27 million Soviet citizens and 6 million Jews. In 1947 Soviet diplomats supported the partition of Palestine, which led to the creation of Israel in 1948. To strengthen Israel, the Soviets transferred Jews from Soviet-occupied territories to Poland, fully expecting them to emigrate. The Soviets instructed Poland, Czechoslovakia, Romania, and Hungary to permit Jewish emigration. From 1948 to 1951, more than 302,000 Jews emigrated from Eastern Europe to Israel. Israel's Jewish population was only 806,000 in 1948, so this was a vital demographic boost.

At Soviet direction, in 1948 Czechoslovakia provided $22 million in arms to Israel, including 50,000 rifles, 6,000 machine guns, 90 million rounds of ammunition, and Supermarine Spitfire and Avia S-199 fighter aircraft. Czech arms played a crucial role in securing air superiority over Israel and halting Arab ground advances in the Israeli War of Independence (1948–1949).

The Soviets may have initially contemplated a strategic alliance with Israel. However, relations deteriorated with the onset of the Cold War when Soviet dictator Joseph Stalin launched an anti-Semitic, anti-Western propaganda campaign. In late 1952 Soviet security services manufactured an alleged conspiracy of Jewish doctors to poison Soviet leaders, and in this atmosphere the Soviet Union broke relations with Israel. Official anti-Semitism eased with the death of Stalin in March 1953. Diplomatic relations with Israel were restored, but Israel had since shifted permanently into the Western camp.

In 1955 Pakistan and Turkey signed a military alliance, followed by an Iranian and Pakistani agreement, and then the Baghdad Pact, which garnered signatures from the governments of the United Kingdom, Iraq, Turkey, Pakistan, and Iran in the Central

Muslims gather for prayer in Termez, Uzbekistan, in the Soviet Union in 1990. Termez is close to the border with Afghanistan. (Reza/Webistan/Corbis)

Treaty Organization. The alliance's ostensible purpose was to contain Soviet advances to the south, but it was unsuccessful and actually prompted movement by Egypt toward the communist bloc.

In the 1950s the United States, Britain, and France sought to maintain an Arab-Israeli arms balance and would not sell advanced weapons to Egypt. Egyptian president Gamal Abdel Nasser approached the Soviets, who agreed in September 1955 to supply arms via Czechoslovakia. This Czech arms deal, as it was known, included 230 tanks, 200 armored personnel carriers, 100 self-propelled guns, 500 artillery pieces, several hundred MiG-15 jet fighters, 50 Il-28 jet bombers, transport aircraft, and assorted naval vessels. This development greatly alarmed Israel as well as Britain and France, which had their own difficulties with Nasser.

Anglo-French tensions with Egypt came to a head in 1956. The United States withdrew funding from the proposed Aswan High Dam project, and in turn Nasser decided to nationalize the Suez Canal, with the revenues to be used to finance the dam. The British, French, and Israelis invaded Egypt in October to regain control of the canal and overthrow Nasser. At that time the Soviets were busy crushing the Hungarian Uprising and in any case had little military capability to intervene on Egypt's behalf. However, the Soviets sent diplomatic notes with veiled threats of force against Britain and France unless they withdrew from Egypt, and proposed a joint U.S.-Soviet military intervention to halt the fighting. Washington rebuffed Soviet threats, rejected the proposal for joint action, and employed political and economic pressure to force Britain and France to abandon their occupation. After the Suez Crisis, the Soviets portrayed themselves as Egypt's friend and protector, even though their bluster had risked nothing and achieved little. During the brief war, British, French, and Israeli forces destroyed large quantities of Soviet-supplied equipment at little cost to themselves. The Soviets attributed this discreditable performance to poorly trained Egyptian operators.

The British and French defeat at Suez facilitated increased Soviet influence in the Middle East. The Soviets agreed to replenish Egypt's lost equipment and supplied more modern MiG-17 and MiG-19 fighters. In 1963 Egypt received first-line T-54/55 tanks, MiG-21 supersonic fighters, Tu-16 bombers, and SA-2 surface-to-air missiles (SAMs). The Soviets provided similar modern equipment to the progressive regimes in Syria and Iraq; the latter's pro-British government was overthrown in 1958. Some 1,300 Soviet and East European advisers trained Egyptian forces to use the new equipment. The number of Soviet tanks and combat aircraft given to the Arabs vastly exceeded Western supplies to Israel, not least because the United States refused to supply significant quantities of modern equipment to Israel before 1967.

Soviet strategy in the Middle East from 1965 to 1973 was subordinate to Soviet strategy toward Indochina. In response to the escalating war in Vietnam after 1965, the Soviets supplied many tens of thousands of tons of weapons and equipment to Hanoi. The overland supply route from the Soviet Union across the People's Republic of China (PRC) to the Democratic Republic of Vietnam (North Vietnam) was not secure because of Sino-Soviet antagonism and the turmoil created by China's Great Proletarian Cultural Revolution. Nor could supplies travel via Vladivostok given the limited capacity of the Trans-Siberian Railroad and the need to increase Soviet forces in the Far East to confront China. Thus, the Soviets shipped supplies to North Vietnam primarily via the Black Sea port of Odessa. The sea route from Odessa to Haiphong via the Cape of Good Hope was more than twice as long as the route via the Suez Canal. Closing the Suez Canal would thus more than halve the quantity of supplies the Soviets could deliver. After the 1967 Six-Day War closed the canal, the Soviets urgently sought to reopen it both by demanding Israeli withdrawal from the canal zone and by arming Egypt to open the canal by force.

The argument that the Soviets instigated the Six-Day War or encouraged Arab aggression in 1967 defies logic. The Soviets wanted to keep the Suez Canal open. Furthermore, Egyptian and Syrian forces had not yet received all the weapons or training that the Soviets intended to provide. The war came about with a third of Egypt's army (55,000 troops, including the best units) deployed in Yemen and thus unavailable to fight Israel. When tensions rose in May 1967, the Soviets warned Egypt that Israel planned to attack Syria. This triggered Nasser's subsequent actions, closing the straits of Tiran and ordering United Nations (UN) peacemakers to leave the Sinai. Possibly, the Soviets hoped that a display of Egyptian resolve would deter Israel from striking Syria, but if so this backfired. Israel chose to interpret these responses as acts of war. On May 26, 1967, the Soviets pressured Egypt and Syria to moderate their rhetoric and prevent armed conflict with Israel by whatever means necessary, but this came too late to prevent Israeli action.

Soviet behavior during the Six-Day War was restrained. The Soviets expressed resolute support for the Arabs, but did not resupply them or risk confrontation with the United States. The Soviets only threatened overt involvement on June 10, when they feared that Israel would take Damascus and overthrow the Syrian government. They broke off relations with Israel and alerted their airborne divisions for deployment, but intervention proved unnecessary when Israel accepted a cease-fire.

After the Six-Day War, the Soviets replaced Egypt's and Syria's lost equipment and dispatched huge quantities of arms to Sudan, Iraq, and Yemen. The Soviets sent 13,000 military advisers to Egypt in late 1967—rising to 20,000 in 1970—with advisers attached to every Egyptian unit down to battalion level. The Soviets demanded an overhaul of the Egyptian high command, and thousands of Egyptian officers visited the Soviet Union for training. Diplomatically, the Soviets continued to insist that Israel withdraw from the canal zone without preconditions. Washington responded that a comprehensive solution to the Arab-Israeli conflict must precede Israeli withdrawal from occupied territories. The Soviets and the East Europeans began to train, fund, and equip terrorist organizations, such as the Palestine Liberation Organization (PLO) and the Popular Front for the Liberation of Palestine (PFLP), to harass Israel, Western Europe, and the United States.

In April 1969 Egypt launched the War of Attrition, which sought to avoid major ground combat while causing continual Israeli casualties. Israel countered with air strikes that destroyed Egypt's air defenses in the canal zone. When this did not force Egypt to desist, Israel began deep-penetration raids throughout Egypt. Egypt then convinced the Soviets to take control of Egypt's air defenses. More than 12,000 Soviet operators manned air defenses that included 85 SA-2 and SA-3 missile sites, radar-guided artillery pieces, and more than 100 MiG-21 fighters with Soviet pilots. Although initially restricted to defense of the Nile River Valley, the Soviets began moving SAM batteries closer to the Suez Canal in July 1970, creating the prospect that Egyptian forces could cross the canal under this umbrella. The United States equipped Israeli aircraft with advanced electronic countermeasures and air-to-surface missiles to defeat the SAM threat.

The effort to put a SAM umbrella over the Suez Canal coincided with a crisis in Jordan. In September 1970 King Hussein violently suppressed increasingly uncontrollable Palestinian guerrilla groups. In response, the Soviets sponsored a brief Syrian invasion of Jordan. Soviet advisers planned the operation and accompanied Syrian tanks until they crossed the border. The Soviets hoped that either Israel would intervene, which would discredit Jordan's King Hussein, or that the Americans would intervene, which would discredit the United States in the Arab world. However, the Jordanian air force smashed Syria's tank columns, making outside intervention unnecessary.

After Nasser's death in September 1970, Egypt's new president, Muhammad Anwar Sadat, sought to improve relations with Western Europe and the United States. When the Soviets tried to influence the Egyptian succession struggle in favor of leftist vice president Ali Sabri, Sadat dismissed and arrested Sabri. More than 100 Nasserist or leftist officials were purged from the Egyptian government in the Corrective Revolution of May 1971. To prevent a complete break in relations, the Soviets demanded—and obtained—a Soviet-Egyptian Treaty of Friendship. The treaty restricted the Soviet role in Egypt to providing military aid and training, and Egypt agreed not to join any anti-Soviet alliance.

Having lost influence in Egypt, the Soviets tried to strengthen their relations with other Arab states through arms deliveries to Syria, Iraq, Somalia, South Yemen, and the Sudan. However, by this time the communist parties in Syria and Iraq were suppressed by the Baathists. Some competition in the form of aid and weapons sales came from China. However, in the Sudan, the Nimeri government cracked down on the substantial Sudanese Communist Party, limiting its influence from that point. The Sudanese communists launched a coup attempt but were crushed. Soviet military advisers were then expelled.

Soviet leader Leonid Brezhnev greets Egyptian president Anwar Sadat, who was in Moscow in October 1971 seeking diplomatic support and military hardware against Israel. (Hulton Archive/Getty Images)

Sadat understood that the Soviets preferred to perpetuate Arab-Israeli antagonism to keep Egypt isolated and dependent on the Soviet Union. He also knew that only the Americans could deliver a political settlement with Israel and the return of the Sinai to Egyptian control. Sadat hoped that Washington could broker a political solution, but American efforts to do so in 1971 and 1972 foundered on Israeli intransigence. Sadat signaled his independence and desire for improved relations with the United States, but was thus breaking with Egypt's long-standing nonalignment policy and strong desire to avoid any measures of foreign control. Sadat's strategy was to prepare for a limited war in the expectation that victory would enable Washington to force Israel to accept a peace agreement and withdraw from the Sinai. Sadat informed the Soviets in February 1973 that he intended to attack Israel, and he demanded their support. The Soviets had little choice but to agree, since failure to support Egypt would destroy Soviet influence in the Middle East. Furthermore, reopening the Suez Canal would facilitate arming Hanoi for a future attack on South Vietnam.

From late June 1967 until early 1973, the Soviets gave Egypt sufficient weaponry to defend itself but not advanced offensive weapons. The Egyptians were especially displeased that the Soviets did not provide their latest MiG-23 and MiG-25 fighters to counter Israeli F-4 Phantoms. Before the October 1973 Yom Kippur (Ramadan) War, the Soviets provided first-line T-62 tanks and large numbers of antiaircraft and antitank missiles, which would enable Egypt to take and hold a bridgehead on the east bank of the Suez against Israeli air and armored counterattacks. Syria and Iraq also received significant quantities of Soviet weapons before the war.

The main Soviet objective before and during the 1973 war was to ensure that the region remained polarized. This required either stampeding Israel into a preemptive attack on Egypt, which would make Sadat's goal of a limited victory over Israel impossible, or prodding Washington into a premature display of full support for Israel, which would ruin Washington's credibility as an honest broker. Moscow tried to provoke Israeli preemption by circulating warnings in the communist press that an attack was imminent and by evacuating Soviet civilians from Egypt and Syria. These gambits failed, not least because the U.S. sternly warned Israel not to preempt.

Once the war began in October 1973, the Soviets sought a cease-fire at the point of maximum Arab gain—when Egypt had taken the east bank of the canal and Syria had taken the Golan Heights—but this effort failed. Israel quickly counterattacked the Syrians, and Moscow asked Egypt to advance in order to divert Israeli attention. The Soviets also began resupplying Syria and Egypt by air and sea and alerted their airborne divisions for deployment to Damascus. Israel, however, stopped short of Damascus and shifted its forces south to inflict a catastrophic defeat on the Egyptians, who had advanced into the Sinai beyond their air-defense umbrella. Israeli forces then crossed the Suez Canal and threatened to destroy Egyptian forces trapped on the east bank. The UN Security Council called for a cease-fire on October 22, 1973, but

Israel disregarded this and continued encircling the Egyptians. The Soviets proposed sending joint U.S.-Soviet military contingents to enforce the cease-fire and threatened to act unilaterally if the United States refused. To emphasize their determination, the Soviets made further preparations to deploy airborne forces, and Soviet troops in Egypt fired two Scud ballistic missiles into Israel. At this point there was a real prospect of renewed fighting and the commitment to nuclear weapons. Washington raised its military alert level, informed Moscow of its willingness to cooperate in maintaining a cease-fire (although not with U.S. troops), asked Sadat to withdraw his request for superpower military intervention (which he did), and demanded that Israel cease operations (which, under extreme duress, it eventually did).

The 1973 war yielded only one positive result for Moscow: the opening of the Suez Canal. Otherwise, the outcome was profoundly negative. Washington reestablished ties with Egypt and excluded Moscow from any substantive role in the Egyptian-Israeli peace process. Moscow's only recourse was to strengthen ties with Syria and to forge a relationship with Libya, which bought $20 billion in Soviet arms from 1974 to 1985.

In 1969 Mohamed Siad Barre seized power in Somalia and proclaimed it a socialist state. Somalia bought Soviet arms and gave the Soviets access to ports on the Indian Ocean and the Gulf of Aden. In 1975 the Ethiopian military seized power and embraced socialism. Two years later Haile Mengistu, the new Ethiopian leader, obtained substantial Soviet military aid. Barre wished to control Ethiopia's ethnically Somalian province of Ogaden and feared that Soviet support for Mengistu would prevent this. Barre rejected Soviet efforts to mediate the Ogaden dispute and appealed to the Americans for military aid. The United States agreed in principle to provide defensive arms, and Barre, assuming that he had secured an alternate arms supplier, invaded Ethiopia in July 1977. In August the United States reversed itself and declined to provide arms to Somalia. Barre begged the Soviets to restore military support but was denied. The Soviets poured $1 billion in military aid into Ethiopia, including 600 tanks, thousands of advisers, and 15,000 Cuban combat troops. These forces drove the Somalians out of Ethiopia by March 1978. Somalia renounced its Treaty of Friendship and Cooperation with the Soviets, expelled Soviet personnel from Somalia, and became a U.S. client state.

After defeating Somalia, Ethiopia focused on suppressing its nationwide internal rebellion. Despite prodigious Soviet military aid worth more than $4 billion from 1978 to 1984, the Ethiopians never managed to crush the rebels. After 1985, reform-minded Soviet leader Mikhail Gorbachev dramatically reduced Soviet aid to Ethiopia, gradually withdrew Soviet advisers, and urged the Ethiopians to negotiate a settlement of their internal disputes.

In 1974 Iran began a determined effort to shift Afghanistan into its orbit. With Iranian assistance, Afghan president Mohammad Daoud Khan lessened his dependence on Moscow and attempted to suppress Afghan communists. To arrest this trend, in April 1978 Moscow approved a coup that killed Daoud and installed

Soviet troops on the Salang Highway during the Soviet Union's military withdrawal from Afghanistan in February 1989. The Soviet invasion and occupation of Afghanistan were contributing factors to the collapse of the Soviet Union in December 1991. (Getty Images)

Nur Muhammad Taraki as president. Afterward, the Soviet political and military presence in Afghanistan rapidly escalated.

In June 1978 a pro-Marxist coup in South Yemen reversed that country's history as a colony of the British. Energetic Soviet-sponsored action in Ethiopia, South Yemen, and Afghanistan in 1978 raised serious questions in the United States regarding the Soviet commitment to détente. Collectively, pro-Soviet regimes in these countries, together with Syria and Iraq, gave the Soviets tremendous potential leverage against the pro-American regimes in Saudi Arabia and Iran.

American efforts to guide Iran from autocracy to constitutional monarchy in the late 1970s completely failed. Opposition to Mohammad Reza Shah Pahlavi grew throughout the 1970s, and he abdicated in early 1979 in the face of revolution. The shah's departure with substantial assets infuriated Iranians, who asked the United States to refuse him entry. When he was permitted entry to the United States for medical care in October 1979, radical Iranian students took over the U.S. embassy in Tehran.

Major U.S. forces began assembling in the region, and the Soviets, perceiving a geopolitical opportunity, warned the Americans not to intervene militarily in Iran. The crisis in Iran coincided with an anticommunist revolt in Afghanistan that the Afghan government was unable to quell. After Hafizullah Amin assassinated

Taraki and became president of Afghanistan in September 1979, the Soviets decided on military action there. In December 1979, 80,000 Soviet troops invaded Afghanistan—and executed Amin—to suppress the revolt and deter a U.S. invasion of Iran, which the Soviets mistakenly believed was imminent.

The Soviet army originally intended to garrison key points and allow the Afghan army to fight the resistance but was soon drawn into combat itself. Soviet equipment and tactics designed for conventional opponents proved poorly suited to fighting guerrillas in rugged Afghan terrain. The indiscriminate use of firepower aroused the intense hatred of the Afghan people and created millions of refugees. With American, British, and Saudi support, Pakistan provided a sanctuary in which resistance fighters could train and launch attacks into Afghanistan. Equipping the resistance fighters with Stinger antiaircraft missiles in 1986 deprived the Soviets of the crucial advantage of low-altitude air support. Soviet general secretary Mikhail Gorbachev finally decided to abandon the debilitating occupation and withdrew Soviet troops in 1989. The Soviet-Afghanistan War cost 15,000 Soviet dead and 470,000 sick and wounded over a 10-year period. Moreover, it nearly bankrupted the Kremlin's already shaky treasury. Afterward, Afghanistan sank into civil war. From a larger perspective, the Soviet war in Afghanistan galvanized American leadership around a global anti-Soviet crusade. The Afghan debacle was in fact a major factor in the collapse of the Soviet Union.

Before 1979 Iraq was a long-standing Soviet military client, receiving 90 percent of its arms from Soviet sources, while Iran was a U.S.-armed client. The fall of the shah of Iran caused Iraq to improve relations with Saudi Arabia, Jordan, and the United States, while Iran strengthened its relations with Syria, Libya, and the Soviets. After Iraq invaded Iran in September 1980, the Soviets tried to manipulate the conflict to bring a pro-Soviet regime to power in Iran. The Soviets believed that Iran's war with Iraq, Iran's need for Soviet arms to fight that war, and the presence of Soviet troops in Afghanistan and American forces in the Persian Gulf would create irresistible pressure on Tehran to turn to Moscow to solve its problems and escape hostile encirclement.

Soviet strategy required time to come to fruition. Moreover, prolonged conflict would weaken Iran and, because Iran could not obtain Western arms, increase its dependence on the Soviet Union. Thus, the Soviets armed both sides to protract the fighting. Some regarded Iraq as an American puppet during the Iran-Iraq War. In fact, the Soviet bloc and its clients provided the vast majority of Iraq's tanks, armored personnel carriers, artillery, small arms, and combat aircraft. At the same time, Soviet clients—Syria, Libya, North Korea, Cuba, and Vietnam—supplied Iran with arms that played a critical role in blunting the initial Iraqi offensive and allowing Iran to counterattack. The Soviets backed Iranian communist resistance groups that three times attempted to overthrow the Khomeini regime, but each time the coups were brutally suppressed. Ultimately, Soviet strategy did not succeed. Only after the end of the Iran-Iraq War, the death of Khomeini, and the Soviet withdrawal from Afghanistan were the Iranians willing to accept a close relationship with Moscow (which persists to this day).

Syrian alignment with Iran in the 1980s created fear of a Syrian attack that Iraq, fully engaged against Iran, could not withstand. The Soviets did not intend to authorize such Syrian action, but Israel, with U.S. backing, moved to pin down the Syrians in any case. Soviet leaders witnessed the Iran-Iraq War in the 1980s and also Israel's powerful incursion into Lebanon in 1982. The minimum Soviet goal during the Israeli invasion of south Lebanon was to ensure that Israel did not totally destroy the Palestinians, or make advances into Syria, although the Soviets took no direct steps to support Syria or counter Israel in Lebanon itself. After the destruction of Syrian air defenses in 1982, the Soviets rebuilt them with the more modern SA-5 SAMs and provided additional modern weapons such as Su-24 and MiG-29 aircraft and T-72 tanks. The Soviet military presence in Syria peaked at 13,000 Soviet and East European advisers in 1984 and declined steadily after 1985.

The Soviets were on the defensive worldwide from 1985 to 1991. This stance was driven by serious internal economic dislocations, political uncertainty, the disastrous Soviet intervention and occupation of Afghanistan, and Soviet leader Mikhail Gorbachev's efforts to reform Soviet society and government (glasnost and perestroika). In the Middle East, the Soviets' willingness to provide unstinting

military largesse to their clients declined, and the Soviets sought to extract themselves from the Afghan quagmire. Diplomatically, the Soviets improved relations with Egypt, Israel, Saudi Arabia, and the Gulf States in the late 1980s and joined the UN consensus in condemning Iraq's invasion of Kuwait in August 1990.

Indeed, Soviet cooperation completely changed the character of the U.S. confrontation with Iraq during 1990–1991, which culminated in the 1991 Persian Gulf War. The Kremlin declined to aid—or even shield—its regional client as it had done during the Cold War. The Persian Gulf War would have in fact been unimaginable at the height of the U.S.-Soviet Cold War rivalry. The movement of major American forces from Germany to Saudi Arabia most certainly would not have been possible during the Cold War. The Soviets attempted to persuade Iraqi strongman Saddam Hussein to withdraw unscathed from Kuwait, but he obstinately refused a diplomatic solution. Thus, the Soviets did not block the use of force in January and February 1991. The Soviet collapse in December 1991 ended four decades of bipolar superpower competition in the Middle East and ushered in a less peaceful and far more unpredictable era in the region.

JAMES D. PERRY AND PAUL G. PIERPAOLI JR.

**See also**

Arab-Israeli Conflict, Overview; Baghdad Pact; DESERT STORM, Operation; Egypt; France, Middle East Policy; Iran; Iran-Iraq War; Iraq, History of, Pre-1990; Iraq, History of, 1990–Present; Israel; Russia, Middle East Policy, 1991–Present; Soviet-Afghanistan War; Suez Crisis; Syria; United Kingdom, Middle East Policy; United States, Middle East Policy, 1945–Present

**References**

Hiro, Dilip. *The Longest War: The Iran-Iraq Military Conflict.* London: Routledge, 1991.
Oren, Michael B. *Six Days of War: June 1967 and the Making of the Modern Middle East.* Novato, CA: Presidio, 2003.
Pollack, Kenneth M. *Arabs at War: Military Effectiveness, 1948–1991.* Lincoln: University of Nebraska Press, 2002.
Thornton, Richard. *The Carter Years.* New York: Paragon House, 1991.
———. *The Nixon-Kissinger Years.* New York: Paragon House, 1989.

## Space Shuttle Atlantis, Military Mission of
### Event Date: 1991

On November 24, 1991, at 6:44 p.m., the U.S. space shuttle Atlantis (OV-104) was launched from Kennedy Space Center, Florida, on Mission STS 44, intended to deploy a U.S. Air Force (USAF) Defense Support Program (DSP) satellite. The satellite was designed to use infrared sensors to detect Earth-based missile launchings, nuclear detonations, and space launches.

The Atlantis crew consisted of mission commander USAF colonel Frederick D. Gregory, USAF pilot Colonel Terence T. Henricks, mission specialist Dr. Story Musgrave, mission specialist Navy Commander Mario Runco Jr., mission specialist Army Lieutenant Colonel James S. Voss, and payload specialist Army Chief Warrant

The launch of space shuttle Atlantis on November 24, 1991, to deploy a Defense Support Program satellite. (NASA)

Officer Thomas J. Hennen. This was the Atlantis's tenth trip into orbital space for the Department of Defense.

The Department of Defense issued the mission execution order (91–7) on October 11, 1991, and the National Aeronautics and Space Administration (NASA) scheduled the launch for November 19, 1991. A problem with the satellite's inertial upper-stage booster delayed the mission for five days, however, while the inertial measurement unit was replaced and tested. The Atlantis successfully launched on November 24, and the crew completed its primary objective of deploying the DSP satellite approximately 6 hours and 18 minutes into the flight.

The DSP satellite was 33 feet long and weighed 5,200 pounds. Its powerful telescope and infrared sensors provided early warning detection and tracking of surface-to-air missiles. Similar satellites played a vital role in the 1991 Persian Gulf War by tracking Iraqi Scud missiles and allowing Patriot missile interceptors extra time to engage them.

In addition to deploying the DSP satellite, the crew completed a number of secondary objectives. An Interim Operational Contamination Monitor (IOCM) measured contamination in the cargo bay during launch. A Terra Scout experiment conducted by Hennen

used the Spaceborne Direct-View Optical System, a telescopic device, to test the ability of a shuttle to serve as an observation station for viewing various sites on Earth. Hennen viewed a number of sites where the USAF had placed large panels in different grid patterns to determine how well observations could be made from space. The Military Man in Space (M88–1) experiment evaluated the ability of a military observer to track troop and equipment movements from space. Another experiment utilized the Shuttle Activation Monitor to measure the onboard radiation environment and its effects on gamma ray detectors. The Cosmic Radiation Effects and Activation Monitor (CREAM) gathered readings on onboard cosmic rays and radioactivity, while the Radiation Monitoring Equipment III (RME III) measured the crew's exposure to ionized radiation.

Two experiments used no onboard equipment; instead, other sites observed the shuttle. The Air Force Maui Optical System (AMOS) experiment used the USAF's electrical-optical system on the Hawaiian island of Maui to observe and evaluate Atlantis's jet firings, water dumps, and encounters with atomic oxygen. The other test involved an Ultraviolet Plume Instrument (UVPI), a sensor on another Department of Defense satellite, which observed Atlantis in order to fine-tune that sensor. In addition, the crew took part in several medical studies. Most of these tests evaluated the effects of prolonged exposure to a weightless environment on the human body and analyzed the effectiveness of various methods in counteracting those effects. One specific experiment used the Visual Function Tester-1 (VFT-1) to study changes that may occur to human vision due to weightlessness.

As a scheduled 10-day mission, STS 44 medical experiments were supposed to aid scientists in preparing for a 13-day mission scheduled for 1992. However, a malfunction in one of the orbiter's three inertial measurement units forced NASA to abort the final three days of the mission. Atlantis successfully landed at Edwards Air Force Base, California, on December 1, 1991, at 2:34 p.m., having completed all the major mission objectives.

Mission STS 44 was the first time that the Department of Defense publicly acknowledged sending a military payload into space on a shuttle mission. Once shrouded in the secrecy of the Cold War, the Pentagon had previously required that all military shuttle flights be subject to an information blackout in protection of national security. The first exception to this policy came in April 1991, when NASA launched a shuttle with a Pentagon experiment for its antimissile program, but the November 1991 launch of Atlantis marked the first time a military satellite was openly sent up through the shuttle program. Financial motivations sparked the policy change from secrecy to openness: the Pentagon saved approximately $80 million per year, money usually spent on spy-proofing military control rooms and test facilities used to develop Department of Defense missions.

This flight was the last military mission aboard a winged spaceship. In its place, the Department of Defense thereafter developed a fleet of unmanned space-launch vehicles to carry payloads into orbit.

By 1996 the Pentagon utilized Pegasus, Taurus, Delta II, Atlas II, and Titan II and IV rockets with Inertial Upper Stage and Centaur upper-stage boosters to deliver military payloads into space.

ADAM P. WILSON

**See also**

Patriot Missile System; Reconnaissance Satellites; Satellites, Use of by Coalition Forces

**References**

Broad, William J. "Shuttle Atlantis Is Launched with Military Satellite." *New York Times,* November 25 1991, 1A.

Cleary, Mark C. *The Cape: Military Space Operations, 1971–1992.* Patrick Air Force Base, FL: 45th Space Wing History Office, 1994.

Department of Defense. "Chapter 23: Space Forces." In *Department of Defense Annual Report, 1996.* Washington, DC: Department of Defense, 1996.

National Aeronautics and Space Administration (NASA). "Space Shuttle Mission STS-44 Press Kit." Washington, DC: NASA Public Affairs Office, November 1991.

---

# Spain, Role in Persian Gulf, Afghanistan, and Iraq Wars

Nation located in the Iberian Peninsula of southwestern Europe, officially known as the Kingdom of Spain. It is bordered by the Bay of Biscay to the north; by France and Andorra to the northeast; by the Balearic Sea to the east; by the Mediterranean Sea, Gibraltar, Straits of Gibraltar, and the Atlantic Ocean to the south; and by the Atlantic Ocean and Portugal to the west. Spain, with a land mass of 194,968 square miles, also controls the Balearic Islands, located about 50 miles off its eastern coast, and the Canary Islands, located about 70 miles off Morocco's western coast. Spain's current population is estimated at 40.41 million people.

In 1975, following the death of longtime dictator General Francisco Franco, Spain adopted a constitutional monarchy led by King Juan Carlos, who is still the Spanish king. Spain has a democratically elected parliament. The monarch is head of state but not of government, although he retains the right to recommend the head of government (prime minister), who is then approved by vote of the National Assembly.

In addition to army, navy, and air force, Spain's armed forces also include the Royal Guards, Civil Guards, Navy Marines, Army Airmobile Force, and the Spanish Legion. The latter three deployed select units to Afghanistan in 2002 and Iraq in 2003. Spain is also a member of the North Atlantic Treaty Organization (NATO) and Eurocorps. During the 1991 Persian Gulf War, Spain dispatched naval forces to assist with the international coalition's naval blockade of Iraq. Furthermore, U.S. military bases in Spain supported supply and logistics operations throughout the war.

Since 1991 Spain has been involved in various NATO and non-NATO operations, including operations in Bosnia Herzegovina (1995), Afghanistan, and Iraq. Most Spanish deployments have been limited in scope, however, with only one brigade sent to

A sailor aboard the Spanish frigate *Vencedora* (F-36) prepares to toss a line to members of a boarding party as they return to the ship in an inflatable boat after inspecting a merchant vessel. The *Vencedora* was one of the ships of the Maritime Interdiction Force (MIF) formed during Operation DESERT SHIELD in 1990 to enforce trade sanctions against Iraq. (U.S. Department of Defense)

Bosnia Herzegovina, and between 550 and 800 troops operating in Afghanistan since the end of 2001. Spain's troops in Afghanistan are incorporated within NATO's International Security Assistance Force–Afghanistan (ISAF), which was created in December 2001 and which coordinates military and military-related activities in Afghanistan. Approximately 750 Spanish troops, including members of the Spanish Legion's 3rd Tercio Juan De Austria, support NATO operations in Afghanistan. The majority of these forces are assigned to a forward support base in Herat, as part of NATO's Regional Command–West, and in Badghis.

As part of the War on Terror, Spain deployed limited naval and air assets to patrol the seas around the Horn of Africa and in the Indian Ocean after the September 11, 2001, terror attacks on the United States. Spanish prime minister José María Aznar and the Spanish government supported the Anglo-American decision to invade Iraq in 2003 to oust Iraqi dictator Saddam Hussein from power. Toward that end, between September 2003 and May 2004, Spain deployed to Iraq some 1,300 troops, including the Spanish

Legion's 3rd Tercio and 4th Tercio (also named Alejandro Farnesio). Spanish forces in Iraq joined with Honduran, Salvadoran, Nicaraguan, Dominican Republican, and Polish troops to form the Multinational Brigade Plus Ultra, which was responsible for military operations and reconstruction operations in Iraq's upper southern region.

On March 11, 2004, just prior to national elections in Spain, terrorist bombings of the Cercenia commuter train system in Madrid killed 191 people and wounded an additional 1,755. A group inspired by Al Qaeda and with connections to other jihadists, but without a direct connection to the group headed by bin Laden, carried out the attack. Three days later, Aznar's central-right Partido Popular (Popular Party) was defeated as a consequence, according to many in Spain, of its initial accusations that the Basque separatist group Euskadi Ta Askatasuna (Basque Homeland and Freedom, or ETA) had carried out the bombings. With Islamists established as the likely suspects, the left-of-center Spanish Socialist Workers' Party came to power. It had criticized Spanish involvement in Iraq. Within days, Spain's new prime minister, José Luis Rodriguez Zapatero, ordered the withdrawal of Spanish troops from Iraq by June 2004.

However, the terrorists did not solely aim to force a withdrawal from Iraq, for on April 2 they made another attempt to bomb a train. On April 3, seven of those involved blew themselves up when the police surrounded their apartment.

Following an investigation of the 11-M, or March 11 attacks, 21 persons were changed with murder, terrorism, or lesser offenses. Seven were found not guilty. Emilio Trashorras, Othman al-Gnaoui, and Jamal Zugam, the main conspirators, received sentences of nearly 40,000 years in prison. The March 11 attacks deeply affected the Spanish people and caused much concern over converts to Islam and the large Muslim immigrant presence in Spain.

The United States decried the precipitous Spanish military withdrawal from Iraq, claiming that it would embolden Al Qaeda and other terrorist groups. Zapatero, however, had campaigned on a promise to withdraw the troops, and he made good on that pledge. U.S.-Spanish relations were thereafter somewhat contentious and became an issue during the 2008 U.S. presidential campaign, when Republican candidate Senator John McCain said that, if elected president, he would not meet with Zapatero.

WYNDHAM WHYNOT

**See also**

Al Qaeda; Global War on Terror; International Security Assistance Force; IRAQI FREEDOM, Operation; North Atlantic Treaty Organization in Afghanistan

**References**

Carr, Raymond. *Modern Spain, 1875–1980.* New York: Oxford University Press 2002.

Gillespie, Richard, Fernando Rodrigo, and Jonathan Story, eds. *Spain, Dictatorship to Democracy.* New York: Routledge, 1995.

Williams, Phil. "In Cold Blood—The Madrid Bombings." *Perspectives on Terrorism* (June 2008): 19–24.

# Special Air Service, United Kingdom

Established in the summer of 1941 in Egypt, the Special Air Service (SAS) is the special forces regiment within the British Army. The regiment saw extensive action during the Persian Gulf War (1990–1991) as well as the wars in Afghanistan (2001–present) and the conflict in Iraq (2003–present).

The SAS consists of four squadrons: A, B, D, and G, as well as a number of smaller specialty units, such as operations Research, Demolitions, Parachute Section, Boat Section, and Army Air Corps Section. The SAS insignia is the winged sword, and its unit motto is "Who Dares Wins."

The SAS has its roots in the Long-Range Desert Group, a group of commandos who fought against Italian forces in North Africa during World War II. Lieutenant Colonel David Stirling, the regiment's founder, began his army career with the Scots Guards in 1939, and thereafter transferred to No. 8 Commando unit in the Middle East. Convinced that small, self-sufficient units of 4 or 5 men each could be more effective than groups of 200, Stirling established the SAS in July 1941. The regiment began with approximately 60 men and a few trucks. By the end of World War II, the force numbered more than 1,000 men.

After the war, the remnants of the SAS (known as the Artists Rifles) were reorganized. Between 1950 and 1966, the SAS carried out combat operations against communist guerrillas in Malaya, and against Indonesian forces and rebel guerrillas in Borneo. Additionally, SAS D-Squadron conducted operations in Jebel Akhdar, Oman, during 1958–1959, and in Aden during 1964–1967. Between 1970 and 1977, the SAS returned to Oman to fight guerrillas there who were attempting to overthrow the government. From the late 1960s, SAS elements also spent 25 years in Northern Ireland, supporting the British army and the Royal Ulster Constabulary (RUC) in their fight against the Provisional Irish Republican Army (PIRA).

In April 1980, back on home soil and under the glare of the world's media, the SAS took a mere 46 minutes to rescue 26 hostages from the Iranian embassy in London, during Operation NIMROD. In May 1982 the SAS carried out operations in the Falkland Islands against Argentine forces during the Falklands War.

In 1990, after the Iraqi invasion of Kuwait and formation of a military coalition spearheaded by the United States to drive out the Iraqis, some 700 men of the SAS (almost the entire regiment) were deployed to Iraq. General Sir Peter de la Billiére, the joint British commander-in-chief in the Persian Gulf, convinced U.S. general H. Norman Schwarzkopf, overall commander of coalition ground forces, to allow the SAS to operate in Iraqi territory. Dividing into separate fighting columns, with 30 SAS men assigned to each, A and D squadrons drove almost 250 miles behind enemy lines.

The SAS operations generally took place under cover of darkness and included missions to interrupt Iraqi communications. Tactics included blowing up underground fiber-optic cables, placing booby traps, and destroying communication towers. In addition to the disruption of Iraqi communication networks, the

SAS destroyed Scud missile launch sites through a series of coordinated attacks.

However, not all SAS missions in Iraq proved successful. Two missions were aborted, and an SAS team known as "Bravo Two Zero" found itself in considerable difficulty behind Iraqi lines. After being discovered by Iraqi forces and splitting into two groups, the team battled harsh weather conditions and hypothermia. Four men were lost in this mission.

After seeing further action in the Balkans and Sierra Leone between 1994 and 2000, SAS units deployed to Afghanistan in 2001 in the ongoing fight against the Taliban and Al Qaeda (Operation ENDURING FREEDOM). Tasked with training the anti-Taliban Northern Alliance, the SAS instructed men in standard British Army assault tactics. The SAS also conducted surveillance and ground assaults on Al Qaeda training camps. Allegedly, during one of these missions in the cave complexes at Tora Bora in late 2001, the SAS believed that it had located the hiding place of Al Qaeda leader Osama bin Laden. However, for political reasons, the SAS operatives withdrew until U.S. forces could arrive, and the chance to capture bin Laden was lost. In addition to their regular assignments, the SAS has undertaken humanitarian assignments in Afghanistan, including locating suitable sites for food aid drops.

In 2003 the SAS returned to Iraq to support the Anglo-American–led military coalition that toppled the Saddam Hussein regime. The SAS deployed units for several operations behind Iraqi lines before the main ground campaign began in March. SAS teams helped to pinpoint the whereabouts of Hussein, who was apprehended in December 2003, and to monitor oil fields. Select SAS units remain in Iraq, although the nature of their work remains, necessarily, guarded.

KIRSTY MONTGOMERY

**See also**

Al Qaeda; Bin Laden, Osama; DESERT STORM, Operation; ENDURING FREEDOM, Operation; Hussein, Saddam; IRAQI FREEDOM, Operation

**References**

Carew, Tom. *Jihad! The Secret War in Afghanistan.* Edinburgh and London: Mainstream Publishing, 2000.

Kemp, Anthony. *The SAS: The Savage Wars of Peace, 1947 to the Present.* London: John Murray, 1994.

McCrery, Nigel. *The Complete History of the SAS: The Full Story of the World's Most Feared Special Forces.* London: Carlton Books, 2003.

Ryan, Mike. *Secret Operations of the SAS.* Barnsley, South Yorkshire: Pen and Sword Books, 2003.

# Special Boat Service, United Kingdom

Established in the summer of 1941 during World War II in the Mediterranean Theater, the Special Boat Service (SBS) is the Royal Marines special forces unit of the British Royal Navy and is the sister unit of the Special Air Service (SAS) regiment of the British Army. The SBS specializes in operations at sea, along coastlines, on rivers, and on dry land. Based in Poole, Dorset, England, the

SBS witnessed extensive action during the 1991 Persian Gulf War, Operation ENDURING FREEDOM in Afghanistan (2001–present), and Operation IRAQI FREEDOM (2003–present).

The SBS consists of four squadrons: C, X, M, and Z, each containing around 60 men. The winged dagger is the insignia of the SBS regiment; the unit motto is "By Strength and Guile." The SBS, or Special Boat Section as it was first known, has its roots in the Long-Range Desert Group, a group of commandos that fought against Axis forces in North Africa during World War II. At first, the chain of command was informal, but by September 1941 the canoeists of the SBS came under the command of Lieutenant Colonel David Stirling, the founder of the Special Air Service (SAS).

In 1950, during the Korean War, the SBS teamed up with U.S. forces to carry out operations against North Korea, launching raids from submarines and warships along the Korean coast. During the Cold War, the renamed Special Boat Squadron played a vital role along the coastlines of Eastern bloc countries. From the late 1960s, the SBS and SAS spent 25 years in Northern Ireland, supporting the British Army and the Royal Ulster Constabulary (RUC) in their fight against the Provisional Irish Republican Army (PIRA). In May 1982 the SBS carried out operations in the Falkland Islands against Argentinean forces. In 1987 the SBS was renamed the Special Boat Service and came under the operational control of the United Kingdom Special Forces.

In 1990, after the Iraqi invasion of Kuwait, an international coalition led by the United States deployed to Iraq. It included some 700 men from the SAS and SBS. Before the war began, British general Sir Peter de la Billiére, the joint British commander in chief in the Persian Gulf, convinced overall commander of coalition forces, U.S. general H. Norman Schwarzkopf, to allow the SAS and SBS to operate in the Iraqi desert. While the SAS covered western Iraq, the SBS covered the east. Operations generally took place under cover of darkness and included missions to interrupt Iraqi communications. Assigned the task of locating and cutting communications cables, SBS employed such tactics as blowing up fiber-optic cables buried underground, placing booby traps, and destroying communication towers.

In the autumn of 2001 SBS units deployed to Afghanistan in the fight against the Taliban and Al Qaeda in Operation ENDURING FREEDOM, a fight that is ongoing. In November 2001 the entire SBS C Squadron was flown in to secure the Bagram air base. Tasked with training the anti-Taliban Northern Alliance, the SBS provided tactical advice. Furthermore, the SBS, along with the SAS, undertook surveillance and ground assaults on Al Qaeda training camps and the cave complexes of Tora Bora, believed to be the hiding place of Al Qaeda leader Osama bin Laden. Later, in 2006, the SBS took part in Operation MEDUSA, a North Atlantic Treaty Organization (NATO)–led operation against the Taliban.

In 2003 the SBS returned to Iraq as part of Operation IRAQI FREEDOM to support coalition efforts there. At the beginning of the conflict, the SBS operated with U.S. Navy SEALS to secure the beaches along the strategic Faw (Fao) peninsula. SBS commandoes also helped to secure Iraq's southern oil fields. The war in Iraq is ongoing, but the role of the SBS since 2003 has been relatively peripheral.

KIRSTY MONTGOMERY

**See also**

DESERT STORM, Operation; ENDURING FREEDOM, Operation; Faw Peninsula; IRAQI FREEDOM, Operation; Special Air Service, United Kingdom; United Kingdom, Navy, Persian Gulf War

**References**

Ladd, James D. *SBS: The Invisible Raiders: The History of the Special Boat Squadron from World War Two to the Present.* London: Arms and Armour, 1983.

Lodwick, John. *Raiders from the Sea: The Story of the Special Boat Service in WWII.* Annapolis: Naval Institute Press, 1990.

Parker, John. *SBS: The Inside Story of the Special Boat Service.* London: Headline, 1997.

Sutherland, David. *He Who Dares: Recollections of Service in the SAS, SBS and M15.* Annapolis: Naval Institute Press, 1999.

# Special Republican Guards

An elite military unit created in 1992 by Iraqi president Saddam Hussein to protect his regime and himself from revolt or assassination by other Iraqi military units. The Special Republican Guards (SRG) was composed of men from clans and towns (such as Tikrit) that were particularly loyal to Hussein. They were better paid and received more benefits than members of the regular army or the Republican Guards, and had the best military equipment at their disposal. After the fall of Hussein's government in April 2003, the SRG was believed to have been responsible for much of the violence of the Iraqi insurgency that followed.

During the 1991 Persian Gulf War, most of Hussein's elite Republican Guard units were decimated. Although those who survived remained loyal to Hussein and helped keep him in power, he apparently feared that some might turn on him. For that reason, in 1992 (some sources say 1995) Hussein created the SRG. From the very beginning, the SRG was intended to protect the regime from internal foes more than from external threat. To ensure loyalty, SRG members were recruited from Hussein's clan and those closely allied to it. The members were also required to be from Tikrit, Bayji, Sharqat, or other smaller towns in the region in which Hussein was born. Recruits were almost always Sunni Muslims, rather than Kurds or Shiites. By insisting on these membership criteria, Hussein was able to better ensure that the SRG would be loyal to him and his family, through ties of family, regional origin, and shared religion. In addition to better pay than their military compatriots, members of the SRG

Iraqi Republican Guard soldiers chant anti-American slogans as they parade outside a Baghdad hotel where members of the foreign media are staying, April 5, 2003. (AP/Wide World Photos)

received enlistment bonuses and subsidized housing, which were not offered to other units.

The SRG was the only armed force allowed to garrison Baghdad. Regular army troops were never stationed in the city, and Republican Guard divisions were stationed in the city's outer defenses. The SRG was not under the authority of the Defense Ministry but rather the State Special Security Apparatus, which was tightly controlled by Hussein himself. Indeed, the commander of the SRG was Qusay Hussein, the dictator's son.

The SRG was originally composed of one brigade, but later was expanded to five brigades with a total of 14 battalions of 1,300 to 1,500 men each. Four of the brigades were mechanized infantry, equipped with the best weapons available in Iraq. A fifth brigade was armored, equipped with T-72 main battle tanks. Antiaircraft weapons were also available, including handheld weapons and antiaircraft artillery. Because the SRG's purpose was to protect the regime, it had to be able to resist assaults by regular military units. At its peak, the SRG numbered about 26,000 men. By March 2003, however, its strength had declined to some 12,000 troops.

The SRG's duties included protecting Hussein's various presidential palaces and residences, along with his farms and other real estate holdings. It also guarded key installations in Baghdad. The 1st Brigade in particular was charged with presidential security. Various units drove and maintained the limousines used by Hussein, and they provided security for motorcades and members of the government and their families. One gruesome task assigned to the 1st Brigade was the apprehension and execution of military officers and government leaders accused of disloyalty to the regime. Other units are believed to have been charged with guarding sites that might have contained weapons of mass destruction (WMDs).

In 1998 a dispute between the Iraqi government and the United Nations (UN) arose when weapons inspectors wanted to examine SRG facilities believed to contain WMDs. Although the situation was resolved without violence, the episode convinced some intelligence experts that Hussein continued to work on forbidden weapons and used his most loyal units to keep prying eyes away.

During the March 2003 Anglo-American–led invasion of Iraq, many American military leaders believed that the SRG would be their most dangerous opponent. While the Republican Guard was largely destroyed outside of Baghdad, the SRG was first encountered in the fighting for Baghdad International Airport on April 4. In a three-hour engagement with troops of the U.S. 3rd Infantry Division, the SRG was soundly defeated. Three tanks were destroyed, and an estimated 250 SRG members were killed; American losses were 1 dead and 8 wounded. Following this battle, the SRG largely melted into the population. Fears that SRG members might fight house-to-house for Baghdad proved unfounded. On May 23, 2003, the provisional Iraqi government ordered the SRG dissolved.

SRG members are believed to have launched the insurgency against coalition forces in the Sunni triangle around Tikrit during the summer of 2003. Ironically, the Sons of Iraq and Anbar Awakening home guard militias that have been funded, trained, and equipped by the Americans beginning in 2007 contain cadres composed of former SRG members.

TIM J. WATTS

**See also**

Anbar Awakening; Baghdad; Baghdad, Battle for; Hussein, Qusay; Hussein, Saddam; Iraq, Army; Iraqi Insurgency; Republican Guard; T-72 Main Battle Tank

**References**

Carlisle, Rodney P. *Iraq War*. New York: Facts on File, 2005.

Keegan, John. *The Iraq War: The Military Offensive, from Victory in 21 Days to the Insurgent Aftermath*. New York: Vintage, 2005.

Woods, Kevin M., and Michael R. Pease. *The Iraqi Perspectives Report: Saddam's Senior Leadership on Operation Iraqi Freedom from the Official U.S. Joint Forces Command Report*. Annapolis, MD: Naval Institute Press, 2006.

---

# Speicher, Michael Scott

**Birth Date: July 12, 1957**
**Death Date: January 17, 1991**

U.S. Navy pilot and the first U.S. casualty of the Persian Gulf War in 1991. Born in Kansas City, Kansas, on July 12, 1957, Michael Scott Speicher moved with his family to Jacksonville, Florida, when he was 15. He graduated from Florida State University in 1980 with a bachelor's degree in business. His father had been a pilot during World War II, and Speicher decided to pursue the same course with the navy. He earned his pilot's wings and spent several years as a flight instructor with the McDonnell Douglas (now Boeing) F/A-18 Hornet. At the beginning of the Persian Gulf War, Lieutenant Commander Speicher was assigned to VFA-81 on the carrier *Saratoga*.

Speicher was flying an F/A-18 when he was shot down on the night of January 16–17, 1991, at the beginning of the Persian Gulf War. His aircraft went down in Anbar Province, some 100 miles west of the Iraqi capital of Baghdad in an area known as Wadi Thumayal. Although the Pentagon claimed at the time that his aircraft had been shot down by a surface-to-air missile (SAM), evidence points to it having been downed by an air-to-air missile from a Mikoyan-Gurevich MiG-25 Foxbat aircraft piloted by Iraqi lieutenant Zuhair Dawood.

Speicher was placed on missing-in-action (MIA) status, the only American serviceman to be so designated during the war. In May 1991 his status was changed to killed in action/body not recovered (KIA/BNR), and in 1992 Speicher's widow remarried.

In December 1992 a military official from Qatar discovered the wreckage of an aircraft in the desert, and this was subsequently identified as Speicher's F/A-18. U.S. spy satellite photography identified symbols in the desert that might have been made by Speicher as a sign that he had survived the crash. The Speicher case was taken up by the National Alliance of Families, which had been active during the Vietnam War in keeping the prisoner of war

(POW) and MIA issues alive. There was also frequent speculation about his fate in the press.

In 2001, therefore, the office of the Secretary of the Navy changed Speicher's status back to MIA, the first time the Defense Department had made such a change. At the same time, Speicher was routinely promoted, first to commander, and then in July 2002 to captain.

Following the U.S. invasion of Iraq in March 2003, Defense Department officials investigated the situation on the ground. At the same time, there was a report that Speicher's initials had been discovered on a prison-cell wall in Baghdad. On August 2, 2009, however, the Navy Department reported that Speicher's remains had been discovered near where he had been shot down and that these had been positively identified. An Iraqi had come forward, informed U.S. officials that Speicher had perished in the crash of his aircraft, and took them to where he had seen the remains being buried by Bedouins.

SPENCER C. TUCKER

**See also**

DESERT STORM, Operation, Coalition Air Campaign

**References**

Shaner, Thom. "U.S. Pilot's Remains Found in Iraq After 18 Years." *New York Times,* August 3, 2009.

Waters Yarsinke, Amy. *No One Left Behind: the Lieutenant Commander Michael Scott Speicher Story.* East Rutherford, NJ: New American Library, 2003.

---

## Standing Naval Force Atlantic

A multinational group of warships representing North American Treaty Organization (NATO) nations bordering the Atlantic Ocean, and a component of the NATO Response Force (NRF) that has been a part of counterterrorism activities since 2001. The core navies contributing to this squadron are those of Canada, the United States, the United Kingdom, Germany, and the Netherlands. The navies of Norway, Denmark, Belgium, Portugal, and Spain are also regular participants in the squadron, which usually comprises from 6 to 10 ships, generally cruisers, destroyers, and frigates, accompanied by a replenishment vessel. Since its inception in 1968 as the Standing Naval Force Atlantic (STANAVFORLANT), this permanent NATO maritime patrol group has provided a flexible response force in the Atlantic, and also has deployed beyond its primary venue when necessary.

As early as 1960, interest had been expressed within NATO in forming a dedicated antisubmarine warfare naval task force,

The Portuguese frigate *Alvares Cabral* moored alongside the Canadian frigate *Nipigon* during a port call, Port Everglades, 1993. Both ships were serving with the North Atlantic Treaty Organization's Standing Naval Force Atlantic. (U.S. Department of Defense)

which came into being in 1965 when the navies of Canada, the Netherlands, the United Kingdom, and the United States each supplied an escort vessel, such as a frigate or destroyer, for a five-month period of joint exercises known as MATCHMAKER I. With the continuing interoperational successes of MATCHMAKER II (1966) and MATCHMAKER III (1967), NATO resolved in December 1967 to establish and deploy STANAVFORLANT beginning in January 1968.

One of the chief advocates for developing STANAVFORLANT was U.S. admiral Richard G. Colbert, whose efforts on behalf of global maritime cooperation earned him the nickname "Mr. International Navy" from Chief of Naval Operations admiral Elmo Zumwalt. Colbert also had supported NATO's multilateral force concept, which would have placed nuclear ballistic missiles on disguised surface ships operated by multinational crews. While this plan was never realized, NATO's Mixed Manning Demonstration (1964–1965) nonetheless tested the feasibility of an international crew aboard one of the U.S. Navy's destroyers operating as a unit of its Atlantic and Mediterranean fleets. Despite that demonstration's overall success, NATO kept to the operational model of mixing ships from various nations in formulating STANAVFORLANT's fundamental characteristics. Each participating ship would be assigned to the force for up to six months, and command of the squadron would rotate on an annual basis among the represented navies. An aspect of Mixed Manning did become a feature of STANAVFORLANT operations: the "cross-polling" (cross-pollinating) exchange of some crew members between ships during exercises, a form of multinational cross-training that continues to enhance the squadron's NATO hallmarks of interoperability, cohesion, and international cooperation.

In addition to participating in NATO training exercises, undertaking humanitarian missions, and making goodwill port calls around the Atlantic, STANAVFORLANT in 1992 joined NATO's STANAVFORMED (Standing Naval Force Mediterranean) and WEU (Western European Union) escort vessels in patrolling the Adriatic Sea during the Kosovo/Yugoslavia conflict in what would become Operation SHARP GUARD. Shipping was monitored but not boarded, and to the extent possible under the prevailing restrictions, maritime aspects of United Nations (UN) Security Council resolutions were enforced. In May 1996 STANAVFORLANT returned primarily to its duties in the Atlantic, but in October 2001, after the September 11 attacks on the United States, the squadron again joined STANAVFORMED in the eastern Mediterranean to guard against and combat terrorism in NATO's Operation ACTIVE ENDEAVOR; the two forces continue to deploy alternately in this theater to ensure an evident and consistent NATO presence.

As of January 2005, the STANAVFORLANT acronym was replaced by SNMG1 (initially, Standing NATO Response Force Maritime Group 1, then simplified to Standing NATO Maritime Group 1). STANAVFORMED, similarly, became known as SNMG2. These changes reflected the more complete integration of the Immediate Reaction Forces (as STANAVFORLANT and STANAVFORMED had been designated) into the NRF structure.

NATO continues to employ both forces in demonstrating its solidarity in the Atlantic, the Mediterranean, and beyond. In 2007 SNMG1 undertook an extraordinary circumnavigation of Africa, and in 2008 the squadron ventured into the Black Sea for naval exercises with Romania and Bulgaria, while SNMG2 transited the Suez Canal for antipiracy duty off Somalia.

GORDON E. HOGG

**See also**

Counterterrorism Strategy; Cruisers, U.S.; Destroyers, Coalition; Destroyers, U.S.; Global War on Terror; North Atlantic Treaty Organization

**References**

Sadlowski, Manfred. *The Navies of NATO: 50 Years SACLANT in NATO.* Bonn, Germany: Monch Publishing Group, 2001.
Sokolsky, Joel J. *The Fraternity of the Blue Uniform: Admiral Richard G. Colbert, U.S. Navy, and Allied Naval Cooperation.* Newport, RI: U.S. Naval War College Press, 1991.
———. *Projecting Stability: NATO and Multilateral Naval Cooperation in the Post-Cold War Era.* Halifax, NS: Centre for Foreign Policy Studies, Dalhousie University, 1998.
Staley, Robert Stephens. *The Wave of the Future: The United Nations and Naval Peacekeeping.* Boulder, CO: Lynne Rienner, 1992.

## *Stark* Incident
### Event Date: May 17, 1987

Iraqi cruise-missile attack on the U.S. Navy Perry-class frigate *Stark* (FFG-31) on May 17, 1987, in the Persian Gulf. The attack occurred during the Iran-Iraq War (1980–1988), which saw Iraq and Iran attacking each other's ships and then routinely firing on cargo and tanker vessels in the Persian Gulf. The Iranians sought to attack ships belonging to Iraqi ally Kuwait, while the Iraqis sought to destroy Iranian tankers and prevent seaborne trade with Iran. More than 200 ships had been attacked since the beginning of the war. Fearing that such activity would disrupt oil supplies to the West, the Ronald Reagan administration dispatched U.S. Navy warships to escort the tankers in the Persian Gulf.

On the night of May 17, 1987, a French-made Iraqi Mirage F-1 fighter aircraft launched two AM-39 Exocet antiship cruise missiles (ASCMs) at a radar contact 36 nautical miles distant. Two minutes later, the missiles struck their target, which turned out to be the *Stark*. Although only one of the missiles detonated, the two severely crippled the frigate and killed 37 crew members and injured another 50.

The Iraqi Mirage involved had departed Iraq's Shaibah Air Base at 8:00 p.m. on a routine antishipping patrol. A U.S. Airborne Warning and Control System (AWACS) aircraft with a combined U.S.-Saudi crew detected the Mirage as it broke over the Persian Gulf 10 minutes later, flying at 5,000 feet and 550 knots. The *Stark* was informed via a tactical link system and itself detected the Mirage at 9:40 p.m., when it was 200 nautical miles distant from

The U.S. Navy guided-missile frigate *Stark* limps to port after being hit by two Iraqi-fired Exocet air-to-surface missiles. The ongoing hostilities between Iran and Iraq affected other nations in the Persian Gulf region, and the U.S. Navy provided a measure of stability and protection to international shipping there, although not without price. (Naval Historical Center)

the ship. The ship's crew considered it a routine night strike against Gulf shipping. No American warship had ever been attacked, and the crew of the *Stark* did not expect this raid to be any different.

Captain Glenn Brindel of the *Stark* was informed of the missile launches, but no special watch or combat conditions were in effect. At 10:09 p.m., the ship's crew warned the Iraqi aircraft that it was approaching an American warship. The Mirage was 12 nautical miles away at that time. What neither Captain Brindel nor his crew realized was that the Mirage had already launched its missiles. The AWACS crew noted that the Mirage made a breakaway maneuver at 10:10 p.m. and was heading for home. A few seconds later, one of the ship's lookouts detected the incoming missiles and notified the ship's Combat Information Center (CIC). By then, it was too late for the crew to take action.

Both of the radar-guided missiles, traveling at Mach 0.8, slammed into the ship's port side. One hit beneath the bridge and the other just aft of the first missile, almost in the superstructure's center. The single warhead detonation all but destroyed the ship's CIC, eliminating most of its combat systems and electronics, and one-third of its firefighting equipment. The crew fought fires throughout the night and ultimately saved the ship. They then took it to Bahrain under its own power.

The subsequent U.S. Navy investigation found several problems with the ship's design and several shortcomings in the ship's operating and training procedures. For example, the ship's electronic countermeasures system had a blind zone off the bow, and it had been facing the Iraqi fighter at the time of the Exocet launch. However, the failure to detect the incoming missiles was as much due to complacency as systems shortcomings. Two critical weapons stations were not manned during the incident, one of them because the assigned watch stander had departed his station to run personal errands. The ship's captain was not called to the CIC, nor kept constantly informed of the situation, until the final moments before the missile struck. More importantly, the ship's executive officer was present in the ship's CIC and neither noticed the empty weapons control stations nor took any action to increase the ship's combat readiness until the incoming missile had been detected.

The *Stark* incident illustrated the deadliness of antiship cruise missiles and proved the "win big or die" nature of modern sea combat. It also triggered political debate in Washington about the wisdom of operating U.S. warships in the Persian Gulf when Europe and Asia received a far greater proportion of their oil from that region than did the United States. However, the Ronald Reagan administration perceived that U.S. credibility was at stake and continued the naval patrols and tanker escorts in the Persian Gulf, soon to be dubbed Operation EARNEST WILL, which would endure until December 1989.

As for the *Stark,* the poststrike investigations forced Brindel's retirement and resulted in letters of reprimand for the executive officer and the tactical action officer on watch that evening as well as disciplinary proceedings against the individual who had departed his assigned watch station. U.S. Navy warships intensified their "quick reaction drills" and other combat readiness training for ships destined for Persian Gulf duty. Also, the Perry-class frigates received upgrades to their electronic warning and countermeasures systems to eliminate blind zones. The severity of the damage to the *Stark* precluded it from returning to service for more than 18 months, and it had to be dispatched onto a special heavy-lift ship and be taken back to a U.S. shipyard for extensive repairs.

CARL OTIS SCHUSTER

**See also**

EARNEST WILL, Operation; Iran-Iraq War; Missiles, Cruise; Persian Gulf

**References**

Cooper, Toni, and Farzad Bishop. *Iran-Iraq War in the Air: 1980–1988.* Atglen, PA: Schiffer Military History, 2000.
Karsh, Efraim. *The Iran-Iraq War, 1980–1988.* Oxford, UK: Osprey, 2002.
Levenson, Jeffrey L., and Randy L. Edwards. *Missile Inbound: The Attack on the Stark in the Persian Gulf.* Annapolis, MD: Naval Institute Press, 1997.
Wise, Harold L. *Inside the Danger Zone: The U.S. Military in the Persian Gulf, 1987–1988.* Annapolis, MD: Naval Institute Press, 2007.

# Starry, Donn Albert
## Birth Date: May 31, 1925

U.S. Army general and one of the most significant reformers of the army following Vietnam. Born on May 31, 1925, in New York City, Donn Albert Starry served as an enlisted soldier during World War II and entered the United States Military Academy, West Point, from the ranks. Graduating in 1948, he was commissioned a second lieutenant in armor. Reporting to Germany for his first assignment as a platoon leader, he served under battalion commander Creighton Abrams, a highly successful tank battalion commander in World War II. An innovative and dynamic military thinker, Abrams was a significant influence on Starry.

Starry served two tours in Vietnam during that war. During his second tour, he commanded the 11th Armored Cavalry Regiment as a colonel, leading it during the 1970 Cambodia incursion, Operation TOAN THANG 43. Following Vietnam, he commanded the Armor School at Fort Knox, Kentucky, as a major general. There

he wrote the influential monograph *Mounted Combat in Vietnam,* part of a series of official U.S. Army studies. He then commanded V Corps in Germany as a lieutenant general.

In 1977 he was promoted to full general and succeeded General William E. DePuy as the second commanding general of the Training and Doctrine Command (TRADOC). With the possible exception of DePuy, Starry was the most influential commander of TRADOC. Seizing upon the deep internal debate and controversy surrounding the 1976 edition of *FM 100-5 Operation* and DePuy's concept of active defense, Starry presided over and personally directed the development of AirLand Battle Doctrine and the long overdue recognition by the U.S. military of the operational level of war. Based heavily on classic German concepts of rapidly moving war fighting, AirLand Battle became the doctrine with which the U.S. Army fought both the 1991 Persian Gulf War and the 2003 Iraq War. While he was TRADOC commander, Starry also introduced the concept of sergeants' business, which became a critical tool in rebuilding the noncommissioned officer (NCO) corps that had been decimated by Vietnam.

Starry retired from the army in 1983. His last assignment was commanding general of the U.S. Army Readiness Command. He is one of a handful of key officers who rebuilt the U.S. Army in the decade following the Vietnam War into a genuine threat to the Soviet Army and the Warsaw Pact.

DAVID T. ZABECKI

**See also**

AirLand Battle Doctrine

**References**

Herbert, Paul H. *Deciding What Has to Be Done: General William E. DePuy and the 1976 Edition of FM 100-5.* Leavenworth Papers, Number 16. Leavenworth, KS: U.S. Army Combat Studies Institute, 1988.
Romjue, John L. *From Active Defense to AirLand Battle: The Development of Army Doctrine, 1973–1982.* Fort Monroe, VA: U.S. Army Training and Doctrine Command Historical Office, 1984.
Starry, Donn A. *Mounted Combat in Vietnam.* Washington, DC: Department of the Army, 1978.
Starry, Donn A., and George F. Hofmann, eds. *From Camp Colt to Desert Storm: The History of the U.S. Armored Forces.* Lexington: University Press of Kentucky, 1999.

# Status of Forces Agreement, U.S.-Iraqi

Bilateral agreement between the governments of the United States and Iraq that set the terms and conditions of the continued American troop presence in Iraq, formally approved by the Iraqi government on December 4, 2008. In early 2008, under pressure from domestic critics as well as the Iraqi government, Washington began negotiations to establish the Status of Forces Agreement, which would not only set the terms of the continued U.S. military presence in Iraq, but would also provide for a definitive exit strategy and a date for the withdrawal of American forces. The George W. Bush administration was especially concerned that an agreement be reached before a new administration took power in January 2009.

The negotiations surrounding the Status of Forces Agreement were fraught with difficulties. Of particular concern to the Nuri al-Maliki government was that early drafts of the proposal ceded too much authority to U.S. forces in Iraq, and that in general the agreement would impinge upon Iraqi sovereignty. Indeed, Maliki was under considerable pressure from various groups in his nation seeking to effect the immediate withdrawal of U.S. troops; other groups did not insist on such a drastic measure, but nevertheless voiced outrage that Washington was dictating terms to Baghdad and that draft proposals seemed to hamper Iraqi sovereignty. A key issue of contention was whether or not U.S. defense contractors would continue to enjoy immunity from prosecution in Iraqi courts for crimes committed against Iraqi citizens. Baghdad insisted that such a policy be abandoned, and Washington reluctantly agreed in the summer of 2008 out of fear that the agreement would not be reached in timely fashion.

In July 2008 the talks hit another snag when Iraq's grand ayatollah, Sayyid Ali Husayn al-Sistani, denounced the draft agreement, asserting that it trampled Iraq's sovereignty. Iraqi government officials, as well as the Iraqi parliament, also came to insist that the agreement contain a definitive date for U.S. troop withdrawal, something that the Bush administration was loath to accede to. By October, however, the two sides had moved closer to an agreement, and the draft proposal was circulated among parliament members and Iraqi government officials.

On November 16, 2008, the Iraqi cabinet approved the status agreement, which called for the withdrawal of U.S. troops from Iraqi cities by December 31, 2009, and the withdrawal of all troops from Iraq by December 31, 2011. On November 27 the Iraqi parliament ratified the agreement, but insisted that withdrawal of U.S. troops from Iraqi cities occur no later than June 30, 2009. The United States accepted the amendment. On December 4, the Iraqi Presidential Council approved the plan, making the agreement final.

The final agreement gave the Iraqi prime minister the ability to negotiate amendments to the agreement based upon the security situation in Iraq. It also forbade U.S. forces from holding Iraqi citizens without formal charges being made, and limited the use of search and seizures by American troops. Coalition forces were now subject to Iraqi law and legal proceedings when off duty and off base, and U.S. defense contractors guilty of committing crimes in Iraq were subject to prosecution in Iraqi courts. Finally, U.S. troops were to vacate all Iraqi cities by June 30, 2009, and were to leave the country entirely by December 31, 2011.

The agreement had many detractors in Iraq, however, who publicly demonstrated in opposition. The government promised to hold a national referendum on the agreement no later than June 20, 2009. Some Iraq experts expect the referendum vote to move up the final withdrawal date to as early as June 2010. The United States would be bound to heed the referendum should that come to pass.

PAUL G. PIERPAOLI JR.

**See also**

Iraq, History of, 1990–Present; Maliki, Nuri Muhammed Kamil Hasan al-; Sistani, Sayyid Ali Husayn al-

**References**

"Iraq, U.S. Reviewing Draft of Status-of-Forces Agreement." CNN .com/world, October 16, 2008, http://www.cnn.com/2008/WORLD/ meast/10/16/iraq.main/index.html.
Rubin, Allisa J. "Troop Pullout to Leave U.S. and Britain as Iraq Force." *New York Times,* December 6, 2008, A7.

# Stealth Technology

Low-observability (LO) technology, also known as stealth technology, utilizes various counterradar measures to minimize the radar cross section (RCS), the thermal and acoustic output, and the radio frequency emissions of a vehicle or aircraft with the goal of making it almost invisible to radar, sonar, and infrared detection.

Designers of LO aircraft and ships take into account the shaping of a ship or aircraft to scatter radar reflection, and they utilize radar-absorbent materials (RAM) to dissipate radar waves and mask radar signatures given off by inlets, exhausts, cockpits, antenna installations, propellers, rotors, and external stores of weapons and fuel in their attempt to decrease the vehicle's RCS. LO technology utilizes a multifaceted "diamond" shape to reduce corner reflections caused when vehicle components form right angles that reflect radar waves directly back to sensors.

One main concern for right angles comes from a plane's tail. Northrop Grumman solved this problem by using a "flying wing" design that completely eliminates the tail. The aircraft is also covered in RAM plates or paint made of carbonyl iron ferrite. The ferrite grains turn radar waves into an alternating magnetic field in the RAM, resulting in the transfer of radar's electromagnetic energy to heat, which then dissipates from the vehicle.

LO plane engines are built to fly at high subsonic speeds in order to avoid tracking by sonic boom and are built within the fuselage to reduce their profile to infrared radar. Additionally, some LO planes cool exhausts to reduce heat signatures. To thwart radio-frequency and electromagnetic tracking, designers use very low-powered computers and eliminate the plane's radar systems to ensure energy use is low enough to avoid detection.

The Lockheed F-117A Nighthawk, also known as the Stealth Fighter, was the first combat aircraft designed around LO technology. In the aftermath of 1970s combat experiences with potent Soviet radar-based air defense systems, the Defense Advanced Research Projects Agency (DARPA) investigated whether it was conceptually possible to develop an aircraft with a low enough RCS to defeat the radar-based defense systems. By 1975 Lockheed

A bow view of the experimental stealth ship *Sea Shadow* underway in San Francisco Bay, 1993. (U.S. Department of Defense)

and Northrop achieved breakthroughs in designing LO aircraft, and in April 1976 the U.S. Air Force (USAF) contracted Lockheed Advanced Development Projects, also known as "Skunk Works," to produce a test aircraft.

Lockheed's demonstrator aircraft was classified under the program name "Have Blue." By mid-1979, Have Blue test flights had proven that Lockheed's design concepts could produce a plane with low radar and infrared signatures that could meet USAF standards and maintain satisfactory flying capabilities. The first test flight of an F-117 came on June 18, 1981, over Nevada test ranges. Production began rapidly after the successful flight, and the first F-117A was delivered in 1982. The 4450th Tactical Group, currently the 49th Fighter Wing, Holloman Air Force Base, New Mexico, achieved operational capability in October 1983.

Although the plane first served in military missions during Operation JUST CAUSE in Panama in 1989, the Nighthawk gained prominence in 1991 during the Persian Gulf War. In the campaign, F-117As proved most valuable in strikes on downtown Baghdad, where it was the only aircraft able to avoid Iraqi surface-to-air missile (SAM) sites. On April 22, 2008, however, the USAF retired the F-117 in favor of the newly developed Lockheed Martin/Boeing F-22 Raptor and the Lockheed Martin/Northrop Grumman/BAE Systems F-35 Lightning II.

Northrop Grumman continued testing LO technology and in 1979 was contracted to produce a stealth bomber. The B-2 Spirit made its first flight on July 17, 1989, and saw first combat in Operation ALLIED FORCE over Kosovo in 1999. Designers of the B-2 contoured the plane into a "flying wing" that hides the bomb bays, engines, and cockpit with RAM and parallel alignment of its external lines to scatter radar waves. The plane's body covers the engine's turbine blades and fan to shield these highly reflective areas from radar. Furthermore, the plane pipes engine exhaust through a long tube covered with heat-absorbing materials to mask its heat signature and to avoid infrared detection. Assigned to the 509th Bomb Wing stationed at Whiteman Air Force Base, Missouri, after being declared fully operational in 2003, B-2s have seen service in three different campaigns.

The B-2 was designed as a long-range bomber and first-strike weapon to knock out important strategic targets, such as communications and radar facilities. The plane performed this role in Afghanistan in 2001 and Iraq in 2003. Designers originally manufactured the B-2 to deliver nuclear payloads in case of intercontinental ballistic missile (ICBM) attack. Most frequently, the B-2 has carried Joint Direct Attack Munitions (JDAMs), a guidance system that converts gravity bombs to guided smart bombs using Global Positioning System (GPS) receivers.

Stealth technology is also employed at sea. The U.S. Navy, DARPA, and Lockheed began the development of stealth ships in the 1980s. They completed construction of the IX-529 *Sea Shadow*, the first stealth ship, in 1985. The *Sea Shadow* takes advantage of the same diamond shaping used in the F-117 and B-2 to reduce its RCS. Additionally, designers utilized a unique double pontoon hull to reduce sonar and infrared detection, along with diminishing the right angles that form and produce radar signatures when the hull enters the water. Known as the small water plane area twin hull (SWATH) configuration, the *Sea Shadow*'s main deck is supported by two thin struts that connect two submerged pontoons. The A-frame shape provides superb stability in rough waters and supplements the ship's stealth.

The *Sea Shadow* was built to test LO technology on ships and has no military capabilities. In April 1993 the navy declassified the *Sea Shadow* and revealed it to the public. After a year of daylight testing, they placed the ship in lay-up status at its home port in San Diego, California, where it stayed for five years until the navy reactivated it in 1999. After reactivation, the *Sea Shadow* participated in tests of new LO technology to be used in the Zumwalt-class destroyer, which the U.S. Navy hopes to commission beginning in 2015.

Presently, the United States, Germany, France, Britain, Sweden, the Netherlands, Norway, Finland, India, and Singapore are utilizing LO technology in military vessels. The U.S. Navy's Zumwalt-class destroyer is planned to utilize a tumblesome wave-piercing hull designed by Northrop Grumman. Designers claim that the hull optimizes the speed and maneuverability of the ship while maintaining the stability of traditional hulls. Additionally, the tumblesome hull uses low angles to reduce the destroyer's RCS and minimizes infrared signatures. The Zumwalt-class is also to employ stealth with an advanced induction motor, an all-electric motor that quiets engine noise. The navy intends the Zumwalt-class destroyer to take on multiple roles of undersea warfare, ship-to-ship combat, antiaircraft support, and long-range surface attacks. Stealth significantly impacts these plans because LO technology would allow the destroyers to avoid detection and to prevent weapons from locking on the ship, greatly increasing its survivability and capabilities as a first-strike weapon.

ADAM P. WILSON

**See also**

B-2 Spirit; Joint Direct Attack Munition and Small Diameter Bomb; Navigation Satellite Timing and Ranging Global Positioning System; United States Air Force, Afghanistan War; United States Air Force, Iraq War; United States Air Force, Persian Gulf War

**References**

Aranstein, David C., and Albert C. Piccirillo. *Have Blue and the F-117A: Evolution of the "Stealth Fighter."* Reston VA: American Institute of Aeronautics and Astronautics, 1997.
Basmadjian, E. E. *The B-2 Spirit.* New York: Rosen, 2003.
Cavas, Christopher P. "Alternatives Suggested for the Next U.S. Cruiser: Navy Prefers Zumwalt-based Ship Design." *Defense News* 22(1) (January 1, 2007): 2–4.

# STEEL CURTAIN, Operation
Start Date: November 5, 2005
End Date: November 22, 2005

A major anti-insurgent operation mounted by U.S. Marines and Iraqi forces during November 5–22, 2005, as part of the broader al-Sayyad operation that aimed to control the resistance in the Euphrates River Valley, deal with Anbar Province, and also establish control by the Iraqi Army in the Al Qaim region. Operation STEEL CURTAIN (also known as Al Hajip Elfulathi) was significant in that it was the first military operation to include significant numbers of Iraqi Army personnel recruited and trained by the coalition government for Iraq. For the first time, Iraqi soldiers took the lead in some of the house-to-house searches and extensively patrolled in insurgent areas. The U.S. command considered the operation to be a success, although it was costly in terms of civilian casualties and the creation of strong tensions.

After the fall of President Saddam Hussein's regime in April 2003, many U.S. leaders considered the war in Iraq to be over. This proved not to be the case when a major insurgency broke out that summer and intensified over the succeeding months. Some of the resistance came from Islamist groups, others did not, but all wanted American troops out of Iraq. The resistance was particularly active in Anbar Province in western Iraq, adjoining the Syrian border, but was not restricted to this area. The Anbar region is dominated by tribes, and the Sunni tribes expected nothing but violence and a diminution of their role in Iraq under a government dominated by Shia groups. This area had also long been used by smugglers. Consisting mostly of rough desert terrain, the province held many routes for men, arms, and supplies to flow from Syria to desert camps and urban locations inside Iraq. Major urban centers included Husaybah, Karabilah, and Ubaydi. Ubaydi in particular was considered a key location for insurgents and was heavily fortified. Indeed the earlier Operation MATADOR in May 2005 had been an attempt to secure Ubaydi. Although coalition forces took the city, they failed to garrison it, and insurgents quickly resumed control over the city.

Most observers believed that coalition success in Iraq would depend upon whether or not a viable Iraqi military could be established. When Hussein was forced from power, the United States took what many now consider to be the unwise course of completely disbanding the Iraqi military as part of the attempt to rid the country of Baathist influences. This decision left a power vacuum that coalition forces could not fill, and it forced the building of a new Iraqi army from scratch. The process was slow and difficult, and Operation STEEL CURTAIN appeared to be an opportunity to speed along the process.

In June 2005 U.S. forces launched Operation SPEAR, an effort to oust insurgents from Anbar Province. In that operation, only 100 Iraqi soldiers participated. By November 2005, however, the number of Iraqi soldiers nationwide had increased dramatically. Special efforts had also been made to recruit and station new units in

A U.S. Marine Corps AH-1W Super Cobra helicopter is prepared for a nighttime takeoff from Forward Operation Base Al Qaim to provide close-air support for coalition forces in Operation STEEL CURTAIN during Operation IRAQI FREEDOM in November 2005. (U.S. Department of Defense)

and around Anbar. Two Iraqi division headquarters were formed, along with four brigade headquarters. Ten infantry battalions were recruited and deployed to Anbar. A total of 15,000 Iraqi soldiers were stationed in the province by November 2005, with 1,000 deployed to help the American troops in Operation STEEL CURTAIN.

The most hopeful sign for the coalition was that some of the new troops were locally recruited. A number were assigned to specially trained Scout Platoons, also known as Desert Protectors. Comparisons were made between the Scout Platoons and Native Americans recruited by the U.S. Cavalry during the 19th-century Native American wars in the American West. Like the Native American units, the Scout Platoons were familiar with the territory in which STEEL CURTAIN took place. They served as a liaison between American units and local tribal leaders, and the Scouts also provided information about which individuals belonged in the area and which individuals might be foreign fighters. American military leaders also viewed the increased number of recruits as a sign that the local population was increasingly unhappy with the foreign fighters, especially members of Al Qaeda.

In July 2005 coalition forces launched Operation HUNTER, which was intended to sweep through the Euphrates River Valley. Coalition planners recognized that in the western provinces most of the insurgents in 2005 were Al Qaeda operatives. The goal

of Operation HUNTER had been to force the insurgents out of the region and cut off the supply lines that funneled fresh resources and men into Iraq and permitted operatives to escape to camps in Syria and beyond. Unlike earlier anti-insurgent campaigns, Operation HUNTER was also expected to establish a permanent Iraqi army presence in the area.

American operational forces for STEEL CURTAIN included marines from the 3rd Battalion, 6th Marine Regiment, and the 2nd Battalion, 1st Marine Regiment. Both were part of the 2nd Marine Division. The marines were reinforced with supporting units and specialists, including forward air controllers, to total approximately 2,500 men.

STEEL CURTAIN began on November 5 with an assault on Husaybah. It took coalition forces four days to clear the city. Many of the insurgents that were forced from Husaybah fled to Karabilah. Another four days were needed to secure Karabilah. The final phase of the operation was to secure Ubaydi. Fighting in this center of Al Qaeda operations was difficult and more protracted, involving house-to-house combat. After seven days, coalition commanders declared the city secure.

From the Iraqi perspective, the operation resulted in hundreds of civilian casualties and destroyed much of Husaybah, including government buildings, schools, and two mosques. Citizens were also very angry and upset because they were not allowed to reclaim their dead.

Operation STEEL CURTAIN officially ended on November 22. Iraqi soldiers were praised for their participation in the operation, especially their work inside the cities. Unlike earlier operations, the coalition forces established forward operating bases in the region as they cleared out the Al Qaeda insurgents. The goal was to establish an ongoing presence that would prevent the return of Al Qaeda.

Coalition losses were relatively light. Ten marines were killed and 30 others were wounded. Losses among the Iraqi troops are unknown. Coalition spokesmen claimed that 139 insurgents were killed and another 256 captured.

Coalition commanders were pleased that five Al Qaeda leaders were killed in the air strikes on Husaybah. Although planners had hoped to capture or kill Jordanian-born Al Qaeda associate Abu Musab al-Zarqawi, he was not among the casualties. He was later killed in an American air strike in June 2006.

Coalition leaders considered the operation a success and held that the new Iraqi Army could now aid in operations against insurgents. Only three weeks after the conclusion of STEEL CURTAIN, the Iraqi provisional government held the first democratic election in years on December 15. A permanent legislative body was elected. Although many in the Al Qaim region and Anbar region refused to vote, the reduction in the harassment and intimidation of voters was considered an important goal of Operation STEEL CURTAIN and similar military operations.

TIM J. WATTS

**See also**

Al Qaeda in Iraq; Iraqi Insurgency; United States Marine Corps, Iraq War

**References**

Benhoff, David A., and Anthony C. Zinni. *Among the People: U.S. Marines in Iraq*. Quantico, VA: Marine Corps University, 2008.

Navarro, Eric. *God Willing: My Wild Ride with the New Iraqi Army*. Washington, DC: Potomac Books, 2008.

West, Bing. *The Strongest Tribe: War, Politics, and the Endgame in Iraq*. New York: Random House, 2008.

# Stryker Brigades

Rapidly deployable, multioperational, highly mobile infantry brigade combat teams. As part of broader Defense Department reform and realignment efforts, the U.S. Army spent much of the 1990s planning a new force structure for the early 21st century. The transformed army would boast new equipment to take advantage of what some saw as a revolution in military affairs. Its units would be more flexible, deployable, and sustainable than those of the Cold War, but every bit as lethal. The Stryker Brigades emerged as a deliberate intermediate step between the Cold War army and this new, objective force.

On October 12, 1999, General Eric K. Shinseki, the U.S. Army's newly appointed chief of staff, delivered the traditional keynote speech to the annual meeting of the Association of the United States Army. In that speech, General Shinseki announced his intent to begin implementing the long-studied reforms. He established many specific goals, including reducing the army's logistics requirements, shrinking the size of support forces, and replacing existing armored vehicles with smaller, lighter counterparts. Army units would adopt a standard modular structure capable of rapid deployment. Most significantly, Shinseki called for the creation of a prototype unit within the next year.

That unit would use readily available equipment to begin moving toward the eventual objective force. It would both validate that future force's design theory and begin providing the army with experience in new operating concepts. By design, the brigade would form both an intermediate step between the existing light and heavy combat brigades and an interim force between the existing and future units. It would be able to deploy almost as quickly as lighter infantry units, but have combat power approaching that of heavier armored units. By using a standard vehicle chassis, state-of-the-art electronics, and a number of other innovations, the new formation would require fewer personnel and supplies.

The 3rd Brigade of the 2nd Infantry Division was selected as the first of seven brigades to adopt the new design. After evaluating 35 U.S. and foreign vehicles, the army settled on a Canadian Light Armored Vehicle as the new unit's mount. In February 2002 this vehicle, modified for the army's needs into several different variations, was officially named to honor two infantrymen with the same last name who had been awarded the Medal of Honor. The Stryker, with eight wheels, became the symbol of the new units, subsequently designated as Stryker Brigade Combat Teams.

The prototype unit technically existed within a year of Shinseki's speech. But it required substantially more time to acquire hundreds of new types of equipment and reconsider the way army brigades traditionally fought. At 19 tons, the basic Stryker infantry carrier provided a medium-weight platform that could be adopted to meet nearly all of the brigade's vehicle needs. The Stryker family included a mortar carrier, a mobile gun system, and reconnaissance, command, fire support, engineering, ambulance, and anti-tank variations. The vehicles and the troops they carried shared information through a sophisticated electronic network. Through experiments, tests, and training the Stryker Brigades learned how to make the most of their new capabilities.

After September 11, 2001, many viewed the new type of brigade as a critical component of the War on Terror. Its new equipment, organization, and techniques theoretically allowed the Stryker Brigade to shoot, move, and communicate with unprecedented ease and coordination. That theory was soon to be tested in combat.

On December 3, 2003, with the beginning of the Iraq War, the first Stryker Brigade crossed the Kuwaiti border bound for the Iraqi city of Mosul. Rapidly changing conditions forced a change in plans while it moved north, and the unit drove into the city of Samarra instead. The brigade's ability to alter plans on the march without pause proved to be but one of its chief assets.

In the course of its initial deployment, the first Stryker Brigade met and exceeded the army's expectations. The medium-weight force proved ideal for a number of missions. With its modern information systems and modular structure, the brigade's subordinate units could be rapidly reconfigured as need arose. Special training and equipment provided for its individual soldiers increased the effectiveness of even the smallest units. The Stryker vehicle itself also offered unexpected advantages in Iraq. While it proved as fast and easy to support as had been hoped, its silence in comparison to tracked vehicles provided a valuable advantage in urban settings. Following the success of the 3rd Brigade, 2nd Infantry Division, additional units completed their conversions into Stryker Brigades and deployed to Iraq.

This did not stop criticism of the Stryker vehicle and the units that used it, however. Many observers, familiar with tactics designed for heavier armored vehicles, have criticized the Stryker's comparative lack of armor and use of wheels rather than tracks. Others have complained about the vehicle's high center of gravity, a deliberate choice to protect its passengers from roadside mines.

Despite such criticisms, the performance of the Stryker Brigades in combat has fulfilled General Shinseki's intent. The new units proved more flexible, deployable, and sustainable than previous designs without sacrificing lethality. Also, techniques and equipment developed for the new brigades quickly found their way into other units. Along the way, the Stryker Brigades and their signature vehicle became an icon of American forces in Iraq since 2003.

JEFFERY A. CHARLSTON

**See also**

United States Department of Defense, Military Reform, Realignment, and Transformation

**References**

Gonzales, Daniel. *Network-Centric Operations Case Study: The Stryker Brigade Combat Team.* Santa Monica, CA: RAND Corporation, 2005.

Peltz, Eric. *Speed and Power: Toward and Expeditionary Army.* Santa Monica, CA: RAND Corporation, 2003.

Reardon, Mark, and Jeffery Charlston. *From Transformation to Combat: The First Stryker Brigade at War.* Washington, DC: Center of Military History, 2007.

# Submarines

Although the Middle East wars have involved neither major naval engagements nor significant antishipping campaigns as did the two world wars, changing technology enables submarines to play an important if nontraditional role in these conflicts. The shallow waters of the Persian Gulf limit the operations of large oceangoing submarines there. However, the advent of submarine-launched cruise missiles gives submarines the capacity to strike targets far inland from the deep ocean areas where they can operate freely.

U.S. Navy submarines launched more than 20 percent of the cruise missiles used against Iraq in the two wars the United States has fought with that country, and they launched the majority of the cruise missiles fired in retaliation for terrorist attacks against the United States between 1992 and 2001. Moreover, the United States and Britain also employed submarines to monitor international shipping in support of United Nations (UN)–mandated sanctions imposed on Iraq before Operation DESERT STORM. Given the enduring tensions between the United States and Iran and their respective submarine fleets, albeit of disparate size and capability, submarines may play an even greater role in any future Middle East wars, particularly since Iran has received or is developing land-attack cruise missiles for its submarines.

Although the primary Western countries involved in the Middle East, the United States and Britain, prefer nuclear-powered submarines, the nature of the Middle Eastern nations' naval-operating areas and the limited size of their defense budgets have driven them to opt for the cheaper and much shorter-ranged diesel-electric models. In fact, prior to the late 1990s they were limited to operating secondhand obsolescent submarines. Since that time, they have acquired increasingly modern top-of-the line, conventionally powered submarines.

With its ports lying up a waterway shared with Iran, Iraq had no submarines for many years. However, its neighbor Iran acquired three Soviet-built Kilo-class diesel submarines in the 1980s and began to build an indigenous class of small shallow-water submarines by the late 1990s. The Kilo-class displaces more than 3,900 tons submerged and has a top underwater speed of 17 knots. The Kilos are armed with 6 21-inch torpedo tubes and 1 surface-to-air missile (SAM) launcher. The first of the Iranian-built Gadir- or Qadir-class boats appeared in 1998. Their precise characteristics are unknown, but most analysts estimate that they displace approximately 200 tons submerged, carry 2 21-inch torpedoes or 4 mines, and are manned by a crew of approximately eight men. Their diesel-electric drive is believed to provide a maximum submerged speed of about 10 knots on batteries and 6–8 knots when snorkeling. Underwater endurance is believed to be approximately 12 hours at 3–5 knots on batteries.

The American Los Angeles–class nuclear-powered attack submarine constitutes the backbone of the American submarine force employed in its Middle Eastern wars. Displacing more than 7,000 tons submerged and having almost unlimited endurance and a top speed of more than 25 knots, the Los Angeles–class boats are regarded as the world's best open-ocean fighting platforms. Their 142-man crews are highly trained, and the submarine's acoustic and electronic sensors enable it to track ships covertly from as far as 50 nautical miles distant. They are also equipped with the extensive command and control systems necessary to communicate with the fleet and forces ashore. These submarines carry 12 Tomahawk Land Attack Missiles (TLAMs) in vertical launch tubes, giving them a significant power-projection capability. However, these submarines' large size, compared to conventional submarines, puts them at a disadvantage in the Persian Gulf's shallow waters and high-density shipping lanes.

The U.S. Navy submarine *Los Angeles* (SSN-688), lead submarine of the Los Angeles class of attack submarines, underway off Oahu, Hawaii. (U.S. Department of Defense)

In fact, two American attack submarines were damaged there between 2003 and 2006 when the venture effect of the ultra-large crude carriers (ULCCs) plying these waters and passing overhead sucked them up into the tankers' bottoms, crunching the submarines' sails.

Although they did not participate in combat operations against Iraq, British submarines were involved in sanctions-enforcement operations. The newest British submarines are the Trafalgar class, of which seven units were in service during Operation DESERT STORM. Slightly smaller than the Los Angeles class at just 5,000 tons submerged, they carry the same sensor load, only with British-built systems. They employ a pump-jet rather than a seven-bladed propeller for propulsion, giving the submarine greater maneuverability and a higher top speed (30 knots). However, the Trafalgar-class lacks the TLAMs and extensive command and control systems found on the U.S. submarines, hence their more limited employment. They have conducted sea control missions in the Atlantic Ocean and Mediterranean Sea.

The Iranian submarines represent the best of the conventionally powered submarine designs in service among Middle Eastern nations, although Egyptian efforts to acquire French- and German-built submarines with air-independent propulsion systems may change that. Once considered obsolete by many American defense analysts, modern diesel submarines are now recognized as a serious threat in constricted waters, such as the Strait of Hormuz and the waters around the Middle East's potential conflict zones. Moreover, modern diesels are quieter when operating on their batteries than are nuclear submarines, and they can remain submerged on their batteries for up to 15 days with the latest air-independent-propulsion systems. Nonetheless, prior to the introduction of submarine-launched land-attack missiles in 1991, submarines traditionally have had their greatest impact in wars that last long enough for attacks on an enemy's fleet and shipping to have a strategic impact on the fighting ashore. Although that has not been the case in the Middle East wars of the last 50 years, Iran's Kilo-class submarines provide Tehran with the capacity to seriously disrupt if not decimate oil shipments coming out of the Persian Gulf.

Carl Otis Schuster

**See also**

Arms Sales, International; Iran, Armed Forces; Israel, Armed Forces; Mines, Sea, Clearing Operations, Persian Gulf and Iraq Wars; Mines, Sea, and Naval Mine Warfare, Persian Gulf and Iraq Wars; Missiles, Cruise; United States Navy, Iraq War; United States Navy, Persian Gulf War

**References**

Finlan, Alastair. *The Gulf War, 1991.* Oxford, UK: Osprey, 2004.

Frieden, David R. *Principles of Naval Weapons Systems.* Annapolis, MD: Naval Institute Press, 1985.

Friedman, Norman. *Ships and Aircraft of the U.S. Fleet.* Annapolis, MD: Naval Institute Press, 1992.

Hooten, Ted. *Jane's Naval Weapons Systems, 2001–2002.* London: Jane's Information Group, 2002.

Katzman, Kenneth. *Iran: U.S. Policy and Options.* Washington, DC: Library of Congress, 2000.

Olsen, John. *Strategic Air Power in Desert Storm.* London: Frank Cass, 2003.

Revelle, Daniel J., and Lora Lumpe. "Third World Submarines." *Scientific American* (August 1994): 16–21.

Sharpe, Richard, ed. *Jane's Fighting Ships: 1991–1992.* London: Jane's Information Group, 1991.

Tripp, Robert. *Lessons Learned from Operation Enduring Freedom.* Santa Monica, CA: RAND Corporation, 2004.

# Sudan

Largest country in Africa, encompassing 967,495 square miles. Sudan, situated in east-central Africa, is the site of a long-standing civil war that includes the bloody Darfur genocide, which began in 2003. It is bordered by Egypt to the north, the Red Sea to the northeast, Eritrea and Ethiopia to the east, Kenya and Uganda to the southeast, the Democratic Republic of the Congo and the Central African Republic to the southwest, Chad to the west, and Libya to the northwest. With a current population of approximately 39.4 million people, Sudan has a tropical climate in the south and an arid desert climate in the north. Despite its natural resources of petroleum, zinc, copper, silver, and gold, Sudan is one of the poorest nations in Africa and has been rocked by civil war and political turmoil in the last several decades.

Some 70 percent of the Sudanese population are farmers, although 66 percent of the population resides in a concentrated area around Khartoum, Omdurman, and Khartoum North. Only a few Sudanese engage in trade and commerce. Most residents lack modern facilities such as electricity, good transportation, and safe drinking water. The population of Sudan is increasing by nearly 6 percent every year, but its gross production has not kept up with this growth, suggesting a difficult future for the country.

Sudan's culture represents those of many different African and Arab peoples and has been influenced by the ancient civilizations of the Kingdom of Kush, Nubia, and Meroe. It has a long and distinguished history dating back several thousand years. The Arabs called Sudan the "Country of the Blacks" (Bilad al-Sud). It was invaded and ruled in the past by the Romans, Egyptians, and British, who controlled it from 1899 to 1955. Sudan was also a hunting place for black slaves, sought by Arab traders. In the past, before modern transportation, Sudan was a transitional depot for Muslim pilgrims from East, Central, and West Africa. They often passed through Port Sudan en route to Mecca for the Islamic pilgrimage.

In 1956 Sudan won its independence from the British and became the Republic of Sudan, with Khartoum as its capital. It has 26 states and a military-rule (transitional) style of government. General Omar al-Bashir is its current president.

Sudan comprises many diverse ethnic groups: Arab, Nubian, Beja, Dinka, Azande, and Zaghawa. Each group speaks a different language, but Arabic is the official language and the one used by the government. The Arabs are the second largest ethnic group, and most are descended from the Jaaliyin and the Juhayna tribes. About 70 percent of Sudanese are Muslims, while 20–25 percent are followers of traditional African religions. Some 5–10 percent of Sudanese are Christians. Sudanese Muslims are Sunnis; however, many of them are members of different mystical, or Sufi, orders. The majority of Sudanese Christians are Roman Catholics.

In 1983 Sudanese president Jafar Nimayri imposed Islamic law (Sharia) over all aspects of life, including civil and criminal laws, which caused a major upheaval that sparked the Second Sudanese Civil War. Prior to that, Sudan had been torn apart by the First Civil War, which raged from 1955 to 1972. Today, Sudan still applies Islamic law to daily life. Many followers of indigenous African religions believe that Muslims and Christians have used religion to oppress them, and they resent the aggressive missionary work of both Muslims and Christians. However, it was the Catholic Church that helped bring the world's attention to the crisis and attendant genocide in Darfur.

Socially, Sudan remains a family-oriented society that cherishes the extended family. The family unit takes care of its elderly and the sick, and watches over the welfare of all. Women are still segregated at many festivities, except for the Western-educated young women who enjoy some limited social and career mobility. Prior to the Bashir regime, many Sudanese women received a modern education and worked as doctors, engineers, and teachers; but with Islamization, an effort began to exclude female workers from many professions, and political purges had the same effect. Unfortunately, nearly all Sudanese women practice a severe form of female circumcision despite its condemnation by the international community, often creating many health problems for them.

Politically, Sudan is divided into southern and northern parts, an artificial creation of the former Egyptian and British colonial regimes. The division was created for political and administrative purposes. A policy of segregation and discrimination against the southerners was carried on after independence and helped fuel the two civil wars, as did competition among northern groups.

Sudan remains an underdeveloped country. A military government backed by the largest Islamic party and headed by Hasan Turabi and Omar al-Bashir came to power in 1989; it put an end to the democratically elected government of President Sadiq al-Mahdi, the leader of the Ummah party, and banned all political parties. Bashir later secured the exit of Turabi from the government. The Sudan had already been involved in a long and bitter civil war primarily between the South and the North. The civil war widened to include western areas like Darfur and also, for some years, efforts to bring down the Bashir government by a coalition of rebels. Sudan's bitter civil wars, which have caused and continue to cause insurmountable problems, have ruined its economy and resulted in the death of more than half a million people. Many Sudanese were forced to flee into neighboring countries to save their lives. Millions of them became refugees in other lands without any hope of returning to Sudan because of the continuing violence and bloodshed.

In August 1998 the U.S. government ordered Operation INFINITE REACH, which featured a preemptory cruise-missile strike on a pharmaceutical factory in Khartoum. The Americans claimed it was a chemical weapons facility with links to Al Qaeda. The strike was controversial, for the facility turned out to be merely a pharmaceutical factory with no links to Al Qaeda.

The Darfur genocide has claimed the lives of as many as 400,000 people and has displaced another 2.5 million. Rather than the religious strife of the two previous civil wars, the catalyst in the Darfur crisis has been ethnic and tribal tensions. Much of the world, including the United States, has denounced the Sudanese government and has labeled the bloodshed genocide. However, with much of the world's attention on conflicts in the Middle East and the War on Terror, little has been done to stop the bloodshed.

Sudan is bitterly divided by elements loyal to the government, freedom fighters (whom the government labels rebels) in the South, inhabitants of the Darfur region to the west, and northerners in opposition to the government. All suspect one another, and efforts to find an amicable solution to the country's problems have all failed. Several local and international conferences have taken place in and outside Sudan to help resolve the problems, and peace treaties have been signed but are then disregarded. Thousands of Sudanese refugees are now living in wretched conditions in refugee camps and are being taken care of by the United Nations (UN) and international charitable organizations.

It should be noted, however, that many of the freedom fighters are Muslims themselves, and not Christians as portrayed in the media. The Arab militias who are fighting them are also Muslim, as well as black. The Arab northerners want to tap the natural resources in the South and rule the country without allowing the indigenous people to benefit from the resources in their own area. The non-Muslim peoples of the South have long opposed the imposition of Islamic law in their region as well. The southerners and people in Darfur believe that the government has marginalized them.

The international community has condemned Sudan for the atrocities committed by the *janjawid*, or fighting groups. Sudan has also been isolated in the past for allegedly sponsoring terrorism, especially with its previous accommodation of Al Qaeda leader Osama bin Laden, and the United States strongly opposes the Islamic nature of the Sudanese government. The international community is currently exerting considerable pressure on Sudan to end the crisis in Darfur, and the U.S. government has sought support for the issue from the UN Security Council. However, many Arab governments oppose pressure on Bashir, and the United States has not received sufficient support in the Security Council for meaningful action, thanks to opposition from the People's Republic of China (PRC), at least in part because the Chinese government imports oil from Darfur and is the major supplier of arms to Sudan.

YUSHAU SODIQ

**See also**

Al Qaeda; Bin Laden, Osama; INFINITE REACH, Operation; Terrorism

**References**

Fadlallah, Mohammad H. *Short History of Sudan.* Lincoln, NE: iUniverse, 2004.

Jok, Madut Jok. *Sudan: Race, Religion, and Violence.* Oxford, UK: Oneworld Publications, 2007.

---

# Suez Crisis
Start Date: July 26, 1956
End Date: March 6, 1957

The Suez Crisis was one of the major events of both the modern Middle East and Cold War as well as of the Arab-Israeli wars. The crisis ended Britain's pretensions to be a world superpower and fatally weakened Britain's hold on what remained of its empire. It also placed a dangerous strain on U.S.-Soviet relations, strengthened the position of Egyptian leader Gamal Abdel Nasser throughout the Middle East, and distracted world attention from the concurrent Soviet military intervention in the Hungarian Revolution.

The Suez Crisis had its origins in the development plans of Gamal Abdel Nasser. In 1952 a reformist and anti-British coup d'état in Egypt, led by young army officers, toppled the government of King Farouk I. During the months that followed, Nasser emerged as the strongman and ultimately became president of Egypt. Nasser hoped to enhance his prestige and improve the quality of life for his nation's burgeoning population by carrying out long-discussed plans to construct a high dam on the upper Nile River south of Aswan to provide electric power. To finance the project, Nasser sought assistance from the Western powers. But Nasser had also been endeavoring to build up and modernize the Egyptian military. Toward that end he had sought to acquire modern weapons from the United States and other Western nations. When the U.S. government refused to supply the advanced arms, which it believed might be used against the State of Israel, Nasser turned to the communist bloc in 1955. In September 1955, with Soviet encouragement, he reached a barter arrangement with Czechoslovakia for substantial quantities of weapons, including jet aircraft and tanks, in return for Egyptian cotton.

This arms deal had an impact on the Aswan High Dam construction project for which Nasser had sought Western financing. In December 1955 Washington declared its willingness to lend $56 million for financing the dam, while Britain pledged $14 million and the World Bank $200 million. The condition to the aid was that Egypt provide matching funds and that it not accept Soviet assistance.

Nasser was unhappy with the attached strings. With Nasser expecting a Soviet offer of assistance, the controlled Egyptian press launched an all-out propaganda offensive against the West, especially the United States. But when no Soviet offer was forthcoming, Nasser finally accepted the Western aid package on July 17, 1956. Much to his chagrin, two days later U.S. secretary of state John Foster Dulles announced that it had been withdrawn. Britain immediately followed suit. The official U.S. reasons for withdrawal were that Egypt had failed to reach agreement with the Sudan over the dam (most of the vast lake created by the dam would be in Sudanese territory), and the Egyptian part of the project's financing had become uncertain. The real reasons were objections from some U.S. congressmen, especially southerners fearful of competition from Egyptian cotton, and Dulles's determination to teach Nasser and other neutralists a lesson. Dulles was angry over Nasser's flirtation with the communist bloc to include the arms purchases and was especially upset over Egypt's recent recognition of the People's Republic of China (PRC).

Nasser's response to this humiliating rebuff came a week later on July 26, when he nationalized the Suez Canal. He had contemplated such a move for some time, but the U.S. decision prompted its timing. In 1955 the canal produced net revenues of nearly $100 million, of which Egypt received only $2 million. Seizure of the canal would not only provide additional funding for the Aswan High Dam project, but it would make Nasser a hero in the eyes of many Arab nationalists.

The British government regarded the sea-level Suez Canal, which connected the eastern Mediterranean with the Red Sea across Egyptian territory, as its lifeline to Middle Eastern oil and the Far East. Indeed, fully 60 percent of all oil consumed in Western Europe passed through the canal. The canal, built by a private company headed by Frenchman Ferdinand de Lesseps, had opened to much fanfare in 1869. It quickly altered the trade routes of the world, and two-thirds of the tonnage passing through the canal was British. Khedive Ismail Pasha, who owned 44 percent of the company shares, plunged Egypt into debt as a result of his profligate spending, and in 1875 the British government stepped in and purchased his shares. In 1878 Britain acquired the island of Cyprus north of Egypt from the Ottoman Empire, further strengthening its position in the eastern Mediterranean north of

Egypt. The British also increased their role in Egyptian financial affairs, and in 1882 they intervened militarily in Egypt, promising to depart once order had been restored. Britain remained in Egypt and in effect controlled its affairs through World War II.

In 1954 Nasser, determined to end British influence in Egypt, succeeded in renegotiating the 1936 treaty with the British to force the withdrawal of British troops from the Suez Canal zone. The last British forces departed the canal zone on June 13, only six weeks before Nasser nationalized the canal.

The British government took the lead in opposing Nasser. London believed that Nasser's growing popularity in the Arab world was encouraging Arab nationalism and threatening to undermine British influence throughout the Middle East. British prime minister Anthony Eden developed a deep and abiding hatred for the Egyptian leader. For Eden, ousting Nasser from power became nothing short of an obsession. In the immediate aftermath of Nasser's nationalization of the canal, the British government called up 200,000 military reservists and dispatched military resources to the eastern Mediterranean.

The French government also had good reason to seek Nasser's removal. Paris sought to protect its own long-standing interests in the Middle East, but more to the point, was then fighting the National Liberation Front (NLF) in Algeria. The Algerian War, which began in November 1954, had greatly expanded and become an imbroglio for the government, now led by socialist premier Guy Mollet. Nasser was a strong and vocal supporter of the NLF, and there were many in the French government and military who believed that overthrowing him would greatly enhance France's chances of winning the Algerian War. This position found considerable support when on October 18, 1956, the French intercepted the Egyptian ship *Athos* and found it loaded with arms and documents proving Egyptian support for the NLF.

Israel formed the third leg in the triad of powers arrayed against Nasser. Egypt had instituted a blockade of Israeli ships at the Gulf of Aqaba, Israel's outlet to the Indian Ocean. Also, Egypt had never recognized the Jewish state and indeed remained at war with it following the Israeli War of Independence (1948–1949). In 1955 Israel mounted a half dozen cross-border raids, while Egypt carried out its own raids into Israeli territory by fedayeen (guerrilla fighters).

Over the months that followed Egyptian nationalization of the Suez Canal, the community of interest among British, French, and Israeli leaders developed into secret planning for a joint military operation to topple Nasser. The U.S. government was not consulted and indeed opposed the use of force. The British and French governments either did not understand the American attitude or, if they did, believed that Washington would give approval after the fact to policies believed by its major allies to be absolutely necessary.

The British government first tried diplomacy. Two conferences in London attended by the representatives of 24 nations using the canal failed to produce agreement on a course of action, and Egypt refused to participate. A proposal by Secretary of State Dulles for a canal users' club of nations failed, as did an appeal to the United Nations (UN) Security Council. On October 1 Dulles announced that the United States was disassociating itself from British and French actions in the Middle East and asserted that the United States intended to play a more independent role.

Meanwhile, secret talks were going forward, first between the British and French for joint military action against Egypt. Military representatives of the two governments met in London on August 10 and hammered out the details of a joint military plan known as MUSKETEER, which would involve occupation of both Alexandria and Port Said. The French then brought the Israeli government in on the plan, and General Maurice Challe, deputy chief of staff of the French Air Force, undertook a secret trip to the Middle East to meet with Israeli government and military leaders. The Israelis were at first skeptical about British and French support. They also had no intention of moving as far as the canal itself. The Israelis stated that their plan was merely to send light detachments to link up with British and French forces. They also insisted that British and French military intervention occur simultaneously with their own attack.

General André Beaufre, the designated French military commander for the operation, then came up with a new plan. Under it, the Israelis would initiate hostilities against Egypt in order to provide the pretext for military intervention by French and British forces to protect the canal. This action would technically be in accord with the terms of the 1954 treaty between Egypt and Britain that had given Britain the right to send forces to occupy the Suez Canal zone in the event of an attack against Egypt by a third power.

On October 23 Mollet and French foreign minister Christian Pineau met in the Paris suburbs at Sévres with Israeli prime minister David Ben-Gurion, defense minister Shimon Peres, and chief of the Israeli General Staff Lieutenant General Moshe Dayan. The French agreed to provide additional air cover for Israel. French ships supposedly searching for Egyptian arms shipments to the Algerian rebels would move to the Israeli coast immediately, and French Mystére aircraft flown by French pilots would be repositioned in Israel. That afternoon British foreign secretary Selwyn Lloyd and Foreign Office undersecretary of state Patrick Dean joined the discussions. The British, while staunchly prointervention, were deeply concerned about their position in the Arab world and were not anxious to be seen in collusion with the Israelis. Thus, an Israeli strike toward the canal through the Sinai would enable the British to have it both ways: they could join the French in demanding of Nasser the right to protect the canal. When he refused, as he certainly would, they could join the French in destroying the Egyptian Air Force, eliminating the one possible

Egyptian Army prisoners of war (POWs) taken by British and French forces stand behind a barbed wire fence during the Suez Crisis, November 3, 1956. Their steel helmets lie in a pile in the foreground. (Israeli Government Press Office)

threat to Israeli success on the ground. All parties agreed to this new plan, informally dubbed the "Treaty of Sévres" and signed by Dean, Pineau, and Ben-Gurion.

On October 23, meanwhile, unrest began in Hungary. The next day Soviet tanks entered Budapest to put down what had become the Hungarian Revolution. French and British planners were delighted at this international distraction that seemed to provide them a degree of freedom of action.

On the afternoon of October 29 Israeli forces began Operation KADESH, the invasion of the Sinai peninsula. Sixteen C-47 transports took off from Israeli fields, each with a paratroop platoon. The objective of the 395-man paratroop battalion was the key Mitla Pass, 156 miles from the Israeli border and only 45 miles from the canal. Meanwhile, the remainder of Colonel Ariel Sharon's 202nd Parachute Brigade would race for the pass in French-provided trucks, linking up with the paratroopers within 36 hours. This operation was designed to trigger a major Egyptian response and threaten the canal in order to trigger the planned British-French response.

The announced objective of Operation KADESH was the eradication of the fedayeen bases, but it was begun so as to appear to the Egyptians as if it were the beginning of an all-out war. Dayan's detailed plan called for nothing less than a weeklong lightning advance that would end with Israeli forces securing the entire Sinai and a total victory over Egypt. The destruction of Nasser's prestige in the Arab world and final Egyptian recognition of the impossibility of an Arab military victory over Israel were the goals, rather than destruction of the Egyptian Army or acquisition of its new Soviet equipment.

A day later, October 30, the British and French governments issued an ultimatum, nominally to both the Egyptian and Israeli governments but in reality only to Egypt, expressing the need to separate the combatants and demanding the right to provide for the security of the Suez Canal. The ultimatum called on both sides to withdraw their forces 10 miles from the canal and gave them 12 hours to reply. The Israelis, of course, immediately accepted the ultimatum, while the Egyptians just as promptly rejected it.

At dusk on October 31, British and French aircraft struck Egyptian airfields and military installations from bases on Cyprus and Malta and from aircraft carriers. The aircraft attacked four Egyptian bases that day and nine the next. On November 1, meanwhile, a British and French naval task force sailed from Malta to join with other ships at Cyprus. In all, the allied landing force numbered some 80,000 men: 50,000 British and 30,000 French. There were 100 British and 30 French warships, including 7 aircraft carriers (5 British) and the French battleship *Jean Bart*; hundreds of landing craft; and some 80 merchant ships carrying 20,000 vehicles and stores. Yet when Eden reported to the House of Commons on events, he encountered a surprisingly strong negative reaction from the opposition Labour Party.

Also, following the initial British and French military action, the Egyptians immediately sank a number of ships in the canal to make it unusable. Meanwhile, the Israelis, battling against ineffective Egyptian forces, swept across the Sinai in only four days. Finally, on November 5, British and French paratroopers carried out a vertical envelopment of Port Said, Egypt, at the Mediterranean terminus of the canal, while at the same time French and British destroyers carried out a shore bombardment against those targets likely to impede a landing. Early on November 6, British troops began coming ashore at Port Said, while the French landed at Port Faud. A single day of fighting saw the ports in allied hands. French and British forces then began a virtually unopposed advance southward along the canal.

U.S. president Dwight D. Eisenhower had already entered the picture. On October 31 he described the British attack as "taken in error." He was personally furious at Eden over events and is supposed to have asked when he first telephoned the British leader, "Anthony, have you gone out of your mind?" The United States applied immediate and heavy financial threats, both on a bilateral basis and through the International Monetary Fund (IMF), to bring the British government to heel. Eisenhower also refused any further dealings with Eden personally.

The Soviets, preoccupied by Hungary, took some five days to come to the conclusion that the United States was actually opposing the British and French action. On November 5, Moscow threatened to send "volunteers" to Egypt. This proved a further embarrassment for the British government, but it was U.S. pressure that was decisive. Nonetheless, the world beheld the strange spectacle of the United States cooperating with the Soviet Union to condemn Britain and France in the UN Security Council and call for an end to the use of force. Although Britain and France vetoed the Security Council resolution, the matter was referred to the General Assembly, which demanded a cease-fire and withdrawal.

Israel and Egypt agreed to a cease-fire on November 4. At midnight on November 6, the day of the U.S. presidential election, the British and French governments also accepted a cease-fire, the French only with the greatest reluctance. By the time the cease-fire went into effect, the French and British controlled about half of the canal's length. French and British losses in the operation were 33 dead and 129 wounded. Egyptian losses are unknown.

A 4,000-man UN Emergency Force, authorized on November 4 and made up of contingents from the Scandinavian countries, Brazil, Colombia, India, and Indonesia, then arrived in Egypt to take up positions to keep Israeli and Egyptian forces separated. At the end of November the British and French governments both agreed to withdraw their forces from Egypt by December 22, and on December 1 Eisenhower announced that he had instructed U.S. oil companies to resume shipping supplies to both Britain and France. Under pressure from both the United States and the UN, Israel withdrew its forces from the Sinai, including the Gaza Strip, during February 5–March 6, 1957. A UN observer force of 3,500 men then took up station in Gaza, at Sharm al-Shaykhh, and along the Sinai border. Although Israel had been assured that Egyptian forces would not return to Gaza, the Egyptians were there within 48 hours of the Israeli withdrawal.

An Egyptian boy stands near a British tank amid the rubble of destroyed buildings in Port Said after the British and French assault on the city during the Suez Crisis, November 1956. (Hulton-Deutsch Collection/Corbis)

Nasser and Arab self-confidence were the chief beneficiaries of the crisis. The abysmal performance of Egyptian military forces in the crisis was forgotten in Nasser's ultimate triumph. Nasser found his prestige dramatically increased throughout the Arab world. Israel also benefited. The presence of the UN force guaranteed an end to the fedayeen raids, and Israel had also broken the Egyptian blockade of the Gulf of Aqaba, although its ships could still not transit the Suez Canal. The crisis also enhanced Soviet prestige in the Middle East, and the UN emerged with enhanced prestige, helping to boost world confidence in that organization.

The Suez Crisis ended Eden's political career. Ill and under tremendous criticism in Parliament from the Labour Party, he resigned from office in January 1957. Events also placed a serious, albeit temporary, strain on U.S.-British relations. More importantly, they revealed the serious limitations in British military strength. Indeed, observers are unanimous in declaring 1956 a seminal date in British imperial history, marking the effective end of Britain's tenure as a great power. The events had less impact in France. Mollet left office in May 1957 but not as a result of the Suez intervention. The crisis was costly to both Britain and France in economic terms, for Saudi Arabia had halted oil shipments to both countries.

Finally, the Suez Crisis could not have come at a worse time for the West because the event diverted world attention from the concurrent brutal Soviet military intervention in Hungary. Eisenhower believed, rightly or wrongly, that without the Suez diversion there would have been far stronger Western reaction to the Soviet invasion of its satellite.

SPENCER C. TUCKER

**See also**

Arab-Israeli Conflict, Overview; Aswan High Dam Project; Baghdad Pact; Dulles, John Foster; Egypt; Eisenhower, Dwight David; France, Middle East Policy; Hussein ibn Talal, King of Jordan; Nasser, Gamal Abdel; Soviet Union, Middle East Policy; United Kingdom, Middle East Policy; United States, Middle East Policy, 1945–Present

**References**

Beaufre, André. *The Suez Expedition, 1956*. Translated by Richard Barry. New York: Praeger, 1969.

Cooper, Chester L. *The Lion's Last Roar: Suez, 1956*. New York: Harper and Row, 1978.

Eden, Anthony. *The Suez Crisis of 1956*. Boston: Beacon, 1968.

Freiberger, Steven Z. *Dawn over Suez: The Rise of American Power in the Middle East, 1953–1957*. Chicago: Ivan R. Dee, 1992.

Gorst, Anthony, and Lewis Johnman. *The Suez Crisis*. London: Routledge, 1997.

Hahn, Peter. *The United States, Great Britain, and Egypt, 1945–1956: Strategy and Diplomacy in the Early Cold War.* Chapel Hill: University of North Carolina Press, 1991.

Kingseed, Cole C. *Eisenhower and the Suez Crisis of 1956.* Baton Rouge: Louisiana State University Press, 1995.

Kyle, Keith. *Suez: Britain's End of Empire in the Middle East.* London: Weidenfeld and Nicolson, 1991.

Louis, William R., and Roger Owen, eds. *Suez, 1956: The Crisis and Its Consequences.* New York: Oxford University Press, 1989.

Lucas, W. Scott. *Divided We Stand: Britain, the United States and the Suez Crisis.* Rev. ed. London: Spectre, 1996.

# Suicide Bombings

Bombings in which an explosive is delivered and detonated by a person or persons who expect to die in the explosion along with the intended target or targets. In recent years the number of suicide bombings or attacks has risen exponentially, and not just in the Middle East. The United States was struck by four hijacked aircraft piloted by Islamic fanatics associated with the Al Qaeda terrorist organization on September 11, 2001, resulting in the deaths of almost 3,000 people. Certainly, this was the worst—and most dramatic—example of a suicide operation. Other shocking attacks took place in Bali, Jakarta, Madrid, London, the Sinai peninsula, and Amman, in addition to those in Iraq, Afghanistan, and Pakistan.

Suicide bombers employ several different techniques. Japanese pilots in World War II were known for crashing their airplanes straight into targets, causing tremendous devastation. These were known as kamikaze ("divine wind"), the name given to a typhoon that destroyed a Mongol invasion fleet off Japan in the 13th century. Kamikazes exacted a heavy toll on Allied warships at the end of World War II, especially off Okinawa. The Tamil Tigers of Sri Lanka utilized suicide bombings during their long struggle against the central government in 1983–2009. Other attackers have employed bombs secured in cars or trucks.

Individual suicide bombers often strap explosives and shrapnel to their bodies and wear vests or belts specially designed for the purpose. They then drive or walk to their targets. Because military targets are heavily defended, typical targets include crowded shopping areas, restaurants, or buses. Suicide bombers may also approach softer targets directly linked to the military or police, such as a line of recruits in the street, as has occurred during the Iraq War. Detonating the explosives kills and injures people in the vicinity and can also destroy notable property, such as religious shrines. One technique is to send two or more suicide bombers against a single target; after the first blast, the second bomber works his way into the crowd of responders and then detonates his explosives.

An explosion in an enclosed area is more destructive than one in the open, and suicide bombers pick their targets accordingly. Forensic investigators at the site of a suicide bombing can usually identify the bomber and the general type of device he or she used. A suicide vest decapitates the bomber; a belt cuts the bomber in two.

The explosive devices themselves are easily constructed. They might include an explosive charge, a battery, a cable, a light switch detonator, and a custom-made belt or vest to hold the explosives. Scrap metal might be employed to act as shrapnel, which in the blast would kill or maim those nearby. Explosives may also be carried in a briefcase or other bag. The bomber sets off the explosive by flipping a switch or pressing a button, sometimes remotely as in the case of a car or truck bombing.

Muslim extremists in the latest wave of violence might leave a written or video *shahada,* which is partially a statement of their intent and partially a will and settlement of any debts. Suicide bombings have been used in the Middle East since the late 1970s. The Islamic resistance employed them in Syria against the Baathist government, although many more conventional attacks also occurred. During the Lebanese civil war, car bombings evolved in some cases into suicide attacks; and in 1981 the Islamic Dawa Party bombed the Iraqi embassy in Beirut.

In response to the Israeli invasion of Lebanon in 1982, the Islamic Resistance, a loosely organized group, formed, and some of its elements planned bombing attacks. In November 1982 an Islamic Resistance suicide bomber destroyed a building in Tyre, Lebanon, and killed 76 Israelis. The Organization of Islamic Jihad and other militant Islamist groups including Hezbollah, as well as numerous Christians, carried out another 50 suicide attacks between 1982 and 1999, when the Israelis withdrew from Lebanon. A massive suicide bombing of their barracks in October 1983 forced American and French troops from Lebanon.

The belief that such attacks bring martyrdom has encouraged suicide bombings in countries all over the world, including Afghanistan, Chechnya, Croatia, Tajikistan, Pakistan, Yemen, Panama, Argentina, and Algeria. In 1995 a suicide bomber dressed as a priest attempted to assassinate Pope John Paul II in Manila.

Suicide attacks by Palestinians began after the First Intifada but were not regular events; however, many more took place during the Second (al-Aqsa) Intifada. The first Palestinian suicide bombing occurred in April 1994 in the West Bank. It killed 8 Israelis and was carried out to avenge the deaths of 25 Muslims who had been praying in the Ibrahimi Mosque when they were killed by Israeli settler Baruch Goldstein. Hamas explained that its basic policy was only to attack Israeli soldiers, but if Palestinian civilians were slaughtered in deliberate attacks, then it would break that policy. There were 198 known suicide-bombing attacks in Israel and Palestine between 1994 and July 2002, which killed 120 people. The bombers died in 136 of those attacks. Because many of the bombers were intercepted and/or the attacks otherwise failed, the numbers of casualties are far lower than in the numerous suicide attacks carried out in Iraq since 2003. Attacks increased after the beginning of the Second Intifada in September 2000. Although suicide bombings comprised only a small percentage of actual attacks launched by Palestinians against Israelis, they accounted for perhaps half the Israelis killed between 2000 and 2002. In 2003 there were 26 attacks killing 144, but in 2004, 15 attacks and 55 dead. In 2005 Hamas ordered a cease-fire, which was, however, not binding on the other groups that had engaged in attacks: the Abu Ali Mustafa Brigades of the Popular Front for the Liberation of Palestine, Islamic Jihad, and the al-Aqsa Martyrs Brigades. During 2005 there were 7 attacks killing 23, and then in 2006 only 2 attacks.

Many of the suicide attackers in Lebanon in the 1980s were Christians; Palestinian suicide bombers have been presumed to be Muslims, although there are many Christians in the Palestinian national movement. A Greek Orthodox religious figure, Archimandrite Theosios Hanna, supported *fida'iyin n shahids* (fighter martyrs) in several speeches. Other Christian leaders have explained the attacks as a desperate response to a brutal military occupation. It is obvious from the Tamil, Japanese, or anarchist violence that the motivation is primarily nationalist, and in fact Islam strictly forbids suicide and engaging recklessly in jihad so as to obtain martyrdom. According to classical doctrine, there are set rules regarding who may participate in jihad, and these exclude children, those with dependants, and also, traditionally, women. The main religious justification is that under circumstances of military occupation, jihad is required of Muslims. In Islam, there is a difference between an individual and a collectively incumbent religious duty. Religious authorities who decry the linkage of Islam with suicide and the killing of innocent people try to convince their audiences that the greater jihad, the striving to be a good Muslim in every possible aspect of life, can substitute for jihad as armed struggle, or that if armed struggle is necessary, it should not involve attacks of this type. Among convocations of clerics who have met on this issue, most acknowledge that jihad is licit for Palestinians, and some believe it is licit in Iraq, although many object to suicide attacks. In 20 books of recantation of violent jihad, the leaders of the Gamaat Islamiya have provided powerful arguments against violence employed for the right reason (in their view) but with the wrong methods, or timing. Not all religious authorities take this position, of course, and unfortunately the televised footage or videos of suicide bombers serve as a recruiting tool for others.

For most Muslims, suicide is anathema; many would-be suicide bombers are motivated by the desire to combat social injustice; others find irresistible the temptation of martyrdom with its promise of rewards in paradise. Martyrdom has its own history in early Islam, and it is believed that martyrs are cleansed of their sins and that they will have special power to intercede on behalf of their relatives and close friends on the Day of Judgment. The families of suicide bombers are often extremely proud of their loved ones and praise them publicly as heroes. Some Palestinian suicide bombers received financial support from the Iraqi government, and in this way were able to provide for their dependants. Suicide bombers also believe that they will be remembered as popular heroes.

Would-be Palestinian suicide bombers have often used the argument that all Israelis serve in the military, at least as reserves, and therefore are combatants and not really civilians. In Iraq, the suicide attacks since the coalition invasion of 2003 were initially

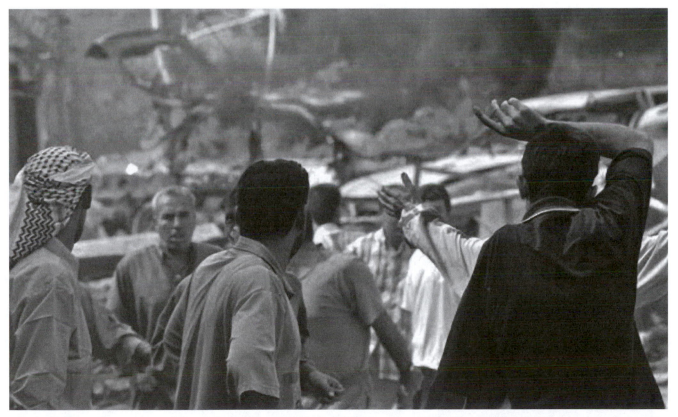

Smoke and flames fill the air after a suicide bomber set off an explosion that killed 33 people and injured another 50 in Tal Afar, Iraq, on October 11, 2005. (U.S. Department of Defense)

directed against coalition forces, but then turned to Iraqi citizens working for the government, police, or military, and also to ordinary civilians. In addition, groups such as al-Qa'ida fi Bilad al-Rafhidayn (Al Qaeda in Mesopotamia) have targeted Shia civilians, declaring them to be "renegades" or apostates and therefore subject to death. The attacks spiked in 2005. In 2003 there were 25 suicide bombings; in 2004, 140; in 2005, 478; in 2006, 300; in 2007, more than 200 suicide bombings; in 2008, more than 115 suicide bombings. Although far fewer, there were a number of costly suicide bombings in the spring of 2009.

Suicide bombings were also employed by insurgents in Afghanistan, although here there were not as many casualties, most probably because the Taliban have chosen to target military personnel or politicians, rather than civilians, and because the planning for them is often poor. Large numbers of civilian casualties have resulted from certain attacks, as in the Baghlan in 2007, where the target was a politician and 70 people died, or when a local miltia leader was targeted at a dogfight in Kandahar in February 2008, and 80 people died.

There are differing attitudes in the various states where suicide attacks have occurred. While most all people fear such attacks, many citizens support the notion of armed resistance. Since Al Qaeda and groups similar to it have been active, counterterrorist agencies, police, and gendarmeries around the world have been focusing on ways to prevent suicide bombings.

Suicide bombings are part of asymmetric warfare. Advantages for any violent radical group employing this tactic are that no escape need be arranged for the bombers and that they are not expected to live to reveal information. Also, the materials for the explosive devices are inexpensive.

Al Qaedist tactics have created a new *fiqh al-jihad*, or rules of jihad, that are somewhat different from the past. For example, in a collective jihad, women, children, and parents of dependant children, or the children of the elderly, were not to volunteer for jihad, but in the five-year period when such attacks were most prevalent in Israel and in the last several years in Iraq, bombers have come from both genders, although most were men. It is a common assumption that suicide bombers are drawn from the poor and desperate, but a careful study of most suicide terrorist acts shows this is untrue; the bombers were, rather, the ideologically committed of different backgrounds. On occasion, Afghani and Iraqi authorities have claimed that mentally impaired people have been induced to be bombers, but this must be only a small number. Sometimes those who were recruited to such actions were chosen for their psychological predispositions not to suicide but to suggestibility, and were prevented, if possible, from contacting their families once their mission was set, so as not to give any hint of their intent. In the case of Palestinian suicide bombers, those attackers who authorities said were traceable to Hamas and Islamic Jihad were persons with no major family responsibilities and who were over the age of 18. In some cases, recruiters sought individuals who could speak Hebrew well.

Understandably, suicide bombings are enormously upsetting to potential civilian victims. Suicide bombers turn up when they are least expected as their victims go about their daily business, and victims and bystanders are taken completely by surprise. The victims are often civilians, and children make up a sizable percentage of those killed. Because the bomber has no concern for his or her own life, it is difficult to prevent such attacks. In Israel and in Iraq, many individuals and businesses have hired security guards who are specially trained to spot potential bombers. Airport and general transport security has now been increased, worldwide.

AMY HACKNEY BLACKWELL AND SHERIFA ZUHUR

**See also**

Hamas; Hezbollah; Intifada, Second; Islamic Jihad, Palestinian; Islamic Radicalism; Jihad; September 11 Attacks

**References**

Aboul-Enein, Youssef H., and Sherifa Zuhur. *Islamic Rulings on Warfare.* Carlisle Barracks, PA: Strategic Studies Institute, 2004.

Friedman, Lauri S. *What Motivates Suicide Bombers?* Farmington Hills, MI: Greenhaven, 2004.

Khosrokhavar, Farhad. *Suicide Bombers: Allah's New Martyrs.* Translated by David Macey. London: Pluto, 2005.

Rosenthal, Franz. "On Suicide in Islam." *Journal of the American Oriental Society* 66 (1946): 239–259.

Skaine, Rosemarie. *Female Suicide Bombers.* Jefferson, NC: McFarland, 2006.

# Suleiman, Michel
## Birth Date: November 21, 1948

Lebanese army officer and president of Lebanon (2008–). Michel Suleiman was born on November 21, 1948, in Amsheet (Amchit), Lebanon, to a Maronite Christian family. He attended Lebanon's military academy, graduating in 1970. Commissioned a second lieutenant in the Lebanese army, he went on to earn a bachelor's degree in political and administrative sciences from Lebanese University. Fluent in Arabic, English, and French, Suleiman—described as having a strong personal presence and firm leadership and management skills—rose steadily through the military hierarchy.

By December 1990 Suleiman had been named chief of the Intelligence Branch of Mount Lebanon, which post he held until August 1991. He then assumed the post of secretary-general of the Army Staff, a position he retained until June 1993. From June 1993 to January 1996, he commanded the 11th Infantry Brigade. During his command, the brigade was heavily involved in fighting in the West Bekáa Valley and in southern Lebanon. Beginning on January 15, 1996, he assumed command of the 6th Infantry Brigade, and in December 1998 he was named commander of Lebanese armed forces, a post he held until he took office as president in May 2008.

As Lebanon's military commander, Suleiman performed admirably while navigating with considerable skill the minefields of Lebanese politics. He managed to keep the public calm during mass demonstrations both for and against Syrian involvement in Lebanese affairs, to diminish sectarian violence, to deploy forces into areas loyal to Hezbollah in southern Lebanon—a first for the Lebanese army—and to help quash Islamic militants in the north of Lebanon in 2000. Suleiman became most celebrated during the clash between the radical Sunni terrorist group Fatah al-Islam and the Lebanese army in northern Lebanon. The conflict began in May 2007 and did not end until September. Suleiman moved with great caution, but nevertheless acquitted himself well, soundly defeating the Fatah al-Islam militants. He also advanced a plan that helped end the Israeli invasion of southern Lebanon in 2006.

In May 2007 political animosity between government loyalists and Hezbollah broke out into open warfare, which lasted until May 2008. Suleiman was careful not to involve the army directly in the clashes, instead seeking to use the armed forces as a mediator and separating the fighters from the political figures they claimed to represent. While some criticized Suleiman for his failure to move with more force to stop the violence, many others lauded his efforts, claiming that his level-headedness and impartiality prevented a more serious civil war.

In November 2007 President Emile Lahoud's tenure in office ended, but the fractured Lebanese political landscape made searching for a new president a tall order. After several months of starts and stops, Lebanon's major political parties had reached a virtual deadlock, as no potential candidate seemed satisfactory enough to hold the vital center of the nation's political hierarchy. By the late winter of 2008, many in Lebanon came to view Suleiman as the only potential candidate who could effectively lead the various political factions in Lebanon. He commanded respect among government loyalists and the opposition, the Arab community, and the international community. On May 25, 2008, following a deal brokered by Arab diplomats, the Lebanese parliament elected Suleiman as president, and three days later he reappointed Fouad Siniora as prime minister. Some in the United States perceived Suleiman's election as a victory for Hezbollah, as he, like General Michel Aoun, is a firm supporter of national unity and Lebanon's basic principle of representation for all national groups. None of the other presidential candidates would have been acceptable to Hezbollah, as well as to other Lebanese parties, unless Aoun had been permitted to stand for election.

PAUL G. PIERPAOLI JR.

**See also**

Hezbollah; Lebanon; Lebanon, Armed Forces

**References**

Fisk, Robert. *Pity the Nation: The Abduction of Lebanon.* 4th ed. New York: Nation Books, 2002.

Rabil, Robert G. *Embattled Neighbors: Syria, Israel, and Lebanon.* Boulder, CO: Lynne Rienner, 2003.

# Sullivan, Gordon R.
## Birth Date: September 25, 1937

U.S. Army general and chief of staff of the army during 1991–1995. Born in Boston, Massachusetts, on September 25, 1937, Gordon R. Sullivan graduated from Norwich University in 1959 with a bachelor's degree in history. Commissioned a second lieutenant of armor through the Reserve Officers' Training Corps (ROTC), he entered the army upon graduation.

Sullivan subsequently earned a master's degree in political science from the University of New Hampshire. In addition to his military branch training, he also graduated from the Army Command and General Staff College and the Army War College.

Overseas assignments included two tours during the Vietnam War, four tours in Europe, and one tour in Korea. His command assignments ranged from platoon through division. He commanded a battalion of the 73rd Armor Regiment and the 1st Brigade of the 3rd Armored Division. He was also assistant commandant of the Armor School at Fort Knox, Kentucky (1983–1985), and was later deputy commandant of the Command and General Staff College, Fort Leavenworth, Kansas (1987–1988). He commanded the 1st Infantry Division (Mechanized) at Fort Riley, Kansas, during 1988–1989. He was then deputy chief of staff for Operations and Plans before being named vice chief of staff of the army as a full (four-star) general. He held this post during the 1991 Persian Gulf War. In the run-up to the war, he intervened personally to speed production of the newer model of the Patriot missile.

General Sullivan became chief of staff of the army in June 1991. His chief task on assuming his post was to oversee the transformation of the army from a Cold War posture into a smaller, more flexible, and technologically advanced force with more of its units stationed in the continental United States, although a sizable force remained in Europe to counter any threat from Russia. Sullivan retired from the army on July 31, 1995. He has coauthored several books, including *Hope Is Not a Method,* which describes the challenges of reshaping the army while he was chief of staff. Sullivan currently serves on the boards of several corporations. He has also served as chairman of the Board of Trustees of Norwich University and is the president and chief operating officer of the Association of the United States Army.

SPENCER C. TUCKER

**See also**

Patriot Missile System

**References**

Dubrick, James M., and Gordon R. Sullivan. *Land Warfare in the 21st Century.* Carlisle Barracks, PA: U.S. Army War College, Strategic Studies Institute, 1993.

———. *War in the Information Age.* Carlisle Barracks, PA: U.S. Army War College, Strategic Studies Institute, 1994.

Scales, Robert H. *Certain Victory: The U.S. Army in the Gulf War.* Washington, DC: Brassey's, 1994.

Sullivan, Gordon R., and Michael V. Harper. *Hope Is Not a Method.* New York: Random House, 1996.

# Sunni Islam

Largest of the two predominant branches of Islam. Approximately 85 percent of Muslims worldwide are adherents of Sunni Islam, although the exact proportions of the two branches are disputed. Muslims themselves seldom used the word "Sunni" prior to the 2003 invasion of Iraq and subsequent occupation or the Islamic Revolution in Iran. It derives from a medieval Arabic phrase, *ahl al-sunnah wa al-jama'a,* meaning those who live according to the Prophet's model, unified in a community. In the early period, this term did not refer to all Muslims but rather to those who were engaged in Islamic scholarship and learning. The *sunnah,* or way, of the Prophet Muhammad refers to his tradition, or practice, of Islam during his 23 years of life following the initial revelation of Allah's words to him. However, "sunnah" generally referred to any tradition of the ancient Arabs.

It is mostly in the West that Muslims are differentiated as Sunnis or Shia. If asked, a Muslim may instead identify himself by a school of Islamic law or jurisprudence, such as the Hanafi school, which was the official legal doctrine of the Ottoman Empire, or of a particular movement. Since the most recent Islamic revival (*sahwa islamiyya*) began in the 1970s, the term *sunniyyun* (plural of *sunni* used interchangeably with *Islamiyyun*) has acquired the meaning of a very devout Muslim, or a *salafi.*

In contrast with the more institutionalized clerics, courts, and systems of Sunni Muslim learning, Sufi Islam is a mystical movement within Islam, the goal of which is the spiritual development of the individual. Sufis seek out personal guides (*shaykh* or *pir*) and are organized into brotherhoods (*tariqat*). There are Shia as well as Sunni Sufi orders. Sufism can be highly ascetic, while mainstream Islam is not. In contemporary times, sometimes even official clerics are also Sufis; however, the *salafists* oppose Sufism.

Sunni Muslims do not adhere to the doctrine of the imams, as do several sects of Shia Muslims (excluding the Zaydiyya). In the past, they generally judged the validity of the caliph (the temporal political and military leader) or the caliphate (Islamic government) itself by his or its adherence to the faith and the order and harmony that he or it maintained. In contrast with the Shia, Sunni Muslims believe that Abu Bakr, Umar, and Uthman—the first three Rashidun caliphs following Muhammad—were legitimate successors of Muhammad and that they are of equal standing with the fourth caliph, Ali, Muhammad's son-in-law. Ali became the fourth caliph in 656 CE after the murder of Caliph Uthman and was himself assassinated in 661. However there were other Muslims, not Ali's supporters, who also opposed the Umayyads, so the political divisions over leadership were complex.

It was not a requirement that the political and religious leadership in Sunni Islam trace its lineage through Ali, although the requirements of a caliph as defined by the scholar Abu al-Hasan Ali Ibn Muhammad Ibn Habib al-Mawardi (972–1058) indicated that he must be of the Prophet Muhammad's Quraysh tribe, male, not physically impaired, and pious. Any link to the Ahl al-Bayt, the immediate family members of the Prophet was, however,

In this scene from the 16th-century manuscript *Life of the Prophet,* Muhammad (whose face is not shown, by Islamic tradition) is accompanied by Abu Bakr and Ali ibn Abu Talib. (The New York Public Library/Art Resource, NY)

highly regarded. The caliphs lost their real authority in 1055. They retained an element of religious authority only in name, as the caliph was mentioned in the Friday prayers. With the Mongol sack of Baghdad in 1258, the caliphs lost all power. For Sunni Muslims, other political leaders were acceptable, though they were supposed to uphold Islamic law. When the Ottoman sultans years later declared themselves to be caliphs in order to wage jihad, other Muslims questioned their religious claim. By the 20th century some Muslims understood the caliphate as an ideal structure but one that could be replaced by other forms of authority. Others supported attempts to restore the caliphate.

In the absence of the caliphate, Muslim politics continued under the precept that other rulers, sultans, or emirs would rule to the best of their ability in accordance with the Sharia (Islamic law) and uphold the *hisba,* the principle of "commanding the good and forbidding the evil," a key principle in Islam. Clerics, or *ulama* (those who possess *'ilm,* religious knowledge), were to be consulted by the ruler, issue fatawa, and help to guide the believers.

To justify Islamic rule the Ottomans, who were Sunni Muslims, later governed under a particular theory called the circle of equity, in which mutual responsibilities were to provide equity, security, and justice. In the 20th century both Sunni and Shia politicized Islamic movements have argued for a more intensely Islamic government. The Muslim Brotherhood, Hamas, Hezbullah, the Gamaat Islamiya, and Al Qaeda have all taken this position. These groups draw on very important arguments about governance and the state that have developed in Islamic history. The Muslim Brotherhood relinquished jihad as armed struggle and sought to change society through *dawa,* a program involving recruitment, education, and social support. Hezbollah and Hamas argue for both armed struggle and *dawa.* Islamic Jihad (in Egypt), Gamaat Islamiya, and Al Qaeda all argue that the groups who only conducted *dawa* are not supporting Muslims, that jihad as armed struggle is necessary. However, the Gamaat Islamiya and Egyptian Islamic Jihad (in Egypt, excluding those members who joined Al Qaeda) recanted their use of jihad beginning in 1997 and reached a truce with the Egyptian government in 1999.

In general, individual interpretations of Islamic law by scholars may vary. There is no pope or central authority in Sunni Islam. In Sunni Islam, unlike Shia Islam, there is no *marjaiyya,* or formal policy of choosing a cleric as a "source of emulation." However there are today many very popular Sunni clerics and preachers whose followers are loyal to their various positions.

The Sunni legal schools employ a principle of lawmaking known as *ijma,* or consensus, that is not employed by the Shia legal schools. However, there are differences in the legal definitions of that consensus. Additionally, a Sunni Muslim could resort to a cleric of one school to obtain a ruling, or fatwa, and is generally expected to adhere to the commonly acknowledged features of his own school. But Muslims may also seek advice from other clerics or authorities, and advice columns in newspapers and on the Internet provide differing opinions, sometimes based on the positions of other legal schools.

Muslims believe that the Qur'an is the literal word of God delivered in Arabic by the angel Gabriel to Muhammad over a period of 23 years. Any desecration of the Qur'an is therefore a desecration of the very words of Allah. Although the Qur'an is the final statement of Allah to humanity, when it does not offer explicit advice on a particular matter, a Muslim may appeal to a jurist to look to the Prophet's *sunnah,* as recorded in the *ahadith,* or collected materials concerning the tradition, behavior, practices, and sayings of the Prophet. They may also use *qiyas,* or a type of analogy, in determining the licitness of any action, or behavior, or the principle of *ijma.*

The *hadith* are always introduced by listing the chain of their transmitters. Ideally, the first transmitter of the text was a companion (*sahabah*) of Muhammad. An important companion was Abu Bakr, also known as "The Most Truthful" (*al-Siddiq*), the first caliph. The next companions in level of importance are the next two caliphs, Umar and Uthman. The Shia reject the *hadith* transmitted by those they call Unjust Companions, who repudiated the leadership of Ali abi Talib. Although these three are important

## Religious Makeup of Selected Middle Eastern and North African Countries

| Country | Sunni Muslims | Shiite Muslims | Other Religions |
|---------|---------------|----------------|-----------------|
| Algeria | 95% | 4% | 1% |
| Bahrain | 30% | 70% | 0% |
| Egypt | 93% | 1% | 6% |
| Iran | 10% | 89% | 1% |
| Iraq | 34% | 63% | 3% |
| Jordan | 92% | 2% | 6% |
| Kuwait | 65% | 35% | 0% |
| Lebanon | 24% | 36% | 40% |
| Libya | 96% | 1% | 3% |
| Morocco | 97% | 2% | 1% |
| Oman | 89% | 10% | 1% |
| Qatar | 60% | 25% | 15% |
| Saudi Arabia | 90% | 10% | 0% |
| Syria | 77% | 13% | 10% |
| Tunisia | 96% | 2% | 2% |
| United Arab Emirates | 82% | 14% | 4% |
| Yemen | 57% | 42% | 1% |

companions, there are ten who are thought to warrant paradise. A much longer list of *sahabah* exist because Sunnis consider anyone who knew or even saw Muhammad, accepted his teachings, and died as a Muslim to be a companion. Early Sunni scholars identified these companions, wrote their biographies, and listed them in various reference texts. This identification was essential because their testimonies and their reputation for veracity affirm and determine the content of the *hadith* and, therefore, the *sunnah.*

There are many collections of these original oral traditions, but they are graded according to their soundness with six respected collections, two of which—that of Muslim and Bukhari—are considered most reliable. However, many Muslims repeat and believe in *hadith* that are not necessarily the most sound, and since the reform movement of the 19th century, some Muslims believe that the *hadith* brought many unwanted innovations or, conversely, too much imitation of tradition (*taqlid*) into Islam. Shia Islamic law generally uses *hadith* that pertain to Muhammad as told to members of Ali's family. These variations lead to some differences in Sunni Islamic law and Shia Islamic law.

Muslims must practice their faith through demonstrated religious rituals and obligations. Many sources speak of five religious practices or duties, often referred to as the Five Pillars. The first pillar is called bearing witness (*shahadah*) and is the recitation of the creed or confession of faith, called the Testimony of Faith: "There is no God, but Allah; and Muhammad is His prophet." The *shahadah* is also uttered as part of the Muslim call (*adhan*) to prayer and is part of the Tashahud, which follows each set of two prayer sequences, when they are recited at least five times daily (at different times two, three, or four sequences are the minimum required). The second pillar is prayer (*salat*), performed at least five times a day (dawn, noon, midafternoon, sunset, and evening). Muslims purify themselves before prayer by washing their hands, face, mouth, nose, ears, and feet. During prayer, all Muslims face

Sunni Muslim men at prayer in the Umayyad Mosque, Damascus, Syria, 2009. (Ryan Rodrick Beiler/Dreamstime.com)

Mecca. The third pillar is fasting (*sawm*) during the daylight hours for all of the month of Ramadan, the ninth month of the Islamic lunar calendar. This fasting means that no food or beverages are consumed and that there is no smoking or sexual intercourse. Those who are sick are excused from fasting and make up their fast. Other days of fasting may be observed, but it is obligatory during Ramadan.

The fourth pillar is almsgiving, effectively a tax (*zakat*) of 2.5 percent calculated on one's income and assets. But unlike a tax, it is supposed to be voluntary. It is used for the community's poor, the promotion of Islam, and the maintenance of the mosque and other religious institutions. The fifth pillar is the required pilgrimage (*hajj*) once in a lifetime to the holy city of Mecca, as commanded in the Qur'an in surah XXII, al-Hajj, 22–33.

The responsibility for performing these duties falls on the individual, but stricter Muslims and Muslim governments hold that it is the duty of the state to command the good and thus to enforce their performance. There are other strictures as well. For example, Muslims must not drink alcohol, not simply as a forbidden substance but because it clouds alertness and judgment and makes it impossible to pray. Pork is forbidden, as are games of chance. Many Muslim women believe that covering their heads is a required individual duty, but others do not. Modest behavior is, however, required of both men and women.

Many Westerners know little about Islam, with the exception of the Five Pillars. Yet ethical behavior is very important to Islamic belief, including the commitment to social justice, as in protection of the weak and aid to the poor and socially disadvantaged. Islam seeks to promote an ethical life lived within a community. It is more difficult in many ways to be a good Muslim while fulfilling one's obligations to family and community than to live as a hermit, and the Prophet Muhammad is said to have promoted marriage and discouraged celibacy or an extreme ascetic lifestyle. Many of the rules regarding relations between men and women, which non-Muslims find very strict and hard to understand, are indeed intended to provide a moral and ethical grounding for the community.

Muslims are concerned with *iman*, or faith, as well as acts of submission (*islam*) and rightful intentions (*ihsan*), and many religio-philosophical principles guide them. The most basic aspect of Islam is belief in Allah and the Oneness (*tawhid*) of Allah. This monotheism is expressed in many ways. Muslims believe in the prophets and believe that they brought important messages to mankind, but Muhammad is considered the Seal of Prophecy, or the last prophet. Nonetheless, Jesus, Moses, Abraham, and others are revered. However, Muslims believe that some Jews did not heed the word of God in his divine message to them. Muslims, who believe that Jesus was only a prophet, also argue that Christians wrongly recognize Christ as Father and Divine Spirit. The doctrine of the Trinity violates the idea of the Oneness of Allah.

Muslims recognize the scriptures as revelations of Allah. Allah was the creator, but he did not simply create the world and humankind and leave humanity to fend for itself. Rather, Allah provided revelations for the guidance of men. The Qur'an is the transcending revelation of Allah that cannot be contradicted by any other revelations of Allah. Still, Muslims recognize other revelations, which include the Jewish and Christian holy scriptures, as well as the Zoroastrian texts.

Muslims believe in the angels (*malaika*), who are the servants of Allah. Angels were not given the free will that Allah granted to humans. Their duties include recording all human deeds, ensouling the fetus at 120 days of gestation (although some Islamic scholars believe ensoulment occurs on the 40th or 80th day), watching over and caring for creation, gathering souls at death, and much more.

All Muslims also believe in the Day of Judgment and in the Resurrection (*qiyama*), when Allah will return to judge all of humanity, Muslim and non-Muslim, including the dead. After the Resurrection, every human is held accountable for his or her deeds. The deeds of each individual are judged by Allah and weighed on a scale. If the good outweighs the evil, then the individual gains entrance into Paradise. If the evil outweighs the good, the individual spends eternity in Hell.

In the pre-Islamic era, referred to as the *jahiliyya* or time of barbarity, people believed entirely in preordination. Islam rejects this passivity because people possess free will and can thus choose to do good or evil and are held accountable for their decisions. At the same time, it is difficult to retain faith in the face of tragedy, poverty, or disaster. The Muslim belief in the omnipotence of God, his transcendence and simultaneous immanence, is meant to solace the believer.

The application of reason, in the form of Hellenic philosophical arguments to theology, philosophy, and the sciences, was prominent in the Golden Age of Islam. Reacting to the philosophers and those who used logical reasoning (*kalam*) were Traditionists, the scholars who focused on *hadith* to determine the *sunnah* and rejected the methodology of logical reasoning.

Multiple Sunni traditions, or schools of law and theology, arose over time. Not all survive today. These schools share the basic theology described above and assert the primacy of the Qur'anic revelation, but there are notable differences.

Sunni Islamic law is based on the Qur'an and the *sunnah*, as nuanced by the particular *hadith* collector and his interpretation. Different scholars using different assumptions, reasoning, hermeneutics (guiding interpretive principles), and source materials arrived at different applications of Islamic law, which were organized into schools known as *madhahib*. Muslims assert that Sharia never changes but that the understanding and application of it into jurisprudence (*fiqh*) does change, since jurisprudence is carried out by human beings. Muslims generally seek to avoid illicit innovation (*bidah*), but many "innovations" have to be

considered. Thus, the Qur'an predates the telegraph. Thus, the application of *fiqh* to adjudicate the use of the telegraph was a matter of interpretation. In addition to the usual sources of law, jurists took into account *maslaha*, public benefit or the common good, in considering new technology.

There are four surviving major schools of law in Sunni Islam. The various schools predominate in different regions. These dominant Sunni schools of law are Hanbali, Hanafi, Maliki, and Shafi, and all use the Qur'an as their primary source.

Hanbali law is the strictest tradition and was practiced by Muslims in Saudi Arabia, Qatar, Syria, Palestine, and elsewhere; with the growth of *salafism* and *neosalafism,* it has expanded. It was founded by Ahmad ibn Hanbal and is the dominant tradition on the Arabian Peninsula, although it has adherents in Iraq, Syria, Jerusalem, and Egypt as well.

The Hanafi *madhhab* may be the largest school. It was founded by Abu Hanifa and encompasses 30 percent of Sunnis. Its adherents are mainly in Turkey, Central Asia, the Balkans, Iraq, Afghanistan, Pakistan, India, Bangladesh, lower Egypt, and in former states of the Soviet Union. Both the Mongol Empire and the Ottoman Empire promoted the Hanafi tradition. When the Ottoman sultan Selim the Grim (1512–1520) captured Palestine, he imposed Hanafi law on the region. The official judicial traditions and systems in contemporary Syria, Jordan, and Palestine are derived from the Hanafi tradition.

The Maliki school has approximately 15 percent of Sunnis as adherents. It was founded by Malik ibn Anas and has adherents in North Africa and West Africa, particularly upper Egypt, Algeria, Tunisia, Morocco, Mauritania, and Libya, as well as in the Sudan, Kuwait, Dubai, and Abu Dhabi. The Maliki school derives its *fiqh* through consensus more than do any of the other traditions. The Maliki system of lawmaking is built on the Qur'an and the *hadith*, supplemented by an interpretation of *ijma* (consensus), as being the consensus or agreed opinion of the People of Medina, and analogy (*qiyas*). In addition, Malik considered the statements of the Prophet's companions and referred to the public good (*maslahah*), customary law (*urf*), common practice (*adat*), and several other legal principles.

The Shafi school was founded by Muhammad ibn Idris al-Shafi and has adherents in the southern Arabian Peninsula, the Hijaz, Palestine, Indonesia, Malaysia, Thailand, Cambodia, parts of India, the Philippines, Sudan, Ethiopia, Somalia, North Yemen, Kurdistan, Sri Lanka, and lower Egypt. The Shafi school utilizes the *usul al-fiqh* (roots of lawmaking) in a way that places *ijma* ahead of analogy.

Historically, there were many Sunni schools and trends in theology. Among the important or well-known trends were the Mutazila, whose doctrine was abandoned, and the Ashariyyah, Maturidiyyah, and Salafism (which has at least two versions).

The Mutazila school was established in Iraq by Wasil bin Ata (699–749). Abbasid caliph al-Mamun (813–827) made Mutazila theology the state religion and persecuted all dissenters. At the time, Muslims had debated the uncreatedness versus the created (manmade) nature of the Qur'an and many other theological questions. Mutazilites rejected the doctrine of the uncreated Qur'an, but with their downfall Muslims accepted precisely that doctrine. The Mutazila's name came from their intermediate position on the question of sin: they asserted that Muslims who commit grave sins and die without repentance cannot be treated as nonbelievers, but judgment must be withheld until the resurrection. The Mutazilites rejected anthropomorphic interpretations of God. For instance, the phrase "hand of God" might refer symbolically to God's power to the Mutazila, whereas their opponents would insist it meant the actual hand of God.

The Ashariyyah school was founded by Abu al-Hasan al-Ashari (873–935) and became the dominant Sunni theology in that era. It emphasizes divine revelation and stresses the understanding of that revelation through the application of human reasoning.

The Maturidiyyah was founded by Abu Mansur al-Maturidi (d. 944). Maturidis believe that the existence of Allah as understood in Islam can be derived through reason alone and that such is true of major concepts of good and evil, legal and illegal.

Salafism, a reform movement in Islam, actually developed in two different contexts in 18th-century Arabia and in 19th-century Egypt and Ottoman Empire. The 19th-century to early 20th-century reformers Jamal al-Din al-Afghani, Muhammad Abduh, Qasim Amin, and Rashid Rida initiated a discussion about the decline of the Muslim world and the reforms it should carry out to overcome the negative influence of Western colonialism and imperialism. While Afghani looked for an Islamic ruler who would stand up to the West and believed that Pan-Islam could solve the problem, Muhammad Abduh, an Egyptian jurist, recommended reform of Islamic education and the methodology of Islamic law in which blind imitation of the past would cease. He thought that Sunni Muslims should consider a return to *ijtihad* (a Shia methodology of lawmaking) to meet contemporary requirements, and he wanted Western sciences introduced into the educational curriculum. Qasim Amin argued for an end to enforced marriages, female seclusion, and lack of education for women, while Rashid Rida pursued a somewhat stricter and more Islamist approach to the proper way of life for Muslims.

Earlier, Muhammad abd al-Wahhab in Arabia promoted a strict monotheism, which he claimed would cleanse Islam of many syncretic traditions that constituted *shirk*, or polytheism. This tradition is referred to by his enemies as Wahhabism, which is the general term used today in the West. The *muwahiddun*, or Unitarians as they call themselves, or Wahhabists who fought as warriors for the Saud tribe, were known as the Ikhwan (brethren). In general, the *muwahiddun* are considered *salafis*, because they wanted to cleanse Islamic practice and society of un-Islamic accretions and innovations (*bida*) that had arisen through cultural synthesis. However, this cleansing is a matter of gradation, so not all Wahhabis, as the West calls them, are either violent purists or

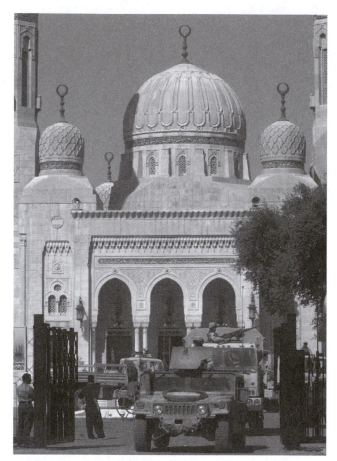

U.S. troops depart following a search operation at the Sunni Ibn Taymiyyah mosque in Baghdad, Iraq. The mosque is attended mainly by Muslims of the Wahhabi sect, 2004. (AP/Wide World Photos)

ardent *salafists*. The Wahhabis adhere to the Hanbali school of law, although some modern *salafis* speak of rejecting all legal tradition and utilizing only the Qur'an and the *sunnah*. The *salafis* were anti-Ottoman, anti-Shia, and anti-Sufi, and opposed such practices as Sufi ceremonies and visiting tombs, even at Mecca. These *salafis* called for jihad in its active form with which they, in alliance with the Saud family, drove out first the Ottomans and then, in a later historical period, the Rashids and the Hashimites.

Terrorist and Al Qaeda leader Osama bin Laden is a *neosalafi* and a Wahhabi. He believes that the Saudi Arabian royal family does not strictly uphold Wahhabi or *salafi* values and should be militantly opposed for its alliance with the West. Other *salafis* have been part of the resistance to U.S. occupation and the new Iraqi government in post-2003 Iraq.

Some *salafis* consider the Shia to be renegades (this refers to a specific denigrating legal epithet given them during the civil wars in Islamic history) or apostates, apostasy being a capital crime in Islam. The Shia had come to fear and hate the Wahhabis because of their raids on Shia areas historically, but this animosity is not true of all Sunnis and Shia who, in general, lived peacefully alongside each other in prewar Iraq. Some charge that the United States and Israel, as well as certain Arab countries, are heightening fears in the region of a Shia crescent of influence, running from Iran to the Shia of Iraq and the Gulf States, and then to the Shia of Lebanon. Such discourse could create more problems among Muslims in the region. Therefore, King Abdullah of Saudi Arabia has spoken out against sectarian discord. Elsewhere leaders such as at al-Azhar try to represent the Jafari *madhhab* as a legitimate legal school of Islam.

RICHARD EDWARDS AND SHERIFA ZUHUR

**See also**
Al Qaeda; Hezbollah; Jihad; Salafism; Sharia; Shia Islam; Wahhabism

**References**
Ahmed, Akbar S. *Islam Today: A Short Introduction to the Muslim World.* Rev. ed. London: I. B. Tauris, 1999.
Armstrong, Karen. *Islam: A Short History.* New York: Modern Library, 2002.
Esposito, John L. *The Oxford History of Islam.* New York: Oxford University Press, 2000.
———. *What Everyone Needs to Know about Islam.* New York: Oxford University Press, 2002.
Fuller, Graham E., and Rend Rahim Francke. *The Arab Shi'a: The Forgotten Muslims.* Hampshire, UK: Palgrave Macmillan, 2001.
Gregorian, Vartan. *Islam: A Mosaic, Not a Monolith.* Baltimore: Brookings Institute Press, 2004.
Sachiko, Muratam, and William C. Chittick. *The Vision of Islam.* New York: Paragon House, 1994.
Salamah, Ahmad Abdullah. *Shia & Sunni Perspective on Islam: An Objective Comparison of the Shia and Sunni Doctrines Based on the Holy Quran and Hadith.* Jedda, Saudi Arabia: Abul-Qasim Publication House, 1991.

# Sunni Triangle

Region of Iraq, populated largely by Sunni Muslims, which has been at the epicenter of the Iraqi insurgency during the Iraq War, which began in 2003. The Sunni Triangle begins near Baghdad, then extends west to Ramadi and north to Tikrit. Each side of the triangle is roughly 125 miles long. This region, which lies generally northwest of the capital city of Baghdad, is densely populated. Tikrit, the birthplace of former Iraqi president Saddam Hussein, has been one of the epicenters of the insurgency since 2003. Also lying within the triangle are the cities of Mosul, Fallujah, Samarra, and Baqubah, all of which have been heavily involved in the insurgency. Hussein's strong tribal and familial connections to the area have traditionally made it the strongest base of support for his regime, and many of his advisers, confidantes, and military commanders hailed from the area.

The term "Sunni Triangle" did not enter the popular lexicon until 2003, after a *New York Times* story that ran on June 10 used it to describe the area in which the growing insurgency was based. The Sunni Triangle witnessed several major offensives conducted by coalition forces designed to flush out and neutralize Iraqi insurgents. The first was Operation RED DAWN, launched in December 2003. Its goal was the capture of the deposed President Hussein. On December 13, 2003, Hussein was found alive and captured in ad-Dawr, a small village not far from his hometown of Tikrit. Hussein's apprehension was a significant public relations and morale boost for coalition forces occupying Iraq.

On April 4, 2004, coalition forces implemented Operation VIGILANT RESOLVE, an attempt to capture control of Fallujah from insurgent forces. The operation precipitated the First Battle of Fallujah, which lasted until May 1, 2004. U.S. forces were unsuccessful in their endeavor, and they sustained 27 killed in the fighting. The prematurely terminated operation proved a public relations nightmare for the United States, as it drove home the notion that its forces were now waging a dangerous and increasingly ineffective counterinsurgency.

During the Second Battle of Fallujah (November 7–December 23, 2004), U.S. forces, working in concert with Iraqi forces, were successful in wresting control of the city from the insurgents. At the time, the Pentagon termed the vicious combat at Fallujah as the worst urban fighting in which American forces had been involved since the January–March 1968 Battle of Hue, during the Tet Offensive of the Vietnam War. The victory was costly, however. U.S. forces suffered 95 killed; Iraqi forces reported 11 killed. At least 1,350 insurgents died in fighting, while another 1,500 were taken captive.

During November 8–16, 2004, American and allied Iraqi Security Forces fought Iraqi insurgents in the Battle of Mosul. It was designed to coincide with the Second Battle of Fallujah. U.S.-led forces were only partly successful in seizing control of Mosul, as a number of insurgents remained in the western third of the city, from which they engaged in hit-and-run tactics. Despite the capture of Fallujah and other counterinsurgency operations, the Sunni Triangle remains among the most dangerous regions of Iraq for U.S. and allied forces.

PAUL G. PIERPAOLI JR.

**See also**
Hussein, Saddam; Iraqi Insurgency; Tikrit

**References**
Buzzell, Colby. *My War: Killing Time in Iraq.* New York: Putnam, 2005.
Keegan, John. *The Iraq War: The Military Offensive, from Victory in 21 Days to the Insurgent Aftermath.* New York: Vintage, 2005.
Ricks, Thomas E. *Fiasco: The American Military Adventure in Iraq.* New York: Penguin, 2006.

# Support and Supply Ships, Strategic

Auxiliary naval vessels of the Maritime Sealift Command (MSC) that transport the supplies, vehicles, weapons, and munitions to sustain projected ground-force operations through high-speed point-to-point sealift. Forward deployed naval squadrons and aircraft carrier battle groups in Operations DESERT SHIELD, DESERT STORM, ENDURING FREEDOM, and IRAQI FREEDOM owed their availability and flexibility to the range of underway replenishment ships gathered around them as they steamed to take up position, and as they subsequently made the transition to a powerful on-station force.

Also of great importance to these campaigns were and are the ships of the MSC's Strategic Sealift Force. These ships are a mixture of commercial cargo types acquired by and converted for the U.S. Navy, predominantly large medium-speed roll-on/roll-off (RO/RO) vehicle cargo ships, container ships, and combination container–RO/RO ships built in the United States and abroad. The RO/RO ships feature large portals with strengthened ramps that allow for quick drive-on loading of battle tanks, armored personnel carriers, rolling artillery pieces, and service vehicles. The container ships and combination container–RO/RO ships are equipped with large heavy-lift cranes that handle the loading and off-loading of their own cargo. MSC's Ready Reserve Force also maintains nine dedicated crane ships to assist chartered merchant vessels in off-loading containers, helicopters, and other heavy loads where port facilities are minimal or lacking.

MSC's three dozen Maritime Prepositioning Force (MPF) ships are distributed into three squadrons, many of whose assets are stationed in the Mediterranean, at Diego Garcia in the Indian Ocean, and in the Pacific at Guam and Saipan. Each MPF squadron has at its disposal the equipment, vehicles, munitions, and supplies necessary to support a U.S. Marine Corps or a U.S. Army brigade for a month. The specifications of the two major MPF vessel types of the MSC are as follows:

**Large Medium-Speed RO/RO Ships**

Gordon class (2 ships: T-AKR-296; T-AKR-298; built in Denmark 1972; MSC 1996–1997). Length 956 feet; beam: 105.9 feet; draft: 35.75 feet; displacement: 55,422 tons (full load); load: 334,000 square feet cargo space; speed: 24 knots; range: 12,000 nautical miles at 24 knots; crew: 26 to 45 civilians.

Shughart class (2 ships: T-AKR-295; T-AKR-297; built in Denmark 1981; MSC 1996–1997). Length: 905.75 feet; beam: 105.5 feet; draft: 35 feet; displacement: 55,298 tons (full load); load: 312,461 square feet cargo space; speed: 24 knots; range: 12,000 nautical miles at 24 knots; crew: 26 to 45 civilians.

Bob Hope class (7 ships: T-AKR-300–T-AKR-306; built by Northrop Grumman, New Orleans, for MSC, 1997–2003). Length: 951.4 feet; beam: 106 feet; draft: 34.6 feet; displacement: 62,069 tons (full load); load: 380,000 square feet cargo space; speed: 24 knots; range: 12,000 nautical miles at 24 knots; crew: 26 to 45 civilians.

Watson class (8 ships: T-AKR-310–T-AKR-317; built by National Steel, San Diego, for MSC, 1997–2002). Length: 951.4 feet; beam: 106 feet; draft: 34 feet; displacement: 62,968 tons (full load); load: 394,000 square feet cargo space; speed: 24 knots; range: 12,700 nautical miles at 24 knots; crew: 26 to 45 civilians.

**Container–RO/RO Ships**

Cpl. Louis J. Hauge Jr. class (5 ships: T-AK-3000–T-AK-3004; built in Denmark 1979; MSC 1984–1985). Length: 755 feet; beam: 90 feet; draft: 32 feet; displacement: 46,552 tons (full load); load: 120,080 square feet cargo space; 332 containers; speed: 17.5 knots; range: 10,800 nautical miles at 17.5 knots; crew: 25 to 32 civilians.

Sgt. Matej Kocak class (3 ships: T-AK-3005–T-AK-3007; built by Sun SDD, PA, and General Dynamics, MA, 1981–1983; MSC 1984–1985). Length: 821 feet; beam: 105.6 feet; draft: 32.2 feet; displacement: 48,754 tons (full load); load: 152,524 square feet cargo space; 540 containers; speed: 20 knots; range: 13,000 nautical miles at 20 knots; crew: 26 to 34 civilians.

2nd Lieutenant John P. Bobo class (5 ships: T-AK-3008–T-AK-3012; built by General Dynamics, MA, 1985–1986 for MSC). Length: 675.2 feet; beam: 105.5 feet; draft: 29.5 feet; displacement: 44,330 tons (full load); load: 162,500 square feet cargo space; 522 containers; speed: 18 knots; range: 11,100 nautical miles at 17.7 knots; crew: 29 to 38 civilians.

The Strategic Sealift Force shares in these maritime assets and also employs some ships from the Ready Reserve Force as fast sealift ships, most prominently the SL-7 type of the USNS Algol (T-AKR-287) class, formerly commercial SeaLand Corporation vessels known as the fastest cargo ships in the world, capable of making 33 knots. Together, the eight Algol-class ships operating during DESERT SHIELD and DESERT STORM—namely, USNS *Algol* (T-AKR-287), USNS *Bellatrix* (T-AKR-288), USNS *Denebola* (T-AKR-289), USNS *Pollux* (T-AKR-290), USNS *Altair* (T-AKR-291), USNS *Regulus* (T-AKR-292), USNS *Capella* (T-AKR-293), and USNS *Antares* (T-AKR-294)—were capable of transporting nearly all the matériel and vehicles required by a U.S. Army mechanized division, including the massive M1A1 Abrams main battle tanks. Their specifications follow:

**Fast Sealift Ships**

Algol class (eight ships: T-AKR-287–T-AKR-294; built 1971–1973 in the Netherlands and Germany; MSC 1984–1986). Length: 946.13 feet; beam: 105.5 feet; draft: 36.66 feet; displacement: 31,017 tons (light load); 55,425 tons (full load); load: 185,000 square feet vehicle space; speed: 33 knots; range: 12,200 nautical miles at 27 knots; crew: 42 civilians.

During DESERT SHIELD's enormous, unprecedented rapid transfer of four divisions' worth of munitions, armaments, armored vehicles, and tanks from the continental United States to the Middle East, MSC was largely successful in mobilizing its fleet of snoozing cargo vessels from Ready Reserve Force status to purposefully

The support and supply ship USNS *2nd Lt. John P. Bobo* (T-AK 3008), under long-term lease to the U.S. Military Sealift Command. (U.S. Department of Defense)

steaming across thousands of miles of ocean. Occasional break-downs were inevitable. In August 1990 *Antares,* loaded with Abrams tanks, lost engine power in midocean and was towed to Spain, where *Altair* took on the heavy cargo for a delayed delivery to Saudi Arabia for DESERT SHIELD preparations. Since the mid-1990s the size of this delivery force has nearly doubled, and it also contributed significantly in the run-up to and the initiation of the Iraq War in 2003. Among the augmented forces assembling for Operation IRAQI FREEDOM were the DESERT SHIELD/DESERT STORM veterans of the Algol class, along with all five ships of the Hauge class, the two Gordon class, the Bob Hope class, the two Shughart ships, the Watson and Bobo classes, and the one-off combination container–RO/RO ship *Lt. Harry L. Martin* (T-AK-3015) and the RO/RO ship *Gunnery Sgt. Fred W. Stockham* (T-AK-3017).

GORDON E. HOGG

**See also**

Fast Combat Support Ships; Military Sealift Command; Repair Ships, U.S.; Underway Replenishment Ships; United States Navy, Iraq War; United States Navy, Persian Gulf War

**References**

Marolda, Edward, and Robert Schneller. *Shield and Sword: The United States Navy and the Persian Gulf War.* Annapolis, MD: U.S. Naval Institute Press, 2001.

Polmar, Norman. *The Naval Institute Guide to the Ships and Aircraft of the U.S. Fleet.* 18th ed. Annapolis, MD: Naval Institute Press, 2005.

Saunders, Stephen, ed. *Jane's Fighting Ships, 2002–2003.* Coulsdon, Surrey, UK, and Alexandria, VA: Jane's Information Group, 2002.

Sharpe, Richard, ed. *Jane's Fighting Ships: 1991–1992.* London: Jane's Information Group, 1991.

# Supporters of Islam

*See* Ansar al-Islam

# Supreme Council for the Islamic Revolution in Iraq

*See* Supreme Iraqi Islamic Council

# Supreme Iraqi Islamic Council

Shia resistance group founded in 1982 and a powerful political party in post-2003 Iraq. The Supreme Iraqi Islamic Council (SIIC) was created and known for decades as the Supreme Council for

Ammar al-Hakim, leader of Iraq's largest Shiite party, the Supreme Iraqi Islamic Council, gives a sermon in Baghdad in September 2009. (AP/Wide World Photos)

the Islamic Revolution in Iraq (SCIRI). It is an Islamist-oriented organization whose goal has been the creation of an Islamic-based regime in Iraq. The group advocates a decentralized Iraqi government and the establishment of an autonomous zone reserved for Shiites in the south of Iraq. The party's name was changed in 2007 to remove the term "Islamic revolution" from the party's official title. This move also seemed to signal a concern on the part of the SIIC to eschew the advocacy of civil and sectarian violence in Iraq, and to draw more Iraqis into its ranks.

The SCIRI was formed in 1982, during the Iran-Iraq War. At that time, the Islamic Dawa Party, Iraq's principal Islamist group, was severely repressed by the Saddam Hussein regime. The SCIRI was formed as a party in exile in Iran, with the backing of the Iranian regime, and contrasted with the Islamic Dawa Party, many of whose members left Iran because they did not wish to fight Iraqis in the Iran-Iraq War. Muhammad Baqir al-Hakim, a member of one of Iraq's most prominent Shia clerical families, came to lead the group. Upon the creation of the party, Hakim made it clear that the primary and immediate goal of the organization was to overthrow Hussein's Baathist regime and to establish an Islamic state in Iraq, along the lines of the regime in Iran. But the SCIRI also became an umbrella organization, allowing other Shia groups to ally with it.

The SCIRI espoused the belief that, ideally, an Islamist regime must be controlled by Islamic scholars (*ulema*), the system that is in operation in Iran. Other Shia Islamist groups, however, did not subscribe to that framework, believing instead that the government should be guided by the whole of the Muslim community (*ummah*). Until the fall of the Hussein regime in 2003, the SCIRI operated largely in exile and along the fringes of Iraqi politics.

That all changed after the Anglo-American–led invasion of Iraq in March 2003, which ousted Hussein from power. Working in tandem with other Shia groups, the SCIRI moved to solidify its base and influence in a nation that had been dominated for many years by the Sunnis. Taking its cues from Islamist organizations in other countries, especially the Muslim Brotherhood and Hamas, the SCIRI gained many adherents by providing humanitarian aid and basic services to displaced and poor Shia Iraqis. The United States became closer to SCIRI than to any of the other Shia parties, for despite its Islamism, the group was well organized, promised to control other Shia militias, and had English-speaking leaders, whom the Americans preferred to Ibrahim al-Jafari of the Islamic Dawa Party. However, other American and British officials have sometimes viewed the party with a weary eye, as the SIIC is likely receiving financial support and, allegedly, weapons from Iran. In an attempt to make itself more credible, the party has soft-pedaled its devotion to revolution and the imposition of an Islamic state in Iraq since the 2003 invasion. Instead, it has stated its commitment to democratic processes and has demonstrated a willingness to cooperate with rival political parties.

Not surprisingly, the SIIC's power base is located in the center and south of Iraq. It competes with other Shia parties, particularly Fadhila in the city of Basra, which has a heavily Shia population. The party maintains an armed militia, known as the Badr Brigades. It is believed that these forces contain from 5,000 to 10,000 well-armed men, the weapons of which have come largely from the Iranians. Badr's headquarters are located in Baghdad.

The party suffered a setback in August 2003 when its leader, Ayatollah Hakim, was killed in Najaf in a car bombing. It has been posited that Al Qaeda in Iraq was behind the murder. Hakim's brother, Abd al-Aziz al-Hakim, then took control of the organization. He died in a Tehran hospital in August 2009 of lung cancer and was succeeded by his son, Ammar al-Hakim.

Currently, the SIIC retains the most seats of any Iraqi political group in the Council of Representatives. In January 2005 it joined forces with the United Iraqi Alliance and captured six of the eight Shia-majority governorates and garnered 40 percent of the votes in Baghdad. Numerous SIIC members have held both official and unofficial positions with the Iraqi government. Hakim was a member of the Iraqi Governing Council, created by the United States, and served as that body's president briefly in late 2003. Hakim has adeptly walked a political tightrope and managed to maintain relatively cordial relations with the United States. Indeed, he has met with numerous high-level U.S. officials, including Secretary of Defense Donald Rumsfeld, and had a one-on-one meeting with President George W. Bush at the White House in December 2006. Nevertheless, SIIC's control of the southern Iraqi governorates has come under fire for alleged corruption and the misdeeds of its Badr organization.

PAUL G. PIERPAOLI JR.

**See also**

Bush, George Walker; Hakim, Abd al-Aziz al-; Hakim, Muhammad Baqir al-; Iraq, History of, Pre-1990; Iraq, History of, 1990–Present; Rumsfeld, Donald Henry

**References**

Nasr, Vali. *The Shia Revival: How Conflicts within Islam Will Shape the Future.* New York: Norton, 2006.

Packer, George. *The Assassins' Gate: America in Iraq.* New York: Farrar, Straus and Giroux, 2005.

Stansfield, Gareth. *Iraq: People, History, Politics.* Cambridge, UK: Polity, 2007.

# Surge, U.S. Troop Deployment, Iraq War

The term "troop surge" refers to the early January 2007 decision by the George W. Bush administration to deploy approximately 20,000 to 30,000 additional American troops to Iraq to arrest insurgent-inspired violence. Those insurgents included both Al Qaeda terrorists and rival Sunni and Shiite sectarian militias. U.S. Army general David Petraeus, commander of U.S. forces in Iraq, is credited with the surge strategy. The impetus for the troop surge was the November 2006 U.S. midterm election, in which the Republican Party lost control of both houses of Congress, largely because of growing public opposition to the Iraq War and dismay with the level of casualties among U.S. soldiers.

With the Democrats having made opposition to the Iraq War the central issue of the 2006 election and calling for a withdrawal of U.S. troops from Iraq, Bush announced a change in strategy to reduce violence and improve security in Iraq. This followed the resignation of Secretary of Defense Donald Rumsfeld, a key architect of the Iraq War, in December 2006. Referring to a "new way forward" in a televised national speech on January 10, 2007, the president announced a plan to secure the capital city, Baghdad, from both Al Qaeda and sectarian militias, and rid Anbar Province (stretching west from Baghdad to the Syrian and Jordanian borders) of Al Qaeda fighters. Approximately 16,000 additional U.S. troops were deployed to secure Baghdad, and another 4,000 troops were sent to Anbar Province.

By June 15, 2007, with these additional troops in place, the surge began in earnest. Instead of simply launching raids against Al Qaeda and sectarian militias, U.S. and Iraqi forces in Baghdad established posts within neighborhoods controlled by these groups. In Anbar Province, because of public outrage sparked by Al Qaeda's murdering of hundreds of Iraqi Muslims, Sunni tribes severed their ties with Al Qaeda and aligned themselves with the Iraqi government and the U.S. military. In so doing, these tribes formed militias ("Sons of Iraq"), comprising some 103,000 men, many of them former insurgents and terrorists, armed and paid by the United States to defend their communities against Al Qaeda. Although this proved effective in rooting out Al Qaeda insurgents in the short term, in the long run these militias will have to be reintegrated into either the Iraqi military or police forces, or find gainful employment elsewhere, in order for them to remain loyal to the Iraqi government.

The surge strategy emerged from the belated recognition that Iraqi security forces were as yet unable to provide security without significant American assistance and support, and that the number of U.S. troops had to be increased to effectively stamp out the insurgency. It was also recognized that to defeat an insurgency, military forces must take up residence and maintain a physical presence within the areas infested by insurgents because, in the words of General Petraeus, "you can't commute to this fight; you must live among the people." Accordingly, the surge increased U.S. troop strength in Baghdad and Anbar Province, the two most violent regions of Iraq, not only to clear but also to hold territory, thus reinforcing Iraqi military and police presence. U.S. troops were also to assist Iraqi forces as they established security. The downside of this strategy was that it prolonged the foreign military presence in the country, which is what had provoked the insurgents and thus gave them cause to continue resistance.

A U.S. Army soldier provides security on a street in Tarmiyah, Iraq, in 2007. The soldier is a member of the 4th Brigade of the 2nd Infantry Division, one of five brigades sent to Iraq as part of the "Iraq troop surge." (U.S. Department of Defense)

Since early 2007, with continued American military assistance, particularly in the form of logistics and air support, Iraqi forces had demonstrated increasing competence and skill in battling insurgents and providing security. In addition, Iraqi prime minister Nuri al-Maliki, a leader of the Islamic Dawa Party, showed a willingness to confront militias, including Shia militias, as evinced by Iraqi military operations in the cities of Basra, Baghdad, and Ninawa. Also, Muqtada al-Sadr, the leader of the powerful Shiite Mahdi Army, agreed not to confront the Iraqi government and U.S. military, and has maintained that promise since mid-June 2007. In both Baghdad and Anbar Province, Al Qaeda was seriously weakened, but unfortunately its signature tactic of inflicting mass casualties through car bombs targeting Shiites, including Shiite mosques, had resumed again in 2009. Coalition efforts in these two areas forced the group to flee to the northern city of Mosul and the surrounding province of Nineveh, as well as to the religiously mixed province of Diyala. Iraqi and U.S. forces then battled Al Qaeda in these new areas. Nonetheless, the situation remained volatile, with Al Qaeda still a dangerous threat and the possibility that any one of the factors that had contributed to the military gains under the surge could be reversed and produce an increase in violence.

The results of the troop surge could be seen in the statistical decline in both Iraqi and U.S. casualties. According to a June 2008 Pentagon report, violence in Iraq dropped between 40 and 80 percent from presurge levels, while the number of violent incidents fell to their lowest point in more than four years. In addition, fewer U.S. troops were killed in May 2008, when 19 died (compared to 126 in May 2007), than in any other month since the invasion of Iraq in March 2003; 29 U.S. troops were killed in June 2008 compared to 101 in June 2007. The Iraqi Body Count, a group that keeps a tally of Iraqi casualties from media reports, noted that 712 Iraqi civilian deaths occurred in June 2008, less than a third of the average during the summer of 2007.

Expanding revenues from the export of Iraqi oil and continued growth in the Iraqi economy (4 percent in 2007) also contributed to a decline in violence in the country, as unemployment dropped. The June 2008 Pentagon report, however, warned that security gains could not be preserved without continued progress in economic development and reconstruction; increasing government services, such as electricity (currently available for a national daily average of only 14.9 hours, including just 13 hours in Baghdad); health care, water, and sewage treatment; and national political reconciliation among Iraq's rival religious and political groups. An important step in political reconciliation was taken with the passage of a long-awaited and needed Amnesty Law on February 26, 2008, for Iraqis accused or convicted of crimes of terrorism. In addition, Iraq's largest Sunni Arab bloc, the Iraqi Accord Front, prepared to rejoin Prime Minister Maliki's cabinet after a yearlong boycott protesting the government's alleged policies of excluding and marginalizing Sunnis. The inclusion of Sunnis into Iraq's government was cited by both the United States and Iraq as a major factor in bringing about national unity. Sunni Arabs had a great deal of power during Saddam Hussein's regime, but became marginalized after he was toppled in 2003. Since then, the Iraqi government has been dominated by Shiites and Kurds.

Despite these developments, however, it was acknowledged that the Iraqi government remained corrupt and inefficient, and that it lacked sufficiently qualified personnel to effectively govern and execute policy and programs.

The surge also entered presidential politics in the United States. In the summer of 2008, Republican candidate John McCain made much of his advocacy of, and support for, the surge. He sought to make the troop surge a major issue in the campaign, attacking his Democratic opponent Barack Obama for his opposition to it. Obama pointed out that it was not just the increase in troop strength but also the reconciliation of the Sunni tribes that had contributed to the decrease in violence. He also noted that McCain had supported the earlier Bush policies that had not worked, whereas he (Obama) had opposed the war from the beginning.

In sum, the surge proved to be successful, but as Petraeus remarked, "we can't kill ourselves out of this endeavor." Ultimately, it is only the Iraqi government that can build a stable, secure, prosperous, and united nation.

STEFAN M. BROOKS

**See also**

Al Qaeda; Al Qaeda in Iraq; Bush, George Walker; Iraq, History of, 1990–Present; Iraqi Insurgency; Mahdi Army; Petraeus, David Howell; Rumsfeld, Donald Henry

**References**

Engel, Richard. *War Journal: My Five Years in Iraq.* New York: Simon and Schuster, 2008.

Galbraith, Peter. *The End of Iraq: How American Incompetence Created a War without End.* New York: Simon and Schuster, 2007.

Isikoff, Michael, and David Corn. *Hubris: The Inside Story of Spin, Scandal, and the Selling of the Iraq War.* New York: Three Rivers/Random House, 2007.

# Suri, Abu Musab al-
## Birth Date: 1958

Nom de guerre of Mustafa Sittmariam Nasar, one of militant Islam's most prolific strategic theorists in the past 30 years and a member of the Al Qaeda terrorist organization. Abu Musab al-Suri was born in Aleppo, Syria, in 1958; his birth name reportedly was Mustafa Sittmariam Nasar. Suri experienced a religious awakening in 1980 after studying engineering at the University of Aleppo for four years. Joining a branch of the Syrian Muslim Brotherhood, he left Syria in 1980 never to return because of the severe repression by the Asad regime of the Islamic opposition. Despite Suri's exile, he maintained his Syrian roots and connections—al-Suri means "the Syrian" in Arabic—and was considered the Syrian representative in Al Qaeda's highest leadership circles.

Suri traveled widely after leaving Syria. He is known to have resided in Jordan, Saudi Arabia, Iraq, and France (mid-1980s), Afghanistan (1987–1992), Spain (1992–1997), and Afghanistan again (1997–2002). While in Spain he married a Spanish woman. During his first visit to Afghanistan he met both Abdallah Azzam and Osama bin Laden, the founders of Al Qaeda. Suri may have received sanctuary in Iran after Operation ENDURING FREEDOM began in late 2001, and he reportedly traveled to Iraq to visit Ansar al-Islam's camp in Kurdistan prior to the U.S.-led invasion of Iraq (Operation IRAQI FREEDOM) in March 2003. In November 2004 the U.S. government offered a $5 million reward for information leading to his capture.

Suri is best known for his prolific theoretical writing and speaking on jihad (holy war) and the appropriate strategies for waging war against the West. His writings are notable for their systematic efforts to learn from past mistakes. His first book, *The Syrian Islamic Jihadist Revolution: Pains and Hopes,* was published around 1990 in Peshawar. In the 1990s, he established a media center called the Islamic Conflict Studies Bureau LTD and was able to create major media opportunities for bin Laden and Al Qaeda leadership in the 1996–1998 period. During this period Suri wrote a number of studies and analyses of jihadist efforts in the Middle East, Central Asia, and South Asia. His 160-page *Musharraf's Pakistan: The Problem and the Solution! And the Necessary Obligation* was published in late 2004. It called for the overthrow of the Pervez Musharraf regime, a call later echoed by Al Qaeda second-in-command Ayman al-Zawahiri. At about the same time, Suri finally completed the 1,600-page *The Call for a Global Islamic Resistance,* a work he had begun in the early 1990s that articulates his ideas for a new global guerrilla warfare strategy based on a decentralized model of organization. He also hoped to write a book on jihad guerrilla strategy titled *The Fundamentals for Jihadi Guerrilla Warfare in Light of the Conditions of the Contemporary American Campaign* and based on his lectures and research in Afghanistan, but he was arrested before the manuscript could be completed. Several transcripts of his lectures on this topic have been released on jihadi Web sites since his arrest.

Suri apparently had strong reservations about the September 11 attacks. On the one hand, he recognized their mobilizing effect on the Islamic community. On the other hand, he also recognized that the attacks provided a justification for U.S. invasion, which shattered the jihadi movement. This recognition led to his publication of *The Call for a Global Islamic Resistance* in which he argued that the old local and regional covert organizations (*tanzims*) were no longer an effective way of conducting revolution. Their large hierarchical organization, firmly rooted geographically, raised too many risks in an era of dominant U.S. military and political influence and active opposition from many local governments. Suri instead argued that a transnational structure based on small cells held together by common doctrine and ideology could carry out terror operations at lower risk. This also would create a deterritorialized jihadist war in which operations are carried out on a global scale and resistance to occupation is not confined to the theater in question.

Suri himself insisted in his writings that he was primarily a theorist and thinker, not an executor of operations. However, he is suspected of having had deep operational involvement in a variety of conflicts and, since 2001, attacks or attempted attacks on Western states. He fought with Al Qaeda and the Taliban in Afghanistan, where his experiences during American air strikes contributed strongly to his reassessment of proper resistance tactics. He was suspected of involvement in the March 2004 Madrid bombing attacks and has been linked in some reports to attacks in London in July 2005. British authorities reportedly suspect that he had some involvement in the 1995 Paris Metro bombings, and he has significant ties with terrorist cells in both Europe and the Maghreb, as well as a record of support for the Algerian terrorist organization Armed Islamic Group (GIA). Some reports also link him with Abu Musab al-Zarqawi, as both men are associated with a virulent dislike of Shia Islam. However, Suri might have acquired this position because of the sectarian situation in Syria. At least one account notes that the intellectually sophisticated and articulate Suri must have had a strong ideological impact on the barely educated Zarqawi.

Suri also ran a major training camp called Al Ghuraba ("The Aliens") in Afghanistan during 2000–2001 that trained foreign fighters for Al Qaeda and the Taliban. Also, he is reported to have assisted in Al Qaeda's experiments with chemical weapons. Suri almost certainly trained Al Qaeda operatives who went back to Europe and created sleeper cells.

Interestingly, Suri was linked with a group of secessionists inside Al Qaeda who reportedly rejected bin Laden's leadership and pledged loyalty to the Taliban. Suri had to take an oath of obedience to Mullah Mohammed Omar, leader of the Taliban, in order to run his training camp. Suri himself denied rumors of a split, however, and emphasized his close links with Al Qaeda leadership, including his invitation to bin Laden's wedding in 2000. The nature of the connection to Al Qaeda is, in some respects, irrelevant, as Suri's writings provide the basis for a school of jihadi strategic studies that have profoundly affected Al Qaeda and other transnational terrorist networks and have raised significant concern for Western analysts and policy makers.

In late 2005 Pakistani security forces reportedly captured Suri in Quetta, Pakistan. He was then allegedly transferred to American custody, but his current location is unknown.

TIMOTHY D. HOYT

**See also**

Al Qaeda; Bin Laden, Osama; Omar, Mohammed; Taliban; Terrorism; Zawahiri, Ayman al-

**References**

Lacey, Jim, ed. *A Terrorist's Call to Global Jihad: Deciphering Abu Musab al-Suri's Islamic Jihad Manifesto.* Annapolis, MD: Naval Institute Press, 2008.

Lia, Brynjar. *Architect of Global Jihad: The Life of Al-Qaeda Strategist Abu Mus'ab Al-Suri.* New York: Columbia University Press, 2008.

---

# Swannack, Charles
## Birth Date: May 9, 1951

U.S. Army general whose last major command was the 82nd Airborne Division during its deployment in Operation IRAQI FREEDOM. Charles Swannack was born on May 9, 1951, in Morristown, New Jersey. When he was nine years old his family moved to Winston-Salem, North Carolina, where he spent his formative years. Swannack graduated from the United States Military Academy, West Point, in 1971 and was commissioned a second lieutenant.

Swannack's first posting was to the American sector of then-divided Berlin, Germany. He then served with the 82nd Airborne Division. Swannack also earned an MS degree in mechanical engineering from Georgia Institute of Technology and then taught at West Point. Following study at the Command and General Staff College, Fort Leavenworth, Kansas, in 1984 Swannack was assigned to the 7th Infantry Division at Fort Ord, California. In 1989 he served in the U.S. invasion of Panama (Operation JUST CAUSE) as commander of an infantry battalion. Swannack then held a series of staff positions and studied at the National War College.

In 1994 Swannack took command of the 2nd Brigade of the 25th Infantry Division. Soon afterward he returned to the 82nd Airborne Division and served as assistant division commander in Operation UPHOLD DEMOCRACY in Haiti. After that he again returned to Washington, D.C., and held several staff positions, including deputy director of Strategy Plans and Policy Directorate in the office of the U.S. Army's deputy chief of staff for operations and plans.

In 1998 Swannack was promoted to brigadier general and took command of the Joint Readiness Training Center in Fort Polk, Louisiana, which trained light infantry forces. In 2001 Swannack assumed command of the Multi-National Force North in Tuzla, Bosnia. This division was integral to North Atlantic Treaty Organization (NATO) efforts to support the Dayton Accords and to ensure the peace in war-torn Bosnia-Herzegovina.

In 2002, Swannack was promoted to major general and was assigned command of the 82nd Airborne Division. This time the

U.S. Army brigadier general Charles H. Swannack, commander of the 82nd Airborne Division during its deployment in Operation IRAQI FREEDOM. (U.S. Department of Defense)

82nd was already engaged in combat operations in Operation IRAQI FREEDOM. When he arrived in theater in October 2002, the 82nd Airborne was part of Task Force All American. Comprising 18,000 soldiers from various units, Task Force All American occupied an area the size of Wyoming in western Iraq. Its area of operations included the city of Fallujah. In the nine months of his command, Swannack endeavored to secure the part of this area under his command while turning over as much responsibility as possible for administering the area to local Iraqi authorities. This plan appeared to be working until the Iraqi insurgency led to a full-scale siege of Fallujah and the April 2004 First Battle of Fallujah.

In May 2004 Swannack became deputy commanding general of the XVIII Airborne Corps. Later in 2004 he retired from active duty. In April 2006 Swannack joined several other retired general officers in calling for the resignation of Defense Secretary Donald Rumsfeld and the reexamination of American tactics and policies in Iraq.

SHAWN LIVINGSTON

**See also**

Fallujah, First Battle of; IRAQI FREEDOM, Operation; Iraqi Insurgency; Rumsfeld, Donald Henry

**References**

Cook, Martin L. "Revolt of the Generals: A Case Study in Professional Ethics." *Parameters: U.S. Army War College* 38(1) (2008): 4–15.

Ledford, Tranette. "Maj. Gen. Charles H. Swannack Jr." *Army Times* 62(41) (2002): 15.

"Retiring 'Swan Dog' Ready for Time Off." *Army Times* 65(18) (2004): 46.

## Swift Boat Veterans for Truth

Political group formed in 2004 in opposition to the presidential campaign of Democratic U.S. senator John F. Kerry, a Vietnam War veteran who had served on swift boats during the conflict. Swift Boat Veterans of Truth (SBVT) was composed chiefly of swift-boat veterans and former Vietnam prisoners of war (POWs). When first conceived, its sole purpose was to prevent Kerry from being elected president. Although it publicized itself as nonpartisan, numerous high-level SBVT members were Republicans or otherwise had close ties to the Republican Party. Among those who made sizable contributions to the organization was Texas oil tycoon T. Boone Pickens.

Only some 250 of the more than 3,500 sailors who had served on swift boats during the war became members of SBVT, and most of those had never served with Kerry. Several of the veterans who joined the group had earlier praised Kerry's performance during the war, including 16 naval officers who had served with Kerry in Coastal Division 11. Only 1 person who had actually served on Kerry's boat joined the group, although he did not have a high profile within the organization. All of the other surviving members of Kerry's crew enthusiastically supported his candidacy.

Among other things, the SBVT charged that Kerry was unfit to serve as president because he had knowingly misrepresented the wartime conduct of other Vietnam War veterans and had either withheld or distorted facts relating to his own conduct during the war. Many of the charges against Kerry were based on Kerry's actions after he returned from the war, including his involvement in Vietnam Veterans Against the War, testimony before the Senate Foreign Relations Committee that was highly critical of the war, and connection to an incident in which he and other veterans threw down their war medals on the steps of the Capitol building, with media cameras recording the action.

Kerry received the Silver Star, Bronze Star, and three Purple Heart medals during his Vietnam tour, but the circumstances surrounding the actions for which he received the awards have generated controversy. For example, his highest award, the Silver Star, was for his action in leaving his boat and shooting a Viet Cong guerrilla who had already been wounded by American automatic weapons fire and may have been helpless. Additionally, at least one of his Purple Heart medals has been questioned for the highly irregular manner in which the award recommendation was processed (it was largely handled by Kerry himself). Since Kerry presented himself as a Vietnam War hero, the SBVT challenged this representation, raising troubling questions.

Perhaps Kerry's most incendiary postwar activity was his involvement in the 1971 Winter Soldier Investigation in which he spearheaded an effort to publicize testimony of some 100 veterans who were alleged to have participated in or witnessed war crimes.

When SBVT went public in May 2004, its allegations against Kerry created few waves, and the media largely ignored it. That all changed, however, when the group produced television ads that began airing on August 5, 2004. These showcased numerous veterans asserting that Kerry was unreliable, dishonest, unfit to be president, and had needlessly besmirched the reputations of thousands of Vietnam War veterans. Interspersed with the interviews were photos of Kerry throwing down his medals and in uniform. A second ad began running on August 24. It showed clips from Kerry's Senate testimony in 1969 and excerpts from the Winter Soldier Investigation. That was followed by two more equally damning commercials that ran into early September.

In August, John O'Neill (SBVT founder) and Jerome E. Corsi published a book titled *Unfit for Command,* published by Regnery Press and featuring a prominent photo of Kerry on the front cover. It reiterated the main selling points of the group's allegations.

Many were aghast at the ad campaign, and Republican senator John S. McCain III strongly rebuked the first ad, saying that it was "very, very wrong." Although McCain challenged President George W. Bush to condemn the ads, neither the president nor the Bush presidential campaign did so. Instead, they merely insisted that they did not endorse the SBVT group and did not question Kerry's patriotism or service in the war.

For Kerry's part, his campaign made the fatal mistake of not immediately and strongly countering the attacks, and by the time the campaign countered the attacks, the damage had already been done. While it is simplistic to say that the television ads alone caused Kerry's defeat in the November 2004 elections, they certainly did not help his chances and managed to plant much doubt in the minds of voters concerning his veracity as a politician and his ability to lead the nation during a time of war.

The SBVT has since changed its name to Swift Vets and POWs for Truth and continues to operate as a nonpartisan organization. In the meantime, the term "swift-boating" entered the American political lexicon as a term describing particularly negative campaign ads. The swift-boat controversy clearly showcased the divisive nature of American politics and demonstrated the continuing centrality of the Vietnam War in contemporary U.S. political discourse.

PAUL G. PIERPAOLI JR.

**See also**

Bush, George Walker; Kerry, John Forbes; McCain, John Sidney, III; United States, National Elections of 2000; United States, National Elections of 2004

**References**

John F. Kennedy School of Government. *Campaign for President: The Managers Look at 2004.* Lanham, MD: Rowman and Littlefield, 2005.

Kranish, Michael, Brian C. Mooney, and Nine J. Easton. *John F. Kerry: The Complete Biography.* New York: PublicAffairs, 2004.

Sabato, Larry J. *Divided States of America: The Slash and Burn Politics of the 2004 Presidential Election.* New York: Longman, 2005.

## Swift Project
### Start Date: 2001
### End Date: Continuing

A secret U.S. government program to trace the financial records of people suspected of having ties to the Al Qaeda terrorist organization. Within weeks of the events of September 11, 2001, the George W. Bush administration launched the project, which has come to be known as the Swift Project. It was named after the Brussels banking consortium Society for Worldwide Interbank Financial Telecommunication (SWIFT). The SWIFT consortium serves as a gatekeeper for electronic transactions among 7,800 international institutions and is owned by a cooperative of more than 2,200 organizations. Every major commercial bank, brokerage house, fund manager, and stock exchange used its services. Because of the top-secret nature of the program, precise details, including the date of implementation, are not known precisely.

The Bush administration entrusted the Central Intelligence Agency (CIA) and the U.S. Treasury Department to set up and run the Swift Project. Legal justification for the implementation of this project was the president's emergency economic powers. American agents used computer programs to wade through huge amounts of sensitive data from the transactions of SWIFT. Treasury officials maintained at the time and since that the Swift Project was exempt from U.S. laws restricting government access to private financial records because the cooperative was classified as a messaging service, not a bank or financial institution. This allowed the U.S. government to track money from bank accounts of suspected terrorists to a source in the United States or elsewhere in the world. It was information of this type that allowed American officials to locate and capture Radwann Isamuddin Hambali, the operations chief of the Indonesian terrorist group Jemah Islamiyya, in Thailand.

News of the Swift Project became public in 2006 and became identified with the surveillance of American citizens by the U.S. government. Members of the Bush administration, especially Vice President Dick Cheney, sharply denounced the media's revelation of the program. Despite considerable negative publicity, the Bush administration continued to use the Swift Project to track the financial records of organizations and people suspected of giving money to Al Qaeda.

STEPHEN E. ATKINS

**See also**

Bush, George Walker; Central Intelligence Agency; Cheney, Richard Bruce

**References**

Bender, Bryan. "Terrorist Funds-Tracking No Secret, Some Say." *Boston Globe,* June 28, 2006, 1.

Bilefsky, Dan. "Bank Consortium Faces Outcry on Data Transfer." *International Herald Tribune,* June 29, 2006, 4.

Lichtblau, Eric, and James Risen. "Bank Data Sifted in Secret by U.S. to Block Terror." *New York Times,* June 23, 2006, 1.

Meyer, Josh, and Greg Miller. "U.S. Secretly Tracks Global Bank Data." *Los Angeles Times,* June 23, 2006, 1.

Stolberg, Sheryl, and Eric Lichtblau. "Cheney Assails Press on Report on Bank Data." *New York Times,* June 24, 2006, 1.

# Sykes, Sir Mark

**Birth Date: March 16, 1879**
**Death Date: February 16, 1919**

Tory member of the British Parliament, expert on the Near East, and perhaps best known for negotiating the secret Sykes-Picot Agreement of 1916 that carved the Middle East into spheres of influence between Britain and France and created the boundaries of many of the present-day Middle Eastern states. Mark Sykes was born in London on March 16, 1879, the child of Sir Tatton Sykes, 5th Baronet. As a youth Mark Sykes spent time in both London and the family estates at Sledmere in Yorkshire.

His wealth and his position as 6th baronet upon his father's death in 1913 left Sykes largely at his own discretion, and he gravitated toward travel and scholarly pursuits. As a young man he became fascinated with Turkey and the entire Near East. He attended Cambridge University for a time and in 1897 joined a reserve battalion of the Princess of Wales' Own Regiment (Yorkshire Regiment). He traveled extensively and published four books while still a young man, three of which were travel narratives dealing with his impressions of Turkey and the Arab world.

Sykes served in the Second Boer War from 1900 to 1902. When he returned home in early 1903 his lineage and background made politics a natural outlet for his talents. During 1904–1905 he served as a parliamentary secretary to George Wyndham, chief secretary of Ireland and the primary British official in Ireland. In 1912 Sykes secured election to Parliament from Hull Central. His father died the following year, making Sykes the 6th Baronet. With the beginning of World War I, Sykes remained a lieutenant colonel with the Green Howards, but given his background as a Turkish and Arab specialist, he secured a post in the War Office. There he helped guide Britain's Near East policies and advised the cabinet on matters pertaining to the region.

World War I had necessitated a shift in British policy toward the Near East. Heretofore, Britain and France had been staunch allies of the waning Ottoman Empire, in part to restrain Russian territorial ambitions in the Balkans and the Near East. However, now Britain and France found themselves at war with the Ottoman Empire and fighting alongside a Russian ally. Arab allies fighting against the Ottomans were of great assistance to the Allies, and many Arabs expected to receive some form of self-determination when the war was over; indeed, once the United States entered World War I in April 1917, self-determination became an ostensible Allied war goal. Numerous pro-Arab Britons with expertise in the region, including T. E. Lawrence, Gertrude Bell, and Sir Percy Cox, desired the breakup of the Ottoman Empire and Arab independence. Sykes, however, tried to steer a middle course that would provide for greater Arab sovereignty but also create a strong Turkey, able to resist future aggression from Russia or other regional powers.

Entente Powers' negotiations over postwar planning for the Near East resulted in the 1916 Sykes-Picot Agreement (Sykes's French counterpart was François Georges Picot), which Sykes had worked on for several months. As France and Britain were clandestinely redrawing the map of the Near East, they consulted with the Russian government, which gave its tacit approval to the arrangements. By 1916, however, Russia was poised on the precipice of civil war, so it could not have asserted itself in the region even if it had disagreed. The agreement gave each of the Allies control over areas of the former Ottoman Empire. Britain would dominate contemporary Jordan and Iraq and a stretch of territory through modern Israel. France would have supervision over southern Turkey, Syria, and Lebanon. Russia was to control Constantinople and the Turkish straits and Armenian territory.

The Sykes-Picot Agreement became a source of embarrassment for the British and French governments after the Bolshevik Revolution and Russia's withdrawal from World War I, when the Bolsheviks published the secret partition treaties. Indeed, the agreement did seem at variance with promises by British officials in Cairo to their Arab allies that they would achieve self-determination, and it certainly flew in the face of U.S. president Woodrow Wilson's Fourteen Points, issued in 1918. The agreement blatantly contradicted Wilson's cherished principle of self-determination.

Sykes may have played a role in the crafting of the 1917 Balfour Declaration. He was a member of the British delegation to the peace negotiations at Paris after World War I that led to the Treaty of Versailles. He was suddenly taken ill with Spanish flu while in Paris and died there on February 16, 1919. The 1916 arrangements for the Near East were approved by the Treaty of Sèvres in August 1920. The basic tenets set forth by the Sykes-Picot Agreement remained, and were approved in the Treaty of Lausanne (1923) in which Turkey recognized the League of Nations mandates given to France and Britain. France's mandate was over Lebanon and Syria, while Britain's was over Iraq and Palestine (at the time Palestine included Jordan as well as present-day Israel and the West Bank). Shortly after World War II, the last of the mandates were given independence, creating the modern states of Iraq, Syria, Lebanon, Jordan, and Israel. Thus, in a real sense Sykes's decisions created many of the nation-states of the modern Middle East and the accompanying problems.

MICHAEL K. BEAUCHAMP

**See also**

France, Middle East Policy; Lausanne, Treaty of; Mandates; Middle East, History of, 1918–1945; Ottoman Empire; Sèvres, Treaty of;

Sykes-Picot Agreement; United Kingdom, Middle East Policy; World War I, Impact of

**References**

Fromkin, David. *A Peace to End All Peace: The Fall of the Ottoman Empire and the Creation of the Modern Middle East.* New York: Henry Holt, 1989.

Lawrence, T. E. *Seven Pillars of Wisdom: A Triumph.* New York: Doubleday, 1935.

Lewis, Bernard. *The Shaping of the Modern Middle East.* New York: Oxford University Press, 1994.

# Sykes-Picot Agreement

Clandestine agreement reached among the British, French, and Russian governments regarding claims of territory belonging to the Ottoman Empire. In the spring of 1915 the British high commissioner in Egypt, Sir Henry McMahon, promised Sharif Hussein ibn Ali of Mecca British support for an Arab state under Hussein in return for Arab military support against the Ottoman Empire. Confident of British assistance, in June 1915 Hussein proclaimed the Arab Revolt. The French government was alarmed over this, and on October 24 McMahon informed Hussein of limitations on a postwar Arab state. Britain was to have direct control of the Baghdad-Basra region so that the area west of Hama, Homa, Aleppo, and Damascus could not be under Arab control. Any Arab state east of the Hama-Damascus area would have to seek British advice. McMahon also warned Hussein that Britain could make no promises that would imperil French interests.

Aware of the British agreement with Hussein, Paris pressed London for recognition of its own claims in the Ottoman Empire. Englishman Sir Mark Sykes and Frenchman François Georges Picot were appointed by their respective governments to conduct the negotiations, and because discussions of the future of Asiatic Turkey necessarily affected the Russians, the two proceeded to Petrograd in the early spring of 1916 and there presented their draft agreement. They secured Russian support in the formal Sazonov-Paléologue Agreement of April 26, 1916, named for Russian foreign minister Sergei D. Sazonov and French ambassador to Russia Georges Maurice Paléologue. It is most often known as the Sykes-Picot Agreement, however. The agreement was officially concluded on May 16, 1916.

The Sykes-Picot Agreement provided extensive territorial concessions to all three powers at the expense of the Ottoman Empire. Russia was to receive the provinces of Erzerum, Trebizond, Van, and Bitlis (known as Turkish Armenia) as well as northern Kurdistan from Mush, Sairt, Ibn Omar, and Amadiyya to the border with Persia (Iran). France would secure the coastal strip of Syria, the vilayet of Adana, and territory extending in the south from Ayntab and Mardin to the future Russian border to a northern line drawn from Ala Dagh through Kaysariyya Ak-Dagh, Jidiz-Dagh, and Zara to Egin-Kharput (the area known as Cilicia). Britain would secure southern Mesopotamia along with Baghdad as well as the ports of Haifa and Acre in Palestine. The zone between the British and French territories would be formed into one or more Arab states, but this was to be divided into British and French spheres of influence. The French sphere would include the Syrian hinterland and the Mosul province of Mesopotamia, while the British would have influence over the territory from Palestine to the Persian border. The agreement also provided that Alexandetta would become a free port, while Jerusalem would be internationalized.

The parties involved agreed to maintain strict secrecy regarding the plan. Despite this, the Italian government learned of its existence by early 1917 and forced the French and British governments to agree in the St. Jean de Maurienne Agreement of April 17, 1917, that Italy would receive a large tract of purely Turkish land in southern Anatolia and a sphere of influence north of Smyrna. This was the final agreement among the Allies regarding the future partition of the Ottoman Empire. It was contingent on the approval of the Russian government, which was not forthcoming because of revolutionary upheaval there. Hussein did not learn of the Sykes-Picot Agreement until December 1917, when the information was published by the Bolshevik government of Russia and relayed to Hussein by the Turks, who vainly hoped thereby to reverse his pro-British stance.

The Sykes-Picot Agreement proved a source of bitter conflict between France and England at the 1919 Paris Peace Conference. French premier Georges Clemenceau expected to receive British support for French claims to Lebanon, Cilicia, and Syria. He based this belief on a December 2, 1918, meeting in London with British prime minister David Lloyd George where, in a verbal understanding without witnesses, Clemenceau agreed to modify the Sykes-Picot Agreement. Recognizing the British role in victory in the Middle East, Clemenceau agreed that the oil-producing area of Mosul, assigned to France in the Sykes-Picot Agreement, would be transferred to the British sphere. Palestine, which had been slated for some form of international status, would also be assigned to the British. In return, Clemenceau believed that Lloyd George had promised British support for French claims to Syria and Cilicia.

At the Paris Peace Conference, however, Lloyd George jettisoned the Sykes-Picot Agreement. Appealing to U.S. president Woodrow Wilson's principles of national self-determination, Lloyd George argued that the Arab Revolt entitled the peoples of Lebanon and Syria to self-rule. Lloyd George wanted Hussein's son Emir Faisal, who was under British influence, to rule Lebanon and Syria. But Lloyd George also insisted that Britain retain control of Iraq and Palestine. Clemenceau protested. The standoff was resolved on April 24, 1920, at the San Remo Conference, whereby the British and French governments reached agreement on mandates in the Middle East. Britain would receive Palestine and Iraq, while France secured Lebanon and Syria. Self-determination in the Middle East was thus rejected.

SPENCER C. TUCKER

**See also**

Mandates; Ottoman Empire; Paris Peace Conference; San Remo Conference; Sykes, Sir Mark

**References**

Andrew, Christopher, and A. F. Kanya-Forstner. *The Climax of French Imperial Expansion, 1914–1924*. Stanford, CA: Stanford University Press, 1981.

Kent, Marian, ed. *The Great Powers and the End of the Ottoman Empire*. London: Routledge, 1996.

Lenczowski, George. *The Middle East in World Affairs*. 4th ed. Ithaca, NY: Cornell University Press, 1980.

Nevakivi, Jukka. *Britain, France and the Arab Middle East, 1914–1920*. London: Athlone, 1969.

Tanenbaum, Jan Karl. *France and the Arab Middle East, 1914–1920*. Philadelphia: American Philosophical Society, 1978.

Tauber, Eliezer. *The Arab Movements in World War I*. London: Frank Cass, 1993.

# Syria

Arab nation in the Middle East covering 71,498 square miles, just slightly larger than the U.S. state of North Dakota. Syria's current population is approximately 19.75 million. The Syrian Arab Republic borders on Jordan and Israel to the south, Beirut and the Mediterranean Sea to the west, Turkey to the north, and Iraq to the east. For much of its history, Syria was dominated by larger powers. Syria was part of the Ottoman Empire until the end of World War I, and the country's economy and educational system had left its populace in relative destitution. In 1920 France received a League of Nations mandate over both Syria and neighboring Lebanon.

French rule resulted in the Great Syrian Revolution (1925–1927) led by a Druze, General Sultan Pasha al-Atrash. The French had to send thousands of troops from Morocco and Senegal to rout the rebels. After a tortuous series of negotiations, Syria was granted considerable autonomy in 1936. Following the defeat of France by Germany in June 1940, Syria was controlled by the Vichy French government, headed by Marshal Henri Philippe Pétain. The Vichy government installed General Henri Dentz as high commissioner to Syria with a cabinet headed by Khalid al-Azm. Pétain ordered Dentz to allow German and Italian aircraft landing rights in Syria on their way to support Rashid Ali al-Gaylani's regime in Iraq.

This situation was intolerable to the Allies. On June 8, 1941, Allied forces that included the British Ninth Army, Australian, and Free French forces, along with troops of the Transjordan Arab Legion, crossed from Palestine into Lebanon and Syria. By June 15 they had reached the Syrian capital of Damascus, which fell on June 21. On July 13 Dentz and the Vichy French forces surrendered, and the next day signed the Acre Convention. The fighting claimed 4,500 Allied and 6,000 Vichy French casualties.

Syria was then turned over to British and Free French authorities even though there were some disputes between these parties.

Aleppo, Syria, one of the world's oldest inhabited cities. (iStockPhoto)

Although the French had announced that they would grant Syria its independence, in fact they continued to occupy the country. They declared martial law, imposed strict press censorship, and arrested political subversives.

In July 1943 under pressure from its allies, the Free French government-in-exile announced new elections in Syria. A nationalist government came to power that August, electing as president Syrian nationalist Shukri al-Quwatli. France granted Syria independence on January 1, 1944, but the country remained under Allied occupation for the remainder of the war. In February 1945 Syria declared war on the Axis powers and then the next month became a member of the United Nations (UN).

In early May 1945 anti-French demonstrations erupted throughout Syria, whereupon French forces bombarded Damascus, killing 400 people before the British intervened. A UN resolution in February 1946 called on France to evacuate the country, and by mid-April all French and British forces had left Syrian soil. Evacuation Day, April 17, 1946, is still celebrated as a Syrian national holiday.

On March 22, 1945, Syria was a cofounder of the Arab League, which advocated Arab nationalism but without the formal unification of Arab states and the resultant problems that such a movement would have witnessed. The Arab League was also aimed at blocking the creation of a Jewish state in Palestine, which the Syrians strongly opposed.

Syria played a relatively small role in the failed Israeli War of Independence (1948–1949) that arose from the creation of the Jewish state in May 1948. At the beginning of the fighting Syria had only some 4,500 troops to commit, almost all of whom were dispatched to the Syrian-Palestinian border. Just six days into the fighting, Syrian troops had been repelled, with heavy casualties. News of the Syrian defeat spread rapidly, and many Syrians blamed Quwatli for the setback. Quwatli reacted by firing his defense minister and chief of staff. As time progressed, however, Syrian troops enjoyed some success and managed to occupy a small strip of Palestinian territory along the border. They also occupied a small piece of land in northeastern Palestine. After these initial successes, the small Syrian military contingent remained rather inactive for the rest of 1948. For Quwatli, whose popularity was quickly eroding, the chief issue of the 1948–1949 war was whether Syria would fight alongside other Arab nations in a show of Pan-Arabism or whether it would fight to retain its Syrian identity. In so doing, he diluted the Syrian effort against the Israelis and engendered opponents in other Arab states.

The Israeli victory in the war and disagreements over Syria's potential union with Iraq torpedoed Quwatli's government. There were three separate coups in 1949, the last one headed by Lieutenant Colonel Adib al-Shishakli, who governed with a heavy hand until 1954. In 1952 after a series of lengthy talks, Shishakli agreed in principle with a U.S. offer that would have brought $400 million in aid to Syria in exchange for Syria's settling of as many as 500,000 displaced Palestinians. The plan was doomed from the start, however, as many Syrians—especially those on the political Left—decried the plan as an attempt to deny Palestinians their right of return to Palestine, which by now had UN backing.

Shishakli was ousted in 1954, and late that year elections were held to determine the makeup of the new government, which would now be civilian. In the end, a three-party coalition (People's Party, National Party, and Baath Party) emerged, with National Party chief Sabri al-Asali as its head. The coalition was a shaky one, and political instability plagued the new government. In the succeeding years the Baathists, who combined Arab nationalism with socialist economic policies, became the most powerful political force in Syria, and Syria gradually entered into economic and military agreements with the Soviet Union.

In February 1958 Syria and Egypt joined to form the United Arab Republic (UAR). Syrian political parties were now supposed to refrain from all political activity. Complete Egyptian domination of the UAR forced yet another coup against the Syrian government in September 1961. Carried out by military officers, the coup plotters promptly pulled Syria out of the UAR and established the Syrian Arab Republic. In December 1961 elections for a national assembly were held, and the body chose two conservative People's Party members to lead the new regime. However, another coup in late 1962 again toppled the government.

In 1963 a joint Baath-military government came to power. The new government nationalized most industrial and large commercial concerns and engaged in land reforms that redistributed land to the peasants. Meanwhile, Syria continued to cultivate relations with the Soviet bloc. A schism in the Baath Party resulted in more instability, and in 1966 the radical wing of the party staged a coup and installed Yussuf Zayan as prime minister. Nur al-Din al-Atasi became president. This new regime tightened Syria's ties with both the Soviets and Egyptians.

Syria fought Israel yet again in the June 1967 Six-Day War, with disastrous consequences. This time, its defeat included the loss of the Golan Heights to the Israelis. The outcome of the war eviscerated the ruling government, and when Syrian forces had to pull back after attempting to aid the Palestinians in Jordan during Black September (1970), the scene had been set for yet another change of government. On November 13, 1970, General Hafiz al-Asad, the minister of defense, seized power in a coup. Asad referred to it as the Corrective Revolution, which essentially ousted from power civilian Baathists in favor of the military Baathists. An ardent nationalist, Asad sought to strengthen ties to other Arab states, de-emphasize Syrian reliance on the Soviet Union, and defeat Israel.

In early 1971 Asad was elected president and immediately began to consolidate his power. He would rule the country until his death in 2000. During the early years of his presidency, he modernized the Syrian Army and engaged in modest economic reforms, while the Baath Party gained even more strength. Befitting his Baathist philosophy, the state played a central role in economic planning and implementation. Asad's tactics could be brutal, and there was little room for dissent or democracy in Syria.

A convoy of armored personnel carriers passes near the mosque of a deserted Syrian village during manuevers in the Golan Heights on August 27, 1997. Although considered Syrian territory after World War I, the Golan Heights have been under Israeli occupation since the Six-Day War in 1967. (AP/Wide World Photos)

Syria joined with Egypt against Israel in the October 1973 Yom Kippur (Ramadan) War. At the beginning of the fighting, Syria launched a massive ground attack that included 1,500 tanks (900 in the initial attack and 600 in reserve) and 144 batteries of artillery in an attempt to retake the Golan Heights. After some initial success and although their forces this time fought quite well, the Syrian attackers were finally driven back beyond their original positions. Syria did not take the Golan Heights but did regain control over a small portion of it as a result of U.S.-led negotiations after the war.

In the late 1970s and 1980s Sunni Muslim fundamentalists began challenging the government's authoritarian rule, as the Sunni majority greatly resented the way they were treated by Alawites who assumed more importance in the government and the military. The Islamic parties opposed the Baath Party's secular outlook. From 1976 to 1982 the cities of Damascus, Homs, Hama, and Aleppo became hotbeds of political unrest. Asad's brother brutally crushed a February 1982 uprising by the Muslim Brotherhood in Hama, and troops killed as many as 30,000 people. Many others who had sympathies with the Islamic parties fled the country.

Asad also sent his army into Lebanon in 1976, ostensibly as a peacekeeping force during the civil war there. The troops stayed on, however, with Asad siding at certain points with the progressive Christian, Druze, and Muslim forces and then later with certain Christian militias. By the mid-1980s Syrian forces in Lebanon were playing both a military and political role in that conflict. The conflict was declared to have ended in 1990, although Syrian troops were not withdrawn from Lebanon until 2005. Syria used Lebanon as both a market and an informal second economy. As a result of the long Syrian presence in Lebanon, many thousands of Syrians moved into Lebanon after the civil war to seek work. Because of special agreements, Syrian produce was cheaper than that grown in Lebanon, which hurt Lebanese farmers. Smuggling, organized by the Syrian military, meanwhile continued from Lebanon into Syria. In 1994 the Lebanese government granted citizenship to 250,000 Syrians, a controversial move for Lebanese.

At the same time, the 1980s saw the Asad regime taking harder-line Arab positions and moving closer to the Soviets. Asad was also courted by the Chinese. His get-tough approach in regional politics included funding and encouragement of terrorism both in the Middle East and internationally. Asad, who was always in the end a pragmatist, sought to ameliorate relations with the West when the Soviet Union began to implode in 1990. When Iraq invaded Kuwait in August 1990, Asad was the first Arab leader to denounce the attack. His government also provided 20,000 troops to the international coalition that defeated Iraqi forces in the 1991 Persian Gulf War.

Asad's frontline stance on the war reflected both his desire to strengthen relations with the West and his strong dislike of Iraqi dictator Saddam Hussein. Although Hussein was a Baathist, he was a direct threat to Asad, who wanted to maintain Syria's position with Saudi Arabia and Egypt as the key decision makers in the region. Syria hosted Iraqi political opposition leaders in exile, and Iraq did the same for Syrian political exiles.

In 1991 Asad's government entered into peace negotiations with Israel, although the process broke down in January 2000 with no firm agreement. Asad died in June 2000 after 30 years in power. He was succeeded by his son, Bashar al-Asad, who had been carefully groomed as the heir apparent after the death of his brother Basil in 1993.

Allegedly a free-market proponent, the younger Asad attempted some economic reforms, but the process has been fraught with setbacks and obstacles. In 1998, 65 percent of all Syrian revenues came from petroleum products. Bashar al-Asad also promised both political and democratic reform, but neither has occurred.

After the September 11, 2001, terror attacks against the United States, Syria pledged its cooperation in the Global War on Terror. But with the beginning of the 2003 Iraq War, which Asad refused to support, U.S.-Syrian relations sharply deteriorated. Syria's continued support, or at least its hosting of militant Palestinian groups and organizations such as Hezbollah, let alone the insurgents fighting U.S. and coalition troops in Iraq, all further strained relations with the United States. Refugees from Iraq, many of them very poor, poured into Syria. And although Syrian troops were out of Lebanon by 2005, there is considerable evidence to suggest that the Syrians continue to involve themselves in the internal politics of that nation. Indeed, most observers agree that Syrian operatives were responsible for the assassination of former Lebanese prime minister Rafic al-Hariri in February 2005, which prompted massive protests in Lebanon and compelled Asad to withdraw all remaining troops from Lebanese soil. These same operatives have likely been responsible for other assassinations of leading Lebanese figures. The assassination of Hariri resulted in the formation of the March 14 coalition, which has been strongly supported by Saudi Arabia and has insisted on further Syrian distancing from Lebanon.

More recently, concerns arose that Syria was attempting to carry out a clandestine nuclear program, possibly with technological assistance from the Democratic People's Republic of Korea (DPRK, North Korea). These concerns were given considerably more credence after a September 2007 Israeli air raid in Syria's Dayr al-Zawr Governate to destroy what was widely believed to be a nuclear reactor under construction. The Syrian government protested the strike, claiming that the site was an agricultural testing facility. At the same time, it hastily removed material from the area.

Beginning in 2007, Syria was involved in secret peace talks with Israel that were coordinated and mediated through the Turkish government. Asad subsequently confirmed these talks and also confirmed that the future of the Golan Heights, which is the primary issue for Syria, was under discussion with Tel Aviv.

The United States has charged that Syria has supported the insurgency in Iraq, funding segments of the insurgency since at least early 2004, and that Syria had allowed an undetermined number of fighters access to Iraq through its border crossings. However, Syria subsequently permitted access by U.S. authorities to its bank records and cooperated in various measures designed to defeat the insurgency. During 2007 and 2008, Syrian diplomats met with Iranian, Iraqi, and U.S. counterparts to discuss ways to curb the Iraq insurgency and quell sectarian violence in Iraq. The extent to which the talks have resulted in a scaling back or elimination of Syrian support for the insurgency remains to be seen, however, and relations between Damascus and Washington continue to be contentious.

PAUL G. PIERPAOLI JR.

**See also**

Arab-Israeli Conflict, Overview; Arab League; Arab Nationalism; Asad, Bashar al-; Asad, Hafiz al-; Baath Party; DESERT STORM, Operation; Global War on Terror; Hezbollah; Iraqi Insurgency; Lebanon; Muslim Brotherhood; Syria, Armed Forces; Terrorism; United Arab Republic

**References**

Lesch, David W. *The New Lion of Damascus: Bashar Al-Assad and Modern Syria*. New Haven, CT: Yale University Press, 2005.

Maoz, Moshe, and Avner Yaniv, eds. *Syria under Assad: Domestic Constraints and Regional Risks*. London: Croom Helm, 1987.

Pipes, Daniel. *Greater Syria: The History of an Ambition*. New York: Oxford University Press, 1990.

Roberts, David. *The Ba'th and the Creation of Modern Syria*. New York: St. Martin's, 1987.

Seale, Patrick. *Asad: The Struggle for the Middle East*. Berkeley: University of California Press, 1990.

# Syria, Armed Forces

Syria has been inhabited continuously for thousands of years and has been the site of dozens of conquests by invading forces. Damascus, the capital of Syria, is one of the oldest-surviving cities in the world. It became a Muslim city in 636 CE and was the heart of the Islamic world until the Abbasid Caliphate was established in Baghdad in the eighth century. By 1517 Syria had been incorporated into the Ottoman Empire, where it remained until World War I. After World War I when the Ottoman Empire was partitioned, Syria became a French protectorate. Syria did not achieve full independence until April 1946.

The modern Syrian Army was first formed as a mandate volunteer force in 1920. Designated the Troupes Spéciales du Levant (Levantine Special Forces) in 1925, all of the unit's officers were originally French. During World War II this force was under Vichy French control until the British occupied Syria. When the force passed to the control of the Free French, it was redesignated the Troupes du Levant (Levantine Forces). When the French finally departed in 1946, the Levantine Force became the Syrian Army, which by 1948 had grown to 12,000 troops.

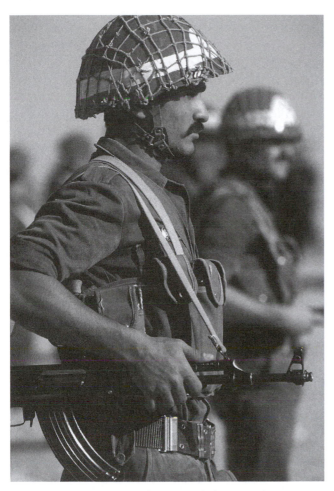

A Syrian honor guard prepares for the arrival of a visiting dignitary during Operation DESERT SHIELD. Despite Syrian animosity toward U.S. ally Israel, it joined the United States in opposing Iraq during the Persian Gulf War of 1991. (U.S. Department of Defense)

In May 1948 the British Mandate for Palestine came to an end. The Jews there declared the independence of the State of Israel, and the forces of Egypt, Iraq, Lebanon, Syria, and Transjordan (later renamed Jordan) immediately invaded Israel.

Syrian involvement in the Israeli War of Independence (1948–1949) began with an advance of infantry and armored vehicles into the Galilee region. The newly established Israel Defense Forces (IDF) had few means to repel armored forces, which it faced on three fronts. The IDF also began the war with no combat aircraft. The Syrian Air Force in 1948 had 50 aircraft, although only 10 were of relatively modern World War II design. French influence on the Syrian military was still significant in 1948. Most Syrian tanks were French models, including the Renault R-35 and R-37. The Syrians also had a small number of French artillery pieces.

The first Syrian advances into Israel targeted the village of Zemach (Samakh), situated at the southern edge of the Sea of Galilee. Despite deploying tanks, armored cars, and artillery against a defensive force armed only with rifles, machine guns, and two small antitank guns, the Syrian Army took three days to capture the village. After the fall of Zemach, the Syrians pushed toward

the Degania Kibbutzim. At Degania A, 70 Israelis armed with rifles and Molotov cocktails repelled a Syrian infantry company reinforced by tanks and artillery. After a similar defeat at Degania B the Syrians withdrew, abandoning all their previous gains and providing a one-month respite to the exhausted Israeli defenders.

On June 10, 1948, Syrian forces successfully forded the Jordan River and attacked Mishmar Hayarden, a kibbutz north of the Sea of Galilee. The Israelis launched a series of fierce counterattacks but could not drive the Syrian Army back from Mishmar Hayarden. From that point on, however, the Syrians were content to consolidate their defensive positions and hold what Israeli territory they had.

The Syrian Army occasionally supported the Arab Liberation Army (ALA), a multinational force commanded by Syria's Fawzi al-Qawuqji. When the IDF launched an offensive to destroy the ALA in October 1948, however, Syria refused to support ALA units or to allow them to withdraw into Syrian territory. On July 20, 1949, Syria and Israel agreed to a cease-fire. Syria withdrew from the Mishmar Hayarden area, which became a demilitarized zone.

Dissatisfaction with the outcome of the Israeli War of Independence ran deep in the Syrian military. Although Syrian president Shukri al-Quwatli envisioned a greater Arab nation encompassing both Syria and Palestine, he also believed in a republican form of government. He was removed from power during a series of military coups that erupted in 1949. In December, Colonel Adib Shishakli seized power. In 1951 he orchestrated his own election as president and dissolved the Syrian parliament. Another coup removed him from power in 1954, and he was replaced by an Arab nationalist coalition. In September 1961 another military coup occurred. Following more turmoil, Syrian Army officers created the National Council of the Revolutionary Command (NCRC), dominated by the Baath Party. The NCRC assumed power on March 8, 1963, and remained in place until 1970, although internal coups changed the face of the NCRC on a regular basis.

Meanwhile, two decades of sporadic raids across the Israeli-Syrian border exploded into an aerial battle over the Golan Heights on April 7, 1967. Israeli aircraft shot down six Syrian Mikoyan-Gurevich MiG-21 fighters, after which IDF warplanes flew over Damascus in a triumphant show of force.

Although the United Arab Republic had dissolved, Egypt and Syria continued to maintain close military ties. On May 30, 1967, Jordan joined the alliance. All three nations began mobilizing their military forces, deploying them to the Israeli border. In response to the overwhelming intelligence indicators, the IDF launched a preemptive strike against Egyptian airfields on June 5, 1967, triggering the Six-Day War. After destroying virtually the entire Egyptian Air Force on the ground, Israeli warplanes launched attacks against Jordanian, Syrian, and Iraqi airfields with much the same results.

With two-thirds of the Syrian Air Force destroyed and the remainder dispersed to distant airfields, Syrian military options against Israel were limited. After an abortive attack on the Tel Dan water plant, Syrian units began shelling Israeli towns from fortified positions atop the Golan Heights. The IDF retaliated with air strikes, attempting to silence Syrian artillery and disorganize or destroy the armored units.

On June 9 Israeli forces broke the Syrian defensive lines atop the Golan Heights plateau. The Syrian Army retreated in disarray, abandoning much of its heavy equipment. When the cease-fire took effect on June 11, IDF troops held the Golan Heights. During the Six-Day War, Israel lost only 141 soldiers on the Syrian front. The war cost Syria 2,500 killed as well as almost all of its equipment that had been deployed on the Golan Heights.

The Israeli occupation of the Golan Heights was a critical factor in the next outbreak of hostilities between the two nations. On October 6, 1973, Egyptian and Syrian forces launched a coordinated surprise attack against Israel. During the Yom Kippur (Ramadan) War, Syria's primary objective was to retake the Golan Heights. Syria also sought to reclaim some measure of the respect it had lost in the humiliating 1967 defeat. During the first two days of fighting Syrian forces made significant advances, regaining much of the lost territory. Syrian tanks outnumbered those of Israel by as much as 10 to 1 in some sectors of the battlefield.

For the IDF the primary front of the war was the Golan Heights, the loss of which would represent the single most serious threat to the security of Israel. Combat against Egypt in the Sinai became the secondary theater, as the IDF rushed reserves to the Northern Front.

Early Syrian advances pushed the IDF back to the outskirts of Nafah. But as the Syrian units advanced, they left the protective umbrella of their antiaircraft defensive network, increasing their own vulnerability to Israeli air attack. By October 8 the initiative and momentum shifted to the Israelis, who began to push the Syrian forces from the Golan Heights and back into Syria. On October 14 Israeli forces began shelling the outskirts of Damascus. Israeli progress was halted by a surprise Iraqi and Jordanian attack into the IDF's flank, but even the combined Arab armies were insufficient to push the IDF out of Syria.

On October 22 the United Nations (UN) imposed a cease-fire on Egypt and Israel. Syria acceded to the cease-fire on October 23. U.S. secretary of state Henry Kissinger engaged in a series of diplomatic meetings in Syria and Israel, eventually brokering a long-term armistice agreement signed on May 31, 1974. Israel agreed to withdraw its forces to the post–Six-Day War border, which left Israel in control of the Golan Heights. Both sides also agreed to the establishment of a demilitarized zone policed by UN troops.

In 1976 Syria sent 40,000 troops into neighboring Lebanon to intervene in the Lebanese Civil War. This led to a 30-year Syrian presence in Lebanon, as Syria sought to impose internal stability while also pursuing its own interests. In 1982 Israel invaded southern Lebanon in an attempt to preempt terrorist attacks across the border, primarily those launched by the Palestine Liberation Organization (PLO). During the first week of Operation PEACE FOR GALILEE, the Syrian Air Force lost 86 aircraft to the Israeli Air Force in the skies over Lebanon. Although the Syrian-Israeli border remained relatively quiet thereafter, the two nations effectively fought a proxy war in Lebanon as Syria funded and trained Lebanese and Palestinian fighters.

During the 1991 Persian Gulf War (Operation DESERT STORM), Syria participated on the side of the UN coalition, led by the United States. This was an abrupt departure from previous Syrian policy, especially considering that Syria had been allied with Iraq in three wars against Israel. Following the Persian Gulf War, Syrian president Hafiz al-Asad, in power since 1970, conducted discreet face-to-face negotiations with the Israeli government. The talks failed to produce a peace settlement, but the Israeli-Syrian border remained relatively peaceful and secure. When Asad died on June 10, 2000, he was succeeded by his son Bashar al-Asad, who has attempted to continue his father's lower-profile policy toward Israel.

Prior to the 1991 Persian Gulf War, Syria imported most of its military technology from the Soviet Union. As a reward for its participation in that war, Syria received financial assistance from several Arab states in the Persian Gulf, including Kuwait and Saudi Arabia. Much of that funding was earmarked for military spending, in part to offset the costs of participation in the war. With the collapse of the Soviet Union, however, and the unwillingness of most Western governments to sell arms to Syria, that nation has experienced difficulty in procuring quality military hardware. Domestic manufacturing of conventional weapons in Syria remains limited primarily to small arms.

Syria currently fields one of the largest military forces in the world and the second-largest Arab force, behind only Egypt. The Syrian military is organized into the Syrian Arab Army, the Syrian Arab Navy, the Syrian Arab Air Force, the Syrian Arab Air Defense Forces, and the Police and Security Force. All Syrian men serve a compulsory 2 years in the Syrian military, beginning at age 18. The officer corps is highly politicized, with membership in the Baath Party being a virtual prerequisite for advancement to flag rank. Annually Syria spends approximately $1 billion on its military, representing almost 6 percent of its gross domestic product (GDP).

The Syrian Army consists of about 200,000 regular troops and 280,000 conscripts organized into seven armored and three mechanized divisions, a Special Forces division, and a Republican Guard division. Its 4,700 main battle tanks included 1,700 Soviet T-72s and 2,000 T-54/55s and T-62s. Many of the T54/55s are emplaced in hull-down static positions in the heavily fortified defensive zone between Damascus and the Golan Heights. Almost all of Syria's armored infantry fighting vehicles and armored personnel carriers are older Soviet BRDMs and BMP-1s. Syria also has significant numbers of field artillery pieces, including the 122-millimeter (mm) 2S-1 and 152-mm 2S-3.

The Syrian Air Force, established in 1948, has some 100,000 regular troops and another 37,000 reservists. Its 1,100 combat aircraft includes Mikoyan-Gurevich MiG-21s, MiG-23s, MiG-25, and MiG-29s and Sukhoi Su-24s. The air force also has some 90 attack helicopters, including Mil Mi-24s. The 65,000-strong Air

Defense Command fields some 25 air defense brigades, each with six surface-to-air missile (SAM) batteries, as well as about 4,000 antiaircraft guns ranging from 23-mm to 100-mm.

The Syrian Navy was established only in 1950. The relatively small force of 4,000 operates some 40 vessels, including 2 older Soviet diesel submarines and 22 missile attack craft. Syria has one of the most advanced unconventional weapons programs of all the Arab nations. Most intelligence assessments agree that Syria has developed, stockpiled, and weaponized a significant amount of chemical agents, including the nerve agents GB (sarin) and VX and the blister agent HD (mustard). Syria's biological warfare agents include anthrax, cholera, and botulism. Syria has a number of delivery options for its chemical weapons, including an arsenal of SAMs. In its pursuit of missile technology, Syria has been aided by shipments of weapons and technological assistance from the Democratic People's Republic of Korea (DPRK, North Korea), which in the 1990s supplied variants of the Scud-C missile, with a range of 300 miles, and the Scud-D, with a range of 430 miles.

PAUL J. SPRINGER AND DAVID T. ZABECKI

**See also**

Arab-Israeli Conflict, Overview; Asad, Bashar al-; Asad, Hafiz al-; Baath Party; Biological Weapons and Warfare; Chemical Weapons and Warfare; DESERT STORM, Operation, Coalition Nations' Contributions to; Lebanon; Syria; United Arab Republic

**References**

Draper, Thomas. *Israel and the Middle East.* New York: H. W. Wilson, 1983.

Herzog, Chaim. *The Arab-Israeli Wars: War and Peace in the Middle East from the War of Independence to Lebanon.* Westminster, MD: Random House, 1984.

Pollack, Kenneth M. *Arabs at War: Military Effectiveness, 1948–1991.* Lincoln: University of Nebraska Press, 2002.

Rabil, Robert G. *Embattled Neighbors: Syria, Israel, and Lebanon.* Boulder, CO: Lynne Rienner, 2003.

Rubin, Barry, and Thomas A. Keaney, eds. *Armed Forces in the Middle East: Politics and Strategy.* Portland, OR: Frank Cass, 2002.

Solomon, Brian. *Chemical and Biological Warfare.* New York: H. W. Wilson, 1999.

Torr, James D. *Weapons of Mass Destruction: Opposing Viewpoints.* San Diego: Greenhaven, 2005.

# Index